THE FOREIGN POLICY

OF

THOMAS FRANCIS BAYARD

J. F. Maynard
1897

The Foreign Policy of Thomas F. Bayard
1885 - 1897

CHARLES CALLAN TANSILL

PROFESSOR OF AMERICAN HISTORY
FORDHAM UNIVERSITY

1940

FORDHAM UNIVERSITY PRESS

NEW YORK

KRAUS REPRINT CO.
New York
1969

L.C. Catalog Card Number 41-2416.

First Edition
Published December, 1940
fsss

Reprinted with the permission of the original publisher
KRAUS REPRINT CO.
A U.S. Division of Kraus-Thomson Organization Limited

Printed in the United States of America

To

Florence Bayard Hilles

PREFACE

SINCE 1933, AMERICAN FOREIGN POLICY HAS TAKEN ON INCREASED SIGnificance, and the decisions that are made by the Department of State are worldwide in their effect. One of the outstanding features of this policy has been the determined effort on the part of the Roosevelt Administration to identify the interests of the United States with those of Great Britain. Few Americans realize that this movement towards Anglo-Saxon unity was first given important impetus by Thomas Francis Bayard while he served as Secretary of State and as our Ambassador to the Court of St. James's. While in London, Bayard bent every effort to establish more intimate bonds between the Englishspeaking peoples, and these endeavors were sharply rebuffed by the American Congress through resolutions of censure. It is evident that Bayard was one of the few Americans of his day who had a clear vision of political realities, and it is high time that his services receive their much-merited recognition in every part of the English-speaking world.

To Bayard it seemed obvious that the United States and Great Britain were the twin conservators of world civilization. In a series of official despatches, in many private letters, and in numerous public addresses, he ardently preached the gospel of Anglo-Saxon unity. Through his efforts the basis of an Anglo-American entente was established, and the way was prepared for the close political concert of the present day. Few Americans, and fewer Britons, realize the fact that it was Bayard, more than any other statesman in our history, who gave real meaning to the familiar phrase, "hands across the sea."

In the writing of this monograph, I have been helped at every turn by the generosity of Florence Bayard Hilles, one of the daughters of Thomas Francis Bayard. Through her unusual kindness, the rich collection of Bayard Papers has been made available for my unrestricted use, and through her constant advice and assistance I have been able to complete this volume that deals with the foreign policy of her distinguished father.

It has been my good fortune to be able to discuss many questionable points in American diplomatic history with Judge John Bassett Moore, who was an intimate friend of Bayard, and who served as the Third Assistant Secretary of State during the years that Bayard formulated the

vii

foreign policy of this country. I am also under obligation to Mr. and Mrs. Hermann G. Place.

No one who has ever been associated with the Reverend Robert I. Gannon, S.J., President of Fordham University, can fail to record the inspiration that flows from his presence. It is largely due to his encouragement that the present task has been completed within this year. To the Reverend Gustave Dumas, S.J., Dean of the Graduate School of Arts and Sciences, Fordham University, I owe a special debt of gratitude. I wish also to record my deep obligation to the Reverend Gerald G. Walsh, S.J., and to express my admiration for his keen understanding of the problems of history. Needless to say, I owe many thanks to the Reverend Robert E. Holland, S.J., the Director of the Fordham University Press.

To the staff of the Library of Congress, my debt is exceedingly large. Dr. Herbert Putnam was unusually helpful, and I received much-needed assistance from Dr. St. George L. Sioussat, Dr. Thomas P. Martin, Mr. Verner W. Clapp, Mr. David C. Mearns, Mr. Henry S. Parsons, Mr. Archibald B. Evans, Miss Grace G. Griffin, and Mr. Vincent L. Eaton.

I am happy to record the numerous obligations that I owe to Dr. R. D. W. Connor, the Archivist of the United States, and to the following members of his able staff: Dr. Philip M. Hamer, Mr. Fred W. Shipman, Dr. Percy S. Flippin, Mrs. Natalia Summers, Miss Edna Vosper, and Miss Julia Bland.

There are many personal friends who have been of great assistance to me. Among them are: Professor Allan Nevins, Mr. Reinhard H. Luthin, Dr. Bernard Mayo, Mr. John S. Enright, Dr. Louis M. Sears, Mr. Samuel E. Collegeman, Mr. and Mrs. X. B. Tansill, Dr. Thomas A. Bailey, Dr. John S. Brooks, Mr. and Mrs. Fred G. Tansill, Mrs. Grace M. Carpenter, Mrs. B. R. Parker, Dr. Ellery C. Stowell, Dr. Curtis W. Garrison, Dr. Samuel F. Bemis, Miss Amy Holland, Miss Hazell Harris, Mr. Raymond T. Parker, and Miss Laura Berrien.

My mother has been deeply interested in this volume and has helped me in numerous ways. My wife has been all that the term helpmate implies. In the research, the organization of data, and in the final drafting of the manuscript, she has been an inspiration and an invaluable co-worker. I am happy to record her devoted service.

CHARLES CALLAN TANSILL

Fordham University

CONTENTS

ix

INTRODUCTION

Early Life—Public Career—Selection as Secretary of State

"HISTORY," SAID SAINT-SIMON, "IS THE BIOGRAPHY OF MIGHT." TO MOST of us it is obvious that this definition is entirely too narrow. History is also the biography of courage and of constant sacrifice for the common good. There are innumerable examples of men who have been moved by the imperatives of patriotism and of the Christian way of life: men who have given personal expression to all the hopes that lie closest to human hearts. In certain nations, during critical periods of their history, unselfish leaders have given authentic illustrations of the manner in which national ends can best be achieved through unvarying adherence to high ideals. They have clearly shown that national achievement is really a thing of the spirit: nations are great only as they contribute to human advancement. This truth had been familiar to Thomas Francis Bayard from the days of his early youth, and his public career was devoted to its confirmation.

Bayard was born in Wilmington, Delaware, on October 29, 1828.[1] His family was one of unusual distinction. The Bayards were famous in French history, the Chevalier Bayard having furnished history with the shining example of the perfect knight. Some of the family became Huguenots and fled to Holland, where their descendants still exist. Early in the seventeenth century, Samuel Bayard married Anna Stuyvesant, sister of the choleric Governor of New Amsterdam. After her husband's death, Anna Bayard, and her three sons, Balthazar, Nicholas, and Petrus, together with a daughter, Catherine, embarked for the New World and landed at New Amsterdam on May 11, 1647.

The three sons married in New Amsterdam and prospered in business. Petrus was more impressionable than his older brothers, and in 1684 he joined the church founded by Jean de Labadie. These Labadists had found a place of refuge in Cecil County, Maryland, where their patron, Ephraim Herrmann, granted them a portion of his fine estate that was called Bohemia Manor. Petrus Bayard followed the Labadists to Maryland, but he became dissatisfied with conditions there

---

1. Bayard's early life and public career will be given extended treatment in a volume that is nearing completion.

and returned to New Amsterdam. In 1698, when the Labadist community was dissolved and their lands were divided, Samuel Bayard, eldest son of Petrus, received a considerable tract as his share.[2] He died in 1721, leaving three sons, Samuel, Peter, and James, and one daughter, Mary Anne.

James Bayard married Mary Asheton, of Virginia, and raised two sons, John and James Asheton. John moved to Philadelphia where he served with distinction as one of the leaders of the Revolutionary movement. James Asheton died in 1769, leaving two sons, John, and James Asheton the second. John identified himself with the patriot cause, and became a colonel in the American army. James Asheton Bayard was too young to take any active part in the struggle for independence, being only nine years old when the Revolution began. After his graduation from Princeton College in 1784, he studied law in the offices of Joseph Reed and Jared Ingersoll. Although he was admitted to the Philadelphia bar in September, 1787, he soon abandoned any attempt to build up a legal practice in that city. Moving to Delaware, he quickly achieved a position of prominence, and on February 11, 1795, he married Ann, daughter of Richard Bassett, at that time serving as the Chief Justice of the State.[3] From 1797 to 1803 he served as a member of the House of Representatives, and in February, 1801, when the Presidential election was thrown into that body for ultimate decision, he took a leading part in the negotiations that led to the choice of Thomas Jefferson.[4] In January, 1805 he took his seat in the United States Senate, where he served until his appointment, in 1813, as one of the commissioners to negotiate the Treaty of Ghent. He returned to the United States in July, 1815, and died the following week, leaving four sons, Richard H., James Asheton, Edward, and Henry M. Bayard, and two daughters.[5]

2. Edward Spencer, *An Outline of the Public Life and Services of Thomas F. Bayard* (N. Y., 1880), chap. 1; B. B. James, *The Labadist Colony in Maryland, The Johns Hopkins University Studies in Historical and Political Science*, 17th series, (Baltimore, 1899), no. vi.

3. Richard Bassett (1745–1815), was a member of the Federal Convention of 1787. From 1789 to 1793 he served in the Senate of the United States; from 1798 to 1801 he was Governor of Delaware; and from 1801 to 1802 he was one of the Associate Justices of the United States Circuit Court.

4. See letters from James A. Bayard to Richard Bassett, February 16, 17, 22, 23, 1801; Bayard to Allan McLane, February 17, 1801; and Bayard to Andrew Bayard, February 22, 1801, "Papers of James A. Bayard, 1796-1815," *Report of American Historical Association, 1913* (Washington, 1915, ed. by Elizabeth Donnan), vol. 2, pp. 126-132.

5. Richard H. Bayard served in the United States Senate during the years 1836–1839, and from 1841 to 1845. He was Minister to Belgium from 1849 to 1852.

James Asheton Bayard, the second son, was one of the ablest lawyers in the history of the Delaware bar. His keen intellect and his spotless character made him a marked man in his state, and he was elected to the United States Senate for successive terms in 1850, 1856, and in 1862. His warm attachment to the American Union was one of the prime factors in defeating the movement towards secession that became manifest in Delaware in the months that just preceded the outbreak of the Civil War. On March 4, 1869, his career as a Senator came to a close. On that same day his son, Thomas Francis Bayard, assumed the duties of that office, and thereby continued the traditions of a family that had been pre-eminent in this country in the important matter of distinguished public service.[6]

Thomas Francis Bayard spent his boyhood years in Wilmington, Delaware, and was sent to private schools which were conducted by the Rev. Richard Newton, and by John S. Beach, who later became an eminent lawyer. At the age of thirteen he was sent to an excellent academy at Flushing, Long Island, where he received instruction from the Rev. Francis L. Hawks. Three years later Bayard was placed in the counting room of his brother-in-law, Augustus Van Cortlandt Schermerhorn, where he became thoroughly familiar with all the intricacies of the importing business and of customhouse regulations. This knowledge was later to stand him in good stead when, as a member of the United States Senate, he made an intensive investigation of customhouse frauds in New York City.[7]

After spending a short time in the mercantile establishment of S. Morris Waln, in Philadelphia, Bayard, at the age of 19, returned to Wilmington, and began the study of law. He was admitted to the Delaware bar in 1851. Two years later he was appointed as the United States District Attorney for Delaware, and a brilliant career appeared to be opening. But Bayard wanted the wide legal training that would come from practice in a larger city, so he resigned his office as District Attorney and went to Philadelphia where he became associated with his friend, William Shippen. When Mr. Shippen died in 1858, Bayard returned to Wilmington and rose rapidly in his profession.

Just previous to the outbreak of the Civil War, a company of

6. Thomas Francis Bayard served in the United States Senate from 1869 to 1885. His great grandfather, Richard Bassett, had served in the U. S. Senate from 1789 to 1793; his grandfather, James A. Bayard held similar office from 1805 to 1813; and his father, James A. Bayard, completed three successive terms in the Senate, from 1851 to 1869.

7. Bayard to William B. Trites, May 31, 1889, *Bayard Papers*, Library of Congress.

militia was organized in Wilmington, with Bayard as a first lieutenant. Owing to the large number of enlistments in the Federal Army, this militia company practically disappeared, although it was never formally disbanded. When an impetuous officer in the Federal Army demanded the surrender of the arms of the company, Bayard refused to accede to this order without some authorization from the Governor of the State or from the General in command of the state militia. The officer persisted in his demands and, breaking down the door of the armory, carried off the muskets. Subsequently, the Federal Government compensated the State of Delaware for the cost of these arms.

At the approach of the Civil War there were many bold spirits in Delaware who favored active participation on the side of the South, but Bayard was strongly opposed to secession. He was hopeful that some compromise could be effected whereby the Federal Union could be preserved, and he was appalled at the prospect of a widespread and destructive civil war. On June 27, 1861, a Peace Convention was held on the village green at Dover, Delaware. In his speech to the convention, Bayard stressed the view that the State of Delaware should have nothing to do with "this secession, or revolution, or rebellion, or by whatever name it may be called." If, however, all peace efforts failed and the Southern States insisted upon their right to secede from the Federal Union, these "erring sisters" should be permitted to depart in peace.[8]

It has been asserted that Bayard's speech "saved Delaware from secession." [9] If this is an overstatement of the situation, it is at least true that his influence helped to defeat any disunion tendency in the State. Both Bayard and his father, James A. Bayard, were warmly devoted to the Union cause, and like War Democrats in many other Northern States, they spared no effort to ensure a victory for the Federal Government. But Bayard had no feeling of vindictiveness towards a fallen foe. As a statesman he wished to restore the old political pattern of national unity, and he clearly realized that it was far better to rebuild the old federal bonds of friendship and mutual dependence than to forge new ties that would hold the Southern States in subjection to the rest of the Union.

As soon as Bayard took his seat in the Senate on March 4, 1869, he

8. Bayard's speech was reprinted in full in the Savannah *Morning News*, March 3, 1880.
9. Edward Spencer, *An Outline of the Public Life and Services of Thomas F. Bayard*, p. 17.

immediately entered upon a prolonged struggle in defence of the constitutional rights of the Southern States. In a powerful speech on December 16, 1869, he sharply attacked the bill introduced by Senator Oliver P. Morton for the purpose of reorganizing and disciplining the Legislature of Georgia.[10] He refused to regard the Southern States as "conquered provinces" that were at the mercy of radical politicians, and he questioned the legality of the Fourteenth and Fifteenth Amendments to the Constitution.

A few weeks later, with reference to the evident determination of the "Radicals" to attach far-reaching conditions to the re-admission of Virginia to her place in the Union, Bayard remarked:

> I came here with the oath upon my lips to sustain the Constitution of the United States. The "United States" means equal States united, and I never will consent that a member of this Union, especially so glorious and respected a member as the State of Virginia, shall come into these Halls, by my vote, anything else than the full peer and equal of any of the rest. For that reason I shall not vote in favor of her inequality.[11]

On February 15, 1870, Bayard waged a similar fight on behalf of the State of Mississippi,[12] and several months later he opposed with great vigor and impressive learning the first Force Bill, which he regarded as an instrument by which the Republican Party would maintain itself in power through a manipulation of the votes of "ignorant and semi-barbarous" negroes.[13] In May, 1872, Bayard exposed the manner in which Federal troops were being used for political purposes in the South,[14] and he indicated the serious constitutional defects in Senator Sumner's "Equal Rights" bill.[15] In February, 1873, he launched a devastating attack upon Senator Carpenter's bill to "establish a Republican form of Government in Louisiana," [16] and two years later, he made one of the most brilliant speeches of his career in a glowing indictment of the use of Federal troops in Louisiana.[17]

Bayard's impassioned defence of the South against the vindictive

10. *Congressional Globe,* 41 Cong., 2 sess., pp. 170-172.
11. *Ibid.,* January 21, 1870, p. 644.
12. *Congressional Globe,* 41 Cong., 2 sess., pp. 1281-1284.
13. *Ibid.,* May 24-25, 1870, pp. 3758, 3803-3806.
14. *Ibid.,* 42 Cong., 2 sess., May 8, 1872, pp. 3175-3176.
15. *Ibid.,* May 9, 1872, pp. 3260-3261.
16. *Ibid.,* 42 Cong., 3 sess., February 27, 1873, p. 1896, and *Appendix,* pp. 184-186.
17. *Ibid.,* 43 Cong., 2 sess., January 8, 1875, pp. 329-335. For an interesting and scholarly survey of the situation in Congress during the Reconstruction Period, see, Dr. Albert V. House, Jr., "Northern Congressional Democrats as Defenders of the South During Reconstruction," *Journal of Southern History,* vol. 6, February, 1940, pp. 46-71.

measures of the Radicals in Congress, was deeply appreciated by the whole population of "Dixie," and in 1896, Representative Tucker paid an eloquent tribute to Bayard's services. From his youth, Tucker had watched Bayard's course

. . . with pride. . . . He needs no eulogy at my hands, for under the fierce light of public and private criticism "he has ever worn the white flower of a blameless life." Nor can I forget that in those dark days that followed the late civil war, when reason was dethroned in these halls and passion was holding high carnival, when my people in the South lay prostrate, bleeding at every pore, with anxious hearts and eager eyes straining to catch the sound of one sympathetic voice amid the roar of unbridled passion, Thomas F. Bayard stepped into the arena almost singlehanded, and alone and cheerfully accepted the gage of battle in behalf of a brave but friendless people. Heaven forgive me, Mr. Speaker, if ever I forget such heroism as his in defense of our suffering people! . . . No Southern man will ever forget it. No man that loves liberty, courage, honor, and justice can forget his matchless fight for this brave people.[18]

In the Presidential election of 1876, Bayard gave his full support to Samuel J. Tilden, and later he served as one of the members of the Electoral Commission. In 1878, Henry Watterson [19] and Manton Marble [20] openly charged that during the election of 1876, Tilden had been betrayed by Bayard, Thurman, and Hewitt. The falsity of these accusations has been clearly demonstrated by Alexander C. Flick [21] and Allan Nevins.[22]

With regard to the role that he played in the election of 1876, Bayard, many years later, remarked:

The election of a President in 1876 was of the deepest interest to me as a citizen, and as a member of the Democratic Party I threw every influence I possessed and every effort I could make, to secure the election of the nominee of my party, who was Mr. Sam'l J. Tilden. My personal acquaintance with him was not intimate. . . . I never wrote a line to Mr. Tilden in my life, nor received one from him. . . . The intimates of Mr. Tilden were not mine, and we were very antipathetic. The fact is, Mr. Tilden lived in quite a different atmosphere of thought and feeling from mine, and I do not think . . . ever comprehended how thoroughly devoid of personal objects

18. *Congressional Record,* 54 Cong., 1 sess., March 19, 1896, p. 2985. In preparing this speech Mr. Tucker had the expert assistance of John Bassett Moore. See, Henry L. Bryan to Bayard, March 10, 1896, *Bayard MS.*
19. Allan Nevins, *Abram S. Hewitt with Some Account of Peter Cooper* (N. Y. 1935), chap. xx.
20. New York *Sun,* August 5, 1878.
21. *Samuel Jones Tilden* (N. Y. 1939), pp. 377ff.
22. *Abram S. Hewitt,* pp. 391-399.

and purposes my action in relation to the Presidency in 1876–1877 was. . . . Nothing influenced me in that great crisis but the intent to prevent my government from falling into confusion and bloody disorder. I would gladly have given my life to prevent the disorders, which must have followed, if a settlement under the forms of law had not been attained.[23]

In 1876 Bayard's name had been placed before the Democratic National Convention, but Tilden easily won the nomination. In 1880 Bayard was once more a candidate for the nomination as President, and if he had been willing to accept certain political "bargains," he might well have been successful.[24] In the Democratic Convention of 1884, he received 170 votes on the first ballot—the South was paying its political debt to Bayard.[25]

The nomination and election of Grover Cleveland, in 1884, restored the Democratic Party to power after a lapse of twenty-four years. Inasmuch as Bayard had served with distinction in the Senate since 1869, there was little doubt that he would be offered a place in President Cleveland's Cabinet. Carl Schurz assumed that the President would call Bayard "to the head of the Cabinet, and as it would be *the* natural thing to do, I expect he will." [26] In the first week of December, 1884, Schurz heard a rumor that Bayard would not accept the nomination as Secretary of State because of the heavy expense that would attend such an office. In great alarm, Schurz inquired of Bayard whether this rumor were true, and if it were, he suggested the acceptance of the office of Secretary of the Treasury. He knew of "no man in America available for that position, who at the head of that Depart-

23. Bayard *Diary,* July 3, 1895, *Bayard MS.*

24. In a long memorandum in the *William McKinley Papers* (Library of Congress), October 4, 1898, Ernest Isitt makes the following assertion: "A competent authority once said—'Nothing but the pride of Mr. Bayard prevented his nomination for the Presidency in 1880.' His refusal to pledge himself to a pre-arranged Cabinet slate was the cause of his failure. It is well known to many politicians still living, that confidential pledges of sufficient votes to nominate Mr. Bayard for President in the Democratic National Convention at Cincinnati had been made. Several of the votes were conditional upon Mr. Bayard's pledge as to two Cabinet places if he was elected. These conditions were presented to Mr. Bayard, but he indignantly refused to ratify them."

25. *Official Proceedings of the Democratic National Convention, 1884,* (N. Y. 1884), p. 227. Just before the meeting of the Democratic National Convention, Carl Schurz, a political "reformer" of the best type, wrote as follows to Bayard: "I should be glad to see you in the Presidential chair on the 4th of March, 1885. . . . If you are nominated, I shall work for your election to the best of my ability. . . . As between you and Cleveland the 'question of merit' is easily decided. Of course, your long and great career gives you the strongest title to the first place. If there is any other question it is that of availability. In that respect the difference between you would probably be slight, but between either of you and any other possible candidate it would be very great." *Schurz MS.*

26. Schurz to Bayard, November 21, 1884, *ibid.*

ment would so universally and unconditionally command the confidence of the country . . . as you would." [27]

Horace White was of a similar opinion, and he strongly urged Bayard to enter President Cleveland's Cabinet:

> I hear . . . that the first place in Governor Cleveland's Cabinet is likely to be tendered to you. I hope that this rumor may prove true. . . . The first place is commonly understood to be the State Department, but is really the Treasury, and if the *option is given* to you, I trust you will consider it your duty to take the latter. My reasons for expressing this hope are various, but the two principal ones are, first, that you hold a position tariff-wise which is not likely to alarm anybody; second, that the Independent Republicans who supported Gr. Cleveland would always feel that they had a *friend* at the head of that great department in the sense of one whose ear would be open to their suggestions.[28]

Bayard was none too anxious to leave the Senate where he had served with real distinction, and moreover, he had only a slight acquaintance with the incoming President. White conveyed to Schurz, Bayard's "disinclination" to enter the President's official family, and Schurz decided to pay a hurried visit to Washington in an attempt to change Bayard's mind.[29] Both Schurz and White still regarded with favor Bayard's nomination as Secretary of the Treasury,[30] but there were certain political forces that prevented any such move. Samuel J. Tilden, and his political lieutenant, Samuel J. Randall, were vehemently opposed to placing in Bayard's hands the control of the patronage that would go along with the office of Secretary of the Treasury.

In December, 1884, Randall sent the following warning to Tilden: "Unless you interfere at once and with determination, I apprehend Mr. B. will be selected as Secy. of Treasury. That means an end of your friends." [31] Tilden promptly selected Daniel Manning, of Albany, New York, as his candidate for the office of Secretary of the Treasury, and

27. Schurz to Bayard, December 2, 1884, *Schurz Papers*, Library of Congress.
28. Horace White to Bayard, December 2, 1884, *Bayard MS*. In a letter to David A. Wells, White remarks: "I hear that the State Department is to be offered to Bayard. I wish it were the Treasury. If you have any conversation with him I wish you would urge this view. The latter is by far the more important office, and I don't know anybody in the country, in either party, who commands in a higher degree the confidence of the business community. Nor do I know anybody in the Democratic party who could handle the patronage more *patriotically*, that is, fight the office-seekers more successfully." *Bayard MS*.
29. Horace White to Schurz, January 5, 1885, *Schurz MS*. Schurz to Bayard, January 10, 1885, *ibid*.
30. Horace White to Schurz, January 13, 1885, *ibid*.
31. Randall to S. J. Tilden, December 17, 1884, *Tilden Papers*, New York Public Library.

Cleveland fell in with this arrangement. When Horace White urged the President-elect to place Bayard at the head of the Treasury Department, Cleveland offered objections because of Bayard's "political affiliations in New York." He feared that the intimate associates of Bayard were "men who believe in patronage as a means of political advancement." While he conceded that Bayard was above "all such base and paltry considerations," he thought that "these men would, nevertheless, have their way with him."

White and Schurz knew the falsity of this viewpoint, and they realized that if Bayard had the slightest inkling of it, he would "sheer the track at once and refuse to come within gunshot of the Cabinet in any capacity." [32] They continued to exert pressure in his behalf, and they realized that Cleveland's disinclination to have Bayard as Secretary of the Treasury was largely due to suggestions from the Tilden wing of the Democratic Party.

Manning himself was anxious to escape the responsibilities of the office of Secretary of the Treasury, and he wrote to Tilden to that effect:

You must release me. The place has been offered, but I have no heart for it. The very thought of it has made me ill for two days. The sacrifice will be too great and I constantly feel that if I make it, I may as well bid good-bye forever to comfort and happiness. I am *so* contented now, and I will always, then, be miserable.[33]

Tilden was insistent upon Manning's acceptance of the Treasury nomination,[34] and the latter reluctantly responded to this pressure and entered upon official duties which he loathed and which soon brought him to an untimely grave.

With the Treasury appointment settled, Cleveland was anxious to have Bayard accept the State Department portfolio.[35] Horace White ardently hoped that Bayard would accede to Cleveland's wishes, for he could see "a foreign policy looming up in the distance at variance with national traditions and involving enormous expenditures and no end

32. White to Schurz, January 24, 1885, *Schurz MS.*
33. Daniel Manning to S. J. Tilden, February 13, 1885, *Tilden MS.* Manning was the President of the National Commercial Bank of Albany, New York.
34. In a letter to Smith M. Weed, Tilden made the following significant comment: "I understand from you that Mr. Manning hesitates about accepting the Treasury. You may tell him for me that I do not think he is quite a free agent in the matter." *Tilden MS.*
35. Horace White to Schurz, January 24, February 1, 1885, *Schurz MS.*

of jobbery. Bayard could put his heel upon it and save us . . . from all entanglements of that kind." [36]

At length, with considerable hesitation, Bayard decided to accept the nomination of Secretary of State. His main consideration in this regard was his desire to give much-needed prestige to the Cleveland Cabinet. In many Democratic circles there was a strong feeling that the Cleveland Cabinet selections had been none too happy, and Bayard received many letters which indicated this sentiment. The following communication from Allen W. Thurman is typical:

> I most sincerely congratulate you, but the country more, upon your appointment to the Department of State. It is the only one that personally I feel very enthusiastic over, and I trust that you will neither consider me presumptuous nor impudent when I tell you the simple truth as to how honest Democrats of Ohio feel concerning the appointment of Messrs. Whitney, Manning, and Vilas. . . . I mean in no way to cast any reflection upon the motives of the President, for I simply don't believe that he knows the true character of these men. . . . We feel now that our only hope is in you.[37]

Installed as Secretary of State, Bayard soon found he was nearly overwhelmed by the flood of applications for offices. The chief diplomatic appointments were soon disposed of. The post of Minister to England was given to Edward J. Phelps, an able Vermont lawyer, who was almost unknown to the general public. Allan Nevins asserts that the appointment of Phelps was a surprise to "everybody, including Bayard." [38] This statement seems hardly correct in view of the following remarks by Abram Hewitt to Bayard on June 15, 1895:

> Mr. Hewitt, among a great many other things, informed the entire company that I was the only man who had ever overcome Mr. Cleveland, and when I said "on what occasion?" he said the English mission in 1885—that Cleveland had intended another person, but that I had insisted upon Mr. Phelps, and he added that he thought I was wholly right.[39]

George H. Pendleton, an indefatigable worker for Civil Service reform and an important member of the Democratic delegation from Ohio, was selected as Minister to Germany,[40] and Robert M. McLane, of Maryland, a seasoned diplomat, was named Minister to France.

---

36. Horace White to Schurz, February 11, 1885, *ibid.*
37. Allen W. Thurman to Bayard, March 5, 1885, *Bayard MS.*
38. *Grover Cleveland*, p. 208.
39. Bayard *Diary*, June 15, 1895.
40. On March 19, 1885, W. S. Groesbeck wrote Bayard a strong testimonial with reference to Pendleton and his standing in Ohio. *Bayard MS.*

Charles Denby was an excellent selection for the mission to China, and the appointments of Lambert Tree to Belgium,[41] Jabez L. M. Curry to Spain, and George V. Lothrop to Russia, were satisfactory. But this important matter of appointments to diplomatic posts did not proceed as smoothly as Bayard had hoped, and he ran into serious difficulties when he approved the nomination of Anthony M. Keiley as Minister to Italy. Mr. Keiley's brother (John D. Keiley) was an important politician in Brooklyn, New York, and the Administration was glad to court his favor. It was also true that Archbishop Gibbons supported the nomination of Anthony M. Keiley to the post in Rome. Responding to this pressure, the President sent Keiley's name to the Senate, and the nomination was approved on April 2, 1885. It was not long before a diplomatic storm seriously disturbed the peace of the Department of State.

On January 12, 1871, at a mass meeting of Catholics in Richmond, Virginia, Keiley made a speech in which he bitterly denounced the "cruel and causeless invasion of the Papal States" by King Victor Emmanuel, and the destruction of the Pope's temporal authority.[42] Neither Bayard nor President Cleveland knew anything of this speech, and they were surprised and embarrassed when the New York *Herald* dug up these long-forgotten remarks and published them.[43] On April

41. Lambert Tree's availability for office was warmly supported by William R. Morrison in a letter to Bayard, April 7, 1885, *ibid.*

42. Richmond *Despatch,* January 13, 1871.

43. New York *Herald,* April 12, 1885. It is very likely that this attack on the appointment of Keiley as Minister to Italy, was engineered by William Henry Hurlburt, a newspaperman who had ardently desired the Roman post for himself. Hurlburt was a very determined seeker for public office, and on March 11, 1885, he wrote to Bayard and modestly admitted that he was just the man for an important diplomatic appointment. *Bayard MS.* Hurlburt then enlisted the assistance of Lucius Q. C. Lamar, who wrote to Bayard about giving him some office: "He is at my room every evening and sometimes in the morning before breakfast. He is nervously and feverishly excited about it and thinks he ought to know what is going to be done with him." Lamar to Bayard, March, 1885, *Bayard MS.*

On March 13, 1885, E. L. Godkin, editor of the New York *Evening Post,* wrote to Bayard to protest against any important appointment being given to Hurlburt: "I have known Mr. Hurlburt for twenty-seven years . . . and have never heard anyone . . . who knew him, speak of him without acknowledging his character to be bad. I know of no one who would take his bond on a matter of any importance, or lend him money with the expectation of being repaid. The City swarms with his angry creditors. . . . In short, I do not hesitate to say that the appointment of such a man would be as insulting to the country to which he was sent as it would be discreditable to his own." *Bayard MS.*

Hurlburt was certain that the appointment of A. M. Keiley as Minister to Italy, was a serious mistake, and he had "good reason to think that the sending of a Catholic to Rome is regarded with extreme dissatisfaction by the able and influential American Protestants

13, Baron Fava, the Italian Minister at Washington, sent a brief note to Bayard inquiring when he could have an interview concerning the alleged remarks of Mr. Keiley.[44] In reply, Bayard stated that the Department of State could not make the editorial of a

. . . newspaper, having no connection whatever with the Government, in relation to the alleged utterances, confessedly made unofficially some fourteen years ago, of a gentleman selected and approved by the Government of the United States to represent it in a foreign country, the basis of discussion with the Minister of that country here resident. In selecting Mr. Keiley as envoy extraordinary and minister plenipotentiary to Italy this Government has sought to fulfil its honorable and amicable duty towards the Government you represent, and cannot enter into discussion in respect of its action.[45]

Bayard wrote to Mr. Keiley and informed him of the request made by the Italian Minister of Foreign Affairs to delay any further action in his case until the matter of the Richmond speech has been "cleared up." [46] In his letter of reply, Keiley avowed "full responsibility" for the remarks that he had made in January, 1871, but he thought that "the progress of events, and the firm establishment of the Italian Kingdom" had removed "all such questions from the realm of discussion." [47] The Italian Secretary of Foreign Affairs thought otherwise, and he instructed Baron Fava to inform Bayard that it would be impossible for Mr. Keiley to be *"persona grata* to our King." [48] In a brief note to Bayard, April 20, 1885, Baron Fava conveyed the general tenor of this instruction, and expressed the hope that Bayard would appoint "another candidate as its representative to Rome instead of Mr. Keiley." [49] The only solution of this difficulty was the resignation of Mr. Keiley, which was forwarded to Bayard on April 28.[50]

On the following day (April 29) Keiley was nominated as Minister to Austria-Hungary, and Bayard expressed to Baron Schaeffer the hope that Keiley would be accorded "that favorable reception at Vienna

who have done and are doing so much to build up Protestant Churches in Rome." Hurlburt to Bayard, April 3, 1885, *ibid.*

44. Baron Fava to Secretary Bayard, April 13, 1885, *Sen. Ex. Doc. 4,* 49 Cong., 1 sess., p. 2.

45. Bayard to Baron Fava, April 13, 1885, *ibid.*, pp. 2-3.

46. Bayard to Keiley, April 17, 1885, *Bayard Letter Book,* vol. 1, *Bayard MS.* See also, Secretary Bayard to Baron Fava, April 17, 1885, *ibid.*

47. Keiley to Secretary Bayard, April 18, 1885, *Sen. Ex. Doc. 4,* 49 Cong., 1 sess., pp. 3-4.

48. Secretary Mancini to Baron Fava, April 19, 1885, *ibid.*, pp. 4-5.

49. Baron Fava to Secretary Bayard, April 20, 1885, *ibid.*, p. 4.

50. Mr. Keiley to Secretary Bayard, April 28, 1885, *ibid.*, p. 5. See also, Bayard to Keiley, April 20, 21, 1885, *Bayard MS.*

which is due to his merits as an American citizen of great ability and character." [51] But this hope was soon blasted by an instruction from Count Kalnoky to Baron Schaeffer, in which objections were raised with regard to the appointment of Keiley as the American Minister at Vienna. There were certain "scruples against this choice," and moreover, the fact that Keiley had been married to a "Jewess by civil marriage" would make his position at Vienna "untenable and even impossible." [52]

When Baron Schaeffer handed to Bayard this telegram from Count Kalnoky, he was immediately informed that the Secretary of State

. . . would not discuss the fact of the religious tenets of Mr. Keiley or those of members of his family. The question is profound and important. Religious liberty is the bedrock of the American system. . . . I told him I had no personal knowledge of Mrs. Keiley's . . . religious beliefs—that her husband was a gentleman of the highest personal character. . . . It was a matter of fact that the highest dignitaries of the Roman Catholic Church in the United States were personally his friends and promoters of his appointment. . . . I said to him that it was the part of men like himself and me, representing the honor and interests of two great . . . nations, not to allow such important relations to be clouded . . . by petty controversies.[53]

In a long letter to Baron Schaeffer, Bayard stated his position with clarity and force. The question raised by the Government of Austria-Hungary had no precedent

. . . in intercourse between friendly nations; and having submitted the matter to the consideration of the President, I am instructed to inform your Government . . . that the ground upon which it is announced, . . . must be emphatically and promptly denied. The supreme law of this land expressly declares that "no religious test shall ever be required as a qualification to any office or public trust under the United States.". . . This is a government of laws, . . . and it is not within the power of the President nor of the Congress . . . to inquire into or decide upon the religious belief of any official, and the proposition to allow this to be done by any foreign Government is necessarily and *a fortiori* inadmissible.[54]

On May 19 Bayard talked the situation over with the Attorney General, A. H. Garland, who expressed the view that

51. Secretary Bayard to Baron Schaeffer, May 4, 1885, *Sen. Ex. Doc. 4*, 49 Cong., 1 sess., p. 6.
52. Count Kalnoky to Baron Schaeffer, May 8, 1885, *ibid.*, p. 7.
53. *Memorandum* written by Bayard after a conversation with Baron Schaeffer, May 9, 1885, *Bayard MS.*
54. Secretary Bayard to Baron Schaeffer, May 18, 1885, *Sen. Ex. Doc. 4*, 49 Cong., 1 sess., pp. 7-9.

. . . while it is in the discretion of the receiving State to refuse the Minister or person sent, this is not an arbitrary discretion. Some good reason must be alleged for the refusal. . . . Indeed, I am of opinion that the rule goes so far as to lay down that unless for very objectionable reasons, of a personal character, if the agent of the country sending is acceptable to that country, the country receiving can make no valid objection.[55]

After receiving this advice from Mr. Garland, Bayard wrote another letter to Baron Schaeffer with regard to the reception by the Austro-Hungarian Government of Mr. Keiley. After a careful search through the records of the Department of State, no case could be found

. . . in which the acceptability of an envoy from the United States was inquired about or ascertained in advance of his appointment to the mission for which he was chosen. . . . If, upon the announcement of a mission, the Government to which the chosen envoy is to be sent objects to him, and declines to receive him on the ground of some vague report to his discredit, probably originating in the disappointment of personal rivalry or in envy, it may result in creating an issue founded upon retaliation, and thus permit petty personal objections to seriously embarrass important public affairs.[56]

On May 26 Bayard sent to Keiley, in the care of the American Embassy at Paris, a telegram informing him of the objections raised by Count Kalnoky.[57] On this same day, Bayard wrote a letter to Keiley and assured him that the Cleveland Administration would

. . . maintain the rights of the American people and of you as their representative. Pending the settlement of the objection of the Austrian Government, I think you will be more comfortable and accessible in Paris, and there I think you had better remain until you hear again from me. . . . I have strong suspicion, amounting to a belief, that personal malevolence has something to do with this Austrian action.[58]

Keiley was greatly surprised to learn, when he reached Paris, of the objections that had been raised by the Austro-Hungarian Government with reference to his appointment of Minister at Vienna. He thought that the position that Count Kalnoky had assumed was an "affront and an anachronism—an insult to a free people and a stupid cowardice before the anti-Semitic barbarity which disgraces Central Europe. My conviction of my duty is quite clear. I shall, unless otherwise ordered,

55. A. H. Garland to Bayard, May 20, 1885, *Personal, Bayard MS.*
56. Secretary Bayard to Baron Schaeffer, May 20, 1885, *Sen. Ex. Doc. 4,* 49 Cong., 1 sess., pp. 10-11.
57. Secretary Bayard to Robert M. McLane, May 26, 1885, *Bayard MS.*
58. Secretary Bayard to Keiley, May 26, 1885, *Bayard Letter Book,* vol. 1, *Bayard MS.* It is clear that Bayard suspected that W. H. Hurlburt was behind this action of the Austro-Hungarian Government.

compel the government of A. H., to assume the responsibility of this extraordinary form of religious hate." [59]

Bayard had no wish for any bold action on the part of Mr. Keiley in the matter of forcing his presence upon the Austro-Hungarian Government. Although he confessed that the Government at Vienna was the "most touchy and technical Court in Europe," he thought it best for Keiley to remain in Paris until he had received further instructions.[60]

In the meantime he had received a note from Baron Schaeffer in which the position of his Government was clearly stated:

> Our objections to Mr. Keiley's appointment as Minister of the United States to the Imperial Court are founded upon want of political tact evinced on his part on a former occasion, in consequence of which a friendly power declined to receive him; and upon the certainty that his domestic relations preclude that reception of him by Vienna society which we judge desirable for the representative of the United States, with which power we wish to continue the friendly relations existing between the two Governments.[61]

Bayard was quick to note that Baron Schaeffer included in his list of objections to Keiley's appointment, the fact that he had evinced a "want of political tact" in consequence of which a friendly power had declined to receive him. It appeared to Bayard that he was not called upon to discuss this complaint because it was "difficult to imagine the basis for such an objection to a gentleman who has as yet never been in Europe nor held official relations to any foreign State." [62]

Bayard believed it was absurd for the Austro-Hungarian Government to refuse to receive Keiley as the American Minister merely because a neighboring friendly power had taken adverse action in his regard. But Italy had recently become a member of the Triple Alliance, and the Court of Vienna was disposed to humor her whims. This fact was clearly indicated in a confidential letter from John M. Francis, the American Minister at Vienna, to Bayard. During a conversation with Mr. Szögyényi, at the Foreign Office, the political aspect of the situation was stressed, and it was flatly stated that the Austro-Hungarian Government was not really concerned over the question of Mr. Keiley's

59. Mr. Keiley to Secretary Bayard, May 27, 1885, *Bayard MS.*
60. Secretary Bayard to Keiley, June 13, 1885, *Bayard Letter Book,* vol. 1, *Bayard MS.*
61. Baron Schaeffer to Secretary Bayard, June 11, 1885, *Sen. Ex. Doc. 4,* 49 Cong., 1 sess., p. 12.
62. Secretary Bayard to Baron Schaeffer, June 15, 1885, *Sen. Ex. Doc. 4,* 49 Cong., 1 sess., pp. 12-13.

marriage to a Jewess, for "Austria is tolerant and liberal in respect of religious matters." [63]

To Mr. Keiley it seemed almost incredible that Count Kalnoky could really be serious in his stand that he could not receive an American Minister who was *non grata* to a neighboring friendly power. To permit

. . . the government of Austria to sit in judgment upon the attitude of a private citizen of the United States towards an historical event connected exclusively with another government, as disclosed by a single utterance in a meeting of private citizens 14 years ago, is to allow to a European Emperor a disfranchising veto upon the privileges of an American citizen. . . . The Government of Austria has no right to embarrass the President and his administration by an objection based upon reasons which not only cannot commend themselves to the approval of the American people, but which must excite their indignation, so soon as they are avowed.[64]

Bayard was in cordial agreement with the opinions of Mr. Keiley, and in a long instruction to Mr. Francis, at Vienna, he expressed his views with force. First, he dealt with the matter of Mr. Keiley's marriage to a Jewess, and indicated the "utter inability of this Government to entertain such a ground of objection." With reference to the possibility that the Court of Vienna could not receive Keiley because of Italian pressure, Bayard thought that this objection was distinctly untenable. It should be remembered that one of "the most acceptable ministers ever sent by the United States to Austria, Mr. John A. Kasson, was first nominated for the Madrid mission, and that Spain objected to receive him because of his alleged public sympathy with the separatist movement in Cuba." It would appear "intolerable" that the good relations between the United States and Austria-Hungary should be embarrassed "by the special prejudices of any third Government." [65]

In a letter to Phelps, at London, Bayard referred to the Keiley incident, and remarked: "*Entre nous*, the objection was that Keiley was 'wedded to a Jewess,' and that objection I took by the throat." [66]

On July 3, Bayard had a long conversation with Baron Schaeffer, and he at once adverted to the position taken by Count Kalnoky that he could not receive Mr. Keiley as American Minister because of

63. John M. Francis to Secretary Bayard, June 17, 1885, *Confidential, Bayard MS.*
64. Keiley to Secretary Bayard, June 29, 1885, *Bayard MS.*
65. Secretary Bayard to John M. Francis, July 1, 1885, *Sen. Ex. Doc. 4,* 49 Cong., 1 sess., pp. 17-20.
66. Secretary Bayard to Phelps, July 1, 1885, *Bayard Letter Book,* vol. 1, *Bayard MS.*

Italian objections. Against such a stand, Bayard entered a vigorous protest, and he assured Baron Schaeffer that

. . . Austria-Hungary had no better friend than the United States, and none more entitled to her good offices and support; that the relations of Italy to Austria-Hungary could not be admitted to give the prejudices or feelings of that government or any of its officials any weight where the United States were concerned in their relations to Austria-Hungary. I [Bayard] then recited the history of the case; the objection on the ground of Mrs. Keiley's religion, and the other questions, and told him that I had written a very full statement of the case to Mr. Francis and desired him to lay it before the Foreign Office, and that I believed that when the statesmen who governed Austria became aware of the facts, they would see that they had acted under a misapprehension when they made their suggestion of objection; and that being so informed, all objection to Mr. Keiley would be withdrawn.[67]

In a note to Phelps, Bayard again sounded a note of optimism concerning the final action of the Austro-Hungarian Government with reference to the reception of Keiley as American Minister: "Austria still flounders in false reasons for objecting to Mr. Keiley, and as yet I cannot obtain a *flat* answer *yes* or *no*. When the correspondence is published, I cannot help thinking they will regret having consented to gratify the small and personal objects of some hangers-on of the Italian Court." [68]

There was little possibility that Count Kalnoky would change his mind about the reception of Keiley, and, on August 4, Bayard received a telegram from Vienna to the effect that Keiley was *non grata*.[69] This information was immediately conveyed to Keiley, in Paris,[70] and he realized that his mission was at an end.[71]

To Bayard it seemed clear that Keiley was a "spirited and honorable man who has been cruelly and wantonly treated by the official insolence of Austria," and he felt certain that American public opinion would sustain the position taken by the Administration.[72] He was gratified, therefore, to receive a note from Francis Wharton, who had

67. *Memorandum* written by Bayard after a conversation with Baron Schaeffer, July 3, 1885, *Bayard MS.*
68. Secretary Bayard to Phelps, July 22, 1885, *Bayard Letter Book*, vol. 1, *Bayard MS.*
69. James Fenner Lee to Secretary Bayard, August 4, 1885, *Sen. Ex. Doc. 4*, 49 Cong., 1 sess., p. 21.
70. Secretary Bayard to Robert M. McLane, August 5, 1885, *Bayard MS.*
71. Mr. Keiley to Secretary Bayard, August 6, 1885, *ibid.*
72. Bayard to President Cleveland, August 18, 1885, *Bayard Letter Book*, vol. 1, *Bayard MS.*

talked with a large number of Democratic politicians who were strongly in support of the policy that had been adopted.[73]

This policy was discussed at great length in an instruction from Bayard to Mr. Lee on August 31, 1885. In conclusion, Bayard stated with trenchant clarity that the Government of the United States would never be placed

... in an attitude of supplication for favor, or become a petitioner for recognition on terms prescribed by any foreign power. It is not the intention of the Government of the United States, as it cannot be the wish of the people of this country, ... to allow the important and dignified objects which diplomatic intercourse was designed to promote, to be lost sight of or subordinated to the prejudices and caprices of a limited social circle.[74]

In a personal letter to Mr. Lee, at Vienna, Bayard expressed himself without reserve:

So long as I am at the head of this Department I shall not give myself the slightest trouble to thwart the small politics or staircase intrigues in Europe, in which we have not the slightest share or interest, and upon which I look with impatience and contempt. ... I want to conduct our relations on the highest plane of honour, good feeling, and good sense, and shall abate no effort in such directions. ... Mr. Francis sent me a report of his final interviews with Count Kalnoky, which gave me a very humble opinion of his theories of what was done to him and for him as an American Minister and a gentleman. The hinges of his knees are too supple in returning profound thanks for social favors. A Minister should never forget he is the representative of a government, an equal member in the family of Nations, entitled to respect not as a favor but a right.[75]

With regard to the Keiley incident, Mr. Lee mentioned the rumor in Vienna that Prince Bismarck was responsible for the action of Count Kalnoky.[76] Bayard promptly rejected this suggestion. The European habit of

... attributing to Prince Bismarck a prowling and predatory disposition is, in my judgment, wholly unjust, and no one would more scornfully deride the suggestion of his stooping to weaken or disturb the amity and comity of the United States with any other Country, than he, himself. He is con-

73. Francis Wharton to Secretary Bayard, August 29, 1885, *ibid.*

74. Secretary Bayard to Mr. Lee, August 31, 1885, *Sen. Ex. Doc. 4,* 49 Cong., 1 sess., pp. 24-27.

74. Secretary Bayard to Mr. Lee, August 31, 1885, *Sen. Ex. Doc. 4,* 49 Cong., 1 sess., pp. *MS.*

76. Mr. Lee to Secretary Bayard, September 16, 1885, *Bayard MS.*

structed on a grand scale, and may be violently wrong, but never small or weak.[77]

On December 14, 1885, President Cleveland sent to the Senate the diplomatic correspondence relative to the Keiley incident, and the Bayard Papers are filled with letters congratulating him upon the manner in which he had handled the whole affair. The Irish and Jewish societies were delighted with the stand that had been taken by the Administration, and the *Christian Advocate* expressed the view that Bayard's correspondence "with the Austrian Government makes the rejection of Minister Keiley because his wife is a daughter of Abraham, look so mean that even a thickheaded Hapsburgher might blush as he reads it." [78]

To Phelps it was apparent that the Austro-Hungarian Government had "no case, and sadly blundered the little material they had. Such seems to be the general impression." [79] Oscar S. Straus assured Bayard that the position he had taken was

. . . universally applauded by all men and women whom I have recently met. It has placed before the eyes of the world the indisputable fact that our Constitutional provisions upon the subject of Religious Liberty are not "glittering generalities," but verities whereby we propose to shape our national affairs. Some few may carp and criticize, but the great mass of the American people will ever be grateful to you for placing before all Europe and all America the full extent and meaning of religious liberty under our Constitution and national polity.[80]

On September 1, 1885, Keiley resigned as Minister to Austria-Hungary, and was subsequently appointed to the international tribunal at Alexandria, Egypt. The Austro-Hungarian Government was anxious to avoid any serious difficulty with the United States with reference to the Keiley incident, and they indicated their hope that the Department of State would soon fill the vacancy at Vienna.[81] After a wait of nearly

77. Secretary Bayard to Mr. Lee, October 2, 1885, *Bayard Letter Book*, vol. 1, *Bayard MS.*
78. S. Pulliam to Bayard, December 28, 1885, *Bayard MS.*
79. Phelps to Secretary Bayard, January 2, 1886, *Bayard MS.*
80. Oscar S. Straus to Bayard, January 29, 1886, *Bayard MS.* On February 6, 1887, the Editorial Board of the *American Hebrew* called Bayard's attention to a statement in the *New Yorker Staats-Zeitung*, to the effect that the Department of State would not recommend for appointment in the diplomatic service, any person who was a Jew. In his letter of reply, February 11, 1887, Bayard denounced the statement in the *Staats-Zeitung* as "wholly and absolutely devoid of truth." *Bayard MS.* In the following month, March 24, 1887, Bayard secured the appointment of Oscar S. Straus, a prominent American Jew, as the Minister to Turkey.
81. In a confidential letter to Bayard, April 3, 1886, Mr. Lee, the chargé d'affaires at

two years, President Cleveland appointed Alexander R. Lawton, of Georgia, (April 15, 1887), as Minister to Austria-Hungary, and the Keiley incident was thus officially closed.[82]

After the unpleasant embarrassment of the Keiley incident had subsided, President Cleveland nominated John B. Stallo as the American Minister to Italy. This appointment was a friendly gesture to the Quirinal, because Stallo, at times, was quite anti-clerical. He was always fearful of some movement to restore diplomatic relations between the United States and the Papacy, and these apprehensions were shared by Baron Fava, the Italian Minister at Washington. On February 18, 1887, Fava had an interview with Bayard, and he inquired whether

. . . there would be any application to the Government of the United States to send a Minister to the Vatican. I [Bayard] told him no such proposition had been or would be made; that the indisposition of the Government of the United States to recognize any particular religion would probably prevent any such application being made; that it would be an anomalous condition of things. He said he was very glad to hear it.[83]

Vienna, indicated the anxiety of the Austro-Hungarian Government to have the United States send a Minister to Vienna. An endeavor to force the hand of the American Government in this matter was made through the adoption of a very snobbish attitude towards the American chargé d'affaires. *Bayard MS.*

82. In 1885, General Lawton was nominated by President Cleveland as Minister to Russia. On April 2, 1885, Bayard received a letter from Senator John Sherman, Chairman of the Senate Committee on Foreign Relations, in which objection was made to Lawton's nomination on the ground that "his disabilities under the third clause of the Fourteenth Amendment, have not been removed by the action of Congress. The pardon granted to him prior to the adoption of the Fourteenth Amendment is not held by the Committee to be a release from or a waiver of the disabilities imposed by the Constitution." *Bayard MS.*

Although Bayard did not accept the interpretation of the Republican Senators with reference to General Lawton's "disabilities" under the Fourteenth Amendment to the Constitution, he nevertheless wrote to Senator Sherman and withdrew General Lawton's nomination from the Senate. (Bayard to Senator Sherman, April 2, 1885, *Sherman MS.*)

When Bayard presented these facts to General Lawton (April 4, 1885), the General sent in his resignation on April 17. (General Lawton to Bayard, April 17, 1885, *Bayard MS.*)

Attorney General A. H. Garland rendered an opinion that the disabilities imposed by the Fourteenth Amendment did not apply to General Lawton, who had served with distinction in the Army of the Confederacy. Carl Schurz, although a close friend of Bayard, disagreed with Garland's opinion. He thought that the Fourteenth Amendment was "designed to disqualify a certain class of men from holding office, and I think that class of men can be relieved of that *constitutional* disqualification by mere presidential pardon, just as little as I would be made eligible to the Senate again by a mere decree of the President, if today an Amendment were added to the Constitution declaring all foreign-born citizens ineligible to office." (Schurz to Bayard, April 15, and May, 1885, *Bayard MS.*)

Bayard did not accept the viewpoint of Schurz, and subsequently, April 15, 1887, Lawton was sent as Minister to Austria-Hungary.

83. *Memorandum* written by Bayard after a conversation with Baron Fava, February 18, 1887, *Bayard MS.*

Although Mr. Stallo was familiar with Bayard's assurances to Baron Fava, he still harbored suspicions of some secret move on the part of the Vatican to prepare the way for the restoration of diplomatic relations with the United States. In a private letter to Bayard, Stallo expresses these suspicions:

Shortly after my arrival in Rome, a Catholic prelate, Rt. Rev. Alysses Mori, now Canon of the Cathedral at Florence, called on me and informed me that he was a naturalized citizen of the United States, and for some years had been Secretary of Archbishop McCloskey. During the winter of 1885–1886, he made several visits to Rome and, while here, became quite an habitué of my house. He proved to be a very entertaining and cultivated gentleman, who spoke nearly all the languages of Europe with great fluency, and who made himself agreeable to my wife and daughter by escorting them to the Vatican galleries and other places of interest in Rome. . . . In time, my original impression that he was an emissary sent to convert the ladies to Catholicism, wore away. . . . In June or July, 1886, he wrote from Florence saying that he was about to go to the United States with his brother on important business, and requested me to send him some letters of introduction which would enable him . . . to secure interviews with you or Governor Porter, Speaker Carlisle, and Mr. Hewitt. . . . In compliance with this request I sent him a number of letters. . . . Although he had not informed me of the nature of his business, I conjectured that he was sent to concert measures for the extinction of the enormous debt . . . left by Archbishop Purcell of the diocese of Cincinnati. . . .

Some time in August, 1886, I learned from a letter of my son that Mori had seen him and opened negotiations on this subject, but shortly thereafter I saw a notice in the American newspapers . . . to the effect that Canon Mori had not been sent to America on any mission whatever. In consequence of this publication, Mori called on me after his return from the United States and, to exculpate himself from the charge of having assumed the role of a Papal agent without authority, produced an autograph letter from Cardinal Jacobini from which, to my astonishment, it appeared that the chief object of his mission had been to persuade the President, yourself, the Speaker of the House, etc., of the propriety of sending a diplomatic representative of the United States to the Holy See. This naturally made me inquisitive as to what had passed between him and the President and yourself, whereupon he admitted that he had discussed the subject at length with both the President and yourself or Governor Porter. Now, it has occurred to me that you and others may have been led into the belief that . . . I had knowledge of his mission and, perhaps, was in sympathy with his scheme. I desire to say, therefore, that if I had possessed that knowledge, I should at once have informed you of my entire disapproval of such a project." [84]

84. J. B. Stallo to Secretary Bayard, April 2, 1887, *Bayard MS.*

Bayard was little concerned over this bit of information from Mr. Stallo, and after waiting four months, he sent a brief reply in which he merely discussed certain editions of the works of Dante, and expressed the hope that Mr. Stallo's "scholarly tastes and literary disposition" would find ample reward in the rich resources in Rome.[85]

If Bayard and President Cleveland had appointed Mr. Stallo to Rome because of his "scholarly tastes," the same could not be said for the appointment of Samuel S. Cox, to Constantinople. Cox had been a newspaperman and a politician, and his nomination was merely a way of paying a debt to a deserving Democrat. He knew little about diplomatic procedure, and did much as he pleased. On June 1, 1886, he informed Bayard that the Sultan of Turkey had bestowed a "decoration" upon Mrs. Cox. If Bayard insisted that this decoration should be returned, it would "upset" Mr. Cox's plans for establishing closer relations between Turkey and the United States. Moreover, the decoration had been bestowed in "such a way and with so much kindness that it was impossible" to decline it.[86]

As soon as Bayard received this letter, he attached a memorandum to it and submitted the matter to the consideration of Mr. Adee. It was Bayard's view that "husband and wife must be held as one in the way of gifts from Foreign Ministers," and American representatives abroad could not receive gifts without the consent of Congress. His view of the matter was given explosive expression in the following words—"Damn Mr. Cox and the Sultan." [87]

Mr. Cox next wrote to Bayard and revealed the Sultan's ardent desire to send a splendid present to Miss Folsom, who was soon to be married to President Cleveland.[88] There seemed to be no limit to the Sultan's generosity! In alarm, Bayard wrote a brief instruction which he hoped would break down certain misapprehensions in Cox's mind:

I do not understand your official report as referring to the Department the propriety of Mrs. Cox accepting the very flattering gift of the grand cordon of the order of the Shefakat. You treat it, on the contrary as *un fait accompli*, which Mrs. Cox has decided for herself, without "coercion" on your part. . . . Had you referred to me the question of *your* own constitutional obligation in the premises, I might have replied that husband and

85. Secretary Bayard to J. B. Stallo, August 13, 1887, *Bayard Letter Book*, vol. 5, *Bayard MS*.
86. S. S. Cox to Secretary Bayard, June 1, 1886, *Bayard MS*.
87. *Bayard MS*.
88. Mr. Cox to Secretary Bayard, June 4, 1886, *ibid*.

wife are one in law. . . . Certainly, I do not desire to see Mrs. Cox deprived of this decoration by *coercion* or threats, . . . and I have no doubt that she will reach her own conclusion in the matter. I telegraphed you of President Cleveland's action a few days ago, in declining the Sultan's friendly tender of a wedding gift although it was offered to "Miss Folsom," not to the wife of the President.[89]

Despite Bayard's instruction, the Sultan insisted upon sending to the President a gift of two beautiful albums filled with photographs of Constantinople. He prudently checked, however, his stream of generosity to Mr. Cox, and he insisted that the American Minister return at once the decoration that had been bestowed upon Mrs. Cox.[90] Exceedingly discomfited by this action, Cox returned to the United States in October, 1886, with the draft of a naturalization treaty which he hoped would prove a diplomatic triumph. But he had made concessions with regard to rights of extra-territoriality which would have exposed American merchants to "great perils," so the Department of State refused to accept the treaty, and Cox's mission came to an inglorious close.[91]

There was little doubt that the ineptitude of Cox was responsible for the failure of the naturalization negotiations with Turkey, but it was not always a matter of diplomatic blundering that brought defeat to some of Bayard's best-laid plans. The extradition treaty with Great Britain is a case in point. On June 25, 1886, Phelps and Lord Rosebery signed an extradition convention which covered cases of manslaughter, embezzlement, larceny, burglary, and malicious injury to property.[92] It was evident that such a treaty would arouse the antagonism of Irish-Americans, and this was soon manifested.

During the course of the negotiations leading up to the signing of the treaty, Phelps wrote some interesting private letters to Bayard with reference to the situation in London. He thought the existing treaty had completely answered

. . . its purpose for more than forty years. . . . But it is now found imperative that it should include the crimes of *larceny* and *embezzlement,* and as the British Government may claim, dynamite offenses. Public justice demands this addition, and demands it speedily, and it is an utter reproach to both Governments that they have now been in negotiation *nearly nine years*

89. Secretary Bayard to Cox, June 16, 1886, *Bayard Letter Book,* vol. 2, *Bayard MS.*
90. Cox to Secretary Bayard, August 18, 1886, *Bayard MS.*
91. Francis Wharton to Bayard, March 11, 1887, *ibid.*
92. Lester B. Shippee, "Thomas Francis Bayard," in *The American Secretaries of State and Their Diplomacy,* vol. 8 (N. Y. 1928), p. 68.

on a subject upon which they are perfectly agreed, without any result, and with very little approximation towards a result. The reason why, is very apparent. Instead of an agreement in a few simple and clear words . . . a long and elaborate new treaty has been proposed, framed on the model of some of those Great Britain has with other nations, and embracing a complete code both of law and procedure and a long list of crimes. . . . It is not surprising that nine years' exertion finds the subject substantially where it began. . . .

I am satisfied I cannot carry through the proposed elaborate treaty without much further delay. . . . The discussion of details is endless. If a treaty is agreed upon, it must pass the Senate. . . . If the treaty is ratified, then a a new Act of Congress is requisite to carry it into effect. Aside from the difficulty of carrying any bill through the House which has neither politics nor money in it, our Irish friends . . . will not let the occasion slip. I doubt . . . if such a bill would succeed. . . .

I propose therefore, . . . the adoption of a short article extending the already existing extradition provisions to the two or three most important crimes to be provided for, without any other change of the stipulation on the subject. Were those crimes already embraced, no proposal for a further treaty would probably have been made. . . . I have sounded Lord Salisbury on this proposal, and he embraces it heartily. . . . Whatever we do, should be done promptly. The present Government may very likely be ousted as the result of the pending elections.[93]

Bayard did not agree with Phelps as to the expediency of acting very promptly in the matter of the extradition treaty with Great Britain, and he felt certain that the American Minister at London would understand the reluctance felt by the Department of State in this matter. This was especially true when one took into consideration the fact that the

. . . Irish question was so burning in England and, of course, here. I regret to say that the temper of the Senate seems averse to the consideration of any public measure from a high or patriotic point of view. . . . As affecting the extradition question and the addition of the two offences proposed, we must expect such opposition as I have described. And as the Dynamite Irish vote has been pretty well captured by Mr. Blaine's party, we must give as little chance for their objective as we can. Therefore, I believe a treaty negotiated with Gladstone's Administration would be less likely to provoke challenge, than the same propositions obtained from Salisbury. There is a slight and temporary lull . . . in the Irish proceedings, which, as I telegraphed you, makes this moment opportune. Now as to Lord Rosebery's suggestion that an *express* exclusion of trial for political offences is useless and objectionable, I think you may say to him that its absence might lead to debate and amendment after signature, and thus delay our object. . . . You can tell

93. Phelps to Secretary Bayard, November 21, 1885, *Bayard MS.*

Lord Rosebery that in all arrangements between the United States and Great Britain, the element of Irish hostility to the latter, is never to be omitted from consideration.[94]

In reply, Phelps assured Bayard that he had

. . . already pressed upon Lord Rosebery the considerations you express in respect to the Irish influence, and the effect of it upon affairs between the two countries. . . . The utterly unscrupulous tactics of Mr. Blaine will be fertile of mischief in this as in so many other matters. And I had fully impressed Lord Rosebery with the importance of clearing out of the way everything that could afford a pretext for dispute. . . .

The extradition treaty I am in daily expectation of bringing to a termination. Only the red-tapery of the Foreign Office is delaying it.[95]

On May 8, Phelps reported that the extradition treaty still

. . . drags, owing to the difficulty of making the subordinates on whom Lord Rosebery depends for his law, comprehend the embarrassment that will follow the insertion in the treaty of various provisions of the British Extradition Act. The provisions themselves as a part of the law here, are all well enough. But if put into the treaty, they become the supreme law in our states and are capable of being so used there as to defeat the whole operation of the treaty on our side.[96]

The treaty was finally signed on June 25, 1886, and sent to the Senate for consideration.[97] Several weeks later, Bayard wrote to inform Phelps that the extradition treaty was being considered by the Senate Committee on Foreign Relations, and "Edmunds (of course) wanted to amend it by limiting the age of the embezzling offenders to all above sixteen years. Was ever such disingenuous nonsense?" [98]

On July 21 the London *Times* published the full text of the extradition treaty which had been secured by some leak in the Senate of the United States. Bayard was not surprised at this breach of confidence, because from "long and sad experience" he had "ceased to expect the observance of honorable secrecy in the Senate in relation to treaties or proceedings in Executive session." [99]

The Republicans in the Senate were strongly opposed to a speedy ratification of the extradition treaty, and they raised many objections

94. Secretary Bayard to Phelps, March 7, 1886, *Bayard Letter Book*, vol. 2, *Bayard MS*.
95. Phelps to Secretary Bayard, March 27, 1886, *Bayard MS*.
96. Phelps to Secretary Bayard, May 8, 1886, *ibid*.
97. In a letter to Bayard, June 26, 1886, Phelps remarks: "You can have no idea of the trouble I have had and the time I have spent in obtaining this short and simple treaty. The difficulty was in *keeping it* short and simple." *Bayard MS*.
98. Secretary Bayard to Phelps, July 17, 1886, *Bayard Letter Book*, vol. 3, *Bayard MS*.
99. Secretary Bayard to Phelps, July 31, 1886, *ibid*.

to the wording of some of the articles. To Phelps these objections were "frivolous beyond credibility," [100] and he thought that the main opposition in America to the treaty came from the Irish. But he believed that

. . . even the Irish, if the question is fairly stated, cannot be opposed to occupy the ground of claiming to protect crime *not political* in its character according to the judgment not of a British, but of an American tribunal. . . . I think if some judicious and competent person is employed quietly to confer with Senators, the confirmation can be easily carried.[101]

This optimism faded when the Senate continued to postpone any final action on the treaty, and on February 11, 1888, Phelps came to the conclusion that the issue had been "dodged in a disgraceful and cowardly manner. . . . I presume it may be ratified next year, if the Irish faction do not acquire complete control of the country." [102]

Under the impact of a flood of protests from Irish clubs and societies, the Senate finally rejected the extradition treaty on February 1, 1889.[103] Phelps was indignant because of the response of the Senate to this Irish "pressure-group," and he felt certain that Irish refugees in the United States had nothing to fear from the provisions of the extradition treaty. It should be remembered, however, that Phelps had little love for the Irish, and his opinion was distinctly biassed.

In the intervals between the handling of major diplomatic issues, Bayard had to settle routine matters that took much of his time. On July 2, 1888, Representative Levi Maish, of the House Committee on Military Affairs, wrote a note informing Bayard that General William T. Sherman had made the assertion that the Cleveland Administration "had not appointed a single true Union man in the Diplomatic service." [104] In answer to this criticism, Bayard pointed out that General Sherman had apparently overlooked the appointments of distinguished Union officers like

. . . General E. S. Bragg (who now represents the United States in Mexico), and Colonel Charles Denby, of Indiana, our Minister in China, as well as General W. B. Franklin, the Commissioner to the Paris Exposition. General

100. Phelps to Secretary Bayard, August 10, 1886, *ibid.*
101. Phelps to Secretary Bayard, October 25, 1887, *Bayard MS.*
102. Phelps to Secretary Bayard, February 11, 1888, *Bayard MS.*
103. *Senate Executive Journal*, vol. 25, pp. 729, 735, 747, 748, 752, 762; vol. 26, pp. 106, 193, 256, 420-421, 435, 445. See also, W. S. Holt, *Treaties Defeated by the Senate* (Baltimore, 1933), pp. 142-143.
104. Levi Maish to Secretary Bayard, July 2, 1888, *Bayard MS.*

George B. McClellan was tendered, but declined the Russian Mission, now as honorably filled by Mr. Lothrop, of Michigan, and many others could be named.[105]

Bayard's attitude towards American economic imperialism in Latin America was clearly indicated shortly after he assumed the office of Secretary of State. Rear Admiral F. C. Stevens was deeply interested in certain mining operations in Honduras, and he was hopeful that a protectorate could be established over that country. Bayard's reply to this inquiry, blasted any such hope:

> Since I came into office it has been my duty and pleasure to tender the moral support of this Government in the cause of peace and good order in Central America, and to deprecate strongly the forcible invasion of one State by another. . . . No scheme looking to the acquisition of territorial sovereignty in Central America would find favor with the present Administration. . . . The prosperity and independence of the Central American States we very much desire, but no entangling alliances with them or any other power.[106]

In July, 1886, Charles Hardinge, the British chargé d'affaires, informed Bayard that he had just learned that the lading of the British steamer *Cydonia*, at New Orleans, was being obstructed by mob violence growing out of strikes at that port. He insisted upon Federal intervention in order that the cargo of the *Cydonia* could be quickly loaded.[107]

There was nothing that Bayard could do in this matter except to send the following short instruction to the British chargé: "The Government of the United States can intervene in such cases only on demand of the Executive of the State and under the limitations prescribed by the Federal Constitution." [108]

There were some minor matters that must have tried Bayard's patience. On December 20, 1886, James Q. Chenoweth, the First Auditor of the Treasury Department, wrote to Bayard and complained about the payment for newspapers at the "ordinary news-stand prices." Thereafter, the Treasury Department would approve vouchers for the

105. Secretary Bayard to Levi Maish, July 5, 1888, *Bayard Letter Book*, vol. 8, *Bayard MS.*
106. Secretary Bayard to Rear Admiral F. C. Stevens, August 25, 1885, *Bayard Letter Book*, vol. 1, *Bayard MS.*
107. Charles Hardinge to Secretary Bayard, July 16, 1886, *Bayard MS.*
108. Secretary Bayard to Charles Hardinge, July 16, 1886, *Bayard Letter Book*, vol. 3, *Bayard MS.*

payment of newspapers only at the "subscription price of said papers." [109]

The tone of this letter aroused Bayard's anger, and he attached to it the following memorandum: "This letter is impudent and insubordinate. What right has this fellow to write direct to the Head of another Department?" Bayard wrote to Secretary Manning about this matter, and it was easily adjusted to his satisfaction.[110]

Some of the patronage letters that came to Bayard's attention, must have afforded him some amusement. The following letter from Paris Haldeman to J. D. Cameron, is typical:

> I enclose a letter from Demerara. Won't you please see Bayard and ask him for God's sake to keep ———— where he is. If he comes here to live, on his farm near Maytown, he will bother your Father, Duffy, and me to death. . . . Tell Bayard, that I, as the defeated Democratic candidate for Congress for this district, won't ask anything from the Administration if they will keep ———— as Consul at Demerara.[111]

Bayard was fortunate in having around him in the Department of State some of the ablest assistants who have ever held Federal office. Alvey A. Adee, the Second Assistant Secretary of State, had been in the diplomatic service since 1870, and had a well-balanced mind and a large fund of information on diplomatic procedure. John Bassett Moore was the Third Assistant Secretary of State.[112] There is no doubt that Mr. Moore had one of the best legal minds in America, and his advice was of great value to Bayard upon innumerable occasions. Francis Wharton, the Solicitor of the Department of State, was a scholar of outstanding ability, one whose able opinions often guided Bayard's course.[113]

With these highly gifted assistants, Bayard was able to conduct the work of the Department of State in an entirely satisfactory manner. One test of his success in the matter of diplomatic appointments was the fact that in August, 1886, he was able to write to Phelps and report

---

109. James Q. Chenoweth to Secretary Bayard, December 20, 1886, *Bayard MS.*
110. Secretary Bayard to Secretary Manning, January 8, 1886, *ibid.*
111. Paris Haldeman to J. D. Cameron, March 19, 1885, *ibid.*
112. On May 27, 1885, Bayard wrote as follows to John Bassett Moore: "I want to get you into this Department. . . . Do not allow the inconvenience or red tape of the Civil Service to deter you from coming down and taking the examination. Dr. Wharton has given the plan of examination, and it is all within your very comfortable and easy response." *Bayard MS.*
113. For Wharton's appointment see his letter to Bayard, March 24, 1885, *Bayard MS.*

that the Senate had not rejected a single one of the nominations that had been sent to it for consideration.[114]

With reference to these diplomatic appointments, John Cadwalader wrote to Bayard and recounted a recent conversation he had had with Andrew D. White, President of Cornell University:

I had a very pleasant interview the other day with President Andrew D. White, of Cornell, and though he is a very strong partisan, even to the extent of sustaining Mr. Blaine, he stated what I think may be interesting to you. Speaking of our Diplomatic Service abroad, he said that he had had a thorough opportunity of testing it, and in his view our Country never before was so well represented throughout Europe. As he was more than once in diplomatic life himself, and as his own qualification entitled him to speak, this seems to be a very satisfactory endorsement of your course and selections.[115]

But despite the high quality of the diplomatic service, and the sage counsel that Bayard received from his assistants in the Department of State, there were many problems that seemed to defy any satisfactory solution. The manner in which Bayard handled these questions, is told in detail in the following chapters.

114. Secretary Bayard to Phelps, August 6, 1886, *Bayard MS.*
115. John Cadwalader to Bayard, March 19, 1888, *Bayard MS.*

The Samoan Question

CHAPTER ONE

The Diplomatic Background of the Samoan Question, 1839-1885

⸺◦⟨∞⟩◦◦⸺

WHEN BAYARD BECAME SECRETARY OF STATE IN MARCH, 1885, HE WAS immediately faced with the task of defining American policy in the Pacific Ocean. This was an assignment that involved not only a careful study of all the precedents in the case, but it was one which required those two essentials of successful diplomacy—patience and persuasion. It was in connection with the Samoan islands that Secretary Bayard first turned his attention to the problems of the Pacific. Although these islands were small and relatively unimportant,[1] they had some strategic value as a possible American naval base. Moreover, they could serve as a convenient port of call for American steamers en route to Australia and New Zealand.

After the turn of the nineteenth century the Samoan islands were increasingly frequented by whalers who sought supplies or who visited them as a pleasant interlude in their long voyages in both the North and South Pacific. In Europe, after 1840, coconut oil began to be used in the manufacture of both candles and soap, and traders came to the islands for the copra which the natives prepared by merely splitting the coconuts and allowing the contents to dry in the sun. When the oil had been extracted from the dried pulp of the coconut, the residue was used as feed for cattle and the fibre of the coconut palm was found of great value in the making of mats.[2]

The main difficulty that stood in the way of an extensive development of the agricultural resources of the Samoan islands was the fact

---

1. The area of the Samoan islands is approximately as follows: Savaii, 660 square miles; Upolu, 340 square miles; Tutuila, 54 square miles; the Manua group, 25 square miles.

2. *House Ex. Doc., 161,* 44 Cong., 1 sess., no. 3, *Parliamentary Papers, 1860,* vol. 65, Cd. 2753; *Parliamentary Papers, 1876,* vol. 76, Cd. 1589; A. W. Murray, *Missions in Western Polynesia* (London, 1863), p. 466.

that the natives did not take kindly to hard work. Living in Arcadian simplicity, with few wants and with no desire to amass any wealth, the average native was content to live in a primitive fashion which required little labor. Their hours of ease were sometimes enlivened by games which they played with great zest. When English settlers introduced cricket to these sport-loving Samoans the result was ruinous. The whole countryside turned out to play, and sometimes a single match lasted for weeks. It would never do to permit these natives to live lives of such pure pleasure, so cricket playing was finally regulated by law.[3]

It fell to the lot of English missionaries to try to teach the Samoans the Christian ideal of work before pleasure. In 1830 the London Missionary Society began to take an active interest in the Samoan islands, and it was not long before the Bible was translated into the Samoan language and a teachers' seminary was founded at Malua.[4] The rapid spread of Christianity [5] meant that the natives were taught the benefits of European civilization and this led to a demand for English-manufactured goods. It was eminently fitting that the *Missionary Magazine* in 1840 should comment upon the fact that the Gospel not only "opens the way to eternal happiness, but is . . . favourable to the cause of social improvement. Numbers of natives display uncommon eagerness to obtain articles of British manufacture." [6]

The natives were soon led to discard loin cloths in favor of shirts, trousers, stockings, and shoes. Apparently, the Samoan women were not taught the evils of feminine vanity, for Lieutenant Wilkes gives us a colorful portrait of a Samoan belle who attended church apparelled in a "red calico gown, four or five petticoats of different colours, woolen socks, green slippers, cap and bonnet, a large plaid blanket shawl, a pair of polar gloves, the whole surmounted by a flaming red silk umbrella." [7]

3. William B. Churchward, *My Consulate in Samoa* (London, 1887), p. 143.

4. John Williams, *A Narrative of Missionary Enterprises in the South Sea Islands* (London, 1838) , chap. i.

5. W. Ellis, *History of the London Missionary Society* (London, 1844), p. 299, estimates that in 1844 there were 40,000 Christians in Samoa. This figure is undoubtedly a great exaggeration. See A. W. Murray, *Missions in Western Polynesia* (London, 1863).

6. Quoted in Sylvia Masterman, *The Origins of International Rivalry in Samoa, 1845–1884* (London, 1934), p. 42.

7. Charles Wilkes, *Narrative of the United States Exploring Expedition during the years, 1838, 1839, 1840, 1841, 1842* (Phila., 1844), vol. 2, p. 80. The close connection between Christianity and trade was clearly indicated by the British missionary John Williams in his *Narrative of Missionary Enterprises in the South Sea Islands,* chap. xxxii, in which he remarks as follows: "Apart entirely from the value of Christianity, no enlightened *statesman* can regard labours which secure such results . . . with indifference, new havens are found in the Antipodes for our fleets, new channels are opened for our commerce."

In Samoa, Christianity and English commerce thus went hand in hand. The political aspect of British missionary enterprise was revealed in 1844, when the chiefs of the island of Tutuila appealed to the British Government for protection. Although Lord Aberdeen decided that it was not "advisable or politic to accept this offer of cession," he also made it plain that Her Majesty's Government would not view "with indifference the assumption by another Power of a Protectorate" over the Samoan islands.[8]

By the middle of the nineteenth century, British interests in the Samoan islands were far larger than those of any other country, and a secure basis had been laid for further British development. The Foreign Office had little fear of encroachment by rival nations. Moreover, the prevailing anti-imperialistic spirit in England led British statesmen to regard somewhat lightly the alleged benefits of a far-flung colonial empire. In view of this situation it was only natural that the British Government should regard with indifference the early attempts of German traders to gain a foothold in the Samoan islands. As early as 1847 certain ships from Hamburg began calling at the port of Apia, and a decade later the German firm of Johann Cesar Godeffroy & Son, established an agency at that port. Under the able direction of Theodor Weber, who served in a dual role as German consul and as head of the agency of Godeffroy & Son, German influence in Samoa grew apace and gave alarm to British officials in the South Pacific.[9]

New Zealand was the British colony most interested in the fate of the Samoan islands. In November, 1871, both Houses of the New Zealand Parliament petitioned Queen Victoria to annex Samoa, and this was merely the beginning of a stream of memoranda that poured into the British Colonial Office in favor of incorporating these islands into the British Empire. The reaction of Lord Kimberley was negative: "I don't see how we are to interfere unless we are to lay down and enforce the doctrine that no European or American Power is to interfere in any part of the South Pacific but ourselves."[10]

8. Sylvia Masterman, *Origins of International Rivalry in Samoa*, p. 50.
9. For German interests in Samoa see Mary E. Townsend, *The Rise and Fall of Germany's Colonial Empire, 1884–1918* (N. Y. 1930), chaps. iii-iv; *Journal of the House of Representatives, New Zealand, 1874, Appendix, South Sea Papers*, p. 2, *Report* by H. B. Sterndale; *Samoa Weissbuch, 1885*, vol. 1, Teil I, 131-177, vol. 2, Teil II, pp. 95-184; *Verhandlungen des Reichstags, 1885, Anl.* vol. 6, *Aktenstueck, No. 63, 167;* H. S. Cooper, *Coral Lands* (London, 1880), vol. 2, chaps. i-iv; and C. F. G. Cummings, *A Lady's Cruise in a French Man-of-War* (Edinburgh, 1882).
10. Sylvia Masterman, *Origins of International Rivalry in Samoa*, p. 93.

This hands-off attitude on the part of the British Colonial Office was continued during the administration of Lord Carnavon who dampened the acquisitive ardor of New Zealand officials by suggesting that they shoulder a portion of the expenses that had grown out of the annexation of the Fiji islands. The canny New Zealand Government promptly rejected such a suggestion: "To ask for contributions from the Colonies was a novel proceeding." They had no intention of subsidizing any colonial ventures and this very fact made their petitions to the Queen less worthy of serious consideration. The agitation for Samoan annexation became less violent, but it persisted nonetheless, and in part it was aimed at the curtailment of American expansion in Pacific waters.[11]

American interests in the South Pacific were chiefly connected with the whaling industry. According to Alexander Starbuck, "so large a portion of our fishing fleet visited the Pacific that the United States was finally forced . . . to send an exploring expedition to those seas." [12] This first expedition to Samoan waters was commanded by Lieutenant Charles Wilkes who was instructed to explore and survey the Southern Ocean with an eye towards "the important interests of our commerce embarked in the whale-fisheries . . . as well as to determine the existence of all doubtful islands and shoals." [13]

Wilkes arrived in Samoan waters in October, 1839, and spent some two weeks on the island of Tutuila making inquiries and surveying the fine harbor of Pago Pago. On November 4, 1839, he appointed a resident Englishman, John C. Williams, as the acting American consul. He next persuaded certain Samoan chiefs to adopt a code of rules governing the relations between American whalers and the natives of the islands. As a farewell gesture of good will he invited these chiefs on board his flagship, the *Vincennes,* and distributed presents as "tokens of friendship." [14]

11. *Ibid.,* p. 130.
12. Alexander Starbuck, *History of the American Whale Fishery from Its Earliest Inception to the year 1876* (Waltham, Mass., 1878), p. 97; Elmo P. Hohman, *The American Whaleman* (N. Y. 1928), pp. 148ff.
13. Secretary Dickerson to Lieutenant Wilkes, August, 1838, *Letters to Officers of Ships of War,* vol. 25, pp. 404-412, Navy Department MS.
14. Lieutenant Wilkes to Secretary Paulding, November 6, 1853, *Wilkes Exploring Expedition,* vol. 1, no. 53, MS Navy Department Archives. The appointment of Williams as acting consul at Apia was never confirmed by the Department of State. In 1844 and again in 1847 he was commissioned as Commercial Agent for the Navigator's Islands, but he did not relish an appointment below the consular grade and he sent in his resignation on June 16, 1848. His last despatch to the Department of State was in April, 1850, prior

The first American citizen to be regularly appointed as American Commercial Agent in the Samoan islands was V. P. Chapin, who arrived in Apia in June, 1853. He held office only a few months and apparently established a precedent for the brief periods of service that were so characteristic of the American representatives in Samoa.[15] It is obvious that the South Pacific was not regarded as a region of much importance to America, and in January, 1869, the Commercial Agent at Apia complained to the Department of State that no American warship had visited that port in "many years."[16]

It was not until the administration of President Grant that the American Government began to take an active interest in the strategic value of the Samoan islands. As usual, "big business" took the initiative in this matter of colonial enterprise. William H. Webb, of New York City, was a well-known shipbuilder who had long been interested in commercial projects in the Pacific Ocean.[17] In 1870 he began to consider the possibility of establishing a steamship line between San Francisco and Australia. In this regard the importance of the Samoan islands as a coaling station immediately engaged his attention. In 1871 he instructed one of his agents, Captain E. Wakeman, to visit the island of Tutuila and report upon the harbor of Pago Pago. Wakeman promptly carried out this direction and wrote to Mr. Webb that Pago Pago was "the most perfectly land-locked harbor that exists in the Pacific Ocean." He then warned Mr. Webb that the German consul at Apia had strongly urged his government to establish a protectorate over the Samoan islands.[18]

This warning of possible German expansion in the Pacific did not reach the Department of State until May, 1872. In the meantime, the American Commercial Agent at Apia had written to Secretary Fish on

to his departure for England. Inasmuch as he did not accept his appointment as Commercial Agent and did not execute a bond in connection therewith, he was not, technically speaking, an official representative of the United States. See Secretary Calhoun to John C. Williams, November 19, 1844, *Instructions to Consuls*, vol. 11, p. 307; Secretary Buchanan to John C. Williams, May 12, 1847, *Instructions to Consuls*, vol. 11, pp. 567-568, MS Dept. of State.

15. George H. Ryden, *The Foreign Policy of the United States in Relation to Samoa* (New Haven, 1933), chap. ii.

16. Jonas M. Coe to Secretary of State, January 2, 1869, *Apia, Consular Despatches*, vol. 3, MS Dept. of State.

17. For W. H. Webb's own account of his interest in Samoa, see New York *Tribune*, December 6, 1887.

18. Captain E. Wakeman to William H. Webb, Sept. 20, 1871, *House Ex. Doc. 161*, 44 Cong., 1 sess., pp. 7-10.

August 30, 1871, and recounted a recent conversation with the German consul. This official had informed him that it was the intention of the German Government "to lay claim to this Group of Islands for the purpose of having a naval station in the Pacific Ocean." [19] Secretary Fish promptly instructed George Bancroft, at Berlin, to inquire at the Foreign Office as to German intentions in the South Pacific.[20] Bancroft replied that Germany had no desire to acquire the Samoan islands,[21] but this assurance failed to quiet the apprehensions of Secretary Fish who again instructed him to make further inquiries about German colonial policy.[22] In March, and in July, 1871, Bancroft sent to the Department of State emphatic denials from the German Government with reference to alleged designs upon Samoa.[23]

These repeated assurances from the German Government were not entirely convincing to Secretary Fish because he had received intimations from many quarters that Germany had ambitious colonial aspirations which she was trying to realize. On August 22, 1871, the American consul at Santo Domingo City sent a despatch to the Department of State which warned of German plans to secure Samaná Bay.[24] Some weeks later the Department of State heard rumors of German attempts to purchase the island of Curaçao.[25] Although Minister Bancroft sent strong denials of these stories of alleged German efforts to acquire naval bases,[26] Secretary Fish still harbored some suspicions of German colonial policy, and this tradition lingered in the minds of State Department officials for many years. It is probably this fact that accounts for the approval, by both the Department of State and the Navy Department, of the action of Commander Meade in

19. Jonas M. Coe to Second Assistant Secretary of State, August 30, 1871, *Apia, Consular Despatches*, vol. 3, MS Dept. of State.

20. Secretary Fish to George Bancroft, October 30, 1871, *Prussia, Instructions*, vol. 15, MS Dept. of State.

21. Bancroft to Secretary Fish, November 29, 1871, December 4, 1871, *Germany, Despatches*, vol. 1, MS Dept. of State.

22. Secretary Fish to George Bancroft, January 8, 1872, *Prussia, Instructions*, vol. 15, MS Dept. of State.

23. Bancroft to Secretary Fish, March 4, 1872, July 29, 1872, *Germany, Despatches*, vol. 1, MS Dept. of State.

24. Fisher Ames to Secretary Fish, August 22, 1871, *Santo Domingo City, Consular Despatches*, vol. 7, MS Dept. of State.

25. Secretary Fish to George Bancroft, November 25, 1871, *Prussia, Instructions*, vol. 15, MS Dept. of State.

26. Bancroft to Secretary Fish, January 5, 1872, *Germany, Despatches*, vol. 1, MS Dept. of State.

signing an agreement on February 17, 1872, with Mauga, the leading chief on the island of Tutuila.

Under the terms of this agreement the United States was given the "exclusive privilege of establishing in the said harbor of Pago Pago . . . a naval station." In return for this concession, the chief and "his people" were to have "the friendship and protection of the great Government of the United States of America." [27]

The impulse behind this action of Commander Meade was supplied by Henry A. Peirce, the American Minister at Honolulu. In a letter to Meade, January 19, 1872, Peirce stressed the importance of placing the Samoan islands under American control, and he assured the Commander that a treaty granting to American citizens "all proper rights and privileges" would "no doubt receive the approval of our Government." [28] This prediction was entirely correct. On May 22, 1872, President Grant sent the agreement between Commander Meade and Chief Mauga to the Senate with a recommendation for its approval on condition that there would be inserted "some modification of the obligation of protection which the agreement imports." [29]

It is evident that President Grant and Secretary Fish were interested in this Meade agreement as a means of promoting American commercial interests in the Pacific, and they had particularly in mind the importance of the harbor of Pago Pago as a port of call for the newly established steamship line of Mr. William H. Webb. The Senate, however, never took any formal action on the agreement between Commander Meade and Chief Mauga, and the exclusive privileges that it conferred upon the United States were thus allowed to lapse. But Mr. Webb still had hopes that the American Government would extend its protection over the Samoan islands. In order to prepare the way for such an event, he persuaded President Grant to appoint Colonel A. B. Steinberger as special commissioner to Samoa with instructions to gather "full and accurate information in regard to the islands." [30]

Colonel Steinberger arrived in Apia on August 14, 1873, and soon won the confidence of the natives. They assumed that he was visiting the islands in response to a petition to the American Government that

27. *House Ex. Doc., 161,* 44 Cong., 1 sess., pp. 6-7.
28. Peirce to Commander Meade, January 19, 1872, enclosed in Peirce to Secretary Fish, January 22, 1872, *Hawaii, Despatches,* vol. 14, MS Dept. of State.
29. *House Ex. Doc., 161,* 44 Cong., 1 sess., pp. 6-7.
30. Secretary Fish to A. B. Steinberger, March 29, 1873, *House Ex. Doc., 161,* 44 Cong., 1 sess., pp. 5 ff.

had been drawn up by the "high chief and rulers" of Samoa in April, 1872, praying that the "protection of the United States of America be extended to this group of islands." At a conference with some Samoan chiefs on August 24, Colonel Steinberger was presented with the Samoan "staff" and "fly-flap." This ceremony, whereby the emblems of Samoan nationality were transferred to the American agent, was a clear indication of the continued desire of the natives for American protection.[31]

Although Colonel Steinberger had no authority to accept in any formal sense this transfer of Samoan sovereignty to the American Government, he did inform the natives that he would present their petition to the President and that he would carry their hopes and their prayers in his "mind and heart."[32] In December, 1873, he was back in San Francisco, and in March of the following year, he was once more in touch with Secretary Fish on Samoan matters. Fish, however, was opposed to a policy of Samoan annexation. He was quick to recognize the commercial and strategic importance of Samoa as far as American interests were concerned, but he was certain that American public opinion was not in favor of such distant colonial acquisitions. The most he was willing to do was to permit Steinberger to return to Samoa as a special agent with assurances to the natives of the "lively interest" of the American Government in "their happiness and welfare."[33]

Colonel Steinberger arrived in Apia on April 1, 1875, and immediately assumed powers that had not been granted to him in his instructions from Secretary Fish. On January 2, 1875, the Samoan chiefs had elected two kings, Malietoa Laupepa and Pulepule. Colonel Steinberger quickly persuaded them to abandon this awkward political arrangement in favor of one king who was to be Malietoa Laupepa. A new constitution was then adopted with a provision for a legislative branch of two houses, the Taimua and the Faipule. There was also to be a Prime Minister, and this office was offered to Colonel Steinberger who promptly accepted it.[34]

This assumption of power by Colonel Steinberger brought him into

31. The *Report* of Colonel Steinberger to Secretary Fish may be found in *Senate Ex. Doc. 45*, 43 Cong., 1 sess., pp. 1-58, and in the *Steinberger Papers, Special Agents*, vols. 28-29, MS Dept. of State.

32. *Steinberger Report, Senate Ex. Doc., 45*, 43 Cong., 1 sess., enclosure C 2.

33. Secretary Fish to A. B. Steinberger, December 11, 1874, *House Ex Doc., 161*, 44 Cong., 1 sess., encl. 17, p. 76.

34. *Report* by George H. Bates, December 10, 1886, *Special Agents*, vol. 33. MS Dept. of State.

sharp conflict with the American consul at Apia, S. S. Foster, who wrote several letters of complaint to Secretary Fish. He suspected that Steinberger had exceeded his instructions, and, without waiting for confirmation from the Department of State, he decided to take the offensive. In December, 1875, he seized Steinberger's yacht and then entered into concert with the acting British consul, S. F. Williams, to make things uncomfortable for the American special agent. King Malietoa was persuaded to come on board the British warship *Barracouta,* and there under the pressure of Captain Stevens and Dr. Turner, of the London Missionary Society, he reluctantly requested the arrest of Steinberger. On the morning of February 8, 1876, Captain Stevens, accompanied by the American consul (Foster), arrested Steinberger and imprisoned him on the *Barracouta.* The Samoan natives were so enraged by the perfidy of Malietoa that they forced him to resign, and when Captain Stevens attempted to re-instate him in power, a fight ensued during which three British citizens were mortally wounded. Steinberger, along with Jonas M. Coe (former American Commercial Agent at Apia), was then taken by force to the Fiji islands. After his release he went to London to press charges against Captain Stevens who was dismissed from the British Navy.[35]

The State Department had no intention of re-instating Colonel Steinberger, who was permitted to drift into obscurity. Foster, however, was removed as American consul at Apia, and Gilderoy W. Griffin took over that office. Griffin soon evinced a warm sympathy for the Steinberger regime which had looked towards an American protectorate over the Samoan islands. After staying at Apia only a few weeks (September 28–November 13, 1876) he decided to return to the United States as an "unofficial agent" of certain Samoan chiefs who were anxious to negotiate a formal treaty with the United States.[36]

On February 10, 1877, James G. Colmesnil arrived at Apia as the American vice-consul.[37] He was not long in discovering that Mr. Liardet, the British consul at Apia, had plans for Samoan annexation to Great Britain. In order to forestall the intrigues of Liardet, Colmesnil

35. *House Ex. Doc. 44,* 44 Cong., 2 sess.; *House Ex. Doc. 161,* 44 Cong., 1 sess.; J. A. Campbell to S. S. Foster, January 12, 1876, *Instructions to Consuls,* vol. 81, MS Dept. of State. See also the *Steinberger Papers, Special Agents,* vols. 28-29, MS Dept. of State.

36. Griffin to Secretary Fish, Washington, February 17, 1877, *Apia, Consular Despatches,* vol. 5, MS Dept. of State.

37. In view of the fact that Colmesnil did not file a bond in accordance with official regulations, he was never recognized by the Department of State as a regular vice-consul.

permitted the Samoan chiefs of the so-called Parliamentary Party to hoist the American flag over their own.[38] This flag-raising episode apparently had the approval of Theodor Weber, the German consul at Apia, who was just as fearful as Colmesnil with reference to British intrigue.[39]

This strong suspicion of British policy in the Samoan islands was shared by Mr. Griffin, who returned to Apia on July 26, 1877, as the American consul. Although he had failed in his efforts to negotiate a treaty between the United States and Samoa, he had been able to induce the Department of State to abandon its attitude of absolute non-interference in Samoan affairs. He was now authorized to co-operate with the Samoan chiefs in order to bring about a stable government.[40]

In carrying out this instruction, Griffin preferred to deal with the Samoans alone and he did not consult with either the German or the English consul at Apia. This policy was very galling to Mr. Liardet, the British consul, who went so far as to encourage a band of ruffians to attack the American consulate. Had it not been for the timely arrival of the French warship, *Le Signelay*, it is very possible that serious injury might have been inflicted upon Mr. Griffin.[41] On another occasion, Mr. Liardet showed his ill will by ordering the arrest of the United States marshal and deputy marshal.[42]

The British Government apologized for the excessive belligerence of its consul at Apia, and gave assurances that Mr. Liardet would be called home to explain his conduct.[43] Sir Arthur H. Gordon, British High Commissioner for the Western Pacific, was sent to Samoa to investigate conditions in the islands, and he also had difficulties with Mr. Griffin.[44] Both Sir Arthur and Theodor Weber, the German consul, endeavored to induce Griffin to join with them in working out a co-

38. Colmesnil to Third Assistant Secretary of State, May 25, 1877, *Apia, Consular Despatches*, vol. 5, MS Dept. of State.
39. *House Ex. Doc. 238*, 50 Cong., 1 sess., p. 198.
40. J. A. Campbell, Third Asst. Secretary of State, to Griffin, July 5, 1877, *Despatches to Consuls*, vol. 86, MS Dept. of State.
41. Griffin to Secretary Evarts, September 29, 1877, *Apia, Consular Despatches*, vol. 5, MS Dept. of State.
42. Griffin to Secretary Evarts, September 14, 1877, *Apia, Consular Despatches*, vol. 5, MS Dept. of State.
43. John Welsh to Secretary Evarts, March 7, 1878, *Great Britain, Despatches*, vol. 133; Secretary Evarts to John Welsh, March 26, 1878, *Great Britain, Instructions*, vol. 25, MS Dept. of State.
44. Mr. Liardet, the British consul, died immediately after the arrival of Sir Arthur Gordon.

operative plan for administering affairs in Samoa, but the American consul resolutely refused to do so. Sir Arthur then exerted strong pressure upon the Samoan chiefs at Apia in order to force them to pay certain dubious financial claims of British citizens, and when compliance was not immediately promised, he seized the Samoan warship *Mulinuu*.[45]

Finally, Sir Arthur's patience was exhausted by Samoan procrastination and he gave the government at Apia until four o'clock on the afternoon of February 23 to accept his terms. On the previous afternoon (February 22), in order to avoid open hostilities, Griffin hoisted the Stars and Stripes over the Samoan flag and sent a note to Sir Arthur, asking him to surrender the *Mulinuu*. Sir Arthur flatly refused to accede to this request, and without more ado, sailed for the Fiji islands. This incident was not closed, however. On March 12, A. P. Maudslay, the new British consul and Deputy Commissioner for the Western Pacific, arrived in Apia, and once more there was a harrowing scene of British bullying. Maudslay demanded the immediate payment of $1,000 as an indemnity for the British sailors who had been killed when Captain Stevens had attempted to reinstate King Malietoa. He also insisted that the Samoan Government surrender all claim to the *Mulinuu* which had been taken to the Fiji islands.

Faced with a threat of bombardment, the Samoan Government at Apia complied with these British demands.[46] Griffin, somewhat discomfited, sent to Washington a full report of the incident. The Department of State would take no action until the matter had been thoroughly investigated. With this end in view, Thomas M. Dawson was sent out to succeed Griffin as consul at Apia, and Gustavus Goward was commissioned to accompany the Samoan Secretary of State, Le Mamea, back to the islands in order to carry out the terms of the recent treaty that had been negotiated with the Samoan Government.[47]

The advantages that the United States derived from the treaty of January 17, 1878, were not far-reaching. In the Meade agreement of 1872 the American Government was given the exclusive right to establish a naval base in Pago Pago harbor. In this new treaty of 1878 it was

45. Griffin to William Hunter, Second Asst. Secretary of State, February 26, 1878, *Apia, Consular Despatches*, vol. 5, MS Dept. of State.

46. Griffin to Third Asst. Secretary of State, March 21, 1878, *Apia, Consular Despatches*, vol. 5, MS Dept. of State.

47. William Hunter to Griffin, June 8, 1878, *Despatches to Consuls*, vol. 89, MS Dept. of State.

specifically provided that an American naval station could be established in Pago Pago harbor, but there was nothing exclusive about this concession. After the American agents had selected their site for naval purposes, the British Government could have their agents select a site in another part of the harbor. In return for this somewhat dubious concession, the American Government promised to "employ its good offices" in the event that disputes should arise between the Samoan Government and other powers.[48]

The conclusion of the Samoan-American treaty of January, 1878, spurred the German consul to renewed activity with reference to a treaty with the Samoan chiefs that would protect German interests. When the Samoan Parliamentary Party evinced little desire to meet the wishes of the consul, he authorized the German warships stationed at Apia to seize the harbors of Saluafata and Falealii until German demands had been satisfied. Under the impact of this pressure, the Samoan Government finally yielded, and a treaty was signed on January 24, 1879.[49] This convention guaranteed to German citizens the "peaceable possession of all lands in Samoa which they have hitherto bought from Samoans in a regular manner." It also provided that German citizens should not be required to pay any tonnage duties, and it granted to the German Government the exclusive use of the harbor of Saluafata as a naval base.[50]

The signature of this German-Samoan treaty indicated the weakness of the Samoan Parliamentary Party. Ever since the deposition of Malietoa Laupepa in February, 1876, the Samoan Parliament (the Taimua and the Faipule) had ruled without any king. Its power was now fast waning, and on May 3, 1879, Malietoa Talavou, the uncle of the deposed Malietoa Laupepa, was brought to Apia by the Puletua, or Royal Party, and was crowned king. But this political change was not accepted by the Parliamentary Party, and civil war soon broke out.[51]

48. William M. Malloy, *Treaties, Conventions,* etc., vol. 2, pp. 1574-1576.

49. Dawson to William Hunter, January 23, 25, 1879, *Apia, Consular Despatches,* vol. 6, MS Dept. of State.

50. *House Ex. Doc. 238,* 50 Cong. 1 sess., pp. 126-129. With reference to the provisions of the German-Samoan treaty, see the remarks of Consul Theodor Weber, *Verhandlungen des Reichstags, 1879,* vol. 6, *Anl. 239,* p. 187.

51. Dawson to Charles Bayson, Third Assistant Secretary of State, September 30, 1878, *Apia, Consular Despatches,* vol. 7, MS Dept. of State. One of the most important acts of the new Samoan Government was the signature on August 28, 1879, of a treaty with Great Britain. In the second article of this Anglo-Samoan treaty the Samoan Government promised not to grant to any other "state any rights, privileges, authority, or predominance in Samoa in excess of such as are or may be accorded to Her Britannic Majesty."

Before hostilities occurred, the foreign consuls in Samoa signed a general convention which provided for the neutralization of the district of Apia. The government of the municipality was placed in the hands of a board consisting of the consuls of those powers which had treaty relations with Samoa. The board was empowered to make and enforce regulations concerning peace, public works, sanitation, and taxation. Although it was expressly provided that this convention should in no way affect the territorial integrity of Samoa, it was obvious that the actual control of the islands would inevitably pass into the hands of the representatives of the United States, Germany, and Great Britain.[52]

This fact of tripartite control in Samoa was clearly indicated by the steps taken to put down the revolution which the Parliamentary Party led against the rule of Malietoa Talavou. During the course of this civil war the neutrality of the municipality of Apia was violated by the rebels. The consular government promptly used force to compel the observance of their regulations, and on December 15, 1879, the representatives of both Samoan factions met on board the German warship *Bismarck* and signed a treaty of peace. According to this instrument, war was to be outlawed in Samoa and arbitration would always be resorted to by the contending parties. Provision was then made for a meeting of a council of chiefs for the purpose of establishing a stable government. At this meeting (December 23) sixteen chiefs, representing all the islands of Samoa, agreed upon a constitution which re-established the Samoan Parliament. Malietoa Talavou was recognized as king, but inasmuch as he was old and infirm, Malietoa Laupepa (his nephew) was appointed as regent and was empowered to carry on the duties of the kingship.[53]

The independence of Samoa was now largely a fiction, and on March 24, 1880, the three consuls signed an agreement which enlarged the tripartite government of the municipality of Apia into a tripartite government for all the Samoan islands.[54] But this political arrangement was none too satisfactory. On November 8, 1880, Malietoa Talavou

---

Great Britain was also given the right to establish a naval base in the harbor of Pago Pago after the American Government had selected a site in the same harbor. Unlike the American and German treaties, the British treaty provided that in all cases, civil or criminal, where British subjects were defendants against Samoan plaintiffs, they should be tried in a British court without any representative of the Samoan Government sitting as an associate judge. See *House Ex. Doc. 238*, 50 Cong., 1 sess., pp. 130-131.

52. *House Ex. Doc. 238*, 50 Cong. 1 sess., pp. 132-134.
53. *Ibid.*, pp. 202-206.
54. *Ibid.*, pp. 207-208.

died, and the question arose as to his successor. There was strong opposition to the elevation of his nephew, Malietoa Laupepa, to the kingship, but with the support of the American and British consuls he was formally installed as the ruler of Samoa on March 19, 1881.

This action was not approved by Captain Zembsch, the German consul-general, who had grown fearful that American influence was growing too strong in the Malietoa government. He began to favor a form of dual government in Samoa with greatly enlarged powers for the party of opposition. Shortly after Malietoa had been crowned king, the opponents of his regime had a conference at which they bestowed a crown upon Tamasese, another Samoan chief.[55] It was obvious to the American and British consuls that civil war in Samoa would result from this political tangle, so they made arrangements with the contending parties in Samoa to meet on board the American warship *Lackawanna* and endeavor to settle all difficulties. After several conferences, a convention was signed on July 12, 1881, which was known as the "Lackawanna agreement." According to its provisions, Malietoa Laupepa was recognized as king, and Tamasese was appointed vice-king. The length of the reign of the king was left to "the determination of the Government."[56] In February, 1883, this article of the agreement was invoked, and Malietoa Laupepa was appointed king for seven more years. At the expiration of this period a new king might be chosen.[57]

On September 2, 1883, the consular convention for the tripartite administration of the district of Apia expired,[58] and the American Government instructed Mr. Canisius (the American consul at Apia) to continue to participate in the consular conferences that had been periodically held since September, 1879. It was apparent that this tripartite administration had accomplished a great deal, and it was the desire of the Department of State that it be continued until some other arrangement could be made.[59] The Department of State also recog-

55. Dawson to Chas. Payson, Third Asst. Secretary of State, April 29, 1881, *Apia, Consular Despatches*, vol. 9, MS Dept. of State.

56. Dawson to Chas. Payson, July 12, 16, 1881, *Apia, Consular Despatches*, vol. 10, MS Dept. of State. Also, *House Ex. Doc. 238*, 50 Cong., 1 sess., pp. 208-209.

57. Theodore Canisius to Alvey A. Adee, February 15, 1883, *Apia, Consular Despatches*, vol. 11, MS Dept. of State.

58. This convention had been signed by the American, the British, and the German consuls at Apia, September 2, 1879. It was never formally approved by the Dept. of State.

59. Before the creation of this consular council for the administration of the district of Apia, the situation in Samoa had been so bad that Apia itself was known as the "Hell of the Pacific." Under the consular administration this state of affairs was quickly remedied, and Apia emerged "into a well-ordered district . . . where property and persons

nized Malietoa Laupepa as *de jure* king, and it clearly indicated that while it would not sanction the use of American military force to sustain him in that position, it would not object if other powers should see fit to employ their armed strength for that purpose.[60]

The attitude of the American Government towards attempts at the annexation of Samoa by foreign powers was unmistakably shown in the fall of 1883. In September of that year, John Lundon, a former member of the New Zealand Parliament, came to Apia and began to work in favor of a program which aimed at the incorporation of Samoa into the British Empire. Thanks to his efforts, King Malietoa sent a petition to Queen Victoria (November 19, 1883) praying for annexation. Lord Derby, realizing that the time was not ripe for annexation projects, refused to answer this petition, and the whole matter was dropped.[61] But before the British Government had taken any action, the American consul at Apia had gotten wind of the affair and had placed the matter before the Department of State at Washington.[62] The answer of John Davis, the Assistant Secretary of State, was terse and clear: "This Government would object to the destruction of the independent existence of any insular community to which we are bound by treaty." [63]

As the fear of Samoan annexation to New Zealand faded away, new apprehensions arose in American minds with reference to German policy in the South Pacific. In 1884 Bismarck was finally ready to give strong support to plans for German colonial expansion, and this radical change in his attitude towards far-reaching projects in distant seas came as a challenge to America. In the years immediately after 1870, Bismarck had shown little interest in economic imperialism, and he had likened German colonies to the silken sables worn by Polish noblemen who had no shirts underneath.[64] In making such a statement Bismarck was simply expressing the anti-imperialistic sentiment commonly held in Europe in the decades just preceding the Franco-Prussian War. In

---

were as safe as they would be anywhere in England." William B. Churchward, *My Consulate in Samoa*, pp. 71-75. John Davis, Acting Secretary of State, to Canisius, August 16, 1883, *Instructions to Consuls*, vol. 108, MS Dept. of State.

60. Secretary Frelinghuysen to Canisius, October 23, 1883, *Instructions to Consuls*, vol. 108, MS Dept. of State.

61. Sylvia Masterman, *Origins of International Rivalry in Samoa*, pp. 174-179.

62. Canisius to Alvey A. Adee, October 28, 1883, *Apia, Consular Despatches*, vol. 12, MS Dept. of State.

63. John Davis to Canisius, December 12, 1883, *Instructions to Consuls*, vol. 109, MS Dept. of State.

64. Moritz Busch, *Bismarck, Some Secret Pages of His History* (N. Y., 1898), vol. 1, p. 552.

England, statesmen like Disraeli and Lord Granville were sharply hostile to colonial dominion, and publicists like George Cornewall Lewis, Goldwin Smith, and Viscount Bury were openly contemptuous of the benefits that were supposed to flow from territories scattered over the seven seas.[65] Men in high office in France shared this same view as to the doubtful value of colonies; their vision was fixed on the lost provinces of Alsace-Lorraine rather than on new lands far away.[66]

After 1870, however, a new economic gospel began to be preached in Europe, and its converts soon included many of those who held the seats of the mighty in England, France, and in Germany. International free trade was abandoned in favor of a policy of protection which was deeply colored by the excessive nationalism of the later decades of the nineteenth century. As the continental nations became more industrialized, the pressure for higher tariffs increased, and a demand arose for colonies that would serve not only as outlets for surplus production but would also produce the essential raw materials necessary for modern manufactures.

In Germany the system of economic nationalism can be traced back to Friedrich List, whose *National System of Political Economy* was published in 1841. Historians like Treitschke and Droysen helped to popularize the views of List, and the rapid expansion of German industry and commerce after 1870 gave strong emphasis to the need of a new national economy. The dynamics of German economic imperialism have been lucidly summarized by Dr. Townsend as follows:

An enchanted national consciousness expressed by Germans both at home and abroad; a swollen purse requiring objects for expenditure, and then a depleted purse in need of large dividends regardless of risk; an abnormally inflated production demanding outlet markets; mushroom industries clamoring for raw materials; an overstocked labor market using emigration as a safety-valve; and finally an ever growing navy promising protection to oversea ventures and investments. Assuredly, such influence would seem to have produced a mental atmosphere most propitious for the growth of any idea of colonialism.[67]

65. R. L. Schuyler, "The Climax of Anti-Imperialism in England," *Political Science Quarterly*, December, 1921, pp. 538ff; C. A. Bodelsen, *Studies in Mid-Victorian Imperialism* (London, 1924); W. F. Monypenny and G. E. Buckle, *The Life of Benjamin Disraeli* (London, 1913–1920), vol. 4, p. 467.

66. Stephen H. Roberts, *History of French Colonial Policy* (London, 1929), vol. 1, pp. 11ff.

67. Mary T. Townsend, *Origins of Modern German Colonialism* (N. Y. 1921), pp. 16-17. See also, Maximilian von Hagen, *Bismarcks Kolonialpolitik* (Stuttgart, 1923), pp. 1-41; P. Decharme, *Compagnies et societies coloniales Allemandes* (Paris, 1903), pp. 24-40.

In the years that immediately followed the founding of the German Empire, Bismarck was opposed to the acquisition of colonies, but in 1876 he confided to the German merchant Lüderitz that "a great nation like Germany could not, in the end, do without colonies." [68] It was evident that the Iron Chancellor was taking more interest in the colonial problem. An important manifestation of this change of attitude was his decision in 1877 to station permanently in the South Pacific two warships for the protection of German trade in that region. Buelow, in explaining this decision to the French Ambassador in Berlin, said that this step was dictated by the necessity of "defending the interests of the merchants of Hamburg, installed in Samoa, against the adventurers from California." [69] Some months later, Buelow again spoke to the French Ambassador about the "firm intention" of the German Government to afford an effective protection to German merchants in Samoa against "American adventurers bearing the titles of colonels or generals." [70]

This act of stationing warships in the South Pacific was followed by a burst of activity in treaty-making. In 1878 German agents negotiated treaties with the inhabitants of the Marshall, the Gilbert, and the Duke of York islands, and on the island of New Britain they secured claims to the harbors of Mioko and Makada.[71] In order to safeguard these new interests the German Government now appointed an Imperial consul-general for the South Seas.

British officials in this region took alarm at this change of attitude on the part of Bismarck, and Buelow endeavored to allay their fears by declaring in the Reichstag that Germany "wants neither to found colonies nor to have a monopoly." She desired merely to have "equal rights for navigation and trade." [72] But there was little doubt that the German Government itself was deeply interested in this question of "trade" in the South Pacific. In 1879 the failure of the trading firm of Godeffroy

68. Maximilian von Hagen, *Bismarcks Kolonialpolitik*, p. 52; Helmuth Rogge, "Bismarcks Kolonialpolitik als aussenpolitisches Problem," *Historische Vierteljahrschrift*, vol. 21, pp. 304-333, 423-443.
69. M. de Sainte Vallier à M. de Waddington, November 21, 1878, *Documents Diplomatiques Français, 1871–1914*, first series, vol. 2, No. 362, p. 402.
70. M. de Sainte Vallier à M. de Waddington, May 5, 1879, *ibid.*, No. 418, p. 487. This reference to "colonels or generals" from America, was evidently a criticism of the activities of Colonel Steinberger.
71. Sylvia Masterman, *Origins of International Rivalry in Samoa*, pp. 157-158.
72. Max von Koschitzky, *Deutsche Kolonialgeschichte*, (Leipzig, 1887–1888), vol. 2, p. 13.

& Son led Bismarck to come out strongly in favor of a government subsidy for this pioneer trading house. Although his "Samoa Bill" was defeated in the Reichstag on April 28, 1880, this was merely a temporary setback.[73] In Germany the tide of sentiment in favor of colonial expansion was rapidly rising, and Bismarck began to push with increasing vigor a program of imperialism.

German acquisition of portions of southwest Africa led to a controversy with Great Britain in which Bismarck sharply complained of the attempt on the part of the British Government to proclaim a Monroe Doctrine for that continent.[74] With reference to the islands in the South Pacific (Samoa), Lord Granville assured Herbert Bismarck that he knew of "no impediment to our coming to a perfect understanding." [75] Some months later, however, Bismarck complained to Count Münster that information had been received from Samoa which indicated that British agents were stirring up trouble between the natives and German residents.[76] Whatever truth there may have been in this charge it is difficult to say, but it is certain that the British officials in the South Pacific were constantly pushing their plans for extensive annexations. To Lord Derby, the colonial secretary, these ambitious schemes of the Australians and the New Zealanders seemed so fantastic that he asked them whether they did not want "another planet all to themselves." [77]

Weary of trying to come to some agreement with Great Britain on colonial questions, Bismarck turned to France in the fall of 1884, and the Ferry Ministry was not averse to a concert with Germany. The Anglo-French entente had broken down in 1882, after the English occupied Egypt in 1882, and for the next twenty years "a fierce antagonism replaced the former cordiality." [78] During the autumn of 1884 and the spring of 1885, Bismarck and Jules Ferry worked together in order to curb British pretensions in Africa,[79] but Ferry was driven from power in March, 1885, and the Iron Chancellor was anxious to restore

73. Mary T. Townsend, *op. cit.*, pp. 113ff.
74. Bismarck to Count Münster, May 5, 1884, *Die Grosse Politik der Europäischen Kabinette, 1871–1914*, vol. 4 (Berlin, 1922), pp. 50-52; Bismarck to Count Münster, June 1, 1884, *Grosse Politik*, vol. 4, pp. 60-61.
75. Lord Granville to Herbert Bismarck, August 20, 1884, *Grosse Politik*, vol. 4, p. 80.
76. Prince Bismarck to Count Münster, December 5, 1884, *Grosse Politik*, vol. 4, p. 92.
77. Lord Derby to Sir Henry Ponsonby, June 29, 1883, *Letters of Queen Victoria*, second series, vol. 3 (London, 1928), p. 432.
78. William L. Langer, *European Alliances and Alignments, 1871–1890* (N. Y. 1931), p. 282.
79. Robert H. Wienefeld, *Franco-German Relations, 1878–1885* (Baltimore, 1929), pp. 137-153.

friendly feelings with the British Government. Even before the fall of Ferry, Bismarck had sent his son Herbert to London as an ambassador of good will, and the tottering Gladstone Ministry welcomed these advances.

On February 5 London was shocked at the news of the fall of Khartoum (January 26, 1885), and the tragic death of that romantic figure, "Chinese Gordon." In the British press Gladstone was sharply censured for his delay in sending a relief expedition to the Sudan, and his popularity vanished overnight. But the disaster at Khartoum was not the only alarming news that caused deep concern to the Gladstone Ministry. On March 30, 1885, Russian troops defeated an Afghan force at Panjdeh, on the Afghan frontier, and British statesmen were now faced with the prospect of a Russian advance upon India. It was high time to come to an understanding with Bismarck.[80]

On March 7, 1885, Count Herbert Bismarck reported from London that Lord Granville was quite conciliatory. With Sir Charles Dilke, Herbert Bismarck had a very pleasant conversation, and Dilke was in favor of important concessions to Germany. With reference to the South Sea Islands (including Samoa), Dilke remarked: "This is the widest field for German colonization, and I shall use all my influence to secure all possible freedom for you. The claims put forward by our Colonies are utterly unreasonable, and we shall pay no attention to them." [81]

The Gladstone Cabinet fell on June 8, 1885, and Lord Salisbury was asked to form a new Conservative Ministry. One of his first acts after assuming office was to assure Count Münster that it was a leading principle of the Conservative Party to maintain a "good understanding with Germany": a friendly relationship such as existed "in the era of Lord Beaconsfield." [82] These assurances of good will were followed by a political concert that had a definite bearing upon the Samoan Question, and without this background of diplomatic bargaining it would be difficult to understand all the implications of the problems that Secretary Bayard faced in dealing with the problems of the Pacific.

80. Lord Edmond Fitzmaurice, *The Life of Lord Granville*, vol. 2, pp. 421ff; Stephen Gwynn and Gertrude M. Tuckwell, *The Life of the Rt. Hon. Sir Charles Dilke* (N. Y. 1917), vol. 2, pp. 111ff; Lord Newton, *Life of Lord Lyons* (N. Y. 1913), vol. 2, p. 349.

81. Count Bismarck to Prince Bismarck, March 7, 1885, *Grosse Politik*, vol. 4, p. 104; *German Diplomatic Documents, 1871–1914* (ed. by E. T. S. Dugdale, London, 1928), vol. 1, p. 192.

82. Count Münster to German Foreign Office, June 26, 1885, *Grosse Politik*, vol. 4, p. 131.

CHAPTER TWO

Bayard Versus Bismarck

······⟨∞⟩······

WHEN BISMARCK DECIDED IN 1884 TO LEND HIS SUPPORT TO AN AMBITIOUS colonial program he had no idea that he was thereby helping to pave the way for serious German-American friction which would eventually lead to open war between the two countries. After securing from the British Government assurances that no attempt would be made to gain control over the Samoan islands,[1] Bismarck began to toy with the idea of annexing these islands to the German Empire. From London he received intimations that the British Foreign Office would not seriously object to such a solution of the Samoan difficulty, but from Washington the news came that the American Government would not agree to any plans for transferring the islands to Germany.[2] German colonial expansion would have to wait upon favorable word from the Department of State, and it was not very likely that this would be forthcoming during the administration of Secretary Bayard. Imperialism began to beckon to America as well as to Germany.

In the very month that Bayard assumed office as Secretary of State, John Fiske, noted American historian and philosopher, brought out an essay entitled "Manifest Destiny." After indicating the upward surge of Anglo-Saxon peoples toward world leadership, Fiske prophesied that the time would come when "every land on the earth's surface that is not already the seat of an old civilization shall become English in its language, in its religion, and its political habits and traditions, and to a predominant extent in the blood of its people."[3]

1. For the Anglo-German correspondence concerning Samoa, see *Parliamentary Papers*, vol. 54, 1884–1885, February, 1885, serial no. 57, Cd. 4273.

2. Count Otto zu Stolberg-Wernigerode, *Germany and the United States of America During the Era of Bismarck* (Phila., 1937), pp. 237-238.

3. *Harper's New Monthly Magazine*, March, 1885, vol. 70, pp. 578-590. Fiske was a

The prophecies of John Fiske were given strong support in the writings of the Rev. Josiah Strong who went so far as to assert that the individual Anglo-Saxon was "divinely commissioned to be, in a peculiar sense, his brother's keeper." There was little doubt in Mr. Strong's mind that the American branch of the Anglo-Saxon race would "move down upon Mexico, down upon Central and South America, out upon the islands of the sea, over upon Africa and beyond. And can any one doubt that the result of this competition of races will be the 'survival of the fittest'?" [4]

While philosophers and theologians were endeavoring to build a broad basis for American imperialism, an able American diplomat at Berlin was writing to Secretary Bayard in favor of a policy of immediate expansion. John A. Kasson had watched with great interest the development of a colonial program in Germany, and he was afraid that if America did not follow in the footsteps of Bismarck, the day would soon come when we would deeply mourn over our lost opportunities. On April 13, 1885, he wrote to Secretary Bayard to express his sorrow "that the blindness, weakness, and timidity of a long-continuing so-called American policy has made our flag on the Pacific Ocean insignificant, and has led foreign nations to ask for our views . . . *after the fait accompli,* instead of before it. . . . The system of Protectorate, as now understood, if adopted by us for such islands as Samoa . . . is well adapted to our situation, and would be of special advantage to the beneficiaries of it." [5]

Some weeks later Kasson sent another despatch to Secretary Bayard in which he deprecated American indifference to colonial dominion. He also sounded an alarm against German designs in Samoa, and he emphasized the importance of keeping a close watch upon the encroachments of German agents in the South Pacific:

Germany, almost unknown in Asia twenty years ago, is now a great moral power there, of which the oldest Asiatic nations stand in awe. . . . At that date unknown in the Pacific ocean, she is now the proprietor of islands and

---

close student of the theories of Charles Darwin, who had paid high tribute to the outstanding qualities of the American people. See Charles Darwin, *The Descent of Man, and Selection in Relation to Sex* (London, 1871, 2 vols.), vol. 1, p. 179.

4. Josiah Strong, *Our Country: Its Possible Future and Its Present Crisis* (N. Y. 1885), pp. 208-227. It is important to note that this volume by Josiah Strong had a circulation of more than 170,000 copies. See Julius W. Pratt, *Expansionists of 1898* (Baltimore, 1936), p. 19.

5. John A. Kasson to Secretary Bayard, April 13, 1885, *Germany, Despatches,* vol. 38, MS Dept. of State.

harbors there for the founding of colonies and for the extension of her commerce. Then known to the United States only as a sympathetic national and commercial friend, and without a navy, she is now known to us by her calculated hostility to our agricultural and commercial development, by her aggressions in the Samoan Islands, and by one of the ships of her navy which in a distant sea illegally violated one of our unarmed commercial vessels, in the absence of any American navy to resent it.[6]

Bayard never became an imperialist, but the growing sentiment in the United States in favor of colonial expansion could not be disregarded, and his reaction to the German program in the South Pacific was not friendly. Alvensleben took care to acquaint him with the rapid development of German economic interests in Samoa. German shipping had increased from eight vessels in 1859 to one hundred and sixty-one in 1883.[7] In 1884 Consul Weber reported to the German Foreign Office that "considering the island region as a whole, German commerce is still leading."[8] In the following year German exports from Samoa totalled "more than three times the value of British exports,"[9] and the value of German plantations in the Samoan islands reached the considerable figure of $588,000.[10]

When these facts were brought to Bayard's attention he was not converted to the view that the preponderance of German economic interests in Samoa should be regarded as a title to political control. In a short memorandum which he wrote after his accession to the office of Secretary of State, he expressed the opinion that "the superior numbers and the greater amount of property held by German subjects in Samoa, cannot be admitted to constitute any claim to greater political predominance."[11]

With Bayard in this frame of mind it was only to be expected that he would resent the maneuvers of Dr. Stübel, the acting German consul at Apia, to secure for Germany certain concessions which would pave

6. John A. Kasson to Secretary Bayard, April 30, 1885, *ibid.* Although Mr. Kasson was sharply critical of German policy in the Pacific he was able to cover this hostility by a screen of discreet silence when he was in Berlin. The German Government regarded him as a friend, and H. von Alvensleben, the German Minister at Washington, called to see Secretary Bayard on March 13, 1885 and "confidentially mentioned that Prince Bismarck would be pleased to have Kasson remain in Berlin." *Memorandum* of Secretary Bayard, March 13, 1885, *Bayard MS.*

7. Sylvia Masterman, *Origins of International Rivalry in Samoa*, pp. 64-65.

8. Count Otto zu Stolberg-Wernigerode, *Germany and the United States of America During the Era of Bismarck*, p. 227.

9. *House Ex Doc. 238*, 50 Cong., 1 sess., p. 281.

10. *Ibid.*, p. 293.   11. *Bayard MS.*

the way for a German protectorate. On November 5, 1884, King Malietoa sent an appeal to the British Government asking that the Samoan islands be taken under the protection of the Crown. On the following day he publicly performed before the German consulate in Apia the most severe abasement which was permitted by Samoan customs. By this act he apparently believed that he would deceive the German consul into believing that the Samoan royal house felt the necessity of keeping on friendly terms with the German Government.[12]

Dr. Stübel was not content with these empty gestures of subordination. Supported by two German warships, he was determined to force a lasting settlement of his difficulties with the Samoan Government. Malietoa was confronted with a treaty which Dr. Stübel wished to have signed at once. When Malietoa requested a copy of the treaty in order that its provisions might be carefully studied, he was informed that such a procedure was not possible, and if the "Government delayed in the matter they would probably soon find trouble brought upon them from the ships of war." [13]

It was under such effective duress that Malietoa signed the treaty of November 10, 1884. It provided for the appointment of a German-Samoan council of state which was empowered to agree upon laws affecting German residents. The membership of this council revealed the extent of the pressure exerted upon Malietoa. It was to consist of the German consul, two Samoans, and two Germans, thus giving a majority of votes to the German element in the islands. The two Germans were to be appointed by the German consul, while the Samoans were to be appointed by the King and Vice-King respectively. Provision was also made for the appointment of a "German officer" who would serve as a "secretary and adviser of the King in all matters in which German residents of Samoa are concerned." [14] Samoan autonomy was to be effectively stifled.

Malietoa now turned to the British consul at Apia and once more

---

12. William B. Churchward, *My Consulate in Samoa*, pp. 372-373.

13. *House Ex. Doc. 238*, 50 Cong., 1 sess., pp. 220-221.

14. *Ibid.*, pp. 6-7. According to the American vice-consul at Auckland, New Zealand, Thomas T. Gamble, it was "reported from Samoa that the knowledge of Mr. Lundon's scheme [for Samoan annexation to Great Britain] incited the German Consul to endeavor to secure the interests of his countrymen by a new convention—and that King Malietoa, who is not overstrong-minded, was bothered on both sides, and so signed both documents as the readiest way out of the difficulty." Jan. 24, 1885, *Auckland, Consular Despatches*, vol. 7, MS Dept. of State.

sent a petition to the British Government praying for protection.[15] A traitor in the service of Malietoa informed the German consul of this petition to Queen Victoria, and Stübel became furious. His anger mounted higher when Malietoa next sent a letter to the German Emperor setting forth the intrigues of Dr. Stübel who was "continually scheming and offering bribes to some Samoan chiefs to induce them to comply with his wishes and thus cause a rebellion in my country." [16]

Stübel retaliated by assuming control over the town and district of Apia. He informed Malietoa that this action was necessary because of repeated infractions of the treaty of November 10.[17] In a proclamation to the people of Samoa, Stübel pointed out how the Government of Germany had been treated by Malietoa with "unkindness and injury." For this reason it had become necessary for the German consul to "take possession of the lands of the village and district of Apia." This meant that "only the Government of Germany will rule for the present over that portion of territory." [18]

A revolution, abetted by Dr. Stübel, immediately broke out against the rule of Malietoa, and the rebel forces proclaimed Tamasese (the Vice-King) as the King of Samoa. The American and British consuls answered this move by issuing a notice that their governments still recognized Malietoa as king, and they announced that the treaties with the existing Samoan Government were still in force.[19]

On February 12 the German Minister conveyed an assurance to Secretary Frelinghuysen that the German Government had no intention of disturbing the *status quo* in Samoa.[20] This statement was confirmed by a despatch from Kasson in Berlin in which he stated that Prince Bismarck had announced that the action of Dr. Stübel would be "disavowed." [21] But the effect of these assurances was greatly weakened by a report from Alvensleben that the German Government intended

15. Malietoa to W. B. Churchward, November 12, 1884; Malietoa to Her Majesty the Queen of Great Britain and Ireland, November 12, 1884, *House Ex. Doc. 238, 50 Cong., 1 sess.*, p. 210.

16. *Ibid.*, p. 225.

17. Stübel to King Malietoa, January 23, 1885, *ibid.*, pp. 212-213.

18. *Ibid.*, p. 212.

19. Canisius to Alvey A. Adee, February 23, 1885, *Apia, Consular Despatches*, vol. 13, MS Dept. of State.

20. State Department *memorandum* written after conversation with Alvensleben, February 12, 1885, *German Legation, Notes from*, MS Dept. of State.

21. Kasson to Secretary Frelinghuysen, February 9, 1885, *Germany, Despatches*, vol. 37, MS Dept. of State.

to ratify the German-Samoan treaty of November 10, 1884, and would "see to it that the provisions of the same are carried out." [22]

The Samoan situation was in this apparently hopeless tangle when Bayard entered upon his duties as Secretary of State, in March, 1885. After a careful study of the correspondence in the Department of State relative to Samoa, Bayard sent a long and carefully reasoned instruction to Berthold Greenebaum, the American consul at Apia. He pointed out that the American Government had never ratified the consular convention of September 2, 1879, which provided for the administration of the district of Apia. It might therefore be "an open question whether our tacit acceptance of that convention, and the entrance *de facto* of our Consul into the municipal council of Apia gives us any right to resent supposed German interference therewith."

This counsel of caution had specific reference to the *municipal administration* of the district of Apia. With reference to the Samoan islands as a whole, Bayard was quick to defend American interests which had been honestly acquired:

The moral interests of the United States with respect to the islands of the Pacific . . . would counsel us to look with concern on any movement by which the independence of those Pacific nationalities might be extinguished by their passage under the domination of a foreign sovereign.

After sounding this clear note against any attempts by foreign powers to annex Pacific islands in which America had long been interested, Bayard referred to the movement in Samoa, sponsored by Dr. Stübel, to drive Malietoa from his throne. While the American Government "could not take the responsibility of interfering with the right of revolution," it should be generally recognized that the United States has a

. . . moral right to expect that no change of native rule shall extinguish the independence of the islands, and if such a change should be brought about by foreign interference and with the ulterior purpose, or result, to transferring the domination over the Samoan group to a single foreign flag, we would feel bound to dissent from such a proceeding.

After these positive declarations that America would not countenance any intrigues by foreign nations looking toward the annexation of the Samoan islands, Bayard called the American consul's attention to the assurances that had been received from both Germany and

22. Alvensleben to Secretary Frelinghuysen, February 24, 1885, *German Legation, Notes from*, MS Dept. of State.

England relative to the independence of those islands. In view of these facts it would be better for Mr. Greenebaum to "avoid any appearance" of taking an active part against Germany. Instead, he should make every effort to maintain "harmony and good will" between the representatives of all the powers having interests in Samoa.[23]

Bayard was anything but a swashbuckler, and he was anxious to find a pacific settlement for all the important questions at issue between the United States and Germany. He also realized that through the operation of certain economic factors a definite friction was being developed between the United States and Germany. The rapid industrial evolution in the German Empire after 1871 had wrought a fundamental change in the economic structure of that state. It soon became necessary to import foodstuffs into Germany, and American grain threatened to supplant German grain even in the home market. American meat products found a growing German market, and when American pork was refused admittance because of alleged dangers from *trichinosis,* a long dispute resulted. German-American tariff controversies helped to sharpen the ill-will between the two countries, and in 1884 things reached such a pass that Mr. Sargent, the American Minister at Berlin, was recalled. To Carl Schurz, a leading German-American and an intimate friend of Bayard, the manner in which the German newspapers had attacked Mr. Sargent was nothing less than "outrageous," and he considered such conduct as a "violation of the laws of hospitality." The ardent friendship that was so characteristic of German-American relations immediately after the Civil War was now a thing of the past.[24]

Bayard was thoroughly familiar with this growing coolness between

23. Secretary Bayard to Berthold Greenebaum, June 19, 1885, *Instructions to Consuls,* vol. 114, pp. 269-275, MS Dept. of State. In the New York *Tribune,* October 16, 1887, there is a short account of the background of Berthold Greenebaum, the American consul at Apia: "Greenebaum is a San Francisco dry-goods merchant whose specialty is a patent overall. His firm had intimate relations with some American merchants in Samoa. Greenebaum had political aspirations, and thought to combine a public with a commercial career in Samoa." His reception by King Malietoa was far from impressive: "After a few minutes walk his guide stepped in front of an unusually large hut, and paralyzed Greenebaum by announcing that it was the royal palace. . . . Just as Greenebaum removed his hat and bowed his head to enter the low doorway, a big hog made a sudden rush from the interior, dashed between Greenebaum's legs and threw the disgusted consul into a heap of kitchen refuse by the side of the door."

24. Carl Schurz to Senator George F. Edmunds, March 9, 1884, *Schurz MS,* Library of Congress. See also, Jeanette Keim, *Forty Years of German-American Political Relations,* chap. iv.; Count Otto zu Stolberg-Wernigerode, *Germany and the United States of America During the Era of Bismarck,* pp. 135-173; and George M. Fisk, "Continental Opinion Regarding a Proposed Middle European Tariff Union," *Johns Hopkins University Studies,* vol. 20.

Germany and the United States, and he made every effort to place German-American relations upon a more friendly footing. He sent to Berlin as the American Minister, George H. Pendleton, an able Ohio politician who was anxious to make his mission a success.[25] Bismarck reciprocated by making things pleasant for Mr. Pendleton who soon felt "quite at home." [26] Bismarck also sent, through Mr. Pendleton, handsome photographs of himself for President Cleveland and Secretary Bayard, and Bayard returned the compliment by forwarding to Berlin pictures of himself and of President Cleveland.[27]

But despite these gestures of good will toward Germany, Bayard had a definite suspicion of Bismarck's program for colonial expansion. In a confidential letter to Pendleton, September 9, 1885, he gives emphatic expression to these doubts:

I wanted in this note to draw your careful attention to a matter which altho' in a hazy condition yet may soon become more defined, and is very grave in its possibilities. That Germany has of late years given evidence of a disposition to cherish schemes of distant annexation & civilization in many quarters of the globe seems unquestionable, and the late attempt to gobble up the Caroline group has given rise to a very excited condition of feeling in Spain. . . .

Rumors of schemes in Central America to obtain political footholds in those regions are not wanting, but the most important suggestion that now and then is in the air, is the possible acquisition of the Antilles by Germany. And as a sequel to a serious collision between Spain & Germany such an event is outlined in a vague way.

I need not say to you how utterly inadmissable is such a plan to this country and how impossible of success. The geographical proximity of Cuba to the United States makes the condition of that Island an especially American question. No other nation has so great an interest in its disposition. . . . This is an old story to you, but it seems to me opportune now to repeat it in order that no possibility of misapprehension may arise in the minds of the Rulers of Germany in relation to the attitude and resolve of the United States in respect to a subject so vital to our safety and welfare.

25. Pendleton was more than a mere politician. See Reginald E. McGrane, "George H. Pendleton," *Dictionary of American Biography*, vol. 14 (N. Y. 1934), pp. 419-420.
26. George H. Pendleton to Secretary Bayard, June 8, 1885, *Personal, Bayard MS;* Secretary Bayard to George H. Pendleton, June 15, 1885, *Personal, Bayard MS.*
27. Pendleton to Secretary Bayard, September 10, 1885, *Personal, Bayard MS;* Bayard to George H. Pendleton, October 21, 1885, *Personal, Bayard MS.* In a personal letter to Mr. Pendleton, November 21, 1885, Bayard refers to the photographs which he is enclosing for Prince Bismarck and makes the following comment: "When you send these photos to Prince Bismarck, accompany that of the President with his compliments and good wishes, and mine with hearty expressions of respect and good will with hopes for his health and happiness." *Bayard MS.*

. . . We cannot see with indifference foreign dominion pushed to our very door. . . . In your residence and friendly exchanges in Germany, . . . the American position in relation to those Islands that lie at the very front door of our home, ought to be made clear to all men.[28]

These suspicions of Bayard relative to German colonial policy were strengthened when he realized that the German Government was inclined to give active support to the provisions of the German-Samoan treaty of November 10, 1884. In order to check German pretensions in the South Pacific, Bayard looked to Great Britain for support, and during the summer of 1885, Sackville-West, the British Minister at Washington, kept Bayard informed as to the attitude of the Foreign Office with regard to German encroachments in Samoa.[29] The British Colonial Office was strongly opposed to any important concessions to Germany in the South Pacific area, but the Foreign Office was doubtful as to the best course to pursue. In a Foreign Office memorandum of December 29, 1885, the situation in Samoa is frankly discussed:

Is it worth while resisting the German desire to take the Samoan administration into their own hands, if we could obtain complete freedom of commerce, most-favored-nation treatment for ourselves and for the colonies, and if the United States agree? . . . The United States have shown anxiety lately to secure in the western Pacific freedom of commerce which they hold should be independent of any one power. We may conclude, I think, that they would be very willing to take common action with us to attain that object. But unless there is a fair prospect of gaining our end, viz., the exclusion of Germany from the sole administration of Samoa, would it not be better to give way at once, and by so doing obtain all we and the colonies can reasonably desire? On the other hand it may be fairly contended that with the United States' aid we might succeed in making arrangements for securing Samoan independence.[30]

In November, 1885, Bayard had a conversation with Sackville-West in which he defined the position of the American Government. After adverting to the commercial importance of the South Sea Islands, he

28. Secretary Bayard to Pendleton, September 9, 1885, *Personal and Confidential, Bayard MS.* In 1884 a rumor was current that Spain was about to cede Cuba to Germany. In order to forestall such a possibility, Secretary Frelinghuysen instructed John W. Foster, at Madrid, to lodge a protest against the transfer of Cuba to any foreign power. If ceded to Germany, or to any important power, Cuba could be converted into a naval base that would menace the independence and peace of the United States. Frelinghuysen to Foster, August 29, 1884, *Confidential, Spain, Instruction,* vol. 19, MS Dept. of State, pp. 642-643.

29. Sackville-West to Secretary Bayard, April 1, April 17, May 5, May 11, June 9, June 23, July 7, and August 5, 1885, *British Legation, Notes from,* vols. 111, 112, MS Dept. of State.

30. Count Otto zu Stolberg-Wernigerode, *Germany and the United States of America During the Era of Bismarck,* p. 239.

declared that the United States could "not allow any one power to have commercial preference" in that area. From the political angle the same thing was true: The United States was anxious to "see independence assured for those islands." [31]

Through these declarations of Bayard the American Government was definitely committed to a co-operative policy with reference to Samoa. This fact was made abundantly clear to Alvensleben, the German Minister, who informed Bayard on December 9, 1885, that the German Government wished to extend its political control over the islands but would be careful to respect all American rights with regard to them. The attitude of the Department of State to this overture was unmistakably negative. The American Government would not agree to a German protectorate over Samoa.[32]

This strong stand with reference to Samoan independence may have deterred the German Government from giving support to some actions of Dr. Stübel which possibly had political significance. In December, 1885, King Malietoa decided to leave his seat of government at Mulinuu Point and take up his residence within the limits of the district of Apia. It is possible that this move was instigated by the British and American consuls. In any event it was deeply distressing to Dr. Stübel to see Malietoa enter Apia and raise the Samoan flag without his permission. He immediately asked the King, in "the most polite manner," to take down his flag, and when this request was not complied with, he called upon the captain of the German cruiser *Albatross* for assistance. A German sailor succeeded in hauling down the Samoan flag which was "carefully folded" and sent to Malietoa.[33]

On December 31, 1885, the American consul at Apia (Greenebaum) cabled to the Department of State and reported that the "King of Samoa has been driven from the seat of Government, and Samoan flag hauled down by German forces from man-of-war." [34] Bayard cabled at once to Pendleton, in Berlin, and instructed him to notify the German Foreign Office that the American Government expected that "nothing will be done to impair rights of the United States under treaty with Samoa as an independent state. United States policy one of guarded reserve.[35]

31. *Ibid.*, p. 239.
32. Alvensleben to Secretary Bayard, December 9, 1885, *German Legation, Notes from,* vol. 18, MS Dept. of State.
33. *Norddeutsche Allgemeine Zeitung,* April 22, 1886; *Berliner Tageblatt,* April 23, 1886.
34. *House Ex. Doc. 238,* 50 Cong., 1 sess., p. 15.
35. Secretary Bayard to Pendleton, January 12, 1886, *Germany, Instructions,* vol. 17, MS Dept. of State.

It is certain that Germany wanted no quarrel with America over Samoa, and on January 16, 1886, Pendleton replied to Bayard that the German Foreign Office was very conciliatory. Count Bismarck stated that he had no information from German officials in Samoa as to events there, but whatever "may have occurred, we intend to maintain the status as it has heretofore existed. . . . If any wrong has been done it shall be righted, and reparation shall be made." [36]

This friendly attitude on the part of Count Bismarck put an end to Bayard's fears of a German *coup d'etat* in Samoa. But he was not allowed to be without some suspicions as to German policy. On February 16 he received from Sackville-West a note which enclosed extracts from a despatch written by the British consul at Apia to the Foreign Office. In this communication there were several references to German intrigue against the rule of King Malietoa, and it was strongly hinted that these German activities would soon lead to open warfare in Samoa.[37]

The situation in the South Pacific looked so threatening to Lord Rosebery, the British Foreign Secretary, that he suggested to Bayard the idea of a tripartite investigation of conditions in Samoa with a report on the best form of government for the islands.[38] Bayard accepted this suggestion at once,[39] but the German Government declined to accede to such a proposal.[40] Bismarck was still seeking some solution of the Samoan difficulties without having recourse to a tripartite investigation which might lead to further troubles. On April 30 Alvensleben had a conversation with Bayard in which he spoke with some feeling against the activities of the British and American consuls in Apia. The only reaction of Bayard to these complaints was a short sentence which he jotted down after the departure of Alvensleben: "*Why German interests should be held in higher consideration than American or British does not appear.*" [41]

A week later (May 5) Alvensleben again called at the Department of State in connection with the Samoan question, and after his conversa-

36. Pendleton to Secretary Bayard, January 16, 1886, *Germany, Despatches*, vol. 40, MS Dept. of State.

37. Sackville-West to Secretary Bayard, February 16, 1886, *British Legation, Notes from*, vol. 112, MS Dept. of State.

38. Sackville-West to Secretary Bayard, March 30, 1886, *British Legation Notes from*, vol. 113, MS Dept. of State.

39. Sackville-West to Secretary Bayard, March 31, 1886, *Bayard MS.*

40. Sackville-West to Secretary Bayard, March 31, 1886, *British Legation, Notes from*, vol. 113, MS Dept. of State.

41. *Memorandum* written after conversation with Alvensleben, April 30, 1886, *Bayard MS.*

tion with Bayard he left a memorandum which represented the views of the German Foreign Office. To the surprise of Bayard this memorandum did *"not* include the proposed substitution of another govt. or Adm. in Samoa than that of Malietoa, which Mr. Alvensleben had verbally informed me was intended." [42]

With Bismarck showing this conciliatory spirit, Bayard was somewhat embarrassed when the news came to him that the American consul at Apia had (May 14) raised the American flag over the Samoan banner and had taken the Samoan islands under American protection.[43] No time was lost in assuring both the German and the British Governments that "no separate protectorate by any nation" was desired. Bayard then suggested that the "German Minister here be authorized to confer with British Minister and me, and arrange that order be established. A competent and acceptable chief to be chosen by natives and upheld by three powers. . . . Joint declaration to be made against annexation or protectorate by any of the three powers." [44]

The British Government immediately replied to this suggestion by indicating their acceptance of it on condition that the German Government would take similar action.[45] The German Government waited a few days before committing itself to the Bayard proposal, but Mr. Adee (Second Assistant Secretary of State) regarded this delay as of no consequence, because Bismarck would probably be glad to receive such a suggestion:

> It gives him a chance to intrigue for Tamasese's election in place of Malietoa, but I see no objection to that if we can get from Germany a cast-iron declaration against annexation.[46]

On June 21 Bayard finally received from Berlin an acceptance of his proposal for a conference at Washington on Samoa.[47] Bismarck, however, desired to postpone the meetings of this conference until he

42. *Memorandum* written by Bayard after conversation with Alvensleben, May 5, 1886, *Bayard MS.*

43. *House Ex. Doc. 238, 50 Cong., 1 sess., p. 291;* Sackville-West to Secretary Bayard, June 1, 1886, *British Legation, Notes from,* vol. 113, MS Dept. of State.

44. Bayard to Pendleton, June 1, 1886, *Germany, Instructions,* vol. 17, MS Dept. of State, p. 650; Bayard to Phelps, June 1, 1886, *Great Britain, Instructions,* vol. 28, MS Dept. of State.

45. Phelps to Secretary Bayard, June 2, 1886, *Great Britain, Despatches,* vol. 153, MS Dept. of State.

46. A. A. Adee to Secretary Bayard, June 6, 1886, *Bayard MS.*

47. Coleman to Secretary Bayard, June 7, 1886, *Germany, Despatches,* vol. 41, MS Dept. of State. See also Bayard to Sackville-West, June 7, 1886, and Bayard to Alvensleben, June 7, 1886, *Bayard MS.*

had received further information from the German consul in Apia, and
he suggested that commissioners "be sent by the three powers to Samoa
to obtain for their Governments full information respecting the status
there." [48] Bayard accepted this suggestion, and he instructed the American Minister at London (Phelps) to inform the British Foreign Office
that an American special agent would probably leave San Francisco, en
route to Apia, on July 31.[49]

This prompt action on the part of the Secretary of State was probably dictated by a desire to show some appreciation of the conciliatory
spirit exhibited by the German consul at Apia in connection with the
disturbances in Samoa. After Greenebaum had raised the American flag
and had taken Samoa under the protection of the United States, Stübel
issued a protest against this action, which he was certain had not been
authorized by the American Government. But Stübel was not unduly
antagonistic in this matter, and on May 27 he joined with the consuls
of Great Britain and the United States in issuing a proclamation which
gave notice that the three powers did not "in any way" recognize
Tamasese as King of Samoa, and all Samoans were ordered to return to
their homes and "remain quiet and peaceable." The German consul
gave further evidences of an accommodating spirit by hauling down
the German flag which he had hoisted at Mulinuu Point on January 23,
1885, and he promised to put pressure upon Tamasese in favor of
peace.[50] In the face of these friendly gestures it was no wonder that
Bayard remarked to Alvensleben that Stübel's actions were dictated by
a "sense of liberality, justice, and good feeling."

On June 28 Alvensleben called at the Department of State and
informed Bayard that Lord Rosebery, the British Foreign Secretary,
had accepted Bismarck's suggestion about sending a commissioner to
Samoa to investigate the situation in the islands. John B. Thurston, the
Governor of the Fiji Islands, had been chosen by Lord Rosebery as the
representative of the British Government in this matter, and Bismarck
had chosen Herr Travers, the German Consul-General at Sydney.[51]

Some two weeks later Lord Rosebery sent an inquiry to Bayard with

48. Coleman to Secretary Bayard, June 18, 1886, *Germany, Despatches*, vol. 41, MS Dept.
of State.

49. Bayard to Phelps, July 7, 1886, *Great Britain, Instructions*, vol. 28, MS Dept. of
State.

50. Bayard to Alvensleben, June 22, 1886 with enclosures A–H, *German Legation, Notes
to*, vol. 10, MS Dept. of State.

51. *Memorandum* written by Bayard after conversation with Alvensleben, June 28,
1886, *Bayard MS.*

reference to the appointment of an American commissioner to Samoa. He was also anxious to ascertain "the proposed bases" of the forthcoming investigation.[52] Bayard replied at once that he was in hopes that an American special agent could leave San Francisco on July 31. The proposed bases of inquiry he understood to be a

. . . thorough examination into the condition of the group and the causes of the late disorders and discontent there, with a view to find a permanent remedy. A report will be made by each Agent to the respective governments, and a status of neutrality to be maintained by the joint counsel and influence of the three powers excluding annexation or predominance by any, and promoting the autonomy and peaceful government of the group by the native authority.[53]

Bayard now turned to his friend George H. Bates, of Delaware, and inquired whether he would be interested in this Samoan mission. On July 17 Bates telegraphed for further details with reference to the compensation that would be paid to the American commissioner, and Bayard replied with some degree of annoyance that

. . . he did not suppose there would be any large pecuniary inducement in the expedition to Samoa, but that no loss should be incurred in a service of no very great difficulty nor one warranting any great outlay of the very limited fund subject to the control of the President for such emergencies. . . . The service in view is not diplomatic nor will the Agent be commissioned. The appointee will be accredited to the Naval Commander, and to the native King of the Islands, but will have none of those incidental expenses which belong to a Resident Minister. . . . His duty will be to examine fully into and report upon the condition of affairs in Samoa, and return home as soon as such information is acquired. His report will be considered together with the separate report of the Agent for Germany, and that of Great Britain. All suggestions accompanying the report will be welcome, but there is no other official duty or responsibility involved. The Ministers Resident at Siam, in Corea . . . receive $5,000 per annum, . . . I had this scale of regulated compensation in mind.[54]

Bates decided to accept the Samoan mission, and on July 22, 1886, Bayard sent him a long letter of instructions. He was authorized to "disavow" the action of Consul Greenebaum in "assuming a protectorate over Samoa in the name of the United States." The American Government was unwilling to take such a step, and it could not agree to any plan whereby the native authority would be replaced by a

52. Charles Hardinge to Secretary Bayard, July 12, 1886, *Bayard MS.*
53. Bayard to Charles Hardinge (British chargé at Washington), July 12, 1886, *Bayard MS.*
54. Bayard to George H. Bates, July 17, 1886, *Personal, Bayard MS.*

permanent tripartite goverment. It did recognize that the temporary situation in the islands might require "the joint effort of the treaty powers to preserve order and insure stable government, in which native interests shall be under autonomous native control, while foreign extra-territorial interests shall remain . . . under the joint care of their several representatives."

None of the three powers

. . . can be supposed to have the slightest concern in the personality of the head of the Samoan native government. Malietoa can no more be the candidate of the United States for absolute kingship than Tamasese can be of Germany, or any other chief might be of Great Britain. . . . Whatever his civil claims may seem to be, any chief in arms is a rebel against the power of the titular government for the time being, and equally so against the concurrent authority of the three powers.[55]

Armed with these instructions which stressed the support of the native Samoan authority in any formula for the solution of the Samoan tangle, Bates arrived in Apia on August 17 and found the German commissioner (Herr G. Travers) awaiting him. John B. Thurston, the British representative, made his appearance at Apia on August 24, and the three commissioners began their inquiry into conditions in the Samoan islands.

It appeared as though the Samoan question was about to be amicably settled when Mr. Greenebaum once more stirred up trouble. Neither the British nor the German Governments wished Greenebaum to return to the islands after his visit to Washington in the summer of 1886. In a note to Charles Hardinge, the British chargé, Bayard had expressed himself (July 12, 1886) in favor of the appointment of new consular agents in Samoa. This point of view was received with favor by the British Legation, and Hardinge was greatly surprised to see in the *Congressional Record* of August 6 that Greenebaum had been confirmed in his position as consul at Apia. In view of the "probability" of explanations being asked for by Lord Iddesleigh, when this announcement appeared in the English press, Hardinge asked Bayard

---

55. Bayard to Bates, July 22, 1886, *Special Missions, Instructions*, vol. 3, MS Dept. of State. For some reason not clearly understood, Bayard failed to advise the British Legation of the appointment of Bates as commissioner to Samoa. On October 24, 1886, Charles Hardinge wrote to Bayard and requested "the name of the gentleman selected as United States Commissioner to take part in the joint inquiry into Samoan Affairs. . . . I see in the papers of today the statement that Mr. George H. Bates of Wilmington was yesterday sent as special envoy to the Samoan Islands, and I shall be very much obliged if you will be so good as to inform me whether this information is authentic." *Bayard MS.*

whether this confirmation of Greenebaum was "merely to satisfy the exigencies of the moment." [56]

Bayard immediately assured Hardinge that there had been no change in his "views and intentions respecting the appointment of new Consuls at this point [Apia] by the three powers." Greenebaum's nomination was not withdrawn from the Senate because it was "not the desire of the President to seem to reflect upon him or suddenly to end his official existence. The confirmation by the Senate will not prolong his stay in Samoa as United States Consul." [57]

Alvensleben was also anxious about Greenebaum's nomination as consul at Apia, and he called at the Department of State to discuss the matter with Bayard. He stated that the "German Government did not make any further complaint . . . against Greenebaum because they understood . . . that he was to be recalled."

Bayard then remarked that "Greenebaum had recalled himself; that he was in this country and had been in the Department yesterday, but I had not seen him; that he would not, however, return to Samoa as Consul of the United States." Alvensleben was pleased to hear this assurance, and he expressed the hope that Greenebaum would stay away from Samoa. Bayard gave him no satisfaction in this regard. Greenebaum was a "free man, and could go where he pleased," but he would not return to Samoa "with any official authority from the United States."

In concluding this interview with Alvensleben, Bayard threw out the following suggestion:

The three consuls to be appointed—American, German and English—ought to have a plan of municipal government for Apia settled and then let them exercise the powers alternately; say, each four months at a time, and then by each of the three powers keeping a man-of-war at Samoa four months in the year. [58]

Some weeks later, Alvensleben reported to Bayard that his suggestion for governing Samoa

. . . by the alternate rule of the three powers—each consul taking four months & so keeping the peace and good order—was acceptable to the Imperial Government of Germany, & that they only would ask that there should be no injury to the interests of Germans under the arrangement.

56. Charles Hardinge to Secretary Bayard, August 9, 1886, *Bayard MS.*

57. Bayard to Hardinge, August 9, 1886, *Bayard MS.*

58. *Memorandum* written by Bayard after interview with Alvensleben, August 20, 1886, *Bayard MS.*

Bayard gave his assurance that "there should be protection to all interests equally with preferences to none." [59] Everything seemed to be progressing satisfactorily when once more Greenebaum created a serious disturbance. Instead of resigning as consul at Apia, as Bayard had expected, Greenebaum returned to Samoa in the autumn of 1886, and during a short stay in Honolulu he persuaded the Hawaiian Government to appoint him as the vice-consul of Hawaii at Apia.[60] The German Government was amazed when it learned of Mr. Greenebaum's activities, and Bismarck asked Mr. Pendleton for an explanation.[61] In answer to Pendleton's telegram of inquiry, Bayard stated that the Department of State had not expected that Greenebaum would "return to Samoa and attempt to exercise any of the functions of his former office." His resignation was now in the hands of Mr. Bates, the American commissioner in Samoa.[62]

The Hawaiian angle of Greenebaum's activities was not so easily settled. On December 20 Bayard received a despatch from Frank P. Hastings, the American vice-consul at Honolulu, to the effect that the Hawaiian Government would soon send a "diplomatic Commissioner or a Consul to reside permanently at the Samoan Islands, and that on the appointment of such representative Mr. Greenebaum's functions as Vice-Consul will cease." [63] Some weeks later the news came to the Department of State that King Kalakaua had commissioned John E. Bush, a half-caste Hawaiian, as "minister plenipotentiary to the Kings of Samoa and Tonga and the independent Chiefs and Peoples of Polynesia." [64]

Although King Malietoa had refused to recognize Greenebaum as a representative of Hawaii, he extended a cordial welcome to Bush (January 7, 1887), who assured the Samoan king of the deep interest that King Kalakaua took in a "kindred race closely allied to the Hawaiians by blood, by language and by historical traditions." After bestowing upon Malietoa the Grand Cross of the Royal Order of the Star of Oceania,

59. *Memorandum* written by Bayard after conversation with Alvensleben, September 27, 1886, *Bayard MS.*

60. George W. Merrill to Secretary Bayard, Honolulu, September 6, 1886, *Hawaii, Despatches,* vol. 22, MS Dept. of State.

61. Pendleton to Secretary Bayard, October 2, 1886, *Germany, Despatches,* vol. 42, MS Dept. of State.

62. *House Ex. Doc., 238, 50 Cong., 1 sess.,* pp. 38-39.

63. F. P. Hastings to Secretary Bayard, November 13, 1886, *Hawaii, Despatches,* vol. 22, MS Dept. of State.

64. Hastings to Secretary Bayard, December 27, 1886, *Hawaii, Despatches,* vol. 22, MS Dept. of State.

Bush opened negotiations for a treaty which was signed on February 17.[65] This treaty was short and to the point. It merely provided that the Samoan Government would enter "into a political confederation with his Majesty Kalakaua," and a pledge was given that King Malietoa would "conform to whatever measures may hereafter be adopted by His Majesty Kalakaua . . . to carry into effect this political confederation, and to maintain it now and forever." [66]

Merrill also informed Bayard that the Hawaiian Government had decided to accede to a request from King Malietoa to commission Mr. Carter, the Hawaiian envoy at Washington, to serve as the representative of the Samoan Government to the United States.[67]

The report of the treaty between King Kalakaua and King Malietoa providing for a Polynesian Confederation, did not reach Bayard until April 1, 1887. In the meantime German activities in Samoa were attracting his attention. In November, 1886, Pendleton, at Berlin, had asked permission for a leave of absence so that he might visit the United States and attend to some personal affairs.[68] This request was granted because Bayard believed that there were no "foreign complications" that required Pendleton's presence in Berlin.[69] In Samoa, however, certain incidents were occurring that soon gave serious concern to the Department of State. If they had arisen sooner it is unlikely that Bayard would have been so willing to let Pendleton absent himself from Berlin.

On January 31, 1887, Malietoa had written to Dr. Becker, the German consul at Apia, to protest against the presence of Herr Brandeis, an Austrian adventurer, in the territory of the rebel chief Tamasese. Becker gave a sharp reply to the note of Malietoa. Brandeis had no appointment of a military character from Tamasese, and inasmuch as he was a "quiet, sensible gentleman," it should be assumed that he would do a great deal of good "for the blessings of Samoa." [70]

65. Merrill to Secretary Bayard, February 15, 1887, *Hawaii, Despatches*, vol. 23, MS Dept. of State.

66. Merrill to Secretary Bayard, March 29, 1887, *Hawaii, Despatches*, vol. 23, MS Dept. of State.

67. Merrill to Secretary Bayard, February 15, 1887, *Hawaii, Despatches*, vol. 23, MS Dept. of State.

68. Pendleton to Secretary Bayard, November 29, 1886, *Bayard MS.*

69. Bayard to Pendleton, December 13, 1886, *Bayard MS.* See also Pendleton to Secretary Bayard, January 17, 1887, *Bayard MS.*

70. Becker to King Malietoa, February 10, 1887, enclosure 5, in despatch from Carter to Bayard, April 2, 1887, *Hawaiian Legation, Notes from*, vol. 3, MS Dept. of State. At this time the office of Minister of Foreign Affairs in Hawaii was held by Walter M. Gibson. In connection with the dubious background of Mr. Gibson, Mr. Thomas Perkins, of Salem,

On February 25 Alvensleben had an interview with Bayard during the course of which he inquired about the rumor "of the Sandwich Islands annexing Samoa." Bayard answered that "it was all nonsense; that Mr. Bush, the Sandwich Island agent, was simply going there rather to evangelize those people than for anything else, and that his visit had no political significance." [71]

Several days later, Bayard sent a note to Alvensleben in which he stated that he had received word from the American vice-consul at Apia that "a Mr. Brandeise" had been sent "under pay and with the title of general to give military instruction to Tamasese in promotion of his rebellion against the Government of Malietoa." Bayard concluded his note with the expression of a hope that "the just and benevolent plan of co-operation by the three powers will not be allowed to be impeded by any such inconsistent and maleficent action as has been so reported." [72]

On March 11 Carter, the Minister from Hawaii, paid a visit to the Department of State and informed Bayard that he had an autograph letter from King Malietoa which commissioned him to serve as the Minister Plenipotentiary and Envoy Extraordinary from Samoa to the United States. Bayard's comments upon this appointment were quite frank:

> I told him that in my judgment it was not wise, as I had already written him, to present himself to me in that capacity; that although he might have authority from Samoa he could have no power, and if the Germans should disregard the wishes of Samoa it might place him in a very embarrassing position, and would probably create an inconsistency in his relations as the Minister of the Sandwich Islands if he mixed himself up officially with Samoa.

Carter then talked "a good deal of the plans of the Germans in Samoa, and said he thought from Dr. Bush's account that the Germans

Massachusetts, wrote as follows to W. C. Endicott, the Secretary of War: "About 1850, an 'adventurer' named Gibson (Walter?) went to the E. Indies in a small craft, imitating, and aspiring no doubt, to be like Rajah Brooke of Borneo. Near the Straits of Borneo, and at some *Dutch* port on the East side of Sumatra, he was accused of meddling, etc., with Malays to the intended detriment of the Dutch, who seized him, and took him to Batavia where he was tried, convicted, and *condemned* to death for the offence. It was exciting, but all said 'served him right.' . . . Somehow while Gibson was in prison, the doors were 'accidentally left open,' and there was no hanging owing to his escape on board ship in harbor. . . . If the Sandwich Island Gibson is the same person *or not,* he can make a better thing out of this new matter than in the Java one." *Bayard MS.*

71. *Memorandum* written by Bayard after conversation with Alvensleben, February 25, 1887, *Bayard MS.*

72. Bayard to Alvensleben, March 2, 1887, *German Legation, Notes to,* vol. 10, MS Dept. of State.

were disposed to stir up strife between Tamasese and Malietoa, . . . and that it ought to be put an end to." At this point Bayard remarked that he had written to Alvensleben "informing him that I had been told that someone attached to the German consulate at Apia had been sent under pay to Tamasese to instruct him in military matters, and that I had said it ought to be stopped, as being in contravention of the plan of mutual support of a native autonomy in Samoa."

In concluding this interview, Carter asked Bayard as "to the course he should pursue." Bayard cautiously replied that he was not "able to give him advice just now," but he did express his "disinclination" to receive Carter as the "Minister of Samoa." [73]

On April 1 Carter had another conversation with Bayard, and startled him with the announcement of a treaty between Hawaii and Samoa. On February 25 Bayard had assured Alvensleben that the rumor about the Sandwich Islands annexing Samoa was "all nonsense."

This assurance to the German Minister had not been founded on fact, and Bayard expressed to Carter his great

. . . surprise at the action of Dr. Bush and said that it was wholly inconsistent with the objects and purposes of his Mission as stated to me, and that it struck me that it would open the Sandwich Islands to a very rude collision with Germany.

When Bayard inquired of Carter as to the reasons why King Kalakaua consented to such an arrangement, the Hawaiian Minister replied that he believed "it was the counsel of Mr. Gibson, the Minister for Foreign Affairs of the King, who had made him believe there was a great deal of glory in the affair."

The remainder of this conversation between Bayard and Carter is full of interest and importance. Carter took this occasion to inform Bayard that

. . . the Hawaiian Government had purchased a vessel and was arming it at an expense of $100,000, at Honolulu, and that it was to be used as a training ship. He also told me [Bayard] that a man of war was ordered in Great Britain. I said "What are they going to do with two armed vessels?" He answered "to send them to Samoa to protect Mr. Bush."

I asked him if he meant to protect Mr. Bush by getting into a conflict with the German man-of-war there. He said he did not know, but that the King was entirely misled by Mr. Gibson, and that his (Mr. Carter's) idea

---

73. Memorandum written by Bayard after conversation with Carter on March 11, 1887, *Bayard MS.*

was that the Hawaiian King wished to become the great leader of the Pacific Islands.

I told him I heard this with astonishment; that I could see nothing in it that had a show of prudence or wisdom; that Samoa had not a breath of power which Germany would care to respect; that the only reason Malietoa had not been driven from the Island was the interest the United States had taken in the matter, and the treaty made with him; that I was acting upon this question on moral grounds, and holding Germany and England to obey the laws of nations with regard to this weak little Kingdom.

At the conclusion of this interview, Bayard repeated to Carter his "amazement" at the actions of the Hawaiian Government, and he warned him that such conduct was "unwise to the last degree." [74]

On the day following this important conversation between Bayard and Carter, the latter sent to the Department of State a note which formally recounted the steps that had been taken by King Kalakaua to effect an alliance with King Malietoa. In his confidential remarks to Bayard on April 1, Carter had stated that Bush, the Hawaiian envoy to Samoa, had "concluded a treaty of alliance between Samoa and Hawaii, and . . . the treaty had been accepted and approved by the Hawaiian Government." In his formal note of April 2, Carter merely says that a "treaty of political alliance and confederation is *proposed* to be entered into by the Hawaiian Government and Samoa," and that this treaty is now "under consideration by the Government of Hawaii." [75]

In his reply of April 12, Bayard again warned the Hawaiian Minister of the serious difficulties that might follow the conclusion of a treaty of alliance between Hawaii and Samoa. It seemed to him that from "every point of view" it would be

. . . ill–advised for Hawaii to take any ground at the present time, and during the pendency of issues in the origin of which the Government of Hawaii could have had no concern, which might tend to bring that Kingdom into conflict in Samoa with other interests directly concerned.[76]

In his instructions to Phelps, at London, and to Pendleton, at Berlin, Bayard repeated the warnings he had given to Carter, and he expressly stated that an alliance between Kalakaua and Malietoa would have such

74. *Memorandum* written by Bayard after an interview with Carter, the Hawaiian Minister, April 1, 1887, *Bayard MS.*

75. Carter to Secretary Bayard, April 2, 1887, *Hawaiian Legation, Notes from,* vol. 3, MS Dept. of State.

76. Bayard to Carter, April 12, 1887, *Hawaiian Legation, Notes to,* vol. 1, MS Dept. of State.

"far-reaching consequences" that he could not bring himself to "regard it with favor." [77]

Towards the end of April, Carter paid a visit to the Department of State and again discussed the Samoan situation with Bayard, who was very frank in stating his opinion:

I told him . . . that I thought the only good in the treaty that I could see was the clause of reservation that it should be subject to the three treaty powers already dealing with Samoan affairs; that it was very plain to me that the wiser course would have been for the envoy from Hawaii to have confined himself to making peace between the various Samoan heads, and that by cultivating harmony between them a nucleus could be formed upon which we could build up something in the shape of a civilized government for Samoa, which would be respected by the powers and prevent the domination and absorption by Germany or Great Britain of the Samoan Group.

He agreed with me entirely and asked me if I would not embody this in a note to him, so that he could send it to the King. . . . I told him that I thought Mr. Bush's action had been very indiscreet; that it could not lessen existing troubles in Samoa, and might create new ones by giving Germany a pretext for breaking the engagement which I considered had been formed with Great Britain and the United States to assist in the control of Samoa under a native autonomy, which was the great object in view. I was afraid that Mr. Bush's action might bring about results which would be very mortifying to Hawaii and might be connected with very serious results.[78]

Bayard kept his promise with Carter and wrote at once to Merrill, in Honolulu, and informed him that he had heard of the Hawaiian-Samoan alliance with "surprise and disquietude," and that he regarded it as "inexpedient." [79]

On August 15 a reply came to the Department of State from Merrill. The Hawaiian Government had recalled its representative from Apia, and the Hawaiian training ship, *Kaimiloa,* would soon leave Samoan waters. These steps would effectually put an end to all the dreams of a Polynesian Confederation.[80] But this reassuring message came to Bayard nearly three weeks after the Washington Conference on Samoa had concluded its sessions. For the present, Bayard would have to meet the sharp attacks of Germany upon Hawaiian meddling in Samoa without

77. Bayard to Phelps, April 12, 1887, *Great Britain, Instructions,* vol. 28, MS Dept. of State.

78. *Memorandum* written by Bayard after an interview with Carter, April 27, 1887, *Bayard MS.*

79. Bayard to Merrill, April 28, 1887, *Hawaii, Instructions,* vol. 3, MS Dept. of State.

80. Merrill to Secretary Bayard, July 13, 1887, received at the Department of State. August 15, 1887, *Hawaii, Despatches,* vol. 23, MS Dept. of State.

any certain knowledge as to the course that King Kalakaua would eventually follow. He also discovered that the British Government was acting in concert with Germany in all matters pertaining to the Samoan Islands.

This Anglo-German concert with reference to the Samoan situation was a direct result of the diplomatic muddle in Europe. In France a spirit of exaggerated nationalism was developing through the activities of Paul Deroulède and Maurice Barrès,[81] and it was given flamboyant expression in the person of General Georges Boulanger who strutted across the French political stage as Genéral Revanche.[82] The reaction in Germany to this French chauvinism was immediate and ominous. During 1886 and 1887 the situation remained delicate, and war constantly threatened.

But these difficulties between France and Germany were not the only shadows that fell across the European landscape. Russian policy in the Near East was viewed with great concern by British statesmen, and the attitude assumed by the French Government with reference to Egypt, and to colonial questions in general, was so unfriendly that Lord Salisbury could hardly restrain a wish for "another Franco-German War to put a stop to this incessant vexation."[83] In August, 1887, Salisbury became so impatient with French diplomacy that he expressed himself with vigor to Sir William White: "For the present the enemy is France. Her conduct is hard to explain on any theory."[84]

In view of the troubled situation on the European continent it seemed expedient to Lord Salisbury to draw closer to Germany, and this fact explains the Anglo-German concert of 1886–1889 with regard to Samoa. On March 19, 1886, Herbert Bismarck complained to Count Hatzfeldt, at London, that British officials in Samoa and in Zanzibar, were sowing suspicions in the "minds of native rulers" against Ger-

---

81. Camille Ducray, *Paul Deroulède* (Paris, 1914); Joachim Kuhn, *Der Patriotismus im Leben der dritten Republik* (Berlin, 1922).

82. Maurice Barrès, *L'Appel au soldat* (Paris, 1900); W. H. Gleadell, "General Boulanger," *Fortnightly Review*, vol. 48 (September, 1887), pp. 360-371; Joseph Reinach, *Le cheval noir* (Paris, 1890); Alexandre Zevaes, *Au temps du Boulangisme* (Paris, 1930).

83. Lord Salisbury to Lord Lyons, Feb. 5, 1887, Lord Newton, *Lord Lyons* (2 vols., London, 1913), vol. 2, p. 386. See also letter from Lord Salisbury to Lord Lyons, July 20, 1887, in which Salisbury remarks: "Can you wonder that there is, to my eyes, a silver lining even to the great black cloud of a Franco-German war?" Gwendolen Cecil, *Life of Robert, Marquis of Salisbury* (4 vols. London, 1922–1932), vol. 4, pp. 48-49.

84. Lord Salisbury to Sir William White, August 10, 1887, Gwendolen Cecil, *op. cit.*, vol. 4, p. 50.

many.[85] In September, 1886, the German Foreign Office was still dissatisfied with British policy in Samoa, and the possibility of armed intervention against King Malietoa was hinted at.[86] On October 14 Prince Bismarck wrote to Count Hatzfeldt and indicated that Germany would support Great Britain in the difficulties arising out of the British occupation of Egypt if the British Government would reciprocate by showing a more friendly attitude towards German aspirations in Samoa.[87]

In reply to this instruction from Prince Bismarck, Count Hatzfeldt expressed the opinion that Germany should "clothe" the concessions it desired from England in such a form that it would be possible for the British Government to grant them "without getting into difficulties with Australia." [88] This Australian angle of the Samoan situation was very evident to Lord Salisbury who advised Sir Philip Currie of the necessity of "sitting upon the Colonial Office" in connection with a too ambitious policy in the South Pacific: "We shall get into a new Angra Pequena trouble if we do not look out. That is to say, we shall force him [Bismarck] into a menacing position upon a matter which we are not prepared to resist him to the end and the result will be a discreditable 'skedaddle.' " [89]

British colonial officials were slow in responding to Foreign Office pressure in favor of a co-operative policy with Germany, and Count Herbert Bismarck wrote to Count Hatzfeldt, to advise him that the situation was regarded as serious. If British officials continued their unfriendly attitude it would be necessary for Germany to withdraw its support of the British position in Egypt.[90] In a second despatch from Count Bismarck to Count Hatzfeldt on March 26, 1887, a note of menace was allowed to creep into the last paragraph: "We are unable to put up with dilatory replies any longer, and I beg you to relieve Lord Salisbury of any doubt, that our policy must be altered in a very short

85. Count Herbert Bismarck, Berlin, to Count Hatzfeldt, London, March 19, 1886, E. T. S. Dugdale, *German Diplomatic Documents, 1871–1914*, vol. 1, pp. 217-218.

86. *Memorandum* by Count zu Rantzau, of the German Foreign Office, September 29, 1886, E. T. S. Dugdale, *op. cit.*, vol. 1, pp. 224-225.

87. Prince Bismarck to Count Hatzfeldt, October 14, 1886, E. T. S. Dugdale, *German Diplomatic Documents, 1871–1914*, vol. 1, p. 226.

88. Count Hatzfeldt to Count Herbert Bismarck, October 20, 1886, E. T. S. Dugdale, *op. cit.*, vol. 1, p. 227.

89. Lord Salisbury to Sir Philip Currie, November 30, 1886, Gwendolen Cecil, *op. cit.*, vol. 4, p. 36.

90. Count Herbert Bismarck to Count Hatzfeldt, March 26, 1887, *Die Grosse Politik der Europäischen Kabinette, 1871–1914*, vol. 4, pp. 165-167.

space of time, unless we can count on England's reciprocity on questions, which are of negligible importance to her in comparison with those of Egypt and the East." [91]

Under the impact of this threat, Lord Salisbury gave way completely, and a memorandum by Count Herbert Bismarck indicates the extent of the British retreat:

Lord Salisbury visited me yesterday afternoon at the Embassy, and the conversation turned first upon Samoa. I have been able repeatedly to ascertain that he attaches no value to Samoa, and that it is only out of consideration for the Australian Colonies that he may not declare this openly. The final solution, that he would prefer, would be for us to take Samoa, England the Tonga Islands, and the United States the Sandwich Islands (Hawaii). He feared that the moment for this solution had not yet arrived, but that perhaps it might come in two or three years. The only course, meanwhile, was to fall in with the wishes of America and make an experiment with the three advisers. [Bismarck: "But not five; leaving out the savages."] As time went on, there would be so many undesirable incidents as to convince even America of the impossibility of maintaining native governments in the Pacific Ocean.

I said to Lord Salisbury that the Americans would have to be restrained in every possible way. They appeared now to interpret the Monroe Doctrine, as though the Pacific Ocean were to be treated as an American Lake; they wished to bring under their exclusive influence not only Hawaii (which was, as Salisbury said, of no interest whatever to England), but also Samoa and Tonga, as stages between the future Panama Canal and Australia. There were even dreamers in America who imagined an eventual Republican brotherhood and a linking up of the various Australian Colonies with the United States.

This suggestion caused Lord Salisbury to pause. He declared that we must keep a sharp eye on American fingers. I then mentioned Malitoa, and Lord Salisbury agreed upon assistance, or at any rate non–interference, by England, in any dealings we undertook with Malitoa. He thought that this would greatly disturb the Australian Colonies, as we were willing to declare solemnly that there was no intention on our part to undertake any alteration of the present constitutional and commercial conditions in Samoa. . . . I thanked Lord Salisbury for his friendly words and informed him that our squadron would shortly deal with Malitoa. I also expressed the hope that the British Government would continue to support us in Samoa as loyally as we had supported it in Egypt. Lord Salisbury replied with a hearty "certainly," and merely added that he hoped we should not make war on Samoa. He was quite pleased when I said—"No, not against Malitoa

91. Count Herbert Bismarck to Count Hatzfeldt, March 26, 1887, E. T. S. Dugdale, *op. cit.*, vol. 1, p. 239; *Die Grosse Politik*, vol. 4, pp. 167-168.

personally, but we wish to see our interests insured against civil war and robbery." [92]

Herr Alvensleben, the German Minister at Washington, was well acquainted with the development of this political concert between Germany and Great Britain, and it naturally stiffened his attitude towards Samoa. On April 11, 1887, he called at the Department of State and handed to Bayard a note which stated that the German Government was not aware "that a certain Mr. Brandeise at Apia sustains, or has sustained, relations with the German consulate at that place, or that he has become associated with Chief Tamasese." In Bayard's note to Alvensleben, March 2, 1887, mention had been made that "Brandeise" was promoting a "rebellion against the Government of Malietoa." Alvensleben said that the German Government took exception to that phrase because they did "not consider Malietoa as the sole monarch of the Island."

Bayard remarked that he had not intended

. . . to make a point of any kind by using the words "rebellion against Malietoa"; that my only intention was, with the aid of the two other powers, Great Britain and Germany, to bring peace and order and civilization to the island by means of a native autonomy, and to use the native material for its own advancement by instructing the people in the arts of peace and good morals so that they could assist themselves. Such was the proposition made by me to the British and German Governments and that was the reason that I reported to the German Government what I thought was inconsistent on the part of its agent. I was very glad to have the report denied.[93]

On April 29, 1887, Alvensleben paid another visit to the Department of State, and upon this occasion he alluded to the treaty between Hawaii and Samoa. Bayard remarked that he had been advised of this convention by Mr. Carter, who would probably write to the German Legation with regard to it. Bayard then stated that he did not regard this arrangement as "a treaty but as a proposition to form a treaty, as it was agreed upon so contingently upon the approval of the three powers; that it was a treaty *in futuro*." In concluding the interview with Alvensleben, Bayard expressed the opinion that

. . . anything that could assist in building up a native civilization in

92. *Memorandum* by Count Herbert Bismarck, August 24, 1887, E. T. S. Dugdale, *op. cit.*, pp. 244-245; *Die Grosse Politik*, vol. 4, pp. 175-177.
93. *Memorandum* written by Bayard after a conversation with Alvensleben, April 11, 1887, *Bayard MS.*

Samoa was highly desirable; that being of the same race with the Sandwich Islanders any advice from them might be taken more sympathetically, and I should be very glad if the Sandwich Islanders could give them any useful hints.[94]

Some weeks later, Alvensleben had a conversation with Bayard in which this matter of a treaty between Hawaii and Samoa was once more discussed. The German Government was now certain of a concert with Great Britain with regard to Samoa, and there was no attempt made to conceal their sharp hostility towards King Malietoa. Alvensleben said that he had been instructed to tell Secretary Bayard that the German Foreign Office regarded the alliance between King Kalakaua and King Malietoa as "a travesty," and that this "political arrangement" would be "entirely ignored" by German officials. At this point Alvensleben spoke so hastily and indistinctly that Bayard

. . . could not understand his exact language, but it was evident from what he said that the German Government was disposed to give no recognition whatever to this alliance between Malietoa and the Sandwich Islands as strengthening in any way the title of Malietoa to be ruler of Samoa.

After referring to certain aspects of the Samoan situation, Bayard then stated that his own views with regard

. . . to the control of the government of these islands had not changed in the least since he first commenced to speak to me on the subject, and that everything I had done had been promptly communicated to him as well as the English Minister, and that nothing I had said or written was inconsistent with what I had told him would be done; that the United States would not desire to see the obliteration of the native control in these Islands; that I thought there was a chance for their advancement, and that I understood the conceded design of the three great powers was to promote that design and not to destroy it.[95]

Some two weeks after this conversation with Alvensleben, Bayard had a long talk with Carter, the Hawaiian Minister, and he informed him that the German Government would ignore the treaty of alliance between Samoa and Hawaii. Carter agreed with Bayard that the policy of the Hawaiian Foreign Office had been very "unwise" with reference to Samoa, and he then remarked

. . . that Gibson, the Minister of Foreign Affairs of Hawaii, had assured

94. *Memorandum* written by Bayard after a conversation with Alvensleben, April 29, 1887, *Bayard MS.*

95. *Memorandum* written by Bayard after a conversation with Alvensleben, May 20, 1887, *Bayard MS.*

him in his private letters that the treaty with Samoa was arranged by Mr. Bush secretly, without his knowledge and by connivance with the King. Bush had been the editor of a paper in Hawaii which was continually harping upon the necessity of the King obtaining the primacy of the Pacific, and had infected the King with that notion, so that the King had been personally disposed to take 400 Hawaiian soldiers and go down to Samoa and help Malietoa. . . . He said he had showered telegrams upon the King in opposition to this movement and thought that had restrained him.

Bayard concluded this conversation by expressing the view that it was "obviously absurd for the King to bring himself in conflict with the wishes of the German Government and I hoped he had not made matters more difficult for the United States to settle favorably with Malietoa." [96]

On June 11 Sackville-West called upon Bayard at the Department of State, and it was soon apparent that he was under pressure from the British Foreign Office in favor of some speedy settlement of Samoan difficulties. When he remarked that "the Germans were impatient" at the way things were going in Samoa, Bayard merely responded that he "could not help that, but would let him know as soon as I could what I proposed to do in the matter." [97]

Three days later, Sackville-West reappeared at the Department of State with an instruction from Lord Salisbury directing him to inform the Government of the United States that the British Foreign Office looked with disapproval upon the treaty of alliance between Hawaii and Samoa. Lord Salisbury felt certain that such an understanding would be

. . . fruitful of disorder and stand in the way of an arrangement being made for peace and good order in Samoa. He proposed that there should be a joint presentation of these views by the three treaty powers to the King of the Sandwich Islands and to Malietoa, disapproving of any such attempted interference by Kalakaua in the affairs of Samoa.

Bayard immediately assured Sackville-West that as soon as he had learned of this treaty between Hawaii and Samoa he had expressed personally to Mr. Carter

. . . very much the same views entertained by Lord Salisbury; I had thought it a most ineffectual proposition in every respect, and one that might be full

96. *Memorandum* written by Bayard after a conversation with Carter, June 3, 1887, *Bayard MS.*

97. *Memorandum* written by Bayard after a conversation with Sackville-West, June 11, 1887, *Bayard MS.*

of difficulty and danger, especially to Hawaii; that the German Minister had also informed me of this arrangement and that his Government would wholly disregard it and would not pay the slightest attention to the proposed interference by the King of Hawaii. I said I had made the same statement to Mr. von Alvensleben . . . but I told him also that upon an inspection of the instrument that it seemed to me entirely conditional upon the approval of the treaty powers, and, as I recollected the document, it so expressly stated that it contemplated only a future action, conditioned upon the approval of the three treaty powers, and therefore I do not look upon it as containing anything that was practicable. I said I would not answer him whether we would join Great Britain and Germany, but having the same views upon the subject I thought we could reach the same object by identic notes to the King of the Sandwich Islands.[98]

A few days after Sackville-West had lodged with Bayard his protest against the treaty between Samoa and Hawaii, Alvensleben called at the Department of State on a similar mission. He complained that Bush, the Hawaiian envoy to Samoa, had carried with him a considerable sum of money which he had spent in giving festivities to the Samoan natives. During these festivities some "very exciting and prejudicial remarks" had been made concerning Germany.

Bayard assured him that the American Government had

. . . instantly expressed its disapproval of the mission of Mr. Bush, and of the treaty, so-called, which he had negotiated in the name of the King of Hawaii with the Samoan Government: that we thought that Hawaii had nothing to do with Samoa, and was perfectly incompetent to deal with its affairs, and that I had informed him such had been the tenor of my remarks to Mr. Carter.

Alvensleben then referred to the warship which the Hawaiian Government had sent to Samoan waters. In this regard Bayard stated that he had understood that this warship

. . . was not seaworthy, and from some defect in her machinery could not go to sea at all, therefore I had no idea she would proceed on a voyage of 2000 miles. I told him also he was probably as well or better aware than I of the condition of affairs in Hawaii so far as the conduct and life of the King was concerned.

Alvensleben also alluded to the serious financial difficulties that were facing King Kalakaua. In view of this fact it seemed to him absurd for the Hawaiian sovereign to embark upon an ambitious role in the South Pacific. Bayard was inclined to agree with Alvensleben in this

98. *Memorandum* written by Bayard after a conversation with Sackville-West, June 14, 1887, *Bayard MS.*

regard, and when the German Minister referred to the necessity for an early conference on Samoa, Bayard stated that he was "nearly prepared to submit in writing a plan for the Government of Samoa." [99] This plan was hurriedly finished and it formed the basis of the discussions that began at the first meeting of the Washington Conference on June 25, 1887. Bayard had now reached the second stage of his Samoan program, and he had been fortunate in holding in check the rising wrath of Bismarck which found partial expression in an outburst to one of his intimate associates:

We should not have to put up with the insolence of the Hawaiians any longer, if a German squadron were at anchor before Samoa. It could sail for Hawaii, and King Kalakaua could be told that unless he desisted from his insolent intrigues in Samoa, we would shoot his legs in two, despite his American protection.[100]

With Bismarck in this frame of mind it was extremely important for Bayard to discover some solution for the Samoan problem. At the six formal sessions of the Washington Conference, June 25–July 26, 1887, he anxiously strove to effect a reconciliation between the idealism of the American plan, and the realism of the plans submitted by Germany and Great Britain. The results of these endeavors are discussed in detail in the following chapter.

99. *Memorandum* written by Bayard after a conversation with Alvensleben, June 20, 1887, *Bayard MS.*

100. Count Otto zu Stolberg-Wernigerode, *Germany and the United States of America During the Era of Bismarck*, p. 247.

CHAPTER THREE

The Washington Conference on Samoa

IT WAS ASSUMED BY SECRETARY BAYARD THAT THE DECISIONS OF THE Washington Conference on Samoa would be definitely colored by the reports submitted by the three commissioners who had been sent to investigate the situation in the South Pacific. The procedure followed by these commissioners in carrying out their investigation clearly revealed the difficulties in the way of formulating a concerted policy for Samoan affairs. When Mr. Bates arrived at Apia on August 17, 1886, he found that Mr. Travers, the German commissioner, had preceded him and had already commenced to study conditions in the islands. Mr. Thurston, the British commissioner, reached Apia on August 24, and the three commissioners held a meeting in order to discuss the "scope" of their instructions. Immediately, serious differences of opinion arose.

Bates and Thurston were of the opinion that their instructions were based upon the assumption that it was desirable to establish an "autonomous native government" in Samoa, to be "supported so far as necessary, by the joint influence and action of the three powers." Travers, however, held to the view that an autonomous native government was not "practicable," and this, apparently was the fixed opinion of the German Government. Bates and Thurston were also inclined to believe that their instructions contemplated a "joint investigation, followed by separate reports." Travers did not disclose the "precise nature" of his instructions, but he did express the opinion that the investigations should be "entirely independent" and the reports "separate." [1]

The report of Bates to Secretary Bayard was dated December 10, 1886, and it was long and carefully written. He was certain that the

1. *Report* of George H. Bates to Secretary Thomas F. Bayard, December 10, 1886, *Special Agents Series*, vol. 2, MS Dept. of State.

natives of Samoa were unable, without long-continued guidance, to "construct or maintain a government which will enforce authority or command respect." The extent of foreign intervention in Samoa would have to be greater than the Department of State had anticipated. The central government would have to be, for some time at least, administered by the "three treaty powers, or through such agencies as they may select." There should be negotiated at once a "quadripartite treaty, to which the three treaty powers and the Government of Samoa should be parties, and which would be practically the constitutional basis of the new government." Under the terms of this treaty, provision should be clearly made for the effective supervision of Samoan affairs by the three treaty powers. Such supervision, however, should not be exercised through the establishment of a tripartite government. This form of government had failed in the past and would lead to serious difficulties in the future. The best solution for the Samoan problem was some form of American control—an American mandate which would not only conserve the rights of the Samoan people but would also further the interests of the British and the German Governments.[2]

The report of Travers to Prince Bismarck was much shorter than that of Bates. After indicating the preponderance of German economic interests in Samoa, Travers came to the conclusion that the government of the islands should be "placed in the hands of but one of the treaty powers, by the consent of the others." That power, of course, should be Germany.[3]

In the report of Thurston to the British Government, emphasis was laid upon the character of the Samoan people. They were described as "excitable," "voluble," and "credulous," and much given to "lying and the circulation of false or extravagant rumors." Not only were they "thieves by instinct," but they were also "eminently lazy" and were often "consumed" with "mutual jealousy." As a people they were "incapable of unity of action," and therefore were neither capable of forming nor maintaining "any form of government worthy of the name."

After this sharp indictment of the many failings of the Samoan people, Thurston expressed the humane view that it was eminently worth while to endeavor to instruct the Samoans in the elements of political science. There was a distinct possibility that the natives could

2. *Ibid.*
3. *Report* of Consul-General Travers to Prince Bismarck, December 8, 1886, *House Ex. Doc., 238,* 50 Cong., 1 sess., pp. 260-267.

be "taught to rule themselves and coalesce in all matters concerning
their common weal." With the assistance of "three foreign members of
Government and a magistrate, for whose services the revenue of the
native government should without difficulty be able to pay, I think it
possible that a native government might in time be established on a
satisfactory footing.[4]

The German Government was exceedingly anxious to ascertain the
views of Mr. Bates with reference to conditions in Samoa, and on
December 3, 1886, Alvensleben called at the Department of State to
make inquiries. Secretary Bayard informed the German Minister that

. . . Mr. Bates had returned from Samoa, and that I had a conversation with
him, but had not yet received his report. . . . He [Mr. Alvensleben] then
asked me about the report of the British agent. I told him that none had
yet been announced to me, and that when it was announced I should prepare
to send a new consul to Apia.[5]

On February 23, 1887, Alvensleben sent a note to Bayard in which
he enclosed an extract from the report of Travers to Prince Bismarck.
In conclusion he expressed the hope that the American Government
would give him some indication of the tenor of the report made by
Bates.[6] Two days later, Sackville-West, the British Minister, paid a visit
to the Department of State to ask about the Samoan situation. He informed Bayard that Alvensleben had given him an extract of the report
of Travers. It was quite probable, he thought, that the British Commissioner had turned in his report. This meant that all three reports
would soon be available for a basis of discussion. Bayard then expressed
the view that

. . . the three reports ought to be considered together, so that a plan of
action for the three consuls could be made. I also told him [Sackville-West]
plainly that I wanted to get an American consul who would command the
respect of all three Gov'ts, because I thought that his decision ought to
weigh more than that of either the English or German consul, for the reason
that our interests in that quarter were less local than those of either Germany
or England.

I told him that I would submit the report as soon as possible, and that
the three reports ought to be submitted simultaneously. . . . He asked me

4. *Report* of John B. Thurston to Mr. Stanhope, October 1, 1886, *House Ex Doc., 238,*
50 Cong., 1 sess., pp. 269-296.

5. *Memorandum* written by Secretary Bayard after a conversation with Mr. Alvensleben,
December 3, 1886, *Bayard MS.*

6. Alvensleben to Secretary Bayard, February 23, 1887, *German Legation, Notes from,*
vol. 18, MS Dept. of State.

in parting if he might tell Lord Salisbury what I said: that the three reports of these three men ought to be made the basis of arrangement. I said "most decidedly he might," and that the three reports would be very valuable in dictating a practical line of operations.[7]

Some three weeks later, Sackville-West again called to see Secretary Bayard with reference to the Samoan question. Bayard frankly informed the British Minister that he had received an extract from the report of Travers. He also stated that the report of Bates was now ready for examination, and this being true, it was important that the British Government send to Washington the report made by Thurston. When Sackville-West inquired as to the next step the American Government would take in this Samoan matter, Bayard replied that he could not make any decision until he had seen the British and German reports. His feeling, however, was

. . . that the American consul, being a worthy and respectable man, ought to be substantially the arbitrator to decide questions that they all three could not agree upon. . . . At the same time there should be a practical commercial neutrality in that Island and I thought it could be done under a native autonomy. I said the American consul should have the main control simply because we had less interest of an individual kind; less property held there by Americans and less commerce than either the Germans or English and were therefore in a position to be disinterested and impartial. I mentioned the fact to him that we had sent a man out there who was thought to be intelligent and capable, and that the Germans, justly or unjustly, conceived the idea that he was not a man of that personal character which gave them confidence in him, and that I at once withdrew him on that account.[8]

In order to evoke some action from the British Government with regard to Samoa, Bayard on March 23, 1887, sent to Sackville-West an extract from the Bates report, and on the same day he sent a similar communication to Alvensleben.[9] In response to this note, Alvensleben called at the Department of State and expressed the hope that they could "get together" and settle the Samoan problem. Bayard's reply was tersely affirmative: "The sooner the better." [10]

7. *Memorandum* written by Secretary Bayard after a conversation with Sackville-West, February 25, 1837, *Bayard MS.*
8. *Memorandum* written by Secretary Bayard after a conversation with Sackville-West, March 18, 1887, *Bayard MS.*
9. Bayard to Alvensleben, March 23, 1887, *German Legation, Notes to,* vol. 10, MS Dept. of State.
10. *Memorandum* written by Secretary Bayard after a conversation with Mr. Alvensleben, April 11, 1887, *Bayard MS.*

The response of the British Government to Bayard's overture was friendly and prompt. On April 19 Sackville-West sent to the Department of State an extract from the report of Thurston, on Samoa, and he indicated that Lord Salisbury hoped that the proposed conference on Samoan affairs would soon be held.[11] Several days later Sackville-West wrote a short note to Bayard to express the "appreciation" of the British Government with reference to the amicable attitude to the Department of State in this Samoan matter.[12]

Before Bayard had been able to read the report of Thurston, Alvensleben paid a visit to the Department of State to inquire about Samoan affairs. After being informed that the British Government had submitted an extract of Thurston's report, Alvensleben then asked Bayard if he "would not prepare a memorandum of some plan to be submitted to the three powers." Bayard replied that he "had no objection to making a memorandum in accordance with the views we had already expressed."[13]

The anxiety of the German Government to arrive at some complete settlement of Samoan difficulties was expressed in the repeated calls of Alvensleben at the Department of State. The diplomatic pressure was somewhat annoying to Bayard, who felt that it was quite unnecessary. On May 20, 1887, the German Minister made one of his frequent visits to the Department of State to discuss the progress of the Samoan negotiations. Bayard informed him that the report of Bates had just come from the printer and that he would send copies to the German and British Legations. Alvensleben then tried to expedite matters by remarking that Sackville-West "would probably go abroad soon to join his daughters." Bayard's reply was tart and to the point: "I answered him that I could not accommodate my public affairs to the private movements of the British Minister."[14]

After provoking this sharp answer from Secretary Bayard, Alvensleben decided to exert pressure upon the Department of State through Sackville-West. On June 11 the British Minister had an interview with Bayard in which he pointedly inquired about the Samoan negotiation.

11. Sackville-West to Secretary Bayard, April 19, 1887, *British Legation, Notes from,* vol. 114, MS Dept. of State.

12. Sackville-West to Secretary Bayard, April 25, 1887, *British Legation, Notes from,* vol. 114, MS Dept. of State.

13. *Memorandum* written by Secretary Bayard after a conversation with Alvensleben, April 29, 1887. *Bayard MS.*

14. *Memorandum* written by Secretary Bayard after a conversation with Alvensleben, May 20, 1887, *Bayard MS.*

Bayard replied very cautiously, and Sackville-West then expressed the view that it "was necessary if we were to make a joint treaty that full powers should be given." This remark drew from Bayard the statement that he was not "prepared to say that the United States would make a joint treaty with anybody—that such a treaty would be against the traditions of this Government; that we would make co-operative treaties and act in co-operation with other Governments, but not ad-jointly with them." Bayard then mentioned the fact that "whether the Germans had done it or not, there had been a disposition to stir up Tamasese in revolt against Malietoa." Sackville-West was of the belief that "there was no question but that the Germans had sent arms and military instructors for that purpose." He concluded his remarks by stating that the German Government was growing impatient about the delay in settling the Samoan imbroglio. Once again Bayard's reply indicated his annoyance at German pressure: "I answered that I could not help that, but would let him [Sackville-West] know as soon as I could, what I proposed to do in the matter." [15]

On June 11 Bayard had a joint conference with Alvensleben and Sackville-West with regard to Samoa. It was in the nature of a preliminary meeting which would lay the basis for subsequent formal conferences. Bayard read at length the instructions he had sent to Pendleton and Bates, and he commented upon the investigations that had been conducted by the special agents of the three powers in Samoa. From the reports of these agents it was evident that the "land claims of the various foreigners in Samoa were in excess of the actual area of the Island group." Even if these claims were scaled down to a considerable extent it would still be true that "there would not be a foot of land left for the natives to live upon." Such a condition of affairs was "scandalous," and it was necessary for the three powers to take prompt action to prevent such a striking injustice.

After Alvensleben and Sackville-West had indicated an immediate assent to these views, Bayard then advocated the establishment of a land commission before which all claimants to lands must present their titles. This commission should consist of five members, one to be appointed by each of the three powers, and the other two to be chosen by the Samoan Government.

The British and German Ministers signified their acceptance of this

15. *Memorandum* written by Bayard after a conversation with Sackville-West, June 11, 1887.

proposal, and Bayard hastened to remind them that in all the treaties concluded between the three powers and Samoa, there was a provision which specifically provided that the Malietoa family was the royal line from which Samoan kings must be chosen. It was important to teach the Samoans the sanctity of treaties, and by this statement Bayard probably implied that the natives should be discouraged from commencing useless revolutions. At this point Alvensleben interrupted Bayard's remarks in order to advance a claim that Malietoa himself was a treaty-breaker. Bayard thought it was inexpedient to enter into a discussion of this point: it was essential that an agreement be reached upon the proposition "that the two Samoan families of Malietoa and Tupua should be the source from which the King and Vice-Kings were obtained."

Although there was no agreement upon this point, Bayard now turned to the question of the administration of justice in Samoa. Owing to the fact that the natives in Samoa lived under a communal system it was obviously unfair to impose pecuniary fines upon lawbreakers. Such a procedure meant that the innocent tribe had to pay for the crimes of reckless individuals. Hearing no objection to this suggestion, Bayard turned to a discussion of the best form of government for the Samoans. He believed that provision should be made for the election of a House of Representatives by direct vote of the Natives. The Representatives should be chosen for a three year term, and they were to be divided into three classes "so that one [class] would go out each year." It was advisable, Bayard thought, to have the Ministers of Foreign Relations, of the Interior, and of the Treasury participate in the sessions of the House of Representatives.

No objection to these suggestions was raised by either Alvensleben or Sackville-West. Alvensleben did, however, express the view that a tripartite form of government for Samoa was an impracticable one, and he cited the report of Bates to sustain his contention. He believed it would be better to provide for the appointment of a Prime Minister by the power which had preponderant interests in Samoa. For the time being this meant German control of the islands. On this point Alvensleben was supported by Sackville-West.

Bayard did not immediately oppose Alvensleben's proposal but he did suggest that

. . . the power to confer the place should also be a power capable to remove in case of necessity, and stated that it must be perceived that the real strength of any government that was created by the arrangement now proposed would consist in the straightforward intent of the three powers to gain no advantage over each other in any way, but to preserve good government and justice in that community. Therefore, if any man who was nominated for the post of Prime Minister should in any way pervert the powers given to him, the Government at whose instance he had been placed there should assist in his removal.

After Alvensleben had given his approval of this suggestion, Bayard reminded both Ministers that the main purpose of the forthcoming Washington Conference was "the preservation of a native autonomy independently of a protectorate or annexation from any of the powers." There was no dissent from this view, and a final agreement was reached on the proposal to separate the consuls of the three powers "from the local and interior government of the country." [16]

On June 20 Alvensleben called at the Department of State to inquire when the first meeting of the Washington Conference would be held. In reply, Bayard stated that

. . . there was nothing to explain about the delay, except the great distance, and the difficulty of dealing with a country of which we had so little knowledge. . . . However, I was very nearly prepared to submit in writing a plan for the Government of Samoa, which I thought we could sustain by co-operative action of the three Governments and I hoped to submit that to him and to Mr. West during the present week.[17]

16. *Minutes* of the preliminary conference on June 11, 1887, *Bayard MS.*
17. *Memorandum* written by Secretary Bayard after a conversation with Alvensleben, June 20, 1887, *Bayard MS.* Bayard's plan for a settlement of the Samoan difficulties was sent to the British and German Ministers some time before June 25. It consisted of the following fifteen points:
　(1) The independence and autonomy of Samoa should be preserved from the control or preponderating influence of any foreign power.
　(2) The three treaty powers should assist the natives of Samoa to form and administer an effective government.
　(3) Recognition should be extended to a native king. Respect for native customs and traditions would seem to require the continuance of Malietoa Laupepa as King, and Tamasese as Vice-King.
　(4) A written constitution should be adopted by the King and his council. Provision should be made for a bicameral legislature.
　(5) Three important Ministers of State should be nominated by the three powers and appointed by the King. They should hold the offices of Minister of Foreign Relations, Minister of the Treasury, and Minister of the Interior. They should also have the right to participate in the sessions of the lower house of the legislature.
　(6) A municipal government should be erected at Apia without any interference from the consuls of the three treaty powers.
　(7) Foreign consuls were to retain criminal jurisdiction over their own countrymen.
　(8) A court for the administration of justice among the natives should be constituted, the judges to be appointed by the King and Council.
　(9) The constitution should prohibit the imposition of pecuniary fines upon the natives.

On June 25 the first session of the Washington Conference on Samoa was opened by an inquiry from Secretary Bayard as to whether the German and British Ministers had received his memorandum. They answered in the affirmative and Alvensleben then produced his own memorandum which he was ready to read "but could not give out of his hand." He was willing, however, to have the views of his Government recorded in the protocol of the Conference.[18]

This attitude on the part of Alvensleben was displeasing to Bayard who indicated that he had submitted to both Ministers a lengthy memorandum setting forth the views of the American Government. He had

(10) The sale of firearms, ammunition, and intoxicating liquors should be prohibited.

(11) A Land Commission should be organized to examine all claims for title to lands in Samoa. The membership of the commission should consist of three foreigners nominated by the three powers and appointed by the King, and two natives chosen by the King.

(12) The salaries of the members of the Land Commission should be paid out of the revenues collected in Samoa.

(13) The Land Commission should set apart certain lands for development of a system of public schools.

(14) Revenue should be raised in Samoa principally through customs and tonnage duties.

(15) Provision should be made by the treaty powers for the stationing of ships of war in Samoa to preserve peace and order.

18. The memorandum of Alvensleben contained the following points:

(1) Inasmuch as King Malietoa was guilty of repeated breaches of his treaties with Germany, and because of the fact that he had comparatively few followers, it was expedient to have a new election for the office of King of Samoa.

(2) With reference to purely native affairs, the administration of the Samoan Government could be conducted by the King and Council.

(3) Provision should be made for the appointment of an Adviser to the King. He should be nominated by the treaty power having "for the time being the preponderating interests in Samoa." The nomination should have the approval of the other two treaty powers, and the tenure of office should be five years. The powers of this Adviser should be extensive. He should have control over "all necessary measures with regard to the maintenance of public order . . . and the security of any kind of property of foreign residents."

(4) In order to secure to the three treaty powers an equality of treatment with respect to commerce, the provisions to that effect in existing treaties should be renewed.

(5) An International Court or Land Commission should be organized to settle disputes relative to land claims.

(6) Special consideration should be given to the problem of raising revenue for the maintenance of the new Samoan Government.

(7) In consideration of the fact that German interests in Samoa were greater than those of the other two treaty powers, the German Government was entitled to nominate the first Adviser to the King.

(8) For the purpose of avoiding any appearance of undue interference in the administration of Samoan affairs, it would be expedient to have a frank acknowledgment on the part of the three treaty powers that the existing treaties are still valid and in force.

turned over this memorandum without any reservations, and it "seemed proper that the views of the other two Governments should be handed to him in the same way."[19]

Alvensleben was not convinced by Bayard's statement, and he flatly refused to submit his memorandum to the Secretary of State. Sackville-West at once followed suit, but he agreed that his statements could be taken down by a stenographer and embodied in the protocol of the conference.[20]

After these memoranda had been read by Alvensleben and Sackville-West, the conference adjourned, in order that Bayard might give careful consideration to the points they had developed. On July 1 Alvensleben paid a visit to the Department of State to inform Bayard that he had received instructions permitting him to come to an agreement with reference to Samoa "by an exchange of notes" with the other two treaty powers. He then indicated that he and Sackville-West would be "ready at any time" to attend further conferences upon the Samoan problem.[21] Later that afternoon, Bayard sent notes to both Alvensleben and Sackville-West in which he fixed July 2 as the date of the second meeting of the Washington Conference.[22]

When the conference re-assembled, Bayard proceeded to indicate

19. *Minutes* of the conference held on June 25, 1887, *Bayard MS.*

20. The memorandum of Sackville-West may be summarized as follows:

(1) Inasmuch as the three treaty powers have no desire to destroy the independence of Samoa, but seek only to establish the right and equality of their commerce, a declaration to this effect might be made as a preliminary step.

(2) It is apparent that the natives of Samoa are incapable of establishing and maintaining a stable and efficient government for the islands. Because of this fact the British Government was ready to agree that one of the treaty powers, as the mandatary of the other two, should have one of its nationals hold the office of Adviser to the King.

(3) In view of the fact that tripartite government in Samoa seems to be impracticable, it might be expedient to have control over the islands vested for a limited period in one of the treaty powers. With regard to this point, the British Government inclined towards the view that "preponderating commercial interests" should be the deciding factor. This, of course, would mean German control.

(4) An International Land Court should be established to have jurisdiction over all disputes involving land titles.

(5) Foreign consuls were to retain criminal jurisdiction over their own countrymen.

(6) Because of the serious dispute in Samoa between Malietoa and Tamasese, it was expedient to have a new royal election. With reference to the probable candidates for election to the office of King, the British Government could only state that it would express no opinion, "favorably or adversely, to the election of Malietoa."

21. *Memorandum* written by Bayard after a conversation with Alvensleben, July 1, 1887, *Bayard MS.*

22. Bayard to Sackville-West, July 1, 1887, *Bayard MS.*

the points upon which all three treaty powers were agreed.[23] One difference of opinion between the United States and the other two treaty powers was with regard to the establishment of a legislative assembly. In order to facilitate agreement between the three powers, the American Government was disposed to abandon the proposal in favor of a Samoan legislature and would consent to the government of the islands by a King and a council of chiefs. In the memorandum presented by the American Government it was proposed that Malietoa be continued as King and Tamasese as Vice-King. In the memoranda presented by the British and German Ministers there was a provision for a new election. For the sake "of coming to an agreement" with the representatives of Great Britain and Germany, Bayard was willing to agree to a new election on condition that it should be "a native election, free, and unawed." At this point Alvensleben inquired whether the newly-elected King should be approved by the powers. Bayard answered with an emphatic negative. Such a provision would "virtually give the powers the choice of a king." The object of the "present arrangement was not to obliterate the rights of the islanders, but to assist them in forming a civilized government; that a virtual neutralization of this group of islands was desirable."

In answer to the German and British proposals that the power having preponderating "commercial interests" in Samoa should have temporary control over the islands, Bayard stated that it seemed to him that such a viewpoint was in direct conflict with the idea of neutralization. The ultimate result of any acceptance of this British-German proposal would be a permanent German control over Samoa. Bayard then indicated why the United States was so interested in these South Pacific islands. American commerce in the Pacific area was bound to increase in a significant manner. The completion of the transcontinental railway lines in the United States and the proposed construction of an isthmian

23. These points upon which the three treaty powers had agreed were: "That there should be no annexation of the islands by any of the treaty powers; that the independence and autonomy of the islands were to be preserved with equality of rights of commerce and navigation for the citizens or subjects of the treaty powers; that a native government was to be established and assisted to maintain itself; that the present jurisdiction of consuls over their own countrymen should be preserved; that the present treaties be maintained, so far as the rights of the three powers under them are concerned; that means of raising revenue for the support of the government should be devised, and that the question of taxing foreigners should be considered; that impost and tonnage duties should be established by identic treaties between the three powers and the Samoan Government; that a land court should be formed to settle titles and holdings of lands in the group."

canal under American auspices would make possible a greatly enlarged American commerce with the Orient. The Samoan islands were needed as an outpost for this expanding foreign trade. It should be remembered, however, that the policies of the United States were "not such as to give the slightest alarm to the commercial interest of any other country." America wished merely to preserve equal opportunities for all the treaty powers in the South Pacific.

A discussion then took place with reference to the validation of titles to land in the Samoan islands. Alvensleben and Sackville-West believed that it would clarify the situation if a Land Commission were established for the purpose of passing upon all titles to lands. In addition to this commission there should also be a Land Court with appellate jurisdiction in disputed cases. Bayard immediately objected to the establishment of both a Land Commission and a Land Court. The matter of claims was not an intricate one, and "if there was the right king, with fair-minded men who would deal with each other with justness between themselves and the people, they would move with more celerity and with more stability than if there were two bodies." Sackville-West, however, supported the viewpoint of Alvensleben, and the discussion then shifted to the question of the Adviser to the King.

Alvensleben presented a long memorandum showing the weakness of the native government. Some form of foreign intervention to Samoa was necessary for the protection of the rights of the nationals of the treaty powers, and inasmuch as Germany had the largest interests in the islands it seemed clear that the German Government "should be given the right to nominate the official whose duty it shall be to control the native government." When Bayard objected that such an arrangement would lead to eventual German control over Samoa, Sackville-West once again came to the aid of Alvensleben. The British Government, he said, supported the idea of foreign control in Samoa "because they thought without it there could be no stable government." They were entirely willing that "this control should be exercised by a person appointed by one of the powers, as the mandatary of the other two."

Bayard refused to be influenced by this apparent British-German accord on Samoan affairs, and he proposed that "in the council of the king there should be three foreigners, a minister of foreign affairs, of the interior, and a treasurer. . . . One might be a German, another an Englishman, and another an American." Only in this way could the native government maintain its independence and the rights of the three treaty powers receive full protection.

After Alvensleben submitted a draft treaty which embodied the German contentions, the conference adjourned. A third meeting was held on July 9 at which the question of the adjudication of land claims once more arose. Bayard was opposed to the establishment of a Land Commission *and* a Land Court. A Land Court was quite sufficient to settle all disputes as to claims, and there was no necessity for the appointment of a commission to make a preliminary report upon cases. Alvensleben was of the opinion that a Land Commission was of great importance, and Sackville-West rushed to his assistance. In a memorandum which he read to the conference, Sackville-West indicated that the British Government was "strongly of the opinion that it will be found necessary to facilitate the leaders of the land court when established." It would be necessary to collect preliminary evidence in order to expedite the final decisions of the Land Court. This work of investigation could best be carried on by a Land Commission. When Bayard remarked that he believed the establishment of a Land Commission would embarrass rather than facilitate the work of a Land Court in Samoa, Sackville-West stated with finality that "his Government were strongly in favor of the commission, and Mr. von Alvensleben's Government was also."

When it was apparent that no agreement could be reached on the question of the adjudication of land titles, the discussion next turned to the matter of what type of foreign intervention in Samoan affairs was to be preferred. Bayard entered a strong objection against the German plan whereby an Adviser to the King would really control the Samoan Government, this Adviser, of course, being appointed by the power with the greatest interests in the islands. Once more Sackville-West came to the support of his German colleague. After asserting that any form of tripartite administration of Samoan affairs was bound to fail, the British Minister stated that Her Majesty's Government was "willing . . . to accord to the German representative the first term of five years as the mandatary of the other two powers." With this declaration of the identity of views on the part of the German and British Governments, the third session of the conference came to a close.

The fourth session of the conference was largely devoted to the important questions of the adjudication of land titles and the type of foreign intervention in Samoan affairs which would best conserve the rights of the nationals of the treaty powers and yet not destroy the independence of the native government. With reference to granting a mandate to the power possessing preponderating interests in the islands, Bayard reminded the conference that the "admitted basis" of their discussions was "the equality of the three powers." This being true, it mattered not "whether the mandatary was an American, or a German, or an Englishman; the result of perpetuating power in the hands of either would have the same result." A perpetual mandate given to any one of the three powers would mean the ascendancy of that power in Samoa. On the other hand, if this mandate should be exercised in alternation, such a procedure would "impose a wholesome check upon a disposition to abuse it."

Alvensleben now inquired whether Bayard had receded from his former stand and was now submitting a "new proposition that the mandatary should be chosen by the powers alternately?" The Secretary of State refrained from giving a direct answer to this question. He merely remarked that he "still believed in the subdivision of powers; that if there were only two ministers . . . there would still be a check upon the disposition to misuse power." Alvensleben interpreted this reply to be a guarded negative to the idea of selecting a mandatary in alternation, and he then submitted a memorandum which attempted to show the weakness of Bayard's original contention that the government of Samoa should be largely carried on by three Ministers of State who would be nominated by the three treaty powers. In order to prove that the tripartite government in Samoa had been a failure, Alvensleben freely quoted from the report of Mr. Bates, the American special agent.

The remainder of the fourth session of the conference was devoted to a discussion as to whether there should be both a Land Commission and a Land Court to pass upon the validity of land titles in Samoa. Bayard voiced strong objections to the establishment of a Land Commission, but Alvensleben and Sackville-West stood their ground in this regard,[24] and finally Bayard remarked that he would "not stand in the way of this piece of machinery if it was considered upon reflection, desirable to the end." Upon this note of apparent compromise the fourth session of the conference was brought to a close.

24. With reference to the attitude of Sackville-West during the Washington Conference, Bayard wrote as follows to E. J. Phelps, November 19, 1888: "In my conferences with him [Sackville-West] and the German Minister on Samoan affairs, he abandoned me entirely and took sides with Germany, although this I always suspected was in accord with Anglo-German understanding." *Bayard Letter Book*, vol. 9, *Bayard MS.*

Shortly after the opening of the fifth session of the conference, on July 21, a sharp division of opinion was apparent with reference to the composition of the Land Court. According to the German plan this court was to be composed of "a judge nominated by the Samoan Government, and of a Consul or of one of the prominent countrymen of the litigant." Such a plan, thought Bayard, would create a special court in each case, and would not lead to that uniformity of decision which was so necessary in order to guard against "hopeless injustice." Alvensleben now hastened to observe that the most pressing problem before the conference was the establishment of some form of government for the Samoan islands, and therefore all the discussions about the adjudication of land titles were only preliminary. Bayard at once replied that the establishment of a Land Court would be a very important function of the new Samoan Government. Alvensleben agreed with this remark, and he assumed that the mandatary power would appoint the judge of the Land Court. To this procedure Bayard entered a most emphatic negative. Such a solution would reduce the matter to "an absolutism."

Bayard now entered into a spirited discussion with Alvensleben concerning the degree of influence to be exercised by Germany in the establishment of the new Samoan Government. He was unalterably opposed to any idea that Germany's preponderant interests in Samoa should give her a special position. The Washington Conference had been called to discover some formula that would protect the equal interests of the three powers in the Samoan islands, and he would not accept any scheme that would pave the way for eventual German control.

The sixth and last session of the Washington Conference on Samoa was held on July 26. Alvensleben read a long paper in which he endeavored to quiet American apprehensions as to German designs upon Samoa. Bayard then read a long memorandum in which the background and purpose of the Washington Conference were carefully discussed. He passed on to a sharp criticism of the plans submitted by Alvensleben for the establishment of a government for Samoa. These plans really amounted to a "virtual displacement of native government, and, instead of native government with foreign assistance, means the absolute and undefined control of the affairs of the islands by a single foreigner." It was apparent to Bayard that

. . . the further this conference has progressed, and the views and objects of the plan presented by the German Minister are developed by him, the further we find ourselves departing from any substantial recognition of a native autonomy for Samoa, and the consequent independence of that island group. The plan as proposed and explained by Mr. von Alvensleben is substantially a foreign autocratic government, based on mercantile interests, and all experience has shown what must necessarily result from such an attempt; and that under it the defeat of the objects we have all distinctly proposed is certain.

In conclusion Bayard proposed that the conference adjourn until the autumn, in order to give the British and German Ministers ample time to submit the protocols to their respective governments and await further instructions. There was no objection to Bayard's proposal and the Washington Conference broke up without arriving at a settlement of the Samoan problem. Its failure to do so soon led to dangerous friction between Germany and the United States in the South Pacific.[25]

25. This account of the Washington Conference on Samoa is based upon the Protocols MSS, in the *Bayard Papers* and in the archives of the Department of State. See also, *S. Ex. Doc., 102,* 50 Cong., 2 sess.

CHAPTER FOUR

War Clouds Over Samoa

----····◆····----

TWO DAYS AFTER THE TERMINATION OF THE WASHINGTON CONFERENCE, Sir John B. Thurston paid a visit to the Department of State to see Secretary Bayard. Thurston had been sent by the British Government to investigate the situation in Samoa, and his report reflected a humanitarian spirit that was noticeably lacking in the written statement that Herr Travers had submitted to the German Foreign Office. Thurston believed that "an earnest attempt to establish the present native Government upon an improved footing was at least worthy of trial." Under the tutelage of foreign advisers the Samoans could be "taught to rule themselves," and he thought that it was quite possible that "a native government might in time be established on a satisfactory footing." [1]

During his conversations with American officials he expressed similar sentiments, and Bayard was greatly attracted to this Britisher who apparently wished to help the natives of Samoa rather than exploit them. In a memorandum written immediately after Thurston's visit, Bayard remarks:

> He [Thurston] expressed to me his strongest approbation of the position that I had taken there on the land question, and gave me his views in full of the extreme injustice and danger of the German proposition. [2]

At the close of his conference with Bayard on July 28, Thurston left a volume containing the laws and regulations adopted by the British Government with reference to the administration of the Fiji Islands. Bayard was deeply impressed with this record of achievement, and he

1. *House Ex. Doc., 238*, 50 Cong. 1 sess., pp. 285-286.
2. *Memorandum* written by Bayard after a conversation with Sir John B. Thurston, July 28, 1887, *Bayard MS.*

expressed to Thurston his high appreciation of the work that had been done on behalf of the natives of those islands. There was an

. . . unmistakable line of morality, good faith and benevolence running through this simple system of government which should commend it to all just-minded men. If such results could only be attained in the Samoan group I would be delighted. The forces of good and the forces of evil are at work in this world, but I recognize in you a valuable ally of the former.[3]

On August 29 Alvensleben called at the Department of State and handed to Bayard a long memorandum which presented the viewpoint of the German Government with reference to the Samoan situation. When Bayard read it he at once realized that Bismarck had sent him a challenge. After expressing regret at the failure of the Washington Conference to come to some agreement with reference to Samoa, the German memorandum announced that King Malietoa would be asked to give immediate reparation for insults offered to German nationals.[4] Satisfaction would also be demanded for the robberies and thefts "committed on German plantations," and for the "systematic refusal of legal protection in cases of criminal offenses committed by Samoans against German subjects." If King Malietoa were

. . . not willing or not powerful enough to give us the necessary satisfaction for the past and sufficient guarantees for the future, [the Imperial Government will] feel obliged to declare war on him and refuse to recognize his government. . . . The Imperial Government is, of course, far from intending to bring about any change in the political relations which the three Powers represented there and connected by friendship, entertain to Samoa, . . . but we are unable to allow the dignity of the German Empire and the security of the German subjects to be any longer slighted in such a manner as has been done by Malietoa.[5]

3. Secretary Bayard to Sir John B. Thurston, July 30, 1887, *Bayard Letter Book*, vol. 5, *Bayard MS.*
4. The "insult" at which the German Government was particularly incensed, was the so-called "affair of the Emperor's birthday." On that day a conflict broke out between some of the followers of Malietoa and certain German residents who were celebrating the birthday of the Emperor. The report of the German consul emphasized the serious nature of this brawl, but the reports of the American and British consuls minimized the importance of the incident. See *Samoa-Weissbuch*, 1889, pt. 5, no. 3; Robert Louis Stevenson, "A Footnote to History," *Letters and Miscellanies*, vol. 19 (N. Y. 1897), pp. 418ff. It is apparent that the German Government did not expect Malietoa to comply with the demands made upon him. In this regard see Lord Salisbury to Sir E. Malet, August 15, 1887, *Accounts and Papers, 1889*, vol. 86, Cd-5629, no. 143.
5. *Memorandum* of the Imperial German Government left with Secretary Bayard by Minister Alvensleben, August 29, 1887, *Bayard MS.* See also *House Ex. Doc., 238*, 50 Cong. 1 sess., pp. 59-60.

Bayard's reaction to this German note is given in a memorandum which he wrote immediately after Alvensleben left the Department of State, August 29, 1887:

> I said to him that I trusted the action of the German Government, whatever it was, would not seek in any way to disturb the absolute neutrality of the Samoan group; that the United States had treaty rights with Samoa for which they expected the fullest respect to be paid. He [Alvensleben] said there was no other design on the part of his government. I told him that I considered it quite as important to German interest as it could be to the United States, that the islands and waters of Samoa should be in a state of peaceful neutrality.[6]

While Bayard was busy contrasting the humane attitude of Sir John B. Thurston with the belligerent demeanor of Alvensleben, the German Government took immediate measures to shatter the American dream of "peaceful neutrality" in Samoa. On August 19, ten days before Alvensleben handed the German memorandum to Secretary Bayard, a German squadron of four warships sailed into Apia harbor. It happened that a Sydney mail packet was due to visit Apia as a port of call, so Commodore Heusner waited until the departure of that steamer on August 23. The next vessel for Australia would not call for several weeks, and a *fait accompli* in Samoa could be accomplished before the outside world got any inkling of what had taken place in the distant South Pacific.

After the Sydney steamer had passed over the horizon, Herr Becker, the German consul at Apia, sent a note to King Malietoa in which he demanded the immediate payment of an indemnity of $13,000 as a form of reparation for repeated thefts from German plantations and for an alleged insult to the German Emperor. It was Becker's personal opinion that there had been "nothing just or correct in Samoa" since the accession of Malietoa to the throne, and he warned the Samoan king to comply with these demands within twenty-four hours. He also indicated that he expected the Samoan king to perform an *ifu,* which meant that he would have to crawl upon his stomach towards the German consul as a token of abject apology.[7]

Malietoa replied at once to Herr Becker's peremptory demands and requested a period of three days grace during which he could consult

6. *Bayard MS.*

7. Consul Becker to King Malietoa, August 23, 1887, enclosed in despatch from Harold M. Sewall, the American Consul-General at Apia, to James D. Porter, Assistant Secretary of State, September 10, 1887, *Apia, Consular Despatches,* vol. 15, MS Dept. of State.

with the Samoan chiefs before taking any final action.[8] Becker refused to grant any extension of time, and on the morning of August 24 some seven hundred German marines landed at Apia and took over the control of affairs. In the face of protests from Sewall, the American Consul-General, Becker announced that war had been declared against Malietoa. The German Government then immediately proceeded to recognize Tamasese as the King of Samoa, and the customary assurances were given that the rights of the treaty powers would be respected.[9]

Sewall responded with a proclamation that the American Government still recognized Malietoa as King of Samoa, but he enjoined all American citizens to offer no opposition to the German military forces.[10] When Commodore Heusner proclaimed martial law on August 27, Sewall warned resident Americans to halt when they were challenged by German sentries, but he sent a strong protest to Consul Becker against the continued presence of armed men within the town and district of Apia.[11]

On August 24 Selu Seananai, the Chief Secretary of the Samoan Government, appealed to Sewall for assistance. He based this appeal upon the language of Article V of the Samoan-American treaty, and he concluded with an expression of trust "in the love of the United States of America towards this weak people." [12] Upon receiving this appeal, Sewall hastened to inform Consul Becker that he had "granted the request of the Samoan Government," and he indicated that he was ready to "proceed to settle the difference on a satisfactory basis." [13] Becker made no formal reply to this communication from Sewall, but he frankly admitted that the German Government wished to take Malietoa into "custody."

When Malietoa fled into the bush, Tamasese, the new king by virtue of German support, issued a proclamation calling upon the chiefs of Samoa to meet in assembly in Mulinuu on September 15. When this *fono*, or assembly, was held, the chiefs were informed by Commodore Heusner that Tamasese had been made King of Samoa, and he sub-

8. King Malietoa to Consul Becker, August 24, 1887, enclosed in Sewall to Porter, Sept. 10, 1887, MS Dept. of State.

9. Consul Becker to Consul-General Sewall, August 24, 25, 1887, *Apia, Consular Despatches*, vol. 15, MS Dept. of State.

10. A copy of this proclamation is contained in the despatch from Sewall to Porter, September 10, 1887, *Apia, Consular Despatches*, vol. 15, MS Dept. of State.

11. Sewall to Becker, August 29, 1887, *ibid.*

12. Selu Seananai to Sewall, August 24, 1887, *ibid.*

13. Sewall to Becker, August 24, 1887, *ibid.*

mitted a document which he instructed them to sign. Inasmuch as they were unarmed and in the presence of superior force, they signed a document whose contents were entirely unknown to them. This document was an official recognition of Tamasese as king, but in view of the fact that it was signed under duress, it had little validity.[14]

At the close of this assembly, Mataafa made a speech in which he informed Commodore Heusner that "neither by birth nor following was Tamasese entitled to be king; that Malietoa was first entitled, and after him he (Mataafa) himself." This was bold talk and Sewall was certain that it marked the beginning of dissension in the ranks of the followers of Tamasese. But German armed power had made such a deep impression upon the Samoan chiefs that they sent messengers to the hiding place of Malietoa and requested that he surrender himself to Consul Becker. This he did on September 17, and after a tearful farewell to his followers, he was hurried on board a German warship, and on the following day the *Adler* carried him to an unknown destination.[15]

With Malietoa out of the way, Consul Becker felt free to assume actual control over Samoa. On October 14 armed sailors from the German squadron were landed in Apia, and the German flag was raised over the headquarters of Tamasese. Becker then informed Sewall that he was obliged to consider the municipal government of Apia "to be provisionally in abeyance." [16] Sewall promptly protested against this peremptory action on the part of the German consul, and he sent a telegram to Secretary Bayard which read: "Tamasese German aid usurps municipal government. Americans unprotected." [17] On October 20 the U.S.S. *Adams* arrived in Apia, and the stage was being prepared for a drama that might take a very serious turn.

The reaction in the United States to these acts of German aggression was outspokenly hostile. The New York *World* believed that the Samoan situation was the result of the "characteristic Bismarckian policy of first picking a quarrel and then rushing in and claiming all that had been decided upon long before the quarrel was started." [18] The New York *Tribune* was fearful that the German intrigues in Samoa were

14. Sewall to Porter, October 8, 1887, *Apia, Consular Despatches,* vol. 15, MS Dept. of State.
15. Sewall to Porter, October 10, 1887, *ibid.*
16. Becker to Sewall, October 14, 1887, enclosed in despatch from Sewall to Porter, November 8, 1887, *Apia, Consular Despatches,* vol. 15, MS Dept. of State.
17. Sewall to Secretary Bayard, Sydney, November 2, 1887, *ibid.*
18. December 13, 1887.

"about to succeed;"[19] the New York *Herald* thought that America's interests were "jeopardized by the recent German interference;"[20] and the San Francisco *Examiner* expressed the opinion that the Germans were "riding a very high horse in Samoa."[21]

Bayard himself was deeply disturbed over the situation in the South Pacific. On September 19 Sackville-West had an interview with Bayard during the course of which he expressed the view that Germany "meant to get control of those [Samoan] Islands." Bayard then remarked that Alvensleben had left at the Department of State

> . . . a note indicating a very hostile disposition on the part of his Gov't. towards Malietoa, and an apparent intention to overthrow him unless he submitted to certain demands—one of which was the payment of a large sum of money, and I did not see how a King whose annual salary was $200 could pay much of a fine, and, therefore, I supposed the intention was to impose upon him impossible conditions, and then place some agent of a German trading company in actual control of that Government.

When Sackville-West inquired if the American Government had taken any action with regard to German aggression in Samoa, Bayard answered in the negative. He did, however, voice the opinion that he had supposed "all Governments owed some allegiance and respect to the opinions of mankind."[22]

Several days later, Alvensleben called at the Department of State for the express purpose of leaving a memorandum with Bayard. According to this document, Germany had declared war on Malietoa because

> . . . he refused to satisfy the just demands which have been stated in a previous communication. . . . As soon as Germany will have obtained by the abdication of Malietoa due satisfaction, the state of war will cease. The speedy restoration of peace and of a better security of the general condition than heretofore, may be foreseen with certainty, if Malietoa does not meet with any encouragement from the Consuls by the prospect of foreign support.

In keeping with the spirit of this memorandum, Alvensleben inquired if Bayard would instruct the American consul at Apia "to withhold from Malietoa any support—moral or other—that would induce him to prolong the conflict, and to inform him of the futility of objecting to the German rule." Bayard immediately replied that he was bound

> . . . in all frankness to say that to impose such a condition upon Malietoa

19. October 16, 1887.   20. October 16, 1887.   21. March 8, 1888.
22. *Memorandum* written by Secretary Bayard after a conversation with Sackville-West, September 19, 1887, *Bayard MS.*

as the payment of pecuniary fines was simply to ask him that which it was impossible for him to comply with; that it was known that he was a poor, half-civilized man, whose annual salary as King was but $200; that he and his people had no money and therefore, to ask them for a large sum of money was to ask them for that which it was perfectly plain they could not comply with. I said that so far as any acts of disrespect to the German Emperor were concerned I had nothing to say except to express sincere regret that they had occurred. . . . As to Germany declaring war against Malietoa, of course the thing had but one side; that it was utterly impossible for the weak King and that little, scattered handful of his subjects to contend with Germany.

I told him he might be assured that no instructions of any kind had been issued by this Department to its new Consul at Samoa, but we had awaited the result of the Conference we were holding, between himself, the British Minister, and myself, the object of which professedly on all hands was to establish a native autonomy in Samoa. . . . I told him that I had received from the American Vice-Consul statements to the effect that the German Commercial Company, established in Samoa, were assuming control in connection with Tamasese—wholly inconsistent with the supremacy of Malietoa, but that I had not brought that to the knowledge of the Conference because I supposed that the object of that Conference was to make such a state of things impossible.

Alvensleben endeavored to obtain from Bayard an expression of approval of the action of the German Government in "suppressing Malietoa." Bayard's reply must have given small satisfaction to the German Minister:

I told him [Alvensleben] . . . that the first allegiance of this Government [the United States] was to right and justice, and that they were not only to consider what were the rights of the German, English, and American Governments in Samoa, but we owed it to ourselves to consider what were the rights of the natives in Samoa.

Bayard then tried to make it very clear to Alvensleben that the Department of State was neither in favor of a tripartite government in Samoa nor a government in which all administrative powers were placed "in the hands of the Germans alone." The German Minister concluded his remarks by expressing the hope that Malietoa would be informed by the American Government that no moral influence would "be used in his behalf." Bayard gave him no assurance in this regard: "I told him I must know more of the facts before I could express an opinion as to what we would do." [23]

23. *Memorandum* written by Secretary Bayard after a conversation with Alvensleben, September 23, 1887, *Bayard MS.*

On September 28 Alvensleben made a formal call on Secretary Bayard to inform him that he was returning to Germany for a visit. Before leaving America he was anxious to have a final discussion of the Samoan situation. He inquired whether Bayard intended to send any new instructions to Apia, and received the reply that the Department of State would take no further action until it was better acquainted with the actual condition of affairs in Samoa. Bayard finally remarked that he had been greatly perturbed over the attitude of the German Government towards King Malietoa. A war with Malietoa

. . . could scarcely be called a conflict with two sides; that he would necessarily be at the mercy of any great power that chose to impose unjust terms upon him or treat him unkindly. I had been impressed by the fact that we could create a respectable gov't. upon a native basis, and I had lately read a book of laws, published in Fiji, which were of a very simple and wholesome morality, within the comprehension of people of low civilization, and I had thought something of that kind could be established and ought to be established in Samoa. I still thought that . . . the trouble was caused by the greed of that commercial company of Germans who virtually represented the German Government in those Islands.[24]

The aggressive actions of the German officials in Samoa were discussed in the American press in the early part of October, 1887, and William C. Whitney, the Secretary of the Navy in President Cleveland's Cabinet, felt so outraged when he saw the newspaper accounts that he sent some clippings to Secretary Bayard with sharp comments. Bayard replied at once that he had already seen the press clippings but had received no official word from Apia since August 16.[25] He then rehearsed for Whitney's benefit the results of the Washington Conference and he also informed him of the tenor of the remarks that had been made by Alvensleben. In the concluding paragraphs of this letter to Whitney, Bayard took issue with the opinion of the Secretary of the Navy relative to the manner in which the Samoan situation had been handled:

Whatever my disappointment in failing to obtain benevolent and generous treatment for these feeble Islanders at the hands of Germany and Great Britain, . . . and however oppressive and unjust I may consider the action of Germany towards Malietoa, . . . I am unaware of the slightest ground for the apprehension you appear to indicate that a "National disgrace" to

24. *Memorandum* written by Secretary Bayard after a conversation with Alvensleben, September 28, 1887, *Bayard MS.*

25. Sewall's despatch of August 16 had been received at the Department of State on September 12.

the United States can be involved in the transactions relating to Samoa.
. . . I may not clearly understand certain expressions in your note, but at
present I will merely say that the action of Germany towards Samoa, as at
present made known to me, violates no treaty stipulations to which the
United States is a party, but so far as I can discover is within the admitted
rights under the law of Nations, and creates no *casus belli*, to any other
government than Samoa.[26]

In contrast to these criticisms of Secretary Whitney with reference
to the Samoan situation, the following remarks from George H. Pendleton must have been comforting to Bayard:

Mr. Scott, the first Secretary of the British Embassy, dined at my house
day before yesterday. . . . He said: "Mr. Bayard got greatly the better of
Alvensleben in the discussions of the [Washington] conference. He was altogether too strong for Alvensleben! . . . He said that full reports were made
to the Foreign Office in London, and by it forwarded to this Embassy, and
they (the members of the Embassy) had read them with great interest, and
were all of the opinion that Alvensleben had not been very successful in his
contentions." [27]

During the course of this dinner at the American Legation in
Berlin, Mr. Pendleton launched into a sharp attack upon the German
Government for its treatment of King Malietoa. He soon discovered
that Mr. Scott took only a "languid interest" in such critical remarks.
If Pendleton had known of the close entente between Germany and
Great Britain with reference to Samoa, he would have understood the
"languor" on the part of the first Secretary of the British Embassy when
German policy in the South Pacific was discussed. In a previous chapter
we have already indicated how Chancellor Bismarck exerted enough
diplomatic pressure upon Lord Salisbury to compel him to favor German plans in Samoa. The length to which Lord Salisbury was willing to
go in this matter of conciliating Germany is clearly shown in a memorandum of Count Herbert Bismarck in which he recounted a recent
conversation with the British Prime Minister:

Lord Salisbury visited me yesterday afternoon at the Embassy, and the
conversation turned first upon Samoa. . . . The final solution that he would
prefer, would be for us to take Samoa, England the Tonga Islands, and the
United States the Sandwich Islands (Hawaii.) . . . I said to Lord Salisbury
that the Americans would have to be restrained in every possible way. They

26. Secretary Bayard to Secretary W. C. Whitney, October 3, 1887, *Bayard Letter Book*,
vol. 6, *Bayard MS.*
27. George H. Pendleton (Berlin) to Secretary Bayard, October 7, 1887, *Personal*,
Bayard MS.

appeared now to interpret the Monroe Doctrine, as though the Pacific Ocean were to be treated as an American Lake. . . . There were even dreamers in America who imagined an eventual Republican brotherhood and a linking up of the various Australian Colonies with the United States. This suggestion caused Lord Salisbury to pause. He declared that we must keep a sharp eye on American fingers. I then mentioned Malitoa. I also expressed the hope that the British Government would continue to support us in Samoa. . . . Lord Salisbury replied with a hearty "certainly." [28]

Apparently, Lord Salisbury was so anxious to demonstrate to Prince Bismarck his desire to follow a co-operative policy in the South Pacific that he hinted that it might be expedient to have a British squadron accompany the German warships in their operations against Malietoa. The German Government preferred to play a lone hand in the punitive measures against Malietoa, but Count Hatzfeldt did request the British Foreign Office to "prevent at all hazards any immediate and serious differences between the British and German representatives in Samoa." Lord Salisbury promised to instruct the British consul at Apia to act in concert with the German representatives, but he refused to "mediate in Washington, on the ground that British-American relations were not particularly good at that time." [29]

Bismarck was somewhat fearful of complications with the United States in this Samoan matter, and he saw to it that the commander of the German fleet in the Pacific received instructions "to avoid conflicts with the Americans." There should be no occupation of Apia by German forces. Even if "no collisions should occur with resident Englishmen and Americans, it will give the press in the Australian colonies and in the United States an opportunity to cast suspicions on our Samoan policy and to insinuate that we intend territorial expansion and violation of the treaty rights of other States interested in the southern Pacific." [30]

On October 10 Bayard received from Sewall, at Apia, a long despatch which treated in detail the aggressions of the German officials in Samoa. A few hours before this despatch reached the Department of State, Bayard had already sent a telegram to Sewall instructing him to "abstain from interference" in Samoa by "favoring or opposing either

28. *Memorandum* by Count Herbert Bismarck, August 24, 1887, E. T. S. Dugdale, *op. cit.*, pp. 244-245; *Die Grosse Politik der Europäischen Kabinette, 1871–1914,* vol. 4, pp. 175-177.
29. Count Otto zu Stolberg-Wernigerode, *Germany and the United States of America During the Era of Bismarck*, p. 249.
30. *Ibid.*, p. 250.

party." [31] On the following day, Bayard sent a brief instruction to Pendleton, in Berlin, in which he referred to the action of the German officials in Samoa, and he emphasized the earnest desire of the American government to "secure a peaceful adjustment" of the difficulties and a "considerate treatment of Samoans." Having in mind the fact that during the sessions of the Washington Conference no serious objections had been raised against the idea of an election by the natives of a King and Vice-King, Bayard now repeated this proposal. [32]

Pendleton replied that he had discussed the matter with Count Bismarck, who showed him a telegram from Apia which indicated that the Samoan chiefs had met in an assembly on September 15 and had "formally recognized Tamasese as king." It was also stated that although the islands were "quiet," a German fleet would remain for a while in Samoan waters "in order, by the moral effect of their presence, to prevent any outbreak." Count Bismarck himself seemed "ignorant of any definite agreement of Conference as to election of King and Vice-King." [33]

Alvey A. Adee decoded this telegram for Bayard and attached the following remarks: "Germany seems to intimate that there is no need of an election (even if one was agreed upon, which she doubts) because it is all over now. The 'moral effect' of the German vessels at Apia is delicious." [34]

On October 13 Pendleton wrote a long despatch to Bayard in which he made a detailed report on the attitude of the German Foreign Office towards the Samoan tangle. Count Bismarck seemed elaborately obtuse in the matter of Bayard's proposal with reference to the election of a King and Vice-King. He assured Pendleton that the idea of a Vice-King was quite "new" to him, but if the Samoans really desired to elect such an officer the German Government would be "happy" to make the necessary arrangements. With reference to the election of a King it was evident that the Samoans had already made a choice. In the telegrams that had been received by the Foreign Office from Apia it was clear that the Samoan chiefs had met in an assembly on September 15 and had

31. Bayard to Sewall, October 10, 1887, *Bayard MS*. This telegram was sent *via* Auckland, New Zealand.

32. Bayard to Pendleton, October 11, 1887, *Germany, Instructions*, vol. 18, MS Dept. of State.

33. Pendleton to Bayard, October 13, 1887, *Germany, Despatches*, vol. 45, MS Dept. of State.

34. Adee to Bayard, October 13, 1887, *Bayard MS*.

formally recognized Tamasese as King. He then had the temerity to congratulate Pendleton upon the alleged fact that the laudable purpose of the American Government

. . . in proposing the immediate election of a King . . . had been anticipated by the Samoans, and that this, having been so readily accomplished and with happy results, there were nothing for the Government to do in that direction.[35]

Bayard's attitude towards German aggression in Samoa was not softened by this despatch from Pendleton. His opinions had already been formed long before the receipt of that communication from Berlin. In a confidential letter to Pendleton he unreservedly expressed his distaste for the way things were being handled in Samoa. He hoped that his suggestion for an immediate election of a King and Vice-King would "force the way to a practical restoration of that native autonomy which at the present writing seems to have disappeared in the smoke of the German guns." He also disclosed his suspicions of British policy:

From our Consul at Apia we have despatches up to September 11th., and he recites certain instructions from the British Government to their Consul at Samoa *not* to stand in the way of the German action at least for a period of six months. As you may gather from the part played by the British Minister in the conference here, . . . such instructions to their Consul at Samoa are not very surprising. The ready consent of Great Britain to the acquisition by Germany of the Solomon and Marshall groups in Polynesia is, I suppose, explicable by the desire to cement their alliance in European affairs. But there is a lack of that honorable frankness towards the United States in the Samoan affair which is our just due, and which I confess is disappointing and displeasing.
 . . . The causes alleged by Germany for this "war upon Malietoa personally" are mere pretexts, and the conditions proposed for its avoidance impossible for him to comply with. . . . All this leads me to believe that men so lofty in their personal characters, so conscious of moral and religious responsibility in their exercise of great powers as the Emperor of Germany and the great statesman at the head of his council, would never suffer such wanton and extreme oppression of a feeble and alien population if the facts could be brought to their personal knowledge.[36]

On the day after this letter to Pendleton was written, the German chargé d'affaires, Baron Zedtwitz, made a formal call at the Department of State. He inquired whether the Department of State would instruct

35. Pendleton to Bayard, October 13, 1887, *Germany, Despatches*, vol. 45, MS Dept. of State.
36. Bayard to Pendleton, October 13, 1887, *Personal and Confidential, Bayard Letter Book*, vol. 6, *Bayard MS.*

the American consul at Apia to "lend his aid to induce Malietoa to abdicate." Bayard's reaction to this request is given in the following memorandum:

> I told him that the United States had acted straightforwardly in this business, from beginning to end, . . . and that I supposed, until I heard of this most unexpected and sudden action of violence of the German Government towards Malietoa, that they were acting with the United States concurrently to create a native autonomy. . . . I said that when I heard that the German Government had landed these forces, burned down native villages, destroyed fruit trees on which these poor people were dependent for their food, it filled me with pain that such measures had been resorted to, and if it was meant that I was asked to approve it I would distinctly answer NO; that the first allegiance of this country was to justice.[37]

Bayard's anger at German policy in Samoa remained at a high pitch throughout October, 1887,[38] and we find him writing a second personal letter to Pendleton in which he expressed himself in no uncertain terms. He found it difficult to keep within "the pale of diplomatic reserve" in any discussion of the Samoan situation, and he paid his respects to the way in which Sackville-West had acted during the sessions of the Washington Conference. If any support had been received from the British Minister it would have been possible for Bayard to secure "some substantial protection against the merciless greed of the German trading company in whose interests the German Government have acted ruthlessly." The protocols of the conference would clearly reveal how Sackville-West had endeavored to "weaken or defeat" every effort made by Bayard to secure a "decent measure of justice and fair play for these defenceless savages." [39]

37. *Memorandum* written by Bayard after a conversation with Zedtwitz, October 14, 1887, *Bayard MS.*

38. In a personal letter to Phelps, October 20, 1887, Bayard alludes to the "unexpected and uncandid treatment of affairs in Samoa by Germany." Even while a conference with the expressed intent to uphold a native autonomy in Samoa by the three powers was progressing, "Germany suddenly announced her intention to overthrow Malietoa, the recognized King, and proceeded to punish him for alleged disrespect to the Emperor, committed six months before, and levy fines for offences committed years ago, and which it was absurd to expect could be paid. I sent you the printed protocols by which you will see the utter insincerity with which Germany has behaved to the United States, and the discreditable acquiescence of the British Minister in all that was done.

". . . It is quite plain that the alliance between Germany and Great Britain is assured and complete, and that in consideration thereof, the latter will connive at any violence or irregularity of acquisition of helpless islanders who cannot resist German invasions." *Bayard Letter Book*, vol. 6, *Bayard MS.*

39. Bayard to Pendleton, October 29, 1887, *Personal, Bayard Letter Book*, vol. 6, *Bayard MS.*

At this moment, more trouble arose in war-torn Samoa. On November 1 Baron Zedtwitz had a conference with John Bassett Moore, the Third Assistant Secretary of State, and informed him that Sewall, at Apia, had given "active expression to his anti-German policy by transgressions of his competency incompatible with neutrality, having under the pretext of formal reference to municipal institutions . . . arbitrarily intervened, liberated prisoners, and consequently forced commander of German squadron to occupy Apia." The German Government requested that Mr. Sewall be "rectified, and also instructed to observe strictly neutral attitude." [40]

On the following day, Zedtwitz made a formal call on Bayard and was assured that Sewall would be instructed by telegram to observe a strict neutrality.[41] Bayard immediately cabled Sewall to maintain a neutral attitude in Samoa, and he instructed Pendleton to take the matter up with the German Foreign Office and have it so arranged that in the discharge of his functions Mr. Sewall would not be "interfered with by German representatives." [42]

After receiving this instruction from Bayard, Coleman, the chargé d'affaires at Berlin, immediately sought an interview with Count Bismarck. He was given assurances that Germany would not interfere with the discharge of Sewall's consular duties. Count Bismarck also informed Mr. Coleman that the Chancellor, greatly regretted that the two nations should "find matter for differences at and about such an inconsiderable out-of-the-way place as Samoa." [43]

In commenting upon this telegram from Coleman, Alvey A. Adee sent the following note to Bayard:

The interview [between Coleman and Count Bismarck] appears to have been talky and vague. I observe that Bismarck wonders why we bother ourselves about those "remote inconsiderable islands." They may be remote and inconsiderable for Germany, but to us they are proximate and considerable, for in the hands of a naval Power they threaten our Pacific flank, and indeed they threaten all the Pacific Coast of South America too, and Hawaii besides. Samoa offsets Pearl Harbor, and Bismarck so intends it.[44]

40. *Memorandum* by John Bassett Moore, November 1, 1887, *Bayard MS.*
41. *Memorandum* written by Secretary Bayard after a conversation with Baron Zedtwitz, November 2, 1887, *Bayard MS.*
42. Bayard to Pendleton, November 2, 1887, *Germany, Instructions,* vol. 18, MS Dept. of State.
43. Chapman Coleman to Bayard, November 4, 1887, *Germany, Despatches,* vol. 45, MS Dept. of State.
44. A. A. Adee to Bayard, November 4, 1887, *Bayard MS.*

On November 4 Baron Zedtwitz called at the Department of State
and handed Bayard a long memorandum which defended the stand Germany had adopted during the sessions of the Washington Conference.[45]
Bayard had proposed the creation of an Executive Council composed of
the King, the Vice-King, and three Ministers to be appointed by the
treaty powers. The memorandum of the German Government attacked
this proposal as entailing too great an expense upon the slender Samoan
revenues, and it also indicated that the three Ministers would probably
devote all their efforts for the advancement of the interests of their
respective nations and in this way would merely perpetuate the difficulties that had arisen from the tri-consular government in Apia.
Moreover, the Ministers appointed by the three treaty powers would
be able to outvote the King and Vice-King, and this arrangement would
probably result "not only in impairing the prestige of the royal office,
but in placing the governmental authority proper in the hands of the
three members." All these objections would be eliminated by the
appointment of a single executive officer like an Adviser to the King
who would serve not as the "representative of any particular power but
. . . as the common mandatary of the three treaty powers."[46]

While Bayard was studying this memorandum of the German Government, Zedtwitz paid another visit to the Department of State in
order to defend German policy in Samoa. He vehemently denied the
reports in the American press that German troops had been cruel to the
Samoan natives, and he complained about the actions of the American
Consul-General at Apia. Sewall, he charged, had concealed King Malietoa in the American consulate after "the declaration of war by the
German Government against him." Bayard's reply to this charge gave
Zedtwitz little satisfaction:

I asked him whether that [charge rested] upon the knowledge or information of the Consul, to which he replied that it was stated upon his
information merely. He seemed disposed to press upon me again the necessity of renewed instructions to our consul. I told him there was no necessity
for such action. . . . The gentleman who had been sent there was a man
of most excellent character and reputation and had considerable experience
as vice-consul at Liverpool. . . . I went on to say that it seemed to me that
the Gov't. of Germany had been very much given over in Samoa to the

45. *Memorandum* written by Bayard after a conversation with Zedtwitz, November 4,
1887, *Bayard MS.*

46. *Memorandum* presented by Baron Zedtwitz to Bayard, November 4, 1887. This
memorandum was dated Berlin, September, 1887, and the original copy is in the *Bayard
MS.* See also *S. Ex. Doc., 31,* 50 Cong., 2 sess., pp. 6-9.

wishes and the interests . . . of a commercial company down there, and that all experience had shown that the only law of a commercial company was the law of its own interest, and if that was to prevail I thought there was little chance of coming to that kind of amicable co-operation which was necessary to preserve the rights of all parties equally.[47]

Pendleton, at Berlin, was sharply critical of German policy in Samoa. In a personal letter to Bayard he freely commented upon the situation in the South Pacific, and he warmly praised the stand taken by Bayard during the sessions of the Washington Conference. It seemed to him that the demands of the German Government indicated

. . . a most grasping spirit for power in the Samoan regime, utterly inconsistent with the professed purpose to maintain an autonomous government in the islands. . . . No one can read those minutes of your discussions without being impressed with the contrast between your frank avowals of a purpose which you consistently pushed and the equally frank avowals of a purpose by your co-conferees which they constantly thwarted by every suggestion as to plan or detail made by either of them. . . . I do not wonder at your indignation at this bold and manifest perversion of your attempt to do a good, humane thing by these defenceless savages, avoiding alike partiality and injury to the three treaty powers, into a grasping and arbitrary control over them in order to satisfy the greed of the German trading Company at their expense.[48]

Bayard's hostile attitude towards German policy in Samoa was confirmed when he received on December 3, a long, personal letter from Sewall, at Apia, in which German aggression in Samoa was frankly rehearsed. German officials had

. . . forcibly overthrown the king and government of Samoa and proclaimed another government against the will of its people. . . . Even our coaling station at Pago-Pago . . . is on German land held by a precarious lease which the owner may terminate at any time. Our treaty itself, now about expiring, Tamasese will refuse to renew, and then . . . the cloak of native government will be thrown off and German supremacy openly asserted. . . . My sympathy for this people is great, and is not lessened by a strong feeling of personal chagrin at the course of events here. It is my firm conviction that the present troubles would never have come upon Malietoa, had it not been for his friendship for the United States. . . . I am sure, Mr. Bayard, that if you could only understand the situation here, there would be little need of my appeal to you in behalf of these people. . . . Although war was declared upon Malietoa personally, it is now over seven weeks since he gave himself up to secure peace for his people, and as yet

47. *Memorandum* written by Bayard after a conversation with Baron Zedtwitz, November 10, 1887, *Bayard MS.*
48. Pendleton to Bayard, November 12, 1887, *Personal, Bayard MS.*

this boon has not been granted to them. . . . Since his deportation his cabinet and chiefs have been hunted down like criminals. . . . If we are to act towards securing them a just and stable government we should act quickly.[49]

In an official despatch of November 8, 1887, Sewall told in great detail of the various steps that German officials in Samoa had taken to overthrow the authority of Malietoa and establish German control over the islands. His account of the manner in which the German consul seized upon a pretext to abolish the tripartite consular administration of Apia, was not pleasant reading for Secretary Bayard.[50] The Tamasese Government was largely under the control of a German adventurer named Brandeis, who had formerly been an officer in the German army. Brandeis had imposed upon the Samoan natives a system of taxation, and he threatened to imprison all who would not promptly meet these exactions. Sewall was deeply disturbed over the effects of this stern regime upon the indolent Samoans who had never been faced with the problem of raising revenues to support an effective administrative system for the islands. He had advised the natives to comply with the regulations that had been promulgated by Brandeis, but it seemed to him that it was obvious that the American Government should not give its approval to such aggressive proceedings.[51]

In the concluding sentence of his personal letter to Bayard (Decem- 6, 1887), Sewall remarked that the Germans in Samoa resented the efforts that were made by Sewall on behalf of the natives of Samoa. This statement was confirmed by Baron Zedtwitz who had a conversation with Bayard on December 9, 1887. Zedtwitz lodged a formal complaint against Sewall, but Bayard replied by criticizing the actions of Consul Becker, who had abolished the tripartite consular administration in Apia and who had assumed an unauthorized control over Samoan affairs. It was "perfectly plain," said Bayard, that this "sort of thing would lead to a great want of harmonious action" in the South Pacific.[52]

At the close of his conversation with Bayard, Zedtwitz left a long letter that Prince Bismarck had sent to him on the Samoan situation. Bismarck first filed an indictment against the "anti-German attitude"

49. Sewall to Bayard, November 7, 1887, (Received, December 3), *Personal, Bayard MS.*
50. Sewall to Bayard, November 8, 1887, *Apia, Consular Despatches,* vol. 15, MS Dept. of State.
51. Sewall to Bayard, December 6, 1887, *Personal, Bayard MS.*
52. *Memorandum* written by Bayard after a conversation with Baron Zedtwitz, December 9, 1887, *Bayard MS.*

of Mr. Sewall at Apia. This attitude was similar to that exhibited by other American consuls who for many years had shown a tendency "to interfere with" German policy in Samoa. In view of the friendly relations that had long existed between the United States and Germany, it was remarkable that "on that remote realm of islands, where neither America nor Germany has any political interests to defend, we are exposed to the continual ill-will of a series of American representatives." Bismarck hoped that when this "strange fact" was brought to the attention of Secretary Bayard he would take immediate steps to remedy the situation.[53]

After giving Bayard several weeks to study the complaints of Prince Bismarck against the anti-German attitude of American consular representatives at Apia, Baron Zedtwitz paid a visit to the Department of State to receive an official reply. He handed to Bayard several documents signed by eight American citizens which indicated that the Tamasese-Brandeis regime was far better than any previous Samoan Government. Bayard immediately pointed out that the

. . . name of one of the men appended to the document—a Mr. Coe—was somewhat familiar. He had been in the service of the Apian Government, and had been connected with certain fraudulent representations to the U. S. Consul, and when it was discovered that his representations were false he was removed from office. I said he could scarcely be considered a reputable person—yet his name was among these, and, of course, could have but little weight. He said he hoped there would be approval by the United States of what had happened there. I said that was impossible.[54]

After concluding this interview with Baron Zedtwitz, Bayard wrote a personal letter to Sewall, at Apia, in which he frankly discussed the Samoan situation. He had received Sewall's personal letter of November 7, and while he was sorry to hear of the "misfortunes of Malietoa," it should be clearly understood that these troubles had not been

. . . caused by his friendship for the United States, nor induced nor aggravated by anything said or done by authority of this government. It was made known to him [Malietoa] at an early day, that . . . none other than moral aid and influence would be extended by the United States. . . . The *proximate* cause of Malietoa's misfortunes was the ill-starred and mischievous mission of Mr. Bush from the King of Hawaii. . . . I was amazed when the Hawaiian Minister, Mr. Carter, informed me that a treaty creating an

53. Prince von Bismarck to Baron Zedtwitz, November 18, 1887, *House Ex. Doc., 238,* 50 Cong. 1 sess., pp. 96-98.

54. *Memorandum* written by Bayard after a conversation with Baron Zedtwitz, January 6, 1888, *Bayard MS.*

alliance, *offensive and defensive,* had been entered into by Malietoa with King Kalakaua. . . . I advised its immediate abandonment and pointed out to Mr. Carter the great danger to *both* these weak governments of exciting the suspicion and hostility of Germany. Although the Bush mission soon collapsed, . . . the evil results of his mission, to poor Malietoa, were soon to bear fruit, and to them I ascribe the scenes witnessed in Samoa since August last.

Throughout your letter of November 7th runs an appeal to me for prompt action to sustain the native government in Samoa and check German aggression. By what reasoning you suppose my power to be able to compass these results I am not informed, but as I have not been able to decide that any violation of international law as affecting the United States or of our treaty rights with Samoa has yet been committed by Germany, it appears to me that to follow your suggestions would lead to a departure from our position as a neutral, and place this government as an ally of Samoa in an attitude of belligerency to Germany. Of the gravity of such action I need not speak, because it is not within the Executive function to make war.

. . . What can be done here to secure a reasonable measure of justice and fair treatment to these innocent and unhappy Islanders, I shall endeavour to do without placing in useless jeopardy the vaster interests of our own countrymen.[55]

Bayard also wrote a note to President Cleveland in which he gave a short survey of the Samoan situation. He would be out of town for several days, but would return to Washington

. . . early Wednesday morning so that on Thursday, at the meeting of the Cabinet, the question of sending more vessels to Samoa can be settled by the light of what we may have learned from Berlin. A private note from Mr. Tree (on his way to St. Petersburg) written at Berlin, gives a very poor account of Mr. Pendleton's health. We have not been very fortunate in that direction, and I cannot help thinking that plain, frank conversation of an *able* man with Prince Bismarck, would help to clear up the situation in Samoa a good deal.

I am apprehensive of great violence in revenge of the German losses, and that there will be a German conquest of the poor natives. I explained to you our treaty rights with that group, and the distinct separation of the island which contains *our* harbor (Pango-pango) from the Island which is the theatre of the present warfare.

If Germany respects our formal rights, as she has professed intention to do, I do not see how we can prevent her oppression of the poor Islanders, for evidently Great Britain means to do nothing.[56]

55. Bayard to Sewall, January 6, 1888, *Personal, Bayard Letter Book,* vol. 6, *Bayard MS.*

56. Bayard to President Cleveland, January 6, 1888, *Cleveland MS.* On December 13, 1887, Bayard had received a letter from Phelps, in London, with reference to the Samoan situation. Phelps was certain that Bayard could expect "no assistance from England. They will simply stand aloof. I intend to send a despatch which I hope may be communicated

On January 17, 1888, Bayard gave his answer to Prince Bismarck's complaints concerning the anti-German attitude of the American consular representatives at Apia.[57] Its eminently fair and restrained tone was a tribute to the judicial temperament of Bayard, and its obvious sincerity carried conviction to all unprejudiced readers. Both he and President Cleveland greatly regretted that the traditionally friendly relations between Germany and the United States should be disturbed by occurrences in the Samoan Islands. The American Government had always endeavored to show a co-operative spirit in dealing with the problems of the South Pacific, and upon occasion had not hesitated to withdraw a consular representative when his actions had created friction in that area. The record of American policy in Samoa was an honorable one, and American efforts had been directed towards assisting the natives to establish an autonomous government under a measure of foreign tutelage. After rehearsing the story of the Washington Conference, Bayard then contrasted the American policy of assistance to the Samoan natives with the German policy of open aggression. It was the opinion of the American Government that

. . . the course taken by Germany in respect to Samoa . . . cannot be regarded as having been marked by that just consideration which the ancient friendship between the United States and Germany entitles this Government to expect; that the present condition of affairs in the Islands cannot, in view of the circumstances under which it was brought about and is still maintained, be regarded by the United States as satisfactory; and that, to the end of creating a more acceptable situation in the Islands, the native government should be placed upon a basis more compatible with independence and impartiality in the discharge of its duties to all the Treaty Powers.[58]

The moderate tone that Bayard adopted in this long defense of American policy in Samoa is in striking contrast with the belligerent

---

to Congress, to the effect that *diplomacy is useless when not backed up by a naval force that can hold its own.* It is well known everywhere that we are absolutely helpless, except to resist invasion, which nobody will even attempt. To oppose power by argument is very pretty in theory, but is of no avail in the intercourse of nations." Phelps to Secretary Bayard, December 3, 1887, *Bayard MS.*

Phelps had an open contempt for the movement in favor of international arbitration. In a letter to President Cleveland, from London, he remarks: "The movement, which is absurd in itself when regarded in the light of experience, has no real backing among men of sense here." Phelps to President Cleveland, November 5, 1887, *Cleveland MS.*

57. For an interesting discussion of the background of German-American friction in Samoa, see Alfred Vagts, *Deutschland und die Vereinigten Staaten in der Weltpolitik*, pp. 656ff.

58. Bayard to Pendleton, January 17, 1888, *Germany, Instructions*, vol. 18, MS Dept. of State.

expressions in the American press. On March 8, 1888, a resolution was adopted by the House of Representatives requesting all information in the possession of the Executive Department with reference to Samoa. Bayard selected the most pertinent correspondence in this regard, and President Cleveland submitted these documents to the House of Representatives on April 2.[59] When these were made available to the American press, a bitter attack upon German aggression in the Samoan Islands was at once launched in many important daily newspapers. The New York *Sun* was openly critical of the course the Administration had followed, and expressed the view that the German program would probably succeed because of American inaction.[60] The San Francisco *Argus* thought that the time had come when the United States would have to assert its rights "even with shot and shell";[61] while the Baltimore *Sun* expressed the view that "German scheming" had caused all the trouble in Samoa.[62]

It seemed to many American editors that Bayard had not defended American interests with enough vigor, and some went so far as to assert that the German Government had violated its treaty engagements with the United States. Even in the President's Cabinet there were some critics like William C. Whitney (Secretary of the Navy) who felt that America had been "disgraced" by submitting to German aggression in Samoa.[63] Bayard anticipated this unjust criticism and tried to avoid it by securing permission from Great Britain and Germany to print the protocols of the Washington Conference.[64] These documents would have given ample proof of the determined stand that he had taken against the predatory policy of Germany, and they would have clearly shown the active support that Great Britain gave to the German plans for the control of Samoa.

Sackville-West objected to the publication of these protocols on the ground that such action "might prejudice the satisfactory solution" of the Samoan question,[65] and Baron von Zedtwitz informed Bayard that the German Government felt that the protocols were "not suited for

---

59. *House Ex. Doc., 238, 50* Cong. 1 sess.
60. April 4, 1888.   61. April 5, 1888.   62. April 3, 1888.
63. See *ante*, p. 75. There was, of course, no treaty between Germany and the United States with reference to Samoa.
64. *Memorandum* written by Bayard after a conversation with Baron von Zedtwitz, March 16, 1888, *Bayard MS.*
65. Sackville-West to Bayard, March 22, 1888, *British Legation, Notes from,* vol. 115, MS Dept. of State.

publication." [66] This action prevented Bayard from appearing in his true light as a sincere and uncompromising champion of the rights of the natives of Samoa, and it gave his Republican foes in the Senate an opportunity to direct an attack upon his policy. The year 1888 would usher in another presidential election, and the petty partisanship of that period would not hesitate to distort the truth in order to gain a political advantage. [67]

At Apia, Sewall was "disappointed beyond measure" that Bayard would not take immediate action against German aggression. To him it appeared as though there would be "no end of the oppression" to which the Samoans were subjected. And yet this cruel regime could be broken down at once by a mere "show of force . . . without danger of a conflict with the Germans." The commander of the American warship *Mohican* had been instructed to refrain from all "interference with matters on shore," but it would be more expedient to give him "discretionary instructions" which would enable him to be of greater service to the Samoans. With "proper encouragement" the native quarrels in Samoa could be quickly composed and a united front be presented to foreign aggressors. [68]

On March 1 Sewall again wrote to Bayard in a very pessimistic tone about conditions in Samoa. The deportation of Samoan chiefs, and the arbitrary actions of

. . . Brandeis and the Germans within the District of the former municipality, have aroused against them among other foreigners intense feeling, and this may at any time manifest itself in violence. The part taken by the German consul in the case of the Pilot Station shows something of the feeling which animates German official action where American interests are concerned. So unreasonable this seems that I am quite aware that I can hardly expect it to be fully comprehended at the Department. But it is real, and is a strong factor in the influences by which it is sought either to drive Americans away from Samoa or to force them to acquiesce in the German plans. . . . Capt. Day of the *Mohican* believes that our rights . . . should be asserted by force. I am convinced that unless force is used, fresh

66. Zedtwitz to Bayard, March 24, 1888, *German Legation, Notes from,* vol. 19, MS Dept. of State.

67. In the New York *Times,* May 20, 1888, there is a pertinent comment upon the partisan tactics of Bayard's foes: "The mischief-making propensities of the Republican Senators have never been held directly responsible for the embarrassing circumstances of the Samoan Islands dispute, yet there appears to be reason for believing that the determination of those Senators to embarrass the administration was very successful in that direction."

68. Sewall to Bayard, February 4, 1888, *Personal, Bayard MS.*

seizures of American property will follow. . . . The German attitude . . .
grows more aggressive every day.[69]

Bayard did not receive this despatch from Sewall until March 24,
and three days later he read it at a Cabinet meeting. But Bayard was
not an alarmist, and he did not permit the situation in Samoa to
arouse in him a militant anti-German spirit. This is very clear when
we read a letter from Bayard to Carl Schurz with reference to the
accession of Frederick III to the German imperial throne. The dignified address of the new Emperor had made a very favorable impression
upon Bayard:

> Compared with the chatter of those who assume to guide the people of
> the United States, the dignified, sober and devout words of the new Emperor,
> contain important food for thought.[70]

It was difficult, however, for Bayard to continue to read the despatches from Sewall, at Apia, and not become increasingly fearful of
German designs in Samoa. These designs were apparently the work
of Theodor Weber, the agent of "Die Deutsche Handels and Plantagen
Gesellschaft für Süd-See Inseln zu Hamburg." This was the German
trading company of which Bayard had spoken so disparagingly in his
conversations with the German Minister. As the successor of the firm
of Godeffroy and Son, the new German corporation had spared no
effort to control the economic situation in Samoa. These efforts had
been directed by Theodor Weber whose conspicuous abilities were
given accurate description by Robert Louis Stevenson:

> He was of an artful and commanding character; in the smallest thing or
> the greatest, without fear or scruple; equally able to affect, equally ready
> to adopt, the most engaging politeness or the most imperious airs of domina-
> tion. It was he who did most damage to rival traders; it was he who most
> harried the Samoans; and yet I never met anyone, white or native, who did
> not respect his memory.[71]

It was through the influence of Theodor Weber that Herr Brandeis
became the adviser to Tamasese, and with respect to the Brandeis
regime, Stevenson remarks: "The more I learn of his brief term of
rule, the more I learn to admire him and to wish we had his like." [72]
In speaking of the opposition of certain Americans to the Brandeis-

69. Sewall to Bayard, March 1, 1888, *Personal, Bayard MS.*
70. Bayard to Schurz, March 31, 1888, *Bayard MS.*
71. *A Footnote to History,* pp. 397-398.
72. *Ibid.,* p. 97.

Tamasese government, Stevenson gives a colorful picture of the Samoan situation during 1888–1889:

From the moment of the declaration of war against Laupepa, we find him [Sewall] standing forth in bold consistent, and sometime rather captious opposition, stirring up his government at home with clear and forcible despatches, and on the spot grasping at every opportunity to thrust a stick into the German wheels. For some while, he and [H. J.] Moors fought their difficult battle in conjunction; . . . and during the consul's absence, there was found an American clerk in Apia, William Blacklock, to perform the duties of the office with remarkable ability and courage.[73]

During the summer of 1888 this conflict against the Brandeis-Tamasese government was carried on by Sewall, Moors, and Blacklock with increasing intensity. In the last part of May, 1888, Sewall informed the Department of State of the plan of Mataafa, one of the principal Samoan chiefs, to lead a movement against the government of Tamasese.[74] In June, a report came from Sewall that Mataafa was "eager for war," and that Brandeis was expecting trouble.[75] Some weeks later the news came to Washington that Brandeis was making numerous arrests of Samoan chiefs in order to avert an uprising against Tamasese,[76] and finally word came from Blacklock, acting as vice-consul at Apia, that open warfare had broken out in Samoa.[77]

Bayard received this telegram from Blacklock on September 15, and he immediately informed President Cleveland of the situation: "From Samoa I hear that the poor natives have risen against Tamasese, the ruler set up by Germany in place of poor Malietoa! I suppose a German gun boat will give them another Ruler." [78]

Bayard also wrote to Secretary Whitney to suggest that a "discreet officer in command of a government vessel be sent to Samoa to protect American interests." [79] Whitney immediately adopted this suggestion, and on September 17 instructions to this effect were sent to Rear Admiral Kimberly.[80] It was important that these instructions should go

73. *Ibid.,* p. 433.
74. Sewall to George L. Rives, Assistant Secretary of State, May 24, 1888, *Apia, Consular Despatches,* vol. 16, MS Dept. of State.
75. Sewall to Rives, June 19, 1888, *ibid.*
76. Sewall to Rives, August 17, 1888, *ibid.*
77. Blacklock to Bayard, telegram, September 4, 1888, *ibid.*
78. Bayard to President Cleveland, September 15, 1888, *Bayard Letter Book,* vol. 8, *Bayard MS.*
79. Bayard to Whitney, September 15, 1888, *Domestic Letters,* vol. 169, MS Dept. of State.
80. Whitney to Bayard, September 17, 1888, *Executive Letter Book,* MS Navy Dept. Archives.

promptly, because Commander Leary, of the U.S.S. *Adams,* had received previous orders to leave Apia. Leary found it necessary to postpone indefinitely his departure from Samoa, and on September 9 he sent a long report to Secretary Whitney on the condition of affairs in those islands. He had sent a protest to Captain Fritze, of the German war ship *Adler,* against a contemplated bombardment of certain villages on the island of Manono, and he had also intervened on behalf of an American citizen whose property was being damaged by the warriors of Tamasese.[81]

Leary made a second report to Secretary Whitney in which he described the complete rout of the Tamasese forces by the revolutionists who installed Mataafa as the King of Samoa.[82] This news was confirmed by a telegram from Blacklock, the vice-consul at Apia, who declared that "nearly the whole population" in Samoa was in favor of Mataafa.[83]

Bayard did not receive this telegram from Blacklock until October 1. On that same day he cabled to Pendleton, in Berlin, to the effect that the American Government would assume that the other treaty powers would, in conformity with their joint understanding, "respect the choice of the Samoan people." [84] Bismarck replied that instructions had been sent to the German consul in Apia to "confine himself to the protection of life and property of German subjects, and to telegraph if they are threatened." It was further indicated that it was a "matter of indifference to the German Government who is the King, if the interests of Germany are protected." [85]

Reassured by this conciliatory telegram from Berlin, Bayard promptly sent instructions to Blacklock to follow a policy of non-interference in the affairs of the Samoan Government, and to reject any idea of an American protectorate over the islands.[86] There is little doubt that Bayard was anxious to avoid any serious trouble with Ger-

81. Commander Leary to Secretary Whitney, September 9, 1888, *S. Ex. Doc., 31,* 50 Cong., 2 sess., pp. 115-116.

82. Leary to Whitney, September 13, 1888, *S. Ex. Doc., 31,* 50 Cong. 2 sess., p. 124.

83. Blacklock to Bayard, September 14, 1888, *Apia, Consular Despatches,* vol. 16, MS Dept. of State.

84. Bayard to Pendleton, October 1, 1888, *Germany, Instructions,* vol. 18, MS Dept. of State.

85. Coleman to Bayard, October 3, 1888, *Bayard MS.* These assurances from Bismarck were sent through the medium of Privy Councillor Holstein.

86. Rives to Blacklock, October 11, 1888, *Instructions to Consuls,* vol. 127, MS Dept. of State.

many concerning Samoa, and he deprecated any loose talk of war. In a letter to E. M. Shepard he clearly voiced his viewpoint:

If peace can be had with honor and without war, what malediction should pursue the man that leads a people into strife? It was the boast of Pericles that he had never caused any Athenian to put on mourning. . . . In these days of pot-house valor and newspaper self-sufficiency, Pericles would have passed for a poor stick. Let us pray that our people may not be led into a career that will end where Germany has ended—an armed camp and a "War Lord" to rule it.[87]

This pacific policy was given further expression in the remarks Bayard made to Sewall, the Consul-General at Apia, who returned to Washington to talk matters over with the Department of State. Sewall had led the fight against German aggression in Samoa, and even Robert Louis Stevenson thought that at times his attitude towards the Germans had been somewhat "captious." If Sewall had expected to convert Bayard into a "warhawk" he was greatly mistaken. Bayard, without any bluster, informed Sewall that the United States had

. . . no policy of annexation or protectorate whatsoever in Samoa or anywhere else; . . . that our object was to be perfectly humane and kind to the natives of those islands, and assist their autonomous government and . . . to neutralize the waters of Samoa for the peaceful commerce of the world. This last I considered a great object. . . . I told him I did not consider the unjust and even cruel treatment of the Samoans by the Germans as a *casus belli* for the United States, and that that fact must be borne distinctly in mind. . . . I told him that no case specifically had ever been brought to my knowledge in which interference by the Government of Germany or German officials with American rights had ever been reported. . . . I explained to him that the Germans had grounds for suspicion of our motives in the Pearl Harbor matter which I thought had caused us to be entirely misunderstood, but thought now, for the purpose of removing suspicion we should deal frankly and kindly with the German officials.[88]

Several days after this conference between Bayard and Sewall, Count von Arco-Valley, the new German Minister, called at the Department of State to discuss the state of affairs in Samoa. He assured Bayard that Count Bismarck was "exceedingly anxious" that no complications

---

87. Bayard to E. M. Shepard, November 8, 1888, *Bayard MS.*
88. *Memorandum* written by Bayard after a conversation with Sewall, November 14, 1888, *Bayard MS.* In a letter to M. V. Byars, November 28, 1888, Bayard expresses himself in a similar vein: "My object has been to maintain a *Native government* in Samoa and neutralize those waters for the protection of peaceful commerce and private property on the high seas. If Germany respects (as hitherto she has) our Treaty rights with Samoa, we cannot regard her action, however unjust and oppressive to *Samoans,* to be a cause of war with *us.*"

of any kind should arise between the two Governments with regard to the problems of the South Pacific. After filing a complaint against the anti-German activities of the American vice-consul at Apia, Count Arco then referred to the fact that the American Government had never recognized the government of Tamasese. Bayard defended the course of the Department of State in this regard, and expressed the view that the recent successful revolt against Tamasese showed the instability of his government. After this explanation of American policy, Bayard asked Count Arco if he could cite any act of an American official which indicated an anti-German bias. The German Minister promptly replied that he had not been informed by his government of "any such act." He had merely wished to "state the desire that care be taken to avoid conflict and friction in those waters."

Bayard, after giving assurances of a strong American desire to avoid all trouble in Samoa, referred to the probable construction of an interoceanic canal through Nicaragua by the United States, and drew Count Arco's attention to the manner in which this great project would give Americans increased interest in the trade of the Pacific area. In this matter of American commerce in the Pacific Ocean it was obvious that the Samoan Islands would have great importance.

Count Arco made no comment upon the question of the increasing interest in America relative to trade with the nations bordering on the Pacific Ocean, but he did refer to the stories in the American press which indicated that Sewall had "very strong anti-German feelings." Bayard stated that Sewall denied the authenticity of these stories, and no matter what might be the personal feelings of either the German or American consuls at Apia, it would be possible to avoid serious difficulties by instructing these officials to refer all questions to their home governments "before undertaking to act themselves."

In concluding this conference with the German Minister, Bayard dwelt upon the fact that his tenure of office as Secretary of State was fast coming to a close, and he expressed a warm desire to "leave a pathway of good understanding and kindly relations" open for his successor, and to "smooth away all friction." [89]

In order to carry out these assurances to Count Arco, Bayard sent

89. *Memorandum* written by Bayard after a conversation with Count von Arco-Valley, November 19, 1888, *Bayard MS.* There is a notation written in Bayard's hand across this memorandum to the effect that it was read at a meeting of the Cabinet, November 20, 1888.

to Chapman Coleman, the American chargé d'affaires in Berlin, a full account of his conversation with the German Minister.[90] He also secured from Sewall a defence of his conduct and an implied promise that he would seek to avoid all friction with German officials in Samoa.[91]

Although Bayard was anxious to leave a "pathway of good understanding" with Germany for his successor in the office of Secretary of State, President Cleveland was not prepared to go as far as his Secretary of State in this policy of conciliation. His impatience at German aggression in Samoa is clearly expressed in a note to Bayard:

> Some time ago when we learned that the King of Samoa had been removed upon a German ship we agreed, I believe, that a more substantial and distinct protest than had heretofore been given by our Government should be interposed to the high-handed proceedings which Germany had indulged it. Am I correct in my supposition that such a thing should be done? And if I am, will you please be prepared at the meeting to tell us the form and time of such protest? [92]

Bayard waited more than a month before he gave his final opinion to the President with reference to Samoa. It was couched in the restrained language he habitually used:

> I have no change to make in the opinion I have heretofore expressed in respect of our rights as a Treaty Power with Samoa. We have no right to control the action of the Treaty Powers with Samoa unless their action controverts or impairs our rights. Germany can make war upon Samoa, and can by negotiation or by conquest annex these islands to the German

90. Bayard to Coleman, November 21, 1888, *Bayard MS.* Throughout the year 1888, Pendleton had been handicapped in the performance of his duties as Minister by serious illness. Alvey A. Adee to Bayard, May 19, 1888; Pendleton to Bayard, May 21, 1888; Bayard to Pendleton, June 7, 1888; Bayard to Lambert Tree, October 6, 1888; Coleman to Bayard October 30, 1888, *Bayard MS.*

91. Sewall to Bayard, November 23, 1888, *Bayard MS.* Sewall was not entirely honest in his relations with Bayard. After talking over with Bayard the situation in Samoa, he had a conference with Senator William P. Frye, a bitter opponent of the Cleveland Administration, and persuaded him to request the Senate Committee on Foreign Relations to investigate the conduct of American foreign policy with regard to Samoa. On December 12 this committee decided to request the presence of Sewall in order to make certain inquiries, and Senator John T. Morgan expressed to Bayard the view that Frye hoped that in this Samoan matter he had stirred up a breeze that he "could fan into a tempest." Morgan to Bayard, December 12, 1888, *Bayard MS.* Bayard replied to Senator Morgan that he was "very desirous of having the fullest light thrown upon the Samoan situation," and that he would be glad to detain Sewall until he had been questioned by the Senate committee. Bayard to Morgan, December 12, 1888, *Bayard MS.* In January, 1889, Sewall had a hearing before a sub-committee of the Senate Committee on Foreign Relations, and freely expressed his views.

92. President Cleveland to Bayard, December 4, 1888, *Bayard MS.*

Empire, as she and France and Great Britain have already done in a score of instances in the Southern Pacific groups. In case Germany does assume a protectorate over Samoa, or makes war, or annexes the territory by conquest, the United States can only demand full respect be paid to their existing treaty rights. This Germany has at all times proposed . . . to do. When Chili made war upon Peru, she took a most valuable part of . . . it. . . . Citizens of Great Britain held large claims against Peru, and the lien of those claims extended over the premises carved by Chili out of . . . Peru. Great Britain never protested against such . . . conquest by Chili. Neither can we find a *casus belli* because of the oppressions or cruelty of Germany towards the unhappy Islanders.[93]

On the day that this memorandum was written (January 5, 1888), a cablegram was received from Samoa with fresh news of German aggression. According to this word from vice-consul Blacklock, three German warships had undertaken to disarm Mataafa. Mataafa's warriors fired upon the German marines, killing twenty and wounding thirty of them. In reprisal the German warships started "shelling and burning indiscriminately, regardless of American property." German officials refused to respect neutral territory, and "Americans in boat flying American flag" were "seized in Apia harbor by armed German boat, but released." [94]

Bayard appreciated at once the dangers of the situation, and he sent a note to Count von Arco-Valley in which he expressed his "great regret" at the news that had just been received by the Department of State relative to the "dangerous and deplorable condition of affairs at Samoa." [95] He also sent an instruction to Pendleton informing him of the action of the German officials in Samoa and requesting him to take the matter up with the German Foreign Office.[96]

On January 8 the German Minister paid a visit to the Department of State to discuss the difficulties that had arisen in Samoa. Bayard was away on a trip to New York City, and George L. Rives, the Acting Secretary of State, received Count von Arco-Valley. Rives was more abrupt in his manner than Bayard, and the conference was far from friendly. The German Minister indicated that he had just received a

93. *Memorandum* written by Bayard and sent to President Cleveland, January 5, 1889, *Bayard MS.*

94. Blacklock to Bayard, dated at Wellington, January 5, 1889, received at Dept. of State, January 5, *Apia, Consular Despatches,* vol. 17, MS Dept. of State.

95. Bayard to Arco-Valley, January 5, 1889, *German Legation, Notes to,* vol. 10, MS Dept. of State.

96. Bayard to Pendleton, January 5, 1889, *Germany, Instructions,* vol. 18, MS Dept. of State.

telegram from Berlin stating that German marines had been landed in Samoa for the protection of German property, and they had been attacked by Samoan rebels "under the command of an American by the name of Klein." He then presented a formal complaint about the action of Mr. Klein.

Before he had completed his remarks he was interrupted by Mr. Rives who observed that it seemed very "remarkable" that the German Government should be making complaints about American citizens in Samoa when the Americans themselves had refrained from filing charges against Herr Brandeis. Count von Arco-Valley replied that Brandeis had never led an attack upon American citizens, but Rives bluntly said that he "did not care to discuss the matter."

The German Minister then stated that his government wished to extend to the United States and Great Britain an invitation to co-operate with Germany in establishing a condition of tranquillity in the Samoan Islands. Rives merely remarked that he would "lay these things before the President at once." Arco-Valley ventured the opinion that the recent disturbances in Samoa were "stirred up by discontented Americans there who seemed to be jealous because the Germans were making more money than they." The reply of Rives was a sharp rebuttal of such charges:

I told him that these allegations seemed to me to be entirely unfounded; that all the testimony from Samoa, most of which was now in print, seemed to be entirely conclusive that the cause of the trouble down there was due to the greed of the Germans, who were trying to get all the trade of the islands into their own hands.[97]

When Bayard returned to the Department of State on January 9, one of his first callers was the German Minister.[98] On the following morning Arco-Valley had a second conference with Bayard with reference to the Samoan situation, and once again he made the statement that when the German marines landed to protect certain German property they were attacked "by a body of natives under an American named Klein." [99] He also, for a second time, extended an invitation to

97. *Memorandum* written by George L. Rives after a conversation with Count von Arco-Valley, January 8, 1889, *Bayard MS*. On this same day (January 8, 1889) Rives wrote to Bayard, who was spending the day in New York City, and after recounting the gist of his conversation with the German Minister, he conveyed the following message: "The President hopes to see you tomorrow morning immediately on your return." *Bayard MS*.
98. Count von Arco-Valley to Bayard, January 9, 1889, *Bayard MS*.
99. In the New York *World*, January 31, 1889, there is the following item concerning Mr. Klein: "In his declaration of war against the Samoans who are now to be subjugated

the American Government to join with Germany "in establishing order in Samoa."

When Arco-Valley had talked with George L. Rives on January 8 in this same connection, he had received scant satisfaction from the abrupt and acid remarks of the Acting Secretary of State. But Bayard was of a different stamp: he had an instinctive courtesy which befitted the office he held and he was far too good a statesman to permit personal pique to affect his relations with the representative of a great power. Upon receiving the complaint from the German Minister relative to the alleged actions of Mr. Klein, Bayard said that the American Government was

. . . totally without knowledge of the nationality of Klein; . . . that he certainly was not connected with this Department, or any branch of the Gov't and never had been. . . . The name Klein was German, not American, and there was more probability that he was German than American.

With regard to Arco-Valley's invitation to the American Government to adopt a co-operative policy in establishing order in Samoa, Bayard replied that such an invitation would be accepted with "readiness," and that the United States would "lend all aid to make life and property safe." [100]

Bayard then gave another indication of his pacific spirit in a reply to an hysterical letter from General I. J. Wistar. Wistar was anxious to have the American Government adopt a belligerent attitude towards Germany. He was certain that a bold, uncompromising policy in Samoa would force German compliance. In the event that the Germans raised "difficulties" in this regard,

. . . nothing would please our people, and every European people, better, for we would then drive their increasing commerce from the Ocean, and cut off all their Colonies in six months. . . . Do read the riot act to them, and inform them that the American people, by their administration, propose to make and run all "kings" in or adjacent to this continent, and will tolerate no European assistance.[101]

---

and robbed, Bismarck refers to an 'unprovoked attack' made upon his sailors by the natives, 'said to have taken place under the leadership of an American named KLEIN.' In his letters to *The World* Mr. Klein emphatically denies that he either led or instigated this attack. He was present in his capacity of a correspondent. We would suggest to Bismarck that when he catches MR. KLEIN it would be well for him to see that he has a fair trial before execution."

100. *Memorandum* written by Bayard after a conversation with Arco-Valley, January 10, 1889, *Bayard MS.*

101. I. J. Wistar to Bayard, January 8, 1889, *Bayard MS.*

Bayard's reply must have disappointed the belligerent General who wished America to run berserk in the broad Pacific:

If, as you say in your note of the 8th, "our masses don't know or care much about international law, or fine shades of fact," it makes it the more necessary that those who are charged with the safe conduct of public affairs should "hold the rudder true" and despite popular clamor or popular ignorance keep the ship of state within the channels of the law.[102]

Bayard's refusal to ride the crest of the anti-German wave that was sweeping over the United States, is an indication of the fine balance he always maintained in his handling of the difficult problems of foreign policy with which he was constantly faced. It took courage to stem this tide of belligerence that was rapidly rising in the early months of 1889, and the American press gave it fresh volume each day.[103] Sewall, without any authorization from Bayard, published a sensational story in the Washington *Post* in which he endeavored to build up a strong sentiment in the United States against any compromise with reference to Samoa. A typical paragraph from this interview will illustrate its tenor:

The condition of affairs is so bad there [Samoa] that the German residents haul down the American flag when it is displayed in public places. They boycott the Americans living there, and are insolent and abusive. . . . It is time a halt was called. The United States should say to oppressors of this poor people, "Stop, you have gone too far." [104]

The New York *Sun* thought that the policy of the Cleveland administration towards Samoa was "unfortunate, if not humiliating." [105] The New York *Herald* was of the opinion that the situation in the South Pacific looked "like war," [106] and it also announced that American naval officers were "sniffing the battle" that would come in Samoan waters.[107] The New York *World* carried a headline about "German Tyranny in Samoa"; [108] the New York *Times* informed its readers that "Germany Grows Insolent"; [109] the San Francisco *Examiner* expressed the view that "Germany in this affair has simply played the highway-

---

102. Bayard to I. J. Wistar, January 10, 1889, *ibid.*

103. Even so cautious a man as E. J. Phelps, the American Minister to Great Britain, believed in the adoption of a bolder attitude with reference to the Samoan situation. In a letter to Bayard, January 9, 1889, he remarks: "I have communicated to the Government your message in regard to Samoa. What a pity we have no Navy, and can only fire blank cartridges." *Bayard MS.*

104. September 21, 1888.   105. November 27, 1888.   106. January 21, 1889.
107. January 22, 1889.   108. January 23, 1889.   109. January 25, 1889.

man"; [110] and the New York *Press* was certain that "international rights are nothing to Germany."

Berthold Greenebaum, whose tenure of office as American consul at Apia had been too colorful to suit the Department of State, rushed into print to tell of his exciting experiences in Samoa. The Germans, of course, were the villains of his story, and he recounted how they had acted towards the Americans in a "most insolent manner." [111]

The Republicans in Congress were eager to derive some advantage from the fast rising wave of public sentiment against German policy in Samoa. On December 10 William P. Frye introduced in the Senate a resolution in favor of a "careful investigation" into Samoan affairs. He was convinced that the attitude of the Department of State was an unfortunate one which had led to an "exceedingly discreditable chapter in the history of American diplomacy." His information on the Samoan situation appears to have been supplied from partisan sources, and his ignorance of the subject was indicated by his persistent misspelling of the names of all the important Samoan chiefs.[112]

Although Senator George Gray denounced the jingoistic character of the Republican attack upon Bayard's Samoan policy,[113] the opposition in the Senate went ahead with their plans and a sub-committee of the Senate Committee on Foreign Relations held hearings to which they invited Harold M. Sewall, the American Consul-General at Apia. It happened that Sewall was a citizen of Maine, and he and Senator Frye soon found many things in common. In his testimony before the Senate sub-committee, Sewall sharply criticized German aggression in Samoa. During the German occupation of Apia

. . . great animosity appeared to be displayed by the Germans towards Americans. The store of one was entered and a woman attendant forced by threats to give up the key of the safe. A sick man for six years . . . was roughly torn from his bed by the German sailors. A German patrol paraded the streets at night and interfered with the passage of peaceful citizens.[114]

110. November 27, 1888.   111. New York *Herald*, January 25, 1889.

112. *Congressional Record,* 50 Cong. 2 sess., vol. 20, pt. 1, pp. 108-109. In the speech of Senator Frye we find that Tamasese masquerades under the name of Tamassi, Malietoa is incorrectly spelled as Milatoa, and Mataafa is made to appear as Madaaffa.

113. *Ibid.,* p. 109.

114. New York *Herald,* January 24, 1889. According to the *Herald,* Sewall was "more severe in his strictures on Mr. Bayard in private conversation than he has been in his testimony." Bayard was justly indignant when he learned of Sewall's criticism of the policy of the Department of State. In a letter to President Cleveland, January 28, 1889, he remarked: "The more I see in the newspapers of Mr. Sewall's line of comment on the State Department in relation to Samoa, the less I am inclined to submit to this 'fire in the

As a result of this anti-German testimony by Sewall, Senator Sherman reported out from the Senate Committee on Foreign Relations two amendments to the consular and diplomatic appropriation bill. One amendment provided for an appropriation of $500,000 for the protection of American interests in the Samoan Islands, and the other one appropriated $100,000 for the survey, improvement, and occupation of the bay and harbor of Pago Pago.[115] These amendments were adopted by Congress and approved by President Cleveland.[116]

In response to this growing interest in Samoan affairs, the President sent to Congress four special messages dealing with the South Pacific.[117] In his message of January 15, 1889, he gave voice to some suspicions of German policy:

> Germany . . . asserts . . . that she has no desire or intention to overturn the native Samoan Government or to ignore our treaty rights, and she still invites our Government to join her in restoring peace and quiet. But thus far her propositions on this subject seem to lead to such a preponderance of German power in Samoa as was never contemplated by us and is inconsistent with every prior agreement or understanding, while her recent conduct as between native warring factions gives rise to the suspicion that she is not content with a neutral position.
>
> Acting within the restraints which our Constitution and laws have placed upon Executive power, I have insisted that the autonomy and independence of Samoa should be scrupulously preserved according to the treaties made with Samoa by the powers named and their agreements and understanding with each other. I have protested against every act apparently tending in an opposite direction, and during the existence of internal disturbance one or more vessels of war have been kept in Samoan waters to protect American citizens and property.[118]

It is evident that President Cleveland was more belligerent than

rear' from one of my subordinates. It is difficult to cope with the Germans and the Republican Senate without having their smaller allies within our own camp." Bayard to Cleveland, *Bayard Letter Book,* vol. 10, *Bayard MS.*

115. *Congressional Record,* January 23, 1889, 50 Cong. 2 sess., vol. 20, pt. 2, p. 1119. With reference to his second amendment to the consular and diplomatic appropriation bill, Senator Sherman expressed the view that the language of the American treaty with Samoa amounted to a "grant *in praesenti,* and operated immediately as far as our rights in Pago Pago were concerned. That was our property just as much as if deeded to us, and a notice to terminate the treaty would not affect a vested right." *Cong. Rec.,* vol. 20, pt. 2, p. 1372.

116. *Statutes at Large of the United States,* February 26, March 2, 1889, vol. 25, pp. 699, 814.

117. James D. Richardson, *Messages and Papers of the Presidents,* vol. 8, pp. 800, 804-805, 806-807, and 810-811. These messages were dated, December 21, 1888, January 15, 30, 1889, and February 8, 1889. See also *Senate Ex. Docs., 31, 68, 92, 102;* 50 Cong., 2 sess.

118. James D. Richardson, *Messages and Papers of the Presidents,* vol. 8, pp. 804-805.

Bayard in his attitude towards Germany, and this was also true of George L. Rives, the Assistant Secretary of State, who expressed the view that the Germans seemed to be "hurling defiance in our teeth." [119] Secretary Whitney was openly critical of the course followed by the Department of State, and on January 5 he sent Bayard a letter in which he bluntly inquired if a fixed Samoan policy had finally been agreed upon. To him it seemed clear

. . . that the conquest of these islands [Samoan] is intended by the German government in the interests of its commercial company, and is being consummated by overt acts, which are multiplying day by day. There is no longer any other pretext upon which can be explained the interference of the German men-of-war in the contest in progress upon the island of Apia. I apprehend that the officers of the Navy will not understand, without definite advices to that effect, what their duty may be under the circumstances as they are developing. . . . The department has heretofore directed the officers of the squadron to act in accordance with the instructions which the Consular agent at Samoa shall receive from the Department of State, but in view of the late advices . . . the department desires to be advised whether it is the purpose of the government to announce any policy regarding the Samoan group of which the officers should be advised.[120]

Bayard was just as anxious as Secretary Whitney that full protection be accorded to all American rights in Samoa. From the viewpoint of International Law none of these rights had been violated, and specific assurances had been received from the German Government that American interests would be adequately safeguarded. There was no reason for the adoption of a reckless policy that would lead to war with Germany, and this was especially true when careful consideration was given to the lack of preparedness on the part of the American Navy. Secretary Whitney's belligerence had a very shaky foundation which was well known to Bayard. The American fleet was no match for that of Germany, and this fact was made uncomfortably clear by Lieutenant W. I. Chambers, who was a member of the staff of Rear

119. New York *Times*, January 25, 1889.
120. New York *Herald*, January 27, 1889. See also New York *World*, January 26, 27, 28, 1889. Secretary Whitney's ignorance of Samoan affairs is indicated by his reference to the "island of Apia." With reference to a division in the Cabinet relative to Samoa, the New York *World*, January 26, 1889, has the following comment: "Secretaries Whitney and Dickinson . . . would serve an immediate warning upon Germany that further interference in the internal affairs of Samoa would be regarded as a violation of our rights under our treaty with Samoa. . . . Secretary Fairchild inclines to Secretary Bayard's policy of caution and so does Secretary Endicott. Attorney-General Garland's position is with the Secretary of State. Secretary Vilas, too, . . . is a man of . . . peace at almost any price."

Admiral Gherardi. In a published statement, Lieutenant Chambers remarked:

> If we go to war with Germany there is an extreme probability that the German fleet may threaten to shell New York. New York is a rich city and could pay a good ransom. We have practically nothing with which to drive the enemy away, and it would take a long time to build anything suitable for that purpose. . . . If Germany were to demand a ransom of say $500,000,000 from New York, we should have to pay it. True, we have the *Vesuvius* and some old monitors, but the former cannot be expected to cope with the whole German fleet, and the latter are slow and their armor protection is comparatively weak.[121]

This statement from Lieutenant Chambers which indicated that in case of war with the United States, Germany would have a "picnic" at American expense, was a clear indication that Bayard was a realist rather than a swashbuckler who loudly called for a war which his country could not afford to wage. When Secretary Whitney urged that instructions be sent to Admiral Kimberly, at Panama, to proceed at once to Samoa, Bayard insisted that a note should also be addressed to Count von Arco-Valley indicating the action taken by the Navy Department.[122] This procedure was followed and Admiral Kimberly was ordered to leave for Samoan waters and to protest against

> . . . the subjection and displacement of native government of Samoa by Germany as in violation of positive agreement and understanding between treaty powers, but inform the representatives of the German and British governments of your readiness to co-operate in causing all treaty rights to be respected and in restoring peace and order on the basis of a recognition of Samoan rights to independence.[123]

On the following day Bayard sent his proposed note to Arco-Valley informing him of the instructions that had been sent to Admiral Kimberly, and suggesting the "free election" by Samoans of a King as a means of putting an end to the "shocking internecine warfare among these Islanders." [124]

It was only too apparent to Bayard that the Republicans in the Senate were anxious to make political capital out of the Samoan situation, and the press throughout the United States was giving effective

121. New York *Herald*, January 28, 1889.
122. *Memorandum* in the *Bayard MS* (undated).
123. Whitney to Admiral Kimberly, January 11, 1889, *S. Ex. Doc., 68*, 50 Cong., 2 sess., pp. 21-22.
124. Bayard to Arco-Valley, January 12, 1889, *German Legation, Notes to*, vol. 10, MS Dept. of State.

assistance to the opponents of Bayard's pacific policy. In a letter to the President, Bayard gave vent to his feelings:

The newspapers, as you see, are full of sound and fury over the Samoan reports. Of these there is nothing we have not had for ten days. I am very glad that the whole story has been placed before the Senate, and I hope that learned body will read it, and that gradually the country may comprehend the necessity of dealing with serious problems in a fitting way. I am sick and weary of the frothy sensationalism with which the most profound results are discussed . . . in the press. The ruthless nature of German rule finds many admirers and would-be imitators in this Country.[125]

In a similar key Bayard also wrote to his old friend Samuel L. Barlow:

I cannot help believing that what I have been doing in the State Department, despite the wretched obstruction and . . . party malignity of the Republican press and Senate, will be better appreciated after a while. To build a coal shed and put some coal in it down in the Samoan Islands is very well, . . . but to appropriate $500,000 to resist Germany by Naval or Military force, is lamentably weak. If a collision should result a good many figures will go back of that sum. . . . It shocks me to read the shallow detestable rapid talk of *War*. How little do these small souls know the horrors of that word.[126]

The partisan "malignity" that was so apparent in the Senate in the early months of 1889, was a heavy burden for Bayard to bear, and this was made all the more uncomfortable when certain Democratic Senators gave a measure of support to Republican tactics of obstruction. On January 23 Bayard received a letter from Senator John T. Morgan, which informed him that the Senate Committee on Foreign Relations had recommended an appropriation of $600,000 to "fit up a Naval station at Pago Pago," and to protect American rights in the Samoan Islands. The Senator was anxious to know whether Bayard preferred that the Senate "should indicate their view on the Samoan situation

125. Bayard to President Cleveland, January 21, 1889, *Bayard Letter Book*, vol. 10, *Bayard MS.*

126. Bayard to S. L. M. Barlow, January 25, 1889, *ibid.* It is interesting to note the role played by certain "pressure groups" with reference to American policy in Samoa. The Chamber of Commerce of San Francisco sent the following petition to Congress on December 20, 1888: "The Chamber . . . respectfully urges upon Congress such a decided policy in Samoa, that American interests may be considered, American citizenship respected and the agreement made by Germany with the Governments of Great Britain and the United States in regard to the independence of the *Samoan Islands* held inviolable. . . . We respectfully represent that the time has arrived, when the United States must maintain its just rights, or sacrifice its self respect." *Miscellaneous Letters*, December, 1888, pt. 2, MS Dept. of State.

and policy as a guide to the Executive, or, rather as a means of presenting a firm and solid front on these matters?" [127]

In reply to this inquiry, Bayard expressed his views with mordant candor:

Undoubtedly it would be most satisfactory to have a firm and solid front presented to Germany and Great Britain . . . in Samoan matters, but my experiences of the last four years have made me hopeless of receiving even ordinary comity or courtesy, much less firm and steady support from the Senate as that body is at present constituted and controlled. . . . If Mr. Frye's opening speech . . . indicates the feeling of that body it would be idle to expect co-operation.[128]

Several days after Bayard had written this letter to Senator Morgan, Senator John Sherman made a speech which indicated that some Republicans were willing to temper their partisanship with a portion of patriotism. The rumors of war that had filled the American press were alarming to Senator Sherman, and he expressed the view that there was no real ground for serious difficulties between Germany and the United States:[129]

It does not seem to me that Germany, whose people are like our own, and Great Britain with their boundless empire, will ever allow the disgrace to be inflicted upon our civilization of having a single man of either of these nations killed in a war or contest over this puerile controversy.[130]

When the Samoan controversy had nearly reached an impasse, Bismarck came forward and suggested a solution. On January 13 he sent word through the German Minister at Washington, that war had been forced upon the German Government by Chief Mataafa. This contest with the Samoan chief would be carried on with "the utmost consider-

127. John T. Morgan to Bayard, January 23, 1889, *Bayard MS.*
128. Bayard to Morgan, January 24, 1889, *ibid.* See also letter from Bayard to Morgan, January 23, 1889, *Bayard MS.*
129. During the course of a conversation with Count von Arco-Valley on February 2, 1889, Bayard remarked that he approved the "general tone" of Senator Sherman's speech. *Memorandum* written by Bayard after a conversation with Arco-Valley, February 2, 1889, *Bayard MS.*
130. *Congressional Record*, January 29, 1889, 50 Cong., 2 sess., vol. 20, pt. 2, p. 1291. Senator Dolph, of Oregon, was much more belligerent in his remarks. He believed that the "sacrifice of the rights of its citizens, the humiliation of its officers in the face of an arrogant power, is worse than war; and I would not submit to it." He also read a letter from John C. Henderson in which it was stated that the Samoan Islands were of "vast importance to the United States in controlling an interoceanic canal. The United States cannot afford to let European military powers own every strategic position commanding the interoceanic canal." *Congressional Record*, January 30, 1889, 50 Cong., 2 sess., vol. 20, pt. 2, p. 1325-1337.

ation for English and American interests." He hoped that the American Government would "furnish the consuls, and the commander of its ships of war in Samoa, with suitable instructions." [131] Following this announcement of war against Mataafa, Bismarck then sent an invitation to the American Government to "take part in a conference on Samoan affairs, to be held in Berlin." [132]

While the American Government was considering this invitation, Arco-Valley had a long conversation with Carl Schurz on the subject of German-American friction with reference to Samoa. Arco-Valley remarked that "according to reliable information received at Berlin, the hostility of the Samoans to the Germans was largely, if not entirely, owing to the constant instigation on the part of the Americans, officials as well as private persons, in Samoa." When Schurz interrupted Arco-Valley long enough to indicate that in the published diplomatic correspondence there was plenty of evidence to show that American officials in Samoa were deeply suspicious of German policy, the conversation was then directed to the "important question what was now best to be done to avoid further difficulty." Arco-Valley was certain that the German Government was "most peaceably disposed," and Schurz assured him that the character "of the American people and the traditions of the government" were also inclined towards peace. Schurz also expressed the view that the American Government was especially anxious that the "autonomy of the Samoan people and the treaty rights of the United States be properly respected." Arco-Valley then inquired if the incoming Republican Administration would be willing to co-operate with Germany in the proposed Berlin Conference with reference to Samoa. Schurz answered that if the German Government made a "fair proposition accompanied with satisfactory assurances," a situation would thereby be created "which would have to be dealt with upon its merits by any administration whatever its party character." [133]

On the day that Bayard received this conciliatory letter from Schurz,

131. Prince Bismarck to Count von Arco-Valley, January 13, 1889, *House Ex. Doc., 118*, 50 Cong., 2 sess., p. 15. Bismarck had already, December 23, 1888, authorized the German representatives in Samoa to call upon the German fleet for assistance in the event that the "outlook for success was assured." *Samoa-Weissbuch*, pt. 5, no. 33.

132. *Memorandum* written by Alvey A. Adee after a conversation with Herr Mumm von Schwartzenstein, January 21, 1889, *Bayard MS*. This invitation was renewed during a conversation between Count von Arco-Valley and Bayard on January 28. See *Memorandum* written by Bayard after a conversation with Arco-Valley, January 28, 1889, *Bayard MS*.

133. Schurz to Bayard, January 30, 1889, *Schurz MS*, Library of Congress.

he also received from the American vice-consul at Apia a telegram to the effect that the German consul had issued a declaration of war against Mataafa and had placed Samoa under martial law.[134] Bayard read this telegram at the Cabinet meeting on January 31,[135] and then turned to Francis Wharton for advice. Wharton promptly submitted a memorandum which discussed the alternatives before the Department of State:

> If we are neutrals, & *Germany* a belligerent (Samoa being the other belligerent) she has a right to search our vessels for contraband or shut them out when attempting to run blockade. If we say, "we are part owners of Samoa and will maintain our rights as such," then we ourselves, by refusing to be searched, take the position of belligerents. My own idea is that it is premature for us to declare our position on this very serious issue. There is a third view possible—that Germany, in seeking to punish those who lately massacred her subjects in Samoa, is doing very much what we did when in 1817 we sent an expedition to break up a nest of pirates in Amelia Island, then under Spanish dominion. . . . . Between these three views I do not think we ought at present to decide. The first means submission to Germany. The second means war. The third means an attitude of jealous watchfulness, not conceding belligerent rights to Germany, not fighting her, but holding her to account for her aggressions, and notifying her how we mean to do so.[136]

Bayard selected the third alternative presented by Wharton, and on January 31 he sent an instruction to Pendleton in which he stated that the American Government assumed that

> . . . German officials will be . . . instructed scrupulously to abstain from interference with American citizens and property in Samoa. No declaration of martial law can confer or expand German jurisdiction over American citizens in Samoa. No such authority will be recognized or conceded by this Government.[137]

Bayard also informed Arco-Valley of the substance of the instruc-

134. Blacklock to Bayard, January 31, 1889, *Bayard MS.*
135. *Memorandum* written by Bayard, January 31, 1889, *Bayard MS.*
136. *Memorandum*, undated, in *Bayard MS.*
137. Bayard to Pendleton, January 31, 1889, *Bayard MS.* In the Bayard manuscripts there is an undated and unsigned memorandum, probably of January 31, 1889, which reads: "Advices from Samoa state that the German officials have given notice that all vessels arriving there will be searched for articles of contraband of war. They have suppressed the *Samoan Times* (an English paper). Passenger on British steamer . . . who visited Mataafa's camp was placed under arrest, but subsequently released in compliance with the demands of British Consul. Mataafa's forces amount to 6,000. They are strongly intrenched and other Samoans are rapidly joining them. Upon the arrival of the Steamer *Richmond* she was boarded and searched by the Germans."

tions that had been sent to Pendleton.[138] The next morning, Arco-Valley called at the Department of State and translated for Bayard an instruction he had just received from Prince Bismarck. The Chancellor expressed the view that the German "military authority" in Samoa had "gone too far," and orders had been sent to the commander of the German forces to "withdraw the part of his proclamation concerning foreigners." Consul Knappe had made a mistake in directing Mataafa to hand over to him the administration of the Samoan Islands. He had been ordered by telegram to "withdraw immediately his command." [139]

These statements of Arco-Valley were confirmed by a telegram from Pendleton who stated that the action of the German consul at Apia was "disavowed" as "entirely contrary to instructions." [140]

Bayard was greatly pleased to learn of Bismarck's conciliatory attitude, and he immediately wrote to Carl Schurz to tell him the good news:

> I am glad to inform you that today Count Arco came with a note-verbale from Berlin . . . to the effect that the extreme action of the German Consul

138. Bayard to Arco-Valley, January 31, 1889, *Bayard MS.*
139. *Memorandum* written by Bayard after a conference with Arco-Valley, February 1, 1889, *ibid.*
140. Pendleton to Bayard, February 1, 1889, *ibid.* See also Bayard to Arco-Valley, February 1, 1889. On the margin of the telegram from the German consul at Apia, January 5, 1889, suggesting annexation of the Samoan Islands, Bismarck wrote: "Out of the question. This seems objectionable to me in the face of increasing American chauvinism and existing agreements. We pledged our word to Great Britain and the United States not to annex Samoa." Bismarck then informed the Foreign Office that he wished the German representatives abroad "to respect international treaties more than the enclosed telegram would indicate. He is surprised that a Prussian official of training would expect him to violate the conventions with America and Great Britain. It is our right to protect property and oppose force by force, but it lies outside political possibilities to break treaties." With reference to Knappe's telegram of January 23, 1889, Bismarck made the following comments: "The protest of your English colleagues against the measures taken is well founded. In the case of conflicts resulting from that occasion, you would be in the wrong. Your demand that Germany take charge of the administration lies outside your instructions and our intentions. Rescind it at once." (Bismarck to Knappe, January 31, 1889). On February 21, 1889, Bismarck rebuked Knappe for the way he had handled the situation in Samoa and inquired why he had not wired to Berlin for instructions: "If such had been the case you would not have got into a situation of having to prove that you were absolutely mistaken, both as regards your own influence on the Samoan parties and the elements of resistance on the side of the opponents, and the country would not have had to pay for your error with a severe sacrifice of lives, whereby, in anticipation of the Imperial martial law, you forced us to make amends and jeopardized our peace with a friendly power." For these comments of Bismarck, see Count Otto zu Stolberg-Wernigerode, *Germany and the United States of America During the Era of Bismarck,* pp. 253-255. See also the *Samoa-Weissbuch,* pt. I, no. 41; pt. II, no. 47; pt. III, nos. 48-49; pt. V, nos. 4, 7, 12, 13, 27, 32-37, 41, 47; and *Verhandlungen des Reichstags,* 1888–1889, Anl. Bd. V, Aktenstueck, no. 138, s. 890, Anl. Bd. VI, Aktenstueck, no. 210, s. 1235.

at Samoa in declaring martial law in that region had been disapproved by his government. . . . This apparent return of Prince Bismarck to the line of the perfectly well understood agreement, that native autonomy and independence should be sustained by the three treaty powers, leads me to be hopeful of a satisfactory adjustment by the conference to which I understood the German Government has decided to invite the United States and Great Britain. . . .

You are perfectly correct in your diagnosis of the case—it is a mercenary clash of rival traders in the cause of which Germany has allowed official action to be too freely employed in the aid of private schemes. . . . I am very sure . . . that the various plans for a native government assisted by the Treaty powers, in which no preponderance of control should be awarded to any one of the three, will under candid treatment yield a just and satisfactory solution of the present unhappy and . . . dangerous condition of affairs. . . .

It is difficult to describe the singular bitterness of feeling which seems to control the Republican Managers, and which has led to a systematic obstruction, misrepresentation, and aspersion of the Administration in every department, and towards none so fiercely as the Department of State in which I am just closing four years of constant duty. They have sought, . . . with too much success, to embarrass me in dealing with Foreign governments, and I was only too glad to see in John Sherman's speech signs of an appreciation of the *responsibility* which approaching power naturally brings. . . .

The Senate Committee [on Foreign Relations] have been examining in *secret* the present Consul [at Apia] to see whether some error or something discreditable to me could not be unearthed. But all I want is the whole history to be made public. . . .

I cannot avoid anxiety lest the indiscretion of some Naval Officer, on one side or the other, may lead to a broil which may expand itself. But I have been so single-minded in pursuing justice and friendly relations with Germany . . . that I believe we will find a clear channel and come to a worthy settlement.[141]

Bayard's desire to have the whole history of the Samoan dispute "made public" was partially fulfilled by President Cleveland's policy of sending to Congress all the important documents in the Department of State which might throw light upon that question. At times this policy of enlightenment raised certain doubts in Bayard's mind. On January 28 Arco-Valley called at the Department of State to leave with Bayard an instruction from Prince Bismarck in answer to a note that Bayard

---

141. Bayard to Schurz, Feb. 1, 1889, *Bayard Letter Book*, vol. 10, *Bayard MS*. In reply, Schurz wrote to Bayard that he was certain that "when the whole history of this business becomes known you will receive full justice at the hands of public opinion. If you could conduct this business to the end, the country might feel perfectly safe." Schurz to Bayard, February 3, 1889, *Schurz MS*.

had sent to Arco-Valley on January 12.[142] Bayard was a little uncertain about the propriety of sending at once to Congress this latest communication from Bismarck, but President Cleveland had no doubts in this regard. In a special message of January 30, Congress was informed of all the latest developments in the Samoan situation, and the pertinent documents were laid before that body for publication.[143] In another message of February 8 the President submitted to Congress the joint protocols of the Washington Conference on Samoa, and now the whole world could see how stubbornly and how effectively Bayard had fought for the rights of the Samoan natives.[144]

The publication of the Samoan correspondence had a salutary effect upon American public opinion, and Wade Hampton sent the following short note to Bayard:

I write now to express my great gratification at your correspondence with Bismarck and to congratulate you heartily on the result of your encounter

142. *Memorandum* written by Bayard after a conversation with Arco-Valley, January 28, 1889, *Bayard MS.*

143. James D. Richardson, *Messages and Papers of the Presidents*, vol. 8, pp. 806-807. In a letter to Bayard, January 29, 1889, President Cleveland stresses the importance of submitting to Congress all important documents relating to Samoan affairs: "We have labored under great disadvantages in so far as an understanding by the American people of the true situation and the theory of our conduct is concerned. My last message to the Congress quite directly puts the responsibility of further action upon that Body. . . . Having put the responsibility upon Congress, all that we desire touching the subject should be immediately put before Congress so that it cannot be said that anything which might influence its action has been withheld. Besides, the transmission of further documents gives an opportunity to make more plain our claim that we have done all we can, and are not to be blamed for anything Congress fails to do. This is very important to us. . . . The thing must be made plain by Executive messages which perhaps will be read and which should be so simple that they *must* be understood. It seems to me that the failure to send to Congress *immediately*, Bismarck's last despatch, is the surrender of the best opportunity to turn the judgment of the people to the proper quarter, we have yet had. I think it will not do to say the purport of it can be spelled out from former communications. . . . I am not afraid of sending too many messages on this subject. There is danger, vexation, and unjust misrepresentation in sending too few. . . . I pray you to earnestly and early reflect upon these suggestions." *Bayard MS.*

144. James D. Richardson, *Messages and Papers of the Presidents*, vol. 8, pp. 810-811. With respect to the evidence of these protocols, Carl Schurz wrote as follows to Bayard on February 27, 1889: "I have read the 'Protocol' with keen interest and cannot refrain from saying that the American side of the question has been represented by you with the most decided and unquestionable superiority in point of argument as well as vigor of debate. I do not wonder that those among your adversaries who still have some respect for the truth, were silenced by the appearance of this document." *Bayard MS.* It was the opinion of President Cleveland that the American position as exhibited by the protocols was "entirely right and unassailable." President Cleveland to Bayard, January 28, 1889, *Bayard MS.* For a conversation between Bayard and Arco-Valley concerning the publication of the protocols, see Bayard *memorandum* of February 2, *Bayard MS.*

with that big bully. You have euchered the Republicans, and I rejoice in your triumph.[145]

Bayard's reply indicated how tired he had grown of the constant struggle he had waged with his Republican opponents who had never cared how low they stooped in order that they might conquer:

I weary so over the tone of our press, and not the press alone, but of men high in the public councils who propose to deal with the vast issues of war or peace between great states in the spirit of prize fighters or scuffling boot blacks. It has been a pitiable sight to witness the conduct of the Senate Committee on Foreign Relations . . . for the past four years. When the record is reviewed, as one day it will be, I believe you will find that I have no cause to be ashamed of the spirit and manner in which I have sought to arrange the relations of the United States with other nations.[146]

In the meantime, on February 4, Arco-Valley paid a visit to the Department of State and showed Bayard some instructions he had just received from Prince Bismarck.[147] The Chancellor expressed the opinion

145. Wade Hampton to Bayard, February 4, 1889, *Bayard MS.*
146. Bayard to Wade Hampton, February 5, 1889, *ibid.*
147. On February 3, 1889 Carl Schurz wrote a very significant letter to Arco-Valley with reference to the possibility of a war between Germany and the United States. He alluded to Germany's excellent army and rapidly developing navy, and he then referred to the fact that although the United States was without large armaments, it did possess considerable wealth, supplies of all kinds, and a patriotism that was willing to make the greatest sacrifices. Because of the width of the Atlantic Ocean, there could be no war on land between the United States and Germany, and during the early part of such a conflict, there could be no great sea battles. The United States could send to sea a large number of commerce destroyers to prey upon the German merchant marine. The Germans could respond by sending a fleet which would attempt to bombard certain American cities. These naval forays, however, were dubious, owing to the fact that an alliance might be concluded between the United States and France. But even if the German fleet could destroy New York, Philadelphia, and Boston, these operations would have no decisive effect upon the result of the war. America would construct a large fleet of her own and the war would drag on for many years.

Arco-Valley sent this letter from Schurz to Prince Bismarck, who sent an interesting answer to the German Minister at Washington. This letter of reply clearly indicates the nervous tension that existed in the Chancellor's office. The race for colonial empire that was so characteristic of the new age of economic imperialism, was very trying upon the nerves of diplomats who were busily studying the formulas of big power politics. It is important to notice that Bismarck did not reject the thought of possible war with the United States because of a dispute over colonial possessions. He readily admitted that the German Government was nervous over the situation. In the event of war with the United States, German commerce destroyers could seriously injure the American merchant marine, and they could bombard American cities along the Atlantic coast. He believed that an alliance between France and the United States would be balanced by one between Germany and England. In concluding his comments he remarked: "Whether the means, of which America would dispose in the case of a war with a European power, would be inexhaustible, I will leave undecided, and I doubt if a strong fleet of battleships with trained crews could be improvised in a year or two, and I suppose that the damage,

that it was the duty of the three treaty powers to put a stop to the "bloody combat" that was taking place in the Samoan Islands. The best means of accomplishing this end was through a resumption of the consultations which had been held in Washington in June and July of 1887. The new conference could best be held in Berlin, and Bismarck extended an urgent invitation to the American Government to send delegates who could continue the discussions of the Samoan problem until some satisfactory solution could be agreed upon.[148]

Bayard's reaction to this invitation is revealed in a memorandum that he wrote after the termination of a conversation with Arco-Valley:

I said that I thought it all important that pending the Conference, matters should remain in *statu quo* in Samoa, and that the war between Tamasese and Mataafa should under no pretext be continued, and I said further, that I did not understand how we were to deal with the question properly if Germany was to conduct military operations by way of revenge or reprisal against native Samoans.

He said that the feeling in Germany was very much aroused by the slaughter of their men and he did not know what would be done in that respect. I said that it was reported that German vessels had indiscriminately shelled the villages of these poor people, and I didn't know with what loss of life or property.

Count Arco answered that the villages were small and insignificant. I said that I understood that, but could not see why their feebleness constituted a ground for such severe retaliation against them. . . . In such a struggle the annihilation of these islanders was certain. He said that Prince Bismarck did not intend or wish such a thing. I said that I thought it would

which we could do to the American commercial emporiums and by destroying the American merchant marine, would be an appreciable one for even the richest country. . . . Also the view, that in a battle with America we should remain alone and would besides have to reckon certainly with French antagonism, would hardly prove to be right. On the contrary, I believe that an American-French alliance would certainly be opposed by a German-English one." See Alfred Vagts, "Hopes and Fears of an American-German War, 1870–1915," *Political Science Quarterly*, December, 1939, pp. 516-519. Also, Alfred Vagts, *Deutschland und die Vereinigten Staaten in der Weltpolitik* (N. Y., 1935), pp. 656-665, and Frederick Bancroft, *Speeches, Correspondence and Political Papers of Carl Schurz* (N. Y., 1913), vol. 5, pp. 1-10.

148. During the course of this conference with Bayard on February 4, 1889, Arco-Valley read some very sharp criticisms that Prince Bismarck had levelled against the conduct of Captain Leary of the U.S.S. *Adams*, and against the actions of Vice-Consul Blacklock. Bayard made no answer to these critical remarks until the following day. In his note of February 5, Bayard stated that the complaints of the German consul at Apia against the conduct of Captain Leary and Vice-Consul Blacklock, did not appear to be "substantiated by an averment of any personal knowledge of the facts, but must have been based upon . . . belief only, or are reported at second hand, and must be classed as merely hearsay evidence." Bayard to Arco-Valley, February 5, 1889, *German Legation, Notes to*, vol. 10, MS Dept. of State.

be more in keeping with this conference that bloodshed should cease and that one word from the three powers jointly would bring about peace. I said that I would give an answer speedily—as soon as the matter could be laid before the President.[149]

On February 5 Bayard wrote to Arco-Valley to express his "acceptance of the proposal of the Government of Germany to resume the consultation held in this city between the representatives of the United States, Germany and Great Britain, which was suspended on the 26th day of July 1887." He then repeated his statements of the previous day with reference to the desirability of terminating at once the bloody struggle between the German military forces and the Samoans.[150]

While Bayard was waiting for further news from Berlin with reference to the date when the proposed conference should assemble,[151] he wrote to several of his friends with regard to the Samoan situation. He was certain that the publication of the protocols of the Washington Conference would disclose the "really hard work" he had performed in trying to

. . . befriend this scanty band of Islanders against the plundering traders of America, Germany, and Great Britain. Civilization has had a rough side to them, and I am not sure whether they will survive its blessings. The *Sun* [Baltimore *Sun*] can do no more important service to the Country than to denounce the dangerous slurs and sneers at Germany which fill the irresponsible press. I am as full of sympathy for the poor Samoans as any man, . . . but we must not forget that fifty German officers and men have been lost in

149. *Memorandum* written by Bayard after a conversation with Arco-Valley, February 4, 1889, *Bayard MS.* See also Arco-Valley to Bayard, February 4, 1889, *German Legation, Notes from,* vol. 20, MS Dept. of State.

150. Bayard to Arco-Valley, February 5, 1889, *German Legation, Notes to,* vol. 10, MS Dept. of State. On February 8 Herr von Mumm, Secretary of the German Legation, called at the Department of State and had a talk with George L. Rives, the Second Assistant Secretary of State. He said that "with reference to Mr. Bayard's note accepting the suggestion for a renewal of the conference at Berlin, they were in some doubt as to whether his suggestion in regard to cessation of hostilities was to be regarded as a condition *sine qua non* or not; but that they had finally determined to telegraph to Berlin the language of the note, and leave the authorities at Berlin to make up their minds as to what it meant." *Memorandum* written by Mr. Rives after a conversation with Herr von Mumm on February 8, 1889, *Bayard MS.*

151. On February 5 Schurz wrote to Bayard to inquire about the feasibility of arranging some settlement of the Samoan question before the Cleveland Administration went out of office. (Schurz to Bayard, February 5, 1889, *Schurz MS.*) Schurz also wrote to Senator John Sherman about the importance of finding a solution for the Samoan problem as speedily as possible. (Schurz to Sherman, February 4, 1889. *Schurz MS.*) Bayard thought that the question of an immediate settlement of the Samoan dispute depended largely upon the attitude that Arco-Valley would assume. Nothing could be done until he had been consulted. (Bayard to Schurz, February 6, 1889, *Bayard MS.*)

conflict with the Natives, and it will require a good deal of magnanimity to restrain the natural desire to avenge them.[152]

To Rodmond Wright he wrote in a similar vein: "Pray do what you can to stop this *dangerous* gabble tending to stir up Germany. In barking at my heels the little dogs may cause a serious accident." [153]

On February 9 he sent a letter to Francis Wharton with reference to the protocols of the Washington Conference on Samoa. He felt that the role he had played during those sessions was that of a "political Missionary to the unclad Samoans." There was still danger that the "gentle Bismarck" would wish "to butcher a hundred or so of the poor natives before he goes into conference to frame a government for them." [154] Several days later he expressed to E. J. Phelps the opinion that he had the Samoan quarrel with Germany "in good trim, altho' (*entre nous*) poor Pendleton's condition has greatly increased my difficulties for eighteen months past." [155]

These "difficulties" were rapidly approaching an end, and the preparations for the Berlin Conference were steadily progressing. In this regard the German Minister paid a formal visit to the Department of State on February 13, and his conference with Bayard is told in detail in a memorandum in the Bayard manuscripts:

> The German Minister called. He opened the conversation by saying that in the newspapers he had observed the statement made that Germany was intentionally delaying the Conference, and that he wished to say that that was a mistake. . . . He asked me whether I had meant that the things that I proposed to be done by Germany should be conditions before the Conference should commence. I answered that I did not think it necessary because I thought they could accompany the Conference. . . . I did not see how he [Prince Bismarck] could invite the United States to assist in the pacification of Samoa while he continued to make Samoa the theatre of war against these people. . . .
>
> I . . . was ready to enter the Conference at once, but he could perceive that the incoming administration might wish to take charge of the negotiation and settlement of the question, and I wished to leave it in as good shape for them as I could. I then told him confidentially that Mr. Pendleton's health was so defective that I thought it would be necessary to have this Government represented at Berlin by another person who would at least assist Mr. Pendleton in the transaction.

152. Bayard to Frederic Emory, February 8, 1889, *Bayard Letter Book,* vol. 10, *Bayard MS.*
153. Bayard to Rodmond Wright, February 8, 1889, *ibid.*
154. Bayard to Francis Wharton, February 9, 1889, *ibid.*
155. Bayard to E. J. Phelps, February 13, 1889, *ibid.*

I then referred to Mr. Sewall, and my discovery that he had not been at all in accord with my wishes and instructions in Samoa. Count Arco replied that Mr. John Sherman had said that Sewall was a fool, and I said I thought Mr. Sherman was right in that opinion. . . .

The interview closed by my telling him that I would endeavor to speak to Mr. Sherman on the subject; that I was a little embarrassed from the fact that Gen. Harrison was not in town, and I did not wish to anticipate the action of Administration; did not wish to make any appointments that were not absolutely necessary; that I would see Mr. Sherman in the next few days, and see what degree of expedition they thought necessary.[156]

Before taking up this matter with Senator Sherman, Bayard wrote a short note to his intimate friend, Samuel Barlow, about the Samoan situation:

I am sorry to know you have been a *whore de combat* (you see I lapse into *French*). Pretty hard on you to be sick and read the Samoan correspondence at the same time. . . . But I *do* want you to read the instalment I now enclose, because it looks mightily as if old Bismarck wanted to bathe his hands in the blood of those poor Islanders before he made peace with what was left of them—when the conference begins. The instructions he sent Count Arco, and the note by me in reply . . . will not make it easy, however, to kill those poor creatures in cold blood. I fear, however, that if the officers and seamen killed and wounded by the Samoans had been Americans, we would have heard a howl for blood all over the broad land! [157]

There was little doubt that many Americans wished to magnify every incident connected with Samoa, and Bayard was not surprised when he received on February 17 a telegram from John C. Klein informing him that the "greatest terror exists [at] Apia." Klein had just arrived at San Francisco, and he inquired whether the Department of State wished him to come at once to Washington to report on conditions in Samoa.[158]

Bayard remembered the sensational stories about Klein's activities in Samoa, and this fact led him to refer this telegram to Senator Sherman with an inquiry as to whether the Senator desired to have Klein summoned to Washington.[159] Sherman had a "general impression" that Klein was a

. . . sensational correspondent who took sides with Mataaffa, and perhaps

156. *Memorandum* written by Bayard after a conversation with Arco-Valley, February 13, 1889, *Bayard MS*.

157. Bayard to Samuel L. Barlow, February 15, 1889, *Bayard Letter Book*, vol. 10, *Bayard MS*.

158. John C. Klein to Bayard, February 17, 1889, *Bayard MS*.

159. Bayard to Sherman, February 17, 1889, *Sherman MS, Library of Congress*.

without fighting himself, encouraged and led the Samoans in the fight. . . . He would like now to be the central figure of a Sensation and pose as a Hero. The Conference is the best solution of the difficulty and I think we had better wait a while without calling Klein here. I will however advise with the Committee tomorrow and inform you of its view.[160]

On the following day Sherman wrote to Bayard that the other members of the Senate Committee on Foreign Relations were "generally disinclined" to summon Mr. Klein to Washington.[161] The fact that a Republican Administration would soon be in power was having a sobering effect upon the partisan group in the Senate which had so loudly called for a decisive policy in Samoa.[162] There was little left for Bayard to do but speed the preparations for the Conference that would be held in Berlin. On February 18 Arco-Valley had a conversation with Bayard with reference to German policy in Samoa. Bayard again emphasized the importance of terminating at once the "bloody combat in Samoa." Arco-Valley then raised the question as to whether the Conference was "conditioned upon the fact that Germany must inflict no punishment upon those who had killed her soldiers." Bayard replied that he was "not prepared to say that," but it was certainly true that "the state of affairs would be thoroughly disturbed if, while proposing pacification, Germany should continue war." [163]

Further details concerning the Berlin Conference were discussed by Bayard and Arco-Valley during a conversation in the Department of State on February 21, 1889. Bayard remarked that he "would have no hesitation in selecting and sending delegates to Berlin if it were not for the fact that such action might seriously interfere with the plans of the incoming administration." Arco-Valley then stated that Mr. Blaine had talked to him "very plainly about his coming in here [to the Department of State]." Bayard confessed that his own relations with Blaine were "the reverse of confidential," but he promised that he would "endeavor to discover whether immediate action could be arranged in the choice of these envoys or persons to represent the United States."

160. Sherman to Bayard, February 17, 1889, *Bayard MS.*
161. Sherman to Bayard, February 18, 1889, *ibid.*
162. The publication of the Samoan correspondence was making it apparent to every impartial person that Bayard had made a valiant fight for Samoan independence. On February 20, 1889, Bayard received a note from J. S. Moore in which he remarked: "The Samoan affair has and will forever bring you admiration from your friends and is most assuredly heaping 'confusion' on a miserable set of partisans. Take my word for it, the American people will know your worth." *Bayard MS.*
163. *Memorandum* written by Bayard after a conversation with Arco-Valley, February 18, 1889, *Bayard MS.*

In concluding his conversation with Bayard, Arco-Valley left at the Department of State a copy of his instructions from Bismarck. They dealt specifically with the calling of the Berlin Conference:

As soon as the United States shall inform Germany when the United States representatives can be expected to arrive at Berlin, the day of the Conference will then be fixed, and telegraphed from Berlin. If the Conference is to be held without delay, the German Government will try to come to an understanding concerning satisfaction for the killing of the German soldiers, only if no agreement is arrived at on this subject between the three powers, or if too great a delay shall occur, Germany shall proceed to take satisfaction according to their own judgment.

Germany does not wish to create armed contention in Samoa, but Germany intends to punish criminals, and cannot renounce this right. The wish expressed in Mr. Bayard's note of February 5th, that orders to suspend belligerent action . . . be telegraphed to the German officials in Samoa, is rendered unnecessary because by the Imperial order of January 12 all further military measures have been put an end to and no other instructions have since been sent.

In spite of the reinforcement of the American squadron in Samoa, which could only be intended to be directed against Germany, the Imperial Government has until the present, not given an order for any new ships to join the squadron at those Islands, because it is the desire of the Imperial Government to keep away from any responsibility of diminishing the reciprocal confidence between the two nations.[164]

After a careful study of Bismarck's instructions to Arco-Valley, Bayard submitted a report to President Cleveland in which he stated that the German Government had indicated a "substantial acceptance" of the suggestions outlined in the American note of February 5. After discussing several points raised in Bismarck's instructions, Bayard recommended the "acceptance on behalf of the United States of the proposal of Germany to allow the Conference to meet in Berlin." It was his belief that "greater expedition in arriving at a decision and settlement of the questions at issue would be much more likely to be secured by holding the next session of the Conference in Berlin, in order to avoid the frequent delays made necessary by the constant reference of the points under discussion by the British and German representatives to their respective Governments."[165]

On February 25 Arco-Valley made a formal call at the Department

164. *Memorandum* written by Bayard after a conversation with Arco-Valley, February 21, 1889, *Bayard MS.*

165. Bayard to President Cleveland, Feb. 27, 1889, *Bayard MS.* See also, *Report Book,* vol. 17, MS Dept. of State.

of State to inquire whether Bayard had selected the American delegates
to the Berlin Conference. Bayard informed him that no appointments
had been made. Arco-Valley then remarked that Mr. Blaine had intimated to him "that the questions between Germany and England ought
to be settled, and that they were in the right way of settlement." Bayard
assented to this view with the comment that he could "scarcely see how
sensible men of either party could have two opinions" on that subject.
In conclusion Bayard promised Arco-Valley to let him know on the
following day "whether the present President would be able before the
incoming Administration to name the men." [166]

After a consultation with President Cleveland, Bayard gave a negative answer to Arco-Valley, and on February 27 the President sent a
special message to the Senate in which he informed them of his decision
to refrain from appointing any delegates to the Berlin Conference. Such
appointments could best be made by the incoming administration.[167]

Bayard was distinctly disappointed at not being able to settle the
Samoan question during his administration as Secretary of State. In a
letter to Carl Schurz he makes a final comment on the handicaps he had
faced in this regard:

> Now that I have succeeded in attracting Prince Bismarck's attention to
> the real condition of Samoa, I find his views and disposition very much as I
> expected them to be—moderate and conciliatory. . . . *Entre nous,* I have
> been crippled a good deal by poor Pendleton's invalid condition, and but
> for that I believe the Berlin conference *in re* Samoa would have been now
> progressing, even probably the matter settled. As it is, Harrison (Blaine alas)
> must appoint the American Envoys, but I do not see how they can fail to
> follow the lines of the protocols as stated by me.[168]

In his letter of reply, Schurz congratulated Bayard upon his record
as Secretary of State and then remarked:

> You have been exposed to uncommon vituperation, but I am sure before

166. *Memorandum* written by Bayard after a conversation with Arco-Valley, February
25, 1889, *Bayard MS.*
167. President Cleveland to the United States Senate, February 27, 1889, *Report Book,*
vol. 17, MS Dept. of State. See also, Bayard to President Cleveland, February 27, 1889,
Bayard Letter Book, vol. 10, *Bayard MS.*
168. Bayard to Schurz, February 28, 1889, *Bayard Letter Book,* vol. 10, *Bayard MS.* In
a conversation with Arco-Valley, March 2, 1889, Bayard expressed himself in much the
same vein: "I said to him [Arco-Valley] confidentially that Mr. Pendleton's ill health was
the only reason why I had not asked him six weeks ago to take the matter up and settle
it. I told him that the reason for the President communicating everything to the Senate
was that there was no one to whom I could speak here; that with my supposed successor,
Mr. Blaine, I could not discuss matters." *Memorandum* written by Bayard after a conversation with Arco-Valley, March 2, 1889, *Bayard MS.*

a year is over, your vindication will be complete, and those who have found fault with you, will have to acknowledge it, at least in their hearts.[169]

Bayard's vindication in the Samoan question came long before the expiration of a year. When the Berlin Conference closed its sessions on June 14, 1889, it was obvious that all the main points that Bayard had stressed during the last two years of his administration were embodied in the terms of the final agreement. The fact that a bitter partisan like Secretary Blaine was willing to accept such a solution was a convincing illustration that Bayard's viewpoint had suddenly become the viewpoint of America.[170]

169. Schurz to Bayard, March 6, 1889, *ibid.*
170. With reference to the Samoan settlement, Bayard's intimate friend, Samuel L. M. Barlow, sent the following comments (March 2, 1889): "One of your bitterest and most malignant opponents in a letter received today says—'I have carefully examined the Samoan papers and I think the conference as developed in the protocols recently published does great credit to Mr. Bayard. His views are broad and sound, his tone temperate and dignified, and his argument both acute and able.'" *Bayard MS.*

The Chinese Question

CHAPTER FIVE

President Cleveland Makes a Bow to Expediency

THE DIPLOMATIC DIFFICULTIES THAT HAD ATTENDED BAYARD'S HANDLING of the Samoan question were also in evidence in the complicated matter of restricting Chinese immigration into the United States. Once again political factors helped to shape the policy pursued by the Administration. From the states that bordered the Pacific Ocean a stream of protests had poured into Congress with reference to the pernicious effects of a steadily increasing influx of Chinese laborers. The advocates of Chinese restriction formed an effective "pressure group" that eventually compelled a reluctant Congress to comply with its demands. The even balance of party strength in the state of the Far West made it necessary for both Republican and Democratic leaders to give a sympathetic hearing to complaints based upon racial considerations. The Solid South had its counterpart in the Solid Pacific States.

The question of Chinese immigration to the Pacific coast was introduced by the discovery of gold in California in 1848. In the provinces of Kwang Tung and Fuh Kien the Chinese laborers were crushed by the desolation that was caused by the Taiping Rebellion, and when they learned of the wealth that could be easily acquired in California, hurried preparations were made to leave their native land.[1] According to Sir Walter Medhurst, these immigrants to the United States were of an eminently "respectable type,"[2] and an outstanding authority like Professor Mary Coolidge has expressed the view that they were of

1. Ludvig V. Helms, *Pioneering in the Far East* (London, 1882), pp. 74-93; Ernest J. Eitel, *Europe in China* (London, 1895), pp. 253-275; S. Wells Williams, *Chinese Immigration* (Saratoga, 1879); William Speer, *The Oldest and the Newest Empire* (San Francisco, 1870), pp. 486-490.

2. "The Chinese as Colonists," *Nineteenth Century*, vol. 4, (1878), p. 519.

"much the same age and class as the German and Irish agricultural immigrants of the same period."[3]

At first they were highly valued as miners, laundrymen, carpenters, and cooks,[4] but as early as April 23, 1852, Governor John Bigler sent a special message to the California legislature in which he called attention to the dangers that threatened from any "wholesale importation" of immigrants from China.[5] As a result of this changing attitude towards Chinese immigration, a large volume of discriminatory legislation was passed, and the hapless Chinese were forced to bear the burden of an excessively heavy load of taxation.[6] But despite this severe treatment, the stream of immigrants from China showed no signs of dwindling. In 1867 it was estimated that in California alone there were some 50,000 Chinese, and a decade later this number had grown to 65,000. Did this increase portend the eventual dominance of the yellow race?[7]

It was inevitable that the influx of Chinese laborers into California would lead to serious racial friction, and when hard times descended upon the state it was only natural to expect that many voices would be raised in favor of a policy of exclusion. In the decade from 1860 to 1870, the construction of the Central Pacific Railroad gave employment to some ten thousand men, nine-tenths of whom were Chinese. When this railroad was completed in 1869, these workers were thrown upon a labor market that could not readily absorb them.[8] Moreover, the shift in transportation facilities from steamship to railroad helped to complicate the labor situation. As a consequence of this economic confusion there developed in California a rapidly rising tide of resentment against Chinese laborers of every description. The question of Chinese immigration soon became a political one.

In 1876 a resolution was adopted by the upper house of the California legislature providing for an investigation of the situation

3. *Chinese Immigration* (N. Y. 1909), p. 21. See also Chester Holcombe, *The Real Chinese Question* (N. Y. 1900), pp. 5ff; Tyler Dennett, *Americans in Eastern Asia* (N. Y. 1922), pp. 535ff.

4. Hubert H. Bancroft, *History of California* (7 vols., San Francisco, 1884–1890), vol. 7, pp. 335-369; James H. Carson, *Life in California* (Stockton, 1852. Reprinted in *The Magazine of History*, vol. 42, no. 4); E. S. Capron, *History of California* (Boston, 1854), p. 277; J. D. Borthwick, *Three Years in California* (London, 1857), pp. 330-331; William Shaw, *Golden Dreams and Waking Realities* (London, 1851), p. 42; Herbert O. Lang, *A History of Tuolumne County* (San Francisco, 1882), p. 5.

5. California, *Senate Journal, 1852*, pp. 373-378.

6. Lucile Eaves, *History of California Labor Legislation* (Berkeley, 1910), pp. 105-125.

7. Mary Coolidge, *Chinese Immigration*, pp. 498-499.

8. Theodore H. Hittell, *History of California* (San Francisco, 1885–1897), vol. 4, chap. v.

resulting from Chinese immigration. A committee was duly appointed and hearings were held. Without going into the partisan character of this investigation, suffice it to say that the report of the committee was bitterly anti-Chinese and reflected anything but an impartial spirit. The economic aspects of Chinese immigration were discussed, and the conclusion was reached that

. . . not less than 180,000,000 in gold have been abstracted from this state [California] alone by Chinese laborers, while they have contributed nothing to the State. . . . It is beyond question that from a purely financial point of view, the United States is loser nearly four hundred millions of dollars by Chinese immigration.

The moral degradation that attended Chinese immigration was far more serious than these economic losses:

Impregnable to all the influences of our Anglo-Saxon life, they remain the same stolid Asiatics that have floated on the rivers and slaved in the fields of China for thirty centuries of time. . . . Among one hundred and twenty-five thousand of them, . . . we have no evidence of a single genuine conversion to Christianity.[9]

The year 1876 was a critical one in the history of the Republican Party. The South was emerging from the disgraceful regime that had been imposed upon that conquered section by Northern "Vindictives." The shadow of a Solid South began to darken Republican prospects for continued control of national politics, and every effort was made to conciliate dissatisfied voters. It was expedient to court the favor of the working classes in California, and in 1876 Congress appointed a special joint committee to investigate the question of Chinese immigration.

The upshot of this situation was that the work of the Congressional committee fell chiefly upon the willing shoulders of two Californians, Senator Sargent and Representative Piper. One of the star witnesses called before the committee was Frank M. Pixley, another Californian. According to Pixley the Chinese were "the lowest of all created intelligence." There were "none so low," and they had had a dubious background of four thousand years of crime.[10]

Other witnesses like Captain Thomas H. King and Dr. Charles C. O'Donnell, told lurid stories of Chinese depravity, and they emphasized the alleged menace of the wholesale contamination of the white race in

9. *Chinese Immigration: Its Social, Moral and Political Effect. Report to the California State Senate of the Special Committee on Chinese Immigration* (Sacramento, 1878), pp. 6-7, 47-48.

10. *Sen. Rept. 689,* 44 Cong., 1 sess., pp. 371-372.

California through association with the dissolute Chinese immigrants. The fact that Captain King was an embezzler, and Dr. O'Donnell a criminal, was lightly regarded by the committee in weighing the evidence that was before them. In the majority report which was largely written by Senator Sargent, a sharp indictment was levelled against the Chinese in California, and strong support was given to a policy of exclusion.[11]

In 1877 hard times struck California and crushed business enterprise. Unemployment was widespread, and the laboring classes hoped to secure some relief through the organization of a Workingmen's Party which would look after their interests. In the fall of 1877 the leaders of this new party held a series of open-air meetings on the sand lots of San Francisco, and the twin evils of capitalists and Chinese were bitterly denounced. The most incendiary speaker at these meetings was one Denis Kearney, who had recently been naturalized. Kearney seemed to walk through life on the easy levels of instinct, and he was an expert in the anatomy of violence. In prosperous times his words would never have taken root, but now they fell on soil made darkly fertile by hunger and desperation.[12]

As a result of this growing pressure from the Workingmen's Party, the California legislature adopted the report of the committee appointed to investigate the question of Chinese immigration, and twenty thousand copies of it were printed and distributed. The effect of this agitation against the Chinese was evident in 1879 when a state constitutional convention agreed upon certain provisions which were patently discriminatory. There was little doubt that a majority of the voters in California were in favor of the slogan, "The Chinese Must Go," and their decison strongly influenced the course taken by Congress.[13]

In the Burlingame Treaty of 1868 it was distinctly stated that the "United States of America and the Emperor of China" cordially recognized the inherent and "inalienable right of man to change his home

11. *Ibid.*, pp. 92-126; 1095-1100, 1114-1121. For some illustrative comments upon this Congressional report, see the pamphlet of S. E. W. Becker, *Humors of a Congressional Committee* (Washington, 1877), pp. 1-36; John W. Foster, *American Diplomacy in the Orient* (N. Y. 1903), pp. 286-293. On the general subject of Chinese immigration, see James A. Whitney, *The Chinese and the Chinese Question* (N. Y. 1888); George F. Seward, *Chinese Immigration in its Social and Economical Aspects* (N. Y. 1881); Roderick D. McKenzie, *Oriental Exclusion* (Chicago, 1928); Tien-Lu Li, *Congressional Policy of Chinese Immigration* (Nashville, 1916).

12. Theodore H. Hittell, *History of California*, vol. 4, pp. 599-609; H. H. Bancroft, *History of California*, vol. 7, pp. 352-362.

13. T. H. Hittell, *History of California*, vol. 4, pp. 615-640.

and allegiance, and also the mutual advantage of the free migration and emigration of their citizens and subjects respectively from the one country to the other." [14] Under the broad provisions of this treaty, Chinese immigrants poured into the United States, and Secretary Seward welcomed their entry. As the two Chinese commissioners, Pao and Li, wrote to Secretary Evarts in 1880:

At the ratification of the treaty [of 1868] the people on both sides of the Pacific Ocean leaped, shouted and clapped their hands with joy and pleasure, friendly relations were firmly established, divisions were obliterated, the people could come and go as they chose, and the governments only heeded the wishes of the people.[15]

On May 15, 1876, Senator Sargent introduced a bill to restrict the immigration of Chinese into the United States,[16] and on December 10, 1877, he introduced a similar measure.[17] The movement in favor of exclusion was growing rapidly, and both political parties were anxious to win votes in California. On December 16, 1878, Eugene Casserly (formerly Senator from California), wrote to Senator Bayard with reference to the "Chinese plague" in California. He feared that, to the people of the East, it might seem "a local issue, yet it is one which at its present rate of growth will ere long threaten our entire social and political fabric from ocean to ocean. I have written to Sam Randall on the subject." [18]

A few days later, Senator Blaine expressed his views very forcefully. He was certain that the continued immigration of Chinese laborers into the United States would mean that the whole Pacific Coast would eventually fall under their control. A people "who eat beef and bread

14. William M. Malloy, *Treaties, Conventions, International Acts, Protocols, and Agreements between the United States and Other Powers, 1776–1909* (Wash., 1910), vol. 1, p. 235.

15. Pao and Li to Secretary Evarts, October 7, 1880, *Foreign Relations, 1881*, pp. 173-174.

16. *Congressional Record*, 44 Cong., 1 sess., vol. 16, p. 3084.

17. *Ibid.*, 45 Cong., 2 sess., vol. 27, p. 81. On November 29, 1877, Senator Sargent wrote to Secretary Evarts to complain that the laws of the United States, and the treaty of 1868, permitted "the influx of vast hordes of people who are alien to our civilization, and our religion; who do not become citizens of the United States, and have no wish to become such; and who bring strange and loathsome diseases among us, corrupt our youth, irritate the artisan classes by substituting for their labor an unambitious and underpaid article, overcrowd localities in our cities and increase in such numbers that it is a very serious problem whether in a quarter of a century at most, our Pacific States and Territories will not become Mongolian instead of remaining American." *Miscellaneous Letters*, MS Dept. of State.

18. Casserly to Bayard, December 16, 1878, *Bayard MS*.

and who drink beer cannot labor alongside of those who live on rice, and if the experiment is attempted on a large scale, the American laborer will have to drop his knife and fork and take up the chop-sticks." [19]

Bayard was thoroughly in favor of some measure of restriction upon the immigration of Chinese laborers into the United States, and he was glad to respond to pressure from his old friend Eugene Casserly who sent him the following telegram: "California intensely unanimous for Chinese house bill. Hear cry of whole people. Fail us not." [20]

In February, 1879, the Fifteen Passenger Bill, which provided that no ship could bring to American ports more than fifteen passengers at any one time, was debated in both houses of Congress. As early as February 20, President Hayes expressed his view of the situation. He was satisfied that "the present Chinese labor invasion . . . is pernicious and should be discouraged." He suspected, however, that the Fifteen Passenger Bill was "inconsistent with our treaty obligations," and if he found out that it violated "the National faith," he was determined to veto it.[21]

On February 21 George William Curtis wrote to Hayes to inform him that he had discovered in New York City

. . . so strong a protest against the Chinese bill as an act of bad faith, and so universal a hope of a veto, that I venture to add my most earnest wish that you may see the bill as I do, as a most flagrant breach of the national faith. If Asiatic immigration be undesirable, this is certainly not the way to apply the remedy: and that the Republican party should be the first to shut the gates of America on mankind is amazing.[22]

Before Hayes had received this letter he had already decided to veto the exclusion bill. On February 23 he made the following illustrative comment in his *Diary*:

19. San Francisco *Chronicle*, December 27, 1878.
20. Eugene Casserly to Bayard, February 14, 1879, *Bayard MS*. Philip A. Roach, of the San Francisco *Examiner*, was anxious for Bayard to write a message to the people of California which would "convince the masses that their relief will be secured only by electing a Democratic President and adhering to Democratic principles. Since the evils of Chinese competition have become known, the Radicals have been in power and have not heeded the many Joint Resolutions passed by the various Legislatures of this State, nor the monster petition of the working men presented in 1870." Roach to Bayard, January 18, 1879, *Bayard MS*.
21. *Diary* of President Hayes, February 20, 1879, *Diary and Letters of Rutherford Birchard Hayes* (Columbus, 1924, ed. by C. R. Williams), vol. 3, p. 522.
22. G. W. Curtis to President Hayes, February 21, 1879, *Rutherford B. Hayes Papers*, Hayes Memorial Library, Fremont, Ohio. During the course of an interview with Secretary Evarts, the Chinese Commissioners denounced the Fifteen Passenger Bill as "insulting." *Chinese Legation, Notes from*, February 18, 1879, vol. 1, MS Dept. of State.

In the maintenance of the national faith, it is in my judgment a plain duty to withhold my approval from this bill. . . . We stand for the sacred observance of treaties. . . . No precedent for such action except in cases which justify war.[23]

He was strengthened in this viewpoint by numerous letters that poured into the White House. The following communication from Henry Ward Beecher is typical:

Should you veto the Chinese Exclusion Bill, you will act in consonance with the profoundest moral and religious convictions of the Nation. Even in California this is true. The Ministers of the Gospel, teachers, and conservative men of property who have a stake in the moral welfare of the community, are not in sympathy with the political rage on this subject. In the North and West, where I am largely acquainted, I hardly know an exception to the feeling of deep moral displeasure at the demands of California politicians. Besides the wrong to the Chinese, the dishonor to our Nation, the great damage to our Commerce, there is a consideration yet more threatening, in my judgment.

You are aware of the progress of Socialism among our laboring population, especially our foreign people. You have seen already the threatening complications arising out of Labor questions. This California craze is another carbuncle. If by combination and by political leverage, the ignorant population can drive competition from their midst, it will give courage all over the land, to men who hold theories of the rights of labor which are destructive of the rights of property, of the freedom of industry, and of the predominance of virtue and intelligence in managing the affairs of the State.[24]

On February 27 the Chamber of Commerce of the State of New York adopted resolutions which declared that it was the "paramount duty of the Government sacredly to fulfil its treaty stipulations with every foreign power." The Chamber deprecated the passage of the Fifteen Passenger Bill as

. . . establishing a bad precedent; as an unworthy political concession to the lawless spirit of a single State, under whose laws the subjects of China have enjoyed neither peace nor safety; as tending to degrade the national character in the sight of all other nations; . . . and, finally, as presenting the hasty action of our Congressional Body in sorry contrast with the more cautious and dignified wisdom of the Heathen Empire.[25]

As a balance to these entreaties to the President to veto the Fifteen

---

23. *Diary* of President Hayes, February 23, 1879, *Diary and Letters of Rutherford Birchard Hayes*, vol. 3, p. 524.
24. Henry Ward Beecher to President Hayes, February 26, 1879, *Hayes MS.*
25. "Resolution of the Chamber of Commerce of the State of New York Relative to Chinese Immigration, February 27, 1879." *Hayes MS.*

Passenger Bill, there were many other communications that vigorously urged the President to sign it. A very significant one in this regard was a memorial from the Legislature of Nevada. This document was a sharp attack upon the Chinese:

> The Legislature of the State of Nevada would respectfully represent that the presence of the Chinese on this coast is an unmitigated evil, that they have no respect or regard for our government; . . . that they are incapable of assimilation with our people either in sentiment, habits of life, or religion; . . . that they are rapidly absorbing all branches of mechanical and manual labor; . . . that they are usually brought in hordes in a condition of semi-slavery; . . . that the privilege accorded to the contracting parties to the treaty aforesaid was upon condition that the immigration to either country by the citizens or subjects of the other should be a voluntary individual act; that China has wholly failed to have that consideration observed.[26]

President Hayes was little influenced by these letters and memorials. He had already made up his mind to veto the bill, and on March 1, 1879, he sent his veto message to the House of Representatives. There was no doubt that the Fifteen Passenger Bill was inconsistent with the provisions of the treaty of 1868, and Hayes was determined that this treaty should not be regarded as a mere scrap of paper. As a concession to the feelings of the exclusionists, he stated that the question of restriction deserved the "most serious attention of the people of the whole country, and a solicitous interest on the part of Congress and the Executive." [27]

This veto message was written by William M. Evarts, the Secretary of State, who was deeply interested in this matter of Chinese exclusion.[28] On March 25, 1879, he submitted to President Hayes a long memorandum that had been received from George F. Seward, the American Minister to China. Seward was thoroughly familiar with

26. *Memorial* from the Legislature of the State of Nevada to President Hayes, February 28, 1879, *Hayes MS.*

27. Veto message of March 1, 1879. J. D. Richardson, *Messages and Papers of the Presidents*, vol. 7, pp. 514-520. In commenting upon the question of Chinese immigration, Professor Richmond Mayo-Smith remarked: "This treaty of 1868 marks the dividing line between two distinct and contradictory policies on the part of the United States toward the Chinese. Up to that time our efforts had been directed toward compelling the Chinese to admit Americans to China for the pursuit of trade and commerce. In this contention we placed ourselves on the broad platform of the right of free migration and the duty of international intercourse. Shortly after this declaration, . . . we turned our backs on the principle of freedom of migration, and passed laws excluding the Chinese as effectually as they had ever excluded foreigners." *Emigration and Immigration* (N. Y., 1895), p. 229.

28. Charles R. Williams, *Life of R. B. Hayes*, vol. 2, pp. 213-217. See also the admirable monograph by Brainerd Dyer, *The Public Career of William M. Evarts* (Berkeley, 1933), pp. 220ff.

every aspect of the immigration problem, and both Hayes and Evarts gave careful consideration to his memorandum. It was apparent, said Seward, that as

. . . the law now stands, no Chinese can land in this country who has not proven before the Consul of the United States at the port of departure, that he is a voluntary emigrant. But this law is a dead letter. Nearly all immigrants come from Hongkong, and the Consul at that port is not provided with a sufficient staff of officers to enable him to make the required examinations. . . . In my opinion these examinations should be made by the Chinese authorities and our own officers acting conjointly. . . .

I take it for granted that there is no person in the land who would be willing to consent to a large immigration of Chinese. This is very decidedly my own sentiment, but I have no fear that we are to witness such a result. . . .

In my view of the matter, no limitations of immigration are necessary beyond those required to provide against importations of laborers and of persons of the pauper and criminal classes. In order to provide for all contingencies, we might go however to the extent of giving notice that we shall propose hereafter, in case of need, a revision of our treaties. . . . I have no hesitation in saying that the Chinese would name a date for this revision of our relations if we should so request.[29]

In accordance with this suggestion, Secretary Evarts instructed Seward to discuss with the Chinese Foreign Office, the question of further restrictions upon Chinese immigration into the United States.[30] After receiving this instruction, Seward canvassed the situation thoroughly but did not come to any definite agreement because he lacked the requisite authority from the Department of State.[31] Secretary Evarts had in mind to appoint a commission that would visit China and arrange for some amendments to the treaty of 1868. On February 18, 1880, he had Senator H. P. Baldwin, of Michigan, write to Dr. James B. Angell and suggest that he make a visit to Washington to talk with the officials of the Department of State about a "matter of much public interest."[32]

Angell, who was President of the University of Michigan, paid the desired visit to Washington and discussed the matter of Chinese immigration with Evarts. Upon his return to Ann Arbor, he wrote to the

29. *Hayes MS.*

30. Secretary Evarts to Seward, April 23, 1879, *China, Instructions,* vol. 3, MS Dept. of State.

31. Seward to Secretary Evarts, June 7, July 21, August 1, and September 9, 1879, *China, Despatches,* vol. 50, MS Dept. of State.

32. H. P. Baldwin to James B. Angell, February 18, 1880, *Angell Papers, Michigan Historical Collections,* University of Michigan.

Secretary of State and outlined his attitude. It appeared to him that one of the ways of settling this important question was to request the Chinese Government to consent to the abrogation of the fifth article of the Burlingame Treaty which permitted Chinese immigration to the United States. But any absolute prohibition of the immigration of Chinese laborers would be

. . . diametrically opposed to all our national traditions and would call down the censure of a very large portion if not a majority of our most intelligent and high-minded citizens. I must confess that personally I am not ready to favor it, until it is *demonstrated* . . . that the necessity for such a step is overwhelming. . . . We might ask that no men without families be permitted to come. It would seem that such a limitation could prevent many evils. . . . A better plan . . . would be to ask the Chinese Government to agree that no Emigrants should come on the present contract system. . . . This regulation . . . would, we may hope, well nigh stop the Emigration. . . .

One of the chief difficulties is found in the fact that almost without exception, the emigrants sail not from a Chinese port, but from the British port of Hongkong. Therefore, the Chinese Government really has nothing to say about the conditions of their emigration.[33]

On March 15 Secretary Evarts wrote to assure Dr. Angell that the "general tone" of his views on the question of Chinese immigration was "quite compatible" with that of the President. Angell was offered an appointment on a proposed mission to China to settle existing difficulties.[34] After he had accepted this appointment,[35] President Hayes added two other members to the commission, John T. Swift, and William H. Trescot. Swift was a Californian who was devoted to the interests of his state, and Trescot was a South Carolinian who had seen previous service as a diplomat.[36]

33. Angell to Secretary Evarts, March 11, 1880, *Angell MS.*
34. Secretary Evarts to James B. Angell, March 15, 1880, *Angell MS.*
35. Angell to Secretary Evarts, March 17, 1880, *ibid.*
36. James B. Angell, in discussing the appointment of the commission, made the following observation: "The Fifteen Passenger Act was clearly in contravention of the Burlingame Treaty, and the veto of President Hayes prevented it from becoming law. The situation was critical. There was, perhaps, danger that some other law in violation of our treaties might be pushed through over a veto. In that case, retaliation on our merchants and missionaries in China might have followed." "Diplomatic Relations Between the United States and China," *Journal of Social Science,* vol. 17, p. 27.

The political motives behind the appointment of this commission are indicated by Chester Holcombe, who served as secretary and interpreter to the commissioners: "The Republican leaders planned a master stroke of policy. A bill was prepared and submitted to Congress directing the appointment of certain Special Commissioners who were to proceed to Peking and there to negotiate such a modification of our treaties with China as would permit of legislation restrictive of the influx of Chinese laborers. While the Democrats grumbled somewhat at the march thus stolen upon them, none ventured to

Before leaving on their mission, Angell and Trescot had several interviews with Secretary Evarts, but no specific instructions were given them.[37] In his formal instruction to the commissioners, Evarts did not include any articles that were absolutely to be insisted upon: they were to have considerable latitude in their efforts to adjust existing difficulties.[38]

When the commissioners reached China they found that the Chinese Foreign Office was willing to consider some limitations with reference to the immigration of Chinese laborers into the United States, but it was strongly opposed to any absolute prohibition of such immigration.[39] After Trescot and Swift had almost given up hope of arriving at any satisfactory understanding, the Foreign Office finally agreed to make some concessions and the treaty of November 17, 1880, was signed. Under its terms the American Government had the right to "regulate, limit, or suspend" the entry of Chinese laborers into the United States, but it could not "absolutely prohibit" such entry. Moreover, it was specifically provided that this "limitation or suspension" should be "reasonable," and should apply only to Chinese who "may go to the United States as laborers, other classes not being included in the limitation." Laborers already in the United States, and all teachers, merchants, and household servants were to be given "all the rights, privileges, immunities and exemptions which are accorded to the citizens and subjects of the most favored nation." In the event that Chinese laborers, or "Chinese of any other class," should meet with "ill treatment" in the United States, the Federal Government would exert "all its power" to devise measures for their protection.[40]

It is apparent that the Chinese commissioners thought they had made an important concession in granting to the American Government the right to *regulate* but not to *prohibit* the entry of Chinese laborers. They had further agreed that the term "laborers" should

oppose the bill, and it was promptly passed." See "The Restriction of Chinese Immigration," *The Outlook*, April 24, 1904, vol. 76, pp. 973-974. For some interesting comments upon the background of the treaty of 1880, see letter of Chester Holcombe to John Russell Young, April 14, 1880, *John Russell Young Papers*, Library of Congress.

37. J. B. Angell, *Reminiscences*, pp. 128ff.

38. Secretary Evarts to Angell, Trescot, and Swift, June 7, 1880, *China, Instructions*, vol. 3, MS Dept. of State.

39. The Commissioners to Secretary Evarts, October 26, 1880, *China, Despatches*, vol. 55, MS Dept. of State.

40. William M. Malloy, *Treaties, Conventions, etc.*, vol. 1, pp. 237-239. For the diplomatic correspondence leading up to this treaty of November 17, 1880, see *China, Despatches*, vols. 55-56, MS Dept. of State.

include both artisans and unskilled laborers. In making these concessions they had understood that the restrictions imposed by the American Government would apply only to these "laborers" and to no other
class.

In later years the Attorney General of the United States rendered an
opinion in which it was stated that the term "laborer" included Chinese other than mere skilled and unskilled workers.[41] Such action was
typical of the confusion that prevailed with regard to the many questions pertaining to Chinese immigration. In the treaty of 1880, the
word "reasonable" had been employed in connection with the period
during which the American Government could restrict the immigration
of Chinese laborers. Mr. Angell inclined towards the view that a period
of *five* years would be a *reasonable* one for Congress to fix by way of
experimentation,[42] but John T. Swift was certain that a period of
restriction as long as *forty* years would be "entirely reasonable."[43]

Congress compromised by passing an act which restricted Chinese
immigration for a period of twenty years. There was no doubt that
Congress had authority to enact such legislation. The only question
that arose was whether this period of twenty years was a "reasonable"
one in view of the language of the treaty of 1880. President Arthur did
not think so, and he vetoed the bill because he believed that it violated
"the faith of the nation as pledged to China."[44] His veto message was
sharply resented by Senator Bayard.

Bayard was a realist who had long recognized the need for some
restriction of Chinese immigration. It was evident to him that an uninterrupted flow of Chinese laborers into the Pacific coast states would
seriously menace White control of that section of the Union. He also
knew that the Burlingame Treaty was the handiwork of a visionary who
allowed his enthusiasm for Chinese culture to run away with his political judgment. It seemed to Bayard that the Burlingame mission to the
Western Powers was much like a "circus," and the treaty that Mr.
Burlingame negotiated with the United States was nothing more than a

41. *Opinions of the Attorney General,* vol. 22, p. 132.
42. James B. Angell, "Diplomatic Relations Between the United States and China,"
Journal of Social Science, (1882) vol. 17, p. 35. For some interesting comments upon the
negotiations leading up to the treaty of 1880, see the *Reminiscences of James B. Angell*
(N. Y. 1912), chap. vi.
43. Mary Coolidge, *Chinese Immigration,* p. 164.
44. Veto message of April 4, 1882. J. D. Richardson, *Messages and Papers of the
Presidents,* vol. 8, pp. 112-118.

"humbug." [45] He believed that a suspension of Chinese immigration for a period of twenty years was not an *unreasonable* restriction, and he strongly denied that this action on the part of Congress had "violated the national faith." The veto message itself was objectionable to many persons not only because of its "coarse language," but also because it really encouraged an immigration which might in time "destroy the labor of our own people." [46]

It was not possible for the opposition in Congress to override the President's veto, so another bill was hurriedly passed. Under its terms all Chinese laborers, "skilled and unskilled and those engaged in mining," were excluded for a period of *ten* years. In order to guard against the admission of any Chinese laborers, a requirement was inserted in the bill whereby Chinese citizens other than laborers were required to bring a certificate defining their status.[47]

The passage of this first exclusion bill seemed merely to open a Pandora's box of further troubles with reference to Chinese immigration. In Congress the representatives from the Pacific coast were clamorous for new legislation that would build even higher the wall of exclusion, and in response to this pressure, Congress passed the law of July 5, 1884. The certificates of the exempt classes were made more precise. The word "merchant" could no longer include hucksters, peddlers, or fishermen. The traveler's certificate was made more detailed, and all certificates would have to be verified by an American diplomatic or consular officer in China.[48]

It was not long before certain defects in the act of July 5, 1884, were made manifest. In accordance with its terms certificates of admission to the United States could be issued to Chinese subjects (other than laborers) who were "departing from a port of China," or to "Chinese

---

45. With reference to the Burlingame Mission, Tyler Dennett in his monograph, *Americans in Eastern Asia*, pp. 379-380, 384-385, remarks: "The Burlingame Mission . . . met in the United States with the heartiest of receptions. The picturesque appearance of the retinue and the moving eloquence of Burlingame, who managed the tour according to the best traditions of the showman's art, captured the imagination of the American people. . . . Mr. Burlingame was an orator, skilled in all the arts of a style of oratory which has now largely passed away. His orations abounded not in logic . . . but in illustrations and flights of eloquence designed not so much to induce a conclusion as to produce an impression. . . . The assertion . . . that China invited the foreign merchants and the foreign missionaries . . . was a travesty of the truth."

46. *Congressional Record*, April 5, 1882, 47 Cong., 1 sess., vol. 13, pt. 3, pp. 2607-2617.

47. Act of May 6, 1882, *U. S. Statutes at Large*, vol. 22, pp. 58-61.

48. *U. S. Statutes at Large*, vol. 23, pp. 115-118. See also, Charles Denby, *China and Her People* (2 vols., Boston, 1906), vol. 2, chap. ix; and John W. Foster, *American Diplomacy in the Orient* (N. Y. 1903), chap. viii.

persons who may at the time be subjects of some foreign Government
other than China, and who may depart for the United States from the
ports of such other foreign Government." Unfortunately, the act made
no provision for Chinese who, "retaining their Chinese subjection in
some countries other than China, desire to come from such countries
to the United States." [49]

This defect in the immigration legislation was disclosed when certain Chinese merchants at Hong Kong, a British colony, desired to
come to the United States. Under the act of July 5 these merchants
would have to secure a certificate issued by an official of the Chinese
Government. Inasmuch as there were no Chinese officials at Hong
Kong, the Treasury Department issued a circular (January 14, 1885)
whereby certificates could be issued to Chinese subjects of the exempt
classes by "the United States consular officer at the port of departure
in the absence of a Chinese diplomatic or consular representative
thereat." Such action was clearly in conflict with the language of the
act of July 5, 1884, and shortly after the Cleveland Administration
assumed office this Treasury Department circular was repealed.[50] This
repeal was forced by the refusal of the American consul at Hong Kong
to carry out the provisions of the circular. The situation is described in
the following note from Alvey A. Adee to Bayard:

> The point in the Chinese correspondence about Hong Kong certificates,
> is perhaps one of policy rather than abstract justice. The Treaty doubtless
> means that non-laboring Chinese, coming from *anywhere,* may enter the
> United States on certification of the fact. The law, passed to execute the
> treaty, seems to refer only to Chinese coming from *China.* The Treasury
> Department's 2nd rule aims to fill the hiatus by giving to consuls of the
> U. S. in other countries the power to issue a sufficient certificate in the
> absence of a Chinese consul there. Now, Mr. Mosby, making a bid for hood-
> lum popularity in San Francisco, where he is about to take up permanent
> residence, made an elaborate argument that the Secretary of the Treasury

49. *Sen. Ex. Doc., 118,* 49 Cong., 1 sess., pp. 1-2.
50. The Chinese question in California was at times mixed up with political factors.
In a letter to Samuel J. Tilden, June 9, 1885, Frank McCoppin, of California, remarks:
"The Chinese question has again disturbed the people, or some of them, upon this Coast.
. . . At one time the President intended to appoint a Californian Minister to China (he
offered it to Mr. S. M. Wilson of this City [San Francisco]), but changed his mind later,
hence the present disturbance." *Samuel J. Tilden Papers,* New York Public Library. See
also a letter from Denis Kearney to Bayard, May 23, 1885, in which Kearney makes the
following statement: "We are very anxious to have one of our people selected as Minister
to China, and look to you to do the square thing for us." *Bayard MS.* At this time
Kearney was running an "Employment and General Business Agency," on Ellis Street in
the city of San Francisco.

has no power under the act, to prescribe a certificate of a Consul in lieu of one issued by the Chinese Government, and that he, Mosby, could not be compelled to issue such a certificate because in doing so he would travel out of his jurisdiction both as to *knowledge* and *fact*. If we contest Mosby's position, we do the just thing, but we run the risk of a little political, or partisan, outburst in California, under Mosby's guerilla leadership.

Other Consuls have given the certificates in accordance with the Treasury Department's circular. . . . Mosby is, so far as I know, the only one who has kicked. If Mosby is right, no Chinaman can come to the U. S. under certificates except from China, or possibly from a port where there is a Chinese Consul.[51]

In this case Mosby was right and the Department of State had to accept the repeal of the Treasury Department circular of January 14, 1885. Such action led to spirited protests from the Chinese Minister, Cheng Tsao Ju.[52] Bayard could only reply that the circular in question "involved the absurdity of a consul certifying, by his *visa*, to the truth and sufficiency of his own certificate; and under it the consul purported to give official evidence of a matter not within his representative competency to certify." The act of July 5, 1884, was so "obscure and defective" that the President would recommend to Congress, "at an early day," legislation "more in harmony with the provisions of the treaty."[53]

In accordance with this promise, the President sent to Congress a special message (April 6, 1886) in which he called attention to the difficulties that stood in the way of Chinese merchants at Hong Kong who desired to visit the United States. Inasmuch as there was not at Hong Kong any "representative of the Government of China competent or authorized to issue the certificate required by the statute," President Cleveland urged that new legislation be enacted so that American consular officials could issue these required documents.[54]

While Congress was considering this question of remedial legislation, the President was spending many anxious hours in an endeavor to settle another problem arising out of Chinese immigration. On September 11, 1885, Cheng Tsao Ju, the Chinese Minister at Washington, wrote to Bayard to complain of an attack upon Chinese residents of

51. A. A. Adee to Bayard, August 11, 1885, *Bayard MS.*
52. Cheng Tsao Ju to Bayard, March 9, 24, 1886, *Chinese Legation, Notes from*, vol. 2, MS Dept. of State.
53. Bayard to Cheng Tsao Ju, March 30, 1886, *Chinese Legation, Notes to*, vol. 1, MS Dept. of State.
54. James D. Richardson, *Messages and Papers of the Presidents*, vol. 8, pp. 390-393.

Rock Springs, Wyoming Territory. This attack had been made by a "mob of American citizens," and not only had many Chinese been killed or wounded, but a large amount of property had been destroyed.[55]

Bayard replied at once and expressed his deep regret at such an occurrence. He also informed the Chinese Minister that two officers of the United States Army had been detailed to accompany and give assistance to the Chinese consuls who were being sent to Rock Springs to investigate the mob attack.[56] While the investigation of the Rock Springs incident was being carried on, another massacre of Chinese citizens occurred. This took place at Seattle, in Washington Territory, on the night of October 7.[57]

Bayard immediately assured the Chinese Minister that every effort would be made to prevent similar occurrences.[58] Hardly had this assurance been given when news was received of an attack upon Chinese laborers at Tacoma, Washington Territory.[59] Bayard returned to the unwelcome task of endeavoring to relieve the apprehensions of the Chinese Minister. The President had issued a proclamation admonishing all citizens of Washington Territory against "aiding, abetting, countenancing, or taking part" in unlawful acts or assemblages, and the Secretary of War had instructed the commandant of the United States troops at Fort Vancouver to "preserve order." [60]

On November 30, 1885, the Chinese Minister sent to Bayard a lengthy note in which he carefully reviewed the background of the attacks made upon Chinese citizens resident in the United States. He referred to the statement of Secretary Evarts which indicated that the Federal Government could not interfere with the administration of the municipal laws of a state of the Union except where the Constitution of the United States expressly so provided.[61] Inasmuch as the Rock

55. Cheng Tsao Ju to Bayard, September 11, 1885, *Chinese Legation, Notes from,* vol. 1, MS Dept. of State.

56. Bayard to Cheng Tsao Ju, September 11, 1885, *Chinese Legation, Notes to,* vol. 1, MS Dept. of State.

57. Cheng Tsao Ju to Bayard, October 17, 1885, *Chinese Legation, Notes from,* vol. 1, MS Dept. of State.

58. Bayard to Cheng Tsao Ju, October 21, 28, and November 2, 1885, *Chinese Legation, Notes to,* vol. 1, MS Dept. of State.

59. Cheng Tsao Ju to Bayard, November 5, 1885, *Chinese Legation, Notes from,* vol. 1, MS Dept. of State.

60. Bayard to Cheng Tsao Ju, November 7, 1885, *Chinese Legation, Notes to,* vol. 1, MS Dept. of State.

61. It was very difficult for the Chinese officials to understand the exact manner in which the American federal government worked. In a personal letter to Bayard, Charles Denby, the American Minister at Peking, recounted a recent conversation with Li Hung

Springs incident occurred within a Federal territory, this principle could not be invoked. Moreover, the Chinese provincial and local authorities had upon several occasions indemnified Americans citizens for losses incurred through riots, and in 1858 a convention had been agreed upon whereby the Chinese Government paid to the United States the sum of $735,258.97 in "full liquidation of all claims of American citizens." In view of this practice, the Chinese Government was certain that the United States would not violate the spirit of the "Golden Rule" by failing to act in a reciprocal manner.[62]

Before Bayard could make an official reply to this note from the Chinese Minister, President Cleveland, in his message to Congress (December 8, 1885), made the following reference to the attacks upon Chinese residents in the Far West:

> The condition of the Chinese question in the Western States and Territories is . . . far from satisfactory. The recent outbreak in Wyoming Territory, . . . and the still more recent threatened outbreak of the same character in Washington Territory, are fresh in the minds of all. . . . All the power of this Government should be exerted to maintain the amplest good faith toward China in the treatment of these men, and the inflexible sternness of the law in bringing the wrongdoers to justice should be insisted upon.[63]

These references to the Chinese question had been drafted by Bayard who was exceedingly anxious to extend all possible protection to the Chinese who were resident in the United States. His attitude in this matter is revealed in a personal letter that he wrote to Denby at Peking:

> After your predecessor, Mr. Young, returned, he was quite ill and I did not see him until . . . lately. He is evidently an intelligent man of the quick and shallow *news writing* school. I was enabled to learn very little from him of China and the real sentiment of the Rulers of the country for us. . . . The condition of business [in America] is very depressed, and much

Chang. Li wanted to know why "the President could not control all questions arising touching the Chinese in America. It required some effort to explain to him our dual form of Government, the powers of the States, and their independence, in local matters, of the Federal Government. You will find during your Administration that the question of the treatment of the Chinese will continually come up. If a foreigner is injured or insulted in China, there is an immediate demand for redress. The Chinese do not understand why our Government does not occupy the same relation to Chinese in America, as the Chinese Government does to Americans here." Denby to Bayard, October 10, 1885, *Bayard MS.*

62. Cheng Tsao Ju to Bayard, November 30, 1885, *Chinese Legation, Notes from,* vol. 1, MS Dept. of State. The enclosures accompanying this note give a full history of the Rock Springs incident.

63. James D. Richardson, *Messages and Papers of the Presidents,* vol. 8, p. 329.

discontent and suffering exists among the laboring classes. All this leads to competition for scant work, and the feeling against "Chinese cheap labor" is strong. I expect more stringent measures to exclude Chinese laborers will be adopted by Congress, but the administration will do everything possible to throw the protection of the law around those who are now here. We expect a new Minister in March, and shall seek kindly intercourse with him.[64]

Before the new Minister arrived,[65] Cheng Tsao Ju wrote to Bayard once more to complain of the "lawless and violent measures" that were being taken against the Chinese in the Far West. He had recently received information which indicated that the situation had grown "deplorable in the extreme." Many telegrams had been sent to him which stated that the Chinese had been driven "by violence out of many places, their dwellings burned, their property robbed, and, in some instances, the people murdered." In order to meet this situation some further action should be taken at once by the Federal Goverment.[66]

On February 18 Bayard sent a long and carefully reasoned reply to these complaints. He assured the Chinese Minister that all "honest and true American citizens" were shocked at the news of the "bloody outrages" that had been inflicted upon the Chinese in Wyoming and Washington Territories. There was nothing to "extenuate such offenses against humanity and law, and not the least of the outrages upon the good name of the law was the wretched travesty of the forms of justice by a certain local officer acting as coroner, and pretending to give a legal account of the manner in which the victims met their death." Bayard's own sense of humanity was aroused to "strong feelings of indignation" at these outrages, and he felt "deep mortification that such a blot should have been cast upon the record of our government of laws." It should be noted, however, that during these outbreaks no representatives of the Government of China or of the United States were involved. There was, therefore, no "official insult or wrong." Whatever occurred was between private individuals wholly devoid of official character.

64. Bayard to Charles Denby, December 26, 1885, *Personal, Bayard Letter Book*, vol. 2, *Bayard MS.*
65. Cheng Tsao Ju was recalled by the Chinese Government in April, 1886. See *Bayard Letter Book*, vol. 2, *Bayard MS.*
66. Cheng Tsao Ju to Bayard, February 15, 1886, *Chinese Legation, Notes from*, vol. 2, MS Dept. of State.

In the states of the Federal Union,

. . . and also in the organized Territories and in the District of Columbia, . . . the conservation of the public peace is committed to the local authorities; and crimes of violence involving the lives and safety or the property of individuals are held to be in violation of the peace, and in derogation of the local laws and jurisdiction. . . . In this respect, the local authority and responsibility is in practice as self-contained in a Territory as in a State. . . .

By argument and analogy you seek to show that a singular and exceptional obligation rests upon the United States toward Chinamen. . . . What are the duties of the Government of the United States under that treaty [of 1880] towards Chinese subjects within their jurisdiction? The Chinese subjects now in the United States are certainly accorded all the rights, privileges, immunities, and exemptions which pertain to the citizens, save in one respect, wherein the Chinese alien is the more favored, since he has the right of option in selecting either a State or a Federal tribunal for the trial of his rights. . . . I think you will thus recognize . . . that none of the protection intended by the law for our own citizens is withheld from your countrymen. . . .

The Government of the United States recognizes in the fullest sense the honorable obligation of its treaty stipulations, . . . but among such obligations are not the reparation of injuries or the satisfaction by indemnity of wrongs inflicted by individuals upon other individuals in violation of the law of the land. Such remedies must be pursued in the proper quarter and through the avenues of justice marked out for the reparation of such wrongs.

The doctrine of the non-liability of the United States for the acts of individuals committed in violation of its laws, is clear as to acts of its own citizens. . . . I am compelled to state most distinctly that I should fail in my duty . . . did I not deny emphatically all liability to indemnify individuals . . . for loss growing out of violations of our public law. . . . Yet, I am frank to say that the circumstances of the case . . . may induce the President to recommend to the Congress, not as under obligation of treaty or principle of international law, but solely from a sentiment of generosity and pity . . . [for] an innocent and unfortunate body of men . . . who . . . were so shockingly outraged, . . . to grant pecuniary relief to the sufferers.[67]

On March 1, 1886, President Cleveland sent to Congress a special message dealing with the Rock Springs incident.[68] Following the line

67. Bayard to Cheng Tsao Ju, February 18, 1886, *Chinese Legation, Notes to,* vol. 1, MS Dept. of State.

68. With reference to this message, Bayard sent to President Cleveland, February 27, 1886, a brief note: "I merely wish to keep you informed and to remark that I think your message proposing benevolent action towards the Chinese, who were so injured in Wyoming Territory, will be very opportune, and may prove a measure of protection to our citizens in China.

"I have just sent copies to the Secretary of the Navy, and suggested the sending of

suggested by Secretary Bayard,[69] he "most emphatically" denied that the United States was under any obligation to indemnify the Chinese citizens for the losses they had sustained as a result of mob outrages. He did, however, submit to the "benevolent consideration" of Congress, the question of giving some assistance to the "innocent and peaceful strangers whose maltreatment has brought discredit upon the country." [70]

While Congress was engaged in this "benevolent consideration," California was seething with anti-Chinese sentiment. A state convention adopted on March 11, 1886, a *Memorial* to Congress which referred to the dangers that threatened America from "the Mongolian hive with its 450 millions of hungry and adventurous inhabitants." With reference to the Chinese laborers resident in California, the *Memorial* stated: "He underbids all white labor and ruthlessly takes its place, and will go on doing so until the white laborer comes down to the scanty food and half-civilized habits of the Chinaman." [71]

In accordance with this viewpoint, Bayard received from W. L. Willis, of Sacramento, California, a long letter in which the question of Chinese immigration was fully discussed. After expressing his high admiration for Bayard, Willis then refers to the situation in the Far West with regard to the Chinese. He was sorry to see that

. . . nearly all the eastern papers misrepresent the attitude and opinions of the best and most conservative men on this coast. I do not speak of the few large capitalists who are opposed to everything that touches their

---

such men-of-war of the East India Squadron as could be so used, to Canton and adjacent ports to give protection and asylum to our citizens assailed by mob violence. The dishonest mission of Burlingame and his treaty are bearing their evil fruits. I shall feel much relieved when I learn that news of your kindly message to Congress shall have been received in China in time to prevent violence." *Cleveland MS.*

69. On February 8, 1886 Bayard sent to President Cleveland the following note: "At one o'clock I am to see the Chinese Minister—no doubt in relation to mob-law in Seattle, Washington Territory, where a systematized action to expel Chinamen is going on. I will come over to see you about this, this P.M. There is a want of statutory power in the Executive to deal with such outbreaks in the territories; at least his power to use the armed forces of the United States in such cases is not clear and satisfactory. I am disposed to think a message will have to go to Congress to provide for the case." *Cleveland Papers.*

70. J. D. Richardson, *Messages and Papers of the Presidents*, vol. 8, pp. 383-386. Bayard sent to Horace White, of the New York *Evening Post*, a copy of the President's message of March 1. On March 13, White sent the following reply: "I thank you for sending me a copy of the President's Message relative to the Chinese Treaty Stipulation. I shall take it home and read it tomorrow, and shall *endeavor* to agree with you, for I always find that a comfort. It is hard to keep civilization going. Sometimes I think that Bismarck's way is the best." *Bayard MS.*

71. *Sen. Misc. Doc.*, *107*, 49 Cong., 1 sess., p. 2.

pockets, . . . but of the business men, the farmers, and those who make up the body of the people. As you well know, California and Oregon are among the doubtful states, and at our last election went Republican. The stand taken by the leaders of the Democratic party at this time can bring them back and make them Democratic states. . . . The Democratic party in California have been for twenty years striving to check Chinese immigration. Could you see with your own eyes, and hear with your own ears, the actual state of affairs in this state, you would scarcely wonder that men of all political creeds . . . have combined to raise a cry for assistance from the government before they are overwhelmed. . . . It has come to be a question of existence with the people of this coast, and they feel that either the Chinese must go, or the white must give way to them, and give up this fair land.[72]

In China there was bitter resentment against the outrages that had been visited upon Chinese resident in the United States, and the American Minister at Peking anxiously strove to prevent any attacks upon American citizens.[73] In a personal letter to Bayard, Denby comments upon the situation in China, and emphasizes the friendly receptions he had received during a tour of many Chinese cities:

I have visited Hong Kong, Canton, Swatow, Amoy, and Foo Chow. I have been everywhere received with the most distinguished consideration. . . . The Viceroys . . . have entertained me in the most lavish manner and with salutes, music, and the enormous dinners of which you have heard. . . . My progress through China has been the signal of festivity in which all foreigners participate. I have found everywhere the most friendly feeling towards the United States. . . . I accomplished a notable feat in the excitable and turbulent city of Canton. I found that the Viceroy who rules the two extreme Southern provinces had never received a foreigner. . . . I set myself to work to have him receive me and return my call. . . . I therefore addressed him a courteous note indicating a day on which I would call on him. . . . He received me and my suite . . . in grand style. . . . He commenced very soon to talk to me about Chinese outrages in the United States. From his province all the Chinese go. I did not like this discussion in the presence of some dozens of Chinese and so many other people. I stated to him that these

72. W. L. Willis to Bayard, March 23, 1886, *Bayard MS.*

73. Denby to Bayard, March 10, 29, 1886, *China, Despatches,* vol. 77, MS Dept. of State. Long before receiving these despatches from Denby, Bayard had been greatly worried about the possibility of attacks upon Americans resident in China, and on February 27, 1886, he recommended to Secretary Whitney that "such American men-of-war as can be made available in the East India Squadron . . . be sent forthwith to Canton and other ports to give what protection and asylum they can to American citizens who may become the objects of mob-assault in that region." *Bayard Letter Book,* vol. 2. *Bayard MS.* On March 5, 1886, Bayard sent to Perry Belmont, Chairman of the Committee on Foreign Affairs, two despatches from Denby relative to the situation of the American missionaries in China. *Bayard Letter Book,* vol. 2, *Bayard MS.*

matters were now the subject of diplomatic correspondence at Washington.
. . . He said he was well aware of that fact, but he desired me to use my
influence to punish the criminals and protect the Chinese. I told him that
the Administration was doing and would do all that it could to protect the
Chinese. . . . He talked a great deal and I endeavoured to change the
subject. . . .
       When he returned my call I received him with a salute of 17 guns. . . .
He . . . commenced on Chinese outrages again and talked with great per-
sistency. He explained to me the difficulty he had in keeping down mobs
and riots owing to the return of Chinese from America who excited the
populace. . . . To switch him off I proposed the health of the Emperor,
and afterwards I asked him the usual questions, how old he was, how many
children he had, how many grand-children, etc. He became interested in
these questions and dropped the outrage topic.[74]

       Bayard was very pleased to learn of the cordial reception that Denby
had received in China, and he indicated that

. . . everything tending to produce the entente cordiale between the United
States and the Chinese government and their Representatives here, has been
sedulously urged by me, and I think I am warranted in saying that I have
obtained the confidence of the Chinese Minister here, and that he is satisfied
of the absolute benevolence of the Administration towards his people and
himself. I had hoped to have it in my power to inform you of the passage
of both houses of Congress of the bill appropriating money to pay for the
losses of the Chinese at Rock Springs, in Wyoming Territory, in October,
1885, in accordance with the President's special message of recommendation.
A measure of this character passed the Senate, and to a moral certainty would
have passed the House also, but for the gorge of business at the close of the
session. . . . I confidently look for its early enactment in December. . . .
The Minister Mr. Cheng is very assiduous in his duties, and our relations
are very pleasant.[75]

       When news came from Denby that in China some attacks had been
made upon foreign missionaries, Bayard expressed the belief that the
claims of American nationals would receive preferred treatment:

The policy and action of the British and French governments towards
China have been aggressively harsh, and ours the direct opposite. I think,

<hr/>

74. Denby to Bayard, May 17, 1886, *Bayard MS*. In a letter to Bayard, June 17, 1886,
Denby again remarks that his trip had been "marked with all possible courtesy on the
part of the Chinese." *Bayard MS*. On May 25, 1886, Senator George Edmunds wrote to
Bayard to inform him that at times a "rabble crowd" was seen "hanging around the
Chinese Minister's house, gazing into the doorway, etc., and at other times following him
or his people about the streets and occasionally doing offensive and improper things."
Bayard at once took the matter up with the chief of police in Washington, who promised
that he would "promptly attend to the matter." *Bayard memorandum*, May 26, 1886,
Bayard MS.
75. Bayard to Denby, August 13, 1886, *Bayard Letter Book*, vol. 3, *Bayard MS*.

therefore, that it is much wiser that claims of American citizens should not be confused with English or French, and I am disposed to believe we shall receive fully as favorable if not better treatment. Your comment upon the influence in China of the reports of the outrages upon Chinese laborers in this country is perfectly just, and the omission by Congress to pass an act of indemnification for the Wyoming mob, was greatly regretted by me in apprehension of the effect upon our citizens resident in China.[76]

To Denby it seemed obvious that the Democratic Party had a glorious opportunity to effect a satisfactory settlement of the question of Chinese immigration and thereby win the favor of Pacific coast voters. If China would "cut the Gordian knot by prohibiting emigration from Hong Kong and elsewhere," he was certain that "an ultimate settlement ensuring peace and quiet is at hand."

But Denby did not devote all his attention to a discussion of the emigration of Chinese laborers. In this personal letter of October 1, he gave an interesting picture of the social life in the Chinese capital:

This winter there will be nine Ministers here [Peking], in lieu of four last winter. Socially there will be innumerable dinners and entertainments. But practically life in these vast compounds is country life. We never see a Chinese socially. The extent of their visiting and receptions is bounded by official calls. Peking is nothing to us. It is by all odds the dustiest and dirtiest city in the world. Its houses are one story. Its streets, except in the business quarter, are bounded by high brick walls. Its public edifices are all in wretched repair. From now until June no drop of rain falls. The dust of these unpaved streets is something inconceivable to an American. There are no walks except by favor on the wall, and all the streets are openly used as privies.[77]

In accordance with Denby's desires the Chinese Government proceeded to cut the Gordian knot that was interfering with Chinese-American relations. The Tsung-li Yamen, or Foreign Office, sent to the American Minister a note which contained the outline of a treaty dealing with Chinese immigration. This note was frankly critical of the American Government for its failure to protect Chinese subjects resident in the United States:

The sufferings of the Chinese [in the United States] have been terrible and the news heartrending to those who have heard of them. . . . China in her treatment toward American citizens follows the treaties as the source or basis of action, but . . . in the United States the treaties can only be regarded as . . . to no purpose.

76. Bayard to Denby, September 25, 1886, *Bayard Letter Book*, vol. 3, *Bayard MS*
77. Denby to Bayard, October 1, 1886, *Bayard MS*.

The Chinese Government now wishes to consider a plan for adopting prohibitory measures herself. Chinese laborers who have never visited the United States shall be strenuously prohibited from proceeding thither. Chinese laborers who have returned to China from the United States and who have no families, valuables, or property there, shall be prohibited from returning to the United States. Chinese laborers who still remain in the United States and those persons who under treaty are allowed to go and return at their own free will and accord, China must request that these shall forever hereafter be treated according to the provisions of existing treaties.[78]

Although this outline of a proposed treaty was received at the Department of State on September 23, 1886, it was not brought to Bayard's attention until some months later. Whether the failure to acquaint Bayard with this important despatch from Denby can be laid at the door of Alvey A. Adee, or some other official in the Department of State, is not clear. At any rate, Bayard knew nothing of its arrival in Washington until some time after he had had a conversation with the Chinese Minister on January 7, 1887. During this conversation one of the topics that received ample discussion was the question of restricting the immigration of Chinese laborers. Chang Yen Hoon inquired whether Bayard had

. . . received from Mr. Denby the results of a communication to him from the Chinese Foreign Office, setting forth the desire of that Government to alleviate the condition of the Chinese here, and to prohibit any further emigration of laborers from China?

Bayard replied that

. . . Mr. Denby had not yet communicated with this Department in regard to the matter. He [the Chinese Minister] informed me that the three points were that no more laborers should come; that those who went away should not return, but that those who had families and property in the United States should be allowed to return and settle up their business.

I stated to him that I thought he and I could find a form of words to bring that about, and that if he would give me the three points I thought I might begin to prepare some amendment to the present treaty which would reach the end desired.[79]

In response to this overture from the Chinese Minister, Bayard sent to the Chinese Legation a *projet* of a treaty which dealt with this question of immigration. According to its terms, the "coming of or

78. Tsung-li Yamen to Denby, August 3, 1886, enclosed in Denby to Bayard, August 4, 1886 (received, September 23, 1886), *China, Despatches*, vol. 78, MS Dept. of State.

79. *Memorandum* written by Bayard after a conversation with Chang Yen Hoon, the Chinese Minister, January 7, 1887, *Bayard MS*.

return to the United States of Chinese laborers shall be absolutely prohibited" for a period of thirty years. If six months before the expiration of the said period of thirty years, neither Government should formally have given notice to the other of an intention to treat such prohibition as at an end, it shall remain in force "for another period of thirty years." It was expressly understood that the provisions of this treaty should not apply to teachers, students, merchants, or travelers.[80]

After having prepared the way for an agreement on the question of immigration, Chang Yen Hoon suddenly became coy, and on January 15 he referred to the fact that no indemnity had as yet been awarded to Chinese sufferers from mob outrages in the Far West. This procrastination on the part of the American Government had placed him in a "rather delicate position," and therefore it seemed "premature" to enter into negotiations for a treaty.[81]

Bayard immediately took the cue from the Chinese Minister in this matter of the indemnity, and on January 20 he wrote to Perry Belmont, the Chairman of the Committee on Foreign Affairs of the House of Representatives, and explained to him the situation:

I would like to say a word to you *confidentially* in respect of the proposed negotiation of a treaty with China to exclude more effectually the laborers of that race. I felt it to be my duty to tell you of my contemplated negotiations in this direction, and that I was inclined to believe my approaches would be favorably met. Intimations, however, have been made to me that the pending claims for indemnity should be favorably acted upon by Congress in advance of further treaty stipulations. Therefore I now say to you *not* to state in debate that this department expects *pending* negotiations to accomplish restrictions. It is my belief, however, that with the indemnity bill *passed,* that negotiations of the desired nature will ensue.[82]

80. Bayard to Chang Yen Hoon, January 12, 1887, *Chinese Legation, Notes to,* vol. 1, MS Dept. of State.
81. Chang Yen Hoon to Bayard, January 15, 1887, *Chinese Legation, Notes from,* vol. 2, MS Dept. of State.
82. Bayard to Perry Belmont, January 20, 1887, *Bayard Letter Book,* vol. 4, *Bayard MS.* In a previous letter to Belmont, July 2, 1886, Bayard also discussed the matter of the payment of an indemnity to China because of the mob outrages in the Far West: "The Chinese Minister has just left me having expressed great solicitude in relation to the matter, and my advices from Col. Denby, who has been visiting Canton, all go to the same result, that some such act of kindness and good will as the Indemnity bill is requisite to set off the effect of the stories of ill-treatment carried back to China by the refugees from the United States, which 'fire the Chinese heart' against our citizens out there." *Bayard Letter Book,* vol. 3, *Bayard MS.*

Bayard was now ready for a conversation with Chang Yen Hoon. When the Chinese Minister called at the Department of State on January 28, Bayard remarked as follows:

I told him . . . that when he first came here I had expressed a desire that he should move about this country as much as he could and carefully note the habits and ways of our people because it would show him the radical difference between the habits and manners of the Americans and Chinese. . . . I said that I did not see how, with systems of Government so different and the presence of Chinese here being intended only to be temporary, that they could assimilate with the habits and ways of our population. I reminded him also that the presence of Americans in China was restricted to certain ports, and that even there to certain localities, and that the treaty expressly provided that, outside of these localities . . . they had no right to be and that the Chinese Government would remove them; that if the same control had been exercised over Chinese in this country by this Government, . . . that the presence of his countrymen, who had been maltreated in the mining regions of the Far West, would not have been allowed . . . simply because we could not reasonably have expected to keep them in safety.

We had no power to order them away from Rock Springs, yet I felt that the fact that the laws had been unable to protect them was a very injurious thing to this country, . . . and that was one reason why I thought we had better not have them come here until we were able to control them for their own protection.

I told him I had been glad to learn from Mr. Belmont that he thought the way was clear to get up for consideration the indemnity bill, and that if it was reached, there seemed to be very little question that it would pass. He [Chang Yen Hoon] expressed a great deal of satisfaction and good will.[83]

On February 8, when the indemnity bill was being discussed on the floor of the House of Representatives, Mr. Morrow asked Mr. Belmont whether, "after this bill has been disposed of, it is proposed to bring forward the bill . . . [to restrict] Chinese immigration?"

Mr. Belmont replied in exactly the manner that Bayard had prescribed in his letter of January 20, 1887:

I do not know how far it would be proper to declare to the House what negotiations there may be pending on this subject; but there have been communications made to Congress which for a time were secret, but from which the seal of secrecy has now been removed, and to those I can refer as indicating the disposition of the Chinese Government; and I can say that nothing has changed in regard to the statements there made by our late Minister to China, Mr. Young. . . . We are assured in this correspondence that the Chinese Government does not desire to embarrass the relations with

83. *Memorandum* written by Bayard after a conversation with Chang Yen Hoon, January 28, 1887, *Bayard MS.*

this country by a continuance of the immigration, and that there is a disposition to modify the treaty to bring about results much more effective than can possibly be accomplished by legislation. Having that in view, the committee do not intend to bring up this matter today.[84]

Thanks to the efforts of both Bayard and Belmont, an indemnity bill was finally passed by Congress and signed by the President on February 24, 1887. It expressly provided for the payment to the Chinese Government of the sum of $147,748.74 in consideration "of the losses unhappily sustained by certain Chinese subjects by mob violence at Rock Springs, in the Territory of Wyoming, September 2, 1885." There was no reference of any kind in this act to the question of *liability* for the losses suffered by the Chinese citizens.[85]

The day after the passage of this act of indemnity, Chang Yen Hoon wrote to Bayard to complain of new mob outrages against Chinese citizens. These attacks were confined to the vicinity of Juneau, Alaska.[86]

It was evident to Bayard that something would have to be done at once with regard to restricting in the most stringent manner the immigration of Chinese laborers. On March 11 he had "rather a satisfactory talk" with the Chinese Minister looking to a "treaty of exclusion of Chinese laborers," [87] and on March 18 Chang Yen Hoon left at the Department of State a long memorandum setting forth the views of his Government.[88] Once more there was sharp criticism of the American Government for its failure to prevent outrages upon Chinese laborers. To the Chinese Minister it seemed as though the "population of the Western Territories have made the ill-treatment of the Chinese

84. *Congressional Record,* 49 Cong., 2 sess., vol. 18, pt. 2, February 8, 1887, p. 1505. See also, Perry Belmont, *An American Democrat: Recollections* (N. Y., 1940), pp. 592-593, for the following remark: "As chairman of the Committee on Foreign Affairs my explanation was equivalent to an official statement of the Administration policy. The Chinese question was a subject of passionate and emotional agitation in the State of California. It might have been expected that such a statement as mine would lead to violent or severe criticism on the part of the California delegation in the House. Morrow, one of its leaders, was a Republican and might have sought some political advantage. Nothing of the sort occurred. My statement was accepted without further discussion."

85. *U. S. Statutes at Large,* vol. 24, p. 418.

86. Chang Yen Hoon to Bayard, February 25, 1887, *Chinese Legation, Notes from,* vol. 2, MS Dept. of State.

87. Bayard to President Cleveland, March 11, 1887, *Bayard Letter Book,* vol. 4, *Bayard MS.*

88. *Memorandum* written by Chang Yen Hoon and left at the Department of State, March 18, 1887, *Chinese Legation, Notes from,* vol. 2, MS Dept. of State. See also a *memorandum* written by Bayard after a conversation with Chang Yen Hoon, March 18, 1887, *Bayard MS.*

a constant practice, and have looked upon the acts of expelling and burning out the Chinese as sources of pleasure." After this acid introduction, the memorandum then set forth certain proposals which could be embodied in a formal treaty. They closely resembled the proposals made by the Tsung-li Yamen to Denby.[89]

Bayard replied with a *projet* of a treaty which incorporated all the proposals of the Chinese Minister except that part of article 1 which gave the Chinese Government the right, on her own accord, to prohibit "from time to time" the "immigration of its subjects into the United States." Under the terms of the Bayard *projet* the "High Contracting parties agree that for a period of twenty years . . . the coming . . . of Chinese laborers to the United States shall be absolutely prohibited." In this way the Chinese Government was deprived of any latitude in the matter of restriction, and a period of twenty years was fixed by treaty.[90]

89. The proposals made in this memorandum of the Chinese Minister were:
   (a) China, having of her own accord prohibited the immigration of its subjects into the United States, will do so from time to time in such manner as may be required by circumstances, there being no necessity for fixing a certain period for that purpose.
   (b) No Chinese laborer who has never been to the United States shall be permitted to go thither.
   (c) Any Chinese laborer who has returned to China from the United States cannot go thither again unless he really has there his family or relations, money, or property, or accounts contracted through him pending settlement.
   (d) Any Chinese laborer who, returning to China from other countries, may desire to pass *in transitu* through the United States should be permitted to do so as hitherto without let or hindrance.
   (e) The exempt class of Chinese subjects, whether proceeding to the United States as teachers, students, merchants, or from curiosity, if possessed with certificates, . . . shall be at once permitted to land without any detention.
   90. The *projet* presented to the Chinese Minister by Bayard, April 11, 1887, contained the following proposals:
   (a) The High Contracting parties agree that for a period of twenty years . . . the coming . . . of Chinese laborers to the United States shall be absolutely prohibited.
   (b) The preceding article shall not apply to the return to the United States of any Chinese subject who has a lawful wife, child, or parent in the United States, or property therein of the value of one thousand dollars, or debts of like amount due him and pending settlement.
   (c) The provisions of this Convention shall not affect the right at present enjoyed of Chinese subjects, being officials, teachers, students, merchants, or travelers for curiosity or pleasure . . . of coming to the United States.
   (d) It is also agreed that Chinese laborers shall continue to enjoy the privilege of transit across the territory of the United States in the course of their journey to or from other countries."
   Bayard to Chang Yen Hoon, April 11, 1887, *Chinese Legation, Notes to,* vol. 2, MS Dept. of State.

On April 13 the Chinese Minister called at the Department of State to discuss the project submitted by Bayard. He thought that both the United States and China

. . . were agreed as to the exclusion of Chinese laborers, but that the point he was not quite satisfied in regard to was the absence in the treaty draft of new stipulations for the personal safety of Chinese in the United States, and he was very much disappointed at our not making an extradition treaty with China.

Bayard replied that the United States "did not have extradition treaties with one half the foreign powers." [91] This fact seemed to mollify the Chinese Minister who wrote to Bayard to record the fact that he had always received from the Secretary of State "the kindest consideration" for which he was "exceedingly grateful." [92] After sending his photograph to Bayard as another gesture of friendship, Chang Yen Hoon left Washington en route for Spain.[93]

Bayard was exceedingly anxious to maintain friendly relations with China, and there is little doubt that he went far out of his way in extending courtesies to the Chinese Minister. Knowing that Chang Yen Hoon was about to undertake a voyage to Spain, Bayard wrote a note to J. L. M. Curry, the American Minister at Madrid, and requested him to show the Chinese Minister special attention. He was disposed to believe that "Orientals are much affected by the minor details, and that personal courtesies and gracious reception count for a great deal with them." [94]

In a letter to Denby, Bayard indicated how the situation stood with reference to Chinese immigration:

Chang Yen Hoon has just gone to Spain, to return here in September. I have tendered him a new treaty of exclusion. . . . When he gets back I

91. *Memorandum* written by Bayard after a conversation with Chang Yen Hoon, April 13, 1887, *Bayard MS.*
92. Chang Yen Hoon to Bayard, April 13, 1887, *Bayard MS.*
93. Bayard to Chang Yen Hoon, April 15, 1887, *ibid.*
94. Bayard to J. L. M. Curry, April 15, 1887, *Bayard MS.* The sincerely cordial feelings that Bayard entertained for China and her representatives in America, is clearly indicated in the following excerpt from a letter he wrote to Cheng Tsao Ju, the former Chinese Minister at Washington, November 26, 1886: "Whatever may be the differences in our systems of government and their policies, both are governments of *men,* and in the hearts of men the Great Creator has implanted certain perceptions of His own attributes, among them Justice and Love. The wisdom of dealing considerately and justly by each other is something that need not be taught or explained by schoolmen, but it is a natural impulse, understood by men all the world over. For you and your country, my good Friend, I have nothing but good will and friendship, and so far as it may be in my power I shall always strive to prove it." *Bayard MS.*

trust we will agree upon its terms, but it seems almost impossible for them to comprehend the limitations upon the power of officials under our system. . . . I found very positive expressions of satisfaction on the part of the present Minister when I paid him the "Rock Springs" fund ($147,000). He at once pressed for a claims convention providing for similar settlement in every case of alleged outrage. I assured him of the impossibility of this, but of our willingness to let each case go to Congress for appropriate relief. The entente cordiale exists between us, and I hope will continue.[95]

This *entente cordiale* between Bayard and Chang Yen Hoon must at times have been somewhat strained.[96] Bayard was naturally a courteous gentleman who invariably observed all the proprieties that hedged in the relations between a Secretary of State and the representatives of other powers. In his correspondence with Chang Yen Hoon his language is restrained and friendly, but the notes from the Chinese Minister are at times so blunt and critical that Bayard's patience must have been sorely tried. In August, 1887, Chang Yen Hoon, soon after his return to the United States, sent a note to Bayard which was distinctly acidulous. He referred to his conversation with Bayard on April 13, and then remarked: "I invited your attention to some articles in the memorandum which I had sent you that you did not agree to, as well as something you subsequently declined to carry out, though you had led me to expect it." [97]

After this undeserved thrust at Bayard, Chang Yen Hoon continued his note in a highly critical tone. He insisted upon the insertion of an article in the proposed treaty whereby ample protection would be assured to Chinese laborers in the United States. In China

. . . not a single American has lost his life by mob violence; while in every case where injury has been done to the property and rights of American citizens by . . . mobs, punishment has been promptly inflicted upon the guilty, and full pecuniary indemnity has been made by the authorities. . . . On the other hand, the correspondence of this Legation shows that in the past three years more than thirty Chinese have been murdered through mobs in the United States, and that so far as known not a single punishment has been inflicted on the murderers. . . .

95. Bayard to Denby, April 18, 1887, *Personal, Bayard MS.*
96. It would be interesting to know to what extent John W. Foster influenced the tone taken by the Chinese Minister in his notes to Bayard. In a letter to Secretary Gresham, January 5, 1895, Bayard stated that he had discovered in 1886 that Foster "was the *real* correspondent in presenting the claims of the Govt. of China." *Bayard Press Copy Book,* vol. 2, *Bayard MS.*
97. In the memorandum which Bayard wrote immediately after this conversation with Chang Yen Hoon there is no promise made that was not subsequently carried out. See Bayard memorandum, April 13, 1887, *Bayard MS.*

All that I sought to obtain by submitting my suggestions as to methods of protection was to secure to Chinese laborers in the United States the same *measure* of protection as is extended to Americans in China. If this is impossible under its system, then it must be inferred that the Government of the United States is impotent to discharge its international obligations.[98]

It is quite probable that this impudent and unfair note from Chang Yen Hoon was sharply resented by Bayard. He had already pointed out to the Chinese Minister the obvious difference between the situation in China and in the United States. In China the Americans were strictly limited as to where they could go: in the United States there was no limitation upon the right of Chinese citizens to travel or reside where they pleased. If American laborers had swarmed by the thousands into the distant provinces of China and had entered into active competition with Chinese laborers in many lucrative lines of endeavor, it is more than likely that they would have been murdered and despoiled on a large scale.[99] It was also true that the imperial authority in China was none too strong in dealing with refractory elements in the outlying provinces. The catalogue of outrages upon foreign missionaries was as long as the Homeric catalogue of ships, and the well-known Boxer Rebellion of a decade later, clearly revealed the growing impotence of the central government.[100]

There is little doubt that the sharp tone adopted by Chang Yen Hoon in his communications to the Department of State grated upon the sensibilities of American officials. An attitude of carping criticism is not calculated to infuse a spirit of cordiality into diplomatic relations. After receiving the Chinese Minister's challenging note of August 16, 1887, the American Government let the matter of an immigration treaty wait for several months before any further step was taken.

98. Chang Yen Hoon to Bayard, August 16, 1887, *Chinese Legation, Notes from,* vol. 2, MS Dept. of State.

99. The difference in the treatment accorded to Americans in China and Chinese in the United States is indicated in a letter from Charles Seymour, the American consul at Canton, to George L. Rives, Mar. 20, 1889: "While Chinese residents in the United States have had the range of the entire Union, and have been at liberty to engage in commerce, mining, and all departments of industry and enterprise, without restriction; the Chinese Authorities claim that under existing treaties foreigners have no right to buy, build, or reside in the interior, and are restricted to the Treaty Ports." *Canton, Consular Despatches,* vol. 11, MS Dept. of State.

100. Hosea B. Morse, *International Relations of the Chinese Empire* (N. Y. 1918), vol. 2, chaps. xi-xiv, xviii-xix, vol. 3, chaps. vi-x; Charles Denby, *China and Her People,* vol. 2, pp. 54-55, 73-84; S. Wells Williams, *The Middle Kingdom,* vol. 2, pp. 700, 705, 709. See also Denby's despatches to Bayard, September 29 and October 9, 1886, *China, Despatches,* vol. 78, MS Dept. of State.

Finally, President Cleveland himself became distinctly exercised over reports that Chinese, in large numbers, were illegally entering the United States. In a letter to Bayard he stated that a recent investigation by an examiner of the Department of Justice had brought to light the manner in which many Chinese were evading the restriction laws. He believed that the "most thorough remedy" for such an abuse was a speedy modification of the treaty with China. It was important to secure an immediate amendment of the restrictive legislation

. . . so that the frauds and evasions now practiced may be prevented. The present conditions should be remedied, or an attempt in that direction made at once and by us, that is *our party*. I am fearful almost to conviction that our people in Congress will so botch and blunder upon the tariff question that all the benefit of the stand already taken will not be realized. If my fears should appear to be well founded, a proper movement upon the Chinese question would furnish a compensation in the way of another string to our bow. And the quicker something in this direction is done the better.[101]

Bayard requested the President to give him all the information that was available

. . . in relation to the fraudulent entry of Chinese into California. It certainly is best to restrict them by treaty, and I will again essay it and at once. From the Department of Justice, of course, I can expect nothing in the way of information or comparison of views.[102]

In a letter to Denby, Bayard spoke of his intention to renew negotiations for

. . . a treaty of greater stringency on the exclusion of his countrymen, the necessity for which has been developed by late occurrences at San Francisco in which the abuse of return certificates has been exposed. His Excellency has proposed to play off his claims for compensation for assaults upon his countrymen in the mining districts as the consideration for increased restriction upon immigration, but this I shall not permit. Our social relations are very friendly, and I lately dined with him on the birthday of the Empress Regent.[103]

On December 28 Bayard wrote to Chang Yen Hoon and stated that apparently "a systematic evasion of the restriction upon the immigration of Chinese laborers . . . has been and continues to be practised by Chinese professing to have gone away from the United States and

101. President Cleveland to Bayard, December 18, 1887, *Confidential, Bayard MS.*

102. Bayard to President Cleveland, December 19, 1887, *Bayard Letter Book,* vol. 6, *Bayard MS.*

103. Bayard to Denby, December 19, 1887, *Personal, Bayard Letter Book,* vol. 6, *Bayard MS.*

claiming the right to return hither." He also complained of the importation of Chinese women into the United States for purposes of immorality. In view of this situation, Bayard invited the Chinese Minister to proceed in the framing of "a just and wise convention in which China and the United States shall deal with this subject in a manner consistent with their sense of mutual respect and duty, and calculated to cement their amicable relations." [104]

In all his relations with Chang Yen Hoon, Bayard showed unusual courtesy, and now he sent to the Chinese Minister a "handsome gift" as a further token of his friendly spirit. In reply, Chang Yen Hoon assured Bayard that he would always remember the "unvarying kindness and courtesy" that had been shown him.[105] But despite these expressions of appreciation, Chang Yen Hoon continued to write notes that were couched in language that was far from conciliatory. After waiting for more than a month, he finally answered Bayard's note of December 28 in a manner that seemed to exclude any possibility of compromise. He quickly dismissed any thought that Chinese laborers were illegally entering the United States in large numbers, and he gave little credence to the reports that Chinese women were being imported for immoral purposes. With regard to a new treaty between the United States and China, he thought it was necessary first to take into consideration the question of including two articles of prime importance—one dealing with the question of affording more adequate protection to Chinese laborers in the United States and the other providing for additional indemnity payments for outrages committed upon Chinese subjects by American mobs.[106]

104. Bayard to Chang Yen Hoon, December 28, 1887, *Chinese Legation, Notes to,* vol. 1, MS Dept. of State. Mary Coolidge, in her monograph *Chinese Immigration,* p. 193, has a criticism of Bayard for not answering the correspondence of Chang Yen Hoon. If she had been acquainted with the actual correspondence in this matter she would not have made her criticism.

On December 26, 1887, J. F. Linthicum, of Sacramento, wrote to Representative Thomas L. Thompson, of California, to complain that apparently nothing was being done by the Administration with reference to restricting Chinese immigration. *Cleveland MS.* When this complaint was brought to Bayard's attention he wrote to President Cleveland, January 5, 1888, as follows: "Correspondence has been going on since last winter with the Chinese Minister at this Capital to *exclude* Chinese laborers by Treaty. The Minister went to Europe and passed the summer, and since then the correspondence has been renewed. This Administration has not been delinquent in essaying a reform in existing treaties made by prior Administrations. As to satisfying the Californians, I fear the effort would be idle, but I am pressing a treaty of exclusion." *Cleveland MS.*

105. Chang Yen Hoon to Bayard, January 25, 1888, *Bayard MS.*

106. Chang Yen Hoon to Bayard, January 30, 1888, *Chinese Legation, Notes from,* vol. 2, MS Dept. of State.

This matter of indemnity payments for acts of violence committed upon Chinese subjects was a very serious one, and to all appearances it seemed as though this question would be an endless one. On February 16 Chang Yen Hoon wrote to Bayard to inform him that ten Chinese laborers had been murdered "in the most horrible manner" on the Snake River, in Oregon.[107] Bayard wearily replied that everything would be done to apprehend the guilty parties,[108] and he tried to accelerate the slow pace of the treaty negotiations.

On February 24 Bayard had a conference with a sub-committee of the Senate Committee on Foreign Relations on the question of Chinese immigration,[109] and it became increasingly obvious that something would have to be done at once. At his request, the Chinese Minister called at the Department of State to discuss the situation.

There are two memoranda which purport to give the substance of the conversation between Bayard and Chang Yen Hoon on February 29, 1888. According to a memorandum kept by Chang Yen Hoon, Bayard opened the interview by alluding to the agitation in the Senate and in the House of Representatives in favor of

. . . more stringent measures to restrict the emigration of the Chinese laborers into the United States. Last year the Congressmen from the Pacific Coast proposed to enact some unreasonable measures for their restriction.

107. Chang Yen Hoon to Bayard, February 16, 1888, *ibid.*
108. Bayard to Chang Yen Hoon, February 23, 1888, *Chinese Legation, Notes to,* vol. 2, MS Dept. of State. With reference to the inclusion of an indemnity provision in the proposed treaty with China, Senator John T. Morgan, of Alabama, wrote to Bayard on February 25, 1888, as follows: "An agreement to pay a certain sum, included in the treaty, would, I have no doubt, be ratified in the Senate, and would be provided for in the 2nd session of the 50th Congress, but, at this session, it might lead to a political debate. The treaty, ratified and proclaimed, would give us a fine send-off, and we can take care of the appropriation later on. I suggest, therefore, that the time of payment be fixed for January, or March, 1889." *Bayard MS.*
109. Senator John Sherman to Bayard, February 22, 1888, and Bayard to Sherman, February 23, 1888, *Bayard MS.* With reference to what transpired at this meeting between the sub-committee of the Senate Committee on Foreign Relations and Bayard, Senator Sherman remarked as follows: "A sub-committee did go to Mr. Bayard and had a conversation with him. I never supposed and never believed that Mr. Bayard gave out any remarks that were made in that conference, because it would have been improper for him to do so, and he is not a man who would do a thing of that kind. The effort was not made with any intention to embarrass the Administration or to embarrass Mr. Bayard in the slightest degree. It was made in the most friendly spirit. Among the members of that sub-committee was the Senator from Alabama (Mr. Morgan), who has been the defender of the Administration. . . . All that was said or all that was proposed by the sub-committee was that if this thing could be brought about by the action of the executive authorities or the treaty-making power, it would be better as an example for the future than for us to assert the power to pass a law without respect to the treaty." *Congressional Record,* September 3, 1888, 50 Cong., 1 sess., vol. 19, pt. 9, p. 8217.

. . . At the present time they are still more active. Unless you [Chang Yen Hoon] and I soon agree upon some satisfactory measures in our negotiations, Congress will certainly enact laws regardless of the treaty stipulations. Should such be the case, they would violate the treaty and the President would of course veto them, but still the Executive would not like to raise any difficulty with the Congress. As the Congress has such an object in view, it would be better to meet its wishes as far as it is possible by agreeing upon some satisfactory measures for the maintenance of the friendly relations between the two nations.[110]

This pledge that the President would veto any laws passed by Congress which were in violation of the treaty of 1880, is *not* contained in the memorandum which Bayard himself wrote after his conversation with the Chinese Minister on February 29, 1888. On this point his memorandum reads as follows:

The Chinese Minister called according to appointment. . . . I stated to him the case fully, and my reasons for desiring, in the interests of amity and mutual respect, that no legislation by Congress, inconsistent with our Treaty stipulations, should be enacted, and I thought it very important that the Chinese question should not in any way be put in issue between the President and one of the political parties of the Country, but that the whole country should be led to act amicably towards the Chinese.

It is evident that this statement was in no sense a pledge of a veto in the event that Congress should pass legislation which ran counter to the provisions of the treaty of 1880. Bayard would not have presumed to speak for the President on such a matter, and his words that he did not wish to have "the Chinese question" be "put in issue between the President and one of the political parties of the Country," could hardly be interpreted as a specific promise of a Presidential veto.

After this introductory statement, Bayard read to Chang Yen Hoon the draft of three additional articles to the *projet* that had already been submitted to the Chinese Government. These new articles were in response to the wishes of the Chinese Minister. Article A provided that Chinese laborers residing in the United States should enjoy "all rights of process that are given by the laws of the United States to citizens of the most favored nation." Article B made provision for an additional indemnity payment to the Chinese Government for losses sustained by Chinese subjects through mob violence, and Article C

110. *Memorandum* kept by Chang Yen Hoon of a conversation with Bayard, February 29, 1888. This memorandum was sent to Bayard by Chang Yen Hoon in a note of February 25, 1889, *Bayard MS.*

dealt with the question of preventing the entry into the United States of Chinese laborers *via* British Columbia.

Bayard indicated to Chang Yen Hoon that the payment of an additional indemnity to the Chinese Government for losses of Chinese subjects sustained through mob violence, was a gesture of friendship. The true remedy in this situation lay in recourse to the courts, and there was no evidence to show that any Chinaman had been denied justice in this regard. Bayard then concluded his remarks by saying that it was "exceedingly important" to conclude a treaty at the earliest possible moment in order to prevent "separate action in the Houses of Congress."

After suggesting two changes, one of which was adopted, Chang Yen Hoon professed to be "very much gratified" with the three new articles proposed by Bayard.[111] But this mood of gratification was short-lived. On March 2 he paid a visit to the Department of State and strongly insisted upon certain amendments to Bayard's proposed new articles. Bayard once more humored the critical Chinaman, and the draft treaty was changed to accord with his new desires.[112] Finally, on

111. *Memorandum* written by Bayard after a conversation with Chang Yen Hoon, February 29, 1888, *Bayard MS.*

112. In a memorandum written by Bayard after his conversation with Chang Yen Hoon, there is a brief account of the final negotiations relative to the immigration treaty:

"The Chinese Minister called in relation to the Treaty, and brought me back the proposed amendments. He seemed to object quite strongly to the proposition that his government should make conventional engagements with the British Government to prevent Chinese laborers coming into the U. S.

"I said I did not know that that was necessary at all, and I did not think I should press the amendment upon him, because in looking at the Treaty draft which we had agreed to, it expressly stated that the Chinese Government desired to co-operate with the United States in prohibiting the immigration of Chinese subjects. That would include co-operation in every way, and when I pointed out to him the debate in the Senate to show how the Chinese streamed in across the borders from British America, [he said] of course, his government would do their best under the treaty to co-operate in preventing it.

"I thought we could perfectly well effectuate what we desired by my writing him a note, after the Treaty was signed, stating what was alleged in regard to the coming of Chinese from Hong Kong, through British Columbia, and that he could write me stating that his government would be glad to do what they could to prevent it.

"He said that was very satisfactory. He then referred to Article A, and proposed an amendment. He had stricken out the words 'all rights of process, etc.,' so as to leave it 'all rights that are given by the laws of the United States to the most favored nations,' and I added the words 'not including the right to become naturalized citizens,' to which he assented. He also put some words at the end as to the re-affirmation by the United States of the obligation to exert all their power to protect the Chinese as stated in Article 3 of the immigration treaty of 1880, to which I made no objection.

"A verbal amendment was added to Article B, which I thought immaterial, but which I amended. It is to the effect that after the recital of injuries to the Chinese by wicked and lawless men, the words were put in 'which unexpected events the Chinese Government

March 12, 1888, a treaty providing for the exclusion of Chinese laborers was signed by Bayard and Chang Yen Hoon, and four days later it was sent to the Senate.[113]

This treaty of March 12, 1888, prohibited, for a period of twenty years, the entry into the United States of Chinese laborers. But this prohibition would not apply to the return of any Chinese laborer who had a lawful wife, child, or parent in the United States, or property therein of the value of one thousand dollars, or debts of like amount due him. Laborers who had once resided in the United States and had returned to China, could not re-enter the United States unless they could meet the above-mentioned qualifications. These restrictions, however, would not affect the right of Chinese subjects who were officials, teachers, students, merchants, or travelers, to visit the United States. In order to ensure adequate protection for the Chinese laborers who still resided in the United States, it was provided that they would enjoy all the rights that were given to the citizens of the most favored nation, excepting the right to become naturalized citizens. As a gesture of friendship, provision was made for the payment to the Chinese Government of an indemnity amounting to $276,619.75 to compensate for the losses sustained by Chinese citizens through mob violence. In the last article of the convention it was stated that the treaty would remain in force for a period of twenty years, and if not denounced by either party, it would remain in force for another period of twenty years.[114]

regrets, and for which it has claimed an indemnity, the legal obligation of which the United States denies, and whereas, etc.' I said I saw no objection to that being inserted, as it placed him in a better position to obey the instructions of his Foreign Office. . . .

"I then told him that I observed that there was a claim he had estimated at $100,000—the death of 40 Chinamen at $2500 apiece—and I wished to draw his attention to the fact that 28 out of that 40 were the victims of the Rock Springs massacre for which the United States had paid in full." *Bayard MS.*

113. Message of March 16, 1888. *Confidential Executive Document O*, 50 Cong., 1 sess., pp. 1-7. In a letter to E. J. Phelps, in London, March 16, 1888, Bayard remarks: "Today a treaty with China goes in, and that has been already dealt with by certain Senators in a way that is simply impossible among gentlemen. But I spare you any further comments, and when you come here you shall see and hear for yourself." *Bayard Letter Book*, vol. 7, *Bayard MS.*

114. *Foreign Relations, 1888*, pt. 1, pp. 393-394. It is interesting to note that Bayard received a letter from the notorious sand-lot agitator, Denis [as signed] Kearney, March 9, 1888, in which he remarked: "I would like to have ten minutes talk with you, at your convenience about Chinese immigration. Your time no doubt is pretty well monopolized. If granted the asked-for interview, I promise not to detain you longer than ten or maybe five minutes although the question is big enough to monopolize one month of your valuable time." *Bayard MS.* There is no record in the *Bayard MSS* of any conversation between Bayard and Kearney.

Now that the treaty with China had been signed, Bayard's main fear was that the Senate, in which the Republican Party had a small majority, would seek to gain some partisan advantage by adopting amendments which would nullify all that he had done to settle the immigration question.[115] In a letter to Denby shortly after the conclusion of the treaty, Bayard remarked:

I send you a copy of the treaty which I hope will attain the end of prohibiting Chinese laborers from coming here, and remove from this Government the reproach for the sufferings of these poor people at the hands of brutal men by paying the full sum asked by the Chinese Minister. . . . I am disposed to believe from the incoherent violence and extreme statements of the Republican leaders that their party organization is disintegrating. It has so terribly deteriorated in all respects that it would be a national calamity were it to be once more potential.[116]

Some weeks later he wrote another letter to Denby in which he expressed the same misgivings as to the action of the Senate:

What will be the fate of the Treaty with China at the hands of the Senate I cannot foretell. The action of the Majority has been wholly devoid of comity, courtesy, or common justice to the Administration. Demagogueism on the subject of the Chinese seems to rule the Pacific Coast, and nothing however serviceable to the Country, but which would also be creditable to the Administration, can run the gauntlet of small politics in the Senate successfully.[117]

There were some well-balanced individuals on the Pacific Coast who refused to allow their prejudices to run away with their judgment. On April 25 John P. Irish, editor of the *Alta California* (San Francisco), wrote to Bayard and expressed approval of the recently signed treaty with China:

115. Many other Democrats had fears similar to those of Bayard. Representative Thomas L. Thompson, in a letter to Dan Lamont, March 25, 1888, voiced his concern as to the attitude of the Republican majority in the Senate with regard to the treaty of March 12: "Friendliness for the Administration and a sincere admiration for the President . . . impels this letter which for obvious reasons I address to you personally. It is patent that the Republican representatives from the Pacific Coast, or at least a majority of them are engaged in what seems to me an unfair endeavor to break the force of the political influence of the new Chinese Treaty on the Pacific States. As I understand it, the essence of the new treaty is recognition of the principle of exclusion. Under its operation any legislation necessary to exclude the further immigration of Chinese laborers to this country may be enacted. This is a step far in advance of what we have had. . . . I have not . . . seen the treaty. Several days ago I called on Secretary Bayard and expressed a desire to learn its contents, but a sense of decorum prevented his informing me as to its provisions." *Cleveland MS.*
116. Bayard to Denby, March 17, 1888, *Bayard Letter Book,* vol. 7, *Bayard MS.*
117. Bayard to Denby, April 21, 1888, *ibid.*

The Chinese treaty is right . . . and should be ratified. I am assured by the Federal Judges here that if it is ratified they will refuse writs of *habeas corpus* to Chinese, leaving the matter of identification and landing to the Treasury authorities. The opposition to the treaty is merely captious and partisan. I know that it will prove to be all that our people want.[118]

The year 1888 was election year, and although John P. Irish regarded the treaty with China as "right," the Republican majority in the Senate was determined to force through certain amendments which might make an appeal to the voters on the Pacific Coast. The amendments were short and without any real value. Article I of the treaty prohibited, for a period of twenty years, the entry of Chinese laborers into the United States. The Senate amendment merely added the superfluous words: "And this prohibition shall extend to the return of Chinese laborers who are not now in the United States, whether holding return certificates under existing laws or not." Article II provided for the issuance of a new form of return certificates to Chinese laborers. Only laborers who had a wife, child, or parent in the United States, or who had property valued at one thousand dollars or debts due him of a like amount, could secure these new return certificates. To the regulations controlling the issuance of these certificates, the Senate added the following amendment: "And no such Chinese laborer shall be permitted to enter the United States by land or sea without producing to the proper officer of the customs the return certificate herein required." [119]

The dubious character of these Senate amendments was clearly indicated by Senator Gray.[120] The Senate majority, however, insisted

118. John P. Irish to Bayard, April 25, 1888, *Bayard MS.*
119. *Foreign Relations, 1888*, pt. 1, pp. 398-399.
120. During a Senate debate on the Chinese treaty (September 3, 1888), Senator Gray remarked as follows: "Article I of the treaty provides: 'The high contracting parties agree that for a period of twenty years . . . the coming, except under conditions hereinafter specified, of Chinese laborers to the United States shall be absolutely prohibited.' That was the wording of Article I as it came to the Senate. The English language could not go further in emphatic words of positive exclusion than this article does. The amendment put upon it by the Senate, which delays its ratification, if it has not destroyed the hope of ratification, is this: 'And this prohibition shall extend to the return of Chinese laborers, who are not now in the United States, whether holding return certificates under existing laws or not.' Now, surely those words added nothing to the prohibitive force of the treaty as it came to the Senate. . . .

"Now, Article II provides that this exclusion shall not apply to the return to the United States of any Chinese laborer who has a lawful wife or child or parent in the United States or property therein of the value of $1,000 or debts of like amount due him and pending settlement. 'Nevertheless,' the article goes on, 'every such Chinese laborer shall, before leaving the United States,' (before he leaves the United States, observe)

upon their adoption, and this course not only helped to delay the transmission of the treaty to the Chinese Government, but it also gave that government an excuse to postpone ratification.

President Cleveland soon got wind of the plan of the Republican leaders to force the adoption of some amendments to the Chinese treaty, and he wrote at once to Bayard with regard to their effect. He was anxious to know whether it would be possible to have

. . . these amendments promptly incorporated in the treaty? If so is it best to try it, or should our people first oppose the amendments, and if they are voted on, oppose the confirmation of the treaty as thus amended? Whatever excuse is put forward for these amendments, of course their object is largely political. My impression is that if we can procure an agreement by the Chinese to these Amendments *quickly* and thus put the treaty in operation quite soon, we shall do more to destroy the plans of political advantage which underlie these Amendments, than can be done in any other way. Have you not any means of estimating the chances of success in securing an agreement to the Amendments by the Chinese Government, or can you gain any hint of the chances? [121]

Bayard replied on the following day that the Senate amendments did not appear to be

. . . much, if at all at variance with the text of the Treaty, and *if* this is to be the extent of the proposed changes I do not apprehend any difficulty in getting the Chinese approval. But I quite agree with you that the amendments are not proposed *bona fide* to improve the treaty, but only to obstruct our negotiations. If our people assent *too readily* to the amendments now proposed, I fear that others will be pressed, and therefore it seems to me to be wiser to let the *Republicans* carry the proposed amendments and if it can *then* be understood that the treaty *as so amended* will be adopted, for the Democrats to assist the confirmation. It is very disheartening to have such

---

'shall deposit, as a condition of his return, with the collector of customs of the district from which he departs, a full description in writing of his family, or property, or debts as aforesaid, and shall be furnished by said collector with such certificate of his right to return under this treaty as the laws of the United States may now or hereafter prescribe and not inconsistent with the provisions of this treaty; and should the written description aforesaid be proved to be false, the right to return thereunder, or of continued residence after return, shall in each case be forfeited.'

"So that the exception from this absolute and universal exclusion is in regard only to those Chinese who have their families here or property here of the value of $1,000 and who have left, first having obtained a certificate such as is described in Article II. Therefore it was idle to argue, and is today idle to argue, that under this treaty a Chinaman who had gone, before this ratification, to China, could return, for it was impossible for him to have had this certificate which it was required he should have in accordance with the laws to be thereafter passed to entitle him to such return." *Congressional Record,* 50 Cong., 1 sess., vol. 19, pt. 9, p. 8220.

121. President Cleveland to Bayard, April 26, 1888, *Bayard MS.*

grave public measures made the sport of small politicians. I hope some member of the Com. on Foreign Relations may give me fuller knowledge of what is going on, but when I inquired of Mr. Paine just now he was wholly unable to tell me anything about it.[122]

On May 4 the Chinese Minister called at the Department of State to discuss the situation with reference to the treaty. Bayard opened the discussion by referring, "confidentially," to the difficulties the treaty was encountering in the Senate where the Republican majority always opposed "everything" that the present Administration introduced. After Chang Yen Hoon remarked that he "thought the Senate had too much power," Bayard stated that the newspapers had reported certain amendments to the treaty with China, and that he

. . . considered those amendments immaterial and unnecessary, because a fair construction of the Treaty would provide for what is stated in the amendments, but that I [Bayard] would not discuss with him today our acceptance of the amendments as they stood, nor say anything about them; because I thought that if it was intimated that he and I would agree upon those amendments, that then others might be proposed by the representatives from the Pacific Coast that we probably would not agree to—to which he assented. . . . I hinted to him that it was necessary for me to exchange ratifications with *him,* and not with the Secretary, and that if I found the Treaty was gotten through the Senate, and sent to the President before he [Chang Yen Hoon] went away from Washington, I would at once let him know, and that if the amendments were not different from those which were reported, I thought we could make short work of them, and that we would not be disposed to allow his work and mine, in behalf of our two countries to be defeated by such amendments as these.[123]

A few days later, the Secretary of the Chinese Legation paid a visit to the Department of State to inform Bayard that the "amendments of the Senate did not change materially the language of the Treaty, and that therefore they were acceptable to him." He also stated that the Minister "would telegraph to Peking the nature of the amendments and say that they were acceptable to him." [124]

122. Bayard to President Cleveland, April 27, 1888, *Bayard Letter Book,* vol. 7, *Bayard MS.*

123. *Memorandum* written by Bayard after a conversation with Chang Yen Hoon, May 4, 1888, *Bayard MS.*

124. *Memorandum* written by Bayard after a conversation with the Secretary of the Chinese Legation, May 9, 1888, *Bayard MS.* With reference to the action of the Chinese Minister in accepting these Senate amendments as not changing "materially the language of the Treaty," Mary Coolidge, in her monograph, *Chinese Immigration,* pp. 195-196, remarks: "Apparently the Chinese Minister did not fully understand the effect of these amendments in shutting out at least twenty thousand Chinese who held certificates of

On May 11 Chang Yen Hoon had a conversation with Bayard, and inquired

. . . why the amendments were made, and said he thought they were very unnecessary. I said I did not think they changed the Treaty in the least and were, therefore, unnecessary, but as the Senate had put them in, they must be considered as in the Treaty. . . . Finally after a great deal of conversation between the Minister and his Secretaries, he told me he had delayed his visit to New York on account of these amendments, and he asked me to send him a copy of the Treaty written out with the amendments in it, marking on the margin where each amendment came in. I told him I would do so and send it to him at once.[125]

Bayard fulfilled this promise and sent very promptly to the Chinese Legation a copy of the treaty as amended by the Senate. In his note of transmittal he remarked that he did not think that these amendments "changed" or added to the "force and effect of the original text of the treaty." [126] Chang Yen Hoon replied on the following day that he had "carefully examined" the amendments, and "as they do not alter the terms of the original treaty, it will give me pleasure to accept them in due form." [127]

After receiving this note from the Chinese Minister, Bayard wrote to President Cleveland and enclosed a copy of it. In his accompanying letter he drew the attention of the President to the fact that Chang Yen Hoon had agreed to the Senate amendments

. . . as not changing in effect the original text of our Treaty. This is a strong commentary upon the Republican insistence upon making these amendments, the only result of which is, not to improve the treaty, but to postpone and delay its operation which they have so clamored for. I think it would be well to have this fact circulated, and the maleficent obstruction of the Senate brought to the knowledge of the people.[128]

In a letter to John P. Irish, on the same day, Bayard repeated his sharp criticisms of the Senate for their obstructive policy in the matter

---

return." This statement shows how completely Miss Coolidge misunderstood the intent of the treaty of March 12, 1888. This instrument shut out the "twenty thousand Chinese who held certificates of return," and it did not require any Senate amendments to give it such an effect. This fact was, of course, clearly understood by the Chinese Minister.

125. *Memorandum* written by Bayard after a conversation with Chang Yen Hoon, May 11, 1888, *Bayard MS.*

126. Bayard to Chang Yen Hoon, May 11, 1888, *Chinese Legation, Notes to,* vol. 1, MS Dept. of State.

127. Chang Yen Hoon to Bayard, May 12, 1888, *Chinese Legation, Notes from,* vol. 2, MS Dept. of State.

128. Bayard to President Cleveland, May 12, 1888, *Bayard Letter Book,* vol. 7, *Bayard MS.*

of amending the treaty with China. He was deeply concerned over the

. . . maleficent results of small Republican interference with the objects of the treaty in the wholly superfluous amendments which they insisted (against Democratic votes) in engrafting upon the original text. I have fortunately just received a letter from the Chinese Minister (with whom I have had several interviews) in which he agrees to accept the amendments "as they do not alter the terms of the original treaty." When the treaty was signed in March, the Chinese counterpart was at once sent to Peking for the Imperial approval, but now come these useless amendments which at my urgent request have been telegraphed by the Minister but which will necessarily delay the exchange of ratifications. . . . The Minister sails for Peru next week and will not return until October, so we must wait.

When one considers the clamorous demand for Chinese exclusion, and the Congressional resolutions and super-activity of the Republican Senators and Representatives hurrying this Department into action, these results of their petty obstructiveness ought to be made known, and charged upon them.[129]

With the Chinese Minister absent in South America, it was inevitable that the movement in favor of a speedy ratification of the treaty should be somewhat slackened. On July 16 the secretary of the Chinese Legation called at the Department of State and inquired whether "any more amendments could be put by Congress to the Treaty." Bayard replied that no further amendments could be adopted by the Senate. The treaty was "now obligatory on the United States if China accepts it."[130]

While the Chinese Government was considering the question of ratification, the Congress of the United States took action and passed a law putting into operation the treaty with China just as soon as that Government ratified it. This bill was presented to the President on September 1, and it received his signature on the thirteenth of the month.[131]

Bayard regarded such action by Congress as "hasty" and "ill-considered." The election of 1888 was close at hand, and he realized how the foreign policy of the Administration could be seriously compromised through political pressure. On September 1 he read in the New York *Herald* a telegram from London which stated that the immigration treaty between the United States and China had been rejected by the

129. Bayard to John P. Irish, May 12, 1888, *ibid.*
130. *Memorandum* written by Bayard after a conversation with the secretary of the Chinese Legation, July 16, 1888, *Bayard MS.*
131. *U. S. Statutes at Large*, vol. 25, pp. 476-479.

Chinese Government. The dangers of the situation were at once apparent to him, and he freely expressed his fears in a letter to John Russell Young:

The sooner our fellow countrymen can be made aware of the abnormal condition of mind into which the Senatorial Cabal have been wrought under the spur of party spirit the better. To-day's *Herald* contains . . . a telegram from London that the pending treaty with China for the exclusion of laborers has been rejected. "The wish is Father to the thought" in British counsels, and a question in the United States just now which ought to be answered is *who* has co-operated here with British influence to bring about the unfortunate defeat of the treaty? If the treaty has been rejected will the amendments of the Republican Committee in the Senate, . . . or the hasty and stringent measure to execute the treaty *in advance* of its ratification, . . . or the possibility of electing to the Presidency a declared opponent to the policy of Chinese exclusion be one of all the accountable causes for the defeat of a most amicable and efficient arrangement tending to shelter the laboring classes of America from dangerous and degrading competition.[132]

Two days later (September 3), in response to an inquiry from Representative Binger Hermann, Bayard stated that he had received "no information whatever from China in relation to the pending Treaty."[133] On that very day, without any previous consultation with Bayard, William L. Scott, chairman of the National Democratic Campaign Committee, and an intimate friend of President Cleveland, introduced a bill in the House of Representatives which proceeded on the theory that the Chinese Government had actually rejected the immigration treaty. If this were true, Chinese laborers with return certificates would soon be coming into American ports. In order to guard against such a possibility, Mr. Scott hastily drafted a bill which provided that after its passage it would be

. . . unlawful for any Chinese laborer who shall at any time heretofore have been or may now or hereafter be a resident within the United States, and who shall have departed or shall depart therefrom, and shall not have returned before the passage of this act, to return to or remain in the United States.

Sec. 2. That no certificates of identity provided for in the fourth or fifth sections of the act to which this is a supplement [May 6, 1882] shall hereafter be issued; and every certificate heretofore issued in pursuance thereof is hereby declared void and of no effect; and the Chinese laborer claiming ad-

132. Bayard to J. R. Young, September 1, 1888, *Bayard Letter Book,* vol. 8, *Bayard MS.* See also Bayard to J. L. Thompson, September 1, 1888, *Bayard Letter Book,* vol. 8, *Bayard MS.*
133. Bayard to Binger Hermann, September 3, 1888, *Bayard MS.*

mission by virtue thereof shall not be permitted to enter the United States.[134]

This bill which would shut out all Chinese laborers applying for entrance into the United States on the basis of return certificates, was rushed through the House of Representatives without a single dissenting vote. There was no debate on the measure, and it was immediately sent to the Senate. Senator George quickly raised objections to the bill because it seemed unfair to exclude Chinese laborers, with return certificates, who were already en route to America:

A Chinaman may be on his way back, he may be almost in sight of our shores, coming under a law and a treaty which allow him to land. It seems to me to be worthy of consideration whether the denial of returning Chinese to come should not be put at a date which would about give them time to get across the Pacific Ocean.[135]

Senator Stewart and his colleagues from the Far West expressed the view that the Chinese laborers with return certificates had been rushing to America ever since the signature of the treaty of March 12, 1888. To them it seemed obvious that these laborers had enjoyed a "pretty good show on the return business. Enough of them have been smuggled in." [136]

Other Senators thought that no action should be taken on the Scott bill until authentic information had been received from China with reference to the alleged rejection of the treaty. In response to this Senatorial pressure, Bayard cabled to Denby on September 4, and inquired what action the Chinese Government had taken with regard to the treaty.[137] Denby replied on the following day that he believed the treaty had been rejected. He had "demanded" that the Foreign Office give him some "positive information" on this point, but he had received no answer to his inquiries. [138]

As soon as Bayard read this cablegram from Denby, he wrote a short note to the President in which he reviewed the situation. He was not surprised at the negative attitude of the Chinese Government:

When one reflects upon the attitude among the family of Nations that China would occupy by consenting in formal treaty to the exclusion of the great body of her people from equal entry into other lands with the popula-

134. *Congressional Record*, September 3, 1888, 50 Cong., 1 sess., vol. 19, pt. 9, p. 8226.
135. *Congressional Record*, 50 Cong., 1 sess., vol. 19, pt. 9, p. 8215.
136. *Ibid.*, p. 8216.
137. Bayard to Denby, September 4, 1888, *China, Instructions*, vol. 4, MS Dept. of State.
138. Denby to Bayard, September 5, 1888, *China, Despatches*, vol. 83, MS Dept. of State.

tions of other countries, it is scarcely to be wondered that they are inclined to withdraw from such a covenant. And yet, but for the delay of the Senate Amendments and the furious haste of anticipatory legislation we should almost certainly have secured the exclusion of this most undesirable class.[139]

On September 6 Denby sent to Bayard a long personal letter in which he expressed himself quite freely:

During the absence of my interpreter for a few days at the hills I learned from the Chinese writer that the late treaty had been rejected. I immediately wrote to the Yamen to ask positive information; up to this time no answer has arrived.

I then called on the Marquis Tseng, who alone of the members of the Yamen speaks English. I put the direct question to the Marquis whether final action had been taken by the Yamen resulting in the rejection of the Treaty. He at first was reticent, said he had not been at the Yamen much lately. I knew that this was not true and I pressed him with searching enquiries. He finally told me that for the first time in the history of treaties the people had protested, that protests had been sent by the Cantonese against the ratification of the Treaty, that a mob had broken the windows of the house of the Chinese Minister at Canton, and that a despatch had been sent to the Minister at Washington that the ratification of the treaty must, for the present, be delayed. I told him I had twice applied to the Yamen to ascertain the facts and that he would confer a favor on me if he would procure the Yamen to send me an immediate answer. . . . I have been awaiting such answer before telegraphing you again.

It is entirely probable that the efforts of the British Minister to procure for the Crown Colonies a similar treaty have induced the Chinese Government to hesitate in the matter of the ratification of our treaty. It would form a precedent that England might insist on. The opposition of the people also goes for a great deal in this form of government. . . .

If this Treaty is finally rejected it will be the beginning of the end of Chinese immigration of any character to the United States. It is the most favorable treaty that China can ever expect. . . . There is little reciprocity in the treatment of the Chinese towards us. Our people are limited to certain treaty ports, manufacturing is prohibited, an innate hostility exists to foreigners all over China, and in some provinces mobs are scarcely restrained from violence. . . . The foreigner in China holds his position by force alone. No good will accompanies him. . . . China day by day, becomes more hostile to foreigners. Even foreign Ministers in Peking never see the inside of a gentleman's house. . . . We must therefore, recognize the fact that kindness to this people goes for little.

. . . A message from the President to Congress informing that body that unreasonable delay has been had in the ratification of the Chinese Treaty, and asserting the necessity of more stringent legislation under the existing

139. Bayard to Cleveland, September 5, 1888, *Bayard Letter Book*, vol. 8, *Bayard MS.*

treaties and avowing his willingness to co-operate in the enactment of any law which will remedy existing evils, will have a fine effect on the country. . . . We may be sure that we are going to receive nothing at the hands of China that she can safely refuse. She will grant no favors. On our part we should look to our own interests only in dealing with China.[140]

On the afternoon of September 6 Denby cabled to Bayard that the treaty was "postponed for further deliberation." [141] As soon as Bayard received this telegram from Denby, he sent a short note of inquiry to the President:

I enclose a copy of a telegram received from Mr. Denby at Peking. Do you not think the substance of this telegram should instantly be sent to the Senate? Few lines in a message would be sufficient, and perhaps it would be well in order to give the Senate *all* the information we have received, that the telegram of day before yesterday should also be communicated.[142]

While the President was considering the advisability of a special message to the Senate with reference to the Chinese treaty, that body passed a resolution (September 11, 1888) requesting the Chief Executive to send to it all the "correspondence or communications by and with the Government of the United States concerning the treaty with China recently ratified by the Senate." On September 18 President Cleveland complied with this request, and the Senate was placed in possession of the diplomatic correspondence between Bayard and the Chinese Minister covering the period from January 12, 1887, to May 14, 1888.[143]

In the meantime Bayard was deeply concerned over the action taken by Congress with regard to the Chinese treaty. The bill introduced by Representative W. L. Scott (September 3, 1888), excluding Chinese laborers with return certificates, had received such strong support that its final enactment was almost certain. The only excuse for its introduction was a statement in the British press that the Chinese Government had rejected the treaty with the United States. Despite this dubious background, the bill had been favorably considered by both Houses of Congress and was on the point of adoption.

Bayard strongly deprecated such hasty action. In a letter to John Russell Young he raised a pertinent question:

140. Denby to Bayard, September 6, 1888, *Bayard MS.*
141. Denby to Bayard, September 6, 1888, *China, Despatches*, vol. 83, MS Dept. of State.
142. Bayard to President Cleveland, September 7, 1888, *Bayard Letter Book*, vol. 8, *Bayard MS.*
143. *Foreign Relations, 1888*, pt. 1, pp. 359-360.

Why cannot Congress legislate on this bill as they did on the other to execute the treaty if accepted, and let their present measure be like the other—conditional upon the fact that the pending treaty is *not* ultimately satisfied.[144]

His open disgust with the way Congress had acted is revealed in a letter to S. D. Warren: "The action of both Houses on matters of national importance is most discreditable and full of evil possibility."[145]

On September 8 the Chinese chargé d'affaires called at the Department of State in "evident distress" about the bill that had been introduced by Representative Scott. He informed Bayard that his government was

. . . most willing to keep their people at home, and joined in the treaty in order to co-operate to that end. He said he had no other belief than that the Treaty as amended would be accepted by his government, and that no intimation to the contrary has been received. . . . The chargé will give me [Bayard] instant knowledge of his news from China, and left me saying that he fully expected the Treaty to be accepted by his government. He was anxious to know what you could do to "stop the bill," but I told him Congress was wholly independent of the Executive, and that you must await the presentation of the bill to you.[146]

In the Senate, a motion to reconsider the vote on the Scott bill was lost on September 14 through the lack of a necessary quorum.[147] This action was discouraging to Bayard, who had hoped that the Senate

144. Bayard to J. R. Young, September 7, 1888, *Bayard Letter Book*, vol. 8, *Bayard MS.*
145. Bayard to S. D. Warren, September 8, 1888, *ibid.*
146. Bayard to President Cleveland, September 8, 1888, *Bayard Letter Book*, vol. 8, *Bayard MS.* Bayard was further disturbed by a mendacious statement made by Senator Dolph on the floor of the Senate. According to the Senator, the negotiations between the United States and China which resulted in the treaty of March 12, 1888, were instituted because of direct Senate pressure. He stated that "it was not until the 16th of March . . . that the treaty was submitted to the Senate by the President of the United States, and I am able to state upon the very best authority that about the time that resolution [the Senate resolution which was adopted on March first] was reported, although there had been some negotiation between the State Department and the Chinese Government some time before, there had been nothing since about the 1st of the preceding May done in regard to that." *Cong. Rec.,* September 7, 1888, 50 Cong., 1 sess., vol. 19, pt. 9, p. 8373. Senator Dolph directly lied in making this statement. Before the introduction of the resolution in the Senate, he had paid a visit to the Department of State and had been assured that negotiations with China were being conducted. He then sponsored a resolution which said the contrary. In a letter to Secretary Gresham, April 11, 1894, Bayard remarked: "I see . . . Mr. Dolph, of Oregon (the same person into whose hands I misplaced, in confidence, the draught of a Chinese Treaty, and who then went back to the Senate and introduced a resolution reflecting upon my want of action on the subject) has introduced a resolution to denounce the Treaty of 1850 with Great Britain." *Bayard Press Copy Book,* vol. 1, *Bayard MS.*
147. *Cong. Rec.,* 50 Cong., 1 sess., vol. 19, pt. 9, p. 8601.

would actually "reconsider the humiliating and disgraceful vote by which the Chinese exclusion bill, in shocking disregard of every conventional and decent restraint, was rushed through." [148]

In a similar vein he wrote to W. L. Putnam:

The treatment of the Chinese question by Congress is most discreditable and mortifying. It has depressed and disgusted me greatly. The truth is that if our relations with foreign nations are to be subjected to such treatment as the Republican Senate have recommended, the United States will stand outside the pale of civilization and the comity of nations. [149]

After a motion to reconsider the vote on the Scott bill failed because of the lack of a quorum, Bayard wrote to President Cleveland with reference to the situation. He thought that the

. . . action of Congress in relation to China is humiliating, and if pursued as is proposed by the Pacific Coast Senators will bring disgrace upon Republican institutions. I observe that Mr. Payne, of Ohio, a member of the For. Rels. Committee voted against the reconsideration of the bill, and that Vest, Turpie, and Walthall also did. Can they not be induced to withhold their votes, if they feel bound to repeat them, if they vote at all? The record of our party on the subject is perfectly clear, and needs no such reckless action as the 'Scott bill' proposes. Perhaps if these gentlemen I have named knew that you had signed the exclusion bill for which they all voted a few days ago [the act of September 13], they would not feel bound *absolutely* to stultify their own record by voting for a totally inconsistent measure. [150]

On September 18 the chargé d'affaires of the Chinese Legation paid a visit to the Department of State to discuss the question of the immigration treaty and the attitude of Congress towards exclusion legislation. The conversation between Bayard and the chargé was set down in a memorandum written by Bayard himself:

They [the chargé d'affaires and his interpreter] were aware that the President had ten days within which to sign this bill [the Scott Act] and asked me if I would use my influence with the President to induce him not to sign it until he had given all the time he could of the ten days, because they

148. Bayard to John Russell Young, September 14, 1888, *Bayard Letter Book*, vol. 8, *Bayard MS.*

149. Bayard to W. L. Putnam, September 13, 1888, *ibid.* In a letter to Bayard, September 11, 1888, Putnam himself made the following comment: "It seems to me that Congress has become pretty thoroughly demoralized, especially over the Chinese question; and the sooner they get away, I should say the better for all concerned." W. L. Putnam to Bayard, September 11, 1888, *Bayard MS.*

150. Bayard to President Cleveland, September 15, 1888, *Bayard Letter Book*, vol. 8, *Bayard MS.*

believed that notification of the ratification would come within that time. . . .

I said that as far as I was personally concerned I did not approve of the present bill [the Scott Act] & that was well known, but that Congress was independent of the Executive, as they were aware, and that the matter was not wholly within his control. He (Mr. Shu) seemed very anxious that the President should not approve this act, but that he should delay his action as long as possible.[151]

On September 17 several members of the Tsung-li Yamen called at the American Legation in Peking and had a long conference with Denby about the immigration question. Denby opened the conference by sharply criticizing the Chinese Government for its failure promptly to ratify the treaty. He considered such conduct to be both "unjust and indefensible." The members of the Tsung-li Yamen replied that their Government had not refused to ratify the treaty: it was "simply considering the question." Denby then referred to the fact that news had been given to the outside world that the treaty had been rejected. Such action was without justification. The Chinese next complained that the legislation that had been passed by Congress would exclude "all Chinese laborers now in China who had certificates." Denby immediately drew their attention to the fact that "the express object of the treaty was to exclude absent laborers from returning." The American Government had been forced to adopt measures that abolished the disgraceful "frauds" connected with the sale, at Hong Kong, of these return certificates. In concluding this conference with the members of the Tsung-li Yamen, Denby frankly informed them that "the thing, the one thing and the only thing to do was to immediately ratify the new treaty." Their reaction to his sharp language he described in a despatch to Bayard: "They were so taken aback by the vigorous onslaught I had made on them . . . that they were in a quandary. The four members of the Yamen left in a demoralized condition." [152]

On September 19 Bayard sent a cablegram to Denby informing him that the Scott bill (providing for the total exclusion of all Chinese laborers from the United States) had been passed by Congress and awaited the President's signature.[153] Denby at once sent a note to the

151. *Memorandum* written by Bayard after a conversation with Mr. Shu, the Chinese chargé d'affaires, and his interpreter, September 18, 1888, *Bayard MS.*

152. Denby to Bayard, September 17, 1888, *China, Despatches,* vol. 83, MS Dept. of State.

153. Bayard to Denby, September 18, 1888, *China, Instructions,* vol. 4, MS Dept. of State.

Tsung-li Yamen in which he set forth the substance of the Bayard cablegram. It was apparent, he thought, that the situation was so "critical" that it could be saved only by an "immediate ratification" of the treaty by the Chinese Government.[154] In reply, the Tsung-li Yamen complained that the Scott bill had been passed by Congress before any action had been taken by the Chinese Government with reference to the treaty. They "certainly had no idea or expected such a thing." It seemed to them that all matters pertaining to treaties between sovereign states should be treated in a most "circumspect" manner. With special reference to the present situation the Chinese Government had to be "extra careful." Before giving their approval to the pending treaty the Tsung-li Yamen would first require that it be amended in certain particulars. These included a reduction of the twenty years limitation upon the immigration of Chinese laborers, and a recognition by the American Government of the right of Chinese laborers, once resident in the United States, to return if they owned any property in the United States.[155]

Denby regarded this reply as a "rejection of the treaty," [156] and he wrote to Bayard in a tone that indicated that he had lost all patience with the Chinese Government. He thought that China was the "last country in the world to complain of exclusion. She excluded all the world from the earliest times. She excludes laborers today by forbidding foreigners to engage in manufacturing in her borders." It was obvious that the new propositions from the Chinese Government would involve fresh negotiations.[157]

These acrid comments of Denby did not reach the Department of State until November 2. In order that Bayard would have some immediate reply to his inquiry of September 19, Denby sent a telegram which reached Washington on the morning of September 21. It was terse and to the point: "Ratification refused unless twenty years' limitation be discussed with a view to shortening. Laborers now abroad owning thousand dollars to return. Provision to be made for laborers now abroad owning less." [158]

---

154. Denby to the Tsung-li Yamen, September 19, 1888, enclosed in Denby to Bayard, September 20, 1888, *China, Despatches,* vol. 83, MS Dept. of State.
155. Tsung-li Yamen to Denby, September 20, 1888, enclosed in Denby to Bayard, September 21, 1888, *China, Despatches,* vol. 83, MS Dept. of State.
156. Denby to the Tsung-li Yamen, September 21, 1888, *ibid.*
157. Denby to Bayard, September 20, 21, 1888, *ibid.*
158. Denby to Bayard, September 21, 1888, *Bayard MS.*

In the meantime, Bayard had made repeated efforts to convince the President that it was unwise for him to sign the Scott bill. It would be far better first to denounce the treaty of 1880, and then proceed to legislate against Chinese immigration. This viewpoint was cogently developed in a memorandum that Bayard prepared for the President on September 18, 1888. He "respectfully and earnestly recommended" that the Scott bill "be returned to the House in which it originated without your approval and accompanied by a statement of your reasons for withholding your approval of the same." These reasons would include the following items: (1) The Scott bill was in "manifest violation of an existing Convention with China"; (2) the Scott bill had not been "passed in accordance with that orderly and deliberate procedure on the part of either House of Congress which the respective rules of the Senate and House of Representatives prescribe"; (3) that the decorum "essential to international proceedings is seriously violated by the enactment, by one of the High Contracting Parties to a Treaty, of a statute clearly inconsistent with the stipulations of a pending convention." It was evident that "international courtesy, good faith, and self-respect" demanded the "disapproval" of the Scott bill.[159]

This advice to President Cleveland fell upon deaf ears. Political considerations bulked largely in his mind, and that is why he had the Scott bill introduced in the House of Representatives without informing Bayard of his intention. This dubious action on the part of the

159. Bayard to President Cleveland, September 18, 1888, *Bayard MS.* Mr. H. W. Pitkin had a similar opinion of the Scott bill. In a letter to Bayard, September 19, 1888, he remarks: "As an Independent I have been fully satisfied with his [Cleveland's] administration and so have all the Independents so far as I have conversed with them. And we shall be reinforced by thousands if he has courage to veto the insane, infamous bill just passed restricting Chinese emigration. . . . If President Cleveland goes back on his record for doing what is right rather than what is expedient, he certainly will impair the confidence of the men whose good opinion he values. I have spent 6 months of the present year in California & Colorado & conversed with hundreds of the best thinking men and I assure you there is a strong reaction setting in there on this question." *Bayard MS.* On September 19, John W. Foster called at the Department of State and had a conversation with John Bassett Moore on the question of Chinese immigration. He declared that "it was not true that the Chinese Government had rejected the treaty and he hoped it would yet be ratified. But opposition had been made to its ratification, which had been postponed. That opposition had come from two quarters. First, from British merchants at Hong Kong engaged in the business of transporting Chinese laborers to the United States, directly and indirectly. Second, and perhaps most effectively, from Canton, where the Chinese merchants, acting in the interest of their Chinese correspondents in San Francisco, had prevailed upon the Governor of the province to send a remonstrance to the Throne against the exchange of ratifications. Notwithstanding these adverse influences, Mr. Foster said he hoped the treaty would yet be ratified." *Memorandum* written by John Bassett Moore after a conversation with John W. Foster, September 19, 1888, *Bayard MS.*

President was a matter of common knowledge in Washington political circles. In the New York *World,* September 6, 1888, there was an interesting article which gave an insight into the situation. According to this article the Scott bill was the work of the White House "kitchen cabinet." Mr. Scott "brought that bill from the White House" to Congress, and secured its immediate passage. Bayard was "out of town and had not been consulted concerning this important action. The first information that he could have received on the subject was from the morning papers." When Mr. Scott introduced the bill in the House of Representatives it "was generally reported . . . that it was an Administration measure and that the bill was written upon Administration paper." The chief purpose of the President and Mr. Scott was to "create popularity on the Pacific Coast" for the Democratic Party. That was the real "meaning of the bill of yesterday. It was this which galloped it through the House without debate or consideration." [160]

There was a large measure of truth in this New York *World* article. It is evident that President Cleveland took action on the matter of the pending Chinese treaty without consulting Bayard.[161] He realized that Bayard would have opposed legislation like the Scott bill, and for political reasons he was determined to make a strong appeal to the voters on the Pacific Coast even though his methods were open to serious question. His stand on this matter was made more palatable to Bayard when the Chinese Government took its unreasonable stand

160. New York *World,* September 6, 1888.

161. In a letter to President Cleveland, September 8, 1888, Bayard speaks of a conversation he had just had with the Chinese chargé d'affaires. The chargé was strongly opposed to the Scott bill and requested Bayard to use his influence to have the bill vetoed. In the last paragraph of his letter to the President, Bayard remarks: "I felt bound to tell him [the chargé] that I had no knowledge whatever of the intention to pass such a bill until it had been hurried through the House of Representatives." *Bayard Letter Book,* vol. 8, *Bayard MS.* With reference to the authorship of the Scott Act, the following comments of Judge John Bassett Moore are pertinent: "In order to understand Bayard's attitude toward the Scott Act, . . . it is necessary to go outside the record. I worked directly with Mr. Bayard in the Chinese matter and drafted some of the papers. The bill for the summary exclusion of the Chinese originated with the Democratic National Committee. The Department of State was not consulted about it. Although Dr. Francis Wharton, who was the Solicitor of the Department of State, was a Pennsylvanian, the matter was not mentioned to him. Those who devised the exclusion bill and those who voted in Congress for its passage were aided by the circumstance that the Chinese Government had asked for modifications of the draft treaty then pending, which would have gone far towards nullifying it. It was considerations such as these that led the President to give the measure his approval after it had passed the Congress. There was then a very substantial financial interest, belonging to what was popularly known as the Six Companies, in the sending of Chinese laborers to the United States, and the notoriety of this fact helped the cause of exclusion." J. B. Moore to C. C. Tansill, June 16, 1939.

with reference to new amendments to the pending treaty. These amendments would have required a reversal of American policy regarding Chinese immigration, and their adoption was unthinkable.

At the President's request, Bayard drafted a message for the President to send to Congress with reference to the Scott bill. In a letter accompanying this draft message, Bayard expressed his views on the situation:

> The status of our affairs with China is far from satisfactory, and I am not free from apprehension as to the results of the manner in which Congress has dealt with the subject. The amendment of the Treaty by the Senate is greatly to be deplored because it was not only useless but most injurious as setting an example of departure from a concluded agreement, of which the Chinese have been prompt to avail themselves. . . . The Chinese propositions are however unwarranted and if granted would leave the question in a worse condition than ever. I am compelled to regard their action as an indefinite prolongation of negotiations, and a subordination of their government to the control of parties interested in Labor Contracts.[162]

On October 1 President Cleveland approved the Scott bill and sent to Congress a special message justifying this action.[163] He thought that the experiment of "blending the social habits and mutual race idiosyncrasies of the Chinese laboring classes with those of the great body of the people of the United States has proved . . . to be in every sense unwise, impolitic, and injurious to both nations." After referring to the negotiations that had led up to the treaty of March 12, 1888, he remarked:

> No information of any definite action upon the treaty by the Chinese Government was received until the 21st ultimo—the day the bill which I have just approved was presented to me—when a telegram from our minister at Peking . . . announced the refusal of the Chinese Government to exchange ratifications of the treaty unless further discussion should be had with a view to shorten the period stipulated in the treaty for the exclusion of Chinese laborers and to change the conditions agreed on, which should

162. Bayard to President Cleveland, September 26, 1888, *Bayard Letter Book*, vol. 8, *Bayard MS.*

163. Bayard did not have any fears that the Chinese Government would suspend diplomatic relations because of the passage of the Scott Act. In a letter to Mrs. Denby, October 2, 1888, he frankly stated that he could not see any "just reason to apprehend that China will resent the passage of the law to which the President has just given his approval, at least in any such mode as would lead to Mr. Denby's return." *Bayard Letter Book*, vol. 9, *Bayard MS.* With reference to the attitude of Congress towards the Scott Act, Bayard wrote to John Russell Young, September 27, 1888, and remarked: "I shall send you something presently on this subject, for the Country *must* be aroused to the consequences of subjecting our international relations to the fires of miserable partisan needs and exigencies." *Bayard MS.*

entitle any Chinese laborer who might go back to China to return again to the United States. . . . I cannot but regard the expressed demand on the part of China for a re-examination and renewed discussion of the topics so completely covered by mutual treaty stipulations as an indefinite postponement and practical abandonment of the objects we have in view, to which the Government of China may justly be considered as pledged.[164]

A few days after President Cleveland signed the Scott bill, the chargé d'affaires of the Chinese Legation wrote to Bayard with reference to the admission of some Chinese laborers who had arrived at San Francisco with return permits.[165] In reply he was advised by Mr. Rives that the Scott Act included certain mandatory provisions which prohibited the landing of Chinese laborers at any American port after the date of the passage of the act. For the enlightenment of the chargé, Rives enclosed in his note a copy of the Scott Act.[166] Rives next informed the Chinese Minister that Congress had appropriated the sum of $276,619.75 in payment for losses sustained by Chinese citizens through mob violence.[167]

When the Chinese Minister paid a visit to the Department of State on November 16, Bayard inquired whether he wished to receive the indemnity payment. Chang Yen Hoon indicated that he had received no instructions from his government in that regard. He did know, however, that there was a "great deal of feeling and excitement in China" with reference to mob outrages in America. The general tenor of this conversation between Bayard and Chang Yen Hoon is revealed in the following excerpts from a memorandum written by Bayard:

He [Chang Yen Hoon] asked me to give him the history of the passage of the exclusion bill. I said I could not give him that because I did not know its actual history; that I had never seen or heard of the act until it had passed the House and gone to the Senate, and, therefore, the history of its passage was as open to him as to me. I showed the Minister the documents containing the President's various communications to Congress, and correspondence between himself and me about the Treaty. I informed him that when it was seen here that there was such a strong opposition to the treaty in China, and that the opposition of the British was understood to be so strong, and when it was discovered that the Treaty could not be confirmed

164. Message of October 1, 1888, James D. Richardson, *Messages and Papers of the Presidents*, vol. 8, pp. 630-635.
165. Shu Cheou Pou to Bayard, October 10, 1888, *Chinese Legation, Notes from*, vol. 2, MS Dept. of State.
166. G. L. Rives to Shu Cheou Pou, October 18, 1888, *Chinese Legation, Notes to*, vol. 1, MS Dept. of State.
167. Rives to Chang Yen Hoon, October 19, 1888, *Chinese Legation, Notes to*, vol. 1, MS Dept. of State.

in China without serious alterations and amendments, . . . that then Congress had apparently resolved to take the Chinese Government on their own terms, and to pass a law in accordance with the instructions that the Tsung-li Yamen had sent to Mr. Denby in January, 1887; . . . that I thought his efforts and views had been defeated in China, and my efforts and views had been largely defeated in the United States.

. . . He heard me throughout, and then his answer was interpreted to me:—he thought I was exactly right, and he agreed in all that I had said. . . . He was exceedingly friendly in demeanor. I told him I was very solicitous that the most perfectly clear understanding should exist between myself and him personally as to all either had intended. He assured me therefore no misunderstanding; that he had entire confidence in what I had said to him.[168]

Bayard's constant courtesy to the Chinese Minister was poorly repaid. Chang Yen Hoon never seemed to understand that impudence is not the usual language of diplomacy. In a note to Bayard (January 26, 1889) he made insinuations that could have resulted in his prompt dismissal. After an extended criticism of the Scott Act he remarked:

I must . . . remind you that in one of the interviews had with you during the negotiation of the unratified treaty, you gave me the assurance that his excellency, the President, would veto any legislation of Congress which violated the existing treaty. I therefore, feel persuaded that in view of the provisions of Article IV . . . I may rely upon your kind interposition with his excellency, the President, with a view to having him recommend to Congress to undo the wrong and hardship which is being inflicted upon my countrymen by the act of October 1.[169]

Bayard's reply was marked by that note of courtesy so characteristic of all his communications. He assumed that the Chinese Minister was laboring under a "misapprehension" of the situation. As Secretary of State he could not have given the alleged assurance referred to by the Minister. It was probable that the misapprehension on the part of the Minister arose from the fact that all conversation between them had passed through an interpreter:

I can only suppose that owing to the indirect nature of our communication through an interpreter you may have misunderstood and mistaken some general and natural expression of a desire and intention of the President to live up to the obligations of treaties; for the statement that he would veto some bill not at that time in existence in case it should be found to contain

168. *Memorandum* written by Bayard after a conversation with the Chinese Minister, November 16, 1888, *Bayard MS.*

169. Chang Yen Hoon to Bayard, January 26, 1889, *Chinese Legation, Notes from,* vol. 2, MS Dept. of State.

anything in contravention of a certain treaty would have been without application, and would scarcely have been intelligible.[170]

Despite the discourteous note he had received from the Chinese Minister, Bayard remained friendly in his attitude towards China, and he deplored the fact that the treaty had not been ratified. His attitude is revealed in a letter he wrote to Denby:

As for our relations with China, I am not so well content because the "Scott law" was a most discreditable action by the Congress, and yet it hardly lies with China to find fault with it. The treaty as signed by the Minister . . . was *their* treaty, made clearly under full powers and after long and full deliberation. The amendments of the Senate did not materially alter its results, as the Minister admitted, but the amendments opened a loophole of escape from the bargain which the Foreign Office took advantage of.

But as it *now* stands, if China should yet ratify the treaty, and send it back and propose to exchange ratifications, it might be agreed to, and if this were done the "Scott law" would be over-ridden by the Treaty of a later date. Therefore I am disposed to wish China would adopt such a course, because it would relieve the situation immensely, and I should feel that a certain stigma was removed from the action of my country.[171]

Bayard's friendly feelings towards China must have been somewhat ruffled when he received on February 26 a long and contentious note from the Chinese Minister. Once more we have a direct reference to Bayard's alleged promise of a Presidential veto in the event that Congress passed any legislation inconsistent with the treaty of 1880. In his note of February 2 Bayard had carefully explained the whole situation and had intimated that the "misapprehension" of the Chinese Minister arose from the fact that the Minister could carry on a conversation only through the agency of an interpreter. In his note of February 25 Chang Yen Hoon did not readily accept this explanation of the difficulties that had arisen. While he did not desire

. . . in the slightest degree to question the sincerity of the disavowal made in your [Bayard's] note of the 2d instant, I think it due to myself that I should state the circumstances under which I received the impression that

170. Bayard to Chang Yen Hoon, February 2, 1889, *Chinese Legation, Notes to*, vol. 1, MS Dept. of State. In order to clear up this misunderstanding with reference to an alleged assurance that President Cleveland would veto any bill in contravention of the treaty of 1880, Bayard enclosed in his note to the Chinese Minister a copy of a memorandum of an interview he had with the Chinese chargé d'affaires, September 18, 1888. He could also have included the memorandum which he made of the conversation he had with the Chinese Minister himself, February 29, 1888. This document was in strong support of Bayard's contention. See *Bayard MS*.

171. Bayard to Denby, February 21, 1889, *Bayard Letter Book*, vol. 10, *Bayard MS*.

the statement of the President's intention cited in my note of the 26th ultimo was made by you. . . : The words used by you in that interview were uttered in the hearing of the three persons named, and were at the time interpreted to me by Mr. Leang. On the same day the interview occurred a memorandum of it was made in writing by Mr. Leang, and on the following morning it was by him read to Messrs. Shu and Bartlett, in order that its correctness might be verified. . . .

I well remember that your statement of the President's intention to veto any act which violated the treaty, as interpreted to me, had a marked influence in inducing me to agree upon the treaty which we soon afterwards signed. While I did not understand you to make it as a promise which you pledged yourself to see fulfilled, I did understand that if we entered into a conventional arrangement upon the subjects then being discussed in Congress, the President would prevent by his veto any contravening act of Congress becoming a law while the treaty was awaiting ratification.[172]

Bayard's term as Secretary of State was fast drawing to a close and he had no desire to enter into a last-minute dispute with the Chinese Minister. He had anxiously striven to remove all major causes of difference between China and the United States, and he had constantly sought to conciliate a nation whose decline as a world power had made it unduly sensitive. In his last note to Chang Yen Hoon he studiously refrained from using the sharp language of reproof which the Chinese Minister's insinuations might easily have provoked. After remarking that he was not disposed to question the "accuracy of the recollection" of Chang Yen Hoon and the gentlemen of his suite, Bayard then went ahead in forthright fashion to give his version of what had happened. Both he and the President had ardently wished to prevent any "breach of treaty engagements," but their efforts had been seriously handicapped by the news that came through British sources that the Chinese Government had rejected the treaty. This news "gave impetus" to the popular belief that certain "influences" had encompassed its defeat. Under this "condition of affairs," an exclusion bill, known as the "Scott bill," was suddenly and without notice brought forward in Congress and "passed with an unanimity in both houses which palpably rendered an interposition by a veto of the Executive wholly futile."[173]

With this explanation, given in good temper and with unquestionable sincerity, Bayard concluded a long and wearisome chapter in

---

172. Chang Yen Hoon to Bayard, February 25, 1889, *Chinese Legation, Notes from,* vol. 2, MS Dept. of State.

173. Bayard to Chang Yen Hoon, February 28, 1889, *Chinese Legation, Notes to,* vol. 1, MS Dept. of State.

American diplomacy in the Orient. The defeat of his efforts to effect an arrangement with China he blamed upon the American Senate rather than upon the Chinese Government. In a letter to W. R. Wright he indicated where he thought the real responsibility lay:

Why the Republican Senate has prevented me from settling several very difficult questions (notably the Canadian Fisheries and the Chinese) is hard to decide. As a result of their obstruction there are serious difficulties in view, all of which I was prepared to adjust and remove. Time will set right much hasty injustice and I must bide my time.[174]

174. Bayard to W. Rodmond Wright, February 8, 1889, *Bayard Letter Book,* vol. 10, *Bayard MS.*

The Fisheries Question

CHAPTER SIX

An Old Problem
Clamors for a New Settlement —
The Fisheries Question

————••◦••————

THE SERIOUS DIFFICULTIES THAT BAYARD HAD TO FACE IN DEALING WITH
the question of Chinese immigration, were a clear indication of the
influence of sectionalism in shaping American foreign policy. But this
feeling of sectionalism was not confined to the Pacific Coast. In his treatment of the problems arising out of the fisheries question, Bayard soon
discovered that Massachusetts was just as local in its outlook as was
California. Loyalties are often regional rather than national.

The "Fisheries Question" is the story of a long and bitter struggle
on the part of the fishermen of New England to preserve certain rights
which they had acquired through age-old visits to the fishing grounds
off the coasts of Canada and the adjacent islands. These fishing grounds
were very extensive. They included the broad reaches of the Gulf of
Saint Lawrence, the more restricted area of the Bay of Fundy, the coast
of Labrador, and the offshore banks of Newfoundland and Nova
Scotia.[1]

Since early colonial days, Yankee fishermen had braved the perils of
storm, fog, and intense cold to collect the cargoes that brought rich
returns from ports in Southern Europe and in the Spanish Main. Any
move to limit their rights to fish in these northern waters, or any serious

1. There are two monumental studies on the general subject of the North Atlantic
fisheries. First, we have the classic study by Lorenzo Sabine, *Report on the Principal Fisheries of the American Seas* (Washington, 1853). The other standard work on the fisheries
question is the co-operative monograph prepared under the direction of the Commissioner
of Fisheries and the Superintendent of the Tenth Census: *The Fisheries and Fishery Industries of the United States* (Washington, 1884–1887). This government report fills seven
volumes which review every aspect of the fisheries of New England. There is a good
survey of the fisheries question in the volume by Professor Raymond McFarland. *A History
of the New England Fisheries* (N. Y. 1911).

attempt to curtail their liberties to use the inshore fisheries, was bound to meet with instant and vehement protest.

The brush of Winslow Homer and the pen of Rudyard Kipling have cast the soft glow of romance over the lives of these hardy seamen who have been given the glib title of "Captains Courageous." But this romantic glamor soon fades when one considers the stark realism of their troubled lives. Long hours of grinding toil, with grave danger as a constant companion, was the usual lot of these fishermen. Some merchant owners and some skippers earned tidy fortunes from this perilous calling, but the majority of those who followed the sea gained only a scanty substance from their efforts.[2]

The American Revolution wrought severe damage to the fishing industry of New England, and it required the adoption of a generous policy by Congress, in 1789, to restore the relative prosperity of colonial days. The bounty system and the development of new fishing grounds helped to revive the fallen fortunes of the hard-pressed fishermen. A third factor that served a useful purpose was the successful diplomacy of John Adams in the treaty negotiations of 1782–1783. According to Article III of the definitive Treaty of Peace that concluded the American Revolution, the people of the United States were to continue to enjoy the right to "take Fish of every kind on the Grand Bank and on all the other Banks of New-foundland, also in the Gulph of St. Lawrence, and at all other Places in the Sea where the Inhabitants of both Countries used at any time heretofore to fish." It was further provided that American fishermen should also have the *liberty* to "take Fish of

2. In the comprehensive and scholarly monograph by George Brown Goode, *The Fisheries and Fishery Industries of the United States* (Washington, 1887), *Section IV*, pp. 9, 11, 95-96, there are the following iluminating comments upon living conditions among the fishermen of New England: "Prior to 1840 almost all the fishing vessels of New England were owned in large part by the fishermen themselves. In 1850, in large ports, like Gloucester, Portland, and Provincetown, the control of the vessels passed to a great extent into the hands of capitalists, or owners, as they are called. . . . At present the majority of the vessels engaged in the Grand Bank and cod fishery, hailing from Provincetown, Plymouth, Beverley, and the ports of Maine, as well as many of those from Gloucester, are manned chiefly by fishermen who are hired by the trip or paid monthly wages. In all the other fisheries, the crew, as a rule, 'go upon shares.' . . . The statistics of the Gloucester fisheries for 1879 show that the average earnings of each fisherman amounted to $175. . . . A capable fisherman, with ordinary success, engaged in fishing at all seasons of the year, should make at least from $300 to $500. It is probable that the fishermen of those New England ports which do not engage in the winter fisheries do not, as a rule, make more than half as much." According to a report from Marblehead in 1834, the fishermen of that port were "always poor." In 1879 the Maine fishermen "did not realize $100 apiece." See also Samuel E. Morison, *The Maritime History of Massachusetts, 1783-1860* (Boston, 1921), pp. 139-143, 311.

every Kind on such part of the Coast of New-foundland as British Fishermen shall use, . . . and also on the Coasts Bays & Creeks of all other of his Britannic Majesty's Dominions in America, and that the American Fishermen shall have Liberty to dry and cure Fish in any of the unsettled Bays Harbours and Creeks of Nova Scotia, Magdalen Islands, and Labrador." [3]

Thanks to these generous terms, American fishermen returned to their old haunts off the coasts of Newfoundland and Nova Scotia, and some of the more venturesome began to frequent the Bay of Chaleur and the Labrador coast. By 1808 three-quarters of the dried fish exported from Massachusetts came from these newly visited regions. British observers began to take alarm at these incursions of Yankee fishermen who "swarmed like flies" in the Gulf of St. Lawrence.[4] But their fears of an undue expansion of the New England fishing industry were soon quieted by the outbreak of the War of 1812. Shortly after its close the British Government insisted upon certain restrictions that seriously curtailed the activities of American fishermen in Canadian waters.[5]

In 1816 several American vessels in the Bay of Fundy were seized by British cruisers and sent to Newfoundland, and in the following year one British sloop of war attracted attention by sending to Halifax twenty American vessels that were fishing along the coast of Nova Scotia.[6] Further seizures brought increased friction, and it was evident to the American Government that some adjustment of the fisheries question would have to be made at once.

In the negotiations leading up to the treaty of October 20, 1818, the British Government held to the view that had been expressed by the British delegation at Ghent in 1814—"all treaties are put an end to by a subsequent war between the same parties." According to Lord Bathurst, the Treaty of Peace of September 3, 1783

. . . contained provisions of different characters—some in their own nature irrevocable, and others of a temporary nature. . . . The nature of the

---

3. Treaty between the United States and Great Britain, September 3, 1783. Hunter Miller, *Treaties and Other International Acts of the United States of America* (Washington, 1931), vol. 2, pp. 153-154.
4. John Quincy Adams, *Duplicate Letters, the Fisheries and the Mississippi,* (Washington, 1822), pp. 210-213.
5. From 1814 to 1817 the tonnage employed by American fishermen in their trips to the Gulf of St. Lawrence and the Labrador coast rose from 17,855 tons to 64,807 tons. See Raymond McFarland, *A History of the New England Fisheries,* p. 156.
6. *Niles' Weekly Register,* vol. 12, p. 299.

liberty to fish within British limits, or to use British territory, is essentially different from the right to independence. . . . In the third article, **Great Britain** acknowledges the *right* of the United States to take fish on the Banks of Newfoundland and other places, . . . but they are to have the *liberty* to cure and dry them in certain unsettled places within His Majesty's territory. If these liberties . . . were to be as perpetual and indefeasible as the rights previously recognized, it is difficult to conceive that the plenipotentiaries of the United States would have admitted a variation of language so adapted to produce a different impression.[7]

This viewpoint of Lord Bathurst was sharply assailed by John Quincy Adams. It was his opinion that under the terms of the third article of the treaty of 1783

. . . it was agreed that the people of the United States should *continue* to enjoy the fisheries of Newfoundland and the Bay of Saint Lawrence, and at all other places in the sea where the inhabitants of both countries *used at any time theretofore to fish;* and also that they should have certain fishing liberties on all the fishing coast within the British jurisdiction of Nova Scotia, Magdalen Islands, and Labrador. The title by which the United States held those fishing rights and liberties was the same. It was the possessory use of the right . . . at any time theretofore, as British subjects, and the acknowledgment by Great Britain of its *continuance* in the people of the United States after the treaty of separation. It was a national right, and . . . the right or liberty to . . . exercise this trade could no more be affected or impaired by a declaration of war than the right to the territory of the nation. . . . The fishery liberties could be lost only by express renunciation of them in the treaty.[8]

The British Government refused to adopt the reasoning of Mr. Adams, and in the first article of the Treaty of 1818 the American negotiators agreed to an abdication of the liberties formerly enjoyed by American fishermen with reference to Canadian *inshore* fisheries. The right to take fish on the banks of Newfoundland, in the Gulf of Saint Lawrence and in the open sea was freely acknowledged, but the United States renounced forever the *liberty* to "take, dry, or cure fish on, or within three marine miles of the coasts, bays, creeks, or harbours of his Britannic Majesty's dominions in America" except in certain specified regions. These regions where Americans could still enjoy the liberty to take fish, were somewhat extensive. They included certain portions of the southern, western, and northern coasts of Newfoundland; the shores of the Magdalen Islands, and the coast of Labrador, eastwardly

---

7. Lord Bathurst to John Quincy Adams, October 30, 1815, *American State Papers, Foreign Relations,* vol. 4, pp. 354-356.
8. John Quincy Adams, *The Fisheries and the Mississippi,* pp. 96, 184-190.

and northwardly from Mount Joly. With reference to drying and curing fish, American fishermen were now limited to the unsettled bays, harbors, and creeks of the southern coast of Newfoundland from Cape Ray to the Rameau Islands, and to the coast of Labrador.[9]

The Treaty of 1818 did not put an end to controversies between Great Britain and the United States with reference to the fisheries. Many important questions remained unsettled. According to the treaty, American fishermen could not frequent the bays or harbors of his Britannic Majesty's dominions in America except for the purpose of "shelter and of repairing damages therein, of purchasing wood, and of obtaining water." Not only did this limitation prevent American fishermen from purchasing bait and other supplies in Canadian harbors, but it also precluded the landing and transshipment of fish from these harbors to other ports. Certain strained interpretations of international law added to the growing confusion. British officials contended that American fishermen could be excluded from *all bays* no matter how wide. They claimed the right to draw lines from headland to headland, and to forbid American vessels to come within three miles of this line. This would mean that not only were American vessels to be excluded from great arms of the sea like the Bay of Fundy and the Bay of Chaleur, but they would also be forbidden to enter all indentations of the coast, such as the north coast of Prince Edward Island from North Cape to East Cape, and the northeast coast of Cape Breton from North Cape to Cow Bay.[10]

In 1841 the Government of Nova Scotia submitted to the law officers of the Crown a series of questions which dealt with the right of American fishermen to navigate the Strait of Canso, to fish in the bays of Fundy and Chaleur, and to land on the coasts of the Magdalen Islands. As might have been expected, the Crown lawyers were in favor

9. Treaty of October 20, 1818. Hunter Miller, *op. cit.*, vol. 2, pp. 658-666. According to Professor Raymond McFarland, *A History of the New England Fisheries*, pp. 158-159, the important differences between the Treaty of 1783 and the Treaty of 1818 were first "that the Americans gave up the inshore fishing along certain parts of the coast, and secondly, that facilities for drying and curing fish were enlarged in favor of American fishermen."

10. John Bassett Moore, *A Digest of International Law*, vol. 1, (Washington, 1906), p. 783; Lorenzo Sabine, *Report on the Principal Fisheries of the American Seas*, pp. 398-476; Charles B. Elliott, *The United States and the Northeastern Fisheries* (Minneapolis, 1887), pp. 106-117; A. H. Marsh, "The Canadian Fisheries Question," *American Law Review*, May–June, 1887, vol. 21; Wallace Graham, "The Fisheries of British North America and the United States Fishermen," *Collections of the Nova Scotia Historical Society*, vol. 14, pp. 215ff.

of restricting in every possible way the operations of American fishermen. They were convinced that these fishermen had neither the right to pass through the Strait of Canso nor to land on the shores of the Magdalen Islands. They also inclined towards the view that the bays of Nova Scotia should be closed to these Yankee interlopers. In a labored justification of their opinion that a line of exclusion should be drawn from headland to headland across these Nova Scotian bays, they referred to the alleged use of the term "headland" in the Treaty of 1818. Inasmuch as this term *does not* appear in the Treaty of 1818 it is evident that the opinion of the Crown lawyers was of little value.[11]

The Nova Scotian authorities gave application to this opinion of the Crown lawyers by seizing on May 10, 1843, the American fishing schooner *Washington*. Captain Darby had anchored the *Washington* in the Bay of Fundy, some ten miles from the shore. She was carried to Yarmouth, Nova Scotia, where the judge of the vice-admiralty court decreed that the seizure was in accordance with the terms of the Treaty of 1818. The *Washington* and her stores were then ordered to be sold, and restitution was not made to the owner until many years later.[12]

There were other seizures of American vessels, and the Canadian Government made preparations to enforce even more effectively her interpretation of the Treaty of 1818. On June 21, 1851, the president of the executive council of Canada and the secretary of Nova Scotia signed an agreement to co-operate in protecting the fisheries from Yankee incursions.[13] Some months later the British Government announced its intention to station along the coasts of Nova Scotia and Prince Edward's Island "such a force of small sailing vessels and steamers as shall be deemed sufficient to prevent the infraction of the treaty [of 1818]."[14]

President Fillmore responded by ordering Commodore Matthew C.

11. Secretary Everett to J. R. Ingersoll, December 4, 1852, *Great Britain, Instructions*, vol. 16, MS Dept. of State. See also J. B. Moore, *Digest of International Law*, vol. 1, p. 785; Charles Isham, *The Fishery Question* (N. Y. 1887), pp. 51-53; Lorenzo Sabine, *Report on the Principal Fisheries of the American Seas, House Ex. Doc. 23*, 32 Cong., 2 sess., pp. 398-476.

12. John Bassett Moore, *History and Digest of the International Arbitrations to which the United States has been a Party* (Washington, 1896, 6 vols.), vol. 4, pp. 4342-4344. In this connection it is significant that the Bay of Fundy is a very large body of water—65 to 75 miles wide, and 130 to 140 miles long. See also, Professor Harold A. Innis, *The Cod Fisheries*, pp. 344-351. For pertinent documents see *Journals of the Assembly, Nova Scotia, 1837, Appendix 75; ibid., 1839, App. 9; ibid., 1841, App. 27; ibid., 1842, App. 75; ibid., 1844, App. 68; ibid., 1846, App. 11; ibid., 1847, App. 75; ibid., 1848, App. 89; ibid., 1852, App. 25.*

13. *Sen. Ex. Doc., 22,* 32 Cong., 2 sess., pp. 436-437.

14. *House Ex. Doc., 120,* 32 Cong., 1 sess., pp. 107-108.

Perry to proceed to the fishing grounds on the coast of the British possessions in North America for the purpose of "protecting the rights of American fishermen under the convention of the 20th of October, 1818." [15] On July 25, 1852, Daniel Webster, Secretary of State, made a speech in which he gave warning to the British Government that American fishermen would be protected "hook and line, and bob and sinker." [16]

It was high time for some peaceful adjustment of this serious controversy, and on June 5, 1854, the Treaty of Washington was signed. Article I of this treaty provided for the admission of American fishermen to the inshore fisheries of Canada, New Brunswick, Nova Scotia, and Prince Edward's Island. This concession was an extremely important one to the fishing industry of New England, and it promptly put an end to the friction which at times had led almost to open warfare.[17]

But this respite from difficulties with Canada over the fisheries question was shortlived. The Treaty of Washington went into effect on March 16, 1855, and was terminated by action of the American Government on March 17, 1866. The protectionist program in Canada whereby increased tariff charges were levied on American goods had given umbrage to American manufacturers. The fact that a large section of British public opinion had favored the cause of the South during the American Civil War gave further irritation to many Americans, and when agents of the Southern Confederacy used Canada as a base from which they launched raids against certain states of the Federal Union, indignation against Great Britain reached a high point. It was also true that after the close of the Civil War protectionist sentiment in the United States was strongly opposed to reciprocity with Canada, and the Treaty of Washington was denounced.[18]

Access to the inshore fisheries of Canada had not been as great a boon to American fishermen as had been anticipated, but after the termination of these liberties in March, 1866, the masters of many American vessels secured licenses from the Canadian Government in

15. *Ibid.*, p. 1.
16. *Sen. Ex. Doc.*, 22, 32 Cong., 2 sess., pp. 444-445.
17. Charles C. Tansill, *The Canadian Reciprocity Treaty of 1854* (Baltimore, 1922), pp. 39-53.
18. Wilfrid Bovey, "Confederate Agents in Canada during the American Civil War," *Canadian Historical Review*, vol. 2, March, 1921, pp. 46-57; Edward Porritt, *Sixty Years of Protection in Canada* (London, 1908), pp. 119-158; Donald C. Masters, *The Reciprocity Treaty of 1854* (N. Y. 1936), pp. 113-173; Lester B. Shippee, *Canadian-American Relations, 1849–1874* (New Haven, 1939), pp. 159-179.

order to continue their fishing operations within the three-mile limit.[19] In 1870 this system of licenses was discontinued by the Dominion Parliament, and American vessels were seized when they entered Canadian harbors for the purpose of purchasing bait.[20] The British Government decided to send a naval contingent to co-operate with the Canadian fleet which was enforcing the provisions of the Treaty of 1818, but the instructions to the British naval unit were conciliatory in tone. Despite this friendly gesture, Secretary Fish was fearful of serious friction with Great Britain over the question of fisheries. When he warned President Grant that the Dominion Government was preparing to exclude American vessels from Canadian bays, the Chief Executive burst out wrathfully: "I will not permit that." [21]

It was apparent to Secretary Fish that some move would have to be made at once to settle all the points at issue between the United States and Great Britain. He found the British Foreign Secretary equally anxious to put an end to the many disputes that were endangering Anglo-American amity, and on May 8, 1871, the well-known Treaty of Washington was signed. Article eighteen restored to American fishermen, for a period of ten years, the liberty to use the inshore fisheries of the provinces of Quebec, Nova Scotia, New Brunswick, and Prince Edward's Island.[22] Inasmuch as these privileges were supposed to be of greater value than those accorded to British subjects under the terms of Articles XIX and XXI, it was provided by Article XXII that commissioners should be appointed to determine the amount of compensation which ought to be paid to the British Government for the liberty to use the Canadian inshore fisheries.[23]

The exact sum that was to be paid for these inshore fishery liberties was left to the determination of a Fisheries Commission of three members; one to be named by the President of the United States, one by the

19. Edward Thornton to Secretary Seward, June 4, 9, 1868, *British Legation, Notes from*, vol. 87, MS Dept. of State; Harold A. Innis, *The Cod Fisheries*, pp. 352-354. See also, *Journals of the Assembly, Nova Scotia, 1866, App. 18.*
20. Ruth F. Grant, *The Canadian Atlantic Fishery* (Toronto, 1934), p. 116.
21. Allan Nevins, *Hamilton Fish* (N. Y., 1937), p. 416.
22. Article XIX admitted, for a period of ten years, British subjects to the inshore fisheries of the United States north of the thirty-ninth parallel of north latitude. Article XXI admitted into the United States free of duty, fish-oil and fish of all kinds (except fish taken from the inland waters) which were the "produce of the fisheries of . . . the Dominion of Canada, or of Prince Edward's Island."
23. William M. Malloy, *Treaties, Conventions*, etc., vol. 1, pp. 700-716. For a scholarly survey of the fisheries question from 1866 to 1877, see Lester B. Shippee, *Canadian-American Relations, 1849-1874*, chaps. xii, xiv-xix.

Queen of England, and the third member by the President and Queen conjointly. The chief difficulty about the personnel of this Commission was with reference to the selection of the third member who was supposed to be impartial in his attitude. Mr. Thornton, the British Minister to the United States, immediately suggested the appointment of M. Delfosse, the Belgian Minister at Washington. Secretary Fish opposed this selection because Delfosse had been "discourteous to the American Government." He also raised the point that Great Britain had guaranteed the neutrality of Belgium and this fact might influence the decision of Delfosse. But the British Government, with its usual tenacity, refused to meet Secretary Fish halfway in this matter of appointment, and Fish finally consented that Delfosse be made a member of the Commission.[24]

This British insistence upon the appointment of Delfosse bore the expected good fruit for the British Government. When the Fisheries Commission finally met in Halifax in 1877, it was decided by a vote of two to one (A. T. Galt, the British Commissioner, and M. Delfosse, the Belgian Commissioner, against E. H. Kellogg, the American Commissioner) that the United States should pay $5,500,000 in gold for the liberty to use the inshore fisheries for the period of twelve years (1873–1885).[25]

There is little doubt that the United States was forced to pay an unfair amount under the terms of this decision. During the ten year period, 1873 to 1882, the total catch of the American fishing fleet within the three-mile limit was only 78,827 barrels of mackerel valued at $598,429. For the twelve years that the treaty provisions were in force the United States, "paid about eight times as much for the privilege as our fishermen secured from it, besides remitting the duty, at one cent per pound, on millions of pounds of Canadian fish imported into the country."[26]

This unjust decision of the Halifax Commission aroused widespread indignation throughout the United States.[27] On March 3, 1883, Congress adopted a resolution which directed the President to give notice

24. Allan Nevins, *Hamilton Fish*, pp. 869-870. See also Secretary Fish to Sir Edward Thornton, August 21, 1873, *British Legation, Notes to*, vol. 16, MS Dept. of State.

25. *Documents and Proceedings of the Halifax Commission, 1847*, House Ex. Doc. 89, 45 Cong., 2 sess., 3 vols.; J. B. Moore, *History and Digest of International Arbitrations*, vol. 1, pp. 703-753.

26. Raymond McFarland, *A History of the New England Fisheries*, pp. 329-330.

27. James M. Callahan, *American Foreign Policy in Canadian Relations* (N. Y., 1937), pp. 362-363.

to the British Government of the termination of Articles XVIII to
XXV, inclusive, and also of Article XXX, of the Treaty of May 8, 1871.
The President carried out this direction, and on July 1, 1885, the
liberty granted to American fishermen to fish within the three-mile
limit along the Canadian coasts came to an end. American statesmen
recognized that the lapse of this concession would adversely affect the
fishing industry, but certain data that had been brought to light minimized the extent of these probable damages. In 1884 Henry Y. Hind,
the British Scientific Witness at the Halifax Fisheries Commission,
published a pamphlet entitled *Fraudulent Official Records of Government*. In this brochure the charge was made that the statistics printed
with the *British Case*, at the meetings of the Commission, were falsified.
He expressly stated that

. . . the Canadian statistics of fish trade with the United States were altered
and adjusted year after year to an enormous extent in favor of Canada, by
the collusion of Canadian officials with the Chief of the United States Bureau
of Statistics. . . . This kind of work was carried on during several years for
purely selfish objects and in the interest of a few individuals.[28]

Many Americans had suspected that the figures presented in the
British Case before the Halifax Commission had been padded, and this
pamphlet by Mr. Hind seemed strong proof that American fishermen
would not greatly suffer through the loss of the Canadian inshore fisheries. It seemed probable, however, that some friction would result
from the fact that these inshore liberties would expire during the middle of the fishing season. In order to avoid any difficulties, Lord Derby,
the British Colonial Secretary, wrote to Lord Lansdowne, the Governor-
General of Canada, on December 4, 1884, and requested a "definite
expression" of policy with reference to the fisheries question. Lansdowne replied that the Dominion Government did not think that it
would be

. . . consistent with the respect which it owes to itself to appear as a suitor
for concessions at the hands of the Government of the United States. It is,
moreover, certainly open to question whether, if negotiations on this subject
are to be approached at all, they will not be approached with a better prospect of success if they are commenced and conducted with the Government
which will assume office next spring rather than with that by which the
articles have been denounced. . . . In another respect . . . the action of
the United States Government is no doubt likely to have inconvenient and

28. J. B. Moore, *History and Digest of International Arbitrations*, vol. 1, pp. 739-740.
There is a copy of this pamphlet in the Library of Congress.

perhaps embarrassing results. . . . The fishery clauses will cease to operate on the 1st of July, 1885. At that time vessels belonging to the United States will be engaged in fishing in Canadian waters. These vessels will have been equipped and fitted out for the season's fishing. . . . If these vessels . . . were either captured for trespass or compelled on pain of seizure to desist from fishing in Canadian waters, considerable loss would be occasioned to the owners and much ill feeling created between the two countries. The Government of the Dominion has no desire to be instrumental in producing such a state of things and I am able to inform your Lordship that should such a course be acceptable to the Government of the United States we shall be prepared to agree to an extension of the operation of the clauses in regard both to "free fishing" and "free fish" until the 1st of January, 1886.[29]

Sackville-West, the British Minister at Washington, discussed with Secretary Frelinghuysen this matter of an extension of the operation of the "free fishing" and "free fish" clauses of the Treaty of Washington until January 1, 1886. After consultation with certain Senators, Frelinghuysen informed Sackville-West that such a suggestion was "impracticable," and a Presidential proclamation was issued on January 31, 1885, warning American fishermen of the approaching expiration of specified articles in the Treaty of Washington.[30] The fisheries question was in this unsettled and unsatisfactory state when Bayard assumed office on March 6, 1885.

On March 12 Sackville-West left with Bayard a memorandum which outlined a proposition very similar to the one he had made to Secretary Frelinghuysen. Once again he inquired whether it would be possible to extend until January 1, 1886, the operation of the treaty clauses dealing with the inshore fisheries and with the admission of Canadian fish into American ports free of duty.[31]

Bayard turned this Sackville-West memorandum over to Alvey A. Adee, who expressed the opinion that the arrangement proposed by the British Minister could not be effected without new legislative action. It implied that the British-American legislation to execute the treaty stipulations

. . . will continue unimpaired, as is naturally the case if that legislation continues with the Treaty and has not been repealed from a day certain by

29. Lord Lansdowne to the Earl of Derby, December 26, 1884, *John Macdonald Papers, Washington Treaty, 1888*, vol. 2, MS Canadian Archives, Ottawa.

30. Secretary Frelinghuysen to Senator Edmunds, January 15, 1885, *Domestic Letters,* vol. 153, MS Dept. of State; Secretary Frelinghuysen to Sackville-West, January 20, 1885, *Great Britain, Notes to,* vol. 19, MS Dept. of State.

31. *Memorandum* of Sackville-West, March 12, 1885, *British Legation, Notes from,* vol. 111, MS Dept. of State.

any subsequent legislative act. The reciprocal legislation of the United States is, however, positively repealed from and after July 1, 1885, and thereafter the British products are to be treated as though no treaty had ever existed; i.e., they again become dutiable. While the Executive (with the Senate, as treaty-making Power) is perfectly competent to continue any provisions of a denounced treaty which are self-executing, . . . it is not, I think, competent to continue such provisions when they depend upon Acts of Congress specifically repealed by Congress.[32]

On March 20, 1885, Bayard sent a short note to Sackville-West in which he apologized for the delay in answering the British Minister's communication of March 12. Such delay should not be attributed to "any want of interest in the highly important subject to which it relates."[33] A week later, Bayard had an interview with Sackville-West and frankly informed him that the American Government had "no power to extend the notice of the abrogation of the Fishing clauses of the Treaty of Washington from July 1, 1885 to January 1, 1886, although it would be very convenient if a little delay could be had."[34]

Bayard next wrote to Captain F. J. Babson, of Gloucester, Massachusetts, and invited him to come to Washington to discuss the question of the value to American fishermen of the Canadian inshore fisheries.[35] Bayard also had some conversations with Sir Ambrose Shea who represented the Government of Newfoundland.[36] After this careful canvass of the fisheries situation, Bayard handed to Sackville-West on April 22 a long memorandum which set forth the attitude of the American Government. Following the opinion expressed by Mr. Adee some weeks earlier, Bayard stated that the President, without new legislation by Congress, was not "constitutionally competent to extend the reciprocal fisheries provisions of the treaty beyond the 1st of July next, the date fixed by action of Congress." It had been suggested by the Province of Newfoundland, and the Dominion of Canada, that in view of the difficulties that would arise if American fishermen were suddenly denied the inshore fishing privileges, it would be expedient to continue those privileges until January 1, 1886. In return for this concession the Governments of Newfoundland and Canada expected the President to

32. *Memorandum* by Alvey A. Adee, March 17, 1885, *Bayard MS.*
33. Bayard to Sackville-West, March 20, 1885, *Bayard Letter Book*, vol. 1, *Bayard MS.*
34. *Memorandum* written by Bayard after a conversation with Sackville-West, March 27, 1885, *Bayard MS.*
35. Bayard to Captain F. J. Babson, April 10, 1885, *Bayard MS.*
36. Bayard to Sir Ambrose Shea, April 14, 1885, *ibid.* See also Bayard to Sackville-West, April 22, 1885, *British Legation, Notes to*, vol. 19, MS Dept. of State.

recommend to Congress the appointment of a commission which would endeavor to effect a settlement of the fisheries question upon an "equitable and honorable basis." President Cleveland was ready to adopt this suggestion upon the understanding that there would be no enforcement of penal laws and regulations against American fishermen who frequented the inshore fisheries.[37]

Sackville-West wrote at once to Lord Lansdowne, in Ottawa, and enclosed a copy of the Bayard memorandum.[38] In reply Landsdowne requested Sackville-West to convey to Bayard the assurance that his proposals would

. . . receive most careful consideration and that the Government of the Dominion is sincerely desirous of placing its relations with the Government of the United States . . . upon a footing advantageous and satisfactory to both and likely to avoid . . . all risk of misunderstanding and annoyance to the individuals concerned therein.[39]

Lord Lansdowne also wrote to the Earl of Derby and discussed the implications of the Bayard memorandum. While the friendly attitude of the American Government in the matter of fisheries was "fully appreciated" in Canada, it was

. . . impossible to exclude from consideration the fact that some hostile criticism is likely to be provoked by an arrangement under which, while persons connected with the fishery imposed duties on entrance into the United States, the same access as heretofore to Canadian waters would be enjoyed by the fishermen of the United States. Mr. Bayard's proposal is however framed in terms which leave no doubt as to the desire of his Government for an amicable understanding with that of the Dominion, and I venture to recommend that Mr. West should be authorized to continue . . . the negotiations.[40]

Lord Derby inquired whether the Dominion Government would concur in the memorandum submitted by Bayard

. . . on the understanding that the arrangement therein proposed is only of a temporary nature and would be assented to strictly on condition that it should not prejudice such equivalents as might be deemed fair to be required

37. *Memorandum* by Bayard, April 22, 1885, *British Legation, Notes to*, vol. 19, MS Dept of State.
38. Sackville-West to Lord Lansdowne, April 23, 1885, *John Macdonald Papers, Washington Treaty, 1888*, vol. 2, MS Canadian Archives.
39. Lord Lansdowne to Sackville-West, April 28, 1885, *John Macdonald Papers, Washington Treaty, 1888*, vol. 2, MS Canadian Archives.
40. Lord Lansdowne to Lord Derby, April 28, 1885, *ibid.*

in the course of negotiations for a more permanent settlement of the Fisheries question.[41]

Lansdowne's answer was unambiguous and affirmative. The Dominion Government was prepared to do "everything within its power" to discourage all friction between American fishermen and Canadian officials. It was entirely willing to agree to a temporary arrangement whereby the inshore fisheries would be granted to American fishermen, but it should be remembered that such a "one-sided" arrangement was bound to arouse some resentment in Canada. The main point which should be emphasized in this whole matter was the readiness of the Dominion Government to make concessions in order that a satisfactory adjustment of existing difficulties could be arrived at. The fact that certain Canadians derived a financial advantage from dealing with American fishermen who frequented Canadian waters, was of no significance whatever. In conclusion, Lansdowne called attention to the fact that there was no mention in the Bayard memorandum of an extension to Canadian fishermen of the liberty to fish in the "territorial waters of the United States." [42]

In America the fishing industry was exceedingly anxious that Canadian fish be subject to a tariff duty after July 1, 1885. On May 10 George Steele wrote to Bayard to express the hope that it would not be "necessary to recommend a continuance of the present policy of admitting Canadian fish free of duty," [43] and a warning was sent by Charles Levi Woodbury that "every fisherman along the shore from Block Island to Eastport" would oppose any postponement of tariff duties on Canadian fish.[44]

Bayard attempted to relieve the apprehensions of Mr. Woodbury by assuring him that there were no negotiations with England relative to admitting Canadian fish free of duty into American ports,[45] and Woodbury replied by stressing the importance of an agreement which would permit American fishermen to "enter colonial bays and ports to buy bait, & ice without seizure or molestation." He was fearful that the new Salisbury Ministry that had just come into power in England

41. Lord Derby to Lord Lansdowne, May 12, 1885, *ibid.*
42. Lord Lansdowne to Lord Derby, May 18, 1885, *John Macdonald Papers, Washington Treaty, 1888,* vol. 2, MS Canadian Archives.
43. George Steele to Bayard, May 10, 1885, *Bayard MS.*
44. Charles L. Woodbury to William C. Endicott, May 11, 1885, *Bayard MS.*
45. Bayard to Charles L. Woodbury, May 16, 1885, *Bayard MS.*

would stir up adverse sentiment in the colonies with reference to concessions to the United States.[46]

These fears of Mr. Woodbury relative to the hostility of the Salisbury Ministry had little foundation. In the summer of 1885 there was a most cordial feeling in most circles in England towards the United States. In a private letter to Bayard, E. J. Phelps, the new American Minister at London, was very voluble in his comments upon the many manifestations of friendship that were showered upon him. When he was received at Court the Queen was "very cordial" and the Prince of Wales was "equally so." The Princess of Wales, the Duchess of Edinburgh, and Lady Granville were courteous "in a marked degree." At the dinner given by the Lord Mayor of London, Phelps was given a "tumultuous" reception. There was no doubt in his mind that the Cleveland Administration was "very popular" in England, and he noticed that there was "much satisfaction" expressed at the selection of Bayard as Secretary of State.[47]

As an expression of this cordial feeling towards the United States, Lord Granville instructed Sackville-West (June 3, 1885) to accede to the temporary arrangement proposed by Secretary Bayard. In conducting negotiations to this end he was to follow "as closely as possible" the wishes of the Government of the Dominion of Canada.[48] In this atmosphere of friendly feelings, Bayard and Sackville-West soon came to an agreement which was recorded in an exchange of notes. It was expressly recognized that the arrangement giving American fishermen access to the Canadian inshore fisheries was "only temporary," and proceeded from the desire of both Governments to "avoid all difficulties which might otherwise arise from the termination of the fishing of 1885 in the midst of the season." Similar inshore fishing privileges were to be extended to British vessels engaged in fishing in the waters of the United States. President Cleveland was to recommend to Congress the appointment of a commission which would deal not only with the fisheries question but with the whole subject of "good neighborhood and intercourse."[49]

46. Charles L. Woodbury to Bayard, June 13, 1885, *ibid.*
47. E. J. Phelps to Bayard, *Private*, June 5, 1885, *ibid.*
48. Sackville-West to Lord Lansdowne, June 5, 1886, *John Macdonald Papers, Washington Treaty, 1888*, vol. 2, MS Canadian Archives.
49. Bayard to Sackville-West, June 19, 20, and 22, 1885; Sackville-West to Bayard, June 20, 22, 1885, *British Legation, Notes to*, vol. 20; *British Legation, Notes from*, vol. 112, MS Dept. of State.

Bayard was well pleased with this arrangement that he had negotiated with Sackville-West. In a letter to Phelps he remarked that he believed it would

. . . enable the fishing transactions in British American waters to be conducted without molestation throughout this season, and the President is to bring the matter before Congress in December and recommend the formation of a joint Commission to arrange some plan of permanent settlement. The agreement as made will lift a rather difficult question out of the reach of personal irritations and controversies, and save a number of our citizens from loss and annoyance. We can better approach the consideration of the subject next winter in an amiable frame of mind. Of course, there are growls, and in Canada much discontent among the set who would have preferred a row.[50]

This feeling of resentment in certain Canadian circles with reference to the fisheries agreement with the United States is well expressed in the following excerpt from a letter written by J. M. Vernon to Sir Charles Tupper:

When the fourth of March arrived without any action of Congress to extend the "Fishery Treaty" I was certain that, as usual, Yankee smartness had outwitted British diplomacy, and this will always occur whenever they get a chance. They have always got the best of England in Treaties and especially whenever Canada was interested. Mr. West and Sir John should have known better and demanded legislation upon the subject.[51]

The British Government was familiar with the criticisms that had been levelled against its policy of conciliation in this matter of the fisheres, and precautions were taken so that in the proposed conference with the United States the Governments of both Canada and Newfoundland should have their views clearly presented.[52] On August 24 Lord Lansdowne wrote a long letter to Sir John Macdonald in which he reviewed the situation with reference to negotiations with the United States. He agreed with Sir John that it would be unwise to "tie

50. Bayard to Phelps, *Private*, June 27, 1885, *Bayard MS.* In another *private* letter to Phelps, July 1, 1885, Bayard again remarks: "By this mail copies of the agreement in relation to the Fisheries will go to you, and I think you will heartily approve it, for it keeps the question in an atmosphere of amity and may save those personal collisions that so often beget national irritation. I am sure English statesmen of both parties will appreciate the feeling which leads this Administration (the State Dept.) to avoid the addition of any new anxieties or embarrassments to those which now surround their government. . . . In Canada some sputterings of discontent are heard, and were to be expected; in the U. S. the satisfaction seems general." *Bayard MS.*

51. J. M. Vernon to Sir Charles Tupper, July 24, 1885, *John Macdonald Papers, Washington Treaty, 1888,* vol. 2, MS Canadian Archives.

52. Julian Pauncefote to the Undersecretary of State, Colonial Office, July 18, 1855, *ibid.*

too directly" the hands of the Canadian representatives upon the proposed commission. He also thought that the British Foreign Office was not acting judiciously in pressing the Dominion Government to "define too precisely the objects with which we shall enter upon the negotiations." It was true, however, that the language of the notes exchanged between Bayard and Sackville-West was so vague that it would be worth while to give to the

. . . Imperial Government a general idea of the direction in which we should like to move. We can at any rate hardly answer Col. Stanley's enquiry by replying that we decline altogether to describe beforehand the kind of bargain we should like to make. The following appear to me to be some of the points in regard to which a general definition of our position might be attempted: As to the Fisheries—1. Do we desire a renewal in substance of the abrogated articles of the Washington Treaty? 2. If so, do we propose a recurrence to arbitration in order to ascertain the value of the concessions made on each side, or shall we be content to admit the Americans to our waters without going into the question of their value? . . . 3. Shall we propose . . . that the "bays" question be disposed of by the commission itself or by arbitration?

As to commercial relations generally, what kind of reciprocity should we desire to see established? Should it be limited to raw materials such as coal and lumber? . . . With regard to Newfoundland, I should be glad to know what you think of the suggestion implied in Col. Stanley's letter that we should agree with the Government of that island upon a common policy.[53]

Macdonald's answer was quite detailed. He believed that it would be advisable to ask for a renewal of the abrogated articles of the Washington Treaty. It was also important to have these treaty provisions extend not only to "free fish and fish-oil" but also to "whale- and seal-oil." An effort should be made to get the Canadian Pacific Coast

. . . marine products included in the Treaty. In 1871 British Columbia was not a portion of the Dominion and did not share in the advantages conferred on Canada by the Treaty. . . . It will be necessary for us to consider whether we cannot use the Fisheries (inshore) of the Hudson and James' Bays and straits as a lever. I believe the American whalers visit these regions to a considerable extent and may be obliged to use our shores and shallow waters for fresh bait, etc. As to the second question, we must ask for a recurrence to arbitration in order to ascertain the value of the concessions made on each side. If the Treaty takes a wider range than Fish and Fisheries, it will be quite open to us to throw our fisheries *in*, in case of a reciprocity treaty being agreed to embracing other articles of commerce.

The question as to Bays will not arise if we have a new Fishery Treaty.

53. Lansdowne to Sir John Macdonald, August 24, 1885, *John Macdonald Papers, Washington Treaty, 1888*, vol. 2, MS Canadian Archives.

If that fails, there will be a mutual exclusion of foreign fishing vessels and the question becomes of importance. It should be settled I think by arbitration. . . . As to general commercial relations, Canada would be satisfied with the terms of the Reciprocity Treaty of 1854, with perhaps some extensions. A Treaty affecting manufactures would not be entertained by the United States, nor I think by England.[54]

Lord Lansdowne was deeply impressed with this letter from Macdonald, and in his note to Lord Stanley, at the Colonial Office, he incorporated most of the suggestions that Sir John had offered. In the event that no understanding could be reached on the fisheries question, the Dominion Government "would probably be prepared to agree that this question should form the subject of arbitration by a neutral power."[55]

From all appearances it seemed as though the chief difficulties in Canadian-American relations would soon be settled to the satisfaction of everyone concerned. In England the most cordial feelings towards the United States were constantly manifested. Shortly after the Salisbury Government assumed office, Sir Stafford H. Northcote (later Lord Iddesleigh) wrote to Bayard in a very friendly vein,[56] and on August 4, he sent a second letter to Bayard in which he commented upon the "strongly marked kindness of feeling exhibited between English and Americans."[57] Phelps, at London, informed Bayard of the cordial attitude of most Britishers towards Americans,[58] and Sir Ambrose Shea gave assurances that the British Government was

. . . much pleased with what has been done as a temporary measure, and we all hope the reference to Congress will be fruitful of satisfactory results. It was fortunate I went to Canada after leaving Washington, for it led to the abandonment of the destructive policy that had been decided on, and on all sides the wisdom of the agreement is freely acknowledged.[59]

It now occurred to David A. Wells, an able American economist

54. Sir John Macdonald to Lansdowne, September 5, 1885, *ibid.*

55. Lansdowne to Colonel Stanley, September 11, 1885, *John Macdonald Papers, Washington Treaty, 1888,* vol. 2, MS Canadian Archives.

56. Sir Stafford H. Northcote to Bayard, June 11, 1885, *Bayard MS.* In a letter to Phelps, June 27, 1885, Bayard states that he had first met Northcote "in 1871 when he was here as the Tory member of the Joint High Commission *in re* the 'Alabama Claims,' and with him and the Marquis of Ripon I have had ever since occasional correspondence." *Bayard MS.* The Salisbury Ministry assumed office during the second week in June, 1885, and Sir Stafford H. Northcote (on July 6 he became Lord Iddesleigh) was given the sinecure office of First Lord of the Treasury.

57. Lord Iddesleigh to Bayard, August 4, 1885, *Bayard MS.*

58. Phelps to Bayard, August 6, 1885, *Private, ibid.*

59. Sir Ambrose Shea to Bayard, August 15, 1885, *ibid.*

and a close friend of Bayard, to visit Newfoundland and discuss with Sir Ambrose Shea the condition of affairs on that island. He found things in a "rather pitiful condition," and felt that American policy towards contiguous countries had been "mean and contemptible." [60]

Bayard had sympathy for these Newfoundlanders whose struggle for bare subsistence was a strenuous one,[61] but his first duty was to American fishermen whose own lot was not easy. There had been some efforts on the part of certain Canadian capitalists to cripple the American menhaden [62] fishery, and Francis Wharton had looked into the matter for Bayard. Wharton grew so angry after reading the correspondence in the Department of State that he expressed to Bayard the desire to "give the British lion a slap with one of our best Manhaydens." [63] Wharton also informed Bayard that in the matter of the award of the Halifax Commission the United States had been "scandalously outwitted." [64]

There was pressing need for a careful and impartial survey of all the varied aspects of the fisheries question, and President Cleveland, in accordance with the promises that Bayard had given to Sackville-West, included in his message to Congress (December 8, 1885) a recommendation for the appointment

> . . . of a commission in which the Governments of the United States and Great Britain shall be respectively represented, charged with the consideration and settlement, upon a just, equitable, and honorable basis, of the entire question of the fishing rights of the two Governments and their respective citizens on the coasts of the United States and British North America.[65]

The rejection by Congress of this recommendation of the Chief Executive led to a renewal of the fisheries dispute and to new friction in Canadian waters. Bayard soon realized that Republican leaders would not hesitate to gain partisan ends through the sacrifice of national interests. Political sabotage became an established practice, and foreign policy was forced to bear the brunt of an attack which drew its chief weapons from the arsenal of brazen mendacity.

60. David A. Wells to Bayard, August 27, 1885, *Bayard MS.* According to Wells the United States exported to Newfoundland each year goods worth some $3,000,000 but imported from that island goods to the value of only $300,000.
61. Bayard to D. A. Wells, August 29, 1885, *Bayard Letter Book,* vol. 1, *Bayard MS.*
62. The name "menhaden" is applied to a species of the herring family.
63. Francis Wharton to Bayard, October 10, 1885, *Bayard MS.*
64. Francis Wharton to Bayard, October 10, 1885, *ibid.*
65. James D. Richardson, *Messages and Papers of the Presidents,* vol. 8, p. 332.

Canada
Proves to be a Troublesome Neighbor

———••◦∞◦••———

THERE WAS LITTLE CHANCE THAT THE SENATE OF THE UNITED STATES, controlled by a safe Republican majority, would approve the recommendation of President Cleveland for a commission that would study and report upon the pressing problems of the fisheries and the establishment of commercial reciprocity with Canada. On December 11 Sackville-West had an interview with Bayard and inquired what action he intended "to take with Congress in order to secure the adoption of the President's recommendations." Bayard replied that a resolution would be introduced in either the Senate or the House of Representatives authorizing the President to appoint a commission. He could not forecast what action Congress would take with reference to this resolution, but he would do "all in his power to carry out the objects indicated in the [President's] message."

Bayard then indicated to Sackville-West the principal reasons that had led the President to approve the policy of a provisional arrangement with Canada. He was anxious not only to "maintain but to increase the existing friendly relations with the Government of the Dominion of Canada"; he believed that it was necessary for both countries to establish their commercial relations upon a "more satisfactory footing," and he thought it was obvious that Canada and the United States would derive mutual advantage from a system "based on the free interstate commerce of the [American] Union."[1]

This desire on the part of the Administration to push through some system of commercial reciprocity with Canada was bitterly opposed by the fishing industry which was willing to "put up with

1. Sackville-West to Lord Salisbury, December 11, 1885, *John Macdonald Papers, Washington Treaty, 1888,* MS Canadian Archives.

the inconveniences of the Treaty of 1818" if the duty on Canadian fish remained in force.[2] The New England press was soon filled with articles opposing any commercial arrangements with Canada, and Bayard was disgusted with all the "pother and rubbish" that was printed with reference to the policy of the Administration. In a letter to David A. Wells he comments upon the false stories that were circulating in New England newspapers, and he thanked Wells for an article in the Boston *Post* in which an attempt was made to picture the situation in its true light. He believed that the fishing industry was

. . . seeking to tax the rest of the country for its own sole advantage, and this mercenary struggle seems to take out of men's hearts all sense of truth, justice, and Christian brotherhood. . . . Stated broadly, the President and his Administration have no public press, and the stipendiaries of the Republican party and its Administrations have not yet given way to new hands. Misrepresentation, downright falsehoods, unjust and ungenerous assaults must be expected, and no efficient and present answer can be given. . . . The cabal in the Senate are thinking only how they can annoy the President and harass and belittle him and his Cabinet, and place him in a false light before the country. The People of this land have different interests and I wish they could speak and be heard.[3]

This Senate cabal, led by Senator William P. Frye, of Maine, was responsible for the introduction of a resolution (January 18, 1886) which opposed the appointment of the commission recommended by President Cleveland. There were certain precedents for this action,[4] but there is little doubt that the chief thought in the minds of many

2. Henry L. Nelson to Bayard, December 21, 1885, *Bayard MS.*

3. Bayard to David A. Wells, January 10, 1886, *Wells Papers*, Library of Congress. In a letter to William Dorsheimer, January 8, 1886, Bayard gave a careful explanation of the arrangement he had effected with Sackville-West in June, 1885, with reference to the fisheries: "By my agreement immunity was secured to our fishermen engaged in *British* waters, and no *actual* equivalent was extended to the British fishermen in American waters, because there was no fishing in American waters desired by the British fishermen. . . . What did the United States give or lose? Not one cent of duty and not one privilege of value. The promise of the President to recommend a Commission to consider and settle the whole controverted question of the Fisheries was all that was agreed to be given, and that was given in his message." *Bayard Letter Book*, vol. 2, *Bayard MS.*

4. President Grant, on June 18, 1874, requested the advice of the Senate with reference to a proposed reciprocity treaty with Canada. (Richardson, *Messages and Papers of the Presidents*, vol. 7, pp. 266-267.) The Senate advised against the negotiation of this treaty. (*Senate Executive Journal*, vol. 19, pp. 355-356, 502.) On June 9, 1884 President Arthur sought the advice of the Senate relative to extending for a period of seven years the existing reciprocity treaty with Hawaii. Once again the Senate indicated its opposition and the question was postponed. (*Sen. Ex. Jo.*, vol. 24, pp. 280, 355, 486.)

Republican Senators was to embarrass the Cleveland Administration. Senator Edmunds expressed the view that the action of Bayard in extending the provisions of the Treaty of Washington presented "a very grave question of the exertion of executive power." [5] Senator Frye was certain that the fishing industry did not need or desire any extension of the Treaty of Washington, and he believed that the matter had been brought about through British influence. It was a "most amazing performance," and he could not understand how it could be "justified." [6]

The significance of this fight against the President's policy was at once manifest to Sackville-West who wrote to Lord Salisbury and explained the situation:

The terms of the resolution [Senator Frye's] indicate the "animus" of the New England Senators against the policy of the present administration, and, it may almost be said, against coming to any amicable agreement with Her Majesty's Government. Their chief arguments were:—1. That the Secretary of State had no right to enter into the temporary agreement without the consent of the Senate. 2. That the fish had for some unexplained reason left Canadian waters and now resorted to American waters and that therefore American fishermen did not require the renewal of fishing privileges which had cost the country $5,500,000. . . . The resolution has without further debate been referred to the Committee on Foreign Relations. . . . The general sentiment is said to have been that the whole subject of the relations of the United States with Canada should receive the careful consideration of Congress.[7]

Some two weeks later, Sackville-West again wrote to Lord Salisbury about the opposition in the Senate to the President's policy concerning the fisheries. He was certain that the statements made by Senators Frye and Edmunds, relative to the indifference of the fishery industry to the extension of the Treaty of Washington, were untrue. He had been informed

. . . that the fish interest both in Boston and Chicago is almost unanimous in favor of the Commission, as well as of reciprocity. In view . . . of what seems to be the general opinion, I propose as soon as the Secretary of State is able to see me, to point out to him again that the fishing season will shortly open, that the temporary arrangement may be said to have ceased on the 1st of January and that the Provincial Government will undoubtedly

5. *Congressional Record*, January 18, 1886, 49 Cong., 1 sess., vol. 17, pt. 1, p. 702.
6. *Ibid.*, p. 703.
7. Sackville-West to Lord Salisbury, January 20, 1886, *John Macdonald Papers, Washington Treaty, 1888*, MS Canadian Archives.

revert to the stipulations of Article I of the Treaty of 1818, the enforcement of which he has repeatedly deprecated as likely to lead to serious difficulties.[8]

On February 19 Sackville-West had an interview with Bayard and embraced the opportunity to indicate to him that the fishing season would soon open and that the temporary arrangement affecting fishing liberties in Canadian waters had expired. Bayard regretted "the animus which had been shown by Congress against the policy of the President, . . . and inveighed bitterly against those who had thwarted it." Although the New England fishermen had been "the foremost to oppose any satisfactory settlement" of the fishery question, Bayard thought it would be expedient to avoid the friction that would inevitably follow any strict enforcement of the provisions of the Treaty of 1818. He also assured Sackville-West of his continued interest in effecting some sort of a commercial reciprocity agreement with Canada.[9]

In a long letter to Phelps, in London, Bayard gave a further outline of his views with regard to the fisheries. He deplored the fact that the

8. Sackville-West to Lord Salisbury, February 2, 1886, *John Macdonald Papers, Washington Treaty, 1888*, MS Canadian Archives.

9. Sackville-West to Lord Rosebery, February 19, 1886, *John Macdonald Papers, Washington Treaty, 1888*, MS Canadian Archives. It was the favorite charge of Republican Senators that Bayard had been outwitted by British and Canadian diplomats. In a despatch to Lord Lansdowne, February 11, 1886, Sackville-West includes a minute of a conversation he had had with Senator Allison on this very point. The minute will clearly indicate the tenor of Republican charges: "The Senator [Allison] commenced by saying that the Senate was considering the Fisheries Question and the President's recommendations for the appointment of a Commission. Mr. Bayard, he thought, in consenting to the temporary arrangement had been 'outwitted' by the Dominion Government and myself [Sackville-West], and by promising to insert the paragraph in the President's message had risked . . . a repetition of the proceedings which led to the Halifax award. 'We cannot with our existing system,' he said, 'contend with the skilled men which your diplomatic profession supplies for the treatment of such questions whenever they may arise, and it is better therefore for us to get along as best we can when they do arise without any definite arrangement which might compromise us.' I expressed my surprise to Mr. Allison that the Senate should entertain the idea which had been put forward by newspaper paragraphs for political purposes, that Mr. Bayard had been 'outwitted by the British Minister.' Congress . . . had precipitately denounced the fishery articles of the Treaty of Washington in the middle of the fishing season and there could be no question of 'outwitting' in endeavouring to avoid a precipitate return to the stipulations of Article I of the Treaty of 1818." *John Macdonald Papers, Washington Treaty, 1888*, MS Canadian Archives. In a letter to Sir John Macdonald, February 2, 1886, Lord Lansdowne makes the following pertinent remark: "It is singular that while we are being abused here for having allowed the Americans to get the better of us, they are accusing their Government of having allowed itself to be outwitted by England and Canada." *John Macdonald Papers, Washington Treaty, 1888*, MS Canadian Archives.

. . . temper of the Senate seems averse to the consideration of any public measure from a high or patriotic point of view, but that blind and obstructive partisanship seems to be the rule of their action. . . . The Irish vote in the United States being very potential, is being sought most vigorously and unscrupulously by the Republican leaders, chief of whom is Mr. Blaine, and . . . every issue will be raised by them by which they can secure the alliance with the Irish vote, and every British question gives a chance for this. The chief struggle between parties in this country is over the retention of the protective tariff duties. On one side it is wholly mercenary, and no other or higher sentiment controls the objects and the methods or the choice of candidates. An illustration is just at hand in the treatment of the Canadian Fisheries question. Last summer a very advantageous, and wholly amicable arrangement was made by me with the British Minister here whereby all the benefits secured to United States fishermen by the treaty of 1872 were to continue for six months, without the corresponding concession of the treaty to the Canadians.

The Americans were thus protected during the season, but no sooner was it over than the very reasonable suggestion of raising a Commission to provide an equitable and just basis for joint use of the fisheries was recommended by the President (in accordance with my promise), than a noisy and vociferous crew came down from Gloucester, with some Democratic Attorneys, and led by Mr. Frye, of Maine, have commenced a wild outcry against the State Department. . . .

Now the *fons et origo* of all this is the fear lest tariff duties will be lowered or abolished, and fearing lest the desire for cheaper food by the manufacturing classes of New England and the United States might have some influence, they combine with a demand for increased "protection to American Industries," a scream against British aggression, hoping thereby to bring the Irish contingent to their aid.[10]

After this sharp thrust at the representatives of the fishing industry, Bayard set forth his views as to the proper interpretation of the Treaty of 1818. He was certain that under the terms of this treaty, Americans had a right to purchase bait in Canadian ports. The legislation in Canada which forbade this practice was not in accordance

. . . with a just or fair construction of the treaty of 1818 read by the light of the treaty of 1783. The release by the United States under the treaty of 1818 was of the right to "*take, dry, and cure* fish," and the restrictions of the treaty should only refer to those three things and not be extended to prohibition to purchase or refit or other things *not* released. I think that . . . a very strong case can be made against the British and Canadian statutes regulating the presence and objects of our fishing vessels in the harbors of British America.[11]

10. Bayard to Phelps, March 7, 1886, *Bayard Letter Book*, vol. 2, *Bayard MS.*
11. Bayard to Phelps, March 7, 1886, *ibid.*

Bayard was apprehensive that serious friction in Canadian waters over fishing rights might provide "Blaine and Company" an opportunity "to stir up feeling against England." He felt somewhat reassured, therefore, when Phelps informed him of the amicable gestures that the Salisbury Government was making towards him. It would be difficult to quarrel with a government that was so effusively friendly. Queen Victoria had accorded a special reception to Mrs. Phelps, and the American Minister and his wife had been invited to spend a night at Windsor Castle.[12]

Phelps lost no time in conveying to Lord Rosebery the apprehensions of Bayard concerning the mixture of politics and diplomacy that was being prepared by Republican leaders. After listening to the American Minister's account of the "utterly unscrupulous tactics of Mr. Blaine," the British Foreign Secretary readily agreed that existing disputes should be speedily settled.[13]

As a step in this direction, Lord Rosebery instructed Sackville-West to inquire if the American Government "intended to give notice to the United States fishermen that they are now precluded from fishing in British North American territorial waters." [14]

Bayard replied that in view "of the enduring nature and important extent of the rights secured to American fishermen in British North American territorial waters under the provisions of the treaty of 1818, to take fish within the three-mile limit on certain defined parts of the British North American coasts," the American Government had "not found it necessary" to give American fishermen any formal notification that the inshore fishery liberties had lapsed.[15]

After sending this short note to Sackville-West, Bayard began an intensive study of all the implications of the fishery question. He had

12. Phelps to Bayard, March 13, 1886, *Private, Bayard MS.* Phelps was quite fearful that the tides of social reform in England were running dangerously high. The time was "ripe for socialistic theories and agitations. And the enlargement of the franchise takes effect at a bad time. Even our election has very sensibly deteriorated the House of Commons, and wild propositions receive much favour there. . . . These signs foreshadow what will take place soon in a House elected by universal suffrage, and which constitutes, without check or restraint, the entire government of England."

13. Phelps to Bayard, March 27, 1886, *Private, Bayard MS.*

14. Sackville-West to Bayard, March 19, 1886, *British Legation, Notes from,* vol. 113, MS Dept. of State. In a personal memorandum which Sackville-West sent to Bayard on March 19, 1886, the fishery question was dealt with in more detail, and a declaration was made that the British Government had done its "utmost" to provide the means for a satisfactory solution of this serious dispute. *Bayard MS.*

15. Bayard to Sackville-West, March 23, 1886, *British Legation, Notes to,* vol. 20, MS Dept. of State.

received a challenging letter from Mr. George Steele, President of
the American Fishing Union, with reference to the policy of the
Administration in the matter of the fisheries. Mr. Steele was particularly interested in the right of American fishermen to purchase bait in
Canadian ports. Bayard turned this letter over to Francis Wharton,
who expressed the view that the refusal to permit the purchase of bait
would be a violation of the Treaty of 1818.[16]

Bayard agreed with this interpretation, and in his letter to Steele
he made a strong presentation of the American viewpoint. Inasmuch
as American fishing vessels sailed not only

. . . under regularly issued domestic fishing licenses (Revised Statutes, secs.
4320, 4321), but also hold the permission to touch and trade at any foreign
port prescribed in Revised Statutes, sec. 4364, they may be regarded either
as fishing vessels or as regularly enrolled trading vessels according to the
circumstances under which they may enter a foreign port or approach
within the three-mile limit of the British American coast. As traders, this
Government must hold that American fishing vessels, so licensed and holding
such permission, have the same right to enter and trade, in any foreign port
of entry that any other American trading vessels have. As to coasts and inshore waters not ports of entry, they have whatever rights of approach,
employment, and sojourn may be secured to them by treaty.

. . . It is . . . quite clear to me that an American fishing vessel, having
obtained permission for foreign trade according to sec. 4364, may rightfully
enter any British North American port of entry, on compliance with the
regular customs formalities, and there purchase any commodity offered for
sale which it may be lawful for any foreign vessel to purchase. The assent
of this Government could not be given to any claim of the Imperial or
Dominion authorities to prohibit the purchase of supplies, such as food, ice,
salt, or bait, by an American fishing vessel in a British North American port
of entry. The rightfulness of any discrimination against them because they
are *fishing* vessels cannot be admitted.

. . . The privilege to purchase bait within the renounced fishing limits
is not reserved by the Treaty. . . . I must hold, however, that this exclusion
of the privilege of purchasing bait only applies to those waters and coasts
where our fishermen have renounced the liberty to take, dry, or cure fish.
. . . Within the renounced fishing limits, not being ports of entry, I must
hold that the renunciation is explicit. . . . Within the waters in which the
liberty is guaranteed forever for the fishing operations of American fishermen, I hold that we have renounced nothing, and are entitled to all facilities
incidental to the enjoyment of the principal rights secured—i.e., of taking
and (on certain described parts of the coast) of curing and drying fish.[17]

16. *Memorandum* by Francis Wharton, March 31, 1886, *Bayard MS.*
17. Bayard to George Steele, March, 1886, *Bayard MS.* The confusion that existed in
Canadian minds with regard to the enforcement of the provisions of the Treaty of 1818

Bayard next wrote to Spencer F. Baird, Director of the United States Commission of Fish and Fisheries, and inquired if bait were needed "under the present methods of fishing only for *open* sea fishing (Cod, Haddock, etc.) and is not needed for *mackerel* fishing, which I understand to be the only kind of fish caught inshore." [18] Baird's reply confirmed, in part, Bayard's viewpoint about the use of bait. He was right

. . . in supposing that the question of obtaining bait in Provincial ports affects only vessels fishing upon the high seas. These usually provide themselves with a partial supply before leaving home, but, owing to the difficulty in keeping it fresh during the entire voyage, they often find it desirable to go into Provincial ports two or three times for additional quantities. . . . Formerly bait was a necessity in the mackerel fishing, but owing to the introduction of the purse-seine it is no longer required. The mackerel fishing is by no means limited to shore waters. . . . The total value of the catch of mackerel by New England fishermen, within three miles of the shore, in the Gulf of St. Lawrence, in 1885, did not exceed $35,000.[19]

While Bayard was gathering this information about fishing bait, the Senate of the United States was debating Mr. Frye's resolution which declared that Congress should not advise the appointment of a joint commission to settle the fisheries question. The President's recommendation in his message of December 8 received but little sup-

and of the Canadian statutes, is revealed in the following excerpt from a despatch sent by M. H. Phelan, United States Consul-General at Halifax, to James D. Porter, Assistant Secretary of State, April 9, 1886. Captain P. A. Scott, in command of the Marine Police, had abruptly ordered all American fishing vessels from Canadian ports and coasts. Phelan immediately asked Captain Scott by what authority "he was acting, as I could find nothing in the published instructions issued by the Minister of Marine and Fisheries, in the Statutes of Canada, or even in the Treaty [of 1818] to warrant such proceedings. He replied that . . . his authority to order vessels from the harbors, bays, or coast would be found in the Statutes of Canada, but an examination of these statutes resulted in a failure to find such authority. The Captain then said that the statutes must have been tampered with. . . . He called the next day to say that he found his authority to order our vessels to sea, in 59. George III, chap. 38 (year 1818). Being informed that this was an Imperial Act and could not be enforced by a local officer unless such officer was commissioned by the Imperial Government, . . . he stated that a mistake had been made by someone and he would do nothing further until the Minister of Marine and Fisheries passed on these questions." *Halifax, Consular Despatches*, vol. 14, MS Dept. of State.

18. Bayard to Professor Spencer F. Baird, April 9, 1886, *Bayard Letter Book*, vol. 2, *Bayard MS*.

19. S. F. Baird to Bayard, April 9, 1886, *Bayard MS*. It is significant to note that the mackerel fisheries declined in an extraordinary manner after 1885. In 1885 the New England catch of salt mackerel amounted to 329,943 barrels. In 1886 the catch slumped to 79,998 barrels, and in 1889 it fell to 21,918 barrels. In 1885 the New England catch of codfish amounted to 902,455 quintals; and in 1889 it declined to 498,989 quintals. Raymond McFarland, *A History of the New England Fisheries*, pp. 369-371.

port even from Democratic Senators, and on April 13 the Frye resolution was adopted by the overwhelming vote of 35 yeas to 10 nays.[20]

To Bayard this debate in the Senate was a "mere blowing of (fish) horns," [21] but this raucous chorus took on a louder note when the Canadian Government began to seize American vessels for alleged infractions of the Treaty of 1818. On May 7 the American schooner, *David J. Adams,* was taken into custody in Digby Harbor and later towed to St. John, New Brunswick, for trial.

In London the news of this seizure became known to Phelps on May 8, and he quickly sent a note to Lord Rosebery expressing his great regret that such action should have been taken "at this juncture when it will be immediately availed of by the party desirous of making trouble with England for the sake of the Irish vote." [22]

In America the news of the seizure of the *David J. Adams* aroused vehement protest, and William C. P. Breckinridge hurriedly wrote to Bayard to find out the best way to circumvent the enemies of the Administration who would undoubtedly try to make capital out of the incident.[23] Bayard was not worried about Congressional resolutions asking for information relative to the seizure of the *Adams.* Everything possible had been done to protect American interests in Canadian waters, and the correspondence in the Department of State would clearly reveal this fact. He would continue his efforts to maintain American rights

. . . and secure our Fishermen from molestation, but the real enemies are in the United States, and in the Radical ranks (tho not wholly). They hate a Democratic Administration more than they love the welfare and honor of the United States.[24]

Bayard then turned to the task of writing a long letter of protest to Sackville-West against the seizure of American vessels for purchasing bait in Canadian ports. On May 9 he turned over to Adee a mass of notes he had made on the subject of American fishing rights. These notes, he thought, could be quickly "trimmed into better shape," and the letter to the British Minister be hurriedly prepared.[25]

20. *Congressional Record,* April 13, 1886, 49 Cong., 1 sess., vol. 17, p. 3440.
21. Bayard to David A. Wells, April 12, 1886, *Bayard Letter Book,* vol 2, *Bayard MS.*
22. Phelps to Bayard, May 8, 1886, *Bayard MS.*
23. W. C. P. Breckinridge to Bayard, May 9, 1886, *ibid.*
24. Bayard to W. C. P. Breckinridge, May 10, 1886, *Bayard Letter Book,* vol. 2, *Bayard MS.*
25. Bayard to A. A. Adee, May 9, 1886, *Bayard MS.*

On the following day the draft of a letter to Sackville-West was submitted to Francis Wharton who regarded it as a "very strong paper." With a few emendations suggested by Wharton,[26] the note to the British Minister was finally completed and sent on the afternoon of May 10. It was long and cogently argued. He first alluded to the recent seizures of American vessels in Canadian waters. Inasmuch as "both these seizures took place in closely land-locked harbors, no invasion of the territorial waters of the British Provinces, with the view of fishing there, could well be imagined. And yet the arrests appear to have been based upon the act of intent of fishing."[27] Bayard next gave a short summary of the legislation of both the American and British Governments with reference to establishing commercial contacts between the United States and the British colonial possessions. This commerce would be seriously interfered with if the restrictive measures recently adopted by the colonial authorities were left unchecked. The Treaty of 1818 was made by America and Great Britain as the contracting parties who "can alone deal responsibly with questions arising thereunder."

The action of the colonial authorities would not only seriously affect the operations of American fishermen on the high seas but would also "practically destroy" the rights of American vessels to visit the inshore waters along the Canadian coast for the objects of "shelter, repair of damages, and purchasing wood and obtaining water." The question of the purchase of bait had reference only to deep-sea fishing outside the three-mile limit, and any action taken to prevent such purchases would be equivalent to expanding the terms of the Treaty of 1818 to objects "wholly beyond its purview, scope, and intent." In view of the fact that there was no longer any inducement for American fishermen to dry and cure fish on the interdicted coasts of the Canadian Provinces, and as bait was no longer used or needed in order to "take" fish in the inshore waters, the recent seizures of American vessels for exercising the "reasonable rights and privileges of trade" in Canadian ports was most annoying.

26. Francis Wharton to Bayard, May 10, 1886, *ibid.*
27. The viewpoint of the Canadian Government is clearly expressed in a note from Lansdowne to Sir John Macdonald, July 5, 1886: "Our contention is, I take it, simply that the purchase of bait does constitute a preparation to fish, that it is not necessary to establish that the fishing for which preparation is made is illegal fishing, that in the case of the 'Nickersen' the court adopted this view, and that we have taken the first opportunity of testing the law." *Governor-General's Correspondence*, vol. 13, *Sir John Macdonald Papers*, MS Canadian Archives.

The customary rights and privileges which should be extended to American vessels in Canadian ports should include the "purchase of ship-supplies of every nature, making repairs, the shipment of crews in whole or part, and the purchase of ice and bait for use in deep-sea fishing." These same rights and privileges have been "freely extended to and are fully enjoyed by the Canadian merchant marine of all occupations, including fishermen, in the ports of the United States."

Everything would be done by the American Government to cause their citizens engaged in fishing "to conform to the obligations of the treaty, and prevent an infraction of the fishing laws of the British Provinces," but it was equally necessary that ordinary commercial intercourse between the United States and the British North American Provinces should be free from "harsh measures and unfriendly administration." [28]

Bayard also sent a telegram to Phelps informing him of the situation. To Phelps it seemed important

. . . to insist not only upon the construction of the language of the treaty for which we contend, but also upon the further point in respect to which I entertain no doubt. That if a technical invalidation of the terms of the treaty in a doubtful particular has been committed, *that does not at all authorize the seizure and confiscation of the vessel.* Neither the provisions of the treaty nor any rule of international law justifies such a proceeding. They might as well hang the crew. The proper course would be an application to our Government to take steps to prevent any further transgressions.[29]

On May 11 Mr. M. H. Phelan, the United States Consul-General at Halifax, sent a telegram to the Department of State in which he declared that the charge against the *Adams* for "violating the Customs was so trifling that it seems they have abandoned it and gone back to the charge of violating the Fishery laws. The officers don't seem to know what to do." [30]

Bayard lost no time in getting in touch with Sackville-West to whom he expressed the opinion that the summary seizure of the *Adams* not only furnished a cause for "retaliatory action" but also created serious "new difficulties." [31] The British Minister promised to tele-

28. Bayard to Sackville-West, May 10, 1886, *British Legation, Notes to,* vol. 20, MS Dept. of State.
29. Phelps to Bayard, May 11, 1886, *Private, Bayard MS.*
30. M. H. Phelan to James D. Porter, May 11, 1886, *ibid.*
31. Bayard to Sackville-West, May 11, 1886, *ibid.*

graph to Lord Lansdowne to see what could be done,[32] and Bayard expressed the hope that the Governor-General would be able to secure "more circumspect and amicable action upon the part of the Canadian officials." [33]

Lansdowne was entirely willing to advise the Canadian officials to be circumspect and amicable in their relations with Americans, but he had no intention of receding from a strong position with respect to Canadian rights. He informed Sackville-West that the *Adams* was to be proceeded against on three counts—violation of the Customs Act of 1883, the Dominion Fishery Act of 1868, and the Treaty of 1818.[34] Two days later he wrote to Sir John Macdonald in connection with the letter Bayard addressed to Sackville-West on May 10. He did not for a moment agree with Bayard's statement that the attitude of the Canadian Government in the matter of the seizure of the *Adams* indicated

. . . an attempt to impede the ordinary commercial intercourse of the two countries. That United States fishing vessels have a right to trade in Canadian ports, in the face of the distinct language of the Convention, merely because during the negotiations of 1818, a proposal was made on the part of Great Britain to expressly exclude them from trading, which proposal was not eventually accepted, seems to me to be altogether unsustainable. . . . Even if it be conceded that there is no use for bait except outside the three-mile limit and that consequently a prohibition to obtain bait would affect not our inshore fisheries but those in the open sea which are *in hypothesi* accessible to all, it does not, I think, follow that such a prohibition would be a "destructive expansion" of the scope of the convention. The object of the convention and of the legislation founded upon it has been to protect British North American fishing interests generally in the same manner as the United States have sought by their system of tariffs to protect and foster the fishing interest of their citizens.

Another point requiring . . . careful attention is that which affects the right of the colonies by legislation of their own to give effect to contracts made between the mother country and foreign powers. You will observe that Mr. Bayard attempts to impugn the authority of our legislation in these matters. That legislation has however been confirmed by the Imperial Government, and is, I apprehend, as effectual and valid as an Imperial Statute.

Mr. Bayard's letter is ably written and the spirit of his argument is not unfriendly. I cannot help hoping that these communications may end in a reasonable and neighbourly adjustment.[35]

32. Sackville-West to Bayard, May 12, 1886, *ibid.*
33. Bayard to Sackville-West, May 12, 1886, *Bayard Letter Book*, vol. 2, *Bayard MS.*
34. Sackville-West to Bayard, May 13, 1886, *Bayard MS.*
35. Lansdowne to Sir John Macdonald, May 15, 1886, *Governor-General's Correspondence*, vol. 13, *John Macdonald Papers*, MS Canadian Archives.

It is very obvious that Lord Lansdowne's political outlook was far broader than that of Sir John Macdonald. Lansdowne kept constantly in mind the needs of the British Empire while Macdonald thought chiefly of Canadian interests. This being the case, it was not long before Macdonald stood sponsor for a bill in the Dominion Parliament which would broaden the provisions of the Act of 1868. Lansdowne thought that such action was not only unnecessary but distinctly inexpedient. In the existing dispute with the United States it was important to exclude all feelings of "bitterness." If at the very outset of the controversy one party

. . . seeks to obtain for itself by a sort of legislative *coup de main,* an advantage not secured to it by existing laws or treaties, will not that party be regarded as wishing to accelerate existing differences instead of removing them? . . . By the action of the United States Government we find ourselves in regard to our fisheries under a condition of things which has twice arisen before. . . . During those periods the law as it now stands sufficed for us. Why do we desire to amend it now? . . . The existing law supplies us with a remedy against the matters of vessels entering our waters in contravention of the convention of 1818. The remedy is a clumsy one, no doubt, but would it not on the whole be better to face its inconveniences than the questions which may be raised by new legislation?
. . . If the amending bill passes we shall by Canadian legislation have placed upon the Convention [of 1818] an interpretation different from and more favorable to ourselves than the interpretation placed upon it by the Imperial Parliament. We are now "in line" with the Mother Country. We shall no longer be "in line" when the bill has become law.[36]

On the following day (May 21) Lansdowne wrote two notes to Sir John Macdonald in an attempt to induce him to follow more moderate measures. He thought it would be possible to include in the proposed fishery legislation a clause to the effect that the measure would not go into effect until approved by the Queen in Council. This procedure would remove any necessity for an explicit royal disallowance in the event that the Colonial Secretary regarded the new law as likely to lead to serious friction with the United States. With reference to the threat of retaliatory legislation on the part of the American Congress, it should be noted that

. . . the bills of Senators Frye and Dingley (the only ones of which I have seen the text) do not go beyond excluding from the same commercial privileges which we may deny to American vessels, vessels of a similar char-

36. Lansdowne to Sir John Macdonald, May 20, 1886, *Governor-General's Correspondence,* vol. 13, *John Macdonald Papers,* MS Canadian Archives.

acter belonging to us. The effect of these bills would therefore . . . be merely to prevent Canadian *fishing* vessels from trading in United States ports: a form of retaliation which could not hurt us and which we could afford to ignore. I should, moreover, like to feel that our warfare was conducted on other principles than those of the Fryes and Dingleys.[37]

Lansdowne was mistaken in believing that American retaliatory legislation of the type introduced by Senator Frye and Representative Dingley would not injure Canadian fishermen. These fishermen had long followed the practice of fitting out their vessels at Gloucester, Massachusetts, where they could purchase supplies more cheaply than in Canadian ports.[38] These commercial privileges, so freely extended to Canadian fishermen who visited American ports, were not only denied to American fishermen who sought to buy bait in Canadian harbors but to masters of American vessels who attempted to purchase herring for export.[39]

Confronted with this situation which constantly grew more serious, Bayard engaged the services of two distinguished lawyers, William L. Putnam, of Portland, Maine, and George W. Biddle, of Philadelphia. They were requested to go at once to Halifax, Nova Scotia, and take part in the case of the *David J. Adams* which was being tried in the vice-admiralty court.[40] Bayard then addressed a note to Sackville-West in which he reviewed new evidence with reference to the summary seizure of the *Adams*. There was little doubt that the circumstances surrounding this seizure were of a character that boded ill for continued friendly relations between Canada and the United States.[41]

37. Lansdowne to Sir John Macdonald, May 21, 1886, *Governor-General's Correspondence*, vol. 13, *John Macdonald Papers*, MS Canadian Archives.

38. Bayard to W. C. P. Breckinridge, May 15, 1886, *Bayard Letter Book*, vol. 2, *Bayard MS*.

39. Bayard to Sackville-West, May 20, 1886, *Bayard Letter Book*, vol. 2, *Bayard MS*. Bayard was specifically referring to the refusal of the authorities at Digby, Nova Scotia, to sell herring for export. Senator W. P. Frye wrote to Bayard on May 20 and protested against such action. Senator W. P. Frye wrote to Bayard on May 20 and protested against such action. Bayard stated that he regarded the adverse attitude of the Canadian officials as "a gross breach of the commercial rights of a citizen of the United States." He assured the importunate Senator that the "interests and honor" of the United States were not suffering through any neglect on the part of the Democratic Administration. Bayard to W. P. Frye, May 20, 1886, *Bayard Letter Book*, vol. 2, *Bayard MS*.

40. Bayard to W. L. Putnam, May 20, 1886, and Bayard to G. W. Biddle, May 20, 1886, *Bayard Letter Book*, vol. 2, *Bayard MS*. See also W. L. Putnam to Bayard, May 22, 1886, and G. W. Biddle to Bayard, May 25, 1886, *Bayard MS*.

41. Bayard to Sackville-West, May 20, 1886, *British Legation, Notes to*, vol. 20, MS Dept. of State. The treatment accorded to the captain and crew of the *David J. Adams* was reviewed by Bayard in this note to Sackville-West: "By the information thus derived it would appear that after four several and distinct visitations by boats' crews from the *Lansdowne*, in Annapolis Basin, Nova Scotia, the *David J. Adams* was summarily taken

On May 21 Bayard had a conference with Sackville-West, who read a telegram from Lord Rosebery that clearly showed the evident eagerness of the British Government to find some formula that would settle the fishery difficulty. Sackville-West himself offered three suggestions: he thought it was expedient to revise the Treaty of 1818; to suspend all retaliatory measures; and to arrive at some sort of commercial reciprocity between the United States and Canada. But Bayard was in no hurry to revise the Treaty of 1818. All that was needed was for the Canadian authorities to construe that convention "in accordance with present circumstances and in recognition of the changes in events since 1818." Sackville-West then inquired whether a *modus vivendi* could be arranged to take care of the situation for the time being. Bayard believed that a temporary settlement could be effected, but he was insistent that it include the right of American fishermen "to go into the ports of entry of Canada, and ship their crews, buy their bait, and do anything else in a fair way to carry on deep-sea fishing without molestation." [42]

The conciliatory attitude of Sackville-West encouraged Bayard to nurse the hope that a speedy solution of the fishery question would be found. In a letter to Phelps he expressed the opinion that the whole matter in dispute was really

---

into custody by the Canadian steamer *Lansdowne* and carried out of the Province of Nova Scotia . . . and into the port of St. John, New Brunswick, and without explanation . . . taken back again by an armed crew to Digby, in Nova Scotia. . . . In Digby the paper alleged to be the legal precept for the capture and detention of the vessel was nailed to her mast in such manner as to prevent its contents being read. . . . Nor was the United States consul-general able to learn from the commander of the *Lansdowne* the nature of the complaint against the vessel."

42. *Memorandum* written by Bayard after a conference with Sackville-West, May 21, 1886, *Bayard MS*. The importance to American fishermen of the right to purchase bait in Canadian ports was obvious. There were few shipments of bait to Gloucester or Boston, and American fishermen were compelled to go to Canadian ports to secure the necessary bait. See L. Saltonstall to Bayard, May 24, 25, 1886, and W. A. Wilcox to E. T. Colby, May 24, 1886, *Bayard MS*. The difference in attitude of the American and the Canadian authorities with reference to right of fishing vessels to carry on commercial operations, was clearly exemplified in a letter that J. B. Richardson wrote to Representative John D. Long, May 16, 1886. It happened that (some years previous) a small vessel from Nova Scotia "put into the port of Gloucester, Massachusetts, where it was learned that the master had on board and had brought into that port a *few pairs of woolen socks*. . . . The whole value of the socks was less than $15 or $20, but they were of Nova Scotia *manufacture* and were *dutiable*, and his, the master's vessel was *less than 100 tons burden*, and for this . . . the *cargo and vessel* were both liable to forfeiture to the United States, and they were libelled and seized. . . . The Secretary of the Treasury . . . after a full investigation, stopped the proceedings for forfeiture, and ordered the vessel and cargo restored to the master after his paying the trifling duty, and the costs of the proceedings." See also John D. Long to Bayard, May 26, 1886, *Bayard MS*.

. . . a question of hostile tariffs and illustrates the evils of a system founded on bending public measures to suit personal interests. . . . I hope you understood my telegram after receipt of yours announcing the tenor of your note to Lord Rosebery. I did not wish him to make public in any way *your* intimation that we had a party here desirous of provoking collision with England. It is perfectly true that the Irish Dynamite element is courted and caressed by Blaine and his fellows, and this of course requires expression by them of animosity to everything British, on every possible occasion.

The developments of dangerous tendencies and anarchical sentiments . . . in the organization of the Knights of Labor, and the suffering and disorders caused by strikes under irresponsible and ignorant leadership, have caused a good deal of reactionary sentiment among the laborers themselves. . . . I hope and pray it may have the effect of diminishing the influence of the noisy demagogues . . . who have tried so hard to stir up difficulty between Great Britain and the United States on this Fishery question.[43]

Two days later (May 23), Sackville-West sent to Bayard a confidential note containing a proposed *modus vivendi*. In view of all the circumstances in the case and taking into consideration

. . . the arguments advanced by both sides on the question of the purchase of bait in Canadian Ports by American vessels, . . . it would seem that the two Governments might formally declare their intention of at once entering into negotiations on the subject, pending which all restrictive and retaliatory actions should be suspended.[44]

Sackville-West also sent to Lord Lansdowne a copy of the proposed *modus vivendi* which he had submitted to Bayard. Lansdowne was very cautious about giving his approval to such a course. It seemed to him that any suggestion of a *modus vivendi* should come "from the Imperial Government or from that of the United States and not from us."[45]

The day before Bayard had received the proposed *modus vivendi* from Sackville-West, he had already outlined its main points in a telegram to Phelps. In this instruction of May 22 he had inquired whether American vessels that had been seized in Canadian waters could be released without prejudice, and orders be given, pending further negotiations, to prevent the enforcement of the Treaty of 1818 except "under Imperial authority."[46]

43. Bayard to Phelps, May 21, 1886, *Bayard Letter Book*, vol. 2, *Bayard MS.*
44. Sackville-West to Bayard, May 23, 1886, *Personal and Confidential, Bayard MS.*
45. Lansdowne to Sir John Macdonald, May 24, 1886, *Governor-General's Correspondence*, vol. 13, *John Macdonald Papers*, MS Canadian Archives.
46. Bayard to Phelps, May 22, 1886, *Great Britain, Instructions*, vol. 28, MS Dept. of State. When Phelps asked Lord Rosebery if the seizures of American vessels in Canadian

Several days later he sent a personal letter to Phelps in which he canvassed the situation in detail. He hoped that Lord Rosebery would be able to bring the Canadian authorities

. . . into line with the Imperial interpretation of the commercial privileges of purchasing bait, ice, supplies, etc., and the right to transship their cargoes in British waters. In volume two (page 1585) of the Award of the Fishery Commission you will find Mr. Dana's argument on this point accepted by the Commission so that the fact is conclusively admitted that these rights are *commercial rights* not created by nor dependent upon the Treaty of Washington nor upon the Treaty of 1818.

. . . Perhaps the granting of exequaturs to our Consuls . . . by the Government of Great Britain to reside and protect commerce in these regions is the simplest proof of the actual state of the law. Two influences are at work—the Tariff combinations and the Irish vote. As you know, the Tariff protectionists maintain each other and vote solidly to prevent that break in the line which they know will precede disintegration.

. . . You saw . . . how decisive was the vote in the Senate rejecting the President's proposition to frame a treaty by the aid of a joint commission. . . . As a *corps de reserve,* ready to march on the minute, is the anti-British vote which was so largely captured by Mr. Blaine in 1884, and with which he maintains a close alliance. Despite the professions which Mr. Bennett's employees are instructed to make, the New York *Herald* is mischievously busy in pointing out the excellent opportunity to secure a collision with Great Britain which can be obtained by a dexterous use of the misunderstandings on the Fisheries question. . . . There can be no doubt that a good deal of excitement exists and there is a diligent mustering of old prejudices against Great Britain. This does not affect my sense of duty or if it does, serves only to make me more alert and determined to counteract all such hateful tendencies.[47]

In order to facilitate the work of George W. Biddle and William L. Putnam, who had been appointed as special counsel to represent the United States in the cases arising out of the seizure of American vessels in Canadian waters, Bayard sent each of them a copy of the *Proceedings* of the Halifax Commission of 1877, with certain marked

---

waters could not be discontinued at once, he received the reply that "Her Majesty's Government would have difficulty in asking the Dominion Government to suspend their legal action if nothing [were] offered as a *quid pro quo.*" Lord Rosebery inquired if some indication could be given of American readiness to negotiate upon the question. In this regard Phelps stated that President Cleveland could "negotiate without consulting Senate and there should be no difficulty in reaching solution." The treaty could be submitted to the Senate in December, "and if good, Senate could not refuse to ratify, or at least give reasons." Lord Granville to Lord Landsdowne, May 25, 1886, *Governor-General's Correspondence,* vol. 13, *John Macdonald Papers,* MS Canadian Archives.

47. Bayard to Phelps, May 27, 1886, *Private and Personal, Bayard Letter Book,* vol. 2, *Bayard MS.*

passages. Their attention was particularly drawn to the explicit orders issued by the British Admiralty in 1870 to the effect that British ships employed in the protection of the fisheries should "not seize any vessel unless it were evident, and could be clearly proved, that the offence of fishing had been committed and the vessel itself captured within three miles of land." Bayard also stated that he had "the distinct authority of Professor S. F. Baird for saying that bait is no longer used for inshore . . . fishing. *Ergo,* the possession of bait or the purchase of bait in Canadian waters is *against* the implication of 'preparing to fish' inshore, but on the contrary implies preparation to fish in the deep sea and not with the marine league." [48]

There was little doubt that from the strictly legal viewpoint the American case was very strong, but the British Government was extremely careful about taking any action that would give offence to Canadian officials. On May 29 Phelps had an interview with Lord Rosebery and complained of the "harsh and unfriendly construction" that the Canadian authorities placed upon the Treaty of 1818. It was a construction that heretofore had been "repudiated by the British Government," and such action had greatly embarrassed the Cleveland Administration which had done everything in its power to find some satisfactory solution for the fishery problem. The unreasonable attitude assumed by the Canadian Government had the effect of excluding American ships "engaged in a perfectly lawful business and doing no harm whatever to British subjects or property, from the right of entry into Canadian ports conceded by all nations to each other in time of peace."

Lord Rosebery was so non-committal that Phelps believed that the American government might have to take "strong and decided ground." [49] Before Bayard could receive this letter he had already sent a telegram to Phelps in which he protested vehemently against a bill

48. Bayard to George W. Biddle and William L. Putnam, May 26, 1886, *Bayard MS.* In a short note to Bayard, May 27, 1886, Mr. Adee remarks as follows: "The more I think of it, the more I am convinced that the dispute turns on the meaning to be attached to the words 'and for no other purpose whatever.' The rational meaning is 'for no other purpose connected with the operation of fishing within the three-mile limit,' and also 'for no other purpose which by law may be forbidden to *all* vessels, whether fishermen or not,' because the police restrictions allowed are expressly to prevent *abuse* of the privilege of resort and by *abuse* must be understood taking, drying, or curing fish within the limit, or doing any *unlawful* act therein. But the Canadian claim would make posting a letter or buying a newspaper on shore an abuse of inshore-waters." *Bayard MS.*

49. Phelps to Bayard, May 29, 1886, *Personal, Bayard MS.*

that was pending in the Canadian Parliament. It was the same bill that had awakened serious apprehensions in the mind of Lord Lansdowne.[50] Phelps was to inform Lord Rosebery that the United States would hold the British Government "liable for all losses which may be sustained by American citizens in the dispossession of their property growing out of the search, seizure, detention or sale of their vessels lawfully within the territorial waters of British North America." [51]

Bayard sent a similar note to Sackville-West in which he expressed the view that this pending legislation in the Canadian Parliament was highly objectionable because it contained the "wholly unwarranted proposition" that Canadian officials could enforce the provisions of the Treaty of 1818 according to their own construction of that convention, and by an

. . . interpretation not claimed or conceded by either party to such treaty, to invade and destroy the commercial rights and privileges of citizens of the United States. . . . Such proceedings I conceive to be flagrantly violative of the reciprocal commercial privileges to which citizens of the United States are lawfully entitled under the statutes of Great Britain and the well-defined and publicly proclaimed authority of both countries.[52]

Phelps immediately replied by telegram that he had seen Lord Rosebery "who did not seem inclined to interfere with Canadian action," and who filed a complaint that the American Government would not negotiate for a settlement. Phelps explained to him that negotiations would be "very difficult under exasperated feeling" produced by "unreasonable seizures." It was unlikely that the Cleveland Administration would risk widespread criticism in the United States by initiating negotiations at the very time when American vessels were being seized.[53]

These strong protests from Bayard against restrictive Canadian legislation were regarded by British officials with increasing alarm.

50. This was House of Commons bill No. 136. It proposed the "forcible search, seizure, and forfeiture of any foreign vessel within any harbor in Canada, or hovering within three marine miles of any of the coasts, bays, creeks, or harbors in Canada, where such vessel has entered such waters for any purpose not permitted by the laws of nations, or by treaty or convention, or by any law of the United Kingdom, or of Canada now in force."

51. Bayard to Phelps, May 29, 1886, *telegram, Great Britain, Instructions,* vol. 28, MS Dept. of State.

52. Bayard to Sackville-West, May 29, 1886, *British Legation, Notes to,* vol. 20, MS Dept. of State.

53. Phelps to Bayard, May 29, 1886, cipher telegram, *Great Britain, Despatches,* vol. 153, MS Dept. of State.

Sackville-West expressed to Lord Lansdowne the opinion that the situation was "serious," [54] and Lord Rosebery who at first upheld the Canadian view of the fishery question,[55] began to have serious doubts as to the expediency of this stand. This new viewpoint was at once communicated to Lord Granville, who telegraphed to Lord Lansdowne that it was important to have the Canadian House of Commons Bill No. 136, set aside for the time being.[56]

After receiving this telegram, Lord Lansdowne thought there was "no course open but to 'reserve' the Bill." Such action, however, should not create "much commotion" in the Canadian Parliament.[57] Sir John Macdonald thought otherwise. It seemed to him

. . . that the Bill should be disallowed by Lord Granville, if he thinks fit, rather than reserved by you. No harm can be done by its being passed here. Its effect will only be to confiscate or rather condemn a vessel on conviction. There can be no conviction for months under the new act and long ere that Lord Granville will have plenty of time to make up his mind on the question of disallowance before the act can be enforced or any claim for redress can rise. In the face of the rather impudent protest of Mr. Bayard it will put us

54. Lansdowne to Sir John Macdonald, May 30, 1886, *Governor-General's Correspondence*, vol. 13, *John Macdonald Papers*, MS Canadian Archives. In a memorandum attached to this note from Lansdowne to Sir John Macdonald, special attention is given to the constitutional aspects of Canadian legislation. With reference to pending House of Commons Bill No. 136, it is stated that this bill is "within the competence of the Canadian Parliament—does not alter or affect the terms of the Convention [of 1818]—and only amends the procedure by which those terms are enforced. The Convention merely states the conditions, but is silent as to the mode of enforcing them. They have been given effect to by Acts passed by the Imperial Parliament, by Congress, and by the Legislatures of the British North American Provinces before Confederation, and since then by the Parliament of Canada. This Provincial and Dominion Legislation has been acted upon for years without objection until now.

"Mr. Bayard apparently misapprehends our Constitution. The Imperial Parliament has delegated to that of Canada the power of legislation on matters specially affecting her rights and interests, and The Queen with the advice of her Canadian Parliament passes the Acts relating to such matters, which thereupon become a portion of the law of the Empire.

"The Government of the United States has long been aware of the necessity of reference to the Dominion Parliament in matters affecting her interests. The Treaties of 1854 and 1871, so far as they related to the Fisheries or trade relations with Canada, were made subject to ratification by Her Legislature. . . . Seizures of goods and vessels for breach of our local customs laws have been made without protest or objection for half a century. The legal tribunals of the Empire and its dependencies recognize the laws of the several states of the Union on matters within their competence as well as the laws of Congress." *Governor-General's Correspondence*, vol. 13, *John Macdonald Papers*, MS Canadian Archives.

55. Lord Granville to Lord Lansdowne, May 25, 1886, *Governor-General's Correspondence*, vol. 13, *John Macdonald Papers*, MS Canadian Archives.

56. Lord Granville to Lord Lansdowne, June 2, 1886, *ibid*.

57. Lansdowne to Sir John Macdonald, June 2, 1886, *ibid*.

in rather a humiliating position. He protests against our power to legislate and we will appear tamely to acquiesce.[58]

Lord Lansdowne was not convinced by Sir John's reasoning. After the receipt of Lord Granville's telegram with respect to the bill there was "no other course open" but to "reserve" it, and he was entirely willing to assume this responsibility.[59] Such action, however, was not enough to satisfy the importunate Granville. In a second telegram he complained that he could not "understand" the position taken by the Dominion Government in the matter of further seizures of American vessels. If this policy were continued it would "necessarily preclude friendly negotiations." [60]

Lansdowne was somewhat piqued at the peremptory tone of Lord Granville's telegram. He was certain that the Colonial Secretary did not fully realize the consequences of an announcement that

. . . no further seizures are to be made, nor does he explain whether his suggestion is that *all* seizures, for whatever contravention of the Treaty, are to be discontinued, or whether he would like us to make the concession only in reference to vessels attempting to buy bait or to enter our harbours for a purpose not specified as lawful. I suspect the latter alternative . . . was present to his mind. . . . I hope we shall not have any more seizures: the two which have been made will be sufficient as test cases, and it appears to me that our police officers should not make further seizures except where the conduct of the trespassing vessels absolutely force them to adopt the extreme course.[61]

58. Sir John Macdonald to Lansdowne, June 2, *Governor-General's Correspondence*, vol. 13, *John Macdonald Papers*, MS Canadian Archives.

59. Lansdowne to Sir John Macdonald, June 2, 1886, *ibid*. In a telegram to Lord Granville, June 2, 1886, Lansdowne remarks: "Please have it clearly explained that bill is reserved solely on the ground mentioned in my telegram of this day: we object altogether to position taken by Bayard in despatch May 29th. Great indignation will be felt here if reservation should be construed as acquiescence by Her Majesty's Government in Bayard's contention as to competence of Canadian Parliament and authorities."

60. Lord Granville to Lansdowne, June 3, 1886, *ibid*.

61. Lansdowne to Sir John Macdonald, June 4, 1886, *Governor-General's Correspondence*, vol. 13, *John Macdonald Papers*, MS Canadian Archives. In a second note to Sir John Macdonald, June 4, 1886, Lansdowne mentions the fact that he had just "got hold of a copy of the customs circular 371 against which Mr. Bayard inveighs so strongly. I do not know whether you had seen it. I am almost sure that I was shewn the 'warning,' but not the circular under cover of which it was enclosed when issued to the collectors. The sting of the circular is in its last clause. . . . The circular goes on to say that 'if such vessel or boat is found fishing, preparing to fish, or violating the provisions of the convention of 1818 *by shipping men or supplies or trading*,' or if hovering within the three-mile limit, does not depart within twenty-four hours after receiving such warning, the customs collector is to place an officer on board and report by telegram to Ottawa. I have no doubt that the words which I have underlined are those which have incensed the United States Government. They assume that the acts described are violations of the convention, and

This impatience on the part of Lord Granville with reference to the repeated seizures of American vessels in Canadian waters is partly accounted for by the strong remonstrances that Bayard sent to the British Government. On June 2 Phelps addressed to Lord Rosebery a long note in which the attitude of the Department was given firm and cogent expression. After a careful appraisal of the situation, Phelps finally remarked:

In any view, therefore, which it seems to me can be taken of this question, I feel justified in pronouncing the action of the Canadian authorities in seizing and still retaining the *David J. Adams*, to be not only unfriendly and discourteous, but altogether unwarrantable.[62]

this is, I take it, that what Mr. Bayard describes as the 'interpolation of language not found in any such treaty.' . . . The effect of this part of the circular is . . . to give the 'hovering' vessels the benefit of a warning, but to render obligatory the detention without warning of vessels fishing, preparing to fish, or violating the convention in the manner described." In reply, Sir John Macdonald remarked: "The Imperial Statute, 59 Geo. III, Cap. 38, 1819, applies to all foreign fishermen, although the second clause seems awkwardly to mix up the Convention with the United States with the exclusion of the fishermen of other nations. It would have been well . . . had the warning and Customs circular been limited to United States fishermen, as no others were troubling our waters. As it is, I shall endeavour to get these papers withdrawn and the two concluding paragraphs of the circular altered as follows: 'Having reference to the above, you are requested to furnish any foreign fishing vessels, boats, or fishermen found within three marine miles of the shore within your district, with a printed copy of the warning enclosed herewith. If any fishing vessel or boat of the United States is found fishing, or to have been fishing, or preparing to fish, or if hovering within the three-mile limit, does not depart within 24 hours after receiving such warning, you will place an officer on board of such vessel and at once telegraph the facts . . . to Ottawa.' It would not do to provide that every vessel which had actually fished or prepared to fish in our waters should get a warning before seizure. . . . The effect of my proposed alteration is that a friendly warning might be given to every foreign fisherman of what the law is, so that he might not unwittingly break it. . . . The circular is silent as to the consequences of entering our harbours and buying bait. I think that had better be omitted until the decision in the *Adams* case is known." Sir John Macdonald to Lansdowne, June 7, 1886, *Governor-General's Correspondence*, vol. 13, *Sir John Macdonald Papers*, MS Canadian Archives.

62. Phelps to Lord Rosebery, June 2, 1886, enclosed in Phelps to Bayard, June 5, 1886, *Great Britain, Despatches*, vol. 153, MS Dept. of State. The argument employed by Phelps in his note to Lord Rosebery was clear and to the point. He did not understand it "to be claimed by the Canadian authorities that the vessel seized has been engaged or was intending to engage in fishing within any limit prohibited by the treaty of 1818. The occupation of the vessel was exclusively deep-sea fishing, a business in which it had a perfect right to be employed. The ground upon which the capture was made was that the master of the vessel had purchased of an inhabitant of Nova Scotia . . . a small quantity of bait to be used in fishing in the deep sea, outside the three-mile limit. The question presented is whether, under the terms of the treaty and the construction placed upon them . . . by the British Government, . . . that transaction affords a sufficient reason for making such a seizure and for proceeding under it to the confiscation of the vessel and its contents. . . .

"Such a literal construction [of the Treaty of 1818] is best refuted by considering its preposterous consequences. If a vessel enters a port to post a letter, or send a telegram,

In a personal letter to Bayard, Phelps explained that he had written his note to Lord Rosebery "in some haste and without access to all the documents" in the case, but he thought that it presented the American viewpoint with "sufficient accuracy and distinctness." [63] Bayard assured him that he had read the note "with much satisfaction," and that the "views and arguments" contained therein were "fully in accord" with the instructions that had already been sent to London.[64]

In the meantime Bayard had warned Sackville-West that there was "no possible justification" for the "harsh and harrassing actions" of the Canadian authorities against "peaceful commerce." [65] Canadian seizures of American fishing vessels were sometimes carried to ridiculous lengths. In a short note to Bayard, Adee indicated just how far Canadian officials would go in enforcing their interpretations of the Treaty of 1818:

I suspect that the potato seizure at Souris will turn out quite a God-send. It may be added . . . that the Prince Edward Islanders were so conscientous in enforcing the Treaty of 1818 that they not only put the potatoes on shore, but administered an emetic to the Captain and landed the mate's ejections so as to make sure that no insular potato should be taken out of port by an American fisherman.[66]

Lansdowne himself recognized how the intemperate zeal of the

---

or buy a newspaper, to obtain a physician in case of illness, . . . to land or bring off a passenger . . . it would, upon this construction, be held to violate the treaty stipulations maintained between two enlightened . . . nations. . . . If a vessel is not engaged in fishing she may enter all ports; but if employed in fishing, not denied to be lawful, she is excluded, though on the most innocent errand. She may buy water, but not food or medicine; wood, but not coal. [The Canadian contention was that an American vessel engaged in fishing was prohibited from entering a Canadian port for any purpose whatever except to obtain wood or water, to repair damages, or to seek shelter.]

". . . At the time of the seizure of the *David J. Adams* and other vessels there was no Act whatever, either of the British or Colonial Parliaments, which made the purchase of bait by those vessels illegal, or provided for any forfeiture, penalty, or proceedings against them for such a transaction. . . . I am informed that since the seizures they have pressed or are pressing through the Canadian Parliament in much haste an Act which is designed for the first time . . . under this Treaty to make the facts upon which the American vessels have been seized, illegal, and to authorize proceedings against them therefor.

". . . Even were it possible to justify on the part of the Canadian Authorities the adoption of a construction of the Treaty entirely different from that which has always heretofore prevailed, and to declare those acts criminal which have hitherto been regarded as innocent, . . . previous notice should have been given . . . to the American fishermen of the new and stringent instructions it was intended to enforce."

63. Phelps to Bayard, June 5, 1886, *Personal, Bayard MS.*

64. Bayard to Phelps, June 18, 1886, *Great Britain, Instructions,* vol. 28, MS Dept. of State.

65. Bayard to Sackville-West, June 1, 1886, *Bayard MS.*

66. A. A. Adee to Bayard, June 1, 1886, *Bayard MS.*

Canadian customs officers had carried them too far. In a note to Sir John Macdonald he deprecated the action of the authorities in this "potato case":

Here is another growl from Bayard. These complaints are very difficult to deal with. There can be no doubt that the action of our police authorities in a case such as that of the *Matthew Kearny* where the offence committed in the purchase of a few potatoes will be regarded as needlessly vexatious. Political capital will be made out of it and our cause will be prejudiced in the eyes of the public. . . . If we pounce upon every boat which spends a few cents in our waters, I fear we shall accumulate against ourselves such a volume of irritation as to render a reasonable settlement unattainable, while the Imperial Government . . . will probably grow weary of defending us against apparently well founded and often reiterated charges of vexatious proceedings.[67]

The Canadian seizures of American fishing vessels were sharply contested by the American Government. Bayard immediately employed special counsel like W. L. Putnam and George W. Biddle to represent the United States in the "hearings" which were scheduled to take place in the Vice-Admiralty Court in Halifax in the cases of the *David J. Adams* and the *Doughty*. After a careful examination of all the facts involved in these two cases, Putnam wrote to Bayard and reported that the

. . . offences of these vessels, even from the standpoint of the Dominion Authorities, seem trivial, and arose mainly if not entirely, through carelessness or ignorance. . . . As to the purchase of bait . . . there seems to be grave doubt whether there is in truth any Statute reaching the matter. . . . Researches have failed to find for me any clear statute rendering it an offence to purchase bait or other supplies in Dominion waters.[68]

In reply, Bayard expressed the view that one of the most important reasons for the difficulties between Canada and the United States was the "rude bluster of some of the political Knights who have assumed to

67. Lansdowne to Sir John Macdonald, June 5, 1886, *Governor-General's Correspondence*, vol. 13, *Sir John Macdonald Papers*, MS Canadian Archives.

68. W. L. Putnam to Bayard, June 4, 1886, *Bayard MS*. See also Bayard to Putnam, June 5, 1886, *Bayard Letter Book*, vol. 2; Putnam to Bayard, June 7, 1886, *Bayard MS*. In a letter to Putnam, June 7, 1886, Bayard states that inasmuch as the seizures of the *Adams* and the *Doughty* had been made the subject of diplomatic representations to the British Government, it would be impossible for the Department of State to urge upon the Dominion Government any remission of penalties. Although the President had no authority to employ counsel to defend private interests, the seizures of American vessels in Canadian waters involved an interpretation of the Treaty of 1818, and for that reason the President had determined that American interests should be represented by able legal talent. This did not mean, however, that the owners of the *Adams* and *Doughty* could not hire private counsel who could co-operate with the counsel employed by the Government.

have a monopoly of regard for the welfare and interests of our fishermen." [69]

It was not only from "political Knights" of Republican complexion that Bayard had to face "bluster" that made his course of conciliation more difficult. Within the President's Cabinet there were at times certain divisions of opinion, and the belligerent Secretary of the Navy, with merely a mosquito fleet, advocated bold gestures towards the troublesome Canadians. On June 4 Whitney suggested the despatch of a squadron of American warships to Canadian waters to protect American interests. Bayard thought that such action might have serious consequences. Knowing that a certain American Rear Admiral had recently used very explosive language in Central American waters in connection with the defense of American rights, there was a possibility that these same "violent expressions" might be used by other naval officers in more northerly latitudes. Before taking any action in this regard, Bayard advised Whitney to bring the matter before the President's Cabinet for careful consideration. [70]

Fortunately, for the cause of peace, the British Government was determined to show a conciliatory attitude in the fisheries dispute, and Lord Granville indicated to Lord Lansdowne his strong objections to further seizures of American vessels. The Governor-General immediately replied that he could not favor any "unconditional engagement" to discontinue these seizures. American fishermen were fully aware of the situation and it was more than likely that they would not frequent Canadian waters except for lawful purposes. He then promised that no further seizures would be made "except for clear and deliberate violations" of the Treaty of 1818 and the Canadian statutes enforcing the treaty. [71]

69. Bayard to W. L. Putnam, June 7, 1886, *Bayard Letter Book*, vol. 2, *Bayard MS.* The private counsel which the owners of the *Adams* and the *Doughty* employed to look out for their interests, consisted of the firm of Meagher, Drysdale, and Newcombe. On June 8 N. H. Meagher wrote to W. L. Putnam concerning the legal points involved in the cases. He stated that the circular issued by the Customs Department notifying foreign fishing vessels that they were required to report to the customs officer, was not put into circulation in Nova Scotia until several days after the seizure of the *Adams*. See also W. L. Putnam to Bayard, June 9, 1886, *Bayard MS.*

70. Bayard to W. C. Whitney, June 5, 1886, *Personal and Confidential, Bayard MS.* It is interesting to note that on June 5, Mr. George Steele, President of the American Fishery Union, addressed a letter to Bayard in which he suggested that American warships be sent to Canadian waters "to protect our flag, our citizens, and their property." *Foreign Relations, 1886*, p. 502.

71. Lansdowne to Granville, June 7, 1886, *Governor-General's Correspondence*, vol. 13, *Sir John Macdonald Papers*, MS Canadian Archives.

Before making this promise to Lord Granville, Lansdowne had conferred with Sir John Macdonald. The Canadian Prime Minister thought that the Dominion Government could not abandon its rights for the rest of the fishing season of 1886. Canada had met "with nothing but ingratitude and discourtesy for . . . doing so last year." [72] He was willing, however, to have instructions issued to Captain Scott "not to seize vessels merely for buying bait." [73] He also indicated to Lansdowne his complete agreement with the view that everything should be done to avoid "all causes of irritation and that the undue zeal of our officers should be restrained." [74]

This amicable attitude on the part of British and Canadian authorities was not regarded by Bayard with any too much optimism. He had a deep and abiding suspicion that Republican leaders would not hesitate to sabotage his efforts to find a satisfactory solution for the fisheries dispute. In a letter to Phelps he clearly voiced his apprehensions:

> You will observe how justly I measured the uses to which the anti-British sentiment would be put by Blaine & Company. The Irish heart (the Irish *vote*) is to be fixed to increase the difficulty of settlement of the Fishery question. It is expected that in addition to his enlightenment of the public mind on the Irish home rule measures, Mr. Blaine is soon to address a public meeting at Portland, Maine, on the Fisheries question. Whether Messrs. Evarts, Edmunds, and Sherman will accept his guidance I do not know, but up to this time I have been able to discover no higher or better rule of action with the Senate Committee on Foreign Relations, to which they belong, and which they control, than to obstruct and oppose anything proposed or approved by the Executive.
>
> Being thoroughly impressed with this belief, it made me hesitate to telegraph you that I fully responded to Lord Rosebery's proposition to make an earnest effort to negotiate, because I thought I ought to intimate how little hope I had of the success of such a treaty as we might sign, meeting fair treatment and decent reception at the hands of a Senate so organized and controlled. But I am satisfied that it is my duty and yours to go straight ahead and do our best to procure a reasonable, equitable, and just settlement of this long vexed question.[75]

72. Sir John Macdonald to Lansdowne, June 5, 1886, *ibid.*
73. Sir John Macdonald to Lansdowne, June 6, 1886, *ibid.*
74. Sir John Macdonald to Lansdowne, June 7, 1886, *ibid.* See also Lansdowne to Sir John Macdonald, June 8, 1886, *ibid.*
75. Bayard to Phelps, June 9, 1886, *Personal, Bayard Letter Book*, vol. 2, *Bayard MS.* In a letter to Lord Lansdowne, June 5, 1886, Sackville-West remarks: "The Secretary of State is accused of not acting with sufficient vigour and if Blaine takes the matter up for electioneering purposes the Senate will refuse to sanction any arrangement simply in order to keep up their irritation." *Governor-General's Correspondence*, vol. 13. *Sir John Macdonald Papers*, MS Canadian Archives. With reference to the interplay of politics and

Phelps was inclined to think that the British Government would be very reluctant to take any action that would be distasteful to the Canadian authorities. He thought that Bayard would have to

. . . take very decided and sharp ground before we shall achieve any result. . . . If we take such a position we must be ready and willing to back it up. . . . It seems to me that upon the question whether we shall take such ground the real state of public sentiment in the United States must be fully considered. . . . If public opinion seems to demand and is likely to justify it, there is much in favour of taking a very decided and peremptory position with the British Government. It would take the wind out of Blaine's sails, would place the Administration in a strong attitude with the country, and would be likely to be effectual. There is no question at all in my mind but that we are entirely in the right in the dispute, and perhaps this is the only way in which we can get justice.[76]

On Bayard's part there was no hesitancy about using strong words in the defense of American rights. When the word came to him that the Canadian authorities were reviving their former pretensions to draw imaginary lines from headland to headland in order to prevent American fishermen from fishing in wide stretches of water like the Gut of Canso and Chaleur Bay, he sent a warning to Sackville-West against such interference "with the unquestionable rights" of American fishermen.[77] His apprehensions about the actions of Canadian officials were relieved when he received a copy of a confidential circular issued by the Commissioner of Customs at Ottawa. He noted with great satisfaction the ". . . phraseology in the order, 'found within three marine miles of the shore,' which I trust will be the unquestioned basis of any

diplomacy, there are two notes which are of some interest. On June 15, 1886, Senator George F. Edmunds sent a short letter to Bayard in which he gave the assurance that "every member of the Committee on Foreign Relations will be glad at any time to receive any suggestions or information, confidential or other, upon this [the fisheries] or any other subject from you in precisely the same spirit as if the Committee and its chairman were your political friends." On June 18 Bayard replied: "I am very glad to receive from you the assurance that the Committee on Foreign Relations will be willing to receive from me information or suggestions confidential or other, and in the same spirit as if they were my political friends. During my service in the Senate and whilst Mr. Fish served as Secretary of State, I was frequently honored by his confidence in public affairs, and it never occurred to me that in the common cause of our country as against foreign governments, there should or could be any other than one party or side for an American." *Bayard Letter Book,* vol. 2, *Bayard MS.*

76. Phelps to Bayard, June 15, 1886, *Personal, Bayard MS.*

77. Bayard to Sackville-West, June 14, 1886, *British Legation, Notes to,* vol. 20, MS Dept. of State.

negotiations we may set on foot, and get rid of the 'imaginary line' from headlands." [78]

This whole question of jurisdiction in the marginal sea along the Canadian coasts was by no means settled by the circular issued confidentially by the Commissioner of Customs at Ottawa. Bayard's note to Sackville-West on June 14 caused no little uneasiness in the mind of the British Minister. He was also fearful of the designs of "Blaine, Frye & Company" whose object was to make it appear that the Dominion Government had been disavowed by the British Ministry. He was certain that Blaine wanted "some foreign question for a 'platform,' and catches at any straw that may be blowing about." [79]

If Blaine had known of certain correspondence that was passing between Bayard and Whitney he might very well have been able to make political capital out of the fishery question. In the summer of 1886, Whitney was making preparations for a cruise of certain American warships in Canadian waters. Such a cruise might produce unpleasant incidents with international complications. For this reason Whitney thought it best to have Professor J. R. Soley accompany the American fleet as an adviser upon questions of International Law. He informed Soley that American relations with Great Britain concerning Canada were moving "satisfactorily at present," but at the same time "we should be prepared for a change." [80] These were ominous words.

When Bayard inquired as to the precise scope of the duties of Professor Soley,[81] Whitney replied that certain incidents might arise while the American fleet was in Canadian waters, and for that reason it was important to attach someone to the staff of the commanding officer in

78. Bayard to Phelps, June 18, 1886, *Personal, Bayard Letter Book,* vol. 2. *Bayard MS.* In this letter to Phelps, Bayard remarks: "You were quite right in thinking the law officers of the Crown should have an opportunity to come to a decision on the proper interpretation to be given to the Treaty of 1818, and of the necessity of Great Britain enforcing upon her provinces a sense of *her* responsibility under it." The Dominion Government was insistent upon its right to pass laws enforcing treaties between the United States and the British Empire. In a letter to Lord Granville, June 7, 1886, Lord Lansdowne observes: "Your Lordship is no doubt aware that legislation of this kind has been frequently resorted to by the Parliament of the Dominion for the purpose of enforcing Treaties. . . . The right of the Dominion Parliament to legislate for these purposes, and the validity of such legislation as against the citizens of a foreign country has . . . not been seriously called in question. Such legislation, unless it is disallowed by the Imperial Government, becomes a part of the law of the Empire." *Governor-General's Correspondence,* vol. 13, *Sir John Macdonald Papers,* MS Canadian Archives.
79. Sackville-West to Lansdowne, June 25, 1886, *ibid.*
80. W. C. Whitney to Bayard, June 27, 1886, *Bayard MS.*
81. Bayard to Whitney, June 28, 1886, *Bayard MS.*

order that no "blunder" would be committed through "ignorance of the law."[82]

At the same time that Secretary Whitney was making preparations to send an American fleet to Canadian waters, Lord Lansdowne was writing to Lord Granville to request the "support of the Queen's ships on the Halifax Station." There was no doubt in Lansdowne's mind that this support would be very "valuable," and he was at great pains to point out to the Colonial Secretary how "much its absence will be felt if it is withheld."[83]

Despite this pressure from Canada, Lord Granville refused to support the request for some of the "Queen's ships" on the Halifax Station.[84] The British Ministry was evidently embarrassed by the attitude of the Dominion officials,[85] and every effort was made to settle a dispute which might easily grow into menacing proportions. It was fortunate that this amicable sentiment existed in British official circles. In America there was a great deal of tinder that needed only a spark to start a blaze of anti-British prejudice that would bring the two nations to the verge of war. Bayard was certain that there was a large class that could be "easily kindled into noisy aggression." The "summary, harsh, and unwarranted arrests" of American fishing vessels in Canadian waters had furnished these belligerent Americans an excellent opportunity to fulminate against Great Britain. The situation had such dangerous possibilities that Bayard was amazed that the British Foreign Office had not been exerting strong pressure upon Canadian officials in favor of a more friendly policy towards American fishermen.[86]

82. Whitney to Bayard, June 28, 1886, *ibid.* On July 5, 1886, Robert Winthrop wrote to Bayard and expressed the view that it would be expedient to have a body of American police "to arrest our Fishermen when they are doing wrong, and to protect them when they are doing right—the arbitrary seizure of American Fishermen by British Cruisers is apt to stir the blood on a 4th of July." *Bayard MS.*

83. Lansdowne to Sir John Macdonald, July 1, 1886, *Governor-General's Correspondence,* vol. 13, *Sir John Macdonald Papers,* MS Canadian Archives.

84. Lansdowne to Macdonald, July 2, 1886, *ibid.*

85. Phelps to Bayard, June 26, 1886, *Personal, Bayard MS.* See also Bayard to G. W. Biddle, June 30, 1886, *ibid.*

86. Bayard to Phelps, July 3, 1886, *Personal, Bayard Letter Book,* vol. 3, *Bayard MS.* The attitude assumed by Bayard with reference to the rights of American fishermen was distinctly colored by the views of Francis Wharton. In a memorandum sent to Bayard in the early days of 1886, Wharton observed as follows: "I am clear as to the following: 1. The Treaty of 1818 does not exclude our fishing vessels, bearing our flag and complying with port laws in the same way as do other trading vessels, from purchasing bait or anything else in ports of entry. 2. By the law of nations, vessels of all kind may visit foreign shores, whether at ports of entry or otherwise, when necessity requires. 3. The treaty of 1818, in renouncing the right to 'take' fish in Canadian territorial waters, reserves,

It was doubtless true that in the United States a strong effort had been made to prevent the public from knowing the many steps the Department of State had taken on behalf of the fishermen. The officers of the American Fishery Union had made haste

. . . to place their cases of complaint before the Department, with urgent demands for specific replies. . . . The replies have been suppressed and intimations of secrecy thrown out, in strong contrast to publicity on all points supposed to be prejudicial to the Department's view of the American case.[87]

Bayard greatly regretted to see the "taunts and sneers of the newspapers and the blustering talk of their correspondents." Such actions would not lead to a peaceful settlement of the fishery controversy. On the other hand, the attitude of the Canadian officials in the enforcement of their restrictive legislation was bound to lead to serious trouble.[88]

by force of the rule 'exclusio unius,' the right to *buy* fish. 4. This 'buying' of fish was held unanimously by the Halifax commissioners not to be a thing for which compensation could be awarded to G. B." *Bayard MS.* After receiving this memorandum from Wharton, Bayard dictated to Adee a memorandum which was closely similar: "Mr. Bayard said that the essential claim of the United States was that *any* vessel, whether a fishing vessel or not, if properly documented by its government, could touch and trade in conformity with revenue laws at any Canadian port of entry and there purchase merchandise or supplies of every description on lawful sale in open market, and ship or discharge seamen: that the reservation, under the treaty of 1818, of the right to enter the inshore waters, for shelter, repairs, wood and water, was intended to secure to all fishing vessels whether carrying permits to trade or not, the right to be within waters not of ports of entry, and where any trading vessel would have no business to be except in stress; that such reserve right of access also gave to such vessels the right to waters of ports of entry for the purposes named in the treaty and no other purpose whatsoever, without requiring of them the formalities of entry or clearance; and that, for all the purposes of the treaty, the purchase of bait, ice, salt, and supplies of every kind essential to the operation of fishing, whether in the inshore waters not renounced by the treaty or on the high seas, was to be regarded as trade, to be conducted only in lawful places and in the usual and customary ways." *Bayard MS.*

87. Bayard to W. L. Putnam, July 7, 1886, *Personal, Bayard Letter Book*, vol. 3, *Bayard MS.*

88. In a personal letter to Bayard, July 8, 1886, W. L. Putnam makes some significant remarks with reference to the enforcement of Canadian restrictive legislation in connection with the fisheries: "The consolidated Customs Act of Canada, of A. D. 1883, may easily be made the means of driving off our fishing vessels under the false cover of protecting the Revenue. The late seizures at Shelburne, Nova Scotia, . . . afford a practical example. . . . These seizures have apparently been made on so narrow grounds and for reasons so obscure, that the owners of our fishing vessels at this port [Portland] are entirely unable to form any opinion of what will be permitted them in Dominion waters. . . . I think the matter would hardly stand today in any worse condition, so far as our fishing vessels are concerned, if they were prohibited in express terms from entering Dominion ports for any purpose whatever. The system of the Dominion Customs Act of A. D. 1883 . . . is very complicated, severe and difficult to understand, and certainly is

This was particularly true of the way in which these Canadian officials acted with reference to the laws and regulations governing fishing operations in Canadian waters. The secretive manner in which the regulations were administered aroused Bayard's indignation:

> Mr. Phelan, our Consul-General at Halifax, found the greatest difficulty in obtaining information of any kind, and was informed by some officials that the orders under which they were acting were "Confidential" and could not be divulged. To hold individuals summarily punishable for violation of secret laws or regulations is something worse than barbaric and is disgraceful to humanity whether professing civilization or no.[89]

In a letter to Phelps, Bayard makes the same complaint:

> The Fishery imbroglio does not improve, and the intentions of Canada seem to be muddy and perhaps intentionally obscured. . . . The *reductio ad absurdum* which you suggested in your note to Lord Rosebery that under the Canadian construction of the Treaty of 1818, *wood* might be obtained but not *coal*, has been gravely verified in the case of the *Novelty* at Pictou. It is reported that her Captain was refused letters at the Post Office—that privilege not being enumerated in the treaty. But a feature more dangerous and reprehensible is the concealment of regulations and the secrecy of the orders given to Customs officers and Captains of the cruisers, and their refusal to divulge them. In fact the conduct of this business seems to have passed into petty, unworthy, and irresponsible hands, who are behaving so disreputably, so harassingly, and wantonly, that serious consequences may result.[90]

Despite the danger of "serious consequences" resulting from the developments in the fishery dispute, the British Government appeared unwilling to take any steps that might give umbrage to Canada. To Phelps it was obvious that the

---

beyond the every-day comprehension of the skippers of fishing vessels, who are very little used to the details of Customs laws.

"I . . . especially refer to sec. 21 and sec. 22, which provide that if any vessel with dutiable goods on board enter any place other than a port of entry, unless from stress of weather or other unavoidable cause, she shall be liable to punishment to the extent of eight hundred dollars. I believe it will be found that under this Customs Act fresh fish are liable to a duty of one cent per pound, so that by the letter of the Statute one of our vessels returning from the Banks with a fare of fish might be claimed liable to this penalty, the only limitations being stress of weather or other unavoidable cause, which, of course, exclude some of the exceptions of the Treaty of A. D. 1818." In another personal letter to Bayard, July 9, 1886, Putnam makes the following pertinent observation: "As I have watched the operations of the Dominion Government, my mind has been quite engrossed with the harshness of its measures and its evasion and lack of frankness. . . . My explanation is in part that the present Dominion Government is under the stress of very severe political attacks." *Bayard MS.*

89. Bayard to W. L. Putnam, July 16, 1886, *Personal, Bayard MS.*

90. Bayard to Phelps, July 17, 1886, *Personal, Bayard Letter Book,* vol. 3, *Bayard MS.*

. . . dignified, friendly, and courteous remonstrance we have made use of, is entirely unavailing. We must either submit to these outrages, or give the British Government distinctly to understand that they will not be submitted to, and that reprisals will be immediately made unless peaceable redress is given. . . . I can only say that we shall not, in my opinion, obtain satisfaction in any other way.[91]

Such a bold course could be successful only in the event that Bayard had the united support of Congress and the country at large. From the Republican majority in the Senate he could expect nothing but political sabotage. On July 10 the Senate passed a resolution which requested the President to communicate any information in the possession of the Government "concerning the alleged seizure of the United States fishing vessel *David J. Adams* while engaged in lawful commerce in one of the ports in the Dominion of Canada."[92] Before President Cleveland made a formal reply to this resolution, Senator William P. Frye wrote to Bayard to inquire whether he had made certain statements which appeared in the Baltimore *Sun*. If he had authorized these statements it would then be necessary for the Senator immediately to reply to them.[93]

Bayard assured Mr. Frye that he had "neither made nor authorized nor approved of any publication whatever in relation to anything connected with my public office or its administration."[94] Three days later, the President sent to the Senate a copy of a report by Bayard with reference to the seizures of American fishing vessels in Canadian waters.[95] But this data was not sufficient for the very active members of the Senate Committee on Foreign Relations, and Bayard was kept busy answering additional requests for information.[96]

These requests were usually related to reports of Canadian seizures of American vessels, and such reports were of frequent occurrence. On July 30 Bayard sent a note of protest to Sackville-West with reference to the illegal action of the customs officer on the northwestern coast of Newfoundland in driving away from the waters of Bonne Bay the American schooner *Thomas F. Bayard*. Under the terms of the Treaty of 1818 these waters were open to American fishermen, and the

91. Phelps to Bayard, July 20, 1886, *Personal, Bayard MS.*
92. *House Ex. Doc. 19*, 49 Cong., 2 sess., p. 141.
93. W. P. Frye to Bayard, July 21, 1886, *Bayard MS.*
94. Bayard to W. P. Frye, July 21, 1886, *ibid.*
95. *House Ex. Doc., 19*, 49 Cong., 2 sess., pp. 140-146.
96. Senator George F. Edmunds to Bayard, July 31, 1886, Bayard to Edmunds, August 2, 1886; Bayard to Sackville-West, August 2, 1886, *Bayard Letter Book*, vol. 3, *Bayard MS.*

expulsion of the schooner was a "flagrant violation" of treaty rights.[97]

Bayard also sent an instruction to Phelps in connection with this incident, and in a personal letter which preceded this instruction he drew attention to the action of Canadian authorities in denying to American fishermen the right to enter Chaleur Bay. Inasmuch as the bay was "over twenty miles wide at its mouth," it was only upon "the 'headland' pretension" that exclusion could be claimed.[98] Bayard then expressed his pleasure at the report that Lord Iddesleigh would be the Secretary for Foreign Affairs in the new British Cabinet. He regarded this appointment as a "good augury" for better relations between England and America. With reference to the American political scene he was somewhat pessimistic. The temper of the Senate Committee on Foreign Relations was

. . . very small and they keep themselves in an attitude of unfriendliness to the Administration. In fact their noble ambition seems to be limited to obstruction and contradiction. I am so much impressed by this belief that I hardly know what treaty negotiated by us would be acceptable to them and meet their party requirements.[99]

While Bayard was endeavoring to find a formula that would satisfy both the Senate and the fishing interests of Canada, certain Canadian

97. Bayard to Sackville-West, July 30, 1886, *British Legation, Notes to,* vol. 20, MS Dept. of State. See also, Charles L. Woodbury to Bayard, July 28, 30, 1866, and Bayard to Woodbury, July 30, 1886, *For. Rel., 1886,* pp. 516-518.

98. With reference to Bayard's protest against the action of Canadian officials in excluding American fishermen from Chaleur Bay, Lord Lansdowne remarks as follows in a note to Lord Granville, August 4, 1886: "It is not necessary upon the present occasion that I should recur to the past history of the 'Headlands Question,' or that I should do more than state that Mr. Bayard's suggestion that the Bay des Chaleurs does not form a part of the waters from which United States fishermen are excluded, is one in which my Government cannot acquiesce. Throughout the negotiations which have at different times taken place in regard to these waters, no such admission has ever been made on the part of the Dominion, or, as far as I am aware, by the Imperial Government. It is therefore wholly incorrect of Mr. Bayard to speak of the question as one which should be included amongst those 'which have been long since settled between the United States and Great Britain.'" *Governor-General's Correspondence,* vol. 13, *Sir John Macdonald Papers,* MS Canadian Archives.

99. Bayard to Phelps, July 29, 1886, *Personal, Bayard Letter Book,* vol. 3, *Bayard MS.* In another letter to Phelps, August 6, 1886, Bayard makes some further comments upon the activities of certain members of the Senate Committee on Foreign Relations like Senator Edmunds: "I enclose two newspaper slips, one from the New York *Tribune* stating a falsehood in relation to you and the other the unmasking of Mr. Edmund's heart in relation to the Administration and the Democratic Party generally. His kindly comments on the 'unfortunate' nature of my selections for office read oddly in connection with the fact that he has practical control of the Committee on Foreign Affairs, and that no single rejection has been voted by a Republican Senate even after a year of deliberation upon many of the cases." *Bayard MS.*

officials were making every effort to discover some basis for agreement. Mr. Foster, the Canadian Minister for Marine and Fisheries, expressed to Sir John Macdonald the fear that if Bayard's "protests are to be heeded we shall soon have no bays, no treaty rights, and no territorial waters." [100] Lansdowne also wrote to Sir John to sound a warning that American fishermen were "following the fish with such pertinacity that we may find it inevitable to take steps in order to determine what are the limits of our territorial waters." [101]

Macdonald deprecated any haste in this matter of passing judgment upon what constituted Canadian territorial waters. He was strongly of the opinion that the

. . . policy of the past should be continued and the settlement of the question postponed; at all events, until all hope of a renewed treaty is abandoned. The subject has been exhaustively discussed by the diplomacy of both nations, and nothing now remains to be said. England and Canada think they are in the right; and the American Government, right or wrong, dare not yield in the face of their fierce democracy. The only solution, therefore, . . . is a reference to a friendly power or a selected jurisconsult. In case of such a reference, should the decision be against the pretensions of the United States, the irritation there fomented by demogogues of the Blaine stamp, would be so great as to preclude the possibility of a friendly negotiation for a Reciprocity Treaty.[102]

Lansdowne did not accept the view that it would be expedient to postpone any decision in the matter of Canadian territorial waters. The presence of large schools of fish in Chaleur Bay would probably induce American fishermen to frequent that body of water. This fact would "in all probability lead to the headlands question being formally raised ere long." The first thing to be done, therefore, was to "arrive at an understanding as to the limits of our territorial waters." [103]

This understanding would have to be arranged through negotiations between England and the United States, and on July 23 Lord Rosebery informed Sackville-West that the British Government was prepared to enter upon "a frank and friendly consideration of the whole question with the most earnest desire to arrive at a settlement consonant alike with the rights and interests of Canada and of the

100. George E. Foster to Sir John Macdonald, June 24, 1886. *Governor-General's Correspondence,* vol. 13, *Sir John Macdonald Papers,* MS Canadian Archives.

101. Lansdowne to Sir. John Macdonald, July 12, 1886, *ibid.*

102. Sir John Macdonald to Lansdowne, July 29, 1886, *Governor-General's Correspondence,* vol. 13, *Sir John Macdonald Papers,* vol. 13, MS Canadian Archives.

103. Lansdowne to Sir John Macdonald, August 2, 1886, *ibid.*

United States." [104] From Phelps came the word that the new British Foreign Secretary, Lord Iddesleigh, would give "favorable consideration" to a plan to end the fisheries dispute. [105] As early as July 1, 1886, Sir John Macdonald had broached to Lord Lansdowne the idea of settling all points in dispute between Canada and the United States by reference to an arbitral commission. [106] Could Bayard prevail upon the Senate finally to agree that such a mode of settlement was desirable? [107]

104. Lord Rosebery to Sackville-West, July 23, 1886, enclosed in note from Charles Hardinge to Bayard, August 2, 1886, *British Legation, Notes from*, vol. 113, MS Dept. of State. In this note from Hardinge to Bayard there was enclosed a lengthy report from George E. Foster, Canadian Minister of Marine and Fisheries, on the fisheries question.

105. Phelps to Bayard, August 10, 1886, *Personal, Bayard MS.*

106. Lansdowne to Sir John Macdonald, July 1, 1886, *Governor-General's Correspondence*, vol. 13, *Sir John Macdonald Papers*, MS Canadian Archives.

107. It might be pertinent to summarize the points at issue between the United States and the Canadian Government in the fisheries dispute. They can be conveniently listed as follows:

(a) *The three-mile limit*. With reference to *bays* the British Government, representing Canada, contended that the line should be drawn from headland to headland, thus excluding American fishermen from the enclosed waters whether large or small. The position of the American Government was clearly stated by Bayard in a note to Mr. Daniel Manning, the Secretary of the Treasury, May 28, 1886: "The position of this department has uniformly been that the sovereignty of the shore does not . . . extend beyond three miles from low water mark, and that the seaward boundary of the zone of territorial waters follows the coast of the mainland, extending where there are islands so as to place around such islands the same belt. This necessarily excludes the position that the seaward boundary is to be drawn from headland to headland, and makes it follow closely, at a distance of three miles, the boundary of the shore of the continent." Francis Wharton, *Digest of International Law* (Washington, 1886), vol. 1, p. 107. According to Charles B. Elliott, *The United States and the Northeastern Fisheries*, p. 111, the position taken by the United States on this question of the extent of the three-mile limit is "supported by every authoritative modern writer on International Law."

(b) *The right to enter Canadian harbors for the purpose of purchasing bait*. The contention of the American Government was that the limitations of the treaty of 1818 had reference only to *inshore* fishing. Since the introduction of purse-seines, this type of fishing no longer required bait, which was used exclusively for deep-sea fishing. In view of this fact it was clear that there was no longer any reason why bait should not be sold to American fishermen whose operations would always be *outside* the three-mile limit. It was important to note that there was no existing legislation, Imperial or Provincial, which contained any provision declaring it illegal to enter a port and purchase bait for deep-sea fishing.

The American claim was based upon the duty of "good neighborhood," and the obligation of international comity. Strictly speaking, the American fishermen had no *right* to purchase bait in Canadian harbors, but it was nonetheless true that the change in the methods of fishing, whereby bait was no longer used in *inshore* fishing operations, did constitute a strong argument against the strict enforcement of Canadian restrictions. In support of the Canadian viewpoint the following excerpt from a report of George E. Foster, Canadian Minister of Marine and Fisheries, June 14, 1886, is pertinent: "It is not the . . . case that the convention of 1818 affected only the inshore fisheries of the British provinces; it was framed with the object of affording a complete and exclusive definition of the rights and liberties which the fishermen of the United States were thenceforward to enjoy in following their vocation, so far as those rights could be affected by facilities for access to the shores and waters of the British provinces, or for intercourse with their people. It is therefore no undue expansion of the scope of that convention to interpret strictly those of its provisions by which such access is denied, except to vessels requiring it for the purposes specifically described. Such an undue expansion would, upon the other hand, certainly take place if, under cover of its provisions, or of any agreement relative to general commercial intercourse which may have since been made, permission were accorded to United States fishermen to resort habitually to the harbors of the Dominion, not for the sake of seeking safety for their vessels or of avoiding risk to human life, but in order to use those harbors as a general base of operations from which to prosecute and organize with greater advantage to themselves the industry in which they are engaged." *House Ex. Doc., 19,* 49 Cong., 2 sess., pp. 29-37.

(c) *The question of commercial privileges for American fishermen in Canadian harbors.* The American Government supported the view that American fishing vessels had a right to purchase bait, ice, or *other supplies* in Canadian harbors. This claim was based upon the obligation of *international comity.* It was given clear and cogent expression in the following excerpt from the report of the House Committee on Foreign Affairs, February 16, 1887, *House Rept. 4087,* 49 Cong., 2 sess., p. 13: "If the privy council and the governor-general of the Canadian Dominion excluded *all* American vessels from all rights of touching and trading in Canadian ports excepting to obtain shelter, repairs, wood, or water, the contention would be logical and more tolerable; but to every American vessel other than a fishing vessel, be the fisherman big or little—a schooner, a sloop, a ship, or a steamer of large tonnage—the Canadian ports seem to be wide open. If, however, she be an American fishing vessel on the high seas, she cannot go into a Canadian bay even to bury those of her dead who in life may have been British subjects. . . . The treaty of 1818 gave rights of fishing independent of general commercial rights, although it may be said that, as to shelter, repairs, wood, and water, the treaty did give to fishermen certain commercial rights, or rather a few rights of humanity. The treaty did not restrain the granting or the exercising of commercial rights. The right, if it be a right, of an American to buy anything in Canada does not come of the inshore fishing treaty of 1818. Your committee are not aware of any Canadian or Newfoundland law which, having been approved by the British Crown, forbids a British subject to there sell ice, or bait, or anything else, to an American, or to trade with him."

(d) *The right to navigate the Gut of Canso.* The navigation of the Gut of Canso had long been regarded by American fishermen as an important right. This strait connects the Atlantic Ocean and the Gulf of St. Lawrence, and the exclusion of American fishermen from its waters would be a serious deprivation. The general rule of international law was clearly stated by A. G. Heffter, in his *Diplomatie de la Mer,* vol. 1, p. 146: "Straits which serve as a means of communication between two seas, should be regarded as free and common to the use of all nations, when they can be passed by vessels beyond the range of cannon placed upon the adjacent shores. . . . No one people can prevent others from the innocent use of these channels of communication."

An important parallel case with reference to the navigation of straits connecting important bodies of water, was the dispute concerning the payment to Denmark of dues on all shipping that passed through the Danish Sound *en route* to the Baltic Sea. Through international pressure, the Danish Government finally agreed in 1857 to consent to the abolition of these dues in consideration for a lump sum to be paid by the principal commercial powers. This sum was to be used for the establishment of a permanent channel service and a system of buoys and lighthouses that would provide adequate safeguards for the commerce passing through the Sound. Great Britain was one of the powers that strongly pressed for the abolition of these Sound dues. The United States agreed to pay $393,011 as its share of the lump sum that was expended for the establishment of this permanent channel service. See Charles E. Hill, *The Danish Sound Dues and the Command of the Baltic* (Durham, 1926).

(e) *Provincial construction of a treaty made between the Governments of Great*

Britain and the United States. There are certain principles of international law which are universally accepted. One of these principles is that "the treaty-making power of government is the power which must answer to the other contracting power for infractions of the treaty. . . . Another equally self-evident principle is that municipal statutes, state or federal, cannot be set up as a defense to a charge of violating a treaty. Consequently the claim of Canada to construe a treaty contracted between the United States and Great Britain, cannot be admitted by the United States. The treaty-making power belongs only to an independent nation." Charles B. Elliott, *The United States and the Northeastern Fisheries*, p. 129.

In confirmation of this viewpoint the American Government cited the note from Earl Kimberley to the Governor-General of Canada in March, 1871, in which the following statement was made: "I think it is right . . . to add that the responsibility of determining what is the true construction of a treaty made by Her Majesty with any foreign power must remain with her Majesty's Government, and that the degree to which this country would make itself a party to the strict enforcement of the treaty rights may depend not only on the literal construction of the treaty, but on the moderation and reasonableness with which these rights are asserted." John Bassett Moore, *Digest of International Law*, vol. 1, p. 825.

In further support of the American position we have an article written by Worthington C. Ford, an intimate friend of Bayard, in *The Forum*, Ocotber, 1886, pp. 174-181, entitled "The Fisheries Dispute." In this article Mr. Ford remarks: "By the Canadian law of 1868, which was revived by the abrogation of the fisheries article in the treaty of Washington, and is pleaded by the Dominion as justifying its attitude toward American fishermen, any commissioned officer of the British navy, any officer of the customs of Canada, or any sheriff or magistrate, may board an American vessel or boat within any harbor in Canada, or hovering within three marine miles of any of the coasts, bays, or creeks, or harbors in Canada, and order it to depart. If the order should not be obeyed within twenty-four hours, the vessel may be brought into port, its cargo and papers examined, and, upon a technical defect, it may be condemned to pay a fine of four hundred dollars. Should the vessel be found fishing or preparing to fish in any position as just described, it becomes subject to forfeiture. This act is a proper cause of complaint on the part of the United States, because it assumes that the Dominion Parliament has the right to construe or interpret the provisions of the treaty of 1818, and that it may exercise that right in such a manner as to defeat the privileges accorded to American fishermen. . . . If under a plea of police regulations, a dependency may nullify solemn treaty obligations entered into by two sovereign powers, it is time to revise our notions of international law, for no treaty could stand under such a ruling."

On the other hand, the Canadian justification for their restrictive legislation was well presented in the report of George E. Foster, Canadian Minister of Marine and Fisheries, June 14, 1886, *House Ex. Doc., 19*, 49 Cong., 2 sess., pp. 29-37: "The authority of the legislatures of the provinces, and, after confederation, the authority of the Parliament of Canada, to make enactments to enforce the provisions of the convention, as well as the authority of Canadian officers to enforce those acts, rests on well-known constitutional principles. Those legislatures existed, and the Parliament of Canada now exists, by the authority of the Parliament of the United Kingdom of Great Britain and Ireland, which is one of the nations referred to by Mr. Bayard as the 'contracting parties.' The colonial statutes have received the sanction of the British sovereign, who, and not the nation, is actually the party with whom the United States made the convention. The officers who are engaged in enforcing the acts of Canada or the laws of the Empire, are Her Majesty's officers. . . . The jurisdiction thus exercised cannot, therefore, be properly described in the language used by Mr. Bayard as a supposed and therefore questionable delegation of jurisdiction by the Imperial Government of Great Britain. Her Majesty governs in Canada as well as in Great Britain; the officers of Canada are her officers; the statutes of Canada are her statutes, passed on the advice of her Parliament sitting in Canada."

CHAPTER EIGHT

Bayard Bends Every Effort to Conciliate Canada

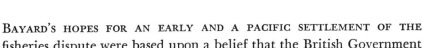

BAYARD'S HOPES FOR AN EARLY AND A PACIFIC SETTLEMENT OF THE fisheries dispute were based upon a belief that the British Government was anxious to find some formula that would be satisfactory both to Canada and to the United States. On July 30, 1886, he sent an instruction to Phelps which contained a strong protest against the action of the authorities on the west coast of Newfoundland in refusing to permit American fishermen to "take fish of every kind" in the harbor of Bonne Bay.[1] In response to this instruction, Phelps lodged a strong complaint with Lord Iddesleigh. The British Government had indicated that it could take no action in the matter of Canadian seizures of American fishing vessels until certain legal proceedings in Canadian courts had been "brought to a conclusion." To this proposition Phelps gave an emphatic negative. The interpretation of a treaty

. . . when it becomes the subject of discussion between two governments is not, I respectfully insist, to be settled by the judicial tribunals of either. That would be placing its construction in the hands of one of the parties to it. It can only be interpreted for such a purpose by the mutual consideration and agreement which were necessary to make it. Questions between individuals arising upon the terms of a treaty may be for the courts to which they resort to adjust. Questions between nations as to national rights secured by treaty are of a very different character and must be solved in another way. The United States Government is no party to the proceedings instituted by the British authorities in Canada. Nor can it consent to become a party. . . . It would be inconsistent with the dignity of a sovereign power to become a party to such proceedings, or to seek redress in any way in the

1. Bayard to Phelps, July 30, 1886, *Great Britain, Instructions,* vol. 28, MS Dept. of State.

courts of another country for what it claims to be the violation of treaty stipulations by the authorities of that country.[2]

The firm stand taken by Phelps in the fisheries controversy had made a deep impression upon the Colonial Office which showed great anxiety to conciliate America.[3] Lord Lansdowne was in London on a visit, and on August 20 he wrote to Sir John Macdonald to complain that all his efforts to induce Her Majesty's Government to send some warships to the Canadian coasts were in vain. All pressure in this regard had met with a "very determined resistance" by both the Foreign and the Colonial Offices on the ground that "the sudden appearance of one of Her Majesty's ships would add to the already existing exasperation and lessen the prospect of the negotiations now in progress leading to a satisfactory result." [4]

In accordance with this pacific program, the Colonial Office immediately sent word to the governments of Canada and Newfoundland with reference to the protests made by Bayard, and attention was called to the fact that "under the treaty of 1818 United States fishermen have the right to fish off the coasts of the Magdalen Islands and off certain coasts of Newfoundland." [5]

This conciliatory attitude on the part of the British Government with reference to the fisheries dispute was an important factor in keeping Canadian-American friction within reasonable bounds. If American protests against the harsh actions of Canadian officials had not been given prompt consideration it is very likely that political pressure would have compelled President Cleveland to adopt strong measures of retaliation. In the late summer of 1886 the Congressional elections were assuming definite importance and the President felt that he could not permit Republican politicians to bring up the charge that the

2. Phelps to Lord Iddesleigh, September 11, 1886, enclosed in despatch from Phelps to Bayard, *Great Britain, Despatches,* vol. 154, MS Dept. of State.

3. In the latter part of August, 1886, Phelps had a conversation with Lord Iddesleigh during which he remarked that the American Government was "not now engaged in making a new Treaty, but in the administration of the existing one, and are asking nothing whatever that we are not already entitled to. . . . I expressed to him my grave apprehensions that unless the conduct of Canadian Authorities is restrained before Congress meets, a war of retaliation will take place which would be very injurious to both sides and to the friendly relations of the Governments." Phelps to Bayard, August 28, 1886, *Personal, Bayard MS.*

4. Lord Lansdowne to Sir John Macdonald, August 20, 1886, *Governor-General's Correspondence,* vol. 13, *Sir John Macdonald Papers,* MS Canadian Archives.

5. Sackville-West to Bayard, September 17, 1886, *Great Britain, Notes from,* vol. 113, MS Dept. of State.

Administration was not looking after the interests of the New England fishermen.[6] On August 14 he had a conversation with Bayard on the question of the fisheries and expressed the desire that the American public be informed of the stand taken by the Department of State in defense of American rights. Bayard gave assurances that the correspondence with the British Foreign Office would clearly indicate the care that had been taken to protect all American fishing interests, and on the following day he promised to send the President a condensed statement of this correspondence. He would also write to Phelps "in a few days and see whether we cannot 'move upon the enemy's works' efficiently." [7]

To the President the fisheries controversy had assumed such importance that he replied at once to Bayard's note:

You were very good to write me your note of today, and I am delighted to see how perfectly you understand what is in my mind and how much better than I could, you express my ideas (as usual). The thing grows on me, and instead of attempting to make our Countrymen understand that we are minding their interests and protecting their rights, through the medium of an interview in the newspapers, . . . I . . . suggest that you send at once a despatch to Phelps expressing the surprise of the President and our Government at the failure of the English Government to recognize and follow the reasonable and just precedent which was established by itself as late as 1871, and that the attempt should now be made to exclude our fishermen from the enjoyment of the purely commercial privileges accorded our other vessels in Canadian ports; that these privileges rest upon other considerations than the stipulations of any treaty and are and should be unaffected by any supposed relation to the question of fishing; that these commercial privileges cannot (or *ought* not) (or *should* not) be the subject of treaty negotiations but should be accorded as growing out of the Commercial relations which should exist between Countries situated as are our domain and the English possessions in Canada; that while we fully concede the right to prohibit such Commercial intercourse, nevertheless if it is denied our citizens and "the usual Commercial facilities and privileges are denied our fishing craft, it will be regarded as an unfriendly course on the part of Canada and the English government, that it will create exasperation and alienation and will oblige this government to a policy of retaliation in kind," and that this policy will be promptly entered upon by the President under the powers recently conferred upon him by Congress.

I want to suggest too that Mr. Phelps be instructed to strongly intimate

6. On July 23, 1886, Senator George F. Edmunds introduced a resolution which instructed the Senate Committee on Foreign Relations to inquire "into the rights" of American fishing vessels and merchant vessels within the North American possessions of the Queen of Great Britain. The resolution was agreed to on the following day. *Congressional Record*, July 23-24, 1886, vol. 17, pt. 7, pp. 7350, 7430.

7. Bayard to President Cleveland, August 15, 1886, *Cleveland MS.*

to the English government in an entirely prudent way, that a persistence in the present course touching this question is furnishing aid and comfort to an element in this Country hostile to everything English and glad of any pretext to fan the flame of hatred and mischief; that while the conservative people are endeavoring to stem this tide it is exceedingly unfortunate that any conduct of any English neighbor should furnish a stumbling block to their efforts.

. . . I confess that I am anxious that when Mr. Blaine makes his much talked of "opening," he may meet minds somewhat pre-possessed with the assurance that everything is being done which can be required by a wise, dignified, and vigorous policy in protecting American rights and securing the privileges which they ought to enjoy.[8]

On August 24, 1886, Blaine made his long-heralded speech which opened the Congressional campaign of 1886. His attack upon the foreign policy of the Cleveland Administration was a vigorous one and it included some pointed paragraphs of criticism on Bayard's handling of the fisheries dispute.[9] It was not the impressive performance that the President had feared, and he wrote to Bayard to assure him that he had never had any doubt that the "Fishery question was in proper shape and had been properly handled." The only reason that he had sent the letter of August 15 was because he was afraid "that there would be too much committal on the part of the press and the people" to the view that the Administration was remiss in its duty to protect American rights in Canadian waters.[10]

Bayard's opinion of Blaine's speech was forcefully expressed in a letter to W. L. Putnam. Perhaps it was from

. . . a conviction long entertained in relation to Mr. Blaine that it is useless to debate with anyone so devoid of self-respect, that it seems almost idle to refute his statements, especially on a complicated public question. To assail the position taken by me in this department, and in the same breath to admit his total and necessary ignorance of it, would have seemed impossible for anyone excepting Mr. Blaine. . . . The phalanx of Protection is very closely organized. . . . The duty on Fish, food for the people, depends upon the maintenance of the banded association at the head of which Mr. Blaine hastens to place himself—fit leader for a simply mercenary force.[11]

Political partisanship in the United States and the "narrow gauge" manner in which public business was being conducted in Canada,[12]

8. President Cleveland to Bayard, August 15, 1886, *Bayard MS.*
9. New York *Tribune*, August 25, 1886.
10. President Cleveland to Bayard, August 26, 1886, *Bayard MS.*
11. Bayard to W. L. Putnam, August 30, 1886, *Bayard Letter Book*, vol. 3, *Bayard MS.*
12. Bayard to W. L. Putnam, September 4, 1886, *ibid.*

did not keep Bayard from making another attempt to arrange a *modus vivendi* which would temporarily settle the most pressing aspects of the fisheries dispute. On September 6 he sent a telegram to W. L. Putnam requesting him to come to Washington as soon as possible in order to discuss plans for an adjustment of the outstanding difficulties with the Canadian Government.[13] A week later he was about ready to send a draft of a proposed *modus vivendi* to Phelps for presentation to Lord Iddesleigh,[14] but Phelps himself had little faith in the efficacy of this pacific procedure. It seemed to him that the Administration would not get any favorable response from the British Government until a "vigorous system of retaliation is commenced."[15] Despite this discouraging opinion from Phelps, Bayard continued to work upon the idea of perfecting a temporary arrangement with the British Government in the matter of Canadian fisheries, and by the last week in September it was almost ready for transmission to London.[16]

But Bayard's efforts to find a solution for the fisheries dispute was made difficult by the attitude of Canadian officials who continued to seize American vessels on the slightest pretext. On October 19 Bayard wrote a long note to Sackville-West to protest against the detention of the American vessel *Everett Steele* on the charge that the captain had failed to report at the customhouse when driven by a storm into the harbor of Shelburne, Nova Scotia.[17] On the following day he sent another note to Sackville-West with reference to the imposition of a large fine upon the American fishing vessel *Pearl Nelson*. This vessel had been compelled by stress of weather, late one night, to seek shelter in the harbor of Arichat, Nova Scotia. At that time the customhouse was closed. The next morning when the captain of the *Pearl Nelson* went ashore to report his arrival, his vessel was seized and he was compelled to pay a fine of $200 because he had permitted his crew to go ashore the previous night *before reporting at the customhouse*.[18]

As a further discouragement to his efforts for a settlement of the fisheries question, Bayard found that the attitude of the Senate

13. Bayard to W. L. Putnam, September 6, 1886, *Bayard MS.*
14. Bayard to Phelps, September 13, 1886, *Bayard Letter Book*, vol. 3, *Bayard MS.*
15. Phelps to Bayard, September 13, 1886, *Personal, Bayard MS.*
16. Bayard to Phelps, September 24, 1886, *Bayard Letter Book*, vol. 3, *Bayard MS.* See also, Bayard to W. L. Putnam, September 25, 1886, *ibid.*
17. Bayard to Sackville-West, October 19, 1886, *Great Britain, Notes to,* vol. 20, MS Dept. of State.
18. Bayard to Sackville-West, October 20, 1886, *Great Britain, Notes to,* vol. 20, MS Dept. of State.

Committee on Foreign Relations was both petty and partisan. The viewpoint of a majority of that committee was "so inimical to our best efforts to reach a settlement that my feelings are the reverse of sanguine in regard to the result." [19]

Perhaps the only way out of these mounting difficulties was to write a strong note to the British Government and indicate in unmistakable terms the necessity of a prompt settlement of the whole fisheries dispute. Bayard sent this note to Phelps on November 6. After referring to recent seizures of American fishing vessels that had entered Canadian harbors merely because of stormy weather on the open seas, Bayard objected vehemently to the action of Captain Quigley, an officer in the Canadian marine, in hauling down the American flag that was flying at the masthead of the *Marion Grimes*.[20]

In a personal letter to Phelps, November 6, 1886, Bayard gave free rein to his feelings in connection with these Canadian seizures of American fishing vessels. The most alarming feature of the whole matter was

. . . the indifference displayed by the British Administration to the insolent provocation and irritating pretensions of the Canadian officials. They have been almost intolerable, and when represented to the British Minister here, make not the slightest impression. . . . I am well aware of the engrossing nature of other questions in Great Britain which have almost convulsed society there and have stirred it to its very depth, but however engrossing they may be, the British Government must now attend to this American question and either assume responsible control over it, or abandon it to the Canadians with whom the United States will then be obliged to deal, and in a practical way.[21]

Although this letter to Phelps had a decidedly threatening tone, Bayard still strove for a friendly adjustment of the fishery difficulties. On November 15 he sent to Phelps an important instruction to which was appended a *modus vivendi* which he ardently hoped would be acceptable to Lord Iddesleigh. In article one of this proposed arrangement it was suggested that a mixed commission be appointed by the President of the United States and the Queen of Great Britain to deal with the questions arising out of the fishery dispute.[22]

19. Bayard to Phelps, November 1, 1886, *Personal, Bayard Letter Book*, vol. 3, *Bayard MS*.

20. Bayard to Phelps, November 6, 1886, *Great Britain, Instructions*, vol. 28, MS Dept. of State.

21. Bayard to Phelps, November 6, 1886, *Personal, Bayard Letter Book*, vol. 3, *Bayard MS*.

22. This mixed commission should agree upon and etstablish by a series of lines the limits which should separate the exclusive from the common right of fishing on the coasts

In a personal letter to Phelps, Bayard remarked that at the

. . . root of the differences between the United States and Canada lies the apparent injustice of not allowing the fish caught by both Canadians and Americans in the waters of the former or by the use of their convenient ports and harbors as a base of fishing operations, to come into the American markets without discriminating duties on the Canadian shore of the catch. . . . Many of the false claims of the advocates of the tax on free fish have been exposed by the occurrences of the season just ended. The "nursery for hardy seamen" means seamen for the British Navy as is shown by the nativities of the crews of captured vessels.

Inasmuch as the recent Congressional elections had "almost destroyed" the Republican majority in the Senate, Bayard had hopes that "something nearer to a just and reasonable treatment of the foreign relations of the country" might be looked for at the hands of remaining Republicans.[23]

Bayard's conciliatory course towards England did not meet with the approval of Phelps who believed that the time had come for America to assert its rights in a decisive manner. He had at last

. . . become satisfied entirely that it is of no use to expect any interference on the part of the British Government with the acts of the Canadian authorities. It is idle and beneath the dignity of the United States to waste

---

and in the adjacent waters of the British North American Colonies, in conformity with the first article of the Treaty of 1818, except that the bays and harbors from which American fishermen were in the future to be excluded, save for the purposes for which entrance into bays and harbors was permitted by said Article, where such bays and harbors as were ten or less than ten miles in width, the distance of three marine miles from such bays or harbors should be measured from a straight line drawn across the bay or harbor, in the part nearest the entrance, at the first point where the width does not exceed ten miles.

The British Government was to agree to instruct the proper colonial and other British officers to abstain from seizing or molesting fishing vessels of the United States unless they are found within three marine miles of the coasts, bays, creeks, and harbors of Her Britannic Majesty's dominions in America, fishing, completing fishing operations, or preparing to fish within those limits.

American fishing vessels should have in the ports of entry of Her Britannic Majesty's dominions in America the same commercial privileges as other vessels of the United States, including the purchase of bait and other supplies.

The British Government should release all American fishing vessels that had been seized by Canadian authorities for failure to report at customhouses when seeking shelter, repairs, or supplies, and to refund all fines exacted for this failure to report. This *modus vivendi* was enclosed in the instruction from Bayard to Phelps, November 15, 1886, *Great Britain, Instructions*, vol. 28, MS Dept. of State. In a letter to W. L. Putnam, November 17, 1886, Bayard remarks: "I believe you will find the *modus vivendi* to contain the points suggested by you, excepting that I thought it wiser not to moot the 'headland line' question, nor the three-mile limit from coasts of the Islands adjacent to the mainland, but to treat those questions as settled in our favor." *Bayard Letter Book*, vol. 3, *Bayard MS.*

23. Bayard to Phelps, November 15, 1886, *Personal, Bayard Letter Book*, vol. 3, *Bayard MS.*

any more argument or importunity on the subject. We do not get the scant courtesy of an adequate reply. We have been forbearing, courteous, kindly, and have made our case perfectly clear by repeated argument. I think the time has now come for decisive action. We must either take that course or submit, and I am sure the country will sustain you in extreme measures when the correspondence is before them.[24]

Some two weeks later, Phelps wrote again to Bayard in the same dubious vein. He thought that the American Government had done everything possible to bring about an adjustment of the fisheries dispute, but he had "little hope of any favourable result until we *compel* it by stringent measures." [25] Bayard was not ready for such action. He still believed that the publication of the correspondence concerning the fisheries question would clarify the situation in the public mind and would lead to some amicable settlement. On December 8, 1886, President Cleveland sent a special message to Congress enclosing a large number of the more important diplomatic notes dealing with the seizures of American fishing vessels in Canadian waters. In this message the President suggested that a commission be authorized by law to take proofs of the losses sustained by these fishermen. He also hinted that it might be necessary for him to make recommendations for "such remedial legislation as may become necessary for the protection of the rights of our citizens engaged in the open-sea fisheries of the North Atlantic waters." [26]

The publication of the fisheries correspondence brought a favorable response from a large section of the press and from many persons in close touch with the fishing industry. The following remarks from Mr. F. B. Goss, of Cape Cod, are typical: "Allow me, a Cape Codman, to thank you for the noble stand you have taken upon the Fisheries question. Your report disarms all criticism and rejoices all hearts here upon the Cape." [27]

This friendly reaction to his efforts on behalf of American fishermen was very heartening to Bayard. In a letter to Phelps he expressed the view that the publication of the fishery correspondence had been "highly beneficial." The noisy misrepresentation and the

24. Phelps to Bayard, November 20, 1886, *Bayard MS.*
25. Phelps to Bayard, December 3, 1886, *ibid.*
26. *House Ex. Doc., 19,* 49 Cong., 2 sess., p. 1.
27. F. B. Goss to Bayard, December 14, 1886, *Bayard MS.* In a letter to Bayard, December 12, 1886, George A. Schuyler made the comment that the New England fishermen seemed "quite surprised to find that their interests have been so much better sustained by you than by blatant newspaper writers." *Bayard MS.*

. . . spattering retraction of the Blaine School aided by the sore-headed spoilsmen and political attornies in New England has been effectively answered and rebuked by the development of our action in relation to the fishery rights. All this will serve to dispel ignorance, and create an interest in the public mind. . . . The truth is . . . whilst we must execute laws and treaties as they stand, yet it seems to me unwise and unreasonable to avoid the plain facts of the case which stand thus—the Canadians owning the territorial, natural, and convenient *base for fishery* operations, . . . and the United States having the natural and *best* market for the product, each possessing something essential for the other.

. . . Knowing . . . the sincere intentions of this Administration to avoid collisions and to strengthen the united forces and elements of civilization and liberty which Great Britain and the United States chiefly contain and represent in the world, I am amazed to see the apparent indifference of British Ministers to such a settlement as will practically make a recourse to retaliatory measures unnecessary and uncalled for.[28]

To Phelps, at London, it appeared obvious that "mere argument" would never settle the fishery question. The British Government should be informed very plainly that America would not submit to a "renewal of the outrages of last season." This firm stand together with the fact that the Canadians themselves had discovered that they had "gone too far" in the matter of seizures of American fishing vessels, might bring about an eventual settlement.[29]

There was some truth in the report that the Canadian Government was disposed to lend a friendly ear to American proposals for a peaceful adjustment of the fishery dispute. Lord Lansdowne expressed to Sir John Macdonald the opinion that Canada had no reason to complain

. . . of the tone of that part of the President's message which has reference to the fisheries dispute. I am indeed surprised at the moderation of his language considering the audience to which he is playing. I observe that he goes out of his way to insist that the negotiations are still proceeding with a prospect of success. I am however not aware of any fact justifying such a conclusion. It may be . . . that the United States Government is meditating a proposal.[30]

The American Government had already submitted a *modus vivendi* (November 15, 1886) to Lord Iddesleigh,[31] who in turn finally placed this proposal before Lord Lansdowne. The Governor-General was not

28. Bayard to Phelps, December 17, 1886, *Bayard Letter Book*, vol. 4, *Bayard MS.*
29. Phelps to Bayard, January 1, 1887, *Bayard MS.*
30. Lord Lansdowne to Sir John Macdonald, December 9, 1886, *Governor-General's Correspondence*, vol. 13, *Sir John Macdonald Papers*, MS Canadian Archives.
31. See *ante*, p. 246.

favorably impressed with Bayard's outline of the terms of this working agreement. From all appearances it was a

. . . one sided and disingenuous proposal, and decides against all the debatable points, and some which are not debatable at all. You will observe that there is not a word in it as to reciprocity. This fact and the recent action of Congress make it, I fear, unlikely that for the present a reciprocity arrangement can be arrived at. If under these circumstances we could obtain the appointment of a mixed commission without the exception of the 10-mile bays, we might by pressing forward the negotiations arrive at a determination of the limits of our territorial waters before another fishing season comes in. This is, however, almost too much to hope for.[32]

Mr. Foster, the Canadian Minister of Marine and Fisheries, was equally dissatisfied with the *modus vivendi* proposed by Bayard. To his mind there was not ". . . the sparkle of a single generous sentiment in it. Mr. Bayard offers nothing, settles most disputed points offhand in his own favour, and sets a machinery in motion by which he hopes to gain the remainder."[33]

It was Lansdowne's view that the peculiar configuration of the Canadian coasts, together with other local circumstances, would be more likely to suggest a fair boundary line than any attempt

. . . to determine such a line with reference to principles of international law. It is my impression that the disputed waters will prove to be less extensive than it is supposed, and that if we could get a good commission and instruct it to lay down (subject to ratification) such a line as that which is

32. Lansdowne to Sir John Macdonald, December 25, 1886, *Governor-General's Correspondence*, vol. 13, *Sir John Macdonald Papers*, MS Canadian Archives.

33. G. E. Foster to Sir John Macdonald, December 28, 1886, *ibid*. In discussing the objections he entertained towards the Bayard *modus vivendi*, Mr. Foster remarks: "In Article I, he [Bayard] cuts off at one stroke the 'Bay' question, proposes to supersede our Customs law . . . and will have a foreign tribunal to establish proceedings and adjudge penalties for violations within the jurisdiction which the Commission shall declare to be our own. In Article II he wipes out at once the limiting provision of Article I of the Treaty of 1818 for so long a time as negotiations may continue, by agreeing to which Canada would furnish him with the strongest argument for his permanent Article IV, and for this he does not offer a suggestion of an equivalent. Article III appears clearly cumbrous and unworkable, even if it could be assented to. But now the question arises as to the creation of a foreign tribunal within which is to be settled our own jurisdiction. Article IV is the permanent version of the temporary arrangement proposed in Article II, and prejudges the whole case in favour of the United States. Article V is . . . the most 'cheeky' of all. These vessels have violated our customs laws, and have been fined lightly, therefore, in some cases, in others had been admonished and let go, and Secretary Bayard proposes now that our customs law shall be practically abrogated as far as United States fishermen go, that we shall declare ourselves to have been wrong, and in so doing shall build up his claim for damages. Might Mr. B. not just as well interfere with our civil and criminal law?"

described in the Kimberley memorandum of 1870, we need not be very apprehensive of the results.[34]

Any possibility of arriving at a speedy adjustment of the fishery dispute was distinctly lessened when the news arrived in the United States that Queen Victoria, on November 26, 1886, had given the royal assent to certain Canadian legislation touching upon the fisheries. This Act of the Dominion legislature had been reserved by Lord Lansdowne on June 2, 1886, for "the signification of the Queen's pleasure thereon." The fact of royal assent was made known in a proclamation issued on December 24. Thereafter, any American fishing vessel that entered Canadian waters "for any purpose not permitted by treaty or convention," could be immediately seized by the Canadian authorities, and "such ship, vessel, or boat, and the tackle, rigging, apparel, furniture, stores, and cargo thereof shall be forfeited."[35]

This action on the part of the British Government awakened instant resentment in the United States. Francis Wharton, the Solicitor of the Department of State, wrote a brief note to Bayard inquiring whether it would not be worth while to get in touch with the Senators from New England and "see what is their idea of a 'Counterpoise' in case the new statute is carried into effect."[36] It was not necessary for Bayard to see the New England Senators with reference to retaliatory legislation. For several weeks Senator Edmunds had been conducting an intensive examination into every aspect of the fisheries question, and on January 19, 1887, he introduced a bill which provided that whenever the President was satisfied that American rights were being violated in Canadian waters he was authorized, by proclamation, to deny to all "vessels, their masters and crews, of the British Dominions of North America, any entrance into the waters, ports, or places of or within the United States."[37] Two days previously, January 17, 1887, Mr. Belmont intro-

34. Lansdowne to Sir John Macdonald, December 29, 1886, *Governor-General's Correspondence*, vol. 13, *Sir John Macdonald Papers*, MS Canadian Archives.

35. *House Report 4087*, 49 Cong., 2 sess., p. 17. According to a summary given in the Boston *Journal*, December 30, 1886, the provisions of the act of 1886 would make it possible "for any petty customs official to bring into port any American vessel found within three miles of the Canadian coast, to search her cargo and to examine her master under oath."

36. Francis Wharton to Bayard, January 3, 1887, *Bayard MS*.

37. *Congressional Record*, January 19, 1887, 49 Cong., 2 sess., vol. 18, pt. 1, p. 793. This bill was S. 3173. It was very distasteful to Bayard who regarded it as "without precedent in the history of our Foreign Affairs." Bayard to W. L. Putnam, January 20, 1887, *Bayard Letter Book*, vol. 4, *Bayard MS*. At Bayard's instigation, Senator Arthur Pue Gorman introduced several amendments to the Edmunds bill, but they were voted down by a large majority. *Cong. Rec.*, January 24, 1887, 49 Cong., 2 sess., vol. 18, pt. 1, pp. 947-952. See also, Francis Wharton to Bayard, January 17, 1887, *Bayard MS*.

duced in the House of Representatives a bill authorizing the President
to forbid the entrance into the United States of "all merchandise coming by land from the provinces of British North America, and may also
forbid the entrance into the United States of the cars, locomotives, or
other rolling stock of any railway company chartered under the laws
of said provinces." [38]

This proposed retaliatory legislation was warmly approved by Phelps
who was certain that Congress was

. . . moving in the right direction. I am perfectly satisfied that we shall
never get any satisfaction till we compel it. And I am equally satisfied that
we shall obtain it the moment we begin to compel it. The trouble is not
with the views of the British Government—it is with their reluctance to
interfere with the Canadian Government. They will never do so as long
as they can help it. The movements towards retaliation that have been
commenced in Congress have done more good than all the argument. If our
Government takes a firm and decided stand, and, if satisfaction is not now
promptly given, retaliates upon Canada *effectually*, we shall very soon see
an end of the difficulty.[39]

On January 28, 1887, Phelps had an interview with the British
Foreign Secretary and presented the American case with vigor. The
result was not satisfactory because the British Government was "unwilling to coerce Canada." Phelps was now more convinced than ever that
retaliation was the "only effectual course." [40]

38. *Cong. Rec.*, January 17, 1887, 49 Cong., 2 sess., vol. 18, pt. 1, p. 737. W. L. Putnam
wrote to Bayard, January 18, 1887, and pointed out that the Belmont bill prohibited the
entrance of the rolling stock of "any railway company chartered under the laws of 'Provinces.' " The railway system of the Lower Provinces consisted of the Intercolonial, which
was a "Dominion" corporation, and of the New Brunswick Railway Company which was
a "Provincial" corporation. It happened, however, that the New Brunswick Railway
Company had been recently acquired by the Canadian Pacific Railway, and therefore, was
no longer a "Provincial" corporation. It was apparent, then, that Mr. Belmont's bill would
not keep out the rolling stock of these railway companies, and Putnam thought that the
bill should be amended in that regard. *Bayard MS.* On February 7, 1887, President Cleveland wrote to Bayard to call attention to the fact that the Belmont bill (H. R. 10786) had
"no provision for seizure and forfeiture of cars and persons of carriage by land nor for
goods brought therein as there is in the case of ships and goods. . . . While the Admiralty
Courts and practice is already adjusted to seizure and forfeiture of ships, etc., it might not
be available for proceedings against cars, etc." *Bayard MS.*

39. Phelps to Bayard, January 25, 1887, *Bayard MS.* In his official despatch to Bayard,
January 27, 1887, Phelps makes similar comments. *Great Britain, Despatches*, vol. 154, MS
Dept. of State. In a personal letter to Bayard, January 8, 1887, Phelps remarks: "It is
embarrassing to deal with Administrations that are struggling for existence and changing
so frequently. We have now the *fourth* Secretary of Foreign Affairs since I came here."
Bayard MS.

40. Phelps to Bayard, February 4, 1887, *Great Britain, Despatches*, vol. 155, MS Dept.
of State.

But Bayard was reluctant to adopt the proposed retaliatory course, and his viewpoint was confirmed by friends like David A. Wells, who believed that the United States was "playing the part of bully to Canada, and are largely in the wrong." [41] Bayard, however, did not agree with Wells in believing that the American Government was "largely in the wrong," but he was strongly of the opinion that the maxim "live and let live" was not only "Christianlike but expedient on the coldest basis of calculation." He also wished to be "proud of our country, and justly to be so, and in order to be so we must deal worthily with all men weak or strong." [42]

These fine maxims were difficult to translate into actual practice in 1887, and in Congress two bills providing for retaliation against Canada had already been introduced. One was sponsored by Senator Edmunds,[43] and it was far-reaching in character. It gave the President power to "deny vessels, their masters and crews of the British Dominions of North America, any entrance into the waters, ports, or places of or within the United States, . . . whether such vessels shall have come directly from said dominions, . . . or by way of some port or place in such destined voyage elsewhere." It also provided that the President could deny entry into any port or place of the United States of fresh fish or salt fish or to any other product of said dominions, or other goods coming from said dominions to the United States."

Perry Belmont, Chairman of the House Committee on Foreign Affairs, had also introduced retaliatory legislation that was very similar to the Edmunds bill, but it was more specific in that it provided for the exclusion of "the cars, locomotives, or other rolling stock of any railroad company" chartered under the laws of the provinces of British North America.[44] In order that the position of the Administration should be clearly understood, President Cleveland invited the Committee on Foreign Affairs to the White House for the purpose of discussing the provisions of the Belmont bill.[45]

Bayard, like the President, preferred the Belmont bill to the one introduced by Senator Edmunds. This preference was based not only on the fact that Belmont was a Democrat, but also because his bill made explicit provision for the prohibition of the entry of Canadian locomo-

41. David A. Wells to Bayard, January 29, 1887, *Bayard MS.*
42. Bayard to David A. Wells, January 31, 1887, *Wells Papers*, Library of Congress.
43. See *Senate Bill 3173*, 49 Cong., 2 sess.
44. See *H. R. 10786*, 49 Cong., 2 sess. See *ante*, pp. 353-354.
45. Perry Belmont, *An American Democrat: Recollections*, pp. 360-361.

tives and rolling stock. Bayard, apparently, did not read the Edmunds
bill with his usual care, and in a letter to Representative J. C. Clements,
he remarked as follows concerning its alleged defects:

> It is not . . . improper to say that the measure of the Senate would seem
> defective because it falls short of a demand for the full extent of our fishery
> rights in British-American waters, and would apparently reduce non-inter-
> course commercially to an exclusion of *Fish* only.[46]

Belmont was quite surprised at this statement of Bayard, and he
wrote at once to Manton Marble to express his displeasure at the way
things were drifting:

> Manning, this morning, in about ten minutes understood all that I
> wanted, and promised he would send an answer tomorrow, although he
> evidently did not want to cross the President or Bayard. Bayard, on the
> other hand, not only did not give *me* a positive answer today, but yesterday
> answered my letters by addressing Clements of the sub-committee with a
> slight criticism of Edmund's Bill, in which he says that the bill simply
> proposes to retaliate on fish (of course it goes much further. Rice, of the
> sub-committee, thinks it goes as far as mine with the exception of the railroad
> clause). This afternoon, Clements and I together went to see Bayard, but
> only got from him the statement that he *preferred* my bill; that if such meas-
> ures were desirable they should be *positive and decisive;* that the Edmunds
> bill simply would irritate, and yet would not give the President sufficient
> power.
> The House undoubtedly will sustain a bill which will go further. With
> the Senate Bill, the trouble I find is that a fair examination of the Edmunds
> bill shows that it is drawn to cover a great deal. . . . Bayard will look upon
> our recommendation of the Edmunds bill (and so will the President) as a
> surrender to Edmunds, and Clements and I have agreed that there is nothing
> for us to do but to advocate my bill, or the Edmunds bill with such amend-
> ments as the Department suggests. . . . The whole difference will eventually
> turn on the *railroad clause* and the *interpretation of Article XXIX.* I can
> not tell you how disappointed I am with Bayard's indecision, and I know
> the same feeling is entertained by the other Democrats of the committee.
> We are, at present, in a bad way, and are drifting towards a very awkward
> situation.[47]

On February 5 Secretary Manning wrote a letter to Belmont in
which he fully discussed every aspect of the proposed retaliatory legislation against Canada. After commenting upon certain ambiguities in the
Belmont and Edmunds bills, he submitted his own draft of a bill which

46. Bayard to J. C. Clements, February 1, 1887, *Bayard Letter Book,* vol. 4, *Bayard MS.*
47. Perry Belmont to Sidney Webster, no date, probably February 2, 1887, *Manton Marble Papers,* Library of Congress.

would be effective and which would also be free from all obscurities in language.[48]

But Bayard was still hopeful that retaliatory legislation against Canada could be avoided, and he sent a telegram to Phelps to that effect.[49] After receiving this word from the Secretary of State, Phelps wrote at once to Lord Salisbury and informed him that Bayard continued to cherish the belief

. . . that the adoption of the *modus vivendi* . . . [might] avert the necessity of measures for which Congress is with almost entire unanimity providing, and which the feeling in the United States, aroused by the conduct of the Canadian authorities, is demanding with an increasing force which no Administration can long resist.[50]

In a long letter to Bayard, Phelps sounds a discouraging note with reference to a continuance of Bayard's conciliatory policy. In his conversations with Lord Salisbury he soon discovered that the British Foreign Secretary was very discursive

. . . and very non-committal. He said that Great Britain stood as a broker between the United States and Canada, and had great difficulty in managing their Canadian clients. In respect to the headland question he had received communications from Canada that led him to believe that that point might be agreed upon. In respect to the purchase of bait he was inclined to take the Canadian view. . . . In reference to the proposed *modus vivendi* plan, he said that he hoped to make me some communication ere long.

This non-committal attitude on the part of Lord Salisbury was very tiresome to Phelps who felt that the British Government had all they could do

. . . to take care of themselves, and have no assurance of remaining in power from one month to another. They are either afraid or unable or unwilling to attempt to coerce Canada. They will do nothing whatever in this business, unless they are compelled to, except Canada first agrees to it. No amount of argument, no appeal to the sense of justice, no considerations of friendship or comity will induce them to take any firm ground antagonistic to Canadian views. . . . In my opinion the only way to prevent collisions next season . . . will be to adopt retaliatory measures so effective and thorough as to bring Canada to terms.[51]

48. Secretary Manning to Perry Belmont, February 5, 1887, enclosed in a letter from Manning to Bayard, February 5, 1887, *Bayard MS.*
49. Bayard to Phelps, February 4, 1887, *Great Britain, Instructions*, vol. 28, MS Dept. of State.
50. Phelps to Lord Salisbury, February 5, 1887, *Bayard MS.*
51. Phelps to Bayard, February 5, 1887, *Bayard MS.*

Despite this long and positive letter from Phelps counselling a policy of retaliation, Bayard still felt a definite reluctance about embarking upon such a course of action. With his ever-present sense of justice and fair play, it was difficult for him to understand why nations should have to argue and quarrel about petty details which in private life gentlemen could settle without the slightest trouble. While he resented the seeming indifference of the British Government to the issues involved in the fisheries dispute, and while he also lost patience with the Canadian officials for their needless harshness in the matter of seizures of American fishing vessels, his chief annoyance was the attitude of the Senate Committee of Foreign Relations towards the Department of State. Senator Edmunds was the most troublesome member of this Committee, and during the summer and fall of 1886 he had frequently called upon Bayard

. . . to furnish him and his committee with information often quite troublesome to procure and which I was under no obligation . . . to provide. But in each case I responded promptly and freely, and when the Committee came to report . . . not a word or line is found which would indicate even the existence of an Executive branch of the government, or that there was a State Department to which they had resorted for the information upon which they reported. The fact, the discreditable fact continues, that since coming into this office in March 1885, not a member of the Committee of either political party has called upon me at the department to confer in respect to any of the important questions before us. . . . In the Senate, the Administration is badly off, and I do not feel that I have a single well-equipped and friendly advocate in the body.

. . . Altho' never a member of that Committee [Senate Committee on Foreign Relations] during my service in the Senate, no one responded more readily than I to the calls of the State Department or gave their measures a more careful consideration and hearty support. I should have been ashamed to have done less, but I cannot fail to contrast my own line of action and feeling with that to which I have been subject by Sherman, Edmunds, Evarts, Harrison & Frye. Of the Democrats I say nothing, for they say nothing, and I may add, do nothing excepting when like Mr. Morgan, of Alabama, they proudly avow their omission to consult the department as to the policy of any measure.[52]

Bayard was also aware of the fact that America's military resources were quite slender, and he was fearful that some strong European Power would cause great devastation in this country "should the issue of arms be ever tendered by us or forced upon us."

52. Bayard to Phelps, February 7, 1887, *Bayard Letter Book*, vol. 4, *Bayard MS.*

But despite the fact that a policy of retaliation against Canada was "repugnant" to Bayard, he was finally compelled by the constant drumfire of advice from Phelps, to come around to that viewpoint.[53] In a letter to Perry Belmont, Chairman of the House Committee on Foreign Affairs, he expressed the opinion that Congress should pass legislation which

. . . should be unquestionable as to its intent, and clear and positive in its prohibitory results. Great Britain evidently is not prepared to *compel* Canada to accept her counsels, or modify her action against our fishermen, but although recognizing the unwisdom and unreasonableness of Canada's action regarding the fishery question, yet prefers to leave repression to the United States, expecting it (as I think) and preferring that the needed discipline should be administered *by us*, rather than by the home Government. Therefore the strong measure is the wise and prudent measure. We *are* in earnest; we *ought to be* in earnest, and in self-defense must create an alternative which "he who runs may read," and heed.[54]

If retaliatory legislation against Canada were the only means of effecting a real settlement of the fishery question, Bayard thought that the action taken by Congress should be far-reaching and unambiguous. Now that the nettle had to be handled, it should be seized

53. In a personal letter to Bayard, February 11, 1887, Phelps repeats his counsel of retaliation. He had become "more and more convinced that our hope of avoiding serious trouble next season lies in such measures toward Canada as will bring that Government to terms. . . . I have . . . learned in an indirect and confidential way that the law officers of the Government when Rosebery was Secretary, found our points (or some of them) incapable of reply, but were unable to control Canada though compelled to back her up." On February 19 Phelps again writes to Bayard in the same strain: "The British Government are so well satisfied that they have nothing to fear from us except argument and remonstrances that I expect from them no step in the direction of an amicable settlement. I cannot too strongly repeat my conviction that nothing short of decided, vigorous, and effective retaliation upon Canada will produce any change in the course pursued by that government toward our fishermen, or obtain from the British Government any attention to our complaints. . . . You may rest assured that considerations of magnanimity, generosity, and reciprocity are utterly thrown away upon the British Government. They will take all they can get. They will concede nothing whatever which they are not compelled to. And they will concede very speedily when they find out they will be compelled to." Three days later (February 22, 1887), Phelps returns to the charge that the British Government will remain indifferent to American rights until a vigorous policy of retaliation is entered upon: "I have nothing from Salisbury. . . . I feel very strongly the course of the British Government in the Fishery business. . . . I can only repeat my conviction that the true hope of peace lies in a vigorous and determined course not of remonstrance but of action." *Bayard MS.*

54. Bayard to Perry Belmont, February 18, 1887, *Bayard Letter Book*, vol. 4, *Bayard MS.* On February 18, 1887, Mr. Belmont had already submitted to Congress a majority and a minority report upon the question of commercial non-intercourse with Canada. Belmont favored a more explicit authorization to the President to cut off Canadian commerce than was contained in Senate bill 3173. In this regard he represented the desire of Bayard and also that of the President.

. . . with a firm grip, and if we are to stop the unjust and unlawful treatment of our fishermen seeking shelter in Canadian bays, we must do it by proving our ability to inflict a greater injury upon Canadian interests by withdrawing from intercourse. I cannot withhold my detestation and want of respect for this line of action, but as the Republican Senators will not assist or permit negotiations and settlement based on mutual concessions, and as we cannot submit to indignity, we must withdraw from business association.[55]

With relations between the United States and Canada growing worse each day, Senator Hoar suddenly made the situation even more strained by introducing a resolution which opposed any reduction in the duties on fish.[56] This action was a direct blow at any attempt on the part of the Administration to settle the fisheries dispute by means of a reciprocity arrangement on the model of the Treaty of Washington of June 5, 1854.

Bayard wrote at once to Senator John T. Morgan, a member of the Senate Committee on Foreign Relations, and expressed his surprise at such action. He was not

. . . aware of any precedent for such a forestalling of action by the Executive within its sole and exclusive prerogative, . . . which it seems to me contains a principle of action at variance with the arrangements of the Constitution.[57]

Bayard also unburdened himself to his close friend, Senator George Gray, of Delaware. He could view the Hoar resolution only as a

. . . derangement of the relative Constitutional functions of the President to negotiate, and the Senate to ratify and confirm, treaties. But if he can thus be forbidden in advance as to our mode of settlement, the exclusion may be extended to all modes or attempts. . . . Having proclaimed the incapacity of a Democratic Administration to conduct our affairs, it is perhaps natural that the Republican statesmen of the Senate should prove it by so obstructing action as to make it impossible. The Senate expressed its views a year ago in opposition to the President's recommendation for a

55. Bayard to Phelps, February 21, 1887, *Bayard Letter Book*, vol. 4, *Bayard MS.*

56. *Congressional Record,* 49 Cong., 2 sess., vol. 18, pt. 3, p. 2191. The text of Senator Hoar's resolution reads as follows: "*Resolved,* That it is the judgment of the Senate that under present circumstances no negotiation should be undertaken with Great Britain in regard to existing difficulties with her province of Canada which has for its object the reduction, change, or abolition of any of our existing duties on imports." The Gloucester fishing industry, of which Senator Hoar was the spokesman, was chiefly interested in retaining the tariff duties on fish.

57. Bayard to John T. Morgan, February 25, 1887, *Bayard Letter Book*, vol. 4, *Bayard MS.*

Commission, but it now invades his prerogative by warning him in advance of an opposition to anything he may propose.[58]

To Senator Beck, Bayard expressed himself along similar lines. The resolution introduced by Senator Hoar proposed

. . . a palpable anticipation and interference with the prerogative of the President. When before was negotiation with a foreign government sought to be forestalled by the action of the Senate? . . . The resolution is only another proof . . . of the reckless, selfish, mercenary spirit of a protective principle of taxation. . . . In December, 1885, the President recommended a joint Commission to consider the question of our relations with Canada. . . . In April, 1886, the Senate (led by Mr. Frye) voted it down, 4 to 1. Now they go a step farther and seek to restrict the prerogative of negotiation by the Executive, an unheard-of and revolutionary suggestion. Followed to its logical consequences nothing more dangerous can be imagined.[59]

On March 3, 1887, President Cleveland approved the bill introduced by Senator Edmunds with reference to establishing commercial non-intercourse with Canada.[60] Whether as a result of this legislation or not, Lord Salisbury on March 24, 1887, indicated that the British Government was prepared to accept Bayard's suggestion for the ap-

58. Bayard to George Gray, February 25, 1887, *ibid.* Bayard believed that the diplomatic situation was "anomalous and awkward. The political relations of Great Britain to Canada have wholly changed since 1818, and the treaty of 1818 is now sought to control what it never contemplated nor in the nature of things could have contemplated. England does not own or practically have any control over all the matters now affected by the treaty. And the United States cannot treat with the government that *does own* and control them. Such an outgrown suit of clothes was never seen before. The Crown lawyers do not answer our points, but hand in Canada's reply which they cannot endorse, but cannot refuse to present." Bayard to W. L. Putnam, February 25, 1887, *Bayard Letter Book,* vol. 4, *Bayard MS.*

59. Bayard to Senator J. M. Beck, February 26, 1887, *Bayard Letter Book,* vol. 4, *Bayard MS.* In a letter to Daniel Manning, Secretary of the Treasury, February 26, 1887, Bayard was equally critical of the implications of the Hoar resolution: "The confusion, disorder, and public injury that must ensue from all attempts of any department of the government to usurp the functions and duties of any co-ordinate branch or departments are readily apparent. The resolution referred to is unprecedented . . . and wholly unwarranted. . . . The Senate majority as at present constituted has exhibited so frequently its intent to ignore or embarrass the Executive in all its departments that I trust for a remedy in public and patriotic opinions just so soon as the situation is realized by our Countrymen." *Bayard Letter Book,* vol. 4, *Bayard MS.*

60. *Foreign Relations,* 1887, pp. 466-467. In commenting upn this legislation, Sidney Webster expressed the view that there was "no use in whining about it, but there was too much politics in 1812, 1814, and in 1818. The politicians of Mr. Madison's Cabinet were scared nearly to death in 1814, and took any arrangement for peace they could get. . . . We have assented to the right of England and Canada to *restrict,* [contenting] ourselves with protesting, and arguing, and appealing to what the average Briton never employs till you have him down or his head 'in chancery.' " Sidney Webster to Bayard, March 4, 1887, *Bayard MS.*

pointment of a mixed commission to consider the best mode of effecting a settlement of the fisheries dispute.[61] He had "no doubt" that Canadian officials would make every effort to enforce their regulations in such a manner as to "cause the smallest amount of inconvenience to fishing vessels entering Canadian ports under stress of weather or for any other legitimate purpose. As a gesture of good will, Lord Salisbury announced that the British Government was willing "to revert for the coming season, and, if necessary, for a further term, to the condition of things existing under the Treaty of Washington, without any suggestion of pecuniary indemnity."[62]

Phelps regarded this note of Lord Salisbury as "uncordial and unfair in its second-hand defense of conduct that is utterly incapable of defense." He was of the opinion, however, that the idea of a mixed commission should be adopted because it seemed "to afford the only probable means of arriving at an agreement on the points in dispute." He thought the commission should hold its meetings in Washington. The question of personnel was most important and he suggested the names of outstanding men like George W. Biddle, William L. Putnam, and James B. Angell.[63]

To John Bassett Moore the offer of Lord Salisbury to revert to the "condition of things existing under the treaty of Washington, without any suggestion of pecuniary indemnity," was of little consequence. If the American Government had not given "notice of the Treaty of 1871, we certainly would have had Lord Salisbury's *boon* without paying a dollar for it." It seemed to him that the opposition that was voiced in New England against Bayard's handling of the fishery question was due to the fact that the fishing interests of that section were annoyed because a serious quarrel had not broken out between Canada and the United States. An open break in relations would "at once shut out Canadian fish." This was exactly what Senators Edmunds, Frye, and Ingalls were driving at, and it was precisely what the Gloucester fishermen wanted.[64]

61. This suggestion was made in the *modus vivendi* proposed by Bayard in his instruction to Phelps, November 15, 1886. *Great Britain, Instructions*, vol. 28, MS Dept. of State.
62. The Marquis of Salisbury to Mr. White, March 24, 1887, enclosed in despatch from Mr. White to Bayard, March 30, 1887, *Great Britain, Despatches*, vol. 155, MS Dept. of State.
63. Phelps to Bayard, March 27, 1887, *Bayard MS.*
64. John Bassett Moore to Bayard, April 25, 1887, *Bayard MS.* According to a report made by Secretary Manning to Perry Belmont, February 5, 1887, the total value of fresh

But this narrow spirit that would favor international discord in order to gain some petty advantage through tariff discrimination, was viewed with contempt by Bayard. In Canada, also, there was a fast growing movement in favor of a vast extension in the commercial relations between the United States and the Dominion, and the leaders of this movement were very anxious to make concessions in the matter of fisheries if thereby they could pave the way for their scheme of commercial union. In the Montreal *Herald*, April 18, 1887, William McDougall, an eminent Canadian lawyer, published a long and closely reasoned letter which favored the American interpretation of Article I of the treaty of 1818.[65] On April 20, the Toronto *Globe* featured an editorial which declared that "an arrangement for unrestricted reciprocity of trade would shelve the fisheries question" and would introduce an era of good feelings between Canada and the United States.[66]

The most indefatigable worker for commercial union between the United States and Canada was Erastus Wiman, who never missed an opportunity to press for such a project. In an open letter to Valancey E. Fuller, Mr. Wiman gave vehement and cogent expression to the view that the abolition of the high tariff walls along the Canadian-American frontier would open to the Canadian farmer "a market such as the world has never equalled.[67] Wiman next wrote to Sir Charles Tupper, a prominent Canadian official, and suggested that he visit Washington for the purpose of discussing in an *informal* manner the questions at issue between the United States and Canada. Tupper adopted this suggestion, and in May, 1887, he talked matters over with Bayard.[68]

It was high time that something was done by Canadian officials to conciliate American opinion. On April 22 Bayard wrote a confidential note to the American Consul-General at Halifax with reference to the

---

fish, including shellfish, admitted *free of duty* into the United States for the fiscal year ending June 30, 1886, amounted to the small sum of $985,573. *House Rept. 4087*, 49 Cong., 2 sess., p. 26.

65. In his letter to the Montreal *Herald*, Mr. McDougall remarked: "I hope, as a Canadian citizen, to express my belief that the contention of our neighbors as to the true meaning and scope of the fishery article of the convention of 1818, cannot be honestly denied."

66. Toronto *Globe*, April 20, 1887.

67. In the *Bayard Papers* there is a copy of this open letter from Wiman to Valancey E. Fuller.

68. See Erastus Wiman to Bayard, April 18, 22, 30, 1887, and Bayard to Wiman, April 23, 1887, *Bayard MS*.

recent refusal "of the Canadian Government to allow American fishing vessels, driven by storm into their ports, to repair damages to their supplies as well as to their . . . rigging, etc. These vessels . . . did not voluntarily put into Halifax, but were compelled to go there. . . . The situation is seriously strained by this action of the Canadian Government." [69] To Phelps, in London, Bayard sent a similar telegram, and on the following day he addressed a long personal letter to Phelps in which he frankly stated that it was "essential that such action on the part of Canada . . . should be stopped." [70]

Phelps, on his part, was worried about the growing irritation in Great Britain with reference to the American habit of passing judgment upon British domestic questions. This unrestrained American criticism of the manner in which the British Government was handling important public questions, was producing "a state of feeling very unfavorable to the maintenance of friendly relations, and calculated very much to embarrass the settlement of any dispute. . . . The point is, that a hostile state of feeling is rapidly growing up in both countries, and a collision on the Fishery question may thereby be brought on." [71]

Bayard could well appreciate these apprehensions of Phelps in regard to American criticisms of the British Government for failing to extend "Home Rule" to Ireland. The American press was

. . . wholly under Irish inspiration and influence. There is no exception to this one-sided system, and the fact that the question of Home Rule in Ireland is only a domestic question for British Legislators, Governors, and other officials, Senators and Representatives in Congress are all one in extravagance and violence. . . . It was this underlying, smouldering sentiment that even more than the narrow selfishness of the Gloucester Fishermen and their Attornies, in and out of Congress, that created difficulties in the way of my obtaining a just and amicable settlement. The perception of these difficulties only increases my desire to overcome them, and my determination to follow our American policy, dictated by the true interests of our own Country. . . . I feel most deeply the distress and anxiety which is today filling the hearts and minds of all who love England and all that makes Britain truly "Great," and have no sympathy with those who mock that distress or seek to increase that anxiety. [72]

Shortly after Bayard and Phelps were exchanging these confidences

69. Bayard to M. H. Phelan, April 22, 1887, *Bayard MS.*
70. Bayard to Phelps, April 23, 1887, *ibid.*
71. Phelps to Bayard, April 23, 1887, *Private and Confidential, Bayard MS.*
72. Bayard to Phelps, May 6, 1887, *Bayard Letter Book*, vol. 5, *Bayard MS.*

about the British political situation, Sir Ambrose Shea,[73] of Newfoundland, wrote to Phelps with reference to the fisheries question. After assuring Phelps that the Government of Newfoundland had "every desire" to remove "all causes of irritation," he then called attention to the fact that an Act had recently been passed by the Colonial Legislature, and confirmed by the Imperial Government, vesting the control of the Newfoundland fisheries in the local government. In view of this legislation there was no reason why the governments of Newfoundland and of the United States should not have a "separate arrangement for fisheries and trade." [74]

Phelps regarded this proposal as a "most important step toward the solution of existing difficulties," and he could not see any valid reason why the American Government should hesitate to accept it.[75] In a personal letter to Bayard, Phelps enlarged upon the advantages that the United States would derive from an acceptance of this offer from Sir Ambrose Shea. If Newfoundland should open her ports to American fishermen, Canada could

. . . hardly stand out after such a rebuke to her narrow policy nor allow Newfoundland to monopolize American trade. . . . It seems to me a very valuable offer. Sir A. Shea will go to Washington if this suggestion finds favour with you.[76]

While Sir Ambrose Shea was making this friendly overture to Phelps, Sir Charles Tupper was holding out an olive branch to Bayard. On May 21, 1887, Sir Charles arrived in Washington and lost no time in calling at the Department of State.[77] Apparently, Bayard greeted Sir Charles with a frank declaration: "The confederation of Canada and the construction of the Canadian Pacific Railway have brought us face

73. According to Alfred B. Morine, a member of the House of Assembly, St. John's, Newfoundland, the reason behind Sir Ambrose Shea's gestures towards Phelps was mainly the hope that he would be able to secure, through American assistance, the position of British Consul-General at New York. Shea had in his possession "a letter from Minister Phelps couched in the most flattering language, and expressing the hope that he will be appointed to this office. I have no doubt that Shea's pliability in 1885 in conceding to the Americans six months extra enjoyment of the privileges exercised by them under the Treaty of Washington has favourably impressed the American Government on His behalf." A. B. Morine to Sir John Macdonald, July 24, 1887, *Governor-General's Correspondence, Sir John Macdonald Papers,* vol. 13, MS Canadian Archives.

74. Sir Ambrose Shea to Phelps, May 10, 1887, *Bayard MS.*

75. Phelps to Bayard, May 11, 1887, *Confidential, ibid.*

76. Phelps to Bayard, May 11, 1887, *ibid.*

77. Sackville-West to Bayard, May 21, 1887, *ibid.* Sir Charles Tupper was at this time acting both as the High Commissioner for Canada in England, and as the Minister of Finance of the Dominion of Canada.

to face with a nation, and we may as well discuss public questions from that point of view." [78]

During the course of the conversation that Bayard had with Sir Charles, the questions at issue between Canada and the United States were thoroughly canvassed. After discussing the matter of commercial reciprocity, the conversation finally turned to the question of the fisheries. Any agreement that would settle this age-old dispute would have to be "carefully considered so as to avoid defeat." One thing was certain —it would not be possible to grant to Canadian fishermen free entry for their catch until Congress authorized such action. Bayard felt sure that he could

. . . satisfy both the Canadian and British governments in regard to the formation of a commission. It is a scheme which will require a great deal of consideration.

Sir C. Tupper.—Suppose then you favor me or Sir J. Macdonald with a plan of the best course that you think would meet the object we have in view, when you have considered the matter?

Mr. Bayard.—I see no reason why that should not be done. We had better remove the location to Washington.

Sir C. Tupper.—I quite agree to that.

Mr. Bayard.—Of course this is unofficial, and I will make my answer in that way.

Sir C. Tupper.—Shall I inform Sir John that your present idea is to have the Commission transferred here?

. . . I think so. I shall want to have a conversation on the subject with the President. [79]

78. Sir Charles Tupper, *Recollections of Sixty Years* (New York, 1914), p. 176.

79. *Memorandum* written by Bayard after a conversation with Sir Charles Tupper, May 21, 1887, *Bayard MS.* On July 18, 1887, Commander C. M. Chester, of the U.S.S. *Galena*, wrote a letter to Rear Admiral S. B. Luce in which he made some interesting comments upon the actual situation of American fishermen in Canadian waters: "They never require bait, but rarely need provisions, and they only take refuge in Canadian ports when needing wood and water or protection from gales, or repairs for damage caused by stress of weather. . . . Thus . . . I do not see that any of the restrictions placed upon our fishing fleet are at all necessary to prevent illegal fishing. The only bait bought is for off-shore (cod or haddock), viz: legal fishing, the mackerel fishermen using no bait. The mackerel fishing . . . is now an off-shore fishing. . . . Our fishermen would be glad if they might be treated with hospitality, allowed to purchase reasonable stores, procure wood and water, land their sick, and seek refuge in cases of bad weather, without being unnecessarily restricted, harassed and illegally warned off the coast." *Bayard MS.*

Another picture of the American fishery industry in actual operation is given in a letter from Commander William B. Hoff, U.S.S. *Ossipee*, to the Secretary of the Navy, July 25, 1887. It was his opinion that the three-mile limit worked but "little hardship to our fishermen, as they are not trawlers but seiners. If there was no rule of limit they would by choice fish out, as they do now. . . . If the prohibition to our fishermen to enter harbors for trade or recreation, bears hardly on them, it bears still more hardly upon the dealers of these maritime provinces. In conversation with people living here, I find that nearly

As a result of this conversation with Sir Charles Tupper, Bayard was more convinced than ever of the necessity of settling all the "irritating issues with Canada." There was little doubt that some settlement would finally be necessary, and it would be better to make this arrangement before Canadian-American relations grew more embittered. It was also apparent to him that the actual carrying out of retaliatory measures against Canadian commerce would "involve very grave results without ensuring the desired end." [80]

In a confidential letter to Phelps, May 30, 1887, Bayard outlined the main points that had been discussed in his conversation with Sir Charles Tupper. It seemed to him that it was well worth while to open negotiations with Canada to settle the more important pending questions, and after a conversation with the President, he was now ready to carry the matter further.[81] On the following day he wrote a long letter to Tupper in which he expressed the view that the best way to attain to a "just and permanent settlement" of the outstanding questions at issue between Canada and the United States was through a "liberal and statesmanlike plan of the entire commercial relations of the two countries." As an indication of his desire to arrive at an amicable understanding with the governments of Canada and Great Britain, he was prepared "to meet the authorised agents of Great Britain at this capital at the earliest possible day, and enter upon negotiations for a settlement of all differences." [82]

In a personal letter to Phelps, Bayard first explained that the time was not ripe to enter upon separate negotiations with Newfoundland. It would be better to negotiate for the settlement of all differences with Canada, and the negotiations should be held in Washington. It was clear that Canada had

. . . outgrown British tutelage and should therefore be caused to realize her own responsibilities. The management of the fisheries is wholly in Canadian control, and if a Canadian Minister is clothed with the powers of a plenipotentiary by Great Britain, the combination of provincial and Imperial authority will yield more immediately responsible results. . . . I realize

---

every one sold to Americans, averaging during the season from twenty dollars worth of bait sold by the poorest fishermen to hundreds of dollars worth sold by the general dealer. . . . This fishing question will settle itself by the revolt of the maritime provinces against the Dominion Government which is starving them out." *Bayard MS.*

80. Bayard to Phelps, May 23, 1887, *Bayard Letter Book*, vol. 5, *Bayard MS.*

81. Bayard to Phelps, May 30, 1887, *Confidential, ibid.*

82. Bayard to Sir Charles Tupper, May 31, 1887, quoted in Sir Charles Tupper, *Recollections of Sixty Years*, pp. 177-180.

in all its force, not only the immediate and widespread disaster to 98 per cent of our commerce with Canada which would occur upon a proclamation of non-intercourse, but that with the passionate elements in our midst the country might enter upon a line of action fraught with misfortune.[83]

On June 1, 1887, Phelps wrote a personal letter to Bayard in which he clearly outlined an argument later elaborated upon by Bayard himself. In his first annual message to Congress, President Cleveland had recommended the appointment of a commission "in which the Goverments of the United States and Great Britain shall be respectively represented, charged with the consideration and settlement . . . of the entire question of the fishing rights of the two Governments and their respective citizens on the coasts of the United States and British North America." [84] Senator Morgan, of Alabama, immediately expressed the view that there was no need for the President to request Congress to authorize the appointment of a commission to deal with the fisheries question. He regarded the President's recommendation as a "mistaken call upon the Congress of the United States for its assistance in conducting this matter. . . . If such a commission is to be provided for at all, let it be done under the constitutional powers of the President. . . . There is no lack of agencies, no lack of power, no lack of authority." [85]

Phelps had views very similar to those of Morgan with reference to the power of the President to appoint commissioners without requesting Congress to authorize such action. He could not see

. . . why the President has not power to appoint them for the purpose of considering and advising a plan of settlement, or as the instruments of obtaining it. I cannot see that any legislation is necessary to enable him to do so. If appointed they would of course act under your immediate control and would have no power to do anything except with your approval. . . . I think the commissioners on our side should insist on, as a *sine qua non,* the extension to our fishermen of the privileges which Newfoundland concedes. This is what we have claimed so decidedly.[86]

In his letter to Sir Charles Tupper (May 31, 1887), Bayard had indicated his hope that Tupper himself would be selected by the British Government as one of the commissioners who would pass upon the chief questions at issue between Canada and the United States. While Tupper indirectly admitted that such a choice would be an admirable

83. Bayard to Phelps, May 31, 1887, *Bayard Letter Book,* vol. 5, *Bayard MS.*
84. James D. Richardson, *Messages and Papers of the Presidents,* vol. 8, p. 332.
85. Henry M. Wriston, *Executive Agents in American Foreign Relations* (Baltimore, 1929), p. 283; *Cong. Rec.,* 49 Cong., 1 sess., vol. 17, pp. 3434-3435.
86. Phelps to Bayard, June 1, 1887, *Bayard MS.*

one, he advised Bayard that the matter of selecting personnel to represent Great Britain on the commission was one which rested entirely with Her Majesty's Government. He was sure, however, that Lord Lansdowne was familiar with every aspect of the situation and would advise the Colonial Secretary as to the best course to pursue.[87]

When Phelps was advised of Bayard's correspondence with Sir Charles Tupper, he had some misgivings. It was distinctly unwise, he believed, to make too many friendly gestures toward Canada. He was certain that the British Government was anxious to have the fisheries dispute ended, and apparently, there was no strong sentiment in London in favor of lending further support to the Canadian contentions. He had received intimations that the British Cabinet would

. . . be glad to have pressure enough put upon Canada to bring them to reasonable terms. This will not invoke any *actual* suspension of intercourse. I am persuaded that if the Canadian authorities are made to understand that such will be the result, they will give in at once. The concession by Newfoundland will much embarrass them. I am assured upon good authority that after that is announced it will be impossible to prevent Nova Scotia from taking the same course. And the influence of the Imperial Government will be in the same direction. It seems to me we should not consent to negotiate in respect to proceedings which we have characterized rightly as outrages, and for which we have given notice we shall demand reparation. We should not now consent to *purchase* exemption from their recurrence.[88]

There was little doubt that Lord Salisbury was desirous of reaching an agreement with the United States with regard to the fisheries question. On July 12 Sackville-West called at the Department of State and showed Bayard a telegram that he had received from the Foreign Office. It was terse and to the point: "If Secretary of State will formally propose the appointment of Commission as suggested in his correspondence with Sir Charles Tupper, Her Majesty's Government will agree with great pleasure."[89]

Bayard immediately sent an instruction to Phelps dealing with the appointment of the mixed commission. The President deemed it of the "highest importance" to reach without further delay a "friendly understanding" with Great Britain in connection with the fisheries

87. Sir Charles Tupper to Bayard, June 6, 1887, quoted in Sir Charles Tupper, *Recollections of Sixty Years*, pp. 181-182.

88. Phelps to Bayard, June 11, 1887, *Bayard MS.*

89. Lord Salisbury to Sackville-West, July 11, 1887, *Bayard MS.* See also *Memorandum* written by Bayard on July 12, 1887, after a conversation with Sackville-West, and telegram from Bayard to Phelps, July 12, 1887, *Bayard MS.*

dispute. In order to expedite this matter, Phelps was instructed to propose to Lord Salisbury the appointment of an Envoy Extraordinary and Minister Plenipotentiary to meet in Washington with a Minister Plenipotentiary of the United States, "both of whom shall be duly authorized to treat of and discuss the mode of settling all questions which have arisen out of the fisheries on the Coasts of British North America." Bayard also inclosed in this instruction a long document arranged in three columns. The first column contained the *modus vivendi* which had been presented to the British Government on November 15, 1886. The second column was devoted to the observations of the British Foreign Office upon the proposed *modus vivendi,* and the third column presented Bayard's reply to the British observations.[90]

While Bayard was awaiting a formal answer from the British Government with regard to the appointment of an Envoy Extraordinary to confer in Washington with a representative of the American Government, he gave some thought to the personnel of the proposed mixed commission. He was of the opinion that it would be expedient to appoint a "moderate Republican" as a member of this body, but it was difficult to select a person who would fit into this category. Judge Gresham was a bold and a patriotic man, but his disregard of party lines impaired his influence with his party. At one time Bayard had thought of appointing Senator John Sherman as a member of the commission, but his recent speeches had indicated that he was "unstable in judgment." It was apparent that the Cleveland Administration could not hope for any "fair dealing" from men of the stamp of Evarts or Edmunds.[91]

In a letter to President Cleveland, Bayard once more expressed his doubts about finding a "moderate Republican" who would be qualified to sit on the mixed commission. If a "frank and fair Republican" could be found who would "treat the welfare of the country as being entitled to preference" over party exigencies in the canvass of 1888, Bayard would be happy to welcome him to a position on the commission.[92]

While Bayard was in this quandary about finding a suitable Republican to sit on the mixed commission, Phelps sent the happy suggestion

90. Bayard to Phelps, July 12, 1887, *Great Britain, Instructions,* vol. 29, MS Dept. of State.

91. Bayard to Phelps, July 14, 1887, *Confidential, Bayard MS.*

92. Bayard to President Cleveland, July 30, 1887, *Bayard Letter Book,* vol. 5, *Bayard MS.*

that James B. Angell, President of the University of Michigan, would be an ideal selection. Although Angell was a Republican, he was also a "level-headed, judicious, and conservative man," who enjoyed the additional distinction of being "friendly to the Administration." [93] Bayard was glad to receive this suggestion about Angell towards whom he was "well inclined." It was also necessary, however, to appoint someone from New England. Bayard himself would be the third American member of the mixed commission. The British representatives would probably include Sackville-West, a "distinguished personage from England," and someone of outstanding ability from Canada. Because of the torrid heat of a Washington summer it would be best to postpone the meetings of the commission until October.[94]

In answer to a question from Phelps, Lord Salisbury promised that the three British members of the mixed commission would be appointed as "soon as possible." [95] A few days later, Salisbury informed Phelps that Joseph Chamberlain had consented to go to Washington as one of the British representatives. To Phelps this appointment seemed a fortunate one. Chamberlain was a "clear-headed, sincere, and upright man, rather an extreme Liberal, though a Unionist and opponent of Gladstone." Phelps believed that he would deal with the "subject as fairly as any man from this side," and would probably be "more acceptable to the American people than a Tory nobleman." [96] After some little delay, the announcement was made that the other members of the British delegation to sit on the mixed commission would be Sir Charles Tupper and Sackville-West.[97]

In the last week in September, 1887, the American press learned that Bayard had selected William L. Putnam, of Maine, and James B. Angell, of Michigan, to sit with him as the representatives of the United States on the mixed commission. Putnam was an outstanding lawyer

93. Phelps to Bayard, August 2, 1887, *Bayard MS.*
94. Bayard to Phelps, August 15, 1887, *ibid.*
95. Phelps to Bayard, August 27, 1887, *ibid.*
96. Phelps to Bayard, August 30, 1887, *Bayard MS.* The Boston *Post,* September 1, 1887, thought that Chamberlain's appointment would be "favorably received" in the United States; the New York *World,* August 30, 1887, expressed the view that the appointment would be "received with satisfaction by the people on this side of the Atlantic"; the New York *Evening Post,* August 31, 1887, was of the opinion that Chamberlain was more "like the typical 'live Yankee' than any other Englishman in public life. . . . He is a republican in principle, and all his political leanings are towards the American type of government."
97. According to the Toronto *Globe,* October 15, 1887, Sir Charles Tupper was "little skilled in the subtle acts of diplomacy. His modes of action are usually coarse almost to brutality."

who had been assisting Bayard for many months as a special counsel with reference to Canadian seizures of American fishing vessels. Angell was a distinguished educator with certain diplomatic experience.[98]

The announcement of the appointment of Joseph Chamberlain as one of the British delegates to sit on the mixed commission, aroused a storm of protest in certain American newspapers. The New York *Tribune* endeavored to convey the idea that the whole idea of a mixed commission to discuss the fisheries question was a triumph for British diplomacy.[99] Other newspapers stressed the view that the appointment of such a commission was an act of defiance in the face of a hostile Senate. In view of this widespread Republican propaganda, Bayard thought it was expedient to give out a statement to the press in which the right of the President to appoint commissioners without consulting the Senate, was strongly supported. There was no doubt in his mind that the President had ample authority

. . . to negotiate any treaty, and in the negotiation he may employ one person or a hundred. . . . About the President's power to negotiate a treaty without instructions from Congress there is no doubt. It is one of his duties. There is no doubt about the power of this Government to negotiate with the English Commission when they come to treat with us. It is our duty and it will be done.[100]

Now that the Administration had decided to have a mixed commission sit in Washington in November, 1887, for the purpose of finding some formula that would settle the fisheries dispute, it was important accurately to define the questions that would come up for consideration. On September 13 Sackville-West called at the Department of State and handed to Bayard a statement suggested by Lord

98. From 1880 to 1882 Angell had been on leave from his duties as President of the University of Michigan to serve on a diplomatic commission that was sent to China to negotiate a treaty for the restriction of Chinese immigration to the United States. His appointment by Bayard in September, 1887, was politically wise, because Angell was a close friend of Senator Edmunds, one of Bayard's most bitter opponents. The American press was outspokenly friendly to the appointments of Angell and Putnam. The New York *Tribune*, September 30, 1887, admitted that the "fitness" of both men for a position on the mixed commission would be recognized by "the country." Angell's letter to Bayard, September 23, 1887, tentatively accepting the appointment until official permission was given by the Board of Regents of the University of Michigan, is in the *Bayard MS.*

99. New York *Tribune*, September 1, 1887.

100. Washington *Post*, September 2, 1887. In order to get around the fact that the Senate had approved by a large majority vote the resolution of Senator Frye (April 13, 1886) against the appointment of a commission to settle the questions at issue between the United States and Canada, Bayard was anxious that the American and British delegations, sitting on the mixed commission, be referred to as "plenipotentiaries" rather than as "commissioners." See Bayard to Sackville-West, September 21, 1887, *Bayard MS.*

Salisbury in regard to the "terms of reference." Bayard proposed some amendments which were quickly agreed to, and the stage was all set for the meetings of the mixed commission.[101]

101. The terms of reference suggested by Lord Salisbury read as follows: "To consider and adjust all or any questions relating to rights of fishery which are in issue between the Governments of Her Britannic Majesty and that of the United States of America and any other questions which may arise in the course of the negotiations and which they may be authorized by their respective Governments to discuss as part of the adjustment." Bayard amended this statement so as to read: "To consider and adjust all or any questions relating to rights of fishery *on the coasts of British North America* which are in *dispute* between the Governments of Her Britannic Majesty and that of the United States of America, and any other questions which may arise in the course of the negotiations, and which they may be authorized by their respective Governments to *consider and adjust.*" The final draft of the terms of reference were phrased as follows: "To consider and adjust all or any questions relating to rights of fishery in the seas adjacent to British North America and Newfoundland which are in dispute between the Governments of Her Britannic Majesty and that of the United States of America, and any other questions which may arise, and which they may be authorized by their respective Governments to consider and adjust." See Bayard to Sackville-West, September 14, 21, and October 19, 1887. See also Sackville-West to Bayard, October 24, 1887, *Bayard MS.*

CHAPTER NINE

Joseph Chamberlain Plays the Dual Role of Lover and Diplomat

AFTER BAYARD HAD SUCCEEDED IN SECURING THE ADOPTION OF HIS PLAN for the meeting of a mixed commission in Washington, he next turned all his energies towards building up a favorable public opinion for an accord with Canada. On October 12, 1887, he wrote a short letter to Samuel L. Barlow, who had intimate connections with the business men of New York City. He was tempted to send to Barlow a "half-open letter in relation to the drift of our relations to Great Britain and our neighbour, the Dominion of Canada." In this way it might be possible that "a few plain and sincere words on this great subject would reach the minds . . . of some intelligent men charged with the care of great pecuniary interests in your Metropolis—C. M. Depew for instance." [1] Barlow replied that he would "gladly do anything you may suggest or think proper *re* Canada and the Fisheries." He was not certain that Chauncey Depew would be "the best man for such a purpose, or even one of the best, but I will see." [2]

Bayard next wrote to Horace White, one of the most influential newspaper men of that day.[3] White was friendly with certain members

1. Bayard to S. L. M. Barlow, October 12, 1887, *Bayard Letter Book*, vol. 6, *Bayard MS.*
2. Barlow to Bayard, October 13, 1887, *Bayard MS.*
3. White was in charge of the financial and economic sections of the New York *Evening Post* and the New York *Nation*. Bayard was not always deeply impressed with the tone of the *Evening Post*. In a letter to Phelps, November 21, 1887, he makes the following trenchant observation: "The *Evening Post* . . . is published upon such a height of superiority and egoism that everything that comes from it towards a Democrat has an insufferable flavor of condescension."
   As early as May 16, 1887, Edward Atkinson wrote to Bayard to suggest that he enlist in the service of the Administration, Franklin Ford, who was supplying a "large number of leading newspapers" with information. In reply, Bayard observed that it might "become very important in the near future that the aid of such a man as you describe Mr. Franklin Ford to be, should be obtained in order to inform the public mind through the agency

of the New York Chamber of Commerce through whom pressure might be exerted upon the New York delegation in Congress. Moreover, through the columns of the New York *Evening Post,* White could clearly present to the voters of that city a clear picture of the selfish forces that were striving to discredit the Cleveland Administration.[4]

When White wrote to inquire just what Bayard wanted him to do, he received the following answer:

I did not have in view anything like an appeal for Republican aid, . . . but only to arouse men's minds to the far-reaching importance of taking steps *only* in the *right* direction so that we should not be called on hereafter to brazen through an untenable demand or submit to the mortification of a compulsory withdrawal. It seems therefore to me that if the broad and general question of the duty and *present necessity* of establishing a well-considered and just and generous policy toward British America could be brought before the public mind, its magnitude and national weight would lead to a . . . condemnation of dealing in small personal and party methods with such vast and palpable public interests. Is there no way of the suggestion reaching the two Senators from the Empire State? The State of New York in the commercial relations of the Nation considerably exceeds that of all the New England Confederacy, and should not be dangled at the tail of the Gloucester kite.[5]

In the meantime, White had talked over the situation with Gustav Schwab, who believed that it was "quite feasible" to secure from the New York Chamber of Commerce "an expression favorable to a settlement of the fishery dispute on the lines which we understand you favor, and to do this in a way that would have an effect upon the New York Senators." [6]

On November 3, 1887, the Chamber of Commerce held its regular monthly meeting and unanimously adopted a resolution in favor of

---

of the press of the true status and tendency of public measures. I am convinced that if the issues involved in the present controversy in relation to the Canadian Fisheries could be properly comprehended by our countrymen, they would sustain the Administration in coming to a just, reasonable and permanent settlement." *Bayard Letter Book,* vol. 5, *Bayard MS.*

4. Bayard to Horace White, October 16, 1887, *Bayard Letter Book,* vol. 6, *Bayard MS.* In this letter, Bayard makes the following significant remarks: "You are very right in denouncing the attempt to transfer to the Executive one of the gravest duties and responsibilities of the Legislative branch. It was wholly unprecedented to invest the President with power in his discretion to declare non-intercourse with a country with whom we were at peace. Heretofore in our history, . . . embargoes and the like were the *acts of Congress,* giving to the Executive power to suspend their operation."

5. Bayard to Horace White, October 21, 1887, *Bayard Letter Book,* vol. 6, *Bayard MS.*

6. Horace White to Bayard, October 21, 1887, *Bayard MS.*

an "early adjustment of the fishery question." [7] The Chamber then appointed a committee to investigate the question of the extension of commercial relations with Canada. Horace White was convinced that it would be possible for Bayard to secure the endorsement of the Chamber for any program that he saw fit to lay before it. If this were done, the New York Senators would be "obliged to give it the most respectful attention." [8]

7. New York *Herald,* November 4, 1887.

8. Horace White to Bayard, November 3, 1887, *Bayard MS.* Bayard was also interested in exerting pressure upon the Senators from Pennsylvania in favor of an accord with Canada. On November 21, 1887, he sent a personal and confidential letter to G. B. Roberts, President of the Pennsylvania Railroad Company, in which he frankly places the real situation before him: "The position you occupy as the head of the greatest association of Capital in this country, is one of vast responsibility for the interests and welfare of so many of our countrymen, that I make no apology for laying before you a condition of affairs in which results of a grave and enduring nature are involved, and upon which you may be enabled to exercise an important influence. I refer to the disputed construction of the the terms of the Treaty between this country and Great Britain of 1818 in relation to the fisheries within the jurisdictional waters of British North America. . . . To settle this question a careful, conscientious attempt is now to be made, and unhappily the fires of political partisanship are suffered to approach it, and animosities growing out of British domestic questions (Home Rule in Ireland) are suffered to interfere. . . . Under these influences there are serious grounds to apprehend obstruction and possible defeat of the efforts now being made to settle amicably, honorably, and permanently the *sole existing question,* out of which collision between the United States and Great Britain can possibly arise. . . . You will not be surprised to learn that the fishing season just closed has been one of daily, almost hourly anxiety to me in view of it being made necessary, in a certain event, for the President to proclaim non-intercourse with Canada, which would have necessarily entailed loss and ruin upon a vast body of our countrymen, and especially upon those engaged in the business of transportation. . . .

"Should we embark upon a policy of retaliation, a war of adverse commercial measures, it is difficult to see, in the event of its being met in like spirit, how it can fail to antagonize the foreign population, whose border extends with our own across the Continent. . . . Consequent and mutual irritation can scarcely fail soon to change a thickly-studded line of rival Customhouses into lines of armed men. . . . It is plain that our relations with the Dominion of Canada must be those of progressive mutual beneficence and good neighborhood, or else 'those of unfriendliness, which awaits but a spark of collision to engender actual strife. . . .

"I feel it to be my duty to place such views before you because the attitude and votes of the two Senators from your State may become highly important in shaping the action of the United States Senate in relation to the results which may be attained by the negotiations about to be commenced. The extremely violent and, as it seems to me, highly dangerous and improper announcements which find their way into the public press . . . to the effect that no matter what arrangement may be agreed upon by the Plenipotentiaries, it will be rejected by the Senate, have induced me to write you thus frankly.

"I hope and believe a reasonable and honorable settlement can be attained. There ought to be no difficulty whatever, and in my judgment it would be discreditable if it is not attained; and if attained, how can its defeat by the Senate be justified before God or man? I know your relations to both the Pennsylvania Senators, and the just influence of your position, and the weight of your personal character and ability with them. Therefore it is that I have yielded to a strong sense of public duty to place before you my views in

This letter from White gave Bayard "great satisfaction." It seemed to him that there was really

. . . but "one thorn in the flesh" in our Canadian relations, but that has rankled so that inflammation is threatened. . . . On what terms we shall live [with Canada] is the question now to be determined, and we are at the initial point and will progress rapidly in the direction of kindly, neighbourly, mutually helpful, and good-natured behavior, or of an embittered and mutually [warring] state, the quasi-war of commercial retaliatory statutes, to be followed probably by armed collision. There is no good reason under God's sunlight for the latter course, but every reason for the former. When we look at the arteries of profitable and amicable intercourse in the shape of railway and artificial waterway communications which today are pulsating between Canada and the United States, . . . it is a cause of wonder that so little interest is expressed and so little positive aid is lent to the direct, straightforward attempts of this Administration to effect a just and permanent settlement on a basis adapted to things as they now exist.

In the Boston *Post* of November 7, a statement had appeared by a "New England Senator" to the effect that the names of the commissioners appointed by President Cleveland to sit on the mixed commission would have to be sent to the Senate for confirmation. The "New England Senator" was certain that these nominations would be rejected. He also believed that inasmuch as the Senate had already expressed its "disapproval of any treaty, . . . it could not endorse the action of this Commission without stultifying itself." [9]

This declaration of hostility by the "New England Senator" against any fishery treaty which resulted from the labors of the mixed commission, aroused the indignation of Bayard. He regarded such action

---

a juncture of deep importance to the welfare of the country of which we both are faithful sons." *Bayard Letter Book*, vol. 6, *Bayard MS*. In his letter of reply, January 13, 1888, Roberts remarked: "I fully share with you the anxiety arising from the unsettled condition of the fishery question and especially in view of the coming presidential election when party feeling runs so high, and the simple politician forgets everything but that which is to the interest of his party. I have had several opportunities (and I have not omitted to avail myself of them) to speak to those whom I thought had not only influence, but who felt sufficient interest in their country to make everything subservient to its welfare. I shall let no opportunity pass, when suitable occasion offers, to do what I can in the direction indicated in your letter." *Bayard MS*.

Through Dr. George L. Miller, a close friend of Daniel Lamont, a friendly approach was made to Jay Gould, President of the Missouri-Pacific Railway Company. Gould's response was immediate and warm. He was "very much gratified" to learn of the President's friendly feelings, which he fully reciprocated. He believed that President Cleveland was "stronger with the business interests of the country than any other person on either political side, and I think we ought all to work to secure his re-election." Gould to G. L. Miller, October 19, 1887, *Cleveland MS*.

9. Boston *Post*, November 7, 1887.

as unprecedented. Surely the President was empowered under the Constitution to negotiate treaties. If

. . . in the present case, to assist in having full consideration to all interests involved in the proposed policy of non-intercourse as a cure of rude treatment, the presence of two honorable and well instructed citizens is invoked, what is to be said of the threat, made in advance of any negotiation, to defeat it whatever it may be. Surely it is time for the Guardians of so much property of their own, and of others, as the Merchants and Bankers of New York City, to make some expression of their interest in these proceedings.[10]

Bayard was not content with these attempts to influence the New York Chamber of Commerce in favor of a treaty with Canada which would bring to an end the long controversy concerning the fisheries. He also made plans to meet the members of the New York Board of Trade and Transportation and lay before them the subject of Canadian-American relations. No effort should be spared in this endeavor to mobilize the sentiment of influential business men in favor of a friendly accord with Canada.[11]

While Bayard was busily engaged in making these gestures towards "big business," he was encouraged by news that came from England. Joseph Chamberlain was evincing a co-operative disposition that augured well for the success of the mixed commission. On August 31 Chamberlain wrote a note to Phelps which revealed a most friendly attitude towards the United States. Although Lord Salisbury's offer of a place on the mixed commission was quite unexpected, Chamberlain felt that

. . . he could not refuse the opportunity of doing something to maintain and confirm the good relations between the United States and Great Britain. You [Phelps] know that my respect and admiration for your country are great and of long standing. And the closer union of all the English-speaking nations is, I am convinced, of far-reaching importance to the civilization and happiness of the world. I am very glad that I shall now be able to make

10. Bayard to Horace White, November 8, 1887, *Bayard Letter Book*, vol. 6, *Bayard MS.*

11. In a letter to Ambrose Snow, President of the New York Board of Trade and Transportation, December 22, 1887, Bayard remarked: "I am at this time . . . engaged in an earnest effort to find a ground of permanent and just settlement of questions having their origin long anterior to the discovery of railways and other modern modes of transportation. . . . It is essential that this important international question [fisheries] should be lifted above the prejudice of heat of party. . . . Public opinion, healthfully and vigorously exerted, can best deal with untechnical questions of widespread and diversified interest, and your important organization, penetrating as it does so wide an area and influentially connecting itself with the occupations and fortunes of so many classes of our Countrymen, can surely be potential in giving expression to such views as are proper to instruct Congressional action." *Bayard Letter Book*, vol. 6, *Bayard MS.*

the personal acquaintance of leading Americans, and that I shall see something of the country and its institutions in which I take so deep an interest.[12]

Bayard was greatly pleased with the tone of this note from Chamberlain, and he confessed to Phelps that his hopes for a successful settlement of the fisheries dispute were founded "mainly upon the breadth and comprehensive justice" of the mind and character of Chamberlain.[13] Sir Charles Tupper was evidently in difficulties, and for a while Bayard was uncertain whether the Canadian Minister of Finance could sit on the mixed commission. According to the American Consul-General at Halifax, the seat of Sir Charles in the Dominion Parliament had

. . . just been declared vacant for bribery by agents at his election. . . . Tupper claims that the Conference [at Washington] is the outcome of his visit to Washington last winter. He is bold and politically unscrupulous, a good debater, fertile in resources, and ingenious in explaining inconsistencies, but lacks the training and legal knowledge of Macdonald.[14]

Sackville-West had long been regarded by Bayard as a "mere postage stamp," and he had written to Phelps to see if a more competent British diplomat could be sent to Washington. After looking over the situation in London, Phelps decided that "it would be of no use" to sound out the Foreign Office on the subject of this change. Sackville-West stood very close to those who held the "seats of the mighty" in England, and it would be quite impossible to displace him as British Minister to the United States.[15]

With Chamberlain as the outstanding member of the British delegation, it was doubly important that no harm should befall him. On October 24 Phelps cabled from London to suggest that special police protection should be given Chamberlain while he was in the United

12. Joseph Chamberlain to Phelps, August 31, 1887, *Bayard MS.*
13. Bayard to Phelps, October 20, 1887, *Bayard Letter Book,* vol. 6, *Bayard MS.*
14. M. H. Phelan to Bayard, October 13, 1887, *Bayard MS.* In the *Daily Sun,* St. John, New Brunswick, October 20, 1887, there is the following pertinent paragraph: "The unseating of Sir Charles Tupper, Mr. McLean, Mr. McDonald, and Mr. Lovitt, and the prospective vacating of several other seats is not a thing to be regretted. . . . Bribery at elections is an unmixed evil. . . . The practice tends to degrade public sentiment by discouraging those who have the highest ideas." In a letter to Bayard, October 21, 1887, W. L. Putnam makes the following observation concerning Sir Charles Tupper: "If he should be finally unseated, I should suppose that according to the practical political theories in Canada, it would affect his standing as a Member of the Commission, and possibly even compel his withdrawal." *Bayard MS.*
15. Phelps to Bayard, March 9, 1887, *Bayard MS.*

States,[16] and Bayard immediately wrote to the Pinkerton Detective Agency and made arrangements for a group of guards to protect the distinguished British visitor.[17]

With regard to Chamberlain's attitude towards the United States, Phelps wrote Bayard a long letter. He thought that Chamberlain felt his position to be

. . . rather that of an arbitrator between the United States and Canada, than that of an advocate. I believe he is quite prepared to conclude that reparation must be made for the injuries sustained by our fishermen from the unwarrantable seizures and prosecutions of the Canadian Government. If this is resolutely insisted on, I think you will obtain it. Of course, the treaty, if you are fortunate enough to make one, will encounter every opposition possible from the Irish party, the adverse majority in the Senate, and the ultra protectionists. And every probable ground of attack that might commend itself to the publick opinion will be tried. It seems to me that as we have characterized the Canadian proceedings as outrages not to be justified, and for which we have demanded reparation, and as Congress and the country have backed us up in this view, we can not now submit to them without reparation or acknowledgment, and purchase exemption from them in the future by concessions to Canada.[18]

To James B. Angell, a member of the mixed commission that was about to begin its proceedings, Phelps gave free expression to his feelings. He thought that it would be better for the Conference to fail

. . . than that its conclusion should not be sustained by the best intelligence of the country. If it is, the Senate must ratify it, or place themselves clearly in the wrong. It will of course be attacked, and efforts made to set publick opinion against it. . . . We have the opposition of the Irish party to contend with. . . . There is also the jealousy of the protectionists. . . . And finally there is the Republican majority in the Senate, to whom the paramount consideration in view of the next Presidential election, is to embarrass and discredit the administration. . . . For all these reasons, and in view of the

16. Phelps to Bayard, October 24, 1887, *ibid.* Daniel Magone took the precaution of writing to Col. D. S. Lamont to warn him about the dangers of "lionizing" Chamberlain. He believed that "worldly wisdom requires that we avoid anything that might tend to excite the Irish." Magone to Lamont, October 29, 1887, *Cleveland MS.*

17. Bayard to Pinkerton's National Detective Agency, New York City, October 25, 1887, *Bayard Letter Book*, vol. 6, *Bayard MS.* Lord Salisbury also sent word through Sackville-West that he would be grateful "if special instructions were given to the New York and Washington Police authorities to watch over the safety of Mr. Chamberlain." Sackville-West to Bayard, October 26, 1887, *Bayard MS.* In the *Bayard Papers* there is a series of reports from the Pinkerton Agency with reference to Chamberlain's activities and the protection that was afforded him.

18. Phelps to Bayard, October 29, 1887, *Bayard MS.*

irritation caused by the hostile conduct of Canada, this did not seem to me the most favorable time to attempt a new treaty. I preferred an *ad interim* arrangement, to tide over the adverse circumstances. . . . But Mr. Bayard has been hopeful that an adjustment can be reached now. . . .

I am sure you will be charmed with Mr. Bayard, and will much enjoy your association with him. . . . Mr. Bayard's only fault in such a matter is that he attributes to the representatives of other nations the same high and magnanimous motives by which he is controlled, and therefore begins with concessions which though right should be held to obtain concessions from them. England will promptly accept everything that magnanimity will give her, but will never give a hair's breadth in return unless compelled.[19]

To Bayard's friends it was only too apparent that no matter what type of treaty was suggested by the mixed commission, there would always be "an ugly opposition in the Senate to deal with."[20] President Cleveland himself was fearful of political sabotage engineered by Republicans in the Senate, and he was fully aware of the danger of accepting any arrangement that was the "result of a Commission with Mr. C[hamberlain] on it."[21]

Bayard clearly recognized the opposition in the United States to Chamberlain's political views concerning Ireland. But Chamberlain's business in the United States had no connection with

. . . home rule in Ireland, and we of course had nothing to do with his selection by his own Government. It would . . . be vain to expect that any but a Unionist should be selected to represent a Unionist Ministry. . . . The root of the matter is very ancient and has stained history in by-gone times with passions of sectarian warfare. You have done nothing to promote but everything to assuage such feelings.[22]

Chamberlain landed in New York City on November 7, and was at once placed under the protection of the Pinkerton guards. Nothing untoward happened at his landing except that a "rough looking man"

19. Phelps to J. B. Angell, October 29, 1887, *Angell Papers, Michigan Historical Collections,* University of Michigan. This estimate of Bayard by Phelps lingered in the memory of Mr. Angell and helped to color his own viewpoint. In his *Reminiscences* (N. Y. 1912), pp. 174-175, he remarks: "I prize especially the acquaintance and friendship I formed with Mr. Bayard. A man of singular personal charm, I have never known one in public life of higher and nobler sense of public duty. He scorned the mean arts of the mere politician and whatever was unworthy in the spirit and policy of his own party. He was so magnanimous to his opponent, that to a certain degree his generosity unfitted him to negotiate with so keen a man as Chamberlain. He was tempted to concede too much." The fallacy of this view will be apparent from a careful reading of this chapter.
20. Carl Schurz to Bayard, November 3, 1887, *Bayard MS.*
21. President Cleveland to Bayard, November 7, 1887, *Bayard MS.*
22. Bayard to President Cleveland, November 7, 1887, *Bayard Letter Book,* vol. 6, *Bayard MS.*

created a diversion by crying: "Three cheers for Gladstone and Parnell."[23] On November 18 Chamberlain, Sir Charles Tupper, and Sackville-West called at the Department of State to see Bayard. When Chamberlain inquired as to the order of proceedings, Bayard courteously replied that this order would be "entirely subject to his convenience." Bayard then invited Chamberlain to dinner on May 26 in order that he could "meet some of the gentlemen connected with the Government here." After this exchange of civilities, the meeting broke up and Bayard made plans to present his visitors to the President on the following day.[24]

On the eve of the meetings of the mixed commission, Bayard felt somewhat optimistic about the results that would probably be obtained. In a letter to Phelps he expressed the opinion that the American position appeared to him to be

. . . stronger and less assailable the more it is considered. The provincialism of Canada (in every sense of the word) and the embarrassment to the Imperial Government caused thereby is an obvious cause of difficulty, but her interests in favor of good commercial relations with the United States are so preponderating that I believe her representative in the Conference will be compelled to abandon the *impossible* construction they have given to our treaty rights. . . .

Frye and "another New England Senator who did not desire his name should be mentioned," have declared the Senate would reject *any* treaty which might come from the present conference! Such an issue has at least the merit of simplification, and upon it I have no objection to go before the American people.[25]

If Bayard felt sanguine of success in this matter of negotiations with the British delegation on the mixed commission, the same might also be said of the feelings of the British delegates themselves. Mr. J. S. D. Thompson, the Canadian Minister of Justice, was certain that Chamberlain was "very keen and shrewd" and was "quite ready for Mr. Bayard." After looking over the situation with care, he assured Sir John

---

23. Robert A. Pinkerton to Bayard, November 7, 11, 12, 1887, *Bayard MS.* According to J. S. Moore, Chamberlain made a very judicious speech at the Chamber of Commerce dinner and became "all at once not only *Persona grata* with the Administration but decidedly so with the majority, and I may say, substantial people of the Metropolis." Moore to Bayard, November 17, 1887, *Bayard MS.*

24. *Memorandum* written by Bayard after meeting Joseph Chamberlain, Sir Charles Tupper, and Sackville-West, November 18, 1887, *Bayard MS.*

25. Bayard to Phelps, November 21, 1887, *Bayard Letter Book,* vol. 6, *Bayard MS.*

Macdonald that "we have much the better team on the British side of the Conference." [26]

When the members of the British delegation called at the Department of State on November 21 it was decided that there should be "absolute secrecy in regard to all that takes place." [27] On the following afternoon the mixed commission held its first meeting in the Department of State. Chamberlain's seat at the table was directly under a portrait of James G. Blaine, whose "black tropical eyes bent down penetratingly upon Mr. Bayard's face." [28]

Perhaps Blaine's spirit as well as his portrait was present at this meeting of the mixed commission. At any rate, it was not long before serious disagreement arose as to the terms of reference which were to guide the deliberations of the commission. [29] The instructions which

26. J. S. D. Thompson to Sir John Macdonald, November 18, 1887, *Washington Treaty, 1888, Sir John Macdonald Papers*, MS Canadian Archives.

27. *Memorandum* dictated by Bayard, November 21, 1887, *Bayard MS*. See also Sir Charles Tupper to Sir John Macdonald, November 21, 1887, E. M. Saunders, *The Life and Letters of Rt. Hon. Sir Charles Tupper* (N. Y. 1916), vol. 2, p. 101.

28. Sir Willoughby Maycock, *With Mr. Chamberlain in the United States and Canada, 1887–1888* (London, 1914), p. 63.

29. When Sir Charles Tupper received a communication from the British Colonial Office indicating the terms of reference which had been agreed upon for the meetings of the mixed commission, he strongly urged that they be amended so as to include the question of seal fisheries in Behring Sea. Sir Charles Tupper to John Bramston, September 22, 1887, *Washington Treaty, 1888, Sir John Macdonald Papers*, MS Canadian Archives. Sir John Macdonald agreed with Sir Charles Tupper with regard to Behring Sea, and he wrote to Lansdowne to express the need of having this question included in the terms of reference. In reply, Lansdowne observes: "Your first point that the restriction of the 'adjustment' to questions actually in dispute may have the effect of excluding completely the consideration of all collateral questions not in dispute, would not occasion me any misgiving but for your experience on a similar occasion of the manner in which United States statesmen have taken advantage of like technicalities. It might, I should think, be argued that if the Commissioners are empowered to consider *and adjust* all questions in dispute, they are thereby also empowered to deal with any matters essential to an adjustment, such as mutual concessions, compensations in money or in privileges conferred, etc. If the 'adjustment' might include these, the 'negotiations' could scarcely exclude them. . . . You have, however, laid your finger upon a much more serious blot when you point out that the limitation of the reference to 'questions respecting fisheries rights in seas adjacent to British North America' will, if literally interpreted, exclude Behring Sea." Lansdowne to Sir John Macdonald, September 26, 1887. *Washington Treaty, 1888, Sir John Macdonald Papers*, MS Canadian Archives. In the actual instructions that were issued to the members of the British delegation, Lord Salisbury indicated that the main question which they would be called upon to settle would be "in connection with the fisheries prosecuted by the citizens of the United States on the Atlantic shores of British North America and Newfoundland. . . . Whilst I have judged it advisable thus in the first place to refer to the questions of the Atlantic coastal fisheries, it is not the wish of Her Majesty's Government that the discussions of the plenipotentiaries should necessarily be confined to that point alone, but full liberty is given to you to enter upon the consideration of any question which may bear upon the issues involved, and to discuss

Lord Salisbury had given to the members of the British delegation were very flexible and would have permitted them to "enter upon the consideration of any questions which may bear upon the issues involved." Bayard knew that the Senate would never approve a treaty which contained any provision for reciprocity with Canada. For that reason he was determined to restrict the discussions of the mixed commission to the sole question of the North Atlantic fisheries, and he flatly refused to go beyond the explicit language of the terms of reference.[30] An intimation was given, however, that if an adjustment of the fisheries question was arrived at, Congress might very well provide for some tariff concessions to Canadian products.[31]

With reference to the fisheries question, Bayard stated that

. . . the privilege of "taking, drying, and curing fish within three miles of the coasts" is *not* the subject of this conference. It was renounced as to the localities described in 1818, and we do not conceive that any difficulty arises at present, nor is there any complaint by reason of the exclusion of United States fishermen from that belt nor of the confiscation when apprehended

---

and treat for any equivalents, whether by means of tariff concessions or otherwise, which the United States' plenipotentiaries may be authorised to consider as a means of settlement. The question of the seal fisheries in the Behring Seas . . . has not been specifically included in the terms of reference." Sir Charles Tupper, *Recollections of Sixty Years*, pp. 186-190.

30. In a letter to Phelps, December 6, 1887, Bayard tells of his struggle with the British delegation with reference to the terms of reference: "Mr. Chamberlain and Sir Charles Tupper verbally gave strong expression to the misapprehension with which they had come hither, and affected to say that an arrangement of more liberal commercial relations between Canada and the United States was the only method by which harmony could be expected to be obtained, or be lost sight of. The 'personal and unofficial' letter from me to Sir Charles Tupper written in June, 1887, . . . was quoted from to give meaning to the terms of reference so carefully prepared and amended by Lord Salisbury, and recited in the powers given to the Plenipotentiaries. Sir Charles even went so far as to seek to control the terms of the conference by what he said verbally to me when he made his unofficial visit to Washington in May last. In the face of the correspondence of 1886–1887, my instructions to you containing the proposal, and Lord Salisbury's acceptance and careful draught of the terms of reference, I need not say that such an attempt at unauthorized substitution was at once stated to be wholly inadmissible, but I confess to you that my surprise was not unmingled with a sentiment of a more positive nature and most unfavorable to the style of diplomacy that admitted such action." *Bayard Letter Book*, vol. 6, *Bayard MS.*

31. In a conversation with Sir Charles Tupper, John G. Carlisle, Speaker of the House of Representatives, stated that the President was willing to put coal, lumber, fish, salt, wool, iron and copper ores on the free list. Carlisle took the ground that "the admission of raw products free was not in antagonism with the protective policy and would assist in reducing the surplus which has become so embarrassing. He said the President told him that he had no intention of sacrificing the whole country to the clamor of a few fishermen, and said the duty on lumber was an injury to the whole country, would rapidly destroy their remaining forests, and at the same time they are paying public money to promote tree planting." Sir Charles Tupper to Sir John Macdonald, November 25, 1887, *Washington Treaty, 1888, Sir John Macdonald Papers*, MS Canadian Archives.

there for fishing. It is the exercise of the express liberties, wholly consistent with abstention from fishing there, that we claim. Canada has imposed such burdens upon the exercise of these liberties that our fishermen find them injuries and not benefits. . . . If American fishermen could exercise their Treaty rights of repairs, wood, and water *only in established ports of entry*, and not frequent for such purposes the unfrequented parts of the coast, would not additional security accrue to Nova Scotia and opportunity for illicit trading be taken away? . . .

Submitting thus to commercial requirements, what possible objection to the usual commercial conveniences [for fishing boats] unless the *open sea* fishing is sought to be *impeded*, and that is a distinct act of unfriendliness and is not warranted by any Treaty nor International Law.[32]

It was soon apparent to both delegations that agreement upon the important questions at issue would come only after many long and arduous sessions of the mixed commission. The second session was set for November 28, but before that date arrived, something occurred which made a fundamental change in the life of Joseph Chamberlain. A widower, nearing the age of fifty-two, with a large family of children, was hardly the person to whom romance would brightly nod. But love has always refused to be confined by conventional patterns, and Chamberlain's heart that had long been closed to thoughts of tender sentiment, suddenly opened wide to the soft strains of a sonnet. On November 26, 1887, Sackville-West gave a large reception in honor of Chamberlain, and the élite of Washington society crowded into the British Legation. Among those in attendance was Mary Endicott, the daughter of William C. Endicott, the Secretary of War in President Cleveland's Cabinet. Immediately after meeting Miss Endicott, Chamberlain was so struck by her beauty and charm that he forgot his duty to the other guests at the Legation and once more the ancient mystery of the way of a maid with a man was enacted on a diplomatic stage.[33]

32. *Memorandum* written by Bayard after the first meeting of the mixed commission, November 22, 1887, *Bayard MS.* In a *memorandum* written on November 23, Bayard observed: "How is it possible that Mr. Chamberlain should be surprised at our bringing before him as a basis of discussion the grounds upon which we had laid our complaints to Great Britain against the Canadians? Do we admit by being silent as to these complaints, that they had not been justified, or that we had abandoned them? . . . Tupper's denial that Canada has sought to use the treaty of 1818 'as a lever' to affect our tariff laws is not credible nor true. He has himself more than hinted it, and his government has expressly argued it." *Bayard MS.*

33. James L. Garvin, *The Life of Joseph Chamberlain* (London, 1933), vol. 2, pp. 335-341; Sir Willoughby Maycock, *With Mr. Chamberlain in the United States and Canada, 1887–1888*, pp. 50-55.

It is quite possible that Chamberlain's instant attraction to Miss Endicott, who later became his wife, softened his attitude towards America and made him more likely to lean towards a compromise. Without denying this possibility, it is quite noticeable, however, that Chamberlain strongly supported the contentions of Canadian statesmen in the meetings of the mixed commission on November 28, 30, and on December 3.[34] Sir Charles Tupper had suggested that inasmuch as the American delegation was opposed to any arrangement for commercial reciprocity between Canada and the United States, it might be possible to agree that Canada and Newfoundland should be a base of supplies for American fishermen in return for the concession that fish, fish-oil, whale-oil and seal-oil from Canada and Newfoundland be permitted to enter the United States free of duty. In addition to this tariff concession the Government of the United States should also be prepared to agree to renounce the privileges which American fishermen had enjoyed under the Treaty of 1818 with reference to the "taking, drying, and curing fish on the shore and coasts of Newfoundland, Labrador, and the Magdalen Islands."

According to Sir Charles Tupper, Chamberlain gave immediate support to this Canadian proposal, and left no doubt in American minds that he was prepared to stand behind the Canadian contentions. He also

. . . cited the dispatches of Lord Rosebery and the Earl of Iddesleigh on this point, and showed clearly that the British Government entirely concurred with the Canadian view on the question in controversy. I [Sir Charles Tupper] had at the previous meeting . . . accepted Mr. Bayard's challenge on this point; but I requested Mr. Chamberlain to take it up, as I felt the response would come with much greater force from him and would meet the evident desire of the United States Plenipotentiaries from the first to draw a distinction between the attitude of Canada and Great Britain. I am bound

34. In a *memorandum* that Bayard wrote shortly after the mixed commission began to hold its meetings, we have a record of Bayard's reaction to the attitude of the British delegation: "A review of the proceedings of this Conference will show that no suggestion of better treatment of our Fishermen, putting in for shelter, or such amelioration of a rigid and harsh interpretation of the Treaty and of future administration of Canadian laws, or of compensation and redress for injuries complained of as having been sustained at the hands of Canadian officials by our Fishermen in 1886–1887, has emanated from the British Plenipotentiaries, and when put forward by the American Plenipotentiaries has been postponed and never renewed. The sole point upon which the negotiation has been hung by the British Plenipotentiaries has been the alteration in the United States Tariff so as to admit all fish free of duty. This has been with them from the first a *sine qua non*, and every proposition submitted by them has contained this feature and made to depend upon its acceptance." *Bayard MS.*

to say Mr. Chamberlain undertook this duty most willingly and discharged it admirably.[35]

In a letter to Phelps, Bayard tells much the same story. After rehearsing what occurred during four meetings of the mixed commission, he alluded to the British offer

. . . to return to the Fishery Articles of 1871, with the condition of considering new commercial arrangements. I can only say to you that this will be declined, and the President will not be asked to enlarge our powers in order to embrace the subject. . . . It may well be that by legislation an expanded *free list* may procure for Canada access to our markets which she has apparently been using a harsh and vexatious administration of her Fishery laws and an extreme interpretation of the treaty of 1818 to obtain, but to establish a reform of the tariff to suit her local interests by means of a Commercial Treaty at this time would be impossible. . . . I do no one an injustice when I say that Canada proposes to "talk shop" and nothing else, and that Mr. Chamberlain's object seems mainly to satisfy Canada. What other suggestions may be made on either side I cannot foretell, but just now the prospects for a just and reasonable interpretation of the vexed provisions of the treaty of 1818 are not very bright.[36]

From the Canadian side, Mr. Thompson was equally critical and pessimistic. In a letter to Sir John Macdonald he complains as follows:

We are not progressing to any appreciable extent. At each meeting of the Conference our American friends conjure up so many fallacies and misstatements that it is difficult to believe that they understand their case. We have kept our Plenipotentiaries with briefs on every imaginable point, and . . . our case seems to grow stronger every day. For example, they contend that by the law of nations a vessel entering port for shelter is free from harbor dues and pilotage, but we find that in every treaty which is made by the United States this is made a matter for express stipulation for either total or partial immunity. We also find that they have seized Spain's fishing vessels on the coast of Florida for not entering at the Custom House although they only came in for provisions.[37]

35. E. M. Saunders, *The Life and Letters of the Right Hon. Sir Charles Tupper*, vol. 2, pp. 101-102. See also the letter from J. S. D. Thompson to Sir John Macdonald, November 28, 1887: "We have all been immensely busy in preparing our Reply to the American Memorandum and its Appendices. . . . As it covers about 300 pages of foolscap, I think that our American friends will have to get a long adjournment in order to read it. I cannot understand why they have opened battle on this line as it is the one which will be most tedious and can lead to nothing. . . . Chamberlain and his English assistants have left the preparation of the Replies implicitly to us, excepting as to a very excellent introduction which Mr. Chamberlain himself prepared." *Washington Treaty, 1888, Sir John Macdonald Papers*, MS Canadian Archives.

36. Bayard to Phelps, December 6, 1887, *Bayard Letter Book*, vol. 6, *Bayard MS.*

37. J. S. D. Thompson to Sir John Macdonald, December 7, 1887, *Washington Treaty, 1888, Sir John Macdonald Papers*, MS Canadian Archives.

After the mixed commission had reached a deadlock in the meeting on December 10, Sir Charles Tupper suggested to Chamberlain the advisability of a private conference with Bayard.[38] This arrangement was gladly acceded to by Bayard, and in a memorandum which he wrote immediately after Chamberlain left, we have a record of the conversation between these two statesmen:

Mr. Chamberlain came as he had proposed in his note, at 4:30. He began by saying—"I suppose I may speak with you confidentially," and I said "Certainly"—that I had no secrets and that my associates knew all that I thought on the subject. He suggested a treaty and handed me a written memo., which he subsequently took away with him. It had four points:

(1) A system of . . . Canadian licenses for American Fishermen—the licenses to be paid so long as Fish were taxed under our Tariff.

(2) Free Fishing for Americans and a base of supplies—the Dominions—with full commercial privileges.

(3) A release by the United States of their rights under Treaty of 1818 to fish along Newfoundland, Magdalen Islands, and Labrador.

(4) Free Fish in United States Markets.

I read it [the memorandum] and told him the latter [point four] was hopeless. . . . After much discussion he said—"How would this do?"—

(1) A Commission of Delimitation, but an agreement in the Treaty as to certain named Bays (Bay des Chaleur) and the Commission to ascertain and limit the ports.

(2) By the treaty to arrange laws of seizures and penalties for Fishing within three miles.

(3) To give full commercial privileges to American Fishermen for supplies—bait, etc.—in Canadian ports, but not the privilege of fishing within three miles of shore.

(4) Free entry for Fish into the United States.

I said that I could not answer, but I would not reject the idea. I stated to him the force of the Irish feeling, and he recognized the truth. He told me John Sherman had told him the Irish influence had prevented the ratification of the Phelps-Rosebery extradition treaty. . . . He spoke gravely of the "ugly" possibilities of the consequences of a failure to agree, etc. Finally, when he put his paper in his pocket he said (taking my hand): "I promise you I will do all that I can," and I answered: "I will do my best to assist in a settlement."

38. This private conference was held at Bayard's residence. In the *Bayard Papers* there is a short note from Chamberlain to Bayard, December 10, 1887, which reads: "Will you give me a personal and purely confidential interview? I think it might facilitate matters somewhat. If so please reserve an hour when I can see you either at your house or here [Arlington Hotel], if you prefer it, as it might excite malice if I were to call on you at the State Department without my colleagues." In reply, Bayard wrote: "At four o'clock this p. m., we can meet at my house (1413 Mass. Ave.) undisturbed. I will await you there and have mentioned your suggestion for this meeting to no one."

He said that Mr. Putnam had said, free coal, lumber might be given by the United States, but not *free fish.* . . . He said he could say privately what he could not say publicly about his opinion of the treatment of our Fishermen by the Canadian Officials.[39]

After Chamberlain had presented his memoranda for discussion, Bayard indicated his personal approval of the following points: (1) The appointment of a commission which would be empowered to settle the difficult question of territorial waters; (2) To give full commercial privileges to American fishing vessels in the territorial waters of Canada and Newfoundland, the American Government, at the same time, renouncing the privileges granted under the Treaty of 1818 with reference to the taking, drying, and curing of fish in the exclusive territorial waters of Canada and Newfoundland: (3) The free importation of fish and fish-oil into the United States. Bayard was also ready to discuss further concessions in connection with the navigation of certain bays or estuaries, like the Bay des Chaleur.[40]

After receiving this favorable response from Bayard, Chamberlain next wished to see President Cleveland before leaving for a trip to Canada where he hoped to persuade Lord Lansdowne and Sir John Macdonald of the necessity of making some concessions to the United States. On December 14 Chamberlain called at the White House and found that the President was in accord with the views of Bayard. Later that afternoon, Chamberlain paid a visit to Bayard's residence and expressed his warm appreciation of the President's "kindness and

39. *Memorandum* written by Bayard after a conversation with Chamberlain, December 10, 1887, *Bayard MS.* In his reply to Chamberlain, Bayard said that he thought that the main question to be settled was one of "good neighborhood," and that he was very anxious that "friendly relations should not be imperilled or impaired without sufficient cause. . . . It must be observed that whilst the stringency of the Canadian construction of the Treaty . . . has increased in 1886–1887, . . . a growing relaxation and liberality of construction has marked the action of the United States Authorities. . . . Whenever the American plenipotentiaries have urged that the same friendly treatment should be given to our Fishermen when they go into Canadian Ports, . . . they present as a reason for withholding it the words of the Treaty connected with four specified purposes—'and for no other purpose whatever.' . . . In effect the Treaty thus becomes wax in the hands of one party, and marble in the hands of the other. . . . The Home Government has indicated its desire to see justice done, . . . *but nothing has been done.* . . . The Great point is the establishment of *an entente cordiale* which is far beyond all the rest, and may not be fully computed." *Memorandum* written by Bayard, December 10, 1887, *Bayard MS.*

40. Sir Charles Tupper to Sir John Macdonald, January 25, 1888, *Washington Treaty 1888, Sir John Macdonald Papers,* MS Canadian Archives; *memorandum* written by Bayard, December 10, 1887, *Bayard MS.* It should always be remembered that Bayard, during these interviews with Chamberlain, spoke only for himself and not for the American delegation as a unit. Bayard made and accepted all suggestions *ad referendum.*

frankness." He then handed Bayard a memorandum, saying that he had

. . . found the President independently giving his approval to what I [Bayard] had outlined as a possible basis of settlement. I told him of the great value the Bay Chaleur had in Canadian views and the insight his securing it exclusively to Canada would have *there*. I then repeated to him the arithmetical features of the case and showed the pecuniary loss to Canada in this item of her business, maintaining the status of the past two years, citing Tariff statistics and the increasing quantity of *free* fish. I again referred to the Retaliation Act, and said that the losses from one day of its operation would cost Canada more than a year's tariff at present rates.[41]

Bayard's outline of the concessions that he favored in order to arrive at an understanding with Canada, was eminently satisfying to Sir Charles Tupper who wrote to Sir John Macdonald that it seemed as though the negotiations were "to have a fair measure of success." [42] But even this "fair measure" of success would be imperilled if Republican partisanship were permitted to play an important part in this matter of a fisheries treaty. Senators like Edmunds and Frye had long been noted for their narrow views, and now a new luminary in Republican ranks began to attract attention. In a letter to Bayard, W. L. Putnam enclosed a copy of the Boston *Record* with an article for which Henry Cabot Lodge was responsible. Putnam's comments upon Lodge anticipate some of the criticisms that were hurled at the Massachusetts legislator at the time of his bitter fight against President Wilson and the League of Nations:

This article exhibits in a moderate degree the perversity of the statements on this subject which he is willing to make, and which his opportunities as an educated man demand he should be held strictly to account for. I think they will satisfy you that he is wholly unsuited for a position on the Committee on Foreign Relations, or indeed for any position where it may ever become necessary to hold the scales with any degree of impartiality.[43]

There was serious danger, of course, that the Canadian demands at the meetings of the mixed commission would be impossible of

41. *Memorandum* written by Bayard after a conversation with Chamberlain, December 14, 1887, *Bayard MS.* See also Chamberlain's letter to Bayard, December 13, 1887, *ibid.* On December 15 Bayard had a conversation with President Cleveland with reference to Chamberlain's proposals and his mission to Canada. In a *memorandum* written on December 15, 1887, Bayard observes: "I read him [the President] the memo. of proposals of Chamberlain and found our minds in agreement generally." *Bayard MS.*

42. E. M. Saunders, *The Life and Letters of the Rt. Hon. Sir Charles Tupper,* vol. 2, p. 105.

43. W. L. Putnam to Bayard, December 16, 1887, *Bayard MS.* In his answering letter to Putnam, December 19, 1887, Bayard gives the assurance that "there is no chance of his [Lodge] obtaining the place on the Committee you refer to." *Bayard MS.*

acceptance, and American public opinion might easily be so aroused over Canadian discourtesy that serious trouble would ensue. To Phelps, in London, the situation had dangerous possibilities:

> The Canadian demand that we should purchase exemption from manifest outrage by modifying our tariff, and be coerced into a new treaty by plain violation of the old one, is what in my judgment neither Congress nor the country will tolerate. And the new imposition by Canada upon the fishing vessels when seeking the necessary shelter to which the treaty entitles them, of a burdensome, compulsory, and unnecessary pilotage, may not unlikely prove the last straw that breaks the camel's back. It is approaching an attempt at conciliation by another step of injustice and wrong.[44]

Chamberlain returned to Washington on January 3, and had a conversation with Bayard, who promptly favored the abolition of the pilotage dues on American vessels driven into Canadian harbors by stress of weather. Bayard also gave his approval to a system of licenses for American fishermen to be in force as long as duties were imposed upon Canadian fish. Through this device it might be possible to induce Congress to remove these duties on fish in the event that the Senate should reject a fisheries treaty.[45]

When Chamberlain was in Ottawa, Canada, the concessions that he obtained from the Dominion Government seemed so far-reaching that he anticipated no trouble in arriving at a satisfactory settlement of Canadian-American difficulties. In a letter to his daughter Beatrice, December 28, 1887, he made the confident statement that he already had the treaty in his "pocket."[46] On January 3, 1888, he was back in Washington and at once addressed a short note to Bayard in which he remarked that he had experienced "some difficulty with the good people on the other side of the border," but he had succeeded in securing their consent to Bayard's proposals "and to a plan for giving them effect."[47]

Bayard assured Chamberlain that he had heard with "the greatest satisfaction that you have succeeded in bringing our Cousins in Canada to take the views outlined in our last personal meeting." He then suggested that Chamberlain come to the Bayard residence on the

---

44. Phelps to Bayard, December 20, 1887, *Bayard MS.*
45. See Chamberlain's secret memoranda of interviews, enclosed in the letter from Sir Charles Tupper to Sir John Macdonald, January 25, 1888, *Washington Treaty, 1888, Sir John Macdonald Papers,* MS Canadian Archives.
46. J. L. Garvin, *The Life of Joseph Chamberlain,* vol. 2, p. 332.
47. Chamberlain to Bayard, January 3, 1888, *Bayard MS.*

morning of January 5, for a conference.[48] After an extended discussion of the points at issue between Canada and the United States, it was finally agreed that the mixed commission would resume its labors on January 9, 1888.

At the meeting of the commission on January 14, Bayard made a frank presentation of the American case against Canada. He made particular reference to the action of the Canadian authorities in

. . . (a) refusing clearances to vessels putting in under the eye of their cruisers for shelter, and compelling them to remain within the 3-mile limit when they wanted to get away; (b) enforcing pilotage upon a fleet of weather-beaten fishing boats putting into Halifax in distress; (c) the obstruction of railway transit on the Manitoba line—refusing the very facilities which the United States were giving freely in San Francisco to British Columbia.

Bayard then expressed the view that Chamberlain was entirely correct in believing that the paramount end in view in holding the meetings of the mixed commission was the "establishment of good

48. Bayard to Chamberlain. January 4, 1888, *ibid.* The main points in this conversation between Bayard and Chamberlain are summarized in a *memorandum* written by Bayard, January 5, 1888: "Mr. Chamberlain came to my house, by appointment, and said he had had a good deal of trouble to bring Sir Chas. Tupper to his views, but he had in the main succeeded. Sir John Macdonald he found a man of breadth and ability. He said the proposal to appoint a skilled Com. to delimit the three-mile line on the '10-mile' basis could be arranged, with Bay Chaleur and one or possibly two other bays which he said he could not remember the names of, but which were unimportant, to be settled in the Treaty. All pilotage charges for fishery vessels to be abolished.

"Objection arose as to the Government vessels of U. S. exercising any jurisdiction in Canadian waters and that it would be better to have a judge of the highest *Provincial* Court to be 'perambulating' and attend wherever called by a case and to decide promptly. If his decision was in favor of the *Vessel* it was to be final, if adverse, then an appeal would be made.

"For 'fishing or preparing to fish,' forfeiture of the vessel not to be relinquished, but no serious application of penalty, and in all cases to be approved by the Governor-General. Minor penalties for infringement of treaty to be arranged by this Commission. Commercial privileges—bait, etc., on one side—free fish and fish-oil on the other. The important feature was, however, that in case the Senate rejected the Treaty, that Canada would still enact by law that Licenses should be granted at a moderate sum to Am. Fishing Vessels with permits to travel and trade, and that *the fees* for such licenses should not be collected whenever free admission of Canadian Fish should be provided by U. S. Laws.

"As an *ad interim* arrangement he believed this would prevent friction and irritation during the next summer, and . . . he recognized that a majority vote in Congress might so modify the Tariff as to satisfy Canadian wishes and views. I strongly expressed approval of keeping the subject on the *train of settlement,* and not leaving it where it was. Mr. C. then asked me how we had better bring the matter before our conference, and said he was willing to state the new proposals and let them come from his side. I told him my colleagues had been informed substantially of all that had passed between him and the President and between him and me. He intimated that he had not spoken so freely to Sir Chas. Tupper. I told him I had rather have an interview and consultation with my colleagues before I answered him as to the mode of renewing our conference." *Bayard MS.*

feeling and friendly relations between the two countries," but he was opposed to carrying this spirit of good will too far. The American plenipotentiaries

. . . must not only consider their own judgments and their willingness to accept any proposal which may be made, but must look beyond and contemplate what would be the result should they fail to obtain two-thirds of the Senate *as now constituted*. . . . The regulation of the fair rights of entry for Fishermen, reserved under the Treaty of 1818, is, as we have good reason to know, the most difficult and certainly the most delicate part of our task. While their recognition should be liberal and substantial, yet we agree that every enlargement should be carefully guarded in Canadian interest and placed under Canadian supervision.[49]

Bayard next endeavored to indicate to the British plenipotentiaries the fact that in the United States

. . . no change in the tariff can be accomplished *by Treaty alone*. The action of the House of Representatives is equally essential in every such case. . . . The issue against excessive Tariff duties has been clearly and unequivocally raised by the Executive in his last message. It has stirred the whole country and the two great parties are aligning themselves upon these lines to contest in a few months the control of the Executive branch and its power. . . . The American Plenipotentiaries have been impressed and wish to impress their associates with the wisdom and expediency of leaving Tariff changes in the interests of reciprocity to be accomplished by concerted legislation. . . . We feel that point arrived at is critical in our conference, and we desire in the spirit I have expressed to come as close to you as we can, so close that you can easily close up the gap.[50]

The day following the meeting of the mixed commission on January 14, was Sunday, but Chamberlain felt so disturbed over the way things were going that he decided to intrude upon the privacy of Bayard's home by sending him a long letter. He could not avoid the feeling

. . . of grave apprehension lest we may have arrived at a point at which

49. *Memorandum* written by Bayard, January 14, 1888, *Bayard MS.*

50. *Memorandum* written by Bayard, January 14, 1888, *Bayard MS.* The House of Representatives had long contended that a treaty cannot change revenue laws without the express sanction of the lower house of Congress. In advising the ratification of the reciprocity treaty with Mexico, January 20, 1883, the Senate had amended the convention by a provision that it should not go into effect "until laws necessary to carry it into operation" had been passed by Congress. See George H. Haynes, *The Senate of the United States* (Boston, 1938), vol. 2, pp. 690ff. In his conversation with Chamberlain, December 14, 1887, President Cleveland had indirectly referred to this practice with reference to reciprocity treaties. See Chamberlain memoranda enclosed in letter from Sir Charles Tupper to Sir John Macdonald, January 25, 1888, *Washington Treaty, 1888, Sir John Macdonald Papers*, MS Canadian Archives.

our efforts to promote an amicable arrangement will utterly break down. In that case the Conference in which we have all bestowed so much thought and labour will have been purely mischievous. . . . To avoid such a result must be your anxious care as well as mine, and I hope I may be permitted at this juncture to remind you of the circumstances which have led up to the present position. When the Conference separated before the Xmas holy days it appeared as though we had arrived at a complete deadlock. . . . It was in this state that I sought a private interview with you in order to submit a new proposition based *inter alia* on a reciprocal arrangement by which the United States and Canada could mutually surrender certain of the rights reserved to each by the Convention of 1818. You frankly told me that this suggestion was inadmissible and proceeded to sketch your own idea of a possible solution which you said must be taken *ad referendum* to the President and your Colleagues. Four days later, on December 14, I waited on the President who spoke very fully and frankly about the Fishery questions and then spontaneously made a proposal for settlement in similar terms to those previously employed by you.

On the same day I reported to you the result of my interview with the President and I submitted to you in writing my understanding of the exact terms of the proposal in order that in my approaching visit to Canada there might be no possibility of misunderstanding. In the meantime you promised to consider whether, if the proposal were by my influence accepted by the Canadian Government, it should be formally made at the next Conference by yourself or by the British Plenipotentiaries. You also expressed the hope that the Senate, having the opportunity of a complete settlement of this long-standing grievance would not allow themselves to be influenced by so paltry a matter as the duty of $190,000 on a few barrels of fish, and in any case you expressed your willingness to take the risk, submitting such an arrangement for their consideration.

Armed in this way with information on your views, I went to Ottawa and not without some difficulty and opposition, and the employment of a little gentle pressure, I succeeded in obtaining the assent of the Governor-General and his Cabinet to the propositions exactly as they stood in the paper, copy of which I had left with you. On January 6th, immediately after my return, I reported to you the success of my efforts at peacemaking. You were good enough to express your satisfaction at the result and you repeated your hope that the Senate would not take the responsibility of rejecting such a settlement. . . . You also mentioned that you had informed Messrs. Putnam and Angell of the nature of our previous communications and of the proposals which I sent to Canada to press on the Colonial Government. . . .

I think you will agree that I have reasons for some little surprise and anxiety on finding that the results of our understanding were not promptly and completely accepted by the United States Plenipotentiaries. I have carried out in the letter and the spirit the agreement at which we happily arrived and which was suggested originally by yourself and the President.[51]

Bayard clearly perceived that Chamberlain was somewhat disingenuous in the way he phrased his letter. As soon as he received the communication, Bayard jotted down a few comments which illustrate his reaction to it:

> Two admitted facts control this question of settling an intricate treaty by conversation and unsigned memos.
>
> 1st. Mr. Chamberlain's visit to Canada was to prepare to make proposals, and was announced to be for that purpose, and with this declaration the conference adjourned, December 9th, to meet January 4. 2nd. After adjt. Mr. C. sought me individually and confidentially and agreed that everything . . . that passed at these interviews was in all cases *ad referendum.*
>
> How then is it possible to treat such discussions as proposals agreed upon and to express suspicion when they are not promptly carried in our meeting?[52]

In his note of reply to Chamberlain, Bayard expressed himself with candor and dignity:

> With full recollection of all that has passed I am not able to agree that you had "reasons for some little surprise" and anxiety in finding that the proposals of the British Plenipotentiaries were not "promptly and completely accepted." I will not here repeat any portion of my statement of yesterday, nor of the full discussion on both sides that followed it, but I do wish to say that I am aware of no alternative in any statements made by me at any time in or out of conference nor of any change in the single-minded way I have endeavoured to treat the difficult questions committed to us, and which I trust will progress towards a settlement in our next conference.[53]

51. Joseph Chamberlain to Bayard, January 15, 1888, *Bayard MS.* In a letter to Sir John Macdonald, January 18, 1888, Sir Charles Tupper stated that Chamberlain was "wildly indignant" about the way the American delegation was acting and had come to the conclusion "that they are a lot of dishonest tricksters." *Washington Treaty, 1888, Sir John Macdonald Papers,* MS Canadian Archives.

52. *Memorandum* written by Bayard, January 15, 1888, *Bayard MS.*

53. Bayard to Chamberlain, January 15, 1888, *ibid.* Sir Willoughby Maycock, in his volume, *With Mr. Chamberlain in the United States and Canada, 1887–1888,* pp. 200-201, gives a highly-colored and dubious account of this disagreement between Bayard and Chamberlain: "It was at this crisis, early in January, that Mr. Chamberlain and I took a walk one morning towards the Washington Memorial. He then told me of his intention to make an announcement in the Plenary Conference that afternoon, that further parley being apparently useless, he had resolved to break off the negotiations and return home. I suggested as an alternative that we might utilise Sir Lionel West: 'Get him to go and see Mr. Bayard at once, with the gloomiest countenance he can assume. Let him tell Mr. Bayard that your patience is exhausted.' . . . Mr. Chamberlain thought this a good idea, and adopted it. West went and saw Bayard, with the result that when the Conference met that afternoon a change had come o'er the spirit of the dream."

In a letter to W. L. Putnam, March 3, 1888, Bayard flatly accuses Chamberlain of being "disingenuous." He also spoke of him as being "uncandid and unsatisfactory." *Bayard MS.*

With matters in this dubious state, Chamberlain sent to Bayard on January 16, a proposal for a *modus vivendi* which would operate in case no treaty could be agreed upon. It provided that American fishing vessels could enter the bays and harbors of Canada and Newfoundland to purchase bait and fishing supplies upon the payment of an annual license fee. In the event that the American import dues on Canadian fish and fish-oil, whale-oil and seal-oil, and other fish products should be removed, the licenses to American fishermen would be granted without charge.[54]

On January 18 Chamberlain thought that the negotiations looked "less promising than at any previous time,"[55] but three days later, Bayard assured President Cleveland that the Conference had "not broken up." Indeed, he thought he could detect a "streak of daylight." [56] Bayard then went to the White House and had a talk with the President who apparently felt that the best way of meeting Chamberlain's display of temperament was by way of reading the riot act to him. He informed

54. Chamberlain to Bayard, January 16, 1888, *Bayard MS.* The proposed *modus vivendi* read as follows:

"1. For a period of three years from the coming into force of the Canadian and New-foundland enactments necessary to carry into effect the provisions herein expressed, the privilege of entering the bays and harbours of Canada and Newfoundland for the purchase of bait and fishing supplies, and to tranship their catch shall be accorded to United States fishing vessels by annual license at a fee of two dollars per ton of the vessel's tonnage. Provided that whenever during the aforesaid period of three years the United States shall, by competent authority, allow fish and fish-oil, whale-oil and seal-oil, and other fish products (the produce of the fisheries engaged in by Canadian and Newfoundland fisher-men) to be imported into the United States free of duty, . . . the license before mentioned shall be granted without charge, and the granting of the same shall be continued during and after the said period of three years without charge, so long as such free admission may continue without interruption.

"2. While the foregoing stipulation shall be in force the provisions of the enactments of Canada and Newfoundland relating to 'Fishing by Foreign Vessels,' which establish the penalty by forfeiture of the vessel for offenses other than those of fishing, having fished, and preparing to fish, shall be suspended, and the penalty for other offenses than those named shall be a fine of $3 per ton of the vessel's tonnage. . . . Purchases of supplies shall not be effected by way of barter or exchange. No other commercial facilities than those conferred by the License are to be exercised.

"3. . . . United States fishing vessels are not to be liable for Pilotage fees when Pilots are not availed of.

"4. If at the end of the period of three years mentioned in Paragraph 1, the Treaty therein referred to shall not have been ratified and proclaimed, or if the free admission mentioned in the Provision in Paragraph 1 shall not have been granted and continued on the part of the United States so as to be then in force, all the foregoing provisions shall cease." *Bayard MS.*

55. J. L. Garvin, *The Life of Joseph Chamberlain*, vol. 2, p. 332.

56. Bayard to President Cleveland, January 21, 1888, *Bayard Letter Book*, vol. 7, *Bayard MS.*

Bayard, who was, of course, to pass the news on to Chamberlain, that under the Retaliation Act, Congress had empowered the President to strike back at Canada. He would not promise any suspension of this law, but the Dominion Government could suspend "her strict and arbitrary action" under the terms of the Treaty of 1818. If the meetings of the mixed commission were a stalemate, he would not appoint a new commission. In view of the possibility that Congress might give certain tariff concessions to Canada, it might be well to adjourn the Conference and "await results."[57]

Bayard himself had grown very weary of the uncompromising attitude of both Sir Charles Tupper and Chamberlain. In a memorandum written after an indecisive meeting of the mixed commission on January 31, Bayard gave expression to his dissatisfaction over the manner in which the members of the British delegation were acting:

> For some reason which I cannot learn, Mr. Chamberlain has yielded the control of the negotiation over to Sir Charles Tupper, who subjects the question to the demands of Canadian politics. Thus, the broad question of establishing good relations and initiating a state of affairs out of which amity and peace will naturally issue, the whole settlement is sought to be based upon . . . dollars and cents, a mercenary basis, forgetting that such matters are easily contained in the establishment of friendly relations.
>
> We heard nothing in the beginning and we hear nothing now but the abolition of tariff duties on fish and fish-oil. In this contest of the counter, the ordinary terms of international amity are overlooked. . . . The commonest rights of food and needed supplies are refused to Am. Fishing vessels *because* they are fishing vessels. We have asked for the right to purchase food in ports of Entry under the eye of Customs Officials, and to purchase such marine supplies as trading vessels ordinarily require, but because the vessels that need them are engaged in Fishing it is denied. . . .
>
> Several times I have reflected upon the singularity of the fate that has committed such complex questions as the relations of Great Britain to Canada and of these two towards the United States, to such a trio as Cham-

57. The gist of Bayard's conversation with the President on January 21, 1888, is given in a *memorandum* written by Bayard on that very day: "The President's idea—First recognizes the law of 1887 and the duties that may accrue to him under it, and as to which no restriction can be agreed. That the whole tariff subject is now before Congress, placed there by the Prest.'s action. That Canada and Newfoundland will be materially affected by what Congress may do, and quite possibly the free list may contain all that Canada and Newfoundland desire to be put in a treaty. Cannot this conference adjourn to await results? or is any such understanding necessary? The Prest. can promise *no suspension* of any law of the United States, but Canada can suspend her strict and arbitrary action under the Treaty. President does not approve of appointing a new Comm. such as he recommended in 1886, and was rejected by Congress. He considers the examination which will necessarily be made by Congress in discussing Tariff reform will include consideration of Canadian and Newfoundland productions and trade relations." *Bayard MS.*

berlain, Sir Charles Tupper, and Sir L. West. At first, and *some* times since,
Mr. Chamberlain was disposed to take an English and liberal view of the
whole question, but he has yielded up point after point to the steady shop-
keeping insistence of his Canadian colleague who sees but the *items* of his
fish bills.

Mr. Chamberlain has exhibited no touch of a wider wisdom, and altho
sometimes disposed to stop chaffering, yet has always been led back to it,
and I have seen and heard and felt the true *Birmingham tone* in his commercial discourse. His nature, or rather, his habit and tone is commercial,
with all its acuteness and hard practical sense but unmoved by anything
higher.

Tupper has never wandered for an instant from his track. He is a *mere*
bargainer, and wants to know and see *what he is to get* for every point
conceded or even softened. He wants *pay* for kindness, for civility, for ab-
stinence of rigid enforcement.[58]

At length, after thirty meetings of the mixed commission, a treaty
was finally signed. First of all, provision was made for the appointment
of a mixed commission which would delimit the British waters along
the coasts of Canada and Newfoundland to which the United States
had, by the Treaty of 1818, renounced forever any liberty to take, dry,
or cure fish. The three-mile limit was to be measured seaward from
the low water mark, but at every bay, creek, or harbor, not otherwise
specially provided for in the treaty, these three marine miles should
be measured seaward from a straight line drawn across the bay, creek,
or harbor, in the part nearest the entrance at the first point where the
width did not exceed ten marine miles. The United States conceded
to Canada the right to regard the waters within the Baie des Chaleurs
and the Bay of Maramichi as territorial waters, but it was expressly
provided that nothing in the treaty should affect the free navigation
of the Strait of Canso by fishing vessels of the United States. American
fishing vessels were to conform to harbor regulations, but they were
not required to report or clear when putting into bays or harbors for
shelter or repairing damages, nor when putting into same, outside the
limits of established ports of entry, for the purpose of purchasing wood
or of obtaining water. They should not be liable for compulsory pilotage, nor for harbor or tonnage dues when entering ports for purposes
of shelter, repairing damages, or for purchasing wood, or obtaining
water. Licenses would be granted, without charge, to American fishing
vessels to purchase needful provisions and supplies. Whenever Congress

58. *Memorandum* written by Bayard, January 31, 1888, *Bayard MS.*

should remove the duty from fish-oil, whale-oil, seal-oil, and fish of all kinds coming from Canada and Newfoundland, the fishing vessels from the United States would be permitted to purchase (by procuring annual licenses, free of charge) provisions, bait, ice, seines, lines, and all other supplies and outfits.[59]

The attitude of the country towards the treaty and the action of the Senate with regard to it will be discussed in detail in the following chapter.

59. *Sen. Ex. Doc. 113*, 50 Cong., 1 sess., pp. 132-138. Accompanying this treaty was a *modus vivendi* which provided that, for a period of two years, American fishing vessels would be granted annual licenses, at a fee of $1.50 per ton, for the purchase of bait, ice, seines, lines, and all other supplies and outfits. The privileges of transshipping their catch and of shipping crews, were also accorded to American fishing vessels. In the event that the American Government would remove the duties on fish, fish-oil, whale- and seal-oil, these licenses would be issued free of charge. American fishing vessels entering Canadian and Newfoundland harbors for the four purposes specified in the Treaty of 1818, would not be required to enter or clear at the custom houses if they did not remain more than twenty-four hours. The penalty of forfeiture would be exacted only for the offences of fishing or preparing to fish in territorial waters.

CHAPTER TEN

Treaty-breaking Powers of the Senate

PRESIDENT CLEVELAND SENT THE FISHERIES TREATY TO THE SENATE ON February 20, 1888, with a message that recommended its approval.[1] On the same day, Bayard addressed a long, confidential letter to Phelps in which he gave a detailed account of the negotiations that produced the treaty. He was certain that the American Government had maintained its position and had

. . . procured such a practical and decent interpretation of the treaty of 1818 as, if observed honorably and honestly, will prevent future friction and allow wholesome and amicable intercourse to progress between the two populations. The process of coming to this arrangement has been difficult, and at several points, seemed hopeless, but the presiding deities in the conference were Conciliation and Justice, and their offspring is the treaty and the proposed *modus*. . . .

1. On February 19, 1888, Bayard sent to President Cleveland a short note in which he observed as follows: "I now send you the supplement to the message on the Fisheries treaty, referring to the tendered *modus vivendi* and the propriety of full publication. The newspaper slip I enclose indicates that Lord Salisbury will lay the treaty before the House of Commons on its arrival in England and like action will be taken in Canada. It is therefore useless and undesirable that the *mock* secrecy of the Senate should be applied to this subject. I will bring the Treaty to you tomorrow by eleven so that it can reach the Senate upon its opening." Bayard to President Cleveland, February 19, 1888, *Cleveland MS.*

In his message to the Senate (February 20, 1888) President Cleveland emphasized the following features of the treaty: "The proposed delimitation of the lines of the exclusive fisheries from the common fisheries will give certainty and security to the area of their legitimate field; the headland theory of imaginary lines is abandoned by Great Britain. . . . The uninterrupted navigation of the Strait of Canso is expressly and for the first time affirmed. . . . The enforcement of penalties for unlawfully fishing or preparing to fish within the inshore and exclusive waters of Canada and Newfoundland is to be accomplished under safeguards against oppressive and arbitrary action. . . . No feature of Canadian administration was more harassing . . . than the compulsion upon our fishing vessels to make formal entry and clearance on every occasion of temporarily seeking shelter in Canadian ports and harbors. Such inconvenience is provided against in the proposed treaty." *Sen. Ex. Doc., 113,* 50 Cong., 1 sess., pp. 127-131.

We have just emerged from this long and weary contention, and it is too soon to conclude about the other side. Of course, Canada had the ultimate decision, and several times the conference was adjourned to await decisions from Ottawa. The conditions of Imperial Federation were curiously illustrated throughout this transaction, and which will is paramount, that of Mother or Child, is still an unsettled question. . . .

As to its reception by the Senate I can only hazard an opinion. The magnitude of the commercial interests threatened with obstruction or ruin by a proclamation of non-intercourse, and the comparative insignificance of the pecuniary interests affected by the present tariff on cured fish, are much better comprehended than two years ago. . . . The phalanx of protected interests moves to the aid of any threatened element, and has but one creed and one sole article to that creed, but in the treaty now submitted the tariff is not touched, and mercenary opposition may not therefore be aroused. But the whole question has been so unfairly dealt with, and such a spattering shown of misrepresentation that, notwithstanding the treaty is unobjectionable on their own showing heretofore, and is so moderate and wise an adjustment of a very sore and long-standing controversy, I fear they may resolve . . . not to permit this administration to succeed in doing right, and to persist in this at the cost of the country. . . .

I suppose there are reasons of decadence, of ill-health with nations and their government as with individuals, and that convalescence may come. But when I consider the vast interests and responsibilities and duties that attach to the management of the affairs of sixty millions of free people, and then contemplate the poor and petty tone of so many charged with high functions, my heart sinks within me.[2]

2. Bayard to Phelps, February 20, 1888, *Confidential and Personal, Bayard Letter Book*, vol. 7, *Bayard MS*. On February 16, 1888, in a letter to Chamberlain, Bayard suggested that it would be an opportune time to discontinue the proceedings in the Vice-Admiralty Court at Halifax against the two fishing smacks, the *David J. Adams*, and the *Ella M. Doughty*. After nearly two years the court appeared "still in doubt, and looking at it from both sides it seems to me that no harm, but possible aid to our treaty might accrue from a discontinuance of the suits, and a discharge of the vessels." On the following day Chamberlain promised to speak to Sir Charles Tupper about the proceedings in the Vice-Admiralty Court and urge the discontinuance of the suits which had been pending since May, 1886. On February 26 Bayard acknowledged the receipt of a letter from Chamberlain enclosing a telegram from Sir John Macdonald stating that the two fishing vessels would be released "on all claims for damages being abandoned." Bayard to Chamberlain, February 26, 1888, *Bayard MS*. On April 25 Sackville-West sent a note to Bayard with an enclosed minute from a report of the Canadian Privy Council, March 8, 1888, recommending the discontinuance of the proceedings against the two fishing boats on condition that the owners surrender all claims for damages or expenses. Thus, after nearly two years, the cases of the *Adams* and the *Doughty* which had deeply stirred the Cleveland Administration in the spring of 1886, were finally settled.

In the *Bayard Papers* there is an enormous amount of correspondence with regard to the *Adams* and the *Doughty*. The more important letters are: W. L. Putnam to Bayard, July 26, August 4, 9, 12, 1886; January 4; February 1; March 14, 18, 24; May 6; June 17, 1887; February 29; March 6, 1888. Bayard to Putnam, February 26; March 3, 1888. Bayard to Phelps, March 10, 1888.

In a second letter to Phelps, February 20, 1888, Bayard complained that "the Senate makes it as troublesome as it can for us to carry on the business of the Country." [3] Phelps shared Bayard's view that the Senate would probably sabotage the treaty for political reasons. He had only a "faint expectation of fair treatment by the Senate." [4] He had no doubt that Bayard would have a fight over the treaty "with the Blaine men in the Senate," but he hoped that the "good sense of the country will insist upon a ratification." [5]

Bayard was somewhat skeptical about a forceful expression of the "good sense of the country" unless this public opinion was properly educated. In a letter to Samuel L. Barlow, who had great influence with important persons in New York City, he remarked:

I want to speak with you freely in relation to the dangers of allowing the fires of small politics to destroy vast interests. I refer to the Fishery treaty which is simply and truly a perfectly just and sensible arrangement, and there is no excuse possible for its rejection. There ought to be some impressive demonstration on the part of the great body of American interests, pecuniary, social, moral, in condemnation of the proposed opposition indicated in the columns of the *Tribune*.[6]

But it was not the *Tribune* alone that opposed the fishery treaty.[7]

3. Bayard to Phelps, February 20, 1888, *Bayard Letter Book*, vol. 7, *Bayard MS.*
4. Phelps to Bayard, February 11, 1888, *Bayard MS.*
5. Phelps to Bayard, February 18, 1888, *ibid.*
6. Bayard to S. L. M. Barlow, February 23, 1888, *Bayard Letter Book*, vol. 7, *Bayard MS.*
7. On February 23, The New York *Tribune* had criticized the fisheries treaty as marking "the lowest point of degradation which American diplomacy has ever reached. . . . The treaty is a shameful one; with the 'modus vivendi' it is an intolerable disgrace. The Senate should make short work of it." The New York *Sun*, March 7, 1888, was equally critical in its comments: "There is in the history of diplomacy no suddener or more incomprehensible surrender of a position deliberately assumed, strenuously maintained up to the last moment, and strong in right, law, and justice. Who abandoned the American case? Was Secretary Bayard betrayed, and, if so, who betrayed him?" Certain prominent individuals did not hesitate to denounce the treaty. Luther Maddocks, secretary of the National Fishery Association, declared that the treaty was a "great disappointment" to him. George Steele, president of the American Fishery Union, was certain that the treaty would do "a great deal more harm than good to American fishermen." Charles Levi Woodbury regarded it as a "shameful surrender." New York *Herald*, February 24, 1888. Senator Frye was bitterly critical of the treaty and drew particular attention to that provision of the treaty wherein American fishing vessels were permitted commercial privileges in Canadian ports upon the payment of a tonnage tax of $1.50 per ton. The Senator then made the astounding statement that the average size of American fishing vessels was 200 tons, and this would mean an annual charge upon them of $300. New York *Tribune*, February 23, 1888.
    In Canada there was a similar chorus of abuse for the treaty. The Toronto *Mail* thought that the Americans had "won their case"; the Montreal *Herald* had no doubt that the "rights, possessions, and interests of Canada are abandoned to the United States";

As the newspapers in other cities took up the fight, some of Bayard's friends began to entertain serious doubts that the treaty would be ratified. James B. Angell, writing from Ann Arbor, Michigan, expressed the fear that

. . . partisan opposition is likely to prevent the ratification of our Treaty at this time, if not reject it altogether. I observe that all the political fishermen and the professional piscatorial agitators like Maddox and Co., are blowing their horns. The better the treaty, the worse it is likely to fare at the hands of the extreme men who do not mean that the Administration shall get any help from it.[8]

Phelps, in London, was increasingly fearful that "no possible treaty could be got through the Senate at this time, actuated as so large a share of its members are by a purely partisan spirit before which the welfare of the country is of no account at all."[9] To W. L. Putnam, in Maine, it was apparent that "the Gloucester people desire no treaty, but wish a

---

and the Ottawa *Free Press* lamented that the "worst apprehensions of the friends of Canada have been realized." New York *Times,* February 23, 1888.

In the United States a large part of the press expressed satisfaction with the terms of the treaty. The New York *Evening Post,* February 22, 1888, believed that the treaty promised "a happy termination of a long and irritating dispute between the United States and Canada. Secretary Bayard is to be congratulated upon completing . . . an agreement that meets every reasonable expectation." The New York *Times,* February 23, 1888, regarded the treaty as "altogether fair and honorable"; the New York *Herald,* February 22, expressed the view that it represented a "victory on all points" for America; the Boston *Post,* February 23, was certain that any opposition to the treaty would be on "purely partisan" grounds; the Barnstable (Massachusetts) *Journal,* March 3, expressed its "hearty approval" of the treaty; the Philadelphia *Enquirer,* March 7, thought that the Senate should approve "the treaty promptly and commend the sagacity and patriotism which Secretary Bayard displayed in procuring it"; and the New York *World,* February 23, was of the opinion that it would be "advantageous to both countries and to our fishing interests if the treaty be promptly ratified."

Hamilton Fish, Secretary of State under President Grant, was quite positive in his belief that Bayard had made a "very successful treaty, and for his sake I am right glad of it, for I do not believe that there is a purer or a better man in public life." New York *Herald,* February 17, 1888. On March 6, Bayard gave an interview to a reporter from the New York *World,* during the course of which he took issue with the statement of Senator Frye that the average size of the fishing vessels in Canadian waters was 200 tons and therefore the license tax of $1.50 per ton would amount to $300 annually. Bayard clearly showed that the average American fishing vessel in Canadian waters was only 75 tons, and the license tax would not amount to more than $115. New York *World,* March 7, 1888.

8. James B. Angell to Bayard, February 24, 1888, *Bayard MS.*

9. Phelps to Bayard, February 25, 1888, *ibid.* In a letter to James B. Angell, February 29, 1888, Phelps writes in a similar vein. He greatly feared the defeat of the treaty in the Senate, and hoped "for its postponement. Partisan warfare is so reckless and shameless. If postponed I think it will be ratified. Whether it is or not, the country will ultimately approve of it, after we shall have gone further and fared worse." *Angell MS, Michigan Historical Collections,* University of Michigan.

state of affairs which will in some way effect an embargo on Dominion fish." [10]

As a relief from this stream of pessimistic comments concerning the fate of the treaty in the Senate, Bayard must have welcomed letters from friends in praise of his conduct of foreign relations. Melville Fuller emphasized the success of American diplomacy through "the astuteness of candor, knowledge, and common sense rather than the effervescing, evanescent brilliancy of pyrotechnics." Bayard's methods were "simply those of candor, honesty, and justice coupled with grasp of the subject matter." [11] George W. Biddle was equally enthusiastic about the treaty which he considered was a "most wise and statesman-like settlement of the points in controversy between the respective governments." [12]

On February 28 Chamberlain paid a farewell visit to Bayard and alluded to certain comments he had heard respecting the treaty. He had made some

. . . appeals to gentlemen here about the Treaty, and . . . a distinguished Republican, who was one of the candidates for the Presidential nomination, had said to him: "The fact is that just now we cannot afford to let this Administration do anything." I [Bayard] said that was very shocking. He agreed with me, and said he felt extremely indignant at the remark. . . . He . . . said in case the Treaty was rejected, that Great Britain and Canada could both feel that they had gone very far to promote an amicable solution, very far, indeed, and that if their efforts were thrown back in their faces by the rejection of this Treaty, he thought the consequences might be most serious.[13]

As the weeks passed on after the signature of the treaty, the opposition to it grew apace, and J. B. Angell was "at times depressed" over the situation,[14] while W. L. Putnam was convinced that the "active opponents" of the treaty were determined to "kill it." [15] Carl Schurz was apprehensive lest an "unscrupulous party spirit" cry the treaty

10. W. L. Putnam to Bayard, February 25, 1888, *Bayard MS.* The leader of this opposition on the part of the Gloucester fishermen was Henry Cabot Lodge, at that time a Representative in Congress from Massachusetts. The attitude of Mr. Lodge was clearly revealed in a statement that appeared in the New York *Tribune,* February 24, 1888: "The more the treaty is considered, the worse it appears for the United States. . . . The Senate, I trust and hope, will reject both protocol and treaty at once. . . . Negotiation has been tried and has failed dismally."

11. Melville W. Fuller to Bayard, February 25, 1888, *Bayard MS.*

12. George W. Biddle to Bayard, February 27, 1888, *ibid.*

13. *Memorandum* written by Bayard, February 28, 1888, *Bayard MS.*

14. J. B. Angell to Bayard, March 4, 1888, *ibid.*

15. W. L. Putnam to Bayard, March 6, 1888, *ibid.*

down,[16] and Samuel L. Barlow was dubious about the fate of the treaty because of the opposition of Anglophobes and "wild Irish."[17]

The first Republican shaft that was fired in the Senate against the Fisheries Treaty took the form of a resolution introduced by Senator Frye on March 15, 1888. It provided that the President be requested to transmit to the Senate copies of the minutes and daily protocols of the meetings of the commissioners who negotiated the treaty signed February 15, 1888. The resolution did not include the usual formula which requested the information on condition that the President believed that the transmission of such correspondence would not be detrimental to the "public service."[18]

Bayard regarded Senator Frye's resolution as

. . . without precedent in form and in substance. The condition "if not in his judgment inconsistent with the public service" is *invariably* found in resolutions of inquiry or asking information of the Executive branch. . . . I may say to you that no stenographer was permitted to be present. . . . I have a great many personal notes of what was discussed in the conference, but I might as well be asked to report to the Senate our verbal conversations and arguments as to give such "minutes."[19]

The partisan spirit that was so clearly revealed in Frye's resolution was very discouraging to Bayard, because it seemed to indicate a "deterioration in tone and moral grade" of the Senate that was "both mystifying and exasperating."[20] He was certain that it would be a "national calamity" if the Republican Party were to be "once more potential."[21] With reference to the Fisheries Treaty, he was inclined to believe that it would be voted upon "in the light of partisanship and not patriotism."[22]

16. Carl Schurz to Bayard, March 7, 1888, *ibid.*
17. Samuel L. Barlow to Bayard, March 8, 1888.
18. *Cong. Rec.*, 50 Cong., 1 sess., vol. 19, p. 2093. See also letter of George Gray to Bayard, March 15, 1888, *Bayard MS.* On March 19, 1888, the New York *Tribune* printed a long letter from Walker Blaine in which the Fisheries Treaty was vehemently attacked, and on March 23 a critical commentary by William H. Trescot was published. Bayard replied to these critics in a letter published in the New York *Times*, March 26, 1888. He was convinced that "the welfare and true interest of our country and a just and wise treatment of the British-American population on our northern frontier alike counsel the adoption of the treaty. In its initiation, negotiation, and conclusion I can truly say for my associates and myself no views but those of single-minded patriotic intent have been allowed place or expression."
19. Bayard to Senator George Gray, March 15, 1888, *Bayard Letter Book,* vol. 7, *Bayard MS.*
20. Bayard to Phelps, March 16, 1888, *ibid.*
21. Bayard to Charles Denby, March 17, 1888, *ibid.*
22. Bayard to W. L. Putnam, March 21, 1888, *ibid.* In a letter to Charles W. Francis,

A serious blow to Bayard's hope for the ratification of the treaty was the resolution of the Chamber of Commerce of the City of New York, March 1, 1888, advising rejection because "the same full and absolute reciprocity to the United States fishing vessels was not accorded in Canada as was permitted at present under United States laws to Canadian fishermen here." [23] After all Bayard's efforts to secure the support of the Chamber of Commerce, this action was most discouraging. Barlow, however, hoped that through the influence of George Bliss, who was a member of the Chamber, something might be accomplished.[24]

In the Senate a serious attack on the Administration's conduct of foreign relations was almost ready to be launched. In a confidential letter to Bayard, Senator John T. Morgan disclosed the ammunition that Republican Senators would use in their assault upon the treaty:

> In the committee of Foreign Relations, it came out clearly this morning that the heavy attack on the Fisheries Treaty will be made on this question: "Has the President the constitutional power to appoint plenipotentiaries without the advice and consent of the Senate." This is the way I state it, for that is the real question, but it is put in connection with the fact that Messrs. Angell and Putnam were appointed just before the meeting of Congress, acted during its Session, signed the treaty and dispersed while the Senate was in session, and their appointment was never notified to the Senate in any form. It appears to be conceded that the President may, in the vacation of the Senate, appoint and commission plenipotentiaries, though this is not expressly admitted. The view of the subject, as presented, includes the point that the constitutional right of the Senate to act upon all appointments to office is disregarded, and that plenipotentiaries are public officers, amenable to impeachment, etc. It is admitted that we could waive all irregularities and accept the treaty, if we approve it, but "should the Senate make a precedent of this sort when there was no necessity, or excuse, to justify an irregular course?" is the way the matter is put.
>
> You will see that the purpose is to avoid a direct issue upon the merits of the treaty and to sink it with this technical question. That course enables the opponents of the treaty to say that it was good enough as a treaty, but came to us in a way that was not permissible. . . .

March 12, 1888, Bayard makes the following comment: "One piece of work just finished is the treaty with Great Britain about the Canadian Fisheries. The settlement is just, equitable, and honorable, and removes a thorn that has been rankling for a century. My task has been performed, and the responsibility is now with the Senate. Should partisan bitterness and unpatriotic folly defeat the treaty, it is my opinion that public indignation will severely visit the men or the party guilty of the act." *Bayard Letter Book*, vol. 7, *Bayard MS*.

23. Bayard to Gustav Schwab, March 10, 1888, *Bayard Letter Book*, vol. 7, *Bayard MS*.
24. Barlow to Bayard, March 21, 1888, *Bayard MS*.

I believe, confidently, that the report of the Committee to the Senate will be a general, adverse report made by a strict party vote. In the Senate the same result will follow unless we can make the argument so strong, and so fortify it with precedents as to the right of the President to appoint these Plenipotentiaries, that the Republicans will be afraid to attempt to avoid responsibility for the defeat of the treaty on this specious ground.[25]

Bayard promised to have a list of precedents prepared which would clearly indicate the power of the President to appoint special agents during a recess of the Senate. If the Republican Senators based their attack upon the alleged lack of Presidential powers in this matter of appointments, Bayard had little doubt that they would be defeated.[26]

There seemed little doubt, however, about the tactics of the Republican majority in the Senate, and Senator Saulsbury requested Bayard to furnish him with a list of the precedents "of the appointment of negotiators without approval of the Senate." [27] Bayard assured Saulsbury that his request would be promptly complied with. He then made a few comments upon the President's control over foreign relations. It appeared to him

. . . preposterous to deny the President the power to commence his making of treaties *when* he sees fit and by what agencies he sees fit, whether the Senate is in session or not and to keep his negotiations absolutely secret until the time arrives for him to submit his work to the Senate for its advice and consent. As I understand the present contention, the President would not be able to frame any treaty by the agency of any other than officers of the United States, until he had received permission from the Senate.[28]

25. John T. Morgan to Bayard, March 23, 1888, *Bayard MS*. As far back as February 21, 1888, Senator J. Z. George had written to Bayard and suggested that it would be well for him to "cause to be furnished to some democratic Senator in whom the administration can rely for friendly support in the Fishery Treaty, a list of the Am. Commissioners, public ministers, etc., which former administrations have appointed in the recess of the Senate." *Bayard MS*. See also Bayard's letter to Senator George, February 22, 1888, *ibid*.

26. Bayard to John T. Morgan, March 23, 1888, *Bayard Letter Book*, vol. 7, *Bayard MS*. On April 7 Bayard sent a letter to Morgan informing him that a "tabulated statement of the appointment of negotiators by the President is nearly completed." *Bayard Letter Book*, vol. 7, *Bayard MS*.

27. Senator Eli Saulsbury to Bayard, March 29, 1888, *Bayard MS*.

28. Bayard to Eli Saulsbury, March 29, 1888, *Bayard Letter Book*, vol. 7, *Bayard MS*. In a letter to Bayard, April 5, 1888, John Bassett Moore observes "I had a very satisfactory conversation with Mr. Saulsbury yesterday evening in regard to the Fisheries Treaty. I found him informed as to the general features of the case and able to discuss it with clearness and certainty. He thoroughly understands the motives of the Gloucester vessel owners and fish dealers in opposing the Treaty. He says he found that every one of them who came before the Edmunds Committee in 1886 desired, first of all, the exclusion of Canadian fish." *Bayard MS*.

It was apparent to Bayard that the report of the Senate Committee
on Foreign Relations with reference to the Fisheries Treaty would be
"strictly on party lines." He could not help believing, however, that
when the issues connected with the treaty were understood throughout
the country there would be a wave of honest indignation "against the
bitter and unpatriotic opposition" to it.[29] It was discouraging, nonetheless, to have to wait for the development of a favorable public
opinion, and, upon occasion, Bayard could not refrain from expressing
his dejected feelings. In a letter to David A. Wells he apologized for
his depressed spirits, but "being knocked down in every round becomes
monotonous. . . . My earnest work is defeated by the Senate so systematically that I am discouraged. But I am not the less determined,
because I am discouraged, and shall go on to make the record just
and 'keep my rudder true.' "[30] To George H. Pendleton he expressed
himself in an equally discouraging vein: "In three years of service in
this office [Secretary of State] no suggestion of comity or co-operation
has come to me from the Foreign Relations Committee of the Senate.
I have six treaties pending consideration, and postponement, defeat,
or obstructive amendment describes the treatment they have met so
far."[31]

At times it seemed to some of Bayard's friends that there was some
hope that the Fisheries Treaty would receive favorable consideration
if action upon it could be postponed. Putnam was certain that the
treaty was "gaining ground with the fishing interests in Maine," and
if the question of ratification "should go over until Autumn, I have
confidence this feeling would develop with great strength."[32] From
George B. Roberts, President of the Pennsylvania Railroad, there came
a friendly letter in which he promised, "at the first opportunity," to
impress upon the two Senators from Pennsylvania his own personal
views and what he believed to be the views "of the better class and
more thoughtful of our people."[33]

But despite these reassuring letters, Bayard still felt apprehensive
about the fate of the Fisheries Treaty. He could only hope that "so

29. Bayard to Samuel L. Barlow, April 18, 1888, *Bayard Letter Book*, vol. 7, *Bayard MS*.
See also Bayard to J. B. Angell, April 23, 1888, *ibid*.
30. Bayard to David A. Wells, April 23, 1888, *Bayard Letter Book*, vol. 7, *Bayard MS*.
31. Bayard to George H. Pendleton, April 28, 1888, *ibid*.
32. W. L. Putnam to Bayard, April 25, 1888, *Bayard MS*.
33. George B. Roberts to Bayard, May 2, 1888, *Bayard MS*. This letter from Roberts
was in response to one from Bayard, April 25, 1888, *Bayard Letter Book*, vol. 7, *Bayard MS*.

fair and just an arrangement" would not be defeated by "party heat and unworthy animosity." One factor in the fight against the treaty was of great importance—the bitter hatred of many Irish-Americans for everything British. There was grave danger that American welfare would be sacrificed by "domestic issues between Great Britain and one of her dependencies, with which we have properly nothing whatever to do." [34]

On the day that Bayard wrote this letter to Judge Stallo (May 7, 1888), the Senate Committee on Foreign Relations submitted two reports on the Fisheries Treaty and the negotiations leading up to it. The majority report, signed by John Sherman, George F. Edmunds, William P. Frye, William M. Evarts,[35] and J. N. Dolph, was sharply critical. Special stress was laid upon the fact that President Cleveland had appointed the American delegation on the mixed commission without any reference to the Senate:

These "plenipotentiaries" came to a conclusion of their labors on the 15th of February, 1888, and the offices of "plenipotentiaries" terminated, and the result was reached without the advice and consent of the Senate having been asked or taken concerning the selection of these public ministers, and without any communication to either house of Congress concerning this most important subject. It is not difficult to see that, in evil times, when the President of the United States may be under influence of foreign and adverse interests, such a course of procedure might result in great disaster to the interests and even the safety of our Government and people. . . . The document submitted to the Senate by the President as the outcome of these negotiations may, it is thought, well illustrate the dangers of such methods.

After this impudent insinuation that President Cleveland might be under "the influence of foreign and adverse interests," the majority report of the committee then gave out a warning to the British Govern-

---

34. Bayard to Judge J. B. Stallo, May 7, 1888, *Bayard Letter Book*, vol. 7, *Bayard MS.* In a letter to Henry White, May 8, 1888, Phelps expresses his fears for the ratification of the treaty: "All my fears as to the fishery matter are in danger of being realized with what consequences can not be foreseen." *Henry White Papers*, Library of Congress.

35. With reference to the attitude of Evarts towards the Fisheries Treaty, Brainerd Dyer, *The Public Career of William M. Evarts*, p. 253, remarks: "Evarts joined with other Republicans in putting strained interpretations on various clauses of the treaty and in refusing to consider amendments proposed by the Democrats to clarify these clauses. He joined in refusing to return the treaty to the Committee on Foreign Relations with instructions to frame amendments adequate to remove the Republican objections, and in refusing to postpone the consideration of the treaty until the election was over and it could be considered on its merits. It may be that even on its merits the treaty would have failed of ratification, but certainly in the midst of an exciting political campaign, . . . no other result was possible."

ment to "take measures to secure justice and fair treatment in her North American dominions to American vessels and American citizens." [36]

The report of the minority of the Senate Committee on Foreign Relations was a detailed rebuttal of all the points raised by the report of the majority. At the close of its report, the minority then expressed the opinion that there was "no fault in the manner of negotiating this treaty, and the President has not in any way exceeded his constitutional powers, or withheld any courtesy due to the Senate in respect of the agents selected by him to conduct the negotiation, or in the time or place of negotiating or concluding the treaty." In a table appended at the close of their report, the minority members of the Senate Committee on Foreign Relations indicated that "the whole number of persons appointed or recognized by the President, without the concurrence or advice of the Senate, or the express authority of Congress, as agents to conduct negotiations and conclude treaties is four hundred and thirty-eight." [37]

This able minority report was written in close collaboration with the Department of State. Bayard's opinion of the majority report was frankly stated in a letter to Senator Morgan: "Is not the position now taken by the majority of the Committee—in effect to give the Senate absolute control over all negotiations by making their advice and consent requisite as a condition precedent for its validity, . . . really preposterous?" [38]

On the following day, in a letter to President Cleveland, Bayard points out a serious defect in the majority report. It appeared to him that it would be expedient for the President to

. . . draw the attention of the North-Western Senators to the extreme and . . . fatal position taken by the majority of the Senate Committee in their report on the Fisheries at page 34. They state *the existing matters* of difficulty "are not subjects for treaty negotiations," and on the next page they propose declining "at whatever cost to enter into any new arrangements." This in effect places us outside the pale of civilized relations, and presents an appeal to force to back up an undefined demand, *for rights never exercised by us nor admitted by our co-contractor.*[39]

36. *Sen. Misc. Doc., 109,* 50 Cong., 1 sess., pp. 17, 38.

37. *Sen. Misc. Doc., 109,* 50 Cong., 1 sess., pp. 103-105. The minority report was signed by John T. Morgan, Eli Saulsbury, Joseph E. Brown, and Henry B. Payne.

38. Bayard to Senator John T. Morgan, May 11, 1888, *Bayard Letter Book,* vol. 7, *Bayard MS.*

39. Bayard to President Cleveland, May 12, 1888, *Bayard Letter Book,* vol. 7, *Bayard MS.* In a letter to John P. Irish, San Francisco, California, May 12, 1888, Bayard repeats

Bayard was hopeful that the consideration of the Fisheries Treaty by the Senate could be postponed until the next session of Congress, and Phelps was very anxious to have this accomplished. He was distinctly apprehensive that if the treaty were rejected "and Blaine elected, we shall have a war with England on the score of these paltry fisheries." [40] There was little doubt that American public opinion should be mobilized in favor of the treaties, and Horace White informed Bayard that he was about to begin a series of articles in the New York *Evening Post* in which he would attack the position taken by the majority of the Senate Committee on Foreign Relations as "immoral, dangerous, and degrading." He thought that it was impossible to

. . . make the public acquainted with the details of the fishery question, because they take no interest in them, but it will not be at all difficult . . . to make them see and appreciate the moral principles underlying the question. I am of your opinion, and have been all the time, that safety lies in postponing action on the treaty until after the election.[41]

On May 24 White wrote to Bayard to inquire whether he was opposed to "the consideration of the treaty with open doors?" [42] The Republicans were anxious to debate the treaty in public sessions of the Senate and thus permit the entire country to follow their attack upon it. It was an unusual procedure, and politics was back of it. But Bayard had no desire for secrecy in this matter, and he assured White that he was in favor of

. . . the open consideration of *this Treaty* although I believe all negotiations are best conducted in that freedom which confidential exchanges most fully secure. But the Treaty *was* confidentially framed and concluded, and it has been . . . published and the reports of all the members of the Committee made public. What remains which ought to be kept secret? . . .

Two copies of the Majority and the Minority reports go to you by mail. . . . I pass over the studied disrespect, injustice, and insulting innuendoes

much of what he wrote to President Cleveland, and then concludes: "I shall indeed be annoyed if the Pacific States shall consent to such a measure of international duty and propriety as the New England Fishing owners have dictated." *Bayard Letter Book,* vol. 7, *Bayard MS.* In a similar letter to Horace White, May 12, 1888, Bayard remarks: "I say nothing of the statement of facts of history by the Majority, which it is difficult to characterize with a pretence of respect, but the position to which the United States would be led by the Majority report would place them outside intercourse with civilized nations." *Ibid.*

40. Phelps to James B. Angell, May 13, 1888, *Angell MS, Michigan Historical Collections,* University of Michigan.

41. Horace White to Bayard, May 15, 1888, *Bayard MS.* These articles by Horace White appeared in the New York *Evening Post* on May 15, 16, and 19, 1888.

42. Horace White to Bayard, May 24, 1888, *Bayard MS.*

towards the Administration (the Secretary of State), and considering its statement . . . of the case and the ultimatum proclaimed in resolving to negotiate no further and to reject the treaty now pending, I think no document so indefensible in morals or reason, or so discreditable on every score, ever emanated from men charged with public duties in the United States. . . .

I am at a loss to account for the apathy, indifference, or it may be gross ignorance, of the Merchants of New York on this question.[43]

The debate in the Senate on the Fisheries Treaty began on May 29, 1888, with Senator Frye leading the attack. It was Frye who had introduced into the Senate a resolution which expressed the opinion that "the appointment of a commission in which the Governments of the United States and Great Britain shall be represented, charged with the consideration and settlement of the fishing rights of the two Governments on the coasts of the United States and British North America ought not to be provided for by Congress." [44] On April 13, 1888, this resolution was adopted by a vote of 35 to 10,[45] and in the face of this adverse action by the Senate, President Cleveland had gone ahead and appointed Thomas F. Bayard, James B. Angell, and William L. Putnam as "plenipotentiaries" to negotiate a treaty with England concerning the fisheries.

The Republicans in the Senate endeavored to make it appear that the procedure followed by President Cleveland in appointing these "plenipotentiaries" without the consent of the Senate, was improper. It was vital for the Democrats to disprove this assertion because

43. Bayard to Horace White, May 25, 1888, *Bayard Letter Book,* vol. 8, *Bayard MS.* In a letter to W. L. Putnam, May 24, 1888, Bayard remarks as follows upon the report of the majority of the Senate Committee on Foreign Relations: "I am prepared upon due reflection to pronounce the said report to be the most discreditable paper that ever emanated from a body of public men in the United States. It is calculated to disgrace our Country and form of government." *Bayard Letter Book,* vol. 7, *Bayard MS.* In a letter to Bayard, May 27, 1888, James B. Angell expresses his interest in what Senator Edmunds "could have to say in answer to that crushing table appended to the minority report showing how the appointments of negotiators have been made. I presume it came from your precincts, but it is overwhelming. Had I supposed final action would have been delayed until now, I should have availed myself of opportunities I have had to make some public defence of the Treaty." *Bayard MS.*

44. *Cong. Rec.,* 49 Cong., 1 sess., vol. 17, p. 3307. In his speech on the Fisheries Treaty, May 29, 1888, Senator Frye sharply denounced the treaty of February 15, 1888: "I have to say about that treaty that it is the most disgraceful, humiliating, and cowardly surrender the American Republic has ever been called upon to submit to, not excepting the treaty of 1818." In a letter to W. L. Putnam, June 1, 1888, Bayard remarks: "I send you with this a copy of the 'Record' containing Mr. Frye's speech on the Treaty, or rather on the 'British Secretary of State,' and other topics. His intemperance and injustice can only injure the cause he advocates." *Bayard Letter Book,* vol. 8, *Bayard MS.*

45. *Cong. Rec.,* 49 Cong., 1 sess., vol. 17, p. 3440.

. . . if the resolution had meant what the majority interpreted it to mean, and the negotiation had been condemned on that ground, it would have been an effective assertion of a right of the Senate to be consulted in advance of any negotiation, thus not only wiping out the practice of using executive agents, but also destroying, or at least crippling, presidential initiative.[46]

Senator Chandler directly challenged the Democratic minority on this very point. To him it was clear that the Fisheries Treaty was a "national dishonor" because two of the "so-called plenipotentiaries, being appointed by the President without the consent of the Senate, were not constitutionally selected." He was certain that it was incorrect to assume that "the power of the President in the first instance to negotiate treaties with foreign powers, to be submitted to the Senate, gives him the right without the consent of the Senate to appoint ambassadors or plenipotentiaries for any such negotiations." The action of President Cleveland in this regard was a "gross violation of the Constitution, wilfully, recklessly, and defiantly perpetrated." [47]

Senator Sherman realized the danger of such an argument and he was careful to disclaim any support of it. In the following excerpt from the *Congressional Record,* his position was clearly defined:

Nor does this treaty turn upon the mode of negotiation. My friend from Alabama has got up a hobby, . . . a moot question, as to whether this treaty could be negotiated by two men who had never been confirmed by the Senate of the United States. I believe in one of his speeches he made the remark that the Committee on Foreign Relations refused to take that view of the question. . . . They expressly declined to do it, and therefore in the report that is made—

MR. MORGAN.—I will state to the Senator that he is quite mistaken about that. . . . If the Senator will consult the report of the minority of that committee he will see that they took just the opposite ground from that.

MR. SHERMAN.—I know myself that I never took that view of it. . . . As to the powers of the President of the United States to negotiate a treaty, I agree with everything that has been said upon that subject. . . . He can take any kind of a man, a dumb man, a blind man, or a deaf man. . . . In my judgment he has a right to use such means as are necessary to bring about any treaty. I suppose that precedents have been quoted by the Senator from Alabama to sustain that position. I do not disagree with him.[48]

46. Henry M. Wriston, *Executive Agents in American Foreign Relations* (Baltimore, 1929), p. 286.

47. *Cong. Rec.*, 50 Cong., 1 sess., vol. 19, pp. 6345-6358.

48. *Ibid.*, p. 7287. In commenting upon this debate in the Senate, Dr. Wriston remarks: "The honors in this debate went to the defenders of the President. His opponents realized it. They were not sincere or candid in the argument. Sherman really gave the case away; the Republicans had set up something to be shot at. On the whole the marksmanship of the Democrats was excellent." *Executive Agents in American Foreign Relations*, p. 291.

Other Republican Senators, taking this cue from Sherman, attacked the treaty from other viewpoints. Senator Riddleberger took the ground that the sixth and twelfth articles of the treaty admitted the Canadians into the coastwise fisheries of the United States. Taking these articles together, there could be no question but that the United States Government "surrenders the entire right of fishing in the Chesapeake Bay up to the Patapsco River, and then along the entire Atlantic coast within 3 miles of that coast." The Senator then took up his usual congenial task of twisting the British lion's tail. In dramatic fashion he asked why America wanted any treaty with England. We should

. . . never have a national government until we have whipped England for her deeds. She never leaves her footprints on any soil where she does not leave them with something that marks the same impress where she can put it down again. Our boasted Monroe doctrine is being annulled and wiped from the face of the earth today, and we find gentlemen on the other side of the Chamber saying we must arbitrate or we must fight. . . . We have nothing before us but the ratification of this treaty which involves everything that is dishonorable to us. . . . I ask why do we want to make a treaty with such a government anyhow? . . . England has never kept a treaty; she has never made one that she did not violate.[49]

Senator Teller was equally intent upon denouncing England and her misdeeds. He agreed with Senator Riddleberger that America would never be a free nation until we whipped England "a third time." Who had forgotten that in all her wars England had been

. . . the most aggressive, the most bloodthirsty, the most destructive of the human race, until it has become a proverb . . . that the Anglo-Saxon is the cruelest of all men? . . . By her course of procedure at one time . . . she [England] put a million and a quarter of Irish people in the grave, starved to death, or dying with sickness from starvation.[50]

Senator Blair poured the vials of his wrath upon President Cleveland whom he described as a "pig-headed Executive," [51] and Senator Hale experienced an overwhelming "sense of shame" when he pondered over the surrender of the Democratic Party to British demands.[52] Senator Hoar regarded the whole temper of the negotiations leading up to the Fisheries Treaty as

. . . feeble, spiritless, ignoble, and timid. The weakest Canadian official laughs in the face of an American complainant when he thinks of Grover Cleveland and Mr. Bayard. . . . What an unwise, blundering, timid, un-

49. *Ibid.,* pp. 7155-7157.   50. *Ibid.,* p. 7220.
51. *Ibid.,* p. 7392.   52. *Ibid.,* pp. 7393-7394.

American diplomacy is that which, when one hundred and fifty American ships cry out to their Government for redress of vexatious treatment in British harbors, . . . to turn wholly away from their injury and suffer Great Britain to discuss over again the interpretation of the treaty of 1818 as to fishing limits, and take down from her walls the rusty, disused weapons of seventy years ago and brandish them again in our faces! What statesmanship, what patriotism is it for President and Secretary and Democratic Senators to set themselves with one voice to arguing the British case! [53]

When Republican Senators grew tired of denouncing President Cleveland and Secretary Bayard, they next resorted to sneering at the Civil War records of Southern Senators.[54] These unfair tactics were met with dignity by Senator Morgan who bore the brunt of the Republican onslaught. With reference to the general attack upon the merits of the treaty and the alleged surrender of the Administration to British demands, Senator Morgan observed:

There was a terrible list of outrages and wrongs, including every phase of what we contend is the misconstruction by Great Britain of the treaty of 1818, carried into actual effect by seizure of our ships . . . year by year. When Mr. Bayard came to treat on this subject he found all this mass of wrong and injustice. . . . It had been practised long, and with perfect impunity, for no administration had resented it. The "grand old party" which was in possession of this Government for twenty-five years did not resent it at all. . . . All was agreeable among the ex-Secretaries and the great men who led the Republican party. . . . Mr. Bayard found it all there. What has he done with it? He has made a means by which it will not occur again.

In order to repel the charge of Democratic subservience to Great Britain, Morgan gave a brief exposé of the final section of the report of the majority of the Senate Committee on Foreign Relations:

This committee, with a stiff presumption . . . set themselves up to advise the British Crown. We beg your Majesty that you will not take this abortion that the President of the United States has negotiated with your commissioners and its rejection as being an evidence on the part of the United States of a hostile purpose. . . . Look at the humiliation of it, begging the British Queen for grace and favor after you have rejected a treaty. . . . This . . . is one of the most humiliating attitudes that a great committee ever took; it is regular toadyism to the British power.

53. *Ibid.*, p. 7518. With reference to Hoar's speech, Bayard made the following comment in a letter to David A. Wells, July 17, 1888: "Did you see Hoar's speech on the Fisheries? I think it about as dishonest and unjust an essay as I ever read. Little 'Bill' Chandler makes no claim to the respect of honorable men, but Hoar does, and how he juggles his conscience is a mystery to me." *Bayard Letter Book*, vol. 8, *Bayard MS.*

54. *Ibid.*, p. 7522.

It was evident to the Senator that the Fisheries Treaty was being attacked in a purely partisan spirit. He was certain that ". . . no measure has ever yet been laid before the Senate of the United States which has received so much of imprecation, so much of abuse, so much that is unjustifiable in thought and utterance, as this treaty.[55]

With particular reference to the assaults that had been made upon Secretary Bayard, Senator Morgan remarked:

> Mr. Bayard is hardly a vain man, but he is a very proud man. I doubt very much if the American family in all of its generations has given birth and nurture and support to a man whose character for integrity, for worth, for excellence in every respect, is higher than that of Thomas F. Bayard. I know . . . that there are men in the United States who hold themselves up very high, who when they come into his presence can not bear the contact. They feel that there is something about him that rebukes them; that there is an atmosphere about him that they can not live in, but I have never heard that man charged by friend or foe, until this debate started, with being anything else than a true man of splendid bearing, of what I might term immaculate honor.[56]

One of the best speeches made in defence of the treaty was that delivered by Senator Gray, of Delaware. Combining common sense with scholarship, he easily disposed of the fears of Senator Riddleberger that the sixth and twelfth articles of the treaty surrendered the inshore fisheries of the United States to Canadian fishermen:

> Ever since this treaty has been before the Senate I have been receiving . . . suggestions . . . that the treaty has in some manner given away the rights of the States to control their own territorial waters. . . . I do not believe that it is within the competence of the Government of the United States under its treaty-making power to confer upon any foreign government . . . the right to participate in the fisheries of the territorial waters of the States that compose this Union. . . . It would hardly be necessary to go further than I have done to show the absurdity of any such interpretation being sought to be attached to this Article XII. But look at its phraseology— "Fishing vessels of Canada and Newfoundland," not "fishermen" but "fishing vessels of Canada and Newfoundland shall have on the Atlantic coast of the United States," what?—"all the privileges reserved and secured by this treaty to the United States fishing vessels in the aforesaid waters of Canada and Newfoundland." What does this mean? Why clearly it means that the privileges that are gained for our fishing vessels in the waters of the North-eastern Provinces, to wit, the right of refuge from storm, to obtain wood, water, and fuel, and commercial privileges to buy on all occasions needful supplies, to be exempt from harassment when resorting to these waters

---

55. *Ibid.*, pp. 7164, 7167.   56. *Ibid.*, p. 7521.

for these purposes—that these and similar privileges, which were the only privileges that are secured by this treaty, shall also attach to Canadian vessels when they visit the waters of the United States on the Atlantic coast.[57]

In spite of the determined opposition on the part of the Republican majority in the Senate, Bayard still had hopes that the business interests of the country would exert such pressure as to compel many Senators to support the treaty. The April issue of the *Rand-McNally Bankers' Monthly*, came out openly in favor of the convention. The opinion was expressed that the

. . . enlightened features which prevailed in the negotiations should go down in history to the great credit of the gentlemen engaged on both sides. . . . It may be well . . . to jot a few leading details of the recent treaty, which we hope the Legislatures of both countries will accept, put in force, and thus give a wholesome lesson to other nations.

On June 4 the Baltimore Board of Trade adopted resolutions which not only approved the Fisheries Treaty but also called upon the Maryland Representatives in Congress to "make no opposition to the 'Fisheries Treaty' now before the Senate." [58]

To Bayard these expressions of friendly opinion with reference to the Fisheries Treaty appeared as most timely, and in a letter to his intimate friend Benoni Lockwood, he inquires about the possibility of enlisting the aid of the New York Chamber of Commerce:

Entre nous, I think some move may be made to reconsider the very inconsiderate resolution adopted by the N. Y. Chamber of Commerce [March 1, 1888] adverse to the Fisheries Treaty. (Are you a member of the Chamber of Commerce?) It is evident now that under the Blaine influence (as voiced by Hale and Frye, the Senators from Maine), the threat of war with Great Britain, under a policy of retaliation against Canada, is to be used in the coming canvass to catch the Hibernian vote. This is very dangerous as well as discreditable.[59]

To David A. Wells he expressed the same idea: "I think if our steady-going, money-getting merchants and 'business-men' could comprehend the dangers into which this country may be drifting, . . . they would raise their voices." [60]

57. *Ibid.,* p. 7477.   58. New York *Evening Post,* June 5, 1888.
59. Bayard to Benoni Lockwood, June 16, 1888, *Bayard Letter Book,* vol. 8, *Bayard MS.*
60. Bayard to David A. Wells, June 20, 1888, *ibid.* In a letter to W. L. Putnam, June 20, 1888, Bayard continues his remarks along the same line: "I am in hopes the Commercial interests along the Atlantic coast may be aroused to a sense of their danger, and that the conscience of the whole Country may be awakened to the crime of inducing an unjustifiable collision between the U. S. and Great Britain." *Ibid.*

After reading a letter which Mr. Gustav Schwab had written to Daniel Magone, Bayard felt a "sense of relief" that there really was an

. . . awakening in the commercial circles of New York to the gravity of the results attendant upon the fate of the Fisheries Treaty with Great Britain now pending in the Senate. . . . I am without that personal knowledge of the members of the Chamber of Commerce . . . which would warrant me in giving advice as to the expediency of proposing at their next meeting in July, to reconsider and rescind the Resolution [March 1, 1888] . . . adopted . . . so hastily and inconsiderately. . . . I have endeavored to do my full share in averting disaster to my country, and at the same time maintain national self-respect on the basis of justice. . . . If the question can only be understood I have no fears that the good sense and patriotism of the American people will prevent them from entering upon a policy of retaliation.[61]

During the course of the fight in the Senate upon the Fisheries Treaty, Bayard had permitted, from time to time, his own views to appear in the press. These press notices had always been moderate in temper and restrained in language. It was somewhat surprising, therefore, when the Baltimore *Sun*, on July 12, 1888, carried a long statement in which Bayard flayed Senator Hoar in trenchant phraseology:

It is hardly worth the trouble to deny the utterances of men who wilfully pervert the truth to suit their own purposes. The remarks of Senator Hoar are disingenuous in the extreme. His statements are most untrue, most unfair. . . . His discourse is more barren of fairness and honesty than any document I have ever known. . . . It is not to be wondered that we failed to consult with the New England Senators as to the nature of the negotiations with the British and Canadian protocolists. . . . Mr. Ingalls on one occasion asked whether it should be blood or negotiation. Mr. Edmunds replied, "Neither." These men were sworn to defeat any attempt to settle existing difficulty. Evidently their purpose was, and is, to embarrass the administration. . . .

Senator Hoar avers that this department declined to furnish the Senate . . . the proposals and counter-proposals made while the joint commission was in session. This is absolutely untrue. . . . I inclose a copy of the papers referred to, and they were printed in the executive document. These were at the disposal of Senator Hoar, and prove his charge to have been utterly unfounded. . . . It is true that I made no attempt to secure the right to fish in the jurisdictional waters of Canada. To obtain this concession it was required that we accede to the demand of the Canadian government that

61. Bayard to D. Magone, June 15, 1888, *Bayard Letter Book*, vol. 8, *Bayard MS*. In a letter to William M. Ivins, June 20, 1888, Bayard further observes: "I have no such knowledge of the temper of the Chamber [of Commerce] as would enable me to pass judgment on the expediency of attempting at this time to reverse its action hitherto, even though such action was admitted to have been inconsiderate." *Ibid*.

its fish and fish-oil be allowed to enter our ports free of duty. I, for one, did not propose to accede to any demand. We determined to obtain our rights, nothing more, and it has cost the United States nothing to do so.[62]

The manner in which this statement was obtained, furnishes a little insight into the methods of newspaper men of that day. In a letter to Frederic Emory, Bayard tells an interesting story:

> You *must* protect me a little more from the indiscretion and inaccuracy of the correspondent who came to me yesterday with some written questions *from you,* which I took time and pains to give him *printed* answers to. To my great regret I find myself advertised in "The Sun" of today [July 12] as "replying to the speech of Senator Hoar." I was only answering *your* inquiries for information. . . . As the correspondent took no notes, and was *expressly* enjoined by me to take his answers from the printed document I gave him, I was surprised and amazed to find that against my intention, . . . my personal views were published.[63]

It was doubtless embarrassing to Bayard to have his "personal views" spread broadcast with his permission, but it must have given him some satisfaction to see in print such a scathing and yet such a truthful appraisal of the attitude of Senator Hoar. He clearly realized by now that the Republican majority in the Senate was partisan rather than patriotic, and the Fisheries Treaty, no matter what its excellences might be, was about to be sacrificed on the altar of party politics. In a letter to Angell, Bayard spoke of the manner in which "the heats of party warp the judgments of men."[64] To Phelps he wrote in the same strain:

> You received the "record" of Congress and have seen the temper and animus of the discussion of the Fisheries. Apart from the acridity of Evarts, Hoar, *et al.,* the main purpose is to attract the "Irish vote" by the promise of a collision with Great Britain. To this end the speeches against the treaty

62. There is little doubt that Hoar's unbridled tongue and partisan spirit gave Bayard great umbrage. In Hoar's speech on the Fisheries Treaty there is one passage of inflated rhetoric which must have jangled upon Democratic nerves: "Those were the days when the flag, beautiful as a flower to those who loved it, . . . floated everywhere in peaceful seas, and was honored everywhere in friendly ports. No petty British officer hauled it down from an American masthead. No Canadian minister of justice laughed in the face of an injured American citizen when Grant was in the White House. . . . I do not like the policy which everywhere robs American citizenship of its glory. I do not like the methods of fraud and crime which have destroyed popular elections in so many Democratic States. . . . I do not like this conspiracy between the old slave-holder and the English manufacturer, to strike down the wages of the American workman and the comfort of the American workman's home. . . . I like no better the present treaty. It leaves the American sailor to be bullied and insulted without redress, and abandons the American right to the fisheries." *Cong. Rec.,* 50 Cong., 1 sess., vol. 19, p. 6060.

63. Bayard to Frederic Emory, July 12, 1888, *Bayard MS.*

64. Bayard to J. B. Angell, July 12, 1888, *Bayard Letter Book,* vol. 8, *Bayard MS.*

have been wholly bereft of all that dignifies or justifies debate. It is this reckless resort to defamation and dangerous alliances which indicate to me the desperation of the Republican organization, which sucked revolution in its cradle and has lived upon it until now. . . . Should you have the opportunity it would be well to let Lord Salisbury understand the serious danger and unwisdom of Canadian Rulers playing into the hands of the Republicans here. . . . I anticipate a rejection of the treaty before the Senate adjourns.[65]

With this idea in mind, it is not likely, therefore, that Bayard was surprised when the Senate did reject the Fisheries Treaty on August 21, 1888, by a vote of Yeas—27, Nays—30, Absent—19.[66] It was a purely partisan vote [67] which rendered futile all of Bayard's anxious efforts to enlist the aid of "big business" on behalf of the treaty.[68] The situation is accurately described by Professor Holt:

> From the moment it entered the Senate the treaty became a political issue and the votes on it followed party lines strictly. . . . The treaty was . . . rejected with thirty Republican senators voting against and twenty-seven Democrats for it. . . . It was then and has since been generally recognized that it was made a political issue, not because of a real difference in policy between the two parties but merely because the treaty happened to be presented during a presidential campaign and one side saw an opportunity of securing some political advantage from it. . . . The risk of further complicating the already critical relations with Great Britain was disregarded for the hope of a political victory.[69]

65. Bayard to Phelps, July 26, 1888, *ibid.*
66. *Cong. Rec.*, 50 Cong., 1 sess., vol. 19, p. 7768.
67. The comments of Cecil Spring Rice, secretary of the British Legation in Washington, with reference to the Fisheries Treaty show how easy it was to recognize the political character of the opposition: "February 10: Our treaty is really progressing but it is sure to be quashed in the Senate, not because the Senate disapproves of it, but because they disapprove of the present Government." On April 27, 1888, he was sure that the "Fisheries Treaty is practically dished," and on May 12 he reports that "the Senate Committee has reported adversely on the Fisheries Treaty by a purely party vote. The reasons given are addressed not to the Senate but to the more bigoted and disagreeable faction of the Republican Party. . . . Every four years politics here become simply the lowest form of personal demagogueism." Stephen Gwynn, *The Letters and Friendships of Sir Cecil Spring Rice* (London, 1929), vol. 1, pp. 85, 90, 93.
68. Immediately after the rejection of the treaty by the Senate, Bayard gave a statement to the press (Philadelphia *Record*, August 22, 1888) in which he remarked: "It is shocking, simply shocking. . . . Our forefathers were not ashamed nor afraid to avow a decent regard for the opinions of mankind, neither were they ashamed nor afraid to do right; but these Republican Senators seem to be men of a different stripe."
69. William S. Holt, *Treaties Defeated by the Senate* (Baltimore, 1933), pp. 143-149. See Sir Charles Tupper, *Recollections of Sixty Years*, p. 192, for an illuminating remark of a leading Republican Senator: "We cannot allow the Democrats to take credit for settling so important a dispute." Also Joseph Chamberlain's statement to Bayard about a comment made to him by a distinguished Republican "who was one of the candidates for the

The President's reaction to this adverse vote upon the Fisheries Treaty was a spirited one. On August 8, W. L. Putnam had anticipated the rejection of the treaty and had advised Bayard to place the responsibility squarely upon the Senate:

> The President ought to send a message throwing the whole responsibility on the Senate, distinctly intimating that, in his view, the necessity for the President's exercising a discretion under the Act of March, 1887, had gone by, as the whole case is now before Congress, and that the Senate, having distinctly declined to unite in adjusting the matter by negotiation, . . . it remains for the Senate to inaugurate such measures in the way of legislation as the case requires.[70]

Cleveland followed this counsel, and on August 23 the Republicans in the Senate were surprised by a special message on the fisheries question. Taken unawares by the President's tactics, Senator Edmunds asked for an immediate adjournment of the Senate in order that his party colleagues could discuss the situation before taking any action. Senator Morgan hoped that the Senate would not adjourn before the President's message was read. There was no justification for such discourtesy, but Senator Edmunds pressed the motion for adjournment which carried by a narrow vote.[71]

On the following day (August 24) the Senate listened to the reading of the President's message which called for retaliatory legislation against Canada that would "subserve the interests of our people and maintain the high standard and the becoming pride of American citizenship."[72]

Presidential nomination": "The fact is that just now we cannot afford to let this Administration do anything." *Memorandum* written by Bayard, February 28, 1888, *Bayard MS*. For further evidence of the partisan character of the Senate opposition, see R. J. Dangerfield, *In Defense of the Senate* (Norman, Oklahoma, 1933), pp. 242-244; and L. B. Shippee, "Thomas F. Bayard," *The American Secretaries of State and Their Diplomacy*, vol. 8, (N. Y., 1928), pp. 63, 336.

70. W. L. Putnam to Bayard, August 8, 1888, *Bayard MS*.

71. *Cong. Rec.*, 50 Cong., 1 sess., vol. 19, p. 7882.

72. In this message of August 23, 1888, the President stressed the following points: "I fully believe that the treaty just rejected by the Senate was well suited to the exigency, and that its provisions were adequate for our security in the future from vexatious incidents and for the promotion of friendly neighborhood and intimacy, without sacrificing in the least our national pride or dignity. . . . It is of importance to note that this treaty has been rejected without any apparent disposition on the part of the Senate to alter or amend its provisions, and with the evident intention . . . that no negotiation should at present be concluded touching the matter at issue. . . . I am by no means disposed to abandon the interests and rights of our people . . . or to neglect their grievances; and I therefore turn to the contemplation of a plan of retaliation as a mode which still remains of treating the situation. . . . These considerations lead me at this time to invoke the aid and counsel of the Congress and its support in such a further grant of power as seems to me necessary and desirable to render effective the policy I

By handing over to the Senate the initiative in this matter of further retaliatory legislation, the President had caught the Republicans off guard.[73] Their chief desire was to carp at Presidential policies and not to formulate constructive programs of their own. Senator Edmunds broke forth into loud complaints that the President had taken no steps to carry out the retaliatory legislation of March 3, 1887:

> Here was a law that he [the President] was to execute when the contingency should arise of the existence of a particular fact. He being satisfied that the fact existed, then it was his duty to take steps to obtain redress in the method that the statute pointed out. . . . Why has he been silent for eighteen months, with the whole power of the law in his hands and the easy means of exerting all the functions that the law imputed to him in such a case? . . . Why has he remained inactive? . . . I must confess . . . my astonishment at such a course of action on the part of the Executive of the United States.[74]

Senator Morgan was not impressed with this catalogue of complaints from Senator Edmunds. He knew only too well that

> . . . in the progress of this whole affair . . . the purpose of all this opposition to the President in respect of his dealing with these fisheries has not been to get the interests of the people of the United States into a better shape, but it has been to entrap the Executive . . . in a political strait-jacket. . . . I think the country appreciates the fortitude of the man who can stand up against the utterances of the honorable Senator from Vermont and with cool, quiet complacency still pursue the line of duty without tremor and without any departure.[75]

In the House of Representatives a bill was introduced (August 23) empowering the President to carry out the provisions of the Act of March 3, 1887, and to authorize him to protect American interests against unjust discrimination in the use of canals in the British dominions of North America.[76] On September 8 a substitute bill of similar

---

have indicated." James D. Richardson, *Messages and Papers of the Presidents*, vol. 8, pp. 620-621.

73. In speaking of the President's special message to the Senate with reference to the enactment of retaliatory legislation, the New York *Herald*, August 24, 1888, was inclined to the view that it was "the greatest *coup d'etat* the Executive has ever had the opportunity to deliver. It makes the success of the Democratic ticket in November absolutely certain"; the New York *Times*, August 24, expressed the opinion that the President's message was an "executive bomb-shell" that took the Republicans by "surprise," and created "consternation"; the Brooklyn *Citizen*, August 25, believed that the President had placed the Senate in a "deep hole"; and even the choleric New York *Sun*, August 25, was moved to exclaim with reference to the message: "It is great, it is glorious, it is patriotic!"

74. *Cong. Rec.*, 50 Cong., 1 sess., vol. 19, pp. 7903-7904.

75. *Ibid.*, pp. 7908-7909.

76. See H. R. 11257, *Cong. Rec.*, 50 Cong., 1 sess., vol. 19, p. 7901.

character was passed by the House of Representatives,[77] but it was not acted upon by the Senate which, controlled by Republicans, was very careful of embarking upon a course of retaliation against Canada. Such a course would mean severe economic loss to the business interests of the northern states from Maine to Minnesota, and it might prove fatal to Republican prospects in the Presidential campaign that was already well under way.[78]

In commenting upon the action of the Senate with regard to the Fisheries Treaty, James C. Welling expressed the fear that if *projects* of treaties were to be distilled

. . . through the alembic of a partisan caucus even before they can be formally acted on by the Senate; if they are to be used as the makeweights of a pending political canvass and not as the solemn engagements of the high contracting parties in whose name they profess to run; if the Senate of the United States, instead of exercising its constitutional function as the *confidential* adviser of the Executive in giving consent to treaties, is to be turned into a public hustings for the Buncombe of the hour, then the difficulties of our situation must be greatly intensified in the eyes of foreign states.[79]

With reference to the President's special message to the Senate, August 23, 1888, the letters to Bayard were highly laudatory. E. Ingersoll thought that the

. . . discussion in the Senate exhibits the partisanship of the majority in no creditable light. As you suggest, I am delighted with Mr. Cleveland's stroke of a day or two ago, and the condition of things reminds me of . . . Gen. Jackson's controversies with the Senate, and I think the result at the polls

77. See H. R. 11309, *ibid.*, pp. 8439-8440. It was significant that this bill passed the House of Representatives by the overwhelming vote of yeas, 176, nays, 4.

78. Press opinion on the rejection of the Fisheries Treaty was largely divided. The New York *Times*, August 22, 1888, expressed the view that the action of the Senate was "perhaps the most remarkable instance of narrow partisanship in the treatment of a great international question ever known in our history"; the Boston *Post*, August 22, sharply condemned the Senate's "wilful obstruction to an honorable settlement of a long standing international difficulty"; the Brooklyn *Citizen*, August 22, thought it was clear that there was "not one man among the Republican Senators who had courage or character enough to refuse to participate in this wretched job to "put the President in a hole"; the New York *Star*, August 22, regarded the rejection of the treaty as a "resort of partisan spite as shortsighted as it is malevolent"; the New York *Herald*, August 24, was certain that the vote in the Senate was a party one which had "little reference to the merits of the case, but was intended to be a blow at a Democratic administration"; and the Philadelphia *Times*, August 23, viewed the defeat of the treaty as an "exhibition of the most dangerous political jingoism." The Republican press, led by the New York *Tribune*, August 22, strongly praised the Senate for casting out "with contempt the most senseless and un-American of treaties."

79. James C. Welling to Bayard, August 23, 1888, *Bayard MS.*

next November will probably be very much the same that it was in his case.[80]

Rodmond Gibbons regarded the political prospect as

. . . glorious. Canada will not revoke the *Modus V;* it would be a losing game for the ex-plotters to instigate fishermen to deviltry; the Irish are satisfied; neither England nor Canada is likely to have any real cause for grievance; the uncrowned King is denuded of his war paint; Cleveland's re-election is assured.[81]

Bayard's own comments upon the attitude of the Senate were caustic in the extreme. He regarded the "rejection of the Fisheries Treaty, coupled with the refusal to amend it or permit negotiation in any shape," as an "unheard-of thing within the pale of civilized governments." [82] To his son-in-law, Samuel D. Warren, he expressed the view that the "more the evidence multiplies of the actual condition of the Republican party, and its utter deliverance over to such a mentally and morally inebriated person as Blaine, the greater the peril appears of placing the affairs of this Country under such control." [83] In a letter to W. L. Putnam he was equally critical:

A partisan majority of the Senate, dominated by the solid New England representation, have deliberately obstructed and thwarted every international arrangement of an important nature yet made or proposed by the present Administration. The men who have done this seem wholly lost to all sense of justice or patriotic feeling.[84]

On March 9, 1889, after he had left office, Bayard gave his final estimate of the Republican majority in the Senate which had opposed all his efforts in a spirit of unusual and malignant hostility:

It is difficult to . . . anyone who was not a daily witness, to comprehend the temper and method in which the Republican Managers of the Senate have dealt with public business wherever the State Department has been concerned. I have closed four years of service without one word of amity, or ordinary courtesy, much less of co-operation, or assistance from any Repub-

---

80. E. Ingersoll to Bayard, August 25, 1888, *Bayard MS.*
81. Rodmond Gibbons to Bayard, August 26, 1888, *ibid.*
82. Bayard to Judge Stallo, September 6, 1888, *Bayard Letter Book,* vol. 8, *Bayard MS.*
83. Bayard to S. D. Warren, September 8, 1888, *ibid.*
84. Bayard to W. L. Putnam, September 13, 1888, *Bayard Letter Book,* vol. 8, *Bayard MS.* In a letter to John Russell Young, September 14, 1888, Bayard remarks: "I think our countrymen do not realize the position in which the United States as a member of the family of Nations, is being placed before the world by the blind desire of the Republican Senators to defeat and disparage even the essential operations of any Representative of our Foreign Relations. It is bankrupting the *firm* to punish a partner." *Bayard Letter Book,* vol. 8, *Bayard MS.*

lican member of the Committee on Foreign Relations. On the contrary, my best efforts and most useful work has been systematically defeated and thwarted at what cost to our Country the sequel must prove.[85]

In such a partisan atmosphere and with such dubious personalities, it was greatly to Bayard's credit that he accomplished as much as he did.[86] Fortunately, the *modus vivendi* which he arranged with reference to the fisheries was highly successful in allaying the difficulties between the United States and Canada that had brought the two countries to the verge of open hostilities. During the last two months of the Cleveland Administration it was a source of some satisfaction to know that, despite the malevolence of Republican leaders, Canadian-American relations had been placed upon a satisfactory footing.

85. Bayard to Carl Schurz, March 9, 1889, *Schurz MS.* In Lady Gwendolen Cecil's *Life of Robert, Marquis of Salisbury*, vol. 4, p. 116, there is a statement which is astonishing in its inaccuracy: "In June '88, the United States Senate had rejected an arbitrated agreement on a Fisheries dispute with Canada which Mr. Chamberlain had negotiated the year before."

86. With reference to the political atmosphere in the fall of 1888, the following letter from Horace White to Carl Schurz, September 16, 1888, is illuminating: "Intelligent Canadians have admitted to me within a few days that there is no justification, either in the treaty of 1818 or out of it, for their refusal to allow fish to be transshipped in bond. The churlishness of their position becomes more marked and gloomy when it is considered that we admit their *fresh* fish duty free. So that when an American and a Canadian are fishing side by side beyond the three-mile limit, the American cannot get his catch into the Boston market under two or three weeks, while the Canadian can put his there within thirty-six hours, and without payment of any duty. Our fishermen are not entitled to any sympathy, however. They 'struck' and they ought to suffer some punishment. They struck for a tariff on fish and it was nothing to them if the country got into a war on their account. Moreover, their abuse of Sec. Bayard has been monstrous even beyond the ordinary license of political warfare. They have certainly lost votes in Maine by the extreme course they have pursued." *Schurz MS.*

Of like tenor is the letter from James B. Angell to Bayard, September 21, 1888: "What is to be the issue of the Canadian and the Chinese difficulties, I can't see. Anything more unworthy than much of the talk and some of the proceedings, I cannot imagine. Both parties are so involved that politically I feel, as Dr. Storrs did, like 'taking to the Woods.' " *Bayard MS.*

In an undated note to Bayard, Manton Marble, in the fall of 1888, remarked: "The Republican party in the Senate has sunk from a useful opposition to a factious cabal. Bound to assist the orderly conduct of government business, it has obstructed what it could not prevent, and has sustained its pretence of an exclusive capacity to govern by a crooked, delayed, or refused co-operation in anything essential to reforms or convenient to current administration." *Bayard MS.*

CHAPTER ELEVEN

Lord Sackville Gains Immortality by Merely Being Stupid

———————•◦∞◦•———————

THE ACTION OF THE SENATE IN REJECTING THE FISHERIES TREATY WAS an impressive illustration of the close connection between politics and diplomacy. It was evident that prominent Republicans could never forgive President Cleveland for removing them from the seats of the mighty to which they had grown so pleasantly accustomed, or for turning the national horn of plenty in the direction of deserving Democrats who for twenty-five years had glumly watched the rich gifts of party patronage pour into receptive Republican laps. In the autumn of 1888 a Presidential election would be held, and early in that year, Republican orators began a campaign of misrepresentation and political sabotage that is unparalleled in American history. It was a slashing attack that appealed to prejudice rather than reason, and because of that very fact it was increasingly difficult to withstand.

The Republican orators were astute politicians who never overlooked an opportunity to gain their ends. There was no trick or political stratagem that was unfamiliar to them, and during the fall of 1888 they projected a scheme that was designed to ruin the career of the British Minister and to encompass the defeat of the Democratic Party. Its effect upon the election returns is difficult to estimate.

In the late eighties the political scales in the United States were so evenly balanced that they could be easily tipped one way or the other by the slightest pressure of racial animosity. In some sections the large Irish vote was a factor of great importance, and many politicians were anxious to court it by assuming a pronounced anti-English attitude. During the summer of 1888 Republican spokesmen advanced the charge that President Cleveland was merely a British dummy who danced at the draw of Lord Salisbury. It was vehemently asserted that the President had given his support to a Fisheries Treaty with England which he had good reason to know was inimical to the fishing industry of New England. So strong were the accusations on this point that the President felt constrained, after the defeat of the treaty in the Senate, to send to Congress on August 23 a message in which he asked for a retaliatory law that would strike a severe blow at Canadian business interests. As a result of this sharp attack upon the British Empire, a flood of congratulatory telegrams poured in upon the White House from loyal sons of Erin the world over.[1] The Irish vote seemed safely Democratic when a blundering British Minister stepped on the political stage and made a little gesture in favor of President Cleveland. The Republicans in the audience welcomed this interlude with fervor, and there is no doubt that they were only too willing to push Sir Lionel Sackville-West into the full glare of the footlights. The story of this inept British actor who fumbled the few lines he should have known by heart, is an interesting chapter in Anglo-American relations.

President Cleveland's message to Congress on August 23, with its sharp challenge to England, had one unlooked-for reverberation. In Pomona, California, a quiet, unassuming fruit-grower named George Osgoodby, began to ponder over the question as to whether the President's message to Congress was a sincere attack upon Canadian business interests or perhaps was nothing more than a political device to win the Irish vote in the United States. As a Republican he was naturally interested in exposing any sham attempt to twist the tail of the British lion.

In the early days of September, 1888, he wrote a letter to the British Minister, Lord Sackville,[2] which he turned over to Mr. P. C. Turner, of Pomona, for examination and comment. Turner immediately copied the letter, and after signing the name of "Charles F. Murchison," he sent it to the British Legation in Washington.[3]

1. Allan Nevins, *Grover Cleveland* (N.Y., 1934), p. 428.
2. In the New York *World*, January 12, 1889, there is an interesting paragraph which might have some validity: "Today [January 11] it was stated that George Osgoodby, on whom the Murchison letter has been fastened, said: 'I did not compose that letter to West. I simply copied it and sent it on in my name. I am willing to make an affidavit to that effect.' The *World* correspondent saw Henry T. Gage, in whose office the remark was made and who is more or less mixed up in the affair. He refused to speak on the subject. All signs point to the fact that Osgoodby is simply a scapegoat. There comes a report from Pomona that years ago, when Osgoodby was a citizen of the State of New York, he played a similar trick on a candidate for Governor, which resulted in the signal defeat of the candidate."
3. See Charles A. Osgoodby to the Smithsonian Institution, February 13, 1931, Library of Congress. Also, Harrison G. Otis (editor of the Los Angeles *Times*) to Senator John

It was a very transparent "decoy" letter with a paragraph of inquiry which should have placed the British Minister on his guard. After referring to President Cleveland's message to Congress of August 23, relative to retaliation against Great Britain, Mr. "Murchison," as a former British citizen, asks Lord Sackville for advice on the question of casting his vote:

. . . I know of no one better able to direct me, sir, and I most respectfully ask your advice in the matter. . . . As you are at the fountainhead of knowledge on the question, and know whether Mr. Cleveland's present policy is temporary only, and whether he will, as soon as he secures another term of four years in the Presidency, suspend it for one of friendship and free trade, I apply to you privately and confidentially for information, which shall in turn be treated as entirely secret. Such information would put me at rest myself, and if favorable to Mr. Cleveland, enable me, on my own responsibility, to assure many of our countrymen that they would do England a service by voting for Cleveland.[4]

The guileless British Minister fell at once into this obvious political trap and sent back the following answer that was hopefully awaited:

You are probably aware that any political party which openly favored the mother country at the present moment would lose popularity, and that the party in power is fully aware of this fact. That party, however, is, I believe, still desirous of maintaining friendly relations with Great Britain. . . . Allowance must, therefore, be made for the political situation as regards the Presidential election, . . . but there is every reason to believe that . . . he [the President] will manifest a spirit of conciliation.[5]

It was unfortunate for Sackville-West that he was deprived of the services of a bright, young secretary at the very moment when he needed him most. In the early months of 1887 Cecil Spring Rice came to Washington to serve as one of the secretaries at the British Legation, and he soon arrived at a shrewd estimate of the political situation. With Henry Adams as one of his mentors he quickly absorbed a great deal of information concerning American habitudes of thought, and there is little wonder that he became somewhat cynical about the "politicos" of that day. Of Bayard he was very fond, and he described to his friends in

---

Sherman, February 19, 1889, *John Sherman MS*, Library of Congress; Los Angeles *Times*, January 8, 1889; and newspaper clippings in the *Bayard MS*, Library of Congress.

4. Mr. Charles F. Murchison to Lord Sackville, September 4, 1888, *House Ex. Doc 1*, *pt. 1*, 50 Cong., 2 sess., pp. 1667-1668.

5. Lord Sackville to Mr. Charles F. Murchison, September 13, 1888, *House Ex. Doc. 1*, *pt. 1*, 50 Cong., 2 sess., pp. 1667-1668.

England the Secretary's "captivating manner and striking appearance." [6] Of Sackville-West he was not so complimentary: "The Americans thoroughly understand him [Sackville-West] and tell him all sorts of things they don't to anyone else. They have a common taste for whiskey, poker, and business." [7]

Spring Rice had few illusions about the high motives which led Republican statesmen to oppose Bayard's conciliatory policy towards England. In his letters to his brother, Stephen, he indicates his contempt for the American system of government: "I think that politics in this country are just as vile and low as anything connected with human baseness can be, and the opinion grows stronger and stronger." [8]

Spring Rice returned to England in the summer of 1888. If he had been with Sackville-West in September of that year he would have strongly protested against any reply to the "Murchison letter." It took a naïve mentality to walk into a trap whose bait was so old and noisome.

After Mr. Osgoodby had received the letter of reply from Sackville-West, he talked the matter over with Mr. Francis G. Haley, of Pomona, and the two of them, on October 18, 1888, took a trip to Los Angeles for the purpose of placing the correspondence in the hands of Mr. Otis, the editor of the Los Angeles *Times*. Failing to find Mr. Otis, they returned to Pomona, and on the following day Mr. W. A. Bell visited Los Angeles and showed the letters to Judge W. F. Fitzgerald, a member of the Republican Executive Committee of California. The Judge was deeply impressed with the political importance of the correspondence and immediately sought a conference with Mr. Otis who advised prompt publication. On October 21 the Los Angeles *Times* printed the letters in full, and the Republican press throughout the North followed suit with hostile comments upon Sackville-West's attempt to influence American elections. [9]

6. Spring Rice to Ferguson, March 18, 1887, *Letters and Friendships of Sir Cecil Spring Rice* (ed. by Stephen Gwynn, London, 1929), vol. 1, p. 57.

7. *Ibid.*, p. 57.

8. Cecil Spring Rice to Stephen Spring Rice, March 30, 1888, *ibid.*, p. 89.

9. Harrison Gray Otis to John Sherman, February 19, 1889, with enclosures, *John Sherman MS*, Library of Congress. Mr. Osgoodby was extremely anxious that no mention be made of his real name until after March 4, 1889. It was impossible, however, to keep his identity secret, and that is the reason why Col. Otis made the whole matter public in the Los Angeles *Times*, on January 8, 1889. It is apparent from the description given of Osgoodby that he was greatly alarmed at the furore that his correspondence had aroused. When he was importuned by a correspondent of the Los Angeles *Times* to disclose his real identity he "flatly refused," and "trembled so from fright that he could hardly talk: 'I don't want my name given to the public for several reasons. In the first place, my

It happened that Bayard was absent from Washington on a vacation when the "Murchison" correspondence was published. Some of the officials admitted to a correspondent from the New York *Herald* that it was "very indiscreet on Minister West's part to confide in writing his opinion about political matters." After eliciting this comment, the *Herald* reporter made a visit to the British Legation to talk the matter over with Sackville-West himself. He at once confirmed the accuracy of the copy of his letter to "Murchison," as published in the press. He then explained that

. . . he did not write letters nor refrain from writing them out of regard to political exigencies within the United States, which were matters that in no way concerned him otherwise than as a friendly and impartial spectator, but solely with reference to what was courteous and proper between himself and those that saw fit to honor him with their communications. . . . He had stated "that any political party which openly favored the mother country at the present moment would lose popularity." Does anybody dispute this attribution of fervid patriotism to the American people? . . . The suggestion that a foreign Ambassador should not write unofficial letters on the domestic politics of the country to which he is accredited was dismissed by Lord Sackville in a summary fashion. It happens constantly, he says, in his intercourse with people that statements are made to him, and information, opinion, and advice asked of him touching matters beyond his sphere and duty as a diplomatic agent of Her Majesty.

When the correspondent from the New York *Herald,* as a parting shot, warned Sackville-West that he would be "severely attacked" in the American press on account of his letter to Mr. "Murchison," the British Minister laughingly replied: "Indeed! Well, let them come on. I read the papers, you know, and I shall enjoy it greatly, I assure you." [10]

To a correspondent from the New York *Tribune,* Sackville-West was equally loquacious. When asked if he felt uneasy about the newspaper comment which pressed for his recall as British Minister to the United States, he smiled and assured the reporter that he was not

wife's parents are from the South, and they are the strongest Democrats you ever saw, and if they learn that I have done this thing to Mr. Cleveland they will take her away from me. My God! I never had any idea that the publication of that Sackville letter would raise such a row. Had I dreamed of such a thing I should have burned it!'" At a second meeting with this correspondent of the Los Angeles *Times,* Mr. Osgoodby still showed his great concern over the stir that had been raised over the Sackville letter. He assured the correspondent that he kept a shotgun ready all the time "for the reason that I have made up my mind not to be taken alive if the Democrats come for me." To quiet his fears he was taken to Los Angeles and kept concealed until after the election was over.

10. New York *Herald,* October 24, 1888.

. . . alarmed at that threat. There has been so much said about me in the past that I have become indifferent to such comment. The man wrote to me asking my advice upon a subject in which he was interested, as he had a perfect right to do. I answered him giving him my views upon the matter, as I had a right to do. That's all there is of it. . . . I have done nothing that is at all prejudicial.

When further questioned about the rejection of the Fisheries Treaty in the Senate he unburdened himself with great freedom:

I understand that both the action of the Senate and the President's letter of retaliation were for political effect. In a general election it is but natural that every point should be seized upon by both parties which would have an effect upon the voters. It is not at all likely that any trouble will result over this Fisheries matter.[11]

On October 23, during a speech delivered at Georgetown, Delaware, Bayard remarked that "without full authentication the private letters of Lord Sackville . . . which upon their face were not intended for publication, could not be noticed by the government."[12] This was a very cautious statement which threw little light upon the course that Bayard would pursue with reference to the correspondence. Other prominent Americans were more outspoken. Professor Simeon Baldwin, of Yale University, was of the opinion that

. . . it was not proper for the British Minister to express himself at all upon the political affairs of this country, but that inasmuch as he probably supposed he was writing a private letter to a trustworthy correspondent, and that it was merely the expression of a private opinion, the United States government would take no notice whatever of it.

Professor Baldwin did not see how the matter could be made "political capital of as there was no harm intended."[13] Colonel Robert Ingersoll was of much the same opinion. He could see

. . . nothing in this for a Republican to complain of. Mr. West . . . wrote a private letter stating his preference for President and saying a good word for Mr. Cleveland. The man to whom the letter was written was probably so flattered and proud that he could not keep it private. . . . The only mistake Minister West made was sending the letter to the wrong man. The matter . . . seems to me of little importance.[14]

On the morning of October 25, Sackville-West called at the Department of State to see Bayard. The Secretary immediately expressed to the

---

11. New York *Tribune*, October 24, 1888.
12. New York *Herald*, October 24, 1888.
13. *Ibid.*, October 25, 1888. 14. *Ibid.*

British Minister his "great surprise" that the letter to Mr. "Murchison" had been written even though it was supposed to be a private communication. Sackville-West then inquired whether Mr. Bayard, if he had been in a similar position, would have answered such a letter. The Secretary's reply was a clear-cut negative:

I answered that in his position I should not have dreamed of doing such a thing, especially as it was in relation to the domestic affairs of the Country to which he had been accredited as Minister. I said that I thought it exceedingly unfortunate that the correspondence had taken place; that I supposed he was aware of how the question of Irish relations to Great Britain was regarded in this country, and how obvious it was that they played an important part in our politics; that now the party led by Mr. Blaine was industriously engaged in fomenting the ill will of the Irish element in the United States against Great Britain.

After this introductory admonition, Bayard then pointed out to Sackville-West the serious imputations that had been made with reference to the sincerity of the President's stand in the matter of retaliatory legislation. It was unfortunate that the British Minister had implied that President Cleveland was not "entirely in earnest" with reference to "Canadian affairs." If such an idea were taken by the American public it would "necessarily cost Mr. Cleveland the respect of men who would think he was trifling with a very grave issue." [15]

After terminating this interview with Sackville-West, Bayard attended a long Cabinet meeting during which the "Murchison" correspondence was the chief topic discussed. At its conclusion, the Secretary gave to the press a statement which expressed the hope that the issues in the campaign of 1888 could be settled without any imputation

. . . of foreign interference or inter-meddling in our domestic affairs. The American people will be prompt to resent and repel as impertinent any such attempts, but they will easily recognize the political pitfall arranged by the California letter, with its object so plainly stamped upon its face. . . . Such petty schemes to break the fall of despairing politicians will be held in proper estimation by popular intelligence.[16]

When Bayard returned to the Department of State he found two notes from Sackville-West awaiting him. One stated that the New York *Herald* had been making inquiries in Los Angeles and had discovered that the "Murchison" letter was "fictitious & concocted by Harrison

15. *Memorandum* written by Bayard at 11 A. M., October 25, 1888, immediately after his conference with Sackville-West. *Bayard MS,* Library of Congress.
16. *Memorandum* of Cabinet decision, October 25, 1888, *Bayard MS.*

Gray Otis in conjunction with the New York Nat. Committee." [17] The second note merely expressed the view that the "whole affair" was a "trick" to make use of the British Minister in order to create political capital. Lord Sackville once more repeated his "disclaimer of any thought or intention of meddling in domestic politics." [18]

In his letter to the President enclosing this second note of October 25 from Sackville-West, Bayard criticized the British Minister for his "fatuity in general." That same evening, to a reporter from the New York *Herald*, he enlarged upon this theme and commented upon the ease with which "Lord Sackville allowed himself to be drawn into the snare. It would seem to me that he had lived in America long enough to imbibe at least a little of our Yankee smartness." [19]

In a cipher telegram to Phelps, the American Minister at London, Bayard gave official expression to the distaste of the American Government for the action of Sackville-West. In the Murchison letter, the British Minister had imputed a lack of sincerity in the President's stand with reference to Canada, and in "newspaper interviews since publication of letter Minister in defence of letter is reported to have greatly reflected upon motives of President and the Senate in their action" in this regard. The American Government could not "regard with indifference interference by foreign ministers in our domestic issues, and you will bring the matter to the attention of Lord Salisbury and say that this Government confidently relies upon disapproval of action of British Minister." [20]

Sackville-West himself remained unperturbed by the excitement that his letter to "Mr. Murchison" had aroused, and he gaily informed a correspondent for the New York *Times* that he had been "annoyed" by the incident but "only to a trifling extent." [21] To a correspondent of the New York *Herald* he was equally buoyant but more expansive. He thought it was absurd to say

. . . that the Minister of a foreign State resident in this country may not at proper times and in proper ways express himself in his private character touching the political affairs of the country. A rule or custom which should prescribe to a member of a foreign legation that he should not, in an individual capacity and in a manner free from influencing circumstances, express

17. Sackville-West to Bayard, October 25, 1888, *Bayard MS.*
18. Sackville-West to Bayard, October 25, 1888, *Cleveland MS.*
19. New York *Herald*, October 26, 1888.
20. Bayard to Phelps, October 25, 1888, *Bayard MS.*
21. New York *Times*, October 26, 1888.

himself as to any matter of fact or opinion concerning the politics of the country to which he is accredited, would create an intolerable position for those subject to such a rule or custom.[22]

When Sackville-West called to see Bayard on the morning of October 26, his high spirits must have been somewhat dampened. He opened the conversation with a question: "I hope you have no hard feelings and are not angry with me?" Bayard replied that he had "no personal feeling on this subject." He was still wondering, however, how Sackville-West could have been "led into so palpable an indiscretion." Moreover, the remarks that the British Minister made during an interview with a correspondent of the New York *Tribune* were "even worse" than the comments in the "Murchison" letter.

Sackville-West promptly fell back upon the excuse that he had been "entirely misrepresented" by the *Tribune* correspondent. Bayard then advised his lordship to read over the statements in the *Tribune,* and, if he chose, to write a private note to the Department of State explaining the circumstances surrounding this published interview. [23]

If Sackville-West had realized the intensity of the political storm that was about to break over his head, his jauntiness of spirit would have rapidly evaporated. The Irish element in New England was ready to launch a few thunderbolts at the head of the hapless British Minister, and in view of the political situation, it was not likely that Sackville-West would remain unscathed. On August 25 John Boyle O'Reilly, editor of the Boston *Pilot,* sent a terse telegram to the President: "British Minister's letter regarded as deep offense—his withdrawal ought to be the consequence." [24]

22. New York *Herald,* October 26, 1888.

23. *Memorandum* written by Bayard after a conference with Sackville-West, October 26, 1888, *Bayard MS.* In this interview with the correspondent of the New York *Tribune,* Sackville-West had remarked as follows: "I understand that both the action of the Senate and the President's letter of retaliation were for political effect. In a general election it is but natural that every point should be seized upon by both parties which would have an effect upon the voters. It is not at all likely that any trouble will result over this Fisheries matter." New York *Tribune,* October 24, 1888. On the afternoon of October 26, Sackville-West sent to Bayard the private note that was suggested in their conversation. In this note Lord Sackville made a "general denial of the accuracy of his alleged statements made not merely to the *Tribune* reporter, but to almost every other reporter who sought him out." Bayard to Phelps, October 26, 1888, *Bayard MS.*

24. John Boyle O'Reilly to President Cleveland, October 25, 1888, *Cleveland MS.* See also the letter to President Cleveland from Mr. J. D. Plunkett, October 26, 1888: "I must raise my voice against the continuance in power here of Lord Sackville. For more reasons than time would warrant here to mention, I am of the opinion that a demand for his recall is the proper thing to do—in this opinion I am supported by the intelligent Irish Citizens of America." *Cleveland MS.*

On the same afternoon, Charles Nordhoff, an influential newspaper man on the staff of the New York *Herald,* sent to Colonel Lamont, the President's secretary, a note of similar tenor: "If the President would ask by cable for the withdrawal of West, & let that be known, & co-incidentally & at the same time fire Mr. Bayard out & get himself an American Secretary of State, he would please a great multitude of his Democratic friends, of whom I am one." [25]

After receiving this telegram from Mr. Nordhoff, Colonel Lamont lost no time in talking over the situation with his friend, Mr. E. A. Moseley, of the Interstate Commerce Commission, who believed that drastic action should be taken at once. He was sure that no one was "nearer the Irish-American pulse than Mr. O'Reilly, and his words are very significant." He felt it in his "bones that if he [Lord Sackville] at least is not figuratively 'kicked' out of Washington it will be bad business for us." He had shown O'Reilly's telegram to Commissioner Bragg who thought that Sackville-West should be recalled at once, and Commissioner Schoonmaker was explosive in his comments upon the British Minister: "If his [Lord Sackville's] backsides are kicked out at once without any delay it will counteract the trouble. If not, things will grow worse." [26]

Under the impact of all this correspondence of so vehement a nature, President Cleveland drafted a short note to Bayard. He was

. . . very much concerned about this matter and almost feel that if this stupid thing does not greatly endanger or wreck our prospects, it will only be because this wretched marplot is recalled. John Boyle O'Reilly of the Boston *Pilot* who is doing good work will falter or worse if this is not done and I am afraid it is too much just what the enemy wants to have him remain here.[27]

25. Charles Nordhoff to Colonel Daniel S. Lamont, October 25, 1888, *Cleveland MS.*

26. E. A. Moseley to Colonel Daniel S. Lamont, October 26, 1888, *Cleveland MS.* Mr. Moseley had taken the trouble to send a telegram to Mr. O'Reilly with reference to Lord Sackville and had received an answering wire.

27. President Cleveland to Bayard, October 26, 1888, *Bayard MS.* At this same time (October 26) Bayard was receiving many letters asking for the immediate recall of Sackville-West. Mr. G. H. Schmidt, of Cincinnati, Ohio, was very much to the point: "Rendez les passe portes à l'ambassadeur Anglais ou nous serons perdus. "*Bayard MS.* Mr. Samuel D. Farling was of the same opinion but more loquacious: "The effect of Lord West's letter regarding President Cleveland, is most terribly destructive to Democratic interests in the coming election and unless something . . . is done . . . it is useless to look for re-election of our noble, true, and able leader. The effect on our Irish Democrats is such as to utterly destroy all hope for us." *Bayard MS.* After the Cabinet meeting on October 26, Bayard remarked to a correspondent of the New York *Herald* that it was almost inconceivable that "in the midst of a heated political canvass Mr. West should have so far forgotten himself as to write such a letter." New York *Herald,* October 27, 1888.

By the late afternoon of October 26 it was evident even to the blunted sensibilities of Sackville-West, that the situation had grown very serious. Calling at Bayard's residence, he inquired if the Department of State had requested his recall. The Secretary replied in a brief negative but gave no assurance for the future.[28] After receiving President Cleveland's note of that day it was apparent to Bayard that some action would have to be taken with reference both to the "Murchison" letter and to Sackville-West's subsequent interviews with newspaper correspondents. Although it was technically true that he had not asked for Sackville-West's recall, he had sent a cipher instruction to Phelps, at London, which suggested his Lordship's removal from Washington. In this instruction he had indicated that

. . . the British Minister has unquestionably impugned motives of President and Senate in relation to Canadian questions, and his usefulness here has ended. Public sentiment here strongly aroused, and no time should be lost in letting Lord Salisbury understand the necessity for immediate action.[29]

In a private letter to Phelps on October 26, Bayard repeated the sentiments of his cipher telegram. It was his opinion that Sackville had unquestionably

. . . made statements capable of no other interpretation than grave impugnment of the integrity and sincerity of the action of the President in his messages, and of the Senate in its action in relation to the Canadian questions. That he has been made the subject of a villainous trick is, I believe, true, but unfortunately other and far more important results are included in the possible effects of his amazing indiscretion and incredible folly. The President feels deeply this conduct of the British Minister and the sentiment of both political parties is in concurrence that his usefulness in this country has ended.[30]

Phelps reported back from London that Lord Salisbury was out of town and that the whole matter of Sackville-West's indiscretion would have to wait until his return.[31] This, of course, meant only a slight delay

28. *Memorandum* written by Bayard at 6:30 P. M., October 26, 1888, *Bayard MS.*

29. Bayard to Phelps, October 26, 1888, *Bayard MS.* Bayard's opinion with reference to Lord Sackville was probably confirmed by the following comments by Francis Wharton, Solicitor of the Department of State: "It seems to me that Lord S's usefulness is now utterly destroyed, & that his staying here can only do harm all around. Unless his govt. itself repudiates & recalls him, is it possible for us to keep him?" Wharton to Bayard, October 26, *Bayard MS.*

30. Bayard to Phelps, *Personal,* October 26, 1888, *Bayard MS.*

31. Phelps to Bayard, *Private,* October 26, 1888, *Bayard MS.* Phelps had an interview with Lord Salisbury, on October 27, 1888, and presented the substance of Bayard's instruction.

in the presentation of Bayard's instruction of October 26, and in Washington it was generally believed that Sackville-West's tenure as Minister was rapidly nearing an end.[32] This belief merged into conviction when it was learned that John Boyle O'Reilly and Congressman Patrick Collins had spent two hours with President Cleveland. According to Mr. O'Reilly, the President gave assurances that Sackville-West would be given his passports if he were not recalled by the British Government within three days.[33]

In the meantime, letters were pouring in upon President Cleveland and Bayard demanding the dismissal of Sackville-West. A. K. McClure advised the President to "knock out Lord Sackville with your biggest boot & best kick, and you've got 'em! *Hesitation is death.*"[34] Nelson J. Waterbury was positive in his opinion that a request should be made upon the British Government for the "immediate recall of Lord Sackville. Not an hour should be lost."[35] Leverett Saltonstall sent word to the President, through Secretary Endicott, that the Irish element in Massachusetts considered the "Murchison" letter as a "very serious matter." He regarded the whole matter as a "nasty business."[36]

Senator John T. Morgan was deeply disturbed about the Sackville incident, and he was very critical of the British Minister for writing the letter to Mr. "Murchison." He suspected that

Mr. West knew that his letter would be published and that it would handicap Mr. Cleveland in his race. He was informed, in the "Murchison" letter, that it was intended to use it in affecting the votes of Britons who had become citizens of the U. S., so he intended it for that use, whether it was printed, or not. He knew that his endorsement of Mr. Cleveland, however slight, would affect the campaign seriously, as it has, to our disadvantage. He deserves no compassion at our hands.[37]

Professor James C. Welling was equally sharp in his criticism of Sackville-West. To advise with a

. . . naturalized British subject, who asks to be *instructed* how he shall vote as a "true Englishman," is to transgress the plainest rules of diplomatic prudence and of national right. The secrecy of the correspondence on the

32. In the New York *World*, October 28, 1888, it was stated that the opinion was unanimous in the Department of State that "Lord Sackville will not long remain in Washington as British Minister."

33. New York *World*, October 28, 1888.

34. A. K. McClure to President Cleveland, October 27, 1888, *Cleveland MS.*

35. Nelson J. Waterbury to President Cleveland, October 27, 1888, *ibid.*

36. Leverett Saltonstall to William C. Endicott, October 27, 1888, *ibid.*

37. Senator John T. Morgan to Bayard, October 27, 1888, *Bayard MS.*

Minister's part, only intensifies the possible wrong that might result to the nation from such wrong-doing on his part. And the fact that the Minister did not *intend* all the mischief that has resulted from his procedure, is no palliation either for his conduct or its consequences. Such a blunder is worse than a crime.[38]

On Sunday afternoon, October 28, a correspondent for the New York *World* paid a visit to the President's countryseat at Oak View, and questioned the Chief Executive about his interview with John Boyle O'Reilly and Patrick Collins. The President was engagingly frank in his remarks concerning his alleged assurances to those gentlemen. He had informed them that they would have "no fault to find with what he had done and the future course to be pursued in the matter." Both of his visitors read into these remarks the meaning they most desired and the subject was "thereupon dropped." [39]

On that same Sunday afternoon, Phelps sent a cipher telegram to Bayard. He had discussed the Sackville incident with Lord Salisbury who thought that the "Murchison" letter was not by itself of sufficient importance to justify the *recall* of the British Minister. A "recall" would probably "terminate" Lord Sackville's diplomatic career. If he were "dismissed" by the American Government it might still be possible to appoint him to some other post. In view of this situation, Phelps believed that it would be best to "act upon the hint of Secretary of State for Foreign Affairs and terminate matters at once." [40]

The following morning (October 29) Phelps telegraphed to Bayard that "all the London papers this morning agree that British Minister must leave. You need not hesitate to act." [41]

In London it was hoped that Sackville-West would tender his resignation and thus put an end to an embarrassing situation,[42] but the British Minister still nursed some hopes of retaining his post at Wash-

38. James C. Welling to Bayard, October 27, 1888, *Bayard MS*. In a note of reply, Bayard expressed the view that "blunders are worse than crimes, and the line between the two is often shadowy." Bayard to J. C. Welling, October 29, 1888, *Bayard MS*.

39. New York *World*, October 29, 1888. In a letter to President Cleveland, October 28, 1888, John Livingston made some interesting remarks about the "Murchison" letter: "Having been one of the Lobby Counsel for Levi P. Morton, in both his Senatorial fights 1885 & 1887, at Albany, when he used his money freely to buy his way into the federal Senate, I am not quite sure that West may not have been subsidized *with money* to write that letter. It would be worth $10,000,000 to England and Canada to get Morton into the Vice-Presidency, with the Garfield precedent in view of filling the higher place." *Cleveland MS*.

40. Phelps to Bayard, October 28, 1888, *Bayard MS*.

41. Phelps to Bayard, October 29, 1888, *Bayard MS*.

42. New York *World*, October 29, 1888.

ington. On October 30 Bayard received a note from Sackville-West in which he "emphatically" denied the truth of the newspaper reports of comments he had made with reference to the "Murchison" letter. He had not "impugned" the action of the President in the matter of his message to Congress in connection with the Fisheries Treaty. He believed that his record in Washington had been "such as to preclude the possibility of my having used such language, but I must succumb I suppose to the consequences of having been made the victim of an infamous plot." [43]

Shortly after this note from Sackville-West had been received at the Department of State, a telegram came to the White House from Daniel W. Voorhees, of Indiana, to the effect that the American people would not " be satisfied" until Sackville-West had either been recalled or had "received his passports, and the more immediate such a conclusion is reached the safer and better it will be for the dignity, honor, and continuance of your administration." [44]

There was little need for all these telegrams and letters of advice. On October 29 Bayard had made a lengthy report to the President on the Sackville incident and raised the question whether the American Government, in keeping with its self-respect, could permit any "further intercourse to be held through the present British Minister at this capital." [45] This report was followed by a note to Sackville-West, October 30, 1888, in which he was informed that the President of the United States had become convinced "that it would be incompatible with the best interests, and detrimental to the good relations of both Governments that you should any longer hold your present official position in the United States." [46]

43. Lord Sackville to Bayard, October 29 (received at the Department of State at 3:25 P. M.), October 30, 1888, *Bayard MS.*

44. Daniel W. Voorhees to President Cleveland, October 30, 1888, *Cleveland MS.* Typical of the letters that the President received from friends and admirers with reference to the recall of Sackville-West is one that came from Mr. John H. James, October 30, 1888. Mr. James believed that it should not be "tolerated that in the crisis of a great Presidential election that the representative of a foreign power shall meddle in any way." A lady with the initials E. A. B. hoped that Mr. Cleveland would give Lord Sackville his passport "at once." Another hour might "prove fatal to your success. . . . I *know* and feel that I am right when I beseech you to dismiss the British Minister." *Cleveland MS.*

45. *Report* of Bayard to President Cleveland, October 29, 1888, *House Ex. Doc. 1, pt. 1,* 50 Cong., 2 sess., pp. 1671-1672.

46. Bayard to Lord Sackville, October 30, 1888, *Bayard MS.* In commenting upon Bayard's note to Lord Sackville, Samuel L. M. Barlow remarked: "The Sackville matter affords food for much reflection. If forty years in diplomacy have taught him nothing, he must be an ass ingrained. The Blaineites thought Mr. Cleveland's Burchard had been

In this official note to Sackville-West, Bayard enclosed a passport "in the customary form," and he assured his Lordship that all the "usual facilities" would be extended to him. In other words, his dismissal would be in strict accordance with the rules governing such actions.

Bayard also sent an instruction to Phelps, in London, informing him that Sackville-West had been advised that his "continuance in his present official position in the United States" was no "longer acceptable" to the American Government. It was necessary, therefore, that "another channel of intercourse between the two governments should be opened."[47]

The decision to send Sackville-West his passport and to inform him that his continuance in office was no longer acceptable to the American Government, was taken at a Cabinet meeting which lasted from eleven a.m. to one-thirty p.m. on October 30. According to the New York *World,* Bayard

. . . was the first to leave the Cabinet room, and as he ran down the main stairway, two steps at a time, there was a grim smile of determination upon his face. Walking rapidly across to the State Department he entered his private room and summoned his aides. After a consultation a draft was made of the report which had been submitted to the President, . . . and with this in his hand the Secretary revisited the White House. The President ran his eye over the report, made a few immaterial corrections, and the Secretary at once returned with it to the Department.[48]

Late in the afternoon of October 30, a statement was given by Secretary Bayard to the press concerning the dismissal of Sackville-West, and once more letters and telegrams came in abundance to the White House and to the Department of State commending this action.[49] On the following day, Bayard sent a long instruction to Phelps giving him the

---

found in Sackville. The result is that the vigorous action which you have taken, gives us help rather than harm. They may reflect, if they are given to such reflection, that they are likely to occupy the position of the man in the Primer:

'He digged a pit, he digged it deep,
He digged it for his brother.
And for his sin, he tumbled in
The pit he digged for t'other.'"

Barlow to Bayard, October 30, 1888, *Bayard MS.*
47. Bayard to Phelps, October 30, 1888, *Bayard MS.*
48. New York *World,* October 31, 1888.
49. The following telegram from Joseph F. Tobias to Bayard, October 31, 1888, is typical of this correspondence: "A thousand cheers for our American President. The old flag still floats triumphantly, even in this Republican stronghold [Philadelphia]. Every one has a smile on his countenance this morning." *Bayard MS.*

complete history of the Sackville incident. The actions of the British Minister were characterized as an

. . . unjustifiable abuse of his Lordship's position here as the accredited Envoy of a friendly power. His conduct was wholly inconsistent with prudent, delicate, and scrupulous abstention from intermeddling with the domestic affairs of the country by whom he had been so kindly and hospitably received.[50]

On the evening of October 31, Bayard made a speech in the Oratorio Hall, in Baltimore, Maryland, and he alluded in scathing terms to the Republican politicians who wished to gain a political advantage by endeavoring to foster the impression that President Cleveland was a tool of England. Bayard had an instinctive pity for an inept diplomat like Sackville-West, but he had nothing but contempt for the men who had made use of him in order to further their political ends:

There are political birds of prey that fatten and rejoice over the carcass of dead and exposed slanders and falsehoods. This country has been the witness, in the last week, of the interruption, for the time being only, of its relations with a foreign and a friendly Power. The act was not the act of the people of the United States, or of any one in sympathy with them. . . . It was the wretched plot of a despairing politician, or a conspiracy of despairing politicians, to bring discredit upon a class of our adopted citizens for the purpose of creating an unjust prejudice in the minds of another class of our adopted citizens. A slander upon the one and a foul attempt to mislead the other.[51]

Judge Allen G. Thurman minced no words in his castigation of Sackville-West. Bayard had purposely refrained from publicly criticizing the British Minister, but Judge Thurman showed little restraint in his comments. After referring to the "Murchison" letter, the Judge then remarked:

It would not require a man with as much brains as are in the skull of a jay bird to read that letter and know that it was a villainous fraud and deception. . . . But yet the British Minister fell into the trap. "How much did he get for it?" Well, that is a question that has been troubling me ever since it was published, and to save my life I cannot make up my mind whether the British Minister was more rascal or more fool.[52]

Frederic R. Coudert, a distinguished authority in International Law, also came to the defence of the Administration, but not in such

---

50. Bayard to Phelps, October 31, 1888, *Great Britain, Instructions,* vol. 28, MS Dept. of State.
51. New York *Herald,* November 1, 1888. 52. *Ibid.*

unrestrained language as that used by Judge Thurman. It seemed to Coudert that Sackville-West has "only himself to blame for the plight that he is in." There might be "some difference of opinion as to the manner of the dismissal," but Coudert was "not disposed to find fault with the administration because of it." [53]

Prominent Republicans were sharply critical of the Democratic Administration for the dismissal of Sackville-West. Hamilton Fish, who had been Secretary of State under President Grant, expressed the opinion that "Sackville tried to help the Democrats and failed, and now the President has turned upon him and kicked him out." [54] James G. Blaine thought that Bayard had placed himself in a very "peculiar position, because if there were a wicked conspiracy of leading Republicans to entrap Lord Sackville into writing an imprudent letter, these conspirators ought to have been punished, but instead of that he punishes Lord Sackville." [55] Senator John Sherman believed that the "trouble is that Mr. West simply told the truth. There is not a word in Mr. West's letter but what every man here knows to be true. . . . If I had been in their place I would have said Mr. West told the truth and we are standing by him through the whole, but they have given Sir Sackville the shake, and now all that remains for you to do is to give Mr. Cleveland the sack." [56]

In Canada, the Prime Minister, Sir John A. Macdonald, thought that "Lord Sackville's indiscretion" was "unfortunate to the last degree." [57] The Toronto *Globe* had little sympathy with the British Minister: "Though Lord Sackville is the victim of a despicable trick he is also the victim of his own folly. The United States Secretary of State argues with great force that the British Ambassador transgressed the amenities and the necessary rules of diplomacy." The Montreal *Herald* also agreed that the "British Minister's answer to the Pomona letter was not only indiscreet, but a blunder that could not be overlooked." [58]

The British press was far more caustic in its comments upon the Sackville incident. The London *Times* admitted that the letter to "Murchison" was an indiscretion that was "indisputable and indefensible," but it also thought that a British Minister might be forgiven if he were not familiar with "all the dirty tricks of American politicians." [59] In a later issue, the London *Times* adopted a more acid tone

53. *Ibid.*   54. N. Y. *Herald*, November 1, 1888.   55. *Ibid.*, November 1, 2, 1888.
56. *Ibid.*   57. *Ibid.*   58. Montreal *Herald*, November 1, 1888.
59. London *Times*, October 29, 1888.

towards America and its political practices. It was convinced that a "more ridiculous spectacle has rarely been witnessed in any civilized country than the flurried and unmannerly haste with which the Government of President Cleveland has endeavoured to put a slight on this country . . . before Her Majesty's ministers could deal, one way or the other, with the alleged indiscretion of the British representative at Washington." [60] The London *Daily Telegraph* confessed that it was too great a friend of America to "enjoy the spectacle of its Government being driven by an ignoble trick and by an election howl to heave good manners and great principles overboard, and for the sake of a handful of votes to adopt a course which in private life would be called by painful names." [61] The London *Standard* was certain that the British Government could not, "without loss of reputation, permit our ambassador at Washington to be expelled from the United States as though he had been guilty of some heinous crime." [62]

The attitude of Lord Salisbury towards the dismissal of Sackville-West is somewhat puzzling. He had discussed the matter with Phelps on October 27, and the American Minister received the impression that Lord Salisbury preferred to have the American Government *dismiss* Sackville-West rather than have the British Foreign Office *recall* him. If he were *recalled* he could not be appointed to another diplomatic post; if he were *dismissed* he would still be eligible for further diplomatic service. Phelps believed that it would be expedient to act upon this "hint" from Lord Salisbury and dismiss Sackville-West at once. [63]

After his interview with Phelps, Lord Salisbury wrote to Sackville-West and informed him that the American Government had presented a request for his recall from Washington. Phelps had not based his request

. . . on the letter which you had written to a resident in California, but on some expressions used subsequently in two interviews with newspaper reporters, which in the opinion of the United States Government, imputed discreditable motives to the President and the Senate. . . . I was glad to find there was no truth in the rumor that any diplomatic representation was to be made in regard to your private letter, which had become public only by a betrayal of confidence. It was, I said, hardly practicable to lay down the principle that a diplomatic representative was prohibited from express-

60. London *Times,* November 1, 1888.
61. London *Daily Telegraph,* November 1, 1888.
62. London *Standard,* November 2, 1888.
63. Phelps to Bayard, October 28, 1888, *Bayard MS.*

ing, even privately, any opinion on the events passing in the country to which he was accredited.

With respect to the language imputed to you in the interviews with newspaper reporters the case is different. You must be taken to have intended it for publication. But to recall you on a formal request from the Government of the United States, made under circumstances of considerable publicity, was a course which implied the censure of two Governments, and therefore before acceding to any such request Her Majesty's Government were bound . . . to satisfy themselves of the objectionable character of the language you had uttered. I accordingly begged Mr. Phelps to be good enough to give me a copy of the expressions imputed to you.[64]

This letter to Sackville-West was written a few hours after Lord Salisbury had talked the matter over with Phelps, and one would naturally suppose that he was capable of reproducing this conversation in an accurate manner. It is significant, however, that Phelps seems to have derived quite a different impression from this conversation of October 27. On the following day he cabled to Bayard that Lord Salisbury "thinks letter ['Murchison' letter] alone insufficient."[65] Nowhere in his cablegram does Phelps give the slightest intimation that he had emphasized the importance of the newspaper interviews as the chief reason for the displeasure of the American Government towards Sackville-West. It would appear that Phelps must have alluded to the indignation aroused in the United States through the publication of the "Murchison" letter.

There is little doubt that Phelps believed that Lord Salisbury would not take any too seriously the dismissal of Sackville-West by the American Government, and that is the reason why he assured Bayard that, from the English point of view, he "need not hesitate to act."[66] The question, therefore, that immediately arises is whether Phelps was an efficient interlocutor between Lord Salisbury and Bayard? Bayard, acting upon these intimations from Phelps, and also responding to pressure from the domestic situation in America, had sent to Sackville-West his letter of dismissal. Was this action in accordance with the real desires of Lord Salisbury, or had Phelps misunderstood the British Prime Minister?

We know now that Queen Victoria asked Lord Salisbury on Oc-

64. Lord Salisbury to Lord Sackville, October 27, 1888, enclosed in despatch from Phelps to Bayard, November 2, 1888, *Great Britain, Despatches*, vol. 159, MS Dept. of State. See also, London *Times*, November 7, 1888, and New York *Herald*, November 7, 1888.
65. Phelps to Bayard, October 28, 1888, *Bayard MS*.
66. Phelps to Bayard, October 29, 1888, *ibid.*

tober 28 what answer he would give to the request of the American Government for the recall of Sackville-West.[67] The reply from Lord Salisbury closely follows the language of his instruction to Sackville-West on the previous day:

> Late last night, Mr. Phelps . . . communicated to me a request for Lord Sackville's recall, not on the ground of his letter which was published, but on the ground of two speeches he made to newspaper reporters which in the opinion of the United States Government imputed discreditable motives to the President and Senate. I asked for a copy of the alleged speeches, as I had not seen them. Mr. Phelps had not seen them either, but promised to procure them. I deferred any answer to his request until we had seen the language imputed to the Minister.[68]

On October 30 Queen Victoria telegraphed to Lord Salisbury and expressed the hope that Lord Sackville would not "be allowed to say he is recalled." [69] Salisbury immediately answered that it was impossible

> . . . to say what ought to be done until we know the precise words to which the United States Government objects. It may be necessary to recall him; but Lord Salisbury has a great repugnance to taking that course on account of the peculiar circumstances. Probably it would in any case suffice for the present to give him leave. As Lord Salisbury has heard nothing from Mr. Phelps, the incriminating speech is probably coming by post.[70]

Two days later, Lord Salisbury sent a short note to the American Minister in which he rehearsed the viewpoint he had given in his letters to Sackville-West and to Queen Victoria. He had understood from Mr. Phelps that Sackville-West had given offence to the American Government through certain comments that had been published in the American press. Inasmuch as the newspapers containing these comments had not been received by the British Foreign Office, no action could be taken.[71]

Phelps promptly replied that he had not intended

> . . . to be understood as saying that the letter of Lord Sackville formed no part of the reasons of the United States Government for desiring his recall; though I did say that the principal reason was the published imputation by

67. Queen Victoria to Lord Salisbury, October 28, 1888, *The Letters of Queen Victoria* (ed. by George E. Buckle, London, 1930), third series, vol. 1, p. 444.
68. Lord Salisbury to Queen Victoria, October 28, 1888, *ibid.*, p. 444.
69. Queen Victoria to Lord Salisbury, October 30, 1888, *ibid.*, p. 444.
70. Lord Salisbury to Queen Victoria, October 30, 1888, *ibid.*, p. 445.
71. Lord Salisbury to Phelps, November 1, 1888, enclosed in a despatch from Phelps to Bayard, November 2, 1888, *Great Britain, Despatches*, vol. 159, MS Dept. of State.

Lord Sackville to the President and to the Senate of discreditable motives in their action touching the subject of the Canadian fisheries.[72]

It is apparent that Phelps felt that he was being pushed pretty hard by Lord Salisbury in this matter of the dismissal of Sackville-West, and he defended his conduct with vigor. In a letter to Bayard he discussed the Sackville-West incident, and expressed the view that there really could be but "one opinion about the inconceivable stupidity of Sackville." The American Government had a right, "even without giving reasons," to ask for the "withdrawal of an unacceptable Minister." Lord Salisbury had made a mistake "in hesitating" before taking any action, and because of this policy of delay, the American Government had a "valid ground" for the course it had taken in the matter.[73]

Once more the question arises as to whether Lord Salisbury would have *hesitated* if Phelps had made it clear to him that the American Government had taken offence not only at the comments of Sackville-West in the American press but also because of the indiscreet "Murchison" letter? It may be significant that Salisbury did not send a cablegram to Sackville-West on October 27, but instead merely sent his letter through the usual channels of communication. This meant that it could not be received in Washington before November 6, which was election day. Did he do this purposely in order to consume time and therefore compel the American Government to take action, or did he fail to take the matter seriously because Phelps had not sufficiently stressed its importance?

Of one thing we can be certain—Lord Salisbury was none too friendly to the American Government, and, at times, he was very willing to concert with Germany in an endeavor to curb American expansion. In August, 1887, he discussed with Count Herbert Bismarck the dangers that threatened both England and Germany in the Pacific as a result of the newly awakened American imperialism. Salisbury thought that both powers would have to "keep a sharp eye on American fingers," and he promised to support the German program in Samoa.[74]

This Anglo-German concert was an important factor in defeating Bayard's plans for working out a satisfactory arrangement whereby

72. Phelps to Lord Salisbury, November 2, 1888, enclosed in a despatch from Phelps to Bayard, November 2, 1888, *Great Britain, Despatches,* vol. 159, MS Dept. of State.

73. Phelps to Bayard, *Private and Confidential,* November 10, 1888, *Bayard MS.*

74. *Memorandum* by Count Herbert Bismarck, August 24, 1887, E. T. S. Dugdale, *German Diplomatic Documents, 1871–1914,* vol. 1, pp. 244-245; *Die Grosse Politik,* vol. 4, pp. 175-177.

the Samoan natives could advance towards self-government with the assistance of friendly foreign tutelage. Bismarck was most favorably impressed with this exercise in co-operative endeavor, and he tried to persuade the British Government to enter into a treaty of alliance with Germany in order to insure protection against American aggression. If England had been allied with Germany, the United States would never have been so bold as to dismiss Sackville-West:

America's demeanor towards England would be more cautious than it was on the Canadian and Sackville questions, if the Americans had to anticipate that they would have to face a break with England in isolation, and without the material or moral assistance of France. The only practical means to prevent America from counting on France in a quarrel with England, is the certainty that France would not be able to undertake an attack on England without being attacked herself by a German army of over a million men. America will not be inclined to give expression by war to the chauvinistic tendencies of her future Government and her former unfriendliness towards England, unless French support is at some time assured to her. British foreign policy will enjoy freedom of movement in all directions, if only she is fully protected from the French war-danger by alliances.[75]

Although the British Government did not accept this German offer of an alliance, Lord Salisbury clearly understood the advantages that could be derived from working in concert with Germany. He had no desire to break these friendly ties which had brought certain benefits to both powers. It is also likely that he gave careful consideration to the possible dangers of a Franco-American concert against England, and the very fact that Bismarck pointedly alluded to the Sackville-West dismissal, is strong evidence that European diplomats were viewing that incident in a much graver light than the American Government suspected. At any rate, Lord Salisbury was distinctly displeased at the action taken by Bayard, and the British press began to reflect the attitude of the Prime Minister.[76]

75. Prince Bismarck to Count Hatzfeldt, January 11, 1889, E. T. S. Dugdale, *German Diplomatic Documents, 1871–1914*, vol. 1, pp. 370-371; *Die Grosse Politik*, vol. 4, pp. 400-403.

76. The attitude of Lord Salisbury towards the United States with reference to the Sackville-West incident is probably well expressed in the biography of Lord Salisbury by his daughter, Lady Gwendolen Cecil. In discussing this incident she remarks: "In November, its Government [the American Government] . . . dismissed Sir Lionel Sackville-West, the British Minister, from Washington with the most summary brutality and without any consultation with his own Government, on the ground of his having interfered in American domestic politics." *Life of Robert, Marquis of Salisbury*, vol. 4, p. 116.

Bismarck regarded the entente between England and Germany as an intimate one

The London *Times* expressed the view that the American Government had shown no real desire to clarify the situation. Lord Salisbury had requested copies of the interviews that Sackville-West had given to the American press, but no effective action had been taken in this regard. It would have been quite simple for the American Department of State to make use of the international cable and thus supply Lord Salisbury with all the information that he needed.[77]

The London *Standard* was certain that the Sackville incident clearly showed that the American Government was in such a great hurry to effect an "electioneering coup" that it failed to "observe the ordinary decencies of international intercourse."[78]

The tone of the British press was deeply disturbing to Phelps. On November 17 he wrote to Bayard that he did not "know yet what the result" would be with regard to the Sackville incident. He had little doubt, however, that "if Her Majesty's Government conclude to establish diplomatic relations, not with the United States but with the Republican party, they will in my opinion make a grave mistake.[79] In order to forestall any such contingency, Phelps had a long talk with Lord Randolph Churchill, with whom he felt that he could talk very freely. He laid before his lordship

. . . the situation of the case as it stood in Washington and pointed out how just & unavoidable was the action of the President and of yourself. I assured him we should not recede a hair's breadth. And that if after a reasonable delay, if a new Minister was not appointed, it should feel bound to ask Lord Salisbury what the intentions of the Government were as to sending one. And should his reply indicate any indisposition to do so, the U. S. Legation here would be at once withdrawn. I showed him also the attitude of the Republican party toward England, and the course of Blaine, the future Sec. of State, and made clear to him what would be the result of Great Britain establishing diplomatic relations not with the United States but with the Republican party, and its affiliations whose capital has been hostility to England, who have rejected the Fishery treaty, entrapped the British Minister & denounced the President all over the country because he did not instantly dismiss Sackville without any communication with his Government. I showed him also the many fissures now being made in the good understanding between the two countries, and how important it is not

with definite political implications: "As long as Bismarck remained in office, . . . an American-German conflict was considered in Berlin as involving also an American-English conflict." Alfred Vagts, *Deutschland und die Vereinigten Staaten in der Weltpolitik*, p. 669.

77. London *Times*, November 7, 1888.
78. London *Standard*, November 7, 1888.
79. Phelps to Bayard, *Private*, November 17, 1888, *Bayard MS*.

to add to or enlarge them. Much of this was new to Lord Randolph. . . .
He promised to do what he could with the government, and if necessary to
take ground in the matter in the House of Commons.[80]

Bayard's own view of the situation was expressed in his *private*
letter to Phelps, November 19, 1888. With reference to the "miserable
Sackville matter," he had no doubt that the Administration had "acted
properly," and would have been "justly subjected to condemnation" if
it had "acted otherwise." Sackville-West knew that the struggle of
Ireland against England for

. . . home rule or a separate government is the controlling question today
in the heart of every man of Irish birth or blood in the United States. He
knew that no man could be advocated by England without losing the vote
of every sympathizer with Ireland in the United States. He knew that
because I as Secretary of State, and you as the American Minister in London,
had maintained absolute reticence in the Irish questions, that we had been
made the target of defamation, detraction, and assault because of our
supposed want of sympathy with Irish demands upon the British Crown.
. . . He knew thoroughly the arguments and efforts made in this canvass to
obtain the Irish vote by alleging British sympathies of the President and his
administration. And so informed, he receives the letter of "Murchison" and
promptly answers in complete sympathy.

And now note that his first newspaper interview, justifying his letter and
impugning the sincerity of the President's action in relation to his message
suggesting Retaliation, and the Senate's action on the Fisheries Treaty, was
also with the New York *Tribune* correspondent. This was the leading paper
of the Republican party, whose columns had been filled for two years past
with daily denunciations of the Secretary of State for his alleged subserviency
to British control. . . . The plot worked to perfection and every conspirator
performed his part with timely precision. . . . In this combination the
British Minister was the *pivot* upon which all revolved.

Now, as to the part of Lord Salisbury, it is plain that your request for
Lord Sackville's recall should have induced him to telegraph the fact to
his Envoy, and let him apply to be withdrawn, or resign, or get himself out
of the way in some efficient mode. But it appears he wrote him by the usual
mail on October 27th, and if the letter left the next day it could not reach
Washington until the day of the election, November 6th. This delay would
have destroyed any attempted remedy of the evil which Lord Sackville had
brought upon the American people by his deliberate interference with their
most sacred and vital affairs.[81]

On November 20 Bayard sent to Phelps some copies of the American newspapers which contained the interviews between Sackville-West

80. Phelps to Bayard, *Private*, November 21, 1888, *Bayard MS.*
81. Bayard to Phelps, *Personal*, November 19, 1888, *Bayard MS.*

and the correspondents of the New York *Tribune,* the New York *Herald,* and the Washington *Post.*[82] As soon as these had arrived in London, Phelps sent them to the Foreign Office with an accompanying letter which reviewed the Sackville incident. The American Government had no choice but to regard Sackville-West's action as "an interference in the political discussions of the United States." In the United States it was generally held that

. . . the acceptance or retention of a Minister was a question solely to be determined, whether with or without the assignment of reasons, by the Government to which he was accredited. And the Government of the United States was not therefore prepared for your Lordship's intimation, that particulars of the language complained of should be furnished, and that the action of Her Majesty's Government in respect to withdrawing the Minister would await the reception of it, and the hearing accorded to the Minister in regard to it.[83]

On this same day (December 4), Phelps sent a *private* letter to Bayard in which he discussed his note to Lord Salisbury and its probable effects. He would do all that he could

. . . consistently with the dignity of our Government, to maintain relations. Perhaps I shall succeed. *But you must be quite prepared for a declaration by the British Government that they will not send a Minister to Washington until after the end of President Cleveland's term.* Should that announcement be made, of course we cannot retain a Minister here. And I shall at once ask for leave of absence in order to return.[84]

By a strange coincidence, Bayard wrote a *personal* letter to Phelps on the very day that Phelps was finishing his *private* note to the Secretary of State. It seemed to Bayard that Phelps had

82. Bayard to Phelps, November 20, 1888, *ibid.*
83. Phelps to the Marquis of Salisbury, December 4, 1888, enclosed in despatch of Phelps to Bayard, December 5, 1888, *Great Britain, Despatches,* vol. 160, MS Dept. of State.
84. Phelps to Bayard, *Private and Confidential,* December 4, 1888, *Bayard MS.* In an editorial in the London *Daily News,* November 27, 1888, there is strong support of the American position in the action taken against Lord Sackville. The First Lord of the Treasury, Mr. Gourley, had announced in the House of Commons (November 26) that the British Government did not intend to take any step "at present" towards filling the vacant post of British Minister at Washington. The *Daily News* regretted this decision on the part of Lord Salisbury and hoped that he might "reconsider it." Lord Sackville had been guilty "of an unpardonable indiscretion. The letter might have been forgiven. But the subsequent interview went beyond all bounds, and would have been tolerated by no European Government. . . . His recall was a matter of course, and ought not to have been resented. National dignity, as well as common sense, forbids the exhibition of a childish sulkiness. Lord Salisbury . . . can not put Lord Sackville in the right, because Lord Sackville is hopelessly in the wrong. Yet, unless he is waiting for the opportunity of a job, these suggestions seem to exhaust the possibility of accounting for a most unwise and unfortunate delay in doing the right thing."

. . . placed the English side of the Sackville case in a nut shell when you told Lord R. that the issue of the hour is whether H. M's. Gov't. will hold diplomatic relations with the Republican party or with the Gov't. of the U. S. . . . I am struck with Lord Salisbury's proposition to convey his views to Lord Sackville by mail—in such an emergency. Perhaps he had *method* in this, and adopted it for his own purposes. . . . After nearly four years of steady resistance to this wild anarchical appeal of Irish hatred and despair for hostile action against Great Britain, I think I am able to judge of the force of the Irish question in American politics, and equally to estimate the apparent want of knowledge of Lord Salisbury and his associates. . . .

I need not say to you that Lord Sackville's personal presence at any time was wholly without value for the purpose of international counsel or discretionary action. I can comprehend the social forces that prevail in England with an equal maleficence as the spoils system in the United States, and nothing but entrenched privilege could ever have sent or maintained such a person as Sackville in a position of so great importance, . . . It is scarcely credible that an intelligent man could find a cause of international offence in our action in sending away such a marplot as Sackville proved himself to be. The time will come soon, if it is not now, that our action will be admitted to be as truly for the interests of G. B. as for our own. . . . I hope there will be no necessity for your withdrawal.[85]

This hope on the part of Bayard was soon dashed by the receipt of a long despatch from Phelps in which he expressed the conviction that the British Government had no intention of appointing a successor to Sackville-West until after the close of President Cleveland's term of office. Under these circumstances he could not doubt that it would

. . . appear clear to the President and yourself, that it is due to the dignity of the Government of the United States, that its representative to this Court should be withdrawn at an early day. . . . I have therefore, respectfully to request that leave of absence for sixty days be granted to me, with liberty to return home.[86]

This determination on the part of Phelps to leave England must have been strengthened when he read over the long note that Lord Salisbury addressed to him on December 24. In this note the British

85. Bayard to Phelps, *Personal*, December 4, 1888, *Bayard MS*. On December 5, 1888, Bayard wrote a short letter to James B. Angell, in which he made the following comments upon the Sackville-West incident: "Our elder and rather pompous Brother John Bull does not like our becoming judges of what is necessary and proper for our own safety and dignity in deciding *who* shall reside among us as Diplomatic Agents. The devolution of Governmental power is accomplished in this Country by the processes of popular election, and for a foreign Minister to interfere with these processes, is absolutely impossible of admission." *Bayard Letter Book*, vol. 9, *Bayard MS*.

86. Phelps to Bayard, December 22, 1888, *Great Britain, Despatches*, vol. 160, MS Dept. of State.

Secretary for Foreign Affairs quoted several lines from Phelps's note of December 4: "It was believed that the acceptance or retention of a Minister was a question solely to be determined, either with or without the assignment of reasons, by the Government to which he was accredited." Lord Salisbury immediately challenged this statement and declared that the British Government could not "assent to the view of international usage which you have here laid down." While it was open to any government to terminate its diplomatic relations with any other state, or with any particular Minister of any other state, it had no claim "to demand that the other state shall make itself the instrument of that proceeding, or concur in it, unless that state is satisfied by reasons, duly produced, of the justice of the grounds on which the demand is made." After referring to certain precedents which appeared to throw some light upon this matter, Lord Salisbury concluded his note with some phrases that were bound to rankle in American minds:

It is sufficient under existing circumstances to say that there was nothing in Lord Sackville's conduct to justify so striking a departure from the circumspect and deliberate procedure by which in such cases it is the usage of friendly states to mark their consideration for each other. I will abstain from comment upon the considerations, not of an international character, to which you refer as having dictated the action of the President.[87]

To present-day students of Anglo-American relations this note of Lord Salisbury to Phelps must seem a striking example of the futility of certain types of diplomatic correspondence. There was little doubt that Sackville-West was an obvious misfit as a diplomat, and the British Government had shown surprising shortsightedness in sending to Washington a man whose incapacity for serious work was widely recognized. The American Government had shown unusual leniency in accepting as British Minister a man whose private life had been notoriously immoral, and whose illegitimate children attempted to carry on the social amenities that were required in the legation at Washington.[88] In America every possible courtesy had been shown to Sackville-West, and for that very reason his amazing indiscretion in the matter of the "Murchison" letter was more deeply resented than otherwise. If Lord Salisbury had been equal to the post of Secretary for Foreign Affairs, and if he had been really desirous of maintaining cordial relations

87. Lord Salisbury to Phelps, December 24, 1888, enclosed in the despatch from Phelps to Bayard, December 29, 1888, *Great Britain, Despatches*, vol. 160, MS Dept. of State.
88. Phelps to Bayard, December 28, 1888, *Bayard MS.*

between America and Great Britain, it would have been very simple for him to use the cable service between London and Washington for the purpose of learning as quickly as possible the real situation. It is true that he might have misunderstood the advice he received from Phelps, but he could have checked that counsel with the information which could have been elicited directly from the Department of State. He must have realized that Sackville-West's usefulness as British Minister in Washington was over in October, 1888, and if he had paid less attention to dubious precedents and had given more consideration to diplomatic realities, the Sackville incident would have been quickly settled.[89]

The last weeks that Phelps spent in London were none too pleasant, and there were many minor irritations that added to the general discomfort. On December 28 he sent a cipher telegram to Bayard in which he referred to certain statements in the Philadelphia *Press* which were reprinted in the London *Daily News.* One of these statements was to the effect that any suggestions made with regard to the withdrawal of Phelps from London should be considered as "the sheerest nonsense." Another statement was to the effect that "as far as the Department of State is concerned, it cares not a rap what England may or may not do." Phelps looked upon these statements as "gravely injurious" to his usefulness in London. Such language, "if not disavowed, will be taken by British Government as adopted by the Department, and will be extremely offensive."[90]

After receiving this telegram from Phelps, Bayard turned to Francis Wharton for advice. Wharton thought that it was unwise to pay any attention to the statements in the Philadelphia *Press,* and he expressed the view that it would be best "to telegraph to Mr. Phelps that the whole thing is below both his notice & ours."[91] Bayard's instinctive courtesy and his desire to meet the wishes of his friend Phelps, led him to "disavow" the expressions "attributed to the Philadelphia *Press,*" but he also adopted the suggestion of Francis Wharton and added the

89. As early as March 7, 1886 Bayard had complained to Phelps about the obvious inefficiency of Sackville-West, and he frankly stated that it was "difficult to transact any business requiring mutual confidence and fairness with the present representative of the British Government here. At least this is the impression he has made upon me, and upon those who assist me in the department." This fact was promptly placed by Phelps before Lord Rosebery who dodged the issue. See Phelps to Bayard, March 27, 1886, *Bayard MS.*
90. For a lurid account of the life of Lord Sackville, see V. Sackville-West, *Pepita* (N. Y., 1937). The account given in *Pepita* of the Sackville incident is without any value.
91. *Memorandum* by Francis Wharton, December 29, 1888, *Bayard MS.*

comment that he really regarded such statements as "unworthy of your notice or mine."[92] Phelps quickly replied that this telegram was "satisfactory and gratifying" and this little irritation to the American Minister at London was quickly allayed.[93]

In a *personal* letter to Phelps on the last day of the year 1888, Bayard sharply castigates Sackville-West's answer to the "Murchison" letter. It was widely known that *C. F. Murchison* was merely a fictitious name employed by

. . . a coterie of the Republican Managers in a scheme to defeat by slanderous misrepresentation the re-election of President Cleveland. To this end the letter to Lord Sackville was concocted and sent, and *his co-operation* became essential for the success of the plot. . . . For this act, and his attendant behaviors, the President asked his instant withdrawal by the Gov't. that had sent him, and finding that nothing but delay was intended, dismissed him (after a hint to that effect) from his official relations to this government. The fraudulent scheme of which the forged letter was the first feature, was thus utilized to its utmost capacity to control the Presidential election. . . . I confess to you my amazement at the dull sense of the British Government and their public press in failing to estimate the dishonor and discredit brought upon Great Britain by such an act of their Minister.[94]

In the meantime, Phelps was making plans to leave England as quickly as possible. His departure from London he regarded as necessary because of the attitude of the British Government. It had been clearly intimated by the Foreign Office that no successor to Sackville-West would be appointed during the continuance of President Cleveland's term of office:

This is . . . universally understood. For us to retain a Minister after that, is humiliating to the national dignity, and exposes us to the just derision of the world. On this subject there are not two opinions on this side of the Atlantic. It has been made known to me in a hundred ways that it is quite understood in all quarters that I cannot remain here under these circumstances. And my departure is universally expected. Farewell dinners & honours and expressions of regret are multiplied.

At this point Phelps' self-esteem came rushing to the front[95] and

92. Bayard to Phelps, December 29, 1888, *ibid.*
93. Phelps to Bayard, January 1, 1889, *ibid.*
94. Bayard to Phelps, December 31, 1888, *Bayard MS.* On January 11, 1889, Phelps telegraphed to Bayard that he heartily concurred "in views expressed in your private letter on December 31st. Hope you will give them full expression in reply to his lordship's note." *Bayard MS.*
95. In a personal letter to Bayard, July 16, 1886, Henry Watterson gives an adverse estimate of Phelps: "I don't like your man Phelps at all. He seems to me a shoppy little

he assures Bayard that "there have never been expressions of regret so hearty and so general upon the departure of any Minister from England" as were pouring in every day upon the American Legation in London. But despite this avalanche of courtesy that was almost overwhelming him, it was impossible to think of staying in London. Not only would it be inconsistent with the dignity of the American Government to do so, but it would also be very difficult for him to maintain his position as Minister on the slender financial resources that were left to him. His expenses had greatly impaired his small private fortune, and it would help him greatly if he could leave London and return to America at once, retaining, of course, his salary as Minister.[96]

When Phelps did not hear from the Department of State at once regarding his proposed leave of absence from London, he went ahead with his plans and engaged passage on a German steamer which left England on January 31. His private affairs in America required "imperative and immediate attention," and he could no longer delay his departure. This urgency, one suspects, definitely colored his eagerness to leave England and made him identify private and public interests. He assured Bayard that his return to America would

. . . have a very decided and salutary effect in stimulating the feeling already aroused in many quarters by Lord Salisbury's course. I hope you will reply to his note. He is altogether wrong in his laws as well as mistaken in his facts. And he is unwise in the course he has taken & in rebuke without any interruption of relations on our part. Meanwhile with the most marked courtesy to myself personally, he has broken off all official intercourse except necessary routine.[97]

Bayard, of course, was glad to accede to the request of Phelps for a leave of absence. But not content with that friendly gesture, Bayard, with characteristic generosity, offered to lend Phelps $5,000 which he could draw upon at once. He also promised to answer Lord Salisbury's note "in due time."[98]

This promise was fulfilled in the last official instruction that Bayard wrote to Phelps. In this state paper Bayard rehearsed the history of the Sackville incident and clearly indicated how the British Minister had

Yankee attorney, quite dizzy over an elevation for which he was unprepared and intoxicated with swelling and swelldom." *Bayard MS.*
96. Phelps to Bayard, *Private,* January 2, 1889, *Bayard MS.*
97. Phelps to Bayard, *Private,* January 9, 1889, *ibid.*
98. Bayard to Phelps, *Personal,* January 15, 1889, *ibid.* In a letter to Bayard, January 26, 1889, Phelps states that he has no "need to avail myself of your offer of pecuniary help, but feel it not the less gratefully than if I had." *Bayard MS.*

interfered in the Presidential election of November, 1888. In the preparation of this instruction, Bayard received assistance from two outstanding experts in the Department of State on questions of International
Law. Francis Wharton had submitted a memorandum which stated
that Lord Salisbury's

> . . . proposition that one sovereign is the sole arbiter of the question how
> far his envoy is entitled to interfere in another sovereign's political affairs is
> too absurd to be controverted except by its statement. In Gouverneur
> Morris's case, Washington did not pretend to consider whether Morris's
> performances in Paris were an interference in French politics—Washington's
> position was "It is enough for you to say so." The textbooks state that the
> dismissal of a Minister for misconduct is a matter of discretion of the
> sovereign dismissing. And a mere announcement of unacceptability is
> conclusive.[99]

John Bassett Moore who had been promoted to the office of Third
Assistant Secretary of State, also submitted a memorandum on the Sackville incident. This memorandum was in the form of a draft instruction
to Phelps. The following excerpts indicate its character:

> Deeply as it must be regretted that there should be occasion for the belief
> that the Minister's correspondence was disingenuously solicited, yet I am
> unable to perceive that its character is in any respect atoned for by his
> assumption that his letter would not be published. That it was to be used to
> influence our elections is patent, for in the "Murchison" letter it was dis-
> tinctly declared that the requested reply was to be so employed. . . . It
> cannot be supposed that if this fact were brought explicitly to the notice of
> Her Majesty's Government, they would find any excuse for their Minister's
> action in the circumstance that he did not suppose his letter would be used
> publicly.[100]

With the assistance of both Wharton and Moore, Secretary Bayard
prepared the instruction of January 30, 1889. After reciting details of
the Sackville incident, Bayard remarked:

> The present issue is not whether it is requisite that a Sovereign asking
> the recall of a foreign minister should give the reasons for the application,
> but whether, when, as in the present case, such recall has been asked on the
> ground of interference in the politics of the country to which he is accred-
> ited, the question of the culpability or degree of such interference is to be
> left not to the decision of the offended Sovereign, but to the determination
> of the Sovereign by whom the offending minister was accredited. It is not
> understood how the latter view can be held by Her Majesty's Government
> to be a principle of the law of nations, for it would be equivalent to saying

99. *Memorandum* of Francis Wharton, *undated, Bayard MS.*
100. *Memorandum* of John Bassett Moore, December 28, 1888, *ibid.*

that, by such law, that Government is entitled to determine how far it will interfere in the politics of foreign States, and what degree of interference by its Ministers in the internal affairs of such States it may see proper to sustain. It would be far better to suspend diplomatic relations entirely than to continue them on the basis of such a right of interference in the domestic politics of other States.

After a pertinent quotation from Calvo's treatise on *International Law*, Bayard concluded with the statement that it could not be "justly regarded as a cause of international offense to request the recall of an envoy whenever it is discovered that his conduct has been such as to unsettle the confidence of the receiving government." [101]

Francis Wharton thought that the instruction of January 30 was "excellent"; [102] Phelps regarded it as "conclusive," [103] while Bayard believed that he had "put Sackville in a condition of permanent rest." [104] He greatly underestimated Sackville-West's extraordinary ability to keep himself in the public eye even though the part he played excited nothing but ridicule. When Bayard was Ambassador to Great Britain, Sackville-West apparently believed that he could stir up trouble for the former American Secretary of State by publishing a full account of the "Murchison affair." His pamphlet was entitled, "My Mission to the United States, 1881–1889," and it was circulated in October, 1895.

It was a sorry affair which had the effect of convincing even the most obdurate Briton that Sackville-West belonged in the pages of *Punch*

101. Bayard to Phelps, January 30, 1889, *Great Britain, Instructions*, vol. 28, MS Dept. of State. On two previous occasions the American Government had dismissed British Ministers at Washington. In the case of Francis James Jackson, in November, 1809, the Secretary of State did not notify the British Government that its envoy was unacceptable, and then proceed to dismiss him. Robert Smith, the Secretary of State, sent a letter of dismissal to Jackson on November 4, and the British Government was later notified of this action. In the case of Mr. Crampton, the British Government was informed that the British Minister had outlived his usefulness in Washington, and when the Secretary for Foreign Affairs failed to take any action, the American Government sent to Crampton a letter of dismissal. See John Bassett Moore, *Digest of International Law*, vol. 4, pp. 511-548; Charles C. Tansill, "Robert Smith," in *American Secretaries of State and Their Diplomacy*, vol. 3 (N. Y. 1928), pp. 165ff; and Henry B. Learned, "William L. Marcy," *ibid.*, vol. 6, pp. 242ff.

102. Francis Wharton to Bayard, February 9, 1889, *Bayard MS.*
103. Phelps to Bayard, *Private*, February 15, 1889, *ibid.*
104. Bayard to David S. Hersey, March 1, 1889, *ibid.* It is pertinent to note that the same decoy trick that worked so well in the case of Lord Sackville, failed dismally in the case of another diplomat. In this same campaign of 1888, Mr. Matias Romero, the Minister to the United States from Mexico, received a letter from an unknown correspondent who asked his opinion about the political situation in the United States. Romero gave this inquisitive correspondent no satisfaction, and he reported the incident to Bayard. *Memorandum* of a conversation between Bayard and Romero, November 16, 1888, *Bayard MS.*

rather than in the diplomatic service. J. R. Roosevelt, the Secretary of the American Embassy in London, wrote a hurried letter to Bayard, who had left London for a brief vacation in the English countryside. Roosevelt was certain that Bayard would refuse to make any statement concerning Sackville-West's brochure, but Ballard Smith, of the New York *World* was anxious to get Bayard's reaction.[105]

Bayard assured Mr. Roosevelt that he regarded the publication of the pamphlet as an "unwise and disreputable" procedure which was entirely beneath his notice.[106] In answer to Ballard Smith's inquiry, Bayard replied that there was nothing to be said upon "an emanation so weak, discreditable, and self-condemnatory." [107]

In a letter to President Cleveland, Bayard gave an interesting review of the situation:

When that melancholy person, Lord Sackville, published his discreditable and incredibly foolish pamphlet, a general descent was made to induce me to come down to his level and assist in the sensational storm they were trying to raise. If you or I ever had any doubt of the wisdom and propriety of giving such a person his passports, a glance at his present pamphlet would relieve us. Nothing so weak, stupid, and mendacious was ever published. . . . You may find it difficult to believe, but the keeper of a dime museum on Broadway wrote to Sackville offering him a salary to exhibit himself daily to the public, and this application Sackville publishes. It has mortified his countrymen, and no reference to it has been made to me in conversation.[108]

It was doubtless true that in the case of Sackville-West, the old adage that a man who is his own lawyer has a fool for a client, was fully exemplified.

105. J. R. Roosevelt to Bayard, October 9, 1895, *Bayard MS.*
106. Bayard to J. R. Roosevelt, October 10, 1895, *ibid.*
107. Bayard to Ballard Smith, October 12, 1895, *ibid.*
108. Bayard to President Cleveland, October 24, 1895, *Bayard Letter Book,* vol. 3, *Bayard MS.* It is pertinent to call attention to the fact that it is extremely difficult to secure a copy of the pamphlet by Sackville-West. It is not available in the Library of Congress nor in the public libraries in the East. Fortunately, excerpts from it appeared in the newspapers of that day.

The Hawaiian Question

CHAPTER TWELVE

America Acquires a Naval Base in the Mid-Pacific

------- ·•◦◦•·· -------

WHILE BAYARD WAS ENDEAVORING TO QUIET THE STORM THAT WAS RAISED by Sackville-West's amazing indiscretions, he was also perfecting a program for the protection of American interests in the Pacific Ocean. It had long been apparent to him that the Hawaiian Islands would serve as an ideal location for a naval base that would confirm America's claim to dominance in the mid-Pacific. He never lost sight of the political aspects of American policy with reference to the Hawaiian Islands, and he laid the basis for their eventual annexation to the United States.

American contact with those islands was first established by fur traders who found a ready market for their pelts in the Chinese port of Canton. Hawaii was a convenient half-way house for weary voyagers from the northwest coast of America to the China Sea, and not only were the sickly crews restored to health in Hawaiian ports, but avaricious captains drove hard bargains for cargoes of sandalwood that brought high prices from eager Chinese customers.[1] When Captain George Vancouver, of the British Navy, visited the islands in 1792, he discovered that American traders had already penetrated to this Paradise of the Pacific. A decade later, Captain Amasa Delano, of Boston, spent some time in Hawaii with Yankee merchants who were growing rich in this far-flung American outpost.[2]

Vancouver readily recognized the importance of the Hawaiian

1. F. W. Howay, "Early Relations Between the Hawaiian Islands and the Northwest Coast," *Hawaii: Early Relations with England-Russia-France. Official Papers Read at the Captain Cook Sesquicentennial Celebration, Honolulu, August 17, 1928* (Honolulu, 1930), pp. 11-38.

2. Captain George Vancouver, *A Voyage of Discovery to the North Pacific Ocean, etc.,* (London, 1801, 6 vols.), vol. 1, pp. 378ff.; Captain Amasa Delano, *Narrative of Voyages and Travels* (Boston, 1818), pp. 387-408; Captain Richard J. Cleveland, *Narrative of Voyages and Commercial Enterprises* (Cambridge, 1842, 2 vols.), vol. 1, pp. 95-106.

Islands as a naval station for Great Britain in the vast expanse of the Pacific, and on February 25, 1794 he persuaded King Kamehameha I to place his kingdom under the protection of the British Crown.[3] The British Government took no steps to confirm this cession, and the matter lapsed through inaction. The same fate followed the attempts of certain Russians to bring the islands under the control of the Czar. Russian ships had visited the islands as early as 1804, and a decade later Alexander Baranov, the governor of the Russian-American Company, sent a vessel to Hawaii to purchase a cargo of supplies. When Baranov learned that this ship had been wrecked, he sent a German doctor in his employ, George A. Scheffer, to the Hawaiian Islands to recover the lost cargo and to acquire, if possible, some measure of control over at least one of the more important islands. Scheffer arrived at Kailua in December, 1815, and through his skill as a physician he soon won the favor of King Kamehameha. In the spring of 1816 he sailed to the island of Kauai, and on May 21, 1816, he secured from King Kaumualii a document whereby the island was placed under the Czar's protection. Angered by this unauthorized act of one of his vassals, King Kamehameha drove the Russians from the islands. When the Czar refused to intervene on behalf of the Russian-American Company this chapter of attempted Russian expansion in the Pacific came to an abrupt close.[4]

In 1819 American whalers began to visit the islands and it was not long before these rough seamen from Nantucket and the hard-fisted traders from Boston were busy debauching and despoiling the native Hawaiians.[5] As a counterbalance to these forces of evil, a band of New

3. George Vancouver, *A Voyage of Discovery*, etc., vol. 5, pp. 27-28, 47-53, 80-81, 88-97; W. D. Westervelt, "Kamehameha's Cession of the Island of Hawaii to Great Britain in 1794," *Papers of the Hawaiian Historical Society*, vol. 22, pp. 19-24.

4. W. D. Alexander, "The Proceedings of the Russians on Kauai, 1814–1816," *Papers of the Hawaiian Historical Society*, vol. 6, pp. 1-17; F. A. Golder, "Proposals for Russian Occupation of the Hawaiian Islands," *Hawaii: Early Relations with England-Russia-France*, etc., *Official Papers Read at the Captain Cook Sesquicentennial Celebration*, Honolulu, *August 17, 1928* (Honolulu, 1930), pp. 39-49; Anatole G. Mazour, "Doctor Yegor Scheffer: Dreamer of a Russian Empire in the Pacific," *Pacific Historical Review*, vol. 6, (March, 1937), pp. 15-20; Paul Gronski, "Les Russes aux iles Hawaii au debut du XIX* siècle," *Le Monde Slave*, vol. 4, no. 10, (October, 1928), pp. 21-39.

5. An interesting picture of American commercial interests in Hawaii in 1829 is given in a letter from John C. Jones, the American agent for commerce and seamen in Hawaii, to Captain W. B. Finch: "The commerce of the United States, which resorts to the Sandwich Islands, may be classed under five heads: First, Those vessels which trade direct from the United States to these islands, for sandalwood, and from hence to China and Manilla. . . . Second, Those vessels which are bound to the Northwest Coast on trading voyages, for furs, and touch here on their outward bound passage. . . . Third, Those vessels, which on their passage from Chili, Peru, Mexico, or California, to China, Manilla

England missionaries landed in Hawaii on April 4, 1820, and immediately undertook the onerous task of regenerating King Liholiho who had shamelessly paraded before the astonished eyes of the newcomers in the scanty attire of a feather wreath, a string of beads, and a loincloth.[6] This shocking disregard of the sartorial possibilities of Massachusetts manufactures made a deep impression upon the Boston missionaries who soon had the warm-blooded natives swathed in "two pairs of pantaloons over a thick woolen shirt, with tight boots and a thick coat or heavy overall."[7]

These stern men of God from Massachusetts strongly disapproved of the Hawaiian design for living with its emphasis upon color rather than sobriety, and they quickly introduced a regime which some Europeans regarded as an "iniquitous combination of the blue laws of Connecticut and the tyranny of a Turkish pasha."[8] Even the American consular agent called them the "bloodsuckers of the community" who had "much better be in their native country gaining their living by the sweat of their brow, than living like lords in this luxurious land, disturbing the minds of these children of Nature with the idea that they are to be eternally damned unless they think and act as they do."[9]

But these sharp criticisms overlooked the fact that the missionaries were perhaps the only foreigners whose entire interest was the welfare of the natives, and it was largely through their constant efforts that the Hawaiians were raised from barbarism to civilization. Secretary Bayard had a high regard for the work of the missionaries in Hawaii, and he expressed to H. A. P. Carter, the Hawaiian Minister at Washington, the belief that their "unselfish and untiring" labors had done "more to

or the East Indies, stop at these islands for refreshments, or repairs. . . . Fourth, Those vessels which are owned by Americans resident at these islands, and employed by them in trading to the Northwest Coast, to California, and Mexico. . . . Fifth, Those vessels which are employed in the whale fishery." C. S. Stewart, *Visit to the South Seas . . . during the years 1829 and 1830* (N. Y. 1831), vol. 2, pp. 213-219.

6. Samuel E. Morison, *The Maritime History of Massachusetts, 1783–1860* (Boston, 1921), pp. 261-262. In the early decades of the nineteenth century the usual costume of the native Hawaiians was limited to a "smile, a malo (girdle), and a cutaneous eruption." William F. Blackman, *The Making of Hawaii* (N. Y. 1899), p. 222.

7. Titus Coan, *Life in Hawaii* (N. Y. 1882), p. 259

8. Foster R. Dulles, *America in the Pacific* (N. Y. 1938), p. 143. See also Alexander Simpson, *The Sandwich Islands: Progress of Events* (London, 1843), p. 40.

9. S. E. Morison, "Boston Traders in Hawaiian Islands, 1789–1823," *Washington Historical Quarterly*, vol. 12, (1921), pp. 166-201. For the work of the American missionaries in Hawaii see Louis B. Wright and Mary I. Fry, *Puritans in the South Seas* (N. Y., 1936).

fit the inhabitants of the Pacific Islands groups for the establishment and enjoyment of civilization, than any other cause." [10]

American missionaries, traders and whalers [11] helped to build up an American interest in the Hawaiian Islands that could not be disregarded by the national government in Washington. On September 19, 1820, John C. Jones was appointed as "agent of the United States for commerce and seamen" at the port of Honolulu. Six years later, Captain Thomas Ap Catesby Jones, commanding the U.S.S. *Peacock,* paid a visit to Honolulu and signed on December 23, 1826, the first treaty negotiated by the Hawaiians with any foreign power. Although this treaty was never ratified by the American Government it nevertheless helped to guide the policy of the two countries.[12]

In 1829 Captain William B. Finch, U.S.S. *Vincennes,* called at the port of Honolulu and read to King Kamehameha II a letter which communicated the good wishes of the President of the United States. There had been some question as to whether citizens of the United States were bound by the laws of Hawaii. All doubts in this regard were banished by the President's declaration that American citizens who violated Hawaiian laws should be censured and punished.[13]

The relations between Great Britain and Hawaii did not follow such a friendly course. In 1836 Richard Charlton, the British Consul-General at Honolulu, was strongly of the opinion that the rights of certain British citizens had been violated by Hawaiian authorities. When Lord Edward Russell, in command of H.B.M.S. *Acteon,* arrived in Honolulu in the autumn of 1836, Charlton immediately filed a list of complaints. Russell not only compelled King Kamahameha to make prompt reparation for these alleged aggressions but he also pushed through a treaty (November 16, 1836) which gave ample protection to British commercial interests.[14]

10. Bayard to H. A. P. Carter, April 12, 1887, *Hawaii, Notes to,* vol. 1, MS Dept. of State.

11. According to John W. Foster, *American Diplomacy in the Orient,* pp. 104-105, the "number of vessels entered at the port of Honolulu for twenty years from 1824 was 2008, of which 1712 were whalers, and more than three-fourths of them were American. The business reached its culmination about 1845, when the local government reported that 497 whalers, manned by 14,905 sailors, refreshed in the ports of the island." See also F. R. Dulles, *America in the Pacific,* p. 145; and Walter S. Tower, *History of the American Whale Fishery* (Phila., 1907), pp. 58-65.

12. *Foreign Relations, 1894, Appendix II,* pp. 8, 35-36.

13. *Ibid.,* p. 8. See also Hiram Bingham, *A Residence of Twenty-One Years in the Hawaiian Islands* (Canandaigua, 1885), p. 353; James J. Jarves, *History of the Hawaiian or Sandwich Islands* (London, 1843), pp. 287, 379.

14. *Foreign Relations, 1894, Appendix II,* pp. 9, 37. Alexander Simpson, *The Sandwich Islands: Progress of Events since Their Discovery by Captain Cook,* pp. 20-22.

This incident was soon followed by French intervention in the islands. In July, 1827, a Catholic missionary party consisting of three priests, Fathers Alexis Bachelot, Abraham Armand, and Patrick Short, together with a choir brother and two lay brothers, landed at Honolulu.[15] In January, 1828, a Catholic chapel was opened for services and soon many of the natives were baptized by the priests. The Protestant missionaries in Hawaii were alarmed by the success of the Catholic clerics, and they inspired the Hawaiian authorities to expel the Catholic mission from the islands. Before this expulsion took place, the natives who had embraced Catholicism were subjected to various punishments to induce them to return to the Protestant persuasion. In April, 1837 Fathers Bachelot and Short returned to Honolulu where they were seized by the authorities and placed on a vessel for deportation. Before this could be carried out, a French warship, *La Venus,* arrived in port and Captain Petit-Thouars caused the two priests to be placed on shore under his protection. In November, 1837, further complications arose when two more priests appeared in Honolulu. Kamehameha III hastened to take action against them and an "Ordinance Rejecting the Catholic Religion" was issued. The French Government promptly sent order to Captain Laplace, commanding the frigate *L'Artemise,* to repair to Honolulu and show the Hawaiian king that it was not wise "to incur the wrath of France." [16]

Captain Laplace arrived in Hawaiian waters in July, 1839, and immediately demanded that the king sign a treaty in which freedom of worship for Catholics should be guaranteed; a site for a Catholic church should be offered, and $20,000 should be advanced as a token of good will. It happened that King Kamehameha was away on a visit when Captain Laplace presented his demands. In the face of an ultimatum from Laplace, the Hawaiian Prime Minister accepted the conditions that had been outlined, and on July 12, 1839, he signed, in the name of the king, a treaty which satisfied all the French demands with reference to full equality for the Catholic Church in the islands. Five days later (July 17, 1839), the Prime Minister signed a second treaty which gave adequate protection to French commercial interests, and which also included an article under whose terms French wines and

15. Ralph S. Kuykendall, *The Hawaiian Kingdom, 1778–1854* (Honolulu, 1938), pp. 139-147; G. V. Blue, "The Project for a French Settlement in the Hawaiian Islands, 1824–1842," *Pacific Historical Review,* vol. 2, pp. 85-99 (March, 1933); Father Reginald Yzendoorn, *History of the Catholic Mission in the Hawaiian Islands* (Honolulu, 1927).
16. R. S. Kuykendall, *The Hawaiian Kingdom, 1778–1854,* pp. 145-152, 163-165.

brandies were admitted upon payment of an import duty not exceeding five per cent.[17]

This successful show of force impressed the Hawaiian Government with the importance of securing recognition of the independence of the islands by Great Britain, France, and the United States. A commission consisting of Mr. William Richards, the missionary adviser to the king, and Timoteo Haalilio, a native chief, arrived in Washington in December, 1842. In a letter to Daniel Webster, Secretary of State, they referred to the treaty that had been concluded on December 23, 1826, between Hawaii and the United States. Although the treaty had never been ratified by the American Government, the King of Hawaii had governed himself by the regulations of that instrument "in all his intercourse with citizens of the United States." Because of the increasing complexity of the international relations of Hawaii, it was exceedingly important to have its independence "*formally* acknowledged by the civilized nations of the world." This should be freely granted by the American Government in view of the fact that the "amount of property belonging to their citizens, which is either landed at or enters the various harbors or roadsteads" of Hawaii, and is therefore dependent upon the protection of the Hawaiian Government, reaches an annual total of "from five to seven millions of dollars." [18]

In reply, Webster admitted that "just acknowledgments" were due to the Government and the inhabitants of the islands for "their numerous acts of hospitality to the citizens of the United States." The President was of the opinion that the Hawaiian Government was one that was "suited to the condition of the people, and resting on their own choice." For these reasons he believed that the interests of

. . . all the commercial nations require that that government should not be interfered with by foreign powers. . . . The United States . . . are more interested in the fate of the islands, and of their Government, than any other nation can be; and this consideration induces the President to be quite willing to declare, as the sense of the Government of the United States, that the Government of the Sandwich Islands ought to be respected; that no power ought either to take possession of the islands as a conquest, or for the purpose of colonization, and that no power ought to seek for any undue

17. *Foreign Relations, 1894, Appendix II*, pp. 9, 37-38. See also, Hiram Bingham, *A Residence of Twenty-One Years in the Hawaiian Island*, p. 536; James J. Jarves, *History of the Hawaiian or Sandwich Islands*, pp. 320ff.

18. William Richards and Timoteo Haalilio to Daniel Webster, December 14, 1842, *Hawaiian Legation, Notes from*, vol. 1, MS Dept. of State.

control over the existing Government, or any exclusive privileges or preferences in matters of commerce.[19]

This unequivocal declaration of America's interest in the Hawaiian Islands was probably the reason why the British Government refused to support the action of Lord George Paulet in taking Hawaii under British protection. The British Consul-General at Honolulu, Richard Charlton, became highly incensed at the attitude of the Hawaiian Government towards certain British claims. He laid his complaints before Lord George Paulet, commanding Her Majesty's ship *Carysfort*, and in February, 1843, this frigate sailed into Honolulu harbor and demanded reparation for alleged insults to the Consul-General and for injuries to British citizens. King Kamehameha III was at a loss to comply with the demands and yet retain Hawaiian independence so he decided to cede the islands to the British Crown in the hope that the British Government would not confirm the cession. He also addressed a letter to President Tyler in which a request was made to interpose "the high influence of the United States with the court of England to grant us an impartial hearing and procure us justice, to induce Her British Majesty to withdraw from the sovereignty of these islands and leave us as we have been—an independent government." [20]

When Lord Paulet accepted the cession of the islands and raised the British standard over the public buildings in Honolulu, a wave of indignation swept through American official circles. Secretary Legaré, in an instruction to Edward Everett, June 13, 1843, expressed the prevailing American view of this high-handed intervention in Hawaiian affairs:

> The subject . . . which for the moment excites more sensation in this country than any other, is the late seizure of the Sandwich Islands by a naval force of Her Britannic Majesty. A solemn protest against this most unexpected and . . . revolting usurpation, has been submitted to this Government by the unfortunate victim of the wrong done, the King of the Islands. I have read it with emotion, and I cannot bring myself to believe that . . . England can possibly sanction the conduct of Lord George Paulet.[21]

19. Daniel Webster to William Richards and Timoteo Haalilio, December 19, 1842, *Foreign Relations, 1894, Appendix II*, pp. 44-45.

20. William Hooper, Acting United States Commercial Agent, to Daniel Webster, March 7, 1843, Honolulu, *Consular Despatches*, vol. 1, MS Dept. of State; R. S. Kuykendall, *The Hawaiian Kingdom, 1778–1854*, pp. 206-226; J. F. B. Marshall, "An Unpublished Chapter of Hawaiian History," *Harper's Magazine*, vol. 67, pp. 511-520 (September, 1883).

21. Secretary H. S. Legaré to Edward Everett, June 13, 1843, *Great Britain, Instructions*, vol. 15, MS Dept. of State.

The British Government disavowed the action of Lord Paulet and on November 28, 1843, joined with the Government of France in a declaration which not only recognized the independence of the Hawaiian Islands but also gave assurances that no further move would be made to take possession of the islands.[22] After this conciliatory gesture, the British Government insisted upon the signature of a treaty which would place British subjects upon the same footing as French citizens. Kamehameha III readily responded to this pressure, and the treaty that was signed on February 12, 1844, provided that British merchandise should pay import duties not exceeding five per cent *ad valorem,* and it included an article to the effect that no British subject accused of any crime should be judged otherwise than by a jury composed of foreign residents proposed by the British consul.[23]

The American Government pursued a far more friendly course toward King Kamehameha III. In an instruction to Mr. Ten Eyck, the second American Commissioner to Hawaii, Secretary Buchanan remarked:

We ardently desire that the Hawaiian Islands may maintain their independence. It would be highly injurious to our interests if, tempted by their weakness, they should be seized by Great Britain or France; more especially so since our recent acquisitions from Mexico on the Pacific Ocean. . . . Having been the first to welcome the Hawaiian Islands into the community of nations, it is our true policy . . . to treat them with as much kindness and forbearance as may be consistent with the maintenance of our own just rights.[24]

On December 20, 1849, at Washington, a treaty was concluded between Hawaii and the United States which clearly expressed the benevolent attitude of the American Government. Unlike the French and British treaties with Hawaii, March 26, 1846, which provided that French or British citizens accused of crime should be tried by juries composed of native residents or of foreigners proposed by the French or British consuls,[25] the American treaty, by way of contrast, included a provision that American citizens were subject "always to the laws and statutes" of Hawaii. By this provision the spirit of the unratified treaty of December 23, 1826, was preserved.[26]

Before this treaty was signed, the situation in the islands was again

22. *Foreign Relations, 1894, Appendix II,* p. 64.   23. *Ibid.,* p. 65.
24. Secretary Buchanan to Mr. Ten Eyck, August 28, 1848, *Hawaii, Instructions,* vol. 2, MS Dept. of State.
25. *Foreign Relations, 1894, Appendix II,* pp. 68-69.   26. *Ibid.,* pp. 79-85.

disturbed by the armed intervention of a European power. On August 13, 1849, Rear Admiral de Tromelin arrived in the port of Honolulu in the French frigate *La Poursuivante*. Upon hearing a list of complaints made by the French consul, Admiral Tromelin, on August 22 made ten formal demands upon the Hawaiian Government and insisted that they be acceded to within three days. After receiving the refusal of King Kamehameha, Admiral Tromelin landed an armed force on August 25 which destroyed some public property and then returned on board ship. On August 28 the Admiral sailed from Honolulu carrying with him the quarrelsome French consul.[27]

In an instruction to William C. Rives, the American Minister to France, Secretary Clayton expressed the opinion that the action of Admiral Tromelin was "unnecessarily harsh." He then instructed Mr. Rives to intimate to the French Minister of Foreign Relations the fact that

. . . the situation of the Sandwich Islands, in respect to our possessions on the Pacific and the bonds commercial and of other descriptions between them and the United States, are such that we could never with indifference allow them to pass under the dominion or exclusive control of any other power.[28]

The French Government did not permit this significant intimation to deter it from renewing pressure upon King Kamehameha in the early months of 1851. As a result of these new demands the Hawaiian King signed a proclamation, March 10, 1851, placing the islands under the protection of the United States.[29] This cession was not accepted by the American Government, but Secretary Webster clearly indicated in an instruction to Mr. Severance, the American Commissioner to Hawaii, the unyielding determination of the United States to preserve Hawaiian independence:

. . . The Hawaiian Islands are ten times nearer to the United States than to any of the powers of Europe. Five-sixths of all their commercial intercourse is with the United States, and these considerations, together with others of a more general character, have fixed the course which the Government of the United States will pursue in regard to them. The annunciation of this policy will not surprise the governments of Europe, . . . and that policy is that

27. Ten Eyck to Commodore Jones, August 31, 1849, enclosed in despatch from Ten Eyck to Secretary Buchanan, September 3, 1849, *Hawaii, Despatches*, vol. 2, MS Dept. of State.

28. Secretary Clayton to W. C. Rives, July 5, 1850, *France, Instructions*, vol. 15, MS Dept. of State.

29. Mr. Severance to Secretary Webster, March 11, 12, 16, 17, 18, 20, and 21, 1851, *Hawaii, Despatches*, vol. 4, MS Dept. of State.

while the Government of the United States . . . scrupulously regards the independence of the Hawaiian Islands, it can never consent to see those islands taken possession of by either of the great commercial powers of Europe, nor can it consent that demands . . . inconsistent with a bona fide independence shall be enforced against that Government.[30]

After Secretary Webster left office his successors did not have the same "scrupulous regard" for the continued independence of the Hawaiian Islands. On December 16, 1853, Secretary William L. Marcy instructed the American Minister at Paris to ascertain the probable course of France "in case of an attempt on the part of the United States to add these islands to our territorial possessions by negotiation or other peaceable means." [31] After convincing himself that the French Government would take no effective action to prevent annexation, Marcy next instructed Mr. Gregg, at Honolulu, to negotiate a treaty of annexation with the Hawaiian King.[32]

Mr. Gregg hastened to comply with these instructions and soon a draft treaty was agreed upon. Two of the articles in this *projet* were not acceptable to Secretary Marcy—Article II, which provided that the Hawaiian Islands should be "incorporated into the American Union as a State," and Article VIII, which bound the American Government to pay annuities of $300,000 to "the King, the Queen, the Crown Prince, . . . the chiefs, and all other persons whom the King may wish to compensate or reward." [33]

While negotiations for an amended draft treaty were in progress, King Kamehameha III died, and inasmuch as his successor was not in favor of the proposed arrangement with the United States, the matter was allowed to drop.[34] Secretary Marcy was able, however, to negotiate

30. Secretary Webster to Luther Severance, July 14, 1851, *Hawaii, Instructions*, vol. 1, MS Dept. of State.

31. Secretary Marcy to John Mason, December 16, 1853, *France, Instructions*, vol. 15, MS Dept. of State.

32. Secretary Marcy to David L. Gregg, April 4, 1854, *Hawaii, Instructions*, vol. 2, MS Dept. of State.

33. David L. Gregg to Secretary Marcy, September 15, 1854, *Hawaii, Despatches*, vol. 5, MS Dept. of State.

34. David L. Gregg to Secretary Marcy, December 19, 29, 1854, *Hawaii, Despatches*, vol. 5, MS Dept. of State; R. S. Kuykendall, *The Hawaiian Kingdom, 1778–1854*, pp. 416-427; W. D. Alexander, "An Account of the Uncompleted Treaty of Annexation between the United States of America and the Hawaiian Kingdom, Negotiated in 1854," *House Ex. Doc.*, 47, 53 Cong., 2 sess., pp. 141-146. In an article, "Great Britain, the United States, and Hawaiian Independence, 1850–1855," *Pacific Historical Review*, vol. 4, (March 1935), pp. 15-24, Professor Richard W. Van Alstyne indicates the vigorous opposition of the British Government to American annexation of Hawaii. With reference to the defeat of Secretary Marcy's policy, he remarks: "The blasting of his hopes in Hawaii was only

with the Hawaiian Government a reciprocity treaty (July 10, 1855) which was rejected by the American Senate "largely on account of the opposition of Senators Benjamin and Slidell, of Louisiana, on the ground that this free sugar would injure the sugar-growing interest of the Southern States." [35]

Another reciprocity treaty with Hawaii was concluded in 1867, but it incurred the hostility of Senator Sumner, Chairman of the Senate Committee on Foreign Relations, and was rejected on June 1, 1870.[36] The economic situation in Hawaii compelled other attempts to negotiate some reciprocal arrangement with the United States. The American Civil War had ruined the whaling industry which had been an important source of wealth to the Hawaiian Islands. On February 10, 1873, Henry A. Pierce, the American Minister at Honolulu, informed Secretary Fish that the subject uppermost in Hawaiian minds was the need of some measure to "stop the decline of the Kingdom in its population, revenue, agricultural productions, and commerce." Public opinion in the islands seemed to regard reciprocity with the United States as the one panacea for these mounting economic difficulties.

As an important *quid pro quo* for American acceptance of a reciprocity treaty with Hawaii, the Hawaiian Government would be willing to permit the United States to establish a naval base at Pearl Harbor.[37] On May 8, 1873, Major-General J. M. Schofield submitted to the Secretary of War a detailed report [38] indicating the importance of Pearl Harbor from the viewpoint of the defence of American interests in the Pacific.[39]

equalled in its completeness by the ascendancy and confidence won by British diplomacy in the islands."

35. Chalfant Robinson, *A History of Two Reciprocity Treaties* (New Haven, 1904), pp. 112-113; O. E. Hooley, "Hawaiian Negotiation for Reciprocity, 1855–1857," *Pacific Historical Review*, vol. 7, (1938), p. 144.

36. *Senate Executive Journal*, vol. 17, pp. 465-466. See also John Patterson, "The United States and Hawaiian Reciprocity, 1867–1870," *Pacific Historical Review*, vol. 7, p. 25.

37. Henry A. Pierce to Secretary Fish, February 10, 1873, *Hawaii, Despatches*, vol. 15, MS Dept. of State.

38. Major-General J. M. Schofield and B. S. Alexander, "Report on Pearl Harbor, 1873," *American Historical Review*, vol. 30, 1925, pp. 561-565.

39. *Foreign Relations*, 1894, pp. 154-158. On March 8, 1873, William Copeland sent a telegram to Senator Bayard in which he asserted that the New York bankers, Seligman & Company, had just received a petition from important interests on the Pacific coast who were strongly opposed to any reciprocal arrangement with Hawaii. Any treaty with Hawaii that would permit the free importation of sugar from the islands would "destroy the most important industry of this [Pacific] coast & the east, the sugar refining business representing millions of dollars & giving employment to thousands of skilled workmen." Copeland to Bayard, March 8, 1873, *Bayard MS*.

On January 30, 1875, a reciprocity treaty between the Hawaiian Islands and the United States was signed at Washington, and although there was no mention of the cession to the United States of Pearl Harbor as a naval base, there was an agreement on the part of the Hawaiian King not to "lease or otherwise dispose of or create any lien upon any port, harbor, or other territory in his dominions, or grant any special privilege or rights of use therein, to any other power, state, or government." [40]

In a report of the Committee on Ways and Means of the House of Representatives, the majority frankly conceded that the main reason why the treaty should be ratified by the United States was on account of the danger of British absorption of the islands. This political factor was of outstanding importance in the eyes of American Congressmen, and there is little doubt that it was responsible for the ratification of the treaty.[41] Senator John T. Morgan, of Alabama, frankly confessed that the treaty had political implications:

The Hawaiian treaty was negotiated for the purpose of securing political control of those islands, making them industrially and commercially, a part of the United States, and preventing any other great power from acquiring a foothold there, which might be adverse to the welfare and safety of our Pacific coast in time of war.[42]

To the Hawaiian planters, the reciprocity treaty proved a tremendous boon which quickly brought them considerable wealth.[43] Far-seeing Americans, like Claus Spreckels, purchased Hawaiian plantations, and by 1883 the value of their investments reached a very respectable figure. In 1877 American imports of sugar from Hawaii amounted to only 30,642,081 pounds. Six years later (1883) these imports increased to 114,132,670 pounds. To the merchants of California, the rapid development of this Hawaiian trade was welcome news, and according to the San Francisco *Merchant,* October 10, 1884, the people of Hawaii were

. . . buying more merchandise of every description in California than any other country in the world, except the opulent and populous British Isles.

40. *Ibid.,* pp. 164-167.
41. J. Laurence Laughlin and H. Parker Willis, *Reciprocity* (N. Y. 1903), pp. 74-83; Chalfant Robinson, *A History of Two Reciprocity Treaties,* pp. 131-140.
42. Chalfant Robinson, *op. cit.,* p. 134.
43. In discussing the effect of reciprocity upon the Hawaiian planters, Professors J. L. Laughlin and H. P. Willis, in their monograph, *Reciprocity,* p. 93, speak of the large profits that were "paid to a little group of planters and producers very limited in number and utterly selfish in their attitude toward the whole question."

And were it not for the wheat export to the United Kingdom, the Hawaiian Islands would stand upon record as a better customer of California merchants even than Great Britain.[44]

The sugar planters of Louisiana were greatly worried over the rapid increase in sugar imports from the Hawaiian Islands, and as early as July 3, 1876, Representative R. L. Gibson wrote to Bayard that

. . . the People of Louisiana are very much opposed to the Hawaiian Treaty, especially those interested in Sugar and Rice. They believe the measure will create a smuggling depot, injure their credit and lower the price of these staples, with no compensations to the Country. If you have no convictions of duty they will feel grateful to you without regard to politics, for any effort you make to secure its defeat.[45]

On March 18, 1875, Bayard had voted in favor of the reciprocity treaty with Hawaii,[46] and despite the pleas of friends like Gibson, he continued to support the idea of intimate commercial connections with the islands. These economic ties would eventually lead to political bonds which would draw Hawaii into the American Union. In this regard, Bayard was in agreement with Blaine who had announced in 1881, in an instruction to Mr. Comly, that the American Government had always "avowed and now repeats that, under no circumstances, will it permit the transfer of the territory or sovereignty of these Islands to any of the great European powers." [47]

On June 9, 1884, President Arthur sent a special message to the Senate in which he requested the advice of that body with reference to negotiating with the Government of Hawaii for an extension of the reciprocity treaty for "a further definite period of seven years." [48] Ten days later (June 19) Senator Miller, of California, reported from the Committee on Foreign Relations, a resolution which not only advised the President to negotiate for an extension of the reciprocity treaty for

44. See also the San Francisco *Merchant,* October 24, 1884, and November 21, 1884.

45. R. L. Gibson to Bayard, July 3, 1876, *Bayard MS.* Bayard was impressed with the statistics quoted in the San Francisco newspapers, and even as late as September 4, 1888, he wrote a letter to General William F. Vilas, in which he made particular reference to the trade relations between the Pacific Coast and the Hawaiian Islands: "You will observe that no note is made of the merchandise so carried but only the profits of *carriage* and the results upon *unprotected* wages. The merchandise so imported gives employment to a vast number of workmen in San Francisco, besides cheapening the cost of living." *William F. Vilas Papers,* Wisconsin Historical Society.

46. *Journal of the Executive Proceedings of the Senate of the United States of America,* vol. 20 (Wash., 1901) , pp. 42-43.

47. Secretary Blaine to Mr. Comly, November 19, 1881, *Hawaii, Instructions,* vol. 2, MS Dept. of State.

48. *Senate Executive Journal,* vol. 24, p. 280.

a period of seven years but which also expressed the opinion that the Hawaiian Government should be requested to permit the establishment of a "naval station for the United States in the vicinity of Honolulu." [49] On a motion by Senator Morrill, the further consideration of the resolution was postponed until the first Monday in December, 1884.[50] On that date (December 2) the President sent to the Senate a supplementary convention extending the duration of the treaty of commercial reciprocity with the Hawaiian Islands.[51] Two days later, Senator Miller presented a memorial from the citizens of California setting forth the benefits that had resulted "from the operations of the reciprocity treaty with the Government of the Hawaiian Islands, and the reasons why reciprocal relations should be continued between the United States and Hawaii." [52] But despite this pressure from Pacific Coast interests, the supplementary convention with Hawaii was not agreed to by the Senate during the continuance of President Arthur's term of office.

While the Senate of the United States was trying to make up its mind with regard to reciprocity with Hawaii, the uncertainty of the situation was reflected in a general business depression throughout the islands.[53] Spurred on by this economic necessity, Mr. Carter, the Hawaiian Minister at Washington, wrote to Bayard and enclosed some statistics which indicated the benefits that had been derived by the citizens of California from the trade with the Hawaiian Islands.[54] Bayard was perfectly willing to recognize that certain economic advantages to American citizens had resulted from commerce with Hawaii, but he also had to take note of the sharp protests that came from certain quarters in America against the continuance of the treaty of 1875. One of the most vigorous opponents of reciprocity with Hawaii was Colonel William R. Morrison, of Illinois, an able and influential member of the Democratic Party. Mr. Morrison was certain that the volume of sugar imports from the Hawaiian Islands would be too small seriously to affect the price of sugar in the United States:

> The import of Sandwich Island sugar is only about one per cent of the consumption of the United States. It can never exceed five or six per cent of our consumption; besides, this being an article of such general consumption, the price will not be reduced. Sandwich Islands producers will, therefore,

49. *Ibid.,* p. 289.   50. *Ibid.,* p. 335.   51. *Ibid.,* p. 375.
52. *Ibid.,* December 11, 1884, p. 383.
53. R. M. Daggett to Secretary Frelinghuysen, January 14, 1885, *Hawaii, Despatches,* vol. 22, MS Dept. of State.
54. H. A. P. Carter to Bayard, December 9, 1884, *Bayard MS.*

always take the very highest prices in our market, and the American consumer can never be benefited by having the price of his sugar reduced by what they can send to him. Yet the government loses the revenue.

To increase the product of sugar on the Islands it is admitted there must be more labor. The only labor available is coolie or imported Chinese labor, which is little other than a form of slavery. Do we propose to tax ourselves to encourage this importation of Chinese into the Islands and strengthen this kind of servile labor?

There is no protection in this treaty, for there are no American interests to be protected. There is no free trade in it, for there is but little trade of any kind, and that is to be made exclusive for one side. There is no reciprocity in it, for much is given and nothing received.[55]

To Bayard, who had assumed the office of Secretary of State in March, 1885, the political factor was the most important one in this equation of Hawaiian-American relations, and this viewpoint is clearly expressed in a confidential note to Mr. Carter, the Hawaiian Minister:

We desire no domination in the Pacific for ourselves nor can we be expected to sanction a doctrine whereby any one among the Powers equally interested in trade and intercourse with those regions, might roam at will over the Pacific seas and absorb the jurisdiction of Islands, because unprotected or unadministered, thence to announce to other nations, whose rights are at least co-equal, the terms on which such islands may be visited or traded with.[56]

In a letter to William R. Morrison, Bayard emphasizes the importance of the political aspect of the Hawaiian situation:

I will not take time to discuss the commercial results of the treaty of January 30, 1875, because they are so infinitely unimportant in comparison with the political interests involved. The competition between the great combination of Refiners of Sugar on the Atlantic seaboard and their rivals on the Pacific Coast is sharp, but the result is to cheapen their product to the U. S. Consumers. I will not deny the obvious selfishness which has controlled the importation of Sugars from the Hawaiian group into California, nor on the other hand do I stop to discuss the arguments and influence of the Protectionist party in the U. S. to prevent freedom of exchanges in this and every other case. But I will draw your attention to *Article 4* of the treaty of 1875 and to that particular clause which binds the Hawaiian government "*not to lease or otherwise dispose of,* or to create any lien upon any port, harbor or other territory in their dominions, *or grant any special privilege or rights of use therein to any other power, state, or government, etc."*

55. J. L. Laughlin and H. P. Willis, *Reciprocity*, pp. 79-82.
56. Bayard to H. A. P. Carter, November 11, 1885, *Hawaiian Legation, Notes to*, vol. 1, MS Dept. of State.

Thus you will perceive how the exclusive commercial privileges exchanged in the treaty, expand themselves into political results of a most important character. The Sandwich Islands are but five days sail from San Francisco, and with swift vessels, the transit will be shortened. . . .

The vast importance, and our close and manifest interest in the commerce of the Pacific Ocean upon which we now hold the most important seaboard, renders the Hawaiian group of essential importance to us on every score, and as a member of the political organization now charged with the administration of our National affairs and interests, I trust you will not allow a commercial question to outweigh political considerations so important as I believe the control of these contiguous Islands on our Pacific Coast to be now, and still more so to be in the near future.[57]

Morrison was not convinced by Bayard's reasoning. From the commercial standpoint the treaty was all

. . . one-sided nor has it resulted in cheaper sugar to the consumer. . . . If we look from the political or international [standpoint] we shall hardly find ourselves justified in incurring a loss of two or more millions per annum for the privilege of landing at the Islands which every other nation may do for nothing. . . . If we have any political rights in the Pacific they should be ours without hiring or paying for them.[58]

Morrison was in touch with John E. Searles, a New York merchant who had recently been sent by the Treasury Department to the Hawaiian Islands to investigate trade conditions. Searles was strongly opposed to the continuance of the reciprocity treaty with Hawaii, and it is not surprising that he was warmly recommended to Bayard by Senators R. L. Gibson,[59] of Louisiana, and Nelson W. Aldrich,[60] of Rhode Island. Gibson and Aldrich were closely allied through economic interests, and they were bitterly opposed to any arrangement whereby California refiners were permitted to make profits out of Hawaiian sugar.

Searles assured Bayard that the better class of Americans were leaving Hawaii as rapidly as they could

. . . divest themselves of property there and the Americans who go there are as a rule not a class of whom we may be proud nor whose loss we need mourn. This condition of things results in giving to foreigners a large bounty from the Treasury of the United States without any adequate compensation

57. Bayard to William M. Morrison, March 16, 1886, *Bayard Letter Book*, vol. 2, *Bayard MS.*
58. Morrison to Bayard, March 16, 1886, *Bayard MS.*
59. R. L. Gibson to Bayard, March 18, 1886, *Bayard MS.*
60. N. W. Aldrich to Bayard, March 18, 1886, *ibid.*

commercially or *politically*. . . . Under existing conditions it is impossible that our people will increase their influence in the affairs of the Islands.[61]

In answer to these criticisms by Searles and Brown, H. A. P. Carter, the Hawaiian Minister in Washington, wrote to Bayard a long letter in which the advantages of American trade with Hawaii were indicated in great detail. Carter first pointed out that

. . . the effect of the Treaty was to open to American enterprise and capital a virgin field of operation. . . . The result has certainly justified the wisdom of the Treaty. The Hawaiian consumer is today the largest consumer per capita of American products of any community outside the limits of the United States. . . . Careful estimates made a year ago in San Francisco, placed the amount of the current loans and advances made by the merchants and bankers of San Francisco at three and a half million. . . . I have chosen to reduce this amount to three million, as it may be that part of the indebtedness has been paid. These amounts are carefully estimated and I believe the statement is a fair and complete statement.

It shows a balance in favor of the United States of over thirty millions during the operation of the Treaty, after paying liberal wages to the working classes in Hawaii, and adding to her material and permanent prosperity. I think that it shows that by investing in a trade essentially natural in its conditions, . . . an amount of twenty three millions in a great variety of articles . . . and eleven millions in coin and exchange, your citizens have withdrawn from Hawaii over fifty millions in articles of necessity to this country, and have acquired vested interests profitable and safe, in Hawaii, to the amount of over fifteen millions more.

The contribution of the United States has been mostly in surplus production, and . . . complaint is made that two dollars of Hawaiian products have been received for one of United States. It is not my intention to convey the idea that this balance is all profit. It has gone largely . . . into the payment of American merchants, factors, mariners, vessels, and other carriers, insurers, bankers, and other money lenders.

. . . If it be objected to the Treaty, that its benefits are limited to one section of the country, I would point out that a good proportion of the imports into Hawaii from the United States are of articles manufactured in the Eastern States.[62]

61. John E. Searles to Bayard, March 23, 1886, *ibid*. In his letter to Bayard, Searles enclosed a copy of a letter from H. A. Brown, of Saxonville, Massachusetts, to Representative William R. Morrison. In this letter to Morrison, Brown makes a sharp attack on the reciprocity treaty and charges that in the fiscal year ending June 30, 1885, the loss in duty on Hawaiian sugar amounted to $4,918,886. Searles himself reported that "since the treaty went into operation, nine years ago, the Custom House has noted the exportation to those islands of American goods to the value of $22,870,000, and has remitted duties amounting to $22,808,000. In other words, if it had made the islands a present of every dollar's worth of goods they bought from this country, and collected duties on their sugars, we should have made no loss."

62. H. A. P. Carter to Bayard, March 22, 1886, *Bayard MS*. On April 21, 1886, William

While this argument about the commercial advantages of a reciprocity treaty with Hawaii was being waged with increasing bitterness, the Senate Committee on Foreign Relations, on April 14, 1886, made a favorable report on the supplementary treaty of December 6, 1884.[63] The committee also suggested an important amendment which would give the United States the right to establish and maintain a naval station at Pearl Harbor, in the island of Oahu.

Although the report of the Senate Committee on Foreign Relations was submitted in executive session, the New York *Tribune* was able to secure a copy of the amended treaty which it published in full on May 6, 1886. In a statement which accompanied the text of the treaty, mention was made of the efforts of the Hawaiian Government to persuade the Cleveland Administration to ratify the treaty without the Pearl Harbor concession. Bayard was reported to be in favor of the amended treaty.[64]

It was soon apparent that the representatives of the New York *Tribune* were in closer touch with the members of the Senate Committee on Foreign Relations than Bayard was. Although Senator Morgan, a Democrat, submitted the amendment with reference to Pearl Harbor, he refrained from acquainting Bayard with the details of his action, and the State Department did not know the exact text of the amended treaty until it was published in the New York *Tribune* on May 6.[65]

On May 7, Mr. Carter, the Hawaiian Minister, called at the Department of State to see Bayard, and the following memorandum gives the gist of their conversation:

N. Armstrong, formerly the Attorney General of the Hawaiian Kingdom, wrote to Bayard to suggest the passage of a law under the terms of which only those Hawaiian articles of commerce which are the actual products of American labor, machinery, and capital should be admitted free of duty. *Bayard MS.*

63. *Senate Executive Journal*, vol. 25, p. 419.

64. New York *Tribune*, May 6, 1886.

65. The lack of intimate communication between Bayard and the Senate Committee on Foreign Relations was certainly not due to any desire on the part of Bayard to run things his own way. On January 16, 1886, Bayard wrote to Senator J. F. Miller, Chairman of the Senate Committee on Foreign Relations, with special reference to the Hawaiian situation: "I observe you are not able to go to your Committee room and that Mr. Edmunds is 'acting chairman' in your absence. There are some interesting matters in which I should like to take counsel with the Committee and to discuss severally with you and Mr. Edmunds and your associates. The growing importance of our Pacific Ocean commerce and the group of Islands which seems just now to be in great demand with some of our Commercial rivals, makes it more than ever of consequence that a steady and well considered line of policy should be entered upon." *Bayard Letter Book*, vol. 2, *Bayard MS.*

Mr. Carter, the Hawaiian Minister, came at 11 o'clock (May 7, 1886) to see me in respect to the publication in the New York *Tribune* of yesterday (May 6) . . . and the statement of my favoring the annexation or lease of Pearl Harbor. . . . I told him that neither in manuscript nor in print had I ever read or seen the proposition published as the treaty with the Sandwich Islands containing the provision relating to Pearl Harbor.

I told him that I had no knowledge that any such paper had ever been signed by himself or Mr. Frelinghuysen. He told me that it had not.

I said that I had been waited on yesterday afternoon by the Agent of a New York paper, who had first showed me this extract from the *Tribune,* and asked me about it; that I naturally and at once, declined to discuss the subject with him, merely saying that treaties were submitted to the Senate by the executive in *confidence,* and that no one had a right to disclose any portion of them. . . .

Mr. Carter then told me in confidence, that when Mr. Edmunds came back from California, he was inspired with the idea of acquiring Pearl Harbor; and that Gen. Miller, the Chairman of the Committee on Foreign Relations, had told this to him (Mr. Carter), and that there was, as Mr. Edmunds thought, a strong feeling in California in favor of the cession of Pearl Harbor to the United States, but that he had understood that the proposition had not been sustained in the Committee on Foreign Relations, Mr. Edmunds being almost alone in favor of it; but that lately, since the finishing of the British railroad to Vancouver's Island, and the alleged subsidy of a line of British steamships coincident with the German aggressions in the South Pacific, that the necessity of the United States owning Pearl Harbor had been ardently proposed by Mr. Edmunds, and he thought that some advance had been made by him; and therefore when he (Mr. C.) saw these statements in the paper, he did not know but that I had yielded to Mr. Edmunds representations.

I told him that there had not been one word written or spoken between me and any member of the Committee on Foreign Relations of the Senate on the subject of the Sandwich Islands, and that if any such new article or amendment had been offered to the treaty, that I had no knowledge of it.

I said to Mr. Carter that . . . the importance of the Sandwich Islands to the United States since the opening and settlement of the Pacific Coast . . . did not require to be stated by me; that it was an open and admitted fact that those Islands could never be allowed to become a menace or source of danger to the United States. . . . I said that I . . . thought it was . . . our policy to strengthen the autonomy of those Islands and do anything we could to promote the mutual prosperity of that Government and our own people.[66]

There was little doubt that the members of the Senate Committee on Foreign Relations were anxious to forestall any attempt by a European

66. *Memorandum* written by Bayard after a conversation with H. A. P. Carter, May 7, 1886, *Bayard MS.*

Power to secure some means of control over Hawaii. The cession of Pearl Harbor as a naval station would definitely place the United States in a position of dominance in the islands, and this very fact accounted for the reluctance of the Hawaiian Government to make a favorable response to this Senate suggestion. On September 1, 1886, King Kalakaua approved an act of the legislative assembly which authorized a loan of two million dollars. To Mr. Merrill, the American Minister at Honolulu, it appeared obvious that the Hawaiian Government wished to have this loan floated by certain English banking houses, and this possibility gave Bayard concern because it might open the way for a measure of British control over the islands.[67]

Bayard was further disturbed by an article in the London *Times* which stated that the Hawaiian Government, fearful that the Cleveland Administration would not ratify the treaty of December 6, 1884, without objectionable amendments, was opening negotiations through the British Colonial Office for a reciprocity treaty with Canada.[68] Although Mr. Carter assured Bayard that "no negotiations or proposals have been initiated by the Hawaiian Government looking forward to a reciprocal arrangement with Canada," [69] the Department of State still had some misgivings about the situation. For this reason, Bayard requested Mr. Carter to call at the Department of State for a conference which was held on November 30, 1886.[70] Bayard informed Carter that he wished to talk with him

67. Merrill to Bayard, September 2, October 14, 19, 1886, *Hawaii, Despatches*, vol. 22, MS Dept. of State. On June 25, 1886, H. A. P. Carter wrote to Bayard to assure him that no money had been spent by the Hawaiian Government for the purpose of influencing American opinion in favor of the reciprocity treaty. *Bayard MS.*

68. September 23, 1886.

69. H. A. P. Carter to Bayard, *Private and Confidential*, October 16, 1886, *Bayard MS.*

70. In his annual message to Congress, December 6, 1886, President Cleveland included the following paragraph concerning the Hawaiian Islands: "I express my unhesitating conviction that the intimacy of our relations with Hawaii should be emphasized. As a result of the reciprocity treaty of 1875, those islands, on the highway of Oriental and Australasian traffic, are virtually an outpost of American commerce and a stepping-stone to the growing trade of the Pacific. The Polynesian Island groups have been so absorbed by other and more powerful governments, that the Hawaiian Islands are left almost alone in the enjoyment of their autonomy, which it is important for us should be preserved. Our treaty is now terminable on one year's notice, but propositions to abrogate it would be, in my judgment, most ill-advised. The paramount influence we have there acquired, once relinquished, could only with difficulty be regained, and a valuable ground of vantage for ourselves might be converted into a stronghold for our commercial competitors. I earnestly recommend that the existing treaty stipulations be extended for a further term of seven years. A recently signed treaty to this end is now before the Senate." *Foreign Relations, 1886*, p. vi.

. . . in consequence of some publications in the San Francisco papers, purporting to give an account of a loan negotiated in England by the Hawaiian Government for about $2,000,000, and to say to him that it had come to the President's ears that it was proposed to pledge the public revenues of the Hawaiian Kingdom as a collateral security for that loan; that it seemed to him that to give even to a set of private creditors the necessary right of inspecting the exercise of the taxing power of a country would virtually be creating a mortgage on that country, or, to use the language of the treaty between Hawaii and the United States, to create a lien in favor of third parties; that it seemed to me that such a course was directly invasive of the rights and liberties of the Kingdom of Hawaii, and indirectly impairing the preferred rights of the United States under their agreement with Hawaii in the treaty of 1875.

I found that Mr. Carter concurred with me as to the unwisdom of such a matter, and he told me that he would communicate with his Government.[71]

Bayard's very frank representations to Mr. Carter made a deep impression upon the Hawaiian Government which quickly modified its policy with reference to securing a loan of $2,000,000. Carter informed Bayard that

. . . the pledge of the revenues of the Sandwich Islands for the payment of this loan had been withdrawn, so that the bond given in advance of the securities to be issued under the loan was simply the pledge of the Minister of Finance, and not a pledge of the taxing powers of the Government. He said that the loan, although nominally for $2,000,000 would in reality not exceed one, and that the result of the operation would be to increase the public debt of the Sandwich Islands about $700,000.

In reply to a question from me he said that the $700,000 was expended in improvements of the harbor of Honolulu and of the island itself.[72]

In response to this friendly gesture by the Hawaiian Government in the matter of the $2,000,000-loan, Bayard wrote to President Cleveland, January 11, 1887, and expressed his opposition to the Senate amendment to the pending Hawaiian treaty with reference to Pearl Harbor. The Hawaiian Government had just taken possession of Midway Island which had

. . . as good a harbor for coaling, etc., as Pearl Harbor. I am disposed to believe there would be no objection to our free use of Midway for such purposes, and it would not involve us or Hawaii with the other treaty powers. . . . The Pearl Harbor is but a very short distance from the sea, and with the present ordnance, would not be tenable against assault unless

71. *Memorandum* written by Bayard after a conversation with Mr. Carter, November 30, 1886, *Bayard MS.*

72. *Memorandum* written by Bayard after a conversation with Mr. Carter, January 7, 1887, *Bayard MS.*

elaborately fortified, so that its control in the event of war would necessarily pass to the stronger *Naval* power, which certainly the U. S. is *not,* at present. Therefore looking at these facts and the disinclination of the Hawaiian Gov't to make the concession, I am opposed to engrafting such an amendment upon a treaty which as at present framed, merely gives a longer life to the present favorable status.[73]

On January 22, 1887, Carter had a conversation with Bayard about the pending Hawaiian treaty. He said that he was aware that Bayard

. . . could not yet have official notice or authentic information of what had been done by the Senate but that the amendment demanding the cession of Pearl Harbor . . . would not have been adopted had it been made public, and an opportunity had been given to the friends of the Sandwich Islands or to the Administration to express an opinion on the subject. . . . He also stated . . . that he did not understand the practical object of the amendment, and said that it seemed to him an Mephistop[helian] act to seek to put that amendment on the treaty.

I [Bayard] told him I did not know what the amendment was, but if it was what the newspapers reported it to be, it was an amendment not germane to the objects of the treaty, but in substance and effect a new treaty altogether—that is to say, a treaty of annexation, and a virtual annexation of this island by the United States Government. . . .

He told me there was no chance of such an amendment being accepted by the Hawaiian Government.[74]

In the meantime, on January 10, 1887, the pending treaty with Hawaii came before the Senate with the amendment relative to Pearl Harbor. Ten days later (January 20) this amendment was agreed to by a close vote of yeas 28, nays 21. This was the last stand of the opponents of the treaty. Later in the day the entire amended treaty was brought to a vote and was approved by the large margin of yeas 43, nays 11.[75] The fate of the treaty was now in the hands of the King of Hawaii and President Cleveland.

The action of the Senate in approving the Pearl Harbor amendment to the pending Hawaiian treaty, was very distasteful to Mr. Carter,

73. Bayard to President Cleveland, January 11, 1887, *Bayard Letter Book,* vol. 4, *Bayard MS.* In the Bayard Papers there is a letter from General N. H. Davis to General J. C. Duane, January 21, 1887, with reference to Pearl Harbor. General Davis thought that it was "all important and a wise national policy that our Govt. should *secure* this harbor as a place of refuge for our Navy in case of war, also as a coaling station & point of rendezvous at *all* times. This appears to be necessary moreover to keep other Govt's from gobbling it up."

74. *Memorandum* written by Bayard after a conversation with Carter, January 22, 1887, *Bayard MS.*

75. *Senate Executive Journal,* vol. 25, pp. 708-710.

who called at the Department of State to discuss the matter with Bayard. He had

. . . ascertained that no motion to reconsider had been entered, and that Senators considered themselves free to speak about the treaty. I told him the President had not considered the action of the Senate, but that it seemed to me [Bayard] that under our arrangement of duties and powers, that the treaty submitted by Mr. Frelinghuysen himself would be considered to have been dropped by the action of the Senate, because it had been acted upon in such a way as to wholly change its original character, and to add features which were not before the negotiators and never had been considered by the Executive.

He drew my attention to the exceedingly vague language of the Edmunds amendment for the cession of Pearl Harbor, by saying that as it stood, at the end of seven years, or the termination of the treaty, the cession of Pearl Harbor would also drop with it, so that no permanent establishment would have been gained by the United States.

I discussed with him informally and personally . . . the general result of substituting the originations of the Senate for the originations of the President. He told me he had written to his Government that he had not the slightest idea that the Executive would consent to be so entirely set aside in the performance of his duties as this action of the Senate would seem to imply, and that he, therefore, thought they might consider this treaty as having been dropped for the present.

. . . He said Mr. Sherman thought, and he believed one of the Senators from Texas was of the same opinion, that the United States should issue a proclamation forbidding in substance the Sandwich Islands from making any alliance with or any concession to any foreign power. I asked him how Mr. Sherman proposed to enforce it, and he answered that he did not know.

I then told him I was unable to answer him yet in regard to his proposition to embrace Midway Island in the domains of Hawaii. . . . I said the United States had definitely taken possession of that Island, and were in possession of it today under international law, but whether they wanted it I did not know. Mr. Carter remarked that it was a singular fact that while the Hawaiians were asking us to cede to them the harbor of Midway Island, the United States were asking from them the cession of Pearl Harbor, and he did not know but an exchange of the two might not be proposed.[76]

Up to this point Bayard had disapproved of the Pearl Harbor amendment to the pending Hawaiian Treaty because he knew that the Hawaiian Government was strongly opposed to it and would probably refuse to ratify the treaty if this amendment were incorporated in it. He had been careful to take no step that would be displeasing to the

76. *Memorandum* written by Bayard after a conversation with Mr. Carter, January 28, 1887, *Bayard MS.*

Hawaiian Government, and he was anxious to secure a renewal of the
reciprocity treaty because it would help to extend and confirm American influence in the islands. In 1874 Kalakaua had been elected King
partly through the efforts of Americans who feared that the election of
Queen Emma would mean an increase in British influence and the
defeat of any attempt to bring about commercial reciprocity with the
United States. It was difficult, however, for the American Government
to continue to look with favor upon the Kalakaua administration, which
was shamelessly corrupt. Led by an astute adventurer, Walter M. Gibson, the King's friends inaugurated a regime in which vice and venality
flourished. In order to gratify his expensive whims, King Kalakaua succeeded in persuading the Legislature to authorize a loan for $2,000,000
which was partly floated by a London syndicate.[77] It was in connection
with this loan that Bayard sent a confidential instruction to Mr. Merrill, the American Minister at Honolulu. It seemed to Bayard that the
terms of this loan were so phrased as to create a right of inspection
and possible control

. . . by foreign creditors, over the financial measures and administration
of the Hawaiian Government, and as such were not in accordance with the
spirit, if not of the letter, of the existing treaty between the Hawaiian
Islands and the United States, which was intended to prevent any cession
of territory or grant of a political nature by Hawaii to any other Government than that of the United States. The reasons for the Treaty of 1875
exist today in increased and still growing force. The political geography of
the United States, and the relations of the island groups of the Pacific Ocean
to our Pacific coast and to the terminal points of its transcontinental railways, have been importantly affected by the progress and natural operation
of events since the formation of that Treaty. . . .

The safety and welfare of the Hawaiian group is obviously more inter-

77. With reference to the condition of affairs in Hawaii from 1874 to 1887, see the
"Statement of Facts Relating to Politics during Kalakaua's Reign," by W. D. Alexander,
Foreign Relations of the United States, 1894, Appendix II, pp. 645-665. See also a "Sketch
of Recent Events," *For. Rel., 1894, App. II*, pp. 793-803. In the *Hawaiian Gazette*, May
24, 1887, there is a lengthy exposé of the rotten conditions in the islands. According to
Professor William F. Blackman, *The Making of Hawaii*, p. 125, Kalakaua was "wanting
in the intellectual ability, the sanity of judgment, the moral fibre, the chiefly dignity,
and sense of responsibility, which had characterized more or less fully all the monarchs
of the Kamahameha line. During five or six years prior to 1887 it was becoming increasingly obvious that his principles and conduct were suffering a relapse into barbarism.
His reign was marked during this period by the gradual assumption of arbitrary powers,
by encroachments on the prerogatives of legislature and people, by unnecessary and
extravagant expenditures and the exploitation and impairment of the public credit, by
shameless corruption in the disposal of government franchises, and by the deterioration
of the civil service."

esting and important to the United States than to any other nation, and for that reason our ties of intercourse and amity should be cherished.[78]

The "safety and welfare" of the Hawaiian Islands were menaced not only by the extravagance and vice of the Kalakaua regime but also by an attempt on the part of the king to bring about an alliance between Hawaii and Samoa. On December 23, 1886, J. E. Bush was commissioned as Envoy Extraordinary and Minister Plenipotentiary to the King of Samoa. Bush, and several boon companions, arrived at Apia on January 3, 1887, and were cordially received by King Malietoa who was presented with the Grand Cross of the Order of Oceania. On February 17 a convention was concluded between Malietoa and Bush, and this was formally ratified by King Kalakaua on March 20, 1887. It provided for the formation of a "political confederation" between Hawaii and Samoa, and it was to be merely the first step in a grandiose scheme to erect a Polynesian League in the Pacific Ocean.[79]

In order to convince King Malietoa that the Hawaiian Government was in earnest about this matter of a Polynesian League, Kalakaua purchased an old steamer which he hastily fitted out as a man-of-war. It was then christened the *Kaimiloa* and put into commission with a motley crew composed mostly of boys from the Honolulu house of correction. On the eve of sailing for Samoa, a serious disorder broke out which resulted in the dismissal of three officers, and when the *Kaimiloa* reached Samoan waters the crew revolted and for a while were in full possession of the ship.

Bayard was seriously disturbed by the reports that came to the Department of State with reference to the Anacreontic activities of King Kalakaua and his companions in vice. On April 8, Senator Morgan expressed to Bayard the view that Kalakaua and Walter M. Gibson were criminals, and that the royal house of Hawaii was afflicted with "moral bankruptcy." [80] Shortly afterwards, Bayard received a private

78. Bayard to Merrill, January 8, 1887, *Hawaii, Instructions*, vol. 3, MS Dept. of State.

79. Merrill to Secretary Bayard, February 15, March 29, 1887, *Hawaii, Despatches*, vol. 23, MS Dept. of State. On January 7, 1887 Carter, the Hawaiian Minister, had a conversation with Bayard with reference to Samoa. In a *memorandum* which Bayard wrote after Carter left the Department of State, he recounted the substance of this conversation: "He [Carter] then spoke in regard to Samoa, and I gave him an idea of my desire to assist as much as possible in having the basis of a native autonomy assisted by the foreign consuls. He said that they were going to send a delegation from Hawaii to assist the native Government there, and suggested to me that it would be a good thing to let the U. S. Consul correspond with the German Minister at Honolulu, so that he might be ready to take an interest in affairs there." *Bayard MS.*

80. John T. Morgan to Bayard, April 8, 1887, *Bayard MS.*

letter from George W. Merrill, at Honolulu, in which mention was made of rumors that persons in high authority in the Hawaiian Government were guilty of receiving bribes in connection "with the issuance of the license for selling opium." [81]

After receiving this letter from Merrill, Bayard responded with an instruction which stated that it was "absolutely necessary" for the protection of the interests of the people of the United States for the Cleveland Administration to know

. . . the true character of the individuals in charge of the governments with whom intercourse is held. Therefore, while not encouraging idle gossip, or irresponsible charges, it is nevertheless our duty, in the line of self-preservation, to sift the truth of serious charges which are made with the deliberation and responsibility you describe. . . . The personal character and conduct of an official entrusted with important public powers is of the most practical interest to those who are called upon to rely upon his statements and promises. Everything, therefore, which tends to certify the truth in connection with such a personage should be made known by you, as a necessary, however unwelcome, part of the confidential duty of a public agent toward his own government.[82]

This growing lack of confidence in the integrity of King Kalakaua and his officials had a distinct effect upon Bayard's attitude toward the efforts of the king to erect a Polynesian League. On February 4, 1887, Carter, the Hawaiian Minister, paid a visit to the Department of State to acquaint Bayard with the news that King Kalakaua was

. . . sending a Commissioner (a Mr. Bush) with a secretary, to Samoa . . . for the purpose of indicating a disposition to place those Islands under a government of laws, with a native autonomy. I [Bayard] told him that it was entirely in the line of my approval, and that I thought the largest amount that could be had of native government there, of a responsible character, the better.[83]

Two weeks later Carter made another visit to the Department of State and first inquired about the pending treaty with Hawaii:

Mr. Carter came to ask my opinion in regard to the condition of the treaty, which was amended by the Senate, and whether I considered that the treaty signed by himself and Mr. Frelinghuysen was at an end because the suggestion had been made to him (this was stated confidentially) that he should simply return that treaty to Hawaii in case the Government of the

81. Merrill to Bayard, April 11, 1887, *Private, ibid.*
82. Bayard to Merrill, April 27, 1887, *Confidential, Bayard MS.*
83. *Memorandum* written by Bayard after a conversation with Mr. Carter, February 4, 1887, *Bayard MS.*

United States refused it. I [Bayard] told him I did not see the necessity for me to come to a decision on that point and to make him an answer; . . . that the consideration of the matter was in some degree before the House of Representatives, whose resolution on the subject was addressed partly to the President and partly to their own Judiciary Committee, asking to obtain in some way a definition of their powers over the question, and I said that until they had ended their consideration of the matter I certainly would not care to express any opinion about it. He said then he supposed it was to be understood the matter was to be left as it was, and I answered that it was . . . best to let it stand.

Bayard then referred for the first time to the corruption that existed in the Hawaiian Government:

I told him Mr. Claus Spreckels was in town and had been to see him. I remarked that he seemed to be a very vigorous man. He said Mr. Spreckels was now convinced that it had been a great mistake for him to have obtained control of the King and legislature of Hawaii by the means that he employed; for he had found that when he sought to stay the current of corruption which he himself had set in motion that it proved too strong for him. He said that he (Spreckels) had discovered that it was a bad thing to be compelled to purchase over again what you had already bought.[84]

Some three weeks later Carter informed Bayard that he had just received an autograph letter from King Malietoa which commissioned him to serve as the Minister Plenipotentiary and Envoy Extraordinary from Samoa to the United States. Bayard at once scented trouble with Germany if Carter should actually assume the duties of Minister from Samoa, and he frankly warned him against taking any action that would bring down German wrath upon Hawaii.[85] It was immediately apparent to Bayard that the relations between Hawaii and Samoa were constantly growing more complicated. On April 1 Carter had a conversation with Bayard in which the startling news was conveyed that a treaty of alliance between Hawaii and Samoa had been "accepted and approved by the Hawaiian Government."

Inasmuch as Bayard had assured Alvensleben, the German Minister, that the rumor about Hawaii annexing Samoa was "all nonsense," this information from Carter about an alliance between the two countries was distinctly embarrassing to the Department of State. Bayard at once expressed his great surprise at this development and

84. *Memorandum* written by Bayard after a conversation with Mr. Carter, February 18, 1887, *Bayard MS.*
85. *Memorandum* written by Bayard after a conversation with Carter, March 11, 1887, *Bayard MS.*

once more warned Carter that this action by the Hawaiian Government might lead "to a very rude collision with Germany." Carter then admitted that

. . . among the letters that had come to him was a copy of the correspondence between Maliatoa and the German Consul, in which the latter had written to Maliatoa, who was complaining that a military instructor had been sent with arms by the German Consul down to Tamatassee to assist him in his insubordination to Maliatoa, and was informed in reply that it was none of his business what the Germans did with Tamatassee, and that if any more complaints were written about what the Germans were doing, he would receive such a letter from him that he would not like.

Bayard concluded the interview by expressing to Carter the view that "an alliance between Hawaii and Samoa would not prevent a repetition of such letters." Indeed, such a step "was unwise to the last degree." [86]

Bayard's repeated warnings to Carter about difficulties between Hawaii and Germany made such a deep impression upon the Minister that he wrote a formal note to the Department of State on April 2 and reversed his statement of the day before. In his confidential remarks to Bayard on April 1, Carter had announced that a treaty of alliance between Samoa and Hawaii had been "accepted and approved by the Hawaiian Government." In his note of April 2 he asserted that a "treaty of political alliance and confederation *is proposed* to be entered into by the Hawaiian Government and Samoa," and that this treaty is now "under consideration by the Government of Hawaii." [87]

In his reply to this note from the Hawaiian Minister, Bayard once more sounded a warning against concluding a treaty of alliance between Hawaii and Samoa. He was certain that from "every point of view" such a step would be "ill-advised." [88] Bayard held to this viewpoint, and when Carter paid a visit to the Department of State on April 27, he was frankly informed that any attempt to forge closer bonds between Hawaii and Samoa "might bring about results which would be very mortifying to Hawaii and might be connected with very serious results." [89]

86. *Memorandum* written by Bayard after a conversation with Carter, April 1, 1887, *Bayard MS.*

87. Carter to Bayard, April 2, 1887, *Hawaiian Legation, Notes from,* vol. 3, MS Dept. of State.

88. Bayard to Carter, April 12, 1887, *Hawaiian Legation, Notes to,* vol. 1, MS Dept. of State.

89. *Memorandum* written by Bayard after a conversation with Carter, April 27, 1887, *Bayard MS.*

After receiving this stern admonition, Carter changed the subject by alluding to the visit of the Queen of Hawaii to Washington. Queen Kapiolani and the Princess Liliuokalani, accompanied by a small retinue, would pass through Washington during the early part of May en route to England where they would attend the celebration of the jubilee held upon the fiftieth anniversary of the accession to the throne of Queen Victoria. Carter believed that

. . . the etiquette abroad was very strict as between crowned heads; that a visiting King did nothing at the capital of the other except what was suggested to him by the authorities there, and did not attempt to give any entertainment whatever himself, but simply accepted such as were tendered him. He said this Queen was a crowned Queen—that is, was crowned at the same time with her husband, which was not the case with Queen Emma, who visited the country some years ago, and that this person was more regal than the former visitor.

When Carter began to outline a series of courtesies that should be extended to the royal party, Bayard dryly remarked that he would "see the Chief Clerk and learn what had been done before." As a "master of ceremonies" he knew "very little and had very little taste for that sort of thing." [90]

As the shadow of a possible conflict between Germany and Hawaii began to darken Bayard's vision of the situation in the Pacific, he started

90. *Memorandum* written by Bayard after a conversation with Carter, April 27, 1887, *Bayard MS.* The schedule of ceremonies was agreed upon during a conversation between Bayard and Carter on April 29. Bayard told Carter that "he, having a knowledge of the habits and tastes of this lady [the Queen], I would be glad to be informed of any particular thing which would be gratifying to her, and would take pleasure in carrying it out if it was in my power; that he might do this privately and consider the matter as originating in my desire to do what was most courteous and agreeable. . . . He said she [the Queen] was not a reigning sovereign, nor was she merely a Queen consort, but was a native-born Sandwich Islander, and was crowned when the King was crowned. . . . He then asked how it would do for Mrs. Cleveland to call upon her. I told him Mrs. Cleveland had no title in the United States; she merely had a social position derived from her husband, but no official rank whatever; . . . that I would not answer in regard to what Mrs. Cleveland might do in the way of calling on the Queen." *Memorandum* written by Bayard after a conversation with Carter, April 29, 1887, *Bayard MS.* In an official instruction to Mr. Merrill, at Honolulu, Bayard gives a few of the details with reference to the ceremonies attendant upon the visit of Queen Kapiolani to Washington, May 3-6, 1887: "Wednesday . . . the Queen and her party were presented to the President and his wife, at the Executive Mansion, and soon thereafter Mrs. Cleveland, accompanied by the wives of several of the Cabinet officers, returned the Queen's visit. . . . Friday morning . . . an excursion was given to Mount Vernon . . . on board of the U. S. S. *Despatch*. . . . Friday evening the Queen and her party were the guests of the President and Mrs. Cleveland at a dinner," Bayard to Merrill, May 26, 1887, *Hawaii, Instructions*, vol. 3, MS Dept. of State. See also Bayard to Carter, April 29, and May 3, 1887, Bayard to President Cleveland, May 3, 1887; Carter to Bayard, April 29, 1887, President Cleveland to Bayard, May 3, 1887, and H. D. Lamar to Bayard, May 3, 1887. *Bayard MS.*

to incline towards the view that it was important to ratify the pending treaty with Hawaii as soon as possible. Such action might discourage a conflict between Germany and the island government. In this connection, Bayard showed Carter a newspaper clipping that indicated a considerable German immigration to the Hawaiian Islands. Further immigration might eventually lead to German control over some of the islands. Faced with this contingency, Bayard thought that Carter should look

. . . the future directly in the face; that just so long as the relations of Hawaii to the United States were in a tentative and doubtful condition, just so long the intrigue of other nations would be encouraged to displace the influence of the United States in these Islands; that the enterprise and prosperity of the Islands would be retarded as stability was essential to commercial prosperity.

I [Bayard] then said that it was in the power of the President, in the event of the treaty that passed the Senate, with the amendment respecting Pearl Harbor, receiving the adhesion of the King of Hawaii (supposing him to be the treaty-making power of that country), to proclaim that treaty and exchange ratifications without again sending it to the Senate, but that it did not seem to me to be wise for the United States, in their position, to tender such a treaty until they were satisfied that it would be accepted.

He [Carter] said that he did not know whether the President of the United States would proclaim that treaty in case it was accepted by Hawaii as it stood. I said I was not prepared to say that; that unquestionably the treaty as it now stood was not the treaty which had been approved by the Executive branch of the government and submitted to the Senate, but that having come back from the Senate with the approval of the Senate as amended, it was in the power of the President, in case it was approved by the Government of Hawaii, to proclaim it and exchange ratifications—of that I had no doubt.

He then said that Canada was holding out to Hawaii all sorts of promises and offers to give them the same advantages, if they would make a treaty of free trade with them, as were now given by Hawaii to the United States. I told him it was not in the power of Canada to give what the United States could.[91]

On May 13 Carter called on Bayard at the Department of State to discuss Hawaiian-American relations. First of all, he drew attention to a recent debate in the British Parliament which seemed to reveal a desire on the part of the British Government to "control the commerce of the Northern Pacific Ocean." Bayard was not greatly disturbed by such revelations. He was certain that

91. *Memorandum* written by Bayard after a conversation with Carter, April 29, 1887, *Bayard MS.*

. . . events would take care of themselves, and when it became necessary for Americans to protect their rights on that Ocean I thought means would be found to do it. He [Carter] then spoke of the Treaty, as ratified by the last Congress, with Hawaii, and the Senate amendment, ceding Pearl Harbor to the United States. He told me he had conversed with the Princess, who was here and Iukla, the aide, and they both told him that the King had frequently expressed to the native Hawaiians in their presence his belief that the United States was the true government for them to have alliance with, and that "Henry," referring to Mr. Carter, "was right about that."

Mr. Carter then said that if it could be understood that the cession of Pearl Harbor would terminate with the Treaty, that is to say, in case the treaty should come to an end, that the cession of Pearl Harbor would come to an end, he thought there would be no difficulty about its ratification by Hawaii. I told him that the more I reflected upon the terms of that cession the less valuable it appeared to me; that I did not believe the United States would send its money and its engineers out there to fortify Pearl Harbor, when so many hundreds more important harbors at home were not fortified; that I did not believe that if the cession were made that any act would be done by the United States to make the use of that harbor more available for U. S. vessels. We had no navy to put in it in the first place, and that our Merchant shipping did not need it.

He then said they would like to have some security for the continuance of the sugar duties. I said there could be no guarantee for the continuance of the sugar duty; that the treaty as he had signed it and as the King had agreed to it, and as Mr. Frelinghuysen had agreed to it, went into force and continued for seven years more; that Pearl Harbor cession made no difference and that no additional guarantee would be given in either case, and that it was not worth while to ask it.[92]

Nearly a month later, Carter had another conversation with Bayard relative to the cession of Pearl Harbor. He believed that the

. . . only question as to the proclamation of the treaty, extending the present condition of things with Hawaii for seven years, combined with the cession of Pearl Harbor to the United States, would be whether that cession was terminable with the treaty; that if it could be understood by an agreement between us that when the treaty ended, the cession of the harbor ended, he thought there would be no difficulty in obtaining the approval of the King of Hawaii to it. He said he had examined the Hawaiian law, and he did not see why it was at all necessary to submit the treaty as it now stood to the Hawaiian Congress, because it did not require any change in existing law.

Bayard repeated to Carter his viewpoint that it was very unlikely that the American Government would, "even in the event of cession,"

92. *Memorandum* written by Bayard after a conversation with Carter, May 13, 1887, *Bayard MS*.

spend any money upon improvements in Pearl Harbor. Carter agreed with this opinion because he thought that the United States "would have no navy within the next twenty years." Bayard was not prepared to go that far, but he did incline towards the view that America did not require "a fortification in the Pacific Ocean."

When the conversation next shifted to the relations between Hawaii and Samoa, Bayard did not hesitate to criticize the attempt of King Kalakaua to bring about a close alliance between himself and King Malietoa. According to Carter, King Kalakaua had been on the point of sending reinforcements to Malietoa to aid him in his struggle with the Germans. Such an act, thought Bayard, would be one of "incredible folly." It was "obviously absurd for the King to bring himself in conflict with the wishes of the German Government." [93]

After waiting a week, Carter again called on Bayard and requested that he be given a written guarantee that Article II of the pending treaty was in no sense intended as an invasion of the sovereignty of the Hawaiian Government. This guarantee should include a statement that "the right to hold Pearl Harbor would end when the commercial treaty was terminated." Bayard immediately replied that he did not think that it

. . . belonged to the Executive Department to interpret the treaty in that way, and I [Bayard] did not mean to say what rights would survive on the termination of the commercial part of the treaty, but I told him in reading the language of the article, I was unable to see that it contained any words which could be construed into a grant of political power within the Kingdom of Hawaii to the United States; that it was simply the right to enter a certain harbor in Hawaii, and to establish there a coaling and repair station for the use of vessels of the United States, and nothing more. I did not see how that could be held to contain any grant of political power. . . .

He [Carter] thought matters stood very well as they are now, and that he thought we might let matters remain as they were. . . . I told him . . . I thought the clause was really of very little value; as we had already a coaling station in Honolulu, and on those docks the jurisdiction of the United States over their own citizens is conceded by Honolulu. We had no trouble at all in getting all facilities for repairing, coaling, etc., and therefore, Pearl Harbor was entirely superfluous as far as that was concerned.[94]

Before any further conversations between Bayard and Carter could take place, a long smoldering revolution broke out in the Hawaiian

93. *Memorandum* written by Bayard after a conversation with Carter, June 3, 1887, *Bayard MS.*

94. *Memorandum* written by Bayard after a conversation with Carter, June 10, 1887, *Bayard MS.*

Islands and the government was overturned. On June 30 a large mass meeting was held in Honolulu, and a list of reforms was demanded. These were promptly agreed to by King Kalakaua, and a new Cabinet was installed.[95] On July 7 a new constitution was proclaimed. Some of the provisions of this instrument were so far-reaching in the curtailment of the King's prerogatives that the constitution was often referred to as the "bayonet constitution. [96]

95. Carter was quite fearful of the situation in Hawaii. On July 6, 1887, in a conversation with Bayard, he expressed the opinion that "the state of affairs in Hawaii was very critical, and that he wished to know what would be the action of the commander of the United States vessels that might go there, or the action of the U. S. Minister, in case the other foreign powers were to land forces for the purpose of protecting their citizens against what he called 'the mob.' He said that if it was true that Kalakaua had sent for 900 stand of arms, and 30,000 rounds of ammunition, he, not having 900 soldiers, might put them in the hands of 'the mob,' and that if that was done, Major Woodhouse, British Minister, . . . who is an aggressive man, would no doubt move very promptly to the defence of his people. Mr. Carter wanted to know what would be the action of our Minister and the Commander of the Naval forces in case of such an event.

"I [Bayard] said it was simply impossible for me to tell; that I could give no information upon a purely supposititious case, but I took it for granted that neither of these officers would see American interests suffer. I asked him whether he thought it would not be wise for him to go out to Honolulu now, for the purpose of procuring the acceptance of the treaty as it passed the Senate, with the Pearl Harbor amendment in it? He said he did not know; that he thought perhaps that until matters had settled down a little it would not be well to give any possible pretext to foreign powers for any interference in Honolulu. I said I could not understand how any pretext could be given; that the treaty was a thing entirely between the Government of Hawaii and the United States.

"Mr. Carter then gave . . . an account of the conduct of the King and of Mr. Gibson. . . . He expressed the most absolute want of confidence in the King's truthfulness, or in his power of memory; that he was either wholly oblivious of his promises or he was wholly indifferent to them. . . . The long and short of what Mr. Carter told me was that corruption, perfidy, and weakness were the chief elements in the Government of Hawaii. He told me more than once that the Pearl Harbor question was not the most important one to consider. I told him I did not care at all for the Pearl Harbor question, but I regretted exceedingly that it had been suffered to cause delay and possibly defeat the treaty; that was the reason why I regretted the interpolation of that amendment." *Memorandum* written by Bayard after a conversation with Carter, July 6, 1887, *Hawaiian Legation, Notes from,* vol. 3, MS Dept. of State.

96. *Foreign Relations, 1894, Appendix, II.* pp. 660-662; 793-817. On February 3, 1894, Charles L. Carter, a son of H. A. P. Carter, wrote a letter to Bayard in which he charged that the Cleveland Administration was at first strongly opposed to any revolution against King Kalakaua. Thus: "In June, 1887, my father, the late H. A. P. Carter, came to Ann Arbor, Michigan, to attend my graduation from the Law School at the place. He was compelled to leave in the midst of the festivities because, as he afterwards told me, he learned that it was the intention of the United States Government to send the warship *Adams* to Honolulu to protect the late King Kalakaua and his government from the anticipated Revolution predicted in the then latest despatches, and he further told me that in consequence of his assurances to you, that the revolution was being conducted by his friends and would be in the best interests of Hawaii, that the orders to Minister Merrill and the warships at Honolulu were not to interfere with those conducting the revolt. . . . I have since learned from those in Honolulu that up to a short time before the revolt consummated, Minister Merrill was indifferent if not hostile to the party of reform, but at the last moment changed in his expressions and did not interpose as had

On July 12 Carter discussed with Bayard the recent revolution in Honolulu. He said that the Queen and her party were "quite hilarious with joy over what had happened in Hawaii, and especially over the deposition of Gibson." He then spoke of the

. . . condition of the Cabinet, and said that his private advices which came by a sailing vessel, . . . were to the effect that the party of revolution there would have gone further and intended to banish the King, but . . . they found it would not be practicable at the moment. He said that the King . . . sent for the foreign Ministers—Mr. Merrill, and the English, French, and Portuguese Ministers and proposed to place the Government in their hands; that they declined it, and suggested making a Government of his own subjects, recognizing the popular demand for reform. . . . He stated that it was the opinion of the gentlemen of the Queen's suite, and his own, that it would not be wise at this time to press the acceptance of the Senate amendment for Pearl Harbor; that it might arouse the jealousy of the natives.[97]

There was one statement that Carter made during his conversation with Bayard that gave great uneasiness to the Department of State. He said that a member of the Queen's party had told him that "Sir William Pauncefote had spoken to him in England advising against the ratification of the Senate amendment ceding Pearl Harbor to the United States." Bayard was quite fearful that the Pearl Harbor amendment would not be acceptable to the Hawaiian Government and therefore the treaty would not be ratified by King Kalakaua. After concluding his conversation with Carter, Bayard drafted a long instruction to Merrill, at Honolulu. While deeply regretting

. . . the existence of domestic disorders in Hawaii, and with no disposition whatever to interfere therein, or to obtrude counsel unasked, yet the consequences which may possibly result to the interests of American citizens, which have grown up under the extension of the commerce between that country and the United States, under the guarantees of existing treaty, must not be jeopardized by internal confusion in the Government of these islands, and it is the duty of the United States to see that these interests are not imperilled or injured. . . . Whilst we abstain from interference with the domestic affairs of Hawaii, . . . obstruction to the channels of legitimate commerce under existing treaty must not be allowed. . . . No other member of the family of nations has so great and immediate an interest in the welfare and prosperity of Hawaii . . . as this Republic.[98]

been feared, which seems to corroborate what I learned from father." *Bayard MS.* There is nothing in the Bayard manuscripts that would confirm this statement of Mr. Carter.

97. *Memorandum* written by Bayard after a conversation with Carter, July 12, 1887, *Bayard MS.*

98. Bayard to Merrill, July 12, 1887, *Hawaii, Instructions*, vol. 3, MS Dept. of State.

Bayard's fears concerning the situation in the Hawaiian Islands are revealed in a memorandum which he wrote on August 12, 1887:

Governor Porter showed me today a letter (confidential) from a Mr. W. R. Castle to the Secretary of the Navy in relation to Hawaiian affairs. The writer had been a Member (Atty Genl) of Kalakaua's Cabinet in 1874, and described the King as utterly profligate, and the condition of affairs as demoralized and consequently insecure. A Republic will probably be proclaimed and a scramble for the domination of the Islands by the great Commercial Powers will ensue.

I am disposed to believe that with the present treaty of the U. S. and Hawaii, the interests of the Sugar growers will tend to alliance with the U. S., *but if our present Sugar Tariff is reduced,* as I think it will be, there is no saying what new trade arrangements will be made with Great Britain or Germany.

The action of the Senate (under the lead of Mr. Edmunds) in amending the renewed treaty by insisting upon a cession of Pearl Harbor, may have important consequences. We had secured an extension of seven years of our present arrangements by the original treaty, and this Pearl Harbor feature was then added against my urgent advice. Mr. Carter has promised to procure the agreement of Hawaii to the Treaty as it has been amended, but it is now rendered doubtful by the late disorders. We must await events (without a Navy).[99]

On September 21 Carter made one of his innumerable visits to the Department of State and expressed the opinion that while the views of the members of the Hawaiian Government were in accord with his concerning the scope of the Pearl Harbor amendment, he thought it

---

With reference to later events in Hawaii, it is important to note that Bayard, in this instruction, distinctly directed that both the American Minister at Honolulu and the naval officers on active duty in Hawaiian waters should "promptly" give their assistance in order to insure the "reign of law and respect for orderly government in Hawaii."

99. *Memorandum* written by Bayard, August 12, 1887, *Bayard MS.* On September 19, 1887, Bayard wrote a confidential letter to Senator James G. Fair, of California, with reference to Mr. Merrill, the American Minister at Honolulu: "Knowing your interest personally in Mr. Merrill, our Minister Resident at Honolulu, as well as your appreciation of the great importance of the maintenance of our interests in that quarter, I feel that I ought to let you know of some statements lately made from private sources to the effect that *conviviality* is sometimes carried too far by Mr. Merrill. The interests entrusted to him are too vast to be jeopardized by indiscretion, and if it be true that Mr. Merrill does not always maintain his self-control, no greater act of friendship could be done by him, or more important service to the office he holds than to administer a word of caution. Affairs in Honolulu have undergone much excitement of late, and a cool head is especially needed there. I write you thus confidentially as I do not wish any correspondence on such a subject to go upon the files of the department." *Bayard Letter Book*, vol. 6, *Bayard MS.* In Senator Fair's letter of reply he states that he had "made close enquiries about Merrill from parties just from the Islands and all speak well of Mr. Merrill. I intend to keep the run of him hereafter and will advise you in case aught goes wrong." James G. Fair to Bayard, November 2, 1887, *Bayard MS.*

was expedient·to have an exchange of notes to the effect that "the jurisdiction of Hawaii was not ceded over Pearl Harbor to the United States, nor was the term of the treaty prolonged by the Pearl Harbor amendment." Bayard replied that there was

. . . no similarity whatever between the precedents cited by him. The Clay-ton-Bulwer arrangement . . . had no similarity to the present state of affairs; that in that case the correspondence was between the two individuals who had negotiated the treaty; that it took place immediately upon the signature of the treaty by them; and that moreover, the correspondence itself, inter-preting the treaty, was instantly submitted to the Senate which had full knowledge of the correspondence and voted with that knowledge in favor of the ratification of the treaty; that, therefore the circumstances of the two cases were wholly dissimilar; that I had no authority in law to give an interpretation to a treaty, but that the Senate must give theirs, or the courts of law would give it subsequently, but that I saw no reason why he should not submit this treaty to his government for its acceptance as amended, and that if they thought it worth while, after consideration, to return it with their approval and acceptance, . . . that they could accompany that accept-ance with a statement of what they held to be an interpretation of the Pearl Harbor amendment. . . . He entirely concurred with that, and said it was what he expected me to say, and that he would carry out the suggestion.[100]

In accordance with Carter's request, Bayard, on September 22, sent to the Hawaiian Legation a note setting forth the situation with refer-ence to the pending treaty. With this formal note he enclosed a copy of the convention as amended by the Senate.[101] In reply, Carter gave a detailed interpretation of what he considered to be the scope of the Pearl Harbor amendment. To him it seemed to be clear

. . . that the question of Hawaiian jurisdiction is left untouched by the article, and that in the event of the United States Government availing itself of the right stipulated for, the autonomous control of the Hawaiian Government remains the same as its control over other harbors in the group where national vessels may be, except that the Article in accordance with Article IV of the existing convention prevents the Hawaiian Government from granting similar exclusive privileges during the continuance of the convention to any other nation.

As no special jurisdiction is stipulated for in the article inserted by the Senate, it cannot be inferred from anything in the article that it was the intention of the Senate to invade the autonomous jurisdiction of Hawaii

100. *Memorandum* written by Bayard after a conversation with Carter, September 21, 1887, *Bayard MS.*
101. Bayard to Carter, September 22, 1887, *Hawaiian Legation, Notes to,* vol. 1, MS Dept. of State.

and to transfer the absolute property in, and jurisdiction over, the harbor to the United States. . . .

Another point which may to some minds be left in doubt would be the duration of the license or right granted by the interpolated Article. The Article mentions no special term for the continuance of the privileges, but . . . it follows, in the absence of any stipulation to the contrary, that its term of duration would be the same as that fixed for the other privileges given by the original convention.[102]

In his answer to Carter's note, Bayard briefly remarked that

. . . the amendment relating to the harbor of Pearl River was adopted, in its executive sessions, by the Senate, and I have no other means of arriving at its intent and meaning than the words employed naturally import. No ambiguity or obscurity in that amendment is observable, and I can discern therein no subtraction from Hawaiian sovereignty over the harbor to which it relates, nor any language importing a longer duration for the interpolated Article II than is provided for in Article I of the supplementary convention.[103]

This exchange of notes removed any objections that still lingered in the minds of the members of the Hawaiian Government, and on November 5 Carter wrote to Bayard to inform him that full powers had been received from Honolulu authorizing the exchange of ratifications of the amended treaty.[104] Five days later, Bayard received a despatch from Merrill, at Honolulu, which enclosed a note from the British Commissioner Resident to the Hawaiian Minister of Foreign Affairs, protesting against the Pearl Harbor concession. The British representative was of the opinion that the acquisition by the United States of a harbor or preferential concession in any part of the Hawaiian Kingdom would "infallibly lead to the loss of its independence and the extinction of the Hawaiian nationality." [105]

On this same day (November 9) Carter read to Bayard a communication he had received from the Hawaiian Government conveying "the great satisfaction felt by the King and by the Gov't. in forming closer

102. Carter to Bayard, September 23, 1887, *Hawaiian Legation, Notes from,* vol 4, MS Dept. of State.

103. Bayard to Carter, September 23, 1887, *Hawaiian Legation, Notes to,* vol. 1, MS Dept. of State.

104. Carter to Bayard, November 5, 1887, *Hawaiian Legation, Notes from,* vol 3, MS Dept. of State.

105. Merrill to Bayard, October 22, 1887 (received November 9), *Hawaii, Despatches,* vol. 23, MS Dept. of State. On November 7 Bayard sent to President Cleveland the Hawaiian Treaty which had just been ratified by the Hawaiian Government. He was "very glad" that this "significant treaty" could soon be proclaimed. Bayard to Cleveland, November 7, 1887, *Bayard Letter Book,* vol. 6, *Bayard MS.*

relations with the United States." Carter also read an instruction from the Hawaiian Minister of Foreign Relations in which he expressed his pleasure

. . . to have procured his Majesty's signature to this treaty in spite "of the influences that might have been exerted against it, and that the British Lion did not know that the treaty had already been signed." . . .

He then said he thought that this treaty would give pretext to Germany for making some trouble if she could with Hawaii. I [Bayard] told him that if that was the state of affairs it was a great deal better that the treaty was made, because we had better know at once what the pretensions of Germany were in the Pacific. . . . Mr. Carter said he had met Mr. West the other day, who had spoken to him about a telegram from Mr. Woodhouse on the subject of the cession of Pearl Harbor, and he (Carter) immediately informed the British Minister that there was no cession of Pearl Harbor, but a mere agreement for its use pending the existence of the treaty; that Mr. West expressed great satisfaction, and asked if he might be at liberty to telegraph that to his Government. Mr. Carter said he might. . . .

Mr. West also said to Mr. Carter that he thought Zedtwitz [the German Minister at Washington] would want to make all the trouble he could about this treaty of Hawaii with the United States, and I [Bayard] answered that there was not the slightest invasion of German rights, but it was best for us to see whether or no we were at liberty to make what arrangements we pleased in regard to Pacific Coasts.[106]

This threat of German interference in the Hawaiian Islands was certainly one of the reasons why the King and the Hawaiian legislative assembly received the news of the ratification of the pending treaty with the United States with "marked manifestations of approval." [107] The German Government was deeply interested in the fate of important islands in the Pacific Ocean, and the claims of the United States were carefully scrutinized. On December 7 Baron Zedtwitz called at the Department of State to discuss the situation with Bayard. Bayard frankly informed him that he could

. . . not understand Prince Bismarck's reference to the Hawaiian Islands. The treaty which Prince Bismarck referred to as giving concessions to the

106. *Memorandum* written by Bayard after a conversation with Carter, November 9, 1887, *Bayard MS*. Bayard was distinctly worried about German expansion in the Pacific. In a letter to Phelps, October 20, 1887, he remarked: "Our want of a Navy makes me groan inwardly. In her Polynesian exploits Germany is very careful to make assurance to the United States that no infraction of their treaty rights, or rights of their citizens, will be allowed, but at the same time we see German power spreading itself in the South Pacific, and you may comprehend that my thoughts are turned anxiously toward the Sandwich Islands where we have very important rights and interests to preserve." *Bayard Letter Book*, vol. 6, *Bayard MS*.

107. Merrill to Bayard, December 16, 1887, *Hawaii, Despatches*, vol. 23, MS Dept. of State.

United States was not signed by me—it had been concluded in 1884; it was nothing but the extension of a commercial arrangement of the greatest importance to Hawaii, and to every person there, and I believed to many Germans, who were getting the advantage of that treaty by having a free market in the U. S. for Hawaiian products. But I wished it understood we did not consider for a moment that the relations of the United States to Hawaii were to be measured at all with those of the other commercial powers; that we considered our interest in Hawaii was manifestly much greater than that of other powers, and our treaties had been made with that view, but there had been no change in treaty from that which had been existing for the last fifteen years—simply an extension.[108]

Bayard could clearly see that the international relations of the Hawaiian Islands were taking on increasing significance, and he quickly discovered that Great Britain, even more than Germany, was anxious to keep them from being annexed by the United States. On January 5, 1888, Carter, accompanied by Samuel G. Wilder, of Honolulu, paid a visit to the Department of State. Apparently, Hawaii was on the eve of another revolution against the authority of King Kalakaua:

He [Carter] said he did not think the King's authority could be long upheld, and that opinion was shared by Mr. Wilder, and that sooner or later the United States might be called upon to assume control of the Islands. Mr. Wilder had told the King that he did not think the monarchy could last much longer. He was strongly in favor of the monarchy, but did not think it possible to keep it up. The fate of Samoa had disturbed him—not that he thought there would be a bold seizure by Germany or any other power of Hawaii, but that he feared there would be a crumbling away of power, and then no one could foretell what would happen. He thought it well to keep Mr. Bayard informed of these possibilities so that he might be prepared to act in case an emergency arose.

They did not like the constant co-operation of the English and American Ministers. For instance, Mr. Woodhouse called on him (Mr. W.) and said he came on behalf of Mr. Merrill to ask if he would take the post of Prime Minister.

Now they (the Hawaiians) wanted the protection of the United States if any protection was needed. Mr. Wilder had advised the King to enter at once into negotiations with the United States to part with the sovereignty

108. *Memorandum* written by Bayard after a conversation with Baron Zedtwitz, December 7, 1887, *Bayard MS.* On December 9, 1887, Bayard wrote to W. C. Whitney, Secretary of the Navy, and remarked that in "view of late occurrences in the Sandwich Islands, and on the movements by Germany in the Samoan Islands, it has occurred to me that it might be well for the United States to make some expressive movement by way of a visit of one of our national vessels to Midway Island—the re-erection of a flag and mast and possibly landing some coal there, which being made publicly known would serve to answer any suggestion of non-use, or abandonment of title by the United States." Bayard to W. C. Whitney, December 9, 1887, *Bayard Letter Book,* vol. 6, *Bayard MS.*

of the country while he was in a position to do so with advantage, and before affairs became more complicated. If there should be a joint protectorate there would be trouble. If several ships' crews of different nationalities should land there would be difficulty in getting them to re-embark.

Mr. Bayard enquired as to the King's habits, and Mr. Wilder said they were not good. He was inclined to drunkenness, and was morose, did not act nicely, although he was more quiet than formerly.

MR. BAYARD.—Do you think there remains in the King that recognized constitutional power to make application to the U. S. Minister alone for protection without asking it from the other powers?

MR. WILDER.—I think so; there have been no steps taken so far which would prevent it.

Mr. Carter said Mr. Wilder had presented a proposition to the King whether it would not be better to sell to the United States, to which Mr. Wilder added that he thought himself justified in saying that should the United States refuse, the other powers would certainly step in. England was very anxious to get possession.[109]

There was little doubt that the British Government was exceedingly anxious to prevent the annexation of the Hawaiian Islands to the United States. On February 9, 1888, Mr. James H. Wodehouse, the British Consul-General at Honolulu, addressed a note to Mr. Austin, the Hawaiian Secretary of Foreign Affairs, in which he registered a protest against the Pearl Harbor concession to the United States. The growing importance of the Hawaiian Islands as a coaling and provision station for ships navigating the Pacific made

109. *Memorandum* written by Bayard after a conversation with Carter and S. G. Wilder, January 5, 1888, *Bayard MS.* On January 7, 1888, Carter again visited the Department of State for a conversation with Bayard: "He said he had brought Mr. Wilder here yesterday at his request in order that he might state his views, in which he (Carter) did not *entirely* concur. . . . After discussing the possible attitude or action of the British, German, French, and other foreign governments in event of open annexation being proposed by the U. S., Mr. Carter evidently thought the growth of such opposition would increase with delay. He told me Mr. Seward had once questioned him as to the policy of the U. S. passing an enabling Act to let Hawaii come into the Union. The doubt was whether this would not annoy the pride and susceptibility of the Hawaiians and throw them into intrigues with other powers. Finally Carter suggested that the King might be sounded confidentially by Merrill or a Special Envoy as to the feasibility of having some declaration made by Hawaii that would be favorable to the entertainment of such a proposal by the U. S.

"I [Bayard] promised to think it over and see him soon. The temper and attitude of the Senate towards the Admn., the faint hope of obtaining any co-operation or assistance from the Representatives, was considered. I wanted an outline in writing. . . . Mr. Carter said it was too indefinite and would make it possible for the King (whom he said was treacherous) to deal with other governments. He feared that Merrill was too much under the influence of Woodhouse, the British Min., and cited the fact of the latter going to the For. Min. at Honolulu with a message from Merrill, looking to a joint protection by *British and American action.*" *Memorandum* written by Bayard after a conversation with Carter, January 7, 1888, *Bayard MS.*

. . . it highly desirable that the harbours of the group should at all times be open equally to the ships of all nations, and as Her Majesty's Government cannot consent to forego the rights and privileges which were expressly conceded to them by the above-mentioned Treaty of 1851, they must still look to the Government of the Hawaiian Islands to maintain unimpaired the rights accorded to Great Britain by that Treaty.[110]

The reply of Secretary Austin must have been disappointing to Mr. Wodehouse. The only thing that had been granted to the United States was

. . . the right to make a harbour at its own expense at a place called Pearl River Harbour, and, having so made it, the exclusive privilege of using it during the continuance of the Treaty. . . . The convention with the United States Government does not involve any Cession of Territory to the United States or any release of Sovereignty or Jurisdiction by this Government. . . . His Majesty's Government regards the question of preferential Concessions in reciprocal Treaties as one which has been thoroughly settled in favour of the right to grant such concessions in return for grants of similar value. . . . The growing importance of the Hawaiian Islands as a coaling station, and provision depot for ships navigating the Pacific, . . . is largely the result of the beneficial influence of the Treaty of Reciprocity between the Governments of the United States and Hawaiian Kingdom.[111]

Bayard himself was equally frank in his correspondence with Sackville-West. On December 23, 1887, Sackville-West handed to Bayard a memorandum which cited the fact that England and France were bound by the convention of November 28, 1843, "never to take possession, either directly or under the title of a protectorate or any other form, of any part" of the Hawaiian Islands. An invitation was then extended to the United States to join with England and Germany in a declaration that would guarantee the "neutrality and equal accessibility of the islands and their harbors to the ships of all nations without preference." [112]

110. James H. Wodehouse to Jonathan Austin, February 9, 1888, enclosed in Merrill to Bayard, February 24, 1888, *Hawaii, Despatches*, vol. 23, MS Dept. of State.
111. Secretary Austin to Consul-General Wodehouse, February 16, 1888, *ibid.*
112. *Memorandum* written by Bayard after a conversation with Sackville-West, Dec. 23, 1887, *British Legation, Notes to*, vol. 115, MS Dept. of State. Bayard informed Sackville-West "that the relations of the United States to the Sandwich Islands were not that of any other nation; that those Islands had an importance to us from their geographical position that they could have to no other nation, and that our treaty of 1875 secured to us an inhibition against any portion of the Sandwich Islands being transferred to any other foreign government." Sackville-West said "that he had explained to Lord Salisbury the meaning of the Pearl Harbor cession, which had been misunderstood, and which Germany considered was an act of acquisition by the United States to create a naval station there; that Mr. Carter had explained the matter to him, and he was perfectly

Bayard made a formal reply to this invitation in a note addressed to Sackville-West, February 15, 1888:

The existing treaties of the United States and Hawaii create . . . special and important reciprocities, to which the present material prosperity of Hawaii may be said to owe its existence, and by one of the articles the cession of any part of the Hawaiian territory to any other government without the consent of the United States is inhibited. In view of such existing arrangements it does not seem needful for the United States to join with other governments in their guaranties to secure the neutrality of Hawaiian territory, nor to provide for that equal accessibility of all nations to those ports which now exists.[113]

The policy that Bayard was following in 1888 was clearly explained by him in a statement which he made in February, 1897. In 1888 America had an interest in the Hawaiian Islands

. . . that no other country could have. A political union would logically and naturally follow, in course of time, the commercial union and dependence which were thus assured. It was my idea that the policy originating in the Fish treaty of the Grant Administration in 1875 should be permitted to work out its proper results. The obvious course was to wait quietly and patiently and let the islands fill up with American planters and American industries until they should be wholly identified in business interests and political sympathies with the United States. It was simply a matter of waiting until the apple should ripen and fall.[114]

This policy of watchful waiting was always attended by certain dangers of revolution which might invite foreign interference in the Hawaiian Islands. On December 12, 1888, Commander I. D. Graham, U.S.S. *Alert*, reported to Secretary Whitney that at the

. . . next election which takes place in February, 1889, there will be an effort made by the natives to overthrow the present Ministry. . . . I am also informed by a prominent American . . . that His Majesty Kalakaua is secretly making efforts to turn the Islands over to the protection of the British Crown. By last steamer a citizen of Honolulu, Mr. W. H. Grenhalgh, who, being deeply involved in debt, by the laws of the country was debarred a passport to leave the kingdom, was granted a passport by the Foreign Office to go to England. . . . It is said that this person though outwardly transacting personal matters for the King, was really the bearer of secret despatches to the English Government. . . .

---

satisfied that the U. S. did not intend to acquire jurisdiction in Hawaii." *British Legation, Notes from,* vol. 115, MS Dept. of State.

113. Bayard to Sackville-West, February 15, 1888, *British Legation, Notes to,* vol. 20, MS Dept. of State.

114. *Sen. Doc. 231,* 56th Cong., 2 sess., pt. 7, p. 260.

Within the next three months I expect to see four of H. B. M.'s ships of war in port, which . . . may be significant.[115]

As soon as Bayard received a copy of this letter of Commander Graham, he requested Mr. Carter to call at the Department of State. After informing Carter of the alleged mission of W. H. Grenhalgh to England to bring about a British protectorate over the Hawaiian Islands, Bayard frankly stated that

. . . such a proposition would be clearly impossible for the United States to submit to, in view of their present Treaty rights with Hawaii, and I [Bayard] wanted to know what knowledge he had, or what his opinion was of these facts, and how much of fire was underneath all this smoke. He told me that on the morning before he had received my letter, he had written three letters to Hawaii: one to his brother (who I understand was Chief Justice), one to a Mr. McFarland, . . . and the third to someone else, and in these letters he had referred to the condition of things there. . . .

He said that the King had transferred all his property to a Commission, and not only that, but he had transferred the crown lands which were attached to his office as King, and which produced an income of forty or fifty thousand dollars a year.

I replied that those crown lands belonged to the Kingdom of Hawaii—that they were not the personal property of the King. Mr. Carter answered that was true; that the action of the King was undoubtedly unconstitutional; . . . that the King had pledged the revenues from the crown lands for ten years in advance, and that he had gotten his sister, who will be his successor to the throne, to agree to this pledge.

I then said to Mr. Carter that if Mr. Grenhalgh had gone to England for the purpose of selling some franchises which he had gotten out of the Hawaiian Government, such as laying down railways and the like, and to create an English syndicate who should take an assignment of the King's property, . . . it would be unfortunate and would be looked upon by this Government with disfavor, because it would be placing the King in a great measure under British influence; . . . that it would be an accession of British influence in Hawaiian affairs, which the United States would look upon with regret and disfavor. . . .

Mr. Carter spoke very freely of Hawaiian affairs, and of the various influences that were there at work tending to throw the King under British control. He said that he had in his mind the suggestion of the United States dealing with this question by means of a treaty through which they could form a protectorate, taking control of the foreign affairs of the Sandwich Islands, and taking charge of their revenues. He said that the present King

115. Commander I. D. Graham to Secretary Whitney, December 12, 1888, *Bayard MS.* In a memorandum attached to this letter, John Bassett Moore expresses to Secretary Bayard the opinion that Commander Graham's remarks indicate "the possibility of more important work for us in Hawaii than in Samoa before many weeks." January 4, 1888, *Bayard MS.*

had the idea that he would receive more personal consideration at the hands of the British Government than at the hands of the United States; that they would probably give him a title—make him a duke or something of that kind, and secure him a better income, but he thought if the United States would keep up his personal dignity and secure as good treatment, that then he would be perfectly willing to act in accordance with their wishes.

Mr. Carter evidently has not the slightest personal respect for the King, and said that this movement of the natives referred to in the meeting held . . . was done for the purpose of restoring the power of the native element . . . but that element had been so filled with corruption that the present Ministry, which was put in power by the Americans, . . . intended to maintain their position and not permit the native rule.

After Bayard indicated to Carter the rapidly growing sentiment in the United States in favor of a policy of expansion, he brought the conversation to a close, but Carter could clearly see that the American mind was in no mood to accept British pretensions in the Pacific.[116]

On February 15 Carter paid a last visit to the Department of State to talk matters over with Bayard. He ardently hoped that in the forthcoming conference in Berlin with reference to Samoa, "there would be no principle laid down that would embarrass Hawaii." He was especially anxious that the American Government refuse any invitation to join with European powers in a guarantee of Hawaiian independence. Bayard assured Carter that the Department of State had drawn the line

. . . sharply between our relations with Hawaii and our relations with the island groups of the South Pacific; that I had expressly stated to the English Minister that we held relations to Hawaii that no other nation had or could have, and that he would observe from my correspondence with Germany that I had never for an instant confused the two or suggested any similarity between the cases of Hawaii and Samoa.[117]

In Bayard's mind Hawaiian annexation to the United States was merely a matter of a comparatively short time. American business enterprise was rapidly preparing the way for intimate political ties. To use

116. *Memorandum* written by Bayard after a conversation with Carter, January 5, 1889, *Bayard MS.*

117. *Memorandum* written by Bayard after a conversation with Carter, February 15, 1889, *Bayard MS.* In a letter from Rear-Admiral L. A. Kimberly, at Honolulu, to Secretary Whitney, November 14, 1887, there is an interesting last paragraph that takes a glance into the future: "Taking into consideration the peculiar conditions of race and interests, and the gradual and sure diminution of the aborigines, there is no doubt but that a day is not far distant, when the line of native kings and royalty will become extinct, and if the Government here does not become republican it will be because the U. S. has neglected her opportunity." *Bayard MS.*

his own words, it was "simply a matter of waiting until the apple should ripen and fall." But the American Minister, John L. Stevens, who represented the United States during the Administration of President Harrison, was fearful that if America waited too long the apple would fall into the lap of Great Britain.[118] In this regard he shared some of the opinions of Bayard himself during the last months he was Secretary of State.

Fortunately for the cause of Hawaiian annexation to the United States, Queen Liliuokalani precipitated matters by setting aside the Constitution of 1887 and proclaiming a new frame of government more in accord with her ideas of royal prerogative. In January, 1893, a revolution, led by the professional and business classes in Honolulu, suddenly broke out, and a provisional government was installed.[119] Shortly afterwards (February 14) a treaty providing for the annexation of the Hawaiian Islands to the United States, was signed in Washington, D. C., and President Harrison hurriedly sent it to the Senate.[120]

On March 4, 1893, President Cleveland assumed the Presidential office for a second time, and his Secretary of State, Walter Q. Gresham, promptly expressed his evident distaste for the Hawaiian treaty. Both Cleveland and Gresham were deeply touched by the appeal of Queen Liliuokalani against the Hawaiian revolutionists.[121] The realities of the situation were overlooked, and the President withdrew the Hawaiian treaty from the Senate. He next appointed James H. Blount, a former Congressman from Georgia, as a special commissioner to visit the islands and report upon the situation. The policy to be pursued by the Administration was still undefined, and President Cleveland wrote to Carl Schurz that he did not regard "annexation in all circumstances and at any time unwise," but he was certain that "we ought to stop and look and think." [122]

118. *Foreign Relations, 1894, Appendix II,* pp. 315-317, 353-354, 362-363, 374-375. See also Alice F. Tyler, *The Foreign Policy of James G. Blaine* (Minneapolis, 1927), pp. 370-372.
119. Julius W. Pratt, *Expansionists of 1898* (Balto., 1936), chaps. i-iii; A. F. Tyler, *The Foreign Policy of James G. Blaine,* chap. viii.
120. *Foreign Relations, 1894, Appendix II,* pp. 197-202.
121. *Ibid.,* pp. 867-868. See also, Allan Nevins, *Grover Cleveland,* pp. 549-553.
122. President Cleveland to Carl Schurz, March 19, 1893, *Schurz MS.* With reference to the general situation regarding Hawaiian annexation, see Matilda Gresham, *Life of Walter Q. Gresham* (Chicago, 1919, 2 vols.), vol. 2, pp. 741ff.; Henry James, *Richard Olney* (N. Y., 1923), pp. 81-95; A. L. P. Dennis, *Adventures in American Diplomacy, 1896–1906* (N. Y., 1928), pp. 101-106; William Castle, Jr., *John W. Foster,* in *The American Secretaries of State and Their Diplomacy* (N. Y., 1928), vol. 8, pp. 242-250.

The report of Mr. Blount to President Cleveland with reference to conditions in Hawaii, was formally submitted on July 17, 1893.[123] It was a sharp indictment of the actions of the American Minister to Hawaii, John L. Stevens. There was little doubt in his mind that Stevens was largely responsible for the revolution against the Queen, and he was certain that the "sentiment of the people" was "for the Queen, against the Provisional Government, and against annexation." He did add, however, that a majority of "the whites, especially Americans, are for annexation." [124]

Bayard's first reaction to the news from Hawaii was far different from that of Gresham. He was still thinking in terms of the political advantages that accrued to the United States from its close association with Hawaii, and he still feared that French and British schemes for colonial expansion might seriously menace the independence of the islands. After referring to a possible conflict between British and French interests in Siam, he remarked:

> The cool manner in which the rights or feelings of weak peoples are disregarded by these self-constituted guardians of the world's property, is most noticeable. It is one diminution of danger in the Sandwich Islands, that they have no near neighbors, no "delimitations of frontier," no "Buffer States" to be formed. It would help you mightily if a submarine telegraph could be constructed from San Francisco to Honolulu. I urged it in 1886 until 1888.[125]

Secretary Gresham was far more concerned with the alleged injustice that had been meted out to Queen Liliuokalani than he was with the international aspects of the Hawaiian situation. He was certain that the constitutional government in Hawaii had not been

> ... overthrown by a revolution of the people on the Islands. On the contrary, the Queen was overawed by the American Minister and the presence of a body of armed troops landed from one of our warships. Her submission was thus coerced. The affair was discreditable to all who engaged in it, including, I fear, some men at this capital. It would lower our national character to endorse a selfish and dishonest scheme of a lot of adventurers.[126]

123. On May 1, 1893, ex-President Harrison wrote to John W. Foster, and remarked: "The pulling down of the flag in Honolulu has created a very intense feeling throughout the country. . . . What a pity that the Senate is not in session that we might draw out from the State Department Mr. Blount's report. They are evidently afraid to give it out." *John W. Foster Papers*, Library of Congress.

124. *Foreign Relations, 1894, Appendix II*, pp. 598-599.

125. Bayard to Secretary Gresham, August 5, 1893, *Bayard Press Copy Book*, vol. 1, *Bayard MS*.

126. Secretary Gresham to Bayard, October 29, 1893, *Gresham Papers*, Library of Congress.

Bayard was entirely in agreement with Gresham in considering the tactics employed by the revolutionists as distinctly questionable. He believed that the United States was "too great and aspires to too high a place in civilization to stoop to the small arts of tricking or bullying a scanty and feeble set of Islanders out of their rights, whatever those rights may be." [127]

In December, 1893, the Hawaiian matter was being ventilated in Congress, much to the disgust of Secretary Gresham, who regarded the opposition in the Senate as motivated by partisan prejudice. But some important Democrats thought that Gresham had been somewhat inept in the way that he had handled the situation. It seemed to John Bassett Moore, that the

. . . publication of Judge Gresham's report to the President was a mistake. Mr. Blount's report should have been published sooner than it was, and Judge Gresham's communication should not have been given to the press at all. That communication suggested much more than was actually contemplated by the President and his Secretary of State, and its somewhat ill-timed publication *necessitated* the publication of the Commissioner's report. I know from your interview of last Saturday that our views on the Hawaiian situation altogether coincide. I told Judge Gresham that I thought the publication of his report was a mistake, and I do not doubt that he thinks so, too. It is unfortunate to let your antagonist get possession of the public mind, and doubly unfortunate to help him to do so. I think that every scrap of correspondence ought to have been sent to Congress the day after it assembled, so that the public poisoning with unfounded charges and suggestions might have been stopped. It is much easier to avoid false impressions than it is to erase them after they have been made.

Only this morning I had a conversation with a very intelligent man, and a supporter of the administration, who was very apprehensive as to the effect of our Hawaiian policy, and I could see that his apprehensions were due to the impression made by Judge Gresham's report, that it was the purpose and present occupation of the administration to bring about the restoration of the Queen in one way or another.[128] I told him that I thought he might be

127. Bayard to Secretary Gresham, November 25, 1893, *Gresham MS*.
128. Gresham's report to the President was made on October 18, 1893. In one paragraph there was a distinct recommendation that force be used to restore the Queen's authority: "Should not the great wrong done to a feeble but independent State by an abuse of the authority of the United States be undone by restoring the legitimate government? Anything short of that will not, I respectfully admit, satisfy the demands of justice." *Foreign Relations, 1894, Appendix II*, pp. 459-463: Matilda Gresham, *Life of W. Q. Gresham*, vol. 2, pp. 746-752. Richard Olney, then holding the office of Attorney General, pointed out that the use of force might lead to open warfare, and before war could be waged the consent of Congress would have to be obtained. Henry James, *Richard Olney*, pp. 85-90.

assured . . . that the administration was proceeding on a broader and more reasonable basis than that.

Mr. Stevens' course was unprincipled, false, and indefensible, but it will not be possible to make out that the leaders in the revolutionary movement were equally censurable, nor is there any reason why we should attempt to do so. Every one at all familiar with Hawaiian affairs for the last ten years has felt that there was room for vast improvement in the government there. I know we felt it very keenly at times, as when Kalakaua assumed the rôle of the protector of the Pacific and got up the famous *Kamiloa* expedition to Samoa, to intervene between that kingdom and Germany. It is true that the constitution of 1887 greatly curtailed the suffrage of the natives, but it was the price Kalakaua paid for the retention of his crown. It was matter of common knowledge, and Mr. Carter exhibited to me what seemed to be satisfactory proofs of the charge, that the same king granted an opium importing privilege for a bribe of thirty thousand dollars. These and other circumstances, including the frequent "revolutions" in the islands, all being matters of public information, make it specially unfortunate that any ground should have been afforded to our people to suppose that the administration was fatuously pursuing a policy that looked solely to the restoration of the Queen.[129]

Although Gresham had to retreat from his policy of restoring Queen Liliuokalani to her throne through the use of pressure that was closely akin to force, he continued to berate the revolutionists and all who aided them. In a plaintive letter to Bayard, December 17, 1893, he poured out his soul as follows:

I have no doubt the thoughtful and patriotic men of the country are with us in the position we have taken, and in the end they control public opinion. It is not true that the sentiment of the country is now against the administration on the Hawaiian question or anything else. The chief trouble is in the Senate, where several Democrats are even malevolent toward the President, but I think the party will be practically unanimous against the annexation treaty and in condemnation of Minister Stevens' action. Even Senator Morgan has admitted to me that the constitutional goverment was overthrown not by a revolution of the people, but by an armed invasion of the United States. . . . If we enter upon a career of acquisition of distant territory, governing it as Great Britain and other European powers govern their dependencies, our republic will not long endure. Should we acquire the Hawiian Islands with their population, we will have a hot bed of corruption.[130]

In response to these letters from Gresham, Bayard clearly indicated

129. John Bassett Moore to Bayard, December 13, 1893, *Bayard MS*.
130. Secretary Gresham to Bayard, December 17, 1893, *Gresham MS*.

his distaste for the way that the advocates of Hawaiian annexation had acted. He realized

. . . fully and painfully the want of co-operative sympathy in the Senate as now composed, and the nature of the opposition you encounter there. I fully agree with you that our great Republic will perish if we embark upon an Imperial system of acquisition of outlying dependencies, and that the methods employed under the late administration in the Hawaiian Kingdom were disgraceful to our Country, and will not be sustained by the American people when they are fairly comprehended. The course of the President and yourself entitled you to the respect of right-minded men everywhere, and of this proof is not wanting.[131]

Apparently, the Senate of the United States was not filled with right-minded men who were in support of the President's Hawaiian policy. The Democrats in the House of Representatives were

. . . practically solid in support of the Administration on the Hawaiian question, but there are some Democrats in the Senate who will antagonize the President in that and all other matters when they think they can afford to do so. It seems to be generally understood that annexation is dead, whatever else may occur. You doubtless know that Senator Morgan introduced a resolution authorizing and directing his committee to take testimony, and report its conclusions upon the action of Mr. Blount and the Administration. Senator Gray informs me that Senator Morgan has thus far examined the witnesses in a very partial and unfair way, evincing a disposition to aid the annexationists and injure the President; and yet he has repeatedly assured me and others that he was satisfied Mr. Blount's report was correct, that he was with the Administration on the question, and the Committee would make a report fully sustaining the position taken by the President in his Special Message. Not a few here, including myself, believe the Senator is insincere and that he means mischief. He is in favor of jingoism and protection, and the Republicans look upon him as being substantially with them.[132]

But it was not only wrong-headed Republicans and sinister Democrats who made diplomatic life difficult for Secretary Gresham. The Provisional Government in Hawaii did not relish the attitude that the Secretary of State had assumed when the Cleveland Administration came into power, and at times they showed an intransigent spirit which

131. Bayard to Secretary Gresham, December 28, 1893, *Gresham MS.*

132. Secretary Gresham to Bayard, January 21, 1894, *Bayard MS.* Bayard agreed with Gresham concerning the unreliability of Senator Morgan: "Your estimate of Mr. Morgan is such as I formed a long time ago. There is something sinister in his disposition, and one can never tell how he will act under any given state of affairs. Mr. Cleveland knew my opinion of him during his first Administration." Bayard to Secretary Gresham, February 6, 1894, *Bayard Press Copy Book*, vol. 1, *Bayard MS.*

greatly taxed Gresham's patience. In one of his numerous letters to Bayard, he lodged the following serious complaint:

The Hawaiian Government is proceeding with a high hand. You have doubtless seen that after detaining one Cranston, an American citizen, in prison for a month, he was forcibly put upon a Canadian steamer at Honolulu and sent to Vancouver. Cranston protested against this, and his request to see the American Minister was refused. This was done without charges being preferred against him and of course without trial, notwithstanding his right to reside and do business in Hawaii under the treaty of 1849. Learning from the British Commissioner that Cranston was about to be deported forcibly, Mr. Willis visited the ship upon which he had been taken, protested against the unauthorized action of the Hawaiian authorities, etc. Smith, the Attorney-General, informed Willis, that Cranston was deported by the Administration in the exercise of the arbitrary power authorized by martial law. I regret that Willis did not have the Commander of the *Philadelphia* take Cranston by force on board his ship and there protect him until instructions should be received. I enclose herewith copy of an instruction sent to Willis, based upon the action of Mr. Thurston, the Hawaiian Minister here. The President could, with propriety, have given him his passports at once. The sentiment in favor of annexation and the sympathy for the present government in Hawaii are obviously on the wane in this country. The second sober thought seems to be coming to people who have taken erroneous views of the situation.[133]

Bayard, of course, sympathized with Secretary Gresham with regard to the partisan attacks that were made upon him, but he never abandoned his opinion that the Hawaiian Islands had distinct importance to the United States from the viewpoint of naval policy in the Pacific. In a letter to Oscar S. Straus, he gave a short review of the Hawaiian situation, and then expressed his ardent hope that a solution would be found that would "not impair the potentiality of the United States over this group." [134]

This American hold upon the islands was strengthened by the outbreak of the Spanish-American War. Dewey's spectacular victory over the Spanish fleet at Manila Bay, May 1, 1898, awakened a new interest in the United States in the problems of the Pacific. In order to conquer the Philippines it would be necessary to use the Hawaiian Islands as a naval base from which supplies could be sent to the Far Pacific. On July 7, 1898, President McKinley signed a joint resolution providing for Hawaiian annexation, and thanks to the war spirit that prevailed

133. Secretary Gresham to Bayard, February 22, 1894, *Bayard MS.*
134. Bayard to O. S. Straus, January 25, 1894, *Bayard Press Copy Book*, vol. 1, *Bayard MS.*

in the United States, this action was warmly approved. It was imperative that Dewey, fighting in Philippine waters, should not be "let
down." The time had finally arrived when it "seemed to the American
people that an independent Hawaii was both an anachronism and a
danger." [135]

In the summer of 1898 Bayard became gravely ill, and he died on
September 28. He did not express himself upon the question of Hawaiian annexation, but ex-President Cleveland, completely out of touch
with the rising tide of imperialistic sentiment, was sharply critical of
the action of the Republican Administration. In a letter to Richard
Olney, he acidly remarked: *"Hawaii is ours.* As I look back upon the
first steps in this miserable business, and as I contemplate the means
used to complete the outrage, I am ashamed of the whole affair." [136]

It is not likely that Bayard would have expressed his opinion in this
petulant language. He had long regarded Hawaiian annexation as
inevitable: it was "simply a matter of waiting until the apple should
ripen and fall." Because of his deep interest in Hawaii as a probable
American outpost in the mid-Pacific, he had rejected a proposal from
the British Government to "neutralize" the islands. America needed a
half-way house on the long trip to the Orient, and the paramount
position that this country had achieved through its contacts and its
treaties with Hawaii, should not be surrendered in favor of some international agreement that would place all nations upon an equal basis.
As Secretary of State, Bayard had favored a policy that would prepare
the way for the ultimate annexation of the islands, and he had strongly
supported the idea of establishing additional ties with Hawaii through
the laying of a cable between San Francisco and Honolulu.[137] In February, 1895, the Senate of the United States was ready to support such a
project with a large appropriation.[138] President Cleveland, however,
was determined not to "boom the annexation craze by entering upon
Government cable building," [139] and the Senate, under the threat of a
veto, receded from its stand. Knight-errant to the bitter end, Cleveland was sadly lacking in the political realism that usually characterized
the policy of Bayard.

135. Thomas A. Bailey, *A Diplomatic History of the American People* (N. Y., 1940),
p. 475.
136. Grover Cleveland to Richard Olney, July 8, 1898, *Cleveland MS.*
137. Bayard to Secretary Gresham, August 5, 1893, *Bayard MS.*
138. *Congressional Record,* 53 Cong., 3 sess., p. 1986.
139. President Cleveland to Bayard, February 13, 1895, *Cleveland MS.*

The Corean Question

CHAPTER THIRTEEN

Bayard Plays the Role of Realist in a Corean Interlude

ALTHOUGH BAYARD WAS DEEPLY INTERESTED IN THE PROBLEMS OF THE
Pacific area, he was a political realist who refused to permit mere
sentiment to control his judgment. This attitude was of particular
importance with reference to American policy towards Corea. In May,
1882, Commodore Shufeldt opened Corea to the nations of the Western
World, and for a short time American influence in the Hermit Kingdom was a significant factor in Far Eastern international relations. But
the American Government did not possess the military strength to
support a positive policy in the Orient, and there would have been little
popular interest in a bold program of colonial expansion. America did
not become colony-conscious until the thunder of Commodore Dewey's
guns at Manila Bay announced the fact that a new world power had
come into existence.

In the United States, the boundless resources of a great continent
had absorbed all the energies of a restless people until the turn of the
twentieth century. In Europe the narrow confines of national territory
had early led to a race for colonial empire, and after 1870, the gospel
of economic imperialism became the accepted creed of the principal
European powers. Undeveloped or backward countries were quickly
partitioned into spheres of influence, and statesmen spent most of their
time exploring the commercial opportunities that beckoned to their
nations. Big business soon made the conduct of foreign relations a mere
essay in dollar diplomacy.

In the United States, during the administrations of Presidents Grant,
Hayes, Arthur, and Cleveland, the first low murmurs of the call of
imperialism began to be heard, but they were too indistinct to awaken
popular interest. America still cherished its doctrine of idealism, and

it continued to express towards backward nations an earnest desire to
help rather than to exploit them. But this assistance was never thought
of in terms of military intervention, and therein lay the weakness of
the American position.

The first indication of American interest in Corea was contained in
a report that was submitted by Edmund Roberts to Secretary McLane,
May 12, 1834. It was the opinion of Roberts that one of the advantages
that might accrue to America through the opening of Japan, was the
possibility that such action would lead to trade with Corea.[1] A similar
viewpoint was entertained by Zadoc Pratt, who introduced into the
House of Representatives (February 12, 1845) a resolution which recommended that immediate steps be taken to open Japan and Corea to
American commerce.[2] After Commodore Perry had carried out the first
item in this program in 1854, it was inevitable that Corea should again
engage the attention of the American Government.

After the close of the American Civil War, Secretary Seward had
ample opportunity to express his deep interest in a policy of expansion.
The purchase of Alaska in 1867 was only one step in a projected American march to the Far East.[3] In August, 1867, the Midway Islands came
under American control,[4] and on September 12, 1867, Seward expressed
to the American representative at Honolulu the opinion that "a lawful
and peaceful annexation of the islands to the United States, with the
consent of the people of the Sandwich Islands, is deemed desirable by
this Government." [5]

In March, 1866, some French Roman Catholic missionaries, and a
large number of their converts, were massacred in Corea. Shortly after
the news of these murders reached China, Rear Admiral Roze, in command of the French Asiatic Squadron, went to Corean waters to investigate the situation and to make a survey of the Corean coast. When he
returned he brought the information that an American vessel, the

1. Tyler Dennett, *Americans in Eastern Asia* (N. Y,, 1922), p. 246.

2. *Congressional Globe,* 38 Cong., 2 sess., vol. 14, p. 294; John W. Foster, *American
Diplomacy in the Orient* (N. Y., 1903), p. 142; William E. Griffis, *Corea, The Hermit
Nation* (N. Y., 1904), p. 390.

3. Tyler Dennett, "Seward's Far Eastern Policy," *American Historical Review,* October,
1922, vol. 28, pp. 45-62; Frederick W. Seward, *Reminiscences of a War-Time Statesman*
(N. Y., 1916), p. 360.

4. John Bassett Moore, *Digest of International Law,* vol. 1, p. 555; *S. Ex. Doc., 79,* 40
Cong., 2 sess.; *S. Rept. 194,* 40 Cong., 3 sess.

5. Secretary Seward to E. M. McCook, September 12, 1867, *Foreign Relations, 1894,
Appendix II,* p. 143.

General Sherman, had been destroyed in the Tai-tong River, Corea, and the crew killed.[6]

Secretary Seward found the news of the murder of the French missionaries and the destruction of the *General Sherman,* "painful and singularly exciting," [7] and he interpreted the sharp notes of protest from the French Minister, at Peking, to Prince Kung, as a clear indication that condign punishment would soon be visited upon the guilty Coreans. Not realizing that the Minister's actions had been taken without consulting the French Government, Seward suggested to Berthemy, the French Minister at Washington, that France and the United States join in a punitive expedition that would compel the Corean authorities in Seoul to give prompt and adequate satisfaction.[8]

After the French Government rejected this overture, Seward next instructed his nephew, Consul-General George F. Seward, at Shanghai, to proceed to Corea and endeavor to conclude a treaty along the lines of the Perry convention of 1854. This visit to Corea was to be a "friendly one," and force was to be used only if found "necessary." [9] George Seward did not undertake this mission because he discovered that his presence in Corean waters would probably lead to new difficulties.

Seward's failure to open Corea did not discourage Secretary Hamilton Fish, who instructed Frederick L. Low, the American Minister at Peking, to make at attempt to establish treaty relations with the Corean Government.[10] In May, 1871, Mr. Low and Rear Admiral John Rodgers entered the River Han with a flotilla of American warships. Low was promptly informed by Corean officials that the King did not wish to sign any treaties with the United States, but he was willing to maintain friendly relations.[11] When Rear Admiral Rodgers ordered two of his warships to survey the Han River, the Coreans responded by firing upon the vessels, and a sharp engagement ensued. After waiting in vain

6. Charles O. Paullin, *Diplomatic Negotiations of American Naval Officers, 1778–1883* (Baltimore, 1912), pp. 283-284; Robert Gale, "The Fate of the General Sherman," *Korean Repository,* vol. 2, No. 7, July, 1895, pp. 253-254; Williams to Secretary Seward, December 16, 1886, *Foreign Relations, 1867, pt. 1,* pp. 426-427. See also, George C. Foulk to Secretary of the Navy Chandler, March 29, 1885, *Corea, Despatches,* vol. 2, MS Dept. of State.

7. Secretary Seward to Williams, November 16, 1866, *Foreign Relations, 1866, pt. 1,* p. 563.

8. Tyler Dennett, "Seward's Far Eastern Policy," *American Historical Review,* vol. 28, pp. 54-56.

9. Tyler Dennett, *Americans in Eastern Asia,* pp. 419-420.

10. Secretary Fish to F. L. Low, April 20, 1870, *Foreign Relations, 1870,* pp. 334-335; F. L. Low to Secretary Fish, November 22, 1870, *ibid.,* 1871, pp. 73-74.

11. F. L. Low to Secretary Fish, May 13, 1871, *For. Rel., 1871,* p. 115.

for a satisfactory apology from the Corean Government, Captain Blake was ordered to destroy the Corean forts. This was easily accomplished and the American expedition returned to China without any success as far as a treaty was concerned.[12]

In the meantime, the Japanese Government was having similar difficulties with Corea. Some of these troubles can be traced to the dynastic situation in Corea. In January, 1864, King Chul-chong had died, and Queen Cho took possession of the royal seal and made Myung-bok, the twelve-year-old son of Prince Heung-sung, the King of Corea. Under the title of Tai-Wen-Kun (Lord of the Great Court), Prince Heung-sung assumed the office of regent, and he ruled with an iron hand. He soon displayed a bitter hostility towards Christianity and towards all foreigners.[13]

It was the Tai-Wen-Kun who inspired the massacre of the French missionaries in 1866, and he regarded the withdrawal of the punitive expedition under Rear Admiral Roze as a signal victory for Corea. His anger was aroused against the Japanese because many of the troops who accompanied Rear Admiral Roze were drawn from the French garrison at Yokohama. For this reason he sharply refused to resume the ancient Corean custom of sending tribute to Japan. Despite this rebuff, the Japanese Government sent two missions to Corea in 1869 for the purpose of establishing closer relations, but they were unsuccessful. This unfriendly attitude on the part of the Tai-Wen-Kun, led the Imperial Government to send, in August, 1871, Hanabusa, Chief Secretary of the Japanese Foreign Office, to Corea to demand better treatment. Although Hanabusa was supported by the guns of two Japanese warships, he accomplished nothing. The Japanese Government now realized that their plans in Corea could be realized only through the employment of military force. After a Japanese surveying party had been fired upon (in September, 1875) by the Coreans near the mouth of the Han River, a large Japanese flotilla was sent to Corean waters and a treaty was signed at Kang-hoa on February 27, 1876. The first item in the Japanese program of expansion in Corea was completed.[14]

12. F. L. Low to Secretary Fish, May 31, June 2, and June 20, 1871, *For. Rel., 1871*, pp. 116-117, 128-129.

13. Joseph H. Longford, *The Story of Korea* (London, 1911), pp. 297-298; F. A. McKenzie, *The Tragedy of Korea* (London, 1908), pp. 12ff.

14. Nagao Ariga, "Diplomacy," in *Japan by the Japanese* (ed. by Alfred Stead, London, 1904), pp. 148-179; Payson J. Treat, *Diplomatic Relations Between the United States and Japan, 1853–1895* (Stanford, 1932), vol. 1, p. 590-593; W. E. Griffis, *Corea, the Hermit Nation*, pp. 422-423; Morse and McNair, *Far Eastern International Relations*, pp. 388-389.

The first article in this treaty was of special significance. It clearly described Corea as an "independent state," which enjoyed the "same sovereign rights as does Japan." This declaration was an open disavowal of any Chinese suzerainty over Corea, and it prepared the way for Japanese penetration of the Corean peninsula.

Corean relations with China date as far back as the year 1122 B.C., and during long periods of time, Corea was regarded by Emperors of China as a tributary state. This was particularly true after 1644. The rulers of Corea received investiture from the Emperor of China, a ceremony which some publicists have asserted was nothing more than the recognition of "a weak sovereign by the most powerful state in Asia."[15] This connection between China and Corea was confirmed by annual embassies that were sent from Seoul to Peking with tribute for the Emperor. This apparent state of vassalage has been explained as merely a part of a familiar Oriental pattern: it was supposed to be similar to the relationship that existed between a younger and an older brother who occupied the position of the head of the house.[16]

When French missionaries were murdered in Corea in 1866, the Chinese Foreign Office promptly disavowed any authority over either the internal affairs or the foreign relations of Corea.[17] In June, 1873, the Chinese Government repeated to the Japanese Ambassador, Soyejima, this disavowal of any responsibility for the "internal administration" and the foreign relations of Corea.[18] The Japanese treaty with Corea (February 27, 1876) put in explicit language these repeated disavowals by the Chinese Government.

It was apparent to the Chinese statesman, Li Hung Chang, that the only way to block Japanese expansion in Corea was for the Chinese Government to adopt a more positive policy.[19] In 1875 a neutral zone some forty miles wide, lying between Corea and China, was cleared of bandits, and in 1877 the frontier was moved twenty miles to the east.[20] Li Hung Chang also made arrangements to have a Superintendent of

15. H. B. Morse, *The International Relations of the Chinese Empire* (N. Y., 1910, 1918, 3 vols.), vol. 3, p. 2.

16. William W. Rockhill, *China's Intercourse with Corea from the XVth Century to 1895* (London, 1905), pp. 3-4.

17. Bellonet to Prince Kung, July 13, 1866, *Foreign Relations, 1867, pt. 1*, p. 421.

18. Nagao Ariga, "Diplomacy," in *Japan by the Japanese*, pp. 159-165.

19. T. C. Lin, "Li Hung Chang: His Korean Policies, 1870–1885," *The Chinese Social and Political Science Review*, vol. 19, No. 2 (July, 1935), pp. 203-219.

20. W. E. Griffis, *Corea, the Hermit Nation*, p. 421.

Trade installed in Seoul, and he warned the Corean Government to be "on the look-out" for Japanese aggression.[21]

One of the ways to provide against Japanese absorption of Corea was through the widening of Corean contacts with the Western World. If strong Western Powers would enter into treaty relations with Corea, it was very likely, if these ties proved advantageous, that these nations would oppose any Japanese schemes to annex the peninsula. It was for this reason that Li Hung Chang turned towards the United States.

On April 8, 1878, Senator Sargent introduced a resolution which authorized the President to appoint a commission to negotiate a treaty with Corea.[22] Although this resolution was not officially acted upon, it may have had some influence upon the Secretary of the Navy (R. W. Thompson), who decided to send Commodore Robert W. Shufeldt on an important commercial and diplomatic mission to several countries, including Corea. Shufeldt found that Japan was reluctant to give him any real assistance in the matter of opening Corea to Western Powers (1880), and he was quick to respond to an invitation from Li Hung Chang to spend some time with him at Tientsin. Li promised to use his influence with the Corean Government to persuade them to open negotiations with the United States in regard to a treaty. After receiving this offer of assistance, Shufeldt returned to the United States.[23]

In June, 1881, Shufeldt returned to China, but he found Li Hung Chang less co-operative than he had hoped. It was not until April of 1882 that Shufeldt was able to discuss with Li the provisions of the proposed treaty which was finally signed on May 22, 1882. The main reason why the signature of the treaty had been so long delayed was because of the insistence of Li that the American Government should recognize Chinese suzerainty over Corea. This could be accomplished by phrasing the first article of the treaty to read as follows: "Chosen, being a dependent state of the Chinese Empire, has nevertheless heretofore exercised her own sovereignty in all matters of internal administration and foreign relations."

Shufeldt refused to sign any treaty which included such an article, but he did agree to accept a letter from the King of Corea to the President of the United States which contained a similar statement. According to Tyler Dennett, this formula, expressed only in the royal letter,

21. Nagao Ariga, *op. cit.,* p. 181.
22. C. O. Paullin, *Diplomatic Negotiations of American Naval Officers, 1778–1883,* p. 293.
23. *Ibid.,* pp. 299-301.

was really worthless.[24] Corea was now launched upon an independent national career, and treaties based upon this American model were soon signed with other powers. As Mr. Pollard significantly remarks:

> The treaty of 1882 is seen to mark an important step in the rivalry of China and Japan over Corea, and in the struggles of European nations for political and commercial advantage in the Far East. It is not too much to say that the American treaty bearing the name of Commodore Shufeldt set in motion the train of circumstances which led first to the Sino-Japanese War, then to the Russo-Japanese War, and finally to the annexation of Corea by Japan.[25]

The signing of the Corean-American treaty of May 22, 1882, led to serious riots in Seoul which apparently were instigated by the Tai-Wen-Kun. The Queen narrowly escaped assassination, and thirteen Japanese were murdered. The Japanese Government quickly sent a punitive expedition which forced compliance with its demands, and peace was restored.[26] Despite this unsettled condition of affairs in Corea, President Arthur, on February 26, 1883, appointed Lucius H. Foote as Envoy Extraordinary and Minister Plenipotentiary to the Corean Government. On May 13, 1883, Foote arrived at Chemulpo, and six days later diplomatic relations were formally established.[27] The Corean Government responded by sending a mission to the United States where it was received with marked cordiality. This was the high point in Corean-American relations.[28]

When the Corean mission was visiting the United States, Ensign George C. Foulk was appointed as one of the escort officers to accompany it, and in June, 1884, Foulk began his duties in Seoul as Naval Attaché. Because of the frequent changes in the diplomatic representatives of the United States at Seoul, Foulk was destined to play a most important role in Corean-American relations from 1884 to 1887. As chargé d'affaires for nearly two years, his responsibilities were very onerous, and his quick, warm sympathies led him to favor a policy of

24. Tyler Dennett, *Americans in Eastern Asia*, p. 460. See also, Robert T. Pollard, "American Relations with Korea, 1882–1895," *Chinese Social and Political Science Review*, vol. 16, No. 3, October, 1932, pp. 426-427; T. C. Lin, "Li Hung Chang: His Korean Policies, 1870–1885," *op. cit.*, pp. 222-224.

25. Robert Pollard, *op. cit.*, p. 425.

26. Tyler Dennett, "American Choices in the Far East in 1882," *American Historical Review*, vol. 30, No. 1, October, 1924, pp. 87-102.

27. Foote to Secretary Frelinghuysen, May 24, 25, 1883, *Foreign Relations, 1883*, pp. 241-244.

28. Robert T. Pollard, "American Relations with Korea, 1882–1895," *Chinese Social and Political Science Review*, vol. 16, pp. 430-432.

effective support to Corean independence. But he underestimated the difficulties that attended every venture in Far Eastern diplomacy, and his failure to take a realistic view of the situation in Corea, caused his efforts to a disappointing end.

In 1884 Corea was a focal point for diplomatic intrigue in the Far East. China was anxious to retain her shadowy control over Corea, and her efforts to do so were vigorously opposed by Japan. Russia realized the importance of Corea as an outpost on the China Sea, and she hoped to increase her influence in the peninsula. Great Britain had two important items in her program of power politics. She not only wished to check the advance of Russia in Corea, but she also expected to divert Chinese attention from the British penetration of Burma. According to Tyler Dennett, England was "even more interested in the Corean question than were the Chinese. From such evidence as is available England appears to have been the initial arch-conspirator." [29]

Whether this analysis is correct or not, it is certain that in the early eighties, China suddenly became anxious to confirm her claim of suzerainty over Corea. The Corean Embassy to the United States was headed by Min Yong Ik, a relative of the Queen, and an important member of the pro-Chinese faction. While in the United States, Min discussed with Secretary Frelinghuysen the matter of sending some eminent American to serve as an adviser to the King of Corea. Min finally approached Shufeldt in this regard, and his reply was so favorable that the members of the Corean Embassy expected his early departure for Seoul where he would not only assume the duties of political adviser but would also serve as the director of military and naval affairs. In addition to these overtures to Shufeldt, Min requested the American Government to permit Ensign George Foulk to serve as Naval Attaché in Seoul.

Shufeldt did not arrive in the Far East until 1886, and he never entered the service of the Corean Government. Min Yong Ik had been interested in both Shufeldt and Foulk because he believed they would be willing to serve as the tools of the pro-Chinese party in Corea, and would play the diplomatic game in accordance with the rules that Li Hung Chang would formulate.[30] When Shufeldt finally arrived in the Far East he evinced strong opposition to China's claim of suzerainty

29. Tyler Dennett, "Early American Policy in Korea, 1883–1887," *Political Science Quarterly*, vol. 38, No. 1, March, 1923, p. 84.

30. With reference to the pressure behind the proposed appointment of Shufeldt, see the letters from E. H. Frazar, Consul-General of Corea in New York City, to Bayard, July 3, October 29, 1885, *Bayard MS.*

over Corea, and Foulk expressed himself in similar fashion. In taking this stand they defeated the hopes of Li Hung Chang, and earned the sharp hostility of the pro-Chinese faction in Seoul.

When Foulk arrived in Corea in June, 1884, he soon discovered that the King and some of his close associates were in no mood to listen to continued Chinese dictation.[31] Li Hung Chang had installed P. G. von Möllendorff as his personal representative in Seoul, and this unmannerly Teuton held the office of Superintendent of Corean Customs and also enjoyed the important position of Vice-President of the Corean Foreign Office. After the outbreak of the Franco-Chinese War in August, 1884, Chinese influence in Seoul diminished for a time, and the Japanese who were resident in Corea began to exert pressure upon the King to declare his independence of China. Finally, on the night of December 4, 1884, the anti-Chinese faction, aided by the Japanese, attempted a coup d'état. Min Yong Ik was severely wounded by the conspirators, and several of his associates were killed. The King hurriedly summoned the Japanese Minister and his armed guard to the palace, and under Japanese direction, he issued a series of decrees, one of which provided for the complete political independence of Corea. The Chinese troops then entered the fray and seized control of the King. The Japanese were driven from Seoul and the revolution was quickly suppressed. The counteraction of the Japanese Government would have been quite far-reaching had it not been for the fact that the Franco-Chinese War came to an end in the spring of 1885, thus leaving China free to oppose Japanese designs in Corea. In the Treaty of Seoul, January 9, 1885, the very modest demands of the Japanese Government were satisfactorily settled, and the contest for Corea was postponed for a decade.[32]

In January, 1885, Mr. Foote left Seoul en route for the United States, leaving Foulk as the chargé d'affaires ad interim. He was destined to hold this office for the next sixteen months. During this interval the Cleveland Administration came into power, and Bayard assumed the duties of Secretary of State in March, 1885. One of the first questions

---

31. In a long report attached to the despatch from Lucius H. Foote to Secretary Frelinghuysen, December 17, 1884, *Corea, Despatches,* vol. 1, MS Dept. of State, Mr. Foulk has an interesting and informing sketch of conditions in Corea. See also, Foulk to W. E. Chandler, Secretary of the Navy, December 23, 1884, *Foulk Papers,* New York Public Library.

32. Foote to Secretary Frelinghuysen, December 5, 17, 1884, *Corea, Despatches,* vol. 2, MS Dept. of State. See also, Nagao Ariga, "Diplomacy," in *Japan by the Japanese,* pp. 189-199; F. A. McKenzie, *The Tragedy of Korea,* pp. 33-36.

that Bayard had to settle with reference to the problems of the Far East, was the appointment of a competent Minister to China. It was finally decided to bestow this important office upon Colonel Charles Denby, of Indiana.

The appointment of Denby was quite reassuring to American "big business" which was looking with acquisitive eyes upon certain commercial opportunities in China. China, with its vast expanse of territory, would soon need a series of railways to meet the growing needs of an important empire. Americans should build these railroads and share in the profits from their successful operation.

On March 17, 1885, Samuel L. Barlow, a typical business "promoter" of New York City, wrote to Bayard about the possibilities of constructing railroads throughout the Chinese Empire. He believed that the Imperial Government was "prepared to begin the building of railroads, and one of the first of her projects is to construct nearly one thousand miles, and she would prefer that this should be done under American auspices, and we could supply rails, cars and the general management."

It was essential that a keen man, with an eye to the expansion of American business opportunities, be selected as the American Minister to China. While the Minister could "take no part in such enterprises, he can do much to this end if he be a wise man." [33]

Big business regarded Denby as distinctly a "wise man" who would aid in the development of business interests in China. General James H. Wilson, of Wilmington, Delaware, was delighted with the appointment. The General was about to leave on a trip to China to survey the situation with special reference to railroad construction. He had learned that the Chinese Government was interested in building "certain important trunk lines of railway at once," and he had been informed that English and German capital, strongly supported by their governments, were endeavoring to secure far-reaching concessions. Wilson was certain that unless American business interests were given prompt support by the Cleveland Administration, through the American Minister to China, they would receive no favors from the Chinese Government. Denby's appointment was particularly pleasing to General Wilson:

33. S. L. M. Barlow to Secretary Bayard, March 17, 1885, *Bayard MS.* See also the strong letters from John W. Foster, June 14, 1885, and from Representative R. W. Townshend, April 3, 1885, approving Denby's appointment as Minister to China. *Bayard MS.*

I have had the pleasure of knowing Colonel Denby for many years, and am sure of his personal help and approval, as far as he can properly give them, and I may add that the selection of a man of his wisdom, prudence and character, has encouraged myself and associates to undergo the expense and take the risk of our proposed venture.[34]

It was not long before General Wilson showed his evident desire to mix business with diplomacy in a way that would be highly beneficial to the interests that he represented. Li Hung Chang, under English inspiration, was making every effort to retain some measure of Chinese control over Corea. The British Government lent support to Li's plans by appointing, as its diplomatic representative at Seoul, a Consul-General who was responsible to the British Minister in Peking. Would it not be wise for the American Government to follow a similar procedure and receive important concessions from Li Hung Chang as a consequence of this team work?

On October 29, 1885, General Wilson sent a telegram to Bayard in which he strongly recommended the appointment of Denby "to Corea as well as China, making this first class mission same English have done." [35] On the following day, Wilson wrote a long letter which explained in detail the position he had taken in his telegram. He believed that Colonel Denby should be accredited as Minister to Corea as well as to China because such action would raise "our mission to a dignity and influence in this Country, which it has not enjoyed since the time of Mr. Burlingame." Moreover, Corea was a very

... poor and backward country with which we are not likely to have a great business at an early day, though her markets for our manufactures will certainly open up in due time. Meanwhile, it is more than probable that all commercial and diplomatic questions arising in or in regard to Corea, will have to be discussed, as well, with the Chinese Government, for the reason that Corea from its geographical position, if not its traditional political subordination to China, will necessarily make its advances under the guidance and perhaps the domination of the Chinese Government, and on the same general line of progress. ...

A Consul, or Consul-General, residing at the Capital or principal seaport of Corea can well look after all our commercial and other interests during Colonel Denby's absence, and being in direct telegraphic communication with Peking, can call him to Corea or ask his instructions in case any emergency demands it. A part of the Salary and nearly all the other expenses of a permanent legation at Seoul, will obviously be saved by carrying into effect

34. General James H. Wilson to Secretary Bayard, August 29, 1885, *Bayard MS.*
35. James H. Wilson to Secretary Bayard, October 29, 1885, *ibid.*

the suggestion which is the occasion of this letter. The British Government has already appointed its minister at Peking to be also minister to Corea. Should our government do the same, it would fully justify you in recommending and Congress in raising the dual or joint mission, to one of the first class.[36]

General Wilson next suggested the advisability of making a loan to the Chinese Government for the purpose of aiding railroad construction. Such a loan would be of great benefit to the United States in many ways. If we could lend American silver dollars

. . . for the purpose of building railroads and developing the other industrial resources of this wonderful country, it would give us practical business control of it, rid our treasury of the silver which burthens it, and at the same time, secure advantages for our skill and enterprize, as well as an almost illimitable market for many of our natural and manufactured products.[37]

Although these letters were written from Tientsin, it is apparent that General Wilson was in close touch with Minister Denby, at Peking. On October 10, 1885, Denby wrote a long personal letter to Bayard in which he reviewed the situation in China. He had enjoyed two interviews with Li Hung Chang, who was the outstanding statesman in China. Their conversation had inevitably drifted towards business topics, and Li had intimated that

. . . in a year there would be Rail Roads in China. I, as delicately as I could, suggested that in the event of building Rail Roads it would be very agreeable to me if American engineers could be employed, and Rail Road supplies purchased in the United States. I understand of course that this is no part of my diplomatic business, and officially I have nothing to do with Rail Roads. But, I presume you will pardon me, if when drinking a glass of wine with the Vice Roy, he chooses to raise this question, I put in, as an American Citizen, a good word for our manufacturers and engineers. I so understood your views and the President's in our conversations. Business is very much done in this manner in China, and there is no place in the world where social influence is so important, and where what you call a "grata persona" may establish personal influence by his manners, habits, and the graces of life.[38]

36. James H. Wilson to Secretary Bayard, October 30, 1885, *Bayard MS.*
37. James H. Wilson to Secretary Bayard, October 31, 1885, *ibid.* In a *memorandum*, written on December 18, 1885, Bayard remarks: "The U. S. Gov't could not regularly make any *loan* to China, altho' doubtless its citizens could and would if the rates *were favorable*. But if the loan was in Standard, legal tender Silver dollars, not one would ever leave the U. S., but would be put in circulation here where their *fiat* power alone is recognized. Otherwise, China would not pay more than the market price of Bullion." *Bayard MS.*
38. Denby to Secretary Bayard, *Personal*, October 10, 1885, *Bayard MS.*

Notwithstanding the fact that Colonel Denby was *persona grata* at Peking, and therefore, in an excellent position to secure important concessions for American corporations, there were certain objections to his being accredited to Corea. They were outlined by Mr. Adee in a memorandum for Bayard:

China has claimed suzerainty over Corea. Our treaty with Corea was negotiated under Viceroy Li's management. When China seemed disposed, afterwards, to intimate that the treaty was made with her consent, we were obliged to intimate pretty strongly that we negotiated with Corea as a Sovereign State. To accredit Col. Denby to Corea also might be construed by China as an acquiescence in her claim of suzerainty. It would almost certainly be distasteful to Japan, which has nearly gone to war with China because of Corea. . . . Unless a Secretary of Legation be provided at Corea, with a living salary, our representation at Seoul would be merely nominal. . . . Col. Denby could only go there semi-occasionally, and at considerable cost for travelling expenses. At other times, diplomatic intercourse with Corea would be practically suspended.[39]

After stating these objections, Adee himself went on record as being "in favor of accrediting Col. Denby to Corea also." Bayard did not accept this advice, and despite the opposition of the Chinese Government, he appointed William H. Parker as the American Minister Resident at Seoul. But Parker did not arrive at his post until June, 1886, and in the interim, Foulk served as the chargé d'affaires. He was nearly engulfed in the tides of diplomatic intrigue that swept through Seoul.

Since December, 1884, there were considerable forces of Japanese and Chinese troops quartered in Seoul, and there was constant danger of open hostilities between them. The Corean Government was anxious to preserve a neutral status in the event of war between Japan and China, but

. . . through fear and weakness, it may not make such a declaration to the Chinese, nor refuse the . . . demands or requests of the Chinese. . . . The Chinese . . . are creating alarms and apprehension among the Coreans tending towards forcing the Corean Government to apply for further Chinese assistance.[40]

In view of the threatening international situation, Foulk believed that it was important for the Corean Government to organize in a more effective fashion its military forces. On October 19, 1883, and again on

39. Adee to Secretary Bayard, October 28, 1885, *ibid.*
40. Foulk to Secretary Frelinghuysen, March 9, 1885, *Corea, Despatches, Confidential,* vol. 2, MS Dept. of State.

September 10, 1884, the Corean Foreign Office had sent, through the agency of the American Minister, appeals to the United States for military instructors. These instructors had not arrived, and the Corean King repeatedly inquired of Foulk when they might be expected.[41] Foulk's inability to name a definite date when the instructors would arrive, had caused him "great embarrassment." The King was disappointed but still hoped that in addition to military instructors, the American Government would send a competent person to serve as an "adviser" to the Corean Foreign Office, and also school teachers and skilled farmers to carry on a broad program of education.[42] The American Presbyterian Board of Missions had already sent an able physician, Dr. H. N. Allen, who had taken charge of the Government hospital in Seoul. American influence in Corea could be extended in a significant manner by the extension of similar services.[43]

But these plans for a peaceful penetration of Corea by well-meaning Americans, were upset by the actions of P. G. von Möllendorff, who held the important post of Vice-President of the Corean Foreign Office. Unknown to his patron, Li Hung Chang, Möllendorff had entered into an agreement with the Russian Government whereby Russian officers were to serve as drill-masters for the Corean army. When the British Government got wind of this arrangement, a fleet was promptly sent to Port Hamilton in April, 1885, and plans were laid to use this as a base against any Russian advance in Corea.[44]

In June, Alexis de Speyer, Secretary of the Russian Legation at Tokio, paid a visit to Seoul, and the negotiations that had been carried on by Möllendorff were thoroughly ventilated. He announced to Foulk that in the event that England continued to occupy Port Hamilton, Russia would insist upon acquiring "ten times as much territory." [45] With reference to the employment of military instructors for the Corean

41. Foulk to Secretary Frelinghuysen, March 12, 1885, *ibid.*

42. Foulk to Secretary Bayard, April 28, 1885, *Corea, Despatches,* vol. 2, MS Dept. of State; Foulk to Secretary Bayard, May 25, 1885, *ibid.*

43. Foulk to Secretary Bayard, May 30, 1885, *Corea, Despatches,* vol. 2, MS Dept. of State. On May 8, 1885 Foulk presented to the King of Corea an autograph letter of good will from President Cleveland. The King pointedly inquired about the arrival of American military instructors, and Foulk replied that he thought he could supply the information "at an early date." Foulk to Bayard, May 9, 1885, *ibid.* On May 13, 1885 Bayard instructed Foulk that Congress had adjourned without acting upon this matter of military instructors for Corea. *Corea, Instructions,* vol. 1, MS Dept. of State.

44. Foulk to Secretary Bayard, May 19, 21, 1885, *Corea, Despatches,* vol. 2, MS Dept. of State.

45. Foulk to Bayard, June 16, 1885, *ibid.*

army, Speyer, in a conversation with officials of the Foreign Office, spoke in the most threatening tone:

If you do not accept the American Army instructors, there would be no loss; but if you do not take the Russian officers, you must lose a great deal. . . . If you break with America in this, there is no loss, but if you do with Russia, trouble lies directly before your eyes.[46] . . . Your Government suspects Russia of a desire to seize territory, and is unwilling to be on friendly and close relations. This is altogether wrong. My country possesses a vast extent of uncultivated land, why then, should she think of seizing any territory belonging to Corea? Supposing that Russia had such a design on Corean territory, and followed England's action in occupying Port Hamilton without giving Corea official notice. Your Government would be perfectly helpless. It is no feeling of fear that keeps my Government from not doing so. . . . America is far away from Corea, and cannot be of any benefit to your country.[47]

The King of Corea denied "all knowledge" of the agreements entered into between Möllendorff and agents of the Russian Government, and in Seoul there was talk of bringing him to trial for "high treason." Foulk advised against this procedure because Möllendorff was a German subject, and he feared trouble with Bismarck. But Foulk was fearful that the Anglo-Russian quarrel might lead to hostilities on Corean soil, so he suggested to the Chinese and Japanese representatives in Seoul that they postpone the contemplated withdrawal of their troops.[48]

To Bayard it was evident that Foulk was taking too active an interest in the diplomatic intrigues in Seoul. The United States was not ready to pursue a bold policy in Corea which might have to be supported by military force. There was a great deal of truth in Speyer's words of warning to the Corean Foreign Office: "America is far away from Corea, and cannot be of any benefit to your country." In his instructions to Foulk, Bayard clearly outlined the policy that should be followed:

I have received . . . your confidential despatch . . . of June 23d last, in regard to the secret negotiations of Mr. P. G. von Möllendorff, for Corea, with Russia. In this connection I desire to advert to the conclusion of your despatch suggesting that the Chinese and Japanese troops should remain longer in Corea, and to remind you that very great discretion is necessary in

46. Foulk to Secretary Bayard, June 18, 23, 26, 1885, *ibid.*
47. Foulk to Secretary Bayard, July 3, 1885, *Corea, Despatches,* vol. 2, MS Dept. of State.
48. Foulk to Secretary Bayard, June 23, 1885, *Corea, Despatches, Confidential,* MS Dept. of State.

making such intimations to the Chinese and Japanese representatives. The Government of the United States has no concern in these matters beyond that of a friendly state which has treated Corea as independent and sovereign and hopes to see her position as such among nations assured.[49]

With reference to the dubious activities of Alexis de Speyer, Bayard again warned Foulk against taking any steps that would impair the impartial attitude of the American Government:

> Seoul is the centre of conflicting and almost hostile intrigues involving the interests of China, Japan, Russia, and England. . . . It is clearly the interest of the United States to hold aloof from all this and do nothing nor be drawn into anything which would look like taking sides with any of the contestants, or entering the lists of intrigue for our own benefit. Hence the exercise of the utmost discretion on your part is necessary. . . . The United States can take no action which might even in appearance seem to favor or oppose the policy of either China or Japan, without impairing the position of friendly impartiality towards all which it is the duty and the pleasure of this nation to maintain.[50]

Speyer himself called at the American Legation in Seoul and explained to Foulk the details of the Möllendorf negotiations. He claimed to have been deceived by Möllendorff as to the real condition of affairs in Corea, and now that the arrangements for Russian military instructors had been completed, it was possible that the Czar's Government would insist that they be carried out.[51]

On July 27 Möllendorff was dismissed from his post in the Corean Foreign Office, and Foulk freely expressed his feelings in a despatch to Bayard. When the Corean Government became aware of Möllendorff's secret negotiations with Speyer,

> . . . a Corean Envoy was despatched to China to report his conduct to Li Hung Chang, the Vice-roy of Chihli, by whom von Möllendorff was placed originally in the service of the Corean Government. This Envoy returned to Corea on the 26th ultimo, and presented to the King a report of charges against von Möllendorff prepared by Li Hung Chang. The conduct of this man would seem to be without a parallel in history. The audacity with which he originated and acted upon schemes of every sort, many of them involving the integrity of the state has been so bold as to create the impression far and wide that he was receiving the actual support of His Majesty, or controlled the powerful influence of the strong pro-Chinese factions in

49. Secretary Bayard to Foulk, August 18, 1885, *Corea, Instructions*, vol. 1, MS Dept. of State.

50. Secretary Bayard to Foulk, August 19, 1885, *Corea, Instructions*, vol. 1, MS Dept. of State.

51. Foulk to Secretary Bayard, July 5, 1885, *Corea, Despatches, Confidential*, vol. 2, MS Dept. of State.

the Government. Nevertheless, I have been long aware that this was not actually the case. . . .

Prior to the revolutionary troubles of December last, von Möllendorff unquestionably was the agent of China, but was held in check by the more enlightened radical progressionists; these having been driven from the country, he began a most extraordinary and high-handed career. He openly denounced the conduct of several of the foreign representatives, more particularly that of the United States.[52]

Möllendorff had also attempted to invalidate a timber contract entered into between certain Corean officials and the American Trading Company, of Yokohama, Japan. Foulk had been able to check this nefarious action through prompt protests to the Corean Foreign Office.

When Foulk's despatch recounting this episode reached the Department of State, Bayard approved his conduct but once more warned the chargé that "in such cases, the settled policy of this Government is not to intervene officially." [53]

Foulk's position was a difficult one. The Corean Government had hoped that the United States would find some means of checking every step taken by both England and Russia that might compromise the sovereignty of Corea.[54] The Chinese and Japanese Governments were also anxious to use the United States, in an indirect way, to further their interests in Corea. They strongly favored the employment of American military instructors for the Corean army, and Li Hung Chang secured the appointment of Americans in important positions in the Corean national administration. O. N. Denny, who had served with credit in the American consular service, was made Adviser to the Corean Foreign Office,[55] and H. F. Merrill was placed in charge of the Corean Customs Service under the general supervision of Sir Robert Hart.[56]

Both Merrill and Denny were supposed to bend all their efforts in the direction of strengthening China's control over Corea, and Foulk could clearly see that Corea had "become more assuredly than heretofore under the control of China." [57] Another step towards establishing

52. Foulk to Secretary Bayard, August 4, 1885, *ibid.*

53. Secretary Bayard to Foulk, September 22, 1885, *Corea, Instructions,* vol. 1, MS Dept. of State.

54. In June, 1885, the Corean Foreign Office addressed a communication to Foulk in which the good offices of the American Government were asked with reference to securing British evacuation of Port Hamilton. Foulk to Secretary Bayard, June 29, 1885, *Corea, Despatches,* vol. 2, MS Dept. of State.

55. Denny did not assume office until February, 1886.

56. Foulk to Secretary Bayard, August 16, 1885, *Corea, Despatches,* vol. 2, MS Dept. of State.

57. Foulk to Secretary Bayard, August 17, 1885, *Confidential, ibid.*

closer bonds between China and Corea, was the proposed construction of a telegraph line between Seoul and Peking to be financed by the Chinese Government.[58] A final item in this program designed for Chinese control over Corea, was the appointment of Yuan Shi Kai to act as a personal representative for Li Hung Chang. It was significant that Yuan Shi Kai brought back with him from China the Tai-Wen-Kun, who was supposed to be wedded to the interests of China.[59]

While Li Hung Chang was perfecting these arrangements that he hoped would cement China's connections with Corea, a new Russian agent came to Seoul and took up temporary residence. Mr. S. Waeber was sent to Corea for the express purpose of exchanging the ratifications of the treaty negotiated during the last year with Corea. He was also instructed to attempt to secure some provision for overland trade between Russia and Corea. Unlike the dictatorial Speyer, Waeber was mild and conciliatory in manner, and created a distinctly favorable impression in Corean circles.[60]

It was only too apparent to Foulk that the contest for the control of Corea was becoming ever more spirited. Not only was China showing new interest in the Corean situation, but other nations were taking steps to increase their influence. Japan had just completed a new legation building in Seoul, and Russia was "about to open an imposing establishment." Since January, 1885, Foulk had served as the American chargé d'affaires, and his salary was so small that he had to live in the most modest manner. It was unfair to American interests to have merely a chargé in Seoul, and Foulk asked to be relieved of his duties.[61]

Foulk had to wait until June, 1886, before being relieved by William H. Parker, the new American Minister Resident. In the meantime he discharged the duties of chargé with ability and discretion, and the increasing complications in the international situation made his role

58. Foulk to Secretary Bayard, September 25, 1885, *Corea, Despatches, Confidential,* vol. 2, MS Dept. of State.

59. With reference to the political implications of the return of the Tai-Wen-Kun, Foulk, in a despatch to Bayard, October 20, 1885, remarks: "The Tai-Won-Kun has been the deadly enemy of the Queen's house, which has endeavored by every possible means to prevent his return to Corea. The Queen and her family are fearful of his further intriguing against them, and a breach has occurred between them and the Chinese over the latter's having returned him to Corea; by this a new phase of Corean politics is presented, the whole power of the Queen's party heretofore having been dependent upon its happy relations with and the manoeuvering support given by China." *Corea, Despatches,* vol. 3, MS Dept. of State.

60. Foulk to Secretary Bayard, October 14, 1885, *Corea, Despatches,* vol. 2, MS Dept. of State.

61. Foulk to Secretary Bayard, October 21, 1885, *ibid.,* vol. 3.

an important one. On November 23 Yuan Shi Kai called upon Foulk and frankly discussed the relations that existed between China and Corea. He first assured Foulk that O. N. Denny was not coming to Corea to act as Adviser to the King, because he was not needed in that capacity. Yuan himself would take over the duties of Adviser, and he hoped to derive much benefit from frequent consultation with Foulk concerning important matters of state. The exact title of Yuan's office in the Corean service was never determined, but by some diplomatic representatives he was spoken of as the Chinese Resident, a term that was probably suggested by British usage in India, where the British representative at a native court was spoken of as a "Resident." [62]

Yuan had expressed the desire to be "guided largely by the United States in Corean matters," but this direction would be assented to only if it was in agreement with the course charted by Li Hung Chang. In the autumn of 1885, Li still hoped to derive assistance from the United States with reference to his plans in Corea, and he continued to exert pressure upon the Corean Foreign Office in regard to securing American military instructors. The fact that he could largely control the granting of important railway concessions in China, was not overlooked by Americans who were anxious to support his policy of establishing Chinese suzerainty over Corea. In December, 1885, the German Minister at Peking was making determined efforts to prevent the extension of any favors to American capitalists,[63] and Samuel Barlow wrote to Bayard to learn if Minister Denby felt "authorized under his instructions to do all that he can in favor of all American enterprises and especially those so important to our people as the building of many miles of railroad." [64]

Bayard assured Barlow that Denby did not "lack friendly instruction in relation to American enterprises of the kind General Wilson alludes to." He was certain that General Wilson, who was in China at that time looking over the situation, had matters "thoroughly in hand" and was ready "to rattle all the china in the National Cupboard." [65]

This china could be rattled in the national cupboard to good effect only so long as Li Hung Chang believed that American and Chinese interests in the Far East were in agreement. In February, 1886, he still

62. Foulk to Secretary Bayard, November 25, 1885, *Corea, Despatches, Confidential,* vol. 3, MS Dept. of State.
63. Denby to Secretary Bayard, December 25, 1885, *Bayard MS.*
64. Samuel L. M. Barlow to Secretary Bayard, February 17, 1886, *Bayard MS.*
65. Bayard to Barlow, February 19, 1886, *Bayard Letter Book,* Vol. 2, *ibid.*

cherished the conviction that it was wise to have Americans in the
Corean service. In February, 1886, despite the loud boasts of Yuan Shi
Kai to the contrary, O. N. Denny arrived in Seoul and was installed as
an adviser in the Corean Foreign Office. It was only natural that a feeling of rivalry should spring up between Denny and Yuan Shi Kai, and
it was not long before Yuan entertained a similar dislike for Foulk.

For a while, cordial relations were maintained between Yuan and
H. F. Merrill, in the Corean Customs Service,[66] but these were seriously
strained when Yuan inspired an attack upon the Customs Service at
Chemulpo. Effective action against repeated assaults of Chinese hood-
lums, was taken only after Merrill had appealed to Li Hung Chang.[67]
Yuan's motive in inciting these disturbances was apparently to register
some strong protest against the payment of any duties upon Chinese
goods entering Corean ports.[68] If Corea was really a tributary state, it
was absurd to expect Chinese goods to be subject to tariff duties.

As a result of this increasing friction, Foulk's health rapidly failed,
and on February 18, 1886, he again requested Secretary Bayard to appoint some officer to relieve him of the responsibilities of chargé d'affaires. There had been no adequate provision for clerical assistance in
the American legation in Seoul, and the salary as chargé had been so
small that Foulk had been compelled to deny himself "reasonable and
necessary comforts of living." [69]

But nothwithstanding this sad state of affairs, Foulk had to discharge
the duties of chargé until the arrival of William H. Parker on June 8.
Foulk's last despatch to Bayard, June 2, 1886, gave a disturbing picture
of the dictatorial manner assumed by Yuan Shi Kai towards the diplomatic representatives of the other powers. In a series of despatches to
the Corean Foreign Office, Yuan emphatically stated that he was in
Seoul to "direct the Corean Government in all its foreign relations."
This action was express violation of the Treaty of Tientsin, April 18,
1885. Under the terms of this treaty, both China and Japan promised
to withdraw their troops from Corea. It was also provided that the King
of Corea should engage military instructors from a third power, and
that in the event of any disturbance of a grave nature in Corea which

66. Foulk to Secretary Bayard, January 18, 1886, *Corea, Despatches, Confidential,* vol. 3,
MS Dept. of State.
67. Foulk to Secretary Bayard, February 1, 1886, *ibid.*
68. Foulk to Secretary Bayard, February 1, 1886, *ibid.*
69. Foulk to Secretary Bayard, February 18, 1886, *Corea, Despatches,* vol. 3, MS Dept.
of State.

required the despatch of troops, each nation would give notice to the other "of their intention so to do." The Japanese viewpoint of this convention had been that it prevented either Japan or China from asserting a claim to any "authority over the rightful sovereignty of the Corean Government."[70]

Yuan Shi Kai's high-handed actions were making inevitable a war between Japan and China over Corea, but this clash of arms did not take place until 1894. During Bayard's term as Secretary of State, Chinese influence in Corea continued to grow, and no serious attempt was made to challenge Li Hung Chang's program of expansion. When Mr. Parker arrived in Seoul as the American Minister Resident, he was given an audience with the King, who went out of his way to show his cordiality. He informed the American Minister that he "looked upon the United States as his best friend," and he expressed the hope that Foulk would remain in Seoul and enter the civil service of Corea.[71]

Foulk had hoped to have a much-needed vacation from diplomatic duties, but Parker turned out to be a confirmed drunkard and a hopeless misfit. On June 27, 1886, Foulk reported to Bayard that Parker had been on a prolonged debauch, and that the effect of the Minister's conduct upon Corean-American relations, was "deplorable beyond expression."[72]

In a letter to Allan McLane, Parker gave a short description of conditions in Seoul. He protested strongly against the fact that he had no secretarial assistance, and had to work eight hours a day. He assured McLane that he used "no liquor, beer, or wine of any description."[73] This must be interpreted as mere diplomatic verbiage, because on July 28 his private secretary wrote to Bayard to complain of Parker's "gross intemperance," and to recommend his immediate recall.[74]

The upshot of the whole matter was that Parker was removed from

70. Foulk to Secretary Bayard, June 2, 1886, *Corea, Despatches, Confidential*, vol. 3, MS Dept. of State; Payson J. Treat, *Diplomatic Relations Between the United States and Japan, 1853–1895* (Stanford, 1932), vol. 2, pp. 216-218.

71. W. H. Parker to Secretary Bayard, June 13, 1886, *Corea, Despatches*, vol. 3, MS Dept. of State.

72. Foulk to Secretary Bayard, June 27, 1886, *ibid.*

73. W. H. Parker to Allan McLane, July 5, 1886, *Bayard MS.*

74. R. J. Travers to Secretary Bayard, July 28, 1886, *ibid.* In a letter to Bayard, August 18, 1886, Allan McLane expresses his great regret over Parker's intemperance, and ascribes it to a "*sudden* temptation and evil impulse which, unfortunately, he was unable to master." In a second letter to Bayard, August 19, 1886, McLane voices the opinion that Parker's conduct was "without palliation," but it was also quite probable that Foulk drew the picture "with all the coloring at Command." *Bayard MS.*

Seoul, and Foulk was ordered to take over once more the duties of chargé d'affaires.[75] General James H. Wilson, who had just returned from China suggested to Bayard the appointment of Mr. Smithers as Minister to Corea, and the appointment of William N. Pethick, vice-consul at Tientsin, to the position of consul. It is interesting to note in this regard that both Smithers and Pethick were friendly with Li Hung Chang, and apparently General Wilson was still hoping to secure concessions by supporting the policies of the powerful viceroy.[76]

Bayard did not accept this advice with reference to Corea, and Foulk remained as chargé d'affaires until December, 1886, when W. W. Rockhill took over that office. In the interim, Foulk had to bear the burden of some very onerous diplomatic duties. In August, 1886, a conspiracy was hatched by Yuan Shi Kai to dethrone the King and elevate the son of the King's eldest brother as the heir-apparent. During the minority of the new King, the Tai-Wen-Kun was to act as the regent.

In a pamphlet entitled, *China and Corea*, published in February, 1888, O. N. Denny told an amazing story of the Chinese design for diplomatic living as conceived in the fertile brain of Yuan Shi Kai. With reference to the plot to dethrone the King of Corea, Denny remarks:

The execution of this diabolical business involved riots, arson, bloodshed, and probable assassinations, besides imperilling the lives of all foreigners in Seoul, as well as those of many of the native people. Every detail of this wicked conspiracy is in the possession of the King, and . . . would have been carried out but for the integrity and loyalty of Prince Min Yong Ik. . . . The most extraordinary part of this infamous business is the draft of it which was to have been and doubtless was submitted to the Viceroy [Li Hung Chang] for his approval or rejection. . . . In one interview, finding that the Viceroy turned a deaf ear to everything reflecting in any way upon Yuan, I was about to dispose of him once for all, as I supposed, by presenting the indisputable evidence of his recent conspiracy, when, to my amazement, the Viceroy coolly informed me that he knew all about the dethronement scheme; that while Yuan was in it, yet it was all the fault of Min Yong Ik, who laid the plot and induced Yuan to go into it, and for his stupidity in letting himself be drawn into such a thing, he had been severely reprimanded. The reprimand was due probably not so much to Yuan's stupidity for being drawn into it, as the Viceroy said, as to the detection and failure of his own wicked conspiracy.[77]

75. Foulk to Secretary Bayard, September 2, 7, 1886, *Corea, Despatches*, vol. 3, MS Dept. of State. In the *Foulk Papers* in the New York Public Library there is a medical certificate from H. N. Allen, June 28, 1886, which indicates the seriously exhausted condition of Foulk and his need for a vacation.

76. James H. Wilson to Secretary Bayard, November 4, 1886, *Bayard MS*.

77. New York *Herald*, August 4, 1888.

These statements of Denny in February, 1888, are largely corroborated in a despatch from Foulk to Bayard, September 8, 1886. On August 16, 1886, Denny had called at the residence of Yuan Shi Kai, who announced in a "wildly excited manner" that he "had accurate knowledge of an agreement in writing, bearing the King's seal, the effect of which was to turn Corea bodily over to Russian protection." He then stated that China would "put an end to such a movement" by sending 70,000 troops into Corea. Yuan also went to the palace and delivered a violent harangue against the alleged agreement between Corea and Russia.

Through Yuan's influence, four prominent Coreans who were friendly to America, were thrown into prison and sentenced to death. Denny was able to save their lives and could have thwarted Yuan's vengeance if the American Minister, W. H. Parker, had not been on a drunken debauch. Despite Denny's strong protests to Li Hung Chang against the conduct of Yuan Shi Kai, the Viceroy took no steps to change his personal representative in Seoul.[78]

The overbearing conduct of Yuan Shi Kai led the King of Corea once more to turn to the United States and request the despatch of military instructors to train the Corean army. On October 3, and in a telegram on the following day, Foulk asked Bayard whether these instructors could be sent soon, and during the course of an audience with the King, His Majesty strongly pressed this inquiry.[79] Owing to lack of Congressional authority, the Cleveland Administration could not respond to this royal request, and this failure to act promptly helped to destroy the few vestiges of American influence that remained

78. Foulk to Secretary Bayard, September 8, 1886, *Corea, Despatches*, vol. 3, MS Dept. of State. In a later despatch to Bayard, Foulk has further comments upon the duplicity of Yuan Shi Kai: "The information I have . . . obtained is fully in harmony with the opinion expressed in my despatch, that the disturbance in Seoul (of August last) was created by the Chinese representative here in an attempt of China to suppress the independent sovereignty of this Kingdom, and that the attempt was frustrated by unexpected complications in Seoul and the fight between sailors of the Chinese fleet at Nagasaki and the police and people of that place. Judge Denny reports that in his earlier interviews the Viceroy was disposed to defend the Chinese representative here, Mr. Yuan, against the charge vigorously brought against him by Judge Denny. . . . The chief charge was that Mr. Yuan had created copies of a purported agreement bearing the seal of the King of Corea by which Corea was turned into a protectorate of Russia. . . . These copies were, however, denounced as forgeries from the beginning by Judge Denny, Mr. Merrill, and several foreign representatives except the Consul-General of England." Foulk to Bayard, *Corea, Despatches, Confidential*, vol. 3, MS Dept. of State.

79. Foulk to Secretary Bayard, October 3, 4, 6, 1886, *Corea, Despatches*, vol. 3, MS Dept. of State.

in Seoul. It was obvious to Foulk that Denny had lost the "support and confidence" of Li Hung Chang, and Foulk himself was cordially disliked by both the Viceroy and Yuan Shi Kai. They had earned this enmity by resolutely opposing the Viceroy's policy of placing Corea definitely under Chinese suzerainty, and they soon had to pay the price for sympathizing with the King's desire to maintain Corean independence.

Unlike Foulk and Denny, the British Consul-General at Seoul had strongly supported the pretensions of Li Hung Chang, and the Viceroy frankly informed Denny that the British Minister in Peking had long been urging the Chinese Government to "incorporate Corea into her own Empire." Foulk believed that it would be expedient for the King of Corea to bring about closer relations with Russia, but owing to English opposition, this would be difficult. England had a "strong hold upon the Peking Government," and would endeavor "to create Chinese suspicion of Russia's good faith." [80]

Realizing that his position as chargé d'affaires had been seriously compromised in Chinese eyes by his support of Corean independence, Foulk asked to be relieved of his diplomatic duties. He was replaced by William W. Rockhill, who arrived in Seoul on December 11, 1886. Foulk remained as Naval Attaché, but he was still under a sharp attack from the pro-Chinese faction.[81]

80. Foulk to Secretary Bayard, October 14, 1886, Corea, Despatches, Confidential, vol. 3, MS Dept. of State. With reference to the entente between England and China, John Russell Young, the retiring American Minister at Peking, wrote as follows to Bayard, March 11, 1885: "I think you will find that every important question has been adjusted, . . . and through the diplomacy of our legation, we have brought our flag back to every port in China. To do this, it has been necessary to adopt an independent policy, and although the policy has met with the animadversions of the English press, the facts remain. If an American minister desires to be popular in China, he has only to make himself an attaché to the British Legation. . . . The only allusion telegraphed here by an English news agency, as to Mr. Cleveland's speech, was that he had declared against Chinese labor. I understand, of course, that the President was speaking of an entirely domestic affair. There was intended mischief in giving it an international importance." Bayard MS.

81. Rockhill's service as chargé d'affaires lasted from December 11, 1886, to April 1, 1887. It is more than likely that Denby, at Peking, was delighted to get rid of Rockhill for a few months. Rockhill was a noted Sinologue, but he could not get along with Denby, and he finally had to resign his post as Secretary of the Legation at Peking. In a letter to Bayard, March 11, 1885, John Russell Young spoke highly of Rockhill's abilities. Bayard MS. On April 2, 1888, Denby wrote to Bayard that Rockhill had left Peking without divulging any information as to where he was going. Denby then spoke in detail of his relations with Rockhill as Secretary of the Legation: "He and I, though not positively unfriendly, have never held towards each other such cordial relations as ought to exist between men in our respective positions. . . . A serious trouble has been that he devoted the greater part of his time to the study of Thibetan, and he twice re̵ ᵈested me to recommend that he should be allowed eight months leave, in order to visit Thibet.

Shortly after Rockhill assumed the duties of chargé, he received a letter from the President of the Corean Foreign Office in which a warm protest was lodged against certain articles that had appeared in one of the Shanghai newspapers. These articles were alleged to have been written by Foulk, and it was claimed that they had "grossly calumniated" the Corean Government.

Foulk promptly denied the authorship of the articles alluded to. He assured Rockhill that he had

. . . never published anything whatever . . . relative to Corea, and it would have been impossible for me to have published articles of the character his Excellency Kim attributes to me. The articles . . . do contain here and there parts of an official letter I sent to our Government more than two years ago. As to how the newspaper people obtained them I am in ignorance. There are also parts of a letter of Minister Foote referred to, but the whole article was written and published by some person unknown to me. . . .

My feelings towards this country have always been warm and disinterested, and I have been proud and grateful for the kindness shown me by its officers and people. . . . Knowing well that the President of my country is the good friend of His Majesty the King of Corea, in my service in Corea as Naval Attaché and Chargé d'Affaires ad interim, I have thought only of the dignity and welfare of His Majesty's Kingdom. Is it that I have thought too much so? [82]

After this exchange of letters, Foulk left Seoul on a short vacation. During his absence, Rockhill attended a reception given by the King of Corea. The attitude of His Majesty towards Foulk is well described in Rockhill's despatch to Bayard:

The King . . . asked if Mr. Foulk would come back to Corea. I replied that I hoped so, that he was sincerely devoted to His Majesty, and had at heart the true interests of the country. The King said that he also hoped that Mr. Foulk would come back. After leaving the King's presence, he called my interpreter back and said to him: "Explain well what I have said

---

I was compelled by a sense of duty to decline these requests. This condition is not at all satisfactory to me." *Bayard MS.* In another letter to Bayard, April 18, 1888, Denby went into further details concerning his relations with Rockhill: "In January of this year it became intolerable to submit to his occupying his own house, and never being in the office. I sent him a written order to occupy the office in the forenoon of each day. This broke up his study of Thibetan in the morning, but he obeyed for some little time until the sickness of his daughter and other causes practically nullified this order." *Bayard MS.* On June 29, 1888, Rockhill had an interview with Bayard, who read him some of the charges made against him by Denby. He expressed "his surprise and great regret, but accepted the situation." *Bayard MS.*

82. W. W. Rockhill to Secretary Bayard, January 3, 1887, *Corea, Despatches,* vol. 4, MS Dept. of State. Foulk to Rockhill, January 2, 1887, enclosed in despatch of Rockhill to Bayard, January 3, 1887.

to Mr. Rockhill so that he may be able to convey to Mr. Foulk the true expression of the kindly and friendly feelings I entertain for him." [83]

The King now devised a plan to secure the services of Foulk. On February 3 Rockhill received a note from the Corean Foreign Office concerning the employment of American military instructors. Rockhill explained that the difficulty was that officers in the Army and Navy of the United States could not accept even temporary service in the armies of other nations without Congressional authorization. If the Corean Government would be willing to accept the services of officers who had resigned from the American Army, the matter could be quickly settled.[84]

The Corean Government was perfectly willing to accept military instructors from the United States who were no longer connected with the American Army. On February 12, 1887, Rockhill wrote to Foulk to inform him that the King of Corea was anxious to secure his services as the chief military instructor of the Corean Army.[85] In a previous letter he had already referred to the possibility of this offer, and he had remarked: "If I had a word of advice to give, it would be, don't take it." [86]

Foulk wisely followed this advice and refused the generous offer from the Corean Government. Rockhill then placed pressure upon the Foreign Office and extracted a letter from Kim Yum Sik which exonerated Foulk from any responsibility with reference to the authorship of the letters that had appeared in the Shanghai *Courier* of January 6.[87]

On April 1, 1887, Hugh A. Dinsmore arrived in Seoul as the American Minister Resident. It was not long before the old charges against

83. Rockhill to Secretary Bayard, January 24, 1887, *Corea, Despatches,* vol. 4, MS Dept. of State. For a similar letter from Rockhill to Foulk, January 24, 1887, see *Foulk MS* New York Public Library.

84. Rockhill to Secretary Bayard, February 13, 1887, *Corea, Despatches,* vol. 4, MS Dept. of State.

85. Rockhill to Foulk, February 12, 1887, *Foulk MS.*

86. Rockhill to Foulk, February 10, 1887, *ibid.*

87. In this letter from Kim Yum Sik to Rockhill, March 28, 1887, the following statements are made: "While Mr. Foulk was in Corea the relations between the two countries were very close, and for this our Ministers were very grateful. While our Ministers had doubts as to Mr. Foulk's being the author of the newspaper articles, . . . the fact of such articles having been published, precluded the possibility of ignoring them. . . . My former despatch (Dec. 29, 1887) was sent before I had come into possession of accurate information. From your last despatch (January 11, 1887) we then first knew that Mr. Foulk did not prompt the articles, and our doubts were all dispelled. . . . I hear that Mr. Foulk has returned from Japan, and I have to request that you explicitly state to him that I know that he had absolutely nothing to do with the publication of these articles." *Foulk MS.*

Foulk were renewed. The President of the Corean Foreign Office paid a visit to the American Legation and once more charged that Foulk was responsible for the letters that had appeared in the Shanghai *Courier* on January 6. Because of this breach of diplomatic propriety, Foulk should leave Corea at once. When Dinsmore showed Kim Yum Sik his letter of retraction (March 28, 1887), he merely replied: "Mr. Foulk did write a letter to his government about Corean officials and according to the translation of this letter by the Chinese, this letter was very detrimental to Corea." Dinsmore then stated that the text of the Foulk letter as published in *Foreign Relations of the United States, 1885,* contained nothing which reflected adversely upon Corea. As for the fact of publication, the United States Government was responsible, and not Foulk.

On the following day the President of the Foreign Office sent a note in which he insisted that the Ministers of State and the people of Corea "do not trust Mr. Foulk" and therefore he should leave the country.

Dinsmore now learned from the Russian chargé, that Yuan Shi Kai had threatened to leave Seoul if Foulk stayed, and the Chinese Commissioner had also spread the rumor that Foulk was "in the habit of going to the palace in disguise and having private audiences with the King." Dinsmore then assured Bayard that Foulk had "not been near His Majesty, nor seen him, nor been within the outer walls of the palace since August of last year." The main source of difficulties in Seoul was Yuan Shi Kai himself, who opposed "every forward" step taken by the King and his Ministers. Should the American Government recall Foulk, it would be "generally accepted by Coreans . . . that it was forced upon us, and upon His Majesty, the King, against his will, and cannot in my belief but prove to be disparaging to the dignity and strength of His Majesty's rule." [88]

On May 27 Dinsmore wrote to Bayard and clearly indicated the successive steps taken by the Chinese Government in their movement towards snuffing out every spark of Corean independence. Yuan Shi Kai dictated and directed everything "under a system of intimidation mixed with an affectation of disinterested kindness." This condition of affairs was given the complete approval of the British Consul-General who was outspoken "in his declaration that Corea is a vassal state and altogether incapable of self-government." The Foreign Office was "abso-

88. Dinsmore to Secretary Bayard, May 3, 1887, *Corea, Despatches,* vol. 3, MS Dept. of State.

lutely under Chinese control insomuch that the Royal pleasure does not seem to be consulted concerning any of the affairs of state of great importance." [89]

It was apparent that Foulk could not remain in Seoul much longer as the Naval Attaché. On June 3 the chargé d'affaires of the Chinese Legation in Washington, called at the Department of State and informed Bayard that he had just received a telegram from Li Hung Chang to the effect that Foulk was creating a "great deal of trouble" in Seoul, and it was hoped that he would be recalled.[90] In response to this pressure, Bayard sent the following instruction to Dinsmore:

> The Chinese chargé d'affaires at this capital, has made oral and written representations to me that the continued residence of Mr. Foulk in Corea was a source of peril to the relations between Corea and China. . . . The situation disclosed by your despatches suggests no such extreme gravity as the statements made here by the Chinese chargé d'affaires would imply. . . . However this may be, the inexpediency of pressing Mr. Foulk further upon the Corean Government as a representative of the United States, is evident. . . . International comity is opposed to any appearance of forcing a government to retain a foreign representative declared by it to be *persona non grata*.[91]

On June 22 Dinsmore sent a telegram to the Department of State saying that "the King and Min Yong Ik entreat Foulk will be allowed to stay. I think it is very advisable for at least some time." [92] Bayard's reply was distinctly negative: "The opposition manifested officially by the Corean Foreign Office to the continued presence of Mr. Foulk must seriously impair his utility in that capacity." [93]

89. Dinsmore to Secretary Bayard, May 27, 1887, *Corea, Despatches*, vol. 3, MS Dept. of State. See also Dinsmore to Bayard, May 30, 1887, and the letter from Yuan Shi Kai to Dinsmore, May 28, 1887, *ibid.*

90. *Memorandum* written by Bayard after a conversation with the Chinese chargé, June 3, 1887, *Bayard MS.*

91. Secretary Bayard to Dinsmore, June 17, 1887, *Corea, Instructions*, vol. 1, MS Dept. of State.

92. Dinsmore to Secretary Bayard, June 22, 1887, *Corea, Despatches*, vol. 3, MS Dept. of State.

93. Secretary Bayard to Dinsmore, June 23, 1887, *Corea, Instructions*, vol. 1, MS Dept. of State. It must not be thought that Bayard's attitude towards Foulk indicated a feeling of hostility. The viewpoint of the Department of State was clearly revealed in a letter written by Alvey A. Adee to the Secretary of the Treasury, July 19, 1890, with reference to the claim of Foulk for salary due him as an officer in the American Navy. In connection with this claim, Mr. Adee remarks as follows: "Mr. Foulk's functions and duties were dual. He was instructed to report both to the Navy Department and the Department of State, and he did so, as I am informed and believe, with great acceptability. . . . He was obliged, at no desire of his own, to perform the duties and maintain the official and social status of a regularly accredited minister, but without adequate means of defraying the

In acknowledging the receipt of this telegram, Dinsmore informed Bayard that he had endeavored to impress upon the Corean officials who were anti-Chinese, the fact that the Corean Foreign Office was "the official medium of communication between the King and foreign legations," and that the American Government "must recognize the demand of the foreign office as authorized by the Corean Government." When these officials insisted that the President of the Foreign Office was "acting under Chinese control and not by the King's orders," Dinsmore replied: "Nevertheless, the King permits his servant to make the demand" upon the American Government.

Although Dinsmore felt that the American Government could not involve itself "in embarrassment with other countries on account of Corea," he did feel genuinely sorry for the King, and he deeply grieved because Foulk was removed as Naval Attaché. In a letter to Foulk, who had left Seoul, Dinsmore remarked:

> It is unnecessary for me to attempt to describe to you my feelings, yet it is no more nor less than I expected. Chun came to see me yesterday from the King to say that there was no further reason for you to remain away. . . . They are calling on me to advise them, but I cannot take the responsibility even if it were lawful to do so. All that I can say is keep cool, do nothing rash and let the King act upon his own judgment and under his own authority.[94]

Thanks to Chinese control, the King of Corea did not dare to "act upon his own judgment." He was only a puppet King who danced at the draw of Li Hung Chang. The Chinese Viceroy continued to make his influence felt in the Corean Foreign Office through pressure exerted by Yuan Shi Kai, and also through his American tool, O. N. Denny. It is significant that Denny made no real effort to save Foulk, and it is more than likely that he was not sorry to see Foulk leave Seoul.[95]

---

necessary incidental expense. . . . He was subject to humiliations, he was compelled to borrow money to maintain his official as well as his personal standing, and there is no doubt that, as he alleges, he suffered both physically and mentally. He was careful, prompt, and intelligent in the discharge of his duties, and the Secretary of State was glad to compliment him officially in unmistakable terms in a letter to the Secretary of the Navy dated November 1, 1887." *House Ex. Doc., 449*, 51 Cong., 1 sess., p. 1-3.

94. Dinsmore to Foulk, June 25, 1887, *Foulk MS*. In a final letter to Foulk, Dinsmore gave the following anecdote: "Min Yong Ik gave a tiffin party last week, at which there was a large company. Amongst others, Yuan. As we were all sitting in the room, I picked up an album and found amongst many other pictures, your own, on the first page. Min spoke out loud in English: "That's Mr. Foulk, and Foulk's a good man. Yes, Foulk's a good man." Dinsmore to Foulk, July 31, 1887, *Foulk MS*.

95. In a letter from W. W. Rockhill to Foulk, February 10, 1887, Rockhill remarks: "Denny and Yuan are now on the best of terms. I met Yuan at Denny's the other day.

The anticlimax of Foulk's career appeals to the dramatic sense of historians. After his removal as Naval Attaché, Foulk went to Japan, married a Japanese, and resigned from the American navy. Tyler Dennett, after making the conjecture that Foulk, "discarded like an old shoe," died in Japan "with a broken heart," draws a comparison between the shabby treatment accorded diplomats by the American Government, and the high honors bestowed by the British Government upon officers who had served it well.[96] There is little doubt that Great Britain has always appreciated the service of its soldiers and diplomats, but this has been an essential part of a long imperial tradition. The United States did not have an empire scattered over the seven seas, and, unlike England, it had not evolved a code which went along with the maintenance of far-flung dominions. The Department of State was not to blame if Foulk permitted his sentiment to cloud his judgment with reference to the strength of the Corean dynasty. Some of his successors made the same mistake, and they were not supported by the American Government because American interests were too small to warrant military intervention. In Bayard's time, the military forces of the United States were quite insignificant, and it would have been the maddest type of folly to support a weak Corean dynasty against the vastly superior armaments of nations that were close enough to Corea to have a vital stake in the fate of that kingdom.

It should also be kept in mind that despite Bayard's acquiescence in the recall of Foulk, the Chinese Government was not able to establish complete control over Corea. Corean independence was not destroyed until 1910, and it was Japan, not China, that pushed through annexation. Both Japan and Russia had long regarded Corea as an essential item in their programs of expansion, and no American Government could have successfully intervened in the face of such military strength.

In the summer of 1887, Li Hung Chang continued to meddle in the affairs of Corea. First he tried to compel the King to vest the Tai-Wen-Kun with dictatorial powers.[97] When this move failed, he tried by other means to prevent the King from sending diplomatic representatives to other countries. During the last week in September a mission to

Denny says his position is stronger in Corea now than it has ever been before." *Foulk MS.*

96. Tyler Dennett, "Early American Policy in Korea, 1883-1887," *Political Science Quarterly*, vol. 38, p. 86.

97. Dinsmore to Secretary Bayard, August 23, 1887, *Corea, Despatches*, vol. 3, MS Dept. of State.

America was ready to leave Seoul, but it was stopped just outside the city by the agents of Yuan Shi Kai. This situation is well described in a despatch from Dinsmore:

When Mr. Pak had gone out of the city gate he was met by Chinese officers, . . . and either by force or intimidation, . . . was induced to delay his departure. He remained outside of the walls . . . two or three days, when he was summoned back by the King who at last is wavering in his purpose. He is extremely anxious to have his Minister go, and has sent me messages every day that he would send him, but he is frightened and has been led to believe that China will make war on him, and he knows that without assistance he could offer but a weak defence. . . . If he would act boldly and promptly and order the Minister to proceed at once, my firm conviction is that China would acquiesce quietly.[98]

On September 27 Dinsmore wrote to Yuan Shi Kai and inquired under what authority the Chinese Commissioner was acting with reference to his attempt to prevent the sailing of the Corean Mission to the United States. Yuan immediately replied that the treaty between the United States and Corea specifically referred to the Hermit Kingdom as a "vassal state" under the suzerainty of China.[99] When Dinsmore challenged the truth of this statement,[100] Yuan then referred to the letter from the King of Corea to the President of the United States, in which it was stated that "from ancient times" Corea had been a "state tributary to China." [101] Yuan carefully refrained from any mention of the fact that in this same letter there was a sentence that read: "Full sovereignty has been exercised by the kings of Chosen in all matters of internal administration and foreign relations."

Tyler Dennett regards this letter from the King of Corea to the President of the United States as "worthless" from the viewpoint of establishing a valid claim of China's suzerainty over Corea.[102] It was certainly a very weak support for Yuan's case, but he tried to make the most of it. Dinsmore, in a note to Yuan, October 7, 1887, frankly acknowledges the fact that he had never heard of the letter to which the Chinese Commissioner had alluded. He then argued that Yuan had been

98. Dinsmore to Bayard, September 30, 1887, *Corea, Despatches,* vol. 3, MS Dept. of State.

99. Yuan Shi Kai to Dinsmore, September 27, 1887, enclosed in Dinsmore to Secretary Bayard, September 30, 1887, *ibid.*

100. Dinsmore to Yuan Shi Kai, October 1, 1887, enclosed in Dinsmore to Secretary Bayard, October 4, 1887, *ibid.*

101. Yuan Shi Kai to Dinsmore, October 3, 1887, *ibid.*

102. *Americans in Eastern Asia,* p. 460.

. . . led to an erroneous conclusion touching the contents of that letter. In any event it would ordinarily seem to me to be unnecessary to suggest to you that the terms of the treaty alone should be considered to ascertain the view held by the Government of the United States of the character and autonomy of the Kingdom of Corea.[103]

Yuan failed to be convinced by such reasoning. He learned with surprise and regreat that Dinsmore had

. . . never been officially informed of the existence of such a letter. . . . As to your statement that it is entirely at variance with international regulations for an independent state to treat with vassals, I believe your Government ought to have formed their opinion long before this, and I can only be surprised that you so suddenly conveyed to me your opinion on such a question. I must inform you that the above-said letter is of the greatest importance, and it alone must be looked to, to ascertain the views held by my Government towards Corea.[104]

Notwithstanding these explanations by Yuan Shi Kai, Dinsmore still harbored his suspicions of the rôle played by the Chinese Commissioner. A printed document had been circulated in Seoul

. . . purporting to be the text of the American-Corean treaty, in the first paragraph of which appears the statement that "the United States recognizes Corea as a dependency of China." I saw one of these in the possession of the acting Consul-General for Great Britain, who notwithstanding my assurance to the contrary, insisted that it was the true reading of the treaty. . . .

Believing that it was not my duty to allow our attitude towards the country thus grossly misrepresented without contradiction, and to allow without opposition our Government to be used as a catspaw to take out the Corean chestnuts for the Chinese, . . . I pursued the course reported. . . . I confess I was taken by surprise when the mission to the United States was interfered with. . . . Even in Mr. Yuan's first note to me, you have observed

103. Dinsmore to Yuan Shi Kai, October 7, 1887, enclosed in Dinsmore to Secretary Bayard, October 15, 1887, *Corea, Despatches*, vol. 3, MS Dept. of State.

104. Yuan Shi Kai to Dinsmore, October 10, 1887, *ibid*. With reference to the attitude of the American Government towards the question of Corean sovereignty in 1882, Alvey A. Adee, the Acting Secretary of State, wrote the following memorandum on July 30, 1895: "We do not, as a government go into the business of 'recognizing' new states *de jure*. What is commonly called *recognition* is that transaction of necessary international business with an evident *de facto* government administering the affairs of the State—we simply deal with the man we find in charge of the shop. Even in concluding a treaty we negotiate with the *de facto* power. The case of Corea is in point. Under Li Hung Chang's initiation, we signed the Corea treaty on the representations of China, as well as Corea, that the latter was independent in her outward relations although in her internal administration a tributary of China. We declined to subscribe, either to the Chinese contention that we had 'recognized' China's suzerainty, or to Corea's claim that we had recognized her independence *de jure*. We simply said that for all international effects of the treaty we could deal only with Corea as a responsible contracting party, not with China as the ultimate sovereign." *Olney Papers*, Library of Congress.

that he did not admit that they had taken a hostile stand against the mission. . . . Now believing that the Minister will not get off before China shall have given her consent, he has grown bold and you will perceive that in his last two despatches to me, . . . he adopts quite an arrogant mode of expression.[105]

In response to telegrams from Dinsmore, Bayard sent an instruction which expressed the "surprise and regret" of the Department of State "at any obstruction by the Chinese Government to the sending of a Corean envoy to the United States under article 2 of the treaty between the United States and Corea, concluded May 22, 1882." [106] Li Hung Chang was evidently impressed by the stand taken by Bayard, and on October 21 Yuan Shi Kai informed the Corean Foreign Office that he had received word from the Viceroy that the Imperial Government would interpose no objections to the Corean Embassy to the United States. This concession was induced by the fact that the Corean Government had expressed "their disposition to obey." [107] It was to be understood, however, that the Corean representatives abroad should not be above the rank of Ministers Resident. In all official and social assemblies the Corean representative should yield precedence to the Chinese Minister, and with reference to affairs of importance, the Corean representative should "always advise with the Chinese minister 'secretly' before taking action." [108]

The Corean Minister to the United States, Pak Chung Yang, was finally able to leave Seoul in November, 1887,[109] and on January 10, 1888, he wrote to Bayard and requested an audience with President Cleveland.[110] Two days later, the Chinese Minister called at the Department of State with reference to the reception of the Minister from Corea. He said his government

. . . had written to him to do everything he could to make things smooth and agreeable to the Corean Envoy, and that was the object he had in view. He was very glad to find what had been done by me [Bayard]. He spoke of

105. Dinsmore to Secretary Bayard, October 15, 1887, *Corea, Despatches,* vol. 3, MS Dept. of State.

106. Secretary Bayard to Dinsmore, October 7, 1887, *Corea, Instructions,* vol. 1, MS Dept. of State.

107. Yuan Shi Kai to the Corean Foreign Office, October 21, 1887, enclosed in Dinsmore to Secretary Bayard, November 11, 1887, *Corea Despatches,* vol. 3, MS Dept. of State.

108. Dinsmore to Secretary Bayard, November 17, 1887, *Corea, Despatches,* vol. 3, MS Dept. of State.

109. Dinsmore to Secretary Bayard, *Personal,* November 10, 1887, *Bayard MS.*

110. Pak Chung Yang to Secretary Bayard, January 10, 1888, *Foreign Relations, 1888,* vol. 1, p. 453.

the great friendship of China and Corea for the United States. . . . This interview tended to impress me that this Corean Mission was exceedingly satisfactory to China, and that what he called for today . . . was to further pave the way to a smooth reception of the Corean [Mission]. . . . The obvious intent of this visit was to connect the Chinese government with the Corean . . . in a friendly way, but to suggest a certain supervision over it, as if the thing had been done with the consent of the Chinese government.[111]

On January 13, 1888, the Corean Minister formally presented his credentials to Bayard at the Department of State,[112] and on January 18 he was received by President Cleveland. It was Dr. Allen, however, and not the Corean Minister who really transacted the affairs of the Corean Legation. On February 1 Dr. Allen paid a visit to the Department of State with reference to securing American capital to develop the mineral resources of Corea. Bayard told him that American citizens must necessarily

. . . be instructed by self-interest, and voluntarily make their engagements; that there was no power of control to prevent them doing so unless something illegal was attempted, which of course this is not. I told him there was nothing in either morals or law to prevent a loan being taken in the United States, whether taken in San Francisco or New York it would be perfectly legitimate. As to the security of such a loan, that was a question on which each man must instruct himself. No official of this govt., as such, could have the slightest possible function with this matter, and the approval of any official would be entirely *ultra vires*. All that we could say to the Corean government would be that we would not allow these people to be arbitrarily dealt with, and that they should be sustained against arbitrary spoliation. . . . I told him this because I wished him to understand that this Gov't did

111. *Memorandum* written by Bayard after a conversation with the Chinese Minister, January 12, 1888, *Bayard MS.* Any misapprehension that might have existed in Bayard's mind as to the exact relations between the Chinese and Corean Governments was probably cleared up by Dr. H. N. Allen, an American medical missionary who had spent some time in Corea, and who was serving as the Secretary of the Corean Legation. In a letter to Bayard, December 6, 1887, Minister R. B. Hubbard, at Tokio, made the following remarks: "I desire especially to commend Dr. Allen, who while nominally only Secretary of Legation, is really, more than any other, the *confidential Agent* of Corea in matters of vital interest to that Kingdom and its future prosperity. He desires, and I have so earnestly advised him, to make proffers to you of his *confidential powers* and to confer and consult freely, without reserve, on the subject of his special and confidential mission to the United States. His influence with the King and the Court and the leading men of Corea, is above that of all other foreigners." *Bayard MS.*

112. In a letter to Denby, at Peking, April 21, 1888, Bayard made the following observation with reference to the reception of the Minister from Corea: "There is some newspaper gossip about the displeasure of Li Hung Chang in relation to the presentation of the Corean credentials without the intervention of the Chinese Minister here, but the latter wrote me waiving his right to be present, and thanking me most effusively for my kindness to the Corean Minister." *Bayard Letter Book,* vol. 7, *Bayard MS.* See also Bayard to Dinsmore, January 26, 1888, *Corea, Instructions,* vol. 1, MS Dept. of State.

not undertake to stand sponsor for every enterprise in which its citizens engage abroad, although just protection would be given them, and there must be no idea of gunboats in the rear of every contract.[113]

In concluding his conversation with Dr. Allen on February 1, Bayard frankly declared that he "was glad to see Corea come into the family of Nations, and had no wish to see them come here under the vassalage of China." Bayard had an instinctive sympathy for weak nations that were sorely pressed to preserve their independence, and he was always ready to extend assistance to backward peoples who were in need of a friendly hand. He had refused to act in accordance with Li Hung Chang's desires in the matter of accrediting Denby to Seoul as well as to Peking, and he had consented to the recall of Foulk only when it was apparent that no other course was really open. In this connection it should also be remembered that in June, 1887, Foulk no longer held a diplomatic post at Seoul, but was designated as a Naval Attaché. The responsibility for his removal from that position could hardly be placed upon Bayard's shoulders alone.

In connection with the conduct of Denby, Bayard was quick to resent any criticism which he regarded as unjust. On June 20, 1888, Senator John H. Mitchell sent a note to Bayard in which there was enclosed a long letter from O. N. Denny, the Confidential Adviser to the King of Corea.[114] This letter was bitterly critical of Denby's alleged interference in the affairs of Corea. Denny believed that if Denby would

. . . pay more attention to the neglected treaty rights of his nationals within his own jurisdiction instead of wasting his time in attempting to prostitute the powers of his high office in tightening the coils of the Celestial anaconda around poor little struggling Corea, his conduct would be more in accord with the objects of his mission. . . . Denby has violated two provisions of the Revised Statutes since he came to Peking. . . . One provision is the one inhibiting any United States official from recommending any person for appointment to office in the government to which he is accredited. The other provision is that no official shall receive any present, reward, or favour from the government to which he is accredited. . . . Denby has recommended for and procured the appointment of his son to a splendid life position in

---

113. *Memorandum* written by Bayard after a conversation with Dr. Allen, February 1, 1888, *Bayard MS.* In another *memorandum* written on February 10 Bayard makes the following statement: "Dr. Allen . . . called. He mentioned that he had been over to New York, but had found no success in his proposal to float a Corean loan there. I told him I thought it would be worth while to make application to some of the men here from the Pacific Coast. I mentioned Senator Stanford." *Bayard MS.*

114. John H. Mitchell to Secretary Bayard, June 20, 1888, *Bayard MS.*

the Royal Chinese Customs Service. In doing this he violated the first-named provision, and in accepting the post for his son or permitting him to accept it, he violated the second. . . .

I, for one, do not propose to submit to his meddlesomeness in this quarter. It seems that nearly every man, high and low, has filed his caveat to pounce upon this little country, but their contract will be too broad before they get through with the job. The Chinese are very uneasy; they do not know just where they will get hit next, but they are looking for a dose from me." [115]

Bayard's reply to these slurs upon Denby, was prompt and vigorous. It was apparent that Denny was

. . . entirely misinformed as to the nature of Col. Denby's communications with this Department in relation to the extension of Chinese control over Corea. The policy of the United States, as Mr. Denby has been instructed, is not averse to the autonomical independence of Corea, and this appears by our present treaty, and the reception of the present Legation. . . . I am sorry that Judge Denny is so obviously prejudiced against this country's representatives in China and Japan. [116]

In Denny's letter to Senator Mitchell he makes the statement that the Chinese were very uneasy. They did not "know just where they will get hit next, but they are looking for a dose from me." On February 3, 1888, Denny had written a sharp critique of Chinese policy in Corea. The New York *Herald* got wind of these criticisms, and on August 4 published some of Denny's acid remarks upon the conduct of Yuan Shi Kai, the personal representative of Li Hung Chang at Seoul. According to Denny, the record of Yuan for brutality and criminality had

. . . seldom if ever been equalled in the annals of international intercourse. With a view to placing the heel of China on the neck of Corea, he has not only opposed almost every effort which has been made in the direction of internal development, but he has, through the mercenary brigade which he always keeps about him, brought failure and ridicule upon almost every effort the better class of Coreans have made to transact business for the government or themselves. [117]

When these published remarks concerning Yuan Shi Kai and Li Hung Chang made their way back to China, the Viceroy demanded

---

115. O. N. Denny to John H. Mitchell, May 13, 1888, enclosed in letter from Mitchell to Bayard, *Bayard MS.*
116. Secretary Bayard to John H. Mitchell, June 22, 1888, *Bayard Letter Book*, vol. 8, *Bayard MS.* In a personal letter to Bayard, November 23, 1888, Denby thanks him for the "marked and amazing kindness" that Bayard has shown in his handling of all questions relating to the conduct of the American Minister at Peking. *Bayard MS.*
117. New York *Herald*, August 4, 1888.

that the King of Corea dismiss Denny from his post in the Foreign Office.[118] This demand could not be refused, and Denny discovered that the "dose" he had prepared for China was now being administered to him.

The dismissal of Denny was an unmistakable indication that the influence of Li Hung Chang was still supreme in Seoul, but it was destined soon to disappear before the rising power of Japan. Chinese ascendancy during the administration of Bayard as Secretary of State, was merely a brief interlude between the acts of a drama that still holds the Far Eastern political stage. It is unlikely that this interlude will ever be presented to another audience.

118. *Ibid.*, November 13, 1888.

Canadian Questions

CHAPTER FOURTEEN

Bayard Clings to the American Doctrine of the Freedom of the Seas

WHILE BAYARD WAS ENDEAVORING TO CONCLUDE HIS CHAPTER ON COREAN-American relations, he was faced with another problem of the Pacific area—the question of the preservation of the fur-seals which were rapidly disappearing under the attack of hunters from Canada. This problem was one whose antecedents went back to the turn of the nineteenth century, when the Czar Paul granted to the Russian American Company, on July 8, 1799, a charter which conferred upon this corporation the use of "all hunting-grounds and establishments now existing on the northeastern coast of America, from the . . . fifty-fifth degree to Behring Strait, and also on the Aleutian, Kurile, and other islands situated in the Northeastern Ocean." [1]

This monopoly of hunting and trading privileges in Russian-America was challenged from time to time by American adventurers who sailed along the Northwest Coast in search of furs for the China trade. In order to prevent these intrusions, the Czar Alexander I, issued on September 16, 1821, another ukase which confirmed the

1. For the text of the ukase of July 8, 1799, see the *Proceedings of the Alaskan Boundary Tribunal* (Washington, 1904, 7 vols.), vol. 2, pp. 23-25. See also, John Bassett Moore, *History and Digest of International Arbitrations to Which the United States Has Been a Party* (Washington, 1898), vol. 1, pp. 755-756; Benjamin P. Thomas, *Russo-American Relations, 1815–1867* (Baltimore, 1930), pp. 40-41.

With reference to the general topic of the fur-seal fisheries, see John Bassett Moore, *History and Digest of International Arbitrations*, vol. 1, pp. 755-961; Joseph B. Lockey, "James Gillespie Blaine," in *American Secretaries of State and Their Diplomacy*, vol. 8, pp. 128-145; William R. Castle, Jr., "John W. Foster," *ibid.,* pp. 193-202; John W. Foster, *Diplomatic Memoirs* (N. Y. 1909), vol. 2, pp. 20-50; Alice F. Tyler, *The Foreign Policy of James G. Blaine* (Minneapolis, 1927), pp. 302-345; John W. Foster, "The Results of the Bering Sea Arbitration," *North American Review*, December, 1895, vol. 161, pp. 693-702; J. B. Henderson, *American Diplomatic Questions* (N. Y., 1901), pp. 3-62; *Fur Seal Arbitration, Proceedings of the Tribunal of Arbitration* (Washington, 1895, 16 vols.), *Senate Ex. Doc. 177,* 53 Cong., 2 sess.

exclusive privileges of the earlier charter, and which fixed the southern limit of Russian possessions at the fifty-first parallel of north latitude. This second ukase also prohibited all foreign vessels from approaching "within less than a hundred Italian miles" of the shores of these Russian possessions.[2]

As a result of spirited protests from both the United States and England, the Russian Government abandoned its pretension to declare any part of the Pacific Ocean a closed sea (*mare clausum*), and on April 17, 1824, a treaty was concluded with the United States which fixed the southern boundary of Russian possessions at fifty-four degrees and forty minutes of north latitude.[3] This treaty also provided that citizens of both countries should have unrestricted liberty to trade with the natives along the unsettled coasts of northwestern America, and they might frequent "without any hindrance whatever, the interior sea, gulfs, harbors, and creeks . . . for the purpose of fishing and trading with the natives of the country."[4]

Under the terms of a treaty of March 30, 1867, the Czar ceded to the United States "all the territory and dominion" which he possessed on the "continent of America and in the adjacent islands."[5] On August 3, 1870, the Acting Secretary of the Treasury, in accordance with the provisions of the Act of July 1, 1870, leased to the Alaska Commercial Company, the privilege of taking fur-seals on the islands of St. Paul and St. George.[6] In March, 1872, Mr. T. G. Phelps called to the attention of the Treasury Department various reports that expeditions were being fitted out in San Francisco, Hawaii, and Australia for the purpose of intercepting the seals at the Aleutian Islands. He then inquired if it was not possible, by means of revenue cutters, to prevent foreigners from doing an irreparable mischief to this "valuable interest." The

2. *Proceeding of the Alaskan Boundary Tribunal*, vol. 2, pp. 25-28; J. C. Hildt, *Early Diplomatic Negotiations of the United States with Russia* (Baltimore, 1906), pp. 158-159.
3. *American State Papers, Foreign Relations* (Washington, 1833-1859, 6 vols.), vol. 5, pp. 433-434.
4. Hunter Miller, *Treaties and Other International Acts of the United States of America* (Washington, 1933), vol. 3, pp. 151-162.
5. William M. Malloy, *Treaties, Conventions, etc.*, vol. 2, pp. 1521-1524.
6. In the *Daily Morning Chronicle* (Washington, D. C.), April 15, 1870, there is the following comment upon the proposal to lease the privilege of taking seals off the islands of St. Paul and St. George: "The Senate Committee on Commerce yesterday held a meeting and had under consideration a petition signed by James Otis, President of the Chamber of Commerce, and fifty-six mercantile firms of the city of San Francisco, California, protesting against the fur-seal monopolies, or the leasing of the islands of Alaska, and in favor of another plan for the preservation of the seal fisheries and protection of the interests of the United States in them."

Secretary of the Treasury replied that he did not see that the United States "would have the jurisdiction or power to drive off parties going up there for that purpose, unless they made such attempts within a marine league of the shore." [7]

A decade later, the Treasury Department took a much stronger stand. On March 12, 1881, Mr. French, the Acting Secretary, wrote a letter to D. A. Ancona in which he took the position that all the waters eastward of the water line in the treaty of 1867 were "comprised within the waters of Alaska Territory." The penalties prescribed by law for the destruction of fur-bearing animals would attach to all violations of this statute within these waters. [8] In March, 1886, a copy of this letter was sent to the Collector of Customs at San Francisco as an indication of the construction placed upon the statutes of the United States by the Treasury Department. [9]

The strict enforcement of these regulations by the Treasury Department seemed to be the only way to preserve the seals in the waters of the North Pacific from complete destruction. In testifying before a Congressional committee in this regard, C. A. Williams remarked:

A large number of British and American vessels, manned by expert Indian seal hunters, have frequented Behring Sea and destroyed hundreds of thousands of fur-seals by shooting them in the water, and securing as many of the carcasses for their skins as they were able to take on board. The testimony of the Government agents shows that of the number of seals killed in the water not more than one in seven, on an average, is secured, for the reason that a wounded seal will sink in the sea; so that for every thousand seal-skins secured in this manner there is a diminution of seal life at these

7. Secretary Boutwell to T. G. Phelps, April 19, 1872, John Bassett Moore, *Digest of International Law*, vol. 1, pp. 894-895.

8. *Senate Ex. Doc. 106*, 50 Cong., 2 sess., pp. 280-281.

9. *House Rept. 3885*, 50 Cong., 2 sess., p. xi. According to a memorandum prepared by Henry W. Elliott for Senator John C. Spooner, January 20, 1905, the following statement is made: "The assertion of our Government that it claimed dominion over the open waters of Behring Sea with reference to the interpretation of 'the waters thereof' of Alaska, as stated in Sec. 1956 of the Revised Statutes, was first made in the winter of 1876 by Acting Secretary H. F. French, U. S. Treasury Dept., in the 'D'Ancona Case': in this ruling the Treasury Department declared that it considered its jurisdiction as ordered by Sec. 1956, to be *over all of the waters of Behring Sea, east of the pelagic boundary in that sea, between Siberia and Alaska, as defined by the terms of the treaty of cession from Russia:* this definition is quoted in full in the 'Sherman Orders,' of April 20, 1877, which forbids the clearance of all American vessels into Behring Sea for pelagic fur-sealing. This ruling in the 'D'Ancona Case' . . . was the warrant which Capt. Bailey used in June, 1876, to seize the American schooner *San Diego*, 20 miles from the nearest land in our part of Behring Sea: this vessel was taken to San Francisco, tried in the U. S. District Court there, found guilty, condemned, her cargo confiscated, etc." *John C. Spooner Papers*, Library of Congress.

rookeries of at least 7,000. . . . During the season of 1885 the number of contraband seal-skins placed on the market was over 13,000; and in 1886, 25,000; in 1887, 34,000; and in 1888 the number . . . was less than 25,000. . . .

From this it appears that, during the last three years, the number of contraband seal-skins placed on the market amounted to over 97,000, and which, according to the testimony, destroyed nearly three-quarters of a million of fur-seals, causing a loss of revenue amounting to over $2,000,000.[10]

George R. Tingle, United States Treasury agent in charge of the fur-seal islands from April, 1885, to August, 1886, expressed the opinion that for every sealskin that was secured by pelagic hunters, nine other seals were destroyed:

The logs of marauding schooners have fallen into my hands, and they have convinced me that they do not secure more than one seal out of every ten that they mortally wound and kill, for the reason that the seals sink very quickly in the water. Allowing one out of ten, there would be 300,000 that they would kill in getting 30,000 skins. . . . You can readily see that this great slaughter of seals will, in a few years, make it impossible for 100,000 skins to be taken on the islands by the lessees. . . . If we did not allow these cheeky, persistent, insolent, British Columbia seamen to go there and defy the United States and its authorities, it would very soon be stopped.[11]

These figures were sharply contested by British and Canadian authorities,[12] but nevertheless they seemed significant to American authorities who feared that this indiscriminate pelagic killing would soon mean the destruction of most of the seals.[13] The Treasury Department decided to prevent this severe blow to American interests by seizing British schooners engaged in pelagic killing, and a new and long chapter in American diplomatic history was thus opened.

On September 27, 1886, Sackville-West, the British Minister at Washington, wrote to Bayard to complain about the seizure of three sealing schooners from British Columbia by the United States revenue cutter *Corwin*. Another protest was sent by Sackville-West on October 21, and on November 12, he left at the Department of State a long note from the Earl of Iddesleigh, the British Foreign Secretary. Accord-

10. *House Ex. Doc. 450,* 51 Cong., 1 sess., p. 17.

11. *Ibid.,* pp. 23-24.

12. Sir Julian Pauncefote to Secretary Blaine, March 9, 1890, with enclosures, *ibid.,* pp. 26-51.

13. Under the terms of its lease to the Alaska Commercial Company, the United States Government received an annual sum of $55,0000, and a tax of $2.62½ on each sealskin taken and shipped. There was also a tax of 55 cents a gallon on each gallon of oil obtained from the seals for sale on the islands or elsewhere.

ing to the depositions of the crews of the Canadian schooners, they were seized by the United States revenue cutter when they were more than sixty miles from the nearest land. The master of the *Thornton* was sentenced to imprisonment for thirty days, and had to pay a fine of $500; the mate of that vessel was also given a sentence that included imprisonment and a fine. In view of this fact, it would appear that certain American officials were laying claim to the sole sovereignty of that part of Behring Sea that lay east of the westerly boundary of Alaska, including a stretch of sea extending some 700 miles from the mainland. Lord Iddesleigh had no doubt that the American Government would disavow these proceedings, and make reparation to the British subjects for the wrongs and losses to which they had been subjected.[14]

During his interview with Sackville-West, on November 12, Bayard said that an apology was due because no reply had been sent to the British Minister's first note. The reason "for not doing so was that I [Bayard] was waiting for a report promised me, of the judicial proceedings of the case which I thought would establish the law and the facts under which U. S. officials had presumed to act and that as soon as I got that I would make reply."[15]

A week later, Sackville-West again called at the Department of State to inquire about the seizure of the British sealers in Alaskan waters. Bayard informed him that he had applied to the "Attorney General to obtain a copy of the judicial proceedings, and had not yet received them." When Sackville-West inquired whether a reply would be made "through him or Mr. Phelps," Bayard replied that "as the inquiry had come through him," the answer would be conveyed through "the same channel."[16] On December 9, Sackville-West made another of his frequent visits to the Department of State, but Bayard merely told him that an answer would be made to Lord Iddesleigh as soon as possible. Alaska was "very remote," and it would take a good deal of time to "learn all about the matter."[17]

In the meantime Bayard had written to Justice Field, of the United States Supreme Court, and had requested a confidential interview with

14. John Bassett Moore, *History and Digest of International Arbitrations*, vol. 1, pp. 770-771. See also, *Senate Ex. Doc. 106*, 50 Cong., 2 sess., pp. 1-7.
15. *Memorandum* written by Bayard after a conversation with Sackville-West, November 12, 1886, *Bayard MS*.
16. *Memorandum* written by Bayard after a conversation with Sackville-West, November 12, 1886, *Bayard MS*.
17. *Ibid.*, December 9, 1886, *Bayard MS*.

reference to the question of American maritime jurisdiction "in the seal fisheries in Behring's Sea." [18] Field replied that he would call at the Department of State during the Christmas recess of the court to discuss the questions arising out of the seizures of the British schooners.[19]

Bayard had also written to George V. N. Lothrop, the American Minister at St. Petersburg, with regard to the Behring Sea situation. He wished particularly to ascertain from Lothrop

. . . the nature and extent of marine jurisdiction actually assumed and enforced by Russia in the Behring Sea. The object of my inquiry relates to the character of maritime jurisdiction in the waters adjacent to the Seal Fisheries, in which are the two Islands of Pribyloff and St. George, formerly exercised by Russia prior to the purchase of Alaska and its dependent groups and marine privileges by the United States. I would like to ascertain whether in the waters in question, . . . Russia was limited to the distance of three miles from the shore of her islands or mainland.

You may have observed that some British vessels engaged in capturing seal in the vicinity of the islands of Pribyloff and St. George, have been seized and condemned in the Judicial Courts of California for violation of the laws of the U. S. respecting seal-taking. The vessels were alleged to have been at the time of capture at a greater distance than three miles from land, and the British government has lodged a complaint and notification of demand for compensation. As the U. S. succeeded to all the rights and powers of Russia in the waters in question, it becomes important to know what jurisdiction was claimed and practically exercised by Russia prior to the transfer. . . . The value permanently of the seal fisheries depends chiefly upon the power to regulate their capture, and this can only be done on land. If they may be shot at sea without discrimination, extermination will follow.[20]

After a careful inquiry, Lothrop could not discover any "case of seizure and adjudication under the Ukase of 1821." [21]

Bayard next turned to Francis Wharton, Solicitor of the Department of State, for advice. On January 11, 1887, he received the following memorandum from Wharton:

I am clear as to three things. (1) Unless under concessions from Great Britain to Russia (passing to us under Alaska treaty), we cannot seize and search (a fortiori, we cannot confiscate), British vessels on the high seas of the Northwest Pacific. (2) Round the sea islands, however, we might establish

18. Bayard to Justice Stephen Field, December 16, 1886, Bayard Letter Book, vol. 4, ibid.
19. Field to Bayard, December 20, 1886, ibid.
20. Secretary Bayard to George V. N. Lothrop, October 29, 1886, Bayard Letter Book, vol. 3, Bayard MS.
21. Lothrop to Secretary Bayard, December 3, 1886, ibid.

a limited police jurisdiction so as to repel intruders say within eight or ten miles. (3) We ought at once to advise the Alaska Seal Company, so that we can understand their case, and not expose ourselves to liability to them on the ground that we gave away their rights. (4) We ought to take a month & consider the matter. I am talking it over with Mr. Moore, and I am about to begin a search into the records of the British correspondence with Russia on this topic. These records are very voluminous. Then we will drive a daring team in which J. Q. Adams and Prince Potemkin will draw double under your whip. But it will take a month to harness and team such steeds.[22]

A few days later, Wharton sent the following memorandum to Bayard:

I find on examination that there were no concessions whatever by G. Britain to Russia by which we as assignees of Russia, can claim any right to seize British sailing vessels on the high seas, outside of the three-mile band. . . . If it should turn out that the seizures . . . were on the high seas, I concur in the belief that honor and policy require that we should take the earliest opportunity to disclaim the arrests, and to frankly and fully express our regret at their having been made.[23]

A third memorandum from Wharton took the ground that it was

. . . far better to abandon even the seal fishery, than to surrender the doctrine of inviolability of national merchant ships on the high seas. I think, however, that for *police purposes* we may repel intruders who come within the range of cannon shot of our shores. As to the seals, I think the only remedy is that you suggest—a joint agreement of maritime powers to protect the rookeries.[24]

While Bayard was gathering all this information, he was being bombarded with notes from the British Minister. On January 9 Sack-

22. Wharton to Secretary Bayard, January 11, 1887, *Bayard MS.* On January 11, 1887, in accordance with this advice from Wharton, Bayard wrote to Charles N. Felton with reference to the operations of the Alaska Commercial Company. He wished to bring to their attention "a question as to the limitation of the marine jurisdiction of the United States over the waters of Behring Sea, which has been very distinctly raised by the Government of Great Britain in the late cases of the seizure and condemnation of certain British-American fishing vessels . . . for an alleged violation of the Statutes of the United States, regulating the seal fisheries in the waters referred to. . . . The Alaska Commercial Company has important interests under its lease from the United States in these seal fisheries of the islands and waters adjacent, in which this business is carried on, and as this Department is now called upon to define the marine jurisdiction, claimed by the Government of the United States over the waters in question, I write you to confer with me on the subject." *Bayard Letter Book*, vol. 4, *Bayard MS.*

23. Wharton to Secretary Bayard, January 17, 1887, *Bayard Letter Book*, vol. 4, *Bayard MS.*

24. Wharton to Secretary Bayard, January 19, 1887, *Bayard MS.* On January 18, President Cleveland wrote a short note to Bayard and informed him that Mr. C. A. Swineford, Governor of Alaska Territory, would soon arrive in Washington. The President thought that if Bayard saw Swineford he might "learn something from him touching the matter discussed today." President Cleveland to Bayard, January 18, 1887, *Bayard MS.*

ville-West again referred to the "grave representations" that had been made by Her Majesty's Government, and he expressed the hope that "the cause of the delay complained of in answering the representations . . . may be speedily removed." [25] Bayard replied that the delay had been caused by the absence of "requisite information as to the facts." He would "diligently endeavor to procure the best evidence possible of the matters inquired of, and will make due response thereupon when the opportunity of decision is afforded to me." [26]

On January 21 Attorney General Garland sent to Bayard some of the papers in the judicial proceedings against the British schooners that had been seized in Alaskan waters,[27] and Bayard wrote to President Cleveland the following day and made a detailed report on the situation:

I submit for your consideration a very important question that has been raised by the Government of Great Britain in relation to the assumed jurisdiction of the United States over vessels navigating the waters of Behring Sea, and engaged in fishing in those waters and taking fur-seals.

The cases which contain the question of the right of the United States to board, search, and seize on the high seas, vessels supposed to be engaged in capturing fur-seal in the waters referred to, have been considered in the United States District Court sitting in the District of Alaska, and judgment of condemnation has been entered in the several cases of the United States vs. "Carolina," "Onward," and "Thornton," being British vessels, and captured by U. S. Revenue Cutter, "Corwin," and brought into the port of Sitka for adjudication.

The cases came on for hearing before Judge LaFayette Dawson, on August 30th last, and resulted in decrees of condemnation of the vessels, and the imposition of sentences for the fine and imprisonment of the officers and crews of the vessels referred to, on the ground of alleged violation of the laws of the United States regulating the fur-seal fishery business in the Alaskan waters.

As I have before informed you, urgent representation has been made to this Department by the British Minister at this Capital, of the grave interest felt by Her Britannic Majesty's Government in the question of the assumed right of search and of jurisdiction of the waters of Behring Sea, and a notification of a reservation of the right for compensation has been given me.

As the season for fur-seal and other fishing in Behring Sea is soon to open, and vessels are now equipping in British Columbia for prosecuting such business in these waters, the Canadian Government is naturally desirous

25. Sackville-West to Secretary Bayard, January 9, 1887, *Senate Ex. Doc. 106*, 50 Cong., 2 sess., p. 7.

26. Secretary Bayard to Sackville-West, January 12, 1887, *ibid.*, p. 11.

27. Garland to Secretary Bayard, January 21, 1887, *Bayard MS.*

of ascertaining whether such vessels, fishing in the open sea and beyond the territorial waters of Alaska, would be exposed to seizure, by the officials of the United States, and consequently Her Britannic Majesty's Government would desire some assurance that, pending a settlement of the question, no such seizures would be made of British vessels in Behring Sea.

It seems necessary, therefore, that the Executive Department of this Government should speedily come to a decision, whether exclusive jurisdiction, and right of search, and police control, extends over the whole area of Behring Sea, or is restricted within that marine league from shore, which in the history of this Government, heretofore, has, in all other localities, been so frequently proclaimed by us as the limit of our territorial control.

This Government has never asserted, but has invariably disclaimed, any pretension to authorize the search by officers of the United States, in time of peace, of foreign vessels on the high seas and outside our jurisdiction, and we have repelled successfully, search of our own vessels, even in the most qualified way, by foreign powers under similar circumstances.

In the cases in Alaska in which, I understand, appeals to the United States Circuit Court are now pending, I gather from the reported language of the Judge of the United States District Court, that the seizures were all made on the high seas, and more than a marine league from any land.

I am aware of the peculiar character of the fur-seal fisheries, and that shooting these animals in the water, necessarily involves their useless slaughter, and will . . . almost inevitably lead to the speedy extermination of the race, and break up the present sole resort of the seal family to the Pribylov Islands in Behring Sea, belonging to the United States. Thus, a valuable source of wealth, giving employment to large numbers of individuals in the United States, would be placed in jeopardy. Without regulation of the method, number, and selection of the seal to be taken, such as is now provided by the laws of the United States, the fur-seal fisheres would soon be in danger of becoming extinct, and certainly would greatly deteriorate in value.

If the United States possess jurisdiction over the entire waters of Behring Sea, it is proper they should actively exert it, and enforce regulations admittedly necessary for the preservation of their fur-seal fisheries. If they do not, and cannot, therefore, exclusively control these waters, it may be practicable to procure the requisite protection by international agreement.

Having had correspondence on the subject with our Minister at St. Petersburg, and made examination of the archives of this Department, I am unable to find satisfactory grounds to warrant me in advising you that the search and seizure of the vessels referred to, and the proceedings against the masters and crews were justified.

Long prior to the acquisition of our present Alaskan possessions from Russia, the Minister of the United States to that country . . . had denied the claims of Russia to such extended exclusive maritime jurisdiction, and by the conventions of 1824 with the United States, and 1825 with Great Britain, such exclusive jurisdiction seems to have been abandoned by Russia. . . .

With the increase of navigation and commerce in the waters of the Pacific Ocean, the rights of free navigation and other attendant and incidental uses of the high seas have become more important, so that the time has arrived when an international understanding must be had.

This Government is one of law, and yields the same voluntary and self-imposed submission to the rules of public international regulation in the use and navigation of the high seas which it requires from other members of the family of nations.

If the conclusion should be reached that the vessels in question were seized outside of the proper marine jurisdiction of the United States, and not in hot pursuit for an offence committed within such jurisdiction, I believe that the honor of the Government, and its consistent and even forcible resistance heretofore to every pretension of other nations to search its vessels on the high seas in time of peace, require that the Attorney General should be requested immediately to direct by telegraph the District Attorney of the United States, having the cases in charge, to discontinue the prosecutions and discharge the vessels from arrest.[28]

The President agreed with the suggestions that Bayard had made in the last paragraph of his letter, and in a note to the British Minister, February 3, 1887, Bayard gave the assurance that orders had been issued "for the discontinuance of all pending proceedings, the discharge of the vessels referred to, and the release of all persons under arrest in connection therewith." [29] A more far-reaching assurance Bayard would not give, even though Sackville-West had pushed hard for a promise that British vessels would not be molested by the revenue cutters of the United States in Alaskan waters.[30] Bayard merely replied that the question of "instructions to Government vessels in regard to preventing the indiscriminate killing of fur-seals," was still under consideration.[31]

Although Bayard was very non-communicative as far as the British Minister was concerned, he prepared a memorandum for the President

28. Secretary Bayard to President Cleveland, January 22, 1887, *Bayard MS.*

29. Secretary Bayard to Sackville-West, February 3, 1887, *Senate Ex. Doc. 106*, 50 Cong., 2 sess., p. 12. See also, John Van Gasken to Bayard, enclosing letter from William Van Gasken to John Van Gasken, March 13, 1887, *Bayard MS.* On March 23, 1887, Francis Wharton sent to Bayard a copy of a letter he had received from Joseph Wharton. It appeared to Joseph Wharton that something should be done at once to save the herds of fur-seals in the North Pacific. The American buffalo had been destroyed to a large extent by "disgusting British hunters," and the seals were "sure to follow them to speedy extinction" if they were not efficiently protected. But Great Britain would not act with the United States in this matter if she were approached with "a show of temper." Diplomatic vinegar never attracted many British flies, and if the Department of State appealed to the British Government "in the interest of comity and reason," there was some hope of a favorable answer." *Bayard MS.*

30. Sackville-West to Secretary Bayard, April 4, 1887, *Senate Ex. Doc. 106*, 50 Cong., 2 sess., pp. 12-13.

31. Secretary Bayard to Sackville-West, April 12, 1887, *ibid.*, p. 13.

along very positive lines. After a careful investigation of the whole question of sealing operations in Behring Sea, he was of the opinion that this body of water was not a

. . . *mare clausum,* but is part of the high seas of the world, and equally open to the navigation of all nations. That being thus an open sea and, as such, part of the great highway of nations, the exclusive property and juris-diction of the United States in the waters thereof, does not extend to a greater distance from the land than is claimed and exercised by the United States . . . over the waters adjacent to its territories on the Atlantic coast. . . .

It is not within my province as Secretary of State to give a construction of the Acts of Congress, . . . but only to submit my opinion in respect to international rights and duties of the United States in relation to the waters of Behring Sea more than three miles from land within the dominion of the United States. . . .

It is believed that a conventional arrangement can be made with other nations, which will secure such co-ordinate and co-operative regulations for the taking of fur-seal as will prevent their indiscriminate slaughter and con-sequent speedy extermination.[32]

To Phelps, in London, Bayard wrote a personal letter along the general lines of this memorandum for the President. He thought he would soon ask Phelps to

. . . make known to Lord Salisbury the necessity for co-operative action of the two governments over their respective citizens, to prevent the annihila-tion of the fur-seals. I do not see how we can maintain Behring's Sea to be a *mare clausum,* or claim an exclusive jurisdiction beyond the three-mile limit. . . . London is the sole place where such furs are dressed and as many subjects are engaged with greater profit in the business as citizens of the United States. The interest therefore of Great Britain in assisting us in regulating on the high seas the killing of fur-seals is as great as our own.[33]

From Russia the word came that the Government of the Czar would be "very glad to co-operate with the United States in any measures for the protection of the legitimate fisheries, and that if the United States

32. *Memorandum* prepared for the President, April 28, 1887, *Bayard MS.*
33. Secretary Bayard to Phelps, May 6, 1887, *Bayard Letter Book,* vol. 5, *Bayard MS.* In another letter to Phelps, May 30, 1887, Bayard remarked: "I am unable to see how we can withdraw from our traditional refusal to admit the right of search and visitation on the high seas, and our insistence upon the restriction of territorial jurisdiction to a marine league from shore. We have compelled Russia in the Sea of Okhotsk and in Behring Sea to abandon a more extensive claim. We did the same thing with Spain in her Cuban waters, and with Great Britain . . . in the Northern Atlantic. But we can make a con-ventional agreement with Great Britain, and if needs be, with other nations that will cause the restraint of its own citizens by each Country to prevent the destruction of our fur-seal fisheries in Behring's Sea." *Bayard Letter Book,* vol. 5, *Bayard MS.*

could see any practicable way, and would take the initiative towards a Convention on the subject, it would be met with a favorable response." [34]

While Bayard was pondering over plans for an international agreement restricting the killing of seals in the North Pacific, the British Minister sent a note of protest against further seizure of British vessels in Behring Sea. Lord Salisbury had expected that the assurances given in Bayard's note of February 3, would prevent any repetition of this drastic action on the part of the American Government.[35] In his reply, Bayard disclaimed having given any blanket assurances in his note of February 3. He had merely stated that the President had issued orders directing the "discontinuance of all pending proceedings, the discharge of the vessels referred to, and the release of all persons under arrest in connection therewith." He had "no knowledge whatever" of the circumstances under which the new seizures had been made.[36]

After sending this non-committal note to the British Minister, Bayard wrote a long personal letter to Phelps, in London. It seemed to him that the British Government was in a

. . . marvellous hurry to have our decisive action in Alaska, and yet after eighteen months, withholds a decision in the two cases of seizure in the Spring of 1886 in Nova Scotia. I expect, however, in a few days to write you, and at the same time and to the same purport, to write our Ministers at Berlin and St. Petersburg, and probably at Stockholm, proposing co-operative action among the governments named and the United States to regulate fur-seal fishing and thus preserve those animals from extermination.

The United States can, of course, control its own citizens on the high seas, but an examination of the history of Behring Sea will not sustain our

34. Lothrop to Secretary Bayard, May 28, 1887, *Bayard MS.* Lothrop further remarked that both Russia and the United States had "asserted jurisdictional rights over this sea [Behring Sea], and it has seemed to me . . . that a Convention might be made without any surrender of these claims. Thus, it could be recited that, by the laws of these countries respectively, this jurisdiction has been asserted and exercised for the protection of the fisheries of Behring Sea, in which both parties were deeply interested, and that for the more efficient exercise of that jurisdiction, and for the necessary protection of the seal fisheries especially, it was deemed expedient to enter into a convention. This would, of course, be binding on the citizens and subjects of the two Powers, and might at least have some influence on the marauding seal hunters of other nationalities."

35. Sackville-West to Secretary Bayard, August 11, 1887, *Senate Ex. Doc. 106,* 50 Cong., 2 sess., pp. 47-48.

36. Secretary Bayard to Sackville-West, August 13, 1887, *ibid.,* p. 49. On August 19, 1887, C. S. Fairchild, Secretary of the Treasury, wrote to Bayard and enclosed copies of the reports of Captain L. G. Shepard, of the Revenue Cutter *Rush,* with reference to the seizures of the British vessels *Anna Beck, W. P. Saynard, Dolphin,* and *Grace,* for seal fishing in Behring Sea in violation of Section 1956 of the Revised Statutes of the United States. *Bayard MS.*

right to exclude other nations from the common right of navigation, fishing, etc., in those waters outside the three-mile line from shore. This announcement has not yet been made by us, but it must be sooner or later, and to control our own citizens, the present Legislation must be amended. . . .

Retaining her possessions on the Eastern Coasts of Behring's Sea, and two Island resorts for fur-seal adjacent, the interest of Russia in the preservation of the seal is identical and almost equal with our own. Already Mr. Lothrop has been sounded by the Russian Minister for Foreign Affairs in relation to our views on the subject. The interests of Great Britain are almost as great as our own, and in a pecuniary point of view, the business is probably more lucrative to the 12- or 13,000 persons engaged in London in preparing the skins for use, than to those who capture the animal.[37]

From a short paragraph that appeared in the New York *Times,* August 19, 1887, Sackville-West learned that the reports of Captain Shepard, of the Revenue Cutter *Rush,* had been received by the Treasury Department. These reports gave the details of the seizures of the British sealing vessels in Behring Sea in July, 1887. Sackville-West was anxious to receive copies of these documents, and he wrote to Bayard to that effect.[38] Bayard replied at once that these reports had just reached his office, and within a "few hours," he would send copies of them to the British Legation.[39]

On August 23 President Cleveland wrote to George A. Jenks, the Acting Attorney General, and instructed him to issue an order "for the release of the officers and other persons employed in the vessels lately seized by the United States Revenue Cutter *Rush* in Behring Sea." But the President included in this note to the Acting Attorney General a distinct reservation to the effect that this order of release which Mr. Jenks should issue would have no effect on the "other questions connected with the alleged violation of the laws of the United States relating to the fur-seal fisheries."[40] In a conference with Bayard and the Acting Attorney General, the President "seemed disposed to delay giving any order that would indicate the restriction of our jurisdiction *to three miles.*"[41]

37. Secretary Bayard to Phelps, August 16, 1887, *Personal, Bayard Letter Book*, vol. 5, *Bayard MS.*
38. Sackville-West to Secretary Bayard, August 19, 1887, *Bayard MS.*
39. Secretary Bayard to Sackville-West, August 20, 1887, *ibid.* See also letters from Barton Atkins, United States Marshal at Sitka, to the Attorney General, August 1, 1887, and G. A. Jenks, Acting Attorney General, to Bayard, August 20, 1887, *ibid.*
40. President Cleveland to George A. Jenks, August 23, 1887, *Bayard MS.*
41. *Memorandum* written by Bayard after a conference with President Cleveland and the Acting Attorney General, August 25, 1887, *ibid.* See also, New York *Times*, August 22, 1887, in which the following statement is made: "It is beyond question that the Govern-

While Bayard had very positive views that the United States had no valid jurisdiction outside the three-mile limit, he did not attempt to impose this opinion upon the President, and inasmuch as no claim had been formally presented by the British Government, there was no immediate necessity for a "precise formulation of our rights in Behring's Sea." [42] But the Acting Attorney General was busily engaged upon research on this very point, and in a letter to Bayard, August 31, 1887, he advanced the following conclusions:

(1) The United States, as sovereign, has the right to protect the fur-seals whose habitat is upon the shores and islands of Alaska, whether within or without the marine belt. (2) Except so far as is necessary to protect such seals, the right to control or forbid the free navigation of the open seas outside the marine belt, in the pursuit of lawful commerce, is not claimed. (3) The limits to which the United States claims the right of protection, . . . are the boundaries set forth in the treaty between the United States and Russia on the twentieth day of June, 1867, for, within those boundaries, the seals found therein have no other habitat than upon the public domain of the United States. [43]

It was evident to Bayard that the President and the Acting Attorney General were very loath to abandon all claims to the protection of seals beyond the three-mile limit, and they had some support from Francis Wharton who wrote an important letter to Bayard on September 4. He thought there was a

. . . good deal worth considering in the position taken by you [Bayard] when we first began to work at the fishery question, that the three-mile zone was not an arbitrary cosmopolitan rule, but a rule adopted by compromise and custom for certain specific coasts, among which that of North East America was conspicuous. I am positive that this is the conclusion we came to, for in making up the *Digest,* after talking with you and Mr. Moore, I was careful to state and restrict the three-mile rule so as to apply it to the N. E. Coast on the basis of custom and diplomatic settlement. In fact, with the authorities before me, I could not do otherwise. Mr. Jefferson, for instance, while adhering to the three-mile rule, as the basis of custom for the N. E. coast, maintained, and so we quoted him, that the territorial waters of the United States extended on the S. E., *for the purposes of police protection,* over the Gulf Stream to Cuba.

Now this does not mean that we are to claim Behring's Sea. That is absurd. But it does mean, I think, that the principle of territorial waters is

---

ment has not abandoned any of its claims over the waters of Behring Sea far beyond the marine league, and that it still treats this as a 'closed area.' "

42. Bayard to Thomas Wright, August 27, 1887, *Bayard Letter Book,* vol. 5, *Bayard MS.*
43. George A. Jenks to Secretary Bayard, August 31, 1887, *ibid.*

that *wherever a sovereign has property, there he is to have sufficient police control over the waters adjacent to such property as to enable him to protect it.* This is the rule of the law of nations, a rule as much growing out of the conditions of the times as did the three-mile rule grow out of the conditions of the times in which it was generated. Observe, I do not say that the three-mile rule is not applicable to the N. E. fisheries. It is, by force of adoption and custom and diplomatic correspondence, but I do not think it applicable to the Seal Fisheries whose protection and preservation require a larger margin. Old precedents do not make present law under conditions to which they are not applicable.

As far as I recollect, the three-mile rule has never applied to the North Pacific. We fought against territorialising of Behring Sea. But we never . . . set up as against it the three-mile rule. As a matter of International Law, . . . I do not think the three-mile rule binds the seal fisheries.[44]

This was a distinct recession from the stand that Wharton had taken in January, 1887, and it indicated to Bayard the necessity of moving slowly in attempting any definition of the attitude of the American Government. The British Government had been very slow in suggesting some worth-while means of settling the troublesome question of the North Atlantic fisheries. If a strong stand were taken in the Behring Sea dispute, it might lead British officials to adopt a more conciliatory attitude, and Phelps, writing from London, threw out the suggestion that the Treasury Department should continue to "hold on to the vessels seized, as the Canadians do to ours." [45]

But the Canadians despised the medicine which they so freely administered to American fishermen in Atlantic waters, and they bitterly criticized the seizures of British schooners in Behring Sea.[46] In response

44. Wharton to Secretary Bayard, September 4, 1887, *Bayard MS.* In the event that the United States attempted to settle the question of the seal fisheries by a treaty with the interested powers, Wharton thought that it would be advisable to extend its terms farther "than the capture of vessels engaged in seal fishing within say 20 or 30 miles from shore. Can we, without sacrificing a great deal now, authorise the search of vessels on the North Pacific to see whether they are on sealing adventures? We agreed to such search within certain zones for slavers." Wharton to Bayard, September 11, 1887, *ibid.*

45. Phelps to Secretary Bayard, August 27, 1887, *Bayard MS.* It is important to note that Judge Dawson, of the United States District Court in Alaska, based his opinions with reference to the condemnation of the British vessels engaged in sealing operations in Behring Sea, upon the data presented by N. L. Jeffries, in his pamphlet, *The Dominion of Behring Sea* (Phila., 1887). Jeffries was the attorney for the Alaska Commercial Company, and was interested in the seizures from the viewpoint of protecting the seal fisheries. In a letter to Bayard, November 14, 1893, John Bassett Moore remarks as follows concerning the appearance of Jeffries: "N. L. Jeffries was in charge of the interests of the Company [Alaska Commercial Company] in Washington, and was the prolific source of most of the articles that appeared in the press—a fat, sleek, oily-faced man, not unsuggestive of a seal." *Bayard MS.*

46. M. H. Phelan to Secretary Bayard, Halifax, September 8, 1887; John Bassett Moore to Francis Wharton, Halifax, August 27, 1887, *Bayard MS.*

to these Canadian complaints, Sackville-West called at the Department of State to inquire about the seizures. With reference to the vessels that had been seized the previous year, Bayard reminded the British Minister that he had been informed that President Cleveland had ordered their release. If they had -

. . . not been taken away by those who owned them it probably was from the insignificant value of the vessels; that I had the impression that they were vessels without a deck, . . . and that I supposed when the crews were landed they found their way home and the owners never put in an appearance or made claim for the vessels.[47]

In a conference with Bayard on September 23, Sackville-West advanced the idea that the Behring Sea dispute could be included in the questions that were to be discussed during the meetings of the Joint High Commission which would hold its sessions in Washington in November, 1887. Bayard immediately rejected this suggestion. The terms of reference for the Joint High Commission had already been agreed upon, and they "did not involve the questions . . . in the Behring Sea operations." [48]

In accordance with instructions from the British Foreign Office, Sackville-West continued to press for the release of the British ships that had been seized in 1886. Apparently, they were still in American custody.[49] When Bayard sent a letter of inquiry to the Attorney General in regard to this fact, he was informed that the United States marshal had suspected that the order of January 26, 1887, directing him to release the vessels, was not genuine, and therefore, he had not acted upon it. A new order had been telegraphed to the marshal, and it was not expected that there would be any further difficulty in that matter.[50]

47. *Memorandum* written by Bayard after a conversation with Sackville-West, September 19, 1887, *Bayard MS.*
48. *Memorandum* written by Bayard after a conversation with Sackville-West, September 23, 1887, *ibid.* In a letter to President Cleveland, September 24, 1887, Bayard made the following comment: "The British Minister, when he handed me the despatch, remarked that he supposed the subject could be considered by the expected Commission, but I told him it stood upon so totally different footing, and was so disconnected with the Canadian questions, that it would be a matter for separate consideration and subsequent decision by the two governments." *Bayard Letter Book,* vol. 6, *ibid.*
49. Sackville-West to Secretary Bayard, September 29, 1887, *Senate Ex. Doc., 106,* 50 Cong., 2 sess., p. 55. See also New York *Herald,* August 27, 1887, for statement of Mr. Foster, the Canadian Minister of Marine and Fisheries.
50. Garland to Secretary Bayard, October 12, 1887, *Senate Ex. Doc., 106,* 50 Cong., 2 sess., p. 56. In a letter to Garland, October 20, 1887, Bayard remarked: "It would be a greater labor than ever Hercules essayed, to keep the tattlers, mischief makers, and fools of the newspaper press, from publishing half truths and whole lies. I told one of these people last night that there was not a particle of foundation for the statement that the

In the meantime, on August 19, Bayard had addressed to the ministers of the United States to France, Germany, Great Britain, Japan, Russia, Sweden, and Norway, an instruction directing them to request the governments to which they were accredited to co-operate with the United States "for the better protection of the fur-seal fisheries in Behring Sea." Bayard had purposely refrained from raising any question as to the

. . . exceptional measures which the peculiar character of the property in question might justify this government in taking, and without reference to any exceptional marine jurisdiction that might properly be claimed for that end. It is deemed advisable, and I am instructed by the President so to inform you, to attain the desired ends by international co-operation.[51]

The French Government expressed a willingness to consider a draft treaty on this subject.[52] The Government of Japan was also interested in such a treaty, but it hoped that the convention could provide for the protection not only of seals in Behring Sea, but also for sea-otter and seals on the coasts of Japan.[53] The Russian Government had no hesitation about indicating its willingness to co-operate with the United States and other powers in the matter of preserving the seals in the North Pacific.[54] Lord Salisbury accepted the idea of co-operative action, and suggested to Phelps that the American Government submit a sketch of a system of regulations for the protection of the fur-seals.[55]

Bayard replied by sending to Phelps (February 7, 1888) a proposal that the interested powers should "take concerted action to prevent their citizens or subjects from killing fur-seals with firearms, or other destructive weapons, north of 50 degrees of north latitude, and between

---

Secretary of State and the Attorney General had any differences in opinion concerning the jurisdiction of the United States in Behring Sea, or anywhere else." *Bayard Letter Book*, vol. 6, *Bayard MS*. There had, however, been a significant difference between the ideas of Bayard and those of the Acting Attorney General, George A. Jenks.

51. *Senate Ex. Doc., 106, 50* Cong., 2 sess., p. 84.

52. *Ibid.,* p. 85.

53. *Ibid.,* p. 107. On October 14, 1887, the Japanese chargé d'affaires had a conversation with Bayard and inquired if the proposed convention could also cover other fur-bearing animals. Bayard said he could "see no reason why it should not be so extended. I thought there had been some misapprehension on the part of Count Ito, as to the proposition of Mr. Hubbard; it was not limited to Behring Sea, but to the protection of fur-seal all over the world, and I thought it was only by international agreement that they could be protected elsewhere." *Memorandum* written by Bayard after a conversation with Shiro Akabane, October 14, 1887, *Bayard MS*.

54. *Senate Ex. Doc., 106, op. cit.,* p. 116. See also *memorandum* written by Bayard after a conversation with the Russian Minister, January 6, 1888, *Bayard MS*.

55. See *memorandum* written by Bayard, December 14, 1887, recounting a conversation with Joseph Chamberlain concerning the fur-seal fisheries, *Bayard MS*.

160 degrees of longitude west and 170 degrees of longitude east from Greenwich, during the period intervening between April 15 and November 1." [56]

Phelps presented Lord Salisbury with a copy of Bayard's instructions, and on February 25 he reported that the British Government was willing to accede to a proposition to establish by mutual arrangement "a close time for fur-seals, between April 15 and November 1, and between 160 degrees of longitude west and 170 degrees of longitude east, in the Behring Sea." The British Government was also willing to join with the United States in any preventive measures that it might be expedient to adopt.[57]

Phelps was about to return to the United States, and Bayard hoped that he would return with an arrangement for policing Behring Sea

. . . so that our Revenue Cutters can arrest the British-American poachers and turn them into their own courts for punishment. I do not want to be obliged to define our claim of jurisdiction, nor on the other hand to claim that sea to be *mare clausum*, because frankly I think such a claim would be not only highly impolitic, but incapable of being sustained. The lines you are now moving on are the best, and I wish, even if nothing else was done before you leave London, that you would impress Lord Salisbury with the importance, pending arrangements, of not allowing clearance in British Columbia for vessels proposing to shoot seal in Behring's Sea. I shall advise

56. Secretary Bayard to Phelps, February 7, 1888, *Senate Ex. Doc., 106,* 50 Cong., 2 sess., p. 88.

57. Phelps to Secretary Bayard, February 25, 1888, *Fur Seal Arbitration,* vol. 5, p. 610. In a letter from N. L. Jeffries and W. W. Eaton to the Secretary of the Treasury, February [no date], 1888, it was stated that in 1887, 150,000 fur-seals had been killed by "English and American traders in Behring Sea, in direct violation of the laws of the United States. . . . The Alaska Commercial Company is permitted to kill 100,000 fur-seals each year, for which privilege it pays to the Government $317,500. . . . Unauthorized persons in violation of law have during the past year taken fully one-half that number of sealskins, on which they pay no tax. . . . It seems clear . . . that the Police power of the Government, and its right to protect its revenue, coupled with its undoubted right to pursue its own property and protect it on the high seas or elsewhere, are sufficient in themselves to correct this evil." *Bayard MS.*

In his report to the Secretary of the Interior for the fiscal year 1887, A. P. Swineford, Governor of Alaska Territory, sharply arraigned the Alaska Commercial Company for flagrant and outrageous abuse of the powers and privileges conferred upon it by the Government of the United States. *Congressional Record,* 50 Cong., 1 sess., vol. 19, pt. 1, pp. 639-640. With regard to these charges, J. S. Moore wrote to Bayard, May 21, 1887, as follows: "In 1875 I was sent to San Francisco to investigate the Alaska Commercial Co. The accusation was that the Company stole fur-seals. My report . . . shows that the Co. did not steal fur-seals, and . . . that the Co. did preserve the Animals, and conducted the business very fairly and honestly in accordance with the Govt. Contract. . . . I reported that this contract was the greatest monopoly ever given by a government to any Company. I showed their then net profit per annum (which has since then doubled), and, lastly, that the whole Pacific Coast was dissatisfied with the contract." *Bayard MS.*

that secret instructions be given to our Revenue cruisers not to molest British vessels at a distance from the shore in Behring's Sea, on the ground that negotiations are now pending for the concerted exercise of jurisdiction over their citizens by the respective governments, for the protection of seal life in certain months and between certain longitudinal lines.[58]

If any arrangement were to be made with the British Government it was necessary that the seizures of British vessels in Behring Sea by United States revenue cutters cease. On April 2 Sackville-West wrote to Bayard that Lord Salisbury had received an intimation from the Canadian Government that orders had been issued by the American Government to continue the seizure of British sealing vessels in Behring Sea.[59] On the following day, Sackville-West called at the Department of State, and Bayard told him that "he could say to Lord Salisbury that no orders had been issued by the Treasury Department on the subject of the sealing in Behring Sea."[60]

But this assurance did not go far enough to please Lord Lansdowne (the Governor-General of Canada) who pressed Sackville-West to secure from Bayard a specific answer to the following question: "May we understand that our sealers will not be molested except within the marine league from the shore?"

Bayard refused to give an affirmative answer to this question when it was placed before him by Sackville-West. He frankly confessed that the important matter of

. . . preserving seal life in Behring Sea might not make it necessary to operate more than a marine league from shore, but I would make no statement on the subject. I said that our object was not to encroach on any British rights whatever, but our action was dictated by good sense and judgment for the preservation of seal life. I did not consider it would be wise to answer Lord Lansdowne's question, and I regretted that he had put it in that way. It was not a narrow technical point of a three-mile limit, but it was a question broadly as to whether we were to act reasonably and moderately for the preservation of seal in those waters. . . . I expressly declined to answer Lord

58. Secretary Bayard to Phelps, March 16, 1888, *Bayard Letter Book*, vol. 7, *Bayard MS.*
59. Sackville-West to Secretary Bayard, April 2, 1888, *Bayard MS.*
60. *Memorandum* written by Bayard after a conversation with Sackville-West, April 3, 1888, *Bayard MS.* On this same day (April 3, 1888), Bayard wrote to Charles S. Fairchild, the Secretary of the Treasury, and recounted his conversation with Sackville-West. He then made the following statement: "As you are already aware, we have proposed, and the British Government has accepted, the proposition that the two governments should legislate concertedly for the protection of Seal life in Behring Sea. Pending this legislative action, I stated to Sir Lionel West that no encouragement of any kind should be given to the depredating sealers of either nation." *Bayard MS.*

Lansdowne's question as to the British Sealers not being molested except within the Marine League. I thought it better not to do so.[61]

With Phelps en route for Washington, Bayard was kept in touch with developments in London through letters from Henry White, who had been left in charge of the American legation. On April 16 White had a conference with Lord Salisbury and M. de Staal, the Russian Ambassador. De Staal stated that his Government was anxious to become a party to some treaty arrangement for the protection of seals in Behring Sea, but it wished to have the

. . . close time for seals extended to the sea of Okhotsk or at least to that part of it in which Robbin Island . . . is situated; as he says that there are many seals there also, under the same circumstances as those in Behring's Sea. I [White] asked whether the Russians expect us and the English to join in policing the Sea of Okhotsk, and he said that his government would do the policing, but that it desires the advantages of the proposed convention as to close time, etc., to extend to the sea above-mentioned. I replied that my instructions did not go beyond the whole of Behring's Sea, and that I could not assent to his proposal without referring to my government. M. de Staal furthermore wants a clause inserted in the Convention prohibiting the importation, for sale to the inhabitants of the islands in the seal protected zone, of alcoholic drinks, fire-arms, gunpowder, and dynamite.

Lord Salisbury said that he would have to consult some of his subordinates before expressing an opinion as to either of the Russian proposals, but added that he saw at the time no objection to including in the Convention the Sea of Okhotsk. He proposed therefore the inclusion of everything north of north latitude 47 degrees (in order to include Robbin Island) without defining the longitude. He assented to the policing by Revenue cutters, and M. de Staal said that, as the Russians have not cruisers enough nor Revenue cutters in those waters, his government would propose to utilize the vessels of a Commercial Company, on board of which they would place government officials. . . . Lord Salisbury also said he had asked Lord Lansdowne, in accordance with his promise to Mr. Phelps, to prevent the clearance of vessels from British Columbia intending to shoot seals in Behring's Sea this summer.

His Lordship seemed to think that it may be necessary to notify the other leading Powers, of this Convention, and to obtain their assent to its provisions. . . . Knowing that you do not wish to define your jurisdiction in Behring's Sea, nor claim the latter to be a *"Mare clausum,"* I made no observations on this subject, save that I should report to you Lord Salisbury's views, in which M. de Staal seemed to concur. . . .

It was finally agreed that Lord Salisbury should communicate with the

61. *Memorandum* written by Bayard after a conversation with Sackville-West, April 6, 1888, *ibid.*

other Departments interested and have a draught convention prepared for submission to the Governments concerned.[62]

In response to a telegram from Bayard requesting copies of any bill introduced in the British Parliament concerning the seal fisheries, White wrote that Lord Salisbury had decided to handle the matter through an Order in Council. This would soon be drafted by the officials in the Colonial Office.[63] White was a little confused in this matter of British procedure, and he had to be put straight through the following note from Eric Barrington:

> Lord Salisbury is afraid he did not make himself understood when last he spoke to you about the Seal Fisheries Convention. An Act of Parliament is necessary to give power to our Authorities to act on the provisions of the Convention when it is signed. The Order in Council will be merely the machinery which the Act will provide for the purpose of bringing its provisions into force.[64]

The chief difficulty in expediting this seal fisheries convention was the fact that Canadian desires had to be consulted,[65] and it was quite possible that the Canadian Government would attempt to postpone any settlement until their viewpoint was adopted.[66] This fear of Canadian procrastination was clearly expressed in White's letter to Bayard of May 2, 1888. He believed that the delay in obtaining drafts of the documents pertaining to the Seal Convention was due to opposition in Canada

> . . . where they probably suspect that we are trying to "do" them out of something. I have seen Lord Salisbury twice in society since writing to you on the 28th, and he implied that Canada is the source of delay. To my question whether he had heard from Canada he replied, "not definitely," from which I inferred that an answer had been received which necessitated another communication from this Government. . . . Lord Salisbury inquired whether I had any instructions as to the *duration* of the proposed Seal Convention. Evidently the Canadians are anxious to cut it as short as possible.

62. Henry White to Secretary Bayard, April 18, 1888, *Bayard MS*. See also, Henry White to Phelps, April 18, 1888, *ibid*.

63. Henry White to Secretary Bayard, April 22, 1888, *ibid*. When White remarked to Lord Salisbury that "all the sea north of 47 degrees would be an immense region to protect," Salisbury "took occasion to say that, upon consulting the map he had observed that on the East his proposal would include a considerable portion of British Columbian coasts for which he saw no necessity, and he is therefore inclined to limit the eastern area of the seal protection to Behring's Sea, as proposed by you, and to let the Russians include as much of their coasts and Sea as they want."

64. Eric Barrington to Henry White, April 28, 1888, *Bayard MS*.

65. Eric Barrington to Henry White, April 27, 1888, *ibid*.

66. Henry White to Secretary Bayard, April 28, 1888, *Bayard MS*.

I said, "as long a time as possible," but no special time had been mentioned in your Instructions. He thought (I fancy, inspired by Canada) about three or five years.[67]

Bayard was annoyed at this obstructive attitude assumed by the Canadian Government, and he thought it was "difficult to see why Great Britain should permit one of her colonies to thwart a plan intended to preserve the race of seals from extermination. Why should Canada any more than India assume to control the treaty-making power of the *Empire* on such a subject?"[68]

His annoyance was increased when he received a letter from Henry White which cast further light upon the situation. White had talked with Lord Salisbury at a dinner given by the Russian Ambassador, and finding

... that he had still nothing from Canada on the seal question, I asked him whether he could not proceed, without waiting any longer, in view of the approach of the seal-shooting season and of the great importance of protecting them this year if possible. He seemed to think this course might be feasible, and a meeting between Lord Salisbury, the Russian Ambassador and myself was arranged for yesterday afternoon, which took place. Unfortunately, however, Lord Salisbury had just received previously a communication from the Canadian Government stating that a memorandum was in course of preparation on the subject and would be shortly forwarded to London; and pending its arrival, Canada begged that nothing would be settled. Under these circumstances Lord Salisbury felt that he could only await this memorandum, of the contents of which he said he was not aware.[69] ...

I succeeded in obtaining an intimation that the probable ground of Canada's objection will be that the proposed Convention would break up an important British Columbian and Canadian trade; as, while we and the Russians have our own islands from which to obtain these animal skins, the former can only get them in the open sea. I was careful at one to reply that the admission of any such plea as that would imply absolute and very speedy extermination of the Seals from both Sea and Islands, which must be prevented, and to this Lord Salisbury seemed quite to agree. I have no idea that the British Govt. will allow objections on the part of Canada to interfere with the Convention; but they feel bound to hear what that Province has to say.[70]

While Bayard was waiting for Lord Salisbury to take some action,

67. Henry White to Secretary Bayard, May 2, 1888, *ibid.*
68. *Memorandum* written by Bayard, May 17, 1888, *ibid.*
69. For this Canadian protest, see Colonial Office to the British Foreign Office, April 25, 1888, *Fur Seal Arbitration*, vol. 5, p. 220.
70. Henry White to Secretary Bayard, May 17, 1888, *Bayard MS.*

Sackville-West called at the Department of State to discuss what course should be followed with reference to the British vessels that had been seized by United States revenue cutters. In a note to Bayard, April 30, 1888, Sackville-West had spoken of the "skippers" of these vessels being in jail. Bayard dismissed this idea as unfounded: he was not "aware that there was any personal imprisonment in the Behring Sea cases." With regard to the possibility that appeals could be taken from the decisions of Judge Dawson, of the United States District Court in Alaska, Bayard believed that the owners of the vessels had permitted too much time to elapse before filing them. He could not see "how the Executive would be able to change the time fixed by law for the taking of the appeals in these cases; that it was a matter regulated by statute, and that we could not change the time or mode of taking the appeal." [71]

After dealing with this legal interlude, Bayard once more looked toward London for some news in connection with the proposed fur-seal convention. Phelps reported on June 23 that he had learned from Henry White that Lord Salisbury was "impatient" with the tactics of delay adopted by the Canadian Government.[72] But this "impatience" did not seem to speed up the wheels of the British Foreign Office, and on July 13 we find Phelps writing to Bayard that there was

. . . no progress in the seal fishery convention, owing solely to the opposition of Canada. England and Russia agree with us. I shall continue to press it, and unless soon disposed of, shall recommend a course in which Russia will join, and to which England will not, I am sure, take much exception— the seizure of all vessels found engaged in the exterminating cruelty which it is sought to put an end to. I do not doubt that such a course may be supported.[73]

Bayard could comprehend the difficulties of the British Government in controlling Canada, but he thought it should be obvious that the

71. *Memorandum* written by Bayard after a conversation with Sackville-West, May 28, 1888, *ibid.* See also Bayard to Sackville-West, May 29, 1888, *ibid.*

72. Phelps to Secretary Bayard, June 23, 1888, *Bayard MS.* This letter was read at the Cabinet meeting on July 5, 1888.

73. Phelps to Secretary Bayard, July 13, 1888, *ibid.* On May 26 Baron Rosen called at the Department of State with reference to the seal fisheries question. He asked "if the arrangement could include Robbin Island, to which Mr. Bayard said there would be no objection to that, as the idea was to protect the whole seal industry—to keep these creatures from being slaughtered while on their way to the breeding places; that we proposed each nation should concurrently legislate to prevent their own citizens from killing seal during certain seasons—we wanted all to join in penalizing the killing of seals on the waters. . . . Baron R. then asked if some arrangment could be made to protect certain parts of the Russian coast from adventurers, to which the Secretary answered that the Russian Government could legislate itself for that purpose." *Memorandum* dictated by Bayard after a conversation with Baron Rosen, May 26, 1888, *ibid.*

Behring Sea convention should not be "impeded by Canadian views. There is no question of territorial waters *there* in which Canada has any pretext of interest, and the Russian co-operation which you suggest, may procure a settlement, and may become necessary."[74]

It was soon evident to Phelps that Canadian opposition was so powerful that the British Government would not go forward in the Behring Sea matter unless the United States and Russia exerted the strongest type of pressure. The only course left to America was the

. . . resolute one of self-defense by seizing vessels engaged in this nefarious business, and holding on to those already captured. This course will save the seal from extermination by the Canadians, and nothing else will. I have no manner of doubt of our right to do it. Russia and probably all nations interested will join us. You may be sure that England will not back up Canada in this business, because she admits it to be wrong, has in vain requested Canada to desist from it, and here our large interests in the business are affected by it very injuriously. I have no doubt it would be satisfactory to the British Government to have us put a stop to it. If you used additional legislation I hope you will ask for it at once and you will doubtless readily obtain it.

In writing the President by this mail, relative to his Canadian message, I have mentioned this subject as very germane, and asked him to read the despatch sent you today, that the whole matter may be dealt with consistently. The London *Times* has already in a leading article pointedly referred to our giving up the vessels seized from seal-poaching as showing that the President's message on the subject of the fisheries is a mere bid for votes, and is not serious. We *must* show Canada that she cannot outrage us with impunity. And the moment we take a firm stand, all the trouble will cease. That is the surest way to avoid difficulty. *And you may be sure it will be satisfactory to the present British Government which is embarrassed by Canadian conduct which she cannot control, and cannot justify and cannot afford to fight for.*[75]

74. Secretary Bayard to Phelps, July 26, 1888, *ibid.* Rosen had another interview with Bayard, who told him that "there was evidently a hitch caused by Canadian matters [with reference to the sealing convention]; that it was not a Canadian question at all, but a British question, and it was very awkward having Canadian interposition paralizing the action of the responsible Government. As long as they were in Canadian waters they were Canadian vessels, but were British vessels when outside Canadian jurisdiction." *Memorandum* dictated by Bayard after a conversation with Baron Rosen, August 3, 1888, *Bayard MS.*

75. Phelps to Secretary Bayard, September 12, 1888, *Bayard MS.* In an official despatch to Bayard on this same day, September 12, Phelps expresses himself in much the same way. He thought there were merely two alternatives for the American Government to take. It would either have to "submit to have these valuable fisheries destroyed or must take measures to prevent their destruction by capturing the vessels employed in it. Between these alternatives it does not appear to me there should be the slightest hesitation. Much learning has been expended upon the discussion of the abstract question of the

Bayard was not ready to adopt the aggressive course outlined in these communications from Phelps, and as late as March 1, 1889, he still clung to the idea that the best way to settle the seal fisheries dispute was through "an international arrangement which would enable the nations to co-operate for the purpose of preventing the destruction of the seal." [76] This international arrangement must have a background of friendly understanding rather than a prelude of sharp friction that might lead to war.

But there were many officials in the Cleveland Administration who shared the views of Phelps with reference to adopting an uncompromising course towards Great Britain in the matter of seal fisheries. With this end in view, a bill was passed by the Senate in February, 1889, providing for the better protection of the salmon fisheries in Alaskan waters. In the House of Representatives an important amendment was added to the bill. Section 1956 of the Revised Statutes of the United States, prohibited the killing of fur-bearing animals "within the limits of Alaska territory, or the waters thereof." According to this House amendment, Section 1956 of the Revised Statutes should be interpreted as applying to all the waters of Behring Sea which were included in the boundaries of the treaty of 1867. The bill as finally passed by Congress and signed by the President, March 2, 1889, declared that the phrase "within the limits of Alaska territory, or the waters thereof," included and applied to all the "dominion of the United States in the waters of the Behring Sea," and it was made the duty of the President to issue a proclamation

. . . warning all persons against entering said waters for the purpose of violating the provisions of said section, and he shall also cause one or more

---

right of *mare clausum*. I do not conceive it to be applicable to the present case. Here is a valuable fishery, and a large and, if properly managed, permanent industry, the property of the nations on whose shores it is carried on. It is proposed by the colony of a foreign nation, in defiance of the joint remonstrance of all the countries interested, to destroy this business by the indiscriminate slaughter and extermination of the animals in question, in the open neighboring sea, . . . when the common dictates of humanity ought to protect them. . . . And it is suggested that we are prevented from defending ourselves against such depredations because the sea at a certain distance from the coast is free. The same line of argument would take under its protection piracy and the slave trade, when prosecuted in the open sea. . . . If precedents are wanting for a defense so necessary and proper, it is because precedents for such a course of conduct are likewise unknown. The best International Law has arisen from precedents that have been established when the just occasion from them arose, undeterred by the discussion of abstract and inadequate rules." "Case of the United States," *Fur Seal Arbitration*, vol. 2, *Appendix 1*, pp. 181-183.

76. *Memorandum* written by Bayard after a conversation with Baron Rosen, March 1, 1889, *Bayard MS.*

vessels of the United States to diligently cruise said waters and arrest all persons, and seize all vessels found to be, or to have been, engaged in any violation of the laws of the United States therein.[77]

The person most responsible for the insertion and adoption of this far-reaching amendment with reference to section 1956 of the *Revised Statutes,* was Mr. Dunn, Chairman of the Committee on Merchant Marine and Fisheries in the House of Representatives. It is quite likely that he had the support of President Cleveland in this matter, and it should be remembered that both the President and the Acting Attorney General had been very loath to adopt Bayard's viewpoint with reference to limiting American jurisdiction in Alaskan waters to the three-mile limit. In the drafting of the Scott Act dealing with Chinese immigration into the United States, Bayard had not been consulted by Administration leaders in Congress, and apparently they followed the same procedure with regard to this fur-seal legislation in March, 1889. This viewpoint is strengthened by the following excerpt from a conversation between Bayard and Baron Rosen on March 1, 1889:

Baron Rosen called, bringing with him a report of Mr. Dunn, on the Alaska fur-seal fisheries. He pointed out to me some of the conclusions reached by Mr. Dunn, in regard to the title of the United States to the waters of Behring Sea being fixed and complete by the cession from Russia. I told him I had examined the book [report]; found it had been reported to the House on the 29th of January, and had not been printed until within the last few days. I told him I had not seen it, and had had no consultation with Mr. Dunn, nor knowledge of what he had reported, and I must distinctly decline being responsible for anything he did.[78]

In three more days, Bayard's term as Secretary of State came to an end, and James G. Blaine succeeded him in that important office. Blaine's failure to find a solution for the Behring Sea dispute, and Bayard's role in its final settlement, are told in the next chapter.

77. John B. Moore, *History and Digest of International Arbitrations, etc.,* vol. 1, pp. 765-767; *Revised Statutes of the United States,* section 1956.

78. *Memorandum* written by Bayard after a conversation with Baron Rosen, March 1, 1889, *Bayard MS.* Carl Russell Fish, in his *American Diplomacy* (N. Y., 1919), p. 378, remarks: "In March, 1889, the House, largely through Blaine's influence, asserted that Behring Sea was under the territorial jurisdiction of the United States. This assertion Blaine undertook to defend." This loose statement is obviously inaccurate.

CHAPTER FIFTEEN

England Wins Another Arbitration

THE PART THAT BLAINE PLAYED IN THE DIPLOMATIC CONTROVERSY RE-
lating to the fur-seal fisheries has been greatly misunderstood, and he
has been unjustly blamed for adopting an aggressive attitude that led
to an inevitable defeat for the United States. As a matter of fact, the
stand that Blaine took, and the arguments he employed, were largely
dictated by the preceding Cleveland Administration.

It should be kept clearly in mind that the seizures in 1886 of British
sealing vessels in Behring Sea, were undertaken by Treasury Department agents without any previous consultation with the Department
of State. Bayard had been disturbed by these actions, and he had persuaded President Cleveland to release the vessels. Other seizures took
place, and Bayard again secured their release. The reason why he had
exerted pressure upon the President in this regard, was because he was
certain that "an examination of the history of Behring Sea will not
sustain our right to exclude other nations from the common right of
navigation, fishing, etc., in those waters outside the three-mile line from
the shore." [1]

This viewpoint was in sharp contrast to the argument advanced by
Francis Wharton, the Solicitor of the Department of State, who contended that the three-mile rule had "never applied to the North Pacific," and had no relevance to the fur-seal fisheries. It was Wharton's
firm belief that the true principle of territorial waters was that "wherever a sovereign has property, there he is to have sufficient police-
control over the waters adjacent to such property as to enable him to
protect it." There was no doubt in his mind that this interpretation
was the proper construction of "the law of nations." [2]

1. Secretary Bayard to Phelps. August 16, 1887, *Bayard Letter Book*, vol. 5, *Bayard MS.*
2. Francis Wharton to Secretary Bayard, September 4, 1887, *Bayard MS.*

It was significant that G. A. Jenks, the Acting Attorney General, shared Wharton's belief that America had certain exclusive rights in Behring Sea. Jenks was in agreement with President Cleveland in this regard, and the memorandum he sent to Bayard did not run counter to the viewpoint of the Chief Executive. He thought that a "qualified property interest" might exist in wild animals, and that "property in the sea which is local and exhaustible is subject to the right of domain." His conclusion was that the United States, as sovereign, had the "right to protect the fur-seals whose habitat is upon the shores and islands of Alaska, whether within or without the marine belt." [3]

This argument of Jenks was later emphasized by Phelps, and it was presented by the American counsel during the arbitration proceedings at Paris, as the most important link in their chain of legal reasoning.

The passage of the Act of March 2, 1889, which declared that the phrase, "within the limits of Alaska territory, or the waters thereof," applied to all the "dominion of the United States in the waters of the Behring Sea," was an assertion, by implication, of the right of American jurisdiction of a large part of the waters of Behring Sea. Blaine was not responsible for this legislation, nor for the seizures of British vessels engaged in pelagic sealing. Unlike Bayard, whose keen legal mind refused to be led astray by legal sophistries, Blaine was determined to defend the dubious practices of the Cleveland Administration, and he chose some of the weapons that had been forged by officials of this same administration. It would have been far better for him if he had adopted

3. G. A. Jenks to Secretary Bayard, August 31, 1887, *Bayard MS.* In his *memorandum,* Jenks outlined the following points: "*First.* The fur-seals within the treaty limits are chiefly begotten and brought forth on the domain of the United States. *Second.* When they leave the land of their birth, they have *animum revertendi.* This is known by their usual custom. *Third.* They are exhaustible, and of commercial value. *Fourth.* They are by nature, impotent for self-protection. . . . *Fifth.* When they leave the place of their birth, and are killed in the open sea, it is a cruel waste and destruction. Legal Propositions. *First.* Animals *ferae naturae,* by prerogative, belong to the sovereign, unless granted out to a subject directly, or as an incident to a grant of land. *Second.* A qualified property may subsist, in a subject, in animals *ferae naturae,* either *per industriam, propter impotentiam,* or *propter previlegium. Third.* Animals *ferae naturae,* are no longer the property of a man than while they are in his keeping or actual possession; but if at any time they regain their natural liberty, his property instantly ceases, *unless they have animum revertendi, which is only to be known by their usual custom of returning. Fourth.* A qualified property may also subsist in relation to animals *ferae naturae, ratione impotentiae,* on account of their own inability. *Fifth.* Property in the sea which is local and exhaustible is subject to the right of domain. *Sixth.* The prerogative right of the sovereign is founded upon the necessity for protection of the several species of those animals which would soon be exhausted by general liberty. Conclusions. *First.* The United States, as sovereign, has the right to protect the fur-seals whose habitat is upon the shores and islands of Alaska, whether within or without the marine belt." *Bayard MS.*

Bayard's tactics, and had refused to be bound by dubious precedents and arguments.

If Blaine had been a little more fortunate in his relations with Russia, the story of the fur-seal dispute would have been quite different. In March, 1889, Baron Rosen, the Russian representative in Washington, began to discuss with Blaine some of the aspects of the fur-seal situation, and it was not long before a detailed outline of a proposed convention was agreed upon. Under its terms, other powers were to be notified that inasmuch as the United States and Russia were the sole owners of the most important breeding grounds of the fur-seal, and whereas the herds of seal were in danger of extermination by the ruthless methods of pelagic killing that were followed by the seal-hunters of certain nations, the two nations had decided, with careful avoidance of all interference with the legitimate trade and commerce of other Maritime Powers, "to exercise their indisputable right to preserve and protect this valuable seal industry." In order to carry out this resolve, the two nations were to issue regulations concerning the number of sealskins to be taken from the islands. There was to be a closed season, and no slaughter of seals would be permitted during the period of migrations. If necessary, these killings would be prevented "by the two Powers with the use of force." [4]

When this proposed convention was submitted to the Russian Foreign Office, objections were at once raised that this joint action by the United States and Russia would lead to serious difficulties with England. Friction with the British Empire had already been felt in the Near East and in Central Asia, and it was not expedient to add to existing disputes. Because of these dangers, the proposed accord with the United States in connection with seal fisheries was dropped, and the first attempt by Blaine to score a diplomatic success at the expense of England, was a complete failure. [5]

Before Blaine had fully recovered from this diplomatic defeat, the British chargé d'affaires presented him with a protest from Lord Salisbury with regard to new seizures of British vessels in the North Pacific. Secretary Bayard had given assurances that there would be no further seizures while the seal fisheries dispute was under discussion. This ap-

4. Alice F. Tyler, *The Foreign Policy of James G. Blaine* (Minneapolis, 1927), pp. 310-315; *Russian Legation, Notes from*, vol. 13, MS Dept. of State. See also, Baron Rosen, *Forty Years of Diplomacy* (N. Y., 1922, 2 vols.), vol. 1, pp. 78ff.
5. Baron Rosen, *Forty Years of Diplomacy*, p. 80.

parent change in policy would hinder, rather than aid, a settlement of the problem.[6]

Blaine promptly replied that the Department of State had heard only rumors concerning the reported seizures of British vessels, but he admitted that these rumors were "probably based on truth." He wished to state, however, that President Harrison desired to reach an understanding with the British Government that would remove all possible ground of misunderstanding in connection with existing troubles in Behring Sea. When Sir Julian Pauncefote reached the United States the Department of State would be glad to arrange for a discussion of the points at issue, and the President believed that an adjustment of the dispute could be quickly reached.[7]

Blaine had "strong confidence" that he would be able to "adjust" this Behring Sea dispute when Lord Pauncefote returned to Washington in October,[8] but Edwardes reported on September 12 that the seizures in Alaskan waters were causing "much excitement both in England and in Canada."[9] Lord Salisbury was apparently somewhat concerned at this rising sentiment, and in a note of October 2, 1889, he referred to the fact that negotiations for a convention to settle the seal fisheries dispute had been "suspended for a time" because of objections raised by the Dominion of Canada, but Her Majesty's Government was "fully sensible" of the importance of this question, and Lord Pauncefote would be "furnished with the requisite instructions in case the Secretary of State should be willing to enter upon the discussion."[10]

When Lord Pauncefote arrived in Washington in the latter part of October, he was especially interested in arranging for some settlement of this controversy, and on November 1 he reported back to Lord Salisbury with reference to a conversation with Secretary Blaine. Blaine did not claim that Behring Sea was a *mare clausum* (closed sea), but he did express the opinion that the American Government had a right to

---

6. H. G. Edwardes to Secretary Blaine, August 24, 1889, *Foreign Relations, 1890*, p. 358.

7. Secretary Blaine to Edwardes, August 24, 1889, *Foreign Relations, 1890*, p. 359. In a note to President Harrison, August 25, 1889, Blaine remarked as follows: "It seems very *Bayardish* for this Government to agree to take no further measures of protection in the Behring Sea 'pending the discussion of the general question' and then allow England to say when that discussion shall be reopened and for how long a time it shall be *drawled* along." Albert T. Volwiler, *The Correspondence Between Benjamin Harrison and James G. Blaine, 1882–1893* (Phila., 1940), p. 79.

8. Secretary Blaine to President Harrison, August 26, 1889, *ibid.*, p. 80.

9. Edwardes to Secretary Blaine, September 12, 1889, *Foreign Relations, 1890*, p. 360.

10. Marquis of Salisbury to Mr. Edwardes, October 2, 1889. There are two notes of this date from Salisbury to Edwardes, *House Ex. Doc. 450*, 51 Cong., 1 sess., pp. 5-6.

protect the fur-seals. Inasmuch as the British Government had suspended the negotiations in May, 1888, at the request of Canada, Blaine felt that Lord Salisbury should now take the initiative in the matter of resuming conversations. But Pauncefote once more alluded to the necessity for securing Canadian advice and assistance before taking any new steps to adjust the dispute, and he pointedly referred to the question of compensation for the Canadian vessels that had been seized in Alaskan waters.[11]

On December 7, 1889, Lord Salisbury sent to Pauncefote, in Washington, an outline of the conditions laid down by Canada with reference to any renewal of negotiations concerning the seal fisheries. They were four in number: (1) The American Government would have to abandon all pretensions to regard Behring Sea as a closed sea *(mare clausum)*, and would also have to revise any legislation based upon that claim. (2) Canada should be represented on any Joint High Commission intrusted with the settlement of the seal fisheries dispute. (3) The proceedings of the Commission should have the approval of Canada. (4) Great Britain and the United States should agree upon the amount of compensation to be paid to British subjects for the seizure of their sealing vessels by American revenue cutters in Alaskan waters.[12]

These conditions were so extreme in their nature that Lord Pauncefote protested that they afforded no real basis for negotiations. They were finally withdrawn, but Canada won her point that no final settlement would be valid until it had received the approval of the Canadian Government. On January 28, 1890, Lord Salisbury sent the terms which he thought should govern the proposed negotiations. The high contracting parties were limited to Great Britain, Russia, and the United States, and the conversations should be conducted at Washington. The question of compensation to the owners of British ships

11. Pauncefote to Lord Salisbury, November 1, 1889, *Fur Seal Arbitration*, vol. 5, p. 386.

12. Marquis of Salisbury to Pauncefote, December 7, 1889, *ibid.*, p. 400. On December 16, 1889, Sir Charles Tupper, in London, wrote to Sir John Macdonald and remarked: "You will observe that Her Majesty's Government are pledged not to conclude any arrangement without securing an adequate public declaration of the United States that Behring Sea is open and free, and stands pledged to us that no agreement as to a close season shall be made without the approval of Canada. Lord Knutsford expects Blaine to abandon in the outset of the negotiations, the pretension that Behring Sea is a *mare clausum*, if he does not formally do so before. . . . Her Majesty's Government cannot but feel that Canada has exhibited great patience under very trying circumstances, and is entitled to the utmost support she can give us." *Sir John Macdonald Papers, Behring Sea,* vol. 2, MS Canadian Archives.

seized in Alaskan waters should be the subject of separate negotiations, and the American Government must give assurances that there would be no further seizures.[13]

Before receiving this note, Blaine sent a long communication to Lord Pauncefote in which he strongly defended the right of the American Government to give adequate protection to the seal fisheries. The taking of seals in the open sea would ruin an industry which had been "carefully developed for more than ninety years under the flags of Russia and the United States." The methods followed by British hunters in Alaskan waters were against the rights of "good morals and of good government the world over" and he expressed "unfeigned surprise" that the British Government should defend the lawless course of these marauders. The "law of the sea is not lawlessness," nor can the law of the sea and the liberty which it confers and which it protects, be perverted to "justify acts which are criminal in themselves, which inevitably tend to results against the interests and against the welfare of mankind." It would not be expedient for the British Government to insist too vigorously upon a strict observance of the three-mile limit, because this narrow restriction might prevent the continuance of proper measures for the protection of the pearl fisheries of Ceylon. It was significant that the sealing ships from Canada had not started on their destructive course until recent years. By what process of reasoning did Her Majesty's Government conclude that an act might be committed with impunity against the rights of the United States which had never been attempted against the same rights when held by the Russian Empire? The President was persuaded that "all friendly nations" would concede to the United States "the same rights and privileges on the lands and in the waters of Alaska which the same friendly nations always conceded to the Empire of Russia." [14]

These interesting legal points in Blaine's note of January 22 did not receive any answer from Lord Salisbury until the latter part of May. In the meantime, conversations had been held in Washington between Blaine, Baron Struve, and Lord Pauncefote. Blaine and Struve proposed that the close season for fur-seals should affect all of the region north of 50 degrees of north latitude, but Pauncefote indicated that the British Colonial Office believed that the restricted zone should be

13. Marquis of Salisbury to Pauncefote, January 28, 1890, *Fur Seal Arbitration*, vol. 5, p. 435.
14. Secretary Blaine to Pauncefote, January 22, 1890, *Foreign Relations, 1890*, pp. 366-370.

in the vicinity of those islands in Behring Sea which were the chief habitat of the seals.[15]

Lord Pauncefote and Blaine discussed in detail the question of the necessity for a close season, and the area that this restriction should affect. Blaine adduced evidence that showed the destructive effect of pelagic sealing as practised by the Canadians, and Pauncefote endeavored to prove that the chief danger to the seal herds was the lack of proper safeguards on the islands that were controlled by the Alaska Commercial Company.[16] In order that Lord Pauncefote would have the proper technical assistance, the Canadian Government sent Mr. Charles Tupper, son of Sir Charles Tupper, to Washington in the spring of 1890.

Tupper discovered that the Russian Minister was supporting the contentions of Secretary Blaine, and he was surprised to find that Pauncefote himself was "much impressed by theory that females are killed in large numbers in open sea, and their nurslings on islands consequently lost." [17] While Blaine had insisted upon a close season for seals, he "practically" refused to discuss its "merits," and strongly pushed for final terms of settlement.[18]

On April 10 Tupper sent to Sir John Macdonald a long letter in which he recounted his troubles in Washington. He had discussed with Sir Julian Pauncefote the terms of the draft convention, and had found him much disappointed in them. He was

. . . more set than ever upon the necessity for *some* close season, with an exhibition of gratification that not only was this the opinion of the people we met, including representatives of other Countries and of the world generally, but Lord Salisbury agreed with him as well. He also, I thought, threw out a hint that he was making propositions on behalf of the British Government, and that he was not speaking for the Canadian Government in this Conference.

He argued quite earnestly in favour of our proposing that the report of the experts should be acted upon in some way so as to make a finality of the question. Sir Julian thinks we should accept and act upon the report if it

15. Colonial Office to the Foreign Office, February 27, 1890, *Fur Seal Arbitration*, vol. 5, pp. 450-454.

16. Secretary Blaine to Pauncefote, March 1, 1890, *House Ex. Doc. 450*, 51 Cong., 1 sess., pp. 14-25; Pauncefote to Secretary Blaine, March 9, 1890, *ibid.*, pp. 26-51.

17. C. H. Tupper to Sir John Macdonald, March 3, 1890, *Sir John Macdonald Papers, Behring Sea*, vol. 2, MS Canadian Archives. Tupper held the office of Minister of Marine and Fisheries.

18. C. H. Tupper to Sir John Macdonald, March 17, 1890, *Sir John Macdonald Papers, Behring Sea*, vol. 2, MS Canadian Archives.

is unanimous, and if the experts disagree, then the question should be decided by some foreign potentate or other person of high standing. He urges further, that we should propose the closure of waters within a radius of some distance from the breeding islands during the investigation, of course guarding ourselves from making an admission of the necessity of such a radius permanently.

I gave him the views of our Government on these points and told him I was quite aware that he was acting directly for the British Government, but that when he consulted me or referred to the Canadian Government, he must expect the Canadian opinion. I explained to him that Mr. Blaine having refused to discuss the merits of the question after inviting a Conference for that purpose, had doubtless tended to reduce the liberality of the draft proposal which my Government was ready to suggest. Sir Julian said he had understood that the Conference was to settle what the close season should be, taking as granted that some season should be agreed upon. I told him that we never understood this nor did we at any time admit that a close season outside the three-mile limit was necessary.

I went on to say that this misunderstanding only showed how carefully we should guard against similar misunderstandings on the part of the proposed experts. . . . I said to him that the report of the experts to be of any value should embrace seal life generally, and that we should learn where regulations were required and what they should be. If the United States proposed to regulate the killing on the Islands, they could not complain if we insisted upon making regulations for our own vessels in the sea. It would be as fitting to leave the regulations to these experts in the one case as in the other. Finally, Sir Julian said he would go over the draft and put it into shape suitable to him from my standpoint, and that we would then look over it again before submitting it to the Conference.

At his request I have agreed to extend the time during which the *modus* shall last by six months, since if the reports are to be made in two years, the *modus* might well give time for action or consideration upon the reports. Sir Julian, I may mention, based his argument in support of his contention that *some* close season is necessary in Behring Sea, on the Convention relating to seal life near Greenland and in the North Sea. I pointed out, however, that this Convention related only to seals which breed upon ice floes and not on land. The danger consisted in both cases in hunting them upon their breeding grounds, in the one case in the open sea upon ice, in the other upon the rookeries in the Islands. He furthermore asserted that experience in connection with marine animals demonstrated the necessity for a close season.

I pointed out that so far from his view being correct, neither Great Britain, Canada, or the United States prescribed a close season for the deep sea fisheries, but that expert opinion in England and the States was decidedly opposed to the idea that regulations were necessary. He then alluded to the Convention between England and France and I reminded him that the Convention regulated the limits of fishing, the policing of the waters, etc., as between the two countries, but prescribed no close season.

Regarding the assessment of damages and the question of liability, I told Sir Julian that we agreed to his endeavouring to reach the amount in consultation with Mr. Blaine, and that if the amount was fixed in this way, the facts of the case should be set out and the question propounded as to whether the conduct of the United States was justified by the principles of International or National Law, for the decision of two eminent jurisconsults—say the Chief Justice of the United States and an eminent Judge in England. Upon this, Sir Julian remarked that Mr. Blaine wanted the jurisconsult to be some European learned in International Law.[19]

In a letter to Sir John Macdonald on the following day (April 11), Tupper gave some further intimate details of his difficulties with Sir Julian, who was inclined to be generous in his concessions to the United States. Sir Julian had read to Mr. Tupper a new draft convention which leaned

. . . more to the side of Concession, and provides that in the event of the disagreement of our Government, on receipt of the report of experts, for a reference to an independent Government to settle the nature of the regulations, if any. The new draft Convention also provides that pending the duration thereof (two years and a half) no sealing by vessels shall be permitted within a radius of fifteen miles from any breeding island.

He also showed me a letter he had written to Lord Salisbury. . . . In this letter he urges that unless we can submit his last draft, . . . the settlement of the question is impossible, and that in his opinion outside criticism will be adverse to our attitude throughout the negotiations. He claims that substantially no injury will be done our sealers by his last Convention, and that if it be not accepted by the United States, our position will then be commended by all disinterested parties.

I need not discuss in this letter the provision regarding the radius. I have already told you we could safely concede 20 miles so far as our sealing operations are concerned; but the other view was put forward, as you will remember, to the effect that the concession of such a radius is unprecedented and means a still further restriction for our sealers at the end of the enquiry.

I entertain strong objections to the clause which puts us at the mercy of a foreign tribunal. If, after scientific and thorough enquiry, we do not believe regulations for the seal hunting are required, it would be humiliating to find that by the *ipse dixit* of a foreign power we were practically excluded from sealing in Behring Sea.

It is in my opinion most unfortunate that he [Sir Julian Pauncefote] had conducted the negotiations in such a way that Mr. Blaine has been able to

19. C. H. Tupper to Sir John Macdonald, April 10, 1890, *Sir John Macdonald Papers, Behring Sea*, vol. 2, MS Canadian Archives.

learn all that he personally was willing to do. The consequence is that he fights now for his own reputation and standing, before Mr. Blaine. It seems clear from the above, that having informally told Mr. Blaine of his intended and very handsome concessions, he dare not retreat.

It may be out of place for me to say it, but I cannot refrain from urging that in future negotiations with the United States, no British Minister at Washington should act for us. It is apparent that there is always present on his part a desire to make his future residence in Washington as pleasant as possible, and he is to that extent, therefore, unable to take and keep a firm and independent position. If Canadians cannot act for Great Britain in the negotiation of Canadian affairs, the Mother Country should at least send out a strong and fearless man from home who would be indifferent to the impression he might personally make upon the United States Administration.[20]

It is possible that Lord Pauncefote being located in Washington, was able to see the realities of the situation more readily than Canadian officials. It happened, however, that even the officials in the British Colonial Office viewed his attitude as too generous, and on April 11 we find Lord Stanley sending a telegram to Washington, warning Pauncefote that concessions to the United States, "if carried too far, would produce most serious consequences in Dominion." [21]

Under this pressure from the British Colonial Office, the position of Lord Pauncefote was anything but pleasant, and Tupper, at times, must have increased this discomfort by his aggressive and self-confident attitude. On April 16 Tupper wrote to Sir John Macdonald and described the procedure at one of the conferences between Blaine, Pauncefote, and M. de Struve, the Russian Minister at Washington. According to Tupper, it had been agreed

. . . by Mr. Blaine, Sir Julian Pauncefote, and Mr. de Struve, that the papers should be fully and thoroughly discussed by them. So soon as my paper was presented, however, Mr. Blaine subsequently refused point blank to discuss the questions raised in his document and my counter-statement, and requested the British Minister to state the best offer he was authorized to make for a close season on behalf of his Government.

In drawing your attention to this phase of the negotiations, I feel sure that you will not suspect me of being vain if I state that the extracts on page 46 of the pamphlet, and indeed all the proof I was able to cull from United States documents, would make it necessary for Mr. Blaine to denounce nearly

20. C. H. Tupper to Sir John Macdonald, April 11, 1890, *Sir John Macdonald Papers, Behring Sea*, vol. 2, MS Canadian Archives.

21. Lord Stanley to Pauncefote, April 11, 1890, *Sir John Macdonald Papers, Behring Sea*, vol. 2, MS Canadian Archives.

every officer who has visited the Islands and without whose evidence he would have nothing to go upon whatever.[22]

In his conversations with Lord Pauncefote, Tupper had insisted that in the draft treaty to be submitted to the United States, there should not be any admission "of any necessity for restrictions of pelagic sealing." When Pauncefote agreed to this, Tupper strongly urged insertion of the

. . . words "and the taking of fur-seals by *land* or sea," in Article VI of the proposed Convention. In doing this, let me again express to you the opinion that no reasonable objection can be urged by the United States Government against the use of these words. The experience of the late lessees of the Pribilov Islands shows that it is not necessary to those enjoying the privilege of taking seals on the Islands, to kill seals between May 1st and 30th of June, or from the 1st of October to the 30th of December, the dates mentioned in Article VI.

It is in the interest of seal life, certainly from the United States' standpoint, not to interfere with the seals on the Islands during these periods. It appears unreasonable to ask our sealers to abstain from killing seals in the open sea at a time when United States lessees may kill and take seals on land.[23]

The draft convention that Pauncefote was about to submit to Blaine, was a patch-work affair that contained suggestions from both the British Colonial Office and from the Canadian Government. As Blaine discussed these points with Pauncefote, he became discouraged as to the outcome of the negotiations. On April 25 Pauncefote reported to Tupper that he had just returned from a conference with Blaine, who was "looking wretched," and who certainly was very "irritable and despondent." Blaine expressed the fear that "nothing was going to come from this Conference after all," but Sir Julian "assured him that his solution of the difficulty would soon be presented." [24]

When this "solution" of Sir Julian's was submitted on April 29, Blaine realized that his prophecy that "nothing was going to come from

22. C. H. Tupper to Sir John Macdonald, April 16, 1890, *Sir John Macdonald Papers, Behring Sea,* vol. 2, MS Canadian Archives.

23. Tupper to Sir Julian Pauncefote, April 26, 1890, *Sir John Macdonald Papers, Behring Sea,* vol. 2, MS Canadian Archives.

24. C. H. Tupper to Sir John Macdonald, April 25, 1890, *Sir John Macdonald Papers, Behring Sea,* vol. 2, MS Canadian Archives. It is apparent that Blaine was often irritable and despondent. His ill-temper is illustrated in the following note he wrote to John W. Foster, December 24, 1891: "Tired and hungry and sick to begin with, I spoke to you rather quickly at the Department. I beg pardon for so doing, and if you had not left so quickly, I would have spoken your pardon there. I have a very quick and very unfortunate temper, but it is over in a minute and hence I write you the first thing after getting home." *Foster MS.*

this Conference," was correct. Article I provided for the appointment of a mixed commission of experts who were to study and report upon (within two years) the following questions: (1) Whether regulations properly enforced upon the breeding islands . . . and in the territorial water surrounding those islands are sufficient for the preservation of the fur-seal species? (2) If not, how far from the islands is it necessary that such regulations should be enforced in order to preserve the species? (3) In either of the above cases, what should such regulations provide? (4) If a close season is required on the breeding islands and territorial waters, what months should it embrace? (5) If a close season is necessary outside of the breeding islands as well, what extent of waters and what period or periods should it embrace?

If the High Contracting Parties were not able to agree upon the regulations to be adopted, the questions of difference should be referred to the arbitration of an impartial government. Pending the report of the Commission, and for six months after the date of such report, the High Contracting Parties should put in force a series of proposed regulations. One of these regulations prohibited the taking of seals by *land*[25] or sea north of certain fixed lines, from May 1 to June 30, and from October 1 to December 30. A protective band of ten miles wide was suggested as a protection against marauders, and the masters of vessels that broke the provisional regulations should be turned over to "the authorities of the nation to which they respectively belong, who shall alone have jurisdiction to try the offence and impose the penalties for the same."[26]

Blaine did not give an immediate answer to the letter from Pauncefote enclosing the draft convention, but during the early days of May, 1890, he treated the British Minister in such a friendly manner that optimism prevailed in the British Legation.[27] On May 10 Blaine informed Pauncefote that he would soon send him a letter concerning the proposed convention submitted on April 29, and that he thought "the proposal was a satisfactory basis for a settlement," but that "some important changes must be made before the United States Government could accept it."[28]

25. This was a suggestion of Mr. Tupper. Tupper's opposition to the submission of differences to the arbitration of an impartial government was unavailing.

26. Pauncefote to Secretary Blaine, April —, 1890, *House Ex. Doc. 450*, 51 Cong., 1 sess., pp. 52-57.

27. C. H. Tupper to Sir John Macdonald, May 9, 1890, *Sir John Macdonald Papers, Behring Sea*, vol. 2, MS Canadian Archives.

28. C. H. Tupper to Sir John Macdonald, May 11, 1890, *ibid.*

On May 22 a statement appeared in the press to the effect that a decision had been made in a Cabinet meeting to reject the proposal of the British Government, and that instructions had been issued to the revenue cutter *Bear* to arrest pelagic sealers in Behring Sea. When Pauncefote repaired at once to the Department of State to investigate the basis for such a statement, Blaine made no attempt to deny its authenticity. He merely remarked that in America the press could not be controlled. With regard to the British proposal, he strongly protested against the regulation which would, within the close season, prohibit the taking of seals *by land* as well as by sea.[29]

On the following day, Pauncefote sent a note of protest against the issuance of instructions directing the revenue cutter *Bear* to seize British vessels engaged in pelagic sealing.[30] In his note of reply, Blaine protested against the course of the British Government "in authorizing, encouraging, and protecting vessels which are not only interfering with American rights in the Behring Sea, but which are doing violence as well to the rights of the civilized world." After this sharp sentence of indictment, Blaine declared that from November 11, 1887, to April 23, 1888, Lord Salisbury had "in every form of speech assented to the necessity of a close season for the protection of seals." During this period negotiations for the settlement of the Behring Sea dispute were progressing satisfactorily, but suddenly, on April 28, the British Government refused to take any further steps until "Canada is heard from." After a wait of several months, the American Minister in London inquired about a resumption of negotiations, but he was met with the reply that Her Majesty's Government was not willing to enter into any convention until its terms had received the approval of the Canadian Government.

This little drama of advance and stop, was repeated in America during the months subsequent to November, 1889. Lord Pauncefote could remember the conversations that had taken place between himself, the Russian Minister, and Secretary Blaine with regard to the protection of seals. He could doubtless recall the occasion when "the lines for a close season in the Behring Sea" laid down by Lord Salisbury "were almost exactly repeated" by the British Minister himself, and were "inscribed on maps which were before us, a copy of which is in

29. J. B. Moore, *History and Digest of International Arbitrations*, vol. 1, p. 789; "Case of Great Britain," *Fur Seal Arbitration*, vol. 5, pp. 515-516.

30. Pauncefote to Secretary Blaine, May 23, 1890, *House Ex. Doc. 450*, 51 Cong., 1 sess., p. 65.

the possession of the Russian Minister, and a copy also in my possession." No obstacles were presented on the American side of the question, and a settlement seemed near at hand when negotiations were suddenly broken off "by the interposition of Canada."

The draft convention and the proposed regulations submitted by Lord Pauncefote were one-sided and inadequate. They would permit the British vessels to kill seals within ten miles of the coast of the Pribilov Islands, whereas Lord Salisbury's proposals of 1888 provided that "no British vessel hunting seals should come nearer to the Pribilov Islands than the 47th parallel of north latitude, about 600 miles." Moreover, the open season proposed by the British draft convention would include the months of July, August, and September. But this open season was the very one "when the areas around the breeding islands are most crowded with seals, and especially crowded with female seals going forth to secure food for the hundreds of thousands of their young."

In conclusion, Blaine stated that he had been instructed by the President to say that while the British proposal of April 30 could not be accepted, the American Government would continue the negotiations in the "hope of reaching an agreement that may conduce to a good understanding and leave no cause for future dispute." [31]

After waiting a few days, Blaine wrote another note to Lord Pauncefote and inquired whether Lord Salisbury would make "for a single season the regulation which in 1888 he offered to make permanent?" [32] Pauncefote supposed that Blaine referred to the "proposal of the United States that British sealing vessels should be entirely excluded from Behring Sea during the seal fishery season." With regard to such a proposal, Pauncefote was certain that Lord Salisbury would now consider that "such an extreme measure as that proposed in 1888 goes far beyond the requirements of the case." [33]

Blaine came back with a note that again endeavored to show that Lord Salisbury had receded from the stand he had taken in 1888, and he expressed the disappointment of the President that Her Majesty's Government was "not willing to suspend, for a single season, the practice which Lord Salisbury described in 1888 as 'the wanton

31. Secretary Blaine to Pauncefote, May 29, 1890, *House Ex. Doc. 450,* 51 Cong., 1 sess., pp. 66-70.
32. Secretary Blaine to Pauncefote, June 2, 1890, *ibid.,* p. 70.
33. Pauncefote to Secretary Blaine, June 3, 1890, *ibid.,* p. 71.

destruction of a valuable industry.' " [34] When Pauncefote replied that it was "entirely beyond the power of Her Majesty's Government to exclude British or Canadian ships from any portion of the high seas, even for an hour, without legislative sanction," [35] Blaine stated that it would satisfy the American Government if "Lord Salisbury would by public proclamation simply request the vessels sailing under the British flag should abstain from entering the Behring Sea for the present season." [36]

The British Government was willing to accede to this request if it were made a part of a general scheme for the settlement of the Behring Sea controversy. The conditions that should serve as the basis for this settlement were then outlined by Pauncefote as follows: (1) The two Governments should agree forthwith to refer to arbitration the question of the legality of the action of the American Government in seizing or otherwise interfering with British vessels operating in Behring Sea, outside territorial waters, during the years 1886, 1887, and 1889. (2)

34. Secretary Blaine to Pauncefote, June 4, 1890, *House Ex. Doc. 450*, 51 Cong., 1 sess., pp. 71-73.

35. Pauncefote to Secretary Blaine, (Received, June 9, 1890), *ibid.*, p. 74. Sir Charles Tupper, in his *Recollections of Sixty Years* (N. Y. 1914), pp. 209-211, has the following comments upon the situation in 1890: "In 1890 the fishery question again caused some anxious hours in both countries. On June 28th of that year Lord Knutsford sent for me, and told me that Lord Salisbury had received a message from Sir Julian Pauncefote, Ambassador at Washington, saying that Mr. Blaine, Secretary of State, had informed him that the Government had sent their cruisers to Behring Sea with instructions to seize any vessels sealing there. The Americans had seized several Canadian vessels some years before, and when called to account by Great Britain, said they claimed Behring Sea as a *mare clausum,* that they were willing to leave that question to an international tribunal, and in the meantime would make no seizures until that question was decided, to which Great Britain agreed. Some delay occurred in arranging that Commission, and they then determined to seize. Lord Knutsford, who was Secretary of State for the Colonies, told me that he had in vain endeavoured to get Lord Salisbury to take prompt action, as the Premier said, the thing having been done, it would involve war with the United States, which was too terrible to contemplate, and that all that he, Knutsford, was to obtain was a promise that he would not answer Pauncefote's message until he had seen me. I went immediately to the Foreign Office, and saw the Under Secretary of State (Sanderson), as Lord Salisbury was not there, with whom I discussed the subject. I told him that I was satisfied the United States would not go to war on a question that every diplomat in the world would feel they were wrong upon, and concluded by saying, 'Tell Lord Salisbury from me that if, under existing circumstances, prompt action is not taken, Canada can only come to the conclusion that the British flag is not strong enough to protect her.'

"The result was that Sir Julian Pauncefote was instructed to say to Mr. Blaine that if the British flag was interfered with, the United States must be prepared for the consequences. The message was no sooner delivered to Mr. Blaine than the fastest ships on the Pacific Coast were directed by telegraph to overhaul the cruisers and withdraw the instructions."

36. Secretary Blaine to Pauncefote, June 11, 1890, *House Ex. Doc. 450*, 51 Cong., 1 sess., pp. 74-75.

Pending the arbitral award, all interference with British sealing vessels shall absolutely cease. (3) The United States Government, if the award should be adverse to them on the question of legal right, will compensate British subjects for the losses which they may sustain by reason of their compliance with the British proclamation.[37]

In the meantime, Pauncefote had turned over to Blaine a long note from Lord Salisbury dated May 22, 1890. With regard to Blaine's contention that the killing of fur-seals in the seas around the Behring Sea island was an offense *contra bonos mores,* Salisbury held that fur-seals "are indisputably animals *ferae naturae,* and these have universally been regarded by jurists as *res nullius* until they are caught." No person could have property in them "until he had actually reduced them into possession by capture." It would require more than a mere declaration "that the Government or citizens of the United States . . . are losers by a certain course of proceedings, to render that course an immoral one."

The action taken by the American Government in instructing revenue cutters to seize British vessels on the high seas, in time of peace, because they were engaged in pelagic sealing, was a violation of International Law, and Her Majesty's Government wished to go on record as strongly opposing all claims "to exclusive privileges in the non-territorial waters of Behring Sea." [38]

In his reply to this blast from Lord Salisbury, Blaine tried to show that the jurisdictional claim of Russia, as expressed in the ukase of 1821, had been acquiesced in by the United States and Great Britain north of the sixtieth parallel of north latitude. According to Blaine's contention, there had been no attempt, in the treaties concluded by the United States and Great Britain with Russia, to regulate or control any "interest in the Russian possessions and the Behring Sea, which lie far to the north and west of the territory which formed the basis of the contention." [39] The protests of John Quincy Adams (as Secretary of

37. Pauncefote to Secretary Blaine, June 27, 1890, *House Ex. Doc. 450.* 51 Cong., 1 sess., pp. 77-78.

38. Marquis of Salisbury to Pauncefote, May 22, 1890, *ibid.,* pp. 60-64.

39. This historical argument of Blaine was very weak. The Russian Government had been quite reluctant to support the sweeping terms of the ukase of 1821, which had probably been pushed through upon the suggestion of the Russian-American Company. There had been very little official consideration given to it, and the American Minister flatly charged that it had been "surreptitiously obtained." *Alaskan Boundary Tribunal Proceedings,* vol. 2, p. 42. The Czar showed no desire to enforce it, and as early as July, 1822, an order was issued to Russian vessels of war, directing them to restrict their activities to the coast, and to exercise surveillance only over the prohibited commerce with actual Russian

State) had been aimed at the extension of Russian jurisdiction in the *Pacific Ocean* and not in Behring Sea, which was regarded as a separate body of water. The terms "Great Ocean," "Pacific Ocean," and "South Sea," which occur in the treaties and diplomatic correspondence of the early decades of the nineteenth century, did not include Behring Sea. With regard to the waters of that sea, the ukase of 1821 stood unchanged, and both the United States and Great Britain had recognized and obeyed it. This same recognition was still due from Great Britain, and it had not been altered by the cession of Russia to the United States.[40]

---

settlements. According to the Russian Chancellor, the "true and only object" of the ukase of 1821, was "to put a stop to enterprises which the laws of all nations recognize as unjust, and to protect interests, whose legality no one can contest." Dexter Perkins, *The Monroe Doctrine, 1823–1826* (Cambridge, 1927), pp. 28-29.

40. Secretary Blaine to Pauncefote, June 30, 1890, *House Ex. Doc. 450, 51* Cong., 1 sess., pp. 78-89. It is more than likely that Blaine drew his inspiration for this argument from Henry W. Elliott, of the Smithsonian Institution. In a letter to Bayard, January 29, 1887, Elliott remarked: "I have been carefully reviewing the entire topic of Russian occupation and control of Behring Sea from the early time of Muscovitic discovery and possession in 1728, up to its transfer to us in 1867. I find it impossible to honestly construe the meaning of that phrase, 'waters commonly known as the North Western Pacific Ocean,' and again, 'the great ocean commonly called the Pacific Ocean or South Sea,' which appear in the protests and treaty stipulations of 1824–1825, to strain these phrases so as to include the Sea of Kamchatka (Behring Sea), since it is beyond cavil or doubt that these 'waters' then 'commonly known as the North Western Pacific Ocean,' are precisely the same waters which we today commonly know as such: the charts, the records of hydrographic survey from 1799 up to date, prove the truth of my statement, beyond all question.

"Therefore, I venture to express the hope that while you carry out the determination which you promptly manifested, of protecting the interests of the Government now in danger on the Seal Islands of Alaska, that no release on our part will be made of our right and title to the full ownership of Behring Sea, east of the pelagic boundary laid down in it by Russia." Bayard MS.

Bayard turned this letter over to John Bassett Moore, who gave it a searching analysis and criticism in a note to Bayard, January 29, 1887. According to Moore, he had "yet to find a single geography, encyclopedia, chart, state paper, or writing of any kind, save the letter of Mr. Elliott . . . that treats the Pacific Ocean or South Seas as not including all the waters on the coasts of Russia (Siberia) and America, clear up to Behring's Straits. The geographies so give it and the *Encyclopedia Britannica* so states it. In the same line are the protests to which Mr. Elliott refers. Mr. Poletica, in his note to Mr. Adams of the 28th of February, 1822, said: 'ought, in the last place, to request you to consider, Sir, that the Russian possessions in the *Pacific Ocean* extend, on the *northwest coast* of America, from *Behring's Strait* to the 51st degree of North Lat., etc.' He says further that 'the extent of sea *of which these possessions form the limits,' might be* treated as shut seas, but that Russia preferred to assert her *'essential rights, without taking advantage of localities.'* Consequently, Russia inhibited approach within *100 Italian miles of those coasts.* . . .

"Nothing could be more conclusive as against Mr. Elliott than the famous ukase of 1821, to which the above correspondence was due. It read as follows: 'Section 1. The transaction of *commerce*, and the pursuit of *whaling* and *fishing*, or any other industry on the *islands*, in the *harbors* and *inlets*, and in general all along the *northwestern coast* of America from *Behring Strait* to the 51st parallel of northern latitude, and likewise on

Blaine followed this dubious note with another of July 19, in which he made an indirect attack upon Lord Salisbury's veracity. In discussing Salisbury's change of heart with reference to the Behring Sea negotiations, Blaine had charged (in his note of May 29, 1890) that the British Government had been on the point of arriving at a settlement of this dispute when the Canadian Government interposed certain objections, and the whole matter was postponed. The basis for Blaine's attack had been a despatch from Phelps to Bayard, February 25, 1888.

Lord Salisbury had replied on June 20 that Blaine was "under a misconception in imagining that I ever gave any verbal assurance, or any promise of any kind, with respect to the terms of the projected convention." [41] Blaine returned to the attack by once more referring to the text of Phelps's despatch of February 25, 1888. The issue lay between the veracity of Phelps and that of Lord Salisbury, and Blaine acridly announced that Phelps had long been known in the United States "as an able lawyer, accurate in the use of words and discriminating in the statement of facts." The Government of the United States reposed "implicit confidence in the literal correctness of the despatch above quoted." [42]

Blaine was pleased with the way that he was able to call Lord Salisbury a liar by means of diplomatic circumlocution, and he wrote to President Harrison that he thought the British Foreign Secretary would be loath "to make a direct issue between Mr. Phelps & himself. . . . We bring him now direct to the explicit agreement of Feby 25—which is clean-cut, sharp-edged, & gives us even more than we need for

the *Aleutian Islands,* and along the *eastern coast* of Siberia, and on the Kurile Islands, . . . are exclusively reserved to the subjects of the Russian Empire.

"Section 2. Accordingly, no foreign vessel shall be allowed either to put to shore 'at any of the *coasts and islands under Russian dominion as specified* in the *preceding section,* or even to approach the *same to within* a distance of less than 100 Italian miles. . . .'

"It appears, therefore, by the only papers upon which Mr. Elliott could rely for his doctrine of shut seas, that the Russian Government not only included in the terms Pacific Ocean and northwestern coast of America, all waters and coasts up to Behring's Strait, but also expressly disclaimed an intention to enforce as to those waters the doctrine that they were *meres fermées.* This is so clear and explicit that argument is unnecessary." *Bayard MS.*

On January 29, 1887, Francis Wharton wrote a short note to Bayard in which he remarked: "I concur with Mr. Moore in the annexed memorandum which I think very valuable." *Bayard MS.*

41. Marquis of Salisbury to Pauncefote, June 20, 1890, *House Ex. Doc. 450,* 51 Cong., 1 sess., pp. 90-92.

42. Secretary Blaine to Pauncefote, July 19, 1890, *ibid.,* pp. 94-96.

the protection of Seals." [43] The President thought that the case had ended "very well for the public, and we can properly wait a response to your last despatch before opening any suggestion of our basis of an arbitration. . . . I am sure the publication of the correspondence will make a favorable impression and will do you great credit. The continued advantage is altogether with you." [44]

This Presidential praise for the way he had handled the Behring Sea dispute was very stimulating to Blaine, who thought that the case for the United States had been strengthened by the "coolness & lack of eagerness" he had displayed in handling the situation. Pauncefote was now "doing the walking," not only "metaphorically but actually." [45]

If Pauncefote was perturbed over Blaine's diplomatic finesse, such was not the case with Lord Salisbury, who carried on the argument with the Secretary of State in another long note of August 2. He sharply challenged Blaine's contention that Behring Sea had not been regarded as an integral part of the Pacific Ocean, and he quoted extracts from the instructions of George Canning (Secretary of Foreign Affairs) to Stratford Canning (British Minister at Washington) to show that England had refused to admit any part of the claim asserted in the ukase of 1821 to an exclusive jurisdiction over a belt of water one hundred miles from the coast, extending from Behring Straits to the fifty-first parallel of north latitude. He also contended that the treaty of 1825 had been regarded by both Russia and Great Britain as a renunciation of the claim advanced in the ukase of 1821. If the American Government continued to adhere to its viewpoint in this question of jurisdiction in Behring Sea, the whole matter could be referred to impartial arbitration.[46]

Blaine waited many months before answering this note from Lord Salisbury, and when he finally wrote his reply it was a weak affair.[47]

43. Secretary Blaine to President Harrison, July 19, 1890, A. T. Volwiler, *Correspondence Between Benjamin Harrison and James G. Blaine, 1882–1893*, pp. 109-110.

44. President Harrison to Secretary Blaine, July 23, 1890, A. T. Volwiler, *op. cit.*, pp. 111-112.

45. Secretary Blaine to President Harrison, July 25, 1890, *ibid.*, pp. 113-114.

46. Marquis of Salisbury to Pauncefote, August 2, 1890, *House Ex. Doc. 144*, 51 Cong., 2 sess., pp. 2-22.

47. Blaine had been worried about the possibility that Joseph Chamberlain might call upon President Harrison in an effort to settle the Behring Sea dispute, and he requested the President to refrain from seeing Chamberlain except when introduced by the Department of State. The President assured Blaine that he would not "be entrapped into any reference to foreign affairs except as they proceed through your department." Blaine to President Harrison, August 19, 1890; President Harrison to Blaine, August 29, 1890, A. T. Volwiler, *op. cit.*, pp. 117-120.

He emphasized the fact that the American Government had never claimed that Behring Sea was a *mare clausum*. Indeed, it had expressly disavowed such a contention. The main question at issue was whether Behring Sea was included in the phrase "Pacific Ocean." The American Government had denied such inclusion, while the British Government had taken an affirmative stand in this regard. If the weight of authority should lean towards the British side, the American Government would have no "well-grounded complaint" against such a decision. But if the United States could prove that the negotiators of the treaties of 1824–1825 had regarded Behring Sea as a separate body of water that was not included in the phrase "Pacific Ocean," then the American case was "complete and undeniable." [48]

48. Secretary Blaine to Pauncefote, December 17, 1890, *House Ex. Doc. 144*, pp. 23-54. In commenting upon Blaine's diplomatic exchanges with Lord Salisbury, John W. Foster, remarks: "In no part of that statesman's career did his devotion to his country more conspicuously rise above partisanship than in that correspondence. It is doubtful if any other living American could have made a more brilliant or effective defense of the action of his government." "Results of the Bering Sea Arbitration," *North American Review*, December, 1895, p. 696.

It cannot be doubted that Blaine was a brilliant and effective orator, but mere oratory was out of place in diplomatic correspondence. While Blaine openly disclaimed any thought that he was contending that Behring Sea was a closed sea (*mare clausum*), yet his argument inevitably led to that very point. He claimed that the United States and Great Britain had recognized the exclusive jurisdiction of Russia over Behring Sea, and that all these Russian rights had passed to the United States as a result of the cession of Alaska in 1867. It was only because of the right of exclusive jurisdiction that the United States could seize British ships on the high seas, and this was equivalent to holding that Behring Sea was a *mare clausum*. Although this right had been exercised only for the protection of fur-seals, it could be extended to cover other important items.

In presenting the claim of the United States before the Paris Tribunal, James C. Carter, one of the counsel for the United States, remarked as follows: "All the doubt and all the controversy which have arisen in reference to this question of the exercise by a nation of the right of self-defense upon the high seas turns upon the validity of regulations of that sort, regulations which go beyond the mere shaping of the right of self-defense and prescribing how it shall be exercised. . . . Let me say that the United States . . . avoids all controversy of that sort. We do not ask for the application of any doctrine . . . to the effect that we can establish any prohibited area on the high seas and exclude the vessels of other nations from it. We do not ask to have it determined that the United States has the right to say that the offense of pelagic sealing when committed by vessels of another nation is a crime for which we can *punish* the officers and crew of such vessel. That would be legislating for the high seas. We do not ask for a decision that the United States can make a law and enforce it, by which she could condemn a vessel that *had been engaged at some past time* in pelagic sealing, if the vessel was not so engaged at the time of seizure. The doctrine maintained by us simply amounts to this, that whenever a vessel is caught red-handed, *flagrante delicto*, in pelagic sealing, the Government of the United States has the right to seize her and capture her; that is to say, it has the right to employ necessary force for the purpose of protecting . . . its property interest in the industry which it maintains upon the islands." John B. Moore, *History and Digest of International Arbitrations*, vol. 1, pp. 869-870.

It is difficult to see how such a right could be maintained except upon the basis of exclusive jurisdiction beyond the three-mile limit in Behring Sea.

Blaine also proposed five questions on which an arbitration might be had. The first four related to the jurisdictional rights of Russia and their transfer to the United States. The fifth had to do with the rights of the United States in the fur-seal fisheries in Behring Sea outside of the ordinary territorial limits.

After waiting some two months, Lord Salisbury delivered a sharp attack upon the Blaine contention that the negotiators of the treaties of 1824–1825 had considered Behring Sea as a separate body of water that was not included in the phrase "Pacific Ocean." He also indicated certain important modifications of the questions that Blaine had drawn up for submission to arbitration.[49]

The stage was now being set for the final act of arbitration of the Behring Sea dispute. On March 15, 1891, Pauncefote urged Blaine to agree to a *modus vivendi* for the approaching sealing-season in Behring Sea, under the terms of which there should be no slaughter of seals on the islands under American jurisdiction, and British subjects should be forbidden to indulge in pelagic sealing. Blaine replied by suggesting the establishment of a twenty-five mile zone around the seal islands in which pelagic sealing would be prohibited, but Pauncefote believed that such a zone would be impracticable, and on April 7 he once more urged Blaine to accept a plan whereby, for the season of 1891, there would be a suspension of all killing of seals upon the islands in Behring Sea or in the waters of the sea. Blaine accepted this suggestion, and Pauncefote immediately advised Lord Salisbury of this agreement.[50] It

49. Marquis of Salisbury to Pauncefote, February 21, 1891, *Foreign Relations, 1891*, p. 542.

50. On November 19, 1890, Elliott, accompanied by Secretary Windom, had called upon Blaine with reference to the seal fisheries. Elliott had just returned from an investigation of these fisheries in Behring Sea, and he pointed out to Blaine that a very serious destruction of the herds of seal would take place unless the American Government soon "came to an agreement with Great Britain. I showed him how absolutely necessary it was to close all of Behring Sea to the pelagic hunter: and, too, how absolutely necessary it was that we reform the work of excessive driving and killing as done on the islands by the lessees." Henry W. Elliott to Senator John C. Spooner, February 4, 1905, *John C. Spooner Papers*, Library of Congress.

In an earlier letter to Secretary Gresham, April 2, 1893, Elliott had given a similar account of his relations with Secretary Blaine in 1890–1891: "In April, 1890, Congress passed after full debate in both Houses, a Special Act for the sole purpose of enabling me to go up to the Seal Islands and make another careful investigation of the condition of the fur-seal herds, just as I had done under authority of a similar Act passed in April, 1874. . . . I finished my work on the islands and returned and had my report with maps and illustrations ready for the printer, November 19, 1890, gave it to Mr. Windom, who at once sent me over to Mr. Blaine with it.

"I found that the seal herds had been as badly injured by abuses on the islands since 1882 as they had been by the shameful waste of killing in the water to which they had

would then appear that Blaine violated this agreement of April 7 by secretly arranging with Charles Foster, Secretary of the Treasury, to issue a permit to the lessees of the seal islands, authorizing them to kill 60,000 seals on the islands "if they can be found." When news of this permit leaked out, Henry W. Elliott and William McKinley, then a member of the House of Representatives, called upon Secretary Foster, who explained that he had issued this order "because Blaine authorizes it, and has told me that Salisbury is ugly and will not stop his people from killing." Elliott then called upon Pauncefote who denied that the

been subjected since 1886, that the killing on land must stop for at least seven years, and the killing in the waters of Behring Sea and portions of the North Pacific Ocean must be forever prohibited, if we ever expected to restore the Pribylov herds to the fine form and number which I recorded of them in 1872–74.

"I stopped the killing on the islands, July 20, 1890, in co-operation with Charles J. Goff, an honest Treasury Agent. . . . At once Mr. Steve Elkins took up his residence in Mr. Blaine's house, bitterly denounced me behind my back, and drew from Mr. Blaine a promise that my order saving the remnant on the Pribylov Islands in 1890, should be repealed in 1891. He actually got the permit before I knew it, on April 14, 1891. I learned of it on the 20th of that month in spite of Charlie Foster's secrecy and trickery, published the shameful truth, and Harrison finding that the job could not be covered, vetoed the license on the 3d of May. . . .

"In short, I may truly say, the whole business, since that day, November 19, 1890, when Mr. Blaine tried to make me suppress the truth as to the abuse on the islands and lay all the blame on the poachers, the whole business has been one of systematic duplicity, pettifogging, and secrecy in the State and Treasury Depts., under Blaine and C. Foster, dominated by Steve Elkins, a silent partner in this present Seal Company." *Gresham MS.*

On May 4, 1891, the Cleveland *Leader and Morning Herald* published a copy of the letter of Henry W. Elliott to the Secretary of the Treasury which transmitted his report on the fur-seal fisheries. On February 10, 1893, the British agent called upon the agent of the United States for a full copy of this report. Both Phelps and Carter opposed the granting of this request, but after some discussion finally stated that they were ready to produce Elliott's report. Their opposition was based on the fact that this report clearly indicated the destructive effect of the seal killings on the islands as well as in the waters of Behring Sea. See John B. Moore, *History and Digest of International Arbitrations*, vol. 1, pp. 904–907.

In a letter to Secretary Gresham, April 13, 1893, Elliott makes the following pertinent comments: "On the 3d inst. I mailed to your address a letter which I deemed my duty to write touching the Behring Sea Commission. Since then the Paris Court has ordered out my report of 1890 touching upon the status of the fur-seal herds of the Government on the Pribylov Islands: No living man possesses the knowledge or the ability to set aside the findings of my investigation, and before the Court adjourns, I shall be honored for doing my duty and telling the truth. I have one request to make of you in order that the business at Paris shall be the more certainly expedited—I respectfully ask that I may be permitted to read the proof of this copy of my report, and be free in my mind as to mutilation or garbling of it. If it is done, I can and will detect it, but that only creates delay and fresh scandal if it should so turn out. I have abundant reason to suspect the present conduct of affairs. . . . The story of my meeting Sir Julian is . . . one that . . . reflects the highest credit on the British Minister and covers Mr. Blaine with disgrace." *Gresham MS.* See also letter from Elliott to Secretary Gresham, May 29, 1893, *ibid.*, and the "Report of Henry W. Elliott on the Condition of the Fur-Seal Fisheries of Alaska," *House Doc. 175*, 54 Cong., 1 sess.

British Government was "ugly" about the matter of prohibiting, for a season, all pelagic sealing. Enraged at what he called Blaine's "venality and duplicity," Elliott published the whole story in the New York *Evening Post* of April 24, 1891, and Blaine was placed upon the defensive.[51]

On this same day (April 24), President Harrison telegraphed to Blaine that the lessees of the islands were bound to feed and care for the natives, and therefore "some seals must be killed for food." He thought it might be practicable for the Secretary of the Treasury to "fix a moderate number under the lease as an independent act of our Government." He also expressed the opinion that "the value of the fisheries would be enhanced by taking none for one season, but as our right to take on the Islands is not in dispute, would prefer to make the prohibition our own act and let E[nglish] action follow on notice of our wishes."[52]

Blaine replied on April 28, that if sealing was "prohibited for season, many obstacles are thrown in the way,"[53] and on the following day he sent a second telegram with these pertinent sentences:

The Secretary of the Treasury has fixed maximum number [of seals] for season at sixty thousand. Revenue Cutter *Rush* is to leave on fourteenth with seal agents for Islands. You do not return here until 15th. Meanwhile British Minister presses agreement to your suggestion that both sides abstain from taking seals this year. British Minister declines to consider the necessity of some seals being taken to support natives and repay company for trouble and expense. They wish entire business to be suspended. . . . It is

51. See sworn statement of Henry W. Elliott, May 2, 1912, in the *W. Q. Gresham Papers,* in the Library of Congress. In a letter from Elliott to Senator John C. Spooner, December 7, 1905, the following statement is made: "Inasmuch as I am the author of that *modus vivendi* of 1891–1893, which caused the clearing of Behring Sea from all pelagic fur-seal hunting by American and British subjects, I know of every detail connected with this joint action by the British Government and my own. . . . I urged the adoption of the *modus vivendi* published as early as March 1, 1891, so as to give due and timely warning to our own people, who as pelagic hunters would be out on the high seas, fully equipped and bound for Behring Sea, by the middle or end of that month. Unless we gave our people such due and timely warning, they would have a just claim for damages, when ordered out of Behring Sea—this rule applied also to the British subjects. For reasons now of official record . . . this *modus vivendi* of 1891 was not published until June 15, 1891, and up to the hour of its publication not a hint ever was given of its adoption. . . . Suddenly, when in the full swing of their season's work, they were warned and ordered out of Behring Sea by U. S. Revenue Marine Cutters, early in July. . . . In this light of the above statements of fact, I believe our pelagic fur-seal hunters of 1891 are entitled to damages only to this extent: They were clearly put out of time and opportunity by the unexpected order of our Government." *John C. Spooner MS.*

52. President Harrison to Secretary Blaine, April 24, 1891, A. T. Volwiler, *Correspondence Between Benjamin Harrison and James G. Blaine, 1882–1893,* pp. 144-145.

53. Secretary Blaine to President Harrison, April 28, 1891, *ibid.,* p. 145.

embarrassing to resist British Minister's position in view of the fact that abstaining from sealing this year was first suggested by yourself.[54]

It is apparent that Blaine was in full retreat from the position he had taken on April 11, when he urged Secretary Foster to issue a permit to the lessees of the seal islands to kill 60,000 seals during the season of 1891.

President Harrison was alive to the situation, and on April 30 he sent a telegram to Blaine in which he expressed the view that, on the whole, it was best to stop the killing of seals "for this season, on proper guarantees."[55] Three days later (May 3), he ordered the cancellation of the permit which would allow the lessees of the islands to kill 60,000 seals for the season of 1891.[56] By these steps he was preparing the way for eventual settlement of the dispute by arbitration. Both President Harrison and Blaine were in favor of permitting the lessees of the seal islands to kill 7,500 seals for the season of 1891. This would mean a cessation of "commercial killings," and would merely provide food for the natives.[57]

Pauncefote was impressed with the generous stand taken by the President, and he sent a telegram to the Colonial Office, in London, expressing the hope that the Canadian Government would accept the American proposal. The rejection of these overtures would give Blaine "a signal triumph and alienate our supporters, who are already irritated by the knowledge that the sealing fleet is mainly equipped by American crews and capital. The Canadian government were prepared for legislation at this season last year. We cannot consistently reply that it is too late now."[58]

President Harrison thought that the Canadian Government was "interposing objections and delays," and that was the reason why Lord Pauncefote would give no definite answer as to the response that might

54. Secretary Blaine to President Harrison, April 29, 1891, *ibid.*, pp. 146-147. This last statement of Blaine's is not correct. Pauncefote had made the suggestion on April 7 that both British and American subjects be prohibited from killing seals, and Blaine had agreed with this suggestion.

55. President Harrison to Secretary Blaine, April 30, 1891, *ibid.*, p. 147.

56. See the sworn statement of Henry W. Elliot, May 2, 1912, *Gresham Papers*. See also the letters from Charles Foster to Elliott, January 11, 23, 1895, *ibid.* It should be said, however, that there is nothing in the tone of President Harrison's communications to Blaine that would indicate any strong disapproval of any action taken by the Department of State with reference to the fur-seal fisheries.

57. President Harrison to Secretary Blaine, April 30, 1891, A. T. Volwiler, *op. cit.*, p. 147; Secretary Blaine to Pauncefote, May 4, 1891, *Foreign Relations, 1891*, p. 552.

58. Lord Pauncefote to Lord Stanley, May 16, 1891, *Sir John Macdonald Papers, Behring Sea*, vol. 3, MS Canadian Archives.

be expected from London in regard to the American proposal.[59] But these delays could not continue indefinitely, and finally, on June 4, the British Minister informed Blaine that Lord Salisbury accepted the proposal of the American Government with the suggestions that British consuls be sent to the islands to study the situation, and that Russian adherence be secured to any agreement that might be reached.[60] These suggestions were not regarded with favor by the Department of State, and conversations continued until the signing of a *modus vivendi* on June 15, 1891.

Under the terms of this arrangement, the British Government undertook to prohibit, until the following May, the killing of seals by British subjects in that part of Behring Sea that lay eastward of the line of demarcation as described in the treaty of 1867 between the United States and Russia. On its part, the American Government was pledged to prohibit the killing of seals in that designated area of Behring Sea, and on the islands this slaughter was limited to 7,500 seals.[61]

The remainder of the year of 1891 was consumed in a discussion of the terms of an arbitration convention. An agreement was reached on February 29, 1892, and the first article of the treaty provided that the questions that had arisen between the two governments "concerning the jurisdictional rights of the United States in the waters of Behring's Sea, and concerning also the preservation of the fur-seal in, or habitually resorting to, the said sea, and the rights of the citizens and subjects of either country as regards the taking of fur-seal in, or habitually resorting to, the said waters," should be submitted to a tribunal of seven arbitrators, two to be named by the President of the United States, two by Her Britannic Majesty, and one each by the President of France, the King of Italy, and the King of Sweden and Norway.[62]

59. President Harrison to Secretary Blaine, May 25, 27, 1891, A. T. Volwiler, *op. cit.*, pp. 152-155.

60. Pauncefote to Secretary Blaine, June 4, 1891, *Foreign Relations, 1891*, p. 358.

61. *Foreign Relations, 1891*, p. 573.

62. For the text of the treaty, see *Foreign Relations, 1891*, pp. 615-619. The questions to be submitted to arbitration were included in Articles VI and VII of the treaty. Article VI reads as follows: "In deciding the matter submitted to the Arbitrators, it is agreed that the following five points shall be submitted to them, in order that their award shall embrace a distinct decision upon each of said five points, to wit: (1) What exclusive jurisdiction in the sea now known as the Behring's Sea, and what exclusive rights in the seal fisheries therein, did Russia assert and exercise prior and up to the time of the cession of Alaska to the United States? (2) How far were these claims of jurisdiction as to the seal fisheries recognized and conceded by Great Britain? (3) Was the body of water now known as the Behring's Sea included in the phrase 'Pacific Ocean,' as used in the Treaty of 1825 between Great Britain and Russia; and what rights, if any, in the Behring's Sea were held

The arbitration treaty was approved by the Senate of the United
States on March 29, 1892, and President Harrison named John M.
Harlan, a justice of the Supreme Court of the United States, and Sena-
tor John T. Morgan, of Alabama, as the American arbitrators. John W.
Foster was appointed as agent for the United States, and Edward J.
Phelps, James C. Carter, Henry W. Blodgett, and F. R. Coudert were
retained as counsel. In the first week of September, 1892,[63] the Case of
the United States was turned over to the arbitrators. On February 3,
1893, the Counter Case of the United States was submitted, and on
February 23 the first session of the tribunal was held in Paris.

The appointment of Phelps as one of the counsel for the United
States in this Behring Sea arbitration, caused little surprise in Democratic circles. In his correspondence with the British Government,
Blaine had repeatedly quoted excerpts from the despatches of Phelps
with reference to the seal fisheries, and it is apparent that both Blaine

---

and exclusively exercised by Russia after said Treaty? (4) Did not all the rights of Russia
as to jurisdiction, and as to the seal fisheries in Behring's Sea east of the water boundary,
in the Treaty between the United States and Russia of the 30th March, 1867, pass unimpaired to the United States under that treaty? (5) Has the United States any right, and if
so, what right of protection or property in the fur-seals frequenting the islands of the
United States in Behring Sea when such seals are found outside the ordinary three-mile
limit?"

63. When the printed *Case of Great Britain* was delivered by the agent of that government, it was discovered that it contained no evidence concerning the nature and habits
of seals, the consideration of which was regarded by the United States as necessary to the
settlement by the tribunal of questions of right as well as of regulations. On September
27 Foster wrote to Michael H. Herbert, the chargé d'affaires of the British Legation, to
complain of this omission of everything pertaining to the American contention of property interest in seals. The President had observed "with surprise and extreme regret" this
dubious action by the British agent. The American Government had furnished in its
printed case all the evidence it planned to offer in defense of its contention, in this way
giving the British Government ample time to prepare its rebuttal. It expected the British
Government to do the same, and was surprised that it had not done so. *Great Britain,
Notes to,* vol. 22, MS Dept. of State. See also, Foster to Robert T. Lincoln, September 29,
1892, *Great Britain, Instructions,* vol. 30, MS Dept. of State; and Foster to Secretary
Gresham, April 17, 1893, *Gresham MS.*

In a personal letter to Henry White, September 29, 1892, J. W. Foster remarked: "I
infer from what you said to me and from what I see in the papers, that Mr. Lincoln will
have left London before this letter and the instruction and letter to Mr. Lincoln about
the Seal Arbitration reaches the Legation. That being the case, you will of course, open
and act upon the letter to him. It affords you a capital opportunity to do a good piece
of work for the Government as well as yourself credit, and I have no doubt you will be
fully alive to the importance of the question. Mr. Phelps is if anything, more positive
than any of us . . . that we should give notice to Great Britain that the Arbitration will
not go forward till this wrong is righted, but we have thought best to give Great Britain
the opportunity . . . to do right. The function of diplomacy is to promote peace and
good understanding, and I hope you can help me to bring about a satisfactory settlement
of this question." *Henry White MS.*

and President Harrison had a high opinion of his abilities. In some of his despatches, Phelps had sharply criticized the policies of the British Government, and this acrid tone had greatly pleased Blaine, who, upon occasion, was not averse to twisting the British lion's tail.

In April, 1891, Phelps published an article in *Harper's Magazine,* in which he dealt with the problem of the seal fisheries. His idea that the American Government had a property right in the seals around the islands in Behring Sea,[64] was one that appealed to Blaine, but it disgusted Bayard who expressed his displeasure in a letter to ex-President Cleveland:

. . . I have yours of the 25th, repeating the current remark: "What is the matter with Phelps?". . . Since Blaine began his maladroit treatment of the Behring Sea matter, I have been importuned to contribute papers on the subject, and have steadily declined. . . . When Mr. Phelps and I met lately in New York, we seemed to be in general accord on the subject, and especially in relation to *not* writing for publication when the question was pending. . . .

In February I was in New Haven at Mr. Phelps's house, and he told me to my surprise that he had sent them [*Harper's Magazine*] an article for their April number, but gave no intimation of his mode of treatment. I remember that I laughed at the idea of controlling the Seals outside our own territory, and likened the case to that of the canvass-back ducks which breed in British America and come down to be shot in Chesapeake Bay!

When his article appeared I knew not what to say, but I began to recall

64. E. J. Phelps, "The Behring Sea Controversy," *Harper's Magazine,* pp. 766-774. The following comment by Phelps is illustrative of his viewpoint: "The freedom of the sea . . . never authorizes injury to the property or just rights of others, which are as sacred at sea as on shore. This colony of seals, making their home on American soil, . . . belong to the proprietors of the soil, and are a part of their property; and do not lose this quality by passing from one part of the territory to another, in a regular and periodic emigration necessary to their life, even though . . . they pass temporarily through water that is more than three miles from shore." *Ibid.,* pp. 768-769.

In a letter to Howard Pyle, January 24, 1891, Bayard refused to write an article for *Harper's Magazine* on the Behring Sea dispute. He also advanced the opinion that Phelps would take a similar stand. The main facts in the dispute had been clearly disclosed in the instruction he had sent to Phelps on February 7, 1888, and nothing had occurred since that date to cause him to alter his judgment "of what ought to be done and the manner of doing it, nor am I aware that the British Government will not proceed to conclude substantially what it then expressed its readiness to do. . . . The issue is not *now* obscure, and partisan prejudice or partisan objects can alone obscure it. . . . If Mr. Phelps *would* write a paper on the subject, no one assuredly could do it better, but I ought to say to you that a short time since I found in conversation with him that (like myself) he had declined to write for publication upon the subject. I hope the Supreme Court may grant the writ and decide the case, and not allow the passions of British politics in connection with the *present burning question of that Kingdom,* to induce the United States to disregard the principles of International Law, and their duty thereunder, in order to curry favor with any class of voters." *Bayard Press Copy Book,* November 11, 1890 to April 15, 1891, *Bayard MS.*

that in his correspondence from London, Mr. Phelps had intimated that the case should be considered and settled on *other grounds* than that of maritime jurisdiction, although he did not define his theory. I was surprised and not satisfied, but nevertheless took my own plan of a conventional arrangement, in which each nation should protect the seal against depredation in water by its own citizens, during the breeding and nursing season. . . .

I remember too, Mr. Phelps explained in private letters his regret at the discharge of the Sealing Vessels in 1887, and I did not find him *heartily* in accord with my methods . . . in settling British matters, and largely with this impression I brought the Fisheries Controversy to Washington for settlement. I did not like the influence which Mr. Smalley, the *Tribune* correspondent in London, seems to have had, and I think he increased Mr. Phelps's irritability towards the British Minister, until he asked urgently to be recalled, and was prepared to come home with or without leave. He always exhibited a disposition for *small* aggressiveness against Great Britain, which I did not consider politic, . . . and now he has exploded most regrettably. . . . The "patent" of the idea of property in the birds of the air and the fish of the sea will not yield much revenue in the way of reputation or contentment.[65]

After learning of his appointment as one of the counsel for the United States in the Behring Sea arbitration, Phelps began to worry about the strength of the American Case. On May 9, 1892, he wrote to Blaine to suggest that "some judicious measures" be taken to counteract the impression in Europe that the American Case would not have much success before the arbitral tribunal. He had learned from Mr. Reid, the late American Minister at Paris, that the

. . . Paris edition of the New York *Herald* has labored persistently against us, as has the *Evening Post* and other newspapers, and they have succeeded in inducing a universal belief that our claim is not regarded in America, nor by American lawyers, as having any foundation, and is only an effort, on the part of President Harrison and yourself, to create some political capital to affect the presidential election, and that we do not expect a decision in our favor. This ought to be met.[66]

Phelps was always complaining about something, and when the sessions of the arbitral commission had finally started, he wrote to Bayard in his usual critical vein:

The arbitration begins its hearing on the 4th, under many embarrassments growing out of the crudeness and imperfections of the treaty, and the previous mistakes in the conduct of the proceedings under it, against which I have remonstrated in vain. I fear the case will be much protracted and

---

65. Bayard to Cleveland, March 27, 1891, *Cleveland MS.*
66. E. J. Phelps to Secretary Blaine, May 9, 1892, *John W. Foster Papers*, Library of Congress.

with arbitrators holding the balance who understand neither the English language nor English law, the result cannot be predicted. We have a powerful case, which may or may not have anything to do with the decision. Of course we have the American press against us, as we should equally have if we were contending for precisely the opposite of what we now claim. If there is anything meaner than the average American newspaper, I hope I shall never find it.[67]

Many American lawyers disagreed with the view of Phelps that the United States had a "powerful case," and this was particularly true with reference to his contention that this country had a distinct right of property in the seals in Behring Sea. In a letter to Secretary Gresham, B. H. Bristow expressed his interest in the American arguments that were being presented before the tribunal in Paris. He was not convinced, however, that the United States had "a property right to unidentified seals in the Pacific Ocean as entitles us to damages for their destruction." [68]

67. Phelps to Ambassador Bayard, April 2, 1893, *Bayard MS.* It is rather a pity that the American press did not get hold of some of the facts with regard to the so-called "experts" who aided the American counsel with their advice. With regard to Mr. J. S. Brown, who served as a seal expert, we have the following description from the unfriendly pen of Henry W. Elliott: "Now comes in Brown, who never has had the faintest natural history training in his life, was and is today a mere type-writer and stenographer. This man is sworn in to carry out the provisions of an Act which he was and is utterly incapable of doing except as he plagiarizes the work of other men. Brown never saw a seal or knew what one looked like until he was sent up there in 1891—sent in shameful violation of the provisions of the Act. He was there only a few weeks in 1891, June 27th to August 18th inclusive. He went up again in 1892 (June and returned in Sept.). He has never passed a consecutive twelve months on the Seal Islands, and thus has never been able to fully observe the landing and departure of the fur-seal herd, yet this man goes to Paris as an 'expert' when there are at least a dozen men who are fitter than he by extended residence among the seals on the islands, all, or any of them, easily obtainable. "Such work as this only makes our case weak and ridiculous when we meet the experts on the other side, in spite of the fact that we have every natural advantage in the controversy." Henry W. Elliott to Secretary Gresham, April 2, 1893, *Gresham MS.*
There were many sharp criticisms in the press in the spring of 1893 concerning the extravagant way that the American Agent in the Behring Sea arbitration, John W. Foster, was spending public funds. In this regard, see Blanton Duncan to Secretary Gresham, March 31, 1893, *Gresham MS.* Mr. Foster bitterly resented these charges of extravagance, and he defended his course in a letter to Secretary Gresham, April 4, 1893. He was certain that "the facts and charges which have been published show that certain information was given out by officials of the State Department. I am quite sure of their origin. Mr. Bryan, whom I notice you have designated (temporarily it is said) as your Private Secretary, has from the days of Secretary Bayard, manifested towards me an unaccountable malignity. I knew when he was called by you to that position he would do me all the damage in his power. Although I knew him to be a 'sneak,' I allowed him to remain in the employ of the Department, because I did not choose to take advantage of my position to resent personal grievances. He doubtless feels that now is his opportunity." *Gresham MS.*
In a second letter to Secretary Gresham, April 17, 1893, Foster recalls these accusations against Mr. Bryan. *Gresham MS.*
68. B. H. Bristow to Secretary Gresham, April 8, 1893, *Gresham MS.*

But John W. Foster (the American agent) was pleased with the way the fur-seal arbitration was progressing. The American counsel had shown themselves "quite able to cope with their adversaries. It is too early to make any prediction as to the result, but nothing has yet occurred to shake our confidence in securing a decision which will give substantial protection to the seals." [69]

On May 1, 1893, ex-President Harrison expressed his pleasure in learning from Foster that the Behring Sea arbitration was "progressing satisfactorily," [70] but John Bassett Moore, after reading of the way that Phelps was conducting himself before the tribunal, voiced his apprehensions that things were not going any too happily:

> If Mr. Phelps has his way, you [Bayard] may be called on to take up the Behring Sea question. He seems to be trying to break up the arbitration. His contradiction of Sir Charles Russell yesterday, when the latter said you had never justified the seizure of British sealers in 1886 on the grounds now alleged by counsel for the United States as justifying those seizures, was extraordinary, and it is not strange that Sir Charles pronounced the interruption of his argument to be unwarranted. This declaration by Messrs. Phelps & Morgan that the United States may refuse to pay damages if the decision of the arbitrators on the question of exclusive right is against us, was not in good taste and was scarcely defensible. It was equivalent to saying to the commission that we will refuse to abide by its decision, if it is against us. While I have felt it to be proper, after the United States have secured an arbitration, to make out the best possible case in support of our pretensions, I have always felt that it was most unfortunate that our Government should have assumed positions against which some of the most glorious parts of our history have been a direct protest.
>
> We have stood as the special champion before the world of the freedom of the seas. And shall it be said for the sake of a few sealskins the United States at the close of the nineteenth century was willing to dishonor its own history and enforce the barbarous doctrine that Great Britain was compelled by us to abandon at the beginning of the century? What would have been our answer if Great Britain in 1871 had said—"We will arbitrate the question of neutral duty in respect to the Alabama Claims, but we will not undertake to pay you damages if the decision is against us?" We should have

69. John W. Foster to Secretary Gresham, April 17, 1893, *Gresham MS*. In a letter to John W. Foster, May 1, 1893, ex-President Harrison makes the following dubious statement: "I have already expressed in a letter to Mr. Halford my disgust at the treatment Judge Gresham gave you. . . . I never knew a man so given to aspersing the motives of other people as he." *J. W. Foster MS*. Foster himself, had a very different view of the way that Gresham had treated him, and in a letter to Gresham, May 5, 1893, he remarked: "I highly appreciate the kindly way in which you refer to my connection with the work of the Arbitration, and the assurance given by you and for the President of your support in my mission." *Gresham MS*.

70. Benjamin Harrison to J. W. Foster, May 1, 1893, *Foster MS*.

pronounced such a declaration as preposterous, and we might have gone further and intimated that it was not compatible with an honest intention to settle the dispute.[71]

Despite these apprehensions of American lawyers that the American case was none too strong and that the manner of presentation was distinctly inept, John W. Foster, the American agent, retained his optimism about the way the arbitration was proceeding. In a letter to Secretary Gresham he gave the following survey of the situation:

The British oral argument has been (to us) unexpectedly prolonged. They are now on their twenty-first day of four-hour sessions and may continue two or three days longer. When we first assembled, the British talked of getting through in a month. . . . They evidently anticipated a "small job," but after examining the Case and hearing Mr. Carter's oral argument, they became satisfied we were making a strong impression on the Tribunal, and hence their prolonged and earnest efforts. They have been hammering away to break the force of our Case, and have displayed great ingenuity and acumen in their attacks, but after these many days of argument we feel as strong as ever in our position—not a single one of our essential claims has been overthrown.

I believe we have the best of the argument on our property-claim to the seals, but it may be the Tribunal will not have the courage to announce a decision which may seem to its members a new declaration of legal principles. But I feel very confident that if we do not secure a recognition of property, we shall obtain regulations which will be an effective protection to the seals and save to our Government the large revenues due from them. . . .

I thought when I left the Department, I was coming over here for a

71. J. B. Moore to Bayard, May 12, 1893, *Bayard MS*. The following excerpt from the argument of Phelps, concerning the right of the United States to protect the seal fisheries, will illustrate his point that the right of self-defense by a nation upon the sea and the right of municipal jurisdiction over adjacent seas were totally distinct: "The ground upon which the destruction of the seal is sought to be justified, is that the open sea is free, and that since this slaughter takes place there, it is done in the exercise of an indefeasible right in the individuals engaged in it; that the nation injured can not defend itself on the sea, and therefore upon the circumstances of this case can not defend itself at all, let the consequences be what they may.

"The United States Government denies this proposition. While conceding, and interested to maintain, the general rule of the freedom of the sea, as established by modern usage and *consensus* of opinion, it asserts that the sea is free only for innocent and inoffensive use, not injurious to the just interests of any nation which borders upon it; that to the invasion of such interests, for the purposes of private gain, it is not free; that the right of self-defense on the part of a nation is a perfect and paramount right to which all others are subordinate, and which upon no admitted theory of International Law has ever been surrendered; that it extends to all the material interests of a nation important to be defended; . . . that it may . . . be exercised upon the high sea as well as upon the land, and even upon the territory of other and friendly nations, provided only that the necessity for it plainly appears." J. B. Moore, *History and Digest of International Arbitrations*, vol. 1, pp. 839-840.

vacation, but I have found my time fully occupied. *The British have assaulted my "case" so vigorously, it has kept me busy defending it by an array of testimony to support it, and putting the latter in shape for our counsel.*[72]

While the British were delivering a frontal assault upon the American position, the Russians were attacking from the rear. When Secretary Gresham called the attention of Prince Cantacuzene (the Russian Minister at Washington) to information received at the Department of State to the effect that Russia was friendly to Great Britain and hostile to the United States in the fur-seal arbitration in Paris, the Prince replied that

. . . the United States declined to allow Russia to become a party to that arbitration, and his Government was therefore obliged to treat independently with Great Britain. He also stated that notwithstanding what had been said from time to time, his Government did not believe the right of property which we had asserted in the fur-seals in the open sea, was well founded; and that his Government could not afford to assert that right. He said that while his Government entertained the most friendly feelings toward the United States, it could not be blamed for taking such action as its own safety seemed to demand; and that when the treaty between Great Britain and Russia was entered into, his Government had given to Great Britain a confidential note admitting that the Behring Sea was an open free sea, and disclaimed jurisdiction over it for any purpose.[73]

It should have been apparent to Secretary Gresham that the American Case, as presented to the arbitral tribunal at Paris, had little chance of winning a favorable award. When this tribunal held its final meeting on August 15, 1893, the award was against the United States on every one of the five questions that were formally submitted to arbitration.[74]

72. John W. Foster to Secretary Gresham, June 20, 1893, *Gresham MS.* On July 19, 1893, Whitelaw Reid wrote to Foster and expressed the opinion that if the decision of the tribunal at Paris was "even moderately favorable to our contentions, you are, I think, much to be congratulated. Certainly, foreign opinion, and even diplomatic opinion, was so strong against us that it is no small triumph to stem the current." *Foster MS.*

73. Secretary Gresham to J. W. Foster, July 14, 1893, *ibid.*

74. For the text of the five questions that were submitted to arbitration, see *ante,* p. 503. The text of the award of the tribunal of arbitration reads as follows: "As to the first of the said five points, We . . . do decide and determine as follows: By the Ukase of 1821, Russia claimed jurisdiction in the sea now known as the Behring's Sea, to the extent of 100 Italian miles from the coasts and islands belonging to her, but, in the course of the negotiations which led to the conclusion of the Treaties of 1824 with the United States and of 1825 with Great Britain, Russia admitted that her jurisdiction in the said sea should be restricted to the reach of cannon shot from shore, and it appears that, from that time up to the time of the cession of Alaska to the United States, Russia never asserted in fact or exercised any exclusive jurisdiction in Behring's Sea or any exclusive rights in the seal fisheries therein beyond the ordinary limits of territorial waters.

"As to the second of the said five points, We . . . do decide and determine that Great

The tribunal also suggested certain regulations which were believed to be necessary for the preservation of the fur-seal fisheries in Behring Sea.[75]

In the United States, public opinion was much divided over the award of the tribunal of arbitration. In a letter to Bayard, H. L. Bryan expressed his criticism of the arguments advanced in the American Case:

> What a "glorious victory" the decision of the Paris Tribunal! How the "property right" in the seals, that pet discovery of Mr. Phelps, has faded away before the breath of the award! And yet the ultra-Republican newspapers are claiming "another triumph of Harrison's and Blaine's Diplomacy." Now we haven't even an undefined right, that might have been useful in sustaining some sort of surveillance. All is gone.[76]

Lambert Tree was glad that the decision had gone against the United States, for victory "would have been worse for us than defeat. We were contending for an utterly unsound principle . . . which as a great maritime nation we could never afford to have established as a rule of International Law." [77]

Gresham accepted the defeat at Paris with as much grace as he could muster, but he retained his suspicions that the British Government would find "excuses and pretexts" for delaying the enforcement of the regulations for preserving the fur-seals that had been adopted by the

---

Britain did not recognize or concede any claim, upon the part of Russia, to exclusive jurisdiction as to the seal fisheries in Behring Sea, outside of ordinary territorial waters.

"As to the third of said five points, . . . We, the said Arbitrators, do unanimously decide and determine that the body of water now known as Behring Sea was included in the phrase 'Pacific Ocean' as used in said Treaty.

"As to . . . the third point, . . . We . . . do decide . . . that no exclusive rights of jurisdiction in Behring Sea and no exclusive rights as to the seal fisheries therein, were held or exercised by Russia outside of ordinary territorial waters under the Treaty of 1825.

"As to the fourth of the said five points, We, . . . decide . . . that all the rights of Russia as to jurisdiction and as to the seal fisheries in Behring Sea, east of the water boundary, in the Treaty between the United States and Russia, of the 30th March 1867, did pass unimpaired to the United States under the said Treaty.

"As to the fifth of the said five points, We . . . do decide . . . that the United States has not any right of protection or property in the fur-seals frequenting the islands of the United States in Behring Sea, when such seals are found outside the ordinary three-mile limit." W. M. Malloy, *Treaties, Conventions, etc.,* vol. 1, pp. 751-754.

75. W. M. Malloy, *Treaties, Conventions, etc,* vol. 1, pp. 754-759.

76. H. L. Bryan to Bayard, August 17, 1893, *Bayard MS.*

77. Lambert Tree to Bayard, August 20, 1893, *ibid.* Don M. Dickinson was equally critical: "Behring Sea, the judgment, Blaine and Phelps! No further comments except to recall the prophecy in my last letter to you, and to express my sympathy for Coudert and Carter, who were forced to pettifog—to pettifog splendidly—but still to pettifog." *Bayard MS.*

arbitral tribunal.[78] In order to ascertain just what the attitude of the British Government was with reference to these regulations, Gresham cabled to Bayard at London and asked him to take the matter up with the Foreign Office.[79]

He also wrote Bayard a letter which indicated his suspicions of British good faith in the matter of agreeing to regulations that would protect the fur-seals. Concurrent legislation

. . . should be obtained and supplemental rules or orders agreed upon and published before the next sealing season. Owners of sealing vessels should know in advance the restrictions under which they will have to act. Will Great Britain unite with us in an honest effort to enforce the regulations in spirit as well as letter? If not, they will be of no avail. The Canadians will doubtless endeavor to induce the British Government to consent to nothing which will make pelagic sealing more hazardous or difficult than heretofore. I fear that whatever is done, Canadians, and perhaps Americans will transfer the ownership of their sealing vessels to citizens or subjects of other powers, thus avoiding the effect of the regulations.[80]

Bayard hastened to carry out Gresham's instructions, and he found that Lord Rosebery concurred in the view that the British and American Government should act promptly in the matter of adopting regulations concerning the fur-seals. Rosebery believed that the negotiations could best be carried on at Washington,[81] but Gresham sent a formal instruction directing Bayard to continue his efforts to arrange matters.[82] When Lord Rosebery again suggested that Washington was the place where the negotiations should be held,[83] Gresham held firm and repeated his instructions of September 16.[84]

The reason for Gresham's insistence upon London as the place where the fur-seal discussions should be held, is explained in a letter to Bayard from H. L. Bryan. Gresham had just informed Bryan that both

78. Secretary Gresham to J. W. Foster, September 11, 1893, *Gresham MS.*
79. Secretary Gresham to Bayard, September 12, 1893, *Foreign Relations, 1894, Appendix I*, pp. 107-108.
80. Secretary Gresham to Bayard, September 13, 1893, *Gresham MS.*
81. Bayard to Secretary Gresham, September 13, 1893, *Foreign Relations, 1894, Appendix I*, pp. 107-108.
82. Secretary Gresham to Bayard, September 16, 1893, *ibid.*, p. 109.
83. Bayard to Secretary Gresham, September 20, 1893, *ibid.*, p. 118.
84. Secretary Gresham to Bayard, October 3, 1893, *ibid.*, pp. 119-120. In a letter to Bayard, October 29, 1893, Secretary Gresham remarked: "Mr. White informed me he saw Lord Rosebery just before he sailed, and after he parted from you, and the Behring Sea regulations at London, adding that Sir Julian had the Canadians somewhat in hand and he (Rosebery) could not get along with them. The President and I thought it better for the United States that you should conduct the negotiations at London." *Bayard MS.* In this same regard, see also, H. L. Bryan to Bayard, October 30, 1893, *ibid.*

the President and himself were aware of Bayard's complete knowledge "of all the questions involved in the Behring Sea matters," and they also believed that "useless correspondence and delay" would be avoided if Bayard would handle the matter through conversations with Lord Rosebery." [85]

Bayard was glad to carry out this instruction, but there would be some delay because of Lord Rosebery's temporary absence from London. He then expressed his inability to understand the rôle played by Phelps at Paris during the sessions of the arbitral tribunal. The only result of his arguments was the fact that the Blaine-Harrison-Foster management had been able

. . . to tie the hands of the United States and Great Britain in seal-protection and advertise to every other nation an opportunity for them to kill seal freely anywhere and at any time three miles from shore. In short, a "spirited policy" has wholly miscarried, and brought humiliation to its proponents. It only makes our duty more difficult, but does not make it less *our duty*.[86]

Gresham did not share with Bayard this harsh judgment upon the arguments of Phelps before the arbitral tribunal. In a letter to John W. Foster, Gresham expressed the view that

. . . our right of property in the fur-seals and our right to protect them, were the most important questions submitted to the Tribunal, and that if the award had been in our favor on those questions there would have been little necessity for regulations. . . . If Great Britain is willing to co-operate cordially with us, the seal industry may be preserved, but I must say I cannot get rid of the impression that various pretexts may be resorted to for delay on the part of that Government. Mr. Bayard is perfectly familiar with the questions submitted to the Tribunal and its action, and the President and I are satisfied that he will be zealous in upholding our interests.[87]

85. H. L. Bryan to Bayard, October 3, 1893, *Bayard MS.*

86. Bayard to President Cleveland, October 3, 1893, *Bayard Press Copy Book*, vol. 1, *Bayard MS.*

87. Secretary Gresham to John W. Foster, October 9, 1893, *Gresham MS.* Robert Lansing, the son-in-law of John W. Foster, was very much afraid that the Department of State would bungle this material of regulations for the fur-seal industry, if it did not have the benefit of expert advice. In a letter to Phelps, October 12, 1893, he remarked: "Since the award of the Tribunal of Arbitration, I have observed certain remarks in the newspapers conveying the idea that the regulations recommended by such award might, through the concurrence of the United States and Great Britain, be modified 'to more satisfactorily meet the requirements of the conditions of seal life.' . . . Of course the two nations have the power by agreement to modify or change the regulations submitted by the Arbitrators; and the danger that some modifications proposed by Great Britain may be adopted, lies in the fact that at present there is no one in the State Department who is sufficiently familiar with the facts of pelagic sealing and seal life to be able to decide what will protect and what will not protect the seal herd, or to detect misstatement from truth. . . . Delay in this matter may be as fatal to seal life as regulations modified at Great

This right of property in fur-seals, and the right to protect these far-ranging animals, had implications of a most serious nature. If the arbitral tribunal had decided in favor of the American contention, it would have meant that the United States had the power to enforce regulations designed to stop the operations of sealing vessels outside the three-mile limit. The exercise of such a power would have constituted a crushing American attack upon the doctrine of the freedom of the seas. In speaking of the award at Paris, John Bassett Moore observed as follows:

The other day President Low [of Columbia University] remarked that, while he was not familiar with the subject, it seemed to him that the tribunal of Paris "had given Great Britain the past and the United States the future." I replied that I scarcely understood how that could be; that on every question of law submitted to arbitration, we had lost; that Great Britain had already consented to joint regulations, and that the United States, instead of getting a close season for seals in the whole of the North Pacific from May till October, which was conceded to you, had got a close season for three months, . . . and after that a sixty-mile zone about the Pribyloff Islands, which was practically worthless. . . . I readily concur in the opinion that the tribunal *saved* the United States the future, by confirming to it and to all other nations the freedom of the seas.[88]

Now that the award had been made by the arbitral tribunal, and certain regulations for the preservation of the fur-seal fisheries had been adopted,[89] Secretary Gresham was exceedingly anxious to have the

---

Britain's suggestion. . . . Any regulations, before adoption by our government, should be submitted to you for approval. . . . Mr. Foster's absence from the country . . . leaves no one in Washington, excepting Senator Morgan to see that everything goes right in the Department and in Congress. A letter from you to Secretary Gresham . . . in relation to this matter, urging no modification, no conditions applicable to the Islands, and the necessity of speedy action, would undoubtedly prevent the result, which, though it may never occur, is certainly possible." *Gresham MS.*

John W. Foster, the American Agent during the Paris arbitration, agreed with Secretary Gresham with regard to the importance of the argument relative to American property in the fur-seals. In his article, "Results of the Behring Sea Arbitration," page 698, he makes the following statement: "It is also notable that the only additional question introduced in the treaty provision for submission to the Tribunal, . . . the right of protection or property in the seals, and which in the judgment of the consul of the United States become the leading, if not the only defence of the seizures, was not advanced in the legal proceedings of 1887."

Mr. Foster declares that the "chief credit for the development of this point" was due to B. F. Tracy, who published an article setting forth this argument in the *North American Review*, in May, 1893. Apparently, Mr. Foster was unacquainted with the article by E. J. Phelps, "The Behring Sea Controversy," *Harpers Magazine*, April, 1891, pp 766-774.

88. J. B. Moore to Bayard, October 14, 1893, *Bayard MS.*

89. Articles I and II of these regulations read as follows: (*Article I*) "The Governments of the United States and of Great Britain shall forbid their citizens and subjects respectively to kill, capture, or pursue at any time and in any manner whatever, the animals

British Government take the steps that were necessary to put these regulations in force. But he found that Lord Rosebery was disposed to delay matters, and Bayard finally sent a telegram on November 23, in which he said that Rosebery had presented to him "impressive reasons" why the negotiations should be conducted in Washington.[90]

In a personal letter to Secretary Gresham, Bayard stated that he was certain that the Behring Sea negotiations would be "continually interrupted and delayed" if carried on in London. If they were transferred to Washington, he could pay a flying visit to the Department of State, and through the medium of diplomatic conversations the whole matter could be speedily settled.[91]

The question of the transfer of the negotiations to Washington, was discussed between H. L. Bryan and Secretary Gresham, and Bryan sent to Bayard a report of this conversation:

> In a private conversation with the Secretary yesterday, he spoke of your cable message stating that Lord R. had suggested cogent reasons for conducting the Behring Sea negotiations at Washington; and the Secretary smilingly said that he thought perhaps your generosity might incline you to admit too readily the strength of these reasons, and that there existed here equally weighty considerations why you should conduct these transactions: one of the strongest being your entire familiarity with the subject, while he would have to take up the study in the midst of other absorbing and delicate questions.[92]

Under continued pressure from Lord Rosebery, Secretary Gresham finally gave way, and consented to transfer the negotiations concerning the fur-seal regulations, to Washington. While Bayard's generous offer of assistance was appreciated by the President, it would be better for him to remain in London in order to look after other diplomatic questions.[93]

---

commonly called fur-seals, within a zone of sixty miles around the Pribilov Islands, inclusive of the territorial waters." (*Article II*) "The two Governments shall forbid their citizens and subjects respectively to kill, capture, or pursue, in any manner whatever, during the season extending, each year, from the 1st of May to the 31st of July, both inclusive, the fur-seals on the high sea, in the part of the Pacific Ocean, inclusive of the Behring Sea, which is situated to the North of the 35th degree of north latitude, and eastward of the 180th degree of longitude from Greenwich till it strikes the water boundary described in Article 1 of the Treaty of 1867, between the United States and Russia, and following that line up to Behring straits."

90. Bayard to Secretary Gresham, November 23, 1893, *Foreign Relations, 1894, Appendix I*, p. 133.

91. Bayard to Secretary Gresham, November 25, 1893, *Gresham MS*.

92. H. L. Bryan to Bayard, December 1, 1893, *Bayard MS*.

93. Secretary Gresham to Bayard, December 4, 1893, *Foreign Relations, 1894, Appendix I*, p. 136.

In a letter to President Cleveland, Bayard expressed the view that Washington was the "proper place" to hold the negotiations, and that a conclusive result would be "sooner reached there than here [London]." [94] He wrote to John Bassett Moore in the same vein, and advanced the opinion that the Department of State would not have any trouble securing the adherence of Japan or Russia to any regulations that were adopted, but he had his doubts about the Canadian Government. The Canadians were "small and sharp—very." As to the actions of Phelps and Carter, he was at a loss to comprehend them, and he had not met "anyone" who did. [95]

Phelps was not aware that his conduct had been so questionable, and he still regarded himself as an expert on everything connected with the fur-seals. In a note to Bayard he complained that the

. . . regulations of the Paris tribunal in respect to the killing of the seals are most flagrantly disregarded. If observed they would be quite sufficient to preserve the seals, and one wiser than you and I would have been glad to obtain [them] in the outset. . . . There are materials enough for trouble if anyone desires to make it. And with ten months of Congress before us, what may happen can not be foretold. [96]

Secretary Gresham shared these fears that there were "materials for trouble" in the Behring Sea negotiations, and he was exceedingly anxious to have everything settled as soon as possible. But the British Government seemed to be in no hurry to arrive at an agreement, even after the negotiations had been transferred to Washington. In a personal letter to Bayard, Gresham stated that he had made

. . . no headway in negotiations with the British Ambassador for an agreement which will make the award of the Paris Tribunal practically effective. The first of the three declarations made by the Tribunal will likely embarrass this government not a little. The arbitrators had no jurisdiction to bind the powers within the limits of their respective sovereignties, and yet the first declaration solemnly declares that the reported regulations should be supplemented by others "applicable within the limits of the sovereignty of the two powers interested, and to be settled by their common agreement." Sir Julian has not said in terms that Great Britain would expect the United States to come to an agreement regulating the taking of seals within our own jurisdiction, but he has intimated as much. I can imagine that later on he will say, "Why should Great Britain be required to protect the zone around

94. Bayard to President Cleveland, December 5, 1893, *Cleveland MS.*
95. Bayard to John B. Moore, December 1, 1893, *Bayard Press Copy Book*, vol. 1, *Bayard MS.*
96. Phelps to Bayard, December 3, 1893, *Bayard MS.*

the Pribylof Islands at joint expense with the United States, unless the latter government agrees to some reasonable restriction as to the number of seals which shall be taken on the islands, as well as in the territorial waters around them?"

Sir Julian is waiting, he says, for a draft of a bill which he expects from London. He was instructed by Lord Rosebery to say Great Britain desired that a Canadian should be admitted as a negotiator, but he was informed that while this government would not object to one or more Canadians being present at the negotiations, it was unwilling to treat with any one except a representative of the British Government.[97]

Bayard's letter of reply showed that he was in full accord with Gresham's views. The award of the arbitral tribunal and the regulations it adopted with reference to pelagic sealing, had created a

. . . separate and distinct obligation upon the two contracting powers of an imperative character, and quite different from the nature of the three "declarations" of the Tribunal which by the text were only "referred" to the United States and Great Britain for "their consideration," and even this reference was qualified by the withholding of the signatures of Lord Hannen and Sir John Thompson from the 2d of the "recommendations.". . . But I still believe it will be wise to insist upon a mutual conventional agreement to accept and execute the *regulations,* which the Tribunal was empowered by the Treaty to make, and which they *did* make. Nor do I think that the *extent* of the interests of either party in the fur-sealing on land, or the preservation of the seal species should control their clear duty and obligation to assist in policing the seas, as is directed in the regulations imposed by the Tribunal equally upon both parties to the submission.

If the Canadians shall honestly accept the decisions of the Tribunal, and the United States will actively patrol the interdicted waters for one year,

97. Secretary Gresham to Bayard, December 17, 1893, *Bayard MS.* The "Declarations" made by the arbitral tribunal at Paris, and referred to the Governments of the United States and Great Britain for their consideration, were three in number. The text of the declarations reads as follows: "(I) The Arbitrators declare that the concurrent Regulations, as determined upon by the Tribunal of Arbitration, by virtue of Article VII of the Treaty of the 29th of February 1892, being applicable to the high sea only, should, in their opinion, be supplemented by other Regulations applicable within the limits of the sovereignty of each of the two Powers interested and to be settled by their common agreement. (II) In view of the critical condition to which it appears certain that the race of fur-seals is now reduced in consequence of circumstances not fully known, the Arbitrators think fit to recommend Governments to come to an understanding in order to prohibit any killing of fur-seals, either on land or at sea, for a period of two or three years, or at least one year, subject to such exceptions as the two Governments might think proper to admit of. Such a measure might be recurred to at occasional intervals if found beneficial. (III) The Arbitrators declare moreover that, in their opinion, the carrying out of the Regulations determined upon by the Tribunal of Arbitration, should be assured by a system of stipulations and measures to be enacted by the two Powers, and that the Tribunal must, in consequence, leave it to the two Powers to decide upon the means for giving effect to the Regulations determined upon by it." W. M. Malloy, *Treaties, Conventions, etc.,* vol. 1, p. 759.

or for two at most, the business of pelagic sealing will cease, for in the absence of fire-arms, nets, etc., it cannot be profitably conducted. As to regulating the catch on the Islands, the interests of the United States are identical with those of England, for the common object of both is to augment the supply, and this can only be accomplished by a restricted mode of killing, regulated as to methods, seasons, and numbers.

You are quite right as to requiring Canada to take part in the negotiations *only* as a dependency of Great Britain. Canadians are British subjects, and *as such* can be empowered as Ministers Plenipotentiary. Thus, Lord Elgin was Governor-General of Canada when he made the treaty in 1854 with Mr. Marcy, so was Sir John Macdonald (a Canadian Minister) when he was a member of the Joint High Commission in 1872, and Sir Charles Tupper in 1888, so also in the Paris Tribunal, but in such case representing Great Britain (and including Canada not named). I do not quite understand Sir Julian waiting for draughts of laws from London, when it was so strongly urged upon me here that the Foreign Office was so "overwhelmed with work" and that Sir Julian personally had the whole business so thoroughly at his fingers' ends.

I still hope you will make a convention and adopt the award and regulations of the Paris Tribunal *ipissimis verbis,* as a first essential, and having clenched those facts, *then* consider what is wise and reasonable in relation to taking seal *on shore* or within the respective jurisdictions. . . . An agreement equally to inhibit the killing of seal on the seas, tells as much against citizens of the United States as against those of Great Britain, and certainly it is the *only* sealing the Treaty of April 1892 had any reference to. . . . A reasonable system of safeguards will be in the line of a just and amicable settlement, and is dictated alike by the interests and self-respect of the United States.[98]

On January 6 Secretary Gresham informed Bayard, by telegram, that the British Ambassador was still urging the American Government to agree that a Canadian should be "admitted as negotiator for concurrent action to make regulations reported by Paris Tribunal effective." But Gresham instructed Bayard that it was the President's wish that he inform Lord Rosebery that the Department of State would "treat with the Imperial Government only." [99] Bayard replied that Lord Rosebery was entirely willing that the British Ambassador at Washington conduct the negotiations without a "Canadian colleague." [100]

Unfortunately for the progress of the negotiations, these concessions of Lord Rosebery were not coupled with instructions to Sir Julian Pauncefote to go ahead with his conversations with Secretary Gresham

98. Bayard to Secretary Gresham, December 28, 1893, *Gresham MS.*
99. Secretary Gresham to Bayard, January 6, 1894, *Foreign Relations, 1894, Appendix I,* p. 140.
100. Bayard to Secretary Gresham, January 8, 1894, *ibid.,* p. 141.

and speedily conclude a convention that would finally settle matters in dispute. On January 21, 1894, Gresham wrote to Bayard and expressed his displeasure with the way things were going. He had spoken to Sir Julian of the time that had already elapsed with reference to the negotiations, and had

... reminded him that the sealing season had commenced and informed him we thought this not a little strange, in view of the earnest desire of his Government that the negotiations should be transferred from London to Washington. He again informed me that he hoped to receive instructions very soon which would enable him to speak more definitely. My confidence in his candor remains unshaken. I think he and Lord Rosebery are embarrassed by the Canadians. While the regulations are not self-executing, I agree with you that the award, including the regulations, is obligatory upon the contracting parties. The three declarations are not part of the award and do not bind the Powers. I will send you tomorrow or the next day copies of a draft of the proposed convention and my note transmitting it to Sir Julian. Until recently he steadily insisted that a convention was unnecessary, asserting that legislation would fully accomplish the end desired. I think, however, he has now changed his mind and sees the necessity of a mutual agreement which will enable us to prevent pelagic sealing during this season. If the Canadians are permitted to have their way, no agreement of any kind will be reached, and the seal herds will speedily disappear.

It was to oblige Sir Julian that you were instructed to inform Lord Rosebery the negotiations must be between the United States and the Imperial Government, and that we would not consent to the introduction of a Canadian as an arbitrator. . . . We were not willing that a Canadian should act with him with authority to vote. He was distinctly informed that we had not the slightest objection to one or more Canadians being present to counsel and otherwise aid him. Sir Julian feared our refusal to treat with a Canadian would be attributed to his influence and he desired a record showing the contrary.[101]

On January 24 Secretary Gresham sent to Lord Pauncefote a draft of a convention between the United States and Great Britain for the purpose of executing the regulations adopted by the Paris Tribunal with regard to fur-seals. The President was increasingly anxious to have some action taken at once, and it was ardently hoped that the British Ambassador would respond to this overture.[102] But Pauncefote paid little attention to this plea to expedite negotiations, and John Bassett Moore concluded that the reason for this procrastination was that pressure was being exerted by the Canadian Government in favor of a

101. Secretary Gresham to Bayard, January 21, 1894, *Bayard MS.*
102. Secretary Gresham to Pauncefote, January 24, 1894, *Foreign Relations, 1894, Appendix I*, pp. 142-146.

policy of inaction. It seemed to Moore that "colonies, like small children, sometimes think it pays to be bad, but their parents ought not to encourage them in such conduct." [103]

At length, on February 22, 1894, Gresham telegraphed to Bayard that the President was unable to understand the do-nothing policy of the British Government, and he wished to have the situation stated "impressively to Her Majesty's Government." [104] Bayard immediately sent a strong note to Lord Rosebery expressing President Cleveland's disappointment at the "unexpected and regretted delay in coming to an agreement for the efficient execution of the regulations for the conduct of fur-seal fishing in Behring Sea." [105] After waiting several days, Bayard had an interview with Rosebery, who "did not seem aware of the proposition for a convention, and asked why the co-operative legislation would not be sufficient." [106] In a note to Bayard, March 2, 1894, Rosebery repeated his belief that a convention was not necessary to carry out the regulations adopted by the Paris Tribunal. This matter could be handled efficiently by mere legislative enactment.[107]

In this note of March 2, 1894, Rosebery frankly admitted that one of the chief reasons why negotiations had not been speedily concluded was on account of the necessity of referring all questions of sealing regulations to the Canadian Government for approval. The British Foreign Office did not seem to realize that the fast-rising tide of resentment in the United States against this policy of delay, might cause an abrupt break in the negotiations at Washington. Some Republican Senators, aided by Senator Morgan, were losing patience with British inaction, and were ready to take matters into their own hands. Secretary Gresham was strongly opposed to any such action, and on February 23 he wrote to Morgan to explain the situation:

I have just read your letter of yesterday. I drafted the bill, a copy of which was sent to you and to Governor McCreary. My idea was that, for the present, we had better not assume Great Britain was not going to meet us in a proper spirit and agree, as the treaty obliges her, to make the reported regulations effective. Of course, I expected you to exercise your own judgment as to the kind of a bill to be introduced. I think you saw the

103. John Bassett Moore to Bayard, February 3, 1894, *Bayard MS.* See also H. L. Bryan to Bayard, February 16, 1894, *ibid.*

104. Secretary Gresham to Bayard, February 22, 1894, *Foreign Relations, 1894, Appendix I,* p. 147.

105. Bayard to Lord Rosebery, February 23, 1894, *ibid.,* pp. 149-150.

106. Bayard to Secretary Gresham, February 28, 1894, *ibid.,* pp. 148-149.

107. Lord Rosebery to Bayard, March 2, 1894, *ibid.,* pp. 151-152.

copy of my note to Sir Julian, enclosing the draft of a treaty strictly within the terms of the convention and the award. It seems to me that we should do nothing of record just now indicating the belief on our part that Great Britain is not going to be fair. I had another interview with Sir Julian yesterday, and he told me he expected to receive instructions from Lord Rosebery in three or four days. I agree with you that I should see Senator Sherman, and I shall ask him to come to the Department tomorrow with you, if you can find time to accompany him. I have an impression I ought to go before your full committee on this question. I am perfectly willing to disclose all that has been done.[108]

The active role that Senator Morgan was playing in the Senate with reference to the fur-seal regulations, was disclosed by Senator George Gray in a short note to Bayard: "Our friend Senator Morgan is stirring up the Behring Sea matter in the Senate, and still wants to insist on 'our right of property in the seals.' His irritable brain is in pernicious activity just now."[109]

It is apparent that many Senators had grown weary of waiting for the British Government to conclude the negotiations at Washington with reference to the execution of the fur-seal regulations. But before they could carry out any program of anti-British legislation, Lord Rosebery was suddenly advanced to the position of Prime Minister (through the resignation of Gladstone), and Lord Kimberley became the new Foreign Secretary. Bayard believed that Kimberley was "a straightforward man of ability and experience," who would not "permit the Canadians to be tricky in relation to Behring Sea." [110]

Kimberley lived up to these expectations, and on April 18 Bayard was able to telegraph to Secretary Gresham that the British Parliament had just passed an act to carry out the regulations adopted by the Paris Tribunal.[111] Almost two weeks earlier, Gresham had informed Bayard that Congress had enacted similar legislation.[112]

This difficult matter of making legislative provision for the execution of the fur-seal regulations was finally settled, and Bayard had

108. Secretary Gresham to John T. Morgan, February 23, 1894, *Gresham MS.* In a letter from H. L. Bryan to Bayard, April 20, 1894, there is the following pertinent sentence: "The Secretary chafed a great deal at the delay Sir Julian was obliged to incur, owing to his instructions and the efforts of the Canadians to have some particular privileges allowed them in the making of the Regulations." *Bayard MS.*

109. George W. Gray to Bayard, March 11, 1894, *Bayard MS.*

110. Bayard to Secretary Gresham, March 7, 1894, *Bayard Press Copy Book,* vol. 1, *Bayard MS.*

111. Bayard to Secretary Gresham, April 18, 1894, *Foreign Relations, 1894, Appendix I,* pp. 178-179.

112. Secretary Gresham to Bayard, April 5, 1894, *ibid.,* p. 165.

played an important part in these negotiations. It appeared to Phelps that Bayard had

. . . adjusted the Behring Sea matter most satisfactorily. The regulations given in the award are ample for the protection of the seals if they are honestly enforced. I thought and still think it was the intention of Great Britain to escape their enforcement for this year at least. But the legislation now adopted would appear sufficient and I hope we shall have no further trouble.[113]

But there was still one phase of the Behring Sea dispute that was left unsettled, and this had to do with the payment of British claims arising out of American seizures of sealing vessels owned by British subjects. On October 28, 1893, Bayard expressed the opinion that there would be "a smart Behring Sea bill to be paid by the United States," [114] and John Bassett Moore assured Bayard that with reference to these claims the American Government would "have a fine sum to pay." [115]

But there were some members of Congress who were strongly opposed to any payment of claims to Great Britain. As early as February 22, 1894, Secretary Gresham wrote to Bayard that Senator Morgan was openly working against such a settlement.[116] John Bassett Moore wrote in a similar vein concerning the actions and views of Morgan:

Remembering the course of Mr. Morgan with respect to the fisheries in 1886, you may not be astonished to learn that he now maintains that the Paris Tribunal did not decide against our claim of property in the seals, and that he also maintains that nothing is due Great Britain for our previous seizures. He argues that the vessels that were seized (sixty miles & more from land), were *hovering* with intent to depredate on our property, and that we therefore had a right to seize them! In matter generally, Mr. Morgan is ranged with the Republicans against the administration, and he is bent on mischief.[117]

Despite this Congressional opposition, Secretary Gresham went ahead, and on August 21, 1894, offered the sum of $425,000 in final settlement of all claims as to American seizures of British sealing ves-

113. Phelps to Bayard, May 2, 1894, *Bayard MS.*
114. Bayard to Frederick Emory, October 28, 1893, *Bayard Press Copy Book*, vol. 1, *Bayard MS.*
115. John B. Moore to Bayard, November 14, 1893, *Bayard MS.*
116. Secretary Gresham to Bayard, February 22, 1894, *Bayard MS.* Gresham had already written to Bayard, October 29, 1893, to inform him that James C. Carter, who had acted as one of the counsel for the United States before the arbitral tribunal at Paris, had remarked that the American Government should treat that "solemn adjudication as amounting to nothing more than the decision of an ordinary court determining a trivial controversy between two individuals." *Ibid.*
117. John B. Moore to Bayard, February 28, 1894, *ibid.*

sels. This offer, of course, was "subject to the action of Congress on the question of appropriating the money." [118] Lord Pauncefote replied at once that the British Government would accept this sum, although the amount was "much below their estimate of the compensation" which was fairly due.[119]

Thanks to the opposition of Senator Morgan, and others of like mind, this appropriation was not passed by Congress, and the matter of unpaid British claims was still unsettled.[120] To Bayard, this action by Congress was most

... humiliating and painful. . . . When I thought last spring that the Canadians were influencing the Imperial government against a full and honorable compliance with the Paris Award, I dwelt with confidence and positiveness to Lord Rosebery and his successor upon the effect of breaches upon the practice of arbitration. And now, "this even-handed justice" commends the chalice to our own lips. I think you cannot be worse off, but will in fact be better off, with a Republican at the head of the Senate Committee on Foreign Relations instead of Mr. Morgan, who is, I think, the most wholly and dangerously unreliable person I ever knew in public life. . . .

I must tell you that when Lord Kimberley spoke to me of his surprise and disappointment caused by the action of Congress in not paying the Canadian damages, he read me a telegram from Sir Julian Pauncefote, in which he stated that you and the President had done everything in your power to have the full appropriation made.[121]

The story of Morgan's tactics was related to Bayard in a letter from John Bassett Moore:

Morgan declares that we don't owe a cent on the claims, and that the decision of the Paris tribunal did not render us liable for them, and he asked leave to read and have printed in the *Record* a letter from Mr. Phelps in support of his views. Objection was made to the printing of Mr. Phelps' screed, and it failed to reach the state of immortality to which Morgan had destined it. For my own part, while I am able to admit that men may honestly differ as to the best mode of settling the claims, I don't think the question of liability is a matter of opinion under the award of the Tribunal of Paris. Even Messrs. Hoar and Higgins supported Judge Gresham's settlement

118. Secretary Gresham to Pauncefote, August 21, 1894, *Foreign Relations, 1894, Appendix* I, pp. 224-225.

119. Pauncefote to Secretary Gresham, August 21, 1894, *ibid.*, pp. 225-226.

120. In a letter to Secretary Gresham, May 25, 1895, Bayard made the following comment upon the attitude of Senator Morgan: "It is greatly to be regretted that your sensible and honorable proposition to settle the Sealing vessels claims, was defeated by the mischievous Morgan, who seems to delight in striking splinters into public questions." *Bayard Press Copy Book,* vol. 2, *Bayard MS.*

121. Bayard to Secretary Gresham, March 9, 1895, *Bayard Press Copy Book,* vol. 2, *Bayard MS.*

on grounds of national honor. Morgan, however, continued to defeat it by parliamentary tactics.[122]

But this long chapter on fur-seal fisheries could not continue forever and on February 8, 1896, a convention was concluded at Washington which made provision for the appointment of a mixed commission to consider the question of claims.[123] William L. Putnam was chosen as the American commissioner, and George E. King was selected to represent Canada. On December 17, 1897, the commissioners made a detailed award, and on June 16, 1898, the Secretary of State delivered to the British Ambassador at Washington a draft for the sum of $473,151.26.[124]

Although this payment put an end to the claims-controversy with reference to American seizures of British sealing vessels, the dispute concerning the fur-seal fisheries dragged on for many years. Pelagic sealing continued until 1911, when a treaty between the United States and Great Britain was concluded which specifically prohibited such operations.[125] On July 7, 1911, a treaty was signed between the United States, Great Britain, Russia, and Japan which bound these four nations to put an end to all pelagic sealing, and to furnish naval patrols that would effectually protect the seals from illegal operations by sealing vessels.[126] In this way a long and, at times, dangerous controversy was finally brought to an amicable conclusion.[127]

122. John B. Moore to Bayard, March 11, 1895, *ibid.* For remarks of Senator Morgan concerning the fur-seal fisheries and the payment of British claims, see, *Congressional Record*, 53 Cong., 2 sess., vol. 27, pp. 2961, 2971, 3040, 3139-3141.
123. W. M. Malloy, *Treaties, Conventions, etc.*, vol. 1, pp. 766-770.
124. John B. Moore, *History and Digest of International Arbitrations*, vol. 2, pp. 2123-2131; *Foreign Relations, 1898*, pp. 371-373.
125. *Treaties, Conventions, etc., Between the United States of America and Other Powers, 1910–1923*, pp. 2629-2632. The date of this convention was February 27, 1911.
126. *Ibid.*, pp. 2966-2972.
127. Thomas A. Bailey, "The North Pacific Sealing Convention of 1911," *Pacific Historical Review*, vol. 4 (1935), pp. 1-14.

CHAPTER SIXTEEN

Goldwin Smith Forsakes the Role of Historian for That of Statesman

THE CATALOGUE OF DIPLOMATIC INCIDENTS CONNECTED WITH CANADIAN-American relations is a long one that has exhausted the patience of a score of American Secretaries of State, and Bayard soon discovered that along with the difficult problems arising out of the North Atlantic and fur-seal fisheries, there was also clamoring for settlement the important question of commercial reciprocity between the United States and Canada. The termination of the Treaty of Washington in March, 1866, was a severe blow to Canadian business, and there were many politicians in the Dominion who hoped to convince the American Government that a prompt renewal of reciprocity would be mutually beneficial.

In 1874 the Canadian Government sent George Brown to Washington with instructions to co-operate with Sir Edward Thornton (the British Minister) in an effort to conclude a far-reaching arrangement that would include many items in addition to those dealing with the fisheries and commercial reciprocity. In spite of the fact that Secretary Fish and President Grant were ready to view this Canadian overture with favor, the Senate adopted a hostile attitude, and the project was defeated.[1]

Although the House Committee on Commerce submitted a report (January, 1876) in favor of reciprocity with Canada, the Canadian Government finally grew weary of empty American gestures, and in March,

1. Lester B. Shippee, *Canadian-American Relations, 1849–1874*, pp. 460-471; Allan Nevins, *Hamilton Fish*, pp. 917-920; James M. Callahan, *American Foreign Policy in Canadian Relations*, pp. 354-356. In addition to providing for a limited commercial reciprocity, this Canadian program included items such as American use of inshore fisheries; reciprocal privileges relating to the coasting trade; enlargement of Canadian canals at Canadian expense; reciprocity in the use of canals; free navigation of Lake Michigan for Canadian vessels; erection and maintenance of lighthouses on the Great Lakes; reciprocal patent laws; and co-operation with regard to the prevention of illicit trade.

1879, a new tariff policy was adopted. One noteworthy item in this tariff law was a clause which provided that in the event the American Government repealed the duties in whole or in part on the natural products of Canada, the Dominion Government would make similar concessions.[2]

There was little disposition in official circles in Washington to conciliate Canada, and on March 3, 1883, Congress adopted a resolution which directed the President to give notice to the British Government of the termination of Articles XVIII to XXV, inclusive, and of Article XXX of the Treaty of Washington. The President carried out this instruction, and on July 1, 1885, the liberty granted to American fishermen to fish within the three-mile limit along the Canadian coasts, came to an end. When Sackville-West inquired whether the "free fishing" and "free fish" clauses of the Treaty of Washington could be extended until January 1, 1886, he was informed by Secretary Frelinghuysen that such a suggestion was "impracticable."[3] On March 27, 1885, Bayard gave a similar answer to the British Minister, but the way was left open for some provisional arrangement that would prevent friction in the North Atlantic fisheries.[4] On April 22 Bayard handed Sackville-West a memorandum which recorded a suggestion by the Governments of Newfoundland and Canada that the American fishermen be permitted to use the inshore fisheries until January 1, 1886, in return for a recommendation by President Cleveland to Congress with reference to the appointment of a commission to study the fisheries question. President Cleveland was ready to adopt this suggestion on condition that there would be no enforcement of the penal laws against American fishermen who frequented the inshore fisheries.[5]

As an indication of British good will towards the United States, Lord Granville instructed Sackville-West (June 3, 1885) to accede to the temporary arrangement proposed by Bayard.[6] Bayard then sent a note to Sackville-West in which a pledge was given that President

2. Edward Porritt, *Sixty Years of Protection in Canada* (London, 1908), pp. 267-273; E. M. Saunders, *Life and Letters of the Right Honorable Sir Charles Tupper* (Toronto, 1912, 2 vols.), vol. 2, pp. 99ff.
3. Secretary Frelinghuysen to Sackville-West, January 20, 1885, *Great Britain, Notes to*, vol. 19, MS Dept. of State.
4. *Memorandum* written by Bayard after a conversation with Sackville-West, March 27, 1885, *Bayard MS.*
5. *Memorandum* written by Bayard, April 22, 1885, *British Legation, Notes to*, vol. 19, MS Dept. of State.
6. Sackville-West to Lord Lansdowne, June 5, 1885, *John Macdonald Papers, Washington Treaty, 1888*, vol. 2, MS Canadian Archives.

Cleveland would recommend to Congress the appointment of a commission that would deal not only with the fisheries question, but with the whole subject of "good neighborhood and intercourse." [7]

Some Americans regarded this arrangement with England as a preparatory step to the conclusion of a convention providing for commercial reciprocity between the United States and Canada. One of the most active of American business men who favored reciprocity, was S. J. Ritchie, of Akron, Ohio. Ritchie was President of the Central Ontario Railway, in Canada, and was the owner of some nickel and copper deposits in the Sudbury region of Ontario Province. He was very anxious to remove the tariff barriers that impeded the flow of goods across the Canadian boundary line, and on August 18, 1885, he wrote to Sir Charles Tupper with reference to the possibility of a reciprocity treaty:

> In the brief moment in which I spoke to you last evening, I had only time to say . . . that I believed there had been a decided change of sentiment at Washington from what existed when you were there a year or more ago, and if you had the time to spare before your return to England, I would be glad to arrange a meeting of yourself and two or three of the leading parties in the Senate at some place satisfactory to you, say in New York, where you could talk over reciprocity matters. As you are aware, our Senate is still Republican, and they will have to deal with the question. Fortunately, those who wield the most influence in that party and who have formerly strongly opposed the measures, now express very friendly feelings towards them. The fact that you are not now in the government, would relieve you and the government of any embarrassment they might experience in opening negotiations in a direct official way, but I feel satisfied that an agreement could be arrived at by which our Congress would pass some measures covering the subject at its next session, and to do this it would only be necessary to have a good understanding with two or three parties in the Senate.[8]

While Ritchie was pressing Sir Charles Tupper to undertake some unofficial negotiations with regard to commercial reciprocity, Lord Lansdowne, the Governor-General of Canada, was writing to Sir John Macdonald in connection with the same problem. Lansdowne agreed with Macdonald that it would be unwise to "tie too directly" the hands of the Canadian representatives who would serve on the proposed commission which President Cleveland would advocate in his message to

7. Bayard to Sackville-West, June 19, 20, 22, 1885; Sackville-West to Bayard, June 20, 22, 1885, *British Legation, Notes to,* vol. 20; *British Legation, Notes from,* vol. 112, MS Dept. of State.

8. S. J. Ritchie to Sir Charles Tupper, August 18, 1885, *John Macdonald Papers, Commercial Union, 1885–1886,* MS Canadian Archives.

Congress. He also believed that the British Foreign Office should not press the Dominion Government to define in too precise a manner "the objects with which we shall enter upon the negotiations." As to commercial relations generally, what kind of reciprocity did Sir John wish to see established? Should it "be limited to raw materials, such as coal and lumber?" In accordance with Canadian tariff legislation, it would be possible "to admit certain United States imports free whenever the United States should do the same." Were these the lines that should be followed in the proposed negotiations? [9]

Macdonald's answer was quite lengthy. He thought it would be advisable to ask for a renewal of the abrogated articles of the Washington Treaty. In this regard, some provision should be made to have these articles extended so as to include "whale- and seal-oil" as well as "free fish and fish-oil." It was also important to have the proposed treaty cover the "marine products" of the Canadian Pacific Coast. As to "general commercial relations, Canada would be satisfied with the terms of the Reciprocity Treaty of 1854, with perhaps some extensions. A Treaty affecting manufactures would not be entertained by the United States, nor, I think, by England." [10]

After receiving these suggestions from Sir John Macdonald, Lansdowne wrote to Lord Stanley, at the British Colonial Office, and pointed out that the interests of Canada and Newfoundland "in regard to the questions which these negotiations will affect are not identical." For this reason there might be "some difficulty in arriving at an understanding with the Government of the Island for a common basis upon which these negotiations might proceed." The exports of Newfoundland were "almost entirely limited to fish and fish-products, while the Dominion has a large interest in promoting the export to the United States of such commodities as cereals and agricultural products of all kinds, lumber and coal." With regard to the proposed negotiations, the Canadian Government was of the opinion that it would be "highly undesirable that it should be publicly committed, previous to the commencement of the negotiations, to a definite statement of the concessions which it seeks to obtain, or those which it is prepared to make." [11]

9. Lansdowne to Sir John Macdonald, August 24, 1885, *John Macdonald Papers, Washington Treaty, 1888,* vol. 2, MS Canadian Archives.
10. Sir John Macdonald to Lansdowne, September 5, 1885, *ibid.*
11. Lansdowne to Lord Stanley, September 11, 1885, *John Macdonald Papers, Washington Treaty, 1888,* vol. 2, MS Canadian Archives.

On December 8, in accordance with the pledge that Bayard had given to Sackville-West, President Cleveland sent a message to Congress in which there was included a recommendation for the appointment of a joint commission which should be charged with the consideration and settlement of "the entire question of the fishing rights of the two Governments and their respective citizens on the coasts of the United States and British North America." Inasmuch as the fishing interests were intimately related to "other general questions dependent upon contiguity and intercourse, consideration thereof . . . might also properly come within the purview of such a commission." [12]

Three days after the President had sent his message to Congress, Sackville-West had an interview with Bayard. When he inquired as to the action that the Department of State would take in order to secure the adoption of the President's recommendations, Bayard replied that

. . . as soon as the Committee of the House of Representatives on Foreign Affairs was constituted, a joint resolution would be moved either in the Senate or the House to authorize the President to appoint a Commission. He could not . . . say what course Congress would pursue, but . . . it was his intention to do all in his power to carry out the objects indicated in the message. He then proceeded to develop the policy which had led to the provisional arrangement: 1st. The desire of the United States Government not only to maintain but to increase the existing friendly relations with the Government of the Dominion of Canada. . . . 2nd. The necessity in the interests of both Governments of establishing the commercial relations between the two Countries on a more satisfactory footing. . . . 3rd. The manifest advantage to both countries of a system based on the free interstate commerce of the Union.[13]

While the American Congress was deliberating as to what course it should pursue concerning reciprocity with Canada, Sir John Macdonald was receiving many letters with regard to the effect of reciprocity upon economic conditions in the Dominion. From British Columbia, word came that the forests and the rich mineral deposits assured that province of

. . . becoming, under favouring circumstances, essentially a manufacturing country, and it is . . . very important that these interests should be guarded by all means consistent with the general welfare. . . . On the whole, I consider it beyond question that any measure of Reciprocity with the United States, acceptable to the Eastern Provinces of the Dominion, would be bene-

---

12. J. D. Richardson, *Messages and Papers of the Presidents,* vol. 8, p. 332.
13. Sackville-West to Lord Salisbury, December 11, 1885, *John Macdonald Papers, Washington Treaty, 1888,* vol. 2, MS Canadian Archives.

ficial to the interests of British Columbia—the products of primary importance which we desire to have admitted into the American market free of
duty being Coal, Lumber, and Fish, and Fish-Oils.[14]

From Fredericton, New Brunswick, Sir John received a report that
Ontario would "favour a Treaty if it will give them free coal and a
free market for their cattle and agricultural produce." Quebec was not
especially interested in securing free entry for fish, but would be
anxious to get the United States market for "their lumber, hay, oats,
and potatoes." The Maritime Provinces wished to have free entry for
their "fish, lumber, and agricultural products." It was well understood
that

. . . in the present unsettled state of affairs in Europe, and with the Irish
difficulties at home, the *Imperial authorities* will be most anxious to have
arrangements made with reference to the Fisheries, and *on almost any terms*.
But our own interests and our patriotism as well, require that *we* should
make some concessions for peace' sake and for the unity of the Empire. . . .
When I met Mr. Evarts in Washington in 1880, and Mr. Blaine in 1881,
they both talked of large reciprocal arrangements, covering a large list of
manufactures, but at the same time imposing a duty on British productions.
. . . This proposition . . . could not be entertained for a moment. The
free admission of manufactures from the United States and a duty on British
manufactures, would be practical independence in the worst form.[15]

From Canada, Bayard received a letter written by the celebrated
publicist, Goldwin Smith, who expressed the belief that the Canadian
people were "about ready for the question of Commercial Union, if it
can be brought before them in a definite and authoritative form."[16]

14. Joseph W. Trutch to Sir John Macdonald, December 24, 1885, *John Macdonald
Papers, Washington Treaty, 1888,* vol. 2, MS Canadian Archives. See also, William Smithe
to Sir John Macdonald, December 28, 1885, in which the following pertinent comments
are made: "Here [British Columbia] we have far richer and immensely more extensive
fishing grounds than you have on the Atlantic seaboard, and so far we have retained them
in our own hands. The importance to the Province and the Dominion of our yet-to-be-
developed fisheries cannot be overestimated. . . . Free interchange of the products of the
sea I think would be a decided advantage to both countries. In so far as reciprocity generally goes, I think it would be decidedly better to have it in all products rather than not
have it in any, but for British Columbia exclusively, it would be best to discriminate. . . .
I think good reasons exist for not having reciprocity in manufactures. Our infantile manu-
factories should have that protection which the weak always require against the strong.
. . . It will be of immense importance to have reciprocity in pig iron and bar steel, lead,
etc. . . . It is scarcely possible to estimate the importance to us of gaining free access to
United States markets for our coal." *Ibid.*
15. T. L. Tilley, to Sir John Macdonald, January 12, 1886, *John Macdonald Papers,
Washington Treaty, 1888,* vol. 2, MS Canadian Archives.
16. Goldwin Smith to Bayard, January 29, 1886, *Bayard MS.*

This proposition was more extensive than that of commercial reciprocity, for it implied a complete demolition of all tariff barriers between Canada and the United States, and it would place the Canadian Provinces on the same footing as the different States in the American Union. Some months earlier, Congressman R. W. Townshend had suggested the establishment of a commercial union that would comprise all the nations "on the American Continent," [17] and in Washington there was a great deal of talk about developing commercial intercourse along more liberal lines. But there were certain Republican leaders in the Senate who were more partisan than patriotic, and Senator Frye introduced on January 18, 1886, a resolution which opposed the appointment of the joint commission to consider the questions at issue between Canada and the United States.[18]

It was apparent to most observers in Washington, including the British Minister, that these Republican Senators were opposed to the negotiations of "any amicable agreement with Her Majesty's Government," [19] and in a letter to Lord Lansdowne he expressed the belief that there was "not much chance of either reciprocity or the appointment of a Commission." [20] During the course of an interview with Sackville-West on February 19, Bayard indicated his regret with reference to the animus that had been shown by Congress

. . . against the policy of the President as indicated by his recommendation for the appointment of a Commission and inveighed bitterly against those who had thwarted it. . . . He [Bayard] begged to assure me that he had not gone back from what he had always said to me with regard to reciprocity, free fish, and free fishing, or from his desire for more intimate commercial relations with Canada, but Congress seemed opposed to reciprocity.[21]

17. R. W. Townshend to Bayard, October 17, 1885, *ibid.*
18. *Congressional Record*, January 18, 1886, 49 Cong., 1 sess., vol. 17, pt. 1, pp. 702-703.
19. Sackville-West to Lord Salisbury, January 20, 1886, *John Macdonald Papers, Washington Treaty, 1888*, vol. 2, MS Canadian Archives.
20. Sackville-West to Lord Lansdowne, February 7, 1886, *ibid.*
21. Sackville-West to Lord Rosebery, February 19, 1886, *John Macdonald Papers, Governor-General's Correspondence*, vol. 13, MS Canadian Archives. In a letter to H. L. Nelson, December 19, 1885, Bayard remarked: "I say nothing of our other commercial relations with Canada whose long frontier renders the frictions of our present tariff laws excessive. We export and import almost an equal amount of some articles, to and from Canada, charging high duties on the same articles *both* ways, and I hope some sensible adjustment may be reached." *Bayard MS*. See also, Bayard to Frederick Fraley, August 1, 1885, *ibid.*

According to a table in the *Bayard Papers*, the total exports and imports between Canada and the United States, during the fiscal year 1886, were as follows:

The Senate opposition was able to have its way, and on April 13 the Frye resolution, against the appointment of a joint commission to deal with Canadian-American disputes, was adopted by a large vote.[22] When this was followed by the seizure of American vessels in Canadian waters for alleged infractions of the Treaty of 1818, a period of tension resulted. Bayard sent a note of protest to Sackville-West,[23] but the Canadian Government remained firm and they were supported with some reluctance by Great Britain.

Sackville-West suggested that the Treaty of 1818 be revised, and that some system of commercial reciprocity be established.[24] Bayard, however, realized that in the face of Senate opposition the question of reciprocity would have to be postponed. All that he could do was to exert pressure upon the British Government in an endeavor to persuade it to induce Canadian officials to be more moderate in their

Imports into the United States from:

(a) Nova Scotia, New Brunswick, Prince Edward Island	....	$ 4,556,980
(b) Quebec, Ontario, Manitoba and Northwest Territory	....	31,263,469
(c) British Columbia	....	1,483,587
(d) Newfoundland and Labrador	....	192,302
	Total....	$37,496,338

Exports from the United States to:

(a) Nova Scotia, New Brunswick, Prince Edward Island	....	$ 2,502,011
(b) Quebec, Ontario, Manitoba and Northwest Territory	....	26,301,962
(c) British Columbia	....	1,840,312
(d) Newfoundland	....	1,308,839
	Total....	$31,953,124

There are comparable figures on imports and exports from Canada in two letters from J. S. Moore to Bayard, May 31, and June 2, 1887, *Bayard MS.*

In a table prepared for Bayard by Worthington C. Ford, for the fiscal year ending June 30, 1886, the following important figures are given:

	Imported into United States		Exported from U. S. to Canada	
Commodity	*Value*	*Duty*	*Value*	*Duty*
Animals (living)	$3,163,740	$632,748	$ 369,633	$ 73,962
Breedstuffs	7,833,100	335,760	2,143,652	335,760
Coal	1,014,116	234,374	6,484,559	1,004,849
Fish	1,105,584	173,189	395,520	56,262
Hay	1,034,496	183,902	6,697	1,339
Provisions and Dairy				
Products	162,805	34,117	1,366,946	324,773
Vegetables	952,216	96,999	150,612	36,378
Wood and wood				
manufactures	7,515,756	751,274	861,127	233,289

22. *Congressional Record*, April 13, 1886, 49 Cong., 1 sess., vol. 17, p. 3440.

23. Secretary Bayard to Sackville-West, May 10, 1886, *British Legation, Notes to,* vol. 20. MS Dept. of State.

24. *Memorandum* written by Bayard after a conversation with Sackville-West, May 21, 1886, *Bayard MS.*

attitude towards the United States. But Bayard was of the opinion that the protectionist element in Congress was also responsible for the strained relations between the United States and Canada. In a letter to Phelps, at London, he alluded to the connection between the American tariff and the unfriendly attitude of Canada:

I have just written out such reference to the fishery subject as I shall advise the President to incorporate in his message to Congress, and in this I have broadly alluded to the general interests of inter-trade between Canada and the United States, and made expressions of favor in relation to a *freer* exchange of the natural productions of the two Countries. At the root of the differences between the United States and Canada lies the apparent injustice of not allowing the fish caught by both Canadians and Americans in the waters of the former, or by the use of their convenient ports and harbors as a base of fishing operations, to come into the American markets without discriminating duties on the Canadian share of the catch. Morrison's bill to reduce the Tariff which was defeated last summer, provided for free fish, and I cannot doubt that when a reformation of the Tariff System is achieved, that no tax on food will be retained.[25]

With relations between Canada and the United States steadily growing more strained as a result of Canadian seizures of American fishing vessels, the business interests of both countries made earnest efforts to find some basis for conciliation. S. J. Ritchie, of Akron, Ohio, who had important business connections in Canada, called on Bayard with a letter of introduction from Senator H. B. Payne,[26] and in the ensuing conversation, Bayard expressed his desire for freer trade relations between Canada and the United States, and assured Ritchie that he would be glad to work for a reciprocity treaty "if he thought the Senate would ratify it." Ritchie believed that a majority of the Senate was in favor of reciprocity, and it only required "someone on the

25. Secretary Bayard to Phelps, November 15, 1886, *Bayard MS.* In another personal letter to Phelps, December 17, 1886, Bayard makes the following similar comments: "The truth is, . . . whilst we must execute laws and treaties as they stand, yet it seems to me unwise and unreasonable to avoid the plain facts of the case which stand thus—the Canadians owning the territorial, natural, and convenient *base for fishery* operations, inshore and open-sea, and the United States having the natural and *best market,* for the product, each possessing something essential for the other. With these two main facts, what so natural, simple, and mutually beneficial as to allow an open market in the United States for fish in consideration of the free use of the bays, ports, waters, and land privileges appurtenant to the convenient prosecution of the business by our Fishermen? With the infinite superiority of our market for all fishery outfit and supplies, superiority in skill, in ship-building, and navigation, . . . is it not discreditable to our Fishermen to deny their ability to catch, carry home, and sell fish here in competition with the Canadians?" *Bayard Letter Book,* vol. 4, *Bayard MS.*

26. H. B. Payne to Bayard, December 8, 1886, *Bayard MS.*

ground thoroughly well-informed, to keep the members of both Houses stirred up and alive to the question." [27]

It was high time that something was done to arrange a settlement of the mounting difficulties between Canada and the United States. In January, 1887, legislation was introduced in Congress providing that whenever the President should be satisfied that American rights were being violated in Canadian waters, he was authorized, by proclamation, to deny to all vessels of the British Dominions of North America, any entrance into the ports of the United States.[28]

Phelps was delighted with this retaliatory legislation, and he expressed to Bayard the belief that Congress was "moving in the right direction." [29] But Bayard was very reluctant to carry out a policy of retaliation against Canada, and he hoped that some amicable solution for existing difficulties could be quickly found.[30] At this juncture, Mr. Ritchie again came into the picture at Washington. On January 31 he wrote a letter to Senator John Sherman, of Ohio, to inform him that he had sent a

. . . large amount of data concerning the trade relations between the United States and Canada to General Swaine, who is arranging it with reference to a bill being prepared by Major Butterworth in the House. I have written him to get all the results and hand them to you. I am greatly pleased with the view you take of this subject, and will perfect arrangements for taking the trip we have talked about.[31]

In accordance with Ritchie's directions, Butterworth introduced a bill in the House of Representatives (February 14, 1887) which provided for unrestricted commercial reciprocity between the United States and Canada.[32] At this time, Ritchie was visiting in Canada, and he immediately wrote to Bayard and enclosed a copy of the Toronto *Mail*. He believed that "unusual significance" was attached to the editorial in the *Mail* because of the fact

. . . that it is not only the leading newspaper in the Dominion but has always been the leading high tariff organ of the government. The proprietor of the New York *Times* told me yesterday that they would support this bill

27. Ritchie to Sir John Macdonald, December 9, 12, 1886, *John Macdonald Papers, Commercial Union, 1886–1887*, MS Canadian Archives.

28. *Congressional Record*, January 19, 1887, 49 Cong., 2 sess., vol. 18, pt. 1, p. 793.

29. Phelps to Secretary Bayard, January 25, 1887, *Bayard MS.*

30. Secretary Bayard to Phelps, February 7, 1887, *ibid.*

31. S. J. Ritchie to Senator John Sherman, January 31, 1887, *John Sherman Papers*, Library of Congress.

32. *Congressional Record*, 49 Cong., 2 sess., p. 1735.

as a solution of the whole difficulty between the U. S. and Canada. Mr. Jones even went so far as to say that "nobody but an idiot" would oppose it.[33]

There were certain Republican Senators who did not desire to have commercial union as a solution of the "whole difficulty" with Canada, and on February 24, 1887, Senator Hoar introduced a resolution which declared that it was the "judgment of the Senate that under present circumstances no negotiation should be undertaken with Great Britain in regard to existing difficulties with her province of Canada which has for its object the reduction, change, or abolition of any of our existing duties on imports."[34]

Senator J. M. Beck sent a copy of this resolution to Bayard, and on the bottom of it he wrote the following message: "I want information so as to resist this *infernal* proposition. It is now before the Finance Committee, and may come up on Monday or Tuesday. Mr. Sherman and Mr. Allison agree with me to oppose."[35]

In his reply to this note, Bayard made a scathing attack upon the Hoar resolution,[36] and in a personal letter to Phelps, he sharply condemned the tactics employed by certain Republican leaders:

You will recall in my personal notes to you, my estimate of the influential part in the Canadian question of the tariff taxation feature, and how the combination of two objects, one wholly mercenary, and the other wholly passionate and vindictive, created the chief, if not the only difficulties in the way of a just and temperate solution of the matters in dispute. The organization of the protected interests, and the organization for the redress of Irish wrongs at the hands of British Rulers are equally alert and vigorous to prevent a settlement that shall not include their respective gratification.

The Resolution introduced by Mr. Hoar, . . . will illustrate one of these objects, and the chorus of the whole Blaine pack, that the administration was cringing to Great Britain, etc., will serve to describe the other. Tariff reform is fast becoming a line of party arrangement, and the grapple with

33. S. J. Ritchie to Secretary Bayard, February 16, 1887, *Bayard MS.*
34. *Senate Misc. Doc. 82,* 49 Cong., 2 sess.
35. J. M. Beck to Secretary Bayard, February 25, 1887, *Bayard MS.* Bayard had long disliked Senator Hoar, and in a letter to David A. Wells, September 4, 1884, he gave the following estimate of the choleric Massachusetts statesman: "I was very glad to get your letter to the immaculate Hoar (I came near commencing the name with a 'W'), of which I had a pretty full extract in the New York *Post.* He is a singularly irritable man, and as *unjust* a man as I ever knew. I mean that it is almost incomprehensible to me that he can be honest." *David A. Wells Papers,* Library of Congress.
36. Bayard believed that the Hoar resolution was "unprecedented and proposes a palpable anticipation and interference with the prerogatives of the President. . . . [It] is only another proof . . . of the reckless, selfish, mercenary spirit of the protective system of taxation." Bayard to J. M. Beck, February 26, 1887, *Daniel Manning Papers,* Library of Congress.

entrenched and unjust privileges sheltered behind statutory taxations must soon take place. Under the light of reason and experience I believe these unjust and unnatural restraints upon the freedom of contact and exchanges, will go down, and should this be so, the exclusion of Canadian-caught fish from the markets of the United States will cease. Every proposed tariff measure introduced within the past four years has placed Fish on the free list.

With this question so imbedded in our domestic affairs, and its solution so provided for in the jurisdiction, it would seem wise and expedient for the British and Canadian governments not to increase the difficulties of those of us who are equally opposed to Dynamite and High duties. As it is, they seem almost designedly to be playing into the hands of the political Blifils and Black Georges.

On the other hand we can see an evidence of the awakening of other interests than those connected with salted fish, in the bill just introduced by Mr. Butterworth (Rep.), of Ohio, for full reciprocity of trade with Canada. He told me that John Sherman approved it, and I believe that to be true.[37]

Under strong pressure from many interests, President Cleveland approved on March 3, 1887, the bill introduced into Congress by Senator Edmunds, under the terms of which the President could establish commercial non-intercourse with Canada.[38] In response to this threat, Lord Salisbury indicated that the British Government was prepared to accept Bayard's suggestion for the appointment of a mixed commission to consider the best mode of effecting a settlement of the fisheries dispute.[39]

This new spirit of conciliation was approved by all Canadians who were interested in reciprocity or in commercial union with the United States. Edward Young, the American Consul at Windsor, Nova Scotia, reported that it was the "earnest desire of both parties, and of almost every individual in this Province, to have more intimate trade relations with the United States." [40] In Nova Scotia the idea of commercial union, as embodied in the Butterworth bill, was being widely discussed, and in the Halifax *Morning Chronicle,* there was a detailed discussion of the whole matter. Since the late election,

. . . many journals throughout the Dominion have been giving considerable attention to the discussion of the question of a commercial union, or as it is

37. Secretary Bayard to Phelps, February 26, 1887, *Bayard Letter Book,* vol. 4, *Bayard MS.*

38. *Foreign Relations, 1887,* pp. 466-467.

39. Marquis of Salisbury to Mr. White, March 24, 1887, enclosed in despatch from White to Secretary Bayard, March 30, 1887, *Great Britain, Despatches,* vol. 155, MS Dept. of State. Bayard's suggestion was made in the *modus vivendi* proposed in the instruction to Phelps, November 15, 1886, *Great Britain, Instructions,* vol. 28, MS Dept. of State.

40. Edward Young to Secretary Bayard, March 19, 1887, *Bayard MS.*

also called a customs union, between Canada and the United States. This union may be fairly described in brief as a reciprocity treaty, which shall provide for the free interchange between the two countries of all their products, both natural and manufactured, without any restrictions or interference of customs laws or customs officials. . . . Whatever views individual writers may have hitherto entertained, the question must now be discussed with constant reference to the bill recently introduced into the United States Congress by Mr. Butterworth, one of the Ohio members of the house of representatives. . . .

This is a larger measure of reciprocity than was ever before formally proposed between the two countries. That the people of this Dominion, and more especially of the lower provinces, have long been warmly in favor of a measure of unrestricted reciprocal trade with the United States there can be no doubt; but that they have seriously contemplated such a sweeping change as this, in the trade relations of the two countries, there is little reason to believe. . . .

The bill contemplates not a division of duties collected by both countries according to the population of each, but that each of the two countries should keep for her own use the duties collected in her own ports. . . . About two-fifths of our imports are from the United States, and of course the duties now paid on these imports would, under the proposed customs union, remain in the pockets of our people, and the Dominion treasury would be so much the poorer. Our customs revenue is now about $20,000,-000. . . . It would be reduced, if other things continued equal, to about $12,000,000. How would they get along on that pittance? [41]

In the United States, one of the most indefatigable supporters of the idea of commercial union was Erastus Wiman, a Canadian who had settled in New York City, and who had prospered in the land of his adoption. Wiman was President of the Great Northwest Telegraph Company which controlled many telegraph lines in Canada, and he was unwearied in his efforts to enlist "big business" in support of closer commercial relations between Canada and the United States. In his many pamphlets and articles, Wiman contended that the prosperity of the United States was largely due to the absence of tariff barriers between the different states. If these same barriers could be removed between Canada and the United States, there would be an enlarged prosperity for both countries. Not only would the American market be of inestimable benefit to the lumber, fishing, and agricultural industries of Canada, but it would also foster the development of Canadian manufactures. [42]

41. Halifax *Morning Chronicle*, March 15, 1887.

42. Wiman published pamphlets entitled *Commercial Union Between the United States and Canada* (Toronto, 1887); *Closest Trade Relations Between the United States*

In an open letter to Valancey E. Fuller, April 26, 1887, Wiman emphasized the view that the abolition of tariff walls along the Canadian-American frontier, would open to the Canadian farmer "a market such as the world has never equalled." All the advantages of an open market, with sixty millions of people, were within the easy grasp of the inhabitants of Canada.[43]

Another ardent advocate of commercial union was Goldwin Smith, a brilliant British historian and publicist who abandoned an Oxford career to settle in the United States and teach in Cornell University. In 1871 he moved to Toronto, Canada, where he founded the *Week* and the *Bystander*. From his editorial desk in Toronto, he spread the gospel of Anglo-Saxon unity on the North American continent. Canada and the United States should form one great nation, and as one of the means to accomplish this end, he strongly supported the idea of commercial union between the two countries.[44]

In Canada the manufacturing interests were opposed to commercial union, and this fact was made abundantly clear by Goldwin Smith. In the United States, however, many of the political leaders who were protectionists, and therefore identified with the manufacturing interests, were open advocates of commercial union. Bayard calls attention to this fact:

A proposition for unlimited reciprocity . . . has been introduced into the House of Representatives by Mr. Butterworth, and he had since been frequently to this department, accompanied by persons interested in the Canadian trade, and it is their purpose to have a great meeting called very shortly in the city of New York which is intended to give voice to a desire for reciprocity and free trade with Canada. The support of this plan is very marked from high protective sources, the Board of Trade in Philadelphia and other cities, and Blaine's . . . man, Hitt, of Illinois, has been very prominent in favoring a Commercial Union with Canada. . . .

If a treaty were now made it could not be confirmed until Congress meets in December, and if the sentiment for reciprocity grows (as seems now to be the case), the result desired by Canada will take place, i.e., free entry

---

and Canada (Toronto, 1892); *Commercial Union in North America* (N. Y. 1888); and several articles, the more important of which are as follows: "The Advantages of Commercial Union to Canada and the United States," *Canadian Leaves* (N. Y., 1887), pp. 269-281; "Can Canada be Coerced?" *North American Review*, January, 1891, vol. 152, pp. 91-102; "What is the Destiny of Canada?" *North American Review*, vol. 148, June, 1889, pp. 665-675; and "Reciprocity with Canada," *Engineering Magazine*, vol. 4, pp. 109-114.

43. *Bayard MS.*

44. Smith's most representative work, with reference to commercial union, was his book entitled *Canada and the Canadian Question* (Toronto, 1891). See also, *A Handbook of Commercial Union* (Toronto, 1888), to which Smith wrote an introduction.

into the United States. The delay in a settlement of the question is wholly attributable to Canadian political exigencies.[45]

Some economists in the United States looked upon the idea of commercial union with undisguised suspicion, and they warned Bayard against it. J. S. Moore was particularly opposed to such an arrangement:

To be perfectly frank, I think a "Zollverein" with Canada, as long as we groan under the present outrageous tariff, would be a misfortune, because we would be asked to carry some 6,000,000 Canadian infants and their infant industries on our backs until they grew up. I can understand a . . . revenue tariff and a "Zollverein," but under the present American tariff such a step simply means strengthening the enemies' camp. I would ere this have had my say, but I simply wish to avoid anything that would trench in the least upon any negotiations or correspondence that you must necessarily have just now.[46]

These counsels of Moore were partially offset by Wiman's numerous letters to Bayard.[47] It was due to Wiman's insistence that Sir Charles Tupper finally visited Washington to have a talk with Bayard. The following excerpts from that conversation are decidedly pertinent:

Sir Charles Tupper said his visit had better be regarded as private. . . . A strong movement was pressing forward reciprocity between Canada and the United States. The great difficulty you [Bayard] will at once see, is of Canada placing herself in a position of virtual hostility to Great Britain which would be done by adopting your tariff as against England, and except we do so, it would be impossible for you to accept a proposal of reciprocity because however carefully restrictions might be imposed, it would be virtually free trade between the United States and Great Britain. Therefore, I [Tupper] do not think the work Mr. Wiman is addressing himself to, is for the best interests of the both countries. But still it is doing good, for it is familiarizing the people with the ideas of reciprocity. . . .

A very great change has taken place in the position of Canada and the United States in regard to trade relations. The reciprocity treaty of 1854 was based upon the products of the farm, forest, and mine. Take the question of mines: After the abrogation of the Treaty of 1854, you imposed a duty upon

45. Secretary Bayard to Phelps, April 23, 1887, *Bayard Letter Book,* vol. 4, *Bayard MS.* Bayard and Smith became close friends, and in his *Reminiscences* (N. Y. 1911), p. 401, the brilliant British publicist makes the following comment upon Bayard: "One of my great friends at Washington was Mr. Bayard, a thoroughly high-bred and honourable politician. He was not the less admirable in my eyes for having at the outbreak of Secession bravely spoken against war; though his voice had been drowned in the roar of onset and he had long suffered in popularity as having been unpatriotic, when in truth he had behaved like the best of patriots. One of his claims to my esteem was that he was a sound free-trader."

46. J. S. Moore to Bayard, April 25, 1887, *Bayard MS.*

47. Erastus Wiman to Bayard, April 18, 22, 30, 1887, *ibid.*

coal and we adopted the same policy. At the same time there was a very important trade in coal between Nova Scotia, and New York and Boston. That has all changed by the natural course of events. Combination between the railway systems and the mines, and the consequent cheapening of transit has so changed affairs that if you made coal free tomorrow we should send comparatively no coal from that point, Nova Scotia, into the United States. Our coal owners would be unwilling to see free trade in coal. Your coal exports to Ontario have increased, notwithstanding the duty. . . . As to *Ores* (Magnetic Iron ores), you are large importers of this product from Canada, and free trade would increase that business to the benefit of your own iron founders. As to the farm, your advantages in that respect are so great that I do not think there would be any disposition to exchange. As to the forest, I think there would be no trouble as regards reciprocity. . . . We want an arrangement that will stand, not for eight or ten years, but forever. . . .

MR. BAYARD.—I may be very frank in stating to you that the feelings of myself and the President are strongly in favor of reciprocity, and that the disposition to a freer trade between the United States and Canada has gained ground with the present Administration. I had hoped at one time that Sir Lionel West would be authorized to make some arrangement with me, an arrangement founded on good will, mutual interests. . . . I do not myself see the slightest necessity for proceeding in a commercial union to the extent advocated by Messrs. Butterworth and Wiman. I suppose London would be selected for the purpose of arranging these matters. If it was only so far as reciprocity is concerned, I think this continent would be the proper place to carry on negotiations. The great point is to get an agreement which shall be the beginning of mutual good feeling and concession. If that can be done I shall be well content.

SIR C. TUPPER.—Great advantage was found in having the last negotiation conducted here. The Imperial Government have but one object—to meet as far as they are able, the views of Canada.

MR. BAYARD.—I have had no correspondence with Mr. West for three months on the subject. There has been no one here representing the government of Great Britain with whom I could have anything to say. . . .

SIR C. TUPPER.—Great as are our interests in reciprocal trade relations, yours are still greater. The people of Canada purchase $9 per head from the United States, while the United States purchase but 52 cents. . . . If, when our House rises, you should think proper to visit Canada, or Sir J. Macdonald or myself to come to see you, we might lay the basis of a treaty that would be mutually agreeable. . . . I must again repeat the desire of Great Britain to remain on friendly terms with the United States.

MR. BAYARD.—Yes; I feel that. We are, of course, the two guardians of the civilization of the world. . . . As far as any scheme or plan of reciprocity is concerned, I think it would be wiser that they should be conducted by a special Commission, which could sift the statistics of production and the present course of trade, which has changed so much in the last five years by the completion of this great road of yours (Canadian Pacific).

Sɪʀ C. Tᴜᴘᴘᴇʀ.—What is the wisest course to be pursued?

Mʀ. Bᴀʏᴀʀᴅ.—I cannot answer that now. I feel sure I can satisfy both Canadian and British Governments in regard to the formation of a commission. . . .

Sɪʀ C. Tᴜᴘᴘᴇʀ.—Suppose, then, you favor me or Sir J. Macdonald with a plan of the best course that you think would meet the object we have in view? . . .

Mʀ. Bᴀʏᴀʀᴅ.—I see no reason why that should not be done. We had better remove the location to Washington.

Sɪʀ C. Tᴜᴘᴘᴇʀ.—I quite agree to that. . . . No action will be taken until I hear from you.[48]

After a conversation with President Cleveland with regard to Canadian-American relations, Bayard wrote to Sir Charles Tupper and gave voice to the opinion that the best way to secure a "just and permanent settlement" of the outstanding questions at issue between the two countries, was through a "liberal and statesmanlike plan of the entire commercial relations of the two countries." In order clearly to show his desire to arrive at a friendly understanding with the governments of Canada and Great Britain, he was ready to "meet the authorized agents of Great Britain at this capital at the earliest possible day, and enter upon negotiations for a settlement of all differences." [49]

While Bayard was waiting upon the British Government to take some action with reference to the appointment of a mixed commission

48. *Memorandum* dictated by Bayard after a conversation with Sir Charles Tupper, May 21, 1887, *Bayard MS*. In a personal letter to Phelps, May 30, 1887, Bayard spoke as follows concerning his conversation with Tupper: "Ten days ago I had a message from West conveying Sir John Macdonald's inquiry whether I would be here, and upon my reply in the affirmative, I was soon called upon by Sir Charles Tupper, who is now the Minister of Finance of the Dominion and also holds the place of High Commissioner to the Imperial Government. . . . He came to propose negotiations, and was, of course, very friendly. He was opposed to a Commercial Union, but willing for reciprocity in certain staple productions. I agreed with him as to the Commercial Union, for it necessarily involves a blending of the systems of taxation, and is 'entangling' in the strongest sense. But he proposed to treat *here*, and after conversation with the President, I have determined to agree to it." *Bayard Letter Book*, vol. 5. *Bayard MS*.

49. Bayard to Sir Charles Tupper, May 31, 1887, quoted in Sir Charles Tupper, *Recollections of Sixty Years*, pp. 177-180. See also *Bayard Letter Book*, vol. 5, *Bayard MS*. In a personal letter to Phelps, May 31, 1887, Bayard informed him of the correspondence with Sir Charles Tupper. In conclusion, Bayard observed: "If the *principle* of a settlement on the basis of reciprocity is agreed upon in the treaty, the schedule of articles can be (must be) regulated by Legislation. If there is anything in John Sherman's profession of a desire for a 'Commercial Union' with Canada, there will be no difficulty in procuring a majority in the Senate for a bill that will include a settlement of the present difficulty." *Bayard Letter Book*, vol. 5, *Bayard MS*.

to deal with questions of dispute between Canada and the United States, he was receiving letters from some of his friends who were opposed to the idea of commercial union with Canada. On May 19, 1887, there was a public meeting in New York City in favor of commercial union, and Congressman Butterworth delivered an address. This meeting was sponsored by the Canadian Club, and it is worth noting that Erastus Wiman was the President of this organization.[50]

It was the opinion of J. S. Moore that this meeting on May 19 had

. . . fallen stale and dead, whilst in Canada it has aroused strong opposition. I don't think we are exactly ripe for anything like that. I have not taken a hand in it, nor do I intend to take one. A "Zollverein" with Canada, I am afraid, would mean to nurse Canadian industry, now that we have outgrown our own *infant industry*. Besides, how can England ever agree to allow American cotton goods to come in free in Canada, and see a duty of 40 per cent against her own manufactures?[51]

From Canada there came many voices that clearly indicated the strength of the movement in support of the idea of commercial union with the United States. Goldwin Smith wrote to Francis Wharton in a vein that could not be misunderstood. In the Dominion the debate on the question of commercial union had

. . . opened in earnest. The voice just heard on the subject is rather adverse, being in fact that of the protected manufacturers who form a compactly organized body ready at once to take the field, while the great natural industries of the country, agriculture, lumbering, mining, and shipping, are without organization and are therefore slow to move. But when the great natural industries are roused to exertion and bring their influence to bear, the result can hardly be doubtful. It is alleged by the Separatists that England would never consent to a measure which would involve discrimination against her goods in favour of those of a foreign country. But Sir Charles Tupper's import duty on iron emphasizes the fact that of the Commercial Unity of the Empire, not a shred remains; and I do not think it will be impossible or even very difficult to convince England that she could be a gainer in the long run by the opening of a free trade between Canada and the United States.

A friendly division of the Empire, such was the footing on which the two

50. Erastus Wiman to Bayard, May 13, 1887, enclosing circulars, *Bayard MS.*

51. J. S. Moore to Bayard, May 21, 1887, *Bayard MS.* In a second letter to Bayard, May 31, 1887, Moore again remarks: "The more I think over this Canadian 'Zollverein,' the more I come to the conclusion of its present impracticability. Under our present tariff system it means protection prolonged, and reminds me very much of the slave States being anxious 40 years ago to plant the slave system in Kansas and other new States. Happily, the Canadians are against it, and England could not think of it. What good can come from such a cynic and man-hater as Professor Goldwin Smith?" *Ibid.*

sections of our race ought to have been placed after the inevitable separation. I do not despair of seeing a return to it.[52]

Press discussion of commercial union did not take place on a wide scale until after the announcement by the British and American Governments of the appointment of a mixed commission to deal with the more important points at issue between Canada and the United States. With regard to reciprocity between the two countries, the Halifax *Morning Herald* called attention to the fact that the United States was "not the chief market for the products of the mines, the forests, or the farms of Nova Scotia." It was essential that the "home market" in Canada should not be injured by any negotiations with the United States.[53] This statement in the Halifax *Herald* aroused the advocates of commercial union into instant activity.

On October 14 Sir Richard Cartwright, one time Finance Minister of the Dominion and an outstanding member of the Liberal Party in Canada, came out strongly in favor of commercial union with the United States: "I have no hesitation in saying frankly that if the United States are willing to deal with us on equitable terms, the advantages of commercial union to both countries, and especially to us, are so great that scarcely any sacrifice is too severe to secure them." [54]

Erastus Wiman rushed into print in an interview with a reporter from the Toronto *Globe*. With regard to commercial union, he believed that in the United States "there was no public sentiment of any weight as yet in regard to the matter." But the Butterworth bill had awakened interest in Congress in unrestricted reciprocity with Canada, and he thought there was a "very good chance" that it might pass the House of Representatives. He hoped that the Senate would regard commercial union "as the best settlement possible of the Fishery question." It was almost certain that this measure was "the only alternative that Secretary Bayard will favor." [55]

Some of the Canadian papers were greatly exercised over Joseph Chamberlain's remark that if Canada desired commercial union "she

52. Goldwin Smith to Francis Wharton, June 11, 1887, *Bayard MS.*
53. October 10, 1887.   54. New York *Times*, October 15, 1887.
55. Toronto *Globe*, October 15, 1887. On April 2, 1887, the *Globe* had published a series of letters from farmers who desired unrestricted reciprocity with the United States. For other comments in the *Globe* on commercial union, see the issues of September 20, October 26, 30, 1887. For other favorable press comments upon commercial union, see the Ottawa *Free Press*, July 19, 1887, the Montreal *Herald*, July 15, 1887, and the Manitoba *Free Press*, July 13, 1887.

must be made to know that it means political separation from Great Britain." In commenting upon this statement, the Toronto *Mail* remarked: "His threat will probably not disturb the friends of Commercial Union, nor diminish the enthusiasm which the movement is evoking in every part of the country." [56] The Montreal *Witness* believed that the only conclusion that could be reached "from Mr. Chamberlain's remarks is either that he has allowed himself flippantly to prejudge the most important matter ever placed before him without weighing his words, or that his solution of Canadian difficulties with the United States is . . . to hand Canada over as a contemptible mischief-maker to the United States." [57]

In commenting upon Chamberlain's remark that commercial union would mean the erection of a protective tariff against Great Britain, Goldwin Smith pointed out that the Dominion had already enacted "a protective tariff against Great Britain, which has recently been extended to iron amidst the wails of British producers, and which it is the constant aim of our protectionists to increase." [58]

According to an Ottawa despatch to the Boston *Herald*, Lord Lansdowne was "strongly in sympathy with the movement towards closer commercial relations with the United States," [59] and at St. John, New Brunswick, the President of the Board of Trade came out in favor of commercial union "because of mutual benefits enjoyed during the previous treaty." [60]

In the United States it was significant that stalwart Republican papers like the *Tribune* were in favor of commercial union with Canada. In passing judgment upon Chamberlain's remarks concerning this close commercial relationship between the United States and Canada, the *Tribune* acidly observed: "As commercial union is now regarded by the leading men and journals of both parties as absolutely necessary for the well-being of Canada, Mr. Chamberlain has succeeded in prejudicing public feeling beyond the frontier strongly against himself. The people of the Dominion look upon reciprocity in the form of

---

56. October 17, 1887.   57. October 17, 1887.
58. Toronto *Mail*, October 18, 1887.   59. October 28, 1887.
60. New York *Herald*, October 30, 1887. In commenting upon the spread of the idea of commercial union in Canada, Erastus Wiman remarked: "The progress of the movement in favor of commercial union in Canada is one of the most remarkable events that has ever occurred in any community. Though originating less than nine months ago in the bill introduced into Congress by Mr. Butterworth, of Ohio, the question is now the most familiar one in Canada." New York *Sun*, October 23, 1887.

commercial union as the only permanent solution of the questions now at issue between them and the United States." [61]

In Portland, Maine, Marshall N. Rich, Secretary of the Board of Trade, expressed the opinion that the people of Maine wanted a "fair reciprocity treaty, and in the course of years we shall get back to it. If commercial union is synonymous with fair reciprocity. I favor commercial union." [62] A. J. Fuller, President of the Bath Board of Trade, openly declared that he was "in favor of a commercial union between the two countries so guarded as to be a mutual benefit to both countries." J. E. Blabon, President of the Portland Board of Trade, was equally desirous of closer commercial relations between Canada and the United States: "I have always believed in reciprocity. . . . I have not studied into the matter of commercial union; but, if it is reciprocity, I believe in it." [63]

In New York City, the Chamber of Commerce held its regular monthly meeting on November 3, 1887, and, under the inspiration of Erastus Wiman, it adopted a resolution which provided for the appointment of a committee to study the question of commercial union.[64] In commenting upon this action, the New York *Evening Post* remarked: "The action taken by the Chamber of Commerce yesterday, . . . is important as showing that this question has penetrated the business community. . . . The treaty may fall short of the wishes of those who advocate complete commercial union, but it will almost certainly lead to such a union in the end." [65]

The New York *Sun* called the attention of its readers to the fact that the Inter-Provincial Conference in Canada had adopted a declaration in favor of commercial union with the United States.[66] The Toronto *Mail* believed that this declaration had "fallen like a bombshell in the opposite camp." Sir Charles Tupper might "poohpooh this important declaration, but neither Mr. Chamberlain nor Lord Salisbury is likely to do so; whilst Mr. Bayard must be more than ever satisfied with the suggestion he made at the outset, namely that the best way out of the difficulties surrounding the fishery question lay in establishing closer trade relations between the two countries." [67]

61. October 24, 1887.   62. Portland *Argus*, October 20, 1887.
63. *Ibid.*, November 5, 1887.   64. New York *Herald*, November 4, 1887.
65. November 4, 1887.   66. November 14, 1887.
67. November 12, 1887. On November 4, the Toronto *Mail* published a long letter from Goldwin Smith which was devoted to the rapid spread in Canada of the idea of commercial union. In this same issue, the *Mail* also published a statement from Mr. Longley,

The movement in favor of commercial union reached its peak on December 28, 1887, when a banquet was held in Boston to which were invited some 250 guests. From Canada there was a large delegation headed by J. W. Longley, the Attorney-General of Nova Scotia, W. Mulloch, Vice-Chancellor of Toronto University, and James Perrault, Vice-President of the Montreal Chamber of Commerce. From Washington the following Congressmen came: Joseph McKenna, J. J. Rogers, William Hitt, W. C. P. Breckinridge, and Nelson Dingley. Jonathan Lane, the President of the Merchants' Association of Boston, made an address in which he dwelt upon the advantages to Boston of commercial union. He was followed by Erastus Wiman, who emphasized the economic blessings that would descend upon both Canada and the United States in the event of commercial union. J. W. Longley publicly proclaimed that he was "both a commercial unionist and an annexationist," and Congressmen Hitt and Rogers promised their continued support of the Butterworth bill then before Congress.[68]

While the press of Canada and the United States was busily discussing reciprocity and commercial union, Bayard was engaged upon the task of preparing for the meeting of the mixed commission that was to settle the outstanding disputes between Canada and the United States. The terms of reference that were finally agreed upon, confined the work of the mixed commission to the adjustment of

. . . all or any questions relating to rights of fishery in the seas adjacent to British North America and Newfoundland which are in dispute between the Governments of Her Britannic Majesty and that of the United States of America, and any other questions which may arise, and which they may be authorized by their respective Governments to consider.[69]

In the interval between the discussion of the terms of reference and

---

the Attorney-General of Nova Scotia, who strongly favored commercial union between Canada and the United States. In the New York *Herald*, December 11, 1887, William McDougall, an eminent Canadian lawyer, was quoted as saying that the idea of commercial union had spread in Canada "as spontaneously as the light of the morning."

On December 13, 1887, Erastus Wiman wrote to Bayard a note which introduced William McDougall. According to Wiman, McDougall was visiting Washington "in the interest of the Great Party in Canada who are desirous of a closer commercial relation with the United States, and his views and information, will, I am sure, be of great value to you. He is not in sympathy with the existing Government, but I am certain that he more correctly represents the state of public sentiment in Canada than any man you have met." *Bayard MS.*

68. In the Boston *Post*, December 29, 1887, there is a full account of this banquet with several of the speeches reproduced in full.

69. Secretary Bayard to Sackville-West, September 14, 21, and October 19, 1887, *Bayard MS.*

the meeting of the mixed commission in Washington, Bayard received many letters relative to reciprocity and commercial union. Bradley T. Johnson, after a vacation in Nova Scotia, wrote to Bayard to inform him that the "protected classes" in Canada opposed commercial union, but the "commercial classes and general public" favored it.[70] Consul M. H. Phelan, at Halifax, assured Bayard that the Liberals in Canada who were

. . . in favor of Commercial Union with the United States, believe that the fishery troubles will aid them in accomplishing it. They are opposed to the Conference because it will remove these troubles. One of the leaders told me that the party would fight it, and would oppose the ratification of any agreement the Conference may arrive at, the more favorable the harder they will fight, as Commercial Union would not only settle the fisheries but all other questions between the two countries.[71]

On October 18 Phelan wrote again to Bayard with reference to J. W. Longley, the Attorney-General of Nova Scotia. Longley was about to leave for Quebec in order to attend the Inter-Provincial conference. After the conference had adjourned, Longley intended to go to

. . . New York to meet Butterworth by appointment, . . . thence to Washington to get your views on the subjects to be discussed at the coming international conference. Longley is one of the leaders of *Commercial Union,* and I believe the father of the movement. He is an *annexationist,* bold and indiscreet in his utterances, and if an opportunity presents itself, you will learn some of the absurdities of Canadian politics.[72]

Through Francis Wharton, Bayard received some further comments by Goldwin Smith. Smith, writing from Toronto, thought there could be

. . . no doubt whatever as to the progress which the movement for Commercial Union is making here. A manufacturer writing in the Toronto *Globe* the other day, stated his conviction that seven-eighths of the people were in

70. Bradley T. Johnson to Bayard, September 7, 1887, *Bayard MS.* In a letter to President Cleveland, September 2, 1887, W. H. Morrell expressed the opinion that "Commercial Union is not yet possible, but extended and enlarged inter-communication is very desirable, and will lead ultimately to free trade with the Dominion, provided they shut out British manufactures." *Cleveland MS.* Erastus Wiman wrote to President Cleveland, September 17, 1887, with regard to commercial union. He was certain that the subject was one of "large importance and deep interest. Its desirability as a mode of settlement of the fishery question, and other causes of friction, between the two countries is apparent; while its practicability at this time seems likely, if the question is approached in a liberal and progressive spirit. Results highly advantageous to the United States, as well as to Canada, would certainly follow its consummation, and it is difficult to definitely designate the interests which would be adversely affected." *Cleveland MS.*
71. M. H. Phelan to Bayard, October 13, 1887, *Bayard MS.*
72. M. H. Phelan to Bayard, October 18, 1887, *Bayard MS.*

favor of the measure. I suspect that he was not far from the mark. Sir Richard Cartwright, our best financier and the real thing, not the nominal leader of the Liberal opposition, as you may perhaps have seen, has come out distinctly on our side. He was a Conservative before he was a Liberal, and he retains much of his conservative feeling against Annexation which will account to you for his dwelling rather dolefully on the danger of that result.[73]

There is little doubt that in certain circles in Canada there was a strong feeling in favor of either commercial union or of some liberal plan for reciprocity with the United States. This favorable view of an enlarged commercial policy was clearly reflected in a confidential despatch from Lord Lansdowne to the Colonial Office. He believed that commercial union would be of distinct benefit to the people of Canada. There could be little doubt that such a system would help Canadian agriculture, but there was also the possibility that it would injure some of the manufacturing industries that had developed as a result of the Canadian protective tariff. With reference to the political implications of commercial union, Lansdowne was of the opinion that if it went into effect, the center "of political activity in regard to all commercial questions affecting the North American Continent would inevitably be at Washington." This would mean, of course, closer ties between Canada and the United States. In the event that the British Government should

. . . deny to Canada the advantages of free trade with the United States, the refusal could be defended only upon what would be regarded as purely selfish grounds. A large section of the Canadian community would no doubt be averse to the change both for sentimental and patriotic reasons, and from dread of its ultimate results; it is however, in my opinion by no means certain that these feelings will prevail in the end, or that, should the constituencies become convinced that Commercial Union is within their reach, and discrimination would enrich their country and relieve them from disagreeable complications with their neighbors, they will have the courage to oppose it. . . .

The different sections of the country are geographically so widely separated from each other and so closely connected with the adjoining portions of the United States, that it is impossible to believe that both do not lose largely by the hindrances which a Customs line with a high tariff, including on each side an infinite number of commodities, imposes upon their commercial transactions, or that each would not gain by the removal of those hindrances and by the unrestricted flow of trade along its natural channels.[74]

73. Goldwin Smith to Francis Wharton, October 18, 1887, *ibid.*
74. Lansdowne to the Colonial Office, October 31, 1887, *John Macdonald Papers, Commercial Union, 1886–1887,* MS Canadian Archives.

Joseph Chamberlain showed a copy of this despatch to Sir Charles Tupper, who forwarded it to Sir John Macdonald. Sir John read the despatch with "some regret, but without surprise," because he had long known that Lansdowne was a "free trader to the bone, and all such men are deaf and blind to any other considerations but the blind teachings of abstract political economy." Macdonald, however, was not much worried about the effect of Lansdowne's despatch. Since November, 1887,

> . . . all the federal elections have gone against Commercial Union. The *Globe* has abandoned it in despair and taken up the harmless cry of free trade. Leading men of the opposition . . . have denounced Commercial Union. . . . Commercial Union is a dead duck, and I think Lord Lansdowne sees now that my policy, as announced to him last spring, of allowing the cry of Commercial Union to blaze, crackle, and go out with a stink, without giving it undue importance, was a wise one.[75]

Joseph Chamberlain landed in New York City on November 7, and on November 15 he had an interview with J. S. D. Thompson, the Canadian Minister of Justice. He informed Thompson that he had

> . . . seen a good many in N. York who referred to the coming conference. Most of them had expressed great doubt that anything would come of it. . . . He had seen some one who professed to be in Mr. Bayard's confidence who stated that Mr. Bayard's view was that the business of the Conference should be confined to a relaxation of the Treaty of 1818. In reply to these suggestions, Mr. Chamberlain had said, in a manner indicating a willingness that it should be communicated to Mr. Bayard, that he could not believe such to be Mr. Bayard's view, "else why should he have put us all to the trouble of coming here?" In this connection Mr. Chamberlain said last night at dinner that the situation could not be improved, even for the Americans, by returning to the treaty of 1783, if they should think of asking for such a thing, because there would be no improvement in substituting for a treaty which the Americans are dissatisfied with, a treaty which we should be dissatisfied with.
>
> Mr. Wiman has been very effusive to Chamberlain, who told him that this was a case in which frankness was a virtue, and that he therefore felt compelled to say that the B. Government would not listen to the proposal for Commercial Union between the United States and Canada while Canada remained in the British Empire. Chamberlain said that he had discussed the matter with Lord Salisbury who held that there could be no doubt about this.[76]

75. Sir John Macdonald to Sir Charles Tupper, January 15, 1888, *John Macdonald Papers, Commercial Union, 1886–1887,* MS Canadian Archives.

76. J. S. D. Thompson to Sir John Macdonald, November 18, 1887, *John Macdonald Papers, Washington Treaty, 1888,* MS Canadian Archives.

At the first meeting of the mixed commission, November 22, 1887, there was serious disagreement as to the scope of the terms of reference. Chamberlain and Tupper had hoped to have the conference deal with the question of commercial relations between the United States and Canada as well as the fisheries question. But Bayard realized that the Senate would not approve a treaty which included a provision for reciprocity with Canada, and he flatly refused to go beyond the explicit language of the terms of reference. An intimation was given, however, to the effect that if a satisfactory adjustment of the fisheries dispute was reached, Congress might be willing to grant some concessions to Canadian products.[77]

On December 10 the commission reached a deadlock, and further meetings were adjourned until January, 1888. This interlude gave Chamberlain an opportunity to visit Canada where he could discuss the fisheries question with Canadian officials. While in Canada, he attended a banquet given by the Toronto Board of Trade. In reply to the toast, "The Commercial Interests of the Empire," he remarked, in part, as follows:

I want to point out to you that we hear a little too much about antagonism of interests. Our interests are your interests and those of the Mother Country, and I will go further and say those of the United States, all lie in the same direction. . . . I refuse to speak or to think of the United States of America as a foreign nation. We are all of the same race and blood. . . . I am in favor of the widest possible commercial union and intercourse not only with the United States, but with all the world. That is the true Unrestricted Reciprocity. There is, however, a restricted reciprocity which would make you dependent for your financial freedom upon the Government of another State, and perhaps pave the way for the surrender of something which is still more important—I mean your political independence.[78]

According to James L. Garvin, the effect of Chamberlain's speech in Toronto, on December 30, 1887, was so overwhelming that it swept from Canadian hearts all further thoughts of commercial union with the United States:

Old eyes were blind with tears, but saw in vision again the island that had bred them long ago and still could breed a leader. It seemed as though the shouting would never end. Of late there had been much talk of slipping into silent secession from the Empire by commercial union with the United

77. See *ante*, p. 529.
78. Toronto *Globe*, December 31, 1887.

States. The morning after this speech that idea was dead in Toronto and weakened throughout the Dominion.[79]

Garvin was very badly mistaken in believing that the idea of commercial union was dead in Toronto after Joseph Chamberlain's speech. In a letter to Bayard, February 20, 1888, Goldwin Smith gave an assurance that commercial union was gaining a

. . . hold on the popular mind. Forty-three of the Farmers' Institutes in this Province have declared in its favor, while only two or three have demurred. Our lumbermen are for it; so indeed are all our natural industries, the only opponents on commercial grounds being our protected manufacturers, and by no means all of these. Could the question be disengaged from party issues and presented directly to our people, there can be little doubt what the verdict would be. If the proposal were made by your people to ours, I do not believe that any Canadian Government would have power to reject it.[80]

The fact that the mixed commission had confined all its efforts to an attempted settlement of the fisheries dispute, was not discouraging to the advocates of commercial union. In the early months of 1888 they redoubled their efforts in its favor. On January 23, Butterworth introduced a resolution which declared that the American Government should, "in the interest of peace and amity between nations, and in response to the demands of our manufacturers," remove all "obstacles and hindrances to complete and unrestricted trade and commerce between the United States and the Dominion of Canada." [81] On February 6, he followed this resolution with a bill which made provision for "full reciprocity" with Canada.[82]

Mr. Hitt, of Illinois, was not to be outdone by Butterworth in his show of zeal for commercial union, so on March 5, 1888, he introduced a joint resolution intended to "promote commercial union with Canada." [83] Ten days later (March 16), Hitt reported his resolution back from the House Committee on Foreign Affairs, with a favorable recommendation,[84] and it finally passed the House of Representatives on March 1, 1889, without a record vote.[85]

79. *The Life of Joseph Chamberlain* (London, 1933), vol. 2, pp. 333-335.
80. Goldwin Smith to Bayard, February 20, 1888, *Bayard MS*.
81. *Congressional Record*, 50 Cong., 1 sess., vol. 19, pt. 1, p. 635. See also, *House Misc. Doc. 133*. On July 19, 1888, the Chicago *Tribune* expressed the view that a number of influential Canadians approved Butterworth's resolution. In the Dominion there was a "powerful and growing sentiment in favor of free trade with the United States and of ultimate annexation."
82. *Congressional Record*, 50 Cong., 1 sess., vol. 19, pt. 1, p. 984.
83. *Ibid.*, pt. 2, p. 1746.
84. *Ibid.*, pt. 3, 2157. See also, *House Report 1183*, 50 Cong., 1 sess.
85. *Ibid.*, 50 Cong., 2 sess., vol. 20, pt. 3, p. 2539.

In the Senate, Mr. Hale, of Maine, introduced a resolution (January 16, 1888) which authorized the admission, duty free, of the products of "certain North American provinces" which may have applied for admission into the American Union.[86] This action served as a prelude to the introduction by Senator Frye of a resolution which called upon the Committee on Foreign Relations to prepare a statement on Canadian trade, population, railroads, canals, and other pertinent topics.[87]

Bayard was bitterly opposed to the resolution introduced by Senator Hale. He regarded it as

. . . an expression of disrespect and unfriendliness to Great Britain, by suggesting a dismemberment of her Empire and a consequent disregard of her laws without her consent or even without consultation with her. It is an intensified expression of the intent we protest against in the action of Canada—that is to *compel* a reduction of our Tariff laws by refusing decent treatment of our Fishermen until we shall admit Canadian Fish free of duty. Hale proposes to keep up the present Tariff until Canadian Provinces shall be compelled to enter the American Union.[88]

It was not always easy, however, for Bayard to retain this objective attitude towards Great Britain and her representatives. During the meetings of the mixed commission, there were moments when his patience was sorely tried by the actions of Chamberlain, Tupper, and Sackville-West. In a memorandum of January 14, 1888, he gives free rein to his feelings:

While partaking fully of the desire to adjust every cause of difficulty in a spirit of the most liberal concession, . . . we should be lacking in that candor and good faith which is essential to all affairs, if we did not bring as impressively as we can to the attention of our associates, the political condition of the case as exhibited by the Act of March last, and to advert to the conservative disposition exhibited by the Executive in not allowing its provisions to be enforced.

We owe nothing to the Canadian govt. during this past December, and their officials here really played into the hands of enemies in the United States in the most amazing manner. Even after Sir Charles Tupper's visit here in May, when negotiations had actually commenced, they seemed anxious to create all the irritation possible—refusing clearance to vessels putting in under the eye of their cruisers for shelter, and compelling them to remain within the three-mile limit when they wanted to get away; enforcing pilotage upon a fleet of weather-beaten fishing boats putting into Halifax in distress, etc. . . .

86. *Congressional Record,* 50 Cong., 1 sess., vol. 19, pt. 1, p. 474.
87. *Ibid.,* p. 789. See also, *Senate Misc. Doc. 43,* 50 Cong., 1 sess.
88. *Memorandum* written by Bayard and undated. *Bayard MS.*

The great and paramount end in view is not a . . . special treaty or agreement, but the establishment of good feeling and friendly relations between the two countries. With *that* once set afoot, the *rest* will come easily, and by easy stages. . . .

We have sought to give you [British representatives], and I believe you now have full knowledge of our views, and of the impossibility of the acceptance by the United States and their people of the Canadian interpretation and application of the Treaty of 1818. It is thus plain that great commercial and material interests, the fortunes of many and the daily occupations of many thousands of worthy people, are imperilled and even more profound and disastrous results may be involved. . . .

It must be always borne in mind that no change in the Tariff can be accomplished by *Treaty alone*. The action of the House of Representatives is equally essential in every such case. No one idea created more resentment in the United States than that the treatment of our Fishermen by Canada was intended to compel Tariff reduction. Lord Lansdowne's despatches plainly stated this, as did the arguments and replies of the Privy Council of the Dominion. I wish to avoid this issue because nothing but danger attends it. In this we submit that this commission will most wisely leave as much as possible of the desired reciprocity in trade to be worked out . . . by Congress.

No view would be broad enough that did not include the condition of *political parties* in the United States, and our action must be instructed by it if we desire to avoid failure. The issue against excessive Tariff duties has been clearly and unequivocally raised by the Executive in his last message. It has stirred the whole country, and the two great parties are aligning themselves upon these lines to contest in a few months the control of the Executive branch and its power.

We need an abatement of *irritation,* if we can with patience deal with existing difficulties. I believe the growth of mutual and inter-dependent interests will heal all wounds. . . .

The American plenipotentiaries have been impressed, and wish to impress their associates, with the wisdom and expediency of leaving Tariff changes in the interests of reciprocity to be accomplished by concerted legislation. Canada has already provided for contingent reciprocity in free entry of certain products. If Fish and Fish-oils can go on the United States free list, Canada will get the benefit *without paying any price for it.*

Commercial Union. We may agree that it is impracticable, yet we will also agree that a liberal system of reciprocity may be obtained by free exchanges, and through voluntary concerted legislation. That a strong disposition exists in the public mind on this subject, has been variously exhibited, and happily, in the United States no party expression has accompanied it. Is it not obvious that if this current of sentiment is not arrested, that much *freer trade* must soon take place between Canada and Newfoundland and the United States? Should anything be done which would tend to check this desirable state of things? . . .

We earnestly desire to seek an opportunity for Canada and Newfoundland to have access to their best and most necessary market, and at the same time to save their govt. all cost of policing their shores at cost greater than the duties they at present pay . . . on their fish, for more than half . . . come in free already. . . .

We feel the point arrived at is critical in our conference, and we desire in the spirit I have expressed, to come as close to you as we can—so close that you can easily close up the gap.[89]

During the meetings of the mixed commission Bayard was conspicuously fair in his attitude towards the questions at issue. On February 15, 1888, the Bayard-Chamberlain treaty for the adjustment of the fisheries dispute was signed, and on February 20, President Cleveland sent it to the Senate. In a letter to W. L. Putnam, Bayard gave an excellent survey of the background of the treaty, and he made some very illustrative comments upon the attitude and actions of Joseph Chamberlain during the sessions of the mixed commission:

The spirit of haste seems to be bred in the bone of our Canadian cousins, and their proposition to discharge the poor little *Adams*, and discontinue proceedings against the *Doughty* on the condition that no damage should be claimed, is a very weak and unwise performance. . . .

I can learn little or nothing here about the prospects of the treaty in the Senate. I sent to the President today the remainder of the correspondence on the subject to date, and the formal (and empty) joint protocols of our conferences. I fear Chamberlain is disingenuous, at least in the matter of papers passed in the conferences, and distinctly agreed to on both sides as part of the record. He has been uncandid and unsatisfactory. With my notes and Mr. Moore's, however, I believe we can establish the true proceedings. Mr. Bergne's memory too was slippery, but he took refuge behind Chamberlain's orders, and remembered only when it was convenient. Enough, however, is in print to make our position throughout perfectly clear and consistent.

Chamberlain told me on the occasion of his farewell call, that a leading Republican Senator, one of the numerous candidates for the Presidency, had told him he had not read the treaty, but that "they (the Reps.) could not afford to allow this Administration to do anything." C. said it made him very angry, as well it might. But he thought they would hesitate long before rejecting.

Do you see the proof of what we told the British Plenipotentiaries about Canada's interests in our tariff, which is shown in the proposed bill from the Committee on Ways and Means? Free wool, free lumber, free vegetables,

89. *Memorandum* written by Bayard on scratch paper, January 14, 1888, *Bayard MS.* It is evident that this memorandum contains the gist of some of the conversations that Bayard had with the British representatives on the mixed commission dealing with the fisheries question.

are worth ten times over free fish to Canada. She fought for the last and did not get it, and the first three will probably come without application. No more severe commentary upon the miserably unwise policy which dictated the treatment of our Fishermen in 1886–7 could be found than in this very tariff bill. Who can doubt that Fish would have been put on the free list but for Canadian action? Whatever may be the present fate of our treaty, a lesson has been given which I believe will be permanently instructive and productive of lasting good results.[90]

In March, 1888, Sir Richard Cartwright introduced into the Canadian House of Commons a resolution which strongly favored commercial union with the United States.[91] On March 26, 1888, Cartwright wrote to Bayard and enclosed a copy of the speech he had made in support of his resolution. He was certain that if Bayard chose to make an inquiry, he would find that the resolution and speech represented

. . . the real wishes of the *people* of Canada very much more than the division thereon in our present House of Commons is likely to do, and that if a vote on the subject were taken in our several local legislatures (which is the nearest approach to a plebiscitum our constitution allows), the majorities in its favour would be overwhelming. Permit me to add that . . . I have often and publickly borne testimony to my high appreciation of the good will and kindly feeling displayed by yourself and the President towards Canada.[92]

In reply to this friendly overture, Bayard stated that there

. . . are necessary results of propinquity which neither can nor ought to be overlooked in framing the regulations for the commercial intercourse between co-terminous States. Such contiguity imposes conditions of its own, and trade regulations are idle that do not respect these conditions. . . . The laws of health, moral no less than physical, demand respect for the nature of man; and two neighboring communities to be happy with each other must be useful to each other. Therefore, all reciprocal commerce and convenience that can be induced and fostered between the people of Canada and those of the United States meets my approval, and to the welfare of both countries I heartily wish God Speed.[93]

It was Goldwin Smith's opinion that the Cartwright resolution would undoubtedly

. . . be defeated at Ottawa and probably the majority against it will be large, but this only means that the present Parliament was elected upon a

90. Bayard to W. L. Putnam, March 3, 1888, *Bayard Letter Book*, vol. 7, *Bayard MS.*
91. Canada, House of Commons, *Debates*, 1888, March 14, 1888, vols. 25-26, pp. 144ff.
92. Sir Richard J. Cartwright to Bayard, March 26, 1888, *Bayard MS.*
93. Bayard to Sir Richard Cartwright, March 31, 1888, *Bayard Letter Book*, vol. 7, *Bayard MS.*

different issue, and that Ministerialists vote with the ministry. The next election, three years hence, may tell a different tale. There has been a meeting of "Imperial Federationists" and Protectionists combined, at Toronto, at which violent appeals were made to my sentiment and angry abuse was showered upon the United States. But this only shows that the Union and Protectionists are claimed by the program of Commercial Union.[94]

When Cartwright's resolution was defeated in the Canadian House of Commons, Smith wrote to Bayard to assure him that this action was not

. . . the decision of the Canadian people, but simply that of a Parliament elected before Commercial Union had come into the field, upon a totally different issue, viz., the North-Western Rebellion and the execution of Riel. Largely also, it is a Parliament elected by corruption, which has prevailed in Canadian politics in the absence of any really great question. The next general election, if I am not much mistaken, will tell a very different tale.

The Commercial Unionists have been gaining victories in the . . . elections notwithstanding the strenuous efforts of the Tory government to crush the movement. . . . Nothing, in my judgment, can prevent the progress of the movement on our side of the line . . . except a false step in the revision of your Tariff.[95]

Cartwright himself was worried over the possibility that President Cleveland might enforce the provisions of the Act of March 3, 1887, which would lead to commercial non-intercourse with Canada. He wrote to Erastus Wiman in this regard,[96] and Wiman drafted a reply which he enclosed in a letter to Bayard. In this reply, Wiman assured Cartwright that he need not have "any apprehension in the matter." If the President would attempt to enforce the Act of March 3, it would "ruin his chances for the Presidency." [97]

Bayard's answer to Wiman was guarded but friendly, and it must have relieved any worries about the President's attitude towards the enforcement of retaliatory legislation. Bayard indicated that he could not forecast what the President's action would be in "a hypothetical case under the law." After this cautious statement, he hurried on to say that he had heard "with sincere satisfaction of the growth of public sentiment upon the lines of neighborly amity and mutual benefit to

94. Goldwin Smith to Bayard, April 3, 1888, ibid.
95. Goldwin Smith to Bayard, April 11, 1888, Bayard MS.
96. Wiman wrote to Bayard on May 29 and stated that there was a "steady growth of the Commercial Union sentiment in the Dominion." Ibid.
97. Erastus Wiman to Sir Richard Cartwright, May 29, 1888, ibid.

the two countries, and trust that nothing may be done to interrupt what I believe to be the natural current of kindly relations." [98]

At this same time, Goldwin Smith continued his correspondence with Bayard concerning the situation in Canada. He was certain that the idea of commercial union was gaining ground in Canada. The last

. . . five bye elections have gone in favour of the Party which has embraced it. That party now commands all the Provincial legislatures except the two of least importance—British Columbia and Prince Edward Island. It is likely to sweep Manitoba in the election impending there. An Ottawa official . . . admitted to me yesterday that the government will not at the present time go to the country with a prospect of success. . . . Their hope is that Commercial Union will blow over. It will blow over when the Map does. [99]

On July 20 Smith wrote again to Bayard to boast of the accuracy of his predictions regarding elections in Canada. The Liberal Party in Manitoba, which was "identified with Commercial Union," had carried

. . . thirty-five elections out of thirty-eight. . . . We do not doubt our success in a general election. Nor do *I* doubt that if anything in the nature of an overture is made by your next Congress, sufficient pressure in the shape of petitions can be brought to bear on the government here to prevent rejection without an appeal to the people. The danger of miscarriage is all on *your* side, and consists in the treatment of Canadian interests by your tariff reformers separately, and not on the principle of Reciprocity. [100]

In the meantime, the debate on the fisheries treaty of February 15, 1888, had been opened on May 29 by Senator Frye in a bitter attack upon its provisions. As the debate proceeded during the summer months of 1888, it was apparent that certain Republican Senators were opposing the treaty because they hoped that Canadian dissatisfaction with the economic situation in the Dominion would lead to a strong movement in favor of annexation to the United States. A settlement of the fisheries dispute, together with commercial reciprocity, would bring prosperity to Canada and remove all desire for annexation.

98. Bayard to Erastus Wiman, May 31, 1888, *ibid.*
99. Goldwin Smith to Bayard, May 31, 1888, *Bayard MS.*
100. Goldwin Smith to Bayard, July 20, 1888, *ibid.* In his *Reminiscences*, p. 446, Goldwin Smith has little to say of his interest in commercial union. The following comments on reciprocity comprise all that he had to say on that topic: "It was as an Englishman that I took part in the movement in favour of Reciprocity with the United States, the manifest dictate, as it seemed to me, of nature and of the interest of the Canadian people. Every movement of this kind is in a line with the free-trade policy which has hitherto been that of Great Britain. But the league of log-rolling monopolies in the United States was too strong for us, and too strong for us and for the real interests of the American and Canadian people to this hour it remains. Of the ultimate triumph of those views I feel no doubt."

On August 7, 1888, John Sherman made a speech in the Senate which revealed the real basis of his opposition to the fisheries treaty. He emphasized the economic ties that bound Canada to the State he represented in the Senate—Ohio. The citizens of Ohio had "large property interests in Canada. They have mines, they have quarries, they have large properties amounting to many millions of dollars. Our intercourse is of the closest character." For this reason, "anything whatever that would tend to promote free commercial intercourse between these countries, yea, anything that will tend to produce a union of Canada with the United States of America will meet my most hearty support." Within ten years Canada would be represented "either in the Imperial Parliament of Great Britain or in the Congress of the United States." He ardently hoped that they would be represented in the American Congress, and he would vote against the pending fisheries treaty because he believed that it would "erect a barrier and prevent the very objects that are sought to be accomplished." Commercial union, of course, would be the economic prelude to political union.[101]

S. J. Ritchie, who represented Ohio "big business" interests in Canada, wrote to Sherman and warmly commended his speech in the Senate. He was confident that there was a rapidly growing sentiment in Canada in favor of annexation, and he believed that it would not be long before several of the leading Canadian newspapers would be

. . . openly throwing this flag to the breeze. Your speech will do very much to aid this. In company recently with a number of leading English Bankers who were large owners of Canadian Pacific Railway securities, the opinion was unanimously expressed that Canada's best interests would be served by a political Union with the States, and at the same time the fear was expressed that the United States did not desire such a union. The idea that Great Britain would interpose serious objection, was scouted by one and all. The agreement between the Premier of Manitoba and the Northern Pacific Railway is here [Montreal] generally interpreted as a bold move in this direction. . . . The mines at Sudbury are now becoming fairly opened, and extension machinery will soon be at work. We hope to be producing copper and nickel, . . . and the ores of both these metals should be placed on the free list. . . . I hope you will have this matter corrected.[102]

Ritchie, with his large interests in Canada, was anxious to have the

101. *Congressional Record*, 50 Cong., 1 sess., vol. 19, pt. 8, p. 7286. See also, Sherman's speech on September 18, 1888, *Cong. Rec.*, 50 Cong., 1 sess., vol. 19, pt. 9, pp. 8666-8671. In his *Recollections of Forty Years* (N. Y., 1895), vol. 2, pp. 1017-1021, Sherman records his change of views with regard to the advisability of Canadian annexation.

102. S. J. Ritchie to Senator John Sherman, August 8, 1888, *John Sherman MS.*

duties on metallic ores removed from the tariff schedules, but many American business men thought otherwise. W. M. Day, editor of the *Iron Trade Review,* was very much worried about Sherman's remarks in the Senate, and he wrote at once to record his objections to any lowering of duties in Canadian ores:

If we have plenty of coal and iron ore in this country now protected with a comparatively low rate of duty, should we disturb it by opening reciprocal relations with Canada? Should not American mine labor be protected against the competition of Canadian mine labor? Will not the same arguments that apply to protection against British competition apply equally well to Canadian-British competition? Has the *proximity* of Canada anything to do with the question? [103]

On August 21, 1888, the Senate defeated the pending fisheries treaty, and the advocates of commercial union now had a splendid opportunity to work for the success of their pet scheme. Benjamin Butterworth lost no time in introducing a joint resolution in the House of Representatives which advocated commercial union with Canada,[104] and on February 19, 1889, he took another step in that direction by introducing a joint resolution authorizing the President to invite a

---

103. W. M. Day to Sherman, August 11, 1888, *John Sherman MS.* From Toronto, Canada, J. D. Edgar wrote to Senator Sherman, August 8, 1888, in warm praise of the idea of commercial union, but from Montreal, A. W. Ogilvie warned Sherman that there was very little annexationist sentiment in Canada: "You would hardly get a corporal's guard of educated men in the Dominion of Canada today, who would be willing to exchange our good old flag even for yours." *Ibid.*

In a newspaper statement that came out in the Baltimore *Sun,* July 12, 1888, Bayard declared: "For my own part, I favor reciprocity with Canada. The existing situation is absurd. . . . Reciprocity has been favored by such men as Webster, Marcy, Everett, Arthur, Frelinghuysen, and many others. . . . It is my hope that all trouble will be ended by the establishment of full reciprocity between Canada and the United States."

On April 10, 1888, Sir Charles Tupper made a speech in the Canadian House of Commons with reference to the Treaty of February 15, 1888. (*Recollections of Sixty Years,* pp. 335-401.) In this speech he made some comments upon the British proposal to settle the fisheries dispute by granting tariff concessions to Canadian products. In connection with Tupper's remarks, Bayard wrote to President Cleveland July 12, 1888, as follows: "Sir Charles Tupper read these proposals in the Ottawa debate and . . . said that I told him the true way to get what reciprocity he wanted was to remove the difficulty (their rough treatment of our fishermen), and that in settling our own tariffs, Canada would be benefited by lowering our duties on raw materials.

"He then referred to the Mills bill putting lumber and bread-stuffs and *wool* on the free list, as proof that the movement was begun. Of course, *he* was defending his own action, and seeking to make his conduct in negotiations appear favorable to Canada. But it is absurd to propose to hold *me* responsible for the language of my opponent. The language of the *treaty* and its provisions are what we stand upon." *Bayard Letter Book,* vol. 8, *Bayard MS.*

104. *Congressional Record,* 50 Cong., 2 sess., vol. 20, pt. 1, p. 234.

large deputation of Canadian officials to the United States as the guests of this nation.[105]

On March 1, 1889, a resolution that had been introduced by Mr. Hitt the previous year, passed the House of Representatives without a record vote.[106] The purpose of the resolution was to "promote commercial union with Canada." In the Senate, this resolution was favorably reported by Senator Sherman, but further action upon it was blocked by Senator Blair.[107]

While the American Congress was wrestling with the problem of commercial union, the Canadian House of Commons was debating a resolution offered by Sir Richard Cartwright, which requested that steps be taken to ascertain what arrangements could be made with the United States in order to establish a system of unrestricted commercial reciprocity between it and Canada. The spirit that animated certain Canadian hearts during this debate, was clearly revealed in the remarks of Mr. George R. Cockburn, of Toronto. He was afraid that Canadians would first be "inveigled" into the American net and then they would

. . . feel in all its force, the "prevailing choice of the people" who have overreached us in almost every transaction, who cheated us by false maps out of the State of Maine, dishonestly pocketed millions of dollars in connection with the Alabama award, and who recently applauded the infamous threat of the Retaliation Bill by a President who had only a few days before, declared publicly that Canada had done everything that was fair, just, and honourable.[108]

Cartwright's resolution was defeated in the Canadian House of Commons by a vote of 121 nays to 77 yeas.[109] This adverse action meant that in Canada the more advanced ideas on commercial union had to give way to a new proposal for unrestricted reciprocity. In the

105. *Ibid.*, vol. 20, pt. 3, p. 2055.
106. *Ibid.*, vol. 20, pt. 3, p. 2539.
107. *Ibid.*, 50 Cong., 1 sess., vol. 19, pt. 9, September 27, 1888, pp. 8979-8980. The plan for commercial union with Canada as outlined by Mr. Hitt, included "the adoption by both countries of precisely the same tariff of duties, or taxes to be levied upon goods coming from abroad, abolishing altogether our line of customhouses on the north by which we collect tariff duties on goods coming from Canada, abolishing their customhouses along the same line by which they collect duties upon goods we send into Canada, and leaving intercourse as unrestricted between this country and Canada as it is between the States. . . . The internal revenue systems of taxes on liquors and tobacco in the two countries would also have to be made uniform in both countries. The proceeds of taxation thus collected would be equitably divided, and the fairest way would seem to be in proportion to population."
108. Canada, House of Commons, *Debates*, March 19, 1889, vol. 27, p. 704.
109. Canada, House of Commons, *Debates*, March 19, 1889, vol. 27, p. 739.

United States there had been no real opportunity for the success of a program providing for commercial union with Canada. This program had been supported by certain representatives of "big business" who hoped thereby to secure important advantages through the development of their mineral holdings in Canada. Other prominent Americans had favored the idea of commercial union merely because they regarded it as a prelude to American annexation of Canada.

Bayard had been not only skeptical of the success of any project that looked towards the establishment of commercial union between Canada and the United States, but he had entertained small hopes even for the enactment of legislation that would prepare the way for commercial reciprocity. Although he had consistently favored the idea of reciprocity with Canada, he had realized only too well, that the protectionists in both Canada and in the United States would defeat any efforts in that direction. Reciprocity would have to rest upon the broad basis of mutual economic interest and of genuine good will. There were few protectionists on either side of the border who could look beyond the items in a tariff schedule to the intangible assets of international understanding.

The Mexican Question

CHAPTER SEVENTEEN

Mexico Merely Gives Lip Service to the "Good Neighbor Policy"

A. Border Incidents

WHILE BAYARD HAD BEEN VAINLY ATTEMPTING TO CARRY OUT A PROGRAM that would provide for commercial reciprocity with Canada, he was also endeavoring to broaden the basis of American relations with Mexico.[1] There was evident need for these friendly efforts. Since the close of the American Civil War, sharp friction had existed along the boundary between the United States and Mexico. Cattle-thieves from Mexico had repeatedly plundered the exposed ranches in lower Texas, and Indians on both sides of the border had taken bloody toll from settlers along the weakly defended frontier.

According to a report made by the commission appointed by President Grant in 1872 to investigate conditions in Texas, the situation was most alarming. Not only was there serious loss of life in Texas, owing to the numerous depredations committed by Mexicans and Indians, but the property loss occasioned by these forays amounted to the large sum of $27,859,363.97. On the other hand, a report submitted

1. The Diaz Government had been very generous in the matter of granting lucrative concessions to American capitalists. Bayard was anxious that these Americans should be protected in their rights. During the course of a conversation with Romero, the Mexican representative in Washington, Bayard stated that he felt "very much concerned that the Mexican Govt. should extend proper protection to the better class of Americans, who took their Capital and moved themselves and their families down in that country. The need of protection was producing a very bad effect. The Americans who went down there developed a great deal of value to Mexico and themselves, and then they became objects of predatory attacks by these brigands, and the Mexican Gov't. had really a moral liability for the safety of these people. I did not wish to state any extreme propositions, and I did not wish to make any claims upon Mexico to recompense these people that I would not respond to myself if made upon the United States." *Memorandum* written by Bayard after a conversation with Romero, January 6, 1888, *Bayard MS.*

by a Mexican commission in 1873, presented a completely different picture.[2]

The exact truth of the situation in Texas is difficult to determine, but there was little doubt that further raids would lead to counter-measures on the part of American troops. This reprisal came in May, 1873, when some Kickapoo Indians made a foray into Texas and escaped with considerable booty. They were promptly pursued into Mexican territory by American soldiers under Colonel R. S. Mac-Kenzie.[3] In 1874–1875 these raids from Mexico continued with increasing frequency, and they led to many counterattacks from the United States.[4] When these punitive expeditions did not put a stop to the Indian forays, it was obvious that some further step would have to be taken. In March, 1877, with the inauguration of President Hayes, a new policy towards Mexico was adopted. Heretofore, with reference to the recognition of new governments, the Department of State had followed a *de facto* principle—governments that rested upon the will of the people were accorded recognition. President Hayes now added a new test for recognition. Governments would not only have to rest upon popular approval, but would also have to possess the strength to fulfil their international obligations.[5]

In accordance with this new attitude towards the Mexican Government, the Hayes Administration decided to give official approval to invasions of Mexican territory by American troops in pursuit of raiders. On June 1, 1877, the Secretary of War issued an order to General Sherman which authorized American troops to follow this doctrine of "hot pursuit" and overtake and "punish" Mexican marauders.[6]

The order of June 1, 1877, aroused violent indignation in Mexico, and the Mexican Minister of Foreign Relations declared that it disre-

2. *Report of the United States Commissioners to Texas appointed under the Joint Resolution of Congress, May 7, 1872* (Washington, 1872); *Report of the Committee of Investigation sent in 1873 by the Mexican Government to the Frontier of Texas* (N. Y., 1875); *House Rept. 701*, 45 Cong., 2 sess., Appendix B.

3. *House Misc. Doc. 64*, 45 Cong., 2 sess., pp. 187-188.

4. J. Fred Rippy, "Some Precedents of the Pershing Expedition into Mexico," *Southwestern Historical Quarterly*, vol. 24, April, 1921, pp. 292-316.

5. See annual message of President Hayes to Congress, December 3, 1877, J. D. Richardson, *Messages and Papers of the Presidents*, vol. 7, pp. 467-468.

6. *House Ex. Doc. 13*, 45 Cong., 1 sess., pp. 14-15; *House Rept. 701*, 45 Cong., 2 sess., p. 241. With reference to this stand taken by the American Government in June, 1877, Brainerd Dyer, in his *Public Career of William M. Evarts*, p. 195, remarks: "There is no more definite policy connected with the Evarts administration of the Department of State than this insistence upon the doctrine of hot pursuit—a doctrine for which a strong case can be made."

garded all the "rules of International Law and the practices of civilized nations, and treated the Mexicans as savages."[7] On June 18 the Minister of War ordered additional troops to the border with instructions to repel any invasions of Mexican territory.[8] In Mexico there was a general impression that war with the United States was inevitable, and "disaffected generals and dilapidated officials" rushed to the Ministry of War to offer their services against "the rapacious northern giant."[9]

The Diaz Government was keen enough to perceive that the attitude of the Hayes Administration towards Mexico was not supported by American public opinion. In July, 1877 Senator Blaine led an attack upon the policy of Secretary Evarts,[10] and Senator Conkling sponsored a Senate investigation of the difficulties with Mexico.[11] President Diaz bestowed important concessions upon American business men, and he made skilful use of propaganda designed to create a favorable impression in the United States with reference to his administration. It was not long before the Department of State had to respond to pressure in favor of the recognition of the Diaz Government, and on March 23, 1878, an instruction to this effect was sent to the American Minister.[12]

The second surrender of the Hayes Administration came on March 1, 1880, when the order of June 1, 1877, was recalled.[13] The Diaz Gov-

7. John W. Foster to Secretary Evarts, June 20, 1877, *Foreign Relations, 1877*, p. 411.
8. Foster to Secretary Evarts, *ibid.*, pp. 416-418.
9. Foster to Secretary Evarts, June 22, 30, 1877, *Mexico, Despatches*, vol. 59, MS Dept. of State.
10. *Harper's Weekly*, July 28, 1877, vol. 21, pp. 578-579.
11. New York *Times*, December 15, 1877.
12. Secretary Evarts to Foster, March 23, 1878, *Foreign Relations, 1878*, pp. 543-544. See also, "Memorandum of Remarks of Mr. Evarts before the Sub-Committee on Foreign Affairs, February 16, 1878," *Mexico, Despatches*, vol. 61; J. F. Rippy, *The United States and Mexico*, pp. 298-310; Foster to Evarts, September 5, October 26, 1878, *Mexico, Despatches*, vols. 63-64; J. M. Callahan, *American Foreign Policy in Mexican Relations*, pp. 369-405; Robert D. Gregg, *The Influence of Border Troubles on Relations between the United States and Mexico, 1876-1910* (Baltimore, 1937), pp. 17-80; Charles W. Hackett, "The Recognition of the Diaz Government by the United States," *Southwestern Historical Quarterly*, vol. 28, July, 1924, pp. 34-56.
A typical concession of the Diaz Government to Americans, was the one granted to James B. Eads for a Ship-Railway across the Isthmus of Tehuantepec. In a letter to Bayard, May 9, 1885, Eads discusses the implications of this concession, and he suggested the importance of an "early negotiation of a treaty between the United States and Mexico, in which the status of each nation with respect to this important work, shall be clearly defined. I have suggested to the President and Secretary of State of Mexico, the importance and propriety of forming such treaty looking to the early completion of the Ship-Railway; and am justified in assuring Your Excellency that a proposition to negotiate such a treaty will meet with a favorable response from Mexico." *Bayard MS.*
13. Secretary Evarts to Foster, March 1, 1880, *Foreign Relations, 1880*, pp. 735-736.

ernment had been completely successful in forcing a reversal of policy on the part of President Hayes with reference both to recognition and to reprisals against border raids. In keeping with this spirit of conciliation, the American Government signed on July 29, 1882, an agreement which provided that "the Regular federal troops of the two Republics may reciprocally cross the boundary line of the two countries, when they are in close pursuit of a band of savage Indians." This agreement was to be in effect for a period of two years.[14]

On October 31, 1884, the reciprocal agreement was renewed for a period of one year, and a similar renewal went into effect on November 1, 1885.[15] This action was rendered necessary by the serious Apache raids during the months from May 1885 to September 1886.[16] Under the famous chief Geronimo, the Apaches left a long trail of destruction until they were finally captured by Brigadier-General Nelson A. Miles in September, 1886. During the course of this campaign a serious incident arose which threatened to disturb the friendly relations that existed between the United States and Mexico. In January 1886, an American detachment under the command of Captain Emmet Crawford was pursuing a band of hostile Indians some fifty miles southwest of Nacori, Mexico. On January 10, the Americans were attacked by Mexican *Nacionales,* and Captain Crawford was killed.

The story of the attack was told in a letter from Lieutenant Marion P. Maus to Captain C. S. Roberts, January 21, 1886. At daylight on the morning of January 10th, the American camp

. . . was alarmed by loud cries from some of the scouts, followed immediately by a shower of bullets into our camp. . . . It was soon discovered that the attacking party was a large force of Mexican soldiers from Chihuahua. . . . They wore no uniform, but I suppose were *Nacionales.* Although we tried in every way by waving handkerchiefs and by calling out in Spanish who we were, they continued a sharp fire for about fifteen minutes. . . . A party of them then approached, and Captain Crawford and I went out about 50 yards from our position in the open and talked with them. . . . I told them in Spanish we were American soldiers, . . . and said we would not fire. They answered they would not fire, but all the time moved toward a hill a short distance away. . . . I am sure that they knew who we were perfectly well at this time. I started back, when again a volley was fired. . . . When

14. W. M. Malloy, *Treaties, Conventions, etc.,* vol. I, pp. 1144-1145. This reciprocal crossing agreement was limited to desert or unpopulated portions of the border.
15. Secretary Bayard to Jackson, October 6, 1885, *Mexico, Instructions,* vol. 21; Jackson to Secretary Bayard, October 17, 1885, *Mexico, Despatches,* vol. 86, MS Dept. of State. See also, Malloy, *op. cit.,* pp. 1162-1163.
16. *Report of the Secretary of War, 1888,* pp. 5-7.

I turned again I saw captain (Crawford) lying on the rocks, with a wound in his head and some of his brains upon the rocks.[17]

When news of this murder reached Washington, James D. Porter, Acting Secretary of State, sent an instruction to the American Minister in Mexico City in which he recounted the incident. He thought it was difficult "to conceive how the allegation of a 'mistake' could be soberly made under such circumstances." In view of this fact he ordered Jackson to make a "searching examination" into every aspect of this "unfortunate occurrence."[18] The American Minister laid the matter before the Mexican Foreign Office,[19] and he was assured that a "very careful investigation" would be made.[20]

On March 20 Bayard wrote to Jackson and complained of the attack upon Captain Crawford as a "gross violation of treaty stipulations and a breach of ordinary comity and international usage between friendly powers." In answer to a suggestion that no Indian scouts be used by American troops because of the likelihood that they might be confused with hostile Indians, Bayard replied: "To abandon the employment of Indian scouts for this especial service would appear to be to relinquish the best known means of giving peace to the borderland between Mexico and the United States, and safety to the inhabitants of both countries."[21]

On March 26, Romero, the Mexican Minister at Washington, paid a formal call at the Department of State. He expressed the view that the Mexicans who had fired upon Captain Crawford were

. . . not only not regular troops of the Mexican Army, but were not even militia under the laws of the locality, but were a body of men who had gathered together to defend their homes against hostile Indians; that the people in Chihuahua had been robbed by these Indians of their stock and property, and when they came upon Captain Crawford's command, they found them in possession of the camp which they knew was the camp of the hostiles, and in possession of the property which had been taken from the Chihuahua people; that, therefore, they supposed them to be the hostiles themselves and that the assault was made in that belief.

17. Lieutenant Marion P. Maus to Captain C. S. Roberts, January 21, 1886, *Foreign Relations, 1886*, pp. 571-572.

18. Acting Secretary James D. Porter to Jackson, February 2, 1886, *Foreign Relations, 1886*, p. 570.

19. Jackson to Secretary Mariscal, February 15, 1886, *ibid.*, p. 574.

20. Secretary Mariscal to Jackson, February 18, 1886, *ibid.*, p. 575.

21. Secretary Bayard to Jackson, March 20, 1886, *ibid.*, pp. 575-576. In this instruction to Jackson, Secretary Bayard enclosed a second letter from Lieutenant Maus, February 23, 1886, and a series of depositions from privates and scouts who were present during the attack upon Captain Crawford.

I [Bayard] told him of the report of Lt. Maus and the fact that he had proven that the Mexicans, after they were informed of the character of the Americans, had not only been very rude and unfriendly in their language, but had detained Lieut. Maus as a prisoner when he went over to see them in regard to some of the animals which they had abandoned, and that that must be followed by some severe punishment and reprobation.[22]

President Diaz did not view the incident which resulted in the death of Captain Crawford in the same light as did Bayard. In a message to the Mexican Congress, on April 1, 1886, he gave his version of the affair:

For my part, and taking into consideration what has been ascertained up to the present time, I have the conviction that in said encounter our troops thought they were fighting the hostile Indians, because they were following the tracks of the savages and of the cattle which had been stolen, and they could not possibly imagine that said Indians had been joined by others of similar aspect, and among whom were very few soldiers or officers of the United States. The killing of the courageous and deserving officers and citizens of both countries is a very lamentable affair, but our troops, which were composed of citizens of the State of Chihuahua, will always have the excuse that they could not take as friends the Indians who were in front, when they well knew that according to the agreement for the passing of troops by the frontier only the regular troops of both Republics can pass reciprocally the boundary line when they are following the trail of the hostile Indians.[23]

After reading these remarks of President Diaz, Bayard addressed a note to Romero, the Mexican Minister at Washington, which clearly indicated that he refused to accept the interpretation of the Mexican Chief Executive with reference to the Crawford incident. Bayard still felt that there was

. . . little room to doubt the hostile and criminal conduct of the officers and men of the Mexican detachment that came into collision with Captain Crawford and killed him and some of his men, besides subsequently grossly insulting by actual arrest and threatened detention Lieutenant Maus and his interpreter *after* their nationality had been perfectly understood.

Bayard concluded his note to Romero by expressing the "confident hope" that the Mexican Government would soon take steps to fulfil the

22. *Memorandum* written by Bayard after a conversation with Romero, March 26, 1886, *Bayard MS.*
23. Excerpts from the speech of President Diaz were enclosed in the note from Romero to Secretary Bayard, April 13, 1886, *Foreign Relations, 1886*, pp. 724-725. See also, Ricardo Rodriguez, *Historia auténtica de la administración del Sr. Gral. Porforio Díaz* (Mexico City, 1904, 2 vols.), vol. 1, pp. 127-128.

"obligations due to a friendly neighbor and bring about the vigorous punishment of the guilty." [24]

In his note of reply, Romero adhered to his belief that the killing of Captain Crawford was "wholly accidental." Unless the Mexican troops had "wholly lost their reason," they would not have fired upon soldiers they knew to be Americans. He was certain that his countrymen were entirely sane, and their action could be explained in terms of mistaken identity. In the event that the Mexican Government discovered that the statements of Lieutenant Maus were correct, it would "act as its duty requires." [25]

Bayard was willing to admit that the first attack upon the American soldiers, under the command of Captain Crawford, might have been accidental. It happened, however, that

. . . there were two distinct attacks upon Captain Crawford's encampment. The first occurred at daylight when a volley was fired into the camp by the Mexicans, and returned. After that, in the open and in daylight, Captain Crawford, with his interpreter, under a white flag of truce, had a conference with the leaders of the Mexican party, and his identity and mission were fully made known. It was not until after that conference that the second attack was made, when Captain Crawford was shot in the open, and in full sight of both camps.

Had you been aware of this, I doubt not you would have suspended judgment and not argued the innocence of the Mexican party from Lieutenant Maus's frank admission that the first attack at daylight may possibly have been due to a mistake as to the identity of his party.[26]

Notwithstanding Bayard's strong presentation of the American case, Romero remained adamant in his belief that the attack upon the American troops was entirely accidental. He was certain that if the Mexican soldiers "had had at least the slightest suspicion that the scouts of the United States Army were there, I surely believe they would not have been attacked." [27]

In the formal note from the Mexican Secretary of Foreign Affairs dealing with this Crawford incident, the responsibility for the death of Captain Crawford is placed squarely upon the shoulders of the American military forces. According to Mariscal, the Americans fired first, and the Mexicans returned this fire. After several Mexicans had been killed, a "beardless young American" came forward and stated that the

24. Secretary Bayard to Romero, April 22, 1886, *Foreign Relations, 1886,* p. 725.
25. Romero to Secretary Bayard, April 29, 1886, *ibid.,* pp. 726-727.
26. Secretary Bayard to Romero, May 4, 1886, *ibid.,* pp. 727-728.
27. Romero to Secretary Bayard, May 5, 1886, *ibid.,* pp. 728-730.

men who were with him "were not hostile Indians, but pursuers of such." It was noted by the Mexicans, that the American officers had with them "no military insignia whatever." The American lieutenant wore merely a "black sack coat without braid," and the Indian scouts who accompanied the American detachment, were dressed in the same manner as the hostile Apache Indians.

It was admitted that Lieutenant Maus was detained for a short while by the Mexican soldiers, but this was because he was not in uniform and his exact identity was not known. During his stay in the Mexican camp he was treated with "great consideration." This considerate attitude was especially commendable in view of the fact that the Indian scouts with the American detachment had committed "all sorts of outrages and assaults" upon unoffending Mexicans. Indeed, these Indian scouts were so untrustworthy that it was more than likely that they had shot Captain Crawford and then blamed this murder upon the Mexican soldiers.[28]

In the face of this conflicting testimony there was nothing for Bayard to do but to refrain from pushing the matter any further. He was confirmed in this do-nothing attitude by an opinion expressed in November, 1887, by General Sheridan, to the effect that the killing of Captain Crawford was an accident. The incident was formally closed by a letter from Secretary Blaine in which the Mexican Government was advised that no demand for an indemnity would be pressed.[29]

As a result of this Crawford incident, the Mexican Government insisted that a very small number of Indian scouts should be attached to American military forces crossing into Mexican territory. The reciprocal crossing agreement expired on November 1, 1886, and in June,

28. Secretary Mariscal to Morgan, Mexico City, May 19, 1886, enclosed in despatch from Morgan to Secretary Bayard, May 25, 1886, *Foreign Relations, 1886,* pp. 587-651, 657-690.

29. Secretary Blaine to Bingham, March 7, 1891, *Domestic Letters,* vol. 181, MS Dept. of State. See also, John Bassett Moore, *Digest of International Law,* vol. 2, p. 425; J. F. Rippy, "Some Precedents of the Pershing Expedition into Mexico," *Southwestern Historical Quarterly,* vol. 24, p. 315.

It is significant to note that the Mexican Government seldom admitted the truth of any of the charges filed by the Department of State. On February 13, 1885, the American Minister to Mexico, Philip H. Morgan, complained to the Mexican Secretary of Foreign Relations about raids into Texas. (Morgan to Secretary Mariscal, February 13, 1885, enclosed in Morgan to Secretary Frelinghuysen, March 3, 1885, *Mexico, Despatches,* vol. 85, MS Dept. of State.) Mariscal replied on July 17, 1885, in a note which recited raids from Texas into Mexico. Mariscal to Jackson, July 17, 1885, enclosed in despatch from Jackson to Secretary Bayard, August 6, 1885, *Mexico, Despatches,* vol. 86, MS Dept. of State.

1887, Bayard was anxious to conclude a renewal of its terms. In a note to Romero he commented upon the existing situation:

It is important in the present emergency that authority should be obtained from Mexico for the pursuit of . . . Indians, and pending a formal arrangement, to that effect between the two governments, I hope it will be in your power to enable me to inform the Secretary of War that such pursuit may be made by the Military forces of the U. S. under the command of Major-General Howard, Pacific Division, U. S. A.

I enclose a copy of the former agreement, and will ask of you a reply at your earliest convenience, as the telegram from General Miles in Arizona indicates the necessity of prompt action.[30]

As soon as Romero received this note he hastened to the Department of State to discuss the situation with Bayard. He said that he would "go at once to see General Sheridan and ask him whether an agreement, excluding the use of Indian Scouts in the United States Army . . . would answer. He said that General Sheridan and General Miles thought that a very small *per centum* of Indian Scouts need be used."[31]

Romero left with Bayard a memorandum which outlined a possible arrangement with reference to the use of Indian scouts in border crossings: "It is understood that no Indian scouts of either Government shall be allowed to cross the boundary line unless they go as guides and traders, and not exceeding in any case five scouts for each Company in each separate command."

After securing the approval of the Secretary of War with regard to this proposed regulation, Bayard then wrote to Romero and inquired if he might consider

"the order, *au fait accompli,* so that the military officers in Arizona may act under it?"[32]

In reply to this request, Romero sent a personal note to Bayard in which he indicated certain limitations upon the powers of President Diaz. The Mexican Constitution required

. . . the consent of the Senate in order that the President may be able to authorize the entrance of foreign troops into the national territory. . . . As the Mexican Senate is not now in session, . . . a serious difficulty arises as regards a speedy determination of this matter. It seems to me certain that, in case that agreement [the crossing arrangement of October 16, 1885] is ex-

30. Secretary Bayard to Romero, June 10, 1887, *Bayard MS.*
31. *Memorandum* written by Bayard after an interview with Romero, June 10, 1887, *Bayard MS.*
32. Secretary Bayard to Romero, June 10, 1887, *Bayard MS.*

tended, or a new one made on account of the expiration of that one, . . . the Government of Mexico will insist upon a stipulation prohibiting the entrance of Indian scouts into its territory, because it so understood the former agreement, and because the entrance of those Indians into Mexico occasioned the unfortunate encounter . . . in which Capt. Mauricio Corredor, of the Mexican Army, and Capt. Emmet Crawford, of the United States Army, were killed.[33]

On June 17 Romero informed Bayard, during the course of an interview, that he was expecting a telegram from the Mexican Foreign Office in answer to Bayard's request for an extension of permission to American troops to cross the Mexican frontier in pursuit of hostile Indians. Bayard then remarked that President Cleveland "was very anxious to know at once, because he desired to put down this Indian revolt with all the expedition possible." Romero concluded the interview with the comment that in Mexico there "was a Congressional Committee in session in the absence of Congress, which he thought had the power to grant permission to cross the boundary." [34]

Two days later (June 19), word came from Secretary Mariscal that the Mexican Government was ready to conclude an arrangement for reciprocal border crossing on the basis which "was accepted on the 10th by the Honorable Secretary of War of the United States." This arrangement, however, would have to be ratified by the Mexican Senate.[35]

It was apparent to Bayard that the matter of reciprocal border crossing would have to be postponed "until the autumn or winter." [36] As a matter of fact, it was postponed until June 25, 1890, when Secretary Blaine finally signed an agreement along the lines that had been indicated by the Mexican Government.[37]

During the pendency of this dispute over the death of Captain Crawford, there was another border incident which was settled in a speedy and satisfactory manner. In March, 1887, Lieutenant Gutierrez, of the Mexican Army, committed an offence in the American section of the town of Nogales. He was promptly arrested and held in custody by the American authorities. On March 3 his superior officer, Colonel

---

33. Romero to Secretary Bayard, June 10, 1887, *ibid.*
34. *Memorandum* written by Bayard after an interview with Romero, June 17, 1887, *Bayard MS.*
35. Romero to Secretary Bayard, June 19, 1887, *ibid.*
36. Secretary Bayard to President Cleveland, June 20, 1887, *Bayard Letter Book,* vol. 5, *Bayard MS.*
37. W. M. Malloy, *Treaties, Conventions, etc.,* vol. 1, pp. 1170-1171.

Arvizu, led his troops into the town and effected the release of Gutierrez.

The Mexican Government realized the serious difficulties that might arise from such an incident, and Secretary Mariscal telegraphed to Romero, at Washington, that an investigation of the incident had been ordered, and that "severe punishment" would be meted out to the guilty officers.[38] On March 7 Romero had an interview with Bayard concerning the rescue of Lieutenant Gutierrez. After recounting the text of the telegram from Mariscal, he was assured by Bayard that the Department of State did not "attribute the slightest national importance to this matter, but considered it some individual affair which would easily be settled."[39]

This settlement, Bayard believed, could be expedited by prompt measures taken by the Mexican Government. The guilty Mexican officers should be punished as soon as possible or they should be turned over to the American authorities in Nogales.[40] Secretary Mariscal shared these sentiments, and he sent word to Bayard that directions had been issued by the Government of Mexico providing for the "instant return to the American authorities of the persons taken from their custody by the Mexicans, and that those who effected the rescue shall be punished."[41]

This was exactly the course that Bayard wished to see followed by the Mexican Government, and during an interview with Romero, he disclosed the fact that an instruction had been forwarded to Mexico City requesting the return of the prisoners who had been taken from the custody of the American authorities in Nogales. With regard to the Mexican soldiers who had effected this rescue, the Mexican Government could "punish them themselves, or if they chose to do so, they could extradite them voluntarily, without application from us, to be punished according to American law."[42]

Romero misunderstood the plain purport of Bayard's statement and sent a despatch to Secretary Mariscal in which he stated that the Department of State had given to the Mexican Government the option

38. Secretary Mariscal to Romero, March 5, 1887, *Bayard MS.*
39. *Memorandum* written by Bayard after a conversation with Romero, March 7, 1887, *Bayard MS.*
40. Secretary Bayard to Manning, March 7, 1887, *Foreign Relations, 1887,* p. 692.
41. Manning to Secretary Bayard, March 8, 1887, *Mexico, Despatches,* vol. 92, MS Dept. of State.
42. *Memorandum* written by Bayard after an interview with Romero, March 8, 1887, *Bayard MS.*

"to deliver the offenders at Nogales to the American authorities for punishment, or for the Mexican Government to inflict adequate punishment."

Mariscal expressed to Manning his deep appreciation of the "kind feeling and moderation" displayed by Secretary Bayard in extending this alleged option, and he indicated that President Diaz would punish the guilty officers, "promptly and adequately." [43]

On March 10 Romero called at the Department of State to show Bayard a telegram from the Governor of Sonora telling of the capture of Lieutenant Gutierrez.[44] The following day he paid another visit to the Department of State and handed to Bayard a memorandum which stated that he had received word from Mariscal that the Mexican Government had not "promised to Mr. Manning to deliver to the local authorities of Arizona, the parties responsible for the encounter at Nogales, Arizona, on the 3d instant, who are now under arrest, and that between the two ways of punishing them, of which the Secretary of State spoke to the Mexican Minister, the Mexican Government prefers to punish in Mexico the guilty parties, with all the severity of the law." [45]

Bayard immediately protested that he thought

. . . it would be more satisfactory to the United States, and that we should require it, that the prisoners taken from the custody of the law on our soil, and carried over into Mexico, should be restored to the custody of the officers from whom they were taken, and that the persons concerned in that rescue, being Mexican soldiers, should be punished by their own Government. He [Romero] asked me if I thought that would be satisfactory. I said it would; that the offence in this case was the invasion of the United States and the deprivation of the officers of the law of a prisoner, and what they should do would be to return the prisoner at once.[46]

To this excellent advice the Mexican Government paid little attention, and Bayard soon discovered that it was impossible to enforce the "requirement" that Lieutenant Gutierrez be turned over to the American authorities at Nogales for punishment. On March 11 Secretary Mariscal informed Manning that Gutierrez would be kept in Mexico

43. Manning to Secretary Bayard, March 9, 1887, *Mexico, Despatches*, vol. 92, MS Dept. of State.
44. L. E. Torres, Governor of Sonora, to Matias Romero, March 10, 1887, *Bayard MS*.
45. *Memorandum* written by Romero, March 11, 1887, *ibid.*
46. *Memorandum* written by Bayard after a conversation with Romero, March 11, 1887, *ibid.*

to await vigorous action by the Mexican Government.[47] He thought that this procedure was in accordance with the wishes of the Department of State as outlined in a communication from Romero.

Both Mariscal and President Diaz had been misled by the misinterpretation that Romero had placed upon Bayard's remarks in the interview on March 8. They believed that Bayard had left the whole matter in their hands and would not insist upon the return of Lieutenant Gutierrez. In an interview with Manning, Mariscal revealed an effusively friendly spirit. In describing this meeting with the Mexican Secretary of Foreign Relations, Manning remarked:

> I think it of sufficient importance to apprise you of the unbounded elation (extravagant, I think) of President Diaz and his Cabinet because of the conciliatory spirit manifested by you in the recent Nogales affair. It is not manifested to me save in the measured language already conveyed to you in my official despatch, but I learn from a private source that the President and his Cabinet have said with gleeful satisfaction that they now felt sure of the pacific and friendly feelings of the U. S. Government. This shows you how deep-seated was the suspicion of a contrary feeling on our part. I trust you will pardon me if I mention that I, in smaller measure, am partaker with you of their trust and newly-awakened confidence.[48]

Before Bayard had received this letter from Manning, he sent to Mexico City the following terse instruction:

> Whether the persons rescued are or are not Mexicans, nothing can satisfy the Government of the United States except the delivery to its authorities of the prisoners who were forcibly taken from the Arizona officials. The alternative offered in my telegram before-mentioned, only concerned the Mexicans who effected the rescue.[49]

On March 19 he sent a long instruction which was equally direct. The alternative offered in the instruction of March 7 referred only to the Mexican soldiers who had rescued Lieutenant Gutierrez. They could either be punished by the Mexican Government or could be turned over to the American authorities at Nogales for appropriate action. But with reference to Gutierrez himself no such alternative had been contemplated or suggested. Armed invasion of American soil and the rescue of a prisoner

. . . from our lawful jurisdiction could confer upon the rescued person no asylum in Mexico, nor bring him within the formalities of extradition. It

---

47. Secretary Mariscal to Manning, March 11, 1887, enclosed in despatch from Manning to Secretary Bayard, March 12, 1887, *Mexico, Despatches,* vol. 92, MS Dept. of State.
48. Manning to Secretary Bayard, *Personal,* March 11, 1887, *Bayard MS.*
49. Secretary Bayard to Manning, March 17, 1887, *Foreign Relations, 1887,* p. 695.

becomes, under such circumstances, the simple international duty of the Mexican Government to undo the wrong committed by its own soldiers, by restoring the rescued prisoners to the jurisdiction from which they had been wrongfully taken; and the obligation to do so was cheerfully admitted by the Mexican Government on the 8th instant, before Señor Mariscal received the apparently misleading telegram of Señor Romero.[50]

Manning lost no time in carrying out this instruction. In a note to Secretary Mariscal he frankly declared that the American Government did not think that it would be "compatible with its dignity to be satisfied with less than the return to its jurisdiction of the prisoners thus rescued, whether they be Mexicans or Americans." [51]

Bayard himself emphasized this viewpoint in a conversation with Romero. He thought there could be no possibility of a mistake as to the position of the Department of State with regard to the return of Lieutenant Gutierrez, and he did not believe that any real difference of opinion existed between the two governments with

. . . regard to the duty of the Government of Mexico to restore to the custody of the American officials [the prisoner who had been rescued]. A possible misunderstanding might have arisen from the words "rescued" and "rescuer." The "rescued" we required to have returned to our custody. The "rescuer" we left Mexico to punish, or to send him to us for punishment.[52]

It was a simple matter for Bayard to lay down conditions for Mexico to fulfil. It was a very different matter for him to secure any real observance of these conditions. On April 6 Manning telegraphed to Bayard that Secretary Mariscal hoped that the United States would "not insist upon its demand that Gutierrez should be delivered up." [53] Bayard, ever conciliatory, responded in the affirmative,[54] and the Mexican Government tried Lieutenant Gutierrez, along with Colonel Arvizu and a private named Valenzuela, before a court martial which promptly passed a sentence of death upon them.[55]

It seemed to Bayard that the action of the court martial was too drastic, and he instructed Manning to inform Secretary Mariscal that the American Government would look with favor upon a mitigation

50. Secretary Bayard to Manning, March 19, 1887, Foreign Relations, 1887, pp. 696-697.
51. Manning to Secretary Mariscal, March 21, 1887, enclosed in Manning to Bayard, March 21, 1887, ibid., pp. 697-698.
52. Memorandum written by Bayard after a conversation with Romero, April 1, 1887, Bayard MS.
53. Manning to Secretary Bayard, April 6, 1887, Mexico, Despatches, vol. 93, MS Dept. of State.
54. Secretary Bayard to Manning, April 8, 1887, Foreign Relations, 1887, p. 710.
55. Manning to Secretary Bayard, May 5, 1887, ibid., p. 719.

of the sentence.[56] Mariscal and President Diaz were deeply touched by the "philanthropic sentiments" of the American Secretary of State,[57] and they finally decided to commute the sentence of the court martial to a term of imprisonment for twenty years.[58] Both Lieutenant Gutierrez and Colonel Arvizu received condign punishment, but this was imposed by México and not by the United States. By insisting upon this procedure the Mexican Government was able to forestall any complaints that it had acted in compliance with American demands, and Bayard was smart enough to realize that in diplomacy results are often achieved by indirection rather than by adherence to the obvious forms of diplomatic practice.[59]

B. The Cutting Case

The most serious crisis in American relations with Mexico during Bayard's term of office as Secretary of State was in connection with the sensational "Cutting Case." Cutting was an American citizen who

56. Secretary Bayard to Manning, *ibid.*, p. 723.

57. Secretary Mariscal to Manning, May 21, 1887, enclosed in despatch of Manning to Secretary Bayard, May 23, 1887, *ibid.*, pp. 728-729.

58. Secretary Mariscal to Bragg, April 27, 1888, enclosed in despatch from Bragg to Secretary Bayard, April 28, 1888, *Foreign Relations, 1888*, p. 1188. See also, Bayard to Bragg, March 22, 1888, *Mexico, Instructions*, vol. 22, MS Dept. of State.

59. There were numerous other incidents that helped to create friction between Mexico and the United States, and if Bayard had wished a pretext for a quarrel he could easily have found one. On November 17, 1887, Romero called at the Department of State and Bayard called his attention to the case of a Mr. Burnett, an American railroad engineer who had killed a Mexican citizen in an accident. Burnett had been immediately imprisoned, and Bayard expressed the view that it would "be of great value to his country and to the good relations between us if, without any correspondence at all, his own Gov't. would voluntarily take up the matter and set the man free, and enable the President to announce it." Bayard thought that such action would "have a very good effect just at this time when so many people were disposed to stir up ill-feeling towards Mexico." *Memorandum* written by Bayard after a conversation with Romero, November 17, 1887, *Bayard MS.* On December 9, 1887, Romero informed Bayard that the American engineer had been "set at liberty," and Bayard requested Romero to give him full particulars in order that they might be incorporated in a letter from the Secretary of State to President Cleveland for the purpose of showing him "how unjust are many of the charges against the Mexicans." *Memorandum* written by Bayard after a conversation with Romero, December 9, 1887, *Bayard MS.*

An important factor that helped to contribute to the tension along the international boundary, was the establishment by the Mexican Government of a Free Zone which followed for several hundred miles the sinuous course of the Rio Grande River. Into this Free Zone, foreign goods could be imported free of duty, and the American Government complained that the zone was used as a vantage point for smuggling large quantities of these goods into the United States. See J. Fred Rippy, *The United States and Mexico* (N. Y., 1926), pp. 282-285; James M. Callahan, *American Foreign Policy in Mexican Relations* (N. Y., 1932), pp. 342-345; Matias Romero, *Mexico and the United States* (N. Y., 1898), pp. 433ff.

served as editor of a newspaper, *El Centinela*, in the Mexican city of Paso del Norte. When Cutting published in his newspaper some strictures upon the character of one Emigdio Medina, the sensitive Mexican haled him into court and forced a withdrawal of these charges in the form of a "reconciliation" which was duly printed in *El Centinela*. But Cutting was far from being reconciled with the litigious Emigdio Medina, and on June 18, 1886, he published, in the El Paso (Texas) *Herald*, an advertisement which accused Medina of being a "fraud" and a "dead-beat." When Cutting returned to Paso del Norte he was arrested (June 23) and taken before Regino Castañeda, the judge of the second court of that city. After a short hearing, during which he did not enjoy the privilege of counsel, Cutting was thrown into a loathsome jail.

Cutting immediately appealed to the American consul at Paso del Norte, J. Harvey Brigham, but all of Brigham's efforts to secure Cutting's release were in vain, and the matter was finally brought before Bayard for action.[60] In the meantime, Henry R. Jackson, the American Minister at Mexico City, had written a strong note of protest to the Mexican Foreign Office,[61] and had received in reply a note from Mariscal which stated that a communication had been addressed to the Governor of Chihuahua recommending that "prompt and due justice be administered" to Cutting.[62]

The summary arrest and imprisonment of Cutting aroused a storm of disapproval in the American press, and tremendous pressure was at once exerted upon the Department of State to secure his immediate release.[63] On July 19 Bayard instructed Jackson, at Mexico City, to

60. Brigham to Secretary Bayard, July 1, 1886, with nine enclosures, *Foreign Relations, 1886*, pp. 691-698.

61. Jackson to Secretary Mariscal, July 6, 1886, enclosed in Jackson to Secretary Bayard, July 8, 1886, *ibid.*, pp. 698-699.

62. Secretary Mariscal to Jackson, July 7, 1886, *ibid.*, p. 699.

63. For a typical account of the "Cutting Incident," see the *Evening Tribune* (El Paso, Texas), July 10, 1886. In the Baltimore *Sun*, July 24, 1886, there is the following moderate presentation of the incident: "The latest report is that Secretary of War Endicott has ordered all available troops in the southwest to report at Fort Bliss. It is the general opinion at El Paso that hostilities are inevitable. . . . It is creditably reported that the Mexican consul at El Paso, in a letter to a Chihuahua orator, complimented him for having said that he would like to have all the American heads in line that with one bee-cut he might sever them all." The papers in Texas threw moderation to the winds and preached a crusade against Mexico. They were strong in their support of the belligerent stand taken by Governor Ireland, who demanded "in the name of the State of Texas and its people, that this wrong by Mexico [the arrest of Cutting] be atoned for and punished." Ireland also issued the following challenge: "If this State and her people must depend upon themselves for protection, the necessary redress can

demand "the instant release" of Cutting,[64] and on the following day he sent a long instruction to the same effect. After discussing the publication by Cutting of the advertisement in the El Paso *Herald* attacking the character of Emigdio Medina, Bayard remarked:

Such a publication would not, even had it been made in Mexico, be the subject of criminal prosecution in that country, according to the Roman common law there in force, nor of any adverse governmental action, unless, perhaps, for the single purpose of requiring security in some small sum to keep the peace. But the paper was not published in Mexico, and the proposition that Mexico can take jurisdiction of its author on account of its publication in Texas is wholly inadmissible and is peremptorily denied by this Government. It is equivalent to asserting that Mexico can take jurisdiction over the authors of the various criticisms of Mexican business operations which appear in the newspapers of the United States. If Mr. Cutting can be tried and imprisoned in Mexico for publishing in the United States a criticism on a Mexican business transaction in which he was concerned, there is not an editor or publisher of a newspaper in the United States who could not, were he found in Mexico, be subjected to like indignities and injuries on the same ground. To an assumption of such jurisdiction by Mexico neither the Government of the United States nor the governments of our several States will submit. . . .

But there is another ground on which this demand may with equal positiveness be based. By the law of nations no punishment can be inflicted by a sovereign on citizens of other countries unless in conformity with those sanctions of justice which all civilized nations hold in common. Among these sanctions are the right of having the facts on which the charge of guilt was made examined by an impartial court, the explanation to the accused of these facts, the opportunity granted to him of counsel, such delay as is necessary to prepare his case, . . . the right to produce his own evidence in exculpation, release even from temporary imprisonment in all cases where the charge is simply one of threatened breach of the peace, and where due security to keep the peace is tendered. All these sanctions were violated in the present case.[65]

---

and will be obtained." In support of Ireland's belligerent language, the Dallas *News* remarked: "Governor Ireland has taken bold steps. If somewhat brusque and irregular, his message to Secretary Bayard is full of genuine Texas spirit. Texas by herself has whipped Mexico, and can do it again with the same sympathetic aid of her American brethren, if necessary. Texans demand nothing less than what Governor Ireland has said to Mr. Bayard, and Texans will be moved as one man in sustaining the State authorities in any practicable and necessary action to force Mexico into measures of redress and justice. No driveling diplomacy at Washington must be allowed." For these excerpts, see, Sam Acheson, *35,000 Days in Texas: A History of the Dallas News* (N. Y., 1938), pp. 112-113.

64. Secretary Bayard to Jackson, July 19, 1886, *Foreign Relations, 1886*, p. 700.
65. Secretary Bayard to Jackson, July 20, 1886, *Foreign Relations, 1886*, pp. 700-702.

582 The Mexican Question

When Jackson conveyed this demand to Secretary Mariscal,[66] he was informed that the Mexican Federal Government did not have the power to direct the officials or the Governor of the State of Chihuahua to release Cutting. Mexico was much like the United States in its federal organization, and the general government was one of definitely limited powers. In view of this fact it would be impossible to put a peremptory stop to legal proceedings in Paso del Norte. It would seem, therefore, that

. . . only the pressure brought to bear by private persons, or perhaps by an ill-informed press, can have been able to bring about the result that a Government friendly to Mexico, and which up to the present has no complaint against this nation for lack of compliance with its international obligations, should demand in an absolute manner what is, in every light, morally impossible.[67]

Along with this news that the Mexican Federal Government could not take the action that was demanded by Secretary Bayard, there was a report from the American consul at Paso del Norte that Mexican troops were being massed at that point.[68] It was apparent to Bayard that serious trouble would result from any clash of troops at the border, and the sensational stories in the American press had evoked a martial ardor in many American hearts that were eager for a conflict with Mexico. The Cutting Case would have to be handled with extreme care, and Bayard turned to Francis Wharton, the Solicitor of the Department of State, for advice. Wharton was sharply critical of the action taken by the Mexican Government. In a memorandum prepared for Bayard he made the following comments:

The offence is one not the subject, in itself, of non-bailable criminal prosecution, being a mere police offence. The proceedings were in defiance of the rules of International Law, counsel and bail being refused, continuance refused, no witnesses produced, no interpreter allowed. The offering now to admit to bail does not purge the outrage. Cutting may be dirty, but he is no dirtier than Don Paapes.

To concede Mex. position is to make the Mexican province's irresponsible despotisms above the law of nations and of treaties. McLeod was arrested and imprisoned in Mr. Van Buren's administration, *by New York authorities*, in violation, as Great Britain claimed, of the law of Nations. Neither Mr. Forsyth nor Mr. Webster, who succeeded, claimed that the United States were not responsible for New York violations of International

66. Jackson to Secretary Mariscal, July 19, 21, 1886, *ibid.*, pp. 703-704.
67. Secretary Mariscal to Jackson, July 21, 1886, *Foreign Relations, 1886*, p. 704.
68. Brigham to Secretary Bayard, July 22, 1886, *ibid.*, p. 705.

Law. On the contrary, this was conceded. To enable the United States to exercise in such matters appellate authority over the States, a statute was passed giving the Supreme Court of the United States appellate authority over State Courts in international matters. The constitutionality of this statute has never been disputed; and it rests on the position that from the nature of things, the United States under the Constituion, is supreme over the States in matters of International Law, and is internationally liable for them.

This is the first time that this impudent and insolent defence has been set up. In innumerable cases which can be cited, Mexico has admitted her liability for provincial outrages. This has been the basis on which we have dealt with her, as accepted by herself. Bail is in itself imprisonment. She cannot *now* sneak out by offering to let Cutting out on bail. She should apologize and give reparation. Otherwise we will be subjected to a settled system of outrages. The political sheep creates the political wolf. If we behave like sheep, Mexico will assume the vulpine position with delight.[69]

On the same day that this memorandum was handed to Bayard by Francis Wharton, Romero, the Mexican Minister, called at the Department of State to discuss the implications of the Cutting Case. He first handed Bayard a copy of Article 186, of the Mexican Penal Code. According to this article it was specifically provided that "any crimes that may be committed on the territory of a foreign state by a Mexican against Mexicans or against foreigners, or by a foreigner against Mexicans, may be punished in Mexico, in conformity with the laws of the country." Under the terms of Article 186, Romero contended that the publication of a libel in Texas was made cognizable and punishable in Mexico, and that Cutting was properly held in prison. Bayard at once "peremptorily and positively" denied this claim of jurisdiction, and he insisted that the United States would never "assent to or permit the existence of such extra-territorial force to be given to Mexican law, nor their own jurisdiction to be so usurped, or their own local justice to be so vicariously executed by a foreign government." He also informed Romero that "the rules of International Law would forbid the assumption of such power by Mexico."

<hr/>

69. Francis Wharton to Secretary Bayard, July 24, 1886, *Bayard MS.* On August 6, 1886, S. S. Green, of St. Louis, Missouri, wrote to Bayard and stated that Cutting "was not a citizen of the United States, but is a British subject, having been born in Canada, and never having, to the personal knowledge of those knowing him for years, taken out any naturalization papers. Cutting came to this country during the late war, landing first in Chicago; thence to this City, where he enlisted in the army, but deserted without having seen service, and returned to Canada, where he remained until the close of the war, when he returned to the United States, locating west of the Mississippi, but never claiming to be a citizen of this country or exercising the right of suffrage." *Bayard MS.*

Bayard then passed on to the general complaint that the American Ministers at Mexico City had repeatedly stated that it was idle to expect justice to American citizens "in cases where they had been wronged by the officials and Government of Mexico." In order to reduce friction between the two countries, it was "essential that a spirit and readiness to redress wrongs and enforce equitable settlements of matters of difference should be constantly and practically manifested." [70]

This firm attitude towards the Mexican Government was necessary not only to secure redress of the many wrongs perpetrated upon American citizens, but also to indicate to the American Congress that the Administration was determined to safeguard American rights in Mexico. On July 26 resolutions were adopted in both the Senate and in the House of Representatives calling for the diplomatic correspondence in connection with the arrest and imprisonment of Cutting.[71] On the following day, Bayard addressed a note to Romero calling his attention to these resolutions. In concluding this communication he remarked: "What answer so creditable to Mexico or desirable for the interests of both countries could be made—as the release of Cutting? I trust I shall be enabled to embody this concluding fact in the reply to the resolutions of Congress." [72]

Romero replied at once that he was expecting a telegram from Secretary Mariscal, and as soon as it arrived he would acquaint the Secretary of State with its contents.[73] This telegram from Mariscal was handed to Bayard on July 29, and it merely stated that the "Supreme Court of Chihuahua is proceeding actively in Cutting's case. Result will depend on its legal decision." [74]

Bayard now went to work to prepare a report to the President on the Cutting Case, and he drew heavily upon the memorandum prepared by Francis Wharton.[75] On August 2 President Cleveland sent this report and certain diplomatic correspondence concerning the Cut-

70. Secretary Bayard to Jackson, July 27, 1886, *Foreign Relations, 1886*, pp. 706-707.
71. The resolution introduced by Senator John J. Ingalls on July 26, 1886, requested the President to furnish information concerning the "illegal detention" of Cutting. The language of the House resolution was similar. See *Congressional Record*, 49 Cong., 1 sess., vol. 17, pp. 7516-7517, 7579.
72. Secretary Bayard to Romero, July 27, 1886, *Bayard Letter Book*, vol. 3, *Bayard MS*.
73. Romero to Secretary Bayard, July 27, 1886, *Bayard MS*.
74. Mariscal to Romero, July 28, 1886, *ibid*.
75. Bayard submitted this report to the President on August 2, 1886. In concluding this report Bayard remarked: "The present case may constitute a precedent fraught with the most serious results." *Congressional Record*, August 3, 1886, vol. 17, p. 7920.

ting Case, to both the Senate and the House of Representatives.[76] They were also given to the press, and their publication clearly indicated the strong stand that Bayard had taken in defense of American rights.[77] Francis Wharton, who was away from Washington for a few days, was very pleased by the tone taken by Bayard. He did not know "which to be most struck with, the ability of your paper, or the folly of Mexico in setting forth the claim of jurisdiction over offences committed in the United States."[78]

But notwithstanding the emphatic tone used by Bayard in his communications to the Mexican Government, the Cutting Case continued to drag along until August 6, when the Mexican Court at Paso del Norte imposed upon the American editor the heavy sentence of imprisonment for one year at hard labor, and a fine of six hundred dollars.[79] On August 7 Bayard received a telegram from Consul Brigham, of Paso del Norte, setting forth the verdict of the court. Brigham also remarked that in Paso del Norte there was "much feeling and excitement."[80]

As soon as Bayard received Brigham's telegram, he wrote a short note to Romero and called his attention to the sentence imposed upon Cutting by Judge Zubia. Romero was then invited to Bayard's residence for an

76. James D. Richardson, *Messages and Papers of the Presidents*, vol. 8, p. 406.

77. In a letter to Bayard, August 7, 1886, George W. Gibbons expressed the belief that the "prompt action in regard to the Canadian and Mexican matters has won for you the affection and loyalty of all true Americans." *Bayard MS*. See also, A. Row to Bayard, August 8, 1886, *Bayard MS*. In an interesting editorial in the Grand Forks (North Dakota) *Herald*, August 13, 1886, reference is made to the support given by the British press to the position of the Mexican Government. England knows "that war with Mexico means that Mexico, and in time, Central America will be annexed to the United States."

A typical letter that came to Bayard after his strong stand in the Cutting Case, was from James A. Reavis, who was travelling in Spain. Reavis wrote from Seville, August 17, 1886, and remarked in part as follows: "Your position in the Cutting matter has greatly added to your former popularity among Americans abroad. As one, I can say that for the first time in my recollection the government of the United States is being recognized abroad as one capable and willing to give protection to her citizens wherever they be. . . . I have traveled many times throughout the Republic of Mexico, . . . noting with sadness the utter abandonment of our government of her citizens that are abroad in Mexico. . . . As traders they are regarded as intruders, and as tourists they are esteemed only fit subjects for the most unreasonable extortions, and upon the least provocation put in prison with an option to pay double and quadruple without available redress." *Bayard MS*.

78. Francis Wharton to Secretary Bayard, August 3, 1886, *ibid*.

79. A copy of the proceedings of the Mexican court is in the *Bayard MS*.

80. Brigham to Secretary Bayard, August 7, 1886, *ibid*.

. . . earnest conference in relation to this case which may be fraught with imporant consequences. Such action as now seems to have been taken by the Mexican authorities presents the contingency which we have heretofore so amicably discussed with the hope and aim of averting, and brings the case into a condition which demands prompt action on the part of the Executive. It is therefore important that I should have an interview with you at as early an hour as is practicable. If agreeable to you I will await you at any hour tomorrow morning at this house (my residence).[81]

Romero had a long conference with Bayard on Sunday, August 8,[82] but nothing definite was settled. On the following day he wrote to Bayard to inform him that the Mexican Constitution empowered the

. . . President to pardon parties found guilty by the Federal Courts. As the case we have been discussing, is before the State Courts, the pardon, if granted, has to come from the Governor of the State. Having inquired yesterday, after our interview, whether the sentence pronounced in the trial of Cutting, at El Paso del Norte . . . was final, I have just received an answer stating that it is not final and it has to be reviewed by the Supreme Court of the State of Chihuahua.[83]

Bayard thought that it was a matter of grave regret that the "pardoning power of the Mexican government should be so inadequate at the present serious juncture,"[84] but Romero endeavored to quiet his fears. The trial of Cutting was "proceeding regularly on appeal in the Supreme Court at Chihuahua," and when the judgment was rendered there would be time "for the consideration of the pardon." Romero was certain that Cutting would be released within a few days.[85]

81. Secretary Bayard to Romero, August 7, 1886, *ibid.*

82. Romero to Secretary Bayard, August 8, 1886, *ibid.* See also, Romero's long despatch to Bayard, Aug. 7, 1886, in which a strong defense is made of the Mexican position, *Foreign Relations, 1886*, pp. 849-856.

83. Romero to Secretary Bayard, August 9, 1886, *Bayard MS.*

84. Secretary Bayard to Romero, August 10, 1886, *Bayard MS.*

85. *Memorandum* written by Bayard after a conversation with Romero, August 11, 1886, *ibid.* On August 11, 1886, James Marr, of the El Paso Bureau of Information, wrote to Bayard to express the opinion that "Mexico must, in the interest of civilization, and humanity, be taught a severe lesson, and if this case of provocation, though it is the least of many that have occurred in the past eight years to my knowledge, is allowed to pass, it will hereafter be a danger and reproach to bear the American name in Mexico." *Bayard MS.*

During his interview with Romero on August 11, 1886, Bayard deprecated "the employment of newspapers as a means of conveying the opinions and personal actions of the representatives of foreign governments pending a transaction." *Bayard MS.* Romero was an old hand at this game of influencing American public opinion through the use of the American press. It is quite probable that the chief agent employed by Romero in this work was John W. Foster, formerly American Minister to Mexico. In a special despatch to the Baltimore *Sun*, August 14, 1886, the following statement is made: "It is broadly asserted that Mexican money is being freely used to defeat the administration

President Cleveland was greatly worried over the dangerous implications in the Cutting Case. If Cutting were not soon released from prison, public opinion in the United States might force the Administration to take some drastic action. On August 14 the President had a conference with Bayard concerning the imprisonment of Cutting,[86] but no definite action was decided upon. With things in this indefinite status, ·Bayard had an interview with Romero on August 17, and he set forth the situation without reserve. Romero indicated that he had written to the Governor of Chihuahua to urge him to speed the trial of Cutting, and if the Supreme Court did not reverse the decision of the lower court, to. issue a pardon "at once." The Governor had expressed himself in agreement with the views of Romero, and this was regarded by the Mexican Minister as a "promise on the part of the government that the pardon would be granted in case the appellate court should affirm the decision convicting Cutting."

Romero endeavored to assure Bayard that the Mexican Government had no wish for war with the United States, and it was making every effort to settle the Cutting Case in an amicable manner. Bayard replied that he took everything that Romero said

. . . as being dictated by good faith and truth, and that I wished that the settlement of Cutting's case could be arrived at as speedily as possible, because there was a great deal of excitement going on in the country; that the matter was being very much discussed, and a great many expressions of excitement were reaching this Department,[87] such as the constant offer of

in the Cutting affair by creating public sentiment in this country hostile to the position assumed by Secretary Bayard. A prominent Republican diplomatist who has criticized the action of the State Department, is said to be an agent of the Mexican government, and a strong effort is being made to work up a feeling in favor of arbitration so as to pave the way for action on the part of the administration which would afterwards be construed by its opponents as a 'back down.'" See also, Francis Wharton to Bayard, September 13, 1886, *Bayard MS.* In reply to this letter from Wharton, Bayard remarks: "I would not waste . . . ammunition on such a flibbertigibbety as Foster, who for $100 will write a reply to his own arguments." *Ibid.*

86. President Cleveland to Secretary Bayard, August 14, 1886, *Bayard MS.* See also, C. M. Handley to Bayard, August 14, 1886, *ibid.*

87. A letter illustrating the excitement in the United States with reference to the Cutting Case, was received by Bayard from Clarence Deringer, August 18, 1886. Deringer thought that Bayard should first investigate and see if the Cutting Case was not a part of a conspiracy "of certain Americans holding interests in Mexico." If Bayard secured conclusive evidence indicating that this case was not a conspiracy, he should then enforce his demand for Cutting's release "at the point of the bayonet." *Bayard MS.*

A very interesting and significant letter was written to Abram S. Hewitt by Edgar B. Bronson, August 21, 1886. According to Bronson, "most of the excitement here [at El Paso, Texas] over the Cutting affair has subsided, except among a few fire-eaters of position and a crowd of adventurers who have everything to gain and nothing to lose

armed force to compel Cutting's release. I said I merely mentioned that to him because it was undoubtedly a fact; that I deprecated all such excitement, and that I was not myself at all affected by them, but that he could see as well as I the disposition to use this case for the purpose of political excitement. Mr. Romero then said he would telegraph the Governor of Chihuahua and urge him to act promptly in the matter.[88]

On August 18 Romero wrote to Bayard to inform him that a telegram had been received from the Governor of Chihuahua stating that the Cutting Case would come before the Supreme Court on August 20.[89] Two days later he called at the Department of State and handed Bayard a copy of a letter from Felix F. Maceyra, the Governor of the State of Chihuahua, to Romero, dated August 13, 1886. Maceyra insisted that the State Government only sought the "triumph of its rights, and it is proper to state, once for all, that its prosecutions are in no wise rancorous. The State would be much pleased if Cutting were acquitted;

---

by war. Cutting is a vagabond journalist devoid of character or honor, who has been publishing a paper in Paso del Norte for some time. Emigdio Medain is a California Mexican who has been resident in Paso del Norte, I believe, about six years. Unless matriculated in Mexico, he is a citizen of the United States. . . . I may say that it is undoubtedly susceptible of absolute proof that Cutting's allegations about Medina were true in every particular, and that he is a 'fraud' and swindler as claimed. . . . From beginning to end Cutting has . . . refused to recognize the jurisdiction of the court before which he was brought, and at examinations and trial alike refused to testify, refused to hire counsel, and when offered the opportunity by the court rather early in the proceedings, refused to accept bail. In short, he declined by his refusal to testify and to employ counsel, to correct or enlighten the court as to the true facts of the case against him. His individual purpose in the matter has been to seek notoriety and to get in such position that he should have a tangible claim for damages against Mexico for false imprisonment." See also, Abram S. Hewitt to Bayard, August 30, 1886, *Bayard MS.* In Bayard's reply to Hewitt, August 31, 1886, he remarked: "I am disposed to believe that greater security to American property and person in Mexico will result from the incident, and that by harmonizing the pretensions of Mexico with the system of local jurisdiction of the United States, our citizens can only be held liable for the violation of laws which they are bound to obey, and that does *not* include the criminal laws of any foreign power." *Bayard Letter Book,* vol. 3, *Bayard MS.*

88. *Memorandum* written by Bayard after a conversation with Romero, August 17, 1886, *Bayard MS.* On the afternoon of August 17 Romero sent to Bayard a copy of the decision of Judge Zubia in the lower Mexican court with reference to the Cutting Case. Romero to Bayard, August 17, 1886, *ibid.*

In a letter to John P. Stockton, August 18, 1886, Bayard made the following comment upon the Cutting Case: "What shifting or changing, under the instruction and suggestion of our fellow citizens here, the Mexican officials may be able to make, I know not. . . . Imprisonment for thirty days without bail or information of a charge, indeed with refusal of both, is not Civilization, and if we do not demand instant release in such case, *when* ought we to?" *Bayard Letter Book,* vol. 3. *Bayard MS.*

89. Romero to Secretary Bayard, August 18, 1886, *Bayard MS.* See also, Bayard to Romero, August 19, 1886, *Bayard Letter Book,* vol. 3, *ibid.*

and if he be condemned, and asks pardon, you may rest assured that it will be granted to him." [90]

Romero concluded this interview of August 20 by informing Bayard that Cutting would not have to ask for the pardon. That formality would be attended to by his attorney, and was of no real importance.[91]

This assurance was comforting to Bayard who was continually receiving letters strongly urging him to take drastic action against Mexico. Even his old, and usually well-balanced friend, Edwards Pierrepont did not escape this contagion. On August 21 he wrote to Bayard in the vein of a dyed-in-the-wool imperialist. He first expressed the view that

. . . the best men of the country without regard to party, heartily approve your course, and with great unanimity, feel that if war results from it, good and not evil will follow.

I think it must be apparent to anyone who has observed the course of events since Louis Napoleon attempted to establish an Empire in Mexico, that some European Power will control Mexico before very long unless the United States take possession of it. Such attempt on the part of any great power in Europe would involve us in war, with that power, but if Mexico, by her own act involves us in war and we acquire the country as we acquired California, we should escape foreign complications and the civilization of the world would be largely advanced.

. . . A just war with Mexico would surely be vastly popular; it would consolidate the Union, and utterly wipe out the last lingering of unpleasant memories of the late civil war, and bring to the Administration, which brought the war to successful issue, imperishable renown.[92]

Because of the strength of this annexationist sentiment, Bayard was vastly relieved when the Supreme Court of Chihuahua, on August 21 ordered the release of Cutting. This decision was based upon the fact that Emigdio Medina had withdrawn his action against Cutting, and as the principal motive of the suit no longer existed, the court decided

90. Governor Maceyra to Romero, August 13, 1886, *ibid.*
91. Secretary Bayard to Romero, August 20, 1886, *Bayard Letter Book*, vol. 3, *ibid.*
92. Edwards Pierrepont to Bayard, August 21, 1886, *Bayard MS.* Among other letters received by Bayard concerning the Cutting Case, was one from John Markham, of Texas. Markham had come to New York City for the purpose of raising recruits for a war with Mexico, and according to a statement in the New York *Daily News*, August 18, 1886, he had gathered some 12,000 men for this adventure. In a letter to Bayard, August 27, 1886, Markham commended Bayard's attitude in the Cutting affair as "that of an American statesman and official, wise, brave, high-minded, patriotic. . . . Allow me to assure you that the bold attitude you assumed from the inception of the controversy to the present, has made you many warm friends in this city [New York]. . . . A new war with Mexico is necessary and just. Only a *foreign war* will save us from a *Social War.*" *Bayard MS.*

that there was no longer any "sufficient ground to continue the case." [93]

The news of the decision of the Supreme Court of Chihuahua was telegraphed immediately to Bayard. Thręe days after the decision had been rendered, Romero sent a formal note to Bayard advising him of Cutting's release.[94] Bayard replied by expressing the hope that "steps will now be promptly taken by the Government of Mexico to harmonize important jurisdictional questions, and remove the present incompatibilities between the laws of the two countries." [95]

Bayard's own feelings in the matter were given full rein in a letter to J. S. Moore. He was

. . . amazed that the danger contained in the broad assumption of Mexico to punish in her tribunals and according to her methods "any crimes committed in the United States upon a Mexican," should not be realized by the common popular sense. With a border line of 2000 miles, rudely and scantily populated, such a pretension by Mexico is a standing menace to the peace of the two Countries, and now that it has been for the *first time* asserted (and promptly denied by me) we must go to work to procure its withdrawal by Mexico by amending her laws.

I confess I was vexed to see in the *Herald* a statement of *my* reply to Blaine, when I had not seen, nor spoken to anyone connected with the *Herald* for weeks, and had never even read Blaine's speech, when I was reported replying to it in the *Herald*. Of Blaine I need say nothing—nothing short of omnipotence could make a gentleman or fair-minded man of him—but he is very shrewd, and in making the protective tariff the *cheval de bataille* of his address, he has assumed the leadership of the best organized, most potent, mercenary, and wholly unscrupulous party in the United States. He is a fit leader, and has a proper following.[96]

President Cleveland himself was very glad that Bayard had gotten "rid of that pestilential business"—the Cutting Case.[97] In reply, Bayard pointed out that the Mexican Government had been deeply impressed with the stand taken by the Department of State in the Cutting matter, and had recently issued a Foreign Office circular which instructed Mex-

93. *Foreign Relations*, 1887, pp. 766-767.
94. Romero to Secretary Bayard, August 24, 1886, *Bayard MS.*
95. Secretary Bayard to Romero, August 26, 1886, *ibid.* After Cutting's release, S. L. M. Barlow wrote to Bayard and remarked: "The release of Cutting will, I assume, put an end to annoyance in that matter and I hope that those who have from the beginning been most unjust and unkind to you, may be brought to recognize the fact that you have simply done your whole duty ably and earnestly; as you were sure to do, on the assumption, doubtless true, that the original arrest was for an offence consummated in the United States." *Ibid.*
96. Bayard to J. S. Moore, August 26, 1886, *ibid.* See also J. S. Moore to Bayard, August 25, 1886, *ibid.*
97. President Cleveland to Bayard, August 26, 1886, *ibid.*

ican courts to observe special care with reference to suits involving the rights of foreigners.[98] To Bayard it seemed impossible to doubt that most Americans would "perceive and sustain the *principle* we have striven for in the case of Cutting. I must now go to work and get Mexico to change her law, and abandon the claim of power to try our citizens for offences against her own laws committed within our jurisdiction."[99]

But before Bayard could turn to this new task he was confronted with a situation that was extremely embarrassing to him. In order to secure a complete and impartial report on all the aspects of the Cutting Case, Bayard sent Arthur G. Sedgwick, a well known New York lawyer, to Mexico as a special agent of the Department of State.[100] It is likely that this appointment was somewhat displeasing to Henry R. Jackson, the American Minister at Mexico City, and to James W. Porch, the American Consul-General at that city. At any rate, on August 31 Porch sent to Bayard a telegram stating that Sedgwick had been found dead drunk "in a house of prostitution and now is the laughing stock of all Mexicans."[101]

Sedgwick immediately denied this charge as "ridiculously false," and Bayard wrote in pencil across this telegram: "Your personal denial is sufficient."[102] Bayard also directed James D. Porter, the Assistant Secretary of State, to send an instruction to Consul Porch, reprimanding him for discussing at a public meeting in Mexico City the telegram he had sent to the Department of State. The instruction to Porch was exceedingly sharp in tone. With reference to Porch's action at the public meeting, the instruction remarked:

98. A copy of this circular was reproduced in the Baltimore *Sun*, August 30, 1886. It should also be noted, however, that on August 30, 1886, Romero sent to Bayard copies of two notes that Secretary Mariscal had sent to him (Mariscal to Romero, August 12, 13, 1886). These notes are long and closely reasoned defences of the position taken by the Mexican Government in the Cutting Case. *Foreign Relations, 1886*, pp. 857-862.

99. Bayard to President Cleveland, August 30, 1886, *Bayard Letter Book*, vol. 3, *Bayard MS*. In a letter to John O. Broadhead, August 30, 1886, Bayard made the following comment: "I have been astounded at the shortsightedness of even the partisans, in their failure to appreciate the importance of the principle involved in the Mexican pretension of extra-territorial force and within the United States of her laws. The case in hand was obscured somewhat by its facts, but the thing contended for was not to be obscured, and I hope now to procure such abatement of the claim contained in the Mexican code as will remove the menace now existing to the peace of the two adjoining countries." *Bayard Letter Book*, vol. 3, *ibid*.

100. Henry M. Wriston, *Executive Agents in American Foreign Relations*, pp. 815-817.

101. James W. Porch to Secretary Bayard, August 31, 1886, *Bayard MS*.

102. A. G. Sedgwick to Secretary Bayard, August 31, 1886, *ibid*.

The Department is at a loss to understand your interference, as Consul-General, in a matter which, whether true or not, in no way was within your official competence, and on the other hand fails to discern your authority to speak as a private individual in representation of the resident American community which, . . . did not share your feelings. The Department of State is abundantly able to protect its own honor, and equally so to defend its representatives from any aspersions which may prove to be unfounded; and must be permitted to judge of the necessity for action.[103]

On September 1 Sedgwick wrote a personal letter to Bayard thanking him for not believing the scandalous stories about his conduct. If Sedgwick were to take the time to refute these stories, he would have no time for official business, but all "the gentlemen" of his acquaintance in Mexico City had assured him that they regarded "the whole thing as a most cruel outrage." [104]

There were some Americans in Mexico City who were not "gentlemen" of Sedgwick's acquaintance, because letters began to pour into the Department of State concerning his conduct in Mexico. On September 7, E. P. Woodward sent the following note to Senator Richard Coke, of Texas, who promptly turned it over to Bayard:

> The Sedgwick affair will be variously reported to you. I have taken pains to inquire into it and find that the conduct of Genl. Sedgwick was horribly disgraceful. He was notoriously and noisily drunk at a Ball given in his honor by an aristocratic club, from which entertainment he went to a Bawdy House and was known to be there until 2 P.M. the next day. All efforts to White Wash Sedgwick ought to fail as they will be based entirely on falsehoods.[105]

In a note to Bayard, Senator Coke stated that Woodward was a "highly esteemed" friend of his who could be "fully relied on." [106] His story of the dubious antics of Sedgwick was corroborated by many other accounts that were sent to Bayard. The despatch from the American Minister, Henry J. Jackson, was very damaging to Sedgwick's reputa-

103. James D. Porter to Porch, September 1, 1886, *Bayard MS.* See also, New York *Herald,* August 31, 1886. At first Bayard had decided not to "notice Mr. Porch's telegram just now, and to await Mr. Sedgwick's return. The episode is not fit for discussion, viewed from any standpoint, and no benefit can result from contributing to the taste for scandalous gossip already so ripe in the Press." *Memorandum* written by Bayard on scratch paper, September 1, 1886, *Bayard MS.* In a letter to President Cleveland, August 30, 1886, Bayard made the following comment about Sedgwick: "I do not credit the statements about Sedgwick's escapade. The press seems as scandalous and false as ever." *Bayard Letter Book,* vol. 3, *Bayard MS.*

104. A. G. Sedgwick to Secretary Bayard, September 1, 1886, *ibid.*

105. E. P. Woodward to Senator Richard Coke, September 7, 1886, *ibid.*

106. Senator Richard Coke to Secretary Bayard, *Bayard MS.*

tion,[107] and the letters of Consul-General Porch left nothing to the imagination.[108]

Bayard's reaction to these letters from Jackson and Porch was strongly negative. He had long been of the opinion that Jackson was not the proper person to represent the United States at Mexico City, and on August 19 he had informed Jackson that the Department of State would place no "obstructions" in the way of his resignation.[109] On September 4 Jackson recounted in detail the reasons for his resignation (which had already been accepted), and on October 7 he presented his letter of recall to the Mexican Foreign Office and terminated his official duties.[110]

Bayard was glad to get rid of Jackson whom he regarded as a person afflicted with a "mental disorder." Jackson's despatches had indicated that far from

107. Jackson to Secretary Bayard, September 9, 1886, *ibid.* In this long despatch, Jackson vehemently denies that he felt any hostility towards Sedgwick because of the latter's appointment as special agent to Mexico. He also states that the "idea that anyone in the American 'colony' in this city [Mexico City] had the slightest disposition to do Mr. Sedgwick harm is simply absurd." With reference to Sedgwick's conduct in Mexico City he is distinctly critical, and he relates what transpired during an interview with Sedgwick at the American Legation after Sedgwick's fall from grace. This interview was "short and painful. He made no formal confession, but he certainly knew that I was advised of the substance of what had transpired and he made no reference to, nor denial of it. I expressed my deep sympathy with him in the calamity which had overtaken him. Shortly after he muttered something about 'cutting his throat,' but finally announced his determination to deny the whole thing." With reference to the telegram that Consul-General Porch sent to the Department of State, Jackson makes the following comment: "While it is true that I declined to sign it with him, it is due to simple justice to say that I am sure it was sent from the purest sense of official duty." *Bayard MS.* In a memorandum attached to this despatch from Jackson, Bayard wrote: "This despatch will not go upon the files."

108. In a letter from Consul-General Porch to J. W. Denver, August 30, 1886, there is the following account of the actions of Sedgwick on the night of August 27: "He commenced drinking toasts with Romero Rubio about ten o'clock, he continued drinking with the wealthy people of this city, and in the morning about six o'clock, he came into the Hotel Iturbide, in company with ten gentlemen belonging to the best families in the City of Mexico. Those Mexican[s] made him dance the *can can* in the patio of the Hotel Iturbide, then marched him into the patio of the Hotel San Carlos, then sang and hollowed hurrah for the great American special agent and hurrahed for Mexico. Then they . . . took off his coat and pulled . . . him all over the parlor floor on his back, then sat down on his stomach and said now we sit down upon the great American Government as we sit upon her agent." *Bayard MS.* See also, New York *World*, September 1, 1886.

In several enclosures in a letter from J. L. Morgan, the secretary of the American Legation in Mexico City, to Bayard, October 1, 1886, there are further accounts of the disgraceful antics of Sedgwick. There is little doubt that the American "colony" in Mexico City was sympathetic towards the American Minister, H. R. Jackson, and bitterly antagonistic towards Sedgwick. *Bayard MS.*

109. Secretary Bayard to Jackson, August 19, 1886, *Mexico, Instructions*, vol. 21, MS Dept. of State.

110. Jackson to Secretary Bayard, September 4, October 7, 1886, *Mexico, Despatches*, vol. 91, MS Dept. of State.

. . . seeking to effect a closer trade union with Mexico, he has inculcated the greatest distrust in that Country and its government. He has pictured in the darkest colors the senility and corruption of the officials, and the hopelessness of dealing with them on a basis of justice and honesty. He has sought to obtain authority to threaten *reprisals* as the only mode to obtain redress for our citizens. . . . He persistently sought the place, and has done nothing but find fault since he went into it. His retirement is a public service.[111]

Jackson's retirement as Minister to Mexico did not put an end to the sharp criticism that continued to circulate concerning the conduct of Sedgwick, and his support by the Cleveland Administration. In a personal letter to Bayard from Mexico City, J. L. Morgan, the secretary of the American Legation, stated that the American "colony" in Mexico strongly resented "the indignity and humiliation which Mr. Sedgwick's conduct imposed upon them," and they were "severely critical" of the attitude taken by the Department of State.[112]

But these criticisms did not prevent Bayard from forcing Consul-General Porch to resign from his post in Mexico City. On December 8 Sedgwick wrote to Bayard and inquired what action would be taken with regard to Porch, who had acted as a "blackguard" in the matter of aspersing Sedgwick's reputation.[113] Bayard immediately took this

111. *Memorandum* written by Bayard and dated, September, 1886, *Bayard MS.* These comments of Bayard with reference to Jackson are very similar to those expressed by M. L. Guiraud during an interview with Bayard. Guiraud, a resident of Mexico City, informed Bayard that Jackson was a "Union-hater. He hates the Constitution and the Government, and has frequently expressed a wish to see it go to pieces. He has not accepted in his heart the result of the war. I once addressed him as 'Mr.' and apologized, changed the address to 'General.' He said, 'My dear fellow, there is no harm in that. I am no general. I cannot wear my uniform.' " Guiraud then asked Bayard if he knew why Jackson had desired the mission to Mexico. When Bayard answered in the negative, Guiraud remarked: "As I said before, he [Jackson] hates the Government of this country and would welcome its overthrow. His idea was to work upon the Mexican feeling of hostility towards the United States; to endeavor to bring about a rupture (in the meantime by means of his position of United States Minister to work himself into close intimacy with the Mexican authorities) and in the event of his efforts in this line being successful, he would take some position in the Mexican service against the United States. Such was his feeling of bitterness towards this Government."

At the conclusion of Guiraud's remarks, Bayard exclaimed: "That is monstrous, and I really cannot credit it. The only way I could possibly give belief to such a thing, is on the supposition that Mr. Jackson is of unsound mind, and I really have thought so at times." *Memorandum* written by Bayard after a conversation with Guiraud, April 9, 1887.

112. J. L. Morgan to Secretary Bayard, October 1, 1886, *Bayard MS.*

113. A. G. Sedgwick to Secretary Bayard, December 8, 1886. In the course of his letter, Sedgwick made the following comments: "When I returned from Mexico you assured me of your sympathy as regarded the attacks of the Press, and spoke most severely of the conduct of the U. S. Consul in the City of Mexico. You said that in your opinion he ought to be removed on the spot, and gave me the impression that this would in all probability be done as soon as the President returned to Washington. Again when I saw you at Mr.

matter up with the President, whose reaction was along the lines expected by Bayard: "There's Porch. I told Vest he would not do this morning and he said he had nothing to say. The whole Mexican business ought to be cleaned up and as quickly as possible. I guess there may be one decent one in the lot, a clerk named Butler. All the rest should go." [114]

Senator Vest wrote to Porch and informed him that the Department of State wished him to send in his resignation, to take effect on April 1, 1887. Senator Cockrell wrote to Porch in a similar vein, and in February, 1887, Bayard inquired through Manning, the new American Minister at Mexico City, if Porch had sent in his resignation. Porch refused to take this action, and President Cleveland removed him by sending to the Senate the nomination of E. G. Love as the new Consul-General.[115]

Barlow's house, you spoke of 'punishing' the Consul for what he had done, as the only proper course for the Government to take. I think under these circumstances that there is no impropriety in my asking you what is going to be done in the matter? If you do nothing, I suffer for it, as the retention of Porch in office is a vindication of his conduct. . . . He persecuted me like a blackguard from one end of Mexico to the other. . . . I am not sufficiently Christian to pass the matter over if I can obtain redress." *Bayard MS.*

114. President Cleveland to Bayard, December 10, 1886, *ibid.*

115. See remarks of J. W. Porch in the newspaper, *Two Republics,* printed in Mexico City, February 9, 1887. In an interview with M. L. Guiraud, April 9, 1887, Bayard made the following comments about Porch: "As regards this man Porch, I thought he was a fool before, but when the Sedgwick case came up I found he was a knave. There was a Minister there with a cipher, and any information he wished to convey to me he could have sent through that secret medium. Instead of that, he gave the matter every possible publicity. He telegraphed to N. Y. *Herald* and published this vile story about a private individual. It was a base and unkind thing to do." *Bayard MS.* See also Bayard's letter to Senator J. R. Hawley, February 28, 1887, in which the same criticism is made of Porch. *Bayard MS.*

Bayard was not completely satisfied with the account given by Sedgwick of his conduct in Mexico City. On February 18, he wrote to Professor Francis Wayland, of Yale University, concerning the Sedgwick affair. The importance of "comprehending the forces at work in Mexico" were of far more importance than any mere personal question. *Bayard MS.* On March 11, 1887, Professor Wayland wrote to Bayard and enclosed a letter from a friend in Mexico City. Wayland believed this correspondent to be a person of "absolute integrity and impartiality." In this letter from Mexico the sharpest criticisms were made of Sedgwick. At a ball given in Mexico City on August 27, 1886, Sedgwick became "intoxicated, so much so that twice during the evening Mexican gentlemen removed their wives from his company. From the ball he went, soon after midnight, with several members of the Jockey Club, to the second or inner 'patio' of the Iturbide Hotel, and here the party engaged for some time in a sort of 'can-can' dance, Mr. S. wearing a wreath of flowers around his neck or shoulders. He fell down several times, and once slightly cut his face." The rest of the letter reveals far more shocking conduct on the part of the American special agent, and the correspondent ended his letter by saying that the American "colony" was unanimous in its support of Porch. *Bayard MS.* Bayard, however, did not believe that Porch should have reported these Anacreontic activities in a telegram to the Department of State which he immediately made public. Bayard to Francis Wayland, March 4, 1887, *Bayard Letter Book,* vol. 4, *Bayard MS.*

But the elimination of Jackson and Porch from the Mexican scene did not mean that things in Mexico City would move with the quiet dignity for which Bayard ardently wished. Once more the shadow of John Barleycorn fell across the threshold of the American Legation. On August 30, 1886, Bayard sent to President Cleveland the commission of Thomas C. Manning as Minister to Mexico. Bayard thought the change in Ministers was "most beneficial, and unless I am greatly mistaken our present selection is wise." Manning had held the high office of Chief Justice of the Louisiana Supreme Court, and appeared to be a man of "dignity and high character." [116]

Manning had been in Mexico only a few weeks when he began to complain about the small sum that was allocated to the Legation for expenses.[117] It seemed to Bayard that "the first thing a man does when he gets into a place is to *complain* of something. . . . I fear we have engaged another grumbler." [118]

It was not long before Manning did far more than mere grumbling. On November 22 word came from Mexico City that Manning had been on a drunken debauch and had disgraced the office of American Minister. Manning himself sent a piteous telegram to Bayard:

A malicious man will send a telegram to a newspaper that I have been drunk. I give you my word of honor that I have not been in public, nor have been seen exposed. I have been in my room and not even in the dining room of the hotel. . . . I drank more than I should have done but privately. Do not let me be ruined for this thing. It shall never occur again. I am in your hands.[119]

Bayard immediately replied that Manning's telegram had caused him "distress and anxiety," and he earnestly requested a full explanation.[120] This explanation came in the form of a telegram from J. L. Morgan, the Secretary of the American Legation. According to Mor-

---

On September 17, 1892, Porch wrote a letter to President Cleveland and reviewed the whole Sedgwick affair. He thought that he had been "ignominiously treated" by Secretary Bayard, and before he would take any active steps to promote the re-election of Cleveland, he wished to have some "expressions of opinion" which would clearly indicate "to what extent" Cleveland had "participated in Mr. Bayard's course." *Cleveland MS.* Needless to say, there is no answer in the Cleveland manuscripts to this letter.

116. Bayard to President Cleveland, August 30, 1886, *Bayard Letter Book*, vol. 3, *Bayard MS.*

117. Manning to Secretary Bayard, November 4, 1886, *Bayard MS.*

118. *Memorandum* written by Bayard, November 12, 1886, *ibid.*

119. Manning to Secretary Bayard, November 22, 1886, *ibid.*

120. Bayard to Manning, November 23, 1886, *Bayard MS.*

gan, Manning was "drunk in his room and unfit for business for four
and one-half days, at times wild. This is generally known here." [121]
It appeared to Mr. Adee that Morgan was a

. . . meddlesome fellow whose "sense of duty" is only too ready to prompt
him to send off just such a telegram as this, to undo any possible lenient and
compassionate feeling that might have been created in your mind by poor
Mr. Manning's piteous telegram. . . . That scoundrel Guiraud . . . is, I
believe, wilfully responsible for this fresh disgrace. He got Sedgwick into his
scrape, and now repeats his game successfully with Manning.[122]

This new scandal in Mexico City depressed Bayard greatly, and he
expressed his feelings in a short memorandum written on scratch paper: "This is indeed a miserable state of affairs. I must await Mr. Manning's letter, but how shall I feel the slightest confidence in him, or
Morgan (who was the selection of Jackson)?" [123]

Bayard's embarrassment was increased when he received on November 26 another telegram from Morgan which said that Manning was
"wildly drunk again yesterday, and thoroughly unfit for business today and possibly for days." [124]

Morgan next secured from Dr. A. W. Parsons, Chief Surgeon of the
Mexican National Railroad, a full statement concerning Manning's
condition which he sent to Bayard on November 30.[125] Before Bayard
had received this letter he instructed Morgan to "protect" the Minister
from any "injurious publicity." Morgan replied that Manning's indiscretion was known by the Mexican Government and by the "public
generally." Americans resident in Mexico City were "intensely mortified." [126] In a letter of November 30 Morgan stated that "no member

121. J. L. Morgan to Secretary Bayard, November 24, 1886, *ibid.* In a letter to Bayard,
November 24, 1886, Morgan elaborates upon his telegram. On November 18 Judge Manning had breakfasted with M. L. Guiraud, and "did not return to the Legation until yesterday morning, 23rd. instant. On Friday evening last, 19th instant, the Manager of the
Hotel at which the Minister lives, sent for Mr. Butler, the Legation Clerk, . . . and told
him the Minister was drinking too much cognac. I was at once advised of the case and
thereafter until the arrival of his family yesterday morning, . . . I had him carefully
watched and attended in order to prevent a public scandal. The affair has become generally known here through the Hotel manager and servants who saw what transpired. . . .
The writing of these lines has cost me intense pain." *Bayard MS.*
122. Alvey A. Adee to Secretary Bayard, November 24, 1886, *ibid.*
123. *Memorandum* written by Bayard, November 25, 1886, *ibid.*
124. J. L. Morgan to Secretary Bayard, November 26, 1886, *ibid.*
125. A. W. Parsons to J. L. Morgan, November 29, 1886, *Bayard MS.* In this report by
Dr. Parsons it appeared that Manning had narrowly escaped an attack of delirium tre-
mens. He was also suffering from a slight attack of pneumonia.
126. Secretary Bayard to J. L. Morgan, November 29, 1886; J. L. Morgan to Secretary
Bayard, November 30, 1886, *Bayard MS.*

of the Government has spoken to me of this regrettable occurrence, but a Cabinet Minister spoke, confidentially, of it to an American friend of mine last week." [127]

Manning could do nothing but throw himself upon the mercy of Bayard. He was certain that Morgan, the Secretary of the Legation, had sought his ruin, "and if he accomplishes it, it will not only be my ruin but that of my family." Morgan was the son-in-law of General John B. Frisbie, who had long wanted to be American Minister to Mexico. He hoped to secure this post through the recall of Manning. [128]

On December 10 President Cleveland wrote to inform Bayard that he was "holding up" Manning's nomination to the Senate as Minister to Mexico. [129] But Manning had strong political support, and Senator R. L. Gibson, of Louisiana, wrote to Bayard that he was certain that the Senate would vote to confirm the nomination. [130] Bayard was glad to receive this news because he had felt a genuine sympathy for Manning. He had steadfastly refused to take the action that certain self-seekers had suggested, and he had kept Manning at his post to the great dismay of John B. Frisbie and J. L. Morgan. [131]

While Bayard was busily engaged in his endeavors to quiet the scandals arising out of the dubious antics of Sedgwick and Manning, he was also occupied with the task of discussing with Mexico the many

127. J. L. Morgan to Bayard, November 30, 1886, *ibid.*

128. Manning to Secretary Bayard, November 30, 1886, *ibid.* In a letter to Bayard, December 5, 1886, M. L. Guiraud echoes these charges of Manning about Morgan and Frisbie. Frisbie had for the past seven years been "a perpetual candidate to the Mexican mission, probably more for the advantage which he could personally derive from it . . . than for the good of either people. . . . In the opinion of unprejudiced Americans here, statements concerning the American Minister are made to favor private interests, to attack the administration, and to compel a change for the benefit of favorites." *Bayard MS.* It was significant that the attacks upon Manning were aired in the columns of the newspaper, *Two Republics,* which was edited by Mr. Mastella Clark, who had married a niece of the former Minister to Mexico, Henry R. Jackson. Clark had been exceedingly bitter in his attacks upon Bayard. See, A. G. Greenwood to Bayard, December 18, 1886, *Bayard MS.* See also, The New Orleans *Daily Picayune,* December 2, 23, 1886.

129. President Cleveland to Bayard, December 10, 1886, *Bayard MS.*

130. R. L. Gibson to Secretary Bayard, December 31, 1886, *Bayard MS.* According to Senator Gibson, Manning's appointment as Minister to Mexico would gratify the people of Louisiana who "believe him to be a high minded and very gifted man, who has been betrayed by his own Secretary. . . . I have conferred with the Members of the Foreign Affairs Committee, especially with Edmunds and Sherman, and I believe there will be no trouble."

131. In a letter to Bayard, March 11, 1887, Manning expressed his gratitude for the support he had received: "I desire to thank the President and yourself for the firm and cordial manner in which both have stood by me in the trying ordeal through which I have passed. I have no fitting words in which to express my gratitude, and I shall let my acts attest it." *Bayard MS.*

complicated legal questions that were connected with the Cutting Case. During an interview with Romero, September 1, 1886, Bayard canvassed many of these legal points. Romero alluded to the fact that Secretary Mariscal had expressed his view of Mexican law and procedure in two notes which had been turned over to the Department of State. Bayard replied that he was aware that Mariscal had published one of these notes in Mexico

. . . before it was possible for me to see it, and that I supposed he did it with a view of satisfying public opinion in Mexico. He said yes; he supposed that was so.

I [Bayard] told him that the opinion had been largely published in this country by those who were desirous of taking the Mexican view of the case, and that when I received through Mr. Sedgwick an authentic statement of what was the Mexican law—Federal and State—and what was the record of the proceedings in Cutting's case, so that there should no longer be any ground for misapprehension of what had been decided and the grounds for the decision, I would then be prepared to submit my view of the transaction.

I told him I could not help thinking that Mr. Mariscal's contention amounted to this: That if any claim of power was put forth which was not absolutely denied by the law of nations, that it became thereby enrolled as a law of nations. I said I thought Mr. M. would find it very difficult to maintain such a proposition; that it was making laws of negation instead of affirmation—a thing I had never heard of before and which I did not believe could exist. . . .

I suggested that as Mr. Mariscal considered Mexico had the power and the claim was repelled by the Government of the United States, that Mexico could retain, if she desired, the claim of such a power over other countries and omit the United States, and that could be effectuated by simply an amendment to their statute and putting in the words "Except the United States of America." That would be perfectly satisfactory to us, and the Mexican Government could continue domination over the countries of Central and South America, or any other country they pleased, although I thought it quite likely that Great Britain would be found as jealous of this jurisdiction as we were. . . .

He said that he was in favor of Mexico taking this action, and I said I hoped they would do it without any pressure or demand on our part; that they would do it voluntarily.[132]

As Bayard had intimated in this conversation with Romero, the Mexican Government had taken its case before the American people by publishing its diplomatic notes before they were sent to the Department of State. This strategy had been quite successful in certain quar-

132. *Memorandum* written by Bayard after a conversation with Romero, September 1, 1886, *Bayard MS.*

ters, and in the American press there were many articles which favored the Mexican contention. In the New York *Evening Post*, August 24, 1886, a letter was published over the initial "D." In this letter it was pointed out that sections 676 and 678 of the Penal Code of New York, were very similar to the provisions of the municipal law of the Mexican State of Chihuahua. Section 676 read as follows: "A person who commits an act without this State which affects persons or property within this State, or the public health, morals, or decency of this State, and which, if committed within this State, would be a crime, is punishable as if the act were committed within this State."

The Mexican statute was more carefully drawn than the New York code. According to section 676, an act committed without the state need not be a crime at all in the place of performance to be punishable in New York, and it would be punished as if the act were committed within the limits of New York. Considering the wording of this section, it seemed obvious that the action of the State of Chihuahua was not so unusual as it first appeared. Suppose one would take the towns of Prescott and Ogdensburg, on opposite sides of the St. Lawrence River. If Cutting had been a Canadian and Medina a New Yorker, and if Cutting had composed and published in Prescott (Canada) a libel on Medina, and had afterwards gone to Ogdensburg (New York), it would have been entirely possible for Medina to have had Cutting arrested and brought to trial in Ogdensburg for criminal libel.[133]

In commenting upon this interpretation, Francis Wharton, the Solicitor of the Department of State, remarked: "We concede that if an offence is started in one country *with intent* that it shall take effect in another, and so takes effect, the latter has cognizance."[134]

It was the contention of the government of the State of Chihuahua that Cutting had published his attack upon Medina for the express purpose of injuring the latter's standing in Mexico. He had been restrained by legal action in Chihuahua from continuing such publications, and he had circumvented this restraint by going to El Paso, Texas, and publishing the libel in that town. If this offence was committed in Texas with the "intent that it shall take effect in another country," and this intent was clearly established, the American case in support of Cutting was somewhat shaky.

According to J. L. Morgan, the Secretary of the American Legation

133. New York *Evening Post*, August 24, 1886.
134. *Memorandum* prepared by Wharton for Bayard, August 27, 1886, *Bayard MS*.

in Mexico, the feeling of Americans in Mexico City was quite hostile to the stand taken by Bayard. These Americans insisted that the laws of Texas and New York were

. . . almost identical with those of Mexico upon the question of extra-territorial jurisdiction; that Cutting being domiciled in Mexico was subject to the jurisdiction of Mexican Courts; that the publication of his article in the El Paso (Texas) *Herald* was but one link in a long chain of facts, and that the circumstances did not warrant the peremptory demand made for his (Cutting's) release. Doubtless, political motives governed some Americans in their opinions; interest, others, but the large majority seem to have given the case careful study and to be conscientious in their expressions that Mexico had won the argument of the case. . . . The Cutting case gave rise to a seemingly honest difference of opinion between a large majority of Americans resident in Mexico and yourself, but little if any feeling entering into the result of a cool judgment.[135]

It is apparent that Bayard was deeply concerned over the implications of the Cutting Case, and he frankly confessed to Wharton that it involved some very "profound questions" of International Law. After careful study he could see its consequences

. . . stretching out in vistas in all directions. Our position of denial of the Mexican claim of jurisdiction was thoroughly sustained by the weight of authority in the French Debates of 1866, when they reformed their old pretensions. In 1852 an act extending this extra-territorial jurisdiction passed the House of Deputies, but was withdrawn in the Senate because of Diplomatic protest. This was Great Britain, of course, and I shall get the correspondence, I think. . . . *One* point, I think, the Mexican case fixes, i.e., that the *existence* of the case against Cutting and its *prosecution* at every stage, was under the thumb and finger of Medina, so that this exercise of International Law and extra-territorial authority was vested in or was controlled by the caprice or desires of a private individual. This is one *reductio ad absurdum*. But graver issues are involved which we will discuss when you come on.[136]

With reference to French precedents in this matter of jurisdiction, Bayard wrote to Robert M. McLane, the American Minister at Paris, and requested him to look into the matter and send a report to the Department of State.[137] He had already received from the Marquis de

135. J. L. Morgan to Secretary Bayard, October 1, 1886, *Personal and Private, Bayard MS.* Romero had sent to Bayard on September 9, 1886, a complete copy of the correspondence published by the Mexican Government relative to the Cutting Case. *Bayard MS.*

136. Bayard to Francis Wharton, September 15, 1886, *Bayard Letter Book,* vol. 3, *Bayard MS.*

137. Bayard to Robert M. McLane, September 13, 1886, *ibid.*

Chambrun a report on the extent of French criminal jurisdiction. After reading this report Bayard was of the opinion that as long as

. . . the tie of citizenship exists, it is natural that the control of the State claiming, and entitled to his allegiance, should be exercised whenever he was found within her territory, but when the supposed offender is *not* a citizen, and owes no allegiance to a Country, the proposition to punish him for acts committed within, and against the laws of the *only* country to whom he owes allegiance *without the consent* of that country, cannot be sustained upon any theory of the independent autonomy of Sovereign states.[138]

Bayard had written to Phelps at London, as well as to McLane, at Paris, with reference to British precedents that might be of service in settling the Cutting Case, and it must have been reassuring to receive from Phelps the opinion that the stand taken by the Department of State was "right beyond question."[139] But there were many doubts as to the attitude of the Mexican Government in this matter. Romero himself tried to relieve Bayard's apprehensions about the probable action of President Diaz. In an interview with Bayard he expressed the view that the

. . . Mexican Government would be disposed to harmonize their laws so as to avoid the conflict with the laws and Government of the United States. I [Bayard] asked him how long it would take. He said it would not be long, as Congress was in session now. I told him I had not examined Mr. Sedgwick's report of the facts in the case, . . . and that as soon as I had read it I might see him again and talk about the matter. He was very friendly. I told him I had the idea that it would be more agreeable to Mexico to change her laws upon her own motion upon being informed of the opinion of the United States Government.[140]

Romero was still optimistic on November 5, when he had another interview with Bayard. He thought there would be "no difficulty in producing a harmonious condition in regard to the contentions of Mexico and the present laws of the United States." Bayard was delighted to receive this assurance, and he made the observation that

. . . Mexico stood alone among nations in contending for such extra-territorial jurisdiction as title 186 implied; that the utmost claim by foreign nations was to punish individuals who outside their territories had committed crimes which threatened the safety of the State, such as forging

138. Bayard to the Marquis de Chambrun, September 15, 1886, *Bayard Letter Book,* vol. 3, *Bayard MS.*

139. Phelps to Secretary Bayard, October 9, 1886, *Bayard MS.*

140. *Memorandum* written by Bayard after a conversation with Romero, October 15, 1886, *ibid.*

National securities; attempting the lives of their rulers by expeditions set on foot in foreign countries, but that in the case of Cutting it was evident that Medina . . . was permitted of his own will to enforce or suspend the penalty.[141]

On November 17 Bayard wrote to A. G. Sedgwick to announce that he had "draughted our position *in re* Cutting," and that he felt "very sure of our worth."[142] He also drafted that part of President Cleveland's message to Congress (December 6, 1886) which referred to the Cutting Case. In concluding this reference the President had expressed the hope that "in the interests of good neighborhood the statute referred to will be so modified as to eliminate the present possibilities of danger to the peace of the two countries."[143]

The President's language in regard to the Cutting Case was so firm and direct that it awakened apprehensions in Mexico City. On February 8, 1887, Manning, the American Minister at Mexico City, had a long interview with the Mexican Secretary of the Interior, and the whole question of Mexican-American relations was discussed in detail. The Secretary of the Interior said that the Mexican Government was

. . . not only desirous that the most cordial relations should exist between it and the United States but they wanted that each should feel that these relations were cordial and were not to be lightly disturbed. He said where real friendship existed some mode could always be found for egress from complications, and difficult questions could easily be settled when both sides were sincerely desirous of settling them. He added I must not understand he was in the least degree impugning the sincerity of my Government in its professions of good will, but as the present Administration was of opposite politics to its several predecessors, many public journals had tried to create the belief that it was less pacific than they.

I replied that it was evident irresponsible newspapers had made more impression upon the Mexican Government than the assurances of the accredited agents of the United States, but since this interview had been sought by him, I would unofficially repeat what I and my predecessors had

141. *Memorandum* written by Bayard after a conversation with Romero, November 5, 1886, *ibid.*

142. Bayard to A. G. Sedgwick, November 17, 1886, *Bayard Letter Book*, vol. 3, *Bayard MS.*

143. *Foreign Relations, 1886*, p. ix. With regard to the Cutting Case the President had also spoken as follows: "This incident has, . . . disclosed a claim of jurisdiction by Mexico, novel in our history, whereby any offense, committed anywhere by a foreigner, penal in the place of its commission, and of which a Mexican is the object, may, if the offender be found in Mexico, be there tried and punished in conformity with Mexican laws. . . . The admission of such a pretension would be attended with serious results, invasive of the jurisdiction of this Government, and highly dangerous to our citizens in foreign lands; therefore I have denied it, and protested against its attempted exercise, as unwarranted by the principles of law and international usages." *Ibid.*, p. viii.

officially said, i.e., that the United States was thoroughly sincere in the expressions of desire to maintain the most cordially friendly relations with the Mexican Government. . . .

He rejoined that the emphasis with which I spoke was an assurance of my sincerity, and he felt sure whenever questions arose . . . the two Governments will amicably adjust them.

I answered by an enquiry: "Do you not think it wise statesmanship as well as neighborly conduct, when two Governments see right before them a question upon which they do radically differ, that they shall adjust and come to an agreement about it before a case arises that presents the question. You have just now alluded to the clause in President Cleveland's Message about Mexico. It was an emphatic declaration that the United States will not tolerate your doctrine of extra-territoriality when applied to Americans. That announcement inspired you with apprehensions of latent ill-feeling. . . . Why do you not abrogate it *quod* Americans? . . ."

Mr. Romero Rubio said we ought not to forget that some of our States had similar provisions and mentioned Texas as one of them. I told him I was more concerned in perpetuating friendly relations and promoting peace than in discussing whether it was right that Texas should copy Mexico in this particular.[144]

This conversation between Manning and the Mexican Secretary of the Interior, must have had some good results, because we find Romero, in an interview with Bayard (May 27, 1887), referring to the "gradual appreciation by Mexico of the kindly intentions" of the Cleveland Administration. Bayard then remarked that he had been at a loss to comprehend

. . . the apparent want of response by Mexico to my [Bayard's] sentiments of friendship for that country, but that I believed now in Mr. Manning we should find an excellent channel of communication, and that he (Mr. M.) being thoroughly well-affected to the Government of Mexico, would be able to convey to them a sense of my straightforward and ingenuous friendship.

Bayard then referred to the Cutting Case and expressed the opinion that the time had come when the

144. Manning to Secretary Bayard, February 9, 1887, *Bayard MS*. Bayard was somewhat displeased at this interview between Manning and the Mexican Secretary of the Interior. In a memorandum which he wrote after reading this letter he expressed himself quite freely: "My comment on this letter is: 1. It was not decorous nor usual for the Minister from a Foreign Country to hold an interview by appointment with any Cabinet officer of Mexico other than the Minister for Foreign Affairs or possibly the President. . . . 5. We have formulated no claim in Cutting's case, and it will be time enough to consider it when we forward the claim for presentation. It is quite plain to me that a great deal of mischief has been sought to be made between Mexico and the United States. . . . The New York *World* has been a shameless libeller of the Administration and especially the State Department since March 1885, and is its assured enemy." *Bayard MS*.

. . . principle contained in the case of Cutting, the extra-territorial power of Mexico over Citizens of the United States for offences committed in this country, ought to be settled. I told him I did not wish to have any triumph over the Mexican Foreign Office, or to obtain any admission of their error in the contention; that I was aware that the Mexican case had been published in Belgium, but I did not propose to publish any contrary case or raise that issue, but that I wanted the claim of jurisdiction by Mexico abandoned; that a very careful examination of international authorities upon the subject had been made, and I believed that Mexico would be found to stand almost . . . alone among modern civilized Governments in the position which Mr. Mariscal had assumed and which was contained in their law; that I believed . . . that Greece and Russia were the only European Governments whose present laws would be found to sustain the broad claim made by Mexican law today in the case of Cutting.

I told him I wished he would think over the matter, because I thought he could make an arrangement with his own Government in their way, and without any sacrifice of their pride; . . . that the great thing between himself and myself should be the removal of all possible causes of friction in advance, so that there should be no ill-feeling in the matter. I pointed out to him that if Mr. Cutting had been an influential and popular citizen of the United States, and Mexico had persisted in an unusual and extreme punishment for an offence committed in the United States, that it was impossible to overestimate the dangerous results.[145]

Despite this constant evidence of good will on the part of Bayard, the Mexican Government showed no disposition to meet him half-way. On June 17 he told Romero that he well appreciated the somewhat

. . . extra-susceptibility of the Mexican people in relation to anything that seemed to invade their jurisdiction in any way at all or to curtail their jurisdiction, and that perhaps it was just as well to let the Cutting incident pass out of sight and out of memory, and treat for a harmonizing of the views of the two governments a little later on—in the meantime the Mexican government abstaining from the exercise of the extra-territorial jurisdiction referred to.[146]

Bayard purposely permitted the Cutting Case to "pass out of sight" for a few months in order to let passions cool,[147] and then on Novem-

145. *Memorandum* written by Bayard after a conversation with Romero, May 27, 1887, *Bayard MS.*

146. *Memorandum* written by Bayard after a conversation with Romero, June 17, 1887, *Bayard MS.*

147. In the summer of 1887 another incident arose which helped to embarrass American relations with Mexico. The American consul at Paso del Norte was J. H. Brigham, who had taken a very active part in the Cutting Case. According to Edgar B. Bronson (Bronson to Abram Hewitt, August 21, 1887, *Bayard MS*), Brigham was "an invalid, irritable and suffering from great physical depression." Judge Zubia was the justice who sat on the lower Mexican court and sentenced Cutting. Apparently, there was no love lost

ber 1, 1887, he sent a long note to the Mexican Government which canvassed the Cutting Case from every viewpoint. After a short résumé of the facts in the case, Bayard stated that the American Government was still

---

between these two individuals, and trouble was brewing. On August 30, 1887, Brigham "made application officially to Judge Zubia concerning certain horses which had crossed the line from a United States reservation. Judge Zubia made an appointment to hear the case, but failed to attend, whereupon Mr. Brigham accompanied by the United States Agent, went to the residence of Judge Zubia, and as a result of the interview left the house, being followed by Judge Zubia, who assaulted Mr. Brigham on the street." Bayard to C. Romero, September 5, 1887, *Bayard Letter Book*, vol. 6, *Bayard MS*. On October 4 Bayard had a conversation with Matias Romero, the Mexican Minister, and he at once brought up the matter of the assault of Judge Zubia upon Consul Brigham. Bayard had asked Consul-General Sutton if Brigham was an "irritable man," and Sutton had replied that Brigham was "a gentleman, and would not intentionally do wrong." Bayard then complained of Judge Zubia's assault upon Brigham as a "gross indecorum." *Memorandum* written by Bayard after a conversation with Romero, October 4, 1887, *Bayard MS*.

On October 6 Romero promised Bayard that he "would do everything he could to make things as we wanted them in the Zubia-Brigham affair." *Memorandum* written by Bayard after a conversation with Romero, October 6, 1887, *ibid*. On October 14 Romero had another conversation with Bayard and explained to him that Judge Zubia had been suffering "from a great deal of domestic distress," and that was the probable reason why he had resented Consul Brigham's manner and had assaulted him. Romero then said that the Mexican authorities "would be very much obliged if the United States could find some other place of occupation for Mr. Brigham." Bayard replied that "making all allowances for Mr. Zubia's domestic distress and Mr. Brigham's possible irritability and roughness of manner in making his demands, that one thing was plain: he had not gone there on his private business for the United States. . . . Therefore, he was strictly right in seeking his remedy, and nothing could excuse the fact that Judge Zubia should rush after him on the public street, and commit there a personal assault, which amounted to a public affront." Bayard finally suggested that the Mexican Government write a note expressing regret at the occurrence, and stating that Judge Zubia had been suspended from office. *Memorandum* written by Bayard after a conversation with Romero, October 14, 1887, *ibid*.

The Mexican Government accepted this suggestion with reference to expressing regret at the conduct of Judge Zubia, and on November 30 Bayard wrote a personal letter to Brigham with reference to his encounter with Zubia. After stating that the Mexican Secretary of Foreign Affairs had criticized Judge Zubia's conduct as "improper and unjustifiable," Bayard then informed Brigham his usefulness as a consular representative of the United States on the Mexican border had been "impaired." This impairment had not been created solely by the unfortunate fight with Judge Zubia, but it was due partly to Brigham's sentiments towards the Mexicans. A "series of untoward events . . . appears to have erected and confirmed in your mind a distrust of the friendliness and motives of the Mexicans which this Government, in the light of its frank and honorable intercourse with the Mexican Government and the numerous proofs of sincerity and good will it has received, cannot share." Because of this unfriendly state of mind towards Mexico, Brigham would have to be given a consular post in some other country. Bayard to J. Harvey Brigham, November 30, 1887, *Bayard Letter Book*, vol. 6, *ibid*.

On January 6, 1888 Bayard told Romero that he thought it was unfortunate that Judge Zubia was in "a position to bring him into contact with American citizens," and on February 10 Romero brought the comforting news that he had just been informed by the Governor of Chihuahua that Zubia "would no longer be in a position where his ill-feeling could affect American Citizens." *Memoranda* written by Bayard after conversations with Romero, January 6, and February 10, 1888, *ibid*.

. . . compelled to deny . . . that a citizen of the United States can be held under the rules of International Law to answer in Mexico for an offense committed in the United States, simply because the object of that offense happens to be a citizen of Mexico. The Government of Mexico has endeavored to sustain this pretension on two grounds: First, that such a claim is justified by the rules of International Law and the positive legislation of various countries; and secondly, on the ground that such a claim being made in the legislation of Mexico, the question is one solely for the decision of Mexican tribunals. In respect to the latter ground it is only necessary to say, that if a Government could set up its own municipal laws as the final test of its international rights and obligations, then the rules of International Law would be but the shadow of a name and would afford no protection either to States or to individuals. . . .

As to the question of International Law, I am unable to discover any principle upon which the assumption of jurisdiction made in Article 186 of the Mexican penal code can be justified. There is no principle better settled than that the penal laws of a country have no extra-territorial force. . . . Such is the consensus of opinion of the leading authorities on International Law at the present day. . . . Criminal offenses committed outside the state by foreigners against its citizens or subjects are not punished under any circumstances or conditions by France, Germany, Belgium, Denmark, Great Britain, Luxembourg, The Netherlands, Portugal, Spain, and Switzerland. . . .

An appeal has been made in the Mexican arguments to the law of France as sustaining Article 186. The error of this is apparent when we observe that the French code authorizes the prosecution of foreigners for offenses outside the territory of France, only in the exceptional cases of crimes against the safety of the state.

In concluding this note to the Mexican Government, Bayard instructed the American representative in Mexico City to inform the Foreign Office that not only should an indemnity be paid to Mr. Cutting for his arrest and detention in Mexico, but also the Mexican statute proposing to confer "extra-territorial jurisdiction should . . . be repealed." [148]

Thomas B. Connery, the American chargé d'affaires at Mexico City, presented the arguments of Bayard to the Mexican Government in a long note of November 15, 1887.[149] On August 12 and 13, 1886, Secretary Mariscal had warmly defended the position of the Mexican Government in the Cutting Case, and he had contended that Article 186

---

148. Bayard to Mr. Connery, November 1, 1887, *Foreign Relations, 1887*, pp. 751-757. See also the long and learned report made by John Bassett Moore on "Extra-territorial Crime and the Cutting Case," *ibid.*, pp. 757-840.

149. Thomas B. Connery to Secretary Mariscal, November 15, 1887, *Foreign Relations, 1887*, pp. 844-849. See also, Connery to Secretary Bayard, December 24, 1887, *Bayard MS.*

of the Mexican penal code was in accord with the principles laid down by a long list of authorities in the field of International Law.[150] On February 10, 1888, Mariscal gave a final answer to the American Government with reference to the arrest and detention of Cutting. It was both voluminous and contentious, and showed no spirit of yielding to the pressure exerted by Bayard with reference to amending the penal code. Mariscal asserted that

. . . the great majority of nations has recognized extra-territorial jurisdiction, it being a matter of free volition on the part of each nation to determine how far each may carry the idea, provided always that the extent of the scope thus allowed has not been specifically condemned by the generality of other states as being contrary to the principles which should govern their mutual relations.

After a long review of the opinions of important authorities which he thought favored the Mexican contention, Mariscal then stated that within the American Union the states of New York and Texas had provisions in their penal codes that were very similar to Article 186 of the penal code of Mexico. Why should the Mexican code be amended and no action be taken with reference to the codes of these two states? The "first condition to an honorable agreement between two independent nations is that there may be perfect reciprocity. No friendly state will insist upon such a proposal, nor will it be admitted by another save at the cost of its national dignity." [151]

In this note Mariscal had specifically refused to amend the penal code or to pay an indemnity for the arrest and detention of Cutting. Connery expressed to Bayard his regret that the Mexican Secretary of Foreign Relations had not met the American proposition in a "spirit of conciliation." Mariscal was merely displaying the same tenacity that had marked all his relations with the United States during Bayard's tenure as Secretary of State. In the matter of Captain Crawford's murder, the American Government finally had to accept the version advanced by the Mexican Government that the death of Crawford was really the result of an "accident." With reference to the rescue of Lieutenant Gutierrez from imprisonment in Nogales, Arizona, Bayard retreated from the strong stand he had taken, and in order to preserve friendly relations with Mexico, he did not insist upon the return of

150. Secretary Mariscal to Romero, August 12, 13, 1886, *Foreign Relations, 1887*, pp. 862.
151. Secretary Mariscal to Mr. Connery, February 10, 1888, *Foreign Relations, 1888*, pp. 1114-1132.

Gutierrez to the custody of American authorities. In the Cutting Case we again find Bayard using strong language but wisely refusing to press his demands to the point of war. He effected the release of Cutting from a Mexican jail, and after securing this concession, he did not feel justified in advising the President to resort to military threats to compel Mexico to amend her penal code. Bayard did, however, flatly warn Romero that if any other American should be thrown into jail under the same circumstances that attended the Cutting Case, he would demand his "instant release." [152]

Fortunately, for the continuance of peaceful relations between the two countries, no other case like that of Mr. Cutting arose during the rest of Bayard's tenure as Secretary of State. Whether he would have carried out his threat to Romero in this regard, is somewhat doubtful in view of his constant desire to settle disputes through pacific means. Moreover, he seems to have entertained a genuine feeling of friendship towards Mexico, and when President Cleveland suggested the name of General E. S. Bragg as the new American Minister to that country, Bayard wrote a short note explaining his views. He thought that the Mexican Mission was one that required

. . . tact and good temper, and if these are not constantly employed, trouble will follow. The present current of our affairs with Mexico is in the right direction, and ought not to be arrested. Should you decide to entrust this mission to General Bragg, he should enter upon it with a full understanding of the requirements, and a resolution to "keep the peace." [153]

In his endeavor to "keep the peace" with Mexico by preventing any repetition of the Cutting Case, Bayard once more discussed with Romero the advisability of amending the Mexican penal code. He wished particularly to impress upon the Mexican Minister the

. . . importance of getting that claim of extra-territorial power out of the way. I [Bayard] told him it was very important between two nations situated as Mexico and the United States were, with a border open for 1500 miles, and a rather lawless set of people on either side, that this contention of Mexico should not be carried into effect. I then illustrated to him the case of a man of wealth and popularity in Texas, for instance, who, having a broil with some Mexican should shoot him, and, not being tried in Texas, should afterwards be arrested in Mexico and his life put in jeopardy, under Mexican forms of trial. In that case I could plainly see this country would be set in a flame, and that there would be an almost unanimous resolve that

152. *Memorandum* written by Bayard after a conversation with Romero, March 5, 1887, *Bayard MS.*
153. Bayard to President Cleveland, January 6, 1888, *Bayard MS.*

the life of an American citizen should not be taken under Mexican law, for an offense wholly committed in the United States. I said I thought if Mr. Mariscal could see the necessary results of such a contention, that he would desire to have the law of Mexico amended; that I esteemed it very fortunate that in the case of Cutting, there was not so much importance in the case itself, and there was some obscurity as to the facts—there had been a joinder of a good with a bad cause of action.[154]

On May 4, 1888, Bayard made a last plea to the Mexican Government to amend Article 186 of its penal code. With reference to Secretary Mariscal's

. . . reference to the codes of New York and Texas, and his expression of surprise that they are not noticed in the report of extra-territorial crime [submitted by John Bassett Moore], it should be observed that they are both discussed at page 25 of that document, and shown to rest, as to the provisions cited by Mr. Mariscal, on a principle precisely opposite to that which he has defended in article 186 of the Mexican penal code.[155]

Mariscal replied some weeks later in a short note which merely promised "carefully to consider" the points indicated in Bayard's instruction of May 4.[156] This communication was the last item in a diplomatic catalogue that was as long and as thoroughly tiresome as the Homeric catalogue of ships. To Bayard it was a clear indication that the Mexican Government had no intention of going out of its way to conciliate American public opinion. But time would bring about a very different story because American investments in Mexico were increasing in such a large volume that they would inevitably lead to annexation. Thus:

. . . Fate has permanently placed the two very dissimilar peoples in contiguity, and great good sense, constant forbearance, and careful self-control are indispensably requisite to keep matters in pacific train between them. The overflow of our population and capital into the bordering States of Mexico, must, sooner or later, saturate these regions with Americanism, and control their political action, but until they are prepared for our laws and institutions, we do not want them, and when they are fit they will find their own way to us. In the meantime we must deal amicably with them, and avoid, as far as possible, all occasions for friction.[157]

154. *Memorandum* written by Bayard after a conversation with Romero, March 23, 1888, *Bayard MS.*
155. Secretary Bayard to Bragg, May 4, 1888, *Foreign Relations, 1888,* pp. 1189-1190.
156. Secretary Mariscal to Bragg, May 29, 1888, *Foreign Relations, 1888,* p. 1202.
157. Secretary Bayard to Bragg, July 11, 1888, *Bayard Letter Book,* vol. 8, *Bayard MS.*
There are a few memoranda in the *Bayard Papers* which shed some additional light upon Bayard's attitude towards Mexico with reference to the boundary dispute between Mexico and Guatemala. Guatemala had long contended that Soconusco, the southern

province of the Mexican State of Chiapas, should belong to her. The claim of Guatemala to Soconusco was distinctly weak, but it had not been abandoned, and this fact was a constant irritant in the relations between Guatemala and Mexico. In May, 1881, Logan, the American Minister to Central America, expressed a fear to Secretary Blaine that Mexico had ambitious plans that contemplated not only an extension of her southern boundary at the expense of Guatemala, but also an attempt to convert the Central American states into a Mexican protectorate. Logan to Blaine, May 24, 1881, *Foreign Relations, 1881*, p. 104. In answer to these fears, Blaine instructed Morgan, the American Minister at Mexico City, to warn Secretary Mariscal against resorting to war with Guatemala. Blaine to Morgan, June 16, 1881, *ibid.*, p. 766. See also, Matias Romero, "Blaine and the Boundary Question between Mexico and Guatemala," *American Geographical Society Journal*, vol. 29, 1897, pp. 281-330.

Blaine was anxious to have the Central American republics adhere to the doctrine of the fixity of their international boundaries, and he suggested to the Mexican Government that the United States would like to act as mediator between Mexico and Guatemala. A. F. Tyler, *The Foreign Policy of James G. Blaine*, pp. 58-59. Secretary Mariscal rejected any suggestion of arbitration with regard to the disputed boundary, and he refused to withdraw Mexican troops from that area. Blaine, however, would not accept this rejection, and on November 28, 1881, he again offered American mediation. Blaine to Morgan, November 28, 1881, *Foreign Relations, 1881*, p. 816. Before any action could be taken on this note, Blaine retired from the office of Secretary of State, and was succeeded by Secretary Frelinghuysen. Freylinghuysen offered to act as umpire on the matter of the boundary between Guatemala and Mexico, but Guatemala relinquished her claims to Soconusco, and consented to a treaty which provided for the delimitation of the boundary line. *Foreign Relations, 1883*, pp. 640ff.

When Bayard came into office this dispute was still unsettled, and Guatemala still had fears that Mexico might harbor an ambitious plan to establish a protectorate over Central America or at least to encroach upon the territory beyond her just claims. Blaine was suspicious of Mexican intentions, but Bayard was not. On May 28, 1888, Romero stated to Bayard that he believed that the American Minister to the Central American States, Henry C. Hall, "was not satisfied as to the good faith of the Mexican attitude towards Guatemala, and thought that Mexico probably had designs upon that country." Bayard told Romero that he was mistaken in this regard. Hall had just paid a visit to the Department of State, and while "he might have heard a good deal of gossip in relation to the matter, I [Bayard] felt sure he had no bias whatever against Mexico, and he certainly had made no such representations to me. I said Mr. Hall was . . . representing very fairly the sentiment which I wished to prevail—and that was that the United States were not disposed to interfere with the local affairs of the governments of other countries. On the contrary, we were disposed to let them go on, and assist them in maintaining their self-respect and local self-government." *Memorandum* written by Bayard after a conversation with Romero, May 28, 1888, *Bayard MS.*

On October 6, 1887, Romero had an interview with Bayard in which he gave a "long account of the proceedings in 1881, in which Mr. Blaine had accepted the statements of the Guatemalan envoy here without asking Mexico for any reply or explanation, and had written them a most unpleasant despatch accusing them of having forcibly acquired the province of Chiapa. . . . He expressed himself well satisfied with the result of the position I [Bayard] had taken in regard to this Guatemalan apprehension." *Memorandum* written by Bayard after a conversation with Romero, October 6, 1887, *ibid.*

More than a year later, Romero again brought up this matter of the difficulties between Mexico and Guatemala relative to the boundary. During an interview with Bayard, he inquired whether any complaint had been made by Guatemala with reference to an "alleged Mexican aggression. . . . He said there was a treaty between the two countries to establish their boundaries by means of a joint Commission, and that those commissioners were pursuing their labors, but that they differed as to the name and locality of a river which was to constitute part of the boundary. . . . I said I trusted that as it was a question of fact to be established by geographical proofs, . . . there ought to be no difficulty

C. THE CASE OF THE *Rebecca*

Another case which led to a long and fruitless controversy between Mexico and the United States was that of the *Rebecca*. This American schooner had cleared at Morgan City, Louisiana, on January 30, 1884, with a cargo of lumber for Tampico, Mexico, but it also had on board six cases of merchandise to be left on the way at Brazos Santiago, Texas. The cases of merchandise were not on the manifest of the cargo for Tampico. While on the way to Brazos, a heavy storm drove the *Rebecca* out of its way and it entered the port of Tampico without having first delivered the cases of merchandise at Brazos. The Tampico customs authorities promptly seized this merchandise and charged that the master of the *Rebecca* was attempting to smuggle them into Mexico. When the charge was heard in the Mexican district court sitting at Tampico, a judgment was rendered that the goods should pay triple

in the matter." *Memorandum* written by Bayard after a conversation with Romero, October 26, 1888, *ibid.*

Some weeks subsequent to this interview, the Guatemalan Minister called at the Department of State and informed Bayard that "the Guatemalan Minister at the City of Mexico reported that he was getting along very well with that Government, and that the Mexican Government had proposed a delay of two years in the work of the commission to establish the boundary between Guatemala and Mexico, and that the Guatemalan Government had assented to that. I told him I was very glad to hear that it was acceptable to both parties, because it kept a boundary question, which is very apt to be a troublesome question, within the domain of friendly diplomatic settlement." *Memorandum* written by Bayard after a conversation with the Minister from Guatemala, November 30, 1888, *Bayard MS.*

On January 21, 1889, Bayard had his last important conversation with Romero on the matter of the relations between Guatemala and Mexico. Bayard also embraced this opportunity to express his friendly feelings for the Mexican Government. Bayard told Romero "that the other day a piece of political gossip had been conveyed to me [Bayard] of an alleged remark by a Mexican Envoy, who was returning to his own Country from Italy . . . to the effect that a Mexican fleet would go to San José in Guatemala and make on the occasion of that visit something of a naval demonstration in Guatemala for the purpose of encouraging the reactionary party against that Government.

"Mr. Romero laughed, and said that to make a naval demonstration it was necessary to have a navy, and Mexico had none. I answered Mr. Romero that I had told my informant not only that, but I had said, between Mr. Romero and myself, and through Mr. Romero, I had with Mr. Mariscal a complete understanding in which I felt absolute reliance, and that was that the Mexican Government had no policy of interference with the domestic affairs of the State of Guatemala, but that they were content to let that State grow and prosper, and be glad that it did prosper, and that I was sure Mexico had no jealousy of Guatemala.

"Mr. Romero said I was perfectly right, and if any change of their feelings towards Guatemala took place, I might be sure I should be the first person to be informed of it." *Memorandum* written by Bayard after a conversation with Romero, January 21, 1889, *ibid.*

duty. When the master refused to comply with this sentence, the goods and the vessel were sold by order of the court.[158]

The main question of law that arose in this case was whether a vessel driven by stress of weather into a foreign port is liable to penal process in such port, either for smuggling or for bringing goods into that port without proper papers. It had been frequently held by the American Government, in conformity with the rulings of American courts, that the *"casus* of unavoidable necessity is a defense to any charge of invasion of customhouse regulations." [159]

In an instruction to the American Minister at Mexico City, Secretary Frelinghuysen had questioned how far it was "compatible with comity, or humanity even, to enforce against the vessels and shipmasters of a friendly state penalties for proven and intentional violation of law, when in fact the vessels, under stress of the elements, may have been forced to deviate from the exact conditions of the voyage prescribed by the ships' papers." [160]

Secretary Mariscal was decidedly skeptical about the statement of the master of the *Rebecca* with reference to being forced by bad weather to abandon his voyage to Brazos, Texas, and first put into the port of Tampico. He thought it was evident that the master of the *Rebecca* had violated the customs regulations of Mexico, and this action was all the more serious in view of the fact that the master had, for many years, been a visitor at Mexican ports. Now that the case had been decided by the Mexican lower court, and no appeal had been taken, the President of Mexico could take no action in the matter.[161]

Before Henry R. Jackson, the American Minister at Mexico City, had received this note from Mariscal, he had already sent to Bayard a long despatch in which a vitriolic attack was made upon the leading officials in Mexico. It was hopeless, he believed, to expect any real redress from such venal politicians.[162] Bayard may have been somewhat influenced by this sharp indictment of Mexican procedure, because in his reply to Jackson he voiced the opinion that it did not seem "hope-

158. Report of Secretary Bayard to President Cleveland, February 26, 1887, *Senate Ex. Doc., 109,* 49 Cong., 2 sess., pp. 1-3.

159. See *memorandum* prepared by John Bassett Moore for the Secretary of State, July 13, 1886, *Bayard MS.* For previous seizures of American vessels by Mexican authorities, see J. B. Moore, *Digest of International Law,* vol. 2, pp. 323-325.

160. Secretary Frelinghuysen to Morgan, April 7, 1884, *House Ex. Doc., 328,* 51 Cong., 1 sess., p. 4.

161. Secretary Mariscal to H. R. Jackson, October 31, 1885, *ibid.,* p. 27.

162. Jackson to Secretary Bayard, August 31, 1885, *Bayard MS.*

ful" to press the case at that time. With reference to Mariscal's charge that the *Rebecca* "could not be deemed to have entered Tampico in distress," Bayard replied that the American Government had never claimed that she did. The position taken by the Department of State was that a storm had prevented the *Rebecca* from reaching Brazos, Texas, and had led the master of the vessel to sail to Tampico. Stress of weather was "the legitimate cause of her variation of course for which the fine was technically imposed, but the point is wholly misunderstood in the Mexican argument." There was little use, therefore, in "formally joining issue with the Mexican Government, after its position has been so distinctly announced, but at some future time the prospects may be more favorable." [163]

Secretary Mariscal defended the position of the Mexican Government by again referring to the fact that the master of the *Rebecca* had not availed himself of the right to appeal from the decision of the Mexican lower court. This failure to take appropriate action had led the Mexican Government to adopt the view that the case had been determined by the judicial branch of the government, and that it was not subject to revision by the Executive. Mariscal did concede, however, that if the documents that were subsequently communicated to the Mexican Government had been known to the court at the time of the trial, the sentence would probably have been quite different.[164]

This admission was viewed by Jackson as a small consolation for the severity of the sentence, and he wrote to Mariscal and threatened "reprisals" for the action against the *Rebecca*.[165] Mariscal contented himself with a reply that the case had been settled by the courts of Mexico and could not be re-opened by the Executive.[166]

Bayard was still hopeful that the discussion might be diverted "into the broader field of equitable consideration as between sovereigns who are and must be jealous of the judicial independence," [167] but he could not help giving expression to his regret that the Mexican Government had not recognized that its course in the case of the *Rebecca* had been "harsh and oppressive." [168]

Bayard was vigorously supported in this criticism of Mexican proce-

163. Bayard to Jackson, December 5, 1885, *Bayard MS.*
164. Mariscal to Jackson, February 9, 1886, *House Ex. Doc.*, *328*, 51 Cong., 1 sess., p. 36.
165. Jackson to Mariscal, February 25, 1886, *Bayard MS.*
166. Mariscal to Morgan, April 2, 1886, *House Ex. Doc.*, *328*, pp. 41-47.
167. Bayard to Jackson, March 9, 1886, *ibid.*, p. 40.
168. Bayard to Morgan, April 27, 1886, *ibid.*, p. 47.

dure by the opinions of Francis Wharton, the Solicitor of the Department of State. He was strongly opposed to the action taken at Tampico with reference to the merchandise destined for Brazos, Texas. Such goods were

. . . no more the subject of Mexican customs penalties, their destiny not being to Mexico, than they would have been had the *Rebecca* been wrecked on the Mexican Coast, and these goods cast ashore in the wreck. . . . Assuming that the *Rebecca* was driven past Brazos by stress of weather, and that the packages in question were retained by her for return to a United States port, I feel bound to assert that the refusal of Mexico to respect the protection given by the flag of the United States to goods so retained under its shelter, and not meant to come under Mexican jurisdiction, was an unjustifiable aggression on the rights of the United States which it is the duty of this department to repel.[169]

In his report to President Cleveland on the *Rebecca* case, Bayard closely followed the argument of Wharton. He expressed the view that the seizure and sale of the *Rebecca* was "a gross breach of comity and hospitality peculiarly unreasonable and unjust." In reviewing the facts in the case, he remarked:

The Mexican Government, while denying that the entrance of the *Rebecca* into Tampico was enforced by stress of weather, has taken the position that the judgment of its courts, ordering the sale of the vessel, is final and conclusive, especially as the master and owners failed to take an appeal from the judgment so rendered to another court, as it is contended might have been done.

This Department has contested and denied the doctrine that a government may set up the judgment of one of its own courts as a bar to an international claim, when such judgment is shown to have been unjust or in violation of the principles of International Law; and has further maintained that, under the circumstances of the case and in view of the fact that the prior proceedings had been so palpably arbitrary and unjust, the master and owners were not bound to attempt further judicial remedies in the local tribunals.[170]

In February, 1887, Senator Joseph E. Brown, of Georgia, led a fight

169. Undated *memorandum* of Francis Wharton, *Bayard MS.* In another memorandum of July 17, 1886, Wharton remarks as follows concerning the *Rebecca* case: "It is said, however, that the parties immediately injured in this case, having submitted themselves to a court of the first instance, are required to press the matter to the final appellate court before diplomatic intervention can be claimed. But this is not the law, even assuming that this is not a case for primary diplomatic intervention, which it is." Wharton then refers to the action taken by Secretary Daniel Webster, January 13, 1851, in an instruction to the American Minister at London. *Bayard MS.*

170. Bayard to President Cleveland, February 26, 1887, *Senate Ex. Doc., 109,* 49 Cong., 2 sess., p. 2.

upon Bayard with a view to compelling the Department of State to publish the complete correspondence concerning the resignation of Henry R. Jackson, the former American Minister to Mexico. Bayard believed that some of the despatches of Jackson, particularly that of August 31, 1885, were so bitterly critical of Mexican officials that their publication would lead to strained relations between Mexico and the United States. For this reason he refused to permit the publication of the entire correspondence with Mexico, and was made the subject of sharp attack by Brown and his friends.[171]

On March 5, 1887, Romero paid a visit to the Department of State, and Bayard then referred to

. . . the resolution in the Senate, debated by Mr. Brown, calling for Mr. Jackson's correspondence. I [Bayard] said that he was able to see from Mr. Brown's statement the line of action that Mr. Jackson evidently proposed in the case of the *Rebecca*. He (Mr. Romero) said it was very evident to him that Mr. Jackson meant to make war, to which statement I made no reply. I said that whatever might be Mr. Jackson's views on this subject, mine were very different, and that I had no object that was inconsistent with the honor and welfare of Mexico, and the peace of that country and the United States.[172]

During the course of another conversation with Romero, Bayard made a final reference to the case of the *Rebecca*. He referred to his relief that Jackson had been superseded in Mexico City by Manning, who was quite friendly to the administration of President Diaz. With Manning as the American representative in Mexico City, Bayard felt that his hopes for friendly relations between the two countries had

. . . been revived. I [Bayard] spoke to him in this way, because while I had not the slightest intention of removing the consideration of the case of the *Rebecca* from Mexico and attempting to discuss it here, yet I felt I must take up the case again for the purpose of settling, in the interests of good understanding between the two countries, the principle upon which I believed the *Rebecca* case to stand; I would not refer to the merits of the case, but merely to the principle which was sought to be established by Mr. Mariscal, . . . and which could not be accepted by the United States— which was the conclusiveness upon the United States of the decision of the municipal tribunals of Mexico in cases represented by the United States Government; that I thought such a principle as not admissible in Interna-

171. Bayard to Senator Joseph E. Brown, February 19, 23, 1887, *Bayard MS.* See also *memorandum* written by Bayard with reference to the publication of this Mexican correspondence, March, 1887, *ibid.*

172. *Memorandum* written by Bayard after a conversation with Romero, March 5, 1887, *Bayard MS.*

tional Law; that I should carefully scrutinize every case that we presented against Mexico, and would encourage no case that was improper and inequitable, but that when we found a case in which justice had been violated, we would expect the Government of Mexico to try that case with us, and not to seek to conclude the United States by the judgment of one of Mexico's own tribunals, and that I thought that when Mr. Manning presented that, that the intention of his presenting it would be thoroughly comprehended and would be met by Mr. Mariscal in a way that would enable us to adjust it and prevent trouble.[173]

On February 17, 1888, Bayard instructed Bragg, the new Minister to Mexico, to press for a settlement of the case of the *Rebecca*,[174] but the mills of Mexican justice ground so slowly that no effective action was taken during the rest of Bayard's tenure as Secretary of State. This failure to respond to American pressure in such an excellent case as the *Rebecca,* is a clear illustration of the determination of the Mexican Government not to concede the smallest point to the Department of State except under threat of actual war. Bayard despised cheap jingoism, and he had no inclination to use a "big stick" to enforce compliance with his requests. He was sincerely anxious to maintain peaceful relations with Mexico even when that nation gave him ample provocation to advocate stern measures of reprisal. If Bayard had been more like Bismarck, American relations with Mexico would have been conducted in a very different spirit, and Mexican replies to American protests would have been realistic instead of academic. In the hands of a less scrupulous Secretary of State, the Cutting Case could have been used as a spark to explode the mass of resentment that had accumulated in many American quarters against Mexico. It is greatly to Bayard's credit that he constantly sought to prevent rather than to manipulate such an explosion.

173. *Memorandum* written by Bayard after a conversation with Romero, May 27, 1887, *Bayard MS.*
174. Secretary Bayard to Bragg, February 17, 1888, *Mexico, Instructions*, vol. 22, MS Dept. of State.

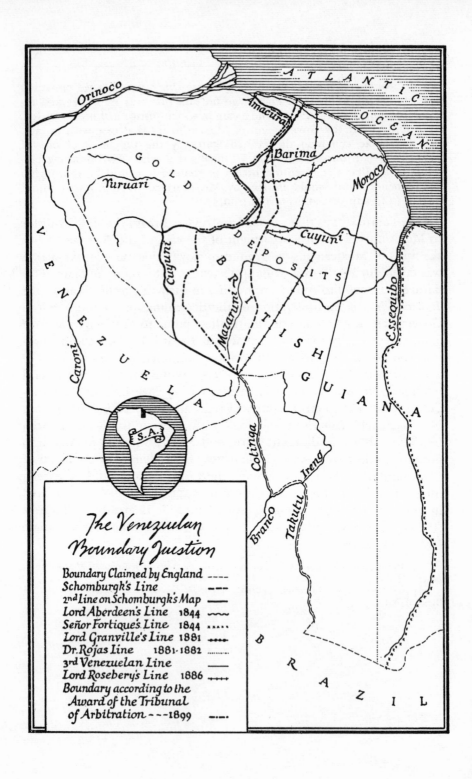

ATLANTIC

OCEAN

Orinoco

Amacura

Barima

GOLD

Yuruari

Moroco

Cuyuni

Cuyuni

DEPOSITS

V
E
N
E
Z
U
E
L
A

B
R
I
T
I
S
H

Mazaruni

Caroni

Essequibo

G
U
I
A
N
A

S.A.

Cotinga

Ireng

Takutu

Branco

B
R
A
Z
I
L

*The Venezuelan
Boundary Question*

Boundary Claimed by England ----
Schomburgk's Line ---
2nd Line on Schomburgk's Map ——
Lord Aberdeen's Line 1844 ～～
Señor Fortique's Line 1844 ·····
Lord Granville's Line 1881 ····
Dr. Rojas Line 1881-1882 ··········
3rd Venezuelan Line ——
Lord Rosebery's Line 1886 ····
Boundary according to the
Award of the Tribunal
of Arbitration ---1899 -·-·-

The Venezuelan Question

CHAPTER EIGHTEEN

Guzmán Blanco
Fears He Is Being Stalked
by a Hungry British Lion

--------••⟨∞⟩••--------

THE CONTROVERSY BETWEEN GREAT BRITAIN AND VENEZUELA OVER THE
extent of the boundaries of British Guiana, had its origins in documents that begin as early as the year 1493. After Pope Alexander VI
had been informed of the results of the first voyage of Columbus, he
issued a bull (May 3, 1493) that confirmed the title of Spain to the new
lands that had been discovered in the Ocean Sea.[1] But Ferdinand of
Spain was anxious to have the Pope issue a bull that was more far-
reaching in its implications, so on September 26, 1493, His Holiness
responded with a bull that laid down for the first time the important
principle that a sovereign's title to new lands had to rest upon effective
occupation in addition to mere discovery.[2] This principle received
Papal confirmation in a bull issued by Pope Leo X on November 3,
1514.[3]

In the meantime, a Papal bull (May 4, 1493) had drawn a line of
demarcation between Spanish and Portuguese territories. This line was
fixed at one hundred leagues west of the Azores or Cape Verde Islands.[4]
Before it could be drawn on contemporary charts, the sovereigns of
Spain and Portugal signed the Treaty of Tordesillas (June 7, 1494)
which advanced the demarcation line to three hundred and seventy
leagues west of the Cape Verde Islands.[5] This change in the demarcation line gave the King of Portugal a valid title to Brazil.

The coast of Venezuela was settled by the Spaniards as early as
1527, and four decades later, Carácas was founded. In 1777, the Cap-

---

1. Frances G. Davenport, *European Treaties Bearing on the History of the United
States and its Dependencies* (Washington, 1917), vol. 1, pp. 56-63.
2. *Ibid.*, pp. 79-83. 3. *Ibid.*, pp. 112-117.
4. *Ibid.*, pp. 71-78. 5. *Ibid.*, pp. 84-100.

taincy-General of Venezuela was established. It was composed of the provinces of Guiana, Cumana, and Maracaibo, together with the islands of Margarita and Trinidad.[6]

While the Spaniards were settling in Venezuela, the Dutch were preparing to lay claim to the coast of Guiana. The Papal bulls of 1493 and 1514 had set forth the principle of effective occupation as the basis for a valid title to territory, and it was certain that the Spaniards had not effectively occupied Guiana. In 1621, the Dutch West India Company was chartered for the express purpose of "attacking Spain's American possessions," and within a few years certain settlements were planted along the west bank of the Essequibo River.[7]

Despite the opposition of the Spanish authorities in Venezuela, the Dutch colonies in Guiana more than held their own, and in the Treaty of Münster, January 30, 1648, the Spanish Government reluctantly recognized the title of the United Provinces of Holland to the towns, castles, fortresses, and countries of the East and West Indies which they had in their possession at the conclusion of the peace.[8]

In the Treaty of Münster no attempt had been made to fix the boundaries of the Spanish and Dutch possessions in Guiana, nor was any subsequent effort made to settle this question through official surveys. There had been repeated efforts by certain cartographers to picture the boundaries in this disputed territory, but this battle of the maps was indecisive.[9] Even when the British Government took over the Dutch claims in Guiana in 1814, it was significant that the treaty of cession (August 13, 1814) did not specify any exact frontier lines for the colonies of Demerara, Essequibo, and Berbice.[10]

In Venezuela, in 1810, a revolution broke out against Spanish rule, and on July 5, 1811, a declaration of independence was adopted. Under the able leadership of Bolívar, the success of the revolutionary movement was assured in 1821, and the surrender of Puerto Cabello in

6. William S. Robertson, *History of the Latin-American Nations* (N. Y., 1932), pp. 82, 106, 116.

7. *Report and Accompanying Papers of the Commission Appointed by the President of the United States "to investigate and report upon the true divisional line between the republic of Venezuela and British Guiana"* (Washington, 1896–1897, 9 vols.), vol. 1, pp. 61, 354-375.

8. F. G. Davenport, *op. cit.*, vol. 1, pp. 353-366. See also, F. G. Davenport, "America and European Diplomacy to 1648," *Rept. of American Historical Association, 1915* (Washington, 1917), pp. 153-161.

9. J. S. T. Sinclair, London *Times*, March 3, 1896.

10. Charles O. Paullin, *European Treaties Bearing on the History of the United States*, vol. 4, pp. 202-203.

November, 1823, brought the war to a close. For a decade, Venezuela was incorporated into the Great Colombian Republic, but in 1830 this union was dissolved, and Venezuela was established as a separate state. This independent status was formally recognized by the United States on February 28, 1835.[11]

In 1831 the settlements of Demerara, Essequibo, and Berbice were united into the colony of British Guiana. Four years later, Robert Schomburgk was sent by the British Government on an exploration trip into the interior of Guiana, and on November 28, 1840, he was appointed as a special commissioner to survey and delimit the boundaries of the colony.[12] On January 13, 1841, the Government of Venezuela was informed of the commission that had been granted to Schomburgk.[13] The Venezuelan Foreign Office replied by proposing the negotiation of a treaty to settle the Guiana boundary,[14] but this suggestion was declined on the ground that Schomburgk had probably started upon his surveying operations.[15]

Schomburgk began his task as surveyor in April 1841, and perceiving at once the great commercial and strategic value of the Orinoco River, he planted boundary posts at Point Barima and at the mouth of the Amacura River.[16] He then proceeded to finish his survey of the boundaries of British Guiana, and submitted to the British Government a report with accompanying maps. This Schomburgk line became the basis of British claims, and it was closely followed by the Tribunal of Arbitration in their award of October 3, 1899.[17]

11. W. S. Robertson, *Hispanic-American Relations with the United States* (N. Y., 1923), pp. 40-41; J. Fred Rippy, *The Historical Evolution of Hispanic America* (N. Y., 1933), pp. 145ff. By a treaty of March 30, 1845, Spain extended recognition to Venezuela. See, Marques de Olivart, *Colleción de los Tratados, Convenios y Documentos Internacionales* (Madrid, 1890–1902, 11 vols.), vol. 1, p. 114.

12. Viscount Palmerston to Sir H. K. Porter, November 28, 1840, *British Parliamentary Papers, Venezuela, 1896*, vol. 97, Cd. 7972 (London, 1896), p. 189.

13. Mr. O'Leary to Señor Smith, January 13, 1841, *ibid.*, p. 189.

14. Señor Smith to Mr. O'Leary, January 28, 1841, *ibid.*, p. 190.

15. Mr. O'Leary to Señor Smith, January 30, 1841, *ibid.*, p. 190. In the memorandum which accompanied the note from José Andrade to Secretary Gresham, March 31, 1894, there is the following statement: "At the latter part of said year she [England] commissioned Sir R. H. Schomburgk, without the knowledge or acquiescence of Venezuela, to examine and lay down the boundaries of British Guiana. . . . The Venezuelan department of foreign relations was kept ignorant of such measures until informed by Her Majesty's consul at Carácas, when they had already been, or were unavoidably to be, carried out." *Foreign Relations, 1894*, p. 813. The dubious nature of this statement is at once apparent.

16. Mr. Schomburgk to Governor Light, June 22, 1841, *British Parliamentary Papers, Venezuela, 1896*, vol. 97, pp. 192-201.

17. For pertinent data on the Guiana boundary, see, Robert H. Schomburgk, *British Guiana* (London, 1840).

On October 5, 1841, the Venezuelan Minister in London, sent a note of inquiry to Lord Aberdeen with reference to the activities of Schomburgk,[18] and after a protracted correspondence, he received the assurance (January 31, 1842) that Schomburgk's boundary posts at the mouth of the Orinoco would be removed.[19] Two years later, the Venezuelan Minister again called the attention of Lord Aberdeen to the Guiana boundary difficulty, and suggested negotiations for a treaty that would fix "definitely the boundary-line that shall divide the two countries." [20]

The claims put forward by Venezuela were so extravagant that they could not be accepted by the British Government, but Lord Aberdeen showed a conciliatory spirit by proposing a compromise line that would give Venezuela the complete control of the mouth of the Orinoco River.[21] The Government of Venezuela did not respond to this friendly overture, and negotiations were suspended.

In 1850 certain gold mines were opened near the Yuruari River, in the disputed territory. Rumors immediately arose that the British Government might occupy this region, and in order to quiet any apprehensions in this regard, the British representative in Carácas, sent to the Government of Venezuela a letter (November 18, 1850) which disavowed any "intention of occupying or encroaching upon the disputed territory; hence, in a like spirit of good faith and friendliness, the Venezuelan Government cannot object to make a similar declaration to Her Majesty's Government." [22] The Venezuelan Foreign Office responded with a similar disavowal,[23] and this meeting of diplomatic minds was afterwards referred to as the Agreement of 1850.

In Venezuela, the two decades that followed the Agreement of 1850 were characterized by domestic turmoil, and negotiations with Great Britain with reference to the Guiana boundary were not resumed until General Guzmán Blanco had crushed all opposition and had become a virtual dictator.[24] On November 14, 1876, the Venezuelan Minister of Foreign Affairs sent a note to Lord Derby (the British Foreign Sec-

18. A. Fortique to Lord Aberdeen, October 5, 1841, *British Parliamentary Papers, Venezuela, 1896*, vol. 97, p. 203.
19. Lord Aberdeen to Señor Fortique, January 31, 1842, *ibid.*, p. 234.
20. Señor Fortique to Lord Aberdeen, January 31, 1844, *ibid.*, pp. 248-251.
21. Lord Aberdeen to Señor Fortique, March 30, 1844, *ibid.*, pp. 251-254.
22. Belford H. Wilson to Señor Lecuna, November 18, 1850, *British Parliamentary Papers, Venezuela, 1896*, vol. 97, pp. 263-264.
23. Secretary Vicente Lecuna to Wilson, December 20, 1850, *ibid.*, p. 265.
24. W. S. Robertson, *History of the Latin-American Nations*, pp. 412-413.

retary) in which he referred to the negotiations of 1841–1844, and expressed the hope that it would be possible to come to some speedy settlement.[25] On this same day (November 14, 1876), the Venezuelan Government sent a note to Secretary Fish in which an appeal for assistance was made to the United States "as the most powerful and the oldest of the Republics of the new continent," whose duty it was to lend "its powerful moral support" to Latin American States in their disputes with European powers.[26]

The Government of Venezuela followed up this overture by sending another note to Lord Derby (February 13, 1877) which recited the claims of Venezuela to certain regions in Guiana, but which closed with a declaration of willingness to "settle this long-pending question in the most amicable manner." [27] The reply of the British Foreign Secretary was not encouraging. The Governor of British Guiana was en route to London, and Lord Derby thought it was best to await his arrival before resuming negotiations relative to the boundary dispute.[28]

The visit of the Governor of British Guiana was apparently a long-deferred affair, and after waiting for more than two years with no word from the British Government, the Venezuelan Minister in London addressed a note to Lord Salisbury which repeated the substance of his previous communication.[29] After a delay of nearly eight months, Lord Salisbury replied that it would be unwise to argue the question of boundary on the ground of strict right. It would be more expedient to attempt to agree upon a "frontier of accommodation which shall satisfy the respective interests of the two countries." Her Majesty's Government was anxious to meet the Government of Venezuela "in a spirit of conciliation, and would be willing . . . to waive a portion of what they consider their strict right, if Venezuela is really disposed to make corresponding concessions on her part." [30]

Venezuela was quite disposed to make concessions in this matter of the Guiana boundary, and in order to arrive at some basis for negotiation, Dr. Rojas inquired if the British Government would accept the

25. Secretary Eduardo Calcaño to Lord Derby, November 14, 1876, *ibid.*, pp. 286-291.
26. Secretary Calcaño to Secretary Fish, November 14, 1876, *Senate Ex. Doc. 226*, 50 Cong., 1 sess., pp. 3-4.
27. Señor José M. Rojas to Lord Derby, February 13, 1877, *British Parliamentary Papers, Venezuela, 1896*, vol. 97, pp. 291-292.
28. Lord Derby to Rojas, March 24, 1877, *ibid.*, p. 293.
29. Rojas to Lord Salisbury, May 19, 1879, *ibid.*, pp. 293-294.
30. Lord Salisbury to Rojas, January 10, 1880, *ibid.*, p. 295.

compromise line offered by Lord Aberdeen on March 30, 1844.[31] Once more the British Government countered with a note which postponed the negotiations until the arrival of an important official from British Guiana.[32]

There is a possibility that this British delay was caused by the news of gold discoveries in the disputed territory.[33] Lord Salisbury may have been eager to learn the value of these discoveries before agreeing to any definitive boundary adjustments. It would seem, however, that the British officials could have conveyed this information in a relatively short time, and the delay in answering the notes of the Venezuelan representatives was too protracted to suit the anxious temperament of the Latin American diplomats. After waiting some five months, Rojas sent a note to Lord Granville (the new British Foreign Secretary) which called attention to the apparent non-arrival of the British officials from Guiana. Would it not be better to stop waiting for these slow-moving British representatives, and resume negotiations at once? In the event that the British Government was willing to renew discussions, Venezuela was "disposed to accept the mouth of the River Moroco as the frontier on the coast." [34] When Lord Granville rejected this suggestion with an indication that he would consider a line farther to the north,[35] Rojas promptly replied with a note that offered a new line commencing on the coast just *one mile* north of the mouth of the Moroco River. In the event that this proposal was unacceptable, Rojas then suggested arbitration of the whole dispute.[36]

The British Foreign Office turned this note over to the Lieutenant-Governor and the Attorney-General of British Guiana, who had finally arrived in England, and they presented an elaborate report which showed the large number of British subjects who resided in the territory that was included in the line proposed by Dr. Rojas. They suggested an alternative line which still gave Venezuela control over the mouth of the Orinoco River, and which considerably reduced the territory that was claimed for England under the Schomburgk line.

31. Rojas to Lord Salisbury, April 12, 1880, *ibid.,* p. 296.
32. Lord Salisbury to Rojas, April 23, 1880, *ibid.,* p. 296.
33. J. Rodway, *Guiana, British, Dutch and French* (London, 1912), p. 129; R. Tennent, *British Guiana and its Resources* (London, 1895), p. 30.
34. Rojas to Lord Granville, September 23, 1880, *British Parliamentary Papers, Venezuela, 1896*, vol. 97, p. 297.
35. Lord Granville to Rojas, February 12, 1881, *ibid.,* p. 298.
36. Rojas to Lord Granville, February 21, 1881, *ibid.,* pp. 298-299.

Lord Granville adopted the suggestion of these British officials, and incorporated it in his note to Dr. Rojas, September 15, 1881.[37]

President Cleveland has spoken of this Granville proposal as "lacking almost every feature of concession," [38] but this indictment is far too severe. It is true that it represented a recession from the line suggested by Lord Aberdeen in 1844, but it is also true that British interests in the disputed area had greatly increased since that time, and the lines proposed by Dr. Rojas showed a far more uncompromising spirit than that suggested by Lord Granville.

Dr. Rojas did not bother to answer this communication from the British Foreign Office, and the Venezuelan Government turned to the United States for assistance. On December 21, 1880, the Venezuelan representative in Washington, addressed a note to Secretary Evarts in which he stated that he had been informed that British officials were erecting a telegraph station at Barima Point.[39] In his reply, Secretary Evarts assured Camacho that

. . . in view of the deep interest which the Government of the United States takes in all transactions tending to attempted encroachments of foreign powers upon the territory of any of the republics of this continent, this Government could not look with indifference to the forcible acquisition of such territory by England. . . . This Government awaits, therefore, with natural concern the more particular statement promised by the Government of Venezuela, which it hopes will not be long delayed.[40]

The statement promised by the Government of Venezuela concerning the erection by British officials of a telegraph station at Barima Point, did not reach Washington until November, 1882, at which time Mr. Frelinghuysen was Secretary of State. It seemed to Frelinghuysen that recourse to arbitration was the best method of settling the dispute between Venezuela and Great Britain, and he frankly stated that the

37. Lord Granville to Rojas, September 15, 1887, *ibid.*, pp. 299-301.
38. "The Venezuelan Boundary Controversy," *Presidential Problems*, p. 207. In certain regards, the statements of ex-President Cleveland are hopelessly incorrect. On pages 174-175 of the "Venezuelan Boundary Controversy," he states that Venezuela declared her independence in 1810 (in reality on July 5, 1811), and in commenting upon the break-up of the Great Colombian Republic, he remarks: "In 1836 this union was dissolved and Venezuela became again a separate and independent republic, being promptly recognized as such by our Government and by other powers." As a matter of fact, the union of the Great Colombian Republic was dissolved in 1830, and Venezuela was recognized by the United States on February 28, 1835.
39. Mr. Camacho to Secretary Evarts, December 21, 1880, *Senate Ex. Doc. 226*, 50 Cong., 1 sess., pp. 12-13.
40. Secretary Evarts to Camacho, January 31, 1881, *ibid.*, p. 14.

American Government would "press upon Great Britain, in a friendly way," the advantages of arbitration.[41]

It was apparent to Venezuelan officials that American intervention in the boundary dispute would probably result in reducing British claims to territory west of the Essequibo River, and in order to strengthen this American interest by giving it an economic basis, the Government of Venezuela granted some very important concessions to American citizens. In September, 1883, Mr. Cyrinius C. Fitzgerald was given the exclusive right to colonize some national lands which extended from the Orinoco River to the mountains of Imataca. In the following year a very extensive concession was granted to one Herbert Gordon.[42]

These concessions were in the disputed territory between Venezuela and British Guiana, and there was little doubt that they would arouse British resentment. It was not long before British officials sent letters warning Fitzgerald and Gordon against any operations within the limits of their concessions. Later, steps were taken to enforce British regulations in those regions.[43]

While this friction was developing along the Guiana boundary, ex-President Guzmán Blanco was accredited as the special representative of the Venezuelan Government to England and to France for the purpose of settling certain disputes. On his way to Europe, he paid a visit to Washington and had several conferences with Secretary Frelinghuysen, who evinced a deep interest in the settlement of the boundary dispute. With a hope of promoting some adjustment of this matter, Frelinghuysen instructed the American Minister at London to express to the British Foreign Office the desire of the American Government to see the dispute settled upon "equitable grounds." Lowell was to embrace the "proper occasion to let Lord Granville know that we are not without concern as to whatever may affect the interests of a sister Republic of the American continent and its position in the family of of nations." [44]

In the meantime, on November 15, 1883,[45] Dr. Rafael Seijas, the

41. Secretary Frelinghuysen to Jehu Baker, January 31, 1883, *Senate Ex. Doc. 226*, 50 Cong., 1 sess., pp. 42-43.
42. *British Parliamentary Papers, 1896, Venezuela*, vol. 97, pp. 314-321.
43. *Ibid.*, pp. 314ff.
44. Secretary Frelinghuysen to Lowell, July 7, 1884, *Senate Ex. Doc., 226*, 50 Cong., 1 sess., pp. 47-48.
45. This note of Dr. Seijas to C. E. Mansfield was in answer to a note from Mansfield, Oct. 15, 1883, with regard to the Guiana boundary.

Venezuelan Minister of Foreign Affairs, submitted to the British Government a proposal to submit to arbitration the question of the title to the territory west of the Essequibo River. Reference was made to the fact that the constitution of Venezuela prohibited the alienation or cession of any of the lands of the republic. This prohibition, however, would not affect a reduction of territory that was brought about by the decision of an arbitral tribunal.[46]

The British Government expressed concern about this article in the Venezuelan constitution. If arbitration was resorted to, and if the decision went against Venezuela, there might be serious difficulty in carrying out the award. Moreover, if the British Government accepted a proposal to arbitrate the title of *all* the territory west of the Essequibo, an adverse decision would affect in a very serious manner the interests of a large number of British subjects. For this reason, the proposal of the Government of Venezuela was rejected.[47]

In discussing this rejection by Great Britain of the Venezuelan proposal of arbitration, ex-President Cleveland becomes somewhat hysterical in his condemnation of British policy. His excited comments are as follows:

Let us pause here for a moment's examination of the surprising refusal of Great Britain to submit this difficulty to arbitration, and the more surprising reasons presented for its justification. The refusal was surprising because the controversy had reached such a stage that arbitration was evidently the only means by which it could be settled consistently with harmonious relations between the two countries.

It was on this ground that Venezuela proposed arbitration; and she strongly urged it on the further ground that inasmuch as the prohibition of her constitution prevented the relinquishment, by treaty of voluntary act, of any part of the territory which her people and their government claimed to be indubitably Venezuelan, such a relinquishment would present no difficulties if it was in obedience to a decree of a tribunal to which the question of ownership had been mutually submitted.

In giving her reasons for rejecting arbitration Great Britain says in effect: The plan you urge for the utter and complete elimination of this constitutional prohibition . . . is objectionable because we fear the prohibition thus eliminated . . . will still be used as a pretext for disobedience to an award. . . .

The remaining objection interposed by Great Britain to the arbitration

46. Dr. Seijas to C. E. Mansfield, November 15, 1883, *Senate Ex. Doc. 226*, 50 Cong., 1 sess., pp. 101-103.

47. Lord Granville to C. E. Mansfield, February 29, 1884, *British Parliamentary Papers, Venezuela, 1896*, vol. 97, pp. 309-310.

requested by Venezuela is based upon the fear that an award might be made in favor of the Venezuela claim. . . .

It first occurs to us that a contention may well be suspected of weakness when its supporters are unwilling to subject it to the test of impartial arbitration.[48]

In discussing this unfair indictment of British policy in connection with the Guiana boundary, one should keep in mind, first of all, the extravagant claims of Venezuela. From the very beginning of the dispute, the Government of Venezuela advanced the most absurd pretensions as to the extent of her territory. In the face of this uncompromising attitude, Lord Aberdeen showed a rare quality of restraint, and the boundary line that he offered in 1844 was unusually generous. This friendly gesture was spurred by the acquisitive Venezuelans, who continued to push their extreme and groundless claims. The line offered by Lord Granville in 1881, was criticized by Cleveland as "lacking almost every feature of concession," but when a student of the Guiana boundary dispute looks through the smoke screen raised by the Cleveland rhetoric, he can clearly perceive that Granville was making a very fair proposal. The real justification of this proposed Granville-line is the fact that the Tribunal of Arbitration closely adhered to it in announcing their award of October 3, 1899.

Cleveland never seemed to understand that the claims of Venezuela were preposterous, and that, in the face of this extravagant attitude, Great Britain could not consent to arbitration. Nations have not been in the habit of placing in the hands of arbitrators the task of drawing important boundary lines. The parties to a dispute have usually arrived at some general agreement, and then have submitted to arbitration merely some specific points which are still in question. The general procedure in this regard was clearly outlined by John Bassett Moore who was then busily engaged upon his monumental work on the history and digest of arbitrations to which the United States had been a party. In a letter to William L. Wilson, Mr. Moore remarks:

We have arbitrated boundary disputes and so has Great Britain, but never, . . . where a line had not previously been agreed upon by direct negotiation. Governments are not in the habit of resigning their functions so completely into the hands of arbitrators as to say, "We have no boundaries; make some for us." In one of our boundary arbitrations, the arbitrator, the King of the Netherlands, being unable to draw the line that had

48. Grover Cleveland, "The Venezuelan Boundary Controversy," *Presidential Problems,* pp. 208-211.

been agreed upon, assumed to draw another, and both parties concurred in setting his award aside. The question was afterwards adjusted by Mr. Webster and Lord Ashburton, in the treaty of 1842. Where lines have previously been agreed upon, we have submitted to arbitral decision specific points of difference as to what was agreed. It would be at least unusual to leave it to arbitrators to make a boundary.[49]

When Lord Granville, on June 10, 1884, once more refused to submit the boundary dispute to arbitration, he was merely following American practice. Granville, however, was sincerely anxious to show a conciliatory spirit towards Venezuela, and during the early months of 1885 he carried on negotiations with General Guzmán Blanco looking towards a general arbitration treaty that would cover all points of dispute between Venezuela and Great Britain.[50] Granville finally reached the point where he was ready to consent to this general arbitration treaty which would include "all differences which *may* arise between the high contracting parties." [51]

At this point, Granville went out of office and was succeeded by Lord Salisbury. On July 27, 1885, Salisbury wrote to Guzmán Blanco and repudiated all the steps that had been taken by Granville with reference to the arbitration treaty. He clearly announced to Blanco that the British Government was "unable to concur in the assent given by their predecessors in office to the general arbitration article proposed by Venezuela. . . . To engage to refer to arbitration all disputes and controversies whatsoever would be without precedent in the treaties made by Great Britain." [52]

In his discussion of the negotiations between Lord Granville and Guzmán Blanco for a general arbitration treaty, ex-President Cleveland makes the following inaccurate comment:

. . . Whatever Lord Granville may have intended by the language used, the Government of Venezuela certainly understood his agreement to include the pending boundary dispute as among the questions that should be submitted to arbitration. . . . The high hopes and joyful anticipations of Venezuela born of this apparently favorable situation were, however, but short-lived. . . . No assertion of the irrevocability of the agreement which Venezuela had made with his predecessor, and no plea or argument of any kind,

49. John Bassett Moore to William L. Wilson, December 10, 1895, *Cleveland MS.*

50. See the notes from Granville to Guzmán Blanco, January 28, February 13, April 2, April 15, June 18, 1885; the notes from Guzmán Blanco to Granville, March 21, April 6, June 8, June 22, 1885. *Senate Ex. Doc. 226, 50 Cong., 1 sess., pp. 114-133.*

51. Granville to Guzmán Blanco, May 15, 1885, *Foreign Relations, 1894, p. 819.*

52. Lord Salisbury to Guzmán Blanco, July 27, 1885, *Senate Ex. Doc. 226, 50 Cong., 1 sess., pp. 133-138.*

availed to save the enlarged terms of this arbitration clause from Lord
Salisbury's destructive insistence.[53]

According to the explicit wording of the arbitration article, the
treaty would apply only to "differences which *may* arise between the
high contracting parties." The Guiana boundary dispute did not come
within the wording of this article which referred only to *future* difficulties. It should also be remembered that Lord Granville had not actually
signed the proposed arbitration treaty with Venezuela. In referring
to the progress of the negotiations between Granville and Guzmán
Blanco, Secretary Olney stated that "a treaty was practically agreed
upon with the Gladstone government in 1886 containing a general
arbitration clause under which the parties might have submitted the
boundary dispute to the decision of a third power." [54]

Secretary Olney was often lost in a mental fog when he dealt with
the Guiana boundary dispute, and this fact is evident when one considers the above statement. The negotiations between Granville and
Guzmán Blanco were concluded in 1885, not in 1886. Moreover, Olney
was badly mistaken in supposing that this treaty contained a clause
"under which the parties might have submitted the boundary dispute
to a third power." As Lord Salisbury clearly pointed out, the proposed
treaty between Great Britain and Venezuela "had reference to *future*
disputes only." [55]

It is apparent that both Secretary Olney and President Cleveland
had little real knowledge of the background of the Guiana boundary
dispute, and their belligerent attitude towards England was based upon
sentiment rather than reason. With Bayard the situation was very different, and the following pages will indicate the progress of Anglo-
Venezuelan relations during the first Cleveland Administration.

When Bayard assumed the office of Secretary of State in March,
1885, the question of the Guiana boundary was soon brought to his
attention. On March 31, 1885, Señor Soteldo, the Venezuelan Minister,
addressed a note to Bayard in which he expressed the hope that he
would soon be able to present information about the "recent attempts
of the British authorities to consummate the usurpation of a great part

53. Grover Cleveland, "The Venezuelan Boundary Controversy," *Presidential Problems*,
pp. 215-216.
54. Secretary Olney to Bayard, July 20, 1895, *Foreign Relations, 1895*, p. 547.
55. Lord Salisbury to Sir Julian Pauncefote, November 26, 1895, *Foreign Relations,
1895*, pp. 573-574.

of Venezuelan Guiana in order to control the mouth of the Orinoco." [56] Some weeks later, Soteldo sent a second note to Bayard about British expansion in Guiana, and he concluded with a statement that his Government wished "to follow the path that may be marked out for it by the great Republic of the North." [57]

In his reply, Bayard pointed out that the President could "not entertain a request to act as umpire unless it should come concurrently from both the contestants." [58]

Bayard also sent an instruction to Phelps, in London, in which he reviewed the situation, and requested information as to the progress that Guzmán Blanco was making in London with regard to a settlement of the boundary dispute. In commenting upon the discussions with the Venezuelan Minister in Washington, Bayard made the following observation:

> The proposals of Venezuela to this Government for an alliance, in return for certain exclusive privileges in the navigation of the Orinoco and other Venezuelan waters, . . . [have] never assumed a definite form. . . . The Venezuelan Government, as you will perceive from the correspondence, has never definitely stated what course it desires this Government to pursue; but on the contrary has expressed a desire to be guided by our counsel, indulging, perhaps, in the hope that we will ultimately act in its behalf to establish its claim against Great Britain.[59]

After sending this instruction to Phelps, Bayard paid little attention to the Guiana boundary dispute until the following year. In the meantime, in England, the negotiations between Lord Rosebery and Guzmán Blanco were fast reaching a stalemate. On June 19, 1886, Blanco wrote to Rosebery with reference to the desirability of reaching an agreement on the boundary dispute,[60] and Rosebery replied at once and suggested a boundary line.[61] Her Majesty's Government was especially anxious to secure undisputed possession of the Guaima River, and it also wished to have the Orinoco "entirely free to commerce and navigation."

56. A. M. Soteldo to Secretary Bayard, March 31, 1885, *Senate Ex. Doc. 226*, 50 Cong., 1 sess., p. 50.

57. Soteldo to Secretary Bayard, April 29, 1885, *ibid.*, pp. 50-52. See also a long note from A. A. Adee to Secretary Bayard, July 14, 1885, *ibid.*, pp. 52-54.

58. Secretary Bayard to Soteldo, July 21, 1885, *ibid.*, pp. 58-59.

59. Secretary Bayard to Phelps, July 20, 1885, *Great Britain, Instructions*, vol. 27, MS Dept. of State.

60. Guzmán Blanco to Lord Rosebery, June 19, 1886, *British Parliamentary Papers, Venezuela, 1896*, pp. 354-355.

61. Lord Rosebery to Guzmán Blanco, July 20, 1886, *ibid.*, pp. 356-357.

The line indicated by Lord Rosebery was more liberal than the one offered by Lord Granville in 1881, and it was distinctly more generous than the line finally agreed upon by the Arbitral Tribunal in 1899. Guzmán Blanco, however, insisted that the arbitration should include all of the territory west of the Essequibo,[62] and this stand was later characterized by Lord Salisbury as a pretension "hardly less exorbitant than would be a refusal by Great Britain to agree to an arbitration on the boundary of British Columbia and Alaska, unless the United States would consent to bring into the question one-half of the whole area of the latter territory." [63]

The British Government showed no sign of meeting these extreme demands of Guzmán Blanco, who soon returned to Venezuela with the belief that British statesmen were harboring designs upon the disputed territory. This feeling of suspicion was confirmed when British officers sailed up the Orinoco and planted posts and fixed placards which indicated the extent of British claims. The next step by the British Government (October, 1886) was the proclamation of the Schomburgk line as the provisional boundary of British Guiana.[64]

To some careful observers in America, it seemed apparent that Great Britain was on the march in Guiana. They regarded as significant the changed wording in the British Colonial Office List for the years 1885–1886. In the edition of 1885, there is the following statement concerning British Guiana: "It is impossible to specify the exact area of the Colony, as its precise boundaries between Venezuela and Brazil, respectively, are undetermined, but it has been computed to be 76,000 square miles." [65] In the edition for the year 1886, the computation of 76,000 was increased to 100,000 square miles.[66] This increase in territorial claims merely meant that in 1886 Great Britain had grown weary of offering compromise lines that Venezuela would not accept, and she was now determined to stand behind the Schomburgk line. The decision of the Arbitral Tribunal showed that this was not an unreasonable position to take.

Venezuelan reluctance to agree upon any compromise line that was really based upon equitable grounds, was paired with a refusal to pay

62. Guzmán Blanco to Lord Rosebery, July 29, 1886, ibid., pp. 365-371.
63. Lord Salisbury to Sir Julian Pauncefote, November 26, 1895, Foreign Relations, 1895, p. 574.
64. Lord Iddesleigh to F. R. St. John, October 23, 1896, British Parliamentary Papers, Venezuela, 1896, vol. 97, p. 372. The proclamation was dated, October 21, 1886.
65. Colonial Office List, 1885, p. 24.   66. Ibid., p. 35.

the monetary claims that were pressed upon her by the British Government. In November, 1886, Sackville-West showed Bayard a copy of a note from F. R. St. John, the British Minister at Carácas, in which he spoke of the "hopelessness of expecting much from the Venezuelan Government as to the payment of British claims." St. John stated that he and Mr. Scott (the American Minister at Carácas) were of the opinion that there should be "a joint presentation by the two Governments to enforce consideration and payment of the claims" due to both countries. Bayard, however, disagreed with this view, but he did think that there "could be a co-operative and concurrent action by each minister that would assist each other in a common object." [67]

There was little likelihood of concurrent action by Scott and St. John with reference to Anglo-American claims against Venezuela. The Venezuelan Government began to bombard the Department of State with notes that conjured up the fearsome bogey of British imperialism in South America, and the political aspect of the situation soon occupied all the attention of American diplomats. On December 13, 1886, Scott informed Bayard of the increasing friction between Great Britain and Venezuela, and he frankly stated that matters looked "very angry and threatening. Moreover, the attempt on the part of Venezuela to take possession of Barima Cape may lead to a collision and an open rupture between the two countries that may lead to war." [68]

This alarming news from Venezuela was confirmed by A. M. Soteldo, the Venezuelan Minister in Washington. On December 29, he called at the Department of State and complained of the "annoyance and provocation" that his country had suffered "at the hands of Great Britain." Bayard's attitude in this matter is clearly revealed in the following excerpt from one of his memoranda:

> I told him [Soteldo] I had no knowledge of the merits of the controversy and had not formed any judgment, but that I had a feeling of interest in maintaining the self-respect of Venezuela, and that I deprecated any undue pressure put by Great Britain upon that Country for any purpose, and that I therefore should probably today send dispatches to our Minister at London proferring the good offices of the United States in favor of a friendly and amicable adjustment of the boundary between Great Britain and Venezuela. I said I did not know what had been done by President Guzmán Blanco in his late visit to Europe, but that the disposition of this Government was the

67. *Memorandum* written by Bayard after a conversation with Sackville-West, November 5, 1886, *Bayard MS.*

68. Scott to Secretary Bayard, December 13, 1886, *Senate Ex. Doc. 226*, 50 Cong., 1 sess., pp. 59-60.

same as it always had been—to see fair play was exhibited towards the South American Republics.[69]

Bayard carried out his promise to Soteldo by writing a long instruction to Phelps on the following day. He directed Phelps to proffer to Lord Salisbury American good offices in the settlement of the Guiana boundary dispute, and he made specific reference to the Monroe Doctrine:

It does not appear that at any time heretofore the good offices of this Government have been actually tendered to avert a rupture between Great Britain and Venezuela. . . . Our inaction in this regard would seem to be due to the reluctance of Venezuela to have the Government of the United States take any steps having relation to the action of the British Government which might in appearance even, prejudice the resort to our arbitration or mediation. Nevertheless, the records abundantly testify our friendly concern in the adjustment of the dispute, and the intelligence now received, warrants me in tendering through you, to Her Majesty's Government, the good offices of the United States to promote an amicable settlement of the respective claims of Great Britain and Venezuela in the premises. . . . Her Majesty's Government will readily understand that this attitude of friendly neutrality and entire impartiality touching the merits of the controversy, . . . is entirely consistent . . . with the sense of responsibility that rests upon the United States in relation to the South American republics. The doctrines we announced two generations ago . . . have lost none of their force . . . in the progress of time.[70]

On January 25, 1887, Phelps wrote to Bayard that he would speak to Lord Salisbury "more plainly" than he was willing to write.[71] His note of February 8 was in no sense inflammatory, and it merely repeated Bayard's instruction of December 30, 1886.[72] Salisbury's reply was negative. The attitude adopted by Guzmán Blanco with regard to the boundary dispute had precluded "Her Majesty's Government from submitting those questions . . . to the arbitration of any third power."[73]

While this correspondence was being carried on, the Venezuelan Minister in Washington was complaining to Bayard about British "usurpations" in the disputed territory along the Guiana boundary.[74]

69. *Memorandum* written by Bayard after a conversation with Soteldo, December 29, 1886, *Bayard MS.*

70. Secretary Bayard to Phelps, December 30, 1886, *Senate Ex. Doc. 226,* 50 Cong., 1 sess., pp. 67-68.

71. Phelps to Secretary Bayard, January 25, 1887, *Bayard MS.*

72. Phelps to Lord Salisbury, February 8, 1887, *Senate Ex. Doc. 226,* 50 Cong., 1 sess., pp. 80-81.

73. Lord Salisbury to Phelps, February 22, 1887, *ibid.,* p. 84.

74. Soteldo to Secretary Bayard, January 4, 1887, *Senate Ex. Doc. 226,* 50 Cong., 1 sess., pp. 69-71.

From Carácas came word that diplomatic relations between Venezuela and Great Britain had been severed. According to the American Minister, the situation looked "very threatening." [75]

On February 2, 1887, Soteldo paid one of his numerous visits to the Department of State for the purpose of presenting further items in his bill of complaints against Great Britain. Bayard told him that he did not

. . . suppose for an instant that the Government of Great Britain had any unfriendly designs upon the territory or the rights of the people of Venezuela; that I [Bayard] did not know anything of the facts of the case and all we had heard was from one side—that of his Government. I said I could imagine, however, that the British traders and merchants in that country were disposed to take anything they could get, . . . and do all in their power to carry the protection of their Government over the lands and property they had acquired, and that perhaps if they had gone beyond what was right and the question was submitted to the British Government, that it would refuse to sustain them.

He asked me about the cessation of diplomatic intercourse between Venezuela and Great Britain, and I told him that it seemed very unwise to take away from Venezuela any opportunity of explanation to the Government of Great Britain, of the true facts of the case. . . . He said they wanted all the moral aid of the United States in the matter, and I told him the United States would be always interested in whatever affected the fate of the South American Republics, and that we had made expressions of that kind to Great Britain, and should make it again, and that we were ever ready to lend our good offices to promote a proper understanding between Venezuela and Great Britain, but that I did not think it would be a wise step for Venezuela to withdraw her diplomatic agent from Great Britain now.[76]

On March 18 Soteldo expressed to Bayard his warm appreciation of the effort that the American Government had made to mediate between

75. Scott to Secretary Bayard, January 21, February 24, 1887, *ibid.* In January 1887, there was a sharp exchange of notes between the Venezuelan Minister of Foreign Affairs and the British Minister at Carácas, F. R. St. John. President Guzmán Blanco was very anxious to erect a lighthouse at Barima Point, but the British Government refused permission unless Guzmán Blanco would "give a formal engagement in writing that the placing of the light will in no way be held as prejudicing the British claim to the territory in dispute." See, Secretary Urbaneja to F. R. St. John, January 8, 26, 1887; F. R. St. John to Urbaneja, January 19, 31, 1887, *British Parliamentary Papers, Venezuela, 1896*, vol. 97, pp. 386-393.

76. *Memorandum* dictated by Bayard after a conversation with Soteldo, the Venezuelan Minister, February 2, 1887, *Bayard MS.* On February 25, Soteldo informed Bayard that he had written privately to President Guzmán Blanco for the purpose of acquainting him with Bayard's view that it was unwise to break off diplomatic relations with Great Britain. *Memorandum* dictated by Bayard after a conversation with Soteldo, February 25, 1887, *Bayard MS.*

Venezuela and Great Britain with regard to the Guiana boundary. He then expressed the hope that some arrangement could be effected whereby the ships of the United States would have the right to enter "the lakes and rivers of Venezuela, and also to . . . participate in the coastwise trade, and that the United States could arrange to give an equivalent." This arrangement would cement the friendly ties that existed between the two nations.[77]

Several days later, Soteldo spoke to Bayard about a British invasion of the territorial waters of Venezuela. Bayard said he had heard nothing about this incident, but he had learned from Phelps that "Great Britain intended to pursue negotiations directly with Venezuela before resorting to arbitration." Bayard thought that this seemed to indicate a friendly attitude on the part of the British Government, and he hoped "the matter would be settled satisfactorily." [78]

In April, 1887, Soteldo was superseded by J. A. Olavarria. On May 2 the new Venezuelan representative paid a visit to the Department of State, and he lost no time in informing Bayard that he was about to send a formal note in which the American Government would be requested to

. . . urge or insist upon arbitration by Great Britain, and also that the Venezuelan Government wished the United States to become the arbitrator. I [Bayard] told him that we should be very glad to lend our good offices in favor of arbitration, but that we could not suggest the United States as arbitrator; that such a suggestion must come from both parties; that at the joint request of both we would be unable to decline, but that we could not propose ourselves upon the recommendation of either. He said he understood that, and that Venezuela would make the suggestion that the United States should be arbitrator.[79]

Olavarria's formal note to Bayard was dated May 4, and it emphasized the opinion that if the American Government would take a bold stand on the basis of the "doctrine of the immortal Monroe," Great Britain would be glad to agree to arbitration.[80] Olavarria followed up

77. *Memorandum* dictated by Bayard after a conversation with Soteldo, March 18, 1887, *Bayard MS.* He also indicated to Bayard that the Venezuelan Government had "not paid him for the last year, and he did not know whether he would go back to Venezuela or not."

78. *Memorandum* written by Bayard after a conversation with Soteldo, March 21, 1887, *Bayard MS.* See also, *memorandum* of March 25, 1887.

79. *Memorandum* written by Bayard after a conversation with Olavarria, May 2, 1887, *Bayard MS.*

80. Olavarria to Secretary Bayard, May 4, 1887, *Senate Ex. Doc. 226*, 50 Cong., 1 sess., pp. 95-96.

this note by another visit to the Department of State. When the question of the Guiana boundary came up for discussion, Bayard told Olavarria that he believed that it was very important to restore diplomatic relations between Venezuela and Great Britain. He had instructed Phelps to make inquiries in this regard, and as soon as he heard from London he would get in touch with Olavarria.[81]

From Carácas, Bayard learned that President Guzmán Blanco was anxious for the American Government once more to proffer its good offices with regard to the boundary dispute. There was a possibility that the British Government might be willing to accept mediation, and this would pave the way for arbitration.[82] When Bayard discussed this despatch with Olavarria, the Venezuelan chargé expressed the view that his Government would not negotiate with England until the disputed territory had been cleared of English officials.[83]

Olavarria then produced a map of Guiana with certain lines that indicated the manner in which the British had extended their boundary line so as to include the important gold mines that had been discovered west of the Essequibo. Bayard was cautious in his comments upon the map. He admitted his surprise at the extent of the boundary line. He had not known that the British had "expanded their boundaries in that way," but he could not "say for a moment whether they had a right to or not." He did not "even feel inclined to form an opinion about it, because it had been suggested that the United States might become the arbitrator between Great Britain and Venezuela to fix the boundary," and in such a case it would never do for him "to form an opinion in advance." [84]

Olavarria was a little puzzled by this impartial attitude, and he wrote to Bayard and strongly pressed the view that the situation in Guiana presented a very opportune time for the United States to demonstrate to Great Britain in an unmistakable way that the "Monroe doctrine is still in full force." [85]

81. *Memorandum* written by Bayard after a conversation with Olavarria, May 18, 1887, *Bayard MS.*
82. Scott to Secretary Bayard, June 21, 1887, *Senate Ex. Doc. 226, 50 Cong., 1 sess.,* pp. 191-192.
83. *Memorandum* written by Bayard after a conversation with Olavarria, July 8, 1887, *Bayard MS.*
84. *Memorandum* written by Bayard after a conversation with Olavarria, July 15, 1887, *ibid.*
85. Olavarria to Secretary Bayard, September 22, 1887, *Senate Ex. Doc. 226, 50 Cong.,* 1 sess., pp. 194-195.

In his note to Bayard (September 22, 1887), Olavarria had not confined himself to protests against the British invasion of the disputed territory along the Guiana border. He also alluded to a fresh difficulty that threatened serious trouble. In May, 1883, two British vessels had been seized by Venezuelan authorities for an alleged invasion of Venezuelan waters. The British Government had resented these seizures and the imprisonment and ill-treatment of the crews. A demand was made upon Venezuela for the payment of an indemnity as compensation to the owners of the British vessels and to the crews that had suffered in Venezuelan jails. Under the threat of British reprisals, this indemnity was paid, but the Venezuelan Government was highly indignant at this action on the part of Great Britain, and it presented to Bayard a statement of the case.[86]

As one reads through the memoranda written by Bayard with reference to this case, it is apparent that he refused to become hysterical about it, despite the insistent pressure of the Venezuelan chargé. Bayard's whole thought concerning this matter was that it might be used as a means of restoring, through American good offices, diplomatic relations between Venezuela and Great Britain. After that was achieved, the way might be open for an arbitral arrangement of the boundary dispute.[87]

While Bayard was endeavoring to find some solution for the difficulties that continued to threaten war between Great Britain and Venezuela, Olavarria sent him a note which contained fresh news of alleged British aggressions in the disputed territory. It seemed to the Venezuelan representative that the British Government was laying claim to

. . . whatever regions may be suggested to her by her insatiate thirst for conquest. She even goes so far as to deny the validity of railway grants comprised within territory where not even the wildest dream of fancy has ever conceived that the day would come when Venezuela's right thereto could be disputed. The fact is that until now, England has relied upon impunity. She beholds in us a weak and unfriended nation, and seeks to make the Venezuelan coast and territories the base of a conquest which, if circumstances are not altered, will have no other bounds than the dictates of her own will.[88]

86. *Senate Ex. Doc. 226*, 50 Cong., 1 sess., pp. 190ff.
87. *Memoranda* written by Bayard after conversations with Olavarria, September 29, 30, October 14, 1887, *Bayard MS.*
88. Olavarria to Secretary Bayard, February 15, 1888, *Senate Ex. Doc. 226*, 50 Cong., 1 sess., pp. 201-202.

Olavarria's note had reference to the fact that British claims in the disputed territory had suddenly mounted in 1887 in a significant manner. On December 31, 1887, the Governor of British Guiana issued a proclamation which denied the validity of a grant made by the Government of Venezuela for the construction of a railroad from Ciudad Bolívar to Guacipati, a city located in the heart of an important gold mining district.[89] According to an article that appeared in the London *Financier,* it was stated that the action of the Governor of British Guiana was a strong indication that the British Government was about to lay claim to the Caratal region in which rich gold mines abounded.[90]

On February 17 Olavarria had a conversation with Bayard concerning British claims in the disputed Guiana territory. It was apparent that these claims had now extended far beyond the Schomburgk line, and Bayard assured Olavarria that he would lay the case before Lord Salisbury "with a request to stop further aggressions of Great Britain on Venezuelan territory." [91] Some hours later, Bayard sent an instruction to Phelps in which he candidly confessed that recent British actions had aroused in him a feeling of

. . . grave disquietude . . . that the territorial claim does not follow historical traditions or evidence, but is apparently indefinite. At no time hitherto does it appear that the district, of which Guacipati is the center, has been claimed as British territory or that such jurisdiction has ever been asserted over its inhabitants. . . . It is true that the line claimed by Great Britain as the western boundary of British Guiana is uncertain and vague. It is only necessary to examine the British colonial office list for a few years back to perceive this.[92] In the issue for 1877 . . . the line runs nearly southwardly from the mouth of the Amacuro to the junction of the Cotinga and Takutu rivers. In the issue for 1887, . . . it makes a wide detour to the westward, following the Yuruari. Guacipati lies considerably to the westward of the line officially claimed in 1887. . . .

It may be well for you to express anew to Lord Salisbury the great gratification it would afford this Government to see the Venezuelan dispute amicably and honorably settled, by arbitration or otherwise, and our readiness to do anything we properly can to assist in that end. . . .

If . . . it should appear that there is no fixed limit to the British bound-

. 89. *Ibid.,* p. 203. 90. *Ibid.,* p. 202.

91. *Memorandum* written by Bayard after a conversation with Olavarria, February 17, 1888, *Bayard MS.*

92. In the *Statesman's Year Book* for 1885, the area of British Guiana was given as 76,000 square miles. In the edition of 1886, the area is fixed at 109,000 square miles, an increase during the year of 33,000 square miles.

ary claim, our good disposition to aid in a settlement might not only be defeated, but be obliged to give place to a feeling of grave concern.[93]

Phelps did not present the contents of this instruction to the British Foreign Office because he believed that "further interference with that subject by our Government" would not serve any useful purpose.[94] This fact remained unknown to President Cleveland,[95] and it later escaped the attention of Secretary Olney who relied upon it in his correspondence with Lord Salisbury.

Phelps was extremely cautious in his actions concerning the Guiana boundary controversy. On March 5, 1888, Guzmán Blanco sent him a draft of a treaty for the settlement of this dispute, and expressed the hope that Phelps would assist in the proposed negotiations.[96] Phelps replied that he had not been authorized by Secretary Bayard to take part in these negotiations. Moreover, it appeared to Phelps that it would be difficult to see "upon what ground the United States Government, though actuated . . . by the most friendly feeling toward the Republic of Venezuela, would be justified in interfering in the matter as it is at present situated." [97]

93. Secretary Bayard to Phelps, February 17, 1888, *Senate Ex. Doc. 226, 50 Cong., 1 sess.*, pp. 204-205. In 1888 Edward D. Matthews published in London a pamphlet entitled, *British Guiana and Venezuela*. Matthews claimed to be familiar with the Caratal gold district, and he asserted that he had been connected with English enterprises in that region. With particular reference to the activities of the Chili Gold Mining Company, he remarked as follows: "The cupidity of the Demerara gold seekers has found a strong supporter in Mr. Hugh Watt, the chairman of the Chili Gold Mining Company. This company was formed about six years ago to purchase mining rights in the auriferous Venezuelan territory of Caratal, and holds its property under Venezuelan titles and Venezuelan law. The business has from first to last been managed most extravagantly, and although a large amount of gold has been taken out of the mine, no dividends have yet been earned. Mr. Hugh Watt was responsible for swelling the capital of the company to the enormous sum of one million sterling, and he has lately been obliged to tell his shareholders that the bulk of their money is lost. He has, therefore, cajoled them into the farce of cutting down their capital by seventy-five per cent, and calling it £250,000 instead of £1,000,000. To assist him in giving a market or fictitious value to this reduced capital, he is, both in Parliament and in the Press, agitating for an attack by England on the Republic of Venezuela in which his valuable property is situated, in the probably delusive belief that should England be unwise enough to attempt to annex the Caratal gold fields, New Chili shares will rise to a respectable position in the Stock Exchange Official List." *British Guiana and Venezuela* (London, 1888), pp. 1ff.

94. Phelps to Secretary Bayard, March 28, 1888, *Great Britain, Despatches*, vol. 157, MS Dept. of State. See also, A. L. P. Dennis, *Adventures in American Diplomacy*, pp. 51-52; Henry James, *Richard Olney*, pp. 221-226.

95. In his essay, "The Venezuelan Boundary Controversy," *Presidential Problems*, pp. 243-244 Cleveland makes the mistake of assuming that Bayard's instruction of February 17, 1888, had actually been presented to the British Foreign Office by Phelps.

96. Guzmán Blanco to Phelps, March 5, 1888, *Bayard MS*.

97. Phelps to Guzmán Blanco, March 12, 1888, *ibid*.

Guzmán Blanco then informed Phelps that Olavarria had sent him several communications which indicated that Bayard was anxious to establish an intimate understanding between Blanco and Phelps.[98] Moreover, it was obvious to Blanco that it was greatly to the interest of the United States not "to allow a European Power like England, and without a shadow of right, to get control of the Orinoco, one of the largest and most important rivers in South America." [99]

Before Bayard could straighten out this diplomatic tangle, Phelps returned to the United States on a visit. On April 23, Olavarria had one of his frequent conversations with Bayard, and he at once inquired

. . . what Mr. Phelps had brought from London in regard to the difficulty between Venezuela and Great Britain. I told him that he had brought nothing. . . . He then asked me what I would advise him to do. I told him that I had had some conversation with a gentleman about Venezuela, who professed to know a great deal on the subject from having lived there, and that I was disposed to believe that there was no design on the part of Great Britain for an extension of her political sovereignty over that Country; that it was the question of the individual interests of certain British subjects, who had gotten possession of large mining possessions and other property in the disputed land, and who were anxious to keep themselves from under the control of the Venezuelan Government; that they feared the exactions of that Government upon them and their property, and wanted to keep themselves under British control because they thought they could conduct their business with more safety. I, therefore, thought the question was rather between Venezuela and certain individuals (who were British subjects) holding property in that disputed country, than between the Government of Venezuela and that of Great Britain; . . . that I did not understand it to be a British invasion of Venezuelan sovereignty or property, but rather a question as to the extent of the duty of Great Britain to protect certain of her subjects in their claims against the government of Venezuela. . . . I did not see how the dignity or self-respect of Venezuela would be impaired by an offer to renew diplomatic relations, and that if such relations were renewed, I had no question that the boundary subject would be a proper

98. Guzmán Blanco was entirely right with reference to Bayard's desires on this point. On October 14, 1887, Bayard, during a conversation with Olavarria, remarked that he was of the opinion "that it might be of great practical importance for Mr. Blanco to go to London and see Mr. Phelps, because it might lead to a restoration of diplomatic relations with England, and with that a settlement of their boundary and other difficulties." The only way "for Mr. Phelps to understand this case would be for Mr. Guzmán Blanco to go to London and give him the facts." *Memorandum* written by Bayard, October 14, 1887, *Bayard MS.* In a conversation with Olavarria, September 30, 1887, Bayard made the following comment: "I told him I thought it would be worth while for him to telegraph to President Guzmán that I considered his presence in London, in order to inform Phelps, necessary at this juncture." *Memorandum* of September 30, 1887, *ibid.*
99. Guzmán Blanco to Phelps, March 14, 1888, *Bayard MS.*

matter for arbitration. . . . When diplomatic relations were restored and Great Britain was ready to treat, the United States would be glad to offer their good offices.[100]

It is significant that Bayard was strongly disposed to believe "that there was no design on the part of Great Britain for an extension of her political sovereignty" over any portion of the rightful territory of Venezuela. He was not, like Cleveland or Olney, easily swayed by the specious pleas of Venezuela, and he instinctively put his trust in the good faith of Great Britain. Because of that trust, he was later to be bitterly attacked by many Senators and Representatives who sought to build up political capital by twisting the long tail of the British Lion.

The political aspect of the Guiana boundary dispute was brought into full view when the Senate of the United States passed, without debate (April 11, 1888), a resolution which requested the President to submit for examination the diplomatic correspondence "concerning the boundaries between British Guiana and Venezuela." [101]

In his letter transmitting this correspondence to President Cleveland (July 26, 1888), Bayard made the following comment:

The Government of the United States has consistently regarded the Anglo-Venezuelan controversy as amenable to decision according to the ordinary rules of historical evidence, and has constantly expressed alike to Venezuela and Great Britain, its earnest desire that arbitration might be resorted to, placing its good offices impartially at the disposal of both contestants to bring about such a result.[102]

There was little chance that arbitration would be resorted to in 1888 for the settlement of the Guiana boundary controversy. British claims were constantly increasing, and war seemed almost inevitable. In June, 1888, the Government of British Guiana announced the creation of a new colonial district which included the territory around Barima Point. Officers were appointed for its permanent occupancy, and money was appropriated for administrative expenses.[103]

Although the Government of Venezuela sent a note of protest to the United States against this new extension of British claims,[104] Bayard sent no further instructions to Phelps concerning British expansion

100. *Memorandum* written by Bayard after a conversation with Olavarria, April 23, 1888, *Bayard MS.*
101. *Congressional Record,* April 11, 1888, 50 Cong., 1 sess., vol. 19, pt. 3, p. 2873.
102. *Senate Ex. Doc.* 226, 50 Cong., 1 sess., pp. 1-2.
103. *Foreign Relations, 1894,* p. 831.
104. Olavarria to Secretary Bayard, June 15, 1888, *Senate Ex. Doc. 226,* p. 208.

in Guiana. Phelps had advised against further pressure with reference to the boundary controversy, and his viewpoint was accepted by the Department of State. Bayard had no intention of presenting an ultimatum to Great Britain which would insist upon arbitration of the dispute with Venezuela. He realized that a treaty between the two countries, fixing the general outlines of the Guiana boundary, was the usual prelude to arbitration which ordinarily dealt with minor points of difference. He was not jingo enough to insist that Great Britain place in the hands of a third party the power to draw a general boundary line between British Guiana and Venezuela.

It should also be remembered that Bayard viewed with some suspicion the long list of items in the Venezuelan catalogue of complaints against Great Britain. In his conversations with the Venezuelan representatives, he had resolutely refused to take sides in the boundary dispute, and he had adverted to the obvious fact that most of the information in the Department of State concerning this controversy, had been supplied by the Government of Venezuela. As an ardent apostle of Anglo-Saxon unity, Bayard looked upon Great Britain and the United States as twin conservators of world civilization. It would have been most difficult for him to regard his kindred across the sea as unprincipled imperialists who sought to take unfair advantage of defenceless South Americans. In weighing the complaints of Venezuela and the assurances of Great Britain, he instinctively inclined towards the British side. As one nowadays looks at the facts of the case with an unprejudiced eye, who can say that this inclination was ill-advised?

After the accession of Blaine to the office of Secretary of State in March, 1889, Great Britain continued to push her claims with respect to the disputed territory along the Guiana boundary. On December 4, 1889, the Government of Demerara issued a proclamation which claimed control over the main mouth of the Orinoco River. In order to confirm this control, the city of Barima was declared to be a British port, and a police station was established there.

The Venezuelan Government promptly protested against this British action, and the United States was informed of this latest development in the boundary dispute. Blaine responded to Venezuelan pressure by instructing Henry White, at London, to confer with Lord Salisbury with reference to the re-establishment of diplomatic relations between Great Britain and Venezuela upon the basis of a temporary return to the *status quo* of former years.[105] When the British Government made no immediate response to this American overture, the Venezuelan Minister, at Washington, appealed to Blaine for assistance. His Government had instructed him to beg "with redoubled earnestness" for American mediation in the Guiana boundary dispute.[106]

After Señor Peraza had made another appeal for American good offices,[107] Blaine instructed Robert T. Lincoln, at London, to endeavor to arrange "some accord between the contestants by which the merits of the controversy may be fairly ascertained and the rights of each party justly confirmed." [108]

In the meantime, Lord Salisbury had written two notes to Señor Urbaneja, the Venezuelan Minister to France, in which he outlined the basis of a possible settlement of the boundary controversy. He made it clear that Her Majesty's Government would not accept as satisfactory any arrangement not admitting as English property the territory included within the line laid down by Sir R. Schomburgk. If arbitration were agreed upon, it could apply only to territory *west* of that line.[109]

In his note to the American Minister, Lord Salisbury referred to the proposals he had made to the Government of Venezuela. When he had received an official answer to this overture, he would reply to the American offer of mediation. It should be understood, however, that arbitration would not apply to all the territory in dispute. The British Government believed that there could be no "reasonable doubt" about the British title to certain lands in the disputed strip. The task of the arbitral tribunal would be limited to an examination of the title to lands that lay outside the confines of this strictly British zone.[110]

In an indirect manner quite characteristic of the practice of diplomacy, Lord Salisbury was informing Mr. Lincoln that the British Government was holding fast to the Schomburgk line as the minimum of British demands. But this attitude did not represent the real spirit of conciliation that had animated British statesmen in their relations with Venezuela, and some months later, Sir T. H. Sanderson, Under-Secretary of State for Foreign Affairs, made a generous proposal to Dr.

105. Secretary Blaine to Henry White, December 30, 1889, *Foreign Relations, 1890*, p. 322.

106. Señor Peraza to Secretary Blaine, February 17, 1890, *ibid.*, pp. 782-783.

107. Señor Peraza to Secretary Blaine, April 24, 1890, *ibid.*, p. 784.

108. Secretary Blaine to R. T. Lincoln, May 6, 1890, *ibid.*, p. 339.

109. Lord Salisbury to R. T. Lincoln, May 26, 1890, *ibid.*, pp. 340-341.

110. Lord Salisbury to Lincoln, May 26, 1890, *Foreign Relations, 1890*, pp. 340-341.

Lucio Pulido, who had replaced Señor Urbaneja as the Venezuelan representative in charge of negotiations with Great Britain. The British Government was now ready to negotiate directly with that of Venezuela for the purpose of establishing a frontier of "mutual convenience between the two Guianas, approaching as far as possible the natural limits," and would "renounce any claim or compensation whatever for the abandonment . . . of the mouths of the Orinoco and the adjoining territories." [111]

Pulido met this friendly gesture with the chilling response that it was not his aim to propose any "adjustment of the difference at once, but to promote a renewal of diplomatic intercourse on condition that the English Government should agree to submit the question to international arbitration." Pulido knew that the British Government had long been anxious to settle the main points of the dispute by direct negotiation, and he fully realized that his non-co-operative attitude would mean an indefinite postponement of any settlement of the controversy. In September, 1890, he returned to Venezuela leaving "the good understanding between the two nations interrupted as before." [112]

In his discussion of the attitude of the British Government in 1890, ex-President Cleveland is so misleading as to be distinctly disingenuous. With reference to Lord Salisbury's proposals to Señor Urbaneja, he makes the following comments:

This scheme, if adopted, would give to England absolutely and without question the large territory between British Guiana's conceded western boundary and the Schomburgk line, with an opportunity to lay claim before a board of arbitration for extensive additional territory beyond the Schomburgk line. This is pitiful. The Schomburgk line, which was declared by the British Government, at the time it was made, to be "merely a preliminary measure, open to further discussion between the Governments of Great Britain and Venezuela," and which had been since largely extended in some mysterious way, is now declared to be a line so well established, so infallible, and so sacred that only the territory that England exorbitantly claims beyond that line is enough in dispute to be submitted to impartial arbitration. The trader is again in evidence.[113]

This language has the ring of a legal brief, and it is apparent that Cleveland is merely making an argument instead of attempting to present in an objective manner the evidence in the case. The Schomburgk line had been drawn on numberless maps and was thoroughly

111. *Foreign Relations, 1894*, p. 834.   112. *Foreign Relations*, 1894, pp. 834-835.
113. Grover Cleveland, "The Venezuelan Boundary Controversy," *Presidential Problems*, pp. 221-222.

familiar to all students of the controversy. It was not true that the British Government had recently extended it in "some mysterious way." There were British claims beyond that line, but the line itself had not been changed. Cleveland's accusation in this regard had a disturbing sinister implication that was thoroughly false. Moreover, the British Government did not look upon the Schomburgk line as "infallible" and "sacred." The Sanderson proposal was a distinct recession from that line, and it represented an earnest attempt to put an end to the dispute in an equitable manner. It is significant that Cleveland suppresses all mention of this proposal.[114]

In the United States no attention was paid to the Sanderson proposal, and Secretary Blaine was ready to take some decisive step that would force a settlement of the boundary dispute. His attitude is revealed in a confidential note to Mr. Scruggs, who was the American representative at Carácas. After a brief recital of the steps that had been taken by the American Government in its efforts to find some solution of the difficulty, Blaine then remarked:

> It is now apparent that all such efforts in the future, as they have been in the past, are likely to prove unavailing. Meanwhile the reports which you and the Minister of Venezuela in Washington have communicated to the Department go to show that Great Britain continues to enlarge its pretensions and extend its occupation within the domain of Venezuela. In the presence of these facts, the President has reached the conclusion, that, by reason of the appeals which Venezuela has made to the United States and of the latter's interest in sustaining republican institutions on the American continents, . . . this government should at an early day take an advanced and decisive step in support of the claims of Venezuela to the territory which Great Britain has, in spite of repeated remonstrances and protest, entered upon, appropriated and fortified.[115]

Blaine's strong language in this instruction to Scruggs may have reflected his desire to use the Guiana boundary dispute as a means of securing British concessions in the fur-seal controversy between the United States and Great Britain. At any rate, Blaine's fast failing health prevented him from carrying out the step he contemplated in this instruction of October 28, 1891. On June 4, 1892, Blaine resigned

114. In the spring of 1901 Cleveland was preparing this essay on "The Venezuelan Boundary Controversy" with occasional assistance from Olney. In a letter to Olney, March 3, 1901, he reveals the spirit in which he wrote his dubious indictment of England: "In reviewing the subject I am surprised to find how mean and hoggish Great Britain really acted; and I like old Mr. Salisbury much less than I did." *Cleveland MS.* This language shows how sophomoric Cleveland actually was in the days of his retirement at Princeton.
115. A. F. Tyler, *Foreign Policy of James G. Blaine*, pp. 86-87.

as Secretary of State, and was succeeded by John W. Foster. Foster was busily engaged upon the task of preparing the case of the United States in the Behring Sea arbitration, and he gave little consideration to the Guiana boundary dispute. It was not until the second Cleveland Administration that this dispute once more engaged the serious attention of the Department of State; at this time Bayard was residing in London as the first American Ambassador to the Court of St. James's.

CHAPTER NINETEEN

Bayard Becomes an Ambassador of Good Will to England

———•◦⟨∞⟩◦•———

A. THE GUIANA BOUNDARY DISPUTE

As BAYARD'S TERM OF OFFICE AS SECRETARY OF STATE DREW TO A CLOSE, he prepared to withdraw to the quiet of private life in Wilmington, Delaware. He had the satisfaction of knowing that he had bent every effort to serve his country to the fullest extent of his ability. His record of achievement had been marred by partisan rancor that reached a point almost unparalleled in our history. In a letter to a favorite uncle, Bayard poured forth his pent-up feelings:

> The last four years my work has been performed under great embarrassments arising from the obstruction in the Senate to nearly all the measures I have felt it my duty to propose and recommend, and I doubt if one of my official predecessors ever experienced so little fair play, or common justice at the hands of a Senate dominated by an opposite party. But the shower of aspersion, misrepresentation, and detraction will pass away, and on the record as it stands I shall willingly await judgment.[1]

To a close friend, W. B. Duncan, he wrote in a similar vein:

> Fisher Ames once spoke of the "sober second thought of the American people," and it is to that that my hopes are directed, and as I have made up my record in black and white, I calmly shall await its inspection by friend and foe, with "a sigh for those who love me, a smile for those who hate." [2]

In the Department of State, Bayard left many devoted friends. Alvey A. Adee, the Second Assistant Secretary of State, was very appreciative of Bayard's kindness to him during the years from 1885 to 1889, and in a letter of November 4, 1895, he remarked: "No matter how

1. Bayard to Dr. Edward Bayard, January 18, 1889, *Bayard Letter Book*, vol. 10, Bayard MS.
2. Bayard to W. B. Duncan, February 9, 1889, *ibid.*

arduous the work is, I find many a chance to think of you and to recall the most agreeable four years of my official life." [3]

Bayard's relations with John Bassett Moore, who held the office of Third Assistant Secretary of State, were most cordial. Judge Moore has been kind enough to give the author innumerable suggestions of great value concerning Bayard's life and public service, and in one of his letters to him, he describes the pleasant hours he enjoyed in Bayard's company:

The fact that Mr. Bayard found me companionable, may be inferred from our especially close relations. I often recall the midsummer nights I spent at his house when his family were away, and the drives we took in the evening. Perhaps towards four o'clock in the afternoon his messenger would bring me a piece of paper, on which was written: "Dear John: Come and spend the night with me and share a cool bottle of wine." I never knew anyone who understood the art of living better than he did. After dinner we would drive through the country, usually by way of the Soldiers' Home, his favorite route. . . . In those drives he would relate his personal experiences, and especially the hard struggles through which he passed in the era of Reconstruction.[4]

His relations with other officials in the Department of State, and with clerks of minor importance, were uniformly friendly. He was extremely kind to Henry L. Bryan, who suffered a serious accident, the attendant expenses being paid by Bayard. In connection with this incident, Francis J. Kieckhoefer wrote as follows to Bayard: "Your kind and affectionate expressions brought tears to his eyes, but made him supremely happy." [5] From Bryan himself came a letter which included a characteristic comment: "My fondest wish is for the possession of sufficient private means, that I could be near you and assist you in my own feeble but devoted way." [6] Beckford Mackey, United States Consul at Juarez, Mexico, was deeply appreciative of the many favors that Bayard had extended to him. In a letter to Bayard, August 28, 1889, he remarked: "I esteem you for your lofty qualities, and I almost love you for your kindness to myself." [7]

In March, 1889 Bayard returned to Wilmington, Delaware, to resume the practice of law. According to the New York *World*, he was

3. A. A. Adee to Bayard, November 4, 1895, *Bayard MS.*
4. Judge John Bassett Moore to the author, July 22, 1939.
5. Francis J. Kieckhoefer to Bayard, March 16, 1894, *Bayard MS.* Kieckhoefer held the position of Chief of the Bureau of Accounts, in the Department of State.
6. Henry L. Bryan to Bayard, January 17, 1896, *Bayard MS.*
7. Beckford Mackey to Bayard, August 28, 1889, *ibid.*

in "very comfortable circumstances," with a fortune estimated at $300,000.[8] Some of his legal fees were quite substantial,[9] but according to Bayard's own figures, his income was distinctly modest.[10] He felt no hesitation, however, about a second marriage which took place on November 7, 1889. The bride was Mary Willing Clymer, a charming cousin who helped to lighten the load of his declining years. In a letter to William F. Vilas, Bayard broke the news of his approaching marriage: "I came to tell you that I am to marry Mary Willing Clymer. . . . My children have so spontaneously and affectionately welcomed the newcomer, that I am sure her gracious presence will cement the happiness of our fireside and dispense joy for all." [11]

Bayard's domestic duties and his legal practice did not divert his attention from foreign affairs, and he kept a close watch on world politics.[12] He also continued to occupy a prominent place in the councils of the Democratic Party, and when Cleveland was elected a second time, in November, 1892, it was obvious that Bayard would receive some high official position. He had not been in strict accord with Cleveland in the Samoan affairs which the Chief Executive, under the influence

8. January 6, 1889.
9. On May 9, 1893, Bayard received from the Secretary of the Virginia Bondholders Committee a single check for $6,000. Hugh R. Garden to Bayard, May 9, 1893, *Bayard MS.*
10. In a memorandum, March 23, 1895, Bayard makes a statement of his financial standing for the year 1894. From rents he received $6,300; from his profession, $2,000, and from interest on bonds, $2,325, a total of $10,625. *Bayard MS.*
11. Bayard to William F. Vilas, May 19, 1889, *Vilas Papers.* In Wilmington Bayard lived in the former home of Myra Clark Gaines, "a cosy old mansion in a splendid lawn of forest trees." New York *World,* January 6, 1889.
12. In a letter to Bayard, August 10, 1889, Horace White remarks: "Your instructive letter of August 6 was duly received. . . . Your diagnosis of the Behring Sea question is certainly the true one. I shall make a discreet use of the facts from time to time. Your management of the State Department will be vindicated by history, and will be better appreciated by your contemporaries when, if ever, Mr. Blaine essays to do something besides peddle consulships to his friends." *Bayard MS.*
On August 4, 1891, Cleveland wrote an interesting letter to Bayard concerning the domestic situation. It seemed to him that "a contagious madness prevails in the land and that the Democratic Constitution or mental condition, especially invite attack. I reflect with unbounded amazement upon what the Democratic party and its representatives have done for the South and the present attitude of many of its leading men. Must we always be borne down by their foolishness? . . . I am much depressed in these days and very uncomfortable. I would be glad to put an end to the talk which connects my name with the campaign of 1892, but the few I have spoken with on the subject, tell me that without regard to . . . my own inclinations, I must not express my feelings or personal desires. They talk to me of duty to the Country and the party; and so I must remain, they think, subject to the violent abuse and most exasperating attack, while the rest of them drift along apparently without responsibility and conducing if not creating mischief—and affairs by such means, assume a shape that would make my nomination a prelude to certain and disastrous defeat." *Bayard MS.*

of W. C. Whitney, would have handled in a much more belligerent manner. In connection with the fur-seal fisheries dispute, and in the matter of Chinese immigration to the United States, Cleveland felt so out of accord with Bayard that he surreptitiously sabotaged the policy of the Department of State. It seemed hardly likely that Bayard would again be tendered the office of Secretary of State for the period of the incoming Administration, but Professor Nevins states that Cleveland made this offer to Bayard, who refused the appointment "because he dreaded the high expense and preferred to be our first Ambassador to Great Britain." [13]

There is nothing in the Bayard Papers that would substantiate such a statement. Bayard spent from January 23 to January 25 with Cleveland, and they had a "very frank and unrestrained talk." According to Cleveland, Bayard left "matters almost entirely in my control." [14] On January 25 Cleveland wrote to Judge Walter Q. Gresham, and offered to him the post of Secretary of State.[15] At first, Judge Gresham refused this appointment.

Meanwhile, important Democrats took it for granted that Bayard would once more enter Cleveland's cabinet, and Wade Hampton wrote that he had heard from "reliable sources of information" that Bayard would again assume the office of Secretary of State.[16] On February 8 Bayard wrote to William F. Vilas with regard to the situation:

> From you, Mr. Cleveland and I have no secrets. . . . It is not possible for me to refuse the best that I can give *to such a man in such a cause,* and this is what I told him, and so the matter was left, and now stands. He will need all the aid he can obtain, and it is a question of ascertaining and distributing forces. If he can find to his own satisfaction someone without my faults, and with more than my character to go into the State Department, I want him to do so, and you, my dear friend, will know that my "if" only means whether he has *time* to look the right man up, for I draw great comfort from the belief that our country does contain a . . . kind of strength in its unknown citizens. You see I cannot tell you positively whether I will

13. Allan Nevins, *Grover Cleveland*, p. 511.
14. Cleveland to L. Clarke Davis, January 25, 1893, *Cleveland MS.*
15. Cleveland to W. Q. Gresham, January 25, 1893, Matilda Gresham, *Life of Walter Quintin Gresham,* vol. 2, p. 679. It is quite probable that Bayard himself proposed the name of Gresham to Cleveland with reference to a Cabinet appointment. In a letter to President Cleveland, May 28, 1895, Bayard makes the following comment: "I never for an instant doubted the wisdom of my selection of Gresham for a place in your cabinet." *Cleveland MS.*
16. Wade Hampton to Bayard, January 29, 1893, *Bayard MS.* See also, Oscar S. Straus to Bayard, January 24, 1893, *ibid.*

be in office again or not, nor will I stop to weigh minor . . . considerations. I only want to do my duty.[17]

After reading this correspondence it would seem apparent that Bayard would have been glad to serve as Secretary of State if Cleveland had expressed any real desire for him to do so. Bayard always placed duty far above any "minor consideration," and it is absurd to believe that he would have permitted any fear of "high expense" to keep him from accepting an appointment which the President believed would be helpful to the American nation. It is far more likely that Cleveland wished to have someone else fill the office of Secretary of State, and there is a strong likelihood that he felt relieved when Gresham's letter of acceptance arrived on February 9.[18]

In order to gild the pill of disappointment to Bayard because of his failure to receive a Cabinet appointment, Cleveland hit upon the happy expedient of raising the rank of diplomatic representation in England from that of Minister to Ambassador. Congress promptly responded to Presidential initiative in this regard, and on March 16 Gresham talked over the situation with Lord Pauncefote.[19] On March 20 Lord Rosebery informed Lord Pauncefote that he had been elevated to the rank of Ambassador.[20] Six days later, President Cleveland wrote to Bayard and formally offered to him the appointment as Ambassador to England.[21]

17. Bayard to William F. Vilas, February 8, 1893, *Vilas MS.*
18. Cleveland to W. Q. Gresham, February 9, 1893, *Cleveland MS.* With regard to Cleveland's attitude towards Bayard in 1893, Judge John Bassett Moore made the following remark in a letter to the author: "I share your impression that Cleveland probably did not desire Bayard as Secretary of State in his second administration." With reference to disagreements between Bayard and Cleveland during the first Administration, Judge Moore further remarks: "There were one or two occasions on which Bayard, except for his loyalty, would have retired. One of these occasions was when Cleveland sent his retaliatory message to Congress in the fisheries dispute. He sent in this message without showing it to Bayard. The most he did was to tell him that he had the subject in hand and hoped that he would permit him to deal with it in his own way. The message was a great blunder, especially as an Act of Congress then existed under which the President had the right to adopt measures of retaliation. The message was written and sent in by Cleveland, largely under the influence of William C. Whitney. . . . In going to London, Bayard no doubt was influenced by various considerations. No doubt the new Mrs. Bayard was very favorable to the step." Judge John Bassett Moore to C. C. Tansill, September 6, 1940.
   George F. Parker, in his article, "Cleveland's Second Administration as President," *Saturday Evening Post*, June 9, 1923, vol. 195, pp. 40-50, states that Cleveland was determined not to reappoint to his second Cabinet any members who held office in his first official family.
19. Julian Pauncefote to Secretary Gresham, March 17, 1893, *Bayard MS.*
20. Julian Pauncefote to Secretary Gresham, March 20, 1893, *ibid.*
21. Bayard had already written to Secretary Gresham, March 13, 1893, to suggest that before Patrick Collins went to London as the "United States Consul, it seems to me highly

The phraseology of Bayard's letter of acceptance creates the impression that there had been no other important office tendered to him, and it is painfully evident that he was very happy to receive this indication of the President's continued trust in him:

> Your letter gratified me, . . . for it confirms my possession of your confidence, . . . and your belief in my absolute fidelity to the cause of our country's welfare to which you are religiously dedicating every faculty with which God has endowed you. . . .
> I have given what thought I could to the situation, and believe I can see the possibility, or probability, of service and aid to you in the scene of duty to which your judgment has assigned me. For the present, at least, the way seems blocked for my entrance upon official duty at home.[22]

On March 30 the news of Bayard's nomination as Ambassador to England appeared in the press, and John Bassett Moore wrote at once to offer his congratulations. To him the all-important consideration was the fact that Bayard had been

> . . . chosen as the custodian of great interests of the Government and people of the United States, and that in no other hands would those interests be so safe as in yours. There are few . . . who now realize the extent to which the *two* great English-speaking nations of the world are indebted to you for

---

important that the President, or you, should impress upon him the imperative necessity of observing a strict neutrality in British politics, which, of course, includes the burning question of 'Irish home rule,' which continues to grow in intensity, and to threaten almost to kindle the flame of a civil war." *Cleveland MS.*

22. Bayard to President Cleveland, March 30, 1893, *Cleveland MS.* When Bayard assumed his duties in London, he continued to write to President Cleveland in friendly terms which clearly indicate that he cherished no resentment at not being appointed to a Cabinet position. On September 1, 1893, Bayard wrote a letter that expressed his anxiety concerning Cleveland's recent operation: "No day has passed since I parted with you in Washington in which I have not felt a desire to be at your side to aid you when I could, and always to sympathize with you in the rugged and difficult task of duty in which your feet were so steadfastly set." *Cleveland MS.* In a letter to George F. Parker, December 19, 1893, Bayard pays the following high tribute to Cleveland's services to the American nation: "When I see him standing in the narrow pass confronting such an army of selfishness, recklessness, and ignorant passions, and almost at the sacrifice of his life, saving the country from a disaster so profound, . . . so fatal to the happiness and prosperity of its people, I find it impossible to estimate the true dimensions of his service, for I can scarcely find in history where one man has rendered greater service to his country and mankind." *Bayard MS.* In another letter to Mr. Parker, March 14, 1894, Bayard remarks: "I chafe a great deal in my isolation here from my friend and chieftain, Mr. Cleveland. Seldom in history has it been given to any man to render more important service to his country than he has rendered since his re-election." *Ibid.*

Cleveland's operation for cancer of the jaw, took place on July 1, 1893, and for at least a month the secret was closely guarded. On July 28 John G. Carlisle, Secretary of the Treasury, wrote as follows to Bayard: "The President has not yet returned from Buzzard's Bay, but is expected the latter part of next week. The newspaper reports in regard to his health are very much exaggerated, as he simply had one of his attacks of rheumatism and suffered somewhat from a decayed tooth." *Bayard MS.*

their present amicable relations. While your specific measures may have been thwarted by unscrupulous partisans and personal enemies, your patriotic firmness saved us from the untold evils of a policy of retaliation, and the peaceful relations of the last eight years are the vindication of your course.[23]

The Senate promptly confirmed Bayard's nomination as Ambassador to England, and Senator George Gray expressed his deep satisfaction at the way the matter was handled:

The post is always one of great opportunity for service, as with that country the issues of peace or war are constantly kept alive by the peculiar relations existing between us. If you accept it, the best and most patriotic sentiment of the country will be behind you, with a trust and confidence that would be given to no one else in such unstinted measure, . . .

The expressions of satisfaction and pleasure with which the announcement was greeted on both sides of the Senate was very emphatic, and was very agreeable to me.[24]

Bayard made hurried preparations to leave for London, and when he arrived in Southampton in the early part of June, 1893, he struck a keynote that he was to sound many times in England. In response to a greeting from the officials of Southampton, Bayard assured them that

. . . he was right glad to set his foot in Old England, and he was glad to breathe the free air of liberty that he breathed at home. . . . As to his ambassadorship, he felt its honour, its dignity, its responsibilities. He valued them chiefly as they should be a means of giving him greater facilities to enable him still more perfectly to bring together into harmony the interests of two great branches of the English-speaking race. Therein he chiefly valued it, and he hoped he might use the power entrusted to him to remove if they should exist, any lingering doubts or misunderstanding between them.[25]

On June 12 Bayard was formally received by Lord Rosebery at the

23. John Bassett Moore to Bayard, March 30, 1893, *Bayard MS.*
24. George Gray to Bayard, March 30, 1893, *Bayard MS.* John Russell Young wrote to Bayard, March 30, 1893, that this new dignity was "a new tie of alliance with the Motherland. Those who like myself, have held you in special honor for these many years, are proud of the President's choice." Lambert Tree assured Secretary Gresham that with reference to Bayard's appointment as Ambassador he did not "know a man in the whole country better equipped for that important post." *Cleveland MS.* One letter that Bayard must have been glad to receive came from J. T. Gause, April 22, 1893, who conveyed the pleasant information that the Harlan and Hollingsworth Company would continue to send him their annual retainer fee of $500. *Bayard MS.*
25. London *Daily News,* June 12, 1893. See also, London *Times,* June 12, 1893. On May 19, 1893, Bayard had already written to Secretary Gresham to thank him for sending to Wilmington the note from Lord Rosebery which expressed the Queen's "particular satisfaction" with Bayard's appointment as Ambassador. Bayard hoped that it might "prove a good augury of friendly settlement of all questions between the two Countries." *Gresham MS.*

Foreign Office, and thus began his official duties as Ambassador.[26] One of the tasks that immediately faced him was the appointment of a new first secretary of the Embassy. Henry White had filled this post to the entire satisfaction of Mr. Lincoln, but he had some enemies in the Cleveland Administration that took office on March 4, 1893. According to Allan Nevins, one of the most important of these enemies was Daniel S. Lamont, who had just been appointed Secretary of War. During a recent visit to London, Lamont felt that he had been slighted by Henry White, and therefore, he was in favor of a change in the personnel of the Embassy.[27]

The difficulties that developed from the forced resignation of White as first secretary of the London Embassy, were very serious for Bayard, and in order to understand the later phases of the Venezuelan boundary controversy it is necessary to discuss the background of this resignation. The following paragraphs from the *Life of Henry White* by Allan Nevins will serve as an introduction to this subject:

> Following Ambassador Bayard's arrival in London in April, 1893, White spared no pains to make him feel at home and to assist him in mastering the technical details of the embassy's work. Himself always candid, friendly, and whole-heartedly helpful, White harbored no suspicion of his new chief and wished only to make himself useful. . . . But despite White's friendliness to his chief, he quickly saw that Bayard was not thoroughly friendly to him. He soon felt a reserve in Bayard's manner; and he had no difficulty in learning the reason from Lloyd Griscom, Bayard's private secretary. The ambassador had come to England convinced that Robert Lincoln had governed the embassy with such a slack hand that little work was done by any of the staff; suspicious that White wished to make use of his position for social advancement, and apprehensive that with his superior experience White would try to "manage" him. Characteristically, White felt most indignant regarding the first of these preconceptions. . . .
>
> By working long hours at the embassy, by showing his grasp of laborious details, and by doing a great deal to enlarge Bayard's social contacts, White partially dispelled the ambassador's prejudices. Bayard was often peppery, would seldom take advice from anyone, and had some irritating mannerisms, such as a way of snatching papers from his assistants' hands. But the first secretary never lost his poise. . . . If Bayard had insisted on White's retention, he might have been kept in London, but Bayard was not a man to insist. . . . Secretary Lamont's prejudice against White marked him for slaughter. Moreover, there was an alert aspirant for his post in James A. Roosevelt of New York. . . . The result was that when in September, 1893,

26. *Westminster Gazette*, June 13, 1893.
27. Allan Nevins, *Henry White* (N. Y., 1930), pp. 73-74.

White prepared to depart for America on leave, Bayard told him that the President wished his resignation.[28]

The first thing that strikes the eye in this excerpt is the statement that Bayard arrived in London in April, 1893. His arrival was in June. The accusation that Bayard was "peppery" and had the unpleasant habit of "snatching papers from his assistants' hands," is distinctly dubious. As we have already seen,[29] Bayard's relations with his subordinates in the Department of State were uniformly courteous and friendly, and it is hardly likely that his disposition fundamentally changed when he reached London. Henry White felt in a critical mood when he lost his London assignment, and he and his friends went to absurd lengths in their campaign of detraction against Bayard.[30]

Just as soon as Bayard had accepted the nomination as Ambassador to England, Daniel S. Lamont wrote to him concerning a change in the position of first secretary of the London Embassy. Lamont inclined to the belief that James R. Roosevelt would fulfil the duties of first secretary more faithfully than Henry White. Bayard replied that he would have to consult President Cleveland before he could make any decision in the matter, but he entertained the view that it might be wise to replace White with Roosevelt.[31]

In the meantime Bayard had received from George L. Rives a letter strongly recommending James R. Roosevelt for the post in London.[32] Lamont then came back with a note which enclosed an unsigned letter from a prominent citizen of New York City in which a sharp attack was

28. *Ibid.*, pp. 96-97.

29. *Ante* p. 651.

30. In the *Henry White*, the *Theodore Roosevelt*, and the *William McKinley Papers*, in the Library of Congress, there are several letters that are bitterly critical of Bayard as Ambassador to England. It was only to be expected that Henry Cabot Lodge and John Hay would vent their spleen upon Bayard, because he did not insist upon the retention of White in his post in the Embassy, but it is a little surprising to see the depth of White's rancor against a man who had treated him with the utmost consideration. It is interesting to note that neither John Hay nor Henry Cabot Lodge trusted each other. In a note to Henry White, February 10, 1901, John Hay remarks: "I return Lodge's letter as you request. It proves anew his selfish treachery. . . . He is not unfriendly to me personally, in the abstract, nor is he to you. But neither you nor I would weigh a feather's weight with him, as against any selfish advantage. He would cut my throat or yours for a favorable notice in a newspaper." *White Papers.* With reference to Lodge, Daniel H. Chamberlain wrote as follows, April 14, 1886, to Henry L. Dawes: "Lodge is absolutely nothing in politics, but what his money gives him. Selfish, ambitious, without deep convictions, and only a *modicum* of ability, he seeks to be and thinks he is even now, a Warwick of Massachusetts." *Henry L. Dawes Papers*, Library of Congress.

31. Bayard to Daniel S. Lamont, April 7, 1893, *Lamont Papers*, Library of Congress.

32. George L. Rives to Bayard, April 4, 1893, *Bayard MS*.

made upon the snobbish attitude of Henry White towards most Americans visiting London.[33]

On April 30, 1893, Roosevelt wrote to Lamont and described an interview with Bayard. Bayard began the conversation by stating that although he was

. . . well aware of White's great competency and usefulness, he recognized the fact, that for certain reasons it was desirable to make a change, and that he should be glad to have me [Roosevelt], therefore, associated with him in London. At the same time, he did not wish to announce this to White in writing, but should prefer to make the communication personally to him after his arrival, and consult his (White's) convenience as to when the change should occur. He suggested that I should proceed to London, according to my intention, advise him of my whereabouts, and that as soon as he had spoken to White he would send for me. . . . He further discussed the affairs of the Legation with me, stating that he wished to get it out of a "rut", . . . and make its members . . . more accessible to Americans. . . . It seems White wrote him about taking a house, and mentioned that its only objection was that it was too near the hotels frequented by Americans. Mr. Bayard said that this was not at all his idea of looking at things.[34]

On August 26, 1893, Bayard finally informed Henry White of the President's desire that he resign his position as first secretary of the London Embassy,[35] and on September 14 he wrote to James R. Roosevelt and outlined the situation.[36] Some weeks later he alluded to the

33. Daniel S. Lamont to Bayard, April 19, 1893, *Lamont MS.*

34. J. R. Roosevelt to Lamont, April 30, 1893, *ibid.*

35. In a memorandum written on August 26, 1893, Bayard recounts his conversation with Henry White: "Today . . . I informed him [White] that the President desired to receive his resignation of the post he now holds. I told him it had been a cause of pain and distress to me personally to be obliged to convey to him this intelligence, but that it had been Mr. Cleveland's wish from the moment of his announcing to me in April last his desire that I should take my present office. I did not intimate in any way *what were* Mr. Cleveland's objections to his remaining *in* office here. I told Mr. White that I had promptly placed before the President his (White's) denial of having expressed himself disrespectfully towards Mr. Cleveland, and that I had placed before the latter the whole of that part of Mr. White's letter to me which related to the subject; that I had waited to receive from Mr. Cleveland his acceptance of Mr. White's denial, but that he had not answered my letter nor given any indication of his change of feeling and opinion on the subject of Mr. White's resignation. . . .

I did not feel justified in withholding from Mr. White any longer, knowledge of the President's wishes, nor to stand in the way of carrying them out. . . . I had felt very uncomfortable about the matter, and wished now to say to him that personally I had entire confidence in his good faith and honor, but felt that the President had a right on every score to make the change. . . . I told Mr. White that Mr. Roosevelt would succeed him here, and that his appointment had been fully understood and agreed to. . . . I expressed the real pain it had given me to convey the President's wishes to him, and that it had worried me ever since my arrival. . . . He thanked me for my courtesy and kindness in the matter. *Bayard MS.*

36. Bayard to James R. Roosevelt, September 14, 1893, *Bayard MS.*

matter in a letter to President Cleveland,[37] and in a letter to Secretary Gresham he discussed in detail the whole question of White's resignation.[38]

White felt deeply chagrined over his forced resignation as first secretary of the London Embassy, and he returned to the United States to sulk and to criticize the actions of "old Bayard." His caustic comments found a ready listener in the person of Secretary Olney, who felt outraged because Bayard would not support with enthusiasm a program of hostility towards England. White and Olney worked in close co-operation during the latter stages of the Venezuelan boundary controversy, and White performed yeoman service in smoothing over the ruffled feelings of British statesmen after they had experienced Olney's strong blasts on the Monroe Doctrine.

Bayard's viewpoint in 1893, with reference to the relations between the United States and South America, was distinctly voiced in a letter to Secretary Gresham. He did not believe that European powers were ready to pounce upon Latin America and carve it up into spheres of influence:

Instability in government in South America has been chronic in all of the present century, and there is nothing known to me to indicate European preference for one form of government there over another, but only that order shall be attained in order that commerce shall not be interrupted. The English view of law, and of international administration, is nearer to our own than those of any other nation, and it is to be regretted that a class or a

37. Bayard to President Cleveland, October 3, 1893, *Bayard Press Copy Book*, vol. 1, *ibid.*

38. In his letter to Secretary Gresham, October 4, 1893, Bayard makes the following comments about Henry White: "That he has always been absolutely and honourably faithful, I have not a shadow of doubt. He has a large fund of physical energy, has great fondness for the social side of his duties, and possesses accomplishments of a really valuable kind for the work. . . . I say all this because Mr. White has asked me to give him a letter to you of such a character as would assist him in seeking other employment under the government. . . . He is most anxious to stay in the service, but has accepted in a fair and manly way the decision for his resignation." *Ibid.* In his letter of reply, Secretary Gresham wrote to Bayard, October 29, 1893, as follows: "Mr. White called at the Department a day or two ago, and handed me his resignation. Also your letter of the tenth instant. He informed me . . . that he had always entertained a high opinion of the President's character and ability, and had never spoken of him otherwise than in commendation. . . . I went to the White House, handed the resignation to the President, and related what Mr. White had said to me. The President directed me to send over for his signature the nomination of Mr. James R. Roosevelt to succeed Mr. White, without saying more. I then informed the President that with his permission, Mr. White would be glad to remain in the public service, and after the President had remained silent for a time, I remarked I would inform Mr. White on his return Monday that his resignation was accepted, and he need not expect to be sent elsewhere. The President replied 'yes' and the interview on that subject ended." *Bayard MS.*

party in the United States are so addicted to irresponsible abuse of everything British, and to seeking every occasion to testify hostility to Great Britain, because it does much to color the public view in both countries and prevent confidential interchanges of intentions or proposed action. It is impossible for the United States to extend over the hemisphere south of us . . . the guarantee of a Republican form of Government which our Constitution secures to each state of our own Union. And yet there really seems to be such a wild idea in the minds of some of our people.

We cannot give to the heterogeneous populations of Mexico, Central America, and South America, the racial qualities, traditions, and education that are the prime bases of a republican state, and all we can do is to so exemplify and illustrate the advantages of peace, order, and prosperity under Republican government, that it will be preferred to any other.[39]

Bayard's instinctive feeling of friendship for England was further expressed in a letter to President Cleveland: "I am very glad to think that since I came here [London] the current of good feeling between the two countries has quickened and deepened." [40] He was very anxious that no important dispute should arise that would imperil this developing *entente cordiale,* and the revival of the Guiana boundary dispute gave him deep concern.

On October 26, 1893, David Lobo, the chargé d'affaires of Venezuela at Washington, sent to Secretary Gresham a long memorandum which recited "prominent facts relating to the boundary question between Venezuela and Great Britain." After building up a strong indictment of British policy in Venezuela, the memorandum closed on the following pacific note: "Venezuela is, and always has been, willing to submit to arbitration." [41]

Some weeks later, Frank C. Partridge, the American Minister at Carácas, informed Secretary Gresham that the Venezuelan Secretary of Foreign Affairs had confided to him that the boundary question had become "very serious," and that "Venezuela's only hope of a favorable settlement is in the friendly offices of the United States." [42] The discussion of this boundary dispute now shifted to Washington. On March 31, 1894, José Andrade sent a note to Gresham which reviewed the general outlines of the controversy, and he enclosed a very long

39. Bayard to Secretary Gresham, December 28, 1893, *Gresham MS.*
40. Bayard to President Cleveland, July 12, 1894, *Cleveland MS.*
41. David Lobo to Secretary Gresham, October 26, 1893, *Venezuela, Notes from,* vol. 7, MS Dept. of State.
42. F. C. Partridge to Secretary Gresham, November 15, 1893, *Venezuela, Despatches,* vol. 44, MS Dept. of State.

memorandum which was a spirited defense of Venezuela's position in this matter.[43]

In London, Bayard was endeavoring to keep the lid firmly down on the tempest that was developing in the Venezuelan teapot, and in a personal letter to Gresham he gave a brief survey of the political situation in England as it affected foreign relations:

Both parties are disposed, and I think equally, to accommodate all questions with the United States, but in view of leaving office, Lord Kimberley would be inclined to take as little trouble and responsibility as possible, and leave matters to his successor (presumably Lord Salisbury).

I have formed a very favorable opinion of Lord Kimberley as an honorable and well-disposed man, but he hardly has that knowledge of the vast and varied mass of facts of this widespread Empire which would enable him to comprehend and settle the complicated questions that surge up from every region of the earth, and in the matters that I present, I find him honest and kind, but *perfunctory*, relying almost wholly upon his official subordinates. This inclines me to advise delay in such matters as may need treatment, because I feel quite sure that before completion, we would find another in office, and the work of explanation and agreement would have to be done over again with the possibility of important changes.

Therefore, I hope we will not be called on to propose any very decisive point until the British elections have been held and we have a permanent and a responsible government in office here—the life of the present hangs on a thread.[44]

After receiving Bayard's letter from London, Gresham wrote him the following mild instruction which was not taken any too seriously. According to Gresham, the President was

. . . inspired by a desire for a peaceable and honorable adjustment of the existing difficulties between an American state and a powerful transatlantic nation, and would be glad to see the re-establishment of such diplomatic relations between them as would promote that end. I [Gresham] can discern but two equitable solutions to the present controversy. One is the arbitral determination of the rights of the disputants as the respective successors to the historical rights of Holland and Spain over the region in question. The other is to create a new boundary line in accordance with the dictates of mutual expediency and consideration. The two Governments having so far been unable to agree on a conventional line, the consistent and conspicuous advocacy by the United States and England of the principle of arbitration, . . . make such a mode of adjustment especially appropriate in the present

43. José Andrade to Secretary Gresham, March 31, 1894, *Venezuela, Notes from,* vol. 7, MS Dept. of State.
44. Bayard to Secretary Gresham, May 27, 1894, *Bayard Press Copy Book,* vol. 1, *Bayard MS.*

instance, and this Government will gladly do what it can to further a determination in that sense. With these considerations I commit the matter to your hands, leaving it to you to avail yourself of any convenient opportunity to advance the adjustment of the dispute in question.[45]

Bayard spent the summer and autumn months of 1894 on a visit to the United States, and in his conversations with Gresham he did not get the impression that there was any haste in this matter of the Venezuelan boundary dispute. In the ordinary course of diplomatic affairs, this controversy would have continued until Venezuela receded from her ridiculous demands for all the territory west of the Essequibo River, and then some compromise line would have been agreed upon. That this line would not have been an unfair one dictated by British greed, is proven by the conciliatory disposition shown by successive British Foreign Secretaries.

In the summer of 1894 the normal course of Anglo-American relations concerning the Venezuelan boundary dispute was sharply changed by the effective use of propaganda. After dealing with the Department of State for several decades in regard to this dispute, the Government of Venezuela suddenly decided, in 1894, to make a direct appeal to American public opinion, and in charge of their propaganda efforts they placed William L. Scruggs, who had recently served as the American Minister at Carácas.[46]

45. Secretary Gresham to Bayard, July 13, 1894, *Great Britain, Instructions*, vol. 30, MS Dept. of State.
46. T. D. Jervey, "William Lindsay Scruggs, a Forgotten Diplomat," *South Atlantic Quarterly*, vol. 27, pp. 292-309. Scruggs had also served as the American Minister to Colombia, and on November 5, 1885, he wrote a letter to Bayard in which he reviewed his political background, and concluded as follows: "Since 1872 I have been out of the country almost continuously in the discharge of my official duties. But had I been at home, I should probably have voted for Tilden in 1876, for Garfield in 1880, and for Cleveland in 1884. And I will here add that I am pleased with Mr. Cleveland's course thus far. . . . Although I have never had the pleasure of meeting you personally, I know you well and favorably (as do thousands of others) in your public character as a statesman." *Bayard MS.*
In a confidential letter to Bayard, April 24, 1885, Bogotá, Scruggs gave a little "inside story" on the situation in Colombia: "When I came hither under a second commission as Minister in 1882, with verbal instructions to 'get the Colombians in good humor with us, and prevent if possible the abrogation of the Treaty of 1846,' I found an ill and suspicious feeling toward us. Efforts were being made by Colombian agents in Europe, and by European agents in Colombia, to bring about a joint guarantee of the neutrality of the Isthmian transit. With that end in view, a resolution had been already introduced in the Colombian Senate, instructing the President to give formal notice of the discontinuance of Article 35, of said treaty. And it is now known, what was then only suspected, that money had been secretly used to stimulate and strengthen this sentiment in Colombia.
"That crisis has happily passed; and were I so authorized, I should now apprehend little difficulty in negotiating a Treaty on the basis of either the Projet of December, 1856, or of the Protocol of February, 1881," *Bayard MS.*

As the legal adviser and special agent of the Government of Venezuela, Scruggs began an intensive campaign to influence every shade of American public opinion. In October, 1894, a pamphlet was published with the title, *British Aggressions in Venezeula, or the Monroe Doctrine on Trial*. It contained a brief outline of the Venezuelan boundary controversy, and it was designed to convince Americans that the British Government was flouting the Monroe Doctrine in a most outrageous fashion. Copies were sent "to the editors of the leading newspapers and magazines both in this country and in England; also to members of Congress, . . . to the Governors and leading members of the general Assemblies of the several States; and to the principal clubs and public libraries in all the large cities." [47] With regard to the applicability of the Monroe Doctrine to the controversy between Venezuela and Great Britain over the Guiana boundary, this pamphlet boldly stated:

> If England should finally decide upon this course, and under the flimsy pretext of a boundary dispute of her own seeking, . . . persist in her efforts to extend her colonial system within the territory and jurisdiction of an independent American Republic, that fact should be but an additional reason . . . why the United States should reaffirm and maintain at all hazards, the principles of the declaration of 1823. The only alternative would be an explicit and final abandonment of those principles; and that would involve a sacrifice of national honor and prestige such as no first-class power is ever likely to make, even for the sake of peace.[48]

The impact of this Scruggs pamphlet was not apparent in the instruction that Gresham sent to Bayard on December 1, 1884. It is distinctly decorous and does not betray any sign of irritation against the British Government. After referring to Bayard's conversations with Señor Andrade in Washington during the summer of 1894, Gresham makes the following mild comments:

> I can not believe Her Majesty's Government will maintain that the validity of their claim to territory long in dispute between the two countries shall be conceded as a condition precedent to the arbitration of the question whether Venezuela is entitled to other territory which, until a very recent period, was never in doubt. Our interest in the question has repeatedly been shown by our friendly efforts to further a settlement alike honorable to both

47. William L. Scruggs, *The Colombian and Venezuelan Republics*, p. 296.
48. William L. Scruggs, *British Aggressions in Venezuela, or the Monroe Doctrine on Trial*, p. 32. In a letter to Secretary Gresham, May 25, 1895, Bayard makes the following observation concerning Mr. Scruggs: "A very inaccurate and foolish publication by Mr. Scruggs, who has gone out of the service of the United States and into that of the Venezuelan Concessionaries, has appeared here [London]." *Bayard Press Copy Book*, vol. 2, *Bayard MS*.

countries, and the President is pleased to know that Venezuela will soon renew her efforts to bring about such an adjustment.

It is not doubted that you will discreetly exert your influence in favor of some plan of honorable settlement.[49]

Two days later, the President sent his annual message to Congress. In a short paragraph of restrained language, he refers to the Guiana boundary dispute:

> The boundary of British Guiana still remains in dispute between Great Britain and Venezuela. Believing that its early settlement on some just basis alike honorable to both parties is in the line of our established policy to remove from this hemisphere all causes of difference with powers beyond the sea, I shall renew the efforts heretofore made to bring about a restoration of diplomatic relations between the disputants and to induce a reference to arbitration.[50]

Mr. Scruggs was not pleased with the pacific tone employed by the President in this message to Congress, and he redoubled his efforts to bring the dispute to the attention of the American public. One effective means of accomplishing this end was through favorable Congressional action, so Scruggs induced Colonel Leonidas F. Livingston, of Georgia, to introduce a resolution which strongly urged that the President's suggestion with reference to submitting the boundary dispute to arbitration, be "earnestly recommended to the consideration of both parties." [51] This resolution received the unanimous approval of the House of Representatives,[52] and on February 13, without a word of debate, the Senate adopted the resolution.[53] A week later, President Cleveland signed the resolution,[54] and Mr. Scruggs was now in a position to exert tremendous pressure upon the Department of State in favor of a more positive policy. Thanks to British policy in Nicaragua, the way was made even easier than he had anticipated.

B. THE NICARAGUA INCIDENT

British interests in Central America were largely confined to three areas: Belize, the Bay Islands, and the Mosquito Shore. During the seventeenth century, British settlements were established along the

---

49. Secretary Gresham to Bayard, December 1, 1894, *Great Britain, Instructions*, vol. 30, MS Dept. of State.

50. Message of December 3, 1894, J. D. Richardson, *Messages and Papers of the Presidents*, vol. 9, p. 526.

51. *Congressional Record*, 53 Cong., 3 sess., vol. 1, p. 837.

52. *Ibid.*, vol. 2, p. 1834.   53. *Ibid.*, vol. 3, p. 2113.   54. *Ibid.*, vol. 3, p. 2642.

Belize River, and the basis was laid for a strong claim to British Honduras. Notwithstanding repeated, and sometimes successful, attacks made by Spanish soldiers, these British settlements continued to expand. In several treaties between England and Spain, the boundaries of Belize were definitely fixed, and Spanish sovereignty over the territory was recognized. After the successful revolution of the Latin American States against the rule of Spain, Belize became practically a British colony, and British interests were extended and strengthened.[55] This situation was not regarded with favor by American statesmen in the decade before the outbreak of the Civil War.

British claims to the Mosquito Shore between Cape Honduras and the mouth of the San Juan River, underwent a similar development. This territory was occupied by a semi-nomadic population called the Mosquitos, who were a mixture of at least three races. Maltreated by Spaniards from Guatemala, the Mosquitos welcomed the British buccaneers who frequented their coast, and as time passed, these British adventurers founded settlements at Cape Gracias á Dios, Bluefields, and at other points. The British Government was quick to see the strategic advantage of supporting these settlements, and in 1740 Captain Robert Hodgson was sent to the Mosquito Shore to take possession of it in the name of the British Sovereign. Under a sharp interpretation of treaties concluded with Spain in 1763 and in 1783, Great Britain was able to retain her hold upon the Mosquito Shore, but the treaty of 1786 was so unequivocal that no subterfuge was possible, and British official protection to the settlements among the Mosquito was withdrawn. This did not mean, however, that British influence in that region was at an end. As in the case of the Belize settlements, the revolt of the Spanish colonies in Latin America against the Mother Country afforded an opportunity to British citizens to regain their hold upon the Mosquito Shore, and in 1848, with British assistance, the King of the Mosquitos seized control over the mouth of the San Juan River. The eastern terminus of any trans-isthmian canal through Nicaragua was now in British hands.[56]

55. Mary W. Williams, *Anglo-American Isthmian Diplomacy, 1815–1915* (Washington, 1916), chaps. i-ii.

56. For a handy outline of the history of British expansion in the Mosquito country, see, M. W. Williams, *Anglo-American Isthmian Diplomacy, 1815–1915*, chaps. 1-11. See also, Samuel A. Bard (E. G. Squier), *Waikna; or Adventures on the Mosquito Shore* (London, 1855); Awnsham and John Churchill, *A Collection of Voyages and Travels* (London, 1752, 8 vols.); Frederick Crowe, *The Gospel in Central America, Containing a Sketch of the Country* (London, 1850); George Henderson, *An Account of the British Settlement of*

The idea of joining the Atlantic and Pacific Oceans by means of a canal goes back to the time of Charles V, and by 1550, the four major canal routes (Darien, Panama, Nicaragua, and Tehuantepec) had already been indicated and discussed.[57] In 1786 Thomas Jefferson expressed the opinion that cutting a canal across the Isthmus would be "a work much less difficult than some even of the inferior canals of France," [58] and William Duane and Richard Bache looked forward to its early completion.[59] Henry Clay's deep interest in a trans-isthmian canal was revealed in his instructions to the American delegates to the Panama Congress.[60] Many other Americans gave careful consideration to the idea of an inter-oceanic canal, and the project was of such evident importance to the American Republic that Goethe remarked in February, 1827, that he would be surprised "if the United States would miss the opportunity of getting such a work into its own hands." [61]

In order to safeguard this important American interest, the American Minister at Bogotá signed, on December 12, 1846, a treaty with the Government of New Granada (later Colombia) which granted a right of way across the Isthmus of Panama. In return for this concession, the United States guaranteed "positively and efficaciously to New Granada, the perfect neutrality of the before-mentioned Isthmus, with the view that the free transit . . . may not be interrupted . . . in any future time while this treaty exists." [62]

The Senate of the United States did not consent to the ratification of this treaty until June 3, 1848, when fears of British intrigue in Central America began to give real concern to American expansionists. With British agents rapidly extending their control over the Mosquito

---

Honduras (London, 1811); E. G. Squier, *Nicaragua, Its People, Scenery, Monuments, and the Proposed Inter-oceanic Canal* (N. Y., 1852, 2 vols.).

57. Willis F. Johnson, *Four Centuries of the Panama Canal* (N. Y., 1906), pp. 18-50; Charles H. Haring, *Trade and Navigation between Spain and the Indies* (Cambridge, 1918), pp. 192-197.

58. Jefferson to M. Le Roy, November 13, 1786, *Writings* (Memorial edition, Washington, 1904, 19 vols.), vol. 5, p. 471.

59. William Duane, *A Visit to Colombia in the Years 1822 and 1823* (Phila., 1826); Richard Bache, *Notes on Colombia Taken in the Years 1822–1823* (Phila., 1827).

60. John Bassett Moore, *Digest of International Law*, vol. 3, p. 2.

61. Johann P. Eckermann, *Gespräche mit Goethe in den letzten Jahren seines Lebens* (Leipzig, 1899), vol. 3, pp. 83-84.

62. Hunter Miller, *Treaties and Other International Acts of the United States of America* (Washington, 1937), vol. 5, pp. 115-160. See also, E. Taylor Parks, *Colombia and the United States, 1765–1934* (Durham, 1935), pp. 202-207; Joseph B. Lockey, "A Neglected Aspect of Isthmian Diplomacy," *American Historical Review*, vol. 41 (1936), pp. 295-305.

Shore and the San Juan River, it was high time that some step be taken to check this advance.[63] After lengthy negotiations, Secretary Clayton signed on April 19, 1850, the famous Clayton-Bulwer Treaty, which bound the United States and Great Britain never to seek exclusive control over an isthmian canal, and never to "erect or maintain any fortifications commanding the same or in the vicinity thereof." These governments would also extend their protection over all communications, "whether by canal or railway, across the isthmus which connect North and South America." With regard to British claims in Central America, the language of the treaty was so ambiguous as to permit the British Government to maintain an indirect control over the Mosquito Shore and the San Juan River.[64] This fact led to renewed American pressure upon the British Government, and finally, on January 28, 1860, in a treaty with Nicaragua, Great Britain abandoned her protectorate over the Mosquito Indians.[65]

It seemed impossible, however, to put an end to British influence along the Mosquito Shore by mere treaties. Many British settlers continued to live with the Mosquito Indians, and numerous quarrels broke out between the Mosquitos and officials of the Nicaraguan Government. In order to put an end to all dispute concerning the meaning of the Treaty of Managua, resort was finally had to arbitration. In July, 1881, the Emperor of Austria-Hungary gave an award that asserted that the sovereignty of Nicaragua, "which was recognized by . . . the treaty of Managua, . . . is not full and unlimited with regard to the territory assigned to the Mosquito Indians, but is limited by the self-government conceded to the Mosquito Indians in Article 3 of this Treaty." Nicaragua was "not entitled to grant concessions for the acquisition of natural products in the territory assigned to the Mosquito Indians," and she could not "regulate the trade of the Mosquito Indians," nor "levy duties on goods imported into or exported from the territory reserved to the Mosquito Indians." [66]

This limited sovereignty of the Government of Nicaragua over the Mosquito Indians led certain British agents to keep a watchful eye

63. Richard W. Van Alstyne, "The Central American Policy of Lord Palmerston, 1846–1848," *Hispanic American Historical Review*, vol. 16 (1936), pp. 339-359.

64. William M. Malloy, *Treaties, etc.*, vol. 1, pp. 659-663. Richard W. Van Alstyne, "British Diplomacy and the Clayton-Bulwer Treaty, 1850–1860," *Journal of Modern History*, vol. 11 (1939), pp. 157ff.

65. *Parliamentary Papers, 1860, Commons*, vol. 68, "Correspondence respecting Central America."

66. *Foreign Relations, 1888*, pt. 1, pp. 763-764.

upon every attempt to strengthen Nicaraguan control over the Mosquito Shore. To the Nicaraguan Government it seemed apparent that Great Britain was really exercising a protectorate over the Mosquitos, and complaints were made to the Department of State. On February 10, 1888, the Venezuelan Minister, at Washington, had an interview with Bayard in connection with the Mosquito territory. He remarked that the Mosquitos were very ungovernable, and he inquired whether Bayard thought

. . . there could be any question on the part of Great Britain to their (the Nicaraguans) undertaking to control these people. I [Bayard] said I did not think so; that the Nicaraguans did not propose to overthrow the tribal relations or legal government of the Mosquito Indians, but they were confessedly under their jurisdiction and under their political control. I said, however, that I thought it would not be wise of the Nicaraguan government to make any show of organized force against these people just now; that this Canal across Lake Nicaragua was commenced, and that it would be under American capital and with the favor and friendship of the Government, and in some degree under its protection; and that I thought that when Americans got down there in force, and this Canal was well under way, that there would be a recognition of it along the whole seacoast upon which these Mosquito Indians live, which would affect the state of affairs very much, and I thought their better way would be to let matters progress as they were now.[67]

This policy of inaction suggested by Bayard was not entirely satisfactory to the Government of Nicaragua. Friction with British citizens in the Mosquito territory was still threatening serious trouble, and on May 25, 1888, Dr. Guzmán once more brought the matter to Bayard's attention. Bayard countered with an expression of surprise that the Nicaraguan Government had made a treaty with Great Britain which provided that the Emperor of Austria-Hungary should act as the arbiter in the dispute concerning the extent of Nicaraguan sovereignty over the Mosquitos. The award of the Austrian Emperor had

---

67. *Memorandum* written by Bayard after a conversation with Dr. Horacio Guzmán, February 10, 1888, *Bayard MS*. In a personal letter to Phelps, at London, May 10, 1888, Bayard made the following observation concerning Senator Edmunds, one of the leaders of the Republican opposition: "Last night at a dinner at the Chinese Legation, he sat opposite me, and between the British Minister and Mr. Belmont, of the House. . . . His chief topic was the Nicaraguan Canal, and he told the British Minister that the United States and Great Britain ought to join in the control of the world's commerce, and that Great Britain should give the United States every aid on the Isthmus of Panama, and that in turn the United States should sustain Great Britain in the control of the Suez Canal." *Bayard Letter Book*, vol. 7, *Bayard MS*.

. . . very seriously impaired the degree of sovereignty which was supposed to have been given to Nicaragua by the Treaty [of Managua]. . . . I could not imagine what the State Department of that day had been about in not insisting upon having that question brought into their consultation. . . . The Clayton-Bulwer arrangement undoubtedly gave them the right to do so, in all matters connected with the control of the Central American States. . . . I had the highest respect for what I believed to be the principle of that Treaty, which was in substance the neutralization of the Central American States. . . . Lately, some case had been presented to this Department, indicating interference by an alleged British official at Bluefields in Mosquito country with an American citizen. . . . I had caused instant representation to be made to the Foreign Office in London, and had received the statement that there was no official control attempted under English authority in that country.[68]

On July 30 Bayard and Señor Guzmán had an extended discussion upon the Mosquito question, and Bayard again expressed his regret that Nicaragua had agreed with Great Britain in 1880 to submit this dispute to the arbitration of the Emperor of Austria-Hungary. Guzmán then inquired about the

. . . Nicaraguan Canal, and about the question of guaranteeing its neutrality by all the European nations. I [Bayard] told him I was not prepared to speak upon that subject. The United States had but one treaty of guarantee of neutrality, and that was over the Isthmus of Panama, and I took it that the Nicaraguan Canal was for the interest of the commerce of the world. But how far that canal could be used in case of war for the passage of warships of other Nations, I was not prepared to say. The United States had a much greater interest in that question than any other Government, and I had no idea that we would consent to any arrangement by which vessels could pass through that canal to assail our Western coast, but this was merely speculation.[69]

In the autumn months of 1888, Guzmán had other conversations with Bayard concerning the Mosquito Shore, and on November 15 he left a copy of a note addressed by J. P. H. Gastrell, the British Minister in Central America, to the Nicaraguan Foreign Office. Gastrell complained that the Government of Nicaragua had established "a post office at Bluefields, thus intervening in the domestic affairs of the reservation." He also stated that "troops and a police force have been stationed, and forts, arsenals, and military posts have been established, or are about to be established by Nicaragua" within the Mosquito ter-

68. *Memorandum* written by Bayard after a conversation with Guzmán, May 25, 1888, *Bayard MS.*

69. *Memorandum* written by Bayard after a conversation with Dr. Guzmán, July 30, 1888, *Bayard MS.*

ritory. These actions, together with the "exercise of military or police authority by Nicaragua within the territory of the reservation," would be inconsistent with the spirit of the treaty of Managua.[70]

In an instruction to Phelps, November 23, 1888, Bayard took direct issue with this British interpretation of the Treaty of Managua. He thought that the Government of Nicaragua was entirely within its treaty rights in establishing post offices and forts within the Mosquito territory. After this positive statement in favor of the Nicaraguan contention, Bayard then made the following significant comments:

> The President cannot but regard the continued exercise of the claim on the part of Great Britain to interfere in behalf of these Indians as the assertion of a British protectorate in another form. . . . The United States can never see with indifference the re-establishment of such a protectorate. Not only would the extension of European influence upon this continent be contrary to the traditional and frequently expressed policy of the United States, but the course of Great Britain in assuming or exercising any dominion over the Mosquito Coast, . . . would be in violation of the express stipulations of the Clayton-Bulwer treaty. . . . I should be wanting in my duty . . . should I fail to bring the matter directly and frankly . . . to the notice of Her Majesty's Government.[71]

This instruction was written during the midst of the difficulties that attended the dismissal of Sackville-West because of the "Murchison" letter, and Phelps believed that the general diplomatic situation was distinctly unpromising. It was not likely that anything "useful" could be done in the Nicaraguan matter in the short period that remained of the Cleveland Administration, and it was evident that any action taken by the Department of State would not "bind those who are to take our places." [72] Despite this feeling of futility concerning diplomatic protests to Great Britain with regard to the Mosquito question, Phelps presented the gist of the Bayard instruction to the Foreign Office, and received a note from Lord Salisbury in which an assurance was given that the British Government had no intention of claiming a protectorate over the Mosquito Shore.[73]

This frank statement from Lord Salisbury quieted any apprehen-

---

70. J. P. H. Gastrell to Señor Zavala, September 10, 1888, *Foreign Relations, 1888,* pt. 1, pp. 767-768.

71. Secretary Bayard to Phelps, November 23, 1888, *Foreign Relations, 1888,* pt. 1, pp. 759-767. See also, *memorandum* dictated by Bayard after a conversation with Dr. Guzmán, November 23, 1888, *Bayard MS.*

72. Phelps to Secretary Bayard, January 2, 1889, *Bayard MS.*

73. Lord Salisbury to H. G. Edwardes, March 7, 1889, *British and Foreign State Papers,* vol. 81, pp. 759-762.

sions that the Department of State may have felt with reference to British intrigue in the Mosquito territory. American capital now became interested in the development of extensive banana plantations in Nicaragua, and it was reported that Bluefields was "American to the core." [74] As the American stake in the Mosquito country became larger, it was inevitable that the American Government would take a more serious view of disorders that would affect these investments. When war broke out in 1894 between Nicaragua and Honduras, there were rumors of a projected Honduran invasion of the land of the Mosquitos. The Government of Nicaragua sent troops into this district, and proclaimed martial law. This action was resented by Americans who requested their government at Washington to send warships for their protection, and in March, 1894, marines were landed from the British cruiser *Cleopatra*.[75] American business interests were opposed to Nicaraguan rule, because they feared it would be a fatal obstacle to their rapid development. They strongly preferred some type of local self-government along the lines indicated in the treaty of Managua. In this regard they were not in support of the contention of the American Government with reference to the rightful control of the disputed territory.

When the news reached Washington that the British marines had landed in Bluefields, Secretary Gresham immediately instructed Bayard to make inquiries at the Foreign Office concerning this intervention.[76] Bayard reported that the British Government had not authorized Captain Howe, of the *Cleopatra*, to take any action at Bluefields. Moreover, Lord Kimberley had given assurances that there was no movement on foot to re-establish the British protectorate over the Mosquito territory.[77] In a personal letter to Secretary Gresham, Bayard made further comments upon the situation at Bluefields. After criticizing the "lower civilization" which dominated the "South American political struggles," Bayard then discussed British policy in Nicaragua:

> The Mosquito incident will not, I think, contain any seeds of trouble. In my last despatch I drew attention to the rather sly action of Great Britain

74. Mary W. Williams, *Anglo-American Isthmian Diplomacy, 1815–1915*, p. 292; Robert N. Keely, "Nicaragua and the Mosquito Coast," *Popular Science Monthly*, vol. 45, pp. 160-175.

75. *Foreign Relations, 1894, Appendix 1*, pp. 234ff.

76. Secretary Gresham to Bayard, March 9, 1894, *Foreign Relations, 1894, Appendix 1*, p. 250.

77. Bayard to Secretary Gresham, March 15, 16, 1894, *ibid.*, pp. 250-252.

and the disingenuous action of Nicaragua in quietly arranging an arbitration by Austria in a purely American case. There was nothing in the diplomatic correspondence on file, nor did I discover until 1888 that such a submission and award had been agreed to and carried out. . . . From my conversation with Lord Kimberley, who is not quite acquainted with the facts and history of the matter, and from General Schenck's correspondence in 1873–74, I believe the English pretension for interference between the Mosquito residents and the government of Nicaragua, was the alleged failure of the latter government to pay the annuity promised to the barefooted King of the Mosquitos of $5,000 per annum for ten years. It had been partly paid, but there remained a balance due. It would seem a very easy thing for Nicaragua now to pay off this balance, and by so doing, put an end to any pretext for British interference. It is, however, owing wholly to the action of the Nicaraguan government in 1879, by submitting her treaty of Managua of 1860 to the sole interpretation of a European Monarchy, that has given a *locus standi* of interfering right to Great Britain, totally unwarranted in my judgment by the Convention of Managua. . . .

Great Britatin has just now her hands very full in other quarters of the globe, and the United States is the last nation on earth with whom the British people or their Rulers desire to quarrel, and of this I have new proofs in my intercourse with them.[78]

This Nicaraguan situation was further confused by the fact that the American Government had become deeply interested in the construction of an interoceanic canal through Nicaraguan territory. Under the terms of the Clayton-Bulwer Treaty, the Governments of the United States and of Great Britain had declared that "neither the one nor the other" would ever obtain or maintain for itself any exclusive control over a ship canal constructed across the Isthmus. But this disclaimer of American intentions to secure sole control over an isthmian canal, was not taken too seriously by certain statesmen. Seward, in 1868–1869, opened negotiations with Colombia for a treaty that conferred upon the United States the right to construct a canal within the territory of that country, and he stated that the American Government would be "unwilling to enter into an entangling alliance with other foreign nations for the construction and maintenance of a passage through the isthmus." [79]

President Grant was quick to catch the accent of the Seward instructions, and he made it clear that he regarded the construction of an

---

78. Bayard to Secretary Gresham, March 21, 1894, *Bayard Press Copy Book*, vol. 1, *Bayard MS*.

79. Dexter Perkins, *The Monroe Doctrine, 1867–1907*, pp. 66-67. See also, Seward to Peter I. Sullivan, March 2, September 17, September 27, October 24, 1868; Seward to Caleb Cushing, November 25, 1868, *Colombia, Instructions*, vol. 16, MS Dept. of State.

isthmian canal as an "American enterprise" to be undertaken under "American auspices." [80] Although nothing came of these negotiations that were undertaken during the Johnson and Grant Administrations, they afford an interesting illustration of the disposition of the Department of State to view the Clayton-Bulwer Treaty as a mere scrap of paper. When the Universal Interoceanic Canal Company was organized by De Lesseps, President Hayes immediately adopted the language of Seward and Grant, and in a message to Congress he clearly outlined his viewpoint: "The policy of this country is a canal under American control. The United States cannot consent to the surrender of this control to any European powers. If existing treaties between the United States and other nations, . . . stand in the way of this policy, . . . suitable steps should be taken . . . to promote and establish the American policy." [81]

In this message to Congress, President Hayes was merely expressing the sentiment of a large number of Americans who regarded the De Lesseps project as an infraction of the Monroe Doctrine. Bayard himself was distinctly fearful of the results that might flow from the completion of an isthmian canal under foreign auspices, and he did not hesitate to announce his views.[82] E. L. Godkin, and other prominent publicists, rushed into print to sound the alarm against any increase in European influence in Central America.[83] The Monroe Doctrine began to enjoy a remarkable revival.[84]

When Blaine became Secretary of State in 1881, he was fully conscious of the strength of American hostility to the De Lesseps canal. He had no doubt that the Monroe Doctrine stood high in popular favor. Hearing rumors that Colombia was seeking to interest European powers in a joint declaration of the neutrality of the Isthmus of Panama, he sent to the ministers of the United States in certain European capitals, a circular letter which plainly stated that the treaty between the United States and Colombia, in 1846, did not require "reinforcement or accession or assent from any other power." With regard to American control over any isthmian canal, Blaine remarked: "During

80. Secretary Fish to Stephen A. Hurlbut, September 4, 1869, *Colombia, Instructions,* vol. 16, MS Dept. of State.
81. Message of March 8, 1880. J. D. Richardson, *Messages and Papers of the Presidents,* vol. 7, pp. 585-586. See also, William F. Johnson, *Four Centuries of the Panama Canal,* pp. 79-81.
82. Dexter Perkins, *op. cit.,* p. 74.
83. *The Nation,* February 5, 1880, vol. 30, pp. 90-91.
84. Dexter Perkins, *The Monroe Doctrine, 1867-1907,* pp. 73-80.

any war to which the United States . . . might be a party, the passage of armed vessels of a hostile nation through the canal would be no more admissible than would the passage of the armed forces of a hostile nation over the railway lines joining the Atlantic and Pacific shores of the United States." [85]

Blaine followed this circular letter of June 24 with an instruction to the American Minister in London which contained a sharp attack upon the Clayton-Bulwer Treaty. This convention was more than thirty years old, and had been negotiated under "exceptional and extraordinary conditions" which no longer existed. The rapid growth of American interests on the Pacific coast had fundamentally altered the situation that had obtained in 1850. Under the terms of the treaty, the American Government was prohibited from maintaining troops within the canal zone. In view of the overwhelming strength of the British Navy this limitation was obviously unfair. Moreover, the "long-established claim of priority" on the part of the United States, conferred upon this country the "right to control the Isthmus transit." The American Government, therefore, wished to be released from the "unequal and unequitable obligations" of the Clayton-Bulwer Treaty. All matters concerning an isthmian canal should be "dealt with and decided by American Powers." [86]

Lord Granville replied that the arguments advanced by Secretary Blaine were based upon principles that were "novel in International Law." A canal across the isthmus of Central America was a concern to the whole world and consequently no single nation should be permitted to gain or exercise exclusive control over it. For this important reason it was advisable that other powers be invited to adhere to the stipulations of the Clayton-Bulwer Treaty.[87]

The reply to Lord Granville devolved upon Secretary Frelinghuysen (Blaine having withdrawn from the President's Cabinet). He stated that the President thought it would be unnecessary and unwise to invite other powers to "guarantee the neutrality of the Isthmus, or to give their navies a pretext for assembling in waters contiguous to our

---

85. *Foreign Relations, 1881*, pp. 537-540. See also, Alice F. Tyler, *The Foreign Policy of James G. Blaine,* pp. 30-35; Lindley M. Keasbey, *The Nicaragua Canal and the Monroe Doctrine* (N. Y., 1896), pp. 394ff.

86. Blaine to Lowell, November 19, 1881, *Senate Doc. 237,* 56 Cong., 1 sess., pp. 384-396.

87. Lord Granville to Sackville-West, January 7, 1882, *Senate Ex. Doc. 194,* 47 Cong., 1 sess., pp. 191-203. See also, Ira D. Travis, *The History of the Clayton-Bulwer Treaty* (Ann Arbor, 1900), pp. 223-226.

shores." More important than any other consideration, was the fact that an international guarantee would be in conflict with the Monroe Doctrine. It was not necessary for the American Government to define or explain that doctrine, but "its history clearly shows that it at least opposes any intervention by European nations in the political affairs of American republics." [88]

Frelinghuysen was so little impressed with Lord Granville's reply,[89] that he went ahead and signed (December 1, 1884) a treaty which provided that the United States would build a canal at its own cost, and under the terms of a "perpetual alliance" with Nicaragua, it would be ready at all times to "protect the integrity of the territory" of that country.[90] Needless to say, this convention openly violated the provisions of the Clayton-Bulwer Treaty, and this may have been the principal reason why it failed to secure the approval of that body. As soon as Bayard assumed the duties of Secretary of State, in March, 1885, he recalled this treaty from the Senate, and it was never revived. His action in this regard is told in a personal letter to Senator Gray:

> In 1885, in Executive Session, the Senate, by a very decided majority, adopted an amendment (proposed by John Sherman) to the then pending treaty with Nicaragua for the construction by the Government of the United States of a Canal, by which existing treaty stipulations with other powers were not to be violated. At first, Mr. Edmunds, of Vermont, and Mr. Morgan violently argued that the Treaty of 1850 was non-existent, and a long paper was gotten up in the State Department to prove that the treaty had been abrogated, but it was not very difficult (for me and others) to prove not only that the treaty was extant, but that the British Government had finally accepted to the full the American construction, and had withdrawn from all attempted control . . . in Central America. I went into office in March, 1885, and very soon withdrew the Frelinghuysen Treaty from the Senate (where . . . it had failed to receive a two-thirds vote and was hanging upon a motion to reconsider the vote by which the treaty was beaten, Mr. Edmunds having changed his vote in order to move to reconsider and thus keep the matter hanging indefinitely).[91]

Senator Edmunds did not lose his interest in an interoceanic canal under American control, and in December, 1888, after the collapse of the De Lesseps project at Panama, he introduced a resolution which expressed the serious concern and disapproval of the Senate with

88. Frelinghuysen to Lowell, May 8, 1882, *Senate Doc. 237*, 56 Cong., 1 sess., pp. 219-231.
89. Lord Granville to Sackville-West, December 30, 1882, *ibid.*, pp. 411-417.
90. John Bassett Moore, *Digest of International Law*, vol. 3, pp. 197-198.
91. Bayard to Senator George Gray, April 28, 1894. *Bayard Press Copy Book*, vol. 1, *Bayard MS.*

regard to "any connection" of "any European government with the construction or control of any ship-canal across the Isthmus of Darien or across Central America." [92] This resolution was not passed by the House of Representatives, but it was approved by the Senate with only three negative votes.[93]

The débâcle at Panama led to a renewed interest in an isthmian canal by way of the Nicaragua route, and in February, 1889, the Maritime Canal Company was chartered by Congress. Although operations were actually started by this company in 1890, lack of funds caused a suspension of activity in 1893, after an expenditure of $6,000,000.[94] An attempt was then made in Congress to provide a limited guarantee for a large block of the bonds of the Maritime Canal Company, and in 1894 a measure to this effect passed the Senate of the United States. Although it failed in the House of Representatives, it was evident that there was widespread interest in the construction, under strictly American auspices, of an interoceanic canal.[95] Events in Nicaragua in the early months of 1894, focussed attention upon the possibility that British opposition to these canal projects might be effective through control over the Mosquito territory.

In January, 1894, hostilities broke out between Honduras and Nicaragua, and there were rumors that Honduran troops would invade the country around Bluefields. The American consular agent at that city sent a telegram to Secretary Gresham requesting the prompt despatch of a man-of-war to Nicaraguan waters for the purpose of protecting the lives and property of American citizens.[96] The U. S. S. *Kearsage* was ordered to report at Bluefields at once,[97] and the American Government decided to keep a watchful eye upon developments along the Mosquito Shore.

When Nicaragua sent troops into the Mosquito reservation in order to prevent an invasion from Honduras, the Mosquito chief, Robert Henry Clarence, vehemently protested against this action as a violation of the treaty rights of the Mosquito Indians.[98] The protest was vigor-

---

92. *Congressional Record*, 50 Cong., 2 sess., December 19, 1888, vol. 20. pt. 1, p. 338.
93. *Ibid.*, January 8, 1889, p. 597.
94. Willis F. Johnson, *Four Centuries of the Panama Canal*, pp. 111-112.
95. Dwight C. Miner, *The Fight for the Panama Route* (N. Y., 1940), pp. 27-32.
96. Mr. Seat to Secretary Gresham, January 25, 1894, *Foreign Relations, 1894, Appendix I*, p. 234.
97. Secretary Herbert to Secretary Gresham, January 27, 1894, *ibid.*, p. 234.
98. Mr. Seat to Mr. Braida, January 22, 1894, *Foreign Relations, 1894, Appendix I*, pp. 235-236.

ously supported by the British Consul at Bluefields (H. F. Bingham), who regarded the presence of Nicaraguan troops in the Mosquito reservation as "meddling with the internal affairs of the Mosquito Indians." [99] In order to give adequate protection to British interests, fifty soldiers from the warship *Cleopatra* were landed at Bluefields,[100] and a provisional government was organized under the control of British and Nicaraguan citizens.[101]

Secretary Gresham was disturbed over reports that British military forces had landed at Bluefields, and he instructed Bayard to "ascertain and report fully by cable the occasion for this action." [102] When Bayard went to the Foreign Office he found that Lord Kimberley was "very willing" to tell all he knew about the situation at Bluefields, but it was soon disclosed that his knowledge was extremely limited. No orders had been issued by the British Government authorizing the landing of troops in the Mosquito reservation, and Kimberley assured Bayard that no steps had been taken with reference to extending a protectorate over the territory around Bluefields.[103]

Two weeks later, Bayard sent a despatch to Secretary Gresham in which he gave further details about the situation in the Mosquito territory. The most influential residents of Bluefields were

. . . traders, English and American, with negroes from the Island of Jamaica. . . . It does not appear that the alleged intervention by the British armed force was for the maintenance of the rights of the Mosquito Indians against alleged Nicaraguan oppressors, but rather, to protect other classes of residents who are not mentioned in the treaty of Managua. . . .

I am disposed to believe that by the exercise of moderation, discretion and just humanity, Nicaragua can remove all vestige of pretext or reason for any foreign intervention for the settlement of questions of a social or political nature between herself and the Mosquito Indians.[104]

It was very evident that the agents of the Nicaraguan Government were despised by American residents in the Mosquito territory, and they were anxious for effective protection whether it was extended by British or American bluejackets. In a statement drawn up by American citizens in March, 1894, there is a sharp indictment of Nicaraguan

99. H. F. Bingham to General Lacayo, February 27, 1894, *ibid.*, pp. 238-239.
100. Mr. Baker to Secretary Gresham, March 6, 1894, *ibid.*, p. 239.
101. José Vita to President Zelaya, March 6, 1894, *ibid.*, p. 249.
102. Secretary Gresham to Bayard, March 9, 1894, *ibid.*, p. 250.
103. Bayard to Secretary Gresham, March 15, 16, 1894, *ibid.*, pp. 250-252.
104. Bayard to Secretary Gresham, March 29, 1894, *Foreign Relations, 1894, Appendix 1,* pp. 258-260.

misrule. When the Nicaraguan soldiers came into the Mosquito reservation they took possession "of all public buildings and property of the Mosquito Government," and they opened the prisons and "set free the felons." The inhabitants of Bluefields were

. . . nigh driven to desperation. . . . The commissioner, although immediately setting about the collection of . . . duties and taxes, refused . . . to recognize the valid obligations of the Mosquito Government. He remarked that he would just run things to suit himself. . . . The commissioner has deceived the people so frequently that they have lost all confidence in him. . . . In Rama the treatment of Americans has been such that we feel assured, should Nicaragua govern the reserve, we would receive the same treatment.[105]

The American citizens who resided in Bluefields wished to have "a local self-government" that would be free from Nicaraguan misrule, but Secretary Gresham had no thought of supporting any movement against Nicaraguan authority. He was anxious to safeguard the sovereignty of Nicaragua in the Mosquito reserve, and he looked with suspicion upon the actions of British agents in the vicinity of Bluefields. These agents had joined with Nicaraguan officials in setting up a provisional government over the Mosquito territory, and Gresham was of the opinion that the British Government was overstepping the limitations of the treaty of Managua. He was

. . . unable to see that this joint assumption of authority by British and Nicaraguan agents is compatible with the stipulations of the treaty of Managua. By that treaty Great Britain renounced all sovereignty over the reservation and recognized the sovereignty of Nicaragua over the same. . . . The agents of the United States in Nicaragua have had no part in framing the reported provisional arrangement, and they have signified their intention not to participate in its administration. The proceeding has not, and cannot have, the sanction of this Government, directly or indirectly. . . .

With the foregoing views and the enclosed papers before you, you are in a position to express to Lord Kimberley the President's hope and expectation that the anomalous situation now disclosed may speedily cease and that no foreign agency shall be permitted to dictate or participate in the administration of affairs in the Mosquito Reservation.[106]

A few days later, Gresham wrote a personal letter to Bayard in which he expressed the view that British participation in the provisional government at Bluefields was

105. Statement of committee of American citizens, March 29, 1894, *ibid.*, pp. 266-267.
106. Secretary Gresham to Bayard, April 30, 1894, *Foreign Relations, 1894, Appendix 1*, pp. 271-273.

. . . hardly consistent with her position as last announced, that the Clayton-Bulwer Treaty is still in force. . . . If that treaty is still in force, the pending Senate bill known as the Morgan bill, which provides that the United States shall guarantee seventy million dollars of the bonds of the Canal Company, ought not to become a law. . . . The bill provides that the bonds shall be secured by a mortgage upon all the property of the Company, and . . . this would give our Government an equitable interest in the canal, which might become a legal one by foreclosure and purchase. Nicaragua has notified the Canal Company that that Government considers the concession forfeited for non-compliance with its provisions. For some reason, the Government of Nicaragua now appears to be unfriendly to the United States, and it is believed here (not without reason), that English interests have brought about this feeling.[107]

In response to the official instruction of April 30, Bayard made inquiries at the Foreign Office and was informed by Lord Kimberley that Great Britain had "no intention or desire to exercise protectorate in any form over any portion of Nicaraguan territory, but to act thoroughly in concert with the United States for maintaining safety of the

107. Secretary Gresham to Bayard, May 2, 1894, *Gresham MS.* On October 14, 1893, John Bassett Moore wrote to Bayard and expressed the following opinion concerning an interoceanic canal: "I have lately been thinking more or less of the Interoceanic Canal Question. The more I reflect on it, the clearer it becomes that our only true policy is neutralization. . . . What I should like to see would be the presentation of the policy of neutralization not only as a just and liberal, but also, as a necessary policy. It would be impossible for any government to hold the canal as part of its defensive system. The moment a canal was opened between the Atlantic and the Pacific, that moment it would become one of the world's highways of commerce, and it would be . . . impossible for any nation to control it for its own purposes." *Bayard MS.*

In a letter to Senator George Gray, April 28, 1894, Bayard commented as follows on the Clayton-Bulwer Treaty: "I see newspaper reports that Mr. Dolph has introduced a resolution to abrogate the . . . Clayton-Bulwer Treaty with Great Britain. . . . I wish simply to say that the Monroe Doctrine (whatever it may be) has never had so practical an aid, so valuable an assistance, as has been derived from the covenants of the Clayton-Bulwer Treaty. My judgment is wholly opposed to releasing Great Britain from . . . that instrument, and should it be done, you may be sure that a crop of questions . . . will arise to plague us and create diplomatic difficulties from which this treaty has been potentially useful in saving us.

"No one wants more than I, an interoceanic avenue, by Canal or Ship-railway, across the Isthmus, but with our own experience of the transcontinental railroads (with their credit-mobiliers, land grants, and infinite corruption), . . . I recoil from embarking the Treasury and Government of the United States in the work of constructing the Canal at Nicaragua or anywhere else. The general principle which enfolds the Convention of 1850 is wise, statesmanlike, and true. Such a work as connecting the two Oceans at the centre of the Western Hemisphere, should be in the interests of the civilized world of commerce." *Bayard Press Copy Book,* vol. 1, *Bayard MS.*

With regard to the Nicaragua Canal, Bayard on November 5, 1887, had written as follows to Hiram Hitchcock: "You may be very sure that the interest of the President and his Administration is sincere in the success of the Nicaraguan Canal. . . . It is a great work and opens up a vista into the realm of possibilities, wonderful indeed. Some day when you are here we will talk about it." *Bayard Letter Book,* vol. 6, *Bayard MS.*

citizens and property of both countries." Kimberley also gave assurances that the British Government was "contemplating no extension of her influence in Nicaraguan territory nor any violation whatever of the Clayton-Bulwer treaty of 1850." [108]

On May 29 Bayard wrote a personal letter to Gresham in which he expressed the opinion that Lord Kimberley was strongly disposed "to accommodate all questions with the United States." It was apparent, however, that a party change in England was imminent, and Bayard hoped that he would not be "called on to propose any very decisive points until after the British elections have been held and we have a permanent and responsible government in office here. The life of the present hangs on a thread." [109]

Gresham was thoroughly in accord with Bayard's views on the Nicaraguan situation, and in a personal letter of June 7, he indicated his approval of the way in which Bayard had handled matters. It was unfortunate that Senator Morgan was chairman of the Senate Committee on Foreign Relations. He could think of nothing but the Nicaragua Canal, and he lost

. . . no opportunity to asperse Great Britain. I have read many times your admirable instruction of November 23, 1888, to Mr. Phelps, and have said to the President that I think this Administration should stand by it. I agree with you that we cannot afford to abandon the Clayton-Bulwer Treaty. It provides for the neutralization of the canal by the two Governments, and I can see no good reason why an effort should not be made to induce other Powers to agree to its neutralization. In an unofficial and confidential conversation with Sir Julian a few days ago, he expressed himself very strongly in favor of neutralizing the Nicaragua canal as the Suez canal was neutralized. The President is in favor of maintaining the Clayton-Bulwer Treaty, and I think he is in favor of neutralization as the best means of securing the speedy construction of a canal.

Sir Julian has repeatedly informed me that, although his Government would like to be rid of any obligation or duty to protect the Mosquito Indians, it cannot, in view of the treaty of Managua, permit Nicaragua to oppress them. I have said to Sir Julian that, by the treaty referred to, Great Britain renounced her sovereignty over the strip and recognized the sovereignty of Nicaragua, the latter Government agreeing that the Indians might govern themselves and others in the strip according to Indian usage and such regulations as they (the Indians) might thereafter adopt, not inconsistent with the sovereignty of Nicaragua; that sovereignty means supremacy

108. Bayard to Secretary Gresham, May 22, 28, 1894, *Foreign Relations, 1894, Appendix 1*, pp. 290-293.
109. Bayard to Secretary Gresham, May 29, 1894, *Bayard Press Copy Book*, vol. 1, *Bayard MS*.

and two sovereigns cannot occupy the same territory at the same time; that Nicaragua cannot be held responsible for anything occurring in the strip when she is not permitted to exercise the ordinary attributes of a sovereign. I cannot see in the treaty anything that justifies Great Britain in insisting that aliens may erect and maintain in Mosquito an independent municipality such as Bluefields. Sir Julian admits that Indian Government in the strip is now a mere fiction. . . . If there is to be any further correspondence with that Government on the subject of the Clayton-Bulwer Treaty, or the treaty of Managua and the right of Great Britain to intervene between Nicaragua and the Indians, it is my desire that you shall conduct it on our part. . . .

I note what you say as to the advisability of going slow in matters connected with the Clayton-Bulwer Treaty and the treaty of Managua until the present administration in England is succeeded by another. In a conversation with Sir Julian a few days ago I suggested that you go slow, and that the two governments exchange as few official notes as possible.[110]

During the summer months of 1894, conditions around Bluefields remained unsettled. The provisional government, which was a strange composite of Nicaraguans and aliens, became increasingly unpopular, and in July a revolution broke out against its arbitrary rule. Robert Henry Clarence, the hereditary Mosquito chief, reassumed his position as King of the Mosquito Indians, and some Americans rallied to his banner.[111] Secretary Gresham had slight sympathy with these rebel Americans, and he was insistent that Nicaraguan sovereignty over the Mosquito reserve be expressly recognized. In setting forth this viewpoint in an instruction to Bayard, Gresham remarked:

My instruction to you of April 30, . . . will have shown that the late attempts to organize through alien intervention, a government for the Mosquito Reservation wholly foreign to the scheme provided by the treaty of Managua, were deemed by us to be at variance with the policy and engagements of half a century. . . . The situation at Bluefields, and elsewhere in the strip, presents no question difficult of solution. The sovereignty of Nicaragua over the whole of the national domain is unquestionable. . . . An alien administration, in other interests than those of the Indians, notoriously exists, especially at Bluefields. . . . No matter how conspicuous the American or other alien interests which have grown up under the fiction of Indian self-government, neither the United States nor Great Britain can fairly sanction or uphold this colorable abuse of the sovereignty of Nicaragua.[112]

110. Secretary Gresham to Bayard, June 7, 1894, *Personal and Confidential, Bayard MS.*
111. Secretary Gresham to Mr. Baker, July 12, 1894; Baker to Secretary Gresham, July 14, 1894, *Foreign Relations, 1894, Appendix 1,* pp. 306-309.
112. Secretary Gresham to Bayard, July 19, 1894, *ibid.,* pp. 311-312. See also, Secretary Gresham to Bayard, July 23, 1894, *ibid.,* p. 313.

Bayard communicated to Lord Kimberley the substance of this instruction from Secretary Gresham, and he emphasized the fact that the United States was "wholly opposed to the employment of the fiction of a Mosquito government to organize an opposition to the Government of Nicaragua." Lord Kimberley replied that the presence of British armed forces in Nicaragua had "no other object or purpose than to protect the lives and property of British residents during a period of lawlessness and strife." The only desire of his Government "beyond that, was to induce the Nicaraguans to treat the Indians with forbearance and moderation, and not shoot them down, as they were very apt to do."

Bayard could appreciate British reluctance to permit the Mosquito Indians to be treated by Nicaraguan agents with "gross injustice and oppression," and he was fully persuaded that, "with good temper and judicious and just treatment of her citizens inhabiting the Mosquito region, Nicaragua will be wholly undisturbed by interference by . . . Great Britain." [113]

British forbearance, however, was based upon the belief that the lives and property of British citizens in the Mosquito territory would be given ample protection by the Nicaraguan officials. During the revolutionary outbreak in July and August of 1894, it was difficult to maintain order in the vicinity of Bluefields, and two American and twelve British citizens were arrested on the charge of having incited the rebellion. The Americans were soon released, but some of the British subjects, including E. D. Hatch, Her Majesty's vice-consul at Bluefields, were imprisoned for a long period.[114]

The American Government was seriously concerned over the unsettled situation that prevailed in the Mosquito country, and on November 23, 1894, Bayard had a conference with Lord Kimberley. The gist of their conversation is given in the following memorandum:

I went to Lord Kimberley at the Foreign Office, by appointment. His subject was Nicaragua, *not* as to the Mosquito question or anything connected therewith politically or jurisdictionally, but merely *internationally* as between Great Britain and Nicaragua [over the] alleged mistreatment of Hatch, a British pro-Consul at Bluefields who had been treated roughly.

113. Bayard to Secretary Gresham, August 10, 1894, *Foreign Relations, 1894, Appendix I*, pp. 322-323.
114. Secretary Gresham to Dr. Guzmán, August 18, 1894; Dr. Guzmán to Secretary Gresham, August 18, 1894; Mr. Baker to Secretary Gresham, August 28, 1894; Mr. Matus to Mr. Baker, August 31, 1894; Dr. Guzmán to Secretary Gresham, September 22, 1894, *ibid.*, pp. 326-343.

Great Britain had waited three months for an explanation, which came only a day or two ago, and then very voluminous, and in Spanish. . . .

Lord Kimberley thinks it possible that Great Britain may require some redress for her grievance, but wishes the United States to understand her action has nothing whatever to do in connection with the Mosquito question or anything *political*. It is simply her insistence upon having her citizens and officials treated respectfully and fairly.

Of course, I [Bayard] disclaimed the slightest intention of interfering with the right of Great Britain to any *just* reclamation, but I did advert to the well known condition of that region and its very imperfect civilization —the frequence of disorder and violence among and between Nicaraguan officials and citizens themselves (Lord Kimberley gave me a late instance where the President of Nicaragua had been fired at five times point blank by a citizen).

I told him of my short interview in October here with Barrios, and what I had said to him, and what I had repeated to Guzmán in Washington, in which I stated that by fairness and just exercise of authority, Nicaragua could secure peace and order in Mosquito and the rest of Nicaragua and be perfectly secure from the slightest interference by Great Britain or the United States. To this Lord Kimberley heartily agreed. The purpose of his seeing me today was to impress upon me that any measures Great Britain might have to adopt to enforce her rights internationally against Nicaragua for ejecting her pro-Consul and citizens, had no connection whatever with any political question with Mosquito or under any treaty with Nicaragua.[115]

Three days later, Bayard had another conversation with Lord Kimberley, who read to him a telegram that had been sent to the British Minister in Nicaragua, instructing him that the

. . . British Government under the Treaty of Managua and the Austrian arbitrament, would not be bound by a number of late decrees made by the Nicaraguan Commission concerning land tables, etc., in Mosquito. Lord Kimberley said this was only intended by his Government as a *caveat*, so that they should not be concluded by any apparent assent to the Nicaraguan decrees in Mosquito. That having waited three months for a reply from the Nicaraguan Government, and their Agent having been most unceremoniously bundled out, they were disposed to concede nothing, and therefore, pending discussion with Nicaragua, they sought to prevent any conclusion against them by giving notice that they would not be bound by the action of the Nicaraguan Commission.

He said no ship of War had been sent to Bluefields, and added that the statements . . . reported by the Nicaraguans . . . were not reliable.[116]

115. *Memorandum* written by Bayard after a conversation with Lord Kimberley, November 23, 1894, *Bayard MS.*

116. *Memorandum* written by Bayard after a conversation with Lord Kimberley, November 26, 1894, *Bayard MS.* See also, Bayard to Secretary Gresham, November 24, 27, 1894, *Foreign Relations, 1894, Appendix 1,* pp. 354-357.

In a personal letter to Secretary Gresham, Bayard gave a brief resume of the situation. Barrios, the Special Envoy of Nicaragua, was about to have an audience with the Queen. Bayard hoped that when Barrios had a talk with Lord Kimberley, he would

. . . prove a sensible man. If the latter is wise, he will let the British relations to Mosquito, "sluff off," and let the Indians who remain, incorporate themselves regularly (or irregularly) with the government of Nicaragua. I have a suspicion that the promoters of . . . the Nicaraguan Canal, at the cost of the government of the United States, are fanning every flame of local excitement at Bluefields in order to stimulate Congress into an anti-British sentiment.[117]

When the news reached London that the Mosquito Indians had declared themselves in favor of incorporation into the Republic of Nicaragua, Bayard thought that this action put an

. . . end to the last pretext of British duty to interfere in any way in local matters in that region, and I think the government here will be very glad of it. What apology or indemnity they will require for the summary ejection of their Agent, Hatch, I do not know, but Nicaragua can better afford to heal his wounds with money, and then ask his immediate withdrawal as *persona non grata*. It will be the simplest and cheapest and most final way of settlement.[118]

Gresham agreed with Bayard that the surrender by the Mosquito Indians of their

. . . right to govern themselves and others in the strip according to Indian custom and usage, removes the last pretext of Great Britain to interfere in the political affairs of Mosquito. . . . I did what I could to induce the Government of Nicaragua, through the Minister here, to revoke its order of banishment against British subjects, including Hatch, the Consul, and Dr. Guzmán finally told me . . . that the order had been revoked.[119]

When Bayard received official information from Nicaragua confirming the news that the Mosquito Indians had been incorporated into the Republic of Nicaragua, he promptly informed Gresham that there "was the most open expression of satisfaction at the foreign office upon the reported voluntary incorporation of the Indians with the rest of Nicaragua, for it was a consummation devoutly to be wished, and they were glad to be free from the subject." [120]

117. Bayard to Secretary Gresham, November 30, 1894, *Bayard Press Copy Book*, vol. 2, *Bayard MS.* See also, Secretary Gresham to Bayard, December 3, 17, 1894, *Foreign Relations, 1894, Appendix 1*, p. 358.
118. Bayard to Secretary Gresham, December 10, 1894, *Bayard MS.*
119. Secretary Gresham to Bayard, December 24, 1894, *Gresham MS.*
120. Bayard to Secretary Gresham, December 22, 1894, *Foreign Relations, 1894, Appendix 1*, pp. 359-360.

Although the British Government was "well pleased" with the incorporation of the Mosquito territory into the Republic of Nicaragua, it had no intention of relieving Nicaragua from the claims that had been filed against it by British citizens. The claims were to be passed upon by a mixed commission, and Bayard resented the fact that no American was to be appointed to serve as a member of this body. He thought this action was "wholly unnecessary, for a word or a sign . . . would have prevented any improper appointment, and as the matter stands, Her Majesty's Government has only given to some mischievous enemy of both countries, a small grievance which may be used to promote friction and misunderstanding between the United States and Great Britain." [121]

The Nicaraguan Government did not agree to recognize these claims or to make any provision for the appointment of the mixed commission until Great Britain began to exert sharp pressure. When this was applied, the Nicaraguan representatives in Washington applied to Secretary Gresham for assistance. In a personal letter to Bayard, Gresham made the following comments:

Señor Barrios and Doctor Guzmán handed me, a day or two after the former's arrival from London, a copy of Lord Kimberley's demand upon Nicaragua. Mr. Barrios seemed to be smarting somewhat under what he termed harsh treatment received from the British foreign office. I distinctly told him and Doctor Guzmán that they must deal directly with Great Britain; that the United States sustained to them no such relation as would authorize us to take their quarrel off their hands, and that we could not take the position that Great Britain could not call Nicaragua to account for an affront without our consent. Notwithstanding this, Doctor Guzmán addressed me a long note . . . in which positions were taken that we could not sustain. I sent for the Doctor and told him that he had made a mistake; that the British note should be answered directly; that after answering it, they could furnish us with a copy and request our good offices, which we should exercise if we thought the situation warranted it. I also suggested that the note had better be withdrawn. It was withdrawn, but a few days later it was sent to me again, and a few days still later, again withdrawn. Doctor Guzmán now tells me his government has answered the note directly, saying that the British subjects, including the Pro-consul, were arrested and expelled, not out of any spirit of resentment towards Great Britain, but in a time of excitement and peril, and because it was believed the expelled persons were inimical to the peace and sovereignty of Nicaragua; that Nicaragua realized she had acted hastily and without proper regard for the rights

121. *Memorandum* written by Bayard after a conversation with Lord Kimberley, March 20, 1895, *Bayard MS.*

of Great Britain, which was regretted; that she would revoke the orders of expulsion, allow the banished persons to return and resume . . . business so long as they obeyed the laws, and refer to arbitration her liability for damages and the amount thereof.

The British note has been published here. Doctor Guzmán denies giving it out, and it is claimed by newspaper men that the British government gave it to the press associations at London. It is unfortunate that Great Britain has taken the position that the third commissioner shall not be a citizen of any American State. That expression is interpreted here quite generally as meaning that he shall not be a citizen of the United States. In view of the well-known fact that the expelled Englishmen . . . did meddle in political affairs in the Strip, and were inimical to Nicaraguan authority, the British demand seems to be harsh.

The concluding paragraph of Lord Kimberley's demand upon Nicaragua implies an intention to reopen the question of Great Britain's right to govern Mosquitia under the pretext of protecting the Indians, and that she means to again assert that right. I hope not.[122]

When the Nicaraguan Government made another appeal for American help in the controversy with Great Britain, Gresham repeated his dictum that "England's demands must be met." In view of the request of the Nicaraguan Minister at Washington for a "fortnight in which to arrange details," Gresham instructed Bayard to ask Lord Kimberley to make this concession.[123]

Bayard immediately sent a personal note to Lord Kimberley in which he paraphrased Gresham's instruction,[124] and Kimberley replied on the same day in a friendly note. The British Government was demanding an indemnity of £15,000 for the detention of Mr. Hatch, the British vice-consul at Bluefields, and they were also insisting upon an agreement for the appointment of a commission to adjust other claims. With regard to these demands, Kimberley remarked as follows:

Many thanks for your friendly note. In the event of the Nicaraguan Government returning an answer to our Admiral intimating compliance with our demands, he has instructions to allow such delay as he may consider reasonable for payment of the indemnity. I may add that we are most anxious to avoid embarrassing or interrupting the commerce of other countries.[125]

Bayard believed that the Nicaraguan Government would comply with the British demands, but he could not "admire the course" that

122. Secretary Gresham to Bayard, March 31, 1895, *Bayard MS.*
123. Secretary Gresham to Bayard, telegram, April 24, 1895, *ibid.*
124. Bayard to Lord Kimberley, April 25, 1895, *ibid.*
125. Lord Kimberley to Bayard, April 25, 1895, *Bayard MS.*

Kimberley had followed. There was a possibility that the Foreign Secretary had

. . . been influenced by party hopes and fears in this country, and there are also some traces of acerbity which I believe are traceable to some of the under-officials of the Department. But the incident will have its uses by throwing a strong light upon the entire situation, and bringing into view the intentions and feelings of the Central American States toward our Government.

I am disposed to believe that no forces would have been landed at Corinto if the British Admiral had been allowed to receive telegrams direct from his government, but the Nicaraguans "sawed off the limb" between themselves and the tree. What a curious exposure of impecuniosity in a government! No wonder it sells "concessions," or anything else that is disposable for cash.

To read poor Mr. Frelinghuysen's treaty of 1884, happily rejected by the Senate and withdrawn in 1885 by the President, in the light of late events, one can see what a mess of corruption and extortion the United States would have found itself in, by covenanting for the . . . right of way around Corinto, and payment of damages *by the United States*, the amount to be ascertained by *Nicaraguan citizens and appointees*. . . . I have noticed in . . . the press that the English protectorate of Mosquito is a thing of past history, and it would be well if Dr. Guzmán would advise his government so to treat it, and to have no more superfluous negotiations about a settled fact.[126]

When the Nicaraguan Government finally complied with the British demands, the marines and sailors that had been landed at Corinto on April 27, were withdrawn, and the port was restored to the control of the Nicaraguan officials. Bayard thought that the Corinto incident had shed a "strong ray of light over Nicaragua, and will be of much assistance in measuring our steps in relation to the South American Republics. The President wrote me a note on May 1st, indicating some anxiety, which, however, must have been speedily dispelled by the withdrawal of the British forces." [127]

The President's suspicions of British policy in Latin America were not immediately dispelled by the withdrawal of British marines from Corinto. They had long been held in check by the conservative hand of Secretary Gresham, whose death on May 28, 1895, was a severe blow to Americans like Bayard, who had implicit faith in British professions of good will toward the United States.

126. Bayard to Secretary Gresham, May 4, 1895, *Bayard Press Copy Book*, vol. 2, *Bayard MS.*

127. Bayard to Secretary Gresham, May 17, 1895, *Bayard Press Copy Book*, vol. 2, *Bayard MS.*

The American press had shared the President's fears that British policy in Latin America had some dangerous implications. The New York *Sun* warned Great Britain in November, 1894, that she must "let Nicaragua alone, or she will have the United States to deal with." [128] In April, 1895, American public opinion was deeply concerned over British pressure upon Nicaragua, and the New York *Tribune* remarked that if England attempted "by bombardment or armed force to bully Nicaragua into paying a bill of damages which has been arbitrarily levied against her, the State Department ought to issue a new edition of the Monroe Doctrine with a marginal reading especially adapted to the case." [129] When the British seized Corinto, American indignation rose to a higher pitch, but John B. McMaster, a leading historian, endeavored to allay this storm of disapproval by stating that the Monroe Doctrine did not commit the United States to

. . . take part in wars between a South American Republic and a European sovereign when the object of the latter is not the founding of a monarchy under a European prince. . . . In the present instance, therefore, the doctrine does not apply so long as England does not hold the ports of Nicaragua longer than is necessary to secure the payment of the sum she is determined to extort.[180]

The New York *Herald* supported this view of Professor McMaster, and in an editorial the opinion was expressed that the Monroe Doctrine did "not cut any figure in this affair." [131] According to the New York *World,* the only question with which the United States was concerned was "how long the English provisional government over an American republic is to last. . . . England cannot have another rood of ground on the American hemisphere, and in the neighborhood of the trans-Isthmian routes she cannot have an inch." [132]

The New York *Tribune* was sharply critical of the way England had acted. The refusal of the British Foreign Office to "submit its claims against Nicaragua and the wanton invasion of Corinto . . . are crimes against civilization." [133] The Baltimore *American* expressed the view that the "conduct of Great Britain towards Nicaragua is brutal and her claim against that country is to a moral certainty, unjust," [134] while the Philadelphia *Press* asked the following question: "If England chooses to hold on, how is she to be dispossessed?" [135]

128. November 29, 1894.   129. April 20, 1895.
130. New York *Herald*, April 28, 1895.   131. New York *Herald*, April 27, 1895.
132. April 26, 1895.   133. April 28, 1895.
134. Quoted in the N. Y. *Tribune*, April 15, 1895.   135. *Ibid.*, April 29, 1895.

The Assembly of the State of New York adopted on May 1, a series of resolutions which denounced the lack of patriotic spirit "which has characterized the Administration at Washington in dealing with this complication at Corinto," and the Senate of the State of Connecticut took similar action.[136]

President Cleveland was always sensitive to outbursts of American public opinion, and there is no doubt that he was affected by these vehement criticisms of British policy. It is more than likely that he took to heart the resolutions of censure that were adopted by the New York State Assembly. With the accession of Olney to the office of Secretary of State on June 8, 1895, the stage was being set for a new political play in which this belligerent Boston lawyer was to play the part of the bold knight that rescued defenceless Venezuela from the clutches of perfidious England. It was a stirring melodrama that captured the fancy of most American audiences, and it was not until later that the public perceived that the Venezuelan maiden was a worthless wench.

C. BAYARD SERVES AS AN ARDENT ADVOCATE OF ANGLO-SAXON UNITY

In order clearly to understand Bayard's attitude during the Guiana boundary dispute, it is necessary to keep in mind the fact that he was an ardent believer in the importance of close co-operation between the English-speaking peoples. When he landed in Southampton in June, 1893, he assured the officials of that city that he was "right glad to set his foot in Old England, and he was glad to breathe the free air of liberty that he breathed at home." [137] Some months later, in a letter to Don Dickinson, he remarked:

> This country is full—fuller than I could conceive—of the accretions, moral, intellectual, physical, of unbroken civilization for centuries. I am stumbling over proofs of all this every day. . . . Generations of cultivated men and women, with enlarged opportunities, and full sense of responsibility for their exercise, have resulted in an accumulation of literary and art treasures . . . almost bewildering.[138]

In November, 1893, Bayard spoke at the unveiling of the Lowell Memorial in the Chapter House at Westminster. His address unmistak-

136. New York *Tribune*, May 1, 2, 1895.
137. London *Daily News*, June 12, 1893.
138. Bayard to Don Dickinson, October 24, 1893, *Bayard MS.*

ably reveals how completely he had responded to the call of English culture:

It is a fine strong saying that "blood is thicker than water," and every day proves how the ties of a common origin and ancestry are stronger than written treaties, and inborn sympathies of race, in the end, can silence international discords and jealousies. It was his [Lowell's] great and honorable purpose to bring the peoples of Great Britain and of the United States into a better comprehension of each other—to replace suspicion by confidence, and ignorant animosity by friendly appreciation. He liked to call himself a "man of letters," and truly was a master of the English tongue, and made his skill and knowledge an agency to interpret the better feelings of both branches of the race who share its glories in common.[139]

Oscar S. Straus regarded Bayard's address at the unveiling of the Lowell Memorial as "very appropriate to the occasion and your official position, serving admirably the useful purpose of cementing the ties of brotherhood between the two great civilizing powers of the earth." Mr. Straus also commented on the fact that he had heard Secretary Gresham speak in the most friendly terms of Bayard, thus indicating that the Secretary of State was in complete accord with Bayard's viewpoint.[140] On June 1, 1894, Straus wrote again to Bayard and remarked that the American press was filled with "reports of your graceful and eloquent speeches in London, and of the commendation of our representative at the Court of St. James. It is agreed on all sides that the best traditions are being fully maintained, and even excelled by you." [141]

A few days later, Secretary Gresham sent a confidential letter to Bayard which concluded with the following compliment: "We hear nothing but glowing accounts of you, and I need not say I have read the speeches which you have made on various social and other occasions with real satisfaction." [142] Wade Hampton was equally enthusiastic about Bayard's course as Ambassador: "Your friends and doubtless the whole country recognize the services you have rendered and are rendering by your presence in England." [143]

Inspired by the friendly words of commendation that he was receiving from his American friends, Bayard continued to deliver speeches in England which stressed the importance of Anglo-Saxon unity. On November 7, 1895, he appeared before the Philosophical Institution

---

139. London *Times*, November 29, 1893.
140. Oscar S. Straus to Bayard, January 8, 1894, *Bayard MS*.
141. Oscar S. Straus to Bayard, June 1, 1894, *ibid.*
142. Secretary Gresham to Bayard, June 7, 1894, *ibid.*
143. Wade Hampton to Bayard, July 23, 1894, *ibid.*

of Edinburgh, and in his address he paid a high tribute to the genius of the Scottish people. He then struck a more somber note when he passed on to discuss the condition of affairs in America. In the United States he had witnessed the insatiable growth of that form of state socialism called "Protection," which had

. . . done more to foster class legislation and create inequality of fortune, to corrupt public life, to banish men of independent mind and character from the public councils, to lower the tone of national representation, blunt public conscience, create false standards in the popular mind, to . . . divorce ethics from politics, and place politics upon the low level of a mercenary scramble, than any other single cause. Step by step . . . it has succeeded in obtaining control of the sovereign power of taxation, never hesitating at any alliance or the resort to any combination that promised to assist its purpose of perverting public taxation from its only true justification and function, of creating revenue for the support of the Government of the whole people into an engine for the selfish and private profit of allied beneficiaries and combinations called "trusts." . . . Thus it has done so much to throw legislation into the political market, where jobbers and chafferers take the place of statesmen.

After this sharp indictment of high protective tariffs in the United States, Bayard then gave a short picture of world politics in the last decade of the nineteenth century. The parallel between conditions then and conditions now, is so striking that some of his paragraphs deserve quotation. His words have such a familiar sound that they might well come from any speaker on the public platform today:

Never since the world was peopled has mankind stood in such anxious expectancy, awaiting the outcome of the immediate future, as in these closing years of the nineteenth century. . . . In some countries consolidation of empire progresses remarkably and impressively, in others disintegration is equally signified. Old dynasties, in sorrowful impotency, are drifting helplessly on the surface of events, or sinking palpably and hopelessly into the sea of time. . . . Other nations appear glowing with sanguine self-confidence, in lusty vigor, and virility. . . . In some nations the hand of autocratic power . . . appears to tighten upon society. . . . Never were the destructive forces of warfare marshaled in such impressive array as we see them today; never before did earth shake under the measured tread of so many men armed and prepared to be armed; never in history were weapons so lethal, missiles so mighty, and explosives so terrific and powerful, or in hands so carefully drilled and instructed in their employment. . . . When I contemplate the autocratic power which is exercised in some countries today, . . . I ask, Where is the safety and personal freedom of the individual? [144]

144. *House Doc. 152*, 54 Cong., 1 sess., pp. 4-23.

E. J. Phelps, who had represented the United States at London during the first Cleveland Administration, had nothing but praise for Bayard's Edinburgh address. He heartily concurred in everything Bayard said about protection, which he regarded as "the worst calamity that ever befell our country." [145] Other prominent Americans were lavish in their praise of addresses that Bayard delivered in many parts of England. The following quotation from a letter of Barrett Wendell is typical:

Let me thank you, too, for the Bristol speech which I welcome doubly, both for itself and because it affords me a chance to tell you with what constant, sympathetic confidence I believe that the real American temper has followed and admired your course in England. The fact for which you have stood before us—the manly, self-respecting friendship of the two great branches of our race, seems to me the fact on which the whole future of the world must turn. If it be preserved, our ideals will dominate; if those who attack it prevail, the ideals we care most for must go. I cannot quite express, then, all the pleasure that such an utterance as your Bristol speech brings me.[146]

But this stream of praise for Bayard's addresses in England, was accompanied by a torrent of abuse from Republicans of every type, who bitterly resented the attacks upon their pet institution of high protective tariffs. Republican politicians had no intention of sitting in silence while Bayard berated them for their selfish outlook. They struck back with vigor, and succeeded in bringing great embarrassment to him at a time when Secretary Olney was engaged in an important enterprise of backstairs diplomacy. Between Olney and Republican politicos, Bayard was due for very difficult days.

D. SECRETARY OLNEY TRAINS HIS TWENTY-INCH GUN UPON GREAT BRITAIN

While Bayard was busily promoting the cause of Anglo-Saxon unity, many British and American publicists were engaged upon a similar mission, and the periodicals of both countries were filled with articles calling attention to the many ties that bound England and America closely together. W. T. Stead,[147] Sir George Clark,[148] A. S.

145. E. J. Phelps to Bayard, December 3, 1895, *Bayard MS.*
146. Barrett Wendell to Bayard, January 18, 1896, *ibid.*
147. Jennie A. Sloan, "Anglo-American Relations and the Venezuelan Boundary Dispute," *Hispanic-American Historical Review*, November, 1938, vol. 18, pp. 488ff.
148. "A Naval Union with Great Britain," *North American Review*, March, 1894, vol. 158, pp. 353-365.

White,[149] Lord Charles Beresford,[150] Lord Brassey,[151] Sir George Grey,[152] Sir Henry Howorth,[153] and Goldwin Smith,[154] rushed into print to preach the importance of establishing more intimate connections between the English-speaking peoples.

Although Andrew Carnegie [155] and Captain A. T. Mahan,[156] joined in this chorus of Anglo-Saxon unity, there were some Americans who still looked with suspicion upon Great Britain. In December, 1895, Theodore Roosevelt was actively denouncing "Anglomaniacs," and Henry Cabot Lodge was so belligerent that President Eliot denounced them both as "degenerated sons of Harvard." [157] In the *North American Review* for June, 1895, Lodge defined his position very clearly with reference to the Anglo-Venezuelan Boundary Controversy:

> Since 1844 England has continually pushed forward the line within which she has declined arbitration, and with each advance she has made an additional claim to more territory about which she would be willing to arbitrate. . . . It is easy also to appreciate England's natural and strong resentment toward a country she has injured as much as she has injured Venezuela. But, at the same time, let England's motives or feelings be what they may, we are concerned for the interests of the United States. . . . All that England has done has been a direct violation of the Monroe Doctrine, and she has quickened and increased her aggressions in proportion as the United States have appeared indifferent. The time has come for decisive action. The United States must either maintain the Monroe Doctrine and treat its infringement as an act of hostility or abandon it. . . . It is not too late to peacefully but firmly put an end to these territorial aggressions of Great Britain and to enforce the Monroe Doctrine so that no other power will be disposed to infringe upon it. But immediate action is necessary.[158]

149. "An Anglo-American Alliance," *ibid.,* April, 1894, vol. 158, pp. 484-493.
150. "Possibilities of an Anglo-American Alliance," *ibid.,* November, 1894, vol. 159, pp. 564-573.
151. "Imperial Federation for Naval Defense," *Nineteenth Century,* January, 1892, vol. 31, pp. 90-100.
152. "Federation for the Anglo-Saxon Race," *Humanitarian,* August, 1894, vol. 5, pp. 85-90.
153. London *Times,* April 25, 1895.
154. "Anglo-Saxon Union," *North American Review,* August, 1893, vol. 157, pp. 170-185.
155. "A Look Ahead," *ibid.,* June, 1893, vol. 156, pp. 685-710.
156. "Possibilities of an Anglo-Saxon Reunion," *ibid.,* November, 1894, vol. 159, pp. 551-563.
157. Henry F. Pringle, *Theodore Roosevelt* (N. Y. 1931), pp. 167-168.
158. H. C. Lodge, "England, Venezuela, and the Monroe Doctrine," *North American Review,* June, 1895, vol. 160, pp. 657-658. It was only to be expected that Theodore Roosevelt would find that Lodge's article in the *North American Review* was admirable, and the "most convincing showing of what England has done." Roosevelt then contacted George W. Smalley, the American correspondent of the London *Times,* and told him "as

In this sharp criticism of British policy in Venezuela, Senator Lodge expressed the views of a large number of Americans whose misgivings about British land-hunger in South America were confirmed by the serious disturbances in Nicaragua. In the spring and summer of 1895, the American press was filled with anti-English articles, and Secretary Gresham himself was becoming convinced that the position taken by Great Britain in the Guiana boundary dispute was both

. . . contradictory and palpably unjust. The British reports show, beyond question, that from time to time Great Britain advanced her pretensions to territory which she previously recognized as belonging to Venezuela. If Great Britain undertakes to maintain her present position on that question, we will be obliged, in view of the almost uniform attitude and policy of our government, to call a halt.[159]

Gresham, however, was not ready to "call a halt" in any peremptory way. He was still hopeful that an amicable solution of the controversy could be found, and he was in no mood to challenge Great Britain on behalf of Venezuela. In a confidential letter to Bayard, he outlined the situation:

Mr. Andrade called a few days ago and asked how you were getting on in London with the Venezuelan question: what progress, if any, you were making in inducing Great Britain to refer the controversy to arbitration. I replied that the controversy was one between Venezuela and Great Britain: that we sustained no such relation to his Government as made it our duty to take its place in the dispute: that whether we intervened or not would depend upon future developments: that we were aware of the efforts which his Government and certain Americans here had made to manufacture a sentiment through the American press which would force this administration to espouse Venezuela's side of the controversy: that Mr. Scruggs, our late Minister to Venezuela, and now employed by his legation here, had been exerting himself in that line.

I also informed him (we had received that information before you imparted it) that apparently in the hope of involving the United States in the controversy, his Government had made concessions to American citizens in the disputed territory. Of course Mr. Scruggs denied all this. I further stated that Venezuela should restore diplomatic relations with Great Britain without delay and proceed in the regular way to adjust the controversy. Certain Republican Senators and Members of the House, I have reason to believe,

---

plainly as mortal can," that the "general sentiment of the country was rather hostile to England and was very strong in support of the Monroe Doctrine." *Selections from the Correspondence of Theodore Roosevelt and Henry Cabot Lodge* (N. Y., 1925, 2 vols.), vol. 1, pp. 148, 168.

159. Secretary Gresham to Bayard, March 31, 1895, *Personal, Bayard MS.*

have encouraged Venezuela . . . in the adoption of policies for no higher purpose than embarrassing this administration. . . .

I must say that it appears to me at times that Lord Kimberley is somewhat of a Jingoist. Perhaps he is talking and acting with reference to the next election in Great Britain. In view of the action of Pro-consul Hatch and the other British subjects expelled from Nicaragua, I think the British demands are harsh. We now have conclusive evidence that the British subjects . . . who were arrested and expelled did encourage and influence others to participate in the disturbances at Bluefields in July, 1894. That Mr. Hatch was largely responsible for the uprising against Nicaragua there can scarcely be a doubt.

I sincerely hope that in dealing with the delicate question, Lord Kimberley will as far as possible avoid action which will embarrass us here.[160]

Bayard was happy to learn that he still retained Gresham's complete confidence, and he expressed his admiration for the "straightforward and disinterested administration" of the Department of State.[161] He little realized that Death was stalking Secretary Gresham, and that, under his successor, the attitude of the Department of State would undergo an abrupt change. In the meantime, Bayard was deeply pleased to learn that John Bassett Moore had written a clear exposition of the Monroe Doctrine for the New York *Evening Post*. It was a badly needed lesson for most Americans, and Mr. Moore himself hoped that a "little historical information (perhaps I might say unmixed with absolute historical ignorance) might have a good effect." [162]

In his article on the true meaning of the Monroe Doctrine, Mr. Moore gave a careful discussion of the background of the doctrine, and then remarked:

The Monroe Doctrine, in all its parts, was based upon the right of American states, whose independence we had acknowledged, to dispose of themselves as they saw fit. It was directed against the interposition of Eu-

160. Secretary Gresham to Bayard, April 23, 1895, *Confidential, Bayard MS*. See also, enclosed *memorandum* of the conversation between Gresham and Dr. Guzmán, April 18, 1895, *ibid*. When Gresham wrote this letter to Bayard he had already received Bayard's despatch of April 5, 1895, which reported that Lord Kimberley had shown him a map of the disputed territory along the Guiana boundary, "on which were delineated, in different colors, the three lines of delimitation. The line coloured in pink was the Schomburgk line, one of the terminal points of which was a short distance inside the mouth of the Orinoco, and which His Lordship stated was conclusively proven and established as a British possession, and would not be submitted to arbitration, but that the ownership of the territory intersected by the other two lines, they would be willing to submit to arbitration." Bayard to Secretary Gresham, April 5, 1895, *Great Britain, Despatches*, vol. 179, MS Dept. of State.

161. Bayard to Secretary Gresham, May 4, 1895, *Bayard Press Copy Book*, vol. 2, *Bayard MS*.

162. John Bassett Moore to Bayard, May 4, 1895, *Bayard MS*.

ropean powers to control their destiny against their will. . . . At the present time an idea seems to prevail that the Monroe Doctrine committed us to a kind of protectorate over the independent states of this hemisphere, in consequence of which we are required to espouse their quarrels, though we cannot control their conduct. To state this theory is to refute it. Like other independent nations, we are at liberty to act with some regard to our own interests. Our position is not that of an involuntary military force, at the beck and call of any American state that may stand in need of it. . . . We have not assumed to forbid European powers to settle their quarrels with American states by the use of force any more than we have hesitated to do so ourselves. . . .

The suggestion has lately been made in various quarters that it is a violation of the Monroe Doctrine for a European power to employ force against an American republic for the purpose of collecting a debt or satisfying a pecuniary demand. . . . There is nothing in President Monroe's declarations even remotely touching this subject. . . . The recent proceedings of the British at Corinto have in nowise involved the Monroe Doctrine.[163]

Bayard was in thorough agreement with this presentation by Mr. Moore of the principles of the Monroe Doctrine, and he was opposed to any needless American participation in the quarrels of the Latin American states. Moreover, he was deeply suspicious of the justice of many of these quarrels. In a letter to Robert T. Lincoln, he referred to the fact that during the years from 1885 to 1889 he had examined with care the Venezuelan situation, and had found that procrastination and insincerity

. . . were the chief stock in trade of our South American cousins. Political expansion in South American regions is not, in my belief, the intention or desire of Great Britain, but where a gold mine is discovered within sight of an ancient line of boundary, the greed of gold will cause that line to deflect. American cupidity is not wanting in the scramble, and there is a vigorous effort to use our flag to assist it in the campaign.[164]

Two days later, Bayard expressed himself along similar lines in a note to President Cleveland. If the Latin American countries were really independent of the United States they would continue to make their own treaties and would have to meet

. . . their own obligations. For the United States to place in the control of such a set of men the virtual control of peace and war with European Powers, would be simple madness. Annexation with responsible control

163. New York *Evening Post*, May 4, 1895.
164. Bayard to Robert T. Lincoln, May 9, 1895, *Bayard Press Copy Book*, vol. 2, *Bayard MS.*

would be better than the quasi-protectorate which Mr. Morgan and other jobbers in Central American interests desire us to assume under the delusion that the "Monroe Doctrine" was intended to lead us to such an impossible conclusion. When our countrymen comprehend the consequences of committing our National welfare to the virtual control of South and Central American politicians and jobbers, they will recoil aghast. As to Mr. Scruggs, I am disposed to have as little as possible to do with him. . . . He is one of Blaine's men and following the moral code of his class, is now acting as the attorney of a foreign government to which he was for years accredited as the confidential envoy of the United States. Such employment is not merely indelicate but dangerous, and dishonorable.

I have sent some despatches to Secretary Gresham which related to the Venezuelan situation, and I wish, in the midst of your many cares, you would read them. If we are to induce confidence in our impartial friendship, and be fitted for the office of Arbitrator, we must be disinterested, i.e., *not* interested in the subject matter in dispute. If Venezuela has granted concession of lands and mines in the disputed territory to citizens of the United States, then our Government is in a degree disqualified for the role of Judge.[165]

President Cleveland did not share Bayard's deep suspicions of South American politicians, and he did not have Bayard's faith in the good intentions of Great Britain. He sharply disapproved of the way the British Government had acted towards Nicaragua, and he let his feelings have full rein in his conversations with his intimate friend, Don M. Dickinson. In a speech in Detroit, in the early part of May, 1895, Dickinson denounced British policy in Nicaragua and in Venezuela, and he made an allusion to Bayard that seemed far from friendly. He thought that Americans might "indulge in a reciprocity of polite phrasing and post-prandial exuberance, if our alert watchmen will meantime keep an eye upon our good friends across the Atlantic, especially when, having appropriated Africa, the islands and even the rocks of the sea, and wherever else force or intrigue may gain a footing, they begin to take an interest, not altogether born of curiosity or of a purely Christianizing spirit, in this hemisphere." [166]

This speech by Dickinson, immediately after a visit to the White House, was regarded as significant in many quarters,[167] and there is

165. Bayard to President Cleveland, May 11, 1895, *Cleveland MS.*
166. Allan Nevins, *Grover Cleveland,* p. 632. See also, Washington *Post,* May 11, 1895.
167. Bayard regarded Dickinson's speech as a "flow of contentious bosh." Bayard to Secretary Gresham, May 25, 1895, *Bayard Press Copy Book,* vol. 2, *Bayard MS.* Dickinson wrote to Bayard to assure him that he had not intended to cast any reflections upon Bayard's conduct as Ambassador, and Bayard replied that it would be quite impossible for him to suppose that Dickinson had "at any time, the slightest intention of saying or

little doubt that the President was getting ready to adopt a more positive tone towards Great Britain with reference to South American problems. As early as March 31, 1895, Gresham had expressed to Bayard the belief that the position taken by Great Britain in the Guiana boundary controversy was "contradictory and palpably unjust." He had also conveyed the warning that if Great Britain maintained "her position on that question," the American Government would have to "call a halt." [168] Cleveland had frequent conversations with Gresham concerning the Venezuelan situation, and on May 9, 1895, he wrote a confidential note to Charles S. Fairchild, in which he confessed that affairs in Venezuela were "liable to assume a condition calling on our part for the greatest care and good management." [169]

Bayard himself realized that in the United States there were many persons who were in favor of "calling a halt" upon British activities in Nicaragua and in Venezuela. If such action were taken, it was possible that a belligerent tone would creep into the notes from the United States to Great Britain, and Bayard deprecated any serious friction between the two countries. The recent utterances of Senator Morgan and his associates were very disquieting, and their

... swords of lath, and shields of pasteboard are so ridiculous and unworthy. The Nicaraguan mountain has brought forth its very little mouse, and if there is any sense of the ludicrous left in the American people, they must be shaking their sides in inextinguishable laughter over Morgan and Calhoun. . . .

I regret very much the vaporing tone of defiance and absurd suspicion towards this Country that so many of our countrymen seem unable to avoid. They are unworthy, and can only impair that position which I am anxious our Country should hold towards the outer world of frank, fearless courtesy and good faith. There is no possible justification for a breach in the friendly relations between this Country and our own.[170]

Bayard did admit, however, that the Nicaraguan episode had

doing anything to give me pain, or reflect unkindly upon what I had done or was doing." Bayard to Dickinson, September 7, 1895, *Bayard Press Copy Book*, vol. 3, *Bayard MS*.
    168. *Ante*, p. 695.
    169. President Cleveland to Charles S. Fairchild, May 9, 1895, Allan Nevins, *Letters of Grover Cleveland, 1850–1908* (N. Y. 1933), pp. 391-392.
    170. Bayard to Senator George Gray, May 18, 1895, *Bayard Press Copy Book*, vol. 2, *Bayard MS*. In a letter to George F. Parker, May 25, 1895, Bayard also remarked: "I can discern no just cause of dissension between the United States and Great Britain, and no intent or purpose of the latter inimical to the happiness, honor, and prosperity of our own. . . . There is no question now open between the United States and Great Britain that needs any but frank, amicable, and just treatment. I deprecate these appeals to excitement and unfounded resentments." *Bayard MS*.

aroused resentment in the United States, and had produced in many quarters a feeling of hostility towards Great Britain. His feelings in this regard were expressed in his last personal letter to Secretary Gresham:

> I wrote you and have written the President since the pasteboard structure of Morgan and his Brother Jingoes has toppled down and the "British occupation of Nicaragua" has passed like a ship in the night. It is amazing what noise a small explosion can produce. There was an element of personal irritability infused into the Nicaraguan episode which cast a disagreeable hue over the British *style* of demand, and the unwisdom of which, I think, came to be felt in the Foreign Office.[171]

This British "style of demand" was not pleasing to Richard Olney, who succeeded Gresham as Secretary of State.[172] Gresham's death was a severe blow to Bayard. Bayard had long been an admirer of Gresham, and had recommended his name to Cleveland as an excellent choice as a member of the Cabinet. Gresham returned this cordial feeling, and he had great respect for Bayard's viewpoint. In his conversations with public men, he invariably spoke in high terms of Bayard, and in this regard the following comment of Oscar S. Straus is revealing: "There is only one man who could replace Mr. Gresham in the Department at this juncture, and I believe that man, he himself would select, if the dead could speak to the living. Of course, I mean you, for I have heard him repeatedly refer with esteem and affection to you, and to the position you had taken in certain matters." [173]

Cleveland had no intention of recalling Bayard from London and making him Secretary of State. He had become accustomed to lean upon Olney for assistance when some Administrative crisis occurred, and the direct and forceful manner of this Boston barrister made a strong appeal to Cleveland who had much the same rough-hewn per-

171. Bayard to Secretary Gresham, May 25, 1895, *Bayard Press Copy Book*, vol. 2, Bayard MS.

172. Olney assumed the office of Secretary of State on June 8, 1895.

173. Oscar S. Straus to Bayard, June 1, 1895, *Bayard MS*. It is significant that Secretary Gresham repeatedly employed John Bassett Moore upon special tasks for which he was so eminently fitted. Moore was a close friend of Bayard, and was an important link between Bayard and Gresham. In a letter to Bayard, August 28, 1894, Henry L. Bryan remarks: "Mr. Moore is still here . . . and is engaged very much with the Secretary in unraveling some of the knotty questions which Nicaragua and Great Britain have each raised, besides lots of others." *Bayard MS*.

In a personal letter to Secretary Olney, June 8, 1895, Bayard expressed his personal gratification that he should "thus be brought into close relations with you in the performance of what are now our joint duties in behalf of our country. . . . I rejoice that you now take his place, and hope it may be in my power to carry into effect those measures of administration which shall be entrusted to me here by the President and yourself." *Bayard Press Copy Book*, vol. 2, *Bayard MS*.

sonality. In the Pullman strike affair, Cleveland had quickly abandoned
his so-called liberalism, and had adopted posthaste the belligerent con-
servatism of Olney. Professor Nevins admits that in this case, Cleveland
did his duty as "Olney unhappily showed it to him." Then in defence
of Cleveland's "unfortunate course," he hastens to add that "this Presidential stand required courage." [174] What he really meant to say was
that in this crisis Cleveland had the courage of Olney's convictions. In
the Venezuelan incident we have another exhibition of this same utter
reliance upon Olney's viewpoint, and once more we find the President
fortifying himself with borrowed courage.

Olney's influence over Cleveland increased as the years passed on,
and in the Guiana boundary controversy it is amazing to see how it
persisted to the end of Cleveland's life. There is no other way to understand the disingenuous, or perhaps merely biased way that Cleveland
treated this controversy in his essay in the volume, *Presidential Problems*. Olney was by far the strongest personality in the Cleveland
Cabinet, and his influence was far-reaching. In all his associations he
had been an aggressive leader who was determined to brush all opposition aside in a most ruthless manner. At home he was a real Autocrat
of the Breakfast Table. His family had to study his moods and gratify
his whims. If he was silent, the family remained mute; if he chose to
talk, he directed the line of conversation. He even carried this domestic
tyranny to the point of forbidding a younger daughter to enter his
home in the event of her marriage, despite the fact that he had encouraged the match. In his business relations, he was cold and reserved,
but his ability and industry brought him reasonable success. His pattern of life was as inflexible and as uniform as the design upon a set
of chinaware, and he despised those little detours along the way of life
that lead to delightful surprises. He was richly endowed with a certain
stubborn quality that is often confused with courage, and he possessed
an abundance of self-confidence that led him to look upon himself as
some modern Ulysses who alone could bend the bow of circumstance
that was thrust into his hands in 1895.[175]

174. Allan Nevins, *Grover Cleveland*, p. 627.
175. In his *Life of Richard Olney* (N. Y. 1923), pp. 12-19, Henry James makes the following comments upon Olney's personality: "Somehow his aspect suggested . . . a man
whom it would be hard to overthrow; . . . a hard-thinking, accomplishing, ruthless being
like one of those modern war-tanks which proceeds across the roughest ground, heedless
of opposition, deaf alike to messages from friends and cries from the foe, able to crush
every person and every obstacle that gets between it and its chosen objective. . . . His
appetite for work and learning amounted to a 'rapacity.' Such elasticity and geniality as

While Olney was studying the documents in the Guiana boundary controversy in preparation for his famous note of July 20, Bayard was still hoping that nothing would arise to disturb the even course of Anglo-American relations. The fact that many Americans were feeling in a belligerent mood towards England was made manifest to him in many ways. On June 24, 1895, in the presence of some English friends, Abram Hewitt asked Bayard if he "felt like going to war with England *now*." Bayard's reaction to this sudden question is given in his *Diary* for that day:

> As I have had to face the loud-voiced mob in my country, and to meet the sneers of Radical Republicans and the foolish Irishmen because I have sought to maintatin "peace with honor" towards Great Britain, it was hardly worth while for one who has never said one word of friendly support of me or of the Administration with which I was associated, to refer to it now. He laid himself open to a sharp reply, but I made none—none whatever.[176]

The fall of the Rosebery Ministry on June 24, 1895, appeared to Bayard as an indication that Anglo-American relations would now enter upon a smoother course.[177] Lord Salisbury was the head of the new Ministry, and he would hold the office of Foreign Secretary. The July elections in England resulted in an overwhelming victory of the Unionist Party, and thus made Salisbury's position a strong one.[178]

On July 10 Bayard paid a visit to the Foreign Office, and was greeted in a "very gracious" manner by Lord Salisbury.[179] In a personal letter to President Cleveland, he gives his impression of the Salisbury Government:

> The Cabinet with Lord Salisbury at its head is an unusually strong one and will have the advantage of united counsels, and not be dependent upon groups of politicians discordant upon so many leading subjects, and with no

---

had been the portion of his youth, dried out of him in those years. . . . The springs never flooded his nature; were never allowed to soften his passions, his resentments, his ambitions. . . . One pities him as the years go on."

176. June 24, 1895, *Bayard MS.*

177. In his *Diary*, July 4, 1895, Bayard remarks as follows: "Lord Peel wears well. He thinks as I do that Rosebery's 'record' as Prime Minister is a very poor one, and his late declaration that his late tenure of office was 'not merely Purgatory—but Hell' was strangely foolish. To me Lord Rosebery seems a spoiled child, and something of an Athenian in his love of novelties. Office is a toy to him, and to win the Derby, a much more serious matter than to carry through an important public measure. Besides all that, surely such a marriage—to secure wealth—is a very poor ideal! Yet, without title and without wealth he would be 'nowhere.' " *Bayard MS.*

178. London *Spectator*, July 20, August 3, 1895.

179. *Memorandum* written by Bayard after a conversation with Lord Salisbury, July 10, 1895, *Bayard MS.*

distinct principle or purpose in view. . . . I am anticipating a more satisfactory condition of things in the treatment and settlement of questions
between the United States and Great Britain, as the present Government,
having a decided majority in Parliament, will feel more secure and consequently able to be more definite in its action. I shall await your instructions
respecting Venezuela with much interest, not to say anxiety.

The condition of Venezuela, like most of the South American Governments, is difficult to comprehend, and may always be considered unreliable.
. . . None of these South American states hesitate, without the slightest
consultation with the United States, to refer to *European* arbitrament
questions of boundary or of any other nature. . . . Their relation to the
United States is very shifting and seems chiefly to be controlled in the use
of our name and national power as a shield against the demands or aggressions of European Powers. . . . If the United States are to have responsibility, they must have conceded power and jurisdiction. Our liabilities
(relative as they are) should be well defined, and the principle upon which
we assume . . . and execute them, should be capable of clear statement, and
worthy of moral, political, and financial support. . . .

I am glad to say that I believe we can deal more satisfactorily, because
more definitely, with the present Government here than with the outgoing
one.[180]

This letter made little impression upon Cleveland, who had now
fallen under the spell of Olney's belligerence. Throughout June, Olney
had been hard at work on the task of drafting a long note which would
sharply challenge the British position in the Guiana boundary dispute.
He was determined to discard the diplomatic language of Secretary
Gresham, and by giving his note the force of an ultimatum, he would
compel the British Government to pay instant heed to the suggestion
of arbitration.[181] After working in Washington until July 2, Olney
carried a draft of his note to Gray Gables and turned it over to President Cleveland. The Cleveland household was somewhat upset over
the arrival of a new member of the family in the shape of a "plump
loud-voiced little girl." Perhaps his fatherly pride strengthened the
President's resolve to take a firm stand with regard to the Venezuelan
boundary question. At any rate, he sent a short note to Olney in which
he gurgled his approval:

I read your deliverance on Venezuelan affairs the day you left it with me.
It's the best thing of the kind I have ever read and it leads to a conclusion
that one cannot escape if he tries—that is, if there is anything of the Monroe

180. Bayard to President Cleveland, July 10, 1895, *Cleveland MS.*
181. According to Mrs. Gresham, *Life of W. Q. Gresham*, vol. 2, pp. 794-795, her husband had not intended to inject any belligerent note in his communication to the British
Government: "There was to be no ultimatum as my husband had prepared it."

Doctrine at all. You show there is a great deal of that and place it, I think, on better and more defensible ground than any of your predecessors— *or mine.*[182]

Although the President thought the note should be softened "here and there," he made very few suggestions, and after consulting with several members of the Cabinet, Olney sent the instruction to Bayard under the date of July 20, 1895. It was a remarkable instruction, and it clearly indicated to all students of the dispute that Olney believed that Great Britain would recoil from a mere show of truculence. In his second paragraph, Olney reveals that he is once more filing a legal brief rather than writing a dispassionate instruction. Speaking of the claims of Venezuela, he said that out of moderation and prudence she has "contented herself with claiming the Essequibo line, the line of the Essequibo River, that is, to be the true boundary between Venezuela and British Guiana."

This claim on the part of Venezuela was absurd, but Olney gives no indication that he so regarded it, and he seems bent upon delivering a broadside against Great Britain. The repeated offers of the British Government to settle the controversy in a fair and friendly spirit, are ignored by Olney, who is interested only in framing an indictment. After a decidedly partisan presentation of the background of the boundary controversy, Olney remarks:

> The accuracy of the foregoing analysis of the existing status cannot, it is believed, be challenged. It shows that status to be such that those charged with the interests of the United States are now forced to determine exactly what those interests are and what course of action they require. It compels them to decide to what extent, if any, the United States may and should intervene in a controversy between and primarily concerning only Great Britain and Venezuela, and to decide how far it is bound to see that the integrity of Venezuela territory is not impaired by the pretensions of its powerful antagonist.

Olney answers this question by declaring that

> . . . there are circumstances under which a nation may justly interpose in a controversy to which two or more other nations are the direct and immediate parties. . . . The doctrine is ordinarily expressed in terms of the most general character and is perhaps incapable of more specific statement. It is declared in substance that a nation may avail itself of this right whenever what is done or proposed by any of the parties primarily concerned is a serious and direct menace to its own integrity, tranquillity, or welfare.

182. Henry James, *Richard Olney*, pp. 110-111.

It was ridiculous to suppose that British possession of some territory along the Venezuelan boundary was a serious menace to American security. But Olney appeared to be in great fright over this British bogey-man, and he decided to banish him by reference to the Monroe Doctrine. After hurriedly passing over the non-colonization principle of that doctrine, he develops at length the principle of non-intervention that was voiced by President Monroe. The precise scope of this rule of non-intervention

. . . cannot be too clearly apprehended. It does not establish any general protectorate by the United States over other American states. It does not relieve any American state from its obligations as fixed by International Law nor prevent any European power directly interested from enforcing obligations or from inflicting merited punishment for the breach of them. It does not contemplate any interference in the internal affairs of any American state or in the relations between it and other American states. It does not justify any attempt on our part to change the established form of government of any American state or to prevent the people of such state from altering that form according to their own will and pleasure. The rule has but a single purpose and object. It is that no Eureopean power or combination of European powers shall forcibly deprive an American state of the right and power of self-government and of shaping for itself its own political fortunes and destinies.

After this cautious statement, Olney becomes more reckless in his language, and declares that the Monroe Doctrine was "unquestionably due to the inspiration of Great Britain, who at once gave to it an open and unqualified adhesion which has never been withdrawn." According to Professor Perkins, this last statement of Olney should "have made George Canning turn in his grave." [183] But Olney did not stop with this bit of misinformation. He went on to assert that this rule of non-intervention had been "acted upon by the executive branch of the Government for more than seventy years." Once more Professor Perkins shows the inaccuracy of this statement by referring to the fact that from 1826 to 1844, the Monroe Doctrine went "unnoticed by the executive. Nor did the Whig administration of Taylor and Fillmore pin its faith to the principles of 1823. No *public* pronouncement on the Doctrine had come from the first administration of that same Grover Cleveland whom the Secretary of State was now engaged in serving." [184]

The same looseness of statement is discernible in Olney's claim that

183. Dexter Perkins, *The Monroe Doctrine, 1867–1907*, p. 157.
184. *Ibid.*, pp. 157-158.

the Monroe Doctrine "was the controlling factor in the emancipation of South America and to it the independent states which now divide that region between them are largely indebted for their very existence." South American independence was really assured in 1822, by the memorable victories of the armies under Bolívar and San Martín. British legionaries and indirect British assistance played a far more important role than any aid that came from the United States.[185] Olney's statement about the importance of the Monroe Doctrine in the South American struggle for freedom is typical of the tone of exaggeration and misrepresentation that permeates his entire note.

Not content with these mistakes, Olney blunders into further historical errors. He dogmatically states that "the most striking single achievement" to be credited to the Monroe Doctrine "is the evacuation of Mexico by the French upon the termination of the civil war." There is little doubt that this statement is quite false,[186] but Olney had small concern for historical accuracy.

After this perversion of history, Olney then proceeds to make some broad statements that were decidedly questionable. He was certain that

. . . distance and three thousand miles of intervening ocean make any permanent political union between an European and an American state unnatural and inexpedient. . . . Each great European power . . . today maintains enormous armies and fleets in self-defense and for protection against any other European power or powers. What have the states of America to do with that condition of things? . . . What is true of the material, is no less true of what may be termed the moral interests involved. . . . Europe as a whole is monarchical, and, . . . is committed to the monarchical principle. America, on the other hand, is devoted to the exactly opposite principle, to the idea that every people has an inalienable right of self-government. . . . If . . . the forcible intrusion of European powers into American politics is to be deprecated, if, as it is to be deprecated, it should be resisted and prevented, such resistance and prevention must come from the United States.

In view of the fact that the British connection with Canada antedated the Monroe Doctrine for more than a half-century and had been a most fortunate bond for both Canada and the Mother Country,

185. A. Hasbrouck, *Foreign Legionaries in the Liberation of Spanish America* (N. Y. 1928).

186. C. A. Duniway, "Reasons for the Withdrawal of the French from Mexico," *Report of American Historical Association, 1902*, vol. 1, pp. 315-328; Dexter Perkins, *The Monroe Doctrine, 1826–1867* (Baltimore, 1933) pp. 515ff; Count Otto zu Stolberg-Wernigerode, *Germany and the United States of America During the Era of Bismarck* (Reading, Pa., 1937), pp. 77-85.

Olney's assertion that this tie was "unnatural and inexpedient" was the height of impudence and diplomatic bad manners.[187] Moreover, it was ridiculous to place England in the class of European monarchical powers who were opposed to democracy. The democratic principle had nothing to fear from British action in Venezuela. Olney, however, was bent upon creating suspicions in the American mind concerning British policy in Latin America, and he strongly intimated that "the safety and welfare of the United States" were menaced by a slight extension of the boundary of British Guiana. England, like other European Powers was "only too liable to succumb to the temptations offered by seeming special opportunities for its own aggrandizement," and this spirit of imperialism would have to be checked as far as South America was concerned. This task of teaching Europe to keep its hands off the Western Hemisphere belonged to the United States: "Today the United States is practically sovereign on this continent, and its fiat is law upon the subjects to which it confines its interposition. . . . Its infinite resources combined with its isolated position render it master of the situation and practically invulnerable as against any or all other powers."

After this sophomoric boasting of American strength, Olney passed on to a criticism of British reluctance to submit to arbitration the question of the title to all the territory in dispute along the Venezuela boundary. The British demand that

. . . her right to a portion of the disputed territory shall be acknowledged before she will consent to an arbitration as to the rest, seems to stand upon nothing but her own *ipse dixit*. She says to Venezuela, in substance: "You can get none of the debatable land by force, because you are not strong enough; you can get none by treaty, because I will not agree; and you can take your chance of getting a portion by arbitration, only if you first agree to abandon to me such other portion as I may designate." It is not perceived how such an attitude can be defended nor how it is reconcilable with that love of justice and fair play so eminently characteristic of the English race.

187. James W. Garner, in his volume entitled *American Foreign Policies* (N. Y. 1928), pp. 113-114, makes the following comments: "Another passage in the note of the Secretary of State which not unnaturally gave offense to the English, because it was regarded as not only out of place but contrary to the facts, was the statement that 'three thousand miles of intervening ocean make any permanent political union between a European and an American state unnatural and inexpedient.' . . . The necessary implication of these words was, that the union between Great Britain and Canada, not to mention others, was both 'inexpedient' and 'unnatural.' It is sufficient to say that the Canadians . . . entertain a contrary opinion; and there is no evidence that they consider their membership in the British Commonwealth of Nations as either unnatural or inexpedient."

. . . It seems therefore quite impossible that this position of Great Britain should be assented to by the United States. . . . In these circumstances, the duty of the President appears to him unmistakable and imperative. Great Britain's assertion of title to the disputed territory, combined with her refusal to have that title investigated, being a substantial appropriation of the territory to her own use, not to protest and give warning that the transaction will be regarded as injurious to the interests of the people of the United States as well as oppressive in itself, would be to ignore an established policy with which the honor and welfare of this country are closely identified. While the measures necessary or proper for the vindication of that policy are to be determined by another branch of the Government, it is clearly for the Executive to leave nothing undone which may tend to render such determination unnecessary.

In the final paragraph of this long instruction, Bayard was directed to lay the matter before Lord Salisbury, and expressed the "earnest hope of the President that the conclusion will be on the side of arbitration." If he were disappointed in this hope, and if Great Britain continued to maintain her position with reference to the Guiana boundary, such action would "greatly embarrass the future relations between this country and Great Britain." [188]

In concluding his argument that ties of a most intimate and indissoluble nature existed between Latin America and the United States, Olney made the following remarkable statement: "The states of America, South as well as North, by geographical proximity, by natural sympathy, by similarity of governmental institutions, are friends and allies, commercially and politically, of the United States." In discussing these remarks, Carl R. Fish expressed the opinion that in this sentence, Secretary Olney could "scarcely have compressed more errors into fewer words." [189]

It was very apparent to any student of the situation, that Olney's note was unique in diplomatic literature. Its patent inaccuracy and its cheap bravado were clear indications that Olney was carrying over into his position as Secretary of State the same spirit of belligerence that was so manifest when he held the office of Attorney General.[190] It was safe

188. Secretary Olney to Bayard, July 20, 1895, *Foreign Relations, 1895,* pt. 1, pp. 545-562.

189. *American Diplomacy* (N. Y. 1919), p. 395. See also, Hiram Bingham, *The Monroe Doctrine; an Obsolete Shibboleth* (New Haven, 1913), pp. 19ff.

190. With regard to Olney and his belligerent attitude towards England, Judge John Bassett Moore, in a letter to the author, July 29, 1939, remarks: "Olney had been urging Cleveland to beat the tomtom in the Venezuelan matter before Gresham died. Gresham was a very honest man, and his instinctive dislike of Olney was not wholly due to his inclination to suspect what he called the 'Yankee character.'"

enough to browbeat railway strikers, but it was a very different matter to treat a great nation like England as though she were some petty culprit caught in the act of thievery. Bayard rightly resented Olney's attitude in this matter, and he hoped that President Cleveland would not lend his support to an anti-English program that pandered to political prejudices.[191] He did not realize how completely the President had fallen under the control of the Secretary of State.

On August 7 Bayard went to the Foreign Office and read to Lord Salisbury the contents of Olney's instruction of July 20. Salisbury expressed his "regret and surprise" that it had been considered

. . . necessary to present so far-reaching and important a principle and such wide and profound policies of international action in relation to a subject so comparatively small. . . . To make proper reply to so able and profound an argument, on a subject so important in its relations, would necessarily involve a great deal of labor, and possibly of time, both of which would be certainly bestowed. . . . He said it was his desire that Great Britain should be perfectly just in the matter, but that arbitration should only apply to cases where there was a real basis of justice and right, and was not demandable for *any* claim that could be set up, for otherwise a nation might be called upon to arbitrate its very existence.

Before closing the interview with Lord Salisbury, Bayard "dwelt upon the expression of the earnest desire of the President to receive a reply in time to enable him to lay the subject before Congress in his next annual message in December." He also alluded to the importance of keeping this question in the "atmosphere of serene and elevated effort."[192]

In a personal letter to President Cleveland, Bayard indicated that he

191. It would be difficult to estimate the effect of political pressure upon Olney in the summer of 1895. A possible straw in the political wind is the following letter from Representative Paschal to Olney, October 23, 1895: "You are right, now go ahead. Turn this Venezuela question up or down, North, South, East, or West, and it is a 'winner'—pardon the slang—morally, legally, politically, or financially, your attitude at this juncture is the trump card. It is, however, when you come to diagnose the country's internal ills that the possibilities of 'blood and iron' loom up immediately.

"Why, Mr. Secretary, just think of how angry the anarchistic, socialistic, and populistic boil appears on our political surface, and who knows how deep its roots extend or ramify? One cannon-shot across the bow of a British boat in defense of this principle will knock more *pus* out of it than would suffice to inoculate and corrupt our people for the next two centuries. . . . I believe scarcely a discordant voice will be heard 'mid the welcoming chorus of applause this country will send up from ocean to ocean, from Lakes to Gulf, the hour the stars and stripes bid defiance to British greed, aggression, and insolence." Matthew Josephson, *The Politicos, 1885–1896* (New York, 1938), pp. 624-625.

192. Bayard to Secretary Olney, August 9, 1895, *Great Britain, Despatches*, vol. 180, MS Dept. of State.

had placed Olney's instruction of July 20 before Lord Salisbury. It was evident that the principles involved were

. . . serious and the facts complicated, as necessarily must be the case where responsibility for the acts and rights of an independent third party is assumed. . . . I drew Lord Salisbury's attention to your desire to have his reply as soon as possible, and when it is received no time shall be lost in placing it before you.[193]

Some weeks later, Bayard wrote to Secretary Olney that he was still awaiting a reply from the Foreign Office to the instruction with reference to the instruction concerning Venezuela:

Anxious as I am to gain the earliest intimation of their intentions, I feel indisposed to express it, or to indicate our apprehension that the representations of my government may not receive their full share of respect and high courtesy. But I shall lose no proper opportunity of obtaining information, nor fail instantly to make it known to you.[194]

In the meantime, in the United States there was a fast-growing spirit of belligerence. This found expression in many speeches which pledged strong support to the Monroe Doctrine. At the patriotic exercises held by Tammany Hall on July 4, 1895, ex-Governor Campbell, of Ohio, expressed the opinion that the policy of Great Britain looked like "an effort to force the United States to abandon the Monroe Doctrine." This effort should be met "in the same spirit" that was so unmistakably shown in 1866, when the French troops of Louis Napoleon were ordered from the soil of Mexico.[195]

Another ex-Governor of Ohio, Joseph B. Foraker, was equally emphatic about the maintenance of the Monroe Doctrine. The American people should stand up "boldly and under all circumstances for the application of the Monroe Doctrine to American affairs throughout the Western Hemisphere. Every Central and South American Republic should be made to feel . . . that it has a friend in the United States, able and willing to protect them at all times from European colonization and oppression." [196]

Even Captain Mahan, who certainly was not anti-English, had no doubt that "an undertaking like that of Great Britain in Egypt, if

193. Bayard to President Cleveland, September 10, 1895, *Bayard Press Copy Book*, vol. 3, *Bayard MS*.

194. Bayard to Secretary Olney, October 21, 1895, *Bayard Press Copy Book*, vol. 3, *Bayard MS*.

195. Philadelphia *North American*, July 5, 1895.

196. Washington *Post*, September 11, 1895.

attempted in this hemisphere, by a non-American State, would not be tolerated by us if able to prevent it." [197]

These expressions of opinion pointed the way towards a strong public sentiment in favor of lending American support to Venezuela in her dispute with England over the Guiana boundary. In the early part of October, 1895, there were many rumors that Secretary Olney had sent a stiff note to Great Britain with reference to this dispute,[198] and the Chicago *Tribune* held to the view that "if President Cleveland has taken the ground it is said that he has, he will have the support of the American people regardless of party." [199]

Just at this time, Lord Pauncefote made a speech in Ottawa, Canada, in which he made a pointed reference to the Guiana boundary dispute:

> Great Britain has certain well defined territory there which has been occupied for generations, about which there can be no successful dispute, and which, of course, would not be submitted to arbitration, as the case does not admit of it, our title being perfectly clear. On the other hand, outside the line at Marchmond, there is territory about which there might possibly be dispute, as the title is not so clearly defined. This, I apprehend, would be a matter for arbitration, and doubtless, if the question arises, will be so submitted.[200]

In commenting upon Pauncefote's speech, the Washington *Post* declared that America's "proper course in this matter . . . is to decide where England's rights end and Venezuela's rights begin, and to plant ourselves upon that line sword in hand." [201]

The Atlanta *Constitution* was just as vehement as the Washington *Post,* and it was certain that "if we do not wake up very soon, England will have all of Central and South America under her control, and the United States will be forced back into the ranks of the third and fourth class commercial powers." [202] The New Orleans *Picayune* thought that the Monroe Doctrine should be the "foundation of the entire foreign policy" of the American Government,[203] and the Chicago *Tribune* had no doubt that in case of emergency the "United States will be found defending the Monroe Doctrine not only with rifles but with cannon, should the necessity arise." [204] The New York *Times* issued a grave warning that the United States "could not with indifference see a

197. A. T. Mahan, "The Future in Relation to American Sea Power," *Harper's New Monthly Magazine,* October, 1895, vol. 91, p. 775. See also, Captain W. D. Puleston, *Mahan* (New Haven, 1939), pp. 168-171.   198. Washington *Post,* October 3, 1895.
199. October 5, 1895.   200. Washington *Post,* October 6, 1895.
201. October 6, 1895.   202. October 13, 1895.
203. October 13, 1895.   204. October 16, 1895.

European power, not even England, invade a weak South American State, and, on no better title than the highwayman establishes to the traveler's purse, rob her of a sixth part of her territory." [205]

The situation was further complicated by a report that the British Government had sent a strong ultimatum to Venezuela with reference to an attack upon some British police near the confluence of the Rivers Cuyuni and Yuruari. Even the London *Times* thought there was "something intensely objectionable" in the idea "of addressing an Ultimatum to Venezuela. Just as no big boy at school will hit a little one unless he is absolutely obliged to do so, so no Great Power likes to hold the muzzle of a pistol at the head of an insignificant State." [206]

On October 22 the New York *World* tried to embarrass Anglo-American relations a little further by publishing a letter from its London correspondent which purported to give an account of Bayard's interview with Lord Salisbury, when he delivered the instruction of July 20. The British Foreign Secretary was reported to have been curt to Bayard upon this occasion, and to have interrupted his reading with the tart remark that England did not recognize the Monroe Doctrine. [207] Bayard promptly denied the authenticity of this report,[208] and the London *Times* assured its readers that the story in the New York *World* was "incorrect." [209]

Despite these denials by Bayard and by the London *Times*, there persisted a feeling in certain American circles that the British Government would pursue its policy in Venezuela without much regard for American opinion. Senator Lodge believed that British actions with

205. October 22, 1895.
206. October 22, 1895. The British Foreign Office hastily assured Bayard that this ultimatum to Venezuela "had nothing to do with the Boundary question and was confined to the matter of the seizure of the British Police and the injuries sustained by British subjects." J. R. Carter to Bayard, October 22, 1895, *Bayard MS.*
207. New York *World*, October 22, 1895.
208. *Ibid.*, October 24, 1895. Ballard Smith, who was responsible for the story in the *World*, came to see Bayard on October 23 with reference to his report of the alleged interview between Bayard and Lord Salisbury. He told Bayard that "he had his information from one who had read Lord Salisbury's memo in his own handwriting. . . . Of course he did not communicate the name of his informant nor did I ask it—I merely said it was a gross breach of trust, at which he smiled. I told him I had . . . made a full memo of all that took place, and with that in mind, repeated my denial of the statements made." *Memorandum* written by Bayard, October 23, 1895, *Bayard MS.* On November 3, 1895, Mr. Terrell, the American Minister at Constantinople, sent Bayard a letter in which he remarked: "I deem it my duty to inform you that one Ballard Smith, the liveried lackey of the Hungarian Jew who owns *The World*, . . . is a scoundrel, who, if you trust, will not scruple to betray you." *Bayard MS.*
209. London *Times*, October 24, 1895.

regard to the Guiana boundary were a "gross violation of the Monroe Doctrine." The President and Congress, Republicans and Democrats, would be united "in resisting at whatever cost any seizure or armed invasion of any American territory." [210] Senator Chandler was in accord with the views of Senator Lodge, and he went so far as to prophesy that "war between England and the United States is inevitable." [211]

With important Republicans talking in terms of war with England, the British Foreign Office should have expedited a reply to Olney's note of July 20. After several intimations to Bayard that he was anxiously awaiting a reply from the British Government, Olney finally sent the following cipher telegram:

Congress meets two weeks from next Monday. President's Message preparing. Without betraying uneasiness, and pursuing dignified attitude hitherto maintained, can you not ascertain and report, whether any immediate answer to my 804 is contemplated, or whether the Eastern Question precludes consideration of all others. If other engrossing question and anxieties prevent answer to my 804 within the time therein requested, surely it would be courteous for the British Government so to state and indicate a not distant time when reply may be expected.[212]

Four days later, Olney again telegraphed to Bayard with regard to England's answer to his instruction of July 20, and in a letter of the same date (November 20) he expressed the view that it "would not be regarded as courteous in this country if the British Government should neither answer the despatch before the assembling of Congress nor give any reason for not answering it." [213]

After Olney had sent this instruction to Bayard, he received a telegram from the American Embassy at London informing him that a copy of the British reply to the American note would be sent the following Saturday (November 23).[214] On November 22 Olney received another telegram from London which stated that Lord Salisbury was

210. New York *World*, October 26, 1895.
211. *Ibid.*, October 29, 1895. Moorfield Storey was quite critical of Roosevelt's attitude on questions of foreign policy. He believed that Roosevelt was "simply repeating views which have been instilled into him by Cabot Lodge. . . . I think it is hardly safe to let the demagogues go too far in the way of rousing the jingo feeling. . . . The real sentiment of the country ought to assert itself." Storey to Carl Schurz, November 11, 1895. In reply, Schurz remarked: "What you say of Roosevelt's article in the *Century* is but too true. He has of late said and written a good many things which it would have been better to have unsaid. He gives too much rein to his restless and combative temperament." *Schurz MS.*
212. Secretary Olney to Bayard, November 16, 1895, cipher telegram, *Bayard MS.*
213. Secretary Olney to Bayard, November 20, 1895, *Olney MS.*
214. Secretary Olney to President Cleveland, November 20, 1895, *ibid.*

busily engaged upon his reply to the American note. This reply would probably not reach the American Embassy before November 25.[215]

On November 23 Bayard sent a long letter to Secretary Olney in which he carefully canvassed the situation in London:

I am thoroughly aware of the desire of the President and yourself to be in possession of Lord Salisbury's reply to your note on the Venezuelan boundary question in time to lay the correspondence before Congress on its convention on December 2d, and I have sought to keep you advised of the unusual pressure upon the present ministry consequent upon the rapid march of events in Turkey and the Far East, and the addition of present domestic difficulties in these kingdoms and their colonies, which have combined to delay the reply of Lord Salisbury to your note.

After his return from the Continent in October, I thought it expedient not to multiply visits at the Foreign Office, until I discovered a sensational effort in the public press to give a false meaning to my absence, and last Wednesday (the regular reception day) when I called, I found six Ambassadors in the ante-chamber awaiting interview. The night before, Lord Salisbury had made an elaborate and important speech at Brighton, embracing an exceptional communication direct from the Sultan of Turkey. . . . The Archbishop of Canterbury thought the occasion opportune to present the difficult problem of denominational education, to which as Prime Minister, a careful reply had been made, so that when my turn for audience came (about five o'clock, p.m.) you may well imagine I found a very weary and overworked man.

Lord Salisbury assured me he had hoped to have sent me his reply to your note last week, but had been summoned to a Royal Council at Windsor and that I should have it "in a day or two." The circumstances which have caused delay are not doubtful, and it would be unjust to suppose that it has arisen from any other than involuntary obstructions.

Having again recalled to his Lordship the short interval that remained before the meeting of Congress, and the strong desire of the President to receive and transmit to Congress the case as it stood, I made my adieux. . . . Today advantage was taken by me of another inquiry at the Foreign Office, . . . and the confidential information was given to Mr. Wells . . . that Lord Salisbury was personally engaged at Hatfield in revising the draught, . . . so that it could hardly reach this Embassy until Monday night.[216]

215. Secretary Olney to President Cleveland, November 22, 1895, *ibid.* See also, David D. Wells to Bayard, November 22, 1895, *Bayard MS.*

216. Bayard to Secretary Olney, November 23, 1895, *Bayard Press Copy Book*, vol. 3, *Bayard MS.* On November 26, 1895, John Bassett Moore wrote a letter to Bayard concerning the war spirit that was abroad in the land: "The present situation makes me apprehensive for the future, and it is certainly one to make every thinking man reflect. Since the panic two years ago, there has grown up quite a war party, which, while professing no actual grievance, thinks that a war would be a good thing for the country. Forgetting the probability of a blockade of our ports in a conflict with any considerable foreign power, they hope for another period of inflation and speculation, like that which

Lord Salisbury finished his instruction to Lord Pauncefote on November 26, and it was sent by steamer the next day.[217] On November 30 James R. Roosevelt, the First Secretary of the American Embassy at London, went to the Foreign Office and had a talk with Mr. Bertie. When the conversation touched upon the Venezuelan situation, Bertie inquired if the substance of Lord Salisbury's note had been cabled to the Department of State

. . . for the use of the President in his message to Congress. I [Roosevelt] said "No," and he then asked "Why not?" I said, in the first place because it was difficult if not impossible to send a correct summary by cable, and in the second place that as we had agreed that the contents of the despatches were to be held as strictly confidential by our Government until they were read by Sir Julian to Mr. Olney, any cable summary sent by us could not be used by the President in his message. He asked "When Congress met," and I said next Monday, the 2nd of December. This seemed to surprise him very much indeed. He said that Lord Salisbury had had the impression that it did not meet until the 9th or 10th. I told him that I had consulted our Statutes, and that it always met on the 1st Monday in December. He said that Lord Salisbury had thought that by allowing us to see the Despatches, and to send a summary by cable, the President could prepare his message before the despatches were read to Mr. Olney by Sir Julian. I said of course this was impossible as they had bound us to consider the despatches as confidential until read to Mr. Olney, that they would not reach Washington until the 7th of December, while the President's message would be sent to Congress on Monday the 2nd. He said, "I must see his Lordship about this, but I fear it is too late!" [218]

Because of this oversight in the part of Lord Salisbury, his instruction to Olney did not reach Washington in time for the President to allude to it in his message to Congress. In this message of December 2,

---

prevailed during and after the Civil War. This is the view of some of the leaders. Others think it good party policy to get up a row with some foreign power. Men who hold this view are not confined to one party; and the thing that makes me apprehensive is, that knowing the susceptibility of even the best men to false counsels in unguarded moments, I think it impossible to predict who may or may not be found in the van when the quiet, honest people who form the unclamorous and uncounted majority, are summoned to participate in a groundless international quarrel, to which, if the merits had even been investigated, it would have been impossible for us to be a party. . . .

"To crown their wicked insanity, some of our leaders are trying to emulate the fatuous fury of the radical French politicians in 1870, when they invited destruction. Our own demagogues, . . . like their French prototypes, are professing to court a conflict with the power which can do us the most harm, but which, somewhat unlike the case of France and her antagonist, is of all powers in the world at least as desirous as any to keep the peace with us." *Bayard MS.*

217. Bayard to Secretary Olney, November 26, 1895, *Olney MS.* See also, James R. Roosevelt to Bayard, November 30, 1895, *Bayard MS.*

218. James R. Roosevelt to Bayard, November 30, 1895, *Bayard MS.*

President Cleveland summarized Olney's instruction of July 20, and stated that the Secretary of State had called upon Great Britain for a definite answer to the question, "whether it would . . . submit the territorial controversy . . . in its entirety to impartial arbitration." [219]

Two days later, Bayard addressed a personal letter to President Cleveland in which he expressed the opinion that

. . . the replies of Lord Salisbury to your Venezuelan instruction are in good temper and moderate in tone. *Our* difficulty lies in the wholly unreliable character of the Venezuelan Rulers and her people, and results in an almost undefinable, and therefore dangerous responsibility for the conduct of them in their own affairs.

I believe, however, that your interposition in this boundary dispute will check efficiently the tendency to "land-grabbing" in South America, which is rather an Anglo-Saxon disposition *everywhere*. Arbitration is a most wise and honorable resort, but it must be conducted and executed in a wise and honorable spirit.[220]

After Cleveland and Olney read the notes of Lord Salisbury, they strongly disagreed with Bayard's view that these communications were "in good temper and moderate in tone." The British Foreign Secretary first dealt with the larger aspects of the controversy. The argument of Secretary Olney was based upon the principles of the Monroe Doctrine, and Salisbury endeavored to show that the Monroe Doctrine was not involved in the Guiana boundary dispute:

The dangers against which President Monroe thought it right to guard were not as imaginary as they would seem at the present day. . . . It was not an imaginary danger that he foresaw, if he feared that the same spirit which had dictated the French expedition into Spain might inspire the more powerful Governments of Europe with the idea of imposing, by the force of European arms, upon the South American communities the form of government and the political connection which they had thrown off. . . . The dangers which were apprehended by President Monroe have no relation to the state of things in which we live at the present day. . . . There is no danger of any European State treating any part of the American Continent as a fit object for European colonization. . . . The British Empire and the Republic of Venezuela are neighbors, and they have differed for some time

219. *Foreign Relations, 1895*, pt. 1, xxviii-xxix. On December 2, 1895, Secretary Olney wrote to Bayard and thanked him for his letter of November 23, which had given a "detailed account of the circumstances which have prevented Lord Salisbury from giving that uninterrupted attention to the Venezuelan question which would have enabled him to forward his views on the subject in time to be considered by the President before sending his Annual Message to Congress." *Bayard MS.*

220. Bayard to President Cleveland, December 4, 1895, *Bayard Press Copy Book*, vol. 3, *Bayard MS.*

past, and continue to differ, as to the line by which their dominions are separated. It is a controversy with which the United States have no apparent practical concern. . . . The disputed frontier of Venezuela has nothing to do with any of the questions dealt with by President Monroe. It is not a question of the colonization by a European Power of any portion of America. It is not a question of the imposition upon the communities of South America of any system of government devised in Europe. It is simply the determination of the frontier of a British possession which belonged to the Throne of England long before the Republic of Venezuela came into existence. . . . The Government of the United States do not say that . . . Venezuela is in the right in the matters that are in issue. But they lay down that the doctrine of President Monroe . . . confers upon them the right of demanding that when a European Power has a frontier difference with a South American community, the European Power shall consent to refer that controversy to arbitration. . . . Whatever may be the authority of the doctrine laid down by President Monroe, there is nothing in his language to show that he ever thought of claiming this novel prerogative for the United States.

Lord Salisbury then entered into a discussion as to whether the Monroe Doctrine

. . . in itself is sound. I must not . . . be understood as expressing any acceptance of it on the part of Her Majesty's Government. It must always be mentioned with respect, . . . but International Law is founded on the general consent of nations; and no statesman, however eminent, and no nation, however powerful, are competent to insert in the code of International Law a novel principle which was never recognized before, and which has not since been accepted by the Government of any other country. . . . The Government of the United States is not entitled to affirm as a universal proposition, with reference to a number of independent States, for whose conduct it assumes no responsibility, that its interests are necessarily concerned in whatever may befall those States simply because they are situated in the Western Hemisphere.[221]

Secretary Olney had based a portion of his argument upon the doctrine of self-preservation. The Monroe Doctrine, he believed, was merely an expression of this widely accepted principle. It was a very far-fetched idea, however, to maintain that an extension of the British boundaries in Guiana would be a direct menace to American security. Equally absurd was Olney's contention that any permanent political

221. With regard to Olney's arguments, Dexter Perkins, *The Monroe Doctrine, 1867–1907*, p. 180, makes the following comments: "Olney had spoken . . . of a rule of 'American public law'; if by this he meant American International Law, he was most certainly in error. How could such a phenomenon exist, or, more puzzling still, how could *American* law, if it did exist, regulate the relations of an American and a European state? Such a contention was little short of ridiculous."

connection between a European and an American state was "unnatural
and inexpedient."

This viewpoint was sharply challenged by Lord Salisbury:

The necessary meaning of these words is that the union between Great
Britain and Canada; between Great Britain and Jamaica and Trinidad;
between Great Britain and British Honduras or British Guiana are "inexpedient and unnatural." President Monroe disclaims any such inference
from his doctrine, . . . and . . . Her Majesty's Government are prepared
emphatically to deny it on behalf of both the British and American people
who are subject to her Crown. . . . They fully concur with the view which
President Monroe apparently entertained, that any disturbance of the existing territorial distribution in that hemisphere by any fresh acquisitions on
the part of any European State would be a highly inexpedient change. But
they are not prepared to admit that the interests of the United States are
necessarily concerned in every frontier dispute which may arise between any
two of the States who possess dominion in the Western Hemisphere.[222]

As Professor Perkins so justly remarks: "Time has done nothing to
indicate that in penning these oft-quoted lines Lord Salisbury was
wrong. They constituted a fitting, indeed, a crushing rebuke to the
imprudent generalizations of the Secretary of State." [223]

John Bassett Moore, then Professor of International Law in Columbia University, had not seen these notes of Lord Salisbury, but had
carefully read the President's message to Congress, and he had caught
the belligerent accents that had been so strongly emphasizd by Secretary Olney. In order to arrest, if possible, this tide towards war with
Great Britain, Professor Moore wrote the following letter to William
L. Wilson, the Postmaster General in Cleveland's Cabinet:

I called at your house on Saturday evening and was very sorry not to find
you at home. Apart from motives of personal respect, I wanted to speak to
you about the Venezuelan matter, which has, I confess, since the President's
message was published, been weighing upon me very heavily. I am apprehensive that, unless great judgment is exercised, the President's announcement will prove to have started us on a course that involves not only the
abandonment of all our traditions, but also our participation in numberless
quarrels. The statement that the question can be reasonably settled only by
such arbitration as Venezuela proposes, certainly was not based on any
examination of the merits of the subject.

222. Lord Salisbury to Sir Julian Pauncefote, November 26, 1895, *Foreign Relations,
1895*, pt. 1, pp. 563-567. In a second note of November 26, 1895, Lord Salisbury gave a
detailed treatment of the Guiana boundary controversy. His outline of this controversy is
a good corrective to the obviously biassed account contained in Olney's instruction of July
20, 1895. *Foreign Relations, 1895*, pt. 1, pp. 567-576.
223. Dexter Perkins, *The Monroe Doctrine, 1867-1907*, pp. 181-182.

The whole system of arbitration presupposes that nations will be reasonable in their claims. The claim of Venezuela to all territory west of the Essequibo is not a scrupulous claim. Her talk about Dutch usurpations is but an admission of English title.

Instead of asserting that arbitration is the only reasonable way of settling the question, I should say that it would be a very unsatisfactory way of attempting it; and in so saying I do not forget that Lord Granville once consented to lump boundary and all other questions in a general arbitration. We have arbitrated boundary disputes and so has Great Britain, but never, so far as I am informed, where a line had not previously been agreed upon by direct negotiation. Governments are not in the habit of resigning their functions so completely into the hands of arbitrators as to say, "We have no boundaries; make some for us." . . .

Venezuela has said, and the New York *Sun* has upheld her in saying, that because her constitutions have adopted as her limits those of the captaincy-general of Venezuela at the date of her declaration of independence, 1810, she cannot by a direct settlement yield any of the national territory. This argument is obviously unsound, and it is false in fact. The captaincy-general of Venezuela, like the rest of the Spanish captaincies-general, had no limits. For this reason, boundaries in South America have almost universally been settled on the basis of *uti possidetis,* as the only practicable basis of peaceful adjustment. . . .

Venezuela has represented again and again that the question of the mouth of the Orinoco is the "knot of the controversy"; and I observe that Mr. Edmunds, . . . said he hoped that the President would not permit Venezuela to be "squeezed" out of the mouth of that river. Yet, it is a fact that Great Britain has again and again offered to yield that point if Venezuela would only settle.

For twenty years Venezuela, instead of settling her boundary dispute, has in various ways, some of them obviously dishonest, been trying to drag the United States into the dispute, and the United States has progressed good-naturedly step by step, without examining the merits of the case, till at length with a sudden impulse, it leaps over the precipice blindly. And what is the position we now hold? It is substantially this: "When a weak American republic asserts a claim to territory in America as against a strong European occupant, and offers to submit its claims to arbitration, the European power, if it refuses the offer, is to be considered as holding the territory by force, and as infringing the Monroe Doctrine." This is the sum and substance of our position. I will not characterize it. . . .

As I happened to be the Counsel to Brazil in the late boundary dispute with the Argentine Republic, . . . I became somewhat familiar with the South American boundary questions. . . . Among the maps we had was a section of that of Olmedilla, cosmographer to the King of Spain about 1770. . . . In the so-called disputed territory east of the Orinoco there is no Spanish settlement. At the mouth of the Pomaron, west of the Essequibo, is the Dutch settlement of New Middleburgh. I have lately examined a French map of the last century, . . . and Dutch Guiana is bounded on the West by a line running from Point Barima, on the Orinoco, south-westerly. I will not refer to the numerous other maps I have examined with substantially the same result. Yet, we now address Venezuela substantially thus: "You are an American republic, and in your claims against European powers we back you. True, you settled your southern boundary directly, on the basis of the *uti possidetis*, but this principle, though applicable everywhere else in South America, is inapplicable to your Eastern boundary. Even the great doctrine of prescription, recognized by every publicist from the time of Grotius, . . . is not applicable to that boundary. Claim what you will and propose arbitration of it, and I will step in and say that it shall be settled in no other way. I know nothing of the merits of the controversy: I am simply backing you. This is according to the Monroe Doctrine." [224]

Olney and Cleveland had taken a most unreasonable position, but they were soon supported by a public opinion that was growing increasingly belligerent. America was spoiling for a fight, and she did not seem to care who was her opponent. As John Bassett Moore again remarks: "We were then entering upon the era of the 'big stick.' We had been so long without a war that our people were growing nervous and irritable lest the world might think us not worth insulting." [225]

The war-spirit found ample expression in the antics of Congress. It

224. John Bassett Moore to William L. Wilson, December 10, 1895, *Cleveland MS.* The very judicial and impartial manner in which Bayard handled the Guiana boundary controversy during his term as Secretary of State, is clearly revealed in the following memorandum written by Bayard after a conversation with Señor Bercerra, the Colombian Minister to the United States, April 15, 1887: "Mr. Bercerra, Colombian Minister called. He said it was vitally important to Colombia that the British should be prevented from holding the mouth of the Orinoco River, and that the attitude of the United States in the matter was generally understood and eminently satisfactory to his country. I said I was very glad to hear it; that while we were not disposed to preserve the balance of power, we wished to preserve the equilibrium of law, whether it related to weak or strong nations, and not to permit any nation to be despoiled because it was weak. He then asked me about the dispute between Venezuela and Great Britain.

"I said I had only seen fit to acquaint myself with the general character of the dispute, which was a dispute in regard to jurisdictional boundaries; that maps had been shown me by Mr. Soteldo, tracing what he said was the just boundary of Venezuela on the one side and British Guiana on the other, but as the United States had offered their good offices to both of these countries to assist in an amicable adjustment, and as that might take the shape of arbitration, and as both countries might desire that the United States should assume that office between them, I thought it was not proper to form any judgment upon the law or the facts of the case in advance, in order that we might stand perfectly free in undertaking arbitration should it be requested of us, or to advise the deposit of this arbitration in the hands of some other party. . . . I said I had no reason to suppose that Great Britain meditated any new acquisition of territory in South America or anywhere on this hemisphere; that I thought she already possessed islands from which she derived no benefit." *Bayard MS.*

225. John Bassett Moore to the author, September 16, 1940. For some illuminating commentaries on the war-spirit in the late nineties, see, Leland H. Jenks, *Our Cuban Colony* (N. Y. 1928), pp. 45-57.

is well to keep in mind the fact that this was a Congress in which the Republican Party made its influence strongly felt. The elections of 1894 had gone heavily against the Democrats, and when the Fifty-fourth Congress convened on December 2, 1895, there were 163 new members. The policies of President Cleveland had been repudiated by the American people, and the Republican Party had the large majority of 140 in the House of Representatives.[226] This rising Republican tide was made manifest when Thomas B. Reed was elected Speaker of the House by an overwhelming vote.[227]

This Republican House of Representatives was anxious to score a partisan success, and they seized upon the text of some of Bayard's speeches in England as a pretext for discrediting the Cleveland Administration. Bayard's Edinburgh Address, in which he criticized the theory and practice of Protection, gave these Republican legislators their opportunity to launch a bitter attack upon Democratic diplomats who talked upon debatable topics. On December 10, 1895, Samuel W. McCall, of Massachusetts, offered a resolution requesting President Cleveland to provide information with respect to Bayard's speeches. The Chief Executive was also asked to inform Congress whether he had taken any steps to "recall or censure" Bayard for his criticisms of Protection.[228]

Not to be outdone in this belligerent clamor, William E. Barrett, also of Massachusetts, introduced a resolution which directed the Committee on Foreign Affairs to ascertain whether Bayard had actually made the statements attributed to him, and if so, to report to the House "such action by impeachment or otherwise, as shall be proper in the premises." [229]

In discussing these resolutions, McCall stated that Bayard's address at Edinburgh was a "violent partisan speech," and his offense was "so astounding that International Law has no name for it." [230] Nelson Dingley, of Maine, had no doubt that Bayard was guilty of an "impeachable offense," [231] and Joseph G. Cannon, of Illinois, thought that if the House of Representatives did not impeach Bayard for his Edinburgh remarks it should at least pass a resolution of censure. [232]

After amendment, the Barrett resolution was agreed to without a

226. New York *World*, December 3, 1895.
227. *Congressional Record*, December 2, 1895, vol. 28, pt. 1, p. 4. Reed received 240 votes to 95 votes cast for Crisp, his Democratic competitor.
228. *Congressional Record*, December 10, 1895, vol. 28, pt. 1, p. 114.
229. *Ibid.*, p. 114.   230. *Ibid.*, p. 117.   231. *Ibid.*, p. 119.   232. *Ibid.*, p. 121.

record vote,[233] and the resolution introduced by McCall was adopted by the House (December 28, 1895), and sent to the president.[234] He responded on January 20, 1896, by sending the text of several speeches delivered by Bayard in England.[235]

In the press there were many editorials which supported the Congressional resolutions attacking Bayard. The Washington *Post* thought that

. . . since the President has not seen fit to recall Mr. Bayard on account of behavior which even his most ardent English admirers admit was a "serious indiscretion," Mr. Bayard should now offer the American people the only reparation in his power and resign. He no longer enjoys popular respect and confidence. . . . He should resign, since we are so merciful as to give him the opportunity. If not, he should be recalled. If not, he should be impeached.[236]

All Americans were not so critical of Bayard's speeches in England. Many of Bayard's friends, including some eminent publicists, wrote to him in commendation of the Edinburgh Address. Edward M. Shepard was delighted and inspired by this address which sounded a

. . . genuine, thrilling note, noble and powerful. It is a refreshment amid the mean and tawdry things which, in this transition time, we must endure. One needs all his belief in God and the worthy destiny of mankind when his ears are filled with the base cries which seem . . . to be dominant. You lift one far enough above, to see truly and to see far beyond.[237]

Oscar S. Straus regarded the Edinburgh Address as a very valuable

. . . contribution towards counteracting the evil forces civilization has to combat. . . . We here feel proud of your magnificent services in the world's capital; your interpretation of the American spirit of patriotism and freedom must augment our prestige as a nation in the family of nations throughout the world.[238]

233. *Ibid.*, p. 126.   234. *Ibid.*, p. 404.

235. *Congressional Record*, December 10, 1895, vol. 28, pt. 1, p. 805.

236. Washington *Post*, December 13, 1895. See also, Washington *Star*, December 13, 1895.

237. Edward M. Shepard to Bayard, December 16, 1895, *Bayard MS*. See also, letters to Bayard from George H. Harrington, December 17, 1895; from John V. Craven, December 20, 1895; and from J. A. Pearce, undated, *Bayard MS*.

238. Oscar S. Straus to Bayard, December 7, 1895, *Ibid.* In this letter to Bayard, Straus makes a comment which is pertinent today: "I take 'no stock' in the 3d term for Cleveland, and without knowing anything regarding Cleveland's views, I predict he would under no circumstances allow the party to nominate him again."

In commenting upon the attacks made upon him in the Philadelphia *Public Ledger*, in November, 1895, Bayard remarked as follows: "The scream of rage that has followed my attack on that form of State Socialism called 'Protection,' has attracted my attention to *the causes* of hostility in the United States to Great Britain. Undoubtedly, the Irish

The convictions of many Democrats, North or South, were given adequate expression in an editorial in the Chicago *Chronicle,* December 12, 1895:

Mr. Bayard's speech was truthful, manly, courageous, timely, even necessary. He might have escaped what a London journal calls an indiscretion by withholding from his address any mention of a conspicuous menace to individual freedom, but had he done so he would have been false to true manhood. It is delightful and reassuring to know that in an age of peculation, bred of debased socialistic policies of the Republican Party, a man of Bayard's position can rise before the whole world and preach the gospel of truth.

It is more than likely that Olney was in sympathy with these attacks upon Bayard. Public sentiment in Massachusetts seemed deeply aroused against Great Britain with reference to the Guiana boundary, and Olney was glad to float upon that belligerent tide. The resolutions in the House of Representatives against Bayard were sponsored by members from Massachusetts, and Henry Cabot Lodge lost no time in the Senate in introducing a resolution confirming the Monroe Doctrine.[239]

As for Cleveland himself, the Boston *Post* believed that his message to Congress on December 3, indicated that he had come "squarely over to the position held by the Republicans."[240] The New York *Herald* regarded Cleveland's message as "firm and strong and true";[241] the New York *Sun* thought that if Cleveland lived up to the words of this message, his Administration would become "truly and illustriously American";[242] the Washington *Post* thought that nothing "more vigorous and assertive could be asked";[243] and the Philadelphia *Enquirer* looked upon the President's references to Venezuela as the "only gleam of intelligent comprehension through the meagre treatment of foreign affairs."[244]

The Washington *Post* stated that Cleveland had followed with deep

---

animosity is the most constant and active, but the *steady* cause is the commercial warfare which the 'Protective' alliance in the United States wages against everything and everybody who proposes to interfere with their gains. This is the mercenary basis of selfish forces and constitutes the 'predatory politics.'

"For instance, here is the Philadelphia *Ledger.* . . . This paper editorially avows a preference for an alliance, armed or otherwise, with Russia, in preference to Great Britain. . . . What does Russia 'stand for'? What is Russian Civilization? What is the basis of the Russian Government? To what do its institutions lead?" *Memorandum* written by Bayard November 20, 1895.

239. *Congressional Record,* December 3, 1895, vol. 28, pt. 1, p. 24.
240. Quoted in the New York *Tribune,* December 6, 1895,
241. New York *Herald,* December 4, 1895.
242. December 4, 1895.   243. December 4, 1895.   244. December 5, 1895.

interest the press comments favoring his message of December 3, and he was reported to have remarked that the country would have no reason to complain of his further attitude in the matter of the Venezuela boundary controversy.[245]

The President was in North Carolina on a hunting trip when the notes from Lord Salisbury arrived in Washington.[246] The New Orleans *Times-Democrat* expressed the view that the President "would do well to give up duck-shooting when he has reason to expect some important communication from Congress or some foreign country," [247] and the Washington *Post* carried a cartoon which depicted Cleveland shooting at ducks (with the caption "Greenbacks") while the British "Lion" was busily at work upon Venezuela.[248]

During the President's absence, Olney drafted a special message that was to be sent to Congress with regard to the Venezuela boundary controversy. On December 15 the Presidential Nimrod returned to the White House. That evening he had a conference with Olney, and he also talked over the situation with Secretary Lamont. After these conversations had been concluded, Cleveland worked for several hours upon Olney's draft of a message to Congress. The next morning he had a second conference with the Secretary of State. On Tuesday morning, at the Cabinet meeting, he read the message, but did not ask for any suggestions.[249] That afternoon the message was sent to Congress.

Cleveland's stature as a President can easily be measured by comparing him with another President who had to make an important decision during a crisis in Anglo-American relations. During the early days of the Civil War, Seward, as Secretary of State, was excessively belligerent, and if his famous instruction of May 21, 1861, had not been toned down by our wise President Lincoln, a serious quarrel with England might have broken out. At that time, war with England would have been fatal to the American Union.[250] In the Venezuela crisis, our duck-hunting President made no move to repress the belligerent spirit of Secretary

245. December 5, 1895.
246. Apparently the President left Washington on December 5th. New York *World*, December 6, 1895.
247. Quoted in the New York *Tribune*, December 10, 1895.
248. December 13, 1895.
249. Henry James, *Richard Olney*, pp. 118-119. See also, George F. Parker, "Cleveland's Second Administration as President," *Saturday Evening Post*, June 9, 1923, vol. 195, pp. 40-50.
250. Ephraim D. Adams, *Great Britain and the American Civil War* (N. Y. 1925), vol. 1, pp. 113-136.

Olney. Instead, he used Olney's draft as the basis of a special message to Congress, and he permitted the martial accents of Olney's language to sound a bold and highly dangerous challenge to the Government of England.

Cleveland began his message by asserting that

. . . the doctrine upon which we stand is strong and sound because its enforcement is important to our peace and safety as a nation, and is essential to the integrity of our free institutions and the tranquil maintenance of our distinctive form of government. . . . If a European power, by an extension of its boundaries, takes possession of the territory of one of our neighboring Republics against its will and in derogation of its rights, it is difficult to see why to that extent such European power does not thereby attempt to extend its system of government to that portion of this continent which is thus taken. . . . The principle for which we contend has peculiar if not exclusive relation to the United States. It may not have been admitted in so many words to the code of International Law, but since in international councils every nation is entitled to the rights belonging to it, if the enforcement of the Monroe Doctrine is something we may justly claim, it has its place in the code of International Law as certainly . . . as if it were specifically mentioned. . . . The Monroe Doctrine finds its recognition in those principles of International Law which are based upon the theory that every nation shall have its rights protected and its just claims enforced. . . . This Government is entirely confident that under the sanction of this doctrine we have clear rights and undoubted claims.

After this strong declaration that the Monroe Doctrine is based upon the age-old principle of the right of self-defense, Cleveland then advances to the ridiculous position that a rectification of the frontiers of British Guiana constituted a threat to American "safety and welfare." The American Government had repeatedly suggested to the British Foreign Office the advisability of arbitrating the controversy with Venezuela, but this proposition had been declined upon grounds which Cleveland regarded as "far from satisfactory." Because of this stubborn and unfair British attitude, there was only one course open to the United States. It was incumbent upon the American Government

. . . to take measures to determine with sufficient certainty for its justification what is the true divisional line between the Republic of Venezuela and British Guiana. The inquiry to that end should of course be conducted carefully and judicially, and due weight should be given to all available evidence records and facts in support of the claims of both parties. In order that such an examination should be prosecuted in a thorough and satisfactory manner, I suggest that the Congress make an adequate appropriation for the expenses of a Commission, to be appointed by the Executive, who shall make the necessary investigation and report upon the matter with the least possible delay. When such report is made and accepted, it will, in my opinion, be the duty of the United States to resist by every means in its power as a wilful aggression upon its rights and interests the appropriation by Great Britain of any lands or the exercise of governmental jurisdiction over any territory, which, after investigation, we have determined of right belongs to Venezuela. In making these recommendations I am fully alive to the responsibility incurred, and keenly realize all the consequences that may follow.[251]

It is difficult to understand just why Cleveland sent this unfortunate message to Congress. During the year 1895 he had watched with painful anxiety the rapidly rising tide of public resentment against the measures that he advocated. His popularity had largely vanished, and even within his own party there was bitter opposition to his leadership.[252] Both he and Olney were well aware of the fact that the jingo spirit in the United States, so apparent throughout the summer of 1895, would send forth a tremendous salvo of approval at any message that echoed the accents of war. Both were probably aware of the fact that there were numerous instances in history where a ruler had recovered lost popularity by shifting the public gaze from the domestic scene to vistas of glory on distant shores.

In Congress the reading of the President's special message evoked instant applause. Republican Senators were warm in their approval. Senator Chandler thought the message was a "courageous paper"; Senator Platt concurred "heartily in all that the President says"; Senator Cullom believed that the message had "a good ring"; to Senator Frye it had a "genuine American tone"; and Senator Lodge was reported to be "bubbling over with delight."[253]

Theodore Roosevelt was so pleased with Cleveland's message that he announced that he would "like to have the last paragraph taught in every school in the country," and Governor William McKinley, of Ohio, was certain that the "President's firm and dignified stand will command the approval of the people of the State of Ohio."[254]

Although many prominent Democrats supported the President's

251. Message of December 17, 1895, *Foreign Relations, 1895*, pt. 1, pp. 542-545. For an interesting account of the spirit in which President Cleveland wrote the message of December 17, 1895, see, A. B. Farquhar to President McKinley, November 10, 1899, *McKinley Papers*, Library of Congress.
252. Allan Nevins, *Grover Cleveland*, pp. 674-675.
253. New York *Tribune*, December 18, 1895.
254. New York *World*, December 18, 1895.

stand in this controversy with England, the Republicans seemed to be more vehement in their praise of the message. The New York *Tribune* thought that Cleveland had spoken "straightforward manly words which are worthy of and which will command the approval and enthusiastic support of the people of the United States." [255] The Chicago *Tribune* was openly belligerent. [256] The Cleveland *Leader* believed that the message meant that "John Bull must either back down or fight," [257] the San Francisco *Chronicle* was of the opinion that the "argument of the President is unanswerable," [258] and the Springfield *Union* uttered a hearty "Good for Mr. Cleveland!" [259]

The Springfield *Republican* strongly deprecated this quarrel over a "beggarly plot of land," [260] and Independent papers like the Providence *Journal*,[261] and the Boston *Herald*,[262] were frankly fearful of the President's course.

In academic circles, the President's message was sharply criticized. Professor Theodore S. Woolsey expressed the belief that the President had gone "gunning without a license. This is not the Monroe Doctrine. It is dictatorship pure and simple." [263] Professor Frank W. Taussig criticized the message as "needlessly bellicose and mischievous," [264] and Professors Hermann von Holst and John Bassett Moore concurred in this view.[265]

Many business leaders in New York City were outspoken in their denunciation of Cleveland's message. Frederick D. Tappen, President of the Gallatin National Bank, regarded Cleveland's action as "most ill-advised"; J. Edward Simmons, President of the Fourth National Bank, thought that the President had been "precipitate," and that the Monroe Doctrine was not applicable to the Guiana boundary controversy. To Charles S. Smith, ex-President of the New York Chamber of Commerce, the stand taken by Cleveland was "not only a blunder, but if pursued to its legitimate end as proposed in his message, it would be the crime of the century"; and George G. Williams, President of the Chemical National Bank, criticized the message as "wicked." [266]

255. December 18, 1895. 256. December 18, 1895. 257. December 18, 1895.
258. December 18, 1895. 259. Quoted in New York *World*, December 19, 1895.
260. December 18, 1895. 261. December 18, 1895. 262. December 18, 1895.
263. New York *World*, December 19, 1895.
264. *Literary Digest*, vol. 12, p. 241.
265. New York *World*, December 19, 1895; New York *Times*, December 19, 1895.
266. *Ibid.*, December 20, 1895. Many of the religious leaders in the New York area were as unsparing in their criticism of Cleveland's message as were the business leaders. In the Plymouth Church, in Brooklyn, there was a strong demonstration against war with Eng-

These business leaders found a ready champion in the New York *Journal of Commerce,* which showed no hesitation in pointing out the dangers of the President's position:

However opinions may differ as to the political value of the Monroe Doctrine, the doubt must be well nigh universal whether this is a time for forcing it to a settlement at the peril of war. The country is still suffering from financial disorganization. . . . We are still borrowing over one hundred millions a year to keep the paper dollar at par and are verging on a crisis. . . . England holds probably 1,500 millions of our securities, which she must be expected to return upon us in vast amounts in the event of war, with the certain result of not only depriving us of our much needed gold . . . but also of overwhelming us in a panic at the moment when the sinews of war were urgently needed. Mr. Cleveland has made a most serious mistake. . . . He has outjingoed the jingoes; and far from being the embodiment of sober judgment, he has become the hasty abettor of political fanaticism.[267]

But despite the loud clamor from the business interests and from the religious press,[268] Mr. Hitt, of Illinois, on December 18, asked the

land. (New York *World,* December 23, 1895). Many ministers were vehement in their criticism of the President. Dr. Parkhurst believed that the United States could not be drawn into war upon a question that was not clearly understood by the great majority of the American people. Rev. Dr. Millington, of Newark, expressed the opinion that "all South America is not worth a drop of blood." (New York *World,* December 23, 1895). Dr. Lyman Abbott was of the same opinion.

267. December 19, 1895. The situation as outlined by the *Journal of Commerce* began to take shape on December 19 and 20, when English owners of American securities began to liquidate their holdings. R. M. McElroy, *Grover Cleveland, the Man and the Statesman* (N. Y. 1923, 2 vols.), vol. 2, pp. 183-186. It is significant, however, that the New York *World,* December 20, 1895, received communications from twenty-five Presidents of Board of Trade throughout the United States in which the position of President Cleveland was approved.

The war spirit in America seemed to reach its peak on December 20, 1895. On the preceding day, the Washington *Post* printed the following inflammatory editorial: "Let but a drum-tap be heard from the White House grounds, and in every city in the land a host will rise and in every rural neighborhood and countryside battalions will start up from the waving fields like shapes in some colossal pantomime. From one seaboard to the other and from the Gulf of Mexico to the chain of lakes, the whole surface of the earth will bristle with moving regiments, the sheen of whose bayonets will pale the stars."

This martial spirit had a most depressing effect upon the stock market, and Friday, December 20, 1895, was long spoken of as "dismal Friday." The fall in securities was estimated at more than $350,000,000. (New York *World,* December 21, 1895). The panic in Wall Street caused severe losses that extended to Berlin, Paris, and Vienna. (London *Times,* December 21, 1895.) There were eight business failures in Wall Street, and the Chicago *Economist* spoke of the situation in the stock market at the "worst this country has ever seen." (December 28, 1895, p. 785). To the London *Times* it seemed clear that "whatever may be the political consequences of the action of President Cleveland, its commercial and financial consequences have been disastrous to the United States." (December 21.)

268. Dexter Perkins, *The Monroe Doctrine, 1867–1907,* pp. 198-199. See also, *The Congregationalist,* vol. 70, December 26, 1895, p. 1028.

unanimous consent of the House of Representatives to the introduction of a bill appropriating $100,000 for the expense of a commission to carry out the recommendations in the President's message to Congress. The bill was passed without a dissenting vote, and on December 19 it was placed before the Senate. After a brief debate in which no word of criticism against the bill was uttered, the Senate approved the measure.[269]

In England the press adopted a moderate tone. The London *Times* thought that a rupture between the two great English-speaking communities "would be a calamity," but nevertheless it regarded the demands of the American Government as too presumptuous to be accepted: "No commission appointed by a Power which is not a party to the dispute will be recognized by us as having a title of any sort to pronounce upon the controverted questions of boundary between the British Empire and Venezuela."[270] The *Daily Graphic* asked whether President Cleveland seriously thought that the "frontiers of European colonies in the Americas are to be held at the good pleasure of a committee of Washington gentlemen."[271] The *Telegraph* and *Standard* took rather a high tone, but the *Daily News*, the *Manchester Guardian*, the *Chronicle*, and the Birmingham *Post* were conciliatory.[272]

Individual Britons were distinctly opposed to war with the United States. Gladstone, after denouncing the "astounding folly" of President Cleveland, expressed the view that "only common sense was required" to find a solution for the difficulty.[273] Catholic prelates like Cardinal Vaughn and the Archbishop of Armagh were anxious for peace, and their sentiments were echoed by dignitaries of the Established Church like Archbishop Plunkett, of Dublin, and the Bishops of Chester, Manchester, and Liverpool. Lord Rosebery believed that a war over the Guiana boundary would "be the greatest crime on record."[274]

On Christmas Day, messages of good will were sent by the Archbishop of Canterbury, and the Bishop of London. From the Duke of York and the Prince of Wales a message was sent that made an enduring impression in America. They could not "but believe the present crisis will

269. *Congressional Record*, 54 Cong., 1 sess., vol. 28, pp. 234-271.
270. December 18, 1895.   271. December 19, 1895.
272. There is a digest of British newspaper opinion in *Public Opinion* (London), December 20, 1895. The British weeklies denounced Cleveland's message but they praised the good sense of the American people and did not anticipate serious trouble. See, the *Statist*, December 1895, p. 660; the *Saturday Review*, December 21, 1895, p. 825.
273. New York *World*, December 22, 1895.   274. *Ibid.*, December 24, 1895.

be arranged in a manner satisfactory to both countries and will be succeeded by the same warm feeling of friendship which has existed between them for so many years." [275]

Cleveland's message of December 17, 1895, was a great shock to Bayard. According to Professor Allan Nevins, after this message had been received in England, Bayard exploded to Henry White "about 'that man Cleveland.' He added that Olney was thwarting all his efforts to maintain good relations 'with this g-r-e-a-t country.' " [276]

It is very probable that Professor Nevins unintentionally misquotes Henry White with regard to Bayard's statement. Bayard's explosion was against "that man Olney," and not against President Cleveland. This anecdote is told in a letter from Henry White to Henry James, June 6, 1922.[277] Bayard retained his respect for Cleveland even after December 17, 1895, and he never criticized him in any regard. On December 18, in a letter to Cleveland, he did, however, express his grave apprehensions that the United States had allowed its interests and welfare to "be imperilled or complicated by such a Government and people as those of Venezuela." [278]

Although Bayard, in his letters to his friends, was careful not to utter any criticism of the President's message to Congress, the private correspondence that poured into the London Embassy was outspoken in its denunciation of the attitude assumed by the President. To Samuel Bancroft it seemed obvious that Olney had hypnotized the President, and he feared that Cleveland had

... thrown away the absolute trust that so many of us have had in him.
... There is a story going about Wilmington that George Gray was said to have told—that Olney had come to him with a draft of a letter to Salisbury that was preposterous, antedating the one that was sent, and told Gray that he would not send it until it had been submitted to the Cabinet. Gray is said to have told him that there were only two members of the Cabinet that he need show such a despatch to, the Secretaries of the Navy and War. Thereupon, Olney took it back and modified it into the shape you know, and in which it is our bane today.[279]

From Lord Pauncefote, the British Ambassador at Washington,

275. New York *World*, December 25, 1895.
276. *Henry White*, p. 112.
277. In this letter from Henry White to Henry James, June 6, 1922, there is the following pertinent passage: "Mr. Bayard detested Mr. Olney after the Venezuela incident and did not think much of him at any time. He once said to me, 'that man Olney is doing all he can to thwart my efforts to keep good relations with this great country!' " *White MS.*
278. Bayard to President Cleveland, December 18, 1895, *Cleveland MS.*
279. Samuel Bancroft to Bayard, December 20, 1895, *Bayard MS.*

there came a note which warmly sympathized with Bayard's stand, and which deprecated the loose criticism that had been showered upon him:

I cannot resist the desire . . . of writing a few lines to you to express my most warm and sincere sympathy for you in relation to the obviously unjust attacks which have lately been made against you in the press of America. The motion of that fellow Barrett in the House of Representatives was simply outrageous, but you have had too long and too brilliant a public career to feel anything but passing annoyance at the folly and ingratitude of these ignorant and irresponsible scribblers and chatterers who have attacked you. You are in my opinion the most popular Representative of the United States that was ever sent to London, and you have certainly done more good work there than the whole of your Predecessors in the great duty of smoothing international acerbities, by your personal influence and great oratorical talent.[280]

Whatever satisfaction Bayard derived from reading this letter was shortlived in the face of a letter he received from the President himself. It dealt with the Venezuelan boundary controversy, and Cleveland tried to make his position very clear. He was confident that the Monroe Doctrine was not obsolete, and he thought it

. . . should be defended and maintained for its value and importance *to our government and welfare,* and that its defence and maintenance involve its application when a state of facts arises requiring it. In this state of mind I can never be made to see why the extension of European systems, territory, and jurisdiction, on our continent, may not be effected as surely and as unwarrantably under the guise of boundary claims as by invasion or any other means. . . . We do not say either that Great Britain's boundary claim is false, nor that the enlargement of her claims toward the centre of Venezuela, as now known, is unjustifiable beyond a doubt, . . . but we do say that these things and others have furnished a controversy in which we were interested, that this controversy was complicated by facts so disputed that it presented a case which . . . should be subjected to the sifting and examination which impartial arbitration affords. The refusal to refer the question to such determination was intensely disappointing. It was disappointing because we cannot see the force of the reasons given for refusal. . . .

Great Britain says she has a flawless case. Our interest in the question led us to ask her to exhibit that case in a tribunal above all others recognized as a proper one for that purpose. . . . Great Britain has refused our request. What is to be done? We certainly ought not, we certainly cannot abandon the case because she says she is right, nor because she refuses arbitration. . . . Instead of threatening war for not arbitrating, we simply say, inasmuch as Great Britain will not aid us in fixing the facts, we . . . do the best we can to discover the true state of facts for ourselves. . . . When with all this

280. Lord Pauncefote to Bayard, December 20, 1895, *ibid.*

we become as certain as we can be . . . that she has seized the territory and superseded the jurisdiction of Venezuela—that is a different matter.[281]

When Cleveland wrote his message to Congress of December 17, and when he wrote this letter to Bayard he had already read John Bassett Moore's letter to W. L. Wilson, December 10, 1895. Moore's viewpoint was that of Bayard. For many years Venezuela "instead of settling her boundary dispute, has in various ways, some of them obviously dishonest, been trying to drag the United States into the dispute." Instead of asserting that arbitration was the only reasonable way of settling the Venezuelan boundary controversy, Moore thought it would be "a very unsatisfactory way of settling the question." America had consented to arbitration of boundary disputes, but never had this been done "where a line had not previously been agreed upon by direct negotiation."

Thanks to Olney's prompting, Cleveland was flying in the face of American practice. Moore had served as an intimate adviser to Bayard and Gresham, but under Olney, W. W. Rockhill had become the Assistant Secretary of State, and he provoked rather than restrained the jingo spirit that prevailed in the Department of State. In a letter to Bayard, Henry L. Bryan gives an intimate picture of the situation that prevailed under Olney's administration:

> It seems rather strange that Mr. Rockhill should have been selected as the Assistant Secretary, for he is not a strong man, intellectually, and fell far short of the abilities expected to be displayed by him when Judge Gresham selected him as the 3d Assistant. But Mr. Rockhill is an opportunist, and when the change was shown in method of treating foreign affairs, leaving the conservative and self-respecting standard of calm and dispassionate adherence to right unmindful of bluster and temporary approval of the noisy shouters for a "firm" policy, he joined with great eagerness in the fray, and has his reward.[282]

Rockhill was very glad to support Olney's so-called "firm policy," and as early as November 7 he revealed his attitude in a letter to Henry White. He stated that his official associates were "much amused at the suggestions contained in the English papers of alliances between Great Britain and the United States, and of the absolute impossibility of our ever coming to blows. . . . England certainly wants alliances of some sort." [283]

During Bayard's term of office as Secretary of State, Rockhill had

281. President Cleveland to Bayard, December 29, 1895, *Bayard MS.*
282. Henry L. Bryan to Bayard, February 14, 1896, *Bayard MS.*
283. W. W. Rockhill to Henry White, November 7, 1895, *White MS.*

served as Secretary of the Legation at Peking. He had constant trouble with Charles Denby, the American Minister, and in June, 1888, Bayard indicated to him that his resignation would be in order. Rockhill did not forget this incident, and was glad to intrigue against Bayard in 1895–1896. He soon had Henry White to help him, and, strange to say, James R. Roosevelt, for whom Bayard had done a great deal, joined in the conspiracy. Roosevelt was on leave of absence from London, where he had displaced Henry White as the First Secretary of the Embassy, but realizing that Olney was unfriendly to Bayard, Roosevelt joined with this little group of Bayard's enemies. Henry L. Bryan, who worked in the Department of State, wrote to Bayard and informed him of the situation:

> What you write me about the Embassy force only confirms what I was loath to believe from the circumstances around the Department during the time when the Venezuelan matter and the Edinburgh address were the topics of discussion, and Mr. Roosevelt was on leave in this city, in repeated conferences with Mr. Rockhill and others who are not at all friendly to you.[284]

When Bayard read President Cleveland's letter of December 29, he read it in connection with all its implications. The background in Washington was only too familiar to him. Needless to say, this letter was very disquieting, and on January 10, 1896, he set down his feelings in a memorandum:

> Brancepeth Castle, Durham. I received Mr. Cleveland's letter yesterday, and carried it in my pocket in the shooting. It depressed me greatly, for it inclines me to the belief that his faculties have been overtasked and his comprehension of the condition of affairs defective. I fear he has made a grave and great error of judgment, and has been too *precipitate,* for I do not see why he should abandon suddenly his attitude of conservatism, and gone apparently into the camp of aggressiveness.
>
> It is true that G. B. has most unwisely disregarded the application so frequently and earnestly put forth by the U. S. to heal this *Venezuela* sore, and relieve V. and the U. S. of the fear that there was an indefinite plan of British occupation in the heart of South America, implying a purpose of extensive domination, originating in private possessions, backed up by Imperial force in the end. It certainly was in the power of Lord S. to have disabused the public mind of any such intent, but several minor events have

284. H. L. Bryan to Bayard, December 25, 1895, *Bayard MS.* In a letter to H. L. Bryan, December 12, 1896, Bayard remarks: "Mr. Roosevelt has suddenly put off to the United States and I believe intends to go to Egypt before he returns here. In the strictest confidence I may say that his absence is not to be regretted. . . . Happily there are no serious questions now which threaten the peace of the two countries, and if there were, Mr. Roosevelt would probably array himself against me, *as he did a year ago.*" *Bayard MS.*

indicated a disposition to press forward without abatement the territorial lines of G. B. There is a profession of continuity of action in the succeeding Administration, but I fear it is only an *aggressive* continuity. Thus in India, . . . in Central America, the proposition to open up the *Mosquito* question, and the refusal to arbitrate or otherwise arrange the Guiana Boundary.

In Africa the only change is to *advance.* . . . If Dr. Jameson had made a successful entry into Johannesburg, I can scarcely doubt the gov't would have sustained him, and yet his act would have been equally *without law.* Perhaps *now* more heed will be given to the remonstrance of the U. S. in the South American case. *That,* I think, should have been the course of the U. S.—earnestly and clearly to have stated the facts of the case, and then to have gravely protested against the refusal of G. B. to submit her unexplained and indefinite claims in the Orinoco region.

I am not prepared to declare the U. S. the guarantor—the Protector—of each South Am. State. They claim to be independent, autonomous, and sovereign, and therefore must be responsible for such engagements as they choose to make. To substitute a European Sovereignty for a South American, is a very different thing, and such an intrusion of the European system into the American would present a very grave question, but that has not yet arisen. One result of the President's action will be undoubtedly to check any such intent for a long time, but in what a position shall we be placed when the Boundary of Guiana shall (may) be declared to be an impairment of Venezuelan rights? That is most serious, and in the meantime, some effort must be made to induce G. B. to have a *line agreed upon.* Will Venezuela agree to *anything* which G. B. can or will accept? And is the U. S. to leave the question of peace or war with G. B. [to be] decided by the will of Venezuela or the interests of Venezuela? To what a condition would this degrade and endanger the world's best hope for peace or progress? [285]

In dealing with Bayard's attitude towards Cleveland, Professor Nevins remarks: "The effect of the message [of December 17] on Bayard had been, as we may imagine, profoundly depressing. He never lost his deep friendship and admiration for Cleveland, but for the moment his faith in him was shaken. Yet in the private memorandum on the subject which he set down at Brancepeth Castle, Durham, he admitted in spite of himself that Cleveland's suspicions of England had much basis." [286]

Professor Nevins is mistaken in believing that this Bayard memorandum had any reference to Cleveland's message to Congress of December 17. Bayard was referring to the personal letter that Cleveland wrote to him on December 29. In his discussion of Olney's attitude towards

---

285. *Memorandum* written by Bayard at Brancepeth Castle, January 10, 1896, *Bayard MS.*

286. *Grover Cleveland,* pp. 643-644.

Bayard, Professor Nevins further remarks: "Olney thought him a misfit, while Lord Salisbury confidentially spoke of him as an 'amateur diplomat'; in growing irritation, Olney concluded during the summer that he [Bayard] ought to be removed and actually proposed the step to the President. But Cleveland, while admitting that Bayard had done badly, thought it was too late to recall him and that it would do more harm than good." [287]

In stating that Lord Salisbury called Bayard an "amateur diplomat," Nevins relies upon a letter from Olney to Cleveland, March 6, 1901. In this letter, Olney makes the following remark:

. . . After your special message to Congress, the first attempts at negotiation were between Mr. Chamberlain and Lord Playfair, on the one side, and Mr. Bayard on the other. . . . Mr. Chamberlain . . . withdrew from the whole affair, . . . [and] about the same time we concluded that negotiations had better be transferred to Washington—to which suggestion Lord Salisbury acceded with cheerfulness—saying to Sir Julian, as Sir Julian confided to me confidentially, that now that the amateur diplomats had got through, perhaps serious negotiations could be set on foot. [288]

Lord Salisbury would never have called Bayard an "amateur diplomat." He was well acquainted with Bayard's splendid service as Secretary of State, and he certainly was not dissatisfied with Bayard as Ambassador to England. Salisbury was referring only to Chamberlain and Lord Playfair, and it is hardly possible that Lord Pauncefote, who thought very highly of Bayard as a statesman, would have conveyed to Olney any remark of Lord Salisbury that would have belittled Bayard.

It is unlikely that Olney sought, as early as the summer of 1895, to have Bayard removed as Ambassador to England. Bayard had done nothing to justify such a radical step. It is also quite unlikely that Cleveland said that Bayard had "done badly" during that same summer. He was hardly that unfair, and his letters to Bayard give no indication that he was displeased with Bayard's actions.

On his part, Bayard was deeply shocked that the Chief Executive could favor Olney's brusque manner of handling delicate diplomatic situations, and he was fearful that war might result from a policy of lending support to a dubious Venezuelan case. In a letter to George F. Parker, Bayard confessed his uneasiness over the outcome of the bound-

287. *Ibid.*, p. 638. There was no desire on the part of Professor Nevins to be unduly critical of Bayard. His account of the Venezuelan boundary controversy is always objective, and his biography of Cleveland is a landmark in American biographical writing.
288. Henry James, *Richard Olney*, pp. 249-250.

ary dispute. He could not easily dismiss these fears because there was "too much at stake even in the remote risk of a collision between the nations who are the main guardians under God of the world's civilization."[289]

The appointment by President Cleveland (January 1, 1896) of the members of the boundary commission had a quieting effect upon the troubled diplomatic waters. The personnel of this commission was distinguished: David J. Brewer, Associate Justice of the United States Supreme Court; Richard H. Alvey, Chief Justice of the Court of Appeals of the District of Columbia; Andrew D. White and Daniel C. Gilman were outstanding educators, and Frederick R. Coudert was an able and well-known lawyer. It is interesting to note that Cleveland did not consult Olney with reference to the selection of the members of this commission.[290]

In England, the news of the appointment of the boundary commission was overshadowed by other complications that attracted public attention. In the Far East, the growing power of the Franco-Russian Alliance awakened British apprehensions with reference to the possible closure of the Chinese market,[291] and certain British periodicals began to look with favor upon closer connections with the United States as a means of meeting this menace. The *Westminster Gazette* called attention to the fact that for many years America had taken a "great interest in the development of China, Japan, and Corea." In the Far East the interests of John Bull and Cousin Jonathan were identical, and the English-speaking peoples could better employ their strength in fortifying their position in the Orient than in "squabbling over such petty matters as the boundaries of Venezuela and Nicaragua." [292]

In the Near East the possible partition of the Ottoman Empire was a question that demanded much of Salisbury's closest scrutiny, and it is the opinion of Professor Langer that "in the years 1895 and 1896 the good old-fashioned Near Eastern crisis probably brought the European nations nearer to war than did any other dispute." [293]

In South Africa, the Jameson Raid (December 29, 1895–January 2, 1896) nearly precipitated a crisis. Emperor Wilhelm, of Germany was

289. Bayard to George F. Parker, December 31, 1895, *Bayard MS.*
290. Allan Nevins, *Grover Cleveland*, p. 645.
291. Philip Joseph, *Foreign Diplomacy in China, 1894–1900* (London, 1928); R. Stanley McCordock, *British Far Eastern Policy, 1894–1900* (N. Y. 1931).
292. Quoted in the New York *World*, October 27, 1895.
293. *The Diplomacy of Imperialism, 1890–1902* (N. Y. 1935), vol. 1, p. 213.

deeply disturbed over the news of this raid, and on January 3, 1896, he sent a telegram to President Kruger, of the Transvaal, congratulating him upon the defeat of this attack upon the "independence" of his country.[294] The reaction in Great Britain to this German gesture of friendship for Kruger, was immediate and unanimous in sharp denunciation. The British press was filled with articles on German perfidy, and the Venezuelan boundary dispute was pushed into the background.[295]

The difference in the British attitude towards Cleveland's message of December 17, and the Kaiser's telegram of January 3, is clearly shown in the following letter from E. Alfred Heath to Bayard:

> I believe the greater part of my countrymen would like to see America and England drawn closer together by the bonds of friendship, and our mutual ties of blood and language. Such statements as those expressed in the "leader" of the New York *Morning Press* and published in the *Daily Telegraph* of yesterday, will do an *immense* amount of good in this country, and was in exact accord with our feelings as a Nation with respect to the *United States* until the late unhappy difference, and even now. I believe, with many it is with a sort of stunned feeling that people think of the matter. They cannot realize a *war with America* is a possibility, looking as we do, on *Americans* as of one blood and language with ourselves, and that the great aim of both nations is civilization and prosperity to all peoples. You will at once see what I mean when you notice the different way in which the words of President Cleveland and the Emperor of Germany have been taken in this country. In the *first,* incredulity, doubt, horror that Englishmen and Americans go to war. In the *second,* the *whole nation* to a man, . . . roused at once to fever heat and ready for anything.[296]

Bayard was in cordial agreement with these views of Mr. Heath, and he bent every effort to find some formula that would settle the Venezuelan boundary dispute. In a letter to Sir Henry H. Howorth, he

294. Friedrich Thimme, "Die Krüger-Depesche," *Europäische Gespräche,* May-June, 1924, pp. 201-244; Raymond Sontag, "The Cowes Interview and the Kruger Telegram," *Political Science Quarterly,* 1925, vol. 40, pp. 217-247.

295. There is an excellent review of this whole subject in W. L. Langer's *The Diplomacy of Imperialism, 1890–1902,* vol. 1, pp. 213-254. An interesting sidelight on the attitude of some British military men towards the Venezuelan dispute, is shown in the following excerpt from a letter sent by Lieutenant-Colonel Thomas Tully to Commander Cowles, January 8, 1896: "We are not taking any stock of possible difficulties with our cousins over the sea. I and other intelligent persons view all this with the most unmitigated contempt. Of course, if we were kicked very hard we should have to bark, but there is no war-talk on this side. We have got another gentleman now to deal with. If he wants to fight we can accommodate him. . . . His name is William, and I can tell you that the English people are pretty angry about this, as to which you will probably forgive us, because I guess we are pretty much of the same family after all." *Bayard MS.*

296. E. Alfred Heath to Bayard, January 11, 1896, *Bayard MS.*

enclosed a copy of his instruction of February 17, 1888, to Phelps, and he indicated his hope that matters would soon be amicably adjusted. In his letter of reply, Howorth expressed his amazement that "the question should have been allowed to smoulder so long and that it should have caused a real strain on the relations between the two countries."[297]

After receiving Bayard's note, Howorth had a long conversation with the editor of the London *Times,* who encouraged him to write a letter on the Venezuelan controversy. Armed with a copy of this letter, which appeared in the *Times* on January 9, David D. Wells, Second Secretary of the American Embassy, paid a visit to the Foreign Office and had a conference with Mr. Wylde. Wylde informed Mr. Wells,

. . . in the *strictest confidence,* that Lord Salisbury had very considerably modified his views in regard to the Venezuelan question, and added that his Lordship did not wish to stir up trouble between England and the United States, and was prepared to "trim" his views to meet the requests of the United States Government in the matter.[298]

The *Saturday Review* was in accord with this changing attitude of Lord Salisbury, and it assured its readers that England could "submit the dispute in Venezuela to arbitration, and American arbitration at that, without loss of self-respect." [299] Professor John Westlake, the eminent British authority on International Law, entertained a similar opinion, and he indicated the manner in which the dispute could be arbitrated to the satisfaction of both England and the United States. The basic principle of this arbitration should be that

. . . neither England or Venezuela should be disturbed in the possession of actual settlements. . . . Having regard to what is known of the facts, is there any reason to believe that either England or Venezuela, by admitting the validity of the actual settlements of the other, would abandon anything which it could possibly maintain in the most unrestricted arbitration.[300]

297. Sir Henry H. Howorth to Bayard, January 7, 1896, *Bayard MS.*
298. David D. Wells to Bayard, January 9, 1896, *ibid.* On January 6 Wells had a previous conversation with Mr. Wylde who had expressed the view that "Her Majesty's Government should give the Venezuelans everything they wanted, as it was only a matter of time, say twenty years, before the disputed territory would drift back to the British Government by purchase or otherwise." *Ibid.*
299. January 4, 1896.
300. London *Times,* January 6, 1896. In commenting upon this proposal by Professor Westlake, the *Times,* January 7, remarked: "There is no particular sanctity in the Schomburgk line, but it was held by Great Britain to mark off practically the settled districts from those which are unoccupied. It ought not to be very difficult to determine what districts . . . have been for some years in the actual occupation of the Venezuelans and the

Impressed with these evidences of British good will, Secretary Olney responded with a friendly gesture. Seven American citizens, including John Hays Hammond, were arrested upon charges of conspiracy in connection with the Jameson Raid in the Transvaal. Upon the suggestion of Lord Pauncefote,[301] Olney instructed Bayard to mention "unofficially to Lord Salisbury that necessary measures for Hammond's protection may be taken through British representative at Pretoria."[302] On the following day, Olney sent another instruction which requested the good offices of British representatives in South Africa for all Americans who had been arrested.[303] Bayard replied that Mr. Chamberlain, the British Colonial Secretary, had assured him that these American requests would be complied with at once.[304]

These instructions of Secretary Olney were interpreted in England as an indication of a friendly spirit, and the London *Speaker* expressed the opinion that "President Cleveland, in taking this step, was wishful to conciliate England."[305] Other British periodicals made similar comments. The *Economist* regarded Olney's instructions as a "compliment" to the British Government;[306] the *Statist* looked upon them as a "friendly act, gracefully done at an opportune moment";[307] while the *Times* thought they were distinctly "encouraging."[308]

These friendly comments were accompanied by a speech made by Arthur Balfour, at Manchester, on January 15. Balfour made a direct reference to the Monroe Doctrine in the following words:

What is the Monroe Doctrine? What is the Doctrine expressed by President Monroe . . . some 70 years and more ago? It was a doctrine in which we at the time . . . heartily concurred, . . . and I have yet to learn that upon the substance of this doctrine the British Government have altered their minds. We have never desired, nor do we now desire, either to interfere with the domestic concerns of any South American State or to acquire for ourselves any territory that belongs to them. . . . The idea of war with the United States of America carries with it something of the unnatural horror of a civil war. May no English statesman and no English party ever have the responsibility of that crime heavy upon their souls.[309]

British respectively, and excluding these, to go to arbitration on the unsettled districts as a whole."

301. John Hays Hammond, *Autobiography* (N. Y. 1935, 2 vols.), vol. 1, p. 361.
302. Secretary Olney to Bayard, January 12, 1896, *Foreign Relations, 1896*, p. 562.
303. Secretary Olney to Bayard, January 13, 1896, *ibid.*, p. 562.
304. Bayard to Secretary Olney, January 13, 1896, *ibid.*, p. 562. See also, John H. Ferguson, *American Diplomacy and the Boer War* (Phila., 1939), pp. 20-24.
305. January 18, 1896, p. 55.   306. January 18, 1896, p. 62.
307. January 18, 1896, p. 72.   308. January 14, 1896.
309. London *Daily Mail*, January 17, 1896.

There were many other important British statesmen and publicists who were seeking some solution of the Venezuelan boundary dispute. In the early part of January, 1896, Sir William Harcourt talked with Joseph Chamberlain in this regard, and he emphasized the importance of making certain concessions to the United States.[310] Chamberlain had long been friendly to America, and his American wife helped to confirm his interest in an amicable settlement of all Anglo-American disputes. Chamberlain now turned to Lord Playfair, who also had an American wife, and, with the consent of Lord Salisbury, the way was now prepared for an unofficial attempt to iron out the Venezuelan difficulty. On January 12, Playfair called at the American Embassy and informed Bayard that he had been commissioned by Lord Salisbury and Joseph Chamberlain to submit a memorandum which outlined a possible solution of the Venezuelan boundary dispute.[311]

310. A. G. Gardiner, *The Life of Sir William Harcourt* (London, 1923, 2 vols.), vol. 2, pp. 395-404.

311. In a memorandum written by Bayard on January 12, 1896, the gist of this conversation with Lord Playfair is summarized as follows: "Lord Playfair came promptly and told me at once he had come at the request of Lord Salisbury and Mr. Chamberlain. He referred to the marked difference expressed throughout this country between the suggestion of war with the United States and war with Germany—the strongest antipathy to the first, and a readiness for the last. He said a way out of the present *impasse* was wanted, and that as Lord Salisbury had sent answers to Mr. Olney, it would seem easy and natural that from the latter, by way of rejoinder, a suggestion for a relief of the situation should be made.

"He said that it would assist a solution if the United States should propose a Conference of the European Powers who have dependencies in the Western Hemisphere, i.e., Great Britain, Spain, France, and Holland, and the United States, to pronounce and formulate the Monroe Doctrine—i.e., that the influence and dominion of none of the European powers should ever be extended beyond its present limits on the American Continent—this, if proposed by the United States, would be accepted by England.

"The possibility of submitting to this Conference the question whether the Venezuelan boundary question comes within the Monroe Doctrine. . . .

"Could not Venezuela and Great Britain agree to an Arbitration thus—As there are no Venezuelan settlements inside the Schomburgk line, and as there are no British settlements beyond the Schomburgk line, could it not be agreed that without regard to the Schomburgk [line], all of those actual occupations by settlement by the respective parties, G. B. and Venezuela, should be excluded from Arbitration, and all the territory not so settled and occupied, but lying between the settlements, be divided by a line drawn by a Court of Arbitration, which line shall be accepted by both Countries.

"To this end, it would be possible to add English and Venezuelan Commissioners to the Commission already appointed by the President, or as that would make the Commission too cumbrous, would it not be better to appoint 2 or 3 from the U. S. Commission to represent the knowledge they have acquired; 2 or 3 from England, 2 or 3 from Venezuela. If the principle were accepted that actual and existing occupations and settlements by Venezuela or by Great Britain should be excluded from Arbitration, but that all other territory not so included should be submitted to Arbitration, there would be no difficulty in settling a line by friendly arbitration. . . .

"Lord P. was very friendly, and remarked upon the different manner in which the Ger-

In this memorandum it was suggested that the American Government should call a conference of the European powers that had American possessions—Great Britain, France, Spain, and Holland. This conference would then deal with the question of the Monroe Doctrine, and would proclaim the principle that "European Powers having interests in America should not seek to extend their influence in . . . [the American] Hemisphere." If the United States would make this proposal, Great Britain would "accept the Monroe doctrine, and it would become International Law between countries named."

With reference to arbitration of the Venezuelan dispute, the Playfair memorandum then suggested that inasmuch as there were

. . . no Venezuelan settlements inside Schomburgk line, and no British settlements beyond that line; therefore, irrespective of that line, mutual condition be accepted, that all British and all Venezuelan settlements be excluded from arbitration, but all country between the settlements be settled by a Court of Arbitration drawing a boundary line which should be accepted by both countries. Such Court of Arbitration to consist of two or three Commissioners from England, two or three from Venezuela, and two or three from present United States Commission.

In concluding this cipher despatch summarizing the Playfair memorandum, Bayard expressed his "positive judgment" that a

. . . proclaimed recognition of Monroe Doctrine as International Law between Powers named would make it binding, not only to them, but practically on all other European Powers, and would end all contemplated plans of future conquest, or intermeddling alliances in the Western Hemisphere by European Powers under any pretext.[312]

man Emperor's action and that of President Cleveland had been received by the people of G. B.—that towards the U. S. expressions were of amazement, disappointment, and pain—the strongest reluctance to assume hostility, but not so towards Germany—but an instant defiance and a readiness to fight." *Bayard MS.* See also, W. Reid, *Memoirs and Correspondence of Lord Playfair* (N. Y. 1899), pp. 416-426.

312. Bayard to Secretary Olney, January 13, 1896, *Bayard MS.* In a private note to Bayard, January 13, 1896, Lord Playfair further remarks: "There is an argument for taking steps to produce an *entente cordiale* between the two countries that I purposely did not urge upon you yesterday, because it is not backed by the same amount of authority that I could claim for the other proposals, but such as it is I mention it to you now.

"I was discussing the advantages with an eminent conservative politician, of the consequences of getting the Monroe Doctrine officially accepted by this country and my friend said: 'Had we been on cordial terms, in what a different position the Armenian question would have been. The European powers were all jealous of each other and would do nothing; and so the concert broke down and thus was a dismal failure. But if the United States, with its splendid missions in Turkey, could have felt sure of being backed by England, how different would have been the results, and how irresistible would have been the conclusion that the cause of humanity and not the love of conquest had inspired the representations of the two powers. That is only one example of what would follow if the two

Olney was utterly opposed to calling a conference of European powers to deal with the Monroe Doctrine, and he informed Bayard that Lord Playfair's suggestions were

. . . highly appreciated, and desire for speedy, as well as rightful, adjustment of Venezuelan boundary controversy fully reciprocated. But the United States is content with existing status of Monroe Doctrine, which, as well as its application to said controversy, it regards as completely and satisfactorily accepted by the people of the Western Continents. It does not favor, therefore, proposed conference of powers. Solution it suggests is this: "Let appropriate clause be added to Behring Sea Convention, or if deemed wisest, let there be an independent Convention, which shall provide for settlement by arbitration of all controversies between the two countries, including Venezuelan boundary, and which, as to that controversy, shall explicitly provide that long-continued occupation of territory by Venezuelans or by British subjects, shall, . . . be given all the weight belonging to it in reason and justice, or by the principles of International Law. Tribunal to consist of two members present American Commission, of two persons chosen by Great Britain, and of a fifth agreed upon by the two Governments, or, in case of failure to agree, nominated by. . . . .[313]

In explanation of his position, Bayard wrote a long despatch to Olney in which he referred to the possible dangers of German interference in Latin American affairs. Consideration of this nature had led him to "believe it would save trouble to future Administrations of the United States if open public notice to all trespassers could be publicly posted on the European side of the Atlantic Ocean." Bayard then inquired if Venezuela was to have any "active participation or voice" in the arbitral tribunal suggested by Secretary Olney in his instruction of January 14.[314] Olney replied with an instruction for Bayard to "com-

---

great English-speaking nations went arm in arm instead of being separated by misunderstanding." *Bayard MS.*

On September 28, 1896, when the Venezuelan boundary dispute was well on the way to satisfactory settlement, Olney wrote a letter to Joseph Chamberlain in which he made the following surprising remarks: "If . . . England should now seriously set about putting the Armenian charnel-house in order, there can be little doubt that the United States would consider the moment opportune for vigorous exertion on behalf of the American citizens and interests in Turkey. It would feel itself entitled to demand full indemnity for past injuries to them as well as adequate security against the like injuries in the future. It would support such demands by all the physical force at its disposal." *Olney MS.* See also, A. L. P. Dennis, *Adventures in American Diplomacy*, pp. 59-61.

313. Secretary Olney to Bayard, January 14, 1896, *Bayard MS.*

314. Bayard to Secretary Olney, January 15, 1896, *Great Britain, Despatches*, vol. 182, MS Dept. of State. On January 3, 1896, Bayard sent a personal note to Olney in which he enclosed copies of a letter he had addressed to the Prince of Wales, December 29, 1895, and the reply of the Prince, December 31, 1895. These letters were written in a friendly vein, and they expressed the hope that nothing would mar the existing good relations that existed between the two countries. *Bayard MS.* On January 15 Olney telegraphed to Bayard

municate contents of my cable of fourteenth without delay, leaving British Government, if it thinks it important, to raise question of Venezuela consent." [315]

On January 17 Lord Playfair came to the American Embassy for a conference with Bayard. He was informed that the "United States did not care to have a conference with the European owners of American colonies," and he immediately remarked that he was quite satisfied "that the conference was not to be held on that subject." After Bayard outlined Olney's proposal for an arbitral commission, Playfair inquired if "Venezuela would consent" to such an arrangement. Bayard answered that he was not ready "to reply just now but that no doubt some arrangement would be made satisfactory to Venezuela." [316]

Bayard reported to Secretary Olney the result of the conference with Lord Playfair,[317] and on January 20 he sent a cipher telegram to the Department of State in which he gave the gist of another meeting with Playfair (January 20). The British Government was prepared to join the United States "in general arbitration of all disputed boundaries, including Venezuela." According to the Foreign Office, there were no British settlements west of the Schomburgk line, and no Venezuelan settlements east of that line. The British Government desired, therefore, that the proposed arbitration would "mutually exclude all occupied settlements of either party," and it was deemed expedient to have some definition of the term "settlements." [318]

---

that the state of feeling in the United States was such that "any publication of such correspondence would be most unfortunate from every point of view." *Olney MS.* Bayard replied that the letter of January 3 and the enclosures were "wholly confidential." *Olney MS.* See also, Bayard's letter to Olney, January 15, 1896, *ibid.*

315. Secretary Olney to Bayard, January 16, 1896, *Bayard MS.*

316. *Memorandum* written by Bayard, January 17, 1896, after a conference with Lord Playfair. *Bayard MS.*

317. Bayard to Secretary Olney, January 17, 1896, telegram, *Olney MS.* See also, confidential letter from Bayard to Secretary Olney, January 18, 1896, *ibid.*

318. Bayard to Secretary Olney, January 20, 1896, *Bayard MS.* At this meeting on January 20, Lord Playfair read to Bayard some excerpts from a note that probably was written by Chamberlain or Lord Salisbury. In this note it was stated that the "Americans would be wrong not to accept a conference to adopt the Monroe Doctrine. Such an international confirmation would tend to clear the air, and remove from the minds of all the American people the idea, so extraordinary to us, that either we or any other European nation covets one additional inch of soil on the American continent. . . . I think there would be no objection to introducing an article to some convention establishing a general arbitration between G. B. and U. S. for all cases of—1. Disputed boundaries in unsettled territories. 2. Complaints by nationals of one side alledging injury by officials of the other. . . .

"The above would of course include the Venezuela coast, in regard to which, however, it would not be enough merely to provide that occupations of disputed districts should

Olney was not inclined to agree to this British proposition to exclude from the arbitration all occupied settlements of either party. He was unable to

. . . comprehend the justice or pertinency of the proposition that mere occupation shall be decisive of title. The time, character, and all circumstances attending such occupation must necessarily be considered and must be interpreted and construed according to the principles of private and public law applicable thereto. Nor does the definition of settlements by agreement in advance seem feasible. Every one of the numerous elements involved in such definition would be subject of debate and of probable disagreement, while, as Venezuela must be consulted at every step, the inevitable delays would be interminable.[319]

In this telegram Olney flatly refused to suggest a definition of "settlements," and he frankly expressed the opinion that it would not be "feasible" to arrive at such a definition in advance of the meeting of the arbitral tribunal. His stand in this regard was distinctly unreasonable, and in the end he had to give way and accept a compromise. His attitude on this and other points, was a revelation to Bayard that Olney was loath to work through him in an attempt to settle the Venezuelan controversy. According to Henry James, "Bayard's ready endorsement of the conference proposal destroyed Olney's confidence in the Ambassador's comprehension of the American policy." [320]

As a matter of fact, Olney's dissatisfaction with Bayard long antedated the proposal for a conference of Powers to deal with the question of the Monroe Doctrine. Olney knew that Bayard had not been in accord with his "stand up and deliver" attitude towards England. Bayard knew that Olney's note was inaccurate and needlessly belligerent. Moreover, it was not in agreement with American practice as concerned the employment of arbitration in the settlement of boundary disputes. Bayard's letters to President Cleveland were a clear indication of Bayard's attitude, and that is the reason why the President wrote his long personal letter to Bayard (December 29, 1895) in which he explained the reasons why he had endorsed Olney's policy. Olney was anxious to get rid of Bayard if he possibly could, but he had no valid excuse for doing so. Balked of his desire in this regard, he indicated his disagreement in his telegrams and instructions, and he made Bayard's

be 'taken into account.' " *Bayard MS.* See also, Bayard to Secretary Olney, January 22, 1896, *Great Britain, Despatches*, vol. 182, MS Dept. of State.
319. Secretary Olney to Bayard, January 22, 1896, *Bayard MS.*
320. *Richard Olney*, p. 127.

position almost unendurable. In a letter to Henry L. Bryan, Bayard describes his feelings:

I need not say to you how distressed and unhappy I have been since December 17, and my path of duty has not always been as clear to me as I would have desired. But *my country* has been before my eyes, and my whole thought has been, can I serve the country best by standing at my post and rendering a possible service in some critical hour, or shall I retire and allow someone holding different views as to the "Monroe Doctrine," or the duties and responsibilities of the United States towards the Republics (so-called) of South America—to come here in my place? I will not embark, however, upon this subject, under which I chafe most painfully.[321]

321. Bayard to H. L. Bryan, January 21, 1896, *Bayard Press Copy Book*, vol. 3, *Bayard MS*. Bayard was also worried about the hostile sentiment in Congress concerning the speeches he had made in England. On January 20, 1896, President Cleveland, in response to a resolution, sent to the House of Representatives copies of Bayard's addresses at Edinburgh and at Boston. *House Doc. 152*, 54 Cong., 1 sess. Sterling J. Morton, Secretary of Agriculture, was full "of sentiments of admiration" with regard to these addresses (H. L. Bryan to Bayard, December 13, 1895, *Bayard MS*), but President Cleveland was much more reserved in his comments (H. L. Bryan to Bayard, January 7, 1896, *Bayard MS*).

The Republicans in the House of Representatives continued their attacks upon Bayard for political reasons, and in February, 1896, the House Committee on Foreign Affairs reported out a resolution of censure. (*House Rept. 520*, 54 Cong., 1 sess.) In the debate that ensued, Bayard was defended by Representatives James B. McCreary, H. St. George Tucker, H. D. Money, and Hugh A. Dinsmore. (See *Congressional Record*, 54 Cong., 1 sess. pp. 2944-48, 2951-55.) The resolution of censure was adopted by the House of Representatives on March 20, 1896, by a vote of 182 yeas, to 72 nays. (*Cong. Rec.*, 54 Cong., 1 sess., vol. 28, p. 3034.)

With regard to these attacks upon Bayard, George Foster Peabody wrote to express his contempt for such proceedings: "I must say that I am sad indeed with many others because of the to me unaccountable and most lamentable extreme of President Cleveland's language with reference to th Venezuelan boundary. . . . I cannot but feel that the position must be trying for you." *Bayard MS*.

Arthur Warren, Editor of the *Ladies Home Journal*, assured Bayard that he was "only too glad to lend my applause to your powerful and wholesome influence. The mission which you have made your own during the whole of your embassy to England is the highest and noblest that a man could undertake in these times." A. Warren to Bayard, January 9, 1896, *Bayard MS*.

Oscar S. Straus wrote his usual comforting and friendly letter. He thought it was "apparent to everybody in this country, that the so-called report of censure upon your address was nothing more than an effort on the part of Republicans to keep themselves busy with something, and to make a little partisan capital. . . . I have heard it more than once stated by men whose opinions are worth something that, 'This attack on Bayard will force him to the Presidency.'" Straus to Bayard, March 3, 1896, *Bayard MS*.

Worthington C. Ford thought that the action with regard to the resolution of censure, was "only one more reason for despising the present Congress, in its insane efforts to make political capital for a few incendiaries, and at the cost of decency and national honor. There is not a dissenting opinion here: that the so-called censure is an act of praise to you. . . . I do not give you my sympathy, for you need none. Not a decent man censures you for what you have said or done; and they are proud to have a man at St. James who represents the best that is of them. But is not this a legitimate outcome of Blaine-Lodge politics? Indeed, I am more severe upon Lodge than on Blaine, for he has less excuse for playing the demagogue. . . . Lodge has no force to make good his utter want of principle.

By the middle of January, 1896, Olney realized that the tone of his instruction of July 20, and that of the President's message of December 17, was too strong, and he was anxious to make some gesture of conciliation. Not caring to do so through Bayard, he began to work through George W. Smalley, the correspondent of the London *Times*. On January 21 he had a conversation with Smalley, who promptly sent a cable to the *Times* which stressed the "friendly spirit prevailing in the White House and the State Department." [322] As the weeks passed on, Olney determined to make more and more use of Smalley's services, and the columns of American correspondence in the London *Times* from January 22 to February 21 are of distinct importance in arriving at a clear understanding of the progress of the negotiations for a settlement of the Venezuelan boundary dispute.

In the meantime, Bayard made every effort to expedite these negotiations. On January 22 he sent a confidential letter to Olney which dealt with his conference with Lord Playfair on January 20. He regretted that his telegram of that day was less definite than he had wished,

. . . but the proceeding as yet is in its tentative stages, and I can perceive from the character of the debate now progressing in the Senate, that conceptions disclosed in the debate of what the "Monroe Doctrine" is supposed to include, and to what vast proportions it is proposed in some quarters to expand and apply it, may possibly, and not unnaturally, delay your reply to the suggestions conveyed to you in the telegram . . . above referred to. The mischievous and reckless sensationalism of the Press in continuing to give currency to rumors calculated to increase irritation in the relations of the two countries—is, I suppose, not to be escaped from. The resources of

---

I have little doubt it was he who inspired the attack upon you, and it was he who has given the cue and tone to the tirades." Ford to Bayard, March 22, 1896, *Bayard MS*.

322. George W. Smalley to Olney, January 22, 1896, *Olney MS*. When Smalley was sent to the United States in May, 1895, to act as the American correspondent of the London *Times*, Bayard wrote him a strong letter of recommendation to President Cleveland. Smalley expressed to Bayard his deep appreciation of this courtesy which he was certain would be of "great value" to him. It would have been a great pleasure to stay in London and see more of Bayard, but "the fates decide otherwise. . . . I should like to congratulate you on your work and success in all ways in London. Nobody but one who has lived long abroad can understand of what moment it is to the United States to be represented with ability and distinction. Yet now I shall look forward selfishly to your return." G. W. Smalley to Bayard, May 23, 1895, *Bayard MS*.

In a letter to President Cleveland, May 24, 1895, Bayard expresses the opinion that Smalley was "diverted of many of his former prejudices and now occupies a position very much in line with that for which you have done so much since 1893. I believe that with his long experience and diminished partisanship, he will do great service to both countries." *Cleveland MS*.

contradiction appear to be inadequate, for the lie proverbially outruns truth, but happily does not outlast it.

I am glad to reaffim the statement contained in my last telegram, that Her Majesty's Government are exceedingly desirous of disabusing the public mind in America of any impression that may exist, of any intention or desire whatsoever on their part, to enlarge their present possessions and jurisdiction in South America. . . .

The individual and property rights of actual settlers in such uncivilized regions are, and should be, carefully protected in all cases, and in my conversation with Lord Playfair, he expressed emphatically the favour and protection that would be exhibited to actual immigration and settlement of such portions of the vast territory which might be adjudged to be within British jurisdiction,—all such present or intending settlers would be welcomed and protected in their property. The great drawback to settlement in the region in dispute, has been the demoralization caused by an absence of settled law, so that adventurers and concessionaries of whatever country, have had no protection and no assured enjoyment.

I feel very hopeful that a boundary line can be fixed, and satisfactorily established for these two disputants.[323]

In order to clarify all the points involved in these discussions with Lord Playfair, Bayard invited his Lordship to another conference, which was held on January 24. What transpired at this conference is made clear in a memorandum written by Bayard:

Lord Playfair came at noon . . . and we discussed the Venezuela matter. He found they were on the track of his negotiation, and that rumor was busy. The improved feeling in the United States was commented upon with satisfaction. . . . He said he had seen Mr. John Morley last night, and that he had expressed great admiration for my instruction of February, 1888. . . .

I told him of the report which Joseph Austin had told me in 1887 he had made to Mr. Gladstone on the disputed territory in Venezuela, and suggested it might be found in the files of the Colonial Office. I then stated my general view of the case, and of the occupation of the seaboard on the Atlantic side of the Guianas by Holland, England, and France, and the occupation by Spain and her Colonial successors . . . of the interior of the continent, embracing the valley of the Orinoco and its confluents. . . . There never was a delimitation by either, no survey, no definite boundary, a semi-savage and scant population, no regular agriculture, no towns, no fortifications. . . .

The region was difficult if not impossible of domestic settlement excepting in scattered points. Then came gold mining and then the corrupt traffic in concessions, in shares and enterprises by the Venezuelan officials, such as Guzmán Blanco and his tribe. I told Lord Playfair of John Chester telling me of the extortion here in London in 1887 or 8, by Guzmán Blanco of £30,000 or £60,000 from a party of British gold mine owners.

323. Bayard to Secretary Olney, January 22, 1896, *Olney MS.*

In such a condition of affairs it was plain that a frontier ought to be marked, and that actual settlers who had *bona fide* paid for their property ought not to be disturbed, and should be allowed to remain under the jurisdiction where they were found, i.e., that no arbitration was needed in these Cases. . . .

Lord Playfair told me the Venezuelans were ready to be bought out, but that Great Britain did not think it would be an honorable mode of settlement. That he still believed the Tribunal of Arbitration could settle it finally, but that Venezuela should be a party. He suggested two U. S. Commissioners, two British Commissioners, and two Venezuelans. . . . But Venezuela was a necessary party, and I do not see how it can be otherwise concluded.[324]

It is apparent that Bayard knew too much about the Venezuelans to have any confidence in their integrity or any sympathy with their extravagant pretensions to all the territory west of the Essequibo. Between Venezuelans and Englishmen there could be but one choice, and Bayard was wholeheartedly in favor of the English. In a letter to W. L. Putnam, he reveals his viewpoint without reserve:

The present imbroglio with the mongrel state of Venezuela, sickens me and I can only ask to be judged as to my share in the treatment of the case by what I have placed upon the record over my own signature. I will not attempt in this note to state my views in full, but I can never give my consent or aid to any plan which places the honour, the interests, and welfare of the people of the United States subject to the decision of one or all of the other governments in this Hemisphere.

There is no pretence of the existence of any plan for the expansion of European system of influence in South America or any part of it. If such attempt should ever be made, we can then make up our minds, and prepare to enforce the decisions which the sense of duty and self-preservation may dictate, but no case exists today calling for any such decision.[325]

Although Bayard had no great liking for the Venezuelans he still thought that they should be represented on any joint commission that would deal with the boundary controversy. This was also the view of Lord Playfair, but Olney sharply disagreed with this viewpoint, and on January 28 he sent to Bayard a new suggestion with regard to the commission:

324. *Memorandum* written by Bayard after a conversation with Lord Playfair, January 24, 1896, *Bayard MS.*
325. Bayard to W. L. Putnam, January 25, 1896, *Bayard Press Copy Book*, vol. 3, *Bayard MS.* In a letter to John Morley, January 24, 1896, Bayard discusses the Venezuelan boundary dispute and concludes: "A contemptible splinter may aggravate a serious inflammation, and I do wish the splinter could be quietly removed and the sore allowed to heal—this is 'common sense.'" *Bayard MS.*

Let there be new Commission—two appointed by United States, probably from present American Commission, two appointed by Great Britain, and if the four divide equally upon results, a fifth to be mutually agreed upon or nominated by.......... This Commission shall report not a line but the facts to the two Governments, which shall thereupon endeavor to fix a line satisfactory to all parties, Venezuela included. The endeavor failing, the facts reported shall be submitted to an arbitral tribunal, consisting of the Chief Justice of England, the Chief Justice of the United States, and a third arbitrator to be mutually agreed upon or nominated by.........., which tribunal shall ascertain and declare such a divisional line as the facts submitted warrant, and which line so ascertained and declared, shall be accepted by and binding upon all parties in interest, Venezuela included.[326]

On January 29, while awaiting a visit from Lord Playfair, Bayard wrote a personal note to Olney in which he made the following statement: "There is a unanimity here in favor of an amicable settlement on grounds consistent with the self-respect and honour alike of the U. S. and G. B., and I believe they are quite ready to meet us halfway, and I trust we can make up the *other* half." [327]

When Lord Playfair arrived at the American Embassy, Bayard showed him Olney's latest proposition, and represented

. . . to him the elevated position it gave to the entire question, and that the *ultimate* power of decision in the hands of the Judiciary in both countries would make it improbable that the case would proceed beyond the *first* step suggested. He has in mind some grant of *mines* by Venezuela that expired in 1883 and was renewed and extended in 1895, which he thinks should be excluded. . . . He will see Chamberlain and Lord Salisbury. He thinks the sub-officials at the Foreign Office will "kick," and I told him they were not the kind of people I would wish in such a case as this—too technical.[328]

While engaged in this negotiation with Lord Playfair, Bayard found time to write a personal letter to President Cleveland with reference to the situation in London. He thought there was an excellent opportunity to arrive at an adjustment of the boundary controversy along lines that would fully accomplish the wish and purpose that lay closest to the President's heart—

326. Secretary Olney to Bayard, January 28, 1896, cipher telegram, *Bayard MS.* On January 28, 1896, George W. Smalley, correspondent for the London *Times*, wrote to Secretary Olney and indicated the manner in which Olney's suggestions were being reported to Mr. Buckle, the editor of the *Times*, for transmission to the British Government. Olney was using Smalley as one channel of information to the British Foreign Office. *Olney MS.*

327. Bayard to Secretary Olney, January 29, 1896, *Olney MS.*

328. *Memorandum* written by Bayard after a conversation with Lord Playfair, January 29, 1896, *Bayard MS.*

. . . the maintenance of friendly competition in the onward march of civilization of the two great branches of the English-speaking people.

I have diligently supplied Mr. Olney with the published expressions of the leading men and journals here, and . . . of the confidential tentative suggestion for a settlement of which Lord Playfair was the proponent. The progress of these suggestions has been somewhat checked by Mr. Olney's apparent subtraction of Venezuela's consent or co-operation from the plan of submission to arbitration—by which I mean that in what has passed in the exchange of telegrams between Mr. Olney and myself, Venezuela seems to be eliminated, although by your message she was distinctly a controlling and independent factor in the settlement of her boundaries.

It is an encouraging feature, and one highly honourable to Great Britain, that there is a ready and friendly co-operation between both political parties to promote an amicable and honourable adjustment of all difficulties with the United States.[329]

On January 29 Bayard sent a telegram to Secretary Olney informing him of the interview that had just been held with Lord Playfair.[330] On the following day, Smalley wrote a note to Olney and outlined the procedure which he thought best in dealing with the British Foreign Office. He also indicated that he had received a telegram from Buckle which stated that he had a strong conviction that he would be able "to send good news."[331] On January 31 Smalley acquainted Olney with the contents of a telegram he had just received from London: "Ultimate binding arbitration will be accepted provided that districts which have been *bona-fide* settled say for ten years by either English or Venezuelans were excluded. Note that we make two great concessions, first, practical admission of your right to intervene, second, abandonment of Schomburgk line."[332]

While Smalley was working with Buckle in an attempt to secure a settlement of the Venezuelan boundary dispute, Bayard had another interview with Lord Playfair on January 31, and assured him that

329. Bayard to President Cleveland, January 29, 1896, *Personal, Cleveland MS.* In a letter to his son Thomas F. Bayard, Jr., January 28, 1896, Bayard remarks: "It gives me great comfort to feel that I have been of service in creating good feeling between this and our country, and I earnestly pray that God may make me an instrumentality for peace and good will. I have no higher, or indeed, other ambition." *Bayard Press Copy Book*, vol. 3, *Bayard MS.*

330. Bayard to Secretary Olney, January 29, 1896, *Olney MS.* On this same day, Sigourney Butler wrote a confidential letter to Olney in which he expressed the opinion that most people had now recovered from "their scare which the Jews rigged up on the New York and London stock market. . . . I expect that England will back down in this matter, and will admit about what we want." *Olney MS.*

331. G. W. Smalley to Secretary Olney, January 30, 1896, *ibid.*

332. G. W. Smalley to Secretary Olney, January 31, 1896, *ibid.*

Secretary Olney disavowed any "arbitral intent or claim of such power by the Commission of the Government of the United States, and stated that I wished Lord Salisbury to appreciate that attitude, and our desire that nothing that could wound the self-respect of the British Government was intended." [333]

On February 3 Lord Playfair and Bayard had another conference, at which Plaiyfair read a letter that he had just received from Joseph Chamberlain. Chamberlain thought that it was important to point out that

. . . although the necessity and practical advantages of confining any inquiry by a Commission or Tribunal of Arbitration to the unsettled lands, . . . has formed a prominent part of every representation you have made to Mr. Bayard, yet there is no allusion to it in the suggestions which come from Washington, although Mr. Bayard says that this condition be believes is understood and desired. In my view it is an essential condition of any-settlement on the lines you have been following.

In this controversy Great Britain has been contending for men and not for territory, for the rights of settlers whom we have encouraged to take up residence and to invest their fortunes in the Colony, and not for a mere question of so many acres more or less of land.

I [Chamberlain] think therefore that the time has come when the tacit understanding on which we have proceeded should be generally confirmed, failing which I fear that there will be no advantage in our continuing our private efforts to find a satisfactory and honorable solution. If, however, this point is accepted on both sides, I believe there will be no difficulty on other heads.[334]

After Bayard had read Chamberlain's letter, he expressed the opinion that "Mr. C's phrase that 'Great Britain has been contending for men and not for territory' was begging the entire question, for the possessions of the men controlled the question of *territory*." Lord Playfair assented to this view, and said he had "authority to strike out these words, and taking a pen did so." Bayard then spoke to Playfair of the "moral impossibility of *such a Tribunal* as Mr. Olney had proposed as the ultimate deciding power, overlooking law and reason and justice in drawing a boundary line which would place *bona fide* settlers, having efficiently occupied the country, outside the jurisdiction of the laws under which they had lived for a reasonable term." [335]

333. *Memorandum* written by Bayard after a conversation with Lord Playfair, January 31, 1896, *Bayard MS.*

334. Joseph Chamberlain to Lord Playfair, February 1, 1896, *Bayard MS.*

335. *Memorandum* written by Bayard after a conversation with Lord Playfair, February 3, 1896, *ibid.*

It is evident that Bayard was wholeheartedly in favor of the British suggestion to exclude from arbitration settled districts in which British colonists had lived for many years. Moreover, he had an unshakeable belief in British honor, which he regarded as a "part of the World's moral wealth," and he was determined not to lose his "share in it." He had no doubt that he could rely with certainty upon seeing this British honor amply "demonstrated in dealing with the debateable land on Venezuela." [336]

British insistence upon some provision in favor of excluding settled districts from arbitration, was clearly indicated to Olney in a telegram from Buckle to Smalley, February 5, 1896:

We object to an arbiter being empowered to evict long established British settlers. Your answer retains this stipulation but proposes that after eviction we may ourselves compensate sufferers, for arbiter has power to determine by which party compensation is to be paid, and might decide that British settlers are on Venezuelan territory through malfeasance of British government, and consequently latter must pay compensation on account of change of jurisdiction. I repeat, reservation of rights of British settlers is strongly insisted on here. If we surrender that, you gain all the material advantages, only giving up your commission, which commission is regarded indefensible here and in Europe and by most of your enlightened men. Remember that in present state feeling abroad towards England, arbiter would probably have anti-English bias.[337]

After receiving another telegram from Buckle which indicated that the British Foreign Office was standing firmly upon the proposition to exclude from arbitration the settled districts along the Guiana boundary, Smalley expressed the opinion that "the settled districts are the crux, and unless some agreement or fresh consideration of that point be possible we are reduced to mere argumentation, and you see how little that has served us." [338]

336. Bayard to James Knowles, January 30, 1896, *Bayard MS.* In a letter to Edward M. Shepard, February 5, 1896, Bayard remarks: "I am and have long been obnoxious to the enemies of international good will between this country and our own, for it is, and will always be, my constant effort to produce good understanding between all the English-speaking peoples, believing the best hopes of civilization and human progress are safest in their hands." *Bayard Press Copy Book*, vol. 3, *Bayard MS.*

337. G. W. Smalley to Secretary Olney, February 5, 1896, enclosing telegram from Buckle of same date, *Olney MS.*

338. G. W. Smalley to Secretary Olney, February 7, 1896, *ibid.* Buckle's telegram to Smalley, February 7, 1896, read in part as follows: "I have not seen my friend again and personally I hardly think cause of peace will be served by negotiations conducted in spirit of your last communication. It will be grave misrepresentation if your friends allege that you alone make concessions and that we refuse them. You have made no concessions in public whatever, whereas Balfour and Chamberlain have publicly accepted Monroe Doc-

Secretary Olney was well aware of the fact that Bayard did not approve of the manner in which the Venezuelan boundary controversy had been handled. He also knew that Bayard was strongly in favor of the British contention as to the exclusion from arbitration of the settled districts, and he resented this attitude. His needless belligerence towards England, and his stand on the settled districts had delayed any settlement of a dispute that could easily been adjusted if Gresham had lived and had continued to serve as Secretary of State. The very fact that his tactless manner had been a diplomatic blunder, must have irritated Olney, and he was determined to vent his spleen upon any American diplomatic officials who did not share his extreme views. James R. Roosevelt, who had displaced Henry White as the First Secretary of the American Embassy in London, paid a visit to Washington during the last months of 1895, and although Bayard had been extremely kind to Roosevelt, this fact seemed to have little weight in the small mind of the First Secretary. He retailed to Olney all the small gossip that he knew about the situation in London, and he was not above attacking Bayard. In January, 1896, when Roosevelt was about to leave for England, he was instructed by Olney to sound out Bayard about having the Venezuelan negotiations removed to Washington. When Roosevelt reached London, he took this matter up with Bayard who said that he had no objection to this transfer of negotiations.[339] Olney was now getting ready to take personal charge of a situation he had badly bungled.

Before taking this step he wrote a long letter to Bayard in which he made a defence of his position with regard to the settled districts. He had noted Bayard's remarks

. . . upon the Venezuelan question "that an amicable settlement on grounds consistent with the self-respect and honor alike of the United States and Great Britain" is unanimously desired in Great Britain. The same desire exists here, probably with the same unanimity. But it is coupled with the strongest conviction that self-respect and honor will not permit the United

---

trine and we have publicly abandoned Schomburgk line. As regards private overtures we . . . offered to agree to a conference to make Monroe Doctrine part of International Law and to resume negotiations direct with Venezuela on basis of excluding only *bona fide* settled districts. You were unable to agree and made a counterproposal which . . . was absolutely accepted here. . . . We are only now at issue on question whether ultimate arbitration should extend to half British Guiana or whether *bona fide* settled districts should be excluded. . . . I have had reluctantly to omit tonight and yesterday some of your strictures on this government which seem to me undeserved and not conducive to success of negotiations." *Olney MS.*

339. J. R. Roosevelt to Secretary Olney, February 7, 1896, *Olney MS.*

States to allow British occupation to be conclusive of British title unless it ought to be so in reason, justice, and by the principles of International Law. The just effect to be given to such occupation—involving its duration, nature, and all its other characteristics—can be determined by only one of three parties—Great Britain, the United States (with Venezuela), or some impartial arbitral tribunal. As it is repugnant to all ideas of justice to let one party to a controversy lay down the rule for its decision, resort to the arbitral tribunal has always seemed to me, and still seems, inevitable. This suggestion has been met with no alternative that I am aware of, except that "settlement" should be defined in advance and as one of the rules of the arbitration. It seemed, and still seems to me, that the attempt at definition would be most difficult, would involve great delays, and would probably prove abortive in the end—leaving the parties more irritated than they are now and the controversy in a more unmanageable shape. It appeared to me, and still appears to me, to be particularly inconsistent with the expressed purpose of the British Government, that the controversy should not "drift." I discern no chance of my being mistaken in this regard unless the British Government is prepared to offer a definition of "settlement" which could be more easily accepted and would be more easily justifiable in reason and on principle and by precedent than I have dared to suppose possible. Do you know what the idea of the Foreign Office on that point is? If so, or if you can find out what it is, I should be glad to be apprised. I should like the information for the information's sake—and if I could make any use of it in the direction of a speedy adjustment of the Venezuelan question, should of course be only too happy to avail myself of it.[340]

As soon as Bayard received Olney's letter he had an interview with Lord Salisbury who promised to send an answer after he had given the matter further consideration.[341] While Bayard was waiting for the For-

340. Secretary Olney to Bayard, February 8, 1896, *Bayard MS*. In a letter to his sister, Mabel Bayard Bird, Bayard reveals his attitude towards the many attacks that had been levelled against him: "Within the last three months I have been the target for a great deal of rancorous assault. . . . Not from many, but from some have come words of gratitude and sympathy, and sometimes of admiration for what they supposed to be the *courage* of my expression, but dear, it required no courage to stand by my faith. . . . I have been made conscious, at times, that my presence here in my office has enabled me to restrain unwise and dangerous forces, and to strengthen those of wisdom and right, and 'lift the world's heart higher.' This thought has given me a serenity and cheerful determination closely akin to real happiness." *Bayard Press Copy Book*, vol. 3, *Bayard MS*.

341. Bayard to Secretary Olney, February 17, 1896, *Olney MS*. On February 12, 1896, George W. Smalley sent to Secretary Olney the following telegram he had just received from Mr. Buckle: "It is thought here that arbitration is not suitable instrument to decide question of settled districts in which there must necessarily be numerous issues of fact each requiring for its decision usual apparatus of claim, defence, examination of oral and written testimony, counsel's speeches and judgment. It would never end. Remember that Delagoa arbitration at Berne has now been going for eight years. It is thought that line between settled and unsettled districts must be matter of negotiation and we are willing to negotiate on this question with you if you adopt Venezuela's cause or we would negotiate through Brazil or Mexico if preferred. My friend believes as he has said in his speech, in negotiation plus arbitration." *Olney MS*.

eign Office to take some action with reference to his representations, he sent a personal letter to President Cleveland. With reference to the much-disputed point about "settled districts," he thought that there could be no doubt that

. . . an "innocent purchaser without notice" is always favored and protected by a court of Equity, and in a Country where no boundaries ever existed and none could be pointed out, and into which men carried their money and labor, such settlers having a reasonably continued occupation, ought to have a voice in the disposition of themselves and their property when the divisional line come to be made. The doctrine of restricting European ownership to *existing* limits, and forbidding its expansion, has now become law by common consent. . . . In other words, settlement should be made as easy as possible, for we have secured the "doctrine" which precludes European increase of influence of control.[342]

It seemed obvious to Bayard that the United States should treat England with more consideration than had been shown by Secretary Olney. This was especially true when one took into consideration the character of the Venezuelans. On February 19 the London papers published accounts of an attempted assassination of President Crespo during his attendance at a bull fight in Carácas. This exhibition of lawlessness made a deep impression upon Bayard, who jotted down some observations upon Venezuelans in general: "What a suggestion it is that the issues of peace and war between the two Trustees of Civilization—the United States and Great Britain—should in any degree be made to depend upon the decision or conduct of such a *menagerie* as a *Venezuelan* Government—the 'Sister Republic,' forsooth!" [343]

In the meantime, Olney was anxious to establish some pretext for

342. Bayard to President Cleveland, February 18, 1896, *Cleveland MS.* In a letter to Senator George Gray, February 18, 1896, Bayard makes the following comments upon British public opinion concerning a settlement of the Venezuelan boundary dispute: "By all this you will see how anxious I am that false issues should not lead us into unsustainable positions. The temper here is very favorable to a permanent and wholesome arrangement. The 'Monroe Doctrine' has been accepted *thoroughly* by the leading and representative men of both parties, and not with stiff and cold formality, but with a warm and friendly meaning that ought to put to shame the blustering bullies who fight so fiercely and at such long range." *Bayard Press Copy Book*, vol. 3, *Bayard MS.*

343. *Memorandum* written by Bayard, February, 1896, *Bayard MS.* With regard to Venezuelan officials, Bayard wrote a personal letter to President Cleveland, February 12, 1896, in which he expresses himself as follows: "Venezuelan Envoys here, and the Administrator of their affairs especially in this unsettled region now in dispute, has left a most unpleasant odor in men's nostrils. It has come to be well understood that *anything* in the way of governmental concessions is for sale in that Country, and the Envoys have usually been the *Brokers*. Speculators in the United States have thrust their soiled hands into the business and sought to embroil the United States in sustaining their corrupt contracts." *Cleveland MS.*

transferring the negotiations to Washington. He had received the letter from James R. Roosevelt, which informed him that Bayard would offer no strenuous opposition to such a transfer.[344] All that Olney had to do now was to pick some alleged flaw in Bayard's conduct of the negotiations in London, and then, in a very abrupt manner, relieve Bayard of all further responsibility in the matter. As a first item in this program, Olney sent Bayard a telegram on February 21 in which he found fault with the fact that he had not received any specific answer to his telegram of January 28. Bayard had written to President Cleveland on January 29 with reference to Olney's proposition, and he had also sent a telegram to Olney on that same day. Bayard was waiting for an answer from the Foreign Office, but Olney endeavored to create the impression that Bayard was at fault because the Foreign Office was not more prompt in its answers. After making this uncalled-for insinuation, Olney then stated that the London *Times* had suggested that the negotiations "should be transferred to Washington," and inasmuch as Venezuela had no representative in London, this suggestion would be adopted by the Department of State.[345]

On February 25 Bayard replied that negotiations had been delayed by Lord Playfair's illness, but he had "renewed pressure" in accordance with Olney's instruction of February 21.[346] A part of this pressure took the form of a letter to Lord Playfair on February 23. The following excerpts will indicate its tenor:

> During the long pause in informal, but most earnest colloquies, it is evident that a strong and most wholesome public sentiment has proved its existence on both sides of the Atlantic [347]—and while it encourages the friend of co-operative international amity, it also notifies the enemies—so that it behooves us to clinch an arrangement without loss of time, and thus prevent the question from being cast into the furnace of the political can-

344. J. R. Roosevelt to Secretary Olney, February 7, 21, 1896, *Olney MS.*
345. Secretary Olney to Bayard, February 21, 1896, *ibid.*
346. Bayard to Secretary Olney, February 25, 1896, *Bayard MS.*
347. In the *North American Review,* February, 1896, pp. 145-153, James Bryce wrote a significant article entitled "British Feeling on the Venezuelan Question." Mr. Bryce remarks that the British public knew very little about Venezuela, and it had regarded the interest of the United States in the boundary question as "entirely indirect and secondary. . . . Nobody had the least idea that your Government considered the matter to be one of immediate and primary importance to America, justifying an ultimatum. That the Monroe Doctrine could be deemed involved had not occurred to our minds. . . . What has astonished us is that the mere empty name of 'republic' should apparently have won much American sympathy for the state which is, in fact, the less free of the two, and the less like your own. . . . Every one desires that an honorable way out of the present difficulty may be found. If the same temper prevails on the other side of the ocean, . . . that way will be found."

vass, upon which the people of the United States will enter in a few short months.

Surely the practicable remedy contained in the suggestions I last made to you—and upon which, when we last met I conceived that we were in substantial accord—ought not to be imperiled or lost because of the conjectural or possible transfer of property rights in the borderless *terra incognita* of Guiana, from one political jurisdiction to another. . . .

I need not say to you that respect for law, with its moral principles and conscience, is equally shared by both branches of our race, and that Spanish-American methods of dealing with property and personal rights would be as little likely to find favour or have influence with the Commissioners on the part of the United States, as with those selected here. So that if there should turn out to be some "hard cases" of honest proprietorship in the disputable region, in which "innocent purchasers without notice" would suffer, . . . provisional arrangements for individual compensation and indemnification for such losses could be made without serious difficulty.

I must say to you that I am impressively instructed to urge co-operation by those in authority here, without loss of time, and with such a spirit as now exists, with such a Commission as is contemplated. . . . If with such methods and machinery, justice is not evolved, where in the range of human nature can it be found? [348]

As Bayard had explained to Secretary Olney, Lord Playfair's illness had delayed negotiations concerning the Venezuelan boundary, and he was still confined to his bed when he received Bayard's letter. He replied on February 25 in a short note which stated that he had been relieved of all further responsibilities in connection with the Venezuelan dispute. The informal negotiations would no longer be carried on, and in explanation of this statement he enclosed a letter from Joseph Chamberlain.[349]

Chamberlain was greatly dissatisfied with the course of the informal negotiations between Bayard and Lord Playfair. He was insistent that adequate consideration be given to the question of "settled districts," and he stated that Lord Playfair had assured him that Bayard believed that the Department of State was in favor of excluding from arbitration all matters referring to these "settled districts." On February 3 Playfair had again stated that he had read all the telegrams that had passed between Bayard and Olney, and in every one he had found that "the principle of settled districts was stated to be the essence of the arbitration." This being true, Chamberlain expressed to Lord Playfair his great surprise upon reading Bayard's letter of February 23, in which

348. Bayard to Lord Playfair, February 23, 1896, *Bayard MS.*
349. Lord Playfair to Bayard, February 25, 1896, *Bayard MS.*

no mention was made of the exclusion of the settled districts from all arbitral proceedings. To surrender this principle would

. . . cut away the ground on which we have sought an amicable compromise, and would stultify the repeated declarations of the British Government from Lord Aberdeen to the present day. As the abstract which I have given of our correspondence shows that this point has from the first been steadily kept before Mr. Olney, I must express my great disappointment that the United States should apparently desire to withdraw from the position which I think we both understood they originally accepted. In this case I can only hope that some other compromise may be found in the course of the negotiations; and, as I understand that these are now officially in progress, I think no object will be served by continuing the informal discussion.[350]

This letter from Joseph Chamberlain is interesting from several angles. It indicates either that Lord Playfair did not report his conversations with Bayard in a correct manner, or that Chamberlain was purposely stupid. While Bayard was not in favor of Olney's stand with reference to "settled districts," he did not fail to make the matter clear to Lord Playfair, and even went so far as to show him the telegrams from Olney in this regard. The real reason why Chamberlain wrote his letter to Lord Playfair was because he had learned that Olney was not friendly to Bayard, and that the negotiations would soon be transferred to Washington.[351] Anticipating this move, he seized an opportunity to go on record in a very emphatic manner, even though he may have misquoted Lord Playfair in doing so.

After reading this letter from Chamberlain, Bayard at once telegraphed to Olney and summarized its contents. He then made reference to Chamberlain's statement that some compromise might be found in the "direct negotiations" which were in progress. With respect to these current negotiations alluded to by Chamberlain, Bayard stated that as yet he had no knowledge of them.[352]

When Olney received this telegram he felt slightly uncomfortable, because it indicated that J. R. Roosevelt had been talking behind Bayard's back concerning the transfer of negotiations to Washington. The only way to answer Bayard was by making another attack upon

350. Joseph Chamberlain to Lord Playfair, February 25, 1896, *Bayard MS.* For other data on Lord Playfair, see, Sir Wemyss Reid, *Memoirs and Correspondence of Lyon Playfair, First Lord Playfair of St. Andrews* (London, 1899), pp. 416ff.

351. J. R. Roosevelt to Secretary Olney, February 21, 1896, *Olney MS.*

352. Bayard to Secretary Olney, February 25, 1896, *Olney MS.* See also, Bayard to Secretary Olney, February 26, 1896, *Great Britain, Despatches*, vol. 183, MS Dept. of State.

his position. On February 26 he sent to London a telegram in which he asked Bayard whether he had acted upon the suggestions made in the instruction of February 8. No answer had been received from the Foreign Office with respect to the meaning of "settlements." If Lord Salisbury insisted that settlements should be excluded from arbitration, and also refused to define the meaning of settlements, there was no "occasion for or utility in negotiations." Because the Foreign Office had delayed sending any definite answer to these questions, it was evident that negotiations should be transferred to Washington, but it should be understood that these same negotiations were not yet "in progress." [353]

Olney had been advised by Bayard that the suggestions in the instruction of February 8 had been brought to the attention of the Foreign Office, and his telegram clearly indicates that he was merely grasping at some excuse that would justify the transfer of the negotiations to Washington.

Bayard lost no time in acquainting Lord Salisbury with Olney's desire to "remove" the negotiations from London. He also made it clear that the Department of State was especially anxious to get as soon as possible a definition of what was meant by the term "settled districts." [354]

353. Secretary Olney to Bayard, February 26, 1896, *Olney MS.*
354. Bayard to Lord Salisbury, February 27, 1896, *Foreign Relations, 1896*, pp. 240-241. In a memorandum written by Bayard after his conversation with Lord Salisbury, February 27, 1896, the following outline is given of the main points that were discussed: "I stated the purpose of my visit. . . . He assented promptly to the commencement of formal negotiations at Washington, and would without delay empower Sir Julian Pauncefote to act for Great Britain, with Mr. Olney for the United States. He said: 'We have no Venezuelan here and you have.'

"I then broached the subject of 'settlements' and asked if he would give us a definition of what was included in that word. He said he would have to go to the Colonial Office for it, and he would *endeavour* to reply, and would write me as soon as he could. He then said our situation resembled two men who wanted to travel together, but one wanted to go all the way to Brighton and the other only so far as Croyden, but they would go as far as they could together.

"He said he would agree to have a Commission appointed composed equally of Americans and Englishmen, who should fully ascertain the *facts*, and all the facts, and should report their findings to the governments. That having these facts in black and white before them, he could not but believe an agreement would be made; that such findings could be the basis of negotiations for a mode of settlement, which he would promptly enter into. He did not promise an arbitration, nor did he decline one. He said that would await the findings of the joint Commission. . . .

"He said the United States liked arbitration more than Great Britain, and he had little fancy for hiring a Foreigner as Umpire. I mentioned that the principles of law recognized in the United States and Great Britain were very similar, indeed, almost the same, to which he concurred." *Bayard MS.*

On February 28, 1896, Mr. Eric Barrington, the private secretary of Lord Salisbury, paid a visit to the American Embassy and informed Bayard that the Foreign Office did

Finding that Lord Salisbury was conciliatory, Bayard sent the following telegram to Secretary Olney:

Interview with Minister for Foreign Affairs, who assented promptly to commence negotiations Venezuelan boundary at Washington; and without delay will empower British Ambassador at Washington to treat with you. After a consultation with Colonial Secretary, he will try to give definition of "settlements." He suggests joint Commission equal number Americans and English, to ascertain all the facts and report to the two Governments, which finding not obligatory, but may enable settlement or become basis for final negotiations.[355]

Olney regarded this suggestion from Lord Salisbury as worthless, and he inquired of Lord Pauncefote if the proposal he made to the British Government on January 28 would be acceptable. This proposal had included a joint fact-finding commission and an arbitral tribunal consisting of the "Chief Justice of England and the Chief Justice of the United States and a third arbitrator mutually agreed upon." This tribunal would act only in the event that England and the United States could not agree upon a boundary line after a study of the report of the fact-finding commission.[356]

Olney now discovered that he could not accelerate the slow diplomatic pace of Lord Salisbury. He had continually found fault with Bayard because of the delays of the Foreign Office, but he soon found out that he could not wring a ready reply from the British Foreign Secretary. On March 3 Lord Salisbury gave a guarded answer to Bayard's note of February 27. The Foreign Office was willing to have the negotiations transferred to Washington, but it would not be rushed in the matter of defining the meaning of the term "settled districts." Moreover, Lord Salisbury was not ready to discuss the question of final arbitration of the boundary dispute. It would be best to appoint a fact-finding commission, and when their report had been submitted, it would then be time to discuss the question of final settlement.[357]

Bayard promptly telegraphed to Secretary Olney the substance of

---

not wish any statements "referring to the informal conversations with Lord Playfair to go upon the record." Bayard immediately assented to this request. *Ibid.*

355. Bayard to Secretary Olney, February 27, 1896, *Bayard MS.* At this point mention should be made of the efforts of Sir William Harcourt to effect some settlement of the Venezuelan boundary dispute. He was particularly fearful of the "obstinacy" of Joseph Chamberlain. See, A. G. Gardiner, *The Life of Sir William Harcourt*, vol. 2, pp. 395ff.

356. Secretary Olney to Lord Pauncefote, February 28, 1896, *Olney MS.*

357. Lord Salisbury to Bayard, March 3, 1896 *Bayard MS.* See also, *Foreign Relations, 1896*, pp. 241-242.

this note from Lord Salisbury.[358] Olney was provoked that he could not move Lord Salisbury with any more despatch than Bayard had been able to do. His irritation was shown in a long personal note to Bayard in which he expressed great surprise and regret that Joseph Chamberlain had apparently been misled. In Bayard's telegram to Olney of February 25, and in his letter on the following day, attention was called to the fact that Chamberlain asserted that he had been allowed to believe that the American Government would agree to the exclusion of "settled districts," and then suddenly, on February 23, his hopes had been dispelled by Bayard's letter to Lord Playfair. It was very possible that Lord Playfair had misinformed Chamberlain on this point, or perhaps the Colonial Secretary had merely been stupid in this matter. Bayard had permitted Playfair to read all the pertinent communications from Secretary Olney with regard to the boundary dispute, and if he reported their contents correctly, Chamberlain should not have been under any misapprehension as to Olney's position. If he did not report correctly, that was not Bayard's fault.[359]

Chamberlain desired to have some scapegoat upon which to fasten the blame for the failure of his informal negotiations, so he quickly picked upon Bayard, and Olney was delighted to have some further opportunity to pick a quarrel. In a personal letter of March 6, Olney launched his attack. He had noted

. . . with surprise and regret the error into which Mr. Chamberlain has been misled, and am quite at a loss to understand how it has happened. Nothing emanating from this side of the water has given the slightest countenance to the idea that this Government would consider for a moment the adoption of what Mr. Chamberlain calls the principle of exclusion—which being interpreted, simply means that what Great Britain has already seized, or what her subjects have already squatted upon, she and they shall be allowed to retain without regard to length of occupation, notice actual or constructive of Venezuela's rights, conditions of the grant or license or material facts under which such occupation or jurisdiction began and has continued, and all the other circumstances qualifying and characterizing it either as a just and equitable basis of title and jurisdiction on the one hand or as of no consequence and significance as regards such title and jurisdiction on the other. Mr. Chamberlain's misconception of our position ought to be removed without delay. While it will of course tend to somewhat prejudice and retard the successful issue of the negotiations about to be

358. Bayard to Secretary Olney, March 4, 1896, *Bayard MS.*

359. In this whole regard it is worth while to read Bayard's long despatches to Secretary Olney, No. 613, February 26, and No. 614, February 29, 1896, *Great Britain, Despatches*, vol. 183, MS Dept. of State.

initiated here, it ought not to render them wholly abortive; while it is obvious that the quicker the correction is made the less mischief the misunderstanding is likely to do. I venture to suggest, therefore, that as soon as practicable after receiving this, you take occasion to point out to Mr. Chamberlain the error into which he has fallen, to state the true position of the United States which I am sure you apprehend, and to add that the position is one from which it is altogether improbable that this Government can be induced to depart.[360]

While this querulous letter was en route to London, Bayard wrote a personal letter to President Cleveland in which he expressed the view that the British Government was animated by a real desire for a "just and satisfactory settlement" of the Venezuelan boundary dispute. In his conversations with Bayard, Lord Salisbury had adverted

. . . to the "isolation" of Great Britain, and their consequent reluctance to place their interests in control of unfriendly parties. It is clearly his belief that a joint American and English Commission will be able to come to an agreement, and if not instantly, yet with reasonable negotiation will accomplish it. The case as stated by Great Britain is meant to be full and fair, and of course must be weighed with the counterstatement of Venezuela.

The appearance of ex-Minister Scruggs as the Agent of Venezuela, confirms the judgment I had long since formed that his leaning against Great Britain at a time when he was the Envoy of the United States at Carácas, had weakened the weight of our tender of disinterested services to that Government. But the desire of this Government to avoid the employment of a European arbiter at this time, will have great weight in inducing them to come to an agreement with the United States *alone*. I will not withhold from you my solicitude that this disposition for settlement should be strengthened by our own action.[361]

On March 17 Bayard received Olney's note of complaint concerning Joseph Chamberlain and his misapprehension of the attitude of the Department of State relative to the "settled districts" in Guiana. Six days later, a cipher telegram was received at the Embassy from Olney in which he instructed Bayard to report what action he had taken with regard to the Chamberlain matter.[362] On the following day, Bayard replied that since the discontinuance of the Playfair negotiations his only channel of communication with Chamberlain was through the

360. Secretary Olney to Bayard, March 6, 1896, *Bayard* MS.

361. Bayard to President Cleveland, March 10, 1896, *Cleveland MS.* On March 18, 1896, Bayard wrote another letter to Cleveland in which he remarked: "I continue to be impressed with the strong desire of Great Britain to settle in a mode satisfactory to the reasonable and equitable judgment of the United States, and avoid a European Umpirage." *Bayard Press Copy Book,* vol. 4, *Bayard* MS.

362. Secretary Olney to Bayard, March 23, 1896, *Bayard* MS.

Foreign Office. This fact made it difficult to avoid delays in getting in touch with the Colonial Secretary. He then stated that he had never misled Chamberlain with reference to the exclusion of settled districts from arbitration, and he thought his letter to Lord Playfair, February 23, 1896, had made that fact clear.[363]

After despatching this telegram, Bayard then wrote a long personal letter to Olney. He thought it best to

. . . recur to the facts which may have become a little confused amid all the arduous labors which have lately been thrown upon you. I have never, at any time, had communication, oral or written with Mr. Chamberlain on the Venezuelan subject, and my informal discussions with Lord Playfair consisted solely of the reception of his memoranda and the communication to him of the counterpropositions and comments as received by me from you. Full and accurate memoranda of what passed between Lord Playfair and myself were duly transmitted to you. As to what passed between Lord Playfair and Mr. Chamberlain, of course, I have no other knowledge than the written memoranda contain, and the general conversation on the subject as reported by Lord Playfair to me.

At no time was there any other communication by me on the subject of the Venezuelan boundary than that of which you have been regularly and carefully informed. Mr. Chamberlain's errors, or misapprehensions, in regard to the acceptance of the principle of exclusion, have not been caused by anything emanating from this Embassy; but, on the contrary, my note to Lord Playfair of February 23d answers, among other things, the fallacy of Mr. Chamberlain's position, as stated in his note of February 1st, that the object for which Her Majesty's Ministers have been contending was "for men, and not territory." . . .

The comment of Mr. Chamberlain . . . in his note to Lord Playfair of February 25th was—"he (Mr. Bayard) goes back to his original proposal, for an open and unconditional arbitration and ignores the insistence *by both you and me* of the principle of exclusion."

It will be perceived that Mr. Chamberlain limits "the insistence upon the principle of exclusion" to himself and Lord Playfair, and states that I "ignored it," and "had gone back to my original proposal for an open and unconditional arbitration."

What Mr. Chamberlain's discussion with Lord Playfair, and his advocacy and strong desire for an exclusion of actual settlements, led him to believe to be hopeful and obtainable grounds of settlement, of course, I have no knowledge, but it is clear and certain that nothing was ever communicated by me, beyond the letter of the written propositions received from you, and that no "principle of exclusion" was intimated, the fact being that I have no knowledge of the population or nature of the occupation of the territory in dispute, and could have expressed no opinion on the subject. . . .

363. Bayard to Secretary Olney, March 24, 1896, *ibid.*

As I have said before in the course of my correspondence, the very *crux* of the case is the question of legal, long-continued, open, effective occupation of an unbounded region, and the definition of such "settlements" was asked for by me of Lord Salisbury, under your instructions, and he promised me in his note of March 3 to "communicate to the Secretary of State for the Colonies" your desire to be informed of the precise meaning attached by Her Majesty's Government to the word "settlements." . . .

Under these circumstances I could not feel that it would be, in any view, judicious or desirable, that I should resort, directly or informally, to the Secretary for the Colonies to encompass an end which was, at my own request, under consideration by the only Department with which I can hold formal communication. . . . The fact stated by Mr. Chamberlain that he was preparing a paper "for the Foreign Office," on the subject of the meaning to be given to the word "settlements," had weight with me in forming my judgment as to the inexpediency of approaching him informally on the subject.[364]

Before Olney could receive this long letter of explanation from Bayard, he sent a cipher telegram to the London Embassy directing Bayard to refute in an emphatic manner any idea that the American Government was willing to exclude from arbitration the settled districts in Guiana. If Bayard could not indirectly get in touch with Chamberlain in order to convey this instruction, he should communicate unofficially with Lord Salisbury to the same effect.[365]

Upon receipt of this instruction from Olney, Bayard at once sought an interview with Mr. Chamberlain in order to make known to him

364. Bayard to Secretary Olney, March 24, 1896, *Bayard Press Copy Book*, vol. 4, *Bayard MS.* On March 25 Olney wrote a note to President Cleveland with reference to Bayard and Chamberlain. It is evident that he wished to pursue the matter to Bayard's disadvantage: "Have you seen the enclosed despatches from Mr. Bayard? . . . The only thing of special interest is the note of Mr. Chamberlain to Lord Playfair of the 25th of February. There is nothing in that, however, that you do not already know except Mr. Chamberlain's attempt to insist that, in the course of the informal negotiations between Mr. Bayard and Lord Playfair, the United States, through Mr. Bayard, committed itself to the principle of the exclusion from arbitration of the settled districts. Mr. Bayard rather vaguely and indefinitely affirms that he had no such concession. . . . As soon as I got this despatch of Mr. Bayard's, to wit, on the 6th of March, I wrote him a personal note asking him to correct the erroneous impression into which Mr. Chamberlain had been led, without loss of time. So far he has not done so, taking the ground . . . that what I asked him to do was not necessary in view of his letter of the 23d of February. On that point I do not agree with him. I do not think the British Government ought to remain under the impression that we agree to things and then withdraw from them, and I have again communicated with Mr. Bayard asking him to make it clear to the British Government that, whatever misapprehensions Lord Playfair may have fallen into, or whatever incorrect reports of Mr. Bayard's attitude he may have communicated, this Government has never entertained the idea of excluding disputed territory from arbitration simply because British settlers are found in occupation." *Cleveland MS.*

365. Secretary Olney to Bayard, March 25, 1896, *Bayard MS.*

Olney's strong "dissent from principle of exclusion of settlements from arbitration." He also took that occasion to deny that he had ever intimated any official withdrawal from that position.[366]

On April 6, in a personal and confidential letter to Bayard, Secretary Olney abandons the sharp tones he had used in official communications, and he explains in a mild manner the reasons for his instructions concerning Chamberlain's misapprehensions.[367] His direct assaults on Bayard suddenly ceased and he now resorted to cheap criticism which he dealt out generously at dinner parties given by Republicans in Washington. One of President Cleveland's pet aversions was Senator Henry Cabot Lodge, but Olney not only visited the Lodge mansion as a dinner guest, but also embraced that occasion to pour into the receptive ears of Henry White a stream of abuse against "old Bayard." [368]

When White responded with his own brand of criticism of Bayard,

366. Bayard to Secretary Olney, March 26, 1896, *ibid*. In a memorandum written after this conversation with Joseph Chamberlain, Bayard remarks: "Thursday 2 P.M. at the Levee finding Lord Salisbury was leaving town, . . . I decided to speak directly to Mr. Chamberlain in accordance with Mr. Olney's expressed wishes. I did so and reminded him that my last note to Lord Playfair had been written on February 23d, and had been answered on the 25th, enclosed his note to Lord P. commenting upon mine of the 23d. I told him that I considered my note to Lord Playfair was a counterproposition that did not embrace 'the principle of exclusion of settlements' from the Arbitration, but that Mr. Olney seemed to desire that Mr. Chamberlain's statements that such a principle of exclusion had at one time been understood and desired, should be more emphatically dissented from and categorically denied by me. Mr. C. then said that nothing in his note to Lord Playfair was intended to bind me or anyone but themselves, and to express his understanding of what he had learned from Lord Playfair.

"I then told him that if Lord Salisbury had been accessible today I would have sought an interview with him at which I would have desired Mr. Chamberlain should be present in order to convey Mr. Olney's distinct dissent from the proposed principle of exclusion of settled districts from the Arbitration, and that I therefore so distinctly informed him and that I denied the statement made in his note to Lord P." *Bayard MS.*

367. Secretary Olney to Bayard, April 6, 1896. In this letter Olney acknowledges Bayard's explanatory letters of March 24 and 27. He greatly regretted the trouble that Bayard had "been put to in the matter to which they relate. I beg you to believe that I should not have asked you to correct Mr. Chamberlain's real or affected misapprehension if I had not had evidence that the leaving it without explicit correction was seriously prejudicing the pending negotiations for the settlement of the Venezuelan Boundary controversy. No other consideration would have led me to notice the matter, since I never imagined for a moment that you had given Lord Playfair or any one else a right to suppose that the United States had assented to or would assent to the principle of the exclusion from arbitration of the 'settled districts' unless the term 'settled' were used in some special and extraordinary sense—a bare possibility which led me to inquire why 'settled districts' had not been defined as promised. I imagine they find it difficult to make a definition which is consistent with any shadow of reasonableness for their claim." *Bayard MS.*

368. Henry White to his wife, May 8, 1896, *White MS.* There was only seven years difference in the ages of Olney and Bayard. In 1896 Olney was sixty-one years old.

Olney conceived an instant affection for him. It is significant to note that the three men in Washington who stood sponsor for Henry White were the very men that President Cleveland regarded with deep suspicion—Henry Cabot Lodge, John Hay, and Henry Adams.[369] It should also be remembered that White had incurred the enmity of Secretary Lamont, and that Cleveland himself, in 1893, had developed a strong dislike for him. But Olney, in his imperious way, brushed aside all these personal factors, and installed White as his chief diplomatic favorite. Within a few weeks after making Olney's acquaintance, White suddenly found himself en route to London, and on this occasion he was entrusted with the important mission of settling the Venezuelan boundary controversy through personal conversations with men high in British public life.[370]

After transferring the Venezuelan negotiations to Washington in February, 1896, Olney discovered that he could not push matters to an early conclusion. He had fumed because Bayard had not speeded up the leisurely pace of Lord Salisbury, and he was disagreeably surprised to discover that his own bluff, belligerent manner did not pay the diplomatic dividends that he had expected. Salisbury had no thought of being hurried by a Boston barrister who had run berserk on the stage of world politics. In the early months of 1896 the troubled waters of European diplomacy became more smooth, and the British Foreign Office had more time in which to make its decisions. In the Near East the tension was relaxed when Russia found out that she could not count upon French assistance to help further her plans against Turkey. Serious friction between England and Germany was averted by a sudden realization on the part of Emperor Wilhelm that it was not expedient to pick a quarrel over British expansion in South Africa.[371]

In May, 1896, Olney had to content himself with a note to Bayard in which he expressed the hope that the British Government would lend its assistance to the American Commission which was gathering data on the Venezuelan boundary.[372] In this letter to Bayard, Olney enclosed a communication from Justice Brewer in which doubt was

---

369. In a letter to Secretary Olney, September 12, 1895, Cleveland makes the following comments about a certain candidate for office: "I learn that he is a good deal of a club man, and, what is a settler with me, that his close intimates are John Hay, Henry Adams, Cabot Lodge, and such." Allan Nevins, *Letters of Grover Cleveland, 1850–1908*, p. 407

370. Allan Nevins, *Henry White*, pp. 111-112.

371. W. L. Langer, *The Diplomacy of Imperialism, 1890–1902*, vol. 1, pp. 206-209, 247-253, 294-295.

372. Secretary Olney to Bayard, May 8, 1896, *Foreign Relations, 1896*, p. 242.

cast upon certain assertions in the *British Blue Book* concerning the establishment by the Dutch Government of a post near the mouth of the Orinoco River.[373]

Lord Salisbury promptly answered Olney's request for assistance. The British Government would be happy to place at the disposal of the American Commission "all the information" which had been gathered with reference the Guiana boundary. After this friendly gesture, Salisbury then proceeded to show that Justice Brewer was badly mistaken in his assertions relative to the extent of the Dutch occupation of Guiana.[374] This didactic note was then followed by an instruction to Lord Pauncefote which outlined a basis for further negotiations. The British Government favored the appointment of a commission to be created by

. . . an agreement between Great Britain and the United States, consisting of four members, namely, two British subjects and two citizens of the United States; the above commission to investigate and to report upon the facts which affect the rights of the United Netherlands and of Spain, respectively, at the date of the acquisition of British Guiana by Great Britain. This commission will only examine into questions of fact without reference to the inferences that may be founded on them; but the finding of a majority of the commission upon those questions shall be binding upon both Governments.

Upon the report of the above commission being issued, the two Governments of Great Britain and Venezuela . . . shall endeavor to agree to a boundary line upon the basis of such report. Failing agreement, the report . . . shall be submitted to a tribunal of three, one nominated by Great Britain, the other by Venezuela, and the third by the two so nominated; which tribunal shall fix the boundary line upon the basis of such report, and the line so fixed shall be binding upon Great Britain and Venezuela. Provided, always, that in fixing such line the tribunal shall not have power to include as the territory of Venezuela any territory which was *bona fide* occupied by subjects of Great Britain on the 1st of January, 1887, or as the territory of Great Britain any territory *bona fide* occupied by Venezuelans at the same date.[375]

Once more the old question of "settled districts" comes to the front, and the British Government wished to exclude from arbitration all territory that had been occupied for as short a period as ten years. This was a direct thrust at the position that had been strongly held by Secretary Olney, whose reply rejected Lord Salisbury's proposals as neither

373. Justice Brewer to Secretary Olney, May 6, 1896, *ibid.*, pp. 242-243.
374. Lord Salisbury to Bayard, May 30, 1896, *Foreign Relations, 1896*, pp. 244-246.
375. Lord Salisbury to Sir Julian Pauncefote, May 22, 1896, *ibid.*, pp. 247-249.

"adapted to bring the Venezuelan boundary dispute to a speedy conclusion or as giving due recognition to the just rights of the parties
concerned." If, however, the proposals of Lord Salisbury were amended
in the following manner, they might prove satisfactory:

The commission upon facts should be so constituted, by adding one or
more members, that it must reach a result and can not become abortive and
possibly mischievous. That commission should have power to report upon
all the facts necessary to the decision of the boundary controversy, including
the facts pertaining to the occupation of the disputed territory by British
subjects.

The proviso by which the boundary line as drawn by the arbitral
tribunal is not to include territory *bona fide* occupied by British subjects or
Venezuelan citizens on the 1st of January, 1887, should be stricken out
altogether, or there might be substituted for it the following: *"Provided
however,* That in fixing such line, if territory of one party be found in the
occupation of the subjects or citizens of the other party, such weight and
effect shall be given to such occupation as reason, justice, the rules of
International Law, and the equities of the particular case may appear to
require.[376]

During the course of these diplomatic exchanges, Bayard remained
on the diplomatic sidelines with little to do. Early in April he received
a letter from John Bassett Moore with reference to the Venezuelan
boundary question. Professor Moore referred to a recent copy of the
London *Times* which contained a pertinent article by an official of the
British Museum. After giving a review of the main facts in the dispute,
this official had inquired as to the cause of

. . . all the "uproar" of the past two months? A very pertinent question
this, indeed. You may have inferred from one or two of my letters that I
have known something of the development of the Venezuelan business. So
I have. But I will not enter upon the subject now. In considering President
Cleveland's character as a statesman, it is, I think, the thing that will give
the historian the most difficulty. . . . Until this miserable Venezuelan fiasco,
engineered by the Yankee attorney-statesman from Boston, it was the steady
support of the thoughtful people that gave President Cleveland his strength.
It is upon such people, who do not need to be daily excited by some new
adventure in foreign politics, that we depend for the success of all wise
movements; and I hope that the movement in behalf of the establishment
of some kind of a tribunal for the adjustment of questions between the
United States and England will . . . accomplish something for the advantage
of mankind.[377]

376. Secretary Olney to Sir Julian Pauncefote, June 12, 1896, *Foreign Relations, 1896,*
pp. 249-252.
377. John Bassett Moore to Bayard, March 20, 1896, *Bayard MS.*

Bayard agreed with Professor Moore that the Venezuelan matter had been a distinct "fiasco," and he assured Senator Gray that he strongly disapproved of "any assumption of responsibility on the part of the United States for the action or liabilities of any other government over which we have no just power or jurisdiction." [378] He would not change this conviction despite any pressure from Washington, and he would not desist from making speeches which reflected his cordial good will towards England. Although Republicans in Congress expressed their vehement dissatisfaction with this course, Bayard went his way unperturbed.

Many Americans warmly approved Bayard's determination to continue his friendly addresses in England. Moncure D. Conway was one of Bayard's staunch supporters. He had resided in England for a quarter of a century, but during his long stay abroad he had never heard "from Minister or Ambassador any utterance which, considering all the circumstances, has so impressed me as the speeches of last evening." [379] Bayard's address at Stratford-on-Avon, April 23, 1896, was particularly pleasing to his friends, and Edward M. Shepard wrote that in the "noble benignity" of Bayard's language he could see the "true America and a vision of its future." [380] Oscar S. Straus was equally enthusiastic about this address. He assured Bayard that he would hasten to paste it in his Shakespeare so that he might not "lose the inspiration" that Bayard's words had brought to him.[381]

While Bayard was enjoying himself making speeches in England,[382] Olney was having a difficult time with the Venezuelan negotiations.

378. Bayard to Senator George Gray, April 15, 1896, *Bayard Press Copy Book*, vol. 4, *Bayard MS.*

379. Moncure D. Conway to Bayard, February 7, 1896, *ibid.*

380. Edward M. Shepard, June 6, 1896, *ibid.*

381. Oscar S. Straus to Bayard, May 13, 1896, *ibid.* In the course of this letter, Mr. Straus finally turned to political questions and made the following interesting comment: "I saw the President some two weeks ago. . . . I doubt if he could under any circumstances be induced to accept another nomination. I very much misjudge him if he could be prevailed upon to accept. I hope not—it may be a fetich, but I own I believe it a great mistake to break down the third-term precedent."

J. M. Forbes was in entire accord with Bayard's viewpoint, and he thought that it was high time for the United States and England to join hands against "their common enemies, the fanatics of all grades whether despots and aristocrats or dynamiters and nihilists." J. M. Forbes to Bayard, May 29, 1896, *Bayard MS.*

382 Olney's venom towards Bayard was clearly revealed in a letter to Maurice Low, November 20, 1899. With reference to Bayard's speeches, Olney remarked: "The constant stream of taffy played by Mr. Bayard upon the English people tickled them as a matter of course—perhaps to some extent sickened them." A. L. P. Dennis, *Adventures in American Diplomacy,* pp. 45-46.

Smalley was discouraged at the prospect, and came to the reluctant conclusion that the Foreign Office was by "nature dawdling and that Salisbury has so many other irons in the fire." [383] In England, Henry White was busy talking with Lord Salisbury, Lord Rothschild, and to Arthur Balfour. With regard to the matter of "settled districts," Lord Salisbury admitted that there was

. . . considerable difficulty in defining them. I [White] urged the impossibility of trusting to the accuracy of the statements, as to population, etc., of subordinate British colonial officials on the spot. . . . I also touched on the importance of keeping the controversy out of the approaching presidential campaign.

Lord Salisbury replied that he would be glad to settle the question, but that he considers compulsory arbitration in matters affecting territory, without any power of appeal, a dangerous precedent to establish. . . .

No reference was made in our conversation to the causes of the delay which has taken place in approaching the settlement of the Venezuelan question. . . . I have good reason to believe that the Government has been advised through American channels, which I have as yet been unable to trace, that, being an eminent lawyer, and not a diplomatist, you are likely to take, in any international difficulty the extreme view of an advocate anxious to win his case in court; . . . that you are animated, moreover, by feelings of hostility to this country. . . . Another reason for delay is . . . the alarm said to have been caused in Canada by the remark in your despatch to Mr. Bayard as to the inexpediency of "any permanent political union between a European and an American state." [384]

The very fact that Lord Salisbury refused to be stampeded into a speedy settlement of the Venezuelan boundary dispute, was very annoying to Olney who complained to his daughter, Mrs. G. R. Minot, that he had been very busy with "that old bull-dog Lord Salisbury." [385] In a letter to his wife he alludes to the hard time he was having with the British Lion which was "switching his tail and grinding his teeth (in the person of Sir Julian) most furiously." [386]

It was quite disconcerting to Olney to have anyone refuse to bend to his will. He had pushed President Cleveland around much as he pleased, but he found that Lord Salisbury was a man of a different stripe. His annoyance at the diplomatic *impasse* he had reached with regard to Venezuela was increased by reading the letters from Henry White. In order to justify his moves behind Bayard's back, White had

383. G. W. Smalley to Secretary Olney, June 10, 1896, *Olney MS.*
384. Henry White to Secretary Olney, June 17, 1896, *ibid.*
385. Secretary Olney to Mrs. G. R. Minot, June 20, 1896, *ibid.*
386. Secretary Olney to Mrs. Olney, June 28, 1896, *ibid.*

to criticize the Ambassador for not expediting Olney's plans. This was quite ungenerous when it is remembered that Olney took everything out of Bayard's hands and kept him in the dark. This fact did not keep Olney from denouncing Bayard as a diplomatic agent who "through sentiment, self-conceit, physical infirmity, and otherwise, has been practically disabled from rendering the services rightfully expected of him."[387]

Despite all of Olney's conferences with Lord Pauncefote, and his indirect overtures through Henry White, the Venezuelan negotiations had reached a "deadlock." [388] Indeed, White reported from London that Joseph Chamberlain had informed him that England would never consent to any arbitration that would include the "settled districts." If the American Government insisted upon its unreasonable stand in this regard, it seemed to Chamberlain that war between the two countries was inevitable.[389]

Before Olney had received this discouraging letter from Henry White, he had already heard from Lord Salisbury to the effect that England would not recede from its determination to exclude from arbitration the settled districts in the Guiana. The claim of Venezuela was so

. . . far-reaching that it brings into question interests and rights which cannot properly be disposed of by an unrestricted arbitration. It extends as far as the Essequibo; it covers two-thirds of British Guiana; it impeaches titles which have been unquestioned for many generations. These districts must be treated separately, and until further inquiry has thrown more light upon the matter it is only by reserving the settled districts generally that this can be done.[390]

In his reply, Olney had advanced the view that the ambitious claims of Venezuela should not be regarded as an

387. Secretary Olney to Henry White, June 30, 1896, *Henry White MS.*
388. Secretary Olney to Henry White, June 30, and July 10, 1896, *ibid.* It is very apparent that the much-advertised services of Henry White in 1896 in the matter of the Venezuelan boundary dispute were largely ineffective. Lord Salisbury was a realist who was seldom swayed by personal considerations. The decision of the British Government to consent to arbitration was finally given in November, 1896, when the result of the elections indicated that a Republican Administration would take over the conduct of foreign relations. Republican leaders were committed to a strong stand on the Monroe Doctrine, and there was little likelihood that they would fail to carry on the Cleveland policy. There was no point in waiting for the installation of the new Administration before coming to an agreement on the Venezuelan boundary.
389. White to Secretary Olney, July 17, 1896, *White MS.*
390. Lord Salisbury to Sir Julian Pauncefote, July 3, 1896, *Foreign Relations, 1896*, pp. 252-253.

. . . insuperable obstacle to unrestricted arbitration. . . . Can it be assumed that Her Majesty's Government would submit to unrestricted arbitration the whole of the territory in dispute provided it be a rule of arbitration, embodied in the arbitral agreement, that territory which has been in the exclusive, notorious, and actual use and occupation of either party for even two generations, or say for sixty years, shall be held by the arbitrators to be the territory of such party? [391]

Olney was growing very weary of his long drawn-out struggle with Lord Salisbury, and he expressed to President Cleveland the belief that the policy of the British Foreign Secretary was a sort of "pettifogging which accomplishes nothing and which is in truth not in keeping with the serious character of the grave issues involved." [392]

At this critical juncture, one of the Republicans whom Cleveland particularly despised, stepped on the English diplomatic stage and recited a few lines for Olney's benefit. John Hay, sojourning in London, had a long conversation with Sir William Harcourt and informed him that a Republican victory in the Presidential election would make no difference in the settlement of the Venezuelan boundary dispute. McKinley would take "no steps backward" from the position that had been assumed by President Cleveland.[393]

Hay also talked with Joseph Chamberlain, who had been strongly opposed to any concession in the matter of "settled districts." Perhaps it was this conversation with Hay that suggested to Chamberlain the expediency of paying a visit to the United States for the purpose of discussing the situation with Olney himself. In the late summer of 1896 he arrived in America, and on September 8 he had an interview with Olney.[394]

391. Secretary Olney to Sir Julian Pauncefote, July 13, 1896, *ibid.,* pp. 253-254.
392. Secretary Olney to President Cleveland, July 16, 1896, *Cleveland MS.*
393. John Hay to Secretary Olney, July 31, 1896, Henry James, *Richard Olney,* pp. 247-248.
394. In a letter from Joseph Chamberlain to Secretary Olney, September 9, 1896, the substance of this conversation is reproduced: "In the interview which you were good enough to give me yesterday I endeavored to make clear to you the objection left by the British Government to unrestricted arbitration in the case of the Venezuelan boundary. This objection arises from the exorbitant character of the Venezuelan claim which includes a large part of the British Colony of Guiana and embraces territory to which we honestly and sincerely believe that we have as much right to as the United States have to the State of Maine.

"To refer the ownership of such territory to a Court whose decision might possibly be governed by the opinion of a Foreign jurist, appointed as umpire by a minor Power, and as to whose qualifications and character it would be almost impossible to have satisfactory evidence beforehand, appears to us to be a course which no great Nation, and least of all the United States, would agree to it in its own case, and which therefore ought not to be urged upon us.

This interview was of no great moment because Chamberlain had no specific instructions from Lord Salisbury, and Olney thought it was wise to continue negotiations through Lord Pauncefote.[395] But Olney's

---

"On the other hand I assured you that, in our desire to arrive at an early and satisfactory arrangement with you, we were ready to negotiate or arbitrate as to a large extent of territory on both sides of the Schomburgk line, to which we believed that our title was just and clear, but as to which, owing to the character of the country and of our occupation, there might be more legitimate subject for investigation.

"I ventured accordingly to suggest that an arrangement might be reached in one of two ways, viz., either by friendly negotiations between the United States and Great Britain with the object of fixing a fair boundary line which might be discussed in a spirit of mutual compromise; or, by an arbitration to be confined to territory situated between two lines which might be drawn so as to exclude the extreme claims on both sides.

"You seemed to fear that the former of those proposals would not lead to any satisfactory result, and you said that the Government of the United States would be very reluctant to take the responsibility of fixing a line which would afterwards have to be imposed on Venezuela.

"As regards the second proposal you urged that it was unnecessary to limit the scope of the arbitration, as it was really impossible to suppose that any Court would adopt the extreme view put forward by Venezuela. I pointed out that, whatever might be the probabilities of the case, there would remain a risk of a gross miscarriage of justice which, as Trustees for the Colony, Her Majesty's Government were not justified in assuming; and that, as we were both agreed that any decision which adopted these extreme claims would be a disastrous one, it would surely be better to exclude them from arbitration, which might be done by confining the subject matter to the territory included between lines to be drawn by us beforehand.

"You appeared, however, to feel that the fixing of such lines might present great difficulties and you said that you had already endeavoured to secure a satisfactory result by suggesting an instruction to the Tribunal that all territory found to be in actual use or occupation by British subjects and Venezuelan citizens respectively for a period of 60 years should be held to be the territory of British Guiana and Venezuela respectively.

"I pointed out to you that . . . this instruction [was] so limited as to be practically useless. In the first place the period of 60 years . . . [is] unnecessarily long and would complicate and prolong the investigations. Secondly, the territory actually used and occupied in an undeveloped country such as British Guiana, was of very small extent. The proposed instruction would therefore leave at the mercy of the arbitrators territory which, although not actually used and occupied, had been under the political and unrestricted control of Great Britain . . . for many years. . . .

"I suggest that the words of the proposed instruction to the Arbitral Tribunal might run to the following effect: 'All territory which has been in the actual use and occupation of British subjects or of citizens of Venezuela respectively, or over which the Governments of the Colony of British Guiana or of Venezuela have exercised unrestricted political control for a continuous period of at least 30 years prior to the date of this Convention, shall be held to be and to form part of British Guiana or Venezuela respectively, as the case may be.'" *Olney MS.*

395. In a letter from Henry James to Henry White, June 3, 1922, Mr. James makes the following comments: "Mr. Endicott has told me how Chamberlain went to see Mr. Olney, taking great pains to be unobserved, even climbing the stairs to his office instead of getting into the elevator, and how angry Mr. Chamberlain was when he returned to the Endicott house by reason of the uncompromising way in which Mr. Olney had refused to discuss the matter as Mr. Chamberlain wanted him to, on the ground that Mr. Chamberlain was not authorized by Lord Salisbury to settle the question. I have no doubt whatever that Olney was determined to keep the negotiations in the channel into which he had led them, i.e., to continue them through Sir Julian Pauncefote—that he did not mean

disinclination to carry on negotiations with Chamberlain did not prevent him from exchanging several letters with the ebullient Colonial Secretary. On September 19 Chamberlain inquired whether Olney would care to express a confidential opinion as to the reception that would be given by the American Government "to any proposition from our side tending to co-operation in regard to Turkey?" [396]

Olney responded to this invitation by writing a long, rambling letter in which he poured the vials of his ready wrath upon "college presidents, pseudo-diplomats, disgruntled office seekers, and cranks of all sorts." It was not long before he denounced Bayard for his speeches, which he thought gave an appearance of "fawning or toadyism." After this outburst, he settled down to a discussion of the bases of Anglo-American relations, and finally reached the startling statement that "nothing would more gratify the mass of the American people than to stand side by side and shoulder to shoulder with England in support of a great cause." Americans were deeply interested in the "advancement of Christian civilization," and if England should actively intervene on behalf of the oppressed Armenians in Turkey, there could be little doubt that the United States "would consider the moment opportune for vigorous exertion on behalf of American citizens and interests in Turkey." [397] Chamberlain was duly impressed with this generous sentiment, and he assured Olney that he firmly believed that "all differences between us, paltry in themselves and only important as they touch the national honour, will be amicably adjusted." [398]

Chamberlain had other conversations with influential Americans, and one result of his visit to the United States was the establishment of a conviction that a Republican victory in the November elections would mean no change in the attitude of the American Government towards the Venezuelan boundary controversy. When he reached England he discussed the situation with Lord Salisbury, who was inclined to allow negotiations to drift until the American elections were over. There was a chance that William Jennings Bryan might be elected President of the United States, and in that event, the Cleveland-Olney policy might be repudiated.

Whether Bryan was elected or not, it was evident to British states-

to let Mr. Chamberlain confuse the wires, and that he gave Mr. Chamberlain to understand that." *White MS.*
396. Joseph Chamberlain to Secretary Olney, September 19, 1896, *Olney MS.*
397. Secretary Olney to Joseph Chamberlain, September 28, 1896, *Olney MS.*
398. Joseph Chamberlain to Secretary Olney, September 28, 1896, *ibid.*

men that President Cleveland was a man "without a party." [399] The "Boy Orator of the Platte" had captured the imagination of the rank and file of the Democratic Party, and many of the leaders had long been hostile to Cleveland. After Bryan's nomination at Chicago, Cleveland's defiance of the age-old principle of party regularity was another factor that added to his unpopularity.

In the summer of 1896 there was scant attention paid to Olney and the Venezuelan boundary controversy. Important domestic issues were stressed in the Presidential campaign, and the situation in Cuba was demanding more and more attention. The "large policy" of 1898 was being rapidly shaped by prominent Republicans who had quickly caught the first, faint tones of the anthem of national expansion that was to burst from American throats in the years just previous to the turn of the twentieth century. Cleveland and Olney had contributed their full share towards the musical education of the American people in this regard. The bold crescendoes in Olney's instructions and in Cleveland's messages to Congress, introduced into millions of American homes a new appreciation of martial music. It was not long before militant maestros like Theodore Roosevelt and Henry Cabot Lodge supplied these popular compositions with the proper warlike pitch. Thanks to the Cuban situation, this aggressive American spirit was diverted from England and finally found belligerent expression in the war with Spain.

Lord Salisbury had read the situation with his usual astuteness. He perceived that there was little danger in postponing the Venezuelan boundary negotiations until after the American elections. When he learned that Mr. McKinley had been returned an easy victor in this contest, he decided to put an end to the dispute which had been so long a cause of friction. On November 12, 1896, Lord Pauncefote and Secretary Olney signed the heads of a proposed treaty which made provision for an arbitral tribunal that would consist of two members nominated by the judges of the Supreme Court of the United States; two members nominated by the judges of the British Supreme Court of Justice, and a fifth member to be selected "by the four persons so nominated." The tribunal would be authorized to investigate and ascertain the extent of the territories belonging to or claimed by the Netherlands and by Spain, respectively, at the time of the acquisition

399. Paxton Hibben, *The Peerless Leader, William Jennings Bryan* (N.Y. 1929), p. 175; Allan Nevins, *Grover Cleveland*, pp. 677-704.

by Great Britain of the colony of British Guiana. Adverse holding during a period of fifty years would make a good title, and the arbitrators might deem exclusive political control of a district, as well as actual settlement thereof, sufficient to constitute adverse holding or to make title by prescription.[400]

In accordance with this arrangement, Great Britain and Venezuela signed on February 2, 1897, a treaty for the settlement of their long-standing boundary controversy. The membership of the arbitral tribunal established under the terms of this treaty, included two American jurists—Chief Justice Fuller, and Justice Brewer, of the Supreme Court. The British members were Lord Herschell and Sir Richard Collins, while F. de Martens, a distinguished authority in International Law, was selected as the presiding member of the tribunal. On October 3, 1899, this arbitral commission concluded its labors and announced an award, by unanimous vote, which gave to Great Britain the major portion of the territory in dispute. Although Venezuela retained control of the mouth of the Orinoco River, her spurious claim to all the lands west of the Essequibo was rejected. The basis of the British claim had long been the famous Schomburgk line. In the award, certain territory east of this line was given to Venezuela, but on the whole, the Schomburgk line was largely followed.[401]

It is obvious that this award was a diplomatic victory for Great Britain, and it also constituted a severe reflection upon the unfortunate policy pursued by President Cleveland and Secretary Olney in the whole matter of the boundary controversy.

Bayard was well pleased with the news of the signing of the preliminary treaty of arbitration on November 12, 1896, and he looked forward to a settlement that would remove all causes of friction between England and the United States. During the last months of his term as Ambassador, he was deeply impressed with the unmistakable evidence of a new spirit of good will between the two countries. In England this friendly feeling took the form of a movement to purchase, through popular subscription, some fitting testimonial of the affection-

400. *Foreign Relations, 1896*, pp. 254-255.
401. For a vast amount of data on the Venezuelan boundary controversy, see, *Report and Accompanying Papers of the Commission Appointed by the President of the United States "to investigate and report upon the true divisional line between the Republic of Venezuela and British Guiana"* (Washington, 1896-1897, 9 vols.). For a discussion of the contents of this report, see, Marcus Baker, "The Venezuelan Boundary Commission and its Work," *National Geographic Magazine*, vol. 8, (1897), pp. 193-201.

ate regard of the British people for Bayard himself. But he realized that this movement was ill-advised, and he wrote to the editor of the *Daily Telegraph* and indicated his objections to it:

On the afternoon of Thursday I returned to London, and then . . . was informed, and through the columns of the *Daily Telegraph,* that . . . a testimonial in the form of two literary treasures was proposed to be presented to me by general subscription, in indication of good will and respect to my Country and to me as its Diplomatic Representative. I was naturally deeply touched and gratified by such a proposal and the generous eulogy contained in the editorial that announced it. Nor was my gratification lessened when your issue of yesterday and that of today contained so many spontaneous tributes of respect and kind feeling from men of all classes of occupation and degrees of fortune.

A few hours of reflection have brought me to the sober judgment that holding my present office, and invested with its discretion and duties I should scrupulously respect and obey the spirit as well as the letter of my country's law, written and unwritten, which inhibits anyone holding office of trust or profit under the United States from accepting "without the consent of Congress any present from any King, Prince, or Government" . . .

While I live I shall not cease to thank the people of these Islands for the whole-hearted, unstinted welcome I have received at their hands, and the warm hospitalities showered upon me and mine since I came among them.[402]

In the United States there were many persons who regarded British good will towards the United States as a product of Bayard's unremitting labors. George F. Peabody was certain that the signing of the provisional treaty adjusting the Venezuelan boundary controversy was made possible through the friendly efforts of Bayard. He had no doubt that the decision of the British Government was "made far more easy by reason of the magnificent work which had been done through your speeches and great presence throughout the length and breadth of the fatherland." [403]

Carl Schurz had followed Bayard's course in England with

. . . the liveliest interest, sympathy, and gratification. It seems to be admitted on all hands that you are the most popular representative this Republic has ever had at the court of St. James, and only our boyish Jingoes who "want a war" and some old demagogues who will be without political capital when they lose all opportunities for twisting the British lion's tail, refuse to recognize the good you have done by fostering the feeling of cordiality between the two countries.[404]

402. Bayard to the Editor of the *Daily Telegraph,* December 5, 1898, *Bayard Press Copy Book,* vol. 5, *Bayard MS.*

403. George F. Peabody to Bayard, November 11, 1896, *Bayard MS.*

404. Carl Schurz to Bayard, January 12, 1897, *Schurz MS.*

Bayard was greatly pleased to learn that his friends were in ardent support of his efforts to cement the ties that bound Britain to the United States, and he was grateful to God that he had been chosen as the instrument to strengthen the "mutual respect and good feeling between the peoples of the two countries." [405] At the banquet given in his honor by the Lord Mayor of London, March 2, 1897, Bayard devoted his last public utterance to this same theme:

I was imbued before I came here, and the feeling has increased since I came here, that there was a plain duty between all the men "who speak the tongue that Shakespeare spoke, the faith and morals hold that Milton held," to stand together and rebuke petty differences, not seeking effusive or emotional alliances, but to stand together for the great purpose for which I believe under God our race has been intended. It is not party politics in either country, it may not be international politics, it is a feeling of conscientious duty that I believe at the bottom underlies the affairs of this great Empire and the country which is my home, the land of my nativity and of my heart. This was my intent, and I weighed the forces for it and against it; and the longer I considered it the plainer it seemed to me that there were currents running too strong to be resisted that would favour the wish of my heart in this respect. I was satisfied that the substructure of our countries is the same; that there is an ingrained affinity of morality, intellectuality, and religion that will carry us necessarily in the same direction; that there is no cause, that there is not today—and I speak it in the presence of those perfectly able to qualify or contradict it—there is not a question for dispute between the people of this country and the people of the United States. [406]

During the early months of 1897, the British press was filled with columns of praise for Bayard. The following excerpt from an editorial in the *Saturday Review,* is typical:

It is within the truth to say that no American Minister or Ambassador has held so high a place in English esteem as Mr. Bayard. To all outward seeming, Mr. Russell Lowell was as well received in England as anyone could be; like Mr. Bayard he was a welcome guest in the best houses; he, too, was asked to Windsor more than once; and when he was entertained in the City, Cabinet Ministers appeared to do him honour. But in Mr. Bayard's reception there was an affectionate cordiality which was not shown to Mr. Russell Lowell, a note of intimate, personal admiration which was never called forth by any other foreigner. . . .

Mr. Bayard came to England as a simple gentleman with no adventitious recommendations, and Englishmen at once recognized him for what he was, and honoured him accordingly. . . . Some time elapsed before ordinary

405. Bayard to Senator George Gray, January 29, 1897, *Bayard Press Copy Book,* vol. 5, *Bayard MS.*
406. *St. James Gazette,* September 29, 1898, p. 12.

Englishmen began to see that Mr. Bayard was a gentleman of a wonderfully fine type. . . . Mr. Bayard had no touch of aristocratic "morgue"; he met everyone with the same gentle courtesy, and his kindliness needed no armour of pride to protect him against liberties which no one thought of taking. . . . Perhaps the rarest quality of the man was his transparent sincerity. . . . He seemed to have nothing to conceal, and nothing that he especially desired to put forward. Even in intimacy no one ever heard him tell a loose tale or touch a "risque" incident. . . . He loved ideals because they appealed to his manhood, and yet he was not lacking in worldly wisdom. He was simply a man of exquisite balance and charming temperament.[407]

John Hay arrived in London on April 21, 1897, to take over the duties of Ambassador at the Court of St. James's. Bayard immediately turned over the Embassy to him, and sailed from England on May 8. Upon his return to the United States he resumed his residence in Wilmington and renewed his acquaintance with old friends who extended a cordial welcome. While still in England he had received a letter from George F. Parker, who recounted a recent conversation with President Cleveland. When Bayard's name was mentioned, the President had spoken of the Ambassador "in the same friendly way with which I have grown familiar."[408] Encouraged by this note, Bayard paid a visit to Princeton in the early part of June, 1897, and spent some pleasant hours with Cleveland, who, despite all the efforts of Olney, retained a warm regard for his old friend.

During the early months of 1898, Bayard carried on a large correspondence with his many American acquaintances, and to no one did he turn with more assurance than to his old comrade-in-arms in the Senate, Carl Schurz. On April 8 he wrote to Schurz and reviewed their long years of friendship:

You and I took our seats in the Senate in March, 1869, so that well-nigh thirty years have passed with all the chances and changes of life in this growing and active Country, and I want to say another word of respect, admiration, and sympathy for the part you have borne, and happily are now taking in the interests of good government and the higher civilization of the Country of which we are both citizens. . . . I remember so well, thirty years ago, when you stepped out "solitary and alone," and struck the shield of organized and corrupt power in the Senate of the United States, and my heart has been with you from that day until this.[409]

In this letter to Schurz, Bayard remarked that he was visiting the

407. March 27, 1897, pp. 308-309.
408. George F. Parker to Bayard, January 13, 1897, *Bayard MS.*
409. Bayard to Carl Schurz, April 8, 1898, *Schurz MS.*

Virginia Hot Springs in an endeavor to regain his health, but he thought that "our grey-bearded Father Time is smiling at the efforts (so futile) to escape the results of his long companionship." The trials and anxieties of his service as Ambassador in London had seriously undermined his constitution, and his letters from England had been filled with references to the many spells of sickness that continually plagued him.

In August, 1898, Bayard went on a visit to the home of his daughter, Mrs. Samuel D. Warren, at Dedham, Massachusetts. It was soon apparent that the sands of his life were fast running out. With increasing difficulty he roused himself from the coma that steadily invaded his waking hours. He knew that he had a rendezvous with Death that could not long be postponed, but conscious of a life that had been dedicated to the service of his country and to the benefit of mankind, he awaited the end with the serene confidence that had marked the demise of another Bayard famous in story, the Chevalier "without fear and without reproach." He died on September 28, and was taken back to Wilmington, Delaware, to be buried with his ancestors in the Old Swedes cemetery. For his epitaph, his family might well have inscribed upon his tombstone the well-known words that describe the career of General Charles G. Gordon: "At all times and everywhere, he gave his strength to the weak, his substance to the poor, his sympathy to the suffering, his heart to God." [410]

410. In some of his letters in the *McKinley Papers*, in the Library of Congress, John Hay sharply critized Bayard. But there was an instinctive gentility about Hay that set him apart from certain other Republicans. When he heard the news of Bayard's death, he issued the following statement: "His scorn of everything mean or base; his disregard of consequences in the pursuit of what he thought right; his frank expectation of that sympathy which he was so ready to give; his belief in the sincerity of others, being himself absolutely sincere—all these qualities, even more than his good looks and gallant bearing, gave the impression not only of a young man, but of one who would always be young. It is hard to think that the rigid limit of three score and ten years should be the term of so much activity and energy. But the fine vitality and power of such a character will survive his death. In the affection of those who knew him, as a model and example to those who admired him, he will live long as an enduring memory and a wholesome inspiration." See, New York *Mail and Express*, October 8, 1898.

It was idle to expect much of Richard Olney. Bayard's death did not put an end to the criticism that he continued to express concerning the manner in which the Venezuelan boundary controversy had been handled. Refusing to acknowledge that the real difficulties were the result of his own mismanagement, he never lost an opportunity, even after Bayard's death, to disparage the achievements of the former Ambassador at the Court of St. James's. In a letter to A. Maurice Low, November 20, 1899, he sneers at Bayard's speeches in England and likens them to a "constant stream of taffy played . . . upon the English people." In a note to Grover Cleveland, March 6, 1901, he resumes this line of attack, and endeavors to convey the impression that Bayard was an "amateur diplomat." *Olney MS.*

In the *McKinley Papers* there is an excellent tribute to Bayard by Ernest Isitt, October 4, 1898: "Mr. Bayard was never subjected to the charge of having narrowly escaped greatness. Mr. Bayard was a great man; in fact, far greater than many public men who were seemingly, but only seemingly, the peer or equal of this eminent son of Delaware. . . . Mr. Bayard honored and dignified the office, no matter whether the office consisted of a Senatorship or an Ambassadorship, instead of the office honoring and dignifying him. A competent authority once said: 'Nothing but the pride of Mr. Bayard prevented his nomination for the Presidency in 1880. His refusal to pledge himself to a pre-arranged Cabinet slate was the cause of his failure.' . . . Not even the almost moral certainty of gaining the highest office on the land could tempt Mr. Bayard to compromise his honor by giving his adherence to the appointment of men whom he discountenanced. . . .

"Mr. Bayard was not a politician of that extremely familiar and contemptible type. He was a politician in the higher, the loftier, the more imperial sense; a statesman such as was represented, in a still greater sense, in the person of a Washington or of a Gladstone; men whose subtle brains successfully clutched the supreme rule, and who became the arbiters of vastly important national events. . . . When Bayard stood before kings the fact of his so standing was merely the world's recognition of a more or less complete life, a life marked by a strong, well-defined character, a life influenced by an unalterable and never-to-be-impeached straightforwardness, and a life that was ever consecrated to the public service without any thought or memory of personal self-interest."

INDEX